The Arthurian
Name Dictionary

Garland Reference Library of the Humanities (Vol. 2063)

The Arthurian
Name Dictionary

Christopher W. Bruce

Garland Publishing, Inc.
A member of the Taylor & Francis Group
New York and London
1999

Library of Congress Cataloging-in-Publication Data

Bruce, Christopher W.
    The Arthurian name dictionary / by Christopher W. Bruce.
        p.   cm. — (Garland reference library of the humanities ; v. 2063)
    ISBN 0-8153-2865-6 (alk. paper)
    1. Arthur, King—Dictionaries.   2. Great Britain—Antiquities, Celtic—Legends—Dictionaries.   3. Great Britain—History—To 1066—Legends—Dictionaries.   4. Britons—Kings and rulers—Folklore—Dictionaries.   5. Names, Geographical—Dictionaries.   6. Arthurian romances—Dictionaries.   7. Mythology, Celtic—Dictionaries.   8. Names, Personal—Dictionaries.   I. Title.   II. Series: Garland reference library of the humanities ; vol. 2063.
DA152.5.A7B78   1999
942.01'4—dc21   98–37750
                                                   CIP

Printed on acid-free, 250-year-life paper
Manufactured in the United States of America

Contents

Foreword

Who are Aamanz, Abastunagio, Bylas, Garengaus, and Iustig? Or Kinkenart and Kinlith and Nestling? And although every reader of Arthurian literature knows of Morgan, who is Morgant? And if you do not happen to know them, how can you find out? Until now such names might be next to impossible to locate; in most cases the effort would require an exhausting search of the index—where one is provided—to the edition of one Arthurian text after another—in Welsh, French, German, Italian, English, and other languages. Now it requires instead a glance at the pages of Christopher Bruce's *Arthurian Name Dictionary*.

When Chris wrote me a couple of years ago to tell me of his project to provide a complete guide to Arthurian characters from the beginning through Tennyson, he asked if I had any advice for him. I replied that he had set himself an immense task and that, in order to complete it, he should consider limiting it significantly, by imposing chronological and perhaps other constraints. I am delighted to note that he chose not to take that part of my advice. Published here, the resulting guide to Arthurian characters is the most ambitious and most nearly complete such name dictionary available—or, I think, even conceivable.

That it is needed will surely be obvious to any serious reader of Arthurian literature. The proliferation of characters in this literature is overwhelming, and even the most diligent and informed scholar cannot easily remember many of the reasonably prominent characters, much less the legions of minor ones. For example, the name index to Garland's *Lancelot-Grail: The Old French Vulgate and Post-Vulgate in Translation* includes well over 2000 names. And there are many hundreds of surviving Arthurian works, some of them rivaling or exceeding the Vulgate and Post-Vulgate in length and complexity.

Names can also change in bewildering ways from text to text; for example, Perceval's father, unnamed in some works, may elsewhere be identified as Bliocadran, Gahmuret, Alain, or Pellinore, or he may bear yet another name in another text. Given both the number and the permutations of names, a comprehensive guide to Arthurian characters can hardly require further justification.

Others have of course made significant efforts in this direction. Ruth Minary and Charles Moorman's *Arthurian Dictionary*, Phyllis Ann Karr's *King Arthur Companion*, and Ronan Coghlan's *Encyclopedia of Arthurian Legends* are all useful volumes that will prove helpful to varying degrees.[1] Yet they are all restricted in certain ways as well. In some cases such volumes draw primarily from Malory (or at best, from the major English and French romances—Malory, Sir Gawain and the Green Knight, Chrétien de Troyes, and the Vulgate Cycle), being therefore of limited value to those working with texts in other languages. They also tend to restrict themselves to the most prominent characters or literary texts. (That, I should note, is also true, by design, of Garland's *New Arthurian Encyclopedia*, which offers entries to only ninety or so of the major characters.)

In some instances, previous reference volumes identify characters by function or genealogy, but without telling us in which works they appear or how their function and identity may change from text to text. For example, the identification of Bedivere as the knight who returns Arthur's sword to the lake is informative, but it can also be misleading if we are left to infer that such a role is originally or universally assigned to him; Bruce thus notes that it was Girflet who disposed of the sword in the French Vulgate *Death of Arthur*. Bedivere assumed Girflet's role in the English tradition. The "movability" of some Arthurian roles is indeed an essential aspect of the legend, and it needs to be documented in all name dictionaries. (In the case at hand, it might be noted in passing that the Girflet/Bedivere role is sometimes taken by yet others, such as Perceval or even Lancelot in some modern novels and films. But that is material for another time and another book.)

The most obvious ways that Chris Bruce's volume distinguishes itself from preceding ones are related to scope, detail, and thoroughness. Instead of a few hundred or even a couple of thousand entries, Bruce offers over 5,600. Indeed, among the volumes mentioned here, Bruce's is the only source of information about the characters whose names stand at the beginning of this foreword.

But Bruce's *Dictionary* is not simply a listing of names. He gives considerable information about important characters and about the episodes and stories in which they appear. The entries on Arthur, Merlin, Morgan, and other major figures run to several pages and constitute small comparative studies of the characters' evolving roles in the elaboration of the legend. Still another particularly valuable feature of this book is Bruce's source table, which provides a quick indication of the sources and contents of a particular narrative and lists the major entries that give information about that narrative or author.

But further description of this admirable book is unnecessary. It will not take long for serious scholars and enthusiastic general readers alike to discover its features and its value. They will appreciate its thoroughness and its usefulness, and they will also find, as I have, that it is fascinating to peruse the volume even when one is not seeking to identify any particular character. And then they will quickly want to make room for it, as I also have, on a shelf that is close at hand.

Professor Norris J. Lacy
Department of French
Pennsylvania State University
August, 1998

---

[1] In a discussion of Arthurian name dictionaries, it would be inexcusable not to mention the two volumes by G.D. West. His *Index of Proper Names in French Arthurian Verse Romances 1150-1300* and *Index of Proper Names in French Arthurian Prose Romances* are thorough and accurate works of scholarship, and they are highly recommended. Yet their scope, too, is limited in the ways indicated by his titles.

Preface

The *Arthurian Name Dictionary* is intended as a general reference for Arthurian scholars, fans, and hobbyists. It lists proper names from nearly every "Arthurian" text written between the sixth century and the nineteenth, and for more than half of these (the most significant texts) is comprehensive, including all characters and places, major and minor, who appear in the texts. (I would have liked to be comprehensive for *all* texts, but the lack of availability of many minor sources prevented it; for more information, see the Sources appendix.) I used Tennyson's *Idylls of the King* as my final source, though the richness and diversity of modern authors' uses of traditional characters deserves its own volume, down the road.

I sincerely hope that this book is valuable to anyone interested in the Arthurian legends. Scholars should find it handy as an "Arthurian desk reference," and readers of modern Arthurian literature should have fun looking up how their favorite characters originated in the traditional legend. (Read T. H. White's depictions of Pellinore and the Questing Beast, then look up the entries here!) In this reference, I have dedicated myself to providing as many characters, places, objects, symbols, and themes—both major and minor—as I could, within reasonable space limitations. I hope, and expect, that what you find here is a more comprehensive catalogue of Arthurian proper names than has ever been published before.

A Few Words from the Author

I've saved most of my acknowledgements for the end of this preface, but right away I have to thank the person most responsible for this dictionary: Sir PETIPACE OF WINCHELSEA.

I first encountered Sir Petipace in Malory's *Le Morte Darthur* when I first read it in 1988. For some reason, out of all the characters listed in the book, his name stuck in my head like a bad song. Years went by before I picked up another Arthurian book, but if someone asked me to name a Knight of the Round Table, I said, "Sir Petipace of Winchelsea."

About 1993, I began studying the Arthurian legends in earnest, and to facilitate my studies, I set out to buy a dictionary or encyclopedia that catalogued Arthurian names. I eventually bought four, and for all of them, Petipace was the acid test. As soon as I opened a book, I would flip to the "P" section and try to find Sir Petipace of Winchelsea.

I never found him.

My first attempt to give Sir Petipace the recognition I thought he deserved, the "Sir Petipace of Winchelsea Society" (SPWS), died a quiet death after only several months despite what I thought was a successful "Petipace Pentecost Party" in 1995.

Next, I thought that Petipace's hometown might want to remember him, but repeated pleas to the officials of the town of Winchelsea, East Sussex, fell on deaf ears. It seems that Petipace had been demonized by those who judge him only by the actions at the end of his life (i.e., conspiring with Mordred and Agravain to expose Lancelot and Guinevere), without any regard to his noble deeds during his prime (i.e., the fight against Sir Tor).

After that, my campaign to promote Petipace took some strange turns. If you happened to be watching Game Three of the 1996 World Series, that was me with the Yankees cap and the cardboard sign that read "Malory I:3:9." ("'And my name,' said the other, 'is Sir Petipace of Winchelsea.'")

Motivated by the belief that poor old Petipace deserved his own entry, I began cataloguing all the proper names in *Le Morte Darthur*, just so I could keep them straight myself. Then, when I started reading Geoffrey of Monmouth, I added his characters to the list. From there, I expanded to other texts, gathered momentum, and three years later, this book rolled off my printer.

Sir Petipace of Winchelsea can be found on page 404. Pay him a visit.

Notes on the Entries

Commonly Used Names

As you read the entries, you may note that there are a number of names, places, phrases, and terms that I sling around without any explanation. For instance, I assume you know who Lancelot, Gawain, and Arthur are, and I assume that you are familiar with the Round Table, the Sword in the Stone, and the Roman War. I have tried to relate each entry to a familiar name, object, or situation, so you can understand the significance of the entry within only a few words.

Therefore, I recommend that you familiarize yourself with the following entries before you read anything else. These are characters, places, and objects central to the Arthurian legends, and most of the other entries try to refer back to one of these:

Arthur	Camlann	Galahad
Arthur's Battles	Chastity Test	Galehaut
Avalon	Corbenic	Gareth
Balin	Culhwch	Gawain
Bedivere	Erec	Girflet
Britain	Excalibur	Glastonbury
Camelot	Fisher King	Grail

Guinevere	Lucius	Rome
Guinglain	Mark	Round Table
Hector of the Fens	Meleagant	Saxons
Hengist	Merlin	Sword in the Stone
Hoel	Mordred	Tristan
Isolde	Morgan le Fay	Urien
Joseph of Arimathea	Palamedes	Uther
Kay	Perceval	Vortigern
Lady of the Lake	Picts	Yvain
Lancelot	Rions	

Designation of Knights

I use a number of phrases to indicate that a person is one of Arthur's knights, including "an Arthurian knight," "a knight in Arthur's service," "a knight of Arthur's court," "one of Arthur's knights," and "Arthur's Sir...." "Knight of the Round Table" is only used to describe knights who are specifically named, in at least one source, as a member of the Round Table fellowship.

"Knight" being a medieval term, the early chronicles and Welsh legends never refer to Arthur's warriors as "knights." Accordingly, all fighters in Arthur's suite that are named exclusively in the Welsh texts or the early chronicles are referred to as "warriors" in this book.

Source Codes

At the end of each entry, in brackets, is a series of codes that identify the Arthurian sources in which the character, place, object, symbol or theme mentioned in the entry appears. Use the "Sources" table at the back of the book to find the full name and description of the text based on the code.

The codes are also designed so, if you prefer, you can easily look up the full description of the source in *The New Arthurian Encyclopedia*. Each code contains just enough letters to identify a unique entry, alphabetically, in the *NAE*.

Translations

It has been my general policy to translate titles and sobriquets, but not proper names. For instance, *Le Chavlier de la Charrette* is listed under "Knight of the Cart," and Isolde *aux blanche mains* is "Isolde of the White Hands." However the knight Orguelleus, whose name means "proud," is still listed under "Orguelleus" because it is a proper name and not a title.

The exception to the translation policy is when an author writing in English has chosen to give a character a foreign language title. Malory does this often (e.g., "Geryne le Gros," "Severauce le Breuse"). These titles are only translated if the characters previously appeared in a non-English source.

Acknowledgements:

I owe thanks to a daunting number of people for their assistance and support with this book. First mention goes to my wife, TERRI, who, in addition to providing me invaluable love and support, also helped me edit the bulk of this book.

Second are the men and women of the INTERLIBRARY LOAN OFFICE at Northeastern University, Boston. I have never seen a more efficient, more productive group of people in my life. I put in request forms for dozens of books at a time, but the Interlibrary Loan Office never failed to find a single text. Some of the volumes they turned up should have been in museums. I was continually having conversations with them like this:

> **Me:** "I need an 1560 edition of *The Book of Taliesin* written in Welsh, in the original manuscript, with none of the pages missing. There are only four in the world. I'd like the one that was owned by Lady Charlotte Guest and has an inscription by Queen Victoria inside the front cover."

> **ILO Staff Person** (typing on his computer): "It'll be here on Tuesday."

PROFESSOR NORRIS J. LACY has my deepest gratitude, both for writing the foreword to this book and for encouraging me, at the beginning, to pursue this project. I would also thank the scholars and students on ARTHURNET, and particularly MICHELLE ZIEGLER, for providing assistance and advice along the way. Thanks to JUDY SHOAF for maintaining this invaluable electronic mailing list.

My appreciation to GARLAND PUBLISHING, and particularly my editor, KRISTI LONG, not only for agreeing to publish my book, but also for making available, to countless students of Arthurian literature, critical editions of dozens of texts.

Finally, I thank my friends and colleagues at the CAMBRIDGE POLICE DEPARTMENT, who, as people uninterested in Arthuriana, were able to provide me with a valuable "outsiders'" point of view, asking me thought-provoking questions like, "Aren't you done with that book yet?" And, "*What* is your book about? Again?" They are the modern-day Knights of the Round Table.

Select Bibliography

Key *primary* sources (i.e., the actual Arthurian texts) are listed in the "Sources" table at the back of this book. Listed below are secondary sources that I consulted and found particularly valuable in explaining origins of characters, places, objects, symbols, and themes.

General Reference

Coghlan, Ronan. *The Illustrated Encyclopedia of the Arthurian Legends*. Shaftesbury, Dorset: Element, 1993.

Lacy, Norris J., ed. *The New Arthurian Encyclopedia*. New York: Garland, 1996.
—, and Geoffrey Ashe. *The Arthurian Handbook*. New York: Garland, 1988.

Minary, Ruth, and Charles Moorman. *An Arthurian Dictionary*. Chicago: Academy Chicago, 1990.

West, G. D. *An Index of Proper Names in French Arthurian Prose Romances*. Toronto: University of Toronto Press, 1978.
—. *An Index of Proper Names in French Arthurian Verse Romances 1150–1300*. Toronto: University of Toronto Press, 1969.

History and Legend

Alcock, Leslie, ed. *Arthur's Britain*. London: Penguin, 1971.

Barber, R. W. *King Arthur: Hero and Legend*. New York: St. Martin, 1986.
—. *The Figure of Arthur*. London: Longman, 1972.

Chambers, E. K. *Arthur of Britain*. London: Sidgwick and Jackson, 1927.

Fletcher, Robert Huntington. *The Arthurian Material in the Chronicles, Especially Those of Great Britain and France*. Boston: Ginn, 1906.

Gilbert, Martin. *Atlas of British History*. New York: Oxford University Press, 1993.

Lindsay, Jack. *Arthur and His Times*. London: Muller, 1958.

MacNiocaill, Gearoid. *Ireland Before the Vikings*. Dublin: Gill and MacMillan, 1972.

Morris, John. *The Age of Arthur*. New York: Scribner, 1973.

Geographic and Topography

Ashe, Geoffrey. *A Guidebook to Arthurian Britain*. Longman: London, 1980.
—. *The Landscape of King Arthur*. New York: Holt, 1988.

—, ed. *The Quest for Arthur's Britain*. London: Praeger, 1968.

Glennie, John S. Stuart. *Arthurian Localities, Their Historical Origin, Chief Country, and Fingalian Relations; with a Map of Arthurian Scotland*. Felinfach: Llanerch, 1994.

Literature and Art

Benson, Larry D. *Malory's "Morte Darthur."* Cambridge: Harvard University Press, 1976.

Brinkley, Roberta F. *Arthurian Legend in the Seventeenth Century*. Baltimore: Johns Hopkins Press, 1932.

Bruce, James Douglas. *The Evolution of Arthurian Romance from the Beginnings Down to the Year 1300*, 2nd ed., 2 vols. Baltimore: Johns Hopkins Press, 1928.

Gardner, Edmund G. *The Arthurian Legend in Italian Literature*. London: Dent, 1930.

Loomis, Roger Sherman, ed. *Arthurian Literature in the Middle Ages: a Collaborative History*. Oxford: Clarendon, 1959.
—. *Arthurian Tradition and Chrétien de Troyes*. New Yor: Columbia University Press, 1949.
—. *The Development of Arthurian Romance*. New York: Harper and Row, 1963.
—. *The Grail: From Celtic Myth to Christian Symbol*. Cardiff: University of Wales Press, 1963.
—, and Laura Hibbard Loomis. *Arthurian Legends in Medieval Art*. London: Oxford University Press, 1938.

Lumiansky, R. M., ed. *Malory's Originality*. Baltimore: Johns Hopkins University Press, 1964.

Maynadier, Howard. *The Arthur of the English Poets*. Boston: Houghton Mifflin, 1907.

Merriman, James Douglas. *The Flower of Kings: a Study of the Arthurian Legend in England Between 1485 and 1835*. Lawrence: University Press of Kansas, 1973.

Murphy, Gerard. *The Ossianic Lore and Romantic Tales of Medieval Ireland*. Dublin: Three Candles, 1961.

Opie, Iona and Peter. *The Classic Fairy Tales*. New York: Oxford University Press, 1974.

Poag, James F. *Wolfram von Eschenbach*. New York: Twayne, 1972.

Weston, Jessie. *From Ritual to Romance*. Cambridge: Cambridge University Press, 1920.

A

AACENA
A forest through which Galahad and Tristan rode during the Grail Quest. [*PostQuest*]

AACHEN
A West German city named in the Alliterative *Morte Arthure* as part of Arthur's vast empire. [*Allit*]

AAMANZ
A knight whose physical similarity to Gawain lent him the nickname "the other Gawain." In pursuit of a knight named Gigamec, who had slain his brother, Aamanz was intercepted and challenged by another knight named Zedoech. The real Gawain happened along and stopped Aamanz as he was about to behead his opponent. Gawain and Aamanz battled, with Gawain emerging as the victor. When Aamanz refused to surrender, Gawain turned him over to Zedoech and Gigamec, who cruelly murdered him as soon as Gawain had left. Gigamec then bore Aamanz's head to Arthur's court, representing it as Gawain's. [*Heinrich*]

AANZIM
Steward of the castle Amonstus and the vassal of Lady Fortune. He hosted Gawain during the knight's visit to the country. [*Heinrich*]

AARON
An ally of Thereus, Arthur's Roman enemy. He ruled the kingdom of Armenia. [*Claris*]

ABADAN
A heathen knight slain by Arthur's Sir Lucan at the first battle of Carhaix. [*Arthour*]

ABAN
A kinsman of Lancelot who joined the Round Table to emulate his famous relative. He participated in the Grail Quest. [*PostQuest*]

ABASTUNAGIO
Son of Galehaut in *La Tavola Ritonda*. He ruled the castle Ferelois, where he held a tournament during the Grail Quest. His counterpart in French romance is GALEHODIN. [*Tavola*]

ABBEY OF THE CROSS
A Scottish abbey that served as the final resting place for Joseph of Arimathea in the Vulgate *Estoire del Saint Graal*. [*VulgEst*]

ABBLASOURE
A place visited by Galahad during the Grail Quest, just prior to his conquest of the Castle of Maidens. [*Malory*]

ABELLEUS [*Abelin]
The object of Tor's first quest. Abelleus stole a white brachet from Arthur's hall; Tor tracked him down and retrieved it. Having promised Abelleus's head to the hound's owner, Tor reluctantly decapitated him. [*PostMer*, *Malory*]

ABER DEU CLEDDYF ("Estuary of the Two Swords")
An estuary in southwest Dyfed (Wales) where Arthur and his warriors journeyed to retrieve the pups of the enchanted hound Rhymi. Obtaining the dogs was one of Culhwch's tasks. Arthur received directions from Tringad, a local resident. [*Culhwch*]

ABER TYWI
A Welsh estuary where the Tywi river empties into the Bristol Channel. Here Arthur and his men fought one of several battles against the boar Twrch Trwyth, and the warriors Cynan and Gwilenhin were slain. From here, the chase moved on to Glynn Ystun. [*Culhwch*]

ABERERCH
The grave site of Rhydderch the Generous, king of Cumbria and brother-in-law of Merlin. [*WelshSG*]

ABESSA
A mute maiden who lived with her blind mother, Corceca, in Spenser's *The Faerie Queene*. In Spenser's allegory, the women are an unflattering portrayal of monasticism. The women lodged Princess Una after she was abandoned by her protector, the Red Cross Knight. Abessa's lover, Kirkrapine, was killed by Una's pet lion when he tried to break into their house. [*Spenser*]

ABILAN OF ESTRANGOT
An Arthurian knight who was unsuccessful in the Perilous Passage adventure. [*Palamedes*]

ABILAS [*Ausile*]

One of four brothers (Abilas, Casibilant, Dion, and Dyonis) who aided their uncle, Duke Calles, in a revolt led by Calles' sons. Abilas and his brothers were joined by Gaheris, Agravain, and Gareth. [*VulgLanc*]

ABINORS

Duke of Scottish Borderlands and the Isles. He made war on Uther Pendragon. Merlin abducted his daughter and imprisoned her on the Turning Island, causing Abinors to die of grief. [*Livre*]

ABIRON

A land of which Segurant, a renowned knight of Uther Pendragon's court, became king. [*Palamedes*]

ABRIORIS

A knight who joined the Round Table after Perceval visited his castle, slew his ferocious lions, defeated him in combat, and sent him to Arthur's court. [*Contin2*]

ABUDAR

Father of Arthur's warrior Regian. [*Wace*]

ACADOES [*Escades*]

A fine knight in the service of King Bagdemagus of Gorre. He guarded the Sword Bridge between Logres and Gorre. When he died, Meleagant assumed his post. [*VulgLanc*]

ACANOR

A black knight from the castle Amalvi. Acanor and his father were both Christians, but Acanor's dark skin led other's to call him the UGLY HERO. Under this alias, he enjoyed many adventures as Arthur's knight. There may be some connection with ESCANOR. [*PostMer*]

ACANTAN THE AGILE

A kinsman of Lancelot who joined the Round Table to emulate his famous relative. He participated in the Grail Quest. He may be the same character as ACORANT. [*PostQuest*]

ACARIVE

A lady from Lyonesse who figures into Tristan's ancestry. Acarive's daughter committed adultery and was executed on the advice of Queen Gloriande of Lyonesse. In revenge, Acarive tried to frame Gloriande for adultery, forging a letter which suggested that Gloriande was having an affair with a knight named Amanz. King Apollo of Lyonesse, Gloriande's wife and Tristan's ancestor, saw through the ploy and executed Acarive. [*ProsTris*]

ACCALON [*Accolon*]

A knight from Gaul. Morgan le Fay, Accalon's lover, used him as an unwilling participant in a plot against Arthur. She provided him with Excalibur, which she had stolen, and arranged for him to champion a knight named Ontzlake against Ontzlake's brother Damas. Meanwhile, however, Damas had tricked Arthur into fighting as *his* champion. Both knights met in combat—Accalon thinking he was fighting Damas, and Arthur thinking he was fighting Ontzlake. Since Arthur had a fake version of Excalibur and its scabbard, and Accalon had the real one, Arthur fared poorly in the battle. As Accalon prepared to deliver the killing blow, Nimue arrived and caused Excalibur to fall from Accalon's hands. Arthur picked up the sword, struck Accalon to the ground, removed his helmet, and realized Morgan's treachery. After receiving Arthur's forgiveness, Accalon died. Arthur had him buried at St. Stephen's church in Camelot. A plot by Morgan to avenge his death failed. [*PostMer, Malory*]

ACCURSED CEMETERY

A graveyard in Ireland visited by Arthur's Sir Cliges in *Les Merveilles de Rigomer*. Cliges learned that any knight who entered the cemetery was bound to die there—a custom that Cliges ended by slaying the lord of the surrounding land. [*Merveil*]

ACECLEDOR

A king in Arthur's service in *Floriant et Florete*. He joined Arthur's campaign against Maragoz, an enemy. [*Floriant*]

ACES [*Acon, Ates*]

A young nobleman from Beaumont in Quimper-Corentin. His father was named Ales and he had a brother named Alon. As a companion of the brothers Yvain, he fought against the Saxons in the early days of Arthur's reign. Arthur knighted him for his service and appointed him to the Round Table. His cousin, Duke Galescalain of Clarence, made him the constable of Clarence. [*VulgMer, Livre, Arthour*]

ACHADENS

A knight who wounded Tristan during a joust. [*ProsTris*]

ACHEFLOUR

Arthur's sister and Perceval's mother in the Middle English *Sir Perceval of Galles*. Her husband, also named Perceval, was slain by the Red Knight, leading Acheflour to raise Perceval ignorant of war and knighthood so that he might avoid the same fate. Eventually, Perceval left for Arthur's court. Acheflour went insane when she mistakenly thought Perceval had been killed. At the end of the romance, however—and in contrast to other Perceval romances in which his mother dies—Perceval and Acheflour are joyously reunited and Acheflour regains her sanity. Her name is probably a corruption of BLANCHEFLOUR. [*SirPerc*]

ACHEN

Father of Arthur's warrior Gusg. [*Culhwch*]

ACHILLES[1]

In *Perlesvaus*, Gawain encounters a descendant of the Greek hero—a knight in the habit of slaying other knights who lodged at his tent. After defeating him, Gawain had to thrust his sword through the sole of the knight's foot in order to kill him. This was apparently the case with all of Achilles' descendants. [*Perlesvaus*]

ACHILLES[2] THE BLOND

A squire of Sir Bors. After many years of faithful service, Bors knighted him and made him lord of the Forbidden Hill castle. [*VulgLanc*]

ACLAMET

A maidservant of Amurfina. She served a love potion to Gawain, which caused him to fall in love with and marry Aclamet's mistress. Aclamet herself loved Arthur's Sir Aumagwin. [*Heinrich*]

ACORANT THE AGILE [*Acorante, Acourant*]

Knight of the Round Table, brother of Danubre the Brave, and kinsman of Lancelot. During the Grail Quest, he was slain by Arpian of the Narrow Mountain, who hated Lancelot's family for their prowess. His death was swiftly avenged by Danubre. He may be the same character as ACANTAN the Agile. [*PostQuest, ProsTris*]

ACORDE THE INSOLENT [*Licoridés*]

One of the noble Byzantine warriors that the knight Alexander brought to Britain from Constantinople. He fought for Arthur in the battle against the traitor Angres of Windsor. [*ChretienC*]

ACORIONDES

One of the noble warriors that the knight Alexander brought to Britain from Constantinople. He fought for Arthur in the battle against the traitor Angres of Windsor. [*ChretienC*]

ACOSTANT

A Knight of the Round Table who participated in the Grail Quest. [*ProsTris*]

ACQUILEIA [*Aquilea*]

An ancient Roman city on the northern edge of the Adriatic Sea, where, according to the chronicles, Maximus was executed after his failed attempt to conquer Rome. Wolfram says that Perceval's paternal uncle Trevrizent explored the city during his travels. [*Gildas, Nennius, Wolfram*]

ACQUILLANS OF THE GREEN MOUNTAIN

Cousin of Arthur's Sir Hervi of Rivel. [*Palamedes*]

ACQUITAIN

In Eilhart von Oberge's *Tristrant*, an evil little dwarf whose astrological powers won him a place in Mark's court. He divined the affair between Tristan and Isolde, and conspired to expose it to Mark. Acquitain appears in Béroul as FROCIN, and in Gottfried von Strassburg as MELOT from Aquitaine. [*Eilhart*]

ACRASIA

A beautiful sorceress in Spenser's *The Faerie Queene* who ruled the Bower of Bliss, a garden that contained all things arousing to the physical senses. Her custom was to lure knights into the Bower and turn them into animals. Gloriana, the Fairy Queen, sent Sir Guyon to destroy the Bower. Guyon resisted Acrasia's seductions, captured her, and destroyed her garden. [*Spenser*]

ACRE

A city on the coast of Israel. Crusaders besieged the city between 1190 and 1191. Many of them were siezed by an illness. In Béroul's *Tristan*, Tristan, disguised as a beggar as part of an elaborate ruse to vindicate Isolde (see MAL PAS), claims that his hands are "stiffened by the illness called 'Mal d'Acre.'" This allusion has been taken by some critics to date the romance later than 1191. [*Beroul, Claris*]

ACRICOR THE HANDSOME

A Knight of the Round Table who participated in the Grail Quest. [*ProsTris*]

ACUBERT

A Saxon knight defeated by Arthur's Sir Hervi. [*Prophecies*]

ADALON

One of the kings of Listenois in *Palamedes*. His brother was the Lord of the Narrow Borderland and his sister was the Queen of Orkney. He was a companion of Hector the Brown. [*Palamedes*]

ADAM THE FAIR [*Adaind, Adayn*]

One of Arthur's knights. He twice accompanied Gawain and a collection of other knights on a quest to find Lancelot. [*VulgLanc*]

ADAMEINS

A British king mentioned in *Arthour and Merlin* among those who could not be counted on to help against the invading heathens. [*Arthour*]

ADAN

The Arabian count of Alarie. At a battle in Damascus, Adan was captured by King Roaz of Glois, who had slain Adan's three brothers. As Roaz's prisoner, Adan was assigned to guard the gates of Roaz's castle. He was freed from this service when Wigalois (Gawain's son) journeyed to Glois and killed Roaz. In gratitude, Adan swore fealty to Wigalois and was baptized. He joined Wigalois in a war against King Lion of Namur, in which Adan's granddaughter, the knight Marnie, was killed by Duke Galopear of Greece. Adan avenged her death by slaying Galopear. [*Wirnt*]

ADDANZ

Perceval's great-grandfather in Wolfram's *Parzvial*. Descended from fairies, he was the son of Lazaliez and the father of Gandin. An active warrior, Addanz died in combat. [*Wolfram*]

ADE

Lancelot's lover in Ulrich's *Lanzelet*. She was the daughter of a the famous huntsman Patricius von den Bigen, and she was raised by her uncle, Linier, in the castle Limors. Lancelot came to Limors during his early adventures, and ran afoul of the ill-tempered Linier even as Ade cast eyes his way. Lancelot ended up killing Linier in combat, and he and Ade became paramours. Ade gave him her brother Tybalt as a squire. During an outing, Lancelot succumbed to the enchantment of the Schatel le Mort, which turned brave knights into cowards. Ade, seeing Lancelot acting cowardly, and not knowing of the enchantment, abandoned him in disgust and never saw him again.

Ade is not found in any other romance. It seems more than a coincidence that Hugh de Morville (who provided Ulrich with his source) had a mother and daughter named Ada. [*UlrichZ*]

ADELONS THE GAY

A knight who fought on the side of King Urien and the King of North Wales during a tournament at the city of Levegnic. [*Palamedes*]

ADELUF III

One of Arthur's sons in Rauf de Boun's *Petit Brut*. His brothers were Morgan the Black and Patrick the Red. Adelufs I and II were kings who preceded Arthur. [*ProsBrut*]

ADIMPONS

A castle where Morgan le Fay once kept Lionel prisoner. [*Palamedes*]

ADNAIN

In *La Tavola Ritonda*, a courteous knight who lodged Tristan during his travels. In return for his hospitality, Tristan forced Adnain's mortal enemy, Count Balie, to make peace. His name bears a similarity to DANAIN THE RED of the *Palamedes*. [*Tavola*]

ADOLANGE

One of Arthur's knights in *La Tavola Ritonda*. He fought in the Leverzep tournament. [*Tavola*]

ADORAS OF THE ISLAND OF THE DOOR

A Knight of the Round Table. [*ProsTris*]

ADRAGAIN THE BROWN [*Adragein)(s*), *Adragenis, Agrauein(s*)]

An early Knight of the Round Table who first served Uther Pendragon. He came from the Black Isle and was the brother of Mador the Black. He fought for Arthur in the early wars against King Rions and the Saxons, and he helped Sir Aglovale defend the Waste Land when Agrippe (Rions' uncle) invaded. He later became a monk in Benoic, and he upbraided Arthur for neglecting to help Kings Ban and Bors when they were attacked by King Claudas. [*VulgLanc, VulgMer, Livre, Arthour*]

ADRIAN

A knight in the service of one of the kings who rebelled against Arthur in the early days of his reign. He was noted for his bravery in a battle against the Saxons near Cambenic. [*VulgMer*]

ADTHERPE

In Malory, a knight who found Isolde weeping in the forest, about to drown herself in a well, after she escaped from an abduction by Palamedes. Adtherpe gave her harbor in his castle, and then rode to fight Palamedes. Palamedes defeated him, and made him reveal Isolde's location. The same character appears in the Prose *Tristan* unnamed; *La Tavola Ritonda* calls him GUIRLANDOT. [*ProsTris, Malory*]

ADVENTUROUS BED

An alternate name for the PERILOUS BED found in the Grail legends. [*VulgLanc*]

ADVENTUROUS CASTLE

Another name for CORBENIC, the Grail Castle. [*ProsTris*]

ADVENTUROUS FORD [*Gué Aventuros*]

A ford in Cornwall. After Tristan and Isolde had lived in the forest of Morrois for a time, Mark agreed to take Isolde back. The exchange took place at the ford. Later, the Adventurous Ford was the location where Isolde proclaimed her innocence before a large assembly. [*Beroul*]

ADVENTUROUS SEATS

According to *La Tavola Ritonda*, the Round Table seats occupied by the knights errant—in contrast to the Royal Seat (occupied by Arthur) and the Perilous Seat (filled by no one until Galahad). [*Tavola*]

ADVENTUROUS SWORD [*Espee Aventureuse*]

The sword that had belonged to Balin the Savage. It appears in several texts, but is not named in all of them.

Balin had received it from a servant of the Lady of the Island of Avalon, and he used it to behead the Lady of the Lake. The Lady of Avalon's messenger told Balin that the sword would bring him sorrow. Later, he used it to kill his brother Balan, receiving a mortal wound himself in the process. This episode occurred on Merlin's Island. Merlin took the sword and thrust it into a block of marble. Gawain saw the sword on the island and was told by a hermit that the weapon, in the hand of his best friend, would cause his death. Evidently, the hermit was referring to Gawain's battle with Lancelot, but if Lancelot ever received the sword, we are not told. Instead, the block of marble floated up to Camelot at the beginning of the Grail Quest. Gawain tried to draw it from the stone, failed, and was informed that he would suffer for having tried. Galahad drew the sword, girded it upon himself, and apparently kept it until he received the Sword of the Strange Hangings. (Possibly, he gave the Adventurous Sword to Lancelot, his father, after receiving the latter.) Fulfilling the second prophecy against Gawain, Galahad struck Gawain down with the sword during the Grail Quest, putting Gawain out of commission for the rest of the adventure. [*VulgLanc, VulgQuest, PostMer*]

AEDAN MAC GABRAIN

Father of Arthur of Dalriada, a possible historical prototype for King Arthur. Aedan ruled the kingdom of Dalriada (modern Argyll and Kintyre) in the late sixth century. He was known for his prolific warfare; and Arthur of Dalriada was killed in one of Aedan's battles against the Picts, at Miathi (Barber, *Figure*, 21–33). Aedan, called "the Wily," appears in a Welsh Triad, in which he visits the court of Rhydderch the Generous, killed all of the beasts, ate all of the food, and drank all of the wine. [*Triads*]

AEDD

A Welsh character adopted from Irish mythology. A Welsh Triad holds that Aedd's son, Prydein, conquered and named Britain. In *Culhwch and Olwen*, two of Arthur's warriors—Gwitart and Odgar—are noted as Aedd's sons, and Aedd himself is called the King of Ireland. [*Triads, Culhwch*]

ÆGELESTHREP [*Ægelsthrep*]

A British plain where in 455, according to the *Anglo-Saxon Chronicle*, Vortigern fought a battle against Horsa and Hengist, and Horsa was killed. Arthurian chroniclers place this battle at EPISFORD. [*Anglo*]

ÆLLE [*Aella*]

A Saxon war-leader who came to Britain from Germany in 477, with his sons Cymen, Wlencing, and Cissa. He landed at Cymenesora and defeated a Briton army at Aldredeslea. In 485, he fought a battle at Mearcredesburna and, in 491, with his son Cissa, he defeated the Britons again at Andredsceaster. The *Anglo-Saxon Chronicle* does not link him to Arthurian tradition, but if Arthur existed, Aelle

would have been his contemporary (and probable opponent). [*Bede, Anglo*]

ÆNEAS

A hero of Greek mythology. As a member of the house of Troy, he journeyed to Italy after the Trojan War and became the ruler of Rome. Nennius and Geoffrey of Monmouth make him the ancestor of Brutus, the first king of Britain. In *King Arthur*, Dryden names him as Arthur's ancestor. [*Nennius, GeoffHR, Dryden*]

ÆSC

A son of Hengist who assisted and succeeded his father in the beginnings of the Saxon conquest of Britain. Æsc joined the war in 456 or 457 and won a battle at Creacanford in Kent. In 465, he again defeated the Britons at Wippedsfleot. He won another victory with his father in 473, and became the ruler of Kent in 488. Mentioned in the non-Arthurian *Anglo-Saxon Chronicle*, he may be identical to EOSA or ASCHIL of Arthurian tradition. [*Anglo*]

AETHLEM

A hound needed by Culhwch, as one of his tasks, to hunt the boar Twrch Trwyth. Other tasks required that Culhwch find certain people to manage Aethlem. Arthur obtained the dog for his kinsman. After the hunt, Aethlem could not be found and was never seen again. [*Culhwch*]

ÆTIUS [*Agitius*]

Historically, a steward of Gaul under the Roman emperor Valentinian in the second quarter of the fifth century. According to the Arthurian chronicles, the Britons entreated him for assistance when, after the Roman withdrawal, Britain was invaded by Picts and Scots. Beset by martial problems at home, Ætius refused to send aid. The Britons took their plea to King Aldroen of Brittany, who sent them his brother, Arthur's grandfather, Constantine. [*Gildas, Nennius, GeoffHR*]

AFANC [*Adanc*]

A lake monster killed by Peredur. In modern Welsh, the word means "beaver," but the *Peredur* creature is a terrible beast that devours maidens and throws poisoned spears at anyone who tries to enter its cave—characteristics uncommon to beavers. On his way to slay the afanc, Peredur met the Empress of Constantinople. She gave him a magic stone, which turned him invisible. He entered the cave unseen and killed the monster with his spear. In another legend, Arthur was said to have slain one of the creatures himself on the shores of LLYN BARFOG. [*Peredur*]

AFAON [*Addaon*]

One of Arthur's warriors in Welsh legend. The son of Taliesin the bard, he was slain by Llawgad or Llongad. The Triads note cryptically that Afaon avenged his death from the grave. [*Triads, Dream*]

AFARNACH

In a poem in the Welsh *Black Book of Carmarthen*, Cei remarks that "though Arthur was but playing, blood was flowing in the hall of Afarnach, fighting with a hag." This passage may recall a familiar legend, represented in *Culhwch and Olwen* when Arthur kills the BLACK HAG. [*WelshPG*]

AFFALACH

The Welsh name for AVALON, but also the name of the Celtic goddess Modron's father, who was said to rule an otherworldly island. William of Malmesbury places his residence at Avalon. His name may be echoed in EVALACH from the Grail histories. [*WilliamM, Triads*]

AFFIBLA DELET

A Knight of the Round Table in Hartmann von Aue's *Erec*. [*HartmannE*]

AFFINAMUS[1] OF AMANTISIN

A duke from the Middle-East or Africa who became the vassal of Feirefiz, Perceval's half-brother. [*Wolfram*]

AFFINAMUS[2] OF CLITIERS

A comrade of Gramoflanz, Gawain's brother-in-law. [*Wolfram*]

AFFRAUDIS

A kingdom to which Tristan journeyed during one of his exiles from Cornwall. He was accompanied by Dinadan and his squire, Alcardo. [*Tavola*]

AFLAWN [*Halwyn*]

Father of Arthur's warrior Huarwar. His name means "not full." [*Culhwch*]

AFRICA

Only Welsh legend suggests that Arthur himself had any involvement with this continent; at least, Arthur's chief gatekeeper Glewlwyd claims to have been in Africa, and possibly implies some Arthurian association. In Geoffrey, the King of Africa, Munstensar, is an ally of the Roman Procurator Lucius and joins the war against Arthur. Wolfram gives Farjelastis, an ally of Perceval's brother Feirefiz, as the Duke of Africa. Gottfried von Strassburg says that King Gurmun of Ireland, Isolde's father, was the son of the King of Africa; and the Norse *Saga of Tristan and Ísönd* names it as Rions' home land. A further Norse Tristan legend says that it was ruled by a King Turnes, who conquered Spain. [*Culhwch, GeoffHR, Wolfram, Gottfried, TrisSaga, SagaTI*]

AGAD

Merlin made the Ship of Joy for the king of Northumberland and his friend Agad. The Ship was used by Tristan and Isolde. [*ProsTris*]

AGALONE

A king in Arthur's service in *La Tavola Ritonda*. Agalone served as steward of Britain, along with a fellow king named Allielle, while Arthur was away in Gaul. He thus occupies the role assigned to CARADOC SHORTARM in the Prose *Tristan*. [*Tavola*]

AGALUS

A vassal of Lord Golagros in the Scots poem of *Golagros*. During the war between Golagros and Arthur, Agalus was captured by Arthur's knights. [*Golagros*]

AGAMANOR

A knight from Normandy who married Phenonee, sister of Arthur's Sir Meliador. [*Froissart*]

AGAMENOR [*Ganemor*]

A Knight of the Round Table and companion of Arpian of the Narrow Mountain and Amatin the Good Jouster. The trio hated any knights of Lancelot's family, and they consequently attacked Acorant the Agile and Danubre the Brave, two of Lancelot's kinsmen, during the Grail Quest. Agamenor and Danubre were the last two survivors of the bloody brawl, and they killed each other. [*PostQuest*]

AGANO

A knight who, with his brother Agion, joined their cousin Harpin in his siege of the Castle of Three Maidens. Sir Hector of the Fens and the King with the Hundred Knights arrived to defend the castle, and Agano and Agion were killed. [*Palamedes*]

AGANOR

A knight in the service of King Mordrain, ruler of the Arabain kingdom of Sarras. When Mordrain left his land to seek Joseph of Arimathea in Britain, he bequeathed his kingdom to Aganor. [*VulgEst*]

AGAR

A healer who treated Tristan after he received a mortal wound at the hands of Bedalis. [*ProsTris*]

AGARAN [*Aguarus, Aragan*]

A young knight whose lands were invaded by the Count of the Valley. Agaran's uncle, a holy man, left his hermitage to come to Agaran's aid. The two of them defeated the Count, but the Count's nephews subsequently slew Agaran's uncle in his cloister. During the Grail Quest, Lancelot visited the hermitage and saw the body. Lancelot's host conjured a devil to explain the circumstances of the man's death. [*VulgQuest, Malory*]

AGARDAS

The home of Hardifius and Elimas, two warriors who participated in King Leigamar's tournament at Sorgarda. [*Heinrich*]

AGARIZ

A vassal of the duke of Aram. He participated in King Leigamar's tournament at Sorgarda. [*Heinrich*]

AGARNICES OF COLOGNE

One of nine clerics sent by Arthur to Sorelois, to help King Galehaut interpret a disturbing dream. [*VulgLanc*]

AGEN

One of Lancelot's French lands. Lancelot appointed Sir Cleges earl of Agen in return for Cleges' support in Lancelot's war against King Arthur. [*Malory*]

AGGA

Attendant to Rowena, Vortigern's wife, in Thelwall's *The Fairy of the Lake*. [*Thelwall*]

AGIA

Tristan's step-mother and Meliadus's second wife in *La Tavola Ritonda*. The daughter of King Bramo, she is unnamed in previous versions of the legend, including the Prose *Tristan*. She hated Tristan because he stood to inherit Lyoness ahead of her own son, Allegreno. Her first attempt to poison Tristan ended in failure when Meliadus nearly drank the poisoned tonic himself, and Agia had to confess her treachery to save her husband. Meliadus sentenced her to die, but the generous Tristan intervened and his father spared her. She tried to murder Tristan a second time, but a nurse accidentally served the potion to young Allegreno, who died. Meliadus did not punish his wife, but he never spoke to her again. [*Tavola*]

AGION

A knight who, with his brother Agano, joined their cousin Harpin in his siege of the Castle of Three Maidens. Sir Hector of the Fens and the King with the Hundred Knights arrived to defend the castle, and Agion and Agano were killed. [*Palamedes*]

AGLANT

A Knight of the Round Table from Brittany. He and Sir Tor sought to learn the fate of Merlin, after he had been imprisoned by Nimue. In their travels, they encountered Bagdemagus, who resented them for having been promoted to the Round Table ahead of him. After defeating them both in joust, Bagdemagus told them of Merlin's fate. [*PostMer*]

AGLEOT

A Saxon king who invaded Scotland. Arthur and Lancelot repelled the invasion at the battle of Arestel. At the battle of the Ford of Blood, Agleot's brother Aramont was captured. [*LancLac, VulgLanc*]

AGLINDA [*Aglinde*]

The maiden daughter of King Nascor. The devil tricked her brother, Nabor, into raping her by a spring, but Aglinda prayed, and Nabor fell dead. In memory of Aglinda's plight, the spring was called the Spring of the Virgin, and it was enchanted to paralyze visiting non-virgin knights. Erec became one of its victims [*PostQuest*]

AGLOANS

In Renaut de Bâgé's *Le Bel Inconnu*, a king from the land of Escoce, in northeastern Scotland. His sister, Margerie, was rescued from two giants by Gawain's son Guinglain. His name may be a variation of ANGUSEL, several of which occur in Renaut's poem. [*Renaut*]

AGLOAS [*Magloas*]

One of Arthur's knights in the Vulgate *Lancelot*. He joined one of Gawain's quests to locate a missing Lancelot. [*LancLac, VulgLanc*]

AGLONDE [*Agloride*]

A river in Gorre visited by Lancelot. There, he met a maiden who later died of love for him. [*VulgLanc*]

AGLONS OF THE VALLEY

A Knight of the Round Table who participated in the Grail Quest. [*ProsTris*]

AGLOVALE [*Agglovale, Agloval, Agravale, Engloval(e)*]

Son of King Pellinore and the Widowed Lady, and brother of Perceval, Lamorat, Meliodam, Alain, Drians, and Tor (all brothers do not appear in the same source). He first appears in the Vulgate *Lancelot*, where his primary function is to convey his young brother Perceval to Arthur's court. In the *Livre d'Artus*, he joins Arthur's service during the Saxon wars. Fourteen of his brothers were killed when King Agrippe invaded the Waste Forest, his mother's home, but Aglovale eventually killed Agrippe in combat. The Dutch romance of *Morien* gives him a son named Morien, fathered by Aglovale on a Moorish princess. In the Dutch tale, Aglovale eventually marries the Saracen woman and becomes king of an Arabian land, but in the Vulgate romances he is slain either by Gawain during the Grail Quest or by Lancelot during the rescue of Guinevere from the stake. In the Third Continuation of Chrétien's *Perceval*, he dies seven years after Perceval becomes the Grail King. His death prompts Perceval to retire to a hermitage. [*VulgLanc, VulgQuest, Contin3, Livre, PostMer, PostMer, PostQuest, Perchevael, Morien, Malory*]

AGNED

A British hill that in Nennius was site of Arthur's eleventh battle against the Saxons (see ARTHUR'S BATTLES). As in all of the twelve battles, Arthur was victorious. Geoffrey of

Monmouth identifies Agned with the Dolorous Mountain, where the CASTLE OF MAIDENS stood. Geoffrey seems to mean Edinburgh in Scotland, though it is unsure whether Nennius intended this identification. Another theory holds that Agned is a corruption of Andegavum, or Angers in France. Some manuscripts of Nennius substitute BREGUOIN for Agned. [Nennius, GeoffHR, TennIK]

AGNENA

The sister of Medea, the lecherous female ruler of Crudele castle. Her other sisters included Lavina, Bresenda, and Pulizena. [Tavola]

AGOSTES

Mother-in-law of Bredbeddle, the Green Knight in *The Grene Knight*. Her daughter loved Gawain, so she provided her son-in-law with the magic to lure Gawain to his castle. She takes the place of MORGAN LE FAY from *Sir Gawain and the Green Knight*. [Grene]

AGOYER THE CRUEL

A peer of Sir Bors who swore fealty to the daughter of King Brandegorre of Estrangorre after a tournament there. He promised to decapitate any knight he defeated, and to send her the head. [VulgLanc]

AGRAVADAIN[1] OF THE VALES OF GALORE

A Knight of the Round Table and brother of Belias. His companions were Moneval and Minoras the Wicked. The trio took a friendly rivalry between the Round Table and the Queen's Knights too far, and they deliberately sought out three Queen's Knights to attack. Agravadain was wounded by Sagremor in the battle, but other knights fortunately intervened before any lives were lost. He died soon afterwards, and was replaced at the Round Table by Banin. "Galore" my indicate Galloway. [VulgLanc, VulgMer, Livre]

AGRAVADAIN[2] THE BLACK

A vassal of Arthur and Lord of the Castle of the Fens. His daughter was desired by Merlin, and then, because of an enchantment cast by Merlin, by King Ban of Benoic, who slept with her and fathered Hector. Because of her lost virginity, Agravadain had to deter any suitors. One of them, Sir Leriador, was so angry that he besieged the Castle of the Fens, but Agravadain triumphed. [VulgMer]

AGRAVAIN [Aggravain, Agrafrayn, Agravan, Agravano, Agreuein, Egrefayn, Engrevain(s), Gefferen, Geffreyn, Griffayn]

A Knight of the Round Table. Son of Lot and Morgause, brother of Gawain, Gaheris, Gareth, and Mordred. First mentioned by Chrétien de Troyes, he has a minor role in *Perceval*. His character was expanded in the Vulgate *Lancelot*, and he becomes a major figure in Malory, as one of the instruments of Arthur's downfall.

He accompanied his brothers when they abandoned their father for service with Arthur. He fought against the Saxons, was knighted by Arthur, and served the king in Gaul and Saxony. He liberated the prisoners of the Hill of Wretches. In Jehan Froissart's *Meliador*, he courts and marries Florée, a princess from Scotland, while in Malory, he marries Laurel, the niece of his sisters-in-law.

Portrayed as egotistical, proud, and uncourtly knight with a misshapen body, Agravain resented any honorable and brave warrior. He was handsome and skilled at arms, but he lacked knightly virtues such as mercy and compassion. He was ignoble towards women, and quarrelsome with his own brothers. His misdeeds include participation in the murder of Lamorat (part of a feud between the families of Pellinore and Lot); the slaying of Dinadan during the Grail Quest, with his brother Mordred; and the abduction of the King of North Wales' daughter, during which he was terribly wounded and had to be cured with the blood of Gawain and Lancelot.

His greatest offense was wrought near the end of Arthur's reign, when he conspired with Mordred to expose the affair between Lancelot and Guinevere. When Arthur was away from court, the two brothers roused a band of knights and captured the lovers *in flagrante delicto* in Guinevere's chambers. Agravain was slain by Lancelot, either at the ensuing battle outside Guinevere's room, when Lancelot rescued Guinevere from execution, or at the siege of Joyous Guard. [ChretienP, LancLac, VulgLanc, VulgMer, Livre, PostMer, PostQuest, PostMort, Tavola, Stanz, Froissart, Malory]

AGRAVAIN'S HILL

A hill formerly known as the HILL OF WRETCHES. Its lords, Druas the Cruel and Sorneham of Newcastle, imprisoned good knights there until it was liberated by Agravain and Gaheris. [VulgLanc]

AGRAVEIL [Agrauel]

A good knight who fought on the side of Arthur and Leodegan in a battle against the Saxons at Camilyard. His mother was known as the Wise Lady of the Forest of No Return. [VulgMer]

AGREGAM THE ANGRY

A Knight of the Round Table who embarked with his fellows on the Grail Quest. [PostQuest]

AGRESIZIA

Perceval's sister in *La Tavola Ritonda*. She accompanied Perceval, Bors, and Galahad during a portion of the Grail Quest. She provided a girdle, fashioned from her own hair, for Galahad's Sword with the Strange Hangings. The questers visited the castle Aspetta Ventura, where the castle's lady, Verdoana, was dying of leprosy. It was said that only the blood of a pure virgin could cure Verdoana, and she asked for some of Agresizia's blood for this purpose. After Galahad, Perceval, and Bors fought valiantly but in vain with the castles knights, Agresizia consented to provide the blood and died during the bleeding. Perceval buried her in the holy city of Sarras.

Agresizia's character appears in the same context, but is unnamed, in the Vulgate *Queste del Saint Graal* and its successors. Perceval's sister is known as DINDRANE in *Perlesvaus*. [*Tavola*]

AGRESTES

An ancient pagan king of Camelot. When Josephus, the son of Joseph of Arimathea, began converting Agrestes' people to Christianity, the king pretended to go along. As soon as Josephus had left, however, Agrestes forced his people back to their heathen religion and killed the disciples that Josephus had left in the city. Following this massacre, Agrestes went mad, began to eat his hands, slaughtered his family, and finally committed suicide by diving into a fire. After his death, Josephus returned and converted Camelot to Christianity for good. [*VulgEst*]

AGRICOL THE WELL-SPOKEN [*Agrocol*]

A peer of Sir Bors. He performed well in a tournament thrown by King Brandegorre of Estrangorre, and he swore fealty to Brandegorre's daughter. [*VulgLanc*]

AGRICOLA

A king who lived in the traditional Arthurian period. John Morris discusses him in *The Age of Arthur*. According to several sources, Agricola liberated Demetia (Dyfed) from the pagan Irish *Ui Liathain* clan, driving them out of Britain. Agricola apparently became king of Dyfed in about AD 500. He was the son of Tribunis (which may have been a title rather than a personal name) and the father of Vortipore. Agricola is one of the few persons spoken of with favor by Gildas. Agricola may have been an ally or even a general of a historical Arthur. [*Gildas*]

AGRIPPE[1] [*Agrippes*]

The King of Mabon Rock. He was besieged by a king named Vadalon, but Agrippe's daughter poisoned the water supply used by the besiegers, and they were forced to abandon the assault. In revenge, Vadalon imprisoned Agrippe's daughter in iron bands, from which she was eventually released by Sir Bors. [*VulgLanc*]

AGRIPPE[2]

Uncle of King Rions, Arthur's enemy. He invaded the Waste Land, owned by Perceval's mother, and killed fourteen of the lady's sons. Aglovale, one of the surviving sons, raised an army of Arthur's knights, encountered Agrippe's forces, and finally killed Agrippe. [*Livre*]

AGRIPPE[3] THE TALL [*Agrippa, Gryp*]

A count or earl whose lands bordered on those of King Hoel of Brittany. Agrippe waged war on Hoel, besieging the town of Alinge and wounding Kahedin, Hoel's son. On the verge of defeat, Hoel enlisted the aid of Tristan, who subsequently killed Agrippe's nephew, Alquin, and spurred Hoel's forces to victory. Agrippe was slain in the battle. The same character is known as ALBROINO in the Italian *La Tavola Ritonda*. [*ProsTris, Malory*]

AGUERISSE

A nobleman who murdered Arthur's Sir Dondinello (Dodinel), and who later died at the hands of Dondinello's son, Carduino. Named as a brother of Gawain, the author likely intended either GARETH or GAHERIS. [*CantariC*]

AGUS OF BOLOAN

One of Arthur's noblemen who fought and died in the Roman War. [*Wace*]

AGUSALE THE DESIRED [*Augusale*]

A knight who fought for Arthur and Leodegan against the Saxons at the first battle of Carhaix. [*VulgMer, Arthour*]

AHARER

A knight from the French romance *Gliglois*. While on his way to join the Knights of the Round Table at the Castle Orgueilleux tournament, Aharer was stopped by Gliglois, a squire, who asked him to escort the lady Beauté (Gliglois's love) to the tournament. Aharer agreed, and gave Beauté a falcon to present to the winner of the tournament. He was mystified, however, by Beauté's cruelty toward Gliglois. [*Gliglois*]

AIFAIES

A broad lake in the Land of Maidens visited by Gawain. A magical mobile island ferried knights across the lake, provided they were pure of heart. [*Heinrich*]

AIGLIN OF THE VALES [*Aglin, Aglu, Aigilin*]

An Arthurian knight introduced in the Vulgate Cycle as the nephew of Kay of Estral. In the early days of Arthur's reign, fought against the Saxons at the battle of Carhaix, against Raolais at Estremores, and against Agrippe in the Waste Land. He participated in quests to learn the fate of Merlin and to locate Lancelot. He brought news of Lancelot's conquest of Dolorous Guard to Arthur's court. He eventually became a companion of Kahedin and Gaheris of Carahew. In *Claris et Laris*, he saves some nuns from a marauder. [*LancLac, VulgLanc, VulgMer, Livre, ProsTris, Claris*]

AIKAN

An Arthurian knight listed in Layamon's *Brut*. [*Layamon*]

AILLEANN

The true name of the GREY-HAMMED LADY in an Irish romance. [*IrishL*]

AIREM

A mythological Irish king, often presented as the Irish counterpart of King Arthur.

AKARINS

A misogynist knight who abused maidens. Aglovale defeated him in combat and sent him as a prisoner to Guinevere. The queen imprisoned him for life. [*ProsTris*]

ALAAZ

A Saxon king who joined King Hargadabran in an attack on Arthur at the battle of Clarence. [*Livre*]

ALADUKE [*Aliduc, Alyduke*]

A knight in Arthur's service who was killed during the Roman War. Geoffrey of Monmouth calls him the Baron of Tintagel while the Alliterative *Morte Arthure* names him as a knight from Turrey who served under King Cador of Cornwall. Malory confusingly seems to place him on the Romans' side, although he also names him as one of the knights rescued from the giant Tericam's prison by Lancelot. [*GeoffHR, Allit, Malory*]

ALAIN¹

Perceval's cousin in *Perlesvaus*. The son of Elinant of Escavalon, Alain was slain by the demonic Knight of the Burning Dragon. His embalmed body was carted around by a maiden, searching for someone to avenge him. Perceval accepted the challenge and slew the fierce knight, but not before the knight blasted Alain's body to ashes with his enchanted shield. A near identical story is told of the unnamed lover of CLAIRE in the Fourth Continuation of Chrétien's *Perceval*. [*Perlesvaus*]

ALAIN²

King of Escavalon and father of Floree, a maiden saved by Gawain from a giant. He ruled the castle Brion and helped Arthur fight the Saxons at the battle of Vambieres. Alain had a nephew named Arquais. [*Livre*]

ALAIN³ [*Aleyn*]

Brother of Drian and, consequently, son of Pellinore and brother of Perceval, Aglovale, Lamorat, and Tor. With his brother Drian, he guarded a tower next to a bridge and made it a custom to joust with any knight who passed that way. He defeated Dinadan in this manner. Alain appears only once in the Prose *Tristan*. Malory includes him as the brother of "Tryan," apparently not making the connection between Alain and Pellinore's family. [*ProsTris, Malory*]

ALAIN³

A knight who fought with his brother, Davis. Arthur's knights Claris, Laris, and Bedivere found them fighting and forced them to reconcile. [*Claris*]

ALAIN⁴

The nephew of Yonet, the servant of Kay's wife Andrivette. Alain is also given as Yonet's surname. [*Girart*]

ALAIN⁵ THE LARGE [**Alain le Gros, Alaine, Alains, Alan, Alein(s), Helain, Hellyas, Julain*]

A Grail character who first appears in Robert de Boron's *Joseph d'Arimathie* as the twelfth son of Bron, Joseph of Arimathea's brother-in-law. Appointed the third Grail keeper, Alain was charged with leading his eleven brothers to Britain. There, his unborn son would become the eternal Grail King. (The mention of Alain's son conflicts with Robert's earlier statement that Alain remained celibate.)

Joseph does not provide the name of Alain's son; we learn this in the Didot-*Perceval*, which was possibly based on a lost romance by Robert. At the beginning of the story, Alain, having received instructions from the Holy Spirit, orders Perceval, his son, to depart for Arthur's court. Thus, unlike Perceval's father in other legends (e.g., BLIOCADRAN and GAHMURET), Alain lived to see his son's youth.

Perlesvaus, written about the same time as *Joseph*, also continues Alain's story past Perceval's birth. Calling his father Gais the Large, the text says that he married Yglais and ruled the castle and valley of Kamaalot. In contrast to the Didot-*Perceval*, Alain opposes Perceval's departure for Arthur's court. As he grew old and infirm, his lands were invaded by the Lord of the Fens. Seeking to avenge his brother Aliban's death, he challenged a giant called the Red Giant. Although he was victorious in the combat, he received a mortal wound and perished.

The Vulgate *Estoire del Saint Graal* expanded and modified the story told by Robert de Boron. In the Vulgate, he is no longer named as Perceval's father, since centuries span Alain's time and Arthur's. Still, however, he is the twelfth son of Bron and the third Grail keeper. He was called the Rich Fisherman (a title given to his father in Robert's version) because he caught a single fish which God multiplied into thousands for Joseph's followers to feast upon. When Josephus, Joseph's son, died, the Grail was passed on to Alain. With 100 people, including his brother Joshua, Alain left the Christian stronghold of Galafort and traveled to the city of Malta in the Strange Land. There, he converted King Calafes to Christianity and used the Grail to heal the king's leprosy. In reward, Calafes built the Grail Castle of Corbenic, where Alain's brother Joshua ruled after his death. Alain was buried in the chapel of Notre Dame in Corbenic.

The Vulgate *Merlin* and the *Livre d'Artus*, probably confused by the change in roles listed above, name him as the FISHER KING in Arthur's time. With his brothers, ruled the lands of Listenois or the Strange Land. He wasted away from an illness, and waited for the best knight in the world to come and ask the Grail Question. His brothers were Pelles and Pellinore. His soldiers fought with Arthur against the Saxons. In other Vulgate tales, however, his brother PELLES is identified with the Fisher King.

Finally, in a brief interpolation at the end of one manuscript of the first continuation of Chrétien's *Perceval*, Alain, named as Perceval's father, is called the husband, and not the son, of Enygeus. [*RobertBorJ, Perlesvaus, Didot, VulgEst, VulgMer, Livre*]

ALAIN[6] THE LARGE [*Alan le Gros*]

A Christian king who was a descendant of the first Nascien, and the ancestor of Lancelot and Galahad. His father was named Nascien and his son was Isaiah. [*VulgEst, Malory*]

ALAIN[7] THE WHITE [*Elaine, Helain(e)(s), (H)elayne, (H)elias*]

Son of Bors, begotten after King Brandegorre of Estrangorre's daughter seduced Bors with a magic ring. Alain arrived at Arthur's court just before the Grail Quest and was knighted by his father. He joined the Round Table shortly. During the Grail Quest, he traveled with Gawain and Hector, and he witnessed a marvelous vision at the Ancient Chapel. He was present at Corbenic when Galahad completed the quest. He eventually became the Emperor of Constantinople. [*VulgLanc, VulgQuest, PostQuest, Malory*]

ALAIN'S POND [*Estanc Alain*]

A lake where Alain the Large, the third Grail keeper, caught a fish which God multiplied into thousands to feed Joseph of Arimathea's company. For this event, Alain became known as the Rich Fisherman. [*VulgEst*]

ALAMAN

A Knight of the Round Table who participated in the Grail Quest. [*PostQuest*]

ALAMIS OF SATARCHJONTE

A duke in the service of Feirefiz, Perceval's half-brother. [*Wolfram*]

ALAN FYRGAN

A warrior listed in the Welsh Triads as having one of the "faithless war-bands." They apparently deserted him before the battle of Camlann and, as a consequence, he was killed there. It is unclear which side he was supporting. The name comes from an actual person—Alannus Fergannus, the Duke of Brittany from 1084 to 1112, who fought against and then allied with William the Conqueror. [*Triads*]

ALAN OF THE MEADOWS

A Knight of the Round Table who participated in the Grail Quest. [*PostQuest*]

ALANTINE

A city in Sorelois, ruled by Galehaut. [*VulgLanc*]

ALARDIN[1] [*Aalardin*]

A knight from whom Caradoc, one of Arthur's knights, rescued a maiden named Guignier. After their duel, Alardin and Caradoc became friends, and Alardin accompanied Caradoc to Arthur's court. He had some knowledge of magic and later, when Guignier lost her breast to a serpent, Alardin provided a magical shield which replaced the lost flesh with gold. Alardin married Guigenor, Arthur's grand-niece. His father was named Guiniacalc. [*Contin1*]

ALARDIN[2] OF THE ISLES

A knight encountered by Gawain during the latter's quest to retrieve a white hart stolen from Arthur's hall. Alardin refused to allow Gawain to cross a river without a battle, and Gawain slew him in the subsequent duel. [*Malory*]

ALARIE

A land, perhaps in the Middle-East, ruled by Count Adan, a knight rescued by Wigalois (Gawain's son). The land was also home to a band of female knights led by Lady Marine. [*Wirnt*]

ALARIS[1]

A knight in the service of King Mark of Cornwall. He was killed in a chance encounter with Sagremor in the forest of Morois. [*ProsTris*]

ALARIS[2]

A knight who cuckolded Sir Claristant by riding off with his *amie*. Claristant caught up with them and engaged Alaris in combat. Alaris was assisted by Claristant's treacherous maiden. Claristant would have been killed, but Kay and Gaswain intervened and saved him. [*ProsTris*]

ALBAGIA

The name given in *La Tavola Ritonda* to the Queen of Orkney. As Gawain's mother and Arthur's half-sister, she is therefore the counterpart of ANNA or MORGAUSE. [*Tavola*]

ALBAN

A knight who challenged Lancelot, when Lancelot was living on the Dry Island and calling himself the Wicked Knight. Lancelot defeated Alban in combat. [*PostMer*]

ALBANA

Grandfather of Albion, the woman who first populated Britain. [*Palamedes*]

ALBANACT[1] [*Alben*]

Son of King Brutus (first king of Britain), brother of Camber and Locrine, and father of Embrunt, Dombart, and Arbrun. Albanact gave his name to Albany (Scotland). His kingdom was invaded by Huns, and Albanact was killed. [*GeoffHR, Wace, Palamedes*]

ALBANACT[2]

Captain of Arthur's guard in Dryden's *King Arthur*. [*Dryden*]

ALBANY [Albanie, Arbanie]

An early name for SCOTLAND, though some texts refer to Albany as a Pictish kingdom within Scotland. Geoffrey of Monmouth says that it was named after Albanact, a son of Brutus. According to *Yder*, Albany was ruled by Nut, Yder's father. [*Yder*]

ALBAO

One of seven brothers, including Ayaò and Dormadat, who usurped the throne of Tristan the Stranger, ruler of Jakobsland. Tristan the Stranger sought out his famous namesake, and the two of them returned and slew the seven brothers. [*SagaTI*]

ALBE

A lovely maiden with whom Danain the Red fell in love. Consequently, Danain became involved in a great feud between Albe's family and the clan of Helyom. [*Palamedes*]

ALBEWIN

A dwarf king in Der Pleier's *Garel*. Albewin's people were terrorized by the giant Purdan. Arthur's Sir Garel saved them by slaying the giant, which the grateful Albewin rewarded by helping Garel kill a demon named Vulganus. Garel appointed Albewin the steward of Anferre. [*PleierG*]

ALBINE[1]

One of the fourteen daughters of King Diodicias of Syria. She married King Sardacia of Damascus. Albine and her sisters revolted against their husbands, planning to form a matriarchy. They failed, and Albine and her sisters were exiled. They came to Britain, which at the time was unpopulated, and Albine named the island Albion after herself. Albine and her sisters became the mistresses of devils and gave birth to a race of giants that Brutus was fated to conquer. [*Palamedes*]

ALBINE[2]

A city in Lyonesse, Tristan's country. [*ProsTris*]

ALBION

The oldest recorded name for the island of Britain, appearing in Roman documents several centuries before Christ (Ashe, *Camelot*, 25). The name may originate with the Latin "albus," meaning "white," referring to the White Cliffs of Dover. According to Geoffrey of Monmouth and other chroniclers, Albion was populated by a race of giants, whom Brutus conquered. Brutus then gave the island his own name: Britain. As for the race of giants, we find in *Palamedes* that they were descended from Albine, an exiled Syrian princess, after whom the island was named. The fourteenth-century *Short Metrical Chronicle* credits the name to the giant Albin, who, like Albine, fathered the giant race conquered by Brutus. [*GeoffHR, Wace, Palamedes, ShortMet*]

ALBIUN

Queen of the Wild Mountain. A malevolent knight named Kurian declared war on her, intending to steal her land. She was saved by Arthur's Sir Tandareis, who defeated Kurian in combat. [*PleierT*]

ALBROINO

Count of the city of Gippa and nephew of King Gilierchino of Brittany, Tristan's father-in-law. He went to war with his uncle and besieged him at the city of Solona. Tristan arrived in the middle of the war, joined Gilierchino's cause, and slew Albroino in combat. Albroino is known as AGRIPPE in the Prose *Tristan*. [*Tavola*]

ALCALEC THE RED [Aucales]

A knight who fought for Arthur and Leodegan against the Saxons at the battle of Carhaix. [*VulgMer, Arthour*]

ALCARDO

Isolde's cousin and Tristan's squire. Tristan eventually knighted him and dubbed him LANTRIS. [*Tavola*]

ALCHENDIC

The giant, pagan king of Sarras in Arthur's time. He withstood an attack by King Richard of Jerusalem, but he was later baptized. [*Prophecies*]

ALCHINO OF LOGRES

A knight liberated from the stronghold of Lucano the Great, a giant, by Tristan. Alchino's wife, Argretta, had been forced to serve as Lucano's concubine. Tristan made him lord of Dianfer, Lucano's stronghold. [*Tavola*]

ALCLUD [Aklud]

An alternate name for DUMBARTON, probably from the river Clyde, which flows through the city. The famed town of ESCALOT may be derived from it.

ALCUS

King of Iceland, who subjugated himself to Arthur in return for Arthur's promise to make his son, Esscol, a knight. Alcus married the daughter of the King of Russia. [*Layamon*]

ALDERLY EDGE

A forest in Cheshire containing a stone wishing well. On the stone is carved a face that local legend holds is Merlin's. An inscription on the well, carved in modern times, reads "Drink of this and take thy fill, for the water falls by the wizard's will." According to a local tale, a farmer encountered Merlin at the well at the close of the seventeenth century. Merlin offered to buy the farmer's horse, saying that one of Arthur's knights needed it. The rock parted, revealing a gate which led into a cavern. Merlin told the farmer that Arthur and his knights were sleeping in the cave. The scared farmer sold the horse to Merlin and ran away. The rock closed behind him, and the cavern has remained hidden ever since (Ashe, *Landscape*, 159).

ALDEWARK

In the fourteenth-century *Short Metrical Chronicle*, the castle that served as Vortigern's burial site. [*ShortMet*]

ALDROEN [*Adroenus, Aldroein*]

A King of Brittany two generations before Arthur. When the Archbishop Guethelin, Aldroen's kinsman, came to Brittany to beg for Aldroen's help in driving the Picts and Huns from Britain, Aldroen sent his brother Constantine, Arthur's grandfather, to accomplish the task and assume the throne of the island. [*GeoffHR, Wace, Layamon*]

ALECYS

A hermit priest encountered by Perceval in a forest, beating a giant cross with a rod. Perceval refrained from punishing this blasphemy only because Alecys looked like a priest. He later discovered that Alecys hated the cross because Christ had died on one, just as one would hate a weapon which had killed one's relative. [*Perlesvaus*]

ALEMANDINE

Queen of the White City on the Island of Beautiful Maidens. A monster terrorized her lands and swallowed her maidens. The creature was slain by Floriant. Alemandine offered herself to Floriant, but he declined and departed. [*Floriant*]

ALEMANNI

The Germanic tribes which inhabited western and central Europe in the Dark Ages. In the story of *Meriadoc*, the Emperor of the Alemanni, at war with King Gundebald of the Land From Which No One Returns, employs the services of Arthur's Meriadoc. Meriadoc rescued the Emperor's daughter from Gundebald, and planned to marry her, but he was betrayed by the Emperor, who wished to use his daughter to seal a truce with the King of Gaul. Meriadoc escaped from his prison, slew the Emperor, and married his daughter. In history, the Alemanni were defeated by King Clovis of the Franks in 506 A.D. The author of *Meriadoc* may have drawn on this history for his Emperor of the Alemanni. [*Historia*]

ALENIE

Greu, a Knight of the Round Table, was the son of the King of Alenie. [*Livre*]

ALEPPO [*Halape*]

A city in northwest Syria; one of many visited by Gahmuret, Perceval's father, during his Arabian adventures. [*Wolfram*]

ALES¹ [*Alles, Alon*]

Father or brother of Arthur's knight Aces. His cousin, Galescalain, made him the seneschal of Clarence. Yvain was another of his cousins. Ales fought in Arthur's wars against the Saxons and in the conflict against Agrippe in the Waste Land. [*VulgMer, Livre*]

ALES²

A knight Tristan defeated in joust by a spring in North Wales. [*Tavola*]

ALESTE

One of the lands ruled by King Malloas. [*PleierM*]

ALEXANDER¹

The Emperor of Greece and Constantinople, husband of Tantalis, and father of Alexander and Alis. He allowed his son Alexander to travel to Britain to earn renown at the court of Arthur. When he died, his sons jointly succeeded him to the throne after some fraternal strife. [*ChretienC, Wolfram*]

ALEXANDER²

Son of the above Emperor Alexander of Greece and Constantinople, and of his queen Tantalis. When he came of age, he left his father's kingdom and brought an army of Greek warriors to the famous court of King Arthur in Britain, where he hoped to win fame and honor. He fell in love with Soredamor, Guinevere's maidservant and Gawain's sister. Though he was reluctant to divulge his feelings, Alexander and Soredamor were wed through Guinevere's intervention, and they had a son named Cliges. In Arthur's service, Alexander and his companions helped to subdue a revolt led by the traitorous Angres of Windsor. Alexander himself captured Angres.

When Alexander's father died, messengers set out to find him to bring him back to Constantinople to be crowned Emperor. The ship bearing the messengers sank and only one man survived. This man favored Alexander's brother Alis, and returned to Constantinople, telling the noblemen that Alexander was dead. Consequently, Alis was crowned emperor. When Alexander learned of this, he left Britain to claim his rightful throne. He became *de facto* emperor of Greece and Constantinople, while Alis retained the ceremonial station.

Before he died of an illness, he charged his son Cliges to go to Britain when he came of age. His wife soon followed him in death, and Cliges had to struggle against Alis for the throne of Constantinople. [*ChretienC*]

ALEXANDER³

A knight captured and imprisoned, along with his brother Floris, by Eskilabon of Belamunt. He was rescued by his uncle, Gilan, and Arthur's Sir Garel. In reward, he fought alongside Garel in a war against King Ekunaver of Kanadic. His father was Duke Retan of Pergalt. [*PleierG*]

ALEXANDER[4]

A prince of India who was enchanted in the form of the CROP-EARED DOG. [IrishD]

ALEXANDER[5] THE GREAT

The French *Perceforest* presents the famed Macedonian king (356–323 BC) as an ancestor of Arthur. A storm drove him to Britain, where he quelled the war-torn island and established secure rulers. He loved Sebille, then the Lady of the Lake. Alexander is only one of many historical and legendary people connected to the Arthurian cycle in various texts. The association was to be expected, given the similarities between the legend of Alexander and the myth of Arthur: both were historical figures to whom fabulous legends were attached; both grew up away from the royal court; both became rulers following the assassinations of their fathers; both endured a period of rebellion before securing the throne; both experienced problems with neighboring barbarians; both conquered most of the known world; both were deified by their countrymen; both had their thrones usurped while leading military expeditions in foreign lands; both were rumored to have died; both returned to their homelands and killed the rebels; both left their countries in anarchy after their deaths; and, finally, both were said to be living in otherwordly kingdoms.

ALEXANDER[6] THE ORPHAN [Alisandre]

Son of Prince Bodwyne and Angledis, and nephew of King Mark of Cornwall. When Mark murdered his father, Angledis and Alexander fled to Sussex to escape Mark's reach. Alexander was raised by Berengier the Constable in the Castle Magance. Upon receiving his knighthood, his mother charged him to avenge his father's death. He soon won fame at a tournament thrown by King Caradoc, and by saving a maiden from the evil Sir Malagrin.

King Mark had put a price on Alexander's head, and it wasn't long before he ran afoul of the minions of Morgan le Fay, Mark's ally. After defeating several of her knights, he eventually ended up, wounded, in her care, at the castle Fair Guard. Though he rejected her advances, he was forced to pledge to remain at Fair Guard for a year, as a condition of Morgan's succor. This oath stood even after the castle's owner, the Count of the Pass, burned it to the ground, and Alexander found himself guarding an empty lot.

A passing maiden, Alice la Belle Pilgrim, heard of his oath, and offered herself to any knight who could defeat him. Many rose to the challenge, but none succeeded. At the end of the year, Alexander left Britain for Benoic, married Alice, and had a son named Bellangere. According to *Palamedes*, he was killed by a knight named Helin, but Malory says that King Mark eventually caught up with him and killed him, and that Bellangere avenged the deaths of his father and grandfather. [*Palamedes, ProsTris, Prophecies, Malory*]

ALEXANDRIA

A Mediterranean seaport, built during the heyday of Rome on the coast of Egypt, near the Nile Delta. Wolfram von Eschenbach records that it was besieged by the Baruc of Baghdad during the reign of Uther in Britain. Perceval's father Gahmuret assisted in the attack. According to the Alliterative *Morte Arthure* and Malory, Alexandria was allied to Lucius, Arthur's enemy in the Roman War. In Heinrich von dem Türlin's *Diu Crône*, its queen is named as Lenomie, Guinevere's sister. [*Wolfram, Heinrich, Allit, Malory*]

ALFAIN

A castle four leagues from Camelot where Lancelot, Hector, and Bors once lodged on their way to Arthur's court. [VulgMort]

ALFRED [Alvrez]

An Irish king and Knight of the Round Table in the romance of *Yder*. Alfred and his two sons, Kamelin and Miroet, discovered Yder after he had been poisoned by Kay. They cured him and returned him to Arthur's court. [Yder]

ALGERE

A knight who served the Duke of Lorraine in a battle against Gawain during the Roman War. His brother, Earl Antele, fought by his side. [Allit]

ALIAUMES

A squire present at the tournament of Lancien, held by King Mark. [Contin4]

ALIBAN

One of Perceval's eleven paternal uncles in *Perlesvaus*. He was the twelfth son of Gais the Large and the brother of Alain. Aliban reigned as lord of the Waste City until slain by the Red Giant. Alain avenged his death. [Perlesvaus]

ALIBANO

A Saxon knight defeated by Lancelot at a fountain. [Novellino]

ALIBEL[1] [Caltbiaus]

A strong knight who served King Claudas of Gaul. His brothers were Brumand, Canart, and Cadant. He fought in Claudas's war against Arthur. [VulgLanc]

ALIBEL[2]

A Knight of the Round Table who participated in the Grail Quest. [ProsTris]

ALIBON[1] OF THE SPUR [Albyon]

A valorous knight who brashly challenged a young Lancelot at the Queen's Ford, where Alibon's father served as vavasor. Lancelot defeated him and sent him to Arthur's court. Alibon later participated in a quest to find Merlin. [*VulgLanc, VulgMer, Livre*]

ALIBON² THE RED

One of the sons of the evil Helin the Red. His brothers were Marin and Helin. Lancelot killed him. [*Palamedes*]

ALIBORC

A knight who fought against the Saxons in the early days of Arthur's reign. Aliborc served the noblemen in rebellion against Arthur. [*VulgMer*]

ALICE THE FAIR PILGRIM [*Aleys, Aylies*]

Daughter of Duke Rancier the Pilgrim, wife of Alexander the Orphan, and mother of Bellangere. She met her future husband after he had sword to guard the castle Belle Regard for a year. She offered herself to any knight who could defeat Alexander, but soon fell in love with him. At the end of the year, no knight had been able to succeed in Alice's challenge, so she brought Alexander to her home in Bovaine or Benoic and married him. [*ProsTris, Prophecies, Malory*]

ALIENOR

Mother of Escanor the Handsome, a knight defeated by Gawain. She was the brother of Escanor the Large and the wife of Bruns the Prophet. [*Girart*]

ALIER¹ [*Al(l)e(r)s*]

An earl defeated by Yvain. The lord had made war against a defenseless countess (called the Lady of Norison in Chrétien's *Yvain*), whom Yvain had agreed to help in return for her healing services. [*ChretienY, Ivens, Ywain*]

ALIER² OF TANNINGUES

One of Arthur's knights who joined the fighting against the Saxons in the early days of Arthur's reign. When fourteen of Alier's sons were killed in a single battle against the Saxons, he retired to a hermitage, giving his remaining son, Marec, to be raised by the Lady of Roestoc. Alier abandoned his robe for his sword when Marec was later dispossessed by Sir Seguarades. [*VulgLanc, Livre*]

ALIFATIMA [*Alipanton, Aliphatim, Aliphatma*]

King of Spain under the Roman Procurator Lucius. He joined Lucius's war against Arthur, bringing soldiers from his nation. He was slain at the battle of Soissons, either by Duke Holdin of Flanders or King Nentres of Garlot. Layamon calls him MEODRAS. The elements of his name— Ali and Fatima—are known in Arabian texts. [*GeoffHR, Wace, VulgMer*]

ALIGRÉS

A knight who served Lord Parsamant, a ravisher. Perceval defeated Aligrés when he conquered Parsamant. [*Contin4*]

ALINGE

A town in King Hoel's Brittany, besieged by Count Agrippe the Tall and saved by Tristan. [*ProsTris*]

ALIPANSIN

One of the Saxon kings who invaded Britain at the beginning of Arthur's reign. Known as the lord of the Grazing Fields, he served King Rions. [*VulgMer*]

ALIS

Emperor of Greece and Constantinople. He ruled jointly with his brother, Alexander, after his parents, Alexander and Tantalis, died. Alis had agreed not to take a wife, so that Alexander's son, Cliges, would rule upon the brothers' deaths. After Alexander's death, however, he broke the pact and married Fenice, the daughter of the Emperor of Germany.

Fenice had fallen in love with the young Cliges, and she had her servant concoct a potion that made Alis think he was making love to her, when in fact he was dreaming. For years, Alis's wife preserved her virginity in this manner. Eventually, she faked her own death and was able to live with Cliges in his stronghold. Alis soon learned the truth, swore vengeance, and Cliges and Fenice were forced to flee Constantinople. Alis was unable to find them, and he eventually died from the obsession consuming him. After his death, Cliges and Fenice returned to Constantinople, where Cliges ruled as Emperor. [*ChretienC*]

ALISTANS

A knight who participated in the Grail Quest. His companion was named Gloans the Red. [*ProsTris*]

ALIXANS THE PROUD

A malevolent knight who invaded the Brown Valley and forced a maiden of the "Brown" family to marry him. Girflet killed him. [*ProsTris*]

ALIZE

The sister of King Hardiz of Gascony. Her first love was King Kaylet of Spain, but she was given by her brother in marriage to Duke Lambekin of Brabant. [*Wolfram*]

ALLEBRAN

A knight saved by Lancelot and Tristan from the prison of the giant of the Dark Forest. Allebran's father, Henry, was a vassal of Lancelot's father, King Ban of Benoic. [*Sala*]

ALLECTUS

In Geoffrey's chronicle, a Roman war leader in the third century who was sent by the Roman senate to deal with Carausius, another Roman who had betrayed the British king and taken the throne for himself. Allectus succeeded in killing Carausius and assuming the throne. He then began to slaughter the Britons in return for their support of Carausius. After several years of this bloody reign,

Allectus was overthrown and killed by the Briton Asclepiodotus, who succeeded him.

These are real people, but Geoffrey has their situation confused. Allectus served as finance minister to Carausius, who was a Roman admiral rather than a British king. Carausius plotted to overthrow the Roman Emperor Diocletian and invaded Gaul. Allectus murdered him, and was himself slain by the Roman general Constantius Chlorus (Lindsay, 10). [*GeoffHR*]

ALLEGRENO

Tristan's half-brother, named only in the Italian *La Tavola Ritonda*, though he appears in the Prose *Tristan* and in Malory's version. He was born to Tristan's father (Meliadus) and stepmother (named as Agia in the *Tavola*). Seeking to move Allegreno in place as Meliadus's heir, Agia prepared a poison potion for Tristan. A nurse accidentally served the concoction to young Allegreno, who perished. [*Tavola*]

ALLIELE

A king in Arthur's service in the Italian *La Tavola Ritonda*. With another king named Agalone, Alliele served as steward of Britain while Arthur was away in Gaul. (He thus occupies the role assigned to the King of Scotland in the Prose *Tristan*.) [*Tavola*]

ALMA¹

A beautiful virgin whose castle was besieged by evil knights, but was rescued by Prince Arthur and Sir Guyon. She welcomed the two knights into her house. The robber knights resumed their siege, but Arthur defeated them for good by slaying their leader, Maleger. [*Spenser*]

ALMA² OF CAMELOT

A Knight of the Round Table who was slain during the Grail Quest. His brothers, Luzes and Tanadal, were also killed. [*PostQuest*]

ALMAIN

A land owned by Tristan in the Middle-English *Sir Tristrem*. [*SirTris*]

ALNWICK

A castle in Northumberland that is one of the possible locations given by Malory for JOYOUS GUARD, Lancelot's castle. It may appear in Girart d'Amien's *Escanor* as ANNUEC. [*Malory*]

ALOHEGRE

A Saxon king killed by Gawain at the siege of Vambieres. [*Livre*]

ALOIS

The King of North Wales in *La Tavola Ritonda*. He went to war with King Amoroldo of Ireland over a castle called Lerline. Lancelot fought as his champion, but the war was settled—through the intervention of Arthur—in Amoroldo's favor. After the Grail Quest, Alois renewed the war, and was killed in combat by Amoroldo. Oddly, one ANSALINERO is named as the king of North Wales in the same story. [*Tavola*]

ALOM

An Arthurian knight defeated in joust by Daniel of the Blossoming Valley. [*Stricker*]

ALON

A knight serving Ladas, a lord defeated by Caradoc, Claris, and Laris. [*Claris*]

ALOUT [*Alous*]

The count of the Land of the Heather. When he died, his brother, Gallidés, made war on his daughters, Amide and the Lady of Hungerford Castle. They were championed by Sir Bors. [*VulgLanc*]

ALPHASAN [*Alfasein, Arfasan*]

The baptismal name of King Calafes, who built the Grail Castle of Corbenic. He was named after the priest who baptized him, a companion of the third Grail keeper, Alain the Large. [*VulgEst*]

ALPHEUS

A Spanish knight slain by Sir Urry of Hungary during a tournament. Alpheus's mother, a sorceress, cast a spell upon Urry so that the wounds he had received wound not heal until examined by the best knight in the world (Lancelot). [*Malory*]

ALQUIN

Nephew of Count Agrippe the Tall. He assisted his uncle in a war against King Hoel of Brittany, and was slain by Tristan during the siege of Alinge. [*ProsTris*]

ALSER

A son of Maelgwn, one of Arthur's chieftains in Welsh legend. He rode a horse named Grey. [*Triads*]

ALTACLARA

According to *La Tavola Ritonda*, the Holy Roman Emperor Charlemagne visited England and found a statue of Lancelot in front of the castle of Leverzep. One of Charlemagne's noblemen took the sword hanging around the statue's neck, naming it Altaclara. [*Tavola*]

ALTAMONDO

A lord of Listenois encountered by Tristan during the Grail Quest. Tristan jousted with, and defeated, one of Altamondo's companions. [*Tavola*]

ALTAN THE HANDSOME

A son of Febus and Florine and brother of Lannor, Siraouc, Argons, and Niatar. [*Palamedes*]

ALTE MONTANJE

A land neighboring Britain under Arthur's control. [*HartmannE*]

ALUN OF DYFED

Son of Seidi, brother of Cas and Cadrieth, and father of Cunyn Cof and Dyfyr (two of Arthur's warriors). Culhwch needed the assistance of one of Alun's sons to hunt the boar Twrch Trwyth. [*Culhwch, Dream*]

ALVERNE

A castle on the island of Effin, ruled by King Flois and Count Blant. It was besieged by a giant named Assiles, and was saved by Gawain. [*Heinrich*]

ALWIN

A Saxon warrior in Thelwall's *The Fairy of the Lake*. He served Queen Rowena, wife of King Vortigern of Britain. [*Thelwall*]

ALYMER

One of Arthur's knights who fought in the war against Mordred. [*Allit*]

ALYNE

In Malory, the daughter of the Lady of the Rule by King Pellinore, who was not aware of her existence. Her betrothed, Sir Myles of Laundis, was mortally wounded in combat with Sir Lorayne the Savage. Her father rode by but, and intent on his quest, did not respond to her cries for help. Myles soon died, and Alyne killed herself. Pellinore came to regret his failure to assist Alyne, particularly when Merlin told him that Alyne was his daughter. Pellinore buried the bodies of the lovers and bore Alyne's head to Camelot in penitence. A similar character appears in the Post-Vulgate *Merlin* continuation, but is unnamed. [*Malory*]

AMABLE

Sister of Carmadan. She healed Lancelot after he drank water from a poisoned well. She fell in love with Lancelot and nearly died from lovesickness, but Lancelot, though he could not become her lover, agreed to become her champion. [*VulgLanc*]

AMADAN THE PROUD

A knight who fought for King Arthur and King Leodegan against the Saxons in the first battle of Carhaix. [*VulgMer, Arthour*]

AMADANT OF THE HILLTOP

One of several of Arthur's knights who embarked on a quest to learn Merlin's fate, after he had been imprisoned by the Lady of the Lake. [*VulgMer*]

AMADIS OF GAUL

Hero of late Medieval Spanish romance, whose legend offers many parallels to the Arthurian cycle. Like Lancelot, Amadis fell in love with the wife of his king, rescued her from a kidnapping, and endured her jealous wrath.

AMADOR[1] OF THE LOVELY HOME

A Knight of the Round Table who embarked on the Grail Quest. He engaged in combat with Sir Bors, who left him wounded at a roadside. Sir Meleagant came upon him and took his lady, for he thought that Amador was near death. When Amador knew his lady was gone, he arose and charged after Meleagant, but in his weakened state, he succeeded only in turning a serious wound into a mortal one. He slew his own lady because he perceived her activities to be the cause of his death. He died in the arms of Galahad. [*PostQuest*]

AMADOR[2] THE WELL-BEHAVED

In *La Tavola Ritonda*, the squire of Belide, a maiden who killed herself out of love for Tristan. Tristan later encountered Amador, knighted, at a tournament in Ireland. He seems to take the place of HEBES in the Prose *Tristan*. [*Tavola*]

AMALVI

A seaside castle ruled by a King Orions in the Post-Vulgate *Suite du Merlin*. When Arthur set hundreds of infants adrift at sea in a vain effort to destroy his incestuous son, Mordred, the boat came ashore at Amalvi. Orions took the children into his care. There is a town called Amalfi on the Gulf of Salerno in southern Italy. [*PostMer*]

AMANDE

Daughter of the king of Spain. She married Sir Manuel of Greece at Arthur's court. [*Manuel*]

AMANGON[1] [*Amagons, Amangons, Amaugon*]

A king in Arthur's service in Renaut de Bâgé's *Le Bel Inconnu*, probably from Chrétien's AMAUGUIN. He suggested a tournament at the Castle of Maidens when Arthur wanted to lure Guinglain, Gawain's son, back to court. Amangon is also mentioned briefly in *La Bataille de Loquifer* and *Les Merveilles de Rigomer*. [*Renaut, Bataille*]

AMANGON[2]

A wicked king who ravaged a collection of well fairies who lived in the Grail kingdom, stealing their golden cups. Other knights followed his example. Afterwards, the kingdom became a waste land, and the Grail Castle was hidden. Amgangon had a son named Pecorins. [*Elucid*]

AMANGON³

The King of Greenland and father of Guenloie, Gawain's love, in *Meriadeuc*. He served Arthur. He is also named as the ruler of the land from which no one returns. [*Meriadeuc*]

AMANT¹ [*Anyause*]

A king who gave all his lands to a noblewoman, but stripped her of them when he discovered her evil nature. Amant then bestowed the realms on the evil woman's maiden sister. When Amant died, his first beneficiary made war on his second. The evil woman's champion, Priadan the Black, was defeated during the Grail Quest by Bors. [*VulgQuest, Malory*]

AMANT²

King of Lambal and enemy of Uther Pendragon, who had robbed Amant of the castle Charroie. When Arthur came to power, Amant saw an opportunity to both avenge himself and reclaim his castle. He marched on Carnelide, where Arthur was battling Saxons. Merlin, however, wove a magical mist which led Amant's army to clash with the forces of King Galahad, a Saxon. Amant's army was decimated. He was later killed in single combat with King Bors of Gannes. His son, Gosengos, inherited his kingdom and swore fealty to Arthur. [*VulgMer*]

AMANT³ [*Armant*]

A Cornish knight who accompanied King Mark on an expedition to Camelot, learning on the way that the purpose of the trip was to kill Tristan. Upon hearing this, Amant and his companion, Berluse, refused to continue. Mark killed Berluse but was convinced to let Amant go on his promise not to reveal Mark's intentions. After burying Berluse, Amant marched to Arthur's court and accused Mark of murder. In a subsequent combat, Mark mortally wounded him. [*ProsTris, Malory*]

AMASPARTINS OF SCHIPELPJONTE

A king in the service of Feirefiz, Perceval's half-brother. [*Wolfram*]

AMATHAON

Son of Dôn and brother of Gofannon. As one of his tasks, Culhwch had to convinced Amathaon to plow the lands of the giant Ysbaddaden. [*Culhwch*]

AMATIN THE GOOD JOUSTER [*Amant*]

A Knight of the Round Table who embarked with the others on the Grail Quest. He joined company with Agamenor and Arpian of the Narrow Mountain. All three knights hated Lancelot's family, so they attacked Galahad, but were defeated. Later, they assaulted Acorante the Agile

and Danubre the Brave, Lancelot's cousins. Amatin was slain by Danubre. [*PostQuest, ProsTris*]

AMAUGUIN THE RED [*Aumagwin*]

A king and Knight of the Round Table in Chrétien's *Erec* and Heinrich's *Diu Crône*. Among the two romances, he appears at a white stag hunt and two chastity tests. His lover, lady Aclamet, failed in one of the latter. He was defeated by Sir Gasozein of Dragoz while traveling in Arthur's company. [*ChretienE, Heinrich*]

AMAURIS¹

An Arthurian knight in *Les Merveilles de Rigomer*. He joined Gawain's quest to conquer Rigomer castle. [*Merveil*]

AMAURIS²

An elderly, honorable knight who served Queen Blanche, a queen saved by Claris and Laris. [*Claris*]

AMAURY OF THE ISLANDS

One of Arthur's knights who fought in the Roman War. He died when a prisoner train that he was accompanying to Paris was attacked by the Romans. [*Wace*]

AMAVIA

A lady who killed herself after her husband, Mordaunt, died. Mordaunt had fallen victim to the sorceress Acrasia in the Bower of Bliss. Sir Guyon was present at Amavia's suicide, and he vowed to destroy the Bower. Amavia's infant son was taken to safety by Guyon. [*Spenser*]

AMAZONS

In a link to Greek mythology, the queen of the Amazons appears in the Italian *I Due Tristani*. She forces herself by enchantment on Tristan, the son of Tristan and Isolde. The young Tristan later saves her from the King of the Idumeans. In the Alliterative *Morte Arthure*, we learn that Lucius the Roman had allies in the land of the Amazons. In Spenser's *The Faerie Queene*, Queen Radigund of the Amazons is slan by the warrior maiden Britomart. FInally, in Johnson's *Tom a Lincolne*, an Amazon is briefly Tom a' Lincoln's lover. [*DueTris, Allit, Spenser, Johnson*]

AMBERVAL

In the First Continuation of Chrétien's *Perceval*, Lionel, Gawain's son, is to go to the wedding of the King of Amberval and to retrieve a magical shield. [*Contin1*]

AMBIGAL OF SALIE

A count who joined Wigalois (Gawain's son) in a war against King Lion of Namur. [*Wirnt*]

AMBRIUS

A monastery near Salisbury, named after its abbot. In Geoffrey's chronicle, it was the location of a battle between Vortigern's Britons and Hengist's Saxons. The two sides had convened to sign a peace treaty, but the Saxons betrayed the Britons and attacked. Eldad, the bishop of Ambrius, buried the victims of the battle. [*GeoffHR*]

AMBROSIUS[1]

A monk at the monastery where Perceval retired after the Grail Quest in Tennyson's *Idylls of the King*. His questioning prompts Perceval's recollection of the Grail story. [*TennIK*]

AMBROSIUS[2] AURELIANUS [*Ambrolius, Ambrose, Ambrosius Aurelius, Aurelius Ambrosius, Aurilambros, Aurlis Brosias, Embres, Emreis, Emrys*]

A historical British war-leader, first mentioned by Gildas. Noting that Ambrosius was of Roman descent, Gildas praised him for organizing the Britons and routing the Saxons in the chaotic years following the Roman departure of Britain. His period of activity was likely somewhere between 435 and 460. He may have led a pro-Roman faction that contended with King Vortigern, and it is not impossible that he became some kind of king after Vortigern's death (Lindsay, 212). Gildas does not mention Vortigern's death or the end of his career, and it is possible (though not likely) that he was the British commander at the decisive battle of Badon. In any event, he is one of the few characters noted favorably in Gildas's diatribe, and later sources were to have Arthur continue the resistance that Ambrosius began.

Bede, writing almost 200 years later, repeats Gildas's account, but Nennius, at the beginning of the ninth century, shows the modifications that centuries of legend made to Ambrosius's character. Using the Welsh form *Emrys*, Nennius agrees with Gildas in one passage that Ambrosius was of Roman blood (specifically, the son of a Roman consul). Nennius's tale of Emrys, however, revolves around the belief of Emrys as a fatherless child.

King Vortigern was informed by his advisors that his fortress at Snowdon—the walls of which kept collapsing each night—could only be built if its foundation was first splattered with the blood of a fatherless child. Vortigern's envoys, searching for such a child, came to the town of Elledi in South Wales, where they heard a bully taunting Emrys for having no father. Upon interrogation, Emrys' mother admitted to an immaculate conception, and Vortigern's men hauled him before the king. Emrys halted his execution by showing Vortigern that an underground lake lay beneath the site of the fortress. Within the lake, they found a chest which contained a cloth with a red and white worm. As Vortigern and his soldiers looked on, the worms fought, and the white defeated the red, which signified, Emrys said, the coming defeat of the Britons by the Saxons. Vortigern bestowed Snowdon upon Emrys and fled north. Curiously, we learn in another passage that Vortigern was afraid of Emrys. Clearly, a memory of

historical events has been uncomfortably merged with legendary material in Nennius's account.

William of Malmesbury's chronicle (1125) ignores Nennius's tale and links Ambrosius, for the first time, to Arthur. Calling him the "lone survivor of the Romans," William says that Ambrosius ruled Britain after Vortigern, and that he drove out the Saxons with the aid of Arthur, apparently Ambrosius's general. The idea of Ambrosius and Arthur as contemporaries does not recur until Thelwall's *The Fairy of the Lake* (1801).

Geoffrey of Monmouth's chronicle (c. 1138) developed the most enduring biography of Ambrosius. Geoffrey assigned Nennius's tale of Emrys to a character largely of Geoffrey's own creation—Merlin—and retained Gildas's and William's picture of Ambrosius as a noble Roman warrior. The son of King Constantine, Ambrosius and his brother Uther were forced to flee Britain after their father was assassinated and their older brother, Constans, was foisted to the throne by a power-hungry Vortigern. They found harbor with King Budec of Brittany. When they came of age, Ambrosius and Uther led an army to Britain, and Ambrosius was almost immediately anointed as king. He destroyed Vortigern at the siege of Ganerew, and soon defeated and executed Hengist and the Saxons at the battle of Consibrough. He then defeated and banished Octa, Hengist's son, and set about constructing a new Britain.

He commissioned Merlin to bring the Giant's Dance—a circle of enormous stones—from Ireland to Amesbury. During the expedition, a new threat arose when Pascentius, Vortigern's son, allied with King Gilloman of Ireland. Ambrosius was assassinated when one of their agents, a Saxon named Eopa, visited his court posing as a doctor. He was buried in Amesbury under the Giant's Dance, and his brother Uther became king.

After Geoffrey's chronicle, Ambrosius disappeared from legend and romance for some time. The authors of the Prose *Merlin* and the Vulgate Cycle renamed him PENDRAGON. He resurfaces in the seventeenth century, most notably in *The Birth of Merlin* (1662), a play attributed apocryphally to Shakespeare, in which his marriage to a Saxon maiden named Artesia jeopardizes the security of his kingdom and causes a rift between Ambrosius and Uther. [*Gildas, Bede, Nennius, WilliamM, Birth, Thelwall*]

AMBYGANYE [*Ambage*]

A country allied to the Roman Emperor Lucius. Warriors from the nation fought in Lucius's war against Arthur. [*Allit, Malory*]

AMELIDE

Cousin of Danain the Red. With her lover, Ernant, she was captured by the giant Trudet. She was freed when Guiron the Courteous killed Trudet. [*Palamedes*]

AMENA

Wife of King Lar of Korntin, and mother of Larie. Her husband was killed by King Roaz of Glois, and Amena was driven to a castle called Roimunt at the edge of Korntin—the only fortress strong enough to withstand Roaz. There she remained for a decade, offering her daughter as a prize to any knight who would kill Roaz. Finally, her lady Nereja brought Wigalois (Gawain's son) from Arthur's court. Wigalois killed Roaz, married Larie, and, although assuming the crown of Korntin for himself, restored Amena to a life of comfort. [*Wirnt*]

AMERCILE

In Heinrich von dem Türlin's *Diu Crône*, a lady at Arthur's court. Her lover was a giant. Both Amerclie and her sister Jare failed a chastity test involving an enchanted goblet. [*Heinrich*]

AMESBURY [*Almesbury, Ambresbury, Aumsbury*]

A city in Wiltshire, on the edge of Salisbury Plain. Merlin set up the Giants' Dance—which he brought from Ireland—here, at the site that became known as Stonehenge. According to several sources, Guinevere retired to a nunnery in Amesbury after Arthur's death. The chronicles suggest that it was named after AMBROSIUS, though Layamon says that its founder was AMBRIUS. [*Geoffrey, Stanz, Malory, TennIK*]

AMICE

A friend of Lady Lidoine. When Lidoine was captured and imprisoned by Belchis, Amice journeyed to Arthur's court to seek assistance. [*Raoul*]

AMIDE

Youngest daughter of Count Alout of the Land of the Heather. Upon Alout's death, Amide's uncle, Gallidés, besieged her in the castle of Hungerford because Amide's sister would not marry Gallidés's seneschal. Amide left the castle to seek out a champion, and she returned with Sir Bors, who defeated Gallidés in combat. [*VulgLanc*]

AMIE

The mother by Gawain of Sir Beaudos. Her father was the King of Wales. [*RobertBlo*]

AMILÍAS

A king slain by Tristan. He made frequent raids on Emperor Donísus of Saxony, who sent for Tristan (then the king of Spain) for assistance. [*SagaTI*]

AMILION [*Amylion, Amylyon*]

An island of fairies west of Britain; home of the fairy lover of Sir Landevale and Sir Lambewell (versions of Launfal) in their respective Middle English romances. The name is probably a variation of AVALON, used by Marie de France in her version of Launfal's story. In Thomas Chestre's tale of *Lanfal*, the island is known as OLÉRON. [*SirLand, SirLamb*]

AMINADAP [*Aminadab*]

One of the early kings of Corbenic, the Grail Castle, in the Vulgate *Estoire del Saint Graal*. His father was Joshua, son of Bron. He married the daughter of the British king Lucius, and his son, Carcelois, reigned after him. His descendants included Pelles, Elaine, and Galahad. John of Glastonbury names him as a maternal ancestor of Arthur. The name is found in Exodus 6:23 as the father-in-law of Aaron. [*VulgEst, JohnG*]

AMINADUC [*Aminaduf, Ammaduc, Minaduc*]

Giant high king of the Saxons and brother of Magaat, Mahaglant, and Maglahant. His son was the Saxon king Oriel, and his nephews were Hargadabran and Hengist. He ruled the country of Hoselice. Aminaduc and the Saxons invade Britain in the early days of Arthur's reign, but were expelled by Arthur and the other British kings. [*VulgMer, Livre*]

AMINCAS OF SOTOFEITITON

A king and vassal of Feirefiz, Perceval's half-brother. [*Wolfram*]

AMINT

A castle near which Sir Tor was conceived when King Pellinore raped the wife of Ares the Cowherd. [*PostMer*]

AMIRAUT

In the Didot-*Perceval*, a pagan ally of Lucius the Roman is known simply as "the Amiraut," or "the Emir." One manuscript calls him the SULTAN. Lucius had married his daughter. The Amiraut was slain by Gawain during the Roman War. [*Didot*]

AMIRE

The King of Libya. His wife, Liamere, was coveted by King Lion of Namur, and Lion killed Amire in a joust. Liamere soon died from sorrow. Amire had been scheduled to attend the wedding of Wigalois (Gawain's son), so when Wigalois learned of Amire's murder, he gathered his knights, waged war on Lion, and avenged Amire by slaying the King of Namur. [*Wirnt*]

AMITE

The mother of Galahad according to the Vulgate *Lancelot*. The daughter of King Pelles, she was one of the most beautiful maidens in Britain. Although called "Amite," her true name was Helizabel. In later stories, her name is changed to ELAINE. [*VulgLanc*]

AMLAWDD [*Anl(l)awd(d)*]

In Welsh legend, a ruler (*wledig*) who was the father of Goleuddydd, Rieingulid, and Igerne, and the grandfather of Arthur and Culhwch. His wife was named Gwen. [*Culhwch*]

AMMILOT

Duke of the Flowers of the Wilderness. He served King Ekunaver of Kanadic and joined Ekunaver's war against Arthur. [*PleierG*]

AMODOR

A knight freed by Tristan from the prison of an island castle. At Tristan's urging, he agreed to become a vassal of Lancelot. [*Povest*]

AMONTSUS

In Heinrich von dem Türlin's *Diu Crône*, a castle in Ordohorht, the land of Lady Fortune. Its steward, Aanzim, gave lodging to Gawain when he visited the country. [*Heinrich*]

AMORAEN

A king who owned the enchanted Sword with Two Rings. Gawain needed the sword so he could trade it for a magic chessboard owned by King Wonder. Amoraen agreed to give the sword to Gawain on the condition that Gawain locate and bring to him the beautiful maiden Ysabele. [*Penninc*]

AMORAT OF SORELOIS

A knight slain by Tristan in a duel at the Plain of Assorted Flowers. [*Sala*]

AMORAVE

The kingdom belonging to Aristor, an enemy of Perceval and his family. Its capital was called Ariste. [*Perlesvaus*]

AMORES THE SWARTHY

A knight who served Arthur and Leodegan in the war against the Saxons. [*VulgMer, Arthour*]

AMORET

A lady who is one of the representatives of chastity in Spenser's *The Faerie Queene*. Amoret and her sister, Belphoebe, were raised by goddesses; Amoret's mistress was Venus. Engaged to Sir Scudamore, she was abducted by the magician Busirane. Britomart, a warrior maiden and friend of Arthur, saved her and became her loyal companion. She was kidnapped again, by the Hairy Churl, and was rescued by her sister and Timias, Arthur's squire. Arthur became her protector and delivered her to Scudamore, whom she finally married. [*Spenser*]

AMOROLDO [*Amoroldino*]

The Italian version of MORHOLT, the Irish giant slain by Tristan. In *La Tavola Ritonda*, the name is also given to Morholt's son, GOLISTANT, when Tristan knighted him and bestowed the kingdom of Ireland upon him. The younger Amoroldo took a queen named Vermiglia, and developed a vast kingdom that included parts of England, Logres, Aquitaine, and Gaul. Arthur eventually made him a Knight of the Round Table. He went to war with King Alois of North Wales over a castle called Lerlinte, enlisting Tristan as his champion, while Alois retained the services of Lancelot. Arthur brokered a peace, but Alois renewed the war after the Grail Quest. In this second campaign, Amoroldo was slain by Lancelot. [*Tavola*]

AMOROTTO OF LISTENOIS

A king in *La Tavola Ritonda*; one possible father of Suziano, a knight slain by Tristan. He gave the rich city of Latinale to Largina, his lover. The same name is used in *Tavola* as the Italian variation of LAMORAT. [*Tavola*]

AMOROUS CITY [*Cité Amoureuse*]

A city in *Le Chevalier du Papegau*, saved by Arthur from the demonic Fish-Knight. It was ruled by the Lady of the Blonde Hair, who fell in love with Arthur. [*ChevPap*]

AMOROUS FORD

A river crossing where Perceval defeated the White Knight, who had defended the ford for seven years. [*Contin2*]

AMOROUS KNIGHT OF THE SAVAGE CASTLE

A knight whom Arthur saved from the jaws of a giant, poisonous serpent. In return, the Amorous Knight cured Arthur of poisonous wounds received in the battle. He also told Arthur how to end the enchantments ensnaring the Kingdom of Damsels. [*ChevPap*]

AMPFLISE[1]

The Queen of France during Uther's time in Wolfram's *Parzival*. She loved and was loved by Perceval's father Gahmuret. When her husband died, she sent envoys to Wales (where she heard Gahmuret was staying to participate in a tournament) to woo Gahmuret back to France; Gahmuret would have gone willingly, but he was bound to marry Queen Herzeloyde of Wales because he had won her tournament. Ampflise gave her foster-son, the ill-fated Schionatulander, to Gahmuret for training in knightly affairs. [*Wolfram*]

AMPFLISE[2]

The beautiful, virtuous daughter of Count Jernis of Ryl. She was a Grail Maiden living at Munsalvæsche and member of the Grail Procession. [*Wolfram*]

AMPHIBALUS

The church in Winchester where Constans, son of Constantine, was raised and educated to become a monk. [*GeoffHR*]

AMR [*Amhar, Anir*]

A son of Arthur who appears in Nennius and Welsh legend. Nennius notes (without explanation) that Arthur killed him and buried him in a tomb in Ercing, called Licat Anir. In the Welsh story of *Geraint*, we learn that Amr served as his father's squire, guarding his bed. [*Nennius, Geraint*]

AMREN THE TALL

Son of Bedwyr, and one of Arthur's warriors. He held the position of chamberlain and guarded Arthur's bed. He accompanied Arthur on an adventure to the cave of the Black Hag in the Valley of Distress. Amren was beaten senseless by the hag. [*Culhwch, Geraint*]

AMURAT

Count of Turtus, husband of Klarine, and father of Duzabel. Sir Garel rescued his daughter when she was captured by a giant named Purdan. Amurat rewarded Garel by bringing his army to Arthur's war against King Ekunaver of Kanadic. [*PleierG*]

AMURELLE

The wife of Blandukors, a nobleman who hosted Gawain during one of his adventures in Heinrich von dem Türlin's *Diu Crône*. She had a daughter named Sgaipegaz. [*Heinrich*]

AMURFINA

Daughter of Lord Laniure of Serre and Ansgien, sister of Sgoidamur, and eventual wife of Gawain in Heinrich's *Diu Crône*. When her father died, Amurfina took possession of a magic bridle that controlled the family fortune, thus disinheriting her sister. In the dispute, both of them solicited Gawain as their champion. While Gawain was visiting her castle, her servant Aclamet served him a love potion which caused him to fall madly in love with Amurfina. They married and Gawain became the lord of Serre. Amurfina's uncle, Gansguoter, was Arthur's step-father. A character of similar nature appears unnamed in *La Mule sans Frein*. [*Heinrich*]

AMUSTAN

The chaplain of King Leodegan of Carmelide (Guinevere's father) in the Vulgate romances. He married Arthur and Guinevere and accompanied them to Arthur's court, where he continued his service as chaplain. He later became a hermit, but he helped Arthur during the False Guinevere episode by identifying the real Guinevere. He be represented in *Lancelot of the Laik* as AMYTANS. [*VulgLanc, VulgMer*]

AMYTANS

In *Lancelot of the Laik*, the name given to the character unnamed in the Vulgate *Lancelot* who, during Arthur's war with Galehaut, upbraids Arthur for his failings, and instructs him on how to be a virtuous and noble king. His name may have been inspired by AMUSTAN in the Vulgate romances. [*LancLaik*]

ANARAUT [*Anavalt, Arnalf, Euerad*]

The Earl of Salisbury under King Arthur. GALLUC is also given this distinction. [*GeoffHR, Wace, Layamon*]

ANAROM THE FAT

A Knight of the Round Table who embarked with the others on the Grail Quest. [*PostQuest*]

ANASCOR [*Anacoron, Nascar*]

A follower of Joseph of Arimathea who, in Sarras, was once charged with guarding the Holy Grail. [*VulgEst*]

ANASTEU

A knight who lived almost a century before Arthur's time. His father, King Assen, strongly disapproved of Anasteu's love for a lowborn woman. Fleeing his father's wrath, Anasteu took his lady into a forest, and carved a home for them out of solid rock, equipping it with various luxuries. Later, this cavern served as Merlin's prison after he was shut up by the Lady of the Lake. [*VulgMer*]

ANATHITES

The Christian bishop left in Sarras by Joseph of Arimathea to preserve the faith. [*VulgEst*]

ANBE

A castle near Camelot. [*PostMer*]

ANCHISES[1]

Seneschal of Queen Lidoine, wife of Sir Meraugis of Portlesguez. [*Raoul*]

ANCHISES[2]

A relative of Sir Bors of Gannes slain by a giant. Bors killed the giant and erected an abbey, called the Abbey of Gannes, on the spot. [*ProsTris*]

ANCIENT CASTLE [**Chastel Anchien*]

A castle on the border of Ireland where Uther Pendragon won a tournament. Leodegan, Guinevere's father, once besieged it. [*Palamedes*]

ANCIENT CHAPEL

A chapel near Salisbury where Arthur was taken after the final battle with Mordred. From there, Arthur departed on the sea with Morgan le Fay. Sir Girflet later found Arthur's "tomb" there, but it contained only his helmet. Girflet retired there as a hermit. [*PostMort*]

ANCISA

A fortress on the Hidden Isle in the Uziano Sea. It was ruled by Lasancis, a knight who tried to massacre the Knights of the Round Table. [*Tavola*]

ANCORE

A forest that Tristan and Galahad traversed during the Grail Quest. [*ProsTris*]

ANDECLIS

In Heinrich von dem Türlin's *Diu Crône*, an allusion is made to Gawain's battle with one Iaphine, who had slain the lover of Lady Andeclis. [*Heinrich*]

ANDELISE

Mother of Sir Durmart by King Jozefent. Her father was the King of Denmark. [*Durmart*]

ANDELIZ

A Knight of the Round Table who participated in the Grail Quest. [*ProsTris*]

ANDIGAMI

One of Arthur's noblemen in the Norse *Erex Saga*. [*Erex*]

ANDOIS

Arthur's host in the Kingdom of Damsels in *Le Chevalier du Papegau*. Arthur came to the kingdom to save its lady, Flor de Mont, from her late father's steward, who had seized the land for himself. Andois declined to help the lady himself because he felt that her father, King Beauvoisin, had not sufficiently rewarded him for his service in foreign wars. [*ChevPap*]

ANDRAGIUS

According to Geoffrey of Monmouth, a king of Britain in the third or second century BC. He was the son of King Cherin. He succeeded his brother, King Eldad, and was succeeded by his son, King Urian. [*GeoffHR*]

ANDRED [*Adreitte, Aldret, Andret, *Andrew, Antret, Audret, Alebruno, Adriecche*]

Nephew of King Mark of Cornwall, cousin of Tristan. In Béroul's *Tristan*, he appears as a good friend of Tristan and Isolde, and he urges Mark not to banish Tristan from the court. In later versions, however, he becomes Mark's sniveling seneschal and spy. Jealous of Tristan's prowess, Andred conspired (with his girlfriend, Girida or Bessille) to entrap the lovers and expose their affair. He succeeded on several occasions. In the Prose *Tristan*, his final tattle leads to Mark's murder of Tristan with a poisoned lance. The Post-Vulgate *Queste del Saint Graal* tells us that Mark raped Andred's wife, Ladiana, begetting Sir Meraugis. In the Italian *La Tavola Ritonda*, Mark, despondent without his nephew and wife, slays Andred for his despicable behavior. In other versions, Andred is executed by Tristan's friends after Mark's death or is drowned while trying to board the ship bringing Isolde to the mortally wounded Tristan. [*Beroul, Eilhart, PostQuest, ProsTris, Tavola, Malory*]

ANDREMO THE OLD OF SOBICIO

Tristan's maternal grandfather. He married Felice, Arthur's sister, and became the father of Elizabeth (Tristan's mother). Andremo was cousin to Ban of Benoic (Lancelot's father). [*Tavola*]

ANDRIVETE [*Androete*]

Daughter of Cador of Northumberland in Girart d'Amien's *Escanor*. Her father threw a tournament at Banborc to find her a husband. Kay distinguished himself in the tournament and fell in love with Andrivete, but, bashful, he returned to Arthur's court without confessing his affections. When her father died, her uncle Ayglin tried to force her to marry a commoner. Kay learned of her plight, returned to Banborc, rescued Andrivete, and married her. In a romance preceding Girart's, Andrivete is proven unfaithful by a chastity test at Arthur's court involving a mantle. [*MantelM, Girart*]

ANDROES

In *La Tavola Ritonda*, the King of Scotland in the time of Uther and in Arthur's early days. He joined King Meliadus of Lyonesse's war against Arthur. [*Tavola*]

ANEBLAYSE [*Danbleys, Danebleise, Denebleise*]

A wealthy city in King Leodegan's Carmelide, featured in the Vulgate *Merlin*. It was besieged by King Rions and the Saxons in the early days of Arthur's reign, but its fortifications were so strong that the defenders only had to worry about being starved out. A combined force of Arthur, Ban, and Bors routed Rions and lifted the siege. The English *Arthour and Merlin* places this battle at CARHAIX. [*VulgMer, Arthour*]

ANED

A hound needed by the warrior Culhwch, as one of tasks, to hunt the boar Twrch Trwyth. Other tasks required that Culhwch find certain people to manage Aned and another hound, Aethlem. Arthur helped Culhwch obtain the hound for the hunt. After the hunt, Aned could not be found and was never seen again. [*Culhwch*]

ANFERGINAN

A valley in Ireland in which a vicious, fire-breathing dragon lived. Tristan slew the dragon, earning him favor at the court of King Gurmun (Isolde's father). [*Gottfried*]

ANFOIES

A knight who participated in the tournament of Sorgarda, won by Gawain. [*Heinrich*]

ANFORTAS

The FISHER KING or Grail King in Wolfram's *Parzival*. The lord of Munsalvæsche, he was Perceval's maternal uncle, son of Frimutel, and brother of Herzeloyde,

Trevrizent, Schoysiane, and Repanse de Schoye. He neglected his duties as Grail King by engaging in a joust for the love of Queen Orgeluse, and was wounded in the groin as punishment. Because of the festering wound, he lived in excruciating pain, but could not die because he was sustained by the Grail. He was cured—after one failed attempt—when Perceval asked the Grail Question. Perceval succeeded him as Grail King. His name may be a variation of the Old French *enfertez* or *enfermetez*, meaning "infirmity" (Bruce, 317n). [*Wolfram*]

ANFROTHIN

In a monologue in Heinrich von dem Türlin's *Diu Crône*, Gawain recounts that he once saved a maiden named Isazanz from abduction by a knight named Anfroihin. [*Heinrich*]

ANGALE [*Orvale*]

The lady of the castle Raguidel and a cousin of Lancelot. Her lord, an evil man named Marigart the Red, was slain by Sir Hector, who later rescued Angale from a pair of lions. [*VulgLanc*]

ANGAN

An Arthurian knight in Wace's *Roman de Brut*. [*Wace*]

ANGARAS

Son of the lord of Karamphi in Heinrich von dem Türlin's *Diu Crône*. Gawain had killed his brother Dahamorht, so he attacked Gawain when the latter was visiting Karamphi. Angaras's father stopped the fight, but as a condition of his freedom, Gawain had to perform a service for Angaras: to learn all that he could about the mystic Grail. At the conclusion of the romance, Gawain satisfied this requirement. Angaras and Gawain became friends, and Angaras was awarded a place at the Round Table. His counterpart in Wolfram von Eschenbach's *Parzival* is VERGULAHT. [*Heinrich*]

ANGAWDD

Son of Caw, one of twenty brothers, and a warrior of King Arthur. [*Culhwch*]

ANGELIS OF THE VAAOS

A Knight of the Round Table who embarked with the others on the Grail Quest. [*PostQuest*]

ANGELA

Saxon queen who was captured by the British. Her armor and enchanted spear were taken by Britomart, the warrior maiden, for her adventures in Fairy Land. [*Spenser*]

ANGELLICA

Daughter of the Earl of London. With Arthur, she had an illegitimate child named Tom a' Lincoln. [*Johnson*]

ANGENIS

The noble king of Iserterre. Allied to King Ekunaver of Kanadic, he joined Ekunaver's war against Arthur, in which he was slain by Duke Gilan of Wales. [*PleierG*]

ANGERS

A region of France, conquered by Arthur and bestowed upon Kay. [*Wace*]

ANGHARAD GOLDEN HAND [*Angharat*]

In the Welsh tale of *Peredur*, a lady at Arthur's court; in Thomas Hughes' play *The Misfortunes of Arthur*, Guinevere's sister. *Peredur* relates how the hero fell in love with her, and vowed not to speak to any Christian man until Angharad professed to love him. For this, he was nicknamed the Mute Knight. Later, Angharad saw Peredur defeat a strong knight in joust. She did not know Peredur's identity, but she went to him and told him she loved him for his knightly prowess. At this, Peredur revealed himself and was able to talk to his companions again. In Hughes' play, Angharad dissuades Guinevere from suicide after the latter has learned that Arthur is returning to Britain to deal with Mordred's treason. [*Peredur, HughesT*]

ANGINON

In Heinrich von dem Türlin's *Diu Crône*, a king and one of Arthur's vassals. [*Heinrich*]

ANGIRON

Arthur's king of Ireland in Heinrich von dem Türlin's *Diu Crône*. [*Heinrich*]

ANGLEDIS

Daugher of Ranner, wife of Prince Bodwyne, and mother of Alexander the Orphan. When Bodwyne was killed by his brother, King Mark, Angledis took Alexander and fled Cornwall. She arrived in Sussex, at the Castle Magance, where she raised Alexander to manhood. Upon his knighting, Angledis charged her son to avenge his father's death. [*ProsTris, Prophecies, Malory*]

ANGLES

A Germanic tribe that invaded and settled in eastern England in the fifth century, during and after the time of King Arthur. The Angles gave their name to England (Angle-Land). William of Malmesbury wrongly calls the war-leaders Hengist, Horsa, and their kinsmen Angles, when in fact they were SAXONS. "Angle" and "Saxon" are often used interchangeably. [*WilliamM*]

ANGLESEY

A large island in the Irish sea of the northern coast of Wales, known as MÔN to the Welsh. A Welsh legend relates how Cei (Kay) went to the island to fight lions and engaged in combat with the fearsome Cath Palug (Clawing Cat). [*WelshPG*]

ANGLITORA

Daughter of Prester John. She loved and had a child with Tom a' Lincoln, Arthur's son, but she scorned Tom when she discovered he was an illegitimate child. She betrayed Tom, and her new lover, a sultan, murdered him. Her son, known as the Black Knight, avenged Tom's death by slaying Anglitora and her lover. [*Johnson*]

ANGNIE

Lady of the Beautiful Forest and wife of Moralde. Her daughter, Claudin, was saved by Arthur's Sir Tandareis. [*PleierT*]

ANGRAM

A city from which Gawain received a dozen lances. [*Wolfram*]

ANGRES

In Chrétien's *Cliges*, a nobleman from Windsor whom Arthur left in charge of Britain during an expedition to Brittany. While Arthur was in Brittany, he received word that Angres had betrayed him and seized the throne. Arthur returned to Britain, raised an army, and began a war against Angres. Eventually, Arthur's army drove Angres back to his castle in Windsor where, at a final battle, the Greek warrior Alexander captured him, but not before Angres killed Alexander's companion Macdor. Arthur executed him. Chrétien has made an obvious thematic connection with MORDRED. [*ChretienC*]

ANGSIR OF SLALOI

In Heinrich von dem Türlin's *Diu Crône*, a reference is made to a tournament fought at Babylon between Arthur and three knights, one of whom was Angsir. [*Heinrich*]

ANGUIGUERRON [*Aguigneron, Anguigeron*]

Seneschal of Clamadeu of the Isles. He appears in Chrétien's *Perceval* and in the Vulgate romances. He was one of a number of rulers that rebelled against King Arthur's ascension to the throne. He also fought the Saxon invasion, leading a battalion at Salisbury. In the service of Clamadeu, he defeated, captured, and imprisoned hundreds of knights from the town of Beaurepaire, in an effort to persuade the lady of the town, Blancheflor, to marry Clamadeu. Perceval agreed to serve as Blancheflor's champion, and he defeated both Anguiguerron and Clamadeu in combat. In some versions, Perceval slays Anguigerron; in others, he sends him to Arthur as a prisoner. Anguigerron's counterpart in Wolfram's *Parzival* is KINGRUN. [*ChretienP, Contin1, VulgMer, PostMer*]

ANGUIN

A knight raised with Lionel and Bors by the Lady of the Lake. His father, Pharien, was a servant of King Bors of Gannes. Anguin and his brother Tantain remained with the Lady after their father's death. [*VulgLanc*]

ANGUISH [*Ang(u)ins, A(n)guisant, Anguisshe, Languis, Hanguin, Lenvis*]

King of Ireland and father of Isolde in the Prose *Tristan* and in Malory. His name could be a derivation of Geoffrey's ANGUSEL of Scotland, though some scholars have suggested a connection with an historical Irish king named ÓENGUS. His counterpart in Gottfried von Strassburg is GURMUN. Malory, perhaps conflating him with ANGUSEL, says that he was one of the kings who rebelled against Arthur, and was defeated with his comrades at Bedegraine. Tennyson gives a similar account, saying that he joined with Urien in an invasion of Carmelide.

His brother-in-law (or nephew), Morholt, was slain in his service by Tristan. When the latter turned up at Anguish's court, Anguish considered killing him but ultimately decided to acquit him over the objections of his wife (variously called Lotta or Isolde). Afterwards, Anguish and Tristan became friends, and Tristan defended the King of Ireland against a murder charge brought by Sir Blamor of Gannes, Lancelot's cousin. Anguish had a dream portending Tristan's affair with Isolde, but still handed his daughter over when Tristan came to collect her for King Mark of Cornwall. [*ProsTris, Tavola, Malory, TennIK*]

ANGUSEL [*A(u)ngel, Aguiflet, Aguillars, Aguisans, Aguisant, A(n)guisel, A(n)guissans, Aguissant, A(n)guizans, Angus, Angvisa(u)nt, Angwisshe, Angwisiez, Auguselus, Aungers*]

King of Scotland, first named by Geoffrey of Monmouth. The numerous variations of his name may include ANGUISH of Ireland. Geoffrey tells us that he was the brother of Urien and Lot, but the Vulgate *Merlin* calls him the son of King Caradoc and one of Arthur's unnamed half-sisters (and therefore Arthur's nephew). In a Welsh adaptation of Geoffrey, his counterpart is ARAWN. He name suggests the common Scottish *Angus*, which belonged to an earl of Moray in the early twelfth century.

In Geoffrey's version, Arthur restores him to his position as king of Scotland after the country was reclaimed from the Saxons. In later works, however, he is portrayed as an early enemy of Arthur. He was one of the kings who rebelled against Arthur's ascension to the throne. Arthur defeated the confederation at the battle of Bedegraine, after which the Saxons invaded Scotland, and Angusel had to return to fortify his city of Caranges. Joined by Kings Urien and Nentres, he successfully fought off the invaders, led by King Oriel. Eventually, Angusel and the other rebelling kings reached a truce with Arthur and together crushed the Saxons at Clarence. He later joined Arthur's wars against Rome, Galehaut, and Claudas. He died fighting Mordred's army at the battle of Richborough or Salisbury, where he led a battalion. Chrétien de Troyes gives him two sons named Cadret and Cuoi, and the *Prophecies de Merlin* assigns him another named Archemais. Thomas Hughes says Gawain inherited his kingdom. [*GeoffHR, ChretienE, Wace, Layamon,*

VulgLanc, VulgMort, VulgMer, Prophecies, Malory, HughesT]

ANJOU [Angeoy, Angers, Anschowe]

This region of western France was the country of Perceval's paternal ancestry in Wolfram's *Parzival*. The country was ruled by Perceval's grandfather Gandin and then by Gandin's son Galoes. The scepter was later passed to Perceval's son Kardeiz. It's capital was Bealzenan.

According to *Arthour and Merlin*, Uther conquered Anjou from Harinan, Igerne's first husband. Geoffrey says that it was conquered by Arthur and given to Kay. Malory says that it was owned by Lancelot, and that Lancelot made Sir Dinas the duke of Anjou in return for Dinas's support in the war against King Arthur. [*Geoffrey, Wace, Layamon, Wolfram, Arthour, Malory*]

ANNA [Anne]

The daughter of Uther and Igerne, wife of Lot, and mother of Gawain and Mordred in Geoffrey's account. The character of MORGAUSE replaced her. *De Ortu Waluuanii* relates how Anna fell in love with Lot, who was staying at Uther's court as a hostage from Norway. They engaged in a clandestine affair, which produced the illegitimate Gawain. Anna, who had kept her pregnancy secret, decided to send Gawain away at his birth to avoid trouble with Uther—but she sent with him a ring and parchment attesting to his lineage, which he later used to gain entry to Arthur's service. In his play *The Misfortunes of Arthur*, Thomas Hughes uses Anna rather than Morgause, but he makes Mordred a product of Anna and Arthur's incest, which Geoffrey does not. [*Geoffrey, DeOrtu, HughesT*]

ANNAS

In two sixteenth-century English versions of Joseph of Arimathea's life, the Jew Annas is one of Joseph's jailers in Jerusalem. Caiaphas, mentioned in the Vulgate texts, is his companion. Annas appears as one of Christ's accusers before Pilate in the apocryphal *Gospel of Nicodemus*. [*HereJoA, LyfeJoA*]

ANNECIANS

A godson of King Bors of Gannes who fought for Arthur at the battle of Bedegraine. [*Malory*]

ANNORE [Anfole]

Queen of Averre in Wolfram's *Parzival*. She was loved by Galoes of Anjou (Perceval's uncle), who died in her service. Der Pleier adds that she was married to King Avenis and had two daughters named Laudamie and Anfole. [*Wolfram, PleierG*]

ANNUEC

The King of Annuec's son took part in the tournament of Banborc, at which Kay met his future wife, Andrivete. Annuec may be ALNWICK in Northumberland. [*Girart*]

ANNWN [Annwf(y)n]

The Celtic otherworld, akin to Hades or Hell, inhabited by fairies, demons, maidens, and warriors. It is variously described as an island, a valley, and an underworld. It is said to have various portals of entry from the mortal world. An early Welsh poem known as *Preiddeu Annwfn* describes an expedition by Arthur and his warriors to the mysterious otherworld, where they defeat 600 warriors and obtain a magic cauldron kept by nine maidens. In the poem, Annwn is called, among other things, a fairy fortress, a glass fortress, and a "fort of carousal." Although three boatloads of warriors went with Arthur to Annwn, only seven men returned. The references to the ships, including Arthur's ship Prydwen, suggests that Annwn is an island. According to *Culhwch and Olwen*, the powers of the demons of Annwn were vested in the warrior Gwynn, son of Nudd. [*Culhwch, Spoils*]

ANNYNAWG [Anynnawg]

One of Arthur's warriors who was the son of Menw. [*Culhwch*]

ANOETH[1]

A British city in which Arthur was imprisoned by Gwen Pendragon for three days, according to a Triad. The word *anoeth* is an intensifier comparable to the English "incredible," possibly meaning either "wonderful" or "difficult." The word is used to describe Arthur's grave in a Welsh poem, which may indicate an early Welsh belief in the mysterious circumstances surrounding Arthur's death (see ARTUR'S GRAVE). [*WelshSG, Triads*]

ANOETH[2] THE BOLD

One of Arthur's warriors. [*Culhwch*]

ANSALINERO

A North Welsh king in *La Tavola Ritonda*. Arthur and King Amoroldo of Ireland appointed him to judge the great tournament at Leverzep. Another king named ALOIS is named as the King of North Wales in the same story. [*Tavola*]

ANSCHOES

A knight present at the Sorgarda tournament in *Diu Crône*. [*Heinrich*]

ANSEÏS [Ossaise]

A knight from Sorelois who fought in the tournament at Sorelois. [*ProsTris, Malory*]

ANSELME

In the Elizabethan play *The Birth of Merlin*, a prophetic hermit who visited Aurelius Ambrosius's court. He condemned Aurelius's marriage to Artesia, a Saxon maiden. [*Birth*]

ANSGAVIN

One of two "toll collectors" from Ansgiure defeated by Gawain in Heinrich von dem Türlin's *Diu Crône*. Ansgavin's brother Salmanide was slain in the battle. [*Heinrich*]

ANSGIEN OF ILERN

The mother of Amurfina (Gawain's wife) and Sgoidamur by Lord Laniure of Serre. Her brother, Gansguoter, was Igerne's second husband. [*Heinrich*]

ANSGIURE

A land visited by Gawain, where he defeated two tyrannical "toll collectors" named Ansgavin and Salmanide. [*Heinrich*]

ANSGOI

The location of Sorgarda Castle, where Gawain won a tournament in Heinrich von dem Türlin's *Diu Crône*. Its lord was named Leigamar. [*Heinrich*]

ANSGÜ

An evil warrior in Heinrich von dem Türlin's *Diu Crône*. His companion, Lohenis of Rahaz, stole Gawain's horse. Ansgü, knowing that Gawain had replaced his warhorse with a nag, challenged him to a joust. Gawain was victorious despite the disadvantage. Ansgü's counterpart in Wolfram von Eschenbach's *Parzival* is FLORANT of Itolac. [*Heinrich*]

ANSOIT OF RIVIERE

A Knight of the Round Table who participated in the Grail Quest. [*ProsTris*]

ANTALINO

The nephew of King Gilierchino of Brittany (Tristan's father-in-law). When Tristan conquered the city of Gippa, he left Antalino as viceroy. [*Tavola*]

ANTANOR THE SILENT

A mute knight in Arthur's court, sworn to refrain from speaking until he saw the best knight in the world. A lady in court, named Cunneware, refrained from laughing for the same reason. When Perceval came to court, Cunneware laughed and was beaten by an insulted Sir Kay. Antanor reproached Kay and predicted retribution for his actions. In response, Kay tanned Antanor. Perceval later revenged Kay's abusive deeds by breaking his arm and collarbone in a joust. Antanor is called KULIANZ the Fool in *Diu Crône*. [*Wolfram*]

ANTELAN

A dwarf king from Scotland who journeyed to Arthur's court to seek adventure. After defeating Perceval, Gawain, and Galleman in combat, he returned home. [*Antelan*]

ANTELE

An earl in the service of the Duke of Lorraine in the Alliterative *Morte Arthure*. With his brother Algere, he fought in a battle against Gawain during the Roman War. Malory includes this character but re-names him ETHELWOLD. [*Allit*]

ANTHEMES [*Alelme, Anslem, Antemes, Anteaumes, Anthiaume*]

Seneschal to King Ban of Benoic in the Vulgate *Merlin*. He fought with Ban and Arthur against the Saxons, and in the wars against King Claudas. He may be identical to the unnamed seneschal in the Vulgate *Lancelot* who betrays Ban by allow Claudas entry into Ban's city of Trebe. [*VulgMer, Livre, Malory*]

ANTHEMIUS

The western Roman emperor between 467 and 472. He was appointed by Emperor Leo I, who ruled in Constantinople. He is not mentioned in Arthurian chronicle or romance, but he figures into the history of Riothamus, a historical British king who many have seen as the origin of Arthur. At the behest of Anthemius, Riothamus brought an army of Britons into Gaul in 468 to drive out the Visigoths. The expedition failed and Riothamus was defeated.

ANTHONJE

Arthur's sister in the Pleier's *Meleranz*, who married the King of Gritenland and became the mother of Gaheris. Gaheris's mother in other romance is usually MORGAUSE, by King Lot. [*PleierM*]

ANTIDOLUS

The seneschal of King Brandon the Saxon. He participated in the Saxon invasion of Britain in the early days of Arthur's reign. He was killed at the siege of Clarence by Arthur's Sir Eliezer. [*VulgMer*]

ANTIKONIE [*Anticoni*]

Sister of King Vergulaht of Ascalun. She became infatuated with Gawain during one of his visits, which caused her brother to attack him. She later married King Dulcemar of Tandernas and gave birth to Tandareis, who became one of Arthur's knights. [*Wolfram, PleierT*]

ANTIUFAIS

An Irish keep visited by Lancelot on his way to Rigomer Castle in *Les Merveilles de Rigomer*. There, he was warmly hosted by Sir Baudris, who provided information on Rigomer. [*Merveil*]

ANTOAGAIS [*Autragais*]

A large knight encountered by Lancelot on his first quest, which was to defend the Lady of Nohaut against an invader. Lancelot wished to steal a glance at Antoagais's lady, but Antoagais refused to let him into her tent. Lancelot fought him for this right, and Antoagais was miserably defeated. Lancelot took his lady after making Antoagais promise to never fight anyone again except in self-defense. Lancelot later learned that the encounter had been arranged by the Lady of Nohaut in order to test the young Lancelot's prowess. [*LancLac*, *VulgLanc*]

ANTONIE

The niece of King Bagdemagus. She lived in Montikluse with her brother, Kandalion. Kandalion imprisoned Tandareis, one of Arthur's knights, and left him to starve, but Antonie kept him alive until her brother decided to free him. She wanted to marry Tandareis, but his betrothal to another prevented it. At his suggestion, she married King Beacurs of Norway, Arthur's nephew. [*PleierT*]

ANTONIO[1]

A knight slain by Tristan during a tournament in Ireland. Antonio's son later encountered Tristan in Cornwall, and tried to slay him with a poisoned arrow. He succeeded only in wounding Tristan, who slew him for the deed. The knight is named only in the Italian *La Tavola Ritonda*, though this episode appears in the Prose *Tristan* and in Malory's version. [*Tavola*]

ANTONIO[2] [*Antoine*]

A bishop from Ireland or Wales who became one of Merlin's scribes. [*VitaMer*, *Prophecies*, *Pieri*]

ANTOR [*Anton, Antore, Antour, Entor*]

Arthur's foster-father, and the father of Kay, in the Prose and Vulgate *Merlins*, the Didot-*Perceval*, and Tennyson. Robert de Boron seems to have originated the character. Renowned as a wise man, Antor raised Arthur after Merlin presented him with the child. When his foster-son became king, Antor joined the wars against the Saxons. His character appears in the Post-Vulgate and Malory as ECTOR. J. D. Bruce suggests, as the origin of his name, a possible corruption of ARTHUR, given the literary tradition of naming children after their foster fathers (cf. GAWAIN in *De Ortu Waluuanii*). [*ProseMer1*, *VulgMer*, *Livre*, *Didot*, *Arthour*, *TennIK*]

ANTORE

The father of Vyolette, a maiden saved from two giants by Guinglain (Gawain's son). In reward for his heroism, Antore gave Guinglain a fine suit of armor. [*ChestreLyb*]

ANTORILAS

A knight in the service of King Claudas (Lancelot's enemy), killed by Gawain in the battle of Trebe. [*VulgMer*]

ANTRIADIN

A castle that King Mark of Cornwall gave to Isolde after she passed a test of chastity at Vermilion Rock. [*Tavola*]

ANTWERP

A city on the coast of Brabant where Loherangrin, Perceval's son, met his future wife. [*Wolfram*]

ANUPLIT

Palamedes' father in the Serbo-Russian *Povest O' Tryshchane*, replacing ASTLABOR from the Prose *Tristan*. [*Povest*]

ANUREZ THE BASTARD

An enemy of Gawain. His brother, Nabigan, was killed by Gawain, so he attacked Gawain and Arthur on their return from a pilgrimage to the Grail Castle. Besieging them in a manor, he had them well trapped, but Sir Meliot of Logres made a timely arrival and killed Anurez in combat. [*Perlesvaus*]

ANWAS THE WINGED

Father of Twrch, and one of Arthur's warriors. [*Culhwch*]

ANZANSNUSE

A lady who, with her husband Rivalin, healed Gawain after he had been injured in a battle with some giants. [*Heinrich*]

ANZILERE

A murderer who figures into Tristan's ancestry. He was born the son of King Clodoveus. His sister was named Cressile or Trasfilas. He slew Appollo, the first King of Lyoness (and Tristan's great-great-great-grandfather), for which his father executed him. Appearing in the Prose *Tristan* and *La Tavola Ritonda*, he is unnamed in the former. [*ProsTris*, *Tavola*]

APLASAT THE LARGE

A Knight of the Round Table who participated in the Grail Quest. [*ProsTris*]

APOLLO [*Apolon*]

The first king of Lyoness, descended from Alexander the Great. He was Tristan's great-great-great grandfather. The son of Sador (son of Bron) and Chelinde, he was abandoned in the forest as an infant by Canor, his stepfather, and was found and raised by Sir Nichoraut of Cornwall and his wife Madule. He grew up to be a good knight but, in a tragic Oedipal situation, he unknowingly killed his father Sador and married his mother Chelinde. St. Augustine converted Apollo to Christianity and revealed these facts to him. Chelinde was killed by a lightning bolt while attempting to murder St. Augustine. Apollo re-married Gloriande and had a son named Candaces, who succeeded him. Apollo was killed by Anzilere, son of the King of Cornwall, who desired his wife. [*ProsTris*, *Tavola*, *Povest*]

APULIA [*Apolon*]

A region of Italy. In *Claris et Laris*, its king, Celias, enters into a brief war with Arthur. [*Claris*]

AQUEON

One of Arthur's castles in Logres. [*Palamedes*]

AQUILIAN

Ruler of the castle Helyn. When Aquilian mistreated Galehaut the Brown, Galehaut killed Aquilian and all of his fourteen sons. [*Palamedes*]

AQUIN OF ORBRIE

One of Arthur's knights. [*Renaut*]

AQUITAINE

Region of southwest France. According to Geoffrey, Duke Guitard ruled it until Duke Hoel conquered it as part of Arthur's campaign in Europe. Gottfried tells us that it was the homeland of the evil dwarf Melot, Tristan's betrayer. In the Vulgate *Lancelot,* it is ruled by King Claudas, and in *La Tavola Ritonda*, King Amoroldo of Ireland holds the dukedom of Aquitaine. [*GeoffHR, Gottfried, VulgLanc, Tavola*]

ARAB THE DWARF

A king who was a vassal of Arthur. [*Heinrich*]

ARABIA

Literally, the peninsula in southwest Asia, between the Red Sea and the Persian Gulf, though some Arthurian authors undoubtedly used it loosely to cover northern Africa as well. Wolfram names the King of Arabia as Zoroaster, a vassal of Perceval's half-brother Feirefiz. The Alliterative *Morte Arthure* suggests that the region was under the control of the Lucius, Arthur's enemy in the Roman War. [*Wolfram, Allit, Malory*]

ARAGON [*Arragon*]

A region of northwest Spain, ruled in Uther's time, according to Wolfram, by King Schaffilor. Chrétien names the son of the king of Aragon among the participants at the Noauz tournament. It is presented in the Pleier's *Tandareis und Flordibel* as a land allied with Arthur, and shows up in *Claris et Laris* as the kingdom ruled by Lempres, an enemy of Arthur. [*ChretienL, Wolfram, PleierT, Claris*]

ARAM¹

An eloquent knight in Arthur's service. Arthur named him as an envoy to Gaul when the land was divided and at war. On Arthur's behalf, Aram proposed Lancelot as Gaul's overlord, which was acceptable to all except King Frollo. Later, Aram participated in the Grail Quest. [*VulgLanc, ProsTris*]

ARAM²

In Heinrich von dem Türlin's *Diu Crône*, the Duke of Aram and his vassals participate in a tournament at Sorgarda. [*Heinrich*]

ARAMONT¹ [*Atramont*]

The King of Brittany in the time of Uther Pendragon. He was the overlord of Gannes, Benoic, and surrounding lands, but King Claudas of Bourges refused to acknowledge him. Aramont went to war with Claudas, but Claudas drew on his allies from Gaul and managed to stalemate Aramont. Aramont then allied with Uther, and together the two kings smashed Claudas, turning his country into a wasteland. After Aramont's death, Claudas returned and waged war on Benoic and Gannes. Aramont was also known as HOEL. It is unclear whether he is identical with FARAMON from the Tristan legends. [*LancLac, VulgLanc*]

ARAMONT²

A Saxon warrior, brother of the Saxon king Agleot. He participated in a Saxon invasion of Scotland, but he was captured by Lancelot while fighting Arthur's men at the Ford of Blood. [*LancLac, VulgLanc*]

ARAN

The Count of Flanders and an ally of King Claudas. Arthur's troops landed in Flanders to go to war against Claudas, and Aran met them in battle. He was slain by Arthur's Sir Patrides. [*VulgLanc*]

ARANDUS

In *La Tavola Ritonda*, a Gaulish king who, along with a king named Brandino, invaded and conquered Benoic—the land of Lancelot's father Ban. Arandus and Brandino replace CLAUDAS, named as Benoic's destroyers in most other versions. [*Tavola*]

ARATINS

One of the many Saxon kings who invaded Britain during Arthur's struggle to establish power. [*Livre*]

ARAVIUS [*Araby, Derane, Ravinity*]

The mountain where Arthur overcame and slew the giant Ritho in Geoffrey's chronicle. The name seems to be a Latin form of ERYRI, the Welsh name for Mount SNOWDON. Layamon calls it "Mount Ravinity," which may be either a corruption or a deliberate variation. [*GeoffHR, Wace, Bek, Malory*]

ARAWN

King of Annwn, the Welsh otherworld, in the non-Arthurian tale of *Pwyll*. After clashing with Pwyll during a hunting incident, the two warriors became friends and agreed to exchange countenances, kingdoms, and wives for a year. Pwyll, however, refused to take advantage of the situation and sleep with Arawn's wife. Arawn's mortally enemy, Hafgan, was killed by Pwyll. R. S. Loomis thought that a number of Arthurian characters showed Arawn's influence, including the GREEN KNIGHT and ORGUELLEUSE. In a Welsh version of Geoffrey of Monmouth, Arawn becomes the counterpart of ANGUSEL, Urien's brother. Arawn may therefore be identical to ARON, Urien's brother and Arthur's knight in the Triads.

ARBRAYE

A castle in Cornwall where Sadoc and Dinas made a pact to defect from the court of King Mark. [*ProsTris, Malory*]

ARBRUN

Grandson of Brutus, son of Albanact, and brother of Embrunt and Dombart. He became king of the Savage Realm and ruled the castle of Sauf. He married the lady Vagés, the companion of a giant he defeated. Arbrun's sons were Brun and Silhaut. [*Palamedes*]

ARCADE

The maiden loved by Pelleas in the Post-Vulgate *Suite du Merlin*. Malory calls her ETTARD. Though Pelleas won a tournament in her honor, Arcade treated him with disdain. He kept attacking her knights and allowing himself to be defeated, just so he could catch a glimpse of her as they threw him in her prison. Gawain learned of his plight and offered to help him by going to Arcade's court and claiming that he had slain Pelleas. What Gawain hoped to accomplish is unclear, but in any event, he abandoned the plan when he saw the lovely Arcade, who responded to his advances and slept with him. Pelleas found them sleeping together and considered killing them, but instead left his sword laying beside them. When Arcade awoke, she realized that Gawain had lied and that Pelleas had spared her life. Gawain confessed his fib and persuaded Arcade to reconcile with Pelleas. The two married and had a son named Guivret the Younger. [*PostMer*]

ARCAN

Brother of the king of the Saxons. He allied with Mordred when the latter revolted against Arthur. He fought in Mordred's army at the battle of Salisbury, where he was slain by Yvain. [*VulgMort*]

ARCELAS [*Celas*]

The King of Trebes slain by Sir Laris during Arthur's war against Thereus of Rome. [*Claris*]

ARCHADE

A knight slain by Palamedes while trying to avenge the death of his brother at Palamedes's hands. [*Malory*]

ARCHAUS

A knight killed by Bleoberis while trying to kidnap a maiden. [*ProsTris*]

ARCHEMAIS [*Archenais*]

Son of King Angusel of Scotland in the *Prophecies de Merlin*. He took part in the expedition to save King Richard of Jerusalem from the King of Baghdad. Archemais succeeded his father to the throne of Scotland. [*Prophecies*]

ARCHEMAN

A cousin and enemy of Tristan. King Mark of Cornwall was his uncle, and the evil Andret was his brother. Tristan killed Archeman at the Fountain of the Lion. [*ProsTris*]

ARCHENIOR OF NOURIENT

A duke and vassal of Feirefiz, Perceval's half-brother. [*Wolfram*]

ARCHIER

The baptismal name of King GURGURAN, after Gawain's example led him to accept Christianity into his kingdom. [*Perlesvaus*]

ARCHIMAGO

An evil magician in *The Faerie Queene* who represents, at various places in Spenser's elaborate allegory, the pope and Satan. Archimago hinders the successes of the heroes Guyon, the Red Cross Knight, and Arthur through sorcery and trickery. The Red Cross Knight throws him into a dungeon, but he manages to escape. [*Spenser*]

ARCHIMEDES

Nephew of King Evalach of Sarras. He led a battalion of Evalach's soldiers against King Tholomer of Babylonia at the battle of La Choine. [*VulgEst*]

ARCIEL

A Knight of the Round Table who killed his brother, Sanades, in combat for the love of a maiden. Arciel received a mortal wound in the fight. As soon as he was aware of it, he tried to slay the maiden to keep any other man from having her, but she fled. Galahad found Arciel in his death throes and had him buried. [*PostQuest*]

ARCOIS

A brave knight from Flanders in the service of King Claudas. Arcois spoke up against Claudas when Claudas suggested that he might go to war with Arthur. Claudas respected Arcois' honesty and sense of justice, and he made Arcois the constable of his court. [*VulgLanc*]

ARDAN[1]

King of Rivelanze. Allied to King Ekunaver of Kanadic, he joined Ekunaver's war against Arthur. Defeated by Sir Garel, he was forgiven by Arthur and awarded a place at the Round Table. [*PleierG*]

ARDAN[2] [Adrawns]

A duke and uncle of Arthur defeated in joust by Palamedes. His son Helis tried to avenge the insult but failed. [Palamedes, ProsTris, Malory]

ARDDUN

Daughter of Eliffer and sister of Peredur and Gwrgi. [Triads]

ARDEROCH AMANDER

A Knight of the Round Table. [HartmannE]

ARDWYAD

Son of Caw, one of twenty brothers, and one of King Arthur's warriors in Welsh legend. His name means "protector" or "sustainer." [Culhwch]

AREBECH [Aresbeth]

A city or castle in Scotland (perhaps in Arestel), besieged by the Saxons during Arthur's reign. Arthur, with the help of Lancelot, drove the Saxons away. [LancLac, VulgLanc]

ARES[1] [Arec, Arel(s), Aret(h)(a), Aries]

One of Arthur's various kings; the father or foster-father of Arthur's knight Tor. In early French romance, he is the king of Autice, and Tor is, in fact, his son. The Post-Vulgate Merlin continuation, alternatively, gives him as poor cowherd who arrived at Camelot on the day of Arthur's wedding and asked Arthur to knight his estranged son, Tor. Arthur complied, and it was later discovered that Tor was in fact the son of King Pellinore by Ares' wife before they were married. [ChretienE, Erex, Yder, LancLac, VulgLanc, PostMer, PostMer, Malory]

ARES[2]

Father of Do and grandfather of Arthur's Sir Girflet. [ProsTris]

ARESTEL

A wooded region in Scotland, known for its fine hunting grounds. During Arthur's reign, it was twice invaded by Saxons. On the fist occasion, King Lot of Lothian called a meeting of all the nobles there, proposing that the princes in rebellion against Arthur ally with him temporarily to face the Saxon threat. On the second invasion, Arthur met the Saxons there (at nearby Saxon Rock) and, with the help of Lancelot, drove them away. [LancLac, VulgLanc, VulgMer]

ARFDERYDD

The site of a battle, probably historical, fought between warring British clans. Scholars have plausibly identified it with Arthuret (no connection to Arthur), eight miles north of Carlisle, in Liddesdale. The Annales Cambriae say that the battle occurred in 573, and the Triads call it "futile," saying that it began over a lark's nest, referring to the Fort of the Lark on the edge of Solway Firth (Ashe, Landscape, 102). At the battle, the warlord Gwenddolau, son of Ceido, opposed a joined force of Peredur and Gwrgi (the sons of Eliffer) and Rhydderch the Generous. Gwenddolau was killed and his warriors kept fighting for a month and a half to honor their slain leader. Merlin was present at the battle, fighting on Gwenddolau's side in the Welsh verses and with Rhydderch and Peredur in Geoffrey's Vita Merlini. He was driven mad—either by the sight of all the dead, by an apparition he saw in the sky blaming him for the deaths, or by the fact that he killed his nephew—and thereafter roamed the Caledonian Wood. [Annales, Triads, Myrddin]

ARFUSAT THE FAT

A peer of Bors who fought in a tournament thrown by King Brandegorre. He swore fealty to the king's daughter, promising never to enter a castle or house until he had fought and defeated half a dozen knights. [VulgLanc]

ARGAN

A knight whose wife, Dyagenne, was loved by Uther Pendragon (after the latter's marriage to Igerne). Argan discovered their affair and challenged Uther, defeating him in combat. Argan spared Uther's life but slew Dyagenne. As a condition of Uther's surrender, Argan made him build an impenetrable castle called Uther's Shame. Argan re-married, but was cuckolded and defeated by Sir Hector. Enraged, Argan built the Red Tower Bridge and tried to defeat any knights who wanted to cross. This custom was continued by his four sons. [ProsTris]

ARGANOR

A Knight of the Round Table who joined in the Grail Quest. [ProsTris]

ARGANT

A king and vassal of King Rions of Ireland, an enemy of Arthur. He assisted Rions in his attack on King Leodegan of Carmelide, which failed. Argant was slain in the battle by Sir Cleodalis, a vassal of Leodegan. [VulgMer]

ARGANTE[1]

Layamon's Queen of Avalon, a "radiant elf" to whom Arthur was taken when mortally wounded from the battle at Camlann. The name Argante may be a corruption of MORGAN, who is traditionally the queen that receives Arthur's body. [Layamon]

ARGANTE[2]

A giantess who was the daughter of a Titan. She lived in incest with her brother, Ollyphant, but her insatiable lust drove her to enslave men whenever she found them. The knight Satyrane tried to slay her but was knocked unconscious. She was pursued by the warrior maiden Pallantine, who was fated to eventually destroy her. [Spenser]

ARGAYLE

According to the Alliterative *Morte Arthure*, one of the lands conquered by Arthur. [*Allit*]

ARGENTIN

A land ruled first by Duke Elimar, who was slain by a giant, and then by Duke Klaris, who was rescued by Arthur's Sir Garel. [*PleierG*]

ARGISTES [*Agristes*]

Gawain's great-grandfather, descended from Joseph of Arimathea. A king, Argistes was the son of Meliant. He married a Saxon noblewoman and had a son named Hedor. [*VulgEst*]

ARGLUD

A forest in Wales (on the Clyde River, at the present location of Dumbarton) where King Meriadoc, as a youth, was supposed to be hanged by his uncle's henchmen. He was saved by his foster-father, Ivor, and later taken to Arthur's court. [*Historia*]

ARGODRAS THE RED

A knight who served King Bagdemagus of Gorre. He arrived at Arthur's court and accused Lancelot of murdering Meleagant, Bagdemgaus's son. Lancelot protested that Meleagant had been killed in a fair fight, but he agreed to meet Argodras in combat at Windesant, Bagdemagus's court. The fight went poorly for Argodras, and he was eventually killed. [*VulgLanc*]

ARGON

The Saracen lord of the Rock, a British castle. Joseph of Arimathea raised Argon from the dead after a wild lion slew him. Beholding this miracle, Argon, his brother Matagran, and all their people converted. [*VulgEst*]

ARGONS¹

Grandfather of Guiron the Courteous. He was the son of Febus and Florine and the father of Fragus. His brothers were Siraouc, Niatar, Altan, and Laimors. [*Palamedes*]

ARGONS² [*Argu(y)s*]

A Cornish knight related to King Mark. He led a company of soldiers against a group of Saxon invaders under Sir Elyas. [*ProsTris*, *Malory*]

ARGRETTA

The beautiful concubine of Lucano the Great, a giant slain by Tristan. When Tristan freed her, she was joyously reunited with her husband, Alchino of Logres. [*Tavola*]

ARGUEL

The King of Escavalon. His son, Galescalain, was the Duke of Clarence and one of Arthur's knights. [*VulgLanc*]

ARGUISIAUS OF CARHAIX

A knight who was defeated and wounded by a marauder named Dragonel the Cruel. Dragonel tried to force Arguisiaus's paramour, Rohais, into marrying him. Perceval arrived, rescued the maiden, and sent Arguisiaus to the castle of Belrepaire for healing. [*Contin4*]

ARGUSTE [*Argustus*]

Son of King Harlon. During the Grail Quest, Argustus led a force of sinful knights, dressed in black, in a tournament against Sir Eliezier, leading good knights dressed in white. Eliezier was winning when Lancelot arrived and began to fight on the side of Argustus, just because he was losing. Lancelot did not realize that the black knights were sinful. The white knights eventually overcame Lancelot, and then defeated Argustus's knights. [*VulgQuest*, *Malory*]

ARGYNGROG

A plain upon which Rhonabwy began his journey during his epic dream. [*Dream*]

ARIDE

King of Galore and an ally of King Rions of Ireland, Arthur's enemy. He joined Rions in a failed invasion of Carmelide. [*VulgMer*]

ARIGIE

Lord of Dusbergo in *La Tavola Ritonda*. He presided over a duel between Lancelot and the Knight of the Ill-Fitting Coat, and he forced them to separate before either suffered serious injury. [*Tavola*]

ARIMATHEA [*Aremathie, Arimatia, Arymathye, B(e)remachie, B(e)remat(h)ie, Bramanzia*]

A city in ancient Palestine that was the homeland of Joseph, the first Grail bearer. The Vulgate *Estoire del Saint Graal* places it "in the land of Ramathaim, beyond the River Jordan." It was ruled in Joseph's time by Elcan, the father of Samuel. [*RobertBor J*, *VulgEst*]

ARIOHAN [*Aroan*]

Father of Frollo, the ruler of Gaul slain by Arthur. After his son's death, he raised an army of Saxons to invade North Wales. Arthur, Meliadus, Pellinore, and the Good Knight Without Fear opposed him, and he was defeated in single combat by Meliadus. He returned home and became ruler of Denmark by marrying the king's daughter. Ogier the Dane was one of his descendants. [*Palamedes*]

ARION

A knight who wished to challenge Lancelot when the latter was living in exile on the Island of Joy. Unfortunately, Arion's horse foundered as he crossed the water to the island, and he was drowned under the weight of his armor. This prompted Lancelot to install a boat at the location. [*PostMer*]

ARISE [Arsie]

One of two rivers in France that flanked Benoic (Lancelot's homeland). The other was the Loire. [LancLac, VulgLanc]

ARISTANT [Arysta(u)nse]

A Knight of the Round Table who fought at the tournament of Sorelois. He was also one of the contestants at the healing of Sir Urry. [ProsTris, Malory]

ARISTE

The castle in the land of Amorave, belonging to Aristor. Aristor kidnapped Perceval's sister, Dandrane, and kept her in Ariste until Perceval rescued her. [Perlesvaus]

ARISTES[1]

Son of Salandres and brother of Dinisordres, Menastide, Nastor, and Gogonne. Perceval defeated the whole family and sent them to Arthur's court as prisoners. [Contin3]

ARISTES[2]

Son of Arthur in the Icelandic Möttuls Saga. His wife was proven unfaithful—along with all the other ladies at court—by an enchanted mantle. [Mottuls]

ARISTOBOKIS

A Knight of the Round Table who fought against the Saxons in the early days of Arthur's reign. He was wounded at the battle of Garlot. [VulgMer]

ARISTOC THE STRONG

A knight who tried to kill Yvain to avenge the death of his father. Yvain defeated him and, because Aristoc refused to yield, killed him. [ProsTris]

ARISTOR

Lord of the castle of Ariste and the land of Amorave. He made a gruesome habit of marrying women and beheading them around their first anniversary. His cousin, the Lord of the Fens, was killed by Perceval, so Aristor decided to take revenge. First, he kidnapped Perceval's sister, Dandrane, intent on forcing her to marry him. Then he murdered Perceval's uncle, Pelles, and killed the Bold Knight, a friend of Perceval's. Perceval journeyed to Ariste and defeated Aristor in combat. He decapitated the wretch, and happily presented his head to Dandrane. [Perlesvaus]

ARISTOT

Father of Corsabrin (a knight slain by Palamedes) and Rechaux. [ProsTris]

ARIUN

Prince of the lands of Medarie and Belakun, and companion of princes Darel and Gamer. Their lord, King Schaffilun, was killed in combat by Wigalois (Gawain's son), to whom the three princes transferred fealty. They accompanied Wigalois in a campaign against the evil King Lion of Namur. [Wirnt]

ARLAC

Lancelot's homeland in several German sources, probably a scribal corruption of "au Lac." [HartmannE, Heinrich]

ARMAGNAC

A region of southwest France owned by Lancelot. Lancelot made Sir Lavaine the Earl of Armagnac in return for Lavaine's support in the war against King Arthur. [Malory]

ARMAND THE HANDSOME

A Knight of the Round Table who participated in the Grail Quest. [ProsTris]

ARMANT [Arduano, Harmaunce, Hermaunce]

King of the Delectable Isle and the Red City. Armant was slain by two treacherous protégés (Helain and an unnamed knight in the Prose Tristan; Passauver and an unnamed knight in La Tavola Ritonda; Helyus and Helake in Malory). After his death, friends bore his body to the mainland, where they encountered Palamedes and convinced him to avenge their master's death. Palamedes journeyed to Armant's kingdom, killed the traitors, and gave the Red City to Marin, Armant's brother. [ProsTris, Tavola, Malory]

ARMENIA [Ermonye]

A former kingdom of Southwest Asia, south of the Caucas mountains. According to the Alliterative Morte Arthure, the land was allied to Lucius, Emperor of Rome, and assisted in Lucius's war against King Arthur. In other legends, its ruler is called King Turcans or King Aaron. [Allit, Malory]

ARMOND

A cowardly knight who roused 50 warriors to attack the noble Galehaut the Brown, who was unarmed. Galehaut killed Armond by strangulation and slew almost 20 more of his attackers before he fell under their blades. [Palamedes]

ARMORICA [Armoryk]

The former Latin name of BRITTANY before it was invaded by the Britons in the fifth century. Geoffrey of Monmouth says that Maximus took it from Duke Inbalt and gave it to Conan Meriadoc, who brought British culture to the region. [GeoffHR]

ARNAL THE HANDSOME [Argas]

A Knight of the Round Table who participated in the Grail Quest. [PostQuest, ProsTris]

ARNIVE

In Wolfram's *Parzival*, the mother of Arthur and wife of Uther Pendragon. Most authors assign this role to IGERNE. Abducted from her husband by the sorcerer Clinschor, she was imprisoned in the Castle of Marvels until rescued and released by Gawain, many years after Uther's death. [*Wolfram*]

ARNOLD[1]

A knight from Cornwall and brother of Sir Gautere. Arnold and Gautere fought against King Arthur in the tournament at the Castle Perilous. [*Malory*]

ARNOLD[2] LE BREUSE

Arnold and his brother Gerard were the first two knights encountered by Gareth on his quest to defeat the Red Knight of the Red Lands. When they opposed his crossing a bridge on the Marcosia River, Gareth slew them both. [*Malory*]

ARNOULLANT THE FAIR

Companion of the mighty Seguarnt the Brown. Arnoullant was eaten by a dragon in the forest of Hurbise. [*Palamedes*]

AROANS OF BETINA

A king and an ally of Arthur's enemy King Rions. With Rions, he opposed Arthur and Leodegan at the second battle of Carhaix, where he was wounded by King Bors of Gannes. [*VulgMer, Arthour*]

ARODALUS THE LARGE

An Arthurian knight who fought against the Saxons at the battle of Vambieres. [*Livre*]

ARODION OF COLOGNE

A scribe at King Arthur's court. Arodion and three other scribes recorded the deeds of Arthur's Knights of the Round Table, including Gawain, Hector, and Lancelot. [*LancLac, VulgLanc*]

AROEL

The Duke of Aroel, who came from Sorelois, was an ally of Lancelot. A skilled and experienced knight, he assisted Lancelot in the battles against King Arthur. [*VulgMort*]

AROIE [*Arroy*]

A Scottish forest through which Perceval, in *Fergus*, pursued a white stag in a long hunt that finally ended in the forest of Ingegal. In the Post-Vulgate *Suite du Merlin*, it is the location of the Forest of Adventures. This was where Gawain, Yvain, and Morholt met with three maidens who led them on separate quests. Scholars have suggested Ayrshire as a possible location. [*Guillaume, PostMer, Malory*]

ARON

Son of Cynfarch and brother of Urien, named in the Welsh Triads as one of Arthur's three Counselor Knights. He may be identical to ARAWN, a king found in non-Arthurian Welsh legend. [*Triads*]

ARONDELE

A maidservant of Lady Galiene of Lothian in Guillaume le Clerc's *Fergus*. She set out to find a champion when Galiene's castle, Roucebourc, was besieged, but, upon arriving at Arthur's court, found that most of Arthur's knights were on a quest to find the absent Sir Fergus. Arondele eventually located Fergus himself, who gladly agreed to serve as Galiene's champion. She is called LUNETTE in the Dutch *Ferguut*. [*Guillaume*]

ARONDIELE

The horse belonging to Arthur's Sir Fergus. It was given to Fergus by his father. The animal was slain during Fergus's combat with the giant of the Dolerous Mount. [*Guillaume*]

ARPHASAR THE UNKNOWN [*Alphazar*]

Brother of Esclabor the Unknown and uncle of Palamedes. [*Palamedes*]

ARPIAN[1] [*Harpin*]

A Knight of the Round Table from the Narrow Mountain or the Strange Mountain. He embarked with the others on the Grail Quest, during which he joined company with Agamenor and Amatin the Good Jouster. All three knights hated Lancelot's family, so they attacked Galahad, but were defeated. Later, they assaulted Acorante the Agile and Danubre the Brave, Lancelot's cousins. Arpian was slain by Danubre. [*PostQuest*]

ARPIAN[2] [*Harpion*]

The Lord of the Treacherous Castle, an evil pagan stronghold, where he imprisoned maidens and killed Arthur's knights. He imprisoned Galahad, Hector, and Meraugis, but was slain by them after a holy cataclysm freed the three knights from his prison. [*PostQuest*]

ARPINELLO

The lord of Bauttiganero. He showed Tristan the way to the castle of Caradoc the Thirteenth. Arpinello had previously been defeated by the mighty Caradoc at the Victorious Tower. Once Tristan had defeated Caradoc, he gave the Victorious Tower to Arpinello. [*Tavola*]

ARQUAIS

Nephew of King Alain of Escavalon. His cousin, Floree, was saved by Gawain from a giant. [*Livre*]

ARRAC

In Heinrich von dem Türlin's *Diu Crône*, the Prince of Arrac is named as one of Arthur's vassals. [*Heinrich*]

ARRAMANT THE FAT [*Atramant*]

A knight defeated by Lancelot after he stole Lancelot's armor and steed, and kidnapped a squire, from Lancelot's lodgings. Lancelot spared his life after receiving Arramant's oath of allegiance. [*VulgLanc*]

ARRANT

A Saxon king of Denmark. He was the son of Magaat and nephew of the Saxon King Aminaduc. As part of the Saxon invasion of Britain at the beginning of Arthur's reign, he was assigned the task of plundering Lothian and Orkney. He was present at the battle of Clarence, the razing of Cardueil, and the plundering of Caradigan. At this final battle, Arthur killed him. [*VulgMer, Livre*]

ARROUANS THE FELON

In *Palamedes*, the father of the evil Breus the Pitiless. Seguarant the Brown killed him. [*Palamedes*]

ARROUSE

An earl from the island of Ponmecainne who fought against Galehaut at the tournament at Sorelois. [*Malory*]

ARROUX [*Aroaise*]

A little river in Benoic where Duke Frollo of Germany encamped before a battle with Arthur. [*VulgMer*]

ARROW

A fine seaside castle in the land of Gorre, where Lancelot once lodged on his way to fight at King Bagdemagus's court. It was well situated in the midst of lush meadows and farmland. [*VulgLanc*]

ARSONNE [*Aisurne*]

A river in Benoic that flowed near King Ban's castle of Trebe. [*VulgMer*]

ART AOINFHEAR

A son of Arthur. [*IrishM*]

ARTEGALL

Champion of justice in Spenser's *The Faerie Queene*. In Spenser's allegory, Artegall is Arthur Lord Grey of Wilton, whom Spenser once served as secretery. Artegall was raised by the goddess Astraea. Glorana, the Fairy Queen, assigned him to liberate the kingdom belonging to the maiden Irena from a giant named Grantorto. The maiden warrior Britomart fell in love with Artegall after seeing an image of him, in Fairy Land, in a mirror. With their faces hidden by visors, Artegall and Britomart encountered each other in duel, but Britomart eventually recognized her opponent and Artegall became entranced by Britomart's beauty. They agreed to marry, but Artegall had to leave Britomart to finish his quest. After several successful adventures, Artegall was enslaved by Queen Radigund of the Amazons. Britomart learned of his plight from his squire, Talus, and rescued him. In further adventures, Artegall was joined by Arthur. Eventually, he arrived at Irena's kingdom and killed Grantorto in combat. [*Spenser*]

ARTEL

A Knight of the Round Table who embarked with the others on the Grail Quest. [*PostQuest*]

ARTESIA

In the Elizabethan play *The Birth of Merlin*, the sister of the Saxon leader Ostorius. She used her wiles to seduce King Aurelius Ambrosius of Britain, blinding him to the gradual Saxon invasion of his kingdom. Uther Pendragon discovered her treachery, but she managed to have Aurelius banish his brother from court. In the end, Artesia and her brother betrayed and murdered Aurelius. When Uther reclaimed the kingdom, he had Artesia executed. [*Birth*]

ARTHGAL [*Algal*]

The Earl of Warwick under Arthur. [*GeoffHR, Wace*]

ARTHGALLO

In Geoffrey of Monmouth's chronicle, a son of King Morvid who succeeded his brother Gorbonian to the throne of Britain in the third century BC. Unlike his brother, he was a tyrant. His nobles eventually deposed him and installed his brother Elidur as king. Elidur reconciled with Arthgallo and forced the nobles to accept him as king again. Arthgallo reigned for another ten years, this time in justice. Elidur succeeded him again when he died. Arthgallo's sons, Margan and Enniaun, were both later kings. [*GeoffHR*]

ARTHINAIL

According to Geoffrey of Monmouth, a king of Britain in the second century BC. He succeeded his brother King Bledgabred and was succeeded by King Eldol. [*GeoffHR*]

ARTHOFILAUS

In Guillaume le Clerc's *Fergus*, the nephew of a malevolent king who besieged Lady Galiene of Lothian in the castle of Rocebourc. Galiene obtained the services of Sir Fergus, Arthur's knight, as her champion. Fergus slew Arthofilaus and defeated his uncle. In the Dutch *Ferguut*, Arthofilaus becomes MACEDONE. [*Guillaume*]

ARTHUR[1] [*Arrtor, Arther, Arthour(e)(s), Arthure, Arthus, A(r)thyr, Artijus, Arto(u)r(et), Artourys, Artouzos, Artui, Artu(u)(r)s, Artusin, Artuxe, Artuz, Hartu, Ortus*]

Legendary British warlord and king. Tales revolving around Arthur, his court, and his knights form the subject matter of the Arthurian Legends. In history, Arthur was likely a Briton war-leader who staved off the Saxon invasion of Britain for a time. In legend, he becomes a great king; the conqueror of dozens of realms; the ruler of the fantasy realm of Camelot; the founder of the Round Table; and the bastion of justice in a "might is right" world. His downfall is wrought by the people closest to him: his wife, Guinevere; his best knight, Lancelot; his nephew, Gawain; his sister, Morgan; and his son, Mordred. He perishes during a great battle against the latter, who has usurped his throne, but legend holds that he still lives on the island of Avalon, from which he will return to lead his people again.

Historicity

Any discussion of the Arthurian mythos must begin with Arthur himself—specifically, whether he existed at all. The answer is an unsatisfying "probably."

The problem is the abysmal lack of historical evidence concerning the period between the end of the Roman rule over Britain (early fifth century) and the end of the Saxon conquest of Britain (late sixth century). There are virtually no surviving written records from Britain during this 150-year period (see BRITAIN). What we do know of this dark age, often called the "Arthurian period," is constructed basically from four sources:

1. *Existing British written sources.* For our purposes, this is only a single source: Gildas's *De Excidio et Conquestu Britanniae* ("Of the Ruin and Conquest of Britain"), written about 540, forty to eighty years after the time of a "historical" Arthur. Unfortunately, Gildas was writing a diatribe, not a history, and he never mentioned Arthur's name. He outlines the Roman and post-Roman era before launching into a tirade against the lechery of rulers living in his own time. Gildas does mention Ambrosius (later to become Arthur's uncle), and probably Vortigern, and other characters who become linked to Arthur in later chronicle and legend. He tells of the great Saxon defeat at Mount Badon, but does not name the British leader. In later sources, this man is to be named as Arthur. Gildas's omission of Arthur's name is frustrating, but is hardly conclusive given the intent and form of his work.

2. *Archaeological Evidence.* Excavations throughout Britain cast light onto living conditions, military circumstances, settlements, and so on. Unfortunately, archaeology cannot, for the most part, provide names. Still, it has contributed valuable information to the Arthurian question. To use one example, sixteenth-century writer John Leland's identification of Camelot with Cadbury is lent support by Leslie Alcock's excavations at Cadbury, which suggest that it was an important military headquarters during the late fifth century.

3. *Continental Sources.* Histories written on the continent during this period provide some slight information on the situation in Britain, though none

of them mention Arthur specifically. Gregory of Tours's *History of the Franks* and Jordanes's *Gothic History* are two examples. The latter provides information about Riothamus, a late fifth-century king of the Britons who some have connected to Arthur. Riothamus reportedly brought an army of Britons into Gaul, at the behest of the Romans, to deal with the Visigoths. Riothamus was defeated. Forced to retreat, he disappeared into Burgundy, near a place called Avallon.

4. *Later British Sources*: Nennius's *Historia Brittonum* and the *Annales Cambriae* are two sources written within 500 years of the Arthurian period that provide information on British history and on Arthur specifically. Nennius lists twelve great battles fought between Arthur against the Saxons, including Badon. the *Annales* also tell of Arthur's victory at Badon and, later, "the strife of Camlann, in which Arthur and Medraut (Mordred) fell..." The problem with this later sources is not only that they were written hundreds of years after the events described, but also that they have become so tainted with legend as to have their historical veracity impeached. Nennius, for instance, says that Arthur killed 960 men by himself at the battle of Badon, and the *Annales* entry prior to Badon tells of a bishop who lived to be 350 years old.

There are three other factors that argue for the existence of an historical figure named "Arthur." The first is literary: around the year 600, a northern bard named Anierin wrote *Y Gododdin*, a lamentation describing the deaths of British warriors against the Angles at the battle of Catraeth. In one stanza, a warrior's prowess is extolled; however, the warrior "was not Arthur," meaning that his skill in battle was second only to a mighty (and presumably famous) warrior named Arthur. Clearly, the audience of the poem was expected to know the identity of "Arthur"; conventional scholarship holds that the reference alludes to the famed battle-leader of a century prior, but some scholars (e.g., Richard Barber, *Figure*, 21–34) have argued that the passage refers to Arthur of Dalriada, a northern figure who lived contemporary to the writing of *Y Gododdin*, and in close geographic proximity to its writer and audience.

It is clear, too, that a great body of Arthurian oral tradition developed among the Celts between the sixth and twelfth centuries. There are allusions to tales in this tradition in the Welsh Triads, the *Black Book of Carmarthen*, the body of literature called the *Mabinogion*, and other sources. Most of these were written late, but they bespeak a much earlier tradition. It is almost inconceivable that some historical figure named Arthur did not exist to inspire an oral tradition of such heroic proportions.

Finally, Arthurian scholars note the increased usage of the name "Arthur" in the two centuries following the "Arthurian period." Irish princes are recorded with the name in the sixth and seventh centuries, as a are Welsh prince who ruled Dyfed in the early seventh century, a

British prince who lived in the seventh century, and another Irishman (Bruce, 6). Logic dictates that some noteworthy historical figure named "Arthur" existed to inspire the subsequent uses of the name.

This can be considered the hypothetical sum of these fragments, investigations, and allusions:

Arthur was a British war-leader who, continuing a revolt begun by Ambrosius before him, battled the Saxon invasions in the late fifth or early sixth century. He may have been a regional ruler, and may have held the title of "king," or he may have been a general under another king or collection of kings. He was almost certainly of Roman descent, with Roman ideas. He may have revived the Roman cavalry in Britain as a means to achieve victory. His headquarters may have been at Cadbury. He enjoyed several successes before he smashed the Saxons at Badon Hill, causing them to retreat to their settlements on the eastern shore. Several decades of relative peace followed, with no further Saxon encroachments. Arthur may have enjoyed further victories in Gaul. He possibly died at a battle called "Camlann," fighting someone named Medraut. On the other hand, if he is indeed identical to **Riothamus**, he eventually led a military excursion into Gaul to help Rome drive away the Visigoths under Euric. He was betrayed by the Roman prefect in Gaul and defeated by the Visigoths. His death is not reported, but he is last recorded in Burgundy near a place called Avallon.

There are a lot of "ifs" in this summary, and it must be considered that "Arthur" may be multiple people (cf. Arthur of Dalriada, Riothamus), fused through legend and hazy history, into a single character.

Name

It is almost certain that *Arthur* is a Celtic form of the Roman *Artorius*, which belonged to several Roman figures and to a *gens*, or clan. It was known in Roman Britain as early as the second century: a officer named Lucius Artorius Castus led a military excursion into Brittany around 150 A.D.

Certain scholars have proposed alternatives to this theory. E. W. B. Nicholson regards *Arthur* as a combination of two Celtic words: *artos* ("bear") and *viros* ("man"), which would make Arthur's name a metaphor for a strong warrior: "Bear-Man." A. Holder proposed a connection with the Irish *art* ("stone"), and M. Müller tried to link Arthur to a culture-divinity in part by noting that the Aryan term for "to plough" is *ar* (Bruce, 4n). None of these theories have won wide acceptance.

Development of the Legend

Early Historical Tradition: About 1138, Geoffrey of Monmouth wrote the history of Britain that brought Arthur to the world. Geoffrey's *Historia Regum Brittaniae*

would be a font of historical information and a masterpiece of historical research and presentation if it were not for the simple fact that he made most of it up, or adopted it irresponsibly from obviously fictional sources. Unfortunately, Geoffrey's chronicle *was* considered genuine history by many people in his day, and almost all Arthurian texts that followed were based on it.

The chronicles that precede Geoffrey are full of odd allusions, enticing pieces of information, and contradictory facts, all of which Geoffrey superceded. These chronicles form the "early tradition" of Arthurian literature. (At the same time, the Welsh built a body of fantastic, supernatural Arthurian literature which is covered in the next section.)

The earliest reference to Arthur, as mentioned before, is in *Y Goddodin* (c. 600), in which a warrior's prowess is compared to Arthur's. But the earliest text to describe Arthur in detail is Nennius's *Historia Brittonum* (early ninth century). The author claimed to have "made a heap" of all the fragments and extracts he found concerning British history. The narrative certainly is a "heap," with little form or structure, but it includes a number of interesting tales, including the story of Ambrosius and Vortigern, and a description of Arthur's twelve great battles against the Saxons. Arthur, whom Nennius describes as the *dux bellorum* or "battle leader" of the British kings, is implicitly not a king himself. *Dux bellorum* may imply some kind of official title, much like the Roman *Dux Brittanium* ("Duke of the Britains").

Arthur was victorious in all of the battles (see ARTHUR'S BATTLES), the last of which was the battle of Badon Hill, where Arthur personally killed 960 opponents, sending the Saxons screaming back to Germany for help. Nennius's narrative dives into genealogies at this point, never returning to Arthur or his fate. However, in an appendix, he describes several *mirabilia* ("miracles") of Britain, two of which cocern Arthur: the tomb of Arthur's son Amr, whom Arthur had killed; and a stone where Arthur's dog, Caval, left a pawprint during the hunt for the boar Troynt. Both Amr and Troynt (Twrch Trwyth) appear in Welsh Arthurian legends and reflect elements of the early legendary tradition about Arthur (see below).

The *Annales Cambriae* date from the late tenth century. This simple list of events by date includes two episodes which concern Arthur: in the year 516, "the battle of Badon, in which Arthur carried the Cross of our Lord Jesus Christ for three days and three nights on his shoulders and the Britons were the victors"; and in the year 537, "the battle of Camlann, in which Arthur and Medraut fell." Both of the dates seem about 20 years too late, and they do not square with Gildas or Nennius. This is the first mention of Camlann, and of Medraut, who was to become Mordred, though it must be noted that the *Annales*, contrary to later tradition, do not specify that Mordred and Arthur were on opposite sides.

The next historical chronicle we need to be concerned with is the *Legenda Sancti Goeznovii* ("Legend of St. Goeznovius") written in Brittany in, according to the text itself, 1019. There has been some debate over the correctness of the date, but modern scholarship seems to regard it as accurate. The text describes, in simple, non-legendary terms, how Vortigern invited too many Saxons to Britain, and how Arthur, in the 460s or 470s, drove them away again. Arthur is said to have been "called from human life" after a number of victories in Britain and Gaul, allowing the Saxons to return. *Goeznovii* specifically calls Arthur "King of the Britons." The importance of this text lies in the fact that it is, as Geoffrey Ashe (Lacy, *NAE*, 204) says, "the only early historical narrative in which Arthur is mentioned plainly, with no obviously dubious or fantastic touches."

We come now to the last important chronicle before Geoffrey of Monmouth: William of Malmesbury's *Gesta Regum Anglorum* (c. 1125). According to William, Arthur was a general under Ambrosius, who staved off the invasion of the "Angles" (rather than the Saxons). William belittles the "trifles" told of Arthur by the Britons, saying that a warrior as great as Arthur deserves to be remembered in authentic history. Given the next "authentic history," Geoffrey of Monmouth's *Historia*, William's statement is thick with unintentional irony.

Early Legendary Tradition: While Nennius, the authors of the *Annales* and *Goeznovii*, and William of Malmesbury were attempting to write authentic histories, the Welsh were building a body of legendary tradition about King Arthur. Evidence shows that Breton *conteurs* carried these legends from Britain to Brittany, and eventually to Gaul and the rest of the continent. These legends, in contrast to the "courtly" French romances which would follow, are characterized by blood, sweat, and tears; by magnificent palaces, fearsome beasts, mysterious otherworlds, supernatural occurrences, hags and giants and sorcerers, bloody battles, and Arthur presiding over all as an "emperor."

The earliest existing example of Welsh legend is a poem known as *The Spoils of Annwn*. Taliesin, an historical northern bard who lived in the century after Arthur, is the supposed narrator. Arthur and three shiploads of warriors sail to Annwn, the Welsh otherworld, for some unclear purpose (to free a prisoner, perhaps, or to find treasure). Arthur returns with a magical cauldron, but only seven warriors have survived the expedition.

Unfortunately, there are few existing cogent narratives to come out of this body of early legend. Complete tales such as *Culhwch and Olwen* (Arthur, presented as an emperor of a vast but realm, helps his nephew Culhwch conquer beasts, witches, and warriors so that he may marry Olwen, the daughter of a giant) are rare. Most of what we have are hints and allusions. One poem tells of the mysterious properties of Arthur's grave, another alludes to Arthur's battles with a hag at the hall of Afarnach, and against the Cudgel-Head at Dissethach, and against the Dog-heads at Mount Eidyn. Bedwyr (Bedivere), Cei (Kay), and Gwalchmei are extolled among his bravest and boldest warriors. The Triads, which are annotations or indices of early legend, talk of Arthur's courts, of his son Llacheu, of his strife with Mordred, of his three wives named Gwenhwyfar, of how one was unfaithful, and of

the battle of Camlann. Most of this material was not written until the twelfth or thirteenth centuries, and some of it shows traces of contamination by Geoffrey of Monmouth, but the majority of it harkens to an earlier era of bold, bloody, and wonderous legend that has since been lost.

Another significant "body" of tradition concerning Arthur is the lives of the Welsh saints, one of which is of particular interest: Caradoc's *Vita Gildae*, which includes an account of the abduction of Guinevere by Melwas of the Summer Region. This seems to be the original abduction story, and is possibly the source of Chrétien de Troyes's tale of Guinevere, Lancelot, and Meleagant.

Geoffrey of Monmouth: Now we come to what is arguably the most important Arthurian text ever written: Geoffrey of Monmouth's *Historia Regum Brittaniae* ("History of the Kings of Britain"), a Latin chronicle from 1138. Beginning with Brutus, the expatriated Roman who conquered Britain (then called Albion) from giants, Geoffrey chronicles a line of British kings through the seventh-century Cadwallar. Though Geoffrey claimed to have adapted his material from an ancient book of British history, it is clear that he embellished or completely invented the main episodes, taking names from wherever he found them: authentic histories, Welsh genealogies, contemporary figures, and his own imagination. Some Celtic material—mostly names—creeps in here and there, such as Arthur's battles with the giant of Mont St. Michel and the giant Ritho.

Geoffrey's book provides the first full "biography" of King Arthur and his famous predecessors. Summarized, it reads something like this:

> After Britain lost support from the Roman military in the early fifth century, the country was beset from all sides by barbarian Picts, Irish, and Huns. The ranks of Britain's warriors had been depleted during Maximus's war with Rome. Rome refused to send aid. With no one else to turn to, the Britons asked King Aldroenus of Brittany for assistance. Aldroenus sent his brother Constantine with legions of warriors. Constantine drove out the barbarians and was crowned king of Britain. He had three sons named Constans (who became a monk), Ambrosius, and Uther. Constantine was assassinated by a Pict. Earl Vortigern of Guent, seeking to increase his own power, removed Constans from his monastery and foisted him to the throne. Once Vortigern had established power as Constans's advisor, he arranged for Constans's assassination. Ambrosius and Uther, just children, fled Britain for Brittany to escape Vortigern's hand. Vortigern ascended to the throne.
>
> Beset with the same barbarian problems, Vortigern hired Saxon mercenaries to swell the ranks of the British army. The Saxons were led by Hengist, who saw a chance to win power and territory. Hengist brought far more Saxons than were needed into Britain, settling in Kent. When

their intentions became obvious, they attacked, decimating the British army at the battle of Amesbury. Vortigern fled into Wales, where he tried to build a fortress at Snowdon and encountered Merlin.

Meanwhile, Ambrosius and Uther raised an army in Brittany and came to Britain. They destroyed Vortigern, killed Hengist, and checked the Saxon advance. Like his father, Ambrosius was poisoned by a Pictish agent. Uther became king and adopted the name Pendragon. He enjoyed further victories against the Saxons. At a victory feast, he fell in love with Igerne, the wife of Duke Gorlois of Cornwall. Gorlois, understanding Uther's intentions, took his wife and left the feast. Uther took affront to this offense and attacked Gorlois, but could not breach the defenses of the castle Tintagel in Cornwall, where Igerne was in safekeeping. Uther called on Merlin's help.

Merlin transformed Uther into the likeness of Gorlois, allowing him to enter Tintagel undetected and to sleep with Igerne, begetting Arthur. Gorlois, meanwhile, was killed fighting Uther's soldiers. Uther married Igerne and had, besides Arthur, a daughter named Anna.

The Saxon wars resumed. Uther fell ill and had to take to the field in a litter. Nevertheless, at the battle of St. Albans, he killed the Saxon leaders Octa and Eosa. Then, like his brother and father, he was poisoned. Arthur was crowned king at the age of 15.

Assisted by Cador of Cornwall and Hoel of Brittany, Arthur resumed the war against the Saxons, now led by Colgrim, Baldulph, and Cheldric. Arthur wielded a sword called Caliburn, fought with a lance called Ron, and carried a shield known as Pridwen. His victories against the Saxons culminated in the battle of Bath (Geoffrey's Badon), in which they were utterly destroyed. Arthur married the lady Guinevere, who had been raised in the house of Cador. Arthur then turned his attention to the Picts and the Irish (led by King Gillamaur), crushing them at Loch Lomond in Scotland.

Having pacified all of Britain, Arthur, in quick succession, conquered Ireland, Iceland, Gothland, and Orkney. Having thus established his power throughout the British Isles, Arthur enjoyed twelve years of relative peace (during which, in the romances, the bulk of the quests and adventures occurred).

After this interval, Arthur proceded to conquer Norway and Denmark. He then conquered Gaul by defeating Frollo, the Roman governor, in single combat. Following this victory, Arthur held a magificent court in Caerleon, establishing bishops, dukes, earls, and kings all over his domain.

During the court, however, a notice came from Emperor Leo of Rome demanding tribute from Arthur. Arthur replied that no tribute was due, and both sides prepared for war. Lucius, the Roman procurator, led the Roman armies and summoned allies from all over the known world. Arthur sailed to Brittany to join forces with his cousin Hoel. When he arrived he learned that Hoel's niece had been kidnapped by the giant of Mont St. Michael. Taking Bedivere and Kay, Arthur went to the mountain and killed the giant, but was too late to save the life of the maiden.

Arthur led his army into Gaul and met Lucius's forces. A meeting to negotiate a truce ended in disaster when Gawain, Arthur's nephew and the best of Arthur's warriors, took offense to a comment by one of Lucius's soldiers and cut off his head. Several battles followed, culminating in the battle of Soissons, where Arthur was victorious and Lucius was killed. Kay and Bedivere also fell in the battle.

Arthur wintered in Gaul and prepared to march on Rome itself, but he received word from Britain that Mordred, his nephew (the son of Anna and the brother of Gawain), whom Arthur had left as regent, had usurped the throne, and had taken Guinevere as his wife. As Arthur prepared to return to Britain to deal with Mordred, Mordred allied with Saxons and swelled his ranks with their numbers. Arthur landed at Richborough, battled Mordred's army, and lost Gawain in the fighting. Guinevere, hearing of Arthur's advance, fled to Caerleon and took the veil.

Pressing on, Arthur encountered Mordred's army again at the river Camel in Cornwall (Geoffrey's version of Camlann). At this final battle, both armies were obliterated. Mordred died, and Arthur received a mortal wound. Before he was taken to the island of Avalon for healing, he bestowed the crown of Britain on Constantine, son of Cador of Cornwall.

No more, then, is Arthur a simple *dux bellorum* who staves of the Saxon invasion of Britain: he is a full-blown emperor; a conqueror of a vast realm who manages to amass enough power to challenge Rome itself. Geoffrey's chronicle was a hit. The British people enjoyed having such a conqueror in their history. The Normans, who had been in power for just over 70 years at the time of Geoffrey's writing, now had an historical claim to the island: they were descendants of Arthur's relatives in Brittany, come again to defeat the Anglo-Saxons. There were skeptics even in Geoffrey's own time, but for the most part, his history was accepted as more-or-less authentic for centuries.

In 1155, Wace adapted Geoffrey's chronicle into the French verse *Roman de Brut* and, for the most part, dropped the pretext of history, infusing the saga with romance and paving the way for the great French romances. Around 1190, Layamon wrote *Brut*, an adaptation of Wace, in English. Though Wace's (and, ultimately, Layamon's) primary source was Geoffrey, both Wace and Layamon show the influence of Celtic and

Breton oral tradition in their versions of Arthur's life. Wace contributed at least one major addition to the Arthurian saga: the Round Table, which, he said, Arthur established to end disputes about precedence among his knights. Wace claimed to have heard of the Round Table from the Bretons. An important addition from Layamon is the statement that Arthur was taken to Avalon by an elfin queen named Argante (probably a corruption of Morgan).

Early French Romances: Wace brought the story of King Arthur across the channel and on to the continent, where it was to remain for the next two centuries.

The lines of transmission have been the subject of much debate. As stated before, Breton storytellers, who traveled far and wide, probably brought Arthurian tales out of Britain for centuries, but very little has survived. Marie de France's lays (c. 1170) were adapted from Breton tales, as were other scattered stories. The tale of Guinevere's abduction reached Modena, Italy as early as 1135, when a sculptor fashioned the Modena Archivolt, depicting the rescue of "Winlogee" (Guinevere) from "Carrado" (Caradoc) and "Mardoc" by "Artus de Bretania" (Arthur), "Isdernus" (Yder), "Galvagin" (Gawain), and "Che" (Kay).

But these tales inspired no body of literature until Wace's *Roman de Brut*, as if French romancers needed Wace's pseudo-historic framework to tell them who Arthur was and to structure their tales. In any event, Arthurian literature exploded in France, Germany, Scandinavia, and Italy over the next 200 years, with the first and most prominent romancer being Chrétien de Troyes.

Chrétien's *Erec, Cliges, Yvain, Lancelot,* and *Perceval,* all composed in the late twelfth century, portray and Arthurian world characterized by courtly love and chivalry, with Arthur's court at the very center of civilization. Arthur himself recedes into the background. He is neither the great general of the chronicles nor the glorious emperor of the Welsh legends; he is a generous, benevolent monarch who supervises the action of the story but rarely participates in it. Sometimes the portrayal of Arthur is negative; he is bland, impotent, passive, selfish, disinterested. And yet, Arthur is regarded with respect and awe, and his court is considered the epitome of civlized society and chivalric virtue.

To analyze each author's treatment of Arthur and his court is beyond the scope of this entry and, indeed, this book. Suffice to say that people and places and themes are introduced in these early romances that will stay with the Arthurian legend to the modern day: the heroes Lancelot, Perceval, Yvain, Yder, Tristan, and Erec; the Grail and the quest to achieve it; the abduction of Guinevere by Meleagant; the affair between Lancelot and Guinevere; Camelot; Chastity Tests; tournaments; and the tale of the Fair Unknown, to name only a few.

Robert de Boron, the Vulgate Romances, and the Post-Vulgate Romances: These texts, written between 1200 and 1240, constitute the last major contributions to the basic text and structure of Arthur's biography. They succeeded, on a grandoise scale, to unite the themes introduced by Chrétien de Troyes and other French writers (the Round Table, the Grail, the affair, the adventures of the heroes) with the history of Arthur's court provided by Geoffrey of Monmouth and Wace. Together, these sources introduced the theme of the Arthur-Grail "cycle," formed of at least four parts: the ancient history of the Grail (Robert de Boron's *Joesph d'Arimathie* and the Vulgate *Estoire del Saint Graal*), the establishment of Arthur and the Round Table (the *Merlins*), the quest for the Grail (Robert de Boron's *Perceval*/Didot-*Perceval* and the Vulgate and Post-Vulgate *Queste del Sainte Graal*), and the downfall and death of Arthur (the *Mort Artus*). The Vulgate Cycle also adds a fifth section that falls between the *Merlin* and the *Queste*: a *Lancelot*, which describes the many adventures of Lancelot and the other Knights of the Round Table. The stories have a religious subtext and portray Arthur's reign in the context of the growth of Christianity throughout the known world.

In a sense, these cycles are the first true "Arthurian" tales because they are the first to show Arthur as an individual rather than as a emperor, conqueror, or kindly old patriarch. For the first time, we see multiple expressions of Arthur's personal joys and woes; his reactions to the events taking place around him.

The prose cycles modify the biography given by Geoffrey of Monmouth considerably and deserve an individual summary:

When Jesus Christ was crucified, Joseph of Arimathea, a soldier of Pontius Pilate and a closet Christian, caught some of the Christ's blood in the cup or dish used at the Last Supper. This became the Holy Grail. Joseph eventually brought the Grail to Britain, and his followers established the Grail Castle at Corbenic. Arthur and his famous knights were descendants of this fellowship.

Merlin is born when a devil lies with a maiden, but he is baptized upon birth and loses his father's evil spirit.

The reign of Vortigern and Ambrosius is described much as in Geoffrey of Monmouth, but Ambrosius becomes "Pendragon" and his brother Constans becomes "Maine." Pendragon and Uther contend with the Saxons as well as with native rebellions.

Uther becomes king after Pendragon dies in battle against the Saxons. Uther falls in love with Igerne, the wife of the duke of Tintagel, and Merlin helps him enter the castle as in Geoffrey of Monmouth, but makes Uther promise to give him the child that is conceived. Uther marries Igerne. Merlin takes Arthur when he is born and gives him to Antor or Ector, a duke, to be raised. Antor has a son named Kay, who becomes Arthur's foster-brother. Uther's vassals revolt against him, and Uther becomes sick and dies. Merlin assures the kings of Britain that God will appoint their new leader at Christmas.

At Christmas, Antor, Kay, and Arthur go to Logres (London) for a tournament. Arthur is Kay's squire. After mass, the nobles exit a church to find a huge stone in the churchyard. A sword (Excalibur) is thrust through the anvil and into the stone, and a message proclaims that the person who draws the sword from the stone will be the new king. All the nobles try to pull it out, but in vain. During the tournament, Kay realizes that he's forgotten his sword, so he sends Arthur to get it. Arthur cannot find it, so he pulls the sword from the stone and gives it to Kay. Antor makes Arthur return it, and Arthur draws it again in front of everyone. At Antor's request, Arthur makes Kay his seneschal. The nobles protest Arthur's appointment at first but eventually accept it.

Some of the more irate kings, with ambitions to the throne themselves, organize a rebellion against Arthur. They include Lot, father of Gawain, and Urien, father of Yvain. At Merlin's advice, Arthur summons help from the French Kings Ban of Benoic and Bors of Gannes, promising to aid them against their mortal enemy, King Claudas, if they assist Arthur against the rebellion. With their assistance, Arthur routs the rebels at the battle of Bedegraine. Arthur unknowingly sleeps with his half-sister, the wife of Lot, and begets Mordred. He has a dream portending the destruction of his kingdom.

The Saxons begin their invasion of Britain anew, and the rebel kings return to their own lands to defend their homes. Arthur meets a maiden named Lisanor and fathers a son named Loholt with her. Gawain, Yvain, and other sons of the rebels break from their fathers and go to join Arthur's forces. Arthur, Merlin, Ban, and Bors go to the kingdom of Carmelide, ruled by Leodegan, and defend it against the Saxon king Rions (Geoffrey's Ritho). Arthur falls in love with Leodegan's daughter, Guinevere, and marries her. As a wedding present, Leodegan gives Arthur the Round Table that had belonged to Uther.

Arthur and his young allies enjoy victory while the rebels are continually defeated. Finally, the rebel kings agree to submit to Arthur, the forces unite, and the Saxons are crushed at the battle of Clarence. Arthur goes to Gaul and defeats King Claudas, who has allied with Romans and with Duke Frollo of Germany. Returning to Britain, Arthur kills Rions in Carmelide. He has pacified Britain.

Rome demands Arthur's submission. Arthur raises an army and goes to Gaul. He stops to kill the giant of Mont St. Michel. Arthur defeats the Roman Emperor Lucius at the battle of Soissons and kills him. Arthur also kills a devil cat at Lake Lausanne, then returns to Britain. Merlin is imprisoned by the Lady of the Lake and disappears from the story.

Arthur's court becomes the most renowned in the world, and it attracks the greatest knights from every kingdom. Lancelot eventually arrives and becomes one of Arthur's most famous and valuable warriors, but he falls in love with Guinevere. Arthur is attacked by an imperialistic lord named Galehaut,

but Lancelot brings an end to the hostilities. The adventures of Lancelot, Gawain, Hector, Balin, Agravain, Sagremor, Gaheris, Gareth, Lionel, Galescalain, Erec, Pelleas, Dodinel, Tristan, Aglovale, Perceval, Tor, Bors, and Yvain are related in detail. Arthur has his own adventures involving Pellinore, Accolon, and the Lady of the Lake. Arthur's half-sister, Morgan le Fay, hates him and tries to kill him. The Saxons invade again, briefly, but are defeated at Saxon Rock. During the invasion, Arthur sleeps with the Saxon sorceress Gamile on the same night that Guinevere is first unfaithful with Lancelot.

Soon afterwards, Guinevere's half-sister, called the False Guinevere, proclaims that she is the true queen and that Guinevere is an impostor. The False Guinevere seduces Arthur, and he exiles the real Guinevere, who goes to live with Lancelot. Eventually, Arthur discovers his mistake; the False Guinevere dies; and the true Guinevere is welcomed back to court. She is later abducted by Meleagant but is rescued by Lancelot.

In Gaul, Claudas has rebuilt his forces. Arthur goes to war with him, defeats him, and Claudas flees Gaul for good.

Galahad, Lancelot's son, arrives at Camelot. The Grail appears to the Knights of the Round Table, and all swear to seek it. Arthur laments because he knows he will lose his best knights in the quest. The quest is eventually completed by Galahad, Perceval, and Bors. Only Bors returns to court. Many knights have been slain. Gawain has murdered over a dozen of them.

Arthur holds a tournament at Winchester to restore the chivalric code, but it is clear that the soul of the court has been lost in the Grail Quest. Knights fight and murder each other; jealousy abounds; Arthur begins to suspect the affair between Lancelot and Guinevere; the queen is accused of murder.

Agravain and Mordred expose the affair by catching the lovers *in flagrante* while Arthur is hunting. Lancelot kills his attackers and flees, and Arthur sentences Guinevere to be burned at the stake. Many Knights of the Round Table join Lancelot's side. Lancelot shows up and rescues Guinevere, slaying more of Arthur's knights, including Gawain's brothers. Arthur, egged on by an infuriated Gawain, pursues Lancelot to his castle at Joyous Guard and fights him there. The pope intervenes and forces Arthur to restore Guinevere as queen. Arthur exiles Lancelot, and Lancelot goes to his homeland of Benoic.

Gawain urges Arthur to war. Leaving Mordred in charge of Britain and the queen, Arthur sails to Benoic with his army and attacks Lancelot. Lancelot tries to make peace; Arthur is tempted, but a vengeful Gawain rejects the proposal and forces Arthur to do the same. Gawain and Lancelot fight single combat, and Gawain is mortally wounded.

Romans invade Gaul. Arthur meets them and slays the emperor, but Kay is killed. News arrives that Mordred has faked Arthur's death, has siezed the throne, and has tried to force Guinevere into marriage. Arthur arrives at Dover and fights Mordred's forces. Gawain dies. Guinevere flees to a nunnery at Amesbury. The fighting reaches Salisbury Plain. The armies are obliterated. Arthur kills Mordred but receives a mortal wound. The only knights remaining are Lucan and Girflet. They bring Arthur to the Ancient Chapel, and Lucan soon dies. Arthur orders Girflet to throw Exclaibur into a lake and, after some hesitation, Girflet complies. Morgan le Fay arrives to bear Arthur away for healing. A body is later buried in the Ancient Chapel, but it is unclear whether it is Arthur's.

Lancelot contends with Mordred's sons and kills them, then retires to a monastery. Arthur's remaining knights do the same. In the Post-Vulgate version, King Mark of Cornwall invades Logres and destroys Camelot and the Round Table.

This version of Arthur's life and death became canonical, and it forms the conext of most of the subsequent romances, such as the Prose *Tristan*, the Italian *Tavola Ritonda*, the English Stanzaic *Le Morte Arthur*, Malory's *Le Morte Darthur*, and, with a few exceptions, most modern texts.

Dates of Reign

No two sources seem to agree as to the date of Arthur's reign. The following facts are noted:

- Gildas places the battle of Badon at around 500. He does not name the British leader, but if it was Arthur, than Arthur flourished at this time. It is uncertain whether, in history, the battle of Badon marked the beginning or end of Arthur's career.

- Nennius places the arrival of the Saxons in King Vortigern's Britain in 428. Arthur's activities seem to lie between 440 and 460.

- The *Annales Cambriae* put Arthur's victory at Badon at 516 and his death at Camlann at 537. These dates seem late.

- The *Legenda Sancti Goeznovii* places Arthur's activities in the 460s or 470s.

- Henry of Huntingdon puts Arthur's twelve battles against the Saxons between 527 and 530. Again, this seems late.

- The *Chronicle of Saint Michael's Mount*, a Breton document likely written in the twelfth century, says that Arthur was king in 421. This date is probably too early.

- Geoffrey of Monmouth has Arthur ruling in Britain while Emperor Leo I reigns in Constantinople. Leo held the throne between 457 and 474. However, Geoffrey gives the date of Arthur's death as 542. Modern scholars believe that Geoffrey made a calculation error and meant to put Arthur's death at 470. Other chronicles were to continue to report Arthur's death at 542, however.

- The Vulgate *Queste del Saint Graal* places the beginning of the Grail Quest at about 475, and Malory ups this by four years.

- The English *Short Metrical Chronicle* puts Arthur's reign during the time of Pope Eleutherius in Rome (c. 175). This of course is far too early. Later, however, the *Chronicle* dates Arthur's coronation at 560, which is almost certainly too late.

- The Italian *La Tavola Ritonda* says that Arthur died in 399, but previously said that the Grail Quest began in about the same year.

- The English ballad "The Legend of King Arthur" places Arthur's reign between 490 and 512.

- Riothamus, who may be Arthur under a different name, reportedly went to Gaul in 468 and was defeated by the Visigoths in 469 or 470.

Character

An analysis of Arthurian texts shows at least eight different descriptions of Arthur's basic character:

1. *British National Hero*. In the the earliest historic traditions, Arthur is presented as a British hero who fought off the Saxon invasions, postponing their conquest of Britain by several decades. In 1125, historian William Malmesbury disparaged the "trifles" told of Arthur by the Bretons, saying that Arthur is "a man who is surely worthy of being described in true histories rather than dreamed about in fallacious myths—for he truly sustained his sinking homeland for a long time and aroused the drooping spirits of his fellow citizens to battle." The historian John Morris, who has no doubt as to Arthur's reality, says, "His triumph was the last victory of western Rome; his short lived empire created the future nations of the English and the Welsh; and it was during his reign and under his authority that the Scots first came to Scotland. His victory and his defeat turned Roman Britain into Great Britain. His name overshadows his age." (Morris, xiii).

2. *World Conqueror*. As an extension of the national hero character, Geoffrey of Monmouth and other chroniclers portrayed Arthur as a great conqueror who brought Britain, the surrounding Islands, Scandinavia, Gaul, and Rome under his control.

Sometimes his empire extends farther, to Africa and the far east. Arthur joins the ranks of such legendary warlords as Julius Caesar and Alexander the Great. In creating this portrayl, Geoffrey gave the British a past "golden age" upon which they might look with pride and for inspiration.

3. *Mythological Emperor*. This portrayal is found in Welsh lore. Arthur presides over a kingdom of Celtic fantasy, full of beast-men, witches, one-eyed giants, dwarves, devils, fairies, and magicians. He sails to the otherworld and leads his army into the highlands of hell. He rules the known world, from Europe to Africa. Arthur and his warriors are giants among men. They can run lightly across the tops of reeds and can hit a fly with an arrow from the other side of the realm. They create fire with their bodies and carry knives as big as bridges and crush mountains under their feet. They are like the gods of classical mythology.

4. *Passive Patriarch*. In the continental romances, Arthur himself yields importance to his famous knights, whose individual adventures occupy the narratives. Arthur seems impotent, confused, and self-absorbed, sitting in the background. Nevertheless, he commands complete respect from his knights, and his court is considered the very center of civilization.

5. *Human High King*. In the French prose cycles and some of their adaptations, including Malory's *Le Morte Darthur*, Arthur becomes a far more human character than in previous texts. He is a fearsome warrior and a respected potentate, but his human failings are all too apparent. He tries to drown his infant son. He is unfaithful to his wife at least twice, with the Saxon sorcereress Gamille and the mother of Arthur the Less. The latter, he rapes. He fails to keep his promise to Kings Ban and Bors and, consequently, they are conquered by Claudas. When he discovers the affair between Lancelot and Guinevere, he handles it poorly and eventually allows himself to be egged into war by his nephew Gawain. These failings are carefully balanced by deeds of nobility and kindess and, in the end, we are forced to conclude that he is a human character placed in a super-human situation. The tragedy of his life, beginning with his incest, is beyond his ability to control; he is almost helpless as his kingdom crumbles around him. Our sympathy for him is increased if our awe is somewhat diminished.

6. *Daring Young Warrior*. In most texts, when Arthur is not fighting wars against Saxons or Romans, he is concerning himself with the duties of holding court. A small number of texts, however, show Arthur donning sword and armor and seeking adventure just as Lancelot or Gawain might do. His knights are amazed and pleased that their mighty king can also be a knight-errant. In the Post-Vulgate *Merlin* continuation, he personally jousts with King Pellinore to avenge a wound Pellinore gave to Girflet; he has further adventures with Merlin. *Le Chevalier du Papegau* describes the adventures of the young king, who goes under the alias the Knight of the Parrot, with fearsome beasts and beautiful ladies. Edmund Spenser's *The Faerie Queene* is largely concerned with the adventures of the dashing young Prince Arthur, a Christ figure, in the realm of Faerie.

7. *God-Appointed Sovereign*. An Arthur of infalliable character, given his throne by the approval of God. Robert de Boron and the author of the Vulgate *Merlin* show signs of leaning towards this portrayal with the Sword in the Stone test, but this characterization is nowhere more obvious than in Tennyson's *Idylls of the King*. Arthur is *not* the son of Uther; he emerges from the waves and washes to shore at Merlin's feet, who makes him Uther's heir. None of his knights can match him in virtue. Guinevere's infidelity is partially inspired by the fact that Arthur is "high, self-contain'd, and passionless"; that she could not endure "that pure severity of perfect light."

8. *Petty, Lecherous Tyrant*. A portrayal found in a minor but significant number of texts. The Welsh saint's lives generally characterize Arthur in an unflattering light. Always the ruler of some small territory, Arthur invariably does something to offend a visiting saint, such as stealing the saint's robe or altar. The saint then, through his superior spirituality, teaches Arthur a much-needed lesson. In these tales, Arthur represents the secular forces at work against God's spiritual mandates. Why the biographers chose Arthur instead of less famous, less-admired figures is unknown, but there may be at work some resentment towards a secular figure eclipsing in fame the legendary St. Patrick or St. Germanus.

The other group of literature to portray Arthur as a tyrant are the Scottish chronicles, which have their own agenda. In Hector Boece's *Scotorum Historiae* (1527), Arthur is a cruel king who never extends his borders beyond the boundaries of Britain. He throws drunken orgies at Christmastime. He names Mordred as his successor but later breaks his promise, causing Mordred's righteous revolt. Mordred, of course, is from Lothian: a Scot. John of Fordun's previous *Chronica Gentis Scotorum* (c. 1385) is nicer to Arthur but agrees that Mordred, as a Scot, had a better claim to Britain than Arthur.

Insignia

In Nennius's description of the battle of the Castle Guinnion, Arthur is said to have "carried an image of St. Mary, the Perpetual Virgin on his shoulders." The *Annales Cambriae* similarly describe the "Battle of Badon, in which Arthur carried the cross of Our Lord Jesus Christ for three days and three nights on his shoulders." Both of these passages, particularly the second, invoke an interesting and somewhat absurd image. It is likely, however, that the sources of both authors intended for Arthur to bear the insignia on his shield, with the Welsh word for "shield" (*yscuit*) mistranslated as "shoulder" (*yscuid*). Geoffrey of Monmouth, consequently, transfers the image of the Virgin Mary back to his shield. In Medieval times, the church of St. Mary of Wedale in Selkirkshire claimed to have a fragment of this emblem; however, it is unlikely that either of these allusions are authentic, since emblems or devices on shields are unknown this early in history (Barber, *Figure*, 101). [*Nennius, Annales, GeoffHR*]

Grave

Given the prolific belief that Arthur would eventually return from the island or valley of Avalon, his grave is rarely mentioned. We first find a reference to it in the early Welsh poem known as *The Stanzas of the Graves*, which discusses the grave sites of famous heroes. The pertinent line reads "anoeth bit bet y Arthur." This line has been translated as "Arthur's grave is hard to find," "a grave for Arthur would be ridiculous," and "the wondrous grave of Arthur." *Anoeth* is the difficult word; it is an intensifier compared to the English "incredible." It could mean that the location of the grave is mysterious, or that the grave itself has mysterious properties. Thus, it is unclear what, exactly, the line is indicating, but it does seems to anticipate later legend in suggesting a enigma surrounding the final resting place of the legendary king. William of Malmesbury, in 1125, wrote that the location of Arthur's grave was unknown and that the Britons expected his eventual return, and this sentiment is echoed throughout the Middle Ages, even after the discovery of his "grave" at Glastonbury (below).

A much clearer description of Arthur's grave was reported by Giraldus Cambrensis in *De Instructione Principum*. About 1190, the monks at Glastonbury Abbey, supposedly directed by Henry II, who had heard tales from bards, located Arthur's grave in the abbey churchyard and exhumed it. The grave, six feet underground in a hollowed oak tree between two stone pyramids, was unmarked on the surface. The Britons had apparently buried Arthur this way so that the Saxons would not defile the sepulcher. A cross, face down atop the wooden coffin, according to Giraldus read: "Here lies buried the famous King Arthur with Wenneveria his second wife on the Island of Avalon." Hence, the identification of Glastonbury with Avalon. Within the oak, two skeletons were found. Arthur's was notable for its enormous bones and a wound in the skull, presumably delivered by Mordred at the final battle. A tuft of golden hair was found on Guinevere's skull, but it crumbled to dust when a monk touched it. The monks moved the bodies to a marble tomb to prevent any violation. Contemporaries of Giraldus also reported the finding; all reports differ in details—some significant, such as the exact writing on the cross—but Giraldus's is the most detailed

Some modern scholars have accused the Glastonbury monks of the twelfth century of deliberate fraud, orchestrated to enhance the reputation of the church and to bring in much needed funds following a disastrous fire.

Such a scheme is not unlikely, but is impossible to prove. The cross itself, whether authentic or a forgery, seems to have existed, but it has been lost. We have a drawing of the artifact in a 1607 book by William Camden, and some scholars have suggested that the words—"Here lies buried the famous King Arthur on the Island of Avalon"—contains antiquated forms and spellings that would have been unknown to a twelfth-century forger.

(The Alliterative *Morte Arthure*, perhaps influenced by the report of the cross, said that Arthur's gravestone read *Hic jacet Arthurus, rex quondam, rexque futurus*—"Here lies Arthur, king that was, king that shall be." Malory reports the same.)

In any event, the report seemed to have little effect on the medieval romances, which continued to describe Arthur's journey to Avalon after the final battle. In the *Vera Historia de Morte Arthuri*, his body is said to disappear from the funeral bier in a mist. Cervantes spoke of the widespread folklore belief that Arthur had been changed into a crow and would some day find his true form again. The great "Briton hope" of Arthur's return thus remained alive. Malory is an exception, and even he hedges, merging both versions of Arthur's end and leaving room for doubt as to whether the body delivered to Glastonbury was truly Arthur's. [*WelshSG, Giraldus, Vera, Allit, Malory, Camden*]

Relatives

Arthur's relatives are listed below. More information can be found under their respective entries.

Parents: Usually, Uther Pendragon and Igerne (or Eigyr in Welsh). In Wolfram's *Parzival*, his mother is named Arnive.

Wives and Lovers: Angellica, Dollalolla, Emmeline, Gamile, Gilaneier, Grey-Hammed Lady, Guinevere, Gwenhwyfar, Inogen, Lady of the Blonde Hair, Lisanor

Sons: Adeluf III, Amr, Aristes, Art Aoinfhear, Arthur the Less, Borre (Bohort), Garnot, Gwydre, Ilinot, Llacheu, Loholt, Mordred, Morgan the Black, Patrick the Red, Tom a' Lincoln

Daughters: Gyneth and Huncamunca

Sisters: Acheflour, Albagia, Anna, Anthonje, Belisent, Blasine, Brimesent, Clarine, Elaine, Felice, Morgan le Fay, Morgause, Olimpia, Orchades, Sangive, and Seife

Brothers: Cador, Gormant, and Madawg

Uncles: Ambrosius, Ardan, Constans, David, Gweir, Gweir False Valor, Gweir Servant of Birds, Gweir White Shaft, Gwrfoddw the Old, Llygadrudd Emys, Maine, Pendragon, Yttra

Aunts: Enfeidas, Goleuddydd

Nephews: Agravain, Beacurs, Borel, Constantine, Gaheris, Galescalain, Gareth, Gawain, Gwidon, Hoel, Lancelot, Meleranz, Mordred, Perceval, Tristan, Yvain

Nieces: Clarissant, Cundrie, Elaine, Elyabel, Itonje, Lore, Soredamor

Grandchildren: Black Knight, Fairy Knight, Melehan

Cousins: Bagdemagus, Borel, Constantine, Culhwch, Helis, Hoel, Illtud, Ither of Gaheviez, Lady of Cabrion, Laris, Leonce, Lidoine, Mark, Mordred, Richard

ARTHUR[2] OF BRITTANY

Hero of a fourteenth-century French romance called *Artus de la Petite Bretagne* and John Bourchier's sixteenth-century English translation, *Arthur of Little Britain*. Arthur of Brittany was a descendant of Lancelot named after Arthur. The tale is otherwise non-Arthurian. Arthur became the greatest knight in the world and married a princess.

ARTHUR[3] OF DALRIADA

Son of King Aedan, who ruled Dalriada (a Scottish kingdom settled by the Irish c. 500) in the final quarter of the sixth century. His existence is attested in the *Life of St. Columba* (c. 700) and other Irish texts. He had several brothers, including Echoid Find and Domingart. Aedan apparently fought a battle against the Picts at Miatha, in which Arthur was killed. Aedan was known as a prolific campaigner, and it is likely that Arthur participated in a number of battles before his death. Some scholars, includng Richard Barber (*The Figure of Arthur*), argue for Arthur of Dalriada as the original prototype of King Arthur. According to this theory, Arthur of Dalriada was the "Arthur" to which *Y Gododdin* (a poem written in the north for northern audiences, contemporary to the life of Arthur of Dalriada) refers; his fame grew in oral legend until he was eventually attached to battles fought before his time, by other warleaders. A less controversial theory holds that some of Arthur of Dalriada's exploits were later conflated with his more famous predecessor's (after whom, presumably, Arthur of Dalriada was named).

ARTHUR[4] OF DYFED

A prince recorded in the genealogies of Dyfed. He was the son of Reitheoir, grandson of Vortipore, and the father of Naiee. He would have lived in the late sixth or early seventh century (Barber, *Figure*, 34–38).

ARTHUR[5] THE LESS

The son of Arthur by the daughter of Tanas, a lovely maiden that Arthur forced himself upon when he encountered her in the forest of Bretheam. Tanas later killed his daughter over an unrelated matter, and abandoned Arthur the Less, still a baby, in the forest. A widow found him and took him in, raising him to the age of fifteen. He was knighted by Tristan, and he soon proved his prowess by defeating both Perceval and Gawain in combat. He called himself "the Unknown Knight" until his true lineage was revealed to him at Arthur's court.

Arthur concealed the fact that Arthur the Less was his son, as he did not want others to know of the rape. Arthur the Less kept the secret, but remained fiercely loyal to his father. He accompanied Galahad during the Grail Quest, and was present at Corbenic, the Grail Castle, to witness Galahad's success. He also helped to repel King Mark's invasion of Camelot. He was slain by Bleoberis, whom he attacked for supporting Lancelot in the war against Arthur. [*PostQuest, ProsTris, PostMort, ProsTris*]

ARTHUR'S BATTLES

The Arthur found in Nennius is not a king, but is called *dux bellorum*, meaning "duke of war," or "war-leader." After the reign of Vortigern, Nennius says, "the Saxons were thriving and increasing in multitudes in Britain." Their leader was Octa (though it is not clear if Octa still holds his position during the wars with Arthur). Arthur appears out of nowhere, leads the British kings in combat, and enjoys twelve victories against the Saxons and nine different locations: the River GLEIN, the River DUBGLAS (four battles here), the River BASSAS, the Forest of CELIDON, the Castle GUINNION, the CITY OF THE LEGION, the River TRIBRUIT, Mount AGNED (or BREGUION), and BADON Hill.

Celidon is the Caledonian Forest in Scotland (Arthur may have been fighting Pictish allies of the Saxons rather than the Saxons themselves), and the City of the Legion is probably Chester. None of the other locations can be identified with any certainty, though many different possibilites have been suggested for each one. Proponents of Arthur as a northern hero locate all of them at northern localities, while other theorists manage to place them in Wales, or Cornwall. The best possibilities for each battle site—Badon at Bath or Badbury Rings, Glein at Glen in Lincolnshire, Agned at Edinburgh, and so on—are all over the British map, leading some scholars to conclude that the battles were fought by different warriors and were later attributed to Arthur as his fame grew. (Others have used this distances as evidence that Artur had revived the cavalry in Britain.) This theory is feasible, but it should be noted that Nennius does not supply a time frame for the twelve battles. We could easily assume that these battles represent a ten or twenty-year career for Arthur, in which case the distances seem less daunting. Another theory holds that the British forces at each battle called themselves "ARTHUR'S MEN," confusing later authors into believing that Arthur himself was present. [*Nennius*]

ARTHUR'S BED

The name given to a group of hills in Cornwall, signifying a local legend about Arthur. [*Topography*]

ARTHUR'S CAVE

Describes at least two caves in which Arthur is said to rest. The first is on the edge of the Forest of Dean in Wales.

The other, in Anglesey, is said to contain a fabulous treasure guarded by spectral creatures. [*Topography*]

ARTHUR'S CHAIR

Refers to four locations in Britain: a rock formation at Tintagel, the saddle between the two highest peaks at Brecon Beacons in Wales, an extinct volcano east of Edinburgh, and a sandstone formation near Hadrian's Wall in Northumberland. The legends associated with these features, if any existed, have been lost. [*Topography*]

ARTHUR'S CUPS AND SAUCERS

Natural rock basins on the side of the headland of Tintagel, on the coast of Cornwall. [*Topography*]

ARTHUR'S MEN

A hypothetical force of British soldiers who may have continued to go by Arthur's name even after the death of the historical Arthur. Geoffrey Ashe (*Handbook*, 370) thought that the appearance of "Arthur's men" at several historical battles may have confused later authors into believing that Arthur himself was present. These battles include Llongborth, which appears in a Welsh poem with Geraint as the hero, and any of the twelve battles listed by Nennius (see ARTHUR'S BATTLES).

ARTHUR'S OVEN

Priests from Laon were supposedly shown a rock formation called "Arthur's Oven" in 1113 in Dumnonia. There is no modern locality with this name, though "King's Oven" on Dartmoor is a possibility. [*Topography*]

ARTHUR'S STONE

Describes several landmarks in Britain. One is on the peninsula of Gower in Wales. Legend has it that Arthur took it from his boot during the battle of Camlann. The "stone" is a boulder, and the legend thus implies that Arthur was a giant. Another "Arthur's Stone" lies in Herefordshire and is reportedly the same stone from which Arthur drew Excalibur. [*Topography*]

ARTHURET

Alternate form of ARFDERYDD, the battle where Myrddin supposedly went insane. Despite the name, it is unrelated to Arthur.

ARTIS THE PALE [*Hartus*]

A Knight of the Round Table who participated in the Grail Quest. [*ProsTris*]

ARTORIUS

A Roman *gens* which seems to have supplied the name ARTHUR. Evidence of the *gens* is found in the first-century writings of the Roman historian Cornelius Tacitus and the Roman poet Juvenal (Decimus Iunius Iuvenalis). The name was known in Roman Britain as early as the second

century: a officer named Lucius Artorius Castus led a military excursion into Brittany around 150 A.D.

ARUN

A river in south West Sussex, along which lies the castle of Arundel. The river was the site of a battle between Arthur's forces and the Saxons in the early days of Arthur's reign. [*VulgMer*]

ARUNDEL [*Arondel, Arundels*]

The duchy ruled by Tristan's father-in-law Jovelin (Havelin), father of Isolde of the White Hands in Gottfried's *Tristan*. Its capital was Karke. Other writers make Isolde's homeland Brittany, but Gottfried apparently changed it to Arundel since he had already given Morgan as the Duke of Brittany. Nevertheless, he erroneously places Arundel next to Brittany and Parmenie, across the English Channel from Britain. The actual Arundel lies along the Arun River in southern West Sussex, England.

The Vulgate *Merlin*, which seems to place Arundel in Wales, says that it was the site of a crucial battle between the kings in rebellion against Arthur—led by King Tradelmant of North Wales—and the Saxons. The Saxons were routed and fled to Saxon Rock. A second battle at Arundel involving King Yder, Yvain, and Gawain against the Saxons resulted in a defeat. Merlin, however, warned Gawain to withdraw his forces from the field in time, and Gawain managed to save the castle and fortify it with a garrison. The story of *Arthour and Merlin*, which equates Arundel with CAMBENIC, places it in Cornwall and gives its ruler as Duke Escant. In *Durmart le Gallois*, it is ruled by Count Briains. [*Gottfried, VulgMer, Durmart, Arthour*]

ARVIRAGUS

One of Britain's kings in Geoffrey's account. He is a historical figure who, according to the Roman historian Juvenal, opposed the Roman rule of Britain. According to Geoffrey, Arviragus was the son of King Cymbeline and the brother of Guiderius. Guiderius became king of Britain after Cymbeline's death. He broke faith with Rome and went to war with Emperor Claudius. When Guiderius was slain in the war, Arviragus ascended the throne, made peace with the empire, and married Claudius's daughter, Genuissa. Arviragus broke with Rome again a few years later, but he was quelled by the Roman General Vespasian. Eventually, he quieted down and became a benevolent, just king. When he died, his son Marius succeeded him. Legend not found in Geoffrey holds that Arviragus gave the city of Glastonbury to Joseph of Arimathea and his followers, allowing Joseph to found an abbey there. [*GeoffHR, HereJoA, TennIK*]

ARWYSTLI

A mountainous region in Wales. While hunting in the area, Merlin and some other warriors encountered a fountain of pure water with apples lying around it. Merlin collected the apples but, finding that there were not enough to go around, generously distributed them to the other warriors and took none for himself. When the other warriors ate the apples, they promptly went insane. Merlin later discovered that a jealous woman—who had desired him but who he had rejected—had deliberately poisoned the apples to take revenge on Merlin. Merlin was later able to heal Maeldinus, one of the unfortunate warriors. [*GeoffVM*]

ASALIM THE POOR [*Anselian*]

A Knight of the Round Table who was slain during the Grail Quest. His brothers, Delimaz the Poor and Caligante the Poor, were also Round Table knights. [*PostQuest*]

ASCALUN [*Ascalon*]

A land ruled by Kingrisin and then his son Vergulaht in Wolfram's *Parzival*. Its capital was Schanpfanzun. Gawain was summoned to the country by Kingrimursel, the landgrave, to answer a murder charge, and became involved in a scuffle with Vergulaht in a misunderstanding involving Kingrisin's sister. In Chrétien's *Perceval*, the land is called ESCAVALON. [*Wolfram, Wirnt, PleierT*]

ASCAMINT

One of Arthur's dukes in the Norse *Erex Saga*. He was present at the wedding of Erec and Enide. [*Erex*]

ASCAMORE [*Achinour, Ascamour(e), Ascomore, Askanere, Askanore, Escamour, Escanor*]

A Knight of the Round Table. He fought in the Roman War and was wounded by the King of Libya. He joined Agravain and Mordred's plot to expose the affair of Lancelot and Guinevere by trapping the two lovers in the queen's chamber. Lancelot killed Ascamore in the ensuing battle. [*Allit, Parlement, Malory*]

ASCANIOR THE FIERCE

An evil giant killed by Guiron the Courteous. Guiron also killed Ascanior's son, Trudet. [*Palamedes*]

ASCHALONE

A knight present at the Sorgarda tournament in *Diu Crône*. [*Heinrich*]

ASCHIL [*Acil, Aescil, Archyl, Aschis, Askil, Echil*]

The King of Denmark who, in Geoffrey of Monmouth's *Historia*, voluntarily subjugated himself to Arthur to avoid being conquered. He fought for Arthur in the invasion of France and in the war against the Roman emperor Lucius, leading a battalion at the battle of Soissons. He was killed fighting Mordred's army at the battle of Camlann. Geoffrey Gaimar, who adapted Geoffrey of Monmouth's chronicle, makes Aschil's brother, Odulf, the king of Denmark under Arthur. Aschil's other brother, Gunter, had previously been king, but Arthur killed him. [*GeoffHR, Gaimar, Wace, HughesT*]

ASCLEPIODOTUS [*Asclepidiot*]

A Briton war leader from the third century who became the choice of the Britons to overthrow the tyrant Roman king Allectus. Asclepiodotus succeeded and became king himself. He ruled fairly and justly for ten years before being conquered by Coel of Kaercolun. Historically, Asclepiodotus was an administrator under a war general named Constantine Chlorus, who, history believes, really re-conquered Britain from Allectus. [*GeoffHR, Wace*]

ASGARES THE SAD

A Knight of the Round Table from Cardueil. He was badly wounded in a battle against Tristan, who was overcome with grief when he learned that Asgares was a Round Table knight. Sir Dodinel bore Asgares to a friend's house for healing. [*PostQuest*]

ASOURE

The name of Yvain's father in the Middle English *Sir Perceval of Galles*. He is usually called URIEN. [*SirPerc*]

ASPETTA VENTURA ("Expected Fortune")

In *La Tavola Ritonda*, a castle visited by Galahad, Perceval, Bors, and Perceval's sister Agresizia during the Grail Quest. It's lady, Verdoana, suffered from a leprosy which could only be cured by the blood of a virgin. All passing ladies were therefore asked to provide a sample of their blood. The three knights fought to protect Agresizia, but she eventually consented and perished during the bleeding. Verdoana, however, was cured. This episode appears in the Vulgate *Queste del Saint Graal* and its other adaptations, but the castle is unnamed. [*Tavola*]

ASPYOL

The noble duke of Tymant in Genewis. He took tentative command of the nation after Lancelot's father, Pant, was deposed and slain. He also cared for Pant's widow, Clarine. When Lancelot returned many years later, Aspyol gladly returned the land to its rightful heir. [*UlrichZ*]

ASSANON

Brother of Senahar, a knight imprisoned by Erec and Galahad. Seeking revenge, Assanon laid an ambush for Galahad, but he planned it badly, and Galahad killed him. [*ProsTris*]

ASSAR

A knight whose sister was raped by King Mark of Cornwall. With his brother Helyas, Assar fled Mark's kingdom for the Island of Two Brothers. The brothers later broke when Helyas abducted Assar's wife. During the war, Assar found Tristan stranded on the Rock of Hermits and rescued him. In gratitude, Tristan agreed to help Assar against Helyas. Tristan killed Helyas in single combat. [*ProsTris*]

ASSE

A British city once inhabited or visited by Arthur's chief gatekeeper Glewlwyd. [*Culhwch*]

ASSEN

A king who ruled the Perilous Forest a century or so before Arthur's time. His son, Anasteu, loved a peasant woman, which sparked Assen's ire. Anasteu fled his father's wrath and carved a home for himself and his lady in a rock. This cavern was later the final resting place of Merlin, when he was imprisoned there by the Ninianne. [*PostMer*]

ASSENTIN

A fierce king. Gawain visited his court seeking the king's maiden daughter, Ysabele, whom Gawain needed as part of an elaborate series of quests designed to obtain the magical Floating Chessboard from King Wonder. Assentin imprisoned Gawain and told his daughter to care for the knight. Later finding the two *in flagrante*, Assentin threw them both in his dungeon, from which they were rescued by the ghost of a knight Gawain had slain. [*Penninc*]

ASSILES

A terrible giant slain by Gawain. He inhabited a desert island and had the strength to move mountains. Assiles and his foster son, Galaas, plagued King Flois of Effin, who enlisted Gawain's services as champion. Gawain's victory against the monster saved the castle of Eigrun. [*Heinrich*]

ASSURNE [*Ausurne*]

A salt-water strait separating Arthur's Britain from Galehaut's land of Sorelois in the Prose *Lancelot*. It could only be crossed by two bridges: the North Wales Bridge and the Irish Bridge, both of which were long, dangerous, and partially submerged. In the midst of the waterway was the Lost Island, where Galehaut had a residence. According to the *Livre d'Artus*, the Assurne separated Britain from Gorre, which has similarities with Sorelois. R. S. Loomis (*Tradition*, 452) thought that it was the river Severn. [*LancLac, VulgLanc, Livre*]

ASTERIAN

In Konrad von Staffelin's *Gauriel*, the Count of Asterian's daughter is kidnapped but rescued by Gauriel, Erec, and Pliamin. [*Konrad*]

ASTOR[1]

The Duke of Lanverunz in the time of Arthur. He was an ally of both King Meljanz (Meliant) of Liz and King Poydiconjunz (Bagdemagus) of Gors. With these two, he

attacked the town of Bearosche but was held off by the opposition of Gawain. [*Wolfram*]

ASTOR[2] OF PANFATIS

An infidel count who served Feirefiz, Perceval's half-brother. [*Wolfram*]

ASUE

A giant fated to be killed by Tristan. He attacked the Dolorous Guard and, as a condition of the castle's surrender, required an annual tribute of a dozen children. [*Palamedes*]

ATALYE

A city in Lombardy where Sir Launfal met Sir Valentyne in joust. [*Launfal*]

ATAMAS

The lord of the Giant's Tower, also called the Knight of the Tower or the Knight of the Spring, after the Spring of Healing which ran near his fortress. He guarded the Spring and fought any knight who came his way. Although he was often less powerful than his opponent, he won the combats because he know the secret of the Spring of Healing. In this manner, he defeated and imprisoned Gawain, Gaheris, Bleoberis, and Sagremor. He was finally defeated by Palamedes during the Grail Quest, and he was forced to free his prisoners, although Palamedes allowed him to continue guarding the Spring. [*PostQuest*]

ATAZ

A Knight of the Round Table who embarked with the others on the Grail Quest. [*PostQuest*]

ATHEAN

A castle near the city of Taneburgh. Hector and Lionel, two of Arthur's knights, lodged at the castle before attending a tournament at Taneburgh. [*VulgMort*]

ATHENS

According to Chrétien de Troyes, this Greek city served as the capital of the empire of Greece and Constantinople. [*ChretienC*]

ATIN

Servant of the brash knight Pyrochles. [*Spenser*]

ATLANTIS

Echoes of the tale of Atlantis—a Utopian Atlantic island which, according to Greek mythology, sank beneath the ocean after an earthquake—can be found in the legend of LYONESSE, the land of Tristan, which supposedly sank beneath the sea between Cornwall and the Isles of Scilly. Only in modern times have occultists and novelists attempted to connect the legend of Atlantis directly to the Arthurian saga.

ATLENDOR

Son of Naf, brother of Gwenwynwyn, and one of Arthur's warriors. [*Culhwch*]

ATROCLAS

A king who enlisted the help of Sir Wigamur, an Arthurian knight, in a combat against King Paldriot of Lendrie. Before the battle, Wigamur discovered that Paldriot was his own father. Wigamur married Atroclas's daughter, Dulceflur. [*Wigamur*]

ATRWM THE TALL

One of Arthur's warriors in Welsh legend. He had an enormous appetite, and could eat all the food from three cantrevs (counties). His companion was Erwm the Tall, who had a similar hunger. [*Culhwch*]

AUBAGU

The name of Arthur's horse in Chrétien's *Erec*. [*ChretienE*]

AUBE

A river in Burgundy where Arthur camped on his way to the Roman War. His forces met with those of King Ban of Benoic and King Bors of Gannes. Arthur later built a castle along the river. [*VulgMer*]

AUDOLUS [*Andalas*]

A knight of great renown who served Arthur. He led an echelon of soldiers in the second battle of Carhaix, in which Arthur and King Leodegan defeated King Rions and the Saxons. [*VulgMer, Arthour*]

AUFERRANTE ("Iron-Shod")

One of Tristan's several horses in *La Tavola Ritonda*. [*Tavola*]

AUFRAT

A dangerous country to which Gawain was directed by a malicious goddess named Giramphiel. [*Heinrich*]

AUGUINTESTER

One of Arthur's knights. [*Heinrich*]

AUGUSTE

A cousin of Morholt of Ireland who plotted to avenge Morholt's death by making Tristan fall into a pit full of vermin. Auguste made the mistake of revealing his plan to Tristan, who was lodging with Auguste incognito. [*ProsTris*]

AUGUSTINE, SAINT

A Roman monk sent by Pope Gregorio to convert the English to Christianity in AD 596. St. Augustine and his companions entered Britain under the authority of King Aethelbert of Kent and established the church at Canterbury. Though he lived a century after the Arthurian period, the Prose *Tristan* says that he converted Lyonesse and Cornwall to Christianity several generations before Arthur's time, and in *Perlesvaus*, Arthur experiences a spiritual rebirth at St. Augustine's chapel in the White Forest. [*Perlesvaus, ProsTris*]

AUGUT

A British castle named after St. Augustine. Sir Bors accidentally killed the son of Augut's lord. He was scheduled to be executed, but he was rescued by Erec. [*PostMer*]

AULA

A forest through which Galahad, Perceval, and Bors rode on the Grail Quest. [*PostQuest*]

AUNOWRE

A great sorceress who, according to Malory, fell in love with Arthur and imprisoned him in her castle in the Perilous Forest. Arthur remained faithful to Guinevere and refused to indulge Aunowre's desires. She plotted to murder him, but Nimue learned of his plight and brought Tristan to rescue him. In the ensuing battle, Arthur awoke from his enchantment and beheaded the enchantress. She is called ELERGIA in *La Tavola Ritonda*. [*Malory*]

AUPATRIS

Father of Lord Caradoc of the Dolorous Tower. An evil giant, Aupatris abducted 12 maidens from the Castle Tarquin annually. Gawain's brother Gaheris sought to end the custom, and he killed the giant. The people of Tarquin erected a statue to commemorate the victory, but it was destroyed by Mordred's sons. [*PostMer*]

AURELIUS

Shortened form of AMBROSIUS AURELIUS; also the name of one of Arthur's warriors in Dryden's *King Arthur*. [*Dryden*]

AURIENCE

Daughter of Lord Boncenes. During the Grail Quest, Galahad visited their castle and convinced Aurience to become a nun. [*ProsTris*]

AURIS

A knight of Arthur's court. [*Merveil*]

AUSTRIA [*Estriche*]

According to the Alliterative *Morte Arthure*, this country was part of Arthur's kingdom. [*Allit*]

AUTECOINE

A river near the Castle Campadoine, which was ruled by Lord Belchis, an enemy of Arthur's knights. [*Raoul*]

AUTICE [Altice]

The land ruled by King Ares, the father of Arthur's Sir Tor. [*LancLac*, *VulgLanc*]

AUTLER [Auter, Haulter]

A knight slain by Lancelot. [*Sala*]

AUTUN

A town along the river Aube in Burgundy where Arthur mustered his forces during the Roman War. [*GeoffHR*, *Wace*]

AUVERGNE [Overgne]

A region in south central France, conquered in Layamon's *Brut* by Hoel of Brittany for Arthur. The Prose *Lancelot* gives King Aramont of Brittany as its overlord. According to Malory, it was one of Lancelot's lands. Lancelot made Sir Gahalantyne the duke of Auvergne in return for Gahalantyne's support in the war against Arthur. [*Layamon*, *LancLac*, *Malory*]

AVADOAN

King of the Isles. He was one of many rulers conquered by Galehaut. There may be some confusion with the King of VALDOAN. [*Livre*]

AVALON [Afallach, Auelon, Avallon, Avalona, Avaron, Aveloun, Avilion, Vallone]

Arthur's final resting place, variously described as an island or valley, from which, according to legend, the king will one day return. Most versions of Arthur's death recount that his sister, Morgan le Fay, carried him to Avalon after he received a mortal wound at the final battle with Mordred.

Geoffrey of Monmouth first introduces this idea at the end of the Arthurian section of his *Historia Regum Britanniae*, where he says that "the glorious King Arthur was mortally wounded, and was carried from [the battlefield of Camlann] to the Isle of Avalon [*Insula Avallonis*], so that his wounds might be healed." In a previous section, Geoffrey notes that Arthur's sword, Caliburn, was forged on the isle of Avalon.

In his *Vita Merlini*, Geoffrey adds further details. Calling it *Insula Pomorum*, or "Apple Island," he says that Merlin and Taliesin brought Arthur to the isle, which was ruled by Morgan and her eight sisters, all adept healers. The island was to the west of Britain. Geoffrey's Avalon is a lush otherworld paradise that produces grain without cultivation and provides longevity to its residents. His descriptions recall the Fortunate Isles of classical myth and, indeed, Geoffrey gives "Fortunate" as an alternate name for the island. Morgan's nine sisters recollect the nine maidens of Annwyn who kept a magic cauldron in *Preiddeu Annwfn* (see also NINE WITCHES).

Given the numerous mythological examples of apples as otherworldly or magical fruits, and given that the Celtic word for "apple" is *avallo*, Geoffrey's equation of "Avalon" to "Apple Island" is probably correct. We must also note, however, the appearance of a ruler named AFFALACH in Celtic myth. Named as the father of Modron—the Celtic progenitor of Morgan le Fay—he is said to rule an island with the qualities of Geoffrey's Avalon. Geoffrey's *Insula Avallonis* equals the Welsh *Ynys Avallach*, which may signify "Apple Island," or may mean "Avallach's Island." Scholars have also pointed out that the Irish sea-god Manannan was said to live on an island called Abhlach ("lush with Apple trees").

"Avallon," however, is also the name of a town in Burgundy. Burgundy, whether coincidentally or not, is near where the British high king called "Riothamus" in continental chronicles ended his career, probably slain in battle against the Visigoths. In their *Arthurian Handbook*, Geoffrey Ashe and Norris Lacy trace the career of Riothamus and argue, as other scholars have done, for an identification between Riothamus and Arthur. If this identification is correct, it adds an entirely new angle to the idea of Avalon or Avallon as Arthur's final resting place.

Successive authors added sporadically to the concept of Geoffrey's *Insula Avallonis*. Wace and Layamon both relate the Briton belief that Arthur would return from Avalon to rule again. Layamon gives its fairy queen's name as Argante rather than Morgan. Chrétien de Troyes names its ruler as Guinguemar, Morgan's lover, while Heinrich von dem Türlin calls its queen Enfeidas, Arthur's aunt. In the Italian *La Tavola Ritonda*, the island, located in the Soriano Sea, is inhabited by a wicked sorceress named Escorducarla. *Durmart le Gallois* names its ruler as King Bangon. The French tale of *Les Merveilles de Rigomer* refers to all of the British Isles as the "Isles of Avalon." Italian legend equates Avalon with the Isle of Sicily.

Perlesvaus reports that Guinevere and Loholt, Arthur's son, were buried there prior to Arthur's own death. (In *Perlesvaus*, Avalon may be identical to Glastonbury.) *Perlesvaus* somewhat strips it of its otherworldly associations by having Lancelot simply happen upon it during his adventures. In Alliterative *Morte Arthure*, Arthur is borne to a manor there, but a surgeon from Salerno fails to cure him and he dies.

In 1191, the monks at Glastonbury Abbey in England supposedly unearthed the bones of Arthur and Guinevere, leading them and several authors, including Giraldus Cambrensis, to conclude that Avalon was Glastonbury—an "island" in the sense that it is surrounded by marshes. This idea caught on with writers of the Grail legend who told of the establishment of Glastonbury Abbey by Joseph of Arimathea. Malory remains divided on the question, saying that Morgan and three other queens took Arthur to Avalon, but later relating how they brought his body to be buried at Glastonbury.

The identification with Glastonbury had the effect of stripping the paradisiacal elements from Avalon, as well as removing the great "Breton hope" of Arthur's return. Consequently, a number of authors rejected it, favoring Geoffrey's celestial description. Tennyson describes Avalon as an "island-valley...where falls not hail, or rain, or snow...[d]eep-meadow'd, happy, fair with orchard lawns" where Arthur is to be healed. [*GeoffHR*, *GeoffVM*, *ChretienE*, *Triads*, *Layamon*, *Giraldus*, *Gottfried*, *Perlesvaus*, *Durmart*, *Merveil*, *Tavola*, *Stanz*, *Allit*, *Malory*, *TennIK*]

AVARICUM

The Roman name for Bourges, a city in Gaul that serves as the setting for Luigi Alamanni's *Avarchide*. The text follows the plot of Homer's *Iliad*, but the characters have Arthurian names; hence, Avaricum is the counterpart of Troy. Arthur appears in the role of Agamemnon, Lancelot takes the place of Achilles, and Gawain assumes the character of Menelaus. A number of other Arthurian characters take part: Claudas as Priam, Meleagant as Ulysses, the Lady of the Lake as Thetis, Galehaut as Patrocles, Tristan and Bors as Ajax and Diomede, Claudin as Paris, Lac as Nestor, and Segurant as Hector. Arthur's forces did, eventually, conquer the city. [*AlamAvar*]

AVARLAN[1]

In the Vulgate *Mort Artu*, a knight who hated Gawain. He poisoned some fruit, which he expected Guinevere to give to Gawain at dinner; Guinevere, however, offered the fruit to Gaheris of Carahew instead. Gaheris died and Guinevere, completely innocent, was accused of murder. Lancelot eventually acquitted her. Malory renamed the character PIONEL. [*VulgMort*]

AVARLAN[2]

A castle in Britain where Gaheris, Gawain's brother, fought a duel against Baudon, the Red Knight. Gaheris was victorious. [*PostMer*]

AVARON

In Robert de Boron's *Joseph d'Arimathie*, Peter, a follower of Joseph of Arimathea, is instructed to journey to the Vale of Avaron to await the coming of Alain's son, probably Perceval. Avaron almost certainly is meant to be AVALON, which would make this romance the first reference of Avalon as a valley rather than an island. [*RobertBorJ*]

AVENABLE ("Lovely")

The daughter of Duke Mathem of Soane. When her father's lands were stolen by Duke Frollo of Germany, Avenable fled to Julius Caesar's Roman court, disguised herself as a man, and called herself GRISANDOLES. Caesar knighted her and made her his seneschal before Merlin exposed her true gender. On Merlin's advice, Caesar married her. Her brother, Patrick, married Caesar's daughter. A similar story is recounted in the romance of SILENCE. [*VulgMer*, *ProsMer2*]

AVENGING LANCE

The name given in the Vulgate Cycle for the BLEEDING LANCE, an artifact from the Grail legends. [*VulgQuest*, *VulgMer*]

AVENIS

King of Averre, husband of Queen Anfole, and father of Anfole and Laudamie. Upon his death, Laudamie became queen of Averre and married Arthur's Sir Garel of the Blossoming Valley. [*PleierG*]

AVERRE [*Anferre*]

The kingdom ruled by Sir Garel, one of Arthur's knights. It was awarded to him after he slew the demon Vulganus and married Queen Laudamie. Previously, it had been ruled by King Avenis and Queen Anfole, Laudamie's parents. Its chief castle was called Muntrogin. [*Wolfram*, *PleierG*]

AVILION

An alternate spelling of AVALON.

AVON

A county of southwest England, on the Severn estuary. The Saxon leader Cheldric fled through Avon after the battle of Bath. [*Layamon*]

AYAÒ

One of seven brothers, including Albaò and Dormadat, who usurped the throne of Tristan the Stranger, ruler of Jakobsland. Tristan the Stranger sought out his famous namesake, and the two of them returned and slew the seven brothers. [*SagaTI*]

AYGLIN

Brother of Cador of Northumberland. When Cador died, Ayglin tried to seize his niece's inheritance by marrying her to a commoner. Kay rescued her and besieged Ayglin. The people of Northumberland forced Ayglin to surrender. [*Girart*]

AYLESFORD

A variation of EPISFORD, where Vortimer fought the Saxons. [*Wace*]

AYMERE [*Eymer(e)*, *Eymur*, *Gaymere*]

In *Sir Degrevant*, the steward of Earl Sere, Degrevant's enemy. Aymere learned of a romance between Degrevant and the earl's daughter. Conspiring to trap the two lovers, he was slain. [*SirDeg*]

AZAGOUC

A land and forest in the Middle East or Africa. The Queen of Zazamanc's suitor, Isenhart, and her prince, Prothizilas, fought each other to their mutual deaths here. Its mightiest prince was named Razalic. It fell under the rule of Perceval's father Gahmuret and then Gahmuret's other son, Feirefiz. Feirefiz later bestowed the land upon Perceval. [*Wolfram*]

Azet

In Heinrich von dem Türlin's *Diu Crône*, a knight named among the lists at Sorgarda, a tournament won by Gawain. [*Heinrich*]

Azinde

In Heinrich von dem Türlin's *Diu Crône*, a knight who appears at Sorgarda, a tournament won by Gawain. [*Heinrich*]

Azzadac

Steward of the castle Roimunt in Korntin. His mistress, Amena, was the mother-in-law of Wigalois, Gawain's son. [*Wirnt*]

B

BAALUS

A king of the Saxons who participated in King Aminaduc's siege at Vambieres. He was slain by Arthur's Sir Aglovale. [*Livre*]

BABEL

A clearing along the river Cordaniste near the city of Orcaut in King Evalach's Sarras. It was the site of a battle between Evalach and King Tholomer of Babylonia. [*VulgEst*]

BABIAN

A beautiful bird native to the land of Cluse (eventually ruled under Arthur by Daniel). During the day, it hovered over the ladies of Cluse, providing shade; at night, it gave off light. It was possessed of a beautiful voice. G. Rosenhagen suggests a derivation from *papegân*, German for "parrot." [*Stricker*]

BABYLON

An ancient city and empire on the Euphrates River in what is now central Iraq, though the use of the name in medieval literature probably refers to Cairo or Egypt. In the time of Joseph of Arimathea, the kingdom was ruled by Tholomer the Fugitive, an enemy of Evalach. Babylon was ruled in Arthur's time, according to Geoffrey of Monmouth, by Micipsa, who was an ally of the Roman Procurator Lucius Hiberius. During the time of Uther, in Wolfram's *Parzival*, Babylon was ruled by two brothers—Pompeius and Ipomidon—who made war on the Baruc of Baghdad. Perceval's father Gahmuret was involved in the war. Heinrich von dem Türlin names Babylon's king as Laamez, who ruled from Baldac, and *Claris et Laris* puts King Datois on the throne of Babylon. Datois was an ally of Thereus, Arthur's Roman enemy. [*GeoffHR, Wolfram, VulgEst, Heinrich*]

BACH BYCHAN ("Small One")

Tristan's page in a Welsh *Tristan* fragment. [*TrisFrag*]

BACINO ("Basin")

A fountain in the forest of Darnantes, where Tristan encountered the Questing Beast. [*Tavola*]

BADE

Capital of the land of Gorre, ruled by King Bagdemagus. Its name is probably taken from Bagdemagus himself, though it may be BATH. [*ChretienL*]

BADON [*Baddon, Baden, Badove, Vaddon*]

A hill or mountain that was the site of Arthur's greatest victory over the Saxons, according to the early chronicles. Gildas, writing in the sixth century, is the first to mention it, placing it at about 500 A.D., at the culmination of the British resistance against the Saxons begun by Ambrosius. Gildas does not name the British commander at Badon—though it is possible, however unlikely, to read Gildas's summary to indicate Ambrosius as this man. Bede, the next writer to mention the battle, dated it at 493 and also excluded Arthur's name.

Both Nennius and the *Annales Cambriae*, however, grant Arthur the distinction as the British victor. Nennius, writing around 800, names Badon as the twelfth and final battle between Arthur and the Saxons, in which "nine hundred and sixty men fell from a single attack of Arthur." The *Annales* date the confrontation at 518, and note that "Arthur carried the cross of Our Lord Jesus Christ for three days and three nights on his shoulders."

According to the Welsh tale of *Breudwyt Rhonabwy*, Osla Big Knife (perhaps a variant of Octa) was Arthur's opponent at Badon, which ended in a truce. Oddly, Osla appears as one of Arthur's warriors in a separate legend.

After the *Annales*, chroniclers modified the location of the battle. Geoffrey of Monmouth places the fight at Bath and makes the Saxon leader Colgrim. In the Vulgate *Merlin*, Arthur smashes the Saxons at CLARENCE. The battle is absent from Malory's novel entirely, returning finally in Tennyson's *Idylls of the King*.

Given its mention in Gildas's early text, Badon was almost certainly an actual battle, though Arthur's connection remains uncertain, as does the actual location of the confrontation. Geoffrey's Bath is a possibility. Other suggestions have included Badbury, Baddington, and Liddington Castle in Wiltshire (near which is another Badbury). In order for the victory to have driven the Saxons back to their southeastern settlements, it would have likely been located in the south-central to southeast area of the island. [*Gildas, Bede, Nennius, Annales, GeoffHR, Dream, Idylls of the King*]

BADUC OF THE PERILOUS CASTLE

A vassal of the Maiden of the Narrow Wood. When the Maiden was besieged by Maduk the Black, an unwanted suitor, Baduc defended her castle. Baduc was slain in battle by Maduk. [*Vengeance*]

BAEDDAN

Father of Arthur's warrior Maelwys in *Culhwch and Olwen*. As Maelwys is the Welsh counterpart of

Meleagant, Baeddan may be the origin of BAGDEMAGUS. [*Culhwch*]

BAGARIM

A Knight of the Round Table who embarked with the others on the Grail Quest. [*PostQuest*]

BAGDEMAGUS [*Bademagu, Bagom(m)edés, Baldemagu, Bandemagu(l), Bando de Magus, Bando di Mago, Bangdemagew, Bano of Magoç Baudemagu, Brandymagus, Poydiconjunz*]

King of Gorre and father of Meleagant, one of Guinevere's abductors. He had brothers named Tarsan and Donadix. He was a cousin of Arthur and the cousin or nephew of King Urien, from who he inherited his kingdom. His first appearance is in Chrétien's *Lancelot*, in which he prevents his son from mistreating the kidnapped Guinevere. He makes a brief appearance in the Second Continuation of Chrétien's *Perceval* as a knight whom Kay hung by his feet from a tree. The Vulgate and Post-Vulgate Cycles expound upon his character, and offer somewhat conflicting stories of his early days. His origin seems to be BAEDDAN in the Welsh *Culhwch and Olwen*, possibly conflated with the name of another character.

The Vulgate version places him in the role of antagonist to Arthur: Bagdemagus's land had been ravaged by Uther Pendragon, so when Uther died, he decided to repopulate it with Uther's former subjects. Any person who strayed into Gorre was forced to stay. He joined his uncle Urien's rebellion against Arthur, eventually forming a tentative peace only when necessary to expel the Saxons. He then allied with Galehaut of Sorelois and opposed Arthur again. He grew more benign with age, and objected to his son's careless activities, including the kidnapping of Guinevere. When his son was killed, Bagdemagus bore no ill will towards Lancelot. His friendship with the knight led to a position at the Round Table.

The Post-Vulgate story, by contrast, presents Bagdemagus as a young companion of Gawain and Yvain. Long before he became the king of Gorre, he was knighted by Arthur and served the King. He was furious when Tor was elevated to the Round Table ahead of him, and he departed Camelot intent on proving his worth—even against Knights of the Round Table. He encountered Merlin, imprisoned in his tomb, and brought news of his fate back to knights searching for the enchanter. Eventually, he reconciled with Arthur and was promoted to the Round Table.

In other adventures, Bagdemagus slept with the wife of King Pellinore, for which Pellinore bound him, beat him, and left him for dead. He was rescued by Gaheris. He fought for Arthur in the wars against King Claudas, and he participated in several tournaments. Malory, in contrast to the Vulgate version, says that Bagdemagus hated Lancelot and plotted, with Sir Galehaut, to kill him; the plan went awry when the two knights attacked Tristan by mistake.

Bagdemagus embarked on the Grail Quest with the others, but he was soon wounded after taking a shield meant for Galahad. Later, he came upon Mordred raping a maiden, and he wounded him in the subsequent combat. Gawain, seeking to avenge his brother's wound, and not knowing the identity of the knight who wounded him, chased after Bagdemagus and challenged him to combat. Bagdemagus was mortally wounded in the subsequent duel. Gawain lamented when he discovered Bagdemagus's identity, and Bagdemagus forgave him before dying. Gawain had him buried in a hermitage. The Stanzaic *Morte Arthur* says that he survived the Grail Quest and joined Lancelot's defection from Arthur's court. [*ChretienL, Contin2, LancLac, VulgLanc, VulgMer, PostMer, PostQuest, Arthour, Stanz, Malory*]

BAGHDAD [*Baldac, Baldake, Bandes, Baudac*]

The capital of modern day Iraq. According to Wolfram, it was invaded by Babylonians in Uther Pendragon's time. Perceval's father Gahmuret aided the Baruc of Baghdad in fighting off the Babylonians and was killed during a battle. The Vulgate *Lancelot* names it as the home of Sapient, one of Arthur's scribes. In the In the Alliterative *Morte Arthure*, it is subject to Lucius of Rome.

In the Prose *Tristan*, the King of Baghdad's daughter is loved by a Sarecen knight named Corsabrin. When she rejects him, he tells people she is insane. The maiden promises herself and her lands to Palamedes if he can defeat Corsabrin in combat, and Palamedes kills him during the tournament at Sorelois. Malory calls the maiden the daughter of "King Bandes."

According to Heinrich von dem Türlin, Arthur and his knights fought in a great tournament in Baghdad against three knights named Ansgir of Slaloi, Gamur the Saracen, and Firus Bahandin. Heinrich calls Baghdad the capital of Babylonia, ruled by King Laamez. [*Wolfram, VulgLanc, ProsTris, Heinrich, Allit*]

BAGOTTA

Galehaut's mother in *La Tavola Ritonda*. She was married to Brunor the Brown and had a daughter named Dalis. Tristan slew her at the Castle of Tears. She is known as the BEAUTIFUL GIANTESS in the Prose *Tristan*. [*Tavola*]

BAINGRANZ OF AINSGALT

The brother of a giant named Galaas, who was slain by Gawain. Baingranz tried to avenge his brother's death, but Gawain defeated him and accepted his surrender. [*Heinrich*]

BAL CATEL

A Roman senator who the Emperor Lucius assigned to liberate a prison train being taken by Arthur's warriors to France. The attempt failed. This character seems to play the same role as Geoffrey's VULTEIUS CATELLUS. [*Layamon*]

BALADINGAN

The homeland of one of King Arthur's knights in Renaut's *The Fair Unknown*. He was known simply as the "Knight of Baladingan." The knight participated in one of the Castle of Maidens tournaments. His character was adapted by Der Stricker as BELADIGANT. [*Renaut*]

BALAN[1] [*Balaan, Balans*]

Ill-fated knight and brother of Sir Balin the Savage in the Post-Vulgate *Suite du Merlin* and Malory's *Le Morte Darthur*. He helped his brother reconcile with King Arthur by capturing King Rions of North Wales, and by joining Arthur's war against Kings Lot and Nero. After the battle of Tarabel, the brothers separated. Balan slew a knight who guarded a bridge to an island. Forced to assume the duties of his victim, he ended up slaying his own brother, who challenged Balan without recognizing him. Tennyson changes the circumstances of their deaths, relating that Balan came upon an unknown knight trampling his shield, finding out that the knight was his brother only after giving and receiving a mortal wound. [*PostMer, Malory, TennIK*]

BALAN[2]

A British count, converted to Christianity by Josephus, the son of Joseph of Arimathea. Balan constructed a chapel that was later occupied by Joseph's follower Parent. [*VulgEst*]

BALANC [*Sabalant*]

A Saxon warrior, slain by Arthur's Sir Ulfin at the battle of Carhaix. [*VulgMer, Arthour*]

BALDAC

Alternate spelling for BAGHDAD.

BALDAS

A Saracen warrior slain by Yvain at the battle of Diana Bridge. [*Arthour*]

BALDULPH[1] [*Balduk, Baldulf, Bladulf, Valence*]

A Saxon leader and brother of Colgrim. He fought alongside his brother against Arthur's Britons after the deaths of Octa and Eosa. During Arthur's siege of York, Baldulph plotted to ambush and slay Arthur, but his plan was foiled by one of his own soldiers—Mauron, who was Arthur's kinsman. Baldulph then disguised himself as a minstrel and was able to sneak into the city to assist his beleaguered brother. Both Saxons were saved by the arrival of Cheldric from Germany. Baldulph continued the war until he and Colgrim were slain by Arthur's forces at Bath. [*GeoffHR, Wace*]

BALDULPH[2] [*Balien, Valence*]

The Earl of Silchester under Arthur. [*Wace, Layamon*]

BALDWIN OF BRITTANY [*Baudewin(s), Baudewyn, Bawdewin, Bawd(e)wyne, Bawdwin, Bodwine*]

A knight or bishop in Arthur's court who pops up in a number of fifteenth-century Middle English verse romances. He is perhaps derived from the Welsh BITWINI. Malory names him as an early supporter of Arthur who fought beside the king against the rebellious British kings at Caerleon and Bedegraine. In reward, Arthur gave Baldwin he title of constable and appointed him regent of Britain during the Roman War (in which the Alliterative *Morte Arthure* says he died). He eventually retired to a hermitage near Camelot.

Baldwin also appears among Arthur's knights in *Sir Gawain and the Green Knight*, *Sir Gawain and the Carl of Carlisle*, *The Carle of Carlisle*, and *The Avowing of King Arthur, Sir Gawain, Sir Kay, and Baldwin of Britain*. Both of the *Carl* romances portray him as a somewhat conceited and churlish bishop. *Avowing*, however, features an episode in which Arthur tests Baldwin, who has resolved never to be jealous over a woman, never to fear death, and never to deny hospitality to anyone who asks for it. Baldwin passes each test. In each of the latter three poems, he appears as a companion of Gawain and Kay. [*Avowing, SirGawain, SyreGaw, Allit, Malory, Carle*]

BALIE

A count who went to war with Adnain, a friend of Tristan's. Tristan defeated him in combat and forced him to make peace. [*Tavola*]

BALIN THE SAVAGE [*Balaa(i)n*]

Ill-fated Arthurian knight who delivered the Dolorous Stroke to King Pellam and slew his own brother, Balan. His story is told in the Post-Vulgate Cycle and in Malory's *Le Morte Darthur*. He may have originated with VARLAN, the king who strikes the Dolorous Stroke in the Vulgate *Queste del Saint Graal*.

A "poor knight" born in Northumberland, Balin had the misfortune of killing a cousin of King Arthur in battle. After serving a year and a half in Arthur's prison, he found difficulty regaining his status as a knight and went around dressed in beggar's clothing. He finally won honor when he alone was able—above all of Arthur's other knights—to draw a sword from a scabbard sent by Lady Lyle of Avalon. When Lyle's messenger asked Balin to return the sword, however, Balin refused, and the lady promised that the weapon would cause him great sorrow.

His triumph was short-lived. The Lady of the Lake arrived at court and asked Arthur for the heads of Balin and Lyle's messenger, citing wrongs they had committed against her family. Balin had his own grievance against the Lady of the Lake: she had killed his mother and a number of noble knights. Moments after Arthur refused the Lady's gruesome request, Balin beheaded her, incurred Arthur's wrath again, and was exiled.

On the road away from Camelot, he was challenged by a knight named Launceor, who was jealous of Balin's prowess and who had obtained Arthur's permission to ride after him. Balin killed Launceor in the first joust. Launceor's lover, Colombe, arrived and, finding her paramour dead, impaled herself on his sword as Balin watched in horror.

Determined to regain the king's favor, Balin hatched a plot to assassinate King Rions of North Wales, who had gone to war against Arthur in order to obtain his beard. He soon met up with his brother Balan, who agreed to help him. They encountered Merlin, who showed them King Rions on his way to his lover's bedside. The brothers ambushed Rions, captured him, and dragged him off to King Arthur. They subsequently assisted Arthur in the battle of Tarabel against Kings Lot and Nero (late in *Le Morte Darthur*, Sir Lamorat claims that Balin killed Lot, a deed formerly attributed to King Pellinore). Arthur praised their skill and welcomed them back to his court.

As Balan embarked on his own adventures, Balin found himself pursuing an invisible knight named Garlon, who happened to be the brother of King Pellam, the Grail King. Using his invisibility as a weapon, Garlon murdered two knights—Sir Harlews and Sir Peryn—right in front of Balin.

Balin caught up with Garlon during a great feast at King Pellam's castle. He was hesitant about whether to confront Garlon in the middle of Pellam's hall. Garlon made the decision easy by smacking Balin in the back of the head, which Balin repaid with a single deadly blow.

Pellam was furious and attacked Balin, shattering Balin's sword. The king then chased Balin all around his castle, as Balin desperately ran from room to room, looking for a weapon. Finding a spear next to a prostate body in a bedchamber, Balin picked it up and thrust it into Pellam. Little did Balin know that his unworthy hands had hefted the holy Bleeding Lance; the spear with which the Roman soldier Longinus had stabbed Jesus Christ on the cross. Known as the Dolorous Stroke, the blow caused Pellam's castle to crumble and caused the surrounding land, Listenois, to become the Waste Land. Merlin pulled Balin from the rubble and sent him on his way.

After leaving the wasted land, Balin encountered Sir Garnysh of the Mount, a despondent lover. Determined to do something right, Balin encouraged the sad knight to visit his paramour's nearby castle. Upon arrival, they found the woman in the arms of another man. Garnysh slew her, cursed Balin, and killed himself.

Coming finally to an island castle, Balin agreed to help the residents by dueling a fierce knight who guarded a bridge to the island. He accepted a new shield for the fight. Unknown to Balin, the guardian was his own brother, who failed to recognize Balin because of the new shield. The brothers fought savagely for hours, learning each other's identity only after they were both mortally wounded. They died alongside each other and were buried in the same tomb. Merlin stuck Balin's cursed sword into a block of marble and set it afloat. The same sword was drawn by Galahad at the beginning of the Grail Quest.

Tennyson portrays Balin as a knight eternally struggling against the "chained rage, which every yelped within him." He tried to emulate Lancelot, whom he saw as gentle, and he had the queen's crown engraved on his shield to remind him to act courtly rather than brutal. Upon learning of their infidelity from Vivien, his savagery ran wild and he destroyed his shield. When his brother Balan saw him trampling the queen's crown, he attacked, leading to the same tragic results. [*PostMer, Malory*]

BALINOR

Son of the King of the Distant Isles. His reputation as a superb knight won him Sir Bors' former Round Table seat after Bors left Arthur's court for Lancelot's. [*VulgMort*]

BALLAD OF THE ROSE

A ballad praising the noble adventures of Gawain's brother, Gaheris. The maidens of Arthur's court wrote the piece, and Tristan scripted the music. [*PostMer*]

BALLDVIN OF GERMANIA

One of Arthur's kings, present at the wedding of Erec and Enide. [*Erex*]

BALLUC

Earl of Guitshire under Arthur. He fought in the Roman War and was slain at the battle of Soissons. [*Wace*]

BALOR

A cyclops in Irish mythology whose eyelids, like Ysbadadden's in *Culhwch and Olwen*, were so heavy that they had to be pried open.

BALSANT

The lord of a castle where Erec lodged after the Sparrowhawk Tournament. [*Erex*]

BAMBURGH

A castle in Northumberland named by Malory as one of the possible locations for Joyous Guard, Lancelot's castle. Though occupied by the Angles, Bamburgh also shows ruins of an earlier British castled called Din Guayrdi. The castle appears in Girart d'Amien's *Escanor* as Banborc. [*Malory, Topography*]

BAN [*Ban(e)(s), Ban(d)o, Liban, Pant*]

Father of Lancelot of the Lake and Hector, son of King Lancelot, brother of King Bors of Gannes, Guinebaut, and Nestor, and husband of Elaine. His earliest existing appearance is found in Chrétien's *Lancelot*, though he probably appeared in the archetypal Lancelot romance (now lost) on which Chrétien's story and the Vulgate *Lancelot* are based. R. S. Loomis argued for a derivation from the Welsh king Bran, particularly since his full name, Ban of Benoic, recalls Bran the Blessed, whose French name would have been *Bran le Benoit*.

Chrétien calls him the king of Gomeret, but he is more widely known, through the Vulgate *Lancelot* and Malory, as the ruler of Benoic in France. The Grail histories trace his lineage to Nascien, Joseph of Arimathea's companion. As allies (or subjects) of Uther Pendragon and Arthur, Ban and his brother Bors helped the Arthur repel the Saxons, quell a rebellion led by several British rulers, and win the war against Rome. In return, the Pendragons assisted the brothers against their mortal enemy, King Claudas of the Land Laid Waste. During his adventures with Arthur, Merlin caused Ban to fall in love with the daughter of the Lord of the Castle of the Fens. Ban slept with the maiden, who later gave birth to Hector.

After crushing Claudas at the battle of Trebe, Arthur became involved with another British insurrection, with the result that Claudas launched a successful invasion of Benoic. Ban embarked for Arthur's court to ask for assistance, but when he saw Claudas burning his beloved city of Trebe behind him, he died of heartbreak. Lancelot, who was still an infant, was carried away by the Lady of the Lake, and Ban's wife retired to a nunnery. Lancelot later returned with Arthur and drove Claudas away.

Ulrich von Zatzikhoven, who uses the form PANT, describes the king as a tryant who was overthrown and slain by his own barons. This characterization of Ban is also found in the *Livre d'Artus*.

Bauduin Butor makes Ban Arthur's great uncle by naming the wife of Constantine, Arthur's grandfather, as Ivoire, Ban's sister. Butor gives Ban a daughter named Libanor with the Lady Sabe. [*ChretienL, UlrichZ, LancLac, VulgLanc, VulgMer, Livre, PostMer, PostQuest, Butor, Arthour, Malory*]

BANADRAB

One of four robber knights slain by Gawain. His companions (and brothers) were Gameranz, Belianz, and Eumenides. [*Heinrich*]

BANBORC

Castle Bamburgh in Northumberland, also called the Castle Orguelleus. Cador of Northumberland held a tournament at Banborc to find a husband for his daughter, Andrivete. Kay distinguished himself in the tournament but was afraid to confess his love for the maiden. When Cador died and his brother tried to marry Andrivete to a commoner, Kay returned and besieged Banborc to rescue her. [*Girart*]

BANGAN

Father of Arthur's warrior Kincar. [*GeoffHR*]

BANGON

King of Avalon in *Durmart le Gallois*. Bangon fought on the side of the Blanches Mores in a tournament against the Roche Lande (and Arthur's knights). [*Durmart*]

BANGOR

Probably Bangor in North Wales. It was the home of King Jozefent, the father of Arthur's Sir Durmart le Gallois. [*Durmart*]

BANIER [*Bannier*]

An Arthurian knight named in "The Marriage of Sir Gawain" and Sir Walter Scott's *The Bridal of Triermain*, perhaps derived from BAN or BANIN. [*Marriage, Scott*]

BANIN

Son of Gratian and godson of King Ban of Benoic. He was raised in Ban's castle of Trebe. He fought in the early wars against King Claudas, Ban's enemy, and his prowess helped to make Trebe the last castle to resist Claudas's invasion. Because of the treachery of Ban's seneschal, Trebe fell to Claudas. Banin entered Claudas's service long enough to challenge and kill the seneschal. He then departed for Arthur's court at Carhaix, where Arthur appointed him to the Knights of the Watch and, later, to the Round Table. He fought for Arthur in the final war against Claudas and participated in the Grail Quest. [*LancLac, VulgLanc, VulgMer, Livre, PostQuest*]

BANTELLAS

A knight of Lord Golagros in *Golagros and Gawain*. In the war between Golagros and Arthur, Bantellas managed to defeat and capture Sir Bedivere. [*Golagros*]

BANW

One of Twrch Trwyth's piglets, killed by Arthur's warriors at Dyffryn Amanw. [*Culhwch*]

BANYERS

A Knight of the Round Table who participated in the Grail Quest. [*ProsTris*]

BARADAM [*Abaradan, Baridan*]

A Knight of the Round Table from Desert. He was one of five cousins who hated Lancelot's family. During the Grail Quest, they foolishly attacked Galahad and were all mortally wounded. [*PostQuest, ProsTris*]

BARADAN THE YOUNG

A Knight of the Round Table who embarked with the others on the Grail Quest. His brother was Angelis of the Vaaos. [*PostQuest*]

BARADIGAN

A land ruled in Arthur's time by Canaan. Mentioned in Renaut de Bâgé's *Le Bel Inconnu*, it may be the same as Chrétien de Troyes's BRANDIGAN, although the rulers are different. In the Second Continuation of Chrétien's *Perceval*, the Lord of Baradigan kills a knight named Sir Caramadis to avenge the death of his cousin, Orguellous. [*Renaut, Contin2*]

BARALIS

Tristan's great-grandfather. The son of King Candaces of Cornwall and Cressille, he inherited the country of Lyoness. He became king of Cornwall when his brother,

Crissidés, died. His two sons were named Feriando and Felix, the latter of whom inherited his kingdoms. [*Tavola*]

BARAM

A Knight of the Round Table killed during the Grail Quest. [*PostQuest*]

BARAMAL [*Baramaus*]

A Saxon king, related to Hengist, who led an echelon of Saxon warriors in a battle against Kings Brandegorre and Caradoc, two lords in rebellion against Arthur. [*VulgMer*]

BARATRON

A king of Russia. He joined King Tallas of Denmark in an attack on King Urien. Arthur's knights came to Urien's defense, and Sir Claris killed Baratron at the siege. [*Claris*]

BARBARY [*Berbana*]

The magician at Corbenic, King Pelles' court, is called a native of Barbary in the Post-Vulgate *Queste del Saint Graal*. This country is also said to supply soldiers to Emperor Filimenis of Constantinople in *Floriant et Florete*. [*PostQuest, ProsTris, Floriant*]

BARBIGOEL

The coastal capital city of Meliant's land of Lis. [*Wolfram*]

BARCINIER

One of Arthur's Knights of the Round Table. [*HartmannE*]

BARDSEY ISLAND

An island off the northwest tip of Wales where Merlin is said to live in a glass fortress full of treasures. [*Topography*]

BARFLEUR [*Barflete*]

A city in Normandy, where Arthur landed on his way to battle Lucius the Roman. [*GeoffHR, Allit*]

BARHAM DOWN [*Barendown, Bareon Downe*]

In the Stanzaic *Morte Arthur* and in Malory, the site of the second battle between Arthur and Mordred, in which many good knights were slain. This followed the battle of Dover and preceded the final battle at Salisbury. [*Stanz, Malory*]

BARINTHUS

An ancient Celtic sea god who, according to Geoffrey of Monmouth in *Vita Merlini*, guided the boat carrying Arthur to Avalon. Geoffrey was probably speaking figuratively. [*GeoffVM*]

BARNAAINS

A knight of Arthur's court in *Les Merveilles de Rigomer*. [*Merveil*]

BARREN WASTELAND

A country visited by Gawain in the Vulgate *Lancelot*. The son of its king had been slain, and the king accused Hasart, his seneschal. Gawain agreed to champion Hasart in judicial combat, while the king secured the services of Gaheris, Gawain's brother. Fortunately, Gawain recognized his brother and ended the combat before either was seriously wounded. [*VulgLanc*]

BARUC[1] OF BAGHDAD

In Wolfram's *Parzival*, this Middle-Eastern leader captured the city of Niniveh from King Ipomidon. In return, the Baruc was invaded by Pompeius's and Ipomidon's Babylonians, but was assisted, for a time, by Perceval's father Gahmuret. [*Wolfram*]

BARUC[2] THE BLACK

A knight who desired to marry Queen Sebille. He ruled the castle of Trion. Known as the Fairy Knight and the Black Knight, he had never been overcome in battle. He killed Sebille's husband out of jealousy, intending to marry the queen by force. Sagremor, Sebille's paramour, championed her against Baruc and defeated him in combat, forcing him to surrender to the queen. [*Livre*]

BARUCH [*Barut(h)*]

A seaside castle in Arabia, owned by the son of King Evalach of Sarras. Nascien, adventuring on the high seas in a holy boat, came to port at Baruch, where he lodged before returning to his own lands. [*VulgEst*]

BARUZ

A knight who competed in the Sorgarda tournament. [*Heinrich*]

BARVELAIN [*Barlonaym*]

A Saxon king killed by Aglovale at the battle of Clarence. [*Livre*]

BASSA

A river which was the site of Arthur's sixth battle against the Saxons, according to Nennius. As in all of the twelve battles, Arthur was victorious. [*Nennius, TennIK*]

BASSE GENT

King Pelles' fife in *Perlesvaus*. As its name seems to signify "low person(s)," it may refer to a populace rather than a piece of land. [*Perlesvaus*]

BASSIANUS

Son of the Roman senator Severus. The Britons wanted to give Bassianus the throne of Britain after the death of Severus in the second century AD. The Romans, however, favored Severus's other son, Geta. Bassianus and Geta fought several battles with each other before Bassianus finally killed Geta and assumed the kingdom. The Roman

Carausius, however, convinced Bassianus's men to turn on him, and Bassianus was killed by his own soldiers during a battle with Carausius. Carausius then assumed the kingdom. [*GeoffHR*, *Wace*]

BAST

The land assigned to King Urien in the Vulgate *Lancelot*. [*VulgLanc*]

BASTARD

Tristan's horse in the Post-Vulgate *Queste del Saint Graal*. [*PostQuest*]

BATH

A city in southwest England. According to Geoffrey of Monmouth, it was founded by King Bladud in the tenth century BC. Bath was besieged by Saxons in Arthur's reign, but Arthur arrived in time to save the city and kill the Saxon leaders Colgrim and Baldulph. Later, Urbgennius served as the Earl of Bath. Geoffrey's use of Bath as the scene of this decisive battle indicates that he believed Bath to be the location of BADON. [*GeoffHR*, *Wace*]

BAUCILLAS

Uther Pendragon's and Arthur's doctor. When the Good Knight Without Fear went insane, Baucillas cured him. [*Palamedes*]

BAUDON

Son of the Duke of Avarlan. Known as the Red Knight, Baudon threw his friend Gallinor into prison after a mistaken dispute over a woman. Gallinor's brother, Gallin, challenged Baudon for Gallinor's release, but Gallin became wounded and infirm. Gaheris, Gawain's brother, promised to fight in Gallinor's stead, and he defeated Baudon, securing Gallinor's release. [*VulgLanc*]

BAUDRIS

An Irish knight who ruled the castle of Antiufais in *Les Merveilles de Rigomer*. He hosted Lancelot during the latter's journey to Rigomer and provided him information on the road ahead. [*Merveil*]

BAUDUINS

The evil lord of Wanglent Castle in Ireland. Gawain encountered him during his quest to conquer Rigomer Castle. Bauduins had come into possession of Fauviel, Gawain's horse, which was stolen from Gawain at keep of Fors Graviers. Gawain slew him with a lance blow and recaptured his steed. [*Merveil*]

BAUFUMES [*Baitramés, Bantrines*]

A Saxon king who joined King Rions of Ireland's invasion of Britain. He was slain by Arthur's knights at the battle of Aneblayse. [*VulgMer*, *Arthour*]

BAULAS

A Knight of the Round Table. [*HartmannE*]

BAYEUX [*Beauce*]

An actual city in northwest France. According to Geoffrey of Monmouth, the city was built by Bedivere's great-grandfather. Bedivere was buried here after his death in the Roman war. The Alliterative *Morte Arthure* transfers this to BAYONNE. [*GeoffHR*, *Wace*]

BAYONNE

An actual city in southwest France near the border of Spain. According to the Alliterative *Morte Arthure,* it was part of Arthur's kingdom and Bedivere's burial place, which suggests that the author was confusing it with BAYEUX. Malory gives it an alternate name for BENOIC. [*Allit*, *Malory*]

BEACURS [*Beatus*]

A son of Lot and Sangive, and brother of Gawain in German romance. His sisters included Cundrie and Itonje. He was the King of Norway and a Knight of the Round Table. He married Antonie, the niece of King Bagdemagus. [*Wolfram*, *PleierG*, *PleierT*]

BEAFLURS ("Beautiful Flower")

A fairy. She was the wife of Pansamurs. Her son, Liahturteltart, was a page to Queen Ampflise of France in the time of Uther. [*Wolfram*]

BEALS

King of Gomoret and one of Arthur's vassals, according to Hartmann von Aue. Beals corresponds with BAN in Chrétien de Troyes's *Erec*. [*HartmannE*]

BEALZENAN

The capital of Anjou, ancestral city of Perceval. It was ruled, in succession, by Gandin, Galoes, Perceval, and Kardeiz. [*Wolfram*]

BEAROSCHE

A city in the realm of Duke Lyppaut. It was the site of a battle between Lyppaut and King Meliant of Lis after Lyppaut's daughter, Obie, refused Meliant as a husband. After a day of fighting in which many good knights were brought down, Gawain, an ally of Lyppaut, forced Obie and Meliant to reconcile, ending the war. [*Wolfram*]

BEAS

A Saracen king, killed by Arthur's Sir Galescalain at the battle of Diana Bridge. [*Arthour*]

BEATRICE

A lady saved by Carduino (son of Arthur's Sir Dondinello) from an evil sorcerer, who had turned her knights into beasts and was trying to force her into marriage. Beatrice and Carduino were later married at Arthur's court. [*CantariC*]

BEATRIS

The niece of the king of Escavalon who married Dinasdarés, an enemy of Gawain. [*Contin1*]

BEAUDOUS [*Biausdous*]

Gawain's son in 'Robert de Blois' FAIR UNKNOWN romance. Born to Amie, the daughter of the king of Wales, Beaudous set out to win fame and fortune when he came of age. He called himself the Knight of Two Shields. By drawing a sword called Honoree from its sheath, he proved himself worthy to marry a princess named Biauté. After saving Biauté from Madoines, a competing suitor, Beaudous married her. [*RobertBlo*]

BEAUMAINS

Kay's derogatory nickname for Gawain's brother Gareth. Meaning "fair hands," it indicated that the young Gareth's hands were untarnished by work or combat. Gareth kept the name throughout his first two years at Arthur's court—one year as a kitchen page, and one as a knight. His mother, Morgause, eventually revealed his true identity while visiting Camelot. The name suggests Malory's familiarity with the *Bel Inconnu* or FAIR UNKNOWN romances, featuring Gawain's son. [*Malory*]

BEAUMONT

City in Quimper-Corentin that was the home of Arthur's Sir Aces. [*VulgMer*]

BEAUNE

An alternate name for BENOIC given by Malory. [*Malory*]

BEAUREGARD

A castle, the bridge to which was guarded by Claudin, son of King Claudas. During the Grail Quest, Galahad defeated Claudin and forced him to relinquish this post. [*ProsTris*]

BEAUREPAIRE ("Beautiful Home") [*Belrapiere, Belrepeire, Biaurepaire*]

A town in the land of Brobarz, ruled by the lady called Blancheflor in Chrétien's *Perceval* and Condwiramurs in Wolfram's *Parzival*. The lady had inherited it from her father, Tampenteire. It was attacked by Clamadeu of the Isles and his seneschal, Anguiguerron, and was on the verge of defeat when Perceval arrived and agreed to act as the lady's champion. Perceval defeated Clamadeu and his seneschal and saved the town. Chrétien says that he turned down Blancheflor's offer to rule the town and departed; Wolfram claims that he married Condwiramurs and became lord of Brobarz. The incident receives little attention in the Post-Vulgate version. In the third

Continuation of Chrétien's *Perceval*, Beaurepaire is attacked a second time by Lord Caridés of Escavalon and is again saved by Perceval. In Heinrich von dem Türlin's *Diu Crône*, it is named as the home of an Arthurian knight named Joranz. [*ChretienP, Contin2, Wolfram, Contin3, Heinrich, PostMer*]

BEAUTÉ[1] [*Belté(s), Beltéz, Bia(l)té(s), Biauté(s), Biautéz*]

A lovely maiden from the castle Landemore. She arrived at Arthur's court at Karahes during a Pentecost feast. Gawain fell in love with her immediately, and presented her to Guinevere. Beauté rebuked Gawain's love, as well as that of Gliglois, Gawain's squire, who was equally smitten upon seeing her. Gawain hoped to win her admiration at the Castle Orgueilleux tournament, but she refused to attend with him, going instead with the knight Aharer, who gave her a falcon to be presented to the winner of the tournament. The love-struck Gliglois, meanwhile, followed Beauté and Aharer, running behind their horses until his feet bled. Beauté finally stopped him and instructed him to take a message to her sister at Landemore. The message revealed to her sister—and to Gliglois—that Beauté truly loved Gliglois but wanted to test him. Her sister knighted Gliglois, who entered the tournament and won—taking the falcon and Beauté as his prizes. Gawain graciously relinquished his love for his former squire's sake. [*Gliglois*]

BEAUTÉ[2] [*Biautei, Biautez*]

Dauther of the King of the Isles. He father decreed that she would be married by the knight who could pull the magnificent sword Honoree from its sheath. Beautés maidservant, Clarete, carried the sword around until Beaudous, the son of Gawain, managed to draw the sword. Meanwhile, Madoines, a jilted suitor of Beauté, invaded her lands. Beaudous arrived at the right time and defeated Madoines. Beauté and Beaudous were married. [*RobertBlo*]

BEAUTIFUL FOREST

The home of Claudin, a maiden saved by Arthur's Sir Tandareis. It was ruled by Claudin's parents, Moralde and Angnie. [*PleierT*]

BEAUTIFUL GIANTESS [**Bele Jaiande*]

The mother of Galehaut and Delice. The Prose *Lancelot* names her land as Estregor, but in the Prose *Tristan*, she inhabits the Castle of Tears, on the Distant Isles, with her husband Brunor. Her husband followed a custom by which he compared a slain foe's lady with the Beautiful Giantess and slew whichever was least beautiful. The Beautiful Giantess invariably won the contest until Tristan came to the island with Isolde. Tristan killed Brunor in combat, and then slew the Beautiful Giantess because Isolde was more beautiful. The Italian *La Tavola Ritonda* gives her the proper name BAGOTTA. [*LancLac, VulgLanc, ProsTris*]

BEAUTIFUL WILDERNESS

A land ruled by Duke Eskilabon, a knight defeated by Arthur's Sir Garel. Its capital was Belamunt. [*PleierG*]

BEAUTY WITHOUT VILLANY [*Belle Sans Villenie*]

Daughter of the Count of Valsin, who came to Arthur's court to beseech Arthur's help in rescuing her lady, the Lady of the Blonde Hair of the Amorous City, from the demonic Fish-Knight. [*ChevPap*]

BEAUVAIS

A European land administered in Arthur's time by Lisavander. [*Wolfram*]

BEAU VIVANT

The name that Sir Breunor gave to his wife, the ILL-SPEAKING MAIDEN, after they were wed. [*Malory*]

BEAUVOISIN OF ILE FORT [*Belnain*]

Ruler of the Kingdom of Damsels. When he died, his steward dispossessed Flor de Mont, his daughter. Beauvoisin's spirit, in the form of a beast, led Arthur to the wicked steward, and Arthur liberated and restored his daughter. [*ChevPap*]

BECLEUS

A castle that serves as the setting for a SPARROWHAWK TOURNAMENT in Renaut de Bâgé's *Le Bel Inconnu*. The castle's lord, Girflet, won the tournament through sheer power of arms even though his lady, Rose Espanie, was clearly unworthy of the sparrowhawk. Gawain's son Guinglain eventually defeated Girflet and won the contest. [*Renaut*]

BEDALIS

One manuscript of the Prose *Tristan*, in departure from the others, describes Tristan's death at the hands of a lord named Bedalis. Tristan had helped his brother-in-law, Kahedins or Ruvalen, arrange a tryst with Gargeolain, Bedalis's wife. To avenge this disgrace, Bedalis tracked Tristan down and mortally wounded him with a poisoned lance. Afterwards, Bedalis became a pirate. He was eventually captured and executed. The romance of *Palamedes* alludes to the same episode. His counterpart in Eilhart von Oberge's *Tristrant* is NAMPETENIS. [*ProsTris*]

BEDEGRAINE [*Beding(r)an, Bedin(g)ham, Bedingram, *Bredigan, Brekenho, Brekingho*]

A castle, city, meadow and forest in Britain where Arthur decisively defeated the kings who rebelled against him at the beginning of his reign. The Vulgate *Lancelot* places it on the border between Ireland and Carmelide, while the *Livre d'Artus* places it on the border of Cornwall. The Vulgate *Merlin* calls it the chief city of Britain and Carmelide. Malory equates it with Sherwood Forest.

Arthour and Merlin places the same battle at ROCKINGHAM. The original form of the name, Bredigan, recalls BRANDIGAN from Chrétien de Troyes's *Erec*.

Arthur's victory at Bedegraine is first mentioned in the Vulgate *Merlin*, and it becomes a major episode in Malory's treatment. Though outnumbered, Arthur won the battle via a combination of creative tactics (including a surprise midnight attack) and a clandestine alliance with the French kings Ban of Benoic and Bors of Gannes.

After suffering the crushing defeat, the rebellious kings were forced to return to their own lands to combat a Saxon invasion. Soon, the kings were forced to ally with Arthur to purge the invaders, and Arthur became the undisputed ruler of Britain.

After the battle, Bedegraine Castle served as one of Arthur's many courts, and was the setting for the bulk of the FALSE GUINEVERE episode. Baudin Butor says that the castle had perviously been one of King Vortigern's courts. [*VulgLanc, VulgMer, Butor, Livre, Malory*]

BEDINOUS

An Arthurian knight in *Les Merveilles de Rigomer*. [*Merveil*]

BEDIONÉS

Lord of the Fres Marés in Ireland. He hosted Lancelot during his journey to Rigomer Castle. [*Merveil*]

BEDIVERE [*Bedevere, Bed(e)wer(e), Bedo(i)er, Bed(o)uer, Bedios, Beduer(e)(s), Beduier(s), Bedver(e), Bedwar, *Bedwyr, Bedyvere*]

A Knight of the Round Table, first found in Welsh legend as Bedwyr. Bedwyr was the son of Pedrawd and father of Amren and the lady Eneuawg. The Welsh legends make Bedwyr one of the best of Arthur's warriors, even though he had only one hand. In addition, he was one of the handsomest men in Britain, behind Arthur himself and Drych. He often appears alongside Cei—a pairing that recurs in Geoffrey of Monmouth. Among his several adventures in *Culhwch and Olwen*, he assists in Culhwch's tasks by tracking down Wrnach the Giant and Dillus the Bearded. A Welsh poem places his grave at Tryfan Hill.

Geoffrey of Monmouth says that Bedivere was Arthur's butler, and that Arthur gave him the country of Normandy. In other sources, he is listed as Arthur's cupbearer, constable, or stable master. He was named after his great-grandfather, who constructed the city of Bayeux in France. Malory names his father as Duke Corneus. He assisted Arthur in the battle against the giant of Mont St. Michel, the conquest of Gaul, and the Roman War. Geoffrey says that he was killed by King Boccus at the battle of Soissons, and was buried in Bayeaux. His nephew, Hirelglas, avenged his death.

In other romances, he survives the Roman campaign and fights in the wars against Lancelot and Mordred. In the Didot-*Perceval*, he dies in the first battle against Mordred. In the Stanzaic *Morte Arthur* (and subsequently in Malory), Bedivere and Lucan are the only knights left alive after the final battle at Salisbury. Assuming the role given to

GIRFLET in the Vulgate *Mort Artu*, he was ordered by Arthur to throw Excalibur into a nearby lake. After twice hiding the sword and enduring Arthur's rebukes, he complied. A lady's hand caught the sword and pulled it beneath the waters. He returned to the chapel where he had left Arthur, and witnessed Arthur's departure to Avalon. He retired to a hermitage with the former Archbishop of Canterbury and wrote down Arthur's story for future generations. The English ballad "King Arthur's Death" says that Bedivere died shortly after Salisbury, and that his brother Lucan performed the feats listed above. [*Culhwch, Geoffrey, Wace, ChretienE, Yder, Layamon, LancLac, VulgMer, Geraint, Stanz, Malory, KingAD, TennIK*]

BEDOIN

The Count of the Castle of the March. He disinherited his own sister, for which he was besieged by Galahad. Bedoin tried to ambush Galahad while he was sleeping. The attack failed, Bedoin was defeated, and Galahad made him restore his sister's lands. [*PostQuest, ProsTris*]

BEDWYR

The original Welsh version of BEDIVERE.

BEDYW

Son of Seithfed, brother of Sinnoch, Naw, and Wadu, and one of Arthur's warriors in Welsh legend. [*Culhwch*]

BÉEARN [*Béarn*]

A region in southwest France, in the Pyrenees, owned by Lancelot. Lancelot made Sir Vyllyers the earl of Béearn in return for Vyllyers' support in the battles against King Arthur. [*Malory*]

BEFORET

The beautiful forest ruled by Iweret, Lancelot's opponent in Ulrich's *Lanzelet*. The forest contained the castle of Dodone. It had once been part of Mabuz's lands, but Iweret annexed it, knowing that Mabuz could not oppose him. Mabuz's mother, a fairy, charged Lancelot, whom she raised, to defeat Iweret in revenge. Beforet is obviously a shortening of *belle forêt*, meaning "beautiful forest," which is its alternate name. The forest was cherished because of its hardy stock of fish, water, and wildlife—including, according to Ulrich, bears, deer, boars, lions, and elephants. [*UlrichZ*]

BEHALIM

A maiden championed by Gawain. A terrible warrior named Reimambram tried to seize the young lady. Her brother Marhardi agreed to champion her, but perished before the combat could take place. Gawain, who had rescued Behalim from a wild woman in the forest, agreed to take the combat in Marhardi's stead. He defeated Reimambram and made him swear fealty to the maiden. [*Heinrich*]

BEHANTIS OF KALOMIDENTE

An infidel count who served Perceval's half-brother Feirefiz. [*Wolfram*]

BEHEADING GAME

Most famously found in *Sir Gawain and the Green Knight*, the Beheading Game typically involves a challenge to a knight. The challenger proposes that the hero strike a blow with an axe to the challenger's head; but the hero has to promise to go to a designated location at the end of a period of time to receive a reciprocal blow. Figuring that if his own strike is accurate enough, he won't have to uphold his end of the promise, the hero accepts the challenge and cleanly beheads the challenger. The hero is astonished, however, when the decapitated knight picks up his head and walks away, disappears, or otherwise suggests that he is not dead and that some enchantment is involved. The poor hero must now go to his certain death or break his vow. Choosing death over dishonor, the hero appears at the designated location, at the designated times. After perhaps a feinted blow or two, the hero is granted a reprieve because he has acquitted himself with honor.

In *Sir Gawain and the Green Knight* and its inferior successor, *The Grene Knight*, the Green Knight, in the service of Morgan le Fay, is the challenger, and Gawain is the hero. This theme is used several times prior to *Gawain* in the First Continuation of Chrétien's *Perceval*, in which Caradoc is the hero and the challenger is his own father, Eliavres; in *Perlesvaus*, in which Lancelot is the hero, and his honorable return saves not only his own life, but also restores the Waste City to prosperity; in *La Mule sans frein*, in which Gawain is challenged to the test by a churl; and in Heinrich von dem Türlin's *Diu Crône* (in an episode based on *La Mule*), in which Gawain's participation in a beheading game against the sorcerer Gansguoter is a condition of his retrieving a magic bridle for the lady Sgoidamur. Probably the most humorous of the pre-*Gawain* beheading games occurs in *Hunbaut*. Gawain, challenged to the contest by a churl, decapitates his opponent with an axe. Gawain, apparently familiar with how the game usually goes, then grabs the churl's body and holds it fast, so that, unable to pick up and refasten his head, the churl dies.

We find a variation in the Middle-English *The Turke and Gawain*. A churl arrives at Arthur's court and offers a non-fatal version of the Beheading Game with fists instead of axes. After allowing Gawain to strike him, the churl insists on delivering the reciprocal blow at a later time, and he leads Gawain on a series of adventures. Finally, on the Isle of Man, the churl insists that Gawain strike him again, but this time with an axe. When Gawain beheads the churl, his companion is released from a curse and becomes the noble Sir Gromer. *The Carle of Carlisle* includes a similar scene in which Gawain's beheading of a bewitched churl transforms him into a nobleman.

The theme ultimately originates in Irish non-Arthurian romance. A tale called *Bricriu's Feast* (c. 1100) contains an episode between the hero Cuchulainn (often seen as the Irish counterpart to Gawain) and a sorcerer that was apparently the inspiration for the test in *Sir Gawain*. [*Contin1, Perlesvaus, Paien, Heinrich, Hunbaut, SirGawain, Grene, Turke, Carle*]

BEJOLARE

The sweet and beautiful mother of Bejolarz, a companion of Wigalois (Gawain's son). [*Wirnt*]

BEJOLARZ OF LEODARZ

Son of Bejolare and Count of Leodarz. As a knight, he served Count Moral, and joined Wigalois (Gawain's son) in his war against King Lion of Namur. [*Wirnt*]

BEL BRULLET

A castle where Guinevere lodged after she was rescued from Brun of Morrois by Sir Durmart. [*Durmart*]

BEL JOEOR

Tristan's horse in Béroul's *Tristan*. [*Beroul*]

BELACANE

The infidel Queen of Zazamanc and first wife of Perceval's father Gahmuret. She had first been loved by a lord named Isenhart. When he died in a combat against a prince named Prothizilas for her love, her kingdom was invaded by Isenhart's friends and allies (led by Vridebrant of Scotland). She faced imminent defeat until the arrival of the noble Gahmuret who beat back the offenders. Ignoring the color of her skin, Gahmuret fell in love with Belacane and married her. They had one pie-bald child name Feirefiz. Eventually, Gahmuret tired of domestic life, abandoned Belacane, and returned to Britain. Belacane soon died from sorrow. [*Wolfram*]

BELADIGANT

The Duke of Zone in Der Stricker's *Daniel*, who took service with Arthur and was appointed Duke of Cluse. He married Sandinose, the Maiden of the Green Meadow. He is found in Renaut's *Le Bel Inconnu* as the Knight of BALADINGAN. [*Stricker*]

BELAKUN

A land ruled by King Schaffilun, who was killed by Wigalois (Gawain's son). Three princes of Belakun were Darel, Gamer, and Ariun. [*Wirnt*]

BELAMIS

A duke in Arthur's service who married the Duchess of the Dark Mountain. [*Stricker*]

BELAMUNT

A castle in the Beautiful Wilderness. In Der Pleier's *Garel*, it was ruled by Duke Eskilabon, who imprisoned many knights until he was defeated by Arthur's Sir Garel. In Wirnt von Grafenberg's *Wigalois*, it was the home of the knight Flojir. [*Wirnt, PleierG*]

BELANDE [*Orlende*]

A city in Northumberland, ruled by King Clarion, an early enemy of Arthur. [*VulgMer, Arthour*]

BELCHIS[1]

The homely lord of the castles Monhaut and Campadoine and father of Espinogres. He kidnapped the Lady Lidoine when he heard that her lover, Meraguis of Portlesguez, was dead. He wanted Lidoine to marry Espinogres, but news of Meraugis's survival forced Belchis to release the woman. [*Raoul*]

BELCHIS[2] [*Belcis*]

King of Denmark in Arthur's service He fought for King Arthur against the Saxons at Vambieres and in the Roman War, leading a battalion of soldiers at the battle of Soissons. [*VulgMer, Livre*]

BELEARE

The Countess of the Castle Joraphas in Korntin and wife of Count Moral. Her husband was carried away by the dragon Pfetan. Wigalois (Gawain's son) found her weeping and agreed to rescue him; he succeeded, but was knocked unconscious during the battle. Beleare managed to locate him after one of her ladies witnessed some peasants stealing his belongings. She brought him back to Joraphas, where he remained until healed. Before Wigalois departed her kingdom, Beleare provided him with a magical suit of armor. [*Wirnt*]

BELEIS THE BLOND [*Ablechin, Beliche*]

A wealthy and powerful knight in the service of King Leodegan of Carmelide. He led an battalion of soldiers against King Rions of Ireland at the battles of Aneblayse and Carhaix. [*VulgMer, Livre, Arthour*]

BELFORTEMUNT

The castle in Trefferin ruled by Queen Dulceflur, whose kingdom was saved by Arthur's nephew Meleranz. [*PleierM*]

BELI[1]

Father of Arthur's warrior Rheidwn Arwy. [*Culhwch*]

BELI[2] ADVER

Father of Arthur's warrior Rhun. [*Culhwch*]

BELI[3] THE GREAT

King of Britain in several non-Arthurian Welsh sources. According to *The Dream of Macsen*, Macsen conquered Britain from Beli; in *Lludd and Llefelys*, however, Beli's son Lludd inherits the rule of the island after Beli's death. Beli's father was Manogan. His other sons were Llefelys, Caswallawn, and Nyniaw. In Welsh mythological genealogies, he is the grandfather of Bran the Blessed and Modron, and is the brother-in-law of the Virgin Mary. He may be the same character later used as the father of Rheidwn or Rhun. He could be a reflection of the pseudo-historical BELINUS (Chambers, 70). Some have seen him as the origin of PELLES, PELLINORE, BILIS, and BELINOR. (Loomis, *Grail*, 111).

BELIAGOG

A giant slain by Tristan [*SirTris*]

BELIANZ THE CRAFTY

One of four miscreant brother knights killed by Gawain in Heinrich von dem Türlin's *Diu Crône*. His brothers were Gameranz, Bandarab, and Eumenides. [*Heinrich*]

BELIAS¹

An enemy of Arthur, known as the Red Knight of Estremores. His brother, Agravadain, was a Knight of the Round Table. [*VulgMer*]

BELIAS² OF DOVES

A duke who joined the rebellion against Arthur in the early days of the king's reign. He later allied with Arthur in order to destroy the Saxons at Clarence. [*VulgMer*]

BELIAS³ THE AMOROUS [*Holias*]

Lord of the Castle of Maidens. In Arthur's service, he led a company of soldiers in the battle of Bedegraine, against kings in rebellion against Arthur, and at Carhaix, against Rions and the Saxons. [*VulgMer, Arthour*]

BELIAS⁴ THE BLACK

A strong knight who guarded the Spring of the Two Sycamores. He detested the Knights of the Round Table because he had been denited admittance to their order. He was an excellent jouster, and he unhorsed, among others, Gawain and Yvain. This prompted a whole host of knights to embark from Arthur's court to find and challenge Belias. One of them, Sarras, led Lancelot to the Spring. After Sarras himself was defeated, Lancelot jousted with Belias and won, mortally wounding him. Lancelot was later challenged by Briadas, Belias's brother, and Broadas, his father. [*VulgLanc*]

BELIDE [*Bellices*]

The daughter of King Faramon of France. She fell in love with Tristan while he was living and serving in Faramon's court. When Tristan did not reciprocate, she became enraged and staged a "rape" scene for which Tristan was convicted and sentenced to execution. Governal, Tristan's tutor, pleaded the truth to Faramon, who in turn coaxed it from his daughter. Acquitted, Tristan left France, and Belide killed herself. [*ProsTris, TristanoR, Tavola*]

BELINANT [*Balinant*]

King of South Wales and father of Arthur's Sir Dodinel in the Vulgate *Merlin*. Though married to a beautiful woman named Eglantine, he fathered Dodinel on his own niece. He ruled Lindesores and the Narrow Borderland, and his brother was King Tradelmant of North Wales. His land was invaded by Saxons, and he allied with other kings (most in rebellion against Arthur) to oppose them. After suffering a defeat at the battle of Clarence, Belinant and the other princes joined with Arthur and expelled the Saxons for good. He later led a battalion of soldiers in Arthur's war against Rome. The Vulgate *Lancelot* lists a King BERNANT of *North* Wales, who may be the same character. There may also be a connetion to CELINANT. [*VulgMer, Livre*]

BELINOR

A dwarf who served Queen Esclarmonde of Iglecele. At Esclarmonde's order, Belinore gave Sir Escanor the Handsome a magnificent horse called Gringolet. The horse later came into the possession of Gawain. There may be some connection with the dwarf BILIS. [*Girart*]

BELINUS [*Bel(l)in(us)*]

In the chronicles, a King of the Britons who preceded Arthur by many centuries. He was the brother of Brennius. When his father, King Dunwallo, died, Belinus and Brennius contended for the throne. After many battles, the brothers reached a truce and divided the island at the river Humber, with Belinus the higher king. Five years later, they went to war again. Brennius was aided by Norweigans, but was still defeated and driven off the island. During the same period, Belinus subjugated Denmark. He was eventually reconciled with his brother. Togehter, they conquered Gaul and Rome. Brennius remained to rule Rome whiel Belinus returned to Britain. His son Gurguint Barbtruc succeeded him.

When Arthur faced war with Rome, he used Belinus's example as justification and inspiration for his own campaign. In the fourteenth-century *Short Metrical Chronicle*, with its confused chronology, Belinus is succeeded by Hengist. He may be reflected in Welsh legend by BELI THE GREAT. [*GeoffHR, Wace, Short*]

BELISENT [*Bellicent*]

Mother of Gawain, Mordred, Gareth, Gaheris, and Agravain in *Arthour and Merlin* and in Tennyson's *Idylls of the King*. She was the daughter of Hoel or Gorlois and Igerne, and the wife of King Lot of Orkney. She encouraged her sons to take service with Arthur. During the Saxon (or Saracen) wars, she was captured by King Taurus, but was rescued by Gawain. A number of other sources name the same character as MORGAUSE, though unlike her counterpart, Belisent is generally portrayed as Arthur's kind and loving sister. [*Arthour, TennIK*]

BELLANGRE LE BEWSE [*Bellangerus*]

Son of Alexander the Orphan and Alice the Fair Pilgrim. Bellangere avenged the death of his father and his grandfather, Prince Bodwyne, by killing King Mark of Cornwall. He later became a Knight of the Round Table.

When Sir Lancelot and Queen Guinevere were accused of treason, Sir Bellangere pledged his support to Lancelot and helped him rescue Guinevere from the stake. He fought alongside Lancelot when Arthur laid siege to Joyous Guard and, later, Benoic. In return for his support, Lancelot made him the Earl of the Laundes. [*Malory*]

BELLEGARDE

A castle in the kingdom of King Lancelot (Lancelot's grandfather), according to the Vulgate *Estoire del Saint Graal*. King Lancelot loved the lady of the castle, who was married, and her husband eventually slew Lancelot in jealousy. In the Vulgate *Lancelot*, the castle is known as the WHITE FORTRESS. [*VulgEst*]

BELLEUS

A knight encountered by Lancelot during his first series of quests. Coming upon Belleus's empty pavilion in a glade, Lancelot went to sleep inside. He awoke to find Belleus, who had returned and mistaken Lancelot for his paramour, kissing him. In the ensuing surprised confusion, Belleus and Lancelot dueled, but settled down after Belleus received a stomach wound. [*Malory*]

BELLIC

The Arabian castle belonging to the first Nascien, before he departed for Britain. [*VulgEst*]

BELLOÉ

A castle in Listenois owned by Lamorat's sister. It was besieged by Count Guiot but was saved by Branor the Brown. It is also the name of a castle, perhaps a different one, that Arthur gave to Erec. There may be a connection with BELOÉ. [*Palamedes*]

BELLYAS THE PROUD

A knight who tried to avenge his brother Frolle's death at the hands of Lamorat. Lamorat defeated Bellyas in combat, granted him mercy, and the two knights became friends. He later became a Knight of the Round Table and was killed fighting Lancelot and his men when they rescued Guinevere from the stake. [*Malory*]

BELNI OF DANOIS

A lady at Arthur's court; one of many who failed a chastity test in Heinrich von dem Türlin's *Diu Crône*. [*Heinrich*]

BELOÉ

A castle in Britain. After the first battle against Mordred, a group of Arthur's knights, who were bearing Gawain's body to Camelot, stopped at Beloé for the night. When the lady of Beloé understood that the corpse was Gawain's, she lamented for the only man she had ever loved. Her husband, who had despised Gawain, struck her with his sword upon hearing this, and she died after requesting burial alongside Gawain. Her death was swiftly avenged by Arthur's knights, and her body was borne to Camelot as she requested. See also BELLOÉ. [*VulgMort*]

BELPHOEBE

A beautiful, brave, and powerful huntress. She was raised by the goddess Diana after she was born through immaculate conception to the virgin Chrysogone. She had a twin sister named Amoret. She found Arthur's squire, Timias, after he had been wounded by some evil foresters, and nursed him back to health. He fell in love with her, and helped her to rescue the maiden Amoret from the Hairy Carl. Belphoebe saw Timias kiss Amoret, accused him of infidelity, and left him. Later, she found Timias living as a hermit, pining over his lost love. Moved by his devotion, she reconciled with him. [*Spenser*]

BELVALIOT [*Belle Valet*]

A castle where Palamedes recovered after a particularly exhausting battle with Lamorat. Arthur gave the castle to Palamedes. [*ProsTris, Malory*]

BEMS-ON-KORCHA

A city in the country of Löver where Arthur was known to sometimes keep his court. [*Wolfram*]

BENCIN

Perceval's nephew in *La Tavola Ritonda*. The son of the Queen of the Waste Land, Bencin served King Pelles. [*Tavola*]

BENDELAYNE

A knight slain in joust by Gareth near the Castle Perilous. A score of Bendelayne's soldiers immediately set upon Gareth in revenge, but Gareth routed them. [*Malory*]

BENE

Daughter of Plippalinot the ferryman, resident of the Castle of Marvels, and friend to Itonje, Gawain's sister. [*Wolfram*]

BENEMIAS OF RAGULEIS

A knight saved from the prison of Eskalibon of Belamunt by Arthur's Sir Garel. In return, he served Garel in the war against King Ekunaver of Kanadic, and was eventually awarded a seat at the Round Table. [*PleierG*]

BENEOIZ [*Beneïz*]

The name given to the magical drinking horn which revealed a woman's chastity, or lack thereof, in the First Continuation of Chrétien's *Perceval*. Banded with gold and embellished with jewels, the horn spilled its wine all over a cuckold, but allowed a man with a faithful wife to drink freely. Arthur's entire court attempted to drink from the horn, but only one, including Arthur, succeeded: Caradoc, whose wife was called Guignier. The same episode appears in Biket's *Lai du Cor* and in numerous subsequent tales, but the horn itself is not named. Beneoiz is probably a form of the French "blessed" (*benoit*) and may have a connection with the blessed horn of King Bran (see THIRTEEN TREASURES). [*Contin1*]

BENIOSUS

In the Icelandic *Saga af Tristram ok Ísodd*, a king who managed to wrest control of Spain (Tristan's homeland) during the chaos that followed the defeat of Biring, Tristan's foster-father, at the hands of King Turnes of Africa. Tristan eventually defeated Beniosus and his companions, Earls Hríngr and Siguròr, and re-conquered Spain. [*SagaTI*]

BENOIC [*Benewic, Benoich, Benoit, Benuic, Benwick*]

Lancelot's homeland in France. It was ruled by his father Ban and later by Lancelot himself. Ulrich von Zatzikhoven called it GENEWIS, a possible variation. The Prose *Lancelot* tells us that Benoic's overlord was first Aramont, then Uther Pendragon, and then Arthur, and that Ban was their vassal. *Lancelot* further tells us that King Claudas invaded and conquered Benoic, causing Ban's death. The Italian *La Tavola Ritonda* recounts a similar story but names King Brandino and King Arandus as those who sacked the city.

The Stanzaic *Morte Arthur* says that Lancelot, during his war with Arthur, bestowed Benoic on his brother Ector. Arthur later laid siege to Benoic for sixth months, but had to depart when Mordred seized the throne of Britain. Malory suggests that Benoic may be located at the city of Bayonne or Beaune; *Lancelot* places it between the Loire and Arise Rivers; and the Vulgate *Merlin* identifies it with Bourges. Possibly, however, "Ban of Benoic" is a scribal corruption of *Bran le Benoit* (Bran the Blessed), a character in Welsh literature. Other scholars have proposed derivations from Gwynedd (North Wales) or Guenet in Brittany. [*UlrichZ, LancLac, VulgLanc, VulgMer, Tavola, Stanz, Malory*]

BENWIG

One of Twrch Trwyth's piglets, killed by Arthur's warriors at Dyffryn Amanw. [*Culhwch*]

BERADE

One of Arthur's knights killed in the Roman War. [*Allit*]

BERALLD

One of Arthur's earls in the Norse *Erex Saga*. He was present at the wedding of Erec and Enide. [*Erex*]

BERCILAK OF THE HIGH DESERT [*Bertilak*]

The true name of the GREEN KNIGHT in *Sir Gawain and the Green Knight*. He inhabited a castle called Hutton. In the later poem, *The Grene Knight*, he is called BREDBEDDLE. Malory's Green Knight, PERTYLOPE, may be

a derivation. L. H. Loomis notes that a similar character in Irish romance is called a *bachlach* ("churl"), which she suggests as the origin of Bercilak's name (Loomis, *Romance*, 531–2). [*SirGawain*]

BERELL

The ghost of Guinevere's mother in *The Awntyrs off Arthure at the Terne Wathelyne* compares herself to an unidentified woman named Berell, claiming to have greater beauty. Berell does not figure into Arthurian legends anywhere else, though Ralph Hanna suggested that the line originally named BRISEN, Elaine's servant (Hahn, 206). [*Awntyrs*]

BERENGIER[1] [*Bellangre*]

Constable of the Castle Magance in Sussex, which he held from his master, Ranner. He raised and trained Alexander the Orphan, Mark's nephew, when Alexander and his mother were forced to flee Cornwall to escape Mark's wrath. [*ProsTris, Prophecies, Malory*]

BERENGIER[2] OF GOMERET

A widower who was the object of desire for Morgan le Fay and her companion Sebille. Morgan kidnapped Berengier's child to extort his love. Flor de Lis, Morgan's maidservant, agreed to help Berengier and his child escape if he would marry her, and Berengier agreed. They fled to safety in his kingdom of Gomeret. [*Prophecies*]

BERHARDIS

A knight slain by Gawain in Heinrich von dem Türlin's *Diu Crône*. He inhabited an enchanted castle in the land of Sere, from which Gawain had to retrieve a bridle. Berhardis was cursed to decapitate any challengers. After Berhardis's death, Gawain discovered that both the castle and the knight were part of his own territory, acquired by his marriage to the lady Amurfina. [*Heinrich*]

BERLIN

A page who served Tydomie, the wife of Arthur's nephew Meleranz. [*PleierM*]

BERLUSE[1] [*Bertelai*]

A Cornish knight and servant of King Mark of Cornwall. When he learned of Mark's plans to slay Tristan, Berluse tried to desert the king, but Mark killed him. He was buried by his companion, Amant. His son, also named Berluse, found harbor with Sir Tor. [*ProsTris, Malory*]

BERLUSE[2] [*Berlet*]

Son of the above Berluse. After his father's death, he found harbor with Arthur's Sir Tor. When he later encountered King Mark, his father's murderer, he engaged in combat but was defeated and saved from death only through the intervention of Sir Dinadan. [*ProsTris, Malory*]

BERNANT

King of North Wales during Arthur's reign. [*VulgLanc*]

BERNARD[1]

Lord of Escalot and father of Elaine, Lancelot's ill-fated admirer, in Malory. He appears unnamed in the Vulgate *Lancelot* and as LANVAL in the Hebrew *Melekh Artus*. His sons were Tirre and Lavaine. Just prior to a great tournament at Camelot, Bernard gave lodging to Lancelot and lent him Tirre's shield to use in the tournament. He later begged Lancelot to marry the love-struck Elaine, but in vain. [*Malory*]

BERNARD[2]

A knight killed in battle by Tristan. [*Sala*]

BERNART

A brief companion of Agravain in *Les Merveilles de Rigomer*. As a vassal of a nobleman named Robert, Bernart and other knights accompanied Agravain on a quest to find Robert's kidnapped wife. [*Merveil*]

BERNELAIN

One of the many Saxon kings who invaded Britain during Arthur's struggle to establish power. [*Livre*]

BERNOUT OF RIVIERS

Count of Ukerlant, son of Count Narant, and companion of King Gramoflanz, Gawain's brother-in-law. [*Wolfram*]

BERRY

A region of central France, conquered for Arthur by Hoel of Brittany, according to Layamon. In the Prose *Lancelot*, Berry and its capital Bourges were ruled by King Claudas, an enemy of Lancelot's family. The country was laid waste by Uther Pendragon and King Aramont of Brittany, and it became known as the Land Laid Waste. [*Layamon*, *LancLac*, *VulgLanc*]

BERTE

The father of Garin, a friend of Gawain. [*ChretienP*]

BERTELAIS

A castle at which the Good Knight Without Fear and Guiron the Courteous killed a tyrannical giant. [*Palamedes*]

BERTELAY [*Berthelai, Bert(h)olai, Bretelai*]

Champion of the False Guinevere, surnamed "the Red" at the beginning of his career and "the Old" at the end. Once a vassal of King Leodegan of Carmelide, he was banished by Arthur and Leodegan after he murdered another knight. In his exile, he met the False Guinevere (Leodegan's daughter and Queen Guinevere's twin half-sister) whom, many years later, he presented at Arthur's court as the true Guinevere. Their claim was that on Arthur's wedding night, his true wife had been taken away and that Arthur's present queen had been substituted in her place. Bertelay offered to fight any of Arthur's knights to prove his case, but he kidnapped Arthur before the combat and fed him a love potion which caused him to accept the False Guinevere as his wife. In the non-cyclical *Lancelot do Lac*, Lancelot championed the real Guinevere against three of Bertelay's knights and won; Bertelay then admitted his guilt and was burned. In the Vulgate *Lancelot*, on the other hand, Arthur remained married to the False Guinevere for several years before both she and Bertelay contracted a mortal illness and confessed their ruse on their deathbeds. [*LancLac*, *VulgLanc*, *VulgMer*]

BERTELOT

Brother of the despised Sir Breus the Pitiless, whom Bertelot often accompanied on his marauding. He was defeated once by Lancelot. [*Malory*]

BERTH

Son of Cadway and one of Arthur's warriors in Welsh legend. [*Culhwch*]

BERTOLES THE BALD

One of Perceval's eleven paternal uncles in *Perlesvaus*. He was the fourth son of Gais the Large and the brother of Alain. He died in combat. [*Perlesvaus*]

BERTRAND[1]

Son of Garin, a friend of Gawain. [*ChretienP*]

BERTRAND[2] OF THRACE

A knight who served Alis, the Emperor of Constantinople. Bertrand discovered Cliges' and Fenice's betrayal of Alis when he found the two lovers sleeping together in a forest. Cliges caught him and cut off one of his legs, but Bertrand managed to get away and to inform Alis of the situation, forcing Cliges and Fenice to flee Greece. His surname refers to an ancient region in the east Balkan peninsula, now divided between Greece and Turkey. [*ChretienC*]

BERWYN

Son of Cerenhyr and one of Arthur's warriors in Welsh legend. [*Culhwch*]

BESSILLE

In the Prose *Tristan*, a Cornish woman who loved Tristan. When Tristan rejected her, she became the paramour of Andred, Tristan's enemy, and conspired to reveal his affair with Isolde to King Mark. She is known as GIRIDA in *La Tavola Ritonda*. [*ProsTris*]

BESTOC

A castle in Gaul where regional lords convened to declare a king of France. Arthur, through his messenger Aram, proposed Lancelot, but Duke Frollo of Germany contested the choice in favor of himself. The Island of Battles, where Arthur later killed Frollo, was nearby. [*VulgLanc*]

BETHANY

A country through which Joseph of Arimathea's followers traveled on the way from Jerusalem to Sarras. [*VulgEst*]

BETICA [*Betike*]

In the Vulgate *Merlin* and *Arthour and Merlin*, the city or land ruled by Duke Nascien, who became a follower of Joseph of Arimathea. In the Vulgate *Estoire del Saint Graal*, however, Nascien's city is ORBERICA. [*VulgMer*, *Arthour*]

BEWFYS ("HANDSOME SON") [*Beau-fyz*]

The name given to GUINGLAIN, Gawain's son, by his mother. When he arrived at Arthur's court, he was dubbed the FAIR UNKNOWN until his true name was revealed. [*ChestreLyb*]

BHALBHUAIDH

Irish form of GAWAIN. His adventures include a quest with the CROP-EARED DOG. [*IrishD*]

BIALES

One of the many Saxon kings who invaded Britain at the beginning of Arthur's reign. He participated in the siege of Vambieres and was killed by Gawain. [*Livre*]

BICANUS

According to Welsh legend, the husband of Rieingulid and father of Saint Illtud, Arthur's cousin. [*SaintsI*]

BIDWINI [*Bytwini*]

Arthur's chief bishop in Cornwall. He blessed the food, drink, and women at Arthur's court. He may be the origin of Bishop BALDWIN of Middle-English romance. [*Culhwch*, *Dream*]

BIEDA

A Saxon warrior, son of Port, who landed in Britain in 501 to join the Saxon conquest. He sailed into Portsmouth with another Saxon named Mægla, and the two warriors killed a British noble there. Bieda would have been a contemporary (and opponent) of a historical Arthur or his allies. [*Anglo*]

BIELMANOIR

The Lord of Bielmanoir ("Fair Manor") is a Knight of the Round Table in *Hunbaut*. [*Hunbaut*]

BIEN PENSANT ("Well Thinking")

The name that Lancelot gave the ILL-SPEAKING MAIDEN after she proved to be a fairly good person. [*Malory*]

BIGAME

The Count of Bigame appears at the tournament of Sorgarda, won by Gawain. His brother was named Sorgarit. [*Heinrich*]

BILAS

An elderly count who tried to force a young maiden into marriage. Arthur's Sir Claris defeated Bilas and imprisoned him, ending his plans. [*Claris*]

BILIS [*Bilei, Ebilis, Wilis*]

A nobleman known as the Lord of the Dwarfs and the King of the Antipodes. He was the shortest of the dwarves, and was the brother of Bliant, the tallest of the dwarves. In Chrétien's *Erec*, Bilis came to the wedding of Erec and Enide and brought his vassals Gribalo and Glodoalan. The Norse *Erex Saga* names his brothers as Brattur and Revellus. R. S. Loomis (*Tradition*, 142) thought that he was to be identified with PELLES, having originated in the Welsh BELI. [*ChretienE, Erex, Heinrich*]

BILLEIUS

Bedivere's nephew in a French chronicle. He is usually called HIRELGLAS. He was said to have married a woman named Fausta, to have had a daughter named Lupa, and to have built the city of Bliriacus. [*Liber*]

BIRDOSWALD

A villiage in Rheged called Camboglanna by the Welsh. It has been suggested as the site of the battle of CAMLANN, though Arthur's death, in both the chronicles and the romances, is almost always located in southern Britain.

BIRÍNG

In the Icelandic *Saga af Tristram ok Ísodd*, the foster-father of both Kalegras (Tristan's father) and Tristan. He became King of Spain after Kalegras's death, but was defeated and deposed by a pirate king from Africa named Turnes. He later joined Tristan at Mark's court in England. [*SagaTI*]

BISCLARET

A Knight of the Round Table present at the Banborc tournament. [*Girart*]

BISHOP OF THE THAMES

In Gottfried's *Tristan*, this oddly-named religious figure advises Mark, who is confused over Isolde's possibly infidelity with Tristan, to ask Isolde to swear before the court that she is innocent. Isolde is able to swear, through a technicality in her speech, that she is faithful to Mark. [*Gottfried*]

BITHYNIA

An ancient country in northwest Asia Minor, in what is now Turkey. It was ruled in Arthur's time by Duke

Politetes, an ally of the Roman Procurator Lucius. [*GeoffHR, Wace*]

BLACK CHAPEL

In the Vulgate *Mort Artu,* the chapel where Girflet and Lucan brought a mortally wounded Arthur after the final battle with Mordred. Lucan perished and was buried there; Arthur was taken away by Morgan le Fay; and Girflet retired as a Black Chapel hermit. It is called the ANCIENT CHAPEL in the Post-Vulgate version. [*VulgMort*]

BLACK CROSS[1]

A monument in Camelot, on which the early pagan king Agrestes slaughtered a dozen followers of Joseph of Arimathea. It was stained black with their blood. It still stood during Arthur's reign, when it served as a rallying point. [*VulgEst, VulgMer*]

BLACK CROSS[2]

An abbey in Cornwall at which Yvain of the White Hands was healed after King Mark injured him. [*ProsTris, Malory*]

BLACK FOREST[1]

A wooded mountain region in southwest Germany. Alis, the Emperor of Constantinople and Greece, fought a battle against the Duke of Saxony in the forest, near the Danube River. The two warriors fought over mutual love for the lady Fenice. Alis, largely because of his nephew Cliges, won the battle. [*ChretienC*]

BLACK FOREST[2]

A forest in Britain inhabited by the Black Knight of the Black Forest. Arthur contended with the Black Knight for ownership of the property. Meriadoc won the combat in Arthur's favor. Perceiving that the rights to the Black Forest truly belonged to the Black Knight, Meriadoc convinced Arthur to abandon his claim. [*Historia*]

BLACK HAG

Daughter of the White Hag who lived in the Valley of Distress. As one of his tasks, the warrior Culhwch had to obtain the Black Hag's blood to straighten the beard of the giant Ysbaddaden. Arthur and his warriors, on Culhwch's behalf, set out for the Black Hag's cave. The first four warriors sent into the cave—Cacamwri, Hwgwydd, Amren the Tall, and Eiddyl the Tall—were beaten half to death. Finally, Arthur himself jumped into the cave and killed the Black Hag with one well-placed throw of his knife, Carnwennan. Caw of Scotland collected her blood and delivered it to Ysbaddaden. An Welsh poem in the *Black Book of Carmarthen* describes a similar battle between Arthur and a hag at AFARNACH. [*Culhwch*]

BLACK HAND

A chapel built by Brangemore of Cornwall, who was slain by her son Espignogrés and buried beneath the chapel's altar. Gawain and Perceval each visited it during their adventures. The mysterious "black hand" within the chapel had slain over 4,000 knights. Perceval discovered that the hand belonged to a devil. He did battle with the hand, and during the combat, lightning struck the chapel and burned it to the ground. Perceval drove away the devil by sanctifying the chapel. [*Contin2, Contin3*]

BLACK HERMIT

A demonic lord encountered by Gawain and Perceval in *Perlesvaus*. He ruled a hellish castle in the Wild Forest, from which he robbed women. One of his victims was the enigmatic Maiden of the Cart, from whom he stole the heads of 152 knights. Gawain learned that the Black Hermit was an earthly manifestation of Lucifer, and that only Perceval could defeat him. At the urging of the Maiden of the Cart, Perceval traveled to the Black Hermit's castle and defeated him in a joust. Seeing their lord fallen, the Black Hermit's own knights threw him into a chasm of filth. [*Perlesvaus*]

BLACK ISLE

See ISLAND OF GLASS.

BLACK ISLES

In *Palamedes,* the kingdom ruled by Lac, Erec's father. [*Palamedes*]

BLACK KNIGHT[1]

An evil warrior who inhabited the White Forest and guarded the glade around the chapel of St. Augustine. He killed Arthur's squire, Cahus, and was himself slain by Arthur. [*Perlesvaus*]

BLACK KNIGHT[2]

A knight defeated by Perceval at a tomb. See the KNIGHT OF THE TOMB. [*Contin2, Didot*]

BLACK KNIGHT[3]

The alias of MADUK THE BLACK. [*Vengeance*]

BLACK KNIGHT[4]

A mighty lord who inhabited Mount Nouquestran (or the Black Mountain) in Scotland, and who guarded a magic horn and wimple. When the young Fergus arrived at Arthur's court, Kay sarcastically suggested that Fergus defeat the Black Knight for his first quest, and Fergus surprised everyone—and humiliated Kay—by doing just that. The Black Knight went to Arthur's court, humbly bearing the horn, wimple, and news of his own defeat. He later fought in the Gedeorde tournament, and was defeated by Fergus again. [*Guillaume*]

BLACK KNIGHT[5]

The name given to Lancelot, when he appeared in disguise (carrying a black shield) at Arthur's second battle against

Lord Galehaut. Lancelot showed so much prowess in the battle that Galehaut called off the war with Arthur in order to win the Black Knight's friendship. [*LancLac*, *VulgLanc*]

BLACK KNIGHT[6]

In the romance of *Yder*, a Black Knight besieges the Castle of Maidens. Arthur ignored the Castle's pleas for help, preferring to direct his attention to a different battle. Later, however, he vowed to punish the Black Knight's outrage. [*Yder*]

BLACK KNIGHT[7]

A nickname given to BARUC THE BLACK, a knight defeated by Sagremor. [*Livre*]

BLACK KNIGHT[8]

A knight in Arthur's service who defeated a knight named Tantalis. [*Floriant*, *Claris*]

BLACK KNIGHT[9]

An alias of the UGLY HERO, one of Arthur's knights. [*Atre*]

BLACK KNIGHT[10]

In the Middle English *Sir Perceval of Galles*, a warrior whose wife a young Perceval met in a forest. Perceval innocently kissed the lady and exchanged rings with her, which the Black Knight interpreted upon his return as adultery. Consequently, the jealous Black Knight tied her to a tree. Perceval encountered them again, as a knight. He defeated the Black Knight in combat, explained the truth of the situation to him, and forced him to reconcile with his wife. The character is known in Chrétien's *Perceval* as ORGELLOUS. [*SirPerc*]

BLACK KNIGHT[11]

Son of Arthur's Tom a' Lincoln by Anglitora. Tom's ghost appeared to his son and related how he had been murdered by Anglitora and her lover. The Black Knight slew the two lovers to avenge his father's death. [*Johnson*]

BLACK KNIGHT[12]

The name adopted by Sir PERARD, one of Gareth's opponents. [*Malory*]

BLACK KNIGHT[13] OF THE BLACK FOREST

A knight who was challenged by Arthur for ownership of the Black Forest. The Black Knight logically contended that since his name was the "Black Knight of the Black Forest," the Black Forest must be his. To win his claim, the Black Knight had to defeat all of Arthur's knights. He came close, but was defeated by Sir Meriadoc. The noble Meriadoc, however, convinced Arthur to return the Black Forest to the Black Knight. [*Historia*]

BLACK KNIGHT[14] OF THE FOUNTAIN

The name given in the Welsh Triads to the Lord of the Fountain defeated by Owain. He is called ESCLADOS by Chrétien de Troyes. [*Triads*]

BLACK KNIGHT[15] OF THE MOUNTAIN

A British knight, enchanted in some manner, who attended the trail of Isolde in Cornwall. [*Beroul*]

BLACK LOWE

The giant of the Black Lowe was once fought by Arthur's Sir Degrane Sans Villany. [*Malory*]

BLACK MOUNTAIN[1]

A Scottish mountain, also called Nouquestran, where Arthur's Sir Fergus defeated the Black Knight, winning a magic horn and wimple. [*Guillaume*]

BLACK MOUNTAIN[2]

In *Tyolet*, the home of a doctor who healed Tyolet after he had been injured in a battle against lions. [*Tyolet*]

BLACK OPPRESSOR

An evil duke who made it a custom to kill any men who came to his court, and to imprison their ladies. He had lost an eye while fighting the Black Serpent of the Barrow. Owain defeated him in combat and made him promise to turn his castle into a place of hospitality. Apparently, this promise was not kept because Peredur was later forced to kill the Black Oppressor to end his wicked ways. [*Owain*, *Peredur*]

BLACK ROCK [*Roche Noire*]

A castle in Cornwall ruled by Dinas, Mark's seneschal. [*ProsTris*]

BLACK SERPENT OF THE BARROW

A vicious snake that inhabited the Mournful Mound and killed or maimed many men. Warriors sought the serpent because it had a magical stone in its tail which caused its bearer to receive any amount of gold he wished. Peredur became interested in killing it during his adventures, but upon arriving at Mournful Mound he was forced to fight a number of other warriors who also wished to kill the beast. Finally, he defeated his competitors, marched up to the serpent, and killed it. Peredur then gave the Serpent's stone to his companion, Edlym Red Sword. [*Peredur*]

BLADUD

According to Geoffrey of Monmouth, king of Britain in the ninth or tenth century BC. He was the son of King Hudibras and the father of King Lear. During his reign, he founded the city of Bath and spread teachings of sorcery throughout Britain. He was killed while attempting to fly. [*GeoffHR*]

BLAES

Son of the Earl of Llychlyn and one of the "three Just Knights" of Arthur's court." He was dedicated to preserving justice through "earthly Law," in contrast to his fellow knights, who followed the Law of the Church and the Law of Arms. There may be a relation between this knight and Merlin's foster father BLAISE. [*Triads*]

BLAHARIS [*Blaaris*]

A Knight of the Round Table defeated and taken prisoner by the Queen's Knights during a tournament. [*VulgLanc*]

BLAIR

A vavasor in Carmelide. Arthur, Merlin, Ban, and Bors lodged with him while they were visiting King Leodegan incognito. His wife was named Leonelle. [*VulgMer, Arthour*]

BLAISE [*Bayses, Blais(s)es, Blasio, Blasy, Blays(e)(s), Bleys(e)*]

Merlin's foster-father in Robert de Boron's *Merlin* and subsequent texts. A holy man and clerk from Northumberland, he heard the confession of Merlin's mother after she was impregnated by an incubus. Blaise divined that Satan was planning to introduce a hideous devil child to the world, in order to counteract the advance of Christianity. Staying by the girl's side, Blaise was on hand to quickly baptize the infant as soon as it was born, driving the devil's nature out of Merlin. He defended Merlin's mother against a group of judges who sought to punish her for perfidy. Serving as Merlin's tutor and companion, Blaise wrote down the many adventures of Merlin, Arthur, and Arthur's knights as Merlin dictated it. Merlin made frequent visits to Blaise to relate new chapters of the Arthurian saga. Blaise also penned a Grail history. The Vulgate Cycle suggests that its romances were descended from Blaise's texts. In the Didot-*Perceval*, Merlin brings Blaise to the Grail Castle to live out his days, while in the Vulgate *Merlin*, Blaise takes up residence in Camelot just prior to Merlin's death.

Certain Arthurian tales—among them Thomas's *Tristan*, the works of Giraldus Cambrensis, the Second Continuation of *Perceval*, and the *Elucidation*—appeal to the authority of a certain "Bleheris" or "Blihis," probably a medieval bard who spread Arthuriana through Britain and Brittany. The character of Blaise, said to have authored Arthur's history, may be a reflection of this historical *conteur* (Loomis, *Romance*, 57n). [*ProsMer1, Didot, VulgMer, PostMer, Arthour, Malory, TennIK*]

BLAKESTAN

The lord of Blakestan was an ally of King Belinant of South Wales. He fought against the Saxons invading Britain in the early days of Arthur's reign. He was present at the battle of Clarence. Blakestan was also the homeland of Guinas, an opponent of Arthur's Sir Hector. [*LancLac, VulgLanc, Livre*]

BLAMOURE OF THE MARSH

A knight who owned a white hart that Gawain pursued on his first adventure. Gawain chased the hart into Blamoure's castle, where Gawain's hounds killed it. This induced Blamoure to slay two of Gawain's hounds. Enraged, Gawain engaged Blamoure in combat, defeated him, and prepared to cut off his head. As Gawain's sword fell, Blamoure's paramour threw herself across her lover's body and was decapitated. Aghast, Gawain granted mercy to Blamoure and sent him to Arthur's court. [*PostMer, Malory*]

BLANCHANDINE

A Hungarian princess and a companion of Florete, the daughter of Emperor Filimenis. When Filimenis went to war with Arthur, Blanchandine and Florete accompanied the emperor's army. The fell in love with Gawain and Floriant, respectively, and defected from Filimenis's camp to Arthur's. Eventually, the war ended and Blanchandine married Gawain. [*Floriant*]

BLANCHE

A queen besieged by Lord Nador. Claris and Laris, two of Arthur's knights, saved her. [*Claris*]

BLANCHEFLOR[1] ("White Flower") [*Blanchefleur, Blancheflour, Blankeflur, Blankiflúr, Blanzifiore*]

Lady of Beaurepaire in Chrétien's *Perceval*. Her town fell into ruin following multiple attacks by Anguiguerron, the seneschal of Clamadeu of the Isles. Perceval wandered into town looking for lodging, and Blancheflor begged him to defend the town. After Perceval defeated both Anguigerron and Clamadeu in combat, Blancheflor would have married him and made him lord of Beaurepaire, but Perceval declined and returned to his adventures. In the third continuation of Chrétien, Perceval returns to defend Blancheflor from another attacker, Caridés of Escavalon, and in the fourth continuation, he finally marries her. Perceval also weds Blancheflor in the Norse *Parcevals Saga*, and in Wolfram von Eschenbach's *Parzival*, where her name is changed to CONDWIRAMURS. In Heinrich von dem Türlin's *Diu Crône*, she later fails in a chastity test at Arthur's court. She is known as LUFAMOUR in the Middle-English *Sir Perceval of Galles*. [*ChretienP, Contin2, Contin3, Contin4, Heinrich, Parceval*]

BLANCHEFLOR[2] [*Blansch(e)flur*]

Mother of Tristan and sister of King Mark of Cornwall. She fell in love with King Rivalin when he came to Cornwall to assist Mark against Ireland. Rivalin fell deathly ill of a painful wound, but the sight and affections of Blancheflor cured him and the two married. She died giving birth to Tristan on the same day that Rivalin was slain. Called BLESINBIL in the Norse version of the legend, her character is replaced in later stories by ELYABEL. [*Eilhart, Gottfried, Tristrem*]

BLANCHEFLOR³

The daughter of King Triamour of Wales. A giant named Urgan attacked her father for the right to possess her, but the giant was slain by Tristan. [*Tristrem*]

BLANCHELES

One of Arthur's knights in the Middle-English *Sir Gawain and the Carl of Carlisle*, likely a variation of BRANDELIS (Hahn, 107). [*SyrGaw*]

BLANCHELAND

The Middle English *Sir Gawain and the Carl of Carlisle* names the Lady of Blancheland, a fairy, as the mother of "The Knyght of Armus Grene" by Sir Ironside. [*SyrGaw*]

BLANCHEMAL THE FAY [*Blancemal*]

The fairy mistress of Gawain, by whom she had a son named Guinglain. She raised Guinglain ignorant of his true name. Upon attaining knighthood, he was forced to adopt the label "The Fair Unknown." Blanchemal lived in the island of Gernemue. [*Renaut*, *Contin4*]

BLANCHES MORES

A castle neighboring the Castle of Ten Maidens. It was the site of a tournament between the Lady of Blanches Mores and the Lady of the Roche Land. The victors of the tournament were to marry the two ladies. Brun of Morrois, and abductor of Guinevere, was the uncle of the Lady of Blanches Mores. [*Durmart*]

BLANDIGAN

The son of Count Blandigan of Iceland or Ireland was defeated by Yvain during the battle at the Castle Orguelleus. [*Contin1*]

BLANDISEN

A fairy who tries to murder Perceval in the Second Continuation of *Perceval* was said to have kidnapped people from the court of King Blandisen. [*Contin2*]

BLANDUKORS

An old nobleman who, in Heinrich von dem Türlin's *Diu Crône*, with his wife Amurelle and his daughter Sgaipegaz, hosted Gawain during one of his adventures. Blandukors lived in the service of a tyrannical giant named Galaas, from whom Gawain freed him. [*Heinrich*]

BLANLIS

A lady at Arthur's court who, along with many others, failed a magical chastity test. [*Heinrich*]

BLANOR [*Blamor*]

A Knight of the Round Table from Benoic or Gannes. He was the son of Nestor, brother of Bleoberis, and cousin of Lancelot. Early in his career, he championed his family

against King Anguisshe of Ireland, whom Blanor had accused of murdering a cousin. Tristan championed Anguisshe and defeated Blanor (*La Tavola Ritonda* assigns this adventure to a knight named BRUNORO). When Lancelot and Guinevere were accused of treason, Blanor joined other knights in pledging his support to Lancelot. In return, Lancelot made him duke of Limousin. After Arthur's death, Blanor became a hermit at Glastonbury and assisted in Lancelot's burial. Once he had stabilized his own lands, he joined Bleoberis, Ector, and Bors on a crusade to Jerusalem, where they died fighting the Turks on Good Friday. [*ProsTris*, *TristanoR*, *Malory*]

BLANQUEMORE VALLEY

A land inherited by Arthur's Sir Meriadeuc from his father, Bleheri. [*Meriadeuc*]

BLANSCHOL

A lady at Arthur's court who, along with many others, failed a chastity test. [*Heinrich*]

BLANT OF ALVERNE

One of Arthur's counts. [*Heinrich*]

BLARIS [*Blaaris*, *Bleherris*, *Bliares*]

Knight and godson of King Bors of Gannes. He fought for Arthur against the rebellion at the beginning of the king's reign, and also against the Saxons at Carmelide and against King Agrippe in the Waste Land. His name seems to possess the same root as BLEOBERIS, to whom Blaris may be identical [*VulgMer*, *Livre*, *Arthour*]

BLASINE

Daughter of Igerne and Hoel, sister of Brimesent, and half-sister of Arthur in the Vulgate *Merlin*. She married King Nentres of Garlot and had a son named Galescalain, whom she encouraged to take service with Arthur. Malory calls her ELAINE. [*VulgMer*, *Arthour*]

BLAT

A wandering squire whose companion was Haupt. Isolde commissioned the two squires to help her cover one of her meetings with Tristan. [*Eilhart*]

BLATHAON

Son of Mwrheth and one of Arthur's warriors in Welsh legend. [*Dream*]

BLAUNCHARD [*Blanchard*]

A magnificent horse given to Sir Launfal by his lover, Triamour. [*ChestreLvl*]

BLEDUD

According to Geoffrey of Monmouth, a king of Britain in the third or second century BC. Bledud succeeded King Merian and was succeeded by King Cap. [*GeoffHR*]

BLEDGABRED

According to Geoffrey of Monmouth, a king of Britain in the second century BC. He succeeded King Sisillius and was succeeded by his brother Arthinail. Bledgabred was renowned as a great singer. [*GeoffHR*]

BLEEDING LANCE

A curious weapon associated with the Grail, appearing first in the Grail Processions of the pre-Robert de Boron Grail romances. Some stories call it the AVENGING LANCE. In Chrétien de Troyes's *Perceval*, the lance follows the Grail Sword and precedes the Grail. Described as pure white, the lance continually dripped blood from its tip. The Welsh *Peredur* likewise describes a "spear of incalculable size with three streams of blood running from the socket to the floor."

Even before Robert de Boron turned the enigmatic Grail into the cup used by Christ at the Last Supper, the Bleeding Lance became identified with the lance of LONGINUS—the Roman solider who, in the Apocrypha, stuck a spear in Christ's side as he hung on the cross. This assertion is found first in the continuations of *Perceval* and the Didot-*Perceval*. In the Christian Grail romances, the blood dripping from the lance's tip is Christ's blood.

According to the Vulgate and Post-Vulgate Cycles, Joseph of Arimathea brought the Bleeding Lance to Britain, and it was kept at Corbenic with the Grail. In one version of the DOLOROUS STROKE, Balin the Savage used it to wound King Pellehan, turning Listenois into the Waste Land. Similarly, Chrétien de Troyes said that it would one day destroy the entire realm of Logres. Galahad later used the blood flowing from the tip to heal Pellehan, the Maimed King. These two properties of the lance—destruction and healing—mirror the two attributes of the Lord in the scriptures.

Galahad brought the Bleeding Lance to Sarras at the conclusion of the Grail Quest, and it was drawn into heaven along with the Grail. It is similarly taken to heaven in the third continuation of Chrétien's *Perceval*.

A second Bleeding Lance (perhaps a symbol for the first) appears in the Vulgate *Estoire del Saint Graal*. Josephus, the son of Joseph of Arimathea, is converting some pagans to Christianity when he learns that another group of pagans, who have refused to convert, are being murdered by their king. He rushes to stop the slaughter, and an angel strikes him through the thighs with a lance to punish him for abandoning the conversions to save the lives of the pagans. Josephus removes the spear from his thighs, but the lance head remains embedded in his flesh. The angel eventually re-appears to remove the point and heal Josephus with some of the blood that drips from its tip.

Proponents of a Celtic origin for the Grail theme have suggested, with marginal success, a connection between the Bleeding Lance and the Luin of Celtchar, a marvelous weapon from Irish legend that supposedly had to be quenched in blood after battle in order to render it safe. [*ChretienP, Contin1, VulgQuest, VulgEst, PostMer, PostQuest, Peredur, Malory*]

BLEHARTIS [*Belchardis, Lectargis*]

One of Arthur's knights in the English *Arthour and Merlin*. His name results from a corruption of *Lait Hardi*, the UGLY HERO. [*Arthour*]

BLEHERI

Father of Arthur's Sir Meriadeuc. He ruled the Lake of Twins and Blanquemore Valley until he was slain by Gawain at the behest of the evil Brien de la Gastine. One of his knights buried him in the Waste Chapel. Lady Lore of Cardigan took his sword and later gave it to Meriadeuc, who used it to avenge his father's death by slaying Brien. [*Meriadeuc*]

BLEIDEN

In Heinrich von dem Türlin's *Diu Crône*, a lady at Arthur's court who failed in a chastity test. [*Heinrich*]

BLENDE OF ALICE

In Heinrich von dem Türlin's *Diu Crône*, a lady at Arthur's court who failed in a chastity test. [*Heinrich*]

BLENZIBLY

Tristan's mother in the Icelandic *Saga af Tristram ok Ísoud*. She replaces BLANCHEFLUR from the earlier German sources and is the counterpart of BLESINBIL in Norse Tristan legend. The daughter of King Philippus and Queen Philippia of England, she revolted against her brother, Mórodd (Mark), when her parents died. The short rebellion ended in a truce. She fell in love with Kalegras, a knight from Spain, with whom she had Tristan. She died soon after her lover. [*SagaTI*]

BLEOBERIS [*Bleoberiis, Bleoberys, Bleriz, Blerois, Bleos of Bliriers, Bliobleherin, Blioble(he)ris, Breoberiis, Briobris, Pliopliheri(n)*]

A Knight of the Round Table from Gannes, first mentioned by Chrétien de Troyes. His name may derive from a twelfth-century storyteller named Bleheris mentioned in several texts. Bleoberis was the son of Nestor, godson of King Bors, brother of Blamor, cousin of Lancelot, father of Nestor of the Fountain, and lord of the Castle of Gannes. Though usually described as skilled and honorable, he is sometimes depicted as malicious—as when he abducts Seguarades's wife and fights with Tristan over her, or when he tries to kill Guinglain (Gawain's son) at the Perilous Ford.

Sometimes called "Bleoberis of the Wilderness," he fought for Arthur against the rebelling kings (at the battle of Bedegraine) and against the Saxons. He also participated in the wars against Agrippe and Claudas and in the Grail Quest. He supported Lancelot when Lancelot and Guinevere were accused of treason, and he helped Lancelot rescue Guinevere from the stake. In return for his support, Lancelot made him the duke of Poitiers.

He was also present at the battle of Salisbury (the final battle against Mordred), and was one of the few survivors. In the aftermath of the battle, he tied Mordred's body to a horse and dragged it around the field until it was torn to pieces. On the battlefield, he constructed the Tower of the Dead, from which he hung Mordred's head.

Searching for Lancelot, he later came across Arthur the Less (King Arthur's son), who attacked Bleoberis for supporting Lancelot in the Lancelot-Arthur conflict. Arthur the Less was slain in the battle.

He retired to a hermitage with the former Archbishop of Canterbury or with Lancelot. After Lancelot's death, Bleoberis took his body to Joyous Guard and buried it. After he stabilized his own lands, he, Blamor, Ector, and Bors traveled to Jerusalem where they died on Good Friday, fighting the Turks. In a variation in Wolfram von Eschenbach's *Parzival*, he is slain by Duke Orguelleuse of La Lande. [*ChretienE, HartmannE, Wolfram, Renaut, VulgLanc, VulgMort, VulgMer, PostQuest, PostMort, ProsTris, Malory*]

BLEODAS

A splendid castle ruled by Lord Blias, an ally of Arthur. [*VulgMer, Arthour*]

BLESINBIL

Tristan's mother in the Norse *Tristrams Saga ok Ísöndar*; the counterpart of BLANCHEFLUR, who appears as Tristan's mother in other versions. The sister of King Mark of Cornwall, she married Canelengres of Brittany and died giving birth to her son. Her Icelandic counterpart is BLENZIBLY. [*TrisSaga*]

BLEVINE [*Benigne*]

The lady of Glocedun castle. Sir Bors rescued her when she was being beaten by a pack of peasants. [*VulgLanc*]

BLI MARADARF

A passage in *Diu Crône* alludes to a combat at Bli Maradarf, by the sea, where Gawain slew a devil named Sarant who had the ability to swallow the sun. [*Heinrich*]

BLIAIRES

A Knight of the Round Table who helped Sir Agloval defeat King Agrippe in the Waste Land. [*Livre*]

BLIANDOIS

A countess who served the duchess of Estrayls. She lost her arm to the Redoubted Giant of the Sure Keep, who was trying to avenge his brother's death at the hands of Arthur and the duchess. [*ChevPap*]

BLIANT[1] [*Brian(s)*]

Tallest of the dwarves and brother of Bilis, shortest of the dwarves. He came to the wedding of Erec and Enide. [*ChretienE, Heinrich*]

BLIANT[2] [*Bryaunt*]

Owner of the White Castle and brother of Celinant. The two brothers found Lancelot, who had gone insane, roaming a forest. They brought him back to their castle for healing, but kept him chained until Lancelot proved his nobility by breaking his chains and saving Bliant from Sir Breus the Pitiless. Lancelot was eventually healed, but he remained with Bliant for a long time, calling himself the Chevalier Malfait. [*VulgLanc, PostMer, Malory*]

BLIAS [*Blios, Blyas*]

Lord of Bleodas, Candaf, or Cloadas. As an ally of Arthur, he led a battalion of soldiers against King Rions at the battle of Aneblayse and fought against King Hargadabran at Vambieres. [*VulgMer, Livre, Arthour*]

BLIOBLIDAS

One of Arthur's knights. He was the son of the King of Galway. [*Meriadeuc*]

BLIOBEL

One of Arthur's knights in *Arthour and Merlin*, who participated in the battle against Rions' Saxons at Carhaix. [*Arthour*]

BLIOCADRAN

Perceval's father, as named in a prequel to Chrétien de Troyes's *Perceval*. Bliocadran's twelve brothers were all killed in tournaments, but Bliocadran refused to pay heed to his wife's pleas to avoid tournaments himself. On the eve of his son's birth, he journeyed to a tournament in Wales and was mortally wounded there. He died as his son Perceval was born. The fate of Bliocadran drove his wife to despair, and she fled her court for the forest, raising Perceval in seclusion, ignorant of knighthood, so that he might avoid his father's fate. Bliocadran's story was recast by Wolfram von Eschenbach as the story of GAHMURET. As Perceval's father, Bliocadran's counterparts also include ALAIN and PELLINORE. [*Bliocadran*]

BLIOS

A knight who loved a maiden named Senehaut. When he suspected her of having an affair with one of her cousins, he beat the cousin, which enraged Senehaut. Sagremor learned of the situation and defeated Blios in combat, forced him to reconcile with his lady, and sent them to Arthur's court. On their way, kinsmen of Senehaut's beaten cousin showed up and sent Blios fleeing into the forest. Sagremor rescued Senehaut from the men and returned her to Blios—but not before sleeping with her and begetting a daughter. [*Livre*]

BLOCCOVIUS [*Boclovius, Boclonius*]

One of Arthur's earls who fought against the Romans at the battle of Soissons and was killed there. [*GeoffHR, Wace, Layamon*]

BLOEQUINZ

A knight from Denmark allied to Escanor the Handsome, an opponent of Gawain. [*Girart*]

BLOIE[1]

A maiden loved by Guiron the Courteous, hero of *Palamedes*. Danain the Red, Guiron's friend, abducted her, but Guiron tracked them down and rescued her. She and Guiron were later thrown into the prison of an evil lord, where Bloie died after giving birth to Galinan, Guiron's son. [*Palamedes, AlamGyr*]

BLOIE[2]

The proper name of the Lady of MALEHAUT, mentioned only once in *Palamedes*. [*Palamedes*]

BLOIESINE

Daughter of Urbin of the Mountain and sister of Brun, a knight killed by Gawain. To avenge her brother, she plotted Gawain's murder, but she eventually fell in love with Gawain. [*Contin4*]

BLOIS[1] [*Bloy, Bloyse*]

A city in central France, on the Loire river, variously given as the homeland of the Arthurian knights Melaldon, Gwyniarte, and Persides, though some of these knights' names were probably, originally, *le blois* ("the pale") rather than *de Blois*. [*VulgLanc, Malory*]

BLOIS[2] OF CASSET [*Bloys de la Case*]

An Arthurian knight who fought in Arthur's ranks at the battle of Bedegraine, and who participated in a quest to learn the fate of Merlin. [*VulgMer, Malory*]

BLOOMING VALLEY [*Blühenden Tal, Flowering Valley, Blossoming Valley*]

A location in German romance: in the Stricker's *Daniel*, it was a land that belonged to Arthur's Sir Daniel, and was ruled previously by Daniel's father, King Mandogran; in the Pleier's *Garel*, it is an island castle given to Sir Garel by Arthur. [*Stricker, PleierG*]

BLOYAS

A knight from Flanders who fought among Arthur's ranks at the battle of Bedegraine. Sir Lucan the Butler saved Bloyas's life in the skirmish. [*Malory*]

BLUAMANS

A Saxon king who was part of King Hargadabran's invasion of Britain. Arthur killed him at the battle of Clarence. [*Livre*]

BLUE FOREST

The wildest forest in the world, located in North Wales. It contained only one house, and was surrounded by a five-league radius of barren, unpopulated land. Sir Sagremor was assaulted by eight knights while traveling through the Blue Forest, but he was rescued by Gawain. [*VulgLanc*]

BLUE KNIGHT

The alias of Sir PERSAUNT, a knight defeated by Gareth in Malory. In Tennyson, he calls himself "The Son of the Morning Star." [*Malory, TennIK*]

BOAR OF CORNWALL

The allusion to King Arthur made by Merlin in his great series of prophecies before King Vortigern and his assembly at Mount Snowdon. Merlin said that the Boar of Cornwall would conquer Britain and Rome. [*GeoffHR*]

BOCCUS [*Boc(l)us, Bokke*]

The King of Media who served the Lucius of Rome. Lucius called upon him to join Rome's war against Arthur. He led a force of soldiers at the battle of Soissons, where he killed or badly wounded Bedivere, and was slain by Bedivere's nephew. [*GeoffHR, Wace, Layamon, VulgMer*]

BODENDR

A page at Arthur's court. [*Mottuls*]

BODWYNE [*Boudin*]

King Mark's brother in Malory's tale of Alexander the Orphan. Unlike Mark, Bodwyne was an honorable knight, loved by the people of Cornwall. He successfully repelled a Saracen invasion of the land, for which he received great praise. Mark, infuriated, slew Bodwyne by stabbing him in the heart with a dagger. Bodwyne's wife, Angledis, and son, Alexander, fled Mark's court. Alexander's son, Bellangere, later avenged his grandfather's murder. The character seems to have been adapted from PERNEHAN, Mark's doomed brother in the Prose *Tristan*. [*Malory*]

BOEOTIA

A region of east central Greece, ruled in Arthur's time by Echion, an ally of Lucius the Roman. [*GeoffHR, Wace*]

BOFOIS [*Boffoi, Boufois*]

A tower belonging to the sorcerer Elïavrés, the father of Sir Caradoc Shortarm. The Castle of Bouffay in Nantes has been suggested as the origin. [*Contin1*]

BOGUDAHT OF PRANZILE

A count defeated by Perceval. [*Wolfram*]

BOILLANDE

A city in Arthur's realm. [*Biket*]

BOLD KNIGHT

The name given by Perceval to the COWARD KNIGHT, after the latter reformed his ways and became brave.

As the Bold Knight, he was slain by Aristor of Amorave. [*Perlesvaus*]

BOLVIN

Counselor to Earl Milon, who desired Enide, Erec's wife. Milon and Bolvin tried to kidnap the woman, but Erec killed them both. [*Erex*]

BONCENES

A lord whose castle was besieged by Lord Guincemain during the Grail Quest. Galahad arrived, slew Guincemain, and ended the siege. Galahad convinced Aurience, Boncenes's daughter, to become a nun. [*ProsTris*]

BONCU

An abominable race of men who battled Arthur's knights at Rigomer Castle. [*Merveil*]

BONIFACE

A Roman cleric who served Arthur. He and other clerics helped Arthur's ally Galehaut interpret a disturbing dream. [*VulgLanc*]

BORDEAUX

According to the Alliterative *Morte Arthure*, this region of southwest France was part of Arthur's kingdom. In the French romances of Huon and Oberon, it is the home of Sir Huon. [*Huon, Allit*]

BORDERLAND[1]

A castle owned by King Brandegorre. He threw a tournament at Borderland, which was won by Sir Bors. [*VulgLanc*]

BORDERLAND[2]

A castle in Benoic ruled by allies of Claudas (the enemy of Lancelot's family). Knights from the Borderland tried to liberate a train of prisoners captured by Arthur in the Roman War. The attack was successfully repelled, and Arthur later had Gawain destroy the castle. [*VulgMer*]

BORDERLANDS

Property held by Arthur. The Borderlands were invaded by Galehaut of Sorelois. [*VulgLanc*]

BORE

One of Arthur's knights in "The Marriage of Sir Gawaine." The author perhaps meant to signify King BORS, Sir BORS, or Sir BORRE. [*Marriage*]

BOREL[1] [*Berell, Berille, Bretel(ot), Dorell*]

Arthur's cousin or nephew, upon whom Arthur bestowed the rulership of Maine or Le Mans. He fought for Arthur in the war against Lucius the Roman, and accompanied a prisoner train through France. The prisoner train was attacked by the Romans, and Borel was slain by King Evander of Syria in the battle. [*GeoffHR, Wace, Layamon, ProsBrut, Allit, Malory*]

BOREL[2]

A Saxon earl killed by Arthur at the battle of Bath with his lance, Ron. [*Layamon*]

BORRE [*Bohort*]

In Malory, the illegitimate son of King Arthur and Lisanor. He became a Knight of the Round Table. In earlier sources, his name is LOHOLT. [*Malory*]

BORS[1] [*Bo(h)(o)ort, Boors, Bordo, Borz*]

The King of Gannes, Gaul, or Gascony, son of King Lancelot, and uncle of Lancelot of the Lake. He had two sons, Bors and Lionel, by his wife, Evaine. He first appears in the Vulgate Cycle, and he is generally described as a good king, though the *Livre d'Artus* calls him a tyrant.

Bors and his brother, King Ban of Benoic, swore fealty to Uther Pendragon in order to defeat their enemy, King Claudas. This allegiance extended to Arthur, and the brother kings therefore journeyed to Britain at his summons to help him subdue a rebellion of British nobles. After defeating the rebels at Bedegraine, Bors and Ban accompanied Arthur to Carmelide, where they fought against King Rions and the Saxons. Bors slew Amant of Lambale, one of Arthur's enemies. Returning to France, the three kings repelled Claudas's invasion. Bors later joined Arthur's campaign against Rome. During Claudas's second invasion, Bors perished of an illness (or of grief) following his brother's death. Claudas conquered his land, but his son Bors later reclaimed it. Bors's wife retired to a nunnery; his sons, raised by the Lady of the Lake, both became Knights of the Round Table.

The origin of his name is uncertain, though a "bohort" (one of the first forms of "Bors") is a type of lance. [*LancLac, VulgLanc, VulgMer, Livre, Malory*]

BORS[2] [*Bohors, Bohort(es), Bo(o)rt, Bo(o)(u)rs, Bordo, Bort, Borz, Bwrt*]

A Knight of the Round Table and cousin of Lancelot who earned fame as one of the successful Grail knights in the Vulgate *Queste del Saint Graal* and adaptations. Although one of the more famous of Arthur's knights, he entered the Arthurian legends comparatively late, first appearing in the Prose *Lancelot*. His character remains relatively unchanged between the Vulgate romances and modern texts.

His parents, King Bors of Gannes and Queen Evaine, died during his childhood. Bors and his brother, Lionel, were raised by Pharien, one of their father's knights, in the court of Claudas, who had conquered his father's land. The children were eventually rescued from Claudas by the Lady of the Lake, who raised them to maturity on her enchanted island. (In Malory, Bors joins Arthur's campaign against Rome, but in the Vulgate stories, the war occurs before Bors' birth.)

The Vulgate and Post-Vulgate romances give Bors innumerable adventures. In one of the earliest episodes, Bors won a tournament at the court of King Brandegorre of Estrangorre. He refused the prize of the tournament, marriage to Brandegorre's daughter, but the maiden's governess gave Bors a magic ring which caused him to fall in love with the girl. He slept with her and fathered Helain the White, who became a Knight of the Round Table. This incident marked Bors' only sexual act. In other adventures, he joined Arthur's war against Claudas and re-conquered his father's kingdom, of which he later became king.

Prior to the beginning of the Grail Quest, Bors visited Corbenic, the Grail Castle, twice, witnessing marvels and miracles on both visits. Bors succeeded in the Grail Quest not because he was a great knight, like Lancelot, or a pure soul, like Galahad, but because he was willing to abandon his worldly values for spiritual ones. To test this resolve, God tested Bors particularly rigorously during the Grail Quest. His first test involved combat with a knight named Priadan the Black, whom Bors defeated but did not kill. In a second trial, Bors had to choose between saving his brother Lionel and rescuing a maiden. He chose the maiden, leaving his brother for dead. The final test took place when a beautiful maiden threatened to kill herself and twelve of her servants unless Bors slept with her. He refused, revealing the maiden as a fiend. Later, he encountered his brother Lionel, furious that Bors and declined to save him during the second test. Bors refused to fight his brother, and Lionel ended up slaying a hermit and another knight who rushed to Bors' defense. Bors prayed, and God came between the brothers, pacifying Lionel. Bors joined Galahad and Perceval on a magic ship and, after several other adventures, the three knights came to Corbenic and attended a Grail mass held by Joseph of Arimathea or his son, Josephus. Galahad performed miracles at Corbenic, and the three knights departed with the Grail to Sarras. After the holy deaths of Galahad and Perceval, Bors returned to Arthur's court to recount their adventures.

In the final days of Arthur's reign, Bors helped Lancelot rescue Guinevere from the stake, although he did not particularly care for the queen. He defected from Arthur's court and joined Lancelot's battles against Arthur at Joyous Guard and Benoic. In return for his support, Lancelot gave him all the lands that he had conquered from King Claudas.

Accounts of his final days vary. In Vulgate *Mort Artu* and the Post-Vulgate *Mort Artu*, Bors helps Lancelot destroy the sons of Mordred, and then joins Sir Bleoberis and the Archbishop of Canterbury in a monastery for the rest of his days. According Malory, he retired with Lancelot to a monastery in Glastonbury, where he remained until Lancelot's death. After he stabilized his own lands, Bors and the other remaining Round Table knights traveled to Jerusalem, where they died fighting against the Turks. [*LancLac*, *VulgLanc*, *VulgQuest*, *VulgMort*, *Contin3*, *PostQuest*, *PostMort*, *Stanz*, *Malory*]

BORTERAMUNT

The capital of Kanadic, ruled by King Ekunaver, who went to war with Arthur. [*PleierG*]

BOSO [*Beof, Bois, Bos, Booz*]

The Earl of Oxford under King Arthur. He accompanied Arthur on the Roman campaign, and was one of the three messengers that Arthur sent to meet with the Roman Procurator Lucius—an effort that resulted in ruin when Gawain killed a Roman warrior. In the ensuing battle, Boso managed to capture the Roman leader Petreius Cotta (or Peredur). He also led a company of soldiers at the final battle at Soissons. His role is taken by BORS in Malory. [*GeoffHR*, *Wace*, *Layamon*, *Allit*]

BOULOGNE

A port in northern France on the English Channel. According to Geoffrey, Arthur conquered it from Frollo as part of his invasion of Gaul, and gave it to either Holdin or Leodegan. In *Arthour and Merlin*, it is one of the lands acquired by Uther Pendragon from King Harinan, Igerne's first husband. [*GeoffHR*, *Wace*, *Arthour*]

BOURGES

A city in central France, capital of the province of Berry. The thirteenth-century *Lancelot do Lac* tells us that it was the birthplace of Uther Pendragon, and that it was ruled by the evil lord Claudas. When Claudas waged war on his overlord, King Aramont of Brittany, Aramont and Uther laid waste to Berry, but spared Bourges because Uther had been born there. [*LancLac*, *VulgLanc*]

BOVAINE

The land ruled by Alice the Fair Pilgrim, who married Alexander the Orphan, in the Prose *Tristan*. Malory changes it to BENOIC. [*ProsTris*]

BOWER OF BLISS

An enchanted garden ruled by the evil sorceress Acrasia. It held every sensual pleasure known to man, and it ensnared many good knights. Gloriana, the Fairy Queen, sent Sir Guyon to destory it. Guyon razed the Bower after resisting its temptations. [*Spenser*]

BOY WITH NO NAME

The nickname given to Gawain when he was growing up ignorant of his real name. Upon achieving knighthood, he became known as the KNIGHT WITH THE SURCOAT. [*DeOrtu*]

BRABANT [*Brabaunt*]

A region of Europe which is now divided between Belgium and the Netherlands. Wace says it was conquered by Arthur during his campaign against Gaul. Wolfram makes Lambekin the Duke of Brabant in Uther's time. Princess Elsam of Brabant, perhaps related to Lambekin, married Perceval's son Loherangrin. [*Wace, Wolfram, Lohengrin, Malory*]

BRADWEN[1]

Son of Iaen; brother of Sulyen, Teregud, Moren, Siawn, and Caradawg; and one of Arthur's warriors from Caer Dathal. He was related to Arthur through Uther. [*Culhwch*]

BRADWEN[2]

An Arthurian warrior who was the son of Moren Mynawg. [*Culhwch*]

BRAGGADOCCHIO

A cowardly peasant who stole Sir Guyon's horse. His companion was Trompart. He carried the "False Florimell," a maiden created by sorcery, away from the son of a witch. Braggadocchio became the False Florimell's "champion," but was eventually exposed for a braggart and a coward, and his maiden melted away. [*Spenser*]

BRAMANGUE [*Bramagnes, Bramague, Bran(d)egue, Brannague*]

A Saxon king who, with other rulers, invaded Britain in the early days of Arthur's reign. He ruled parts of Denmark and Ireland. After suffering a defeat at Saxon Rock, Bramangue commanded plundering parties and ordered the siege of Vambieres. His sons, Haram, Orient, and Daril, also contributed to the invasion. He was slain by Sir Sagremor, either at Vambieres or on the the Rier Vargonche. [*VulgMer, Livre, Arthour*]

BRAMANTE

A duke and friend of Meliadus and Tristan in *La Tavola Ritonda*. He ruled the city of Teneson and had a brother named King Bramo. Bramante assisted Meliadus in a war against Arthur, and he presented Tristan with a magnificent warhorse named Piantagiorno. Tristan slew a giant named Urgano the Hairy that plagued Bramante. He occupies the role given to GILAN in Gottfried's *Tristan*. [*Tavola*]

BRAMO

A king who was the father of Agia, Tristan's step-mother. His brother, Duke Bramante, was a friend of Tristan and Meliadus. [*Tavola*]

BRAN THE BLESSED

A king of Britain in ancient Welsh legend. E. K. Chambers thought that he might be a manifestation of the pseudo-historic BRENINUS. His name means "Raven," and it matches an Irish God of that name. Bran was the son of Llyr the sea god and is often described as a giant. In the non-Arthurian Welsh story of *Branwen*, Bran forms an uneasy alliance with Ireland through the marriage of his sister Branwen to the Irish king. Eventually, he goes to war with Ireland, destroys the island, suffers devastating losses, and is mortally wounded in the foot by a poisoned spear, which causes his land to fail. Aspects of his Irish war parallel Arthur's adventures in *The Spoils of Annwn* and in *Culhwch and Olwen*, including the journey to an island, the recovery of a cauldron, and the survival of only seven warriors.

According to the Welsh Triads, Bran's head was buried in the White Hill, near London, to protect Britain from foreign invaders. Arthur reportedly dug up the head because he wanted to be Britain's only protector.

The figure of Bran likely inspired several Arthurian characters, including BAN OF BENOIC (a corruption of "Bran le Benoit"), BRANDEGORRE, BRAN DE LIS, and BRANDELIDELIN. (R. S. Loomis thought that a great number of characters in French romance owed their origins to Bran.) Most importantly, however, Bran may be the origin of BRON, the Fisher King in the Robert de Boron Grail legends. A Welsh triad names Bron as "one of the three blissful rulers of the Island of Britain, who first brought the faith of Christ to the nation of Cymry from Rome, where he was seven years a hostage for his son Caradawc." Along with this religious connection, we have the episode of Bran's maiming (in *Branwen*), his ownership of a magical vessel (the cauldron) which provided bounty to worthy warriors, and the decay of his land following his wound. [*Triads*]

BRANDALUS

One of Perceval's eleven paternal uncles in *Perlesvaus*. He was the fifth son of Gais le Gros and the brother of Alain. He resided in Wales and was slain at a young age. [*Perlesvaus*]

BRANDEBAN [*Brandelis*]

The Duke of Tannings. Sir Sagremor championed him against Meliadus the Black on the Dry Island. Sagremor later fought a dozen of Brandeban's men who were trying to abduct a lady. [*VulgLanc*]

BRANDEGORRE[1] [*Brandagoras, Bran(de)gor(is), Brango(i)r(i)(e)(s)*]

The King of Estrangorre who joined the rebellious kings in their second campaign against King Arthur. He led a battalion in the battle of Bedegraine, where he was defeated by Arthur, Ban, and Bors. Later, he allied with Arthur in order to expel the Saxons from Britain, and he also joined Arthur in the war against Claudas. He married the daughter of the Emperor of Constantinople and had a beautiful daughter, upon whom Sir Bors fathered Helain the White. He also had a son named Evadeam, known as the Dwarf Knight. His wife had a son from a previous marriage named Sagremor—later a Knight of the Round Table. His name was probably originally *Bran de Gorre*; perhaps a reference to the BRAN of Welsh legend and the land of GORRE invented by Chrétien de Troyes. [*VulgLanc, VulgMer, Malory*]

BRANDEGORRE²

A Saxon high king who, with others, invaded Britain in the early days of Arthur's reign. He led a battalion against Arthur's lords at the battle of Garlot, and was killed there. [*VulgMer, Arthour*]

BRANDELIDELIN

The King of Punturteis in Uther's time. He was the maternal uncle of Gramoflanz. Brandelidelin participated in a tournament at the Welsh city of Kanvoleis, thrown by Perceval's mother Queen Herzeloyde. Later, as an ally of Arthur, he had a hand in stopping a battle between King Gramoflanz and Gawain. He may be connected to BRANDELIS of French romance. [*Wolfram*]

BRANDELIS¹ [*Brandalis, Brandaliz, Brand(e)les, Brandeliz, Brandellis, Brandiles, Brandyles, Bra(n)s de Lis, Brasdelis*]

An Arthurian knight upon whose sister, Guilorete, Gawain begot one or two sons. He first appears in the first continuation of Chrétien de Troyes's *Perceval*. Gawain, in escaping from his tryst with the maiden, had slain Bran's father, Norroiz, and two brothers. Bran fought with him as well, but agreed to postpone the combat until later, as Gawain had been wounded in one of the previous duels. They met five years later at the Castle of Lis. When the intervention of Gawain's young son, Lionel, failed to stop their combat, Arthur ordered a halt to the hostilities, and the two knights became friends.

Among his adventures in the Vulgate Cycle (and subsequently in Malory), he was imprisoned by some enemies and rescued by Gaheris; was imprisoned again by Tericam of the Impenetrable Forest and was freed by Lancelot; participated in a quest to find Lancelot; fought in the wars against Claudas and Galehaut; and helped Erec slay Montenart of the Isle Reposte. During the Grail Quest, he fought with and was defeated by Galahad. He either perished fighting Lancelot during Guinevere's rescue from the stake, or died at the battle of Salisbury against Mordred's army.

In *Claris et Laris*, Brandelis becomes a friend of Claris after Claris rescues him from the evil Red Knight. He is later imprisoned by Lord Thoas, an enemy of Arthur's court, but is eventually freed. After receiving guidance from Merlin, he releases Laris, Claris's friend, from the prison of King Tallas of Denmark.

A Middle English tale called *The Jeaste of Sir Gawain* recalls Brandelis's first appearance, relating how Gawain defeated Brandelis's father, Gilbert, and his two brothers, Gyamoure and Tyrry, after sleeping with his sister in a forest pavilion. Again, Brandelis fights Gawain to a draw. Contrary to the *Perceval* continuation, however, *Jeaste* says that Brandelis and Gawain never met again after their first duel.

Originally separated as Bran de Lis, this character may have a connection with the Welsh god BRAN. His surname may come from the French *lis* ("lily"), the Welsh *llys* ("castle"), or from a corruption of the French *iles* ("isles").

Note also the characters BRIAN OF THE ISLES, BRANDALUS, BLANCHELES, BRANDILIAS, and BRANDELIDELIN, who may have the same roots. [*Contin1, LancLac, VulgLanc, PostQuest, PostMort, Claris, Malory, Jeaste*]

BRANDELIS² [*Brandalis*]

A knight in the service of King Amant, an opponent of Arthur. When Amant was slain by King Bors of Gannes, Brandelis swore eternal enmity towards Arthur. [*VulgMer*]

BRANDELIS³ [*Brandalis*]

A Saxon king who fought Arthur's forces at the battle of Cambenic. Gawain cut his arm off. [*VulgMer*]

BRANDELIS⁴

Son of Lac, brother of Erec, and a Knight of the Round Table. He intervened in a fight between Tristan and Palamedes. [*Palamedes, DueTris*]

BRANDES [*Banderous, Branles*]

The Count of Colchester of Linis, present at the wedding of Erec and Enide. [*ChretienE, HartmannE, Heinrich*]

BRANDIGAN¹

A king who was Gawain's grandfather. [*Contin2*]

BRANDIGAN² [*Bardiga, Brandiganz, Prandigan*]

A beautiful British castle and town ruled by King Evrain. The town was on an island in the middle of a lake, and possessed marvelous fortifications, partially because of its geographical setting. It was the setting of a dangerous adventure known as the Joy of the Court; many knights died attempting it, and Brandigan became the new home of the slain knights' ladies. Erec eventually completed the adventure and brought a better mood to the castle. In Wolfram's *Parzival*, Clamide is once mentioned as the King of Brandigan. It may be the origin of BEDEGRAINE. [*ChretienE, Wolfram, Ivens*]

BRANDILIAS [*Brandris*]

A knight who served one of the princes rebelling against Arthur. He fought against the Saxons at Clarence. [*VulgMer, Arthour*]

BRANDIN OF THE ISLES [*Branduz*]

Lord of the Dolorous Guard. When the Saxons invaded Britain at the beginning of Arthur's reign, Brandin joined them against Arthur. Niniane, the Lady of the Lake, was briefly his paramour and taught him some enchantments that he applied to his castle. He trapped many knights and ladies in the Dolorous Guard before it was liberated by Lancelot. Lancelot also forced him to release Gawain and a number of other prisoners from the Dolorous Prison, a jail located in another of Brandin's castles. [*LancLac, VulgLanc, Livre*]

BRANDINO

A Gaulish king in *La Tavola Ritonda*. With another king named Arandus, he invaded and conquered the city of Benoic while its ruler, King Ban (Lancelot's father), was in Britain. The two kings occupy the role given to CLAUDAS in the Prose *Lancelot*. [*Tavola*]

BRANDINOR

A Knight of the Round Table who participated in the Grail Quest. He is named as the brother of Hector. [*PostQuest*]

BRANDOINES

A vassal of the King with a Hundred Knights. He fought at King Mark's tournament at Lancien. [*Contin4*]

BRANDON [*Braidon*]

A Saxon king who, with others, invaded Britain in the early days of Arthur's reign. He plundered several northern countries, including Scotland and Garlot. He was killed by Gawain. [*VulgMer*]

BRANES

A vassal of the King with a Hundred Knights. He fought at King Mark's tournament at Lancien. [*Contin4*]

BRANGAIN [*Braginja, Brandina, Brangane, Brangæne, Brangene, Brangien, Branguina, Brangwaine, Brengain, Brengvien, Brengwain, Bríngven, Bringvet, Bringwain*]

Isolde's faithful and beautiful maidservant in almost all of the Tristan legends. She had two brothers named Mathael and Perynin, whom she presented to Tristan as servants. When Tristan came to Ireland to escort Isolde to King Mark of Cornwall to be wed, Isolde's mother gave Brangain a love potion intended for Mark and Isolde on their wedding day. Tristan and Isolde accidentally drank it on the way, however, and fell in love with each other. On Isolde's wedding night, she substituted Brangain, under the cover of darkness, in Mark's bedroom, since Isolde was no longer a virgin. Isolde then tried to have Brangain killed to hide the secret; the attempt failed when the assigned killers took pity on her. Isolde regretted the attempt, and she and Brangain were eventually reconciled, but not before Brangain was kidnapped by Palamedes and used as a tool to get to Isolde. (In Malory, Brangain's murder is plotted by two jealous maidservants rather than by Isolde herself.) Thomas says that Brangain had an affair with Kahedins of Brittany—who fell in love with her upon seeing her statue in Tristan's Hall of Statues—but became enraged when Mariadoc, a cowardly and dishonest knight, reported that Kahedins had fled from him in combat. Some versions of the legend suggest that Brangain was infatuated with Tristan. Eilhart von Oberge says that she died before Isolde and Tristan, but does not name the cause. In *La Tavola Ritonda*, she perishes from sorrow after Mark forcibly retrieves Isolde from the castle of Joyous Guard, where she was living with Tristan. In some other Italian texts, she marries Governal, Tristan's tutor, and becomes the queen of Lyonesse. [*Thomas, Beroul, Eilhart, Gottfried, ProsTris, TrisSaga, TristanoR, Tavola, SagaTI, Malory*]

BRANGEMUER

A knight who was the offspring of a fairy (*Brange*part) and a man (Guinga*muer*). He ruled an otherworldly island. His body was borne to Camelot in a swan boat after the servant of a lord called the Little Knight slew him with a lance. Gareth agreed to avenge Brangemuer's death with the lance head. After Gareth accomplished his mission, Brangemuer's spirit returned to the realm of his mother. [*Contin1*]

BRANGEPART [*Brang(u)espart*]

A fairy who was the mother by Guingamuer of Brangemuer, a knight avenged by Gareth. [*Contin1*]

BRANGIEN

Maidservant of Lady Lore of Cardigan, probably suggested by BRANGAIN. [*Meriadeuc*]

BRANGOIRE

A king allied to Arthur, probably identical to BRANDEGORRE. [*Floriant, Claris*]

BRANGUEMORE OF CORNWALL [*Blancemor(n)e*]

A sorceress who built the Chapel of the Black Hand. Her son Espignogrés murdered her and buried her beneath the chapel's altar. The chapel became inhabited by a demon that slew many knights until it was vanquished by Perceval. [*Contin3*]

BRANIE OF THE HIGH MOUNTAIN

A lady at Arthur's court. Both Branie and her sister, Clameroi, failed a chastity test. [*Heinrich*]

BRANLANT [*Bralant, Branclant, Branlanc, Branland, Branlang, Branslant, Bre(n)lant*]

A Scottish stronghold that was the home of Sir Brun and Lady Lore. A "Lady of Branlant," possibly Lore, was loved by Waldin of the Fearsome Vales, who tried to marry her by force. In *Arthour and Merlin*, the husband of the lady is himself called Duke Branland. [*Renaut, Contin1, VulgMer, Livre, Arthour*]

BRANO

A nephew of King Faramon of France in *La Tavola Ritonda*. He was accused of theft at the same time that Faramon's daughter, Belide, falsely accused Tristan of rape. Faramon offered Belide a choice of saving either Brano or Tristan; when she chose Tristan, he knew she was lying about the crime. The same character is named MELIANT in the Prose *Tristan*. [*Tavola*]

BRANOR THE BROWN

A famous knight of Uther Pendragon's table, hailed in *Palamedes*. He was the son of Ellain the Brown, the brother of Bruhalt and Hector, and the uncle of Segurant the Brown. When he was about 120 years old, he visited Arthur's court and defeated almost all of Arthur's knights in joust, including Arthur, Lancelot, Palamedes, and Gawain. The episode is recounted in the Greek romance *Ho Presbys Hippotes*, though Branor is not named. [*Palamedes, Presbys*]

BRANTRIVIERS

An Arthurian knight in Hartmann von Aue's *Erec* and Heinrich von dem Türlin's *Diu Crône*. [*HartmannE, Heinrich*]

BRAOLANT [*Braolans*]

A Saxon king who, with other Saxon rulers, invaded Britain in the early days of Arthur's reign. [*VulgMer*]

BRATHACH

Son of Gwawrddur Hunchback, brother of Duach, Nerthach, and the lady Gwenwledyr, and one of Arthur's warriors. According to *Culhwch and Olwen*, Brathach and his brothers were "sprung from the Highlands of Hell." [*Culhwch*]

BRATTICE

A mountainous castle. The daughter of its lord was forced to live like a chambermaid by her cruel husband, but Gareth killed him and rescued the lady. [*VulgLanc*]

BRATTUR

One of Arthur's noblemen. He was the brother of Bilis, the dwarf king, and Revellus. [*Erex*]

BRAVAIN [*Brainons*]

One of Arthur's Knights of the Round Table. [*ChretienE, Heinrich*]

BRECKHAM [*Brequeham*]

A forest divided between Cambenic and North Wales, near Escavalon. In the early days of Arthur's reign, a group of Britons, led by King Clarion and Duke Escant of Cambenic, ambushed a party of Saxons in Breckham and slaughtered them. The forest, which was the site of one of Gawain's many adventures (the rescue of the maiden Florée), contained the Good Deed monastery, the castle of Leverzep, and three hermitages: the Cross, the Crossing, and the Restful Hermitage. It also held the Heath of the Crossroads, a place of adventures. Its name may be a variation of BEDEGRAINE. [*VulgLanc, VulgMer, Livre*]

BRECKNOCK

A property ruled by King Brychan—whose wife, Gwladys, was abducted by Gwynnlyw and later lusted after by Arthur. These events are related in the Welsh life of Saint Cadoc. [*SaintsCad*]

BREDBEDDLE

The true name of the GREEN KNIGHT in *The Greene Knight*; the counterpart of BERTILAK of *Sir Gawain and the Green Knight*. His sorceress step-mother, Agostes, sent him to Arthur's court in order to lure Gawain to Bredbeddle's castle, as Agostes' daughter (Bredbeddle's wife) was secretly in love with him. As in *Gawain*, Gawain accepted Bredbeddle's Beheading Game challenge and met him a year later at the Green Chapel, where Bredbeddle spared Gawain's life. Bredbeddle later appears in the ballad of *King Arthur and King Cornwall* as one of Arthur's knights. He tamed a fiend known as the Burlow-Beanie, which helped Arthur to slay the sorcerer Cornwall. [*Grene, KingA&C*]

BREFENY

An Irish forest traversed by Lancelot on his way to Rigomer Castle. It lay between the kingdoms of Connaught and Meath. [*Merveil*]

BREGION

The site of one of Arthur's battles against the Saxons, according to Nennius. In some manuscripts, the name of the mountain is AGNED. William Camden though that Mount Bregion (*Cath-Bregion*) was located at CADBURY. Nennius may have been connecting to Arthur a victory actually achieved by Urien at *Brewyn* (Loomis, *Romance*, 7). [*Nennius, Camden*]

BREMEINS

A British king, mentioned in *Arthour and Merlin* among those who could not be counted on to help the rebellious kings against the invading heathens. [*Arthour*]

BRENDAN [*Brandain*]

In the *Bliocadran Prologue* to Chrétien de Troyes *Perceval*, Perceval's mother, after her husband's death, tells her court that she is going to visit St. Brendan, when in actuality she plans to flee into the forest with her son. Presented as a Scottish saint in *Bliocadran*, St. Brendan was actually an Irish missionary who lived c. 484–577, which would place him slightly later than the Arthurian time frame. His church in Scotland serves as the burial place of the Red Knight (killed by Perceval) in the Fourth Continuation of Chrétien's *Perceval*. [*Bliocadran, Contin4*]

BRENNIUS [*Bremin, Brenne*]

An historic Gallic king who conquered Rome in the fourth century BC. Geoffrey of Monmouth expands his legend, saying that he was the son of King Dunwallo of Britain and the brother of Belinus. Brennius and Belinus went to war after their father's death, and Brennius was defeated. Retreating to Gaul, he became the duke of

Burgundy. Eventually, the brothers were reconciled and, together, they conquered Gaul and Rome. Brennius stayed to rule Rome while Belinus returned to Britain. Brennius may be reflected in the Welsh god BRAN. [*GeoffHR*, *Wace*]

BREONS

A Knight of the Round Table who was the son of Canodan. [*ChretienE*]

BRENT KNOLL

A hill in Somerset near the Bristol Channel that features the remains of an Iron-Age fortress. An interpolation in William of Malmesbury's *Historia Rerum Anglicarum* tells of an expedition by Arthur to destroy three giants on the hill. Yder, one of Arthur's young warriors, went ahead of his companions and encountered the giants alone. When Arthur arrived, Yder had slain all the giants but had received a serious wound and was unconscious. [*WilliamM*, *Topography*]

BREQUEAN

A Knight of the Round Table killed during the Grail Quest. [*PostQuest*]

BRESENDA

The sister of Medea, the lecherous female ruler of Crudele castle. Her other sisters included Lavina, Agnena, and Pulizena. [*Tavola*]

BRETHEAM

A forest near one of Arthur's courts, possibly identical to the forest of BRECKHAM. While hunting in it, Arthur met a beautiful maiden and forced himself upon her, begetting Arthur the Less. [*PostQuest*]

BRETIAUS[1]

In the Didot-*Perceval*, the brother of Lucius, Arthur's Roman enemy. He was killed during the Roman War. [*Didot*]

BRETIAUS[2]

An Arthurian knight who successfully defended himself against a false charge that he murdered another knight's pet wolf. [*Claris*]

BRETON GATE

The city gate in King Bors' Gannes. It faced Brittany. [*VulgLanc*]

BREUS THE PITILESS [Bereuse, Brehu(s), Breunis, Breusso, Breuz, *Brun sans Pitié]

The antithesis of knighthood in French romance—a murderer, rapist, thief, coward, and traitor—featured in the Prose *Tristan*, *Palamedes*, and Malory's *Le Morte Darthur*. His tactics included attacking by surprise, killing maidens (because his father, Brun or Arrouans, was killed through the treachery of a maiden), trampling knights with his horse, and running away whenever any knight challenged him. A pervasive character, he first appears in the First Continuation of Chrétien's *Perceval* as one of Arthur's knights. He next shows up in the Prose *Lancelot* as a tormentor of Gawain during the latter's quest to find Lancelot. According to the Vulgate *Merlin*, he served Clarion and Escant, two of the northern kings who rebelled against Arthur, and the *Livre d'Artus* has him joining the Saxons against Arthur. In *L'Atre Perilleux*, he is called the King of the Red City. Gawain defeats him in combat. Girart d'Amiens gives him a brother named Colivre, and Malory makes him the brother of Bertelot. In *Palamedes*, he discovers the tomb of Febus, a great ancestor of Guiron the Courteous. In *Tavola*, he has a lady—of whom he is extremely jealous—named Galiena. Many knights, including Tristan, Lancelot, Dinadan, Palamedes, Gaheris, and Bleoberis, chased Breus in vain. If caught, Breus used trickery to escape. After he stole a shield that the Lady of the Lake sent by messenger to Lancelot, Lancelot tracked him down and finally slew him. [*Contin1*, *Contin2*, *LancLac*, *VulgLanc*, *VulgMer*, *ProsTris*, *Contin4*, *Atre*, *Girart*, *Tavola*, *Malory*]

BRIADAN

One of two knights who murdered the Good Knight Without Fear. His companion was Ferrant. [*Palamedes*]

BRIADAS THE UNDEFEATED [Briadan]

A powerful jouster who guarded the Spring of the Two Sycamores. He was considered undefeatable; he had even knocked down Gawain. This lasted until he was conquered by Lancelot and received a mortal wound. His brother, Belyas the Black, and father, Broadas, were also slain by Lancelot. [*VulgLanc*]

BRIAINS OF ROCHIERS

A knight who joined Nogant in an assault on Queen Fenise of Ireland. [*Durmart*]

BRIAMONT

A knight of Arthur's from Cardueil who participated in a quest to learn the fate of Merlin. [*VulgMer*]

BRIAN[1] [Briien]

A Knight of the Round Table found in Hartmann von Aue's *Erec*. He may be identical to one of the other Brians. Any of the Brians may be literary descendants of the Welsh BRAN. [*HartmannE*, *Heinrich*]

BRIAN[2] [Brien]

Brother of the Arabian warlord Larner. He killed his brother for a magnificent suit of armor, which he then brought to the country of Korntin. It eventually fell into the hands of Wigalois (Gawain's son). [*Wirnt*]

BRIAN³

An Arthurian knight who participated in the Roman War. [*Allit*]

BRIAN⁴

A Knight of the Round Table from Listenois. He was liberated from the dungeon of Lord Tericam by Lancelot. [*Malory*]

BRIAN⁵ OF MEZ

One of Arthur's knights. [*Girart*]

BRIAN⁶ OF THE FOREST

A knight that Gawain encountered in his first quest. Sir Brian was fighting with his brother, Sir Sorlouse of the forest, over who would chase the hart that Gawain was pursuing. Gawain told them the hart quest was his, and they yielded quickly to him rather than fight him. Gawain sent the two brothers to King Arthur. [*Malory*]

BRIAN⁷ OF THE GASTINE [*Brien*]

A malevolent knight. He elicited a rash promise from Arthur, which turned out to be the unconditional services of Gawain. Brian invaded the Lake of Twins, and forced Gawain to slay Lord Bleheri, who ruled the land. With Bleheri dead, Brien took over all of his former lands and castles, and imprisoned their knights and ladies. Meriadeuc, Bleheri's son, learned of the injustice from his mother and killed Brien to avenge his father's death. Brien's son, Galien, continued to plague Meriadeuc's family but was slain by Gawain. [*Meriadeuc*]

BRIAN⁸ OF THE ISLES [*Brien*]

In *Perlesvaus*, the ruler of Brittany and an enemy of Arthur. He harbored Kay when Kay defected from Arthur's court, and also joined forces with Meliant, an enemy of Lancelot. The three knights invaded Britain while Arthur was on a pilgrimage to the Grail Castle. Pillaging and burning, Brian marched his army to Cardueil, where he was defeated and captured by the combined prowess of Gawain, Lancelot, and Arthur. After he was healed, Brian took Kay's place as Arthur's seneschal. He professed loyalty to Arthur, although in truth he had little love for the king, and harbored a burning hatred of Lancelot—fueled in part by a secret alliance with Claudas, Lancelot's mortal foe. He tricked Arthur into throwing Lancelot into prison. When Arthur relented and freed Lancelot, Brian defected and joined Claudas. The two later invaded Scotland. The epilogue to *Perlesvaus* suggests that he killed, or was killed by, Lancelot. [*Perlesvaus*]

BRIAN⁹ OF THE ISLES [*Brien*]

A knight who loved the Lady of the Isles. She would only marry the best knight in Britain, who she perceived as Gawain. To prove his superiority, Brian set out to conquer Gawain. He found Gawain, without armor, near Arthur's court. Brian insisted on fighting him anyway and seriously wounded him. Brian, believing he had killed Gawain, returned to the Isles and informed the Lady of his success. The Lady prepared to marry him, but Gawain, healed, showed up on their wedding day and ended the marriage. Gawain defeated Brian in combat and sent him to Arthur's court, where he became one of Arthur's knights. Not wishing to reveal his own name, he adopted the alias "Handsome Prisoner." [*Meriadeuc*]

BRIAN¹⁰ OF THE ISLES

Brother of Mellot of Logres and cousin of Nimue. He disliked Arthur and imprisoned many Knights of the Round Table in his Castle Pendragon. Lancelot eventually defeated him and drove him from the castle. His character recalls BRANDIN OF THE ISLES from the Vulgate *Lancelot*. [*Malory*]

BRIAN¹¹ THE LESSER

An Arthurian knight in Heinrich von dem Türlin's *Diu Crône*. [*Heinrich*]

BRIANS

A knight present at the tournament of Sorgarda, won by Gawain. He was a vassal of the Duke of Aram. [*Heinrich*]

BRIANT¹ OF NORTH WALES [*Bryaunt*]

A knight with whom Sir Lancelot jousted—and defeated—before the Castle of Maidens tournament. [*Malory*]

BRIANT² OF THE RED ISLAND

A king who married Mariole, a maiden with a magical golden circlet. They had a daughter named Tristouse. When Mariole's magic circlet was stolen, Briant died. Tristouse later had a son named Torec, who defeated Arthur's knights. [*Maerlant*]

BRICE

A city in Logres in the Vulgate *Merlin*. The Archbishop of Brice presided at Uther's funeral and supported the young Arthur's claim to the throne by excommunicating the rebellious leaders who opposed Arthur, and by validating the sword-in-the-stone test. The author of *Merlin* probably misinterpreted Archbishop *du Brice* from Wace's Archbishop DUBRIC. [*VulgMer*, *Arthour*]

BRICKUS

Arthur's grandfather and Uther's father in Wolfram's *Parzival*. His brother Lazaliez was Perceval's great-great-grandfather. His parents, Mazadan and Terdelaschoye, were both fairies. His role as Arthur's grandfather generally belongs to CONSTANTINE. [*Wolfram*]

BRICOUNE GATE

One of the gates in Arthur's city of Logres. [*VulgMer*]

BRIDALAM

A Knight of the Round Table killed during the Grail Quest. [*PostQuest*]

BRIDAS

A vassal of King Mark of Cornwall who participated in Mark's tournament at Lancien. [*Contin4*]

BRIDGE OF THE GIANT

The custom of the bridge was that its guardian must remain there until he was defeated by another knight or until four months had passed. A knight named Golistan served as its guardian for a while, but he was defeated by Seguarant the Brown. Another guardian was Sir Neroneus of the Isle. [*Palamedes, ProsTris*]

BRIDGE OF THE NEEDLE

A pencil-thin bridge which crossed a chasm to the Grail Castle. Gawain decided to brave the bridge and, upon stepping on it, found that it was really just as wide as any other bridge. [*Perlesvaus*]

BRIDLAW

A warrior of Arthur and companion of Bedwyr. [*WelshPG*]

BRIÉBRAS

The surname of Arthur's Sir Caradoc, meaning "short arm." In *Les Merveilles de Rigomer*, it is a knight's entire name. [*Merveil*]

BRIET OF GONEFORT

One of Arthur's knights. [*Renaut*]

BRIGHT FOUNTAIN

A land terrorized by a fierce demon with no torso, bearing a gorgon-like head that turned all people to stone. Sir Daniel of the Blossoming Valley defeated the demon—as Perseus conquered Medusa—by looking at his opponent only through a reflection in a mirror. The Count of the Bright Fountain became Daniel's faithful companion. Daniel later saved him from beheading at the hands of a giant. [*Stricker*]

BRIMEHOLZ

A fairy companion of Madoine. Madoine loved Arthur's Sir Laris. [*Claris*]

BRIMESENT [*Hermesent(e)*]

Arthur's sister in the Vulgate *Merlin*. The daughter of Hoel and Igerne, she married King Urien and had a son named Yvain. Her sister was called Blasine. She encouraged her son to take service with Arthur. Her role is assumed by MORGAN LE FAY in the Post-Vulgate. [*VulgMer, Arthour*]

BRINEMANS [*Brincians*]

One of several knights defeated by Lancelot on his way to Rigomer Castle. Lancelot sent him to Guinevere as a prisoner. [*Merveil*]

BRINOL OF THE HEDGED MANOR [*Brinos, Bromel la Pleche*]

A knight, also called Brinol the Pleasant, who began his career as a member of Arthur's army fighting the Saxons. Some time after the Saxon wars, Guinevere, traveling through the forest, saw Brinol and his brother abusing another knight. Taking pity on the beaten knight, Guinevere ordered her knights to save him. In the ensuing combat, two of Brinol's brothers were killed. After this, Brinol hated Guinevere and attacked any knight who claimed to serve her, wounding, among others, Dodinel. Finally, he was defeated by Lancelot and forced to reconcile with the queen. Later, however, he fell in love with Elaine of Corbenic and renewed his hate for Arthur's court, as Elaine would not return Brinol's love because of her love for Lancelot. He refused to let any of Arthur's knights enter Corbenic for months, but he was eventually defeated by Bors, who made him surrender to Lancelot. He then re-entered Arthur's fellowship and fought in the war against Claudas. [*VulgLanc, Livre, Malory*]

BRIODA

In *La Tavola Ritonda*, a castle inhabited by relatives of Tristan. These relatives slew Meliadus, Tristan's father, and Tristan later invaded the castle and killed the murderers. In the Prose *Tristan*, these villains come from NORHOLT. [*Tavola*]

BRIOL OF THE FOREST ARSEE [*Briot*]

A knight encountered by Perceval in his quest for the Grail. Briol lodged him, gave him directions to the Fisher King's castle, and told him of an upcoming tournament at the Castle Orguelleus. [*Contin2*]

BRIOLLO

A Saracen king, killed by Gaheris (Gawain's brother) at the battle of Diana Bridge. [*Arthour*]

BRION[1]

A castle in France near the home of the Lady of the Lake. It was separated from the castle Charosque by the forest of Briosque. [*VulgLanc*]

BRION[2]

Castle belonging to Alain of Escavalon. Alain once lodged Gawain at the castle, and Gawain slept with Alain's daughter, Florée, begetting a son. [*Livre*]

BRIOS[1] OF MONTASCON

A wounded knight encountered by Lancelot on his way to Rigomer Castle. Brios had been injured at Rigomer, and was fated to never heal until a "faultless" knight examined his wounds. The story infers that Gawain is this "faultless" knight, but Brios does not appear again in the story. Brios gave Lancelot some information about Rigomer. [*Merveil*]

BRIOS² OF THE EMPLACEMENT

A knight who served King Caradoc of Estrangorre. He fought in the wars against the Saxons in the early days of Arthur's reign. [*VulgMer*]

BRIOSQUE [*Brioke*]

A fertile French forest in Benoic and Burgundy which contained the lake that was the home of the Lady of the Lake. Merlin first encountered her there. It was the rallying point for Arthur's forces before the war with Claudas, and the site of a battle between the two kings' armies. It was named after the two castles on either side of it: Brion and Charosque. [*VulgLanc, VulgMer, ProsMer2*]

BRISEN [*Bris(i)ane*]

A lady and servant of King Pelles, with whom she conspired to have Lancelot sleep with Elaine. Through enchantment, Brisen got Lancelot drunk and sent him off to the Castle of Case, where Guinevere was supposedly waiting for him. They put Elaine in Guinevere's place, knowing that Lancelot, in his drunken state and in the dark, would mistake Elaine for Guinevere. The plan worked, and Galahad was conceived. Brisen later helped Elaine trick Lancelot into sleeping with her a second time, at Camelot. [*VulgLanc, Malory*]

BRISTOL

In *Arthour and Merlin*, the site of a battle fought by Pendragon and Merlin against invading Saxons or Saracens. The Saxons, led by Maladors and Gamor, were defeated, but Pendragon was slain. [*Arthour*]

BRITAIN [*Breta(i)(n)gne*]

The largest British island, including the modern countries of England, Scotland and Wales. It is the kingdom most often associated with Arthur, though some authors—particularly continental ones—seem confused as to its location and boundaries. It is often difficult to distinguish between Britain and BRITTANY. According to Nennius, Britain was named after Brutus, the island's first king, who conquered it after arriving from Greece (prior to Brutus, the island was called ALBION). More likely, however, it is a variation of PRYDEIN, which is Britain's name in Welsh texts.

The origins of Arthur are woven inextricably into the backdrop of British history in the fifth century. Briefly summarized, this history, from what we can piece together, is as follows:

Rome came to Britain in the first century, uniting the island, pushing the native Celts into the hills of Wales and the highlands of Scotland, and establishing Roman customs and laws. For three hundred years, Rome and Britain were one and the same. During this time, there were occasional battles to be fought against barbarian Picts in the north, Irish raiders in the west, and Germanic pirates in the east.

In the late fourth century and early fifth century, the *pax Romana* collapsed. First, a succession of Brito-Roman generals broke from the western empire and invaded Gaul. The most illustrious of these were Maximus—who deposed Emperor Gratian in 383—and Constantine III, who invaded Gaul in the first decade of the fifth century.

These aspiring usurpers of Britain were only part of Rome's worries. The empire was already collapsing from within, and enemies were closing on all sides. Rome withdrew its military and administrative support for Britain in about 410. Britain was left largely defenseless, most of its warriors having been withdrawn to deal with the barbarian invasions of the continental territories, or siphoned away by Constantine III. Rome's withdraw opened Britain to more frequent and devestating raids from its traditional Picitish and Irish enemies. It appears that a British high king, popularly called Vortigern, ruling sometime before 450, attempted an old Roman trick: the hiring of one group of barbarians to fight another. In this case, Vortigern employed Saxons (who may or may not have already settled in parts of eastern Britain) against the Picts. The Saxons grew in number and power, however, and they established permanent settlements on the eastern shores. Eventually, they revolted and attacked the British, with more and more of their kinsman arriving from Germany each year. The Saxons completed the conquest towards the end of the sixth century, and the remaining native Britons were forced into enclaves in Wales, Cornwall, and the north. The Saxons retained control over the island for about 500 years, until the Norman conquest in 1066.

It appears that in the late fifth century, the Saxon advances were checked, for a few decades, by a British resurgence, begun by a Roman descendant named Ambrosius Aurelianus. There appears to have been a battle called Badon which delivered a heavy blow to the Saxons and forced them to retreat to their settelements on the shore for twenty or thirty years, during which Britain was ruled independently by the British. Contemporary accounts show, however, that the British were unable to remain united, and that regional feuds allowed the island to fall to the English relatively quickly.

Arthur's place—in legend, if not in history—belongs to the few decades (c. 460–520) in which the British were able to stop the Saxon encroachments. We find him named as the great British general at Mount Badon, and, as legend progresses, as the king of Britain during this temporary—and final—British revival.

BRITHAEL [*Bertel, Bertil, Brastias, Bretel, Bricel, Bricot, Britael*]

An Arthurian knight who originally belonged to Gorlois, the Duke of Cornwall. One source names him as the Duke's cupbearer. When Uther wanted to sneak into the castle of Tintagel to sleep with Igerne, Gorlois' wife, Merlin magically disguised Uther as the duke and himself (or Sir Ulfin) as Brithael to get past the guards. Later, Brithael became Uther's vassal and fought in the battle of Saint Albans. As Arthur's knight, he participated in the battles against the rebelling kings at Caerleon and Bedegraine. He also helped defeat the Saxons at Carhaix, and participated in the campaign against Claudas. Through Merlin, Brithael and Ulfin learned of the first plot to replace Guinevere with the False Guinevere and foiled it. Arthur made him warden of the northern lands. In time, he retired to a hermitage near Windsor. [GeoffHR, Wace, Layamon, VulgMer, Livre, Arthour, Malory, TennIK]

BRITOMART

A female knight who exemplifies chastity in Spenser's *The Faerie Queene*. In Spenser's allegory, Britomart is one representative of Queen Elizabeth. She was the daughter of King Rions of South Wales. She fell in love with a knight named Artegall after seeing a vision of him in a mirror. Traveling to Fairy Land to find him, she became the companion of Prince Arthur, Sir Guyon, and the Red Cross Knight, the latter of whom she helped to escape from the Castle Joyous. Among other adventures, she encountered Merlin and heard his prophecies of the future of Britain, and she rescued the maiden Amoret from the prison of the sorcerer Busirane. Britomart and Amoret encountered Artegall and Scudamore (Amoret's *amie*) with visors over their faces, and Britomart fought both of them, defeating Scudamore and fighting Artegall to a draw. Their identities were revealed. Britomart and Artegall fell in love and were swiftly betrothed, but Artegall had to leave to finish a quest assigned to him by Gloriana, the Fairy Queen. He was later captured and imprisoned by Queen Radigund of the Amazons. Britomart heard of his plight from his squire Talus, and she freed him by slaying Radigund. [Spenser]

BRITON

To those living in Britain, the Britons referred specifically the early Celtic people living in South Britain that had driven the Picts into Ireland and Scotland. To foreigners, the term *Briton* casually meant any habitant of the island of Britain. Compare with PICT, SCOT, and CELT.

BRITTANY [Breta(i)gne, Bretan, Breteyn, Bretland]

A region of northwest France, directly across the channel from Britain. The area was once called Armorica. The chronicles contend that the first British conqueror of the area was Maximus, and that Conan Meriadoc was its first ruler. Conan, a Briton by birth, tried to bring British customs to the region by importing British citizens—especially women. For this reason, Brittany became known as "Other Britain," "Little Britain," or "Lesser Britain." The account given by the chronicles is a condensation of historical events: the anarchy in Britain after the Roman withdrawal, the Pictish threat, and the Saxon invasion led to a migration of Britons across the channel and a resettlement of British culture in Brittany.

Rulers of Brittany in the Arthurian age are variously given as Hoel (whose wife, the duchess of Brittany, was kidnapped by the giant of Mont St. Michel), Brian of the Isles, Aramont, Fflergant, Caradoc, and Peissawg the Tall. Arthur is often named as Brittany's overlord. In Middle High German romance, Brittany is often noted as Arthur's primary kingdom, with its capital at Nantes. [Culhwch, GeoffHR, LancLac, Dream, PleierG, Malory]

BRITTO

As related by Nennius, an alternate name for BRUTUS. [Nennius]

BRIZILJAN [Breziljan, Brizljan, Priziljan]

German version of BROCELIANDE, an Arthurian forest.

BROADAS [Broadés]

A large knight who inhabited the Spring of the Two Sycamores. Lancelot killed both of his sons, Belias the Black and Briadas the Undefeated. Broadas tried to throw Lancelot in a well, but Lancelot killed him. [VulgLanc]

BROBARZ

A land ruled by Tampenteire and then by his daughter, Condwiramurs. Its main castle was Beaurepaire. The land was invaded and besieged by Clamadeu and his seneschal Kingrun, who wanted the land and the lady. Just as it looked as if Condwiramurs would lose, Perceval arrived and defeated Clamadeu and Kingrun. After he married Condwiramurs, Perceval became lord of Brobarz. Perceval bequeathed the scepter of Brobarz—along with his other secular kingdoms—to his son Kardeiz. [Wolfram]

BROCAIRE [Brocaie]

A forest near Penning Castle, through which Gawain, Mordred, and Yvain traveled on their way back from a tournament. [VulgLanc]

BROCELIANDE [Brecheliande, Brocheland, Brocheliande, Brockland]

A forest in Brittany that often appears in Arthurian romance, after Wace described its marvels (including an enchanted fountain) in his *Roman de Rou*. It was the location of the fountain where Yvain defeated Esclados the Red in Chrétien's *Yvain* and its adaptations. The forest contained the strongholds of New Castle and Lindesores. It was the site of important meetings and troop movements during the early rebellions against Arthur, and during the Saxon wars. In the Vulgate *Merlin* and Tennyson's *Idylls*, it served as the place of Merlin's imprisonment by the Lady of the Lake. French romance seems to be largely unaware, however, that a channel separates Broceliande from the rest of Britain. German romance, which calls it BRIZILJAN, places it in the country of Löver near Dinazarun. [ChretienY, HartmannI, VulgMer, PleierG, ProsMer2, TennIK]

BROCHEFORT

A forest through which Pendragon and Uther were traveling when they first encountered Merlin. [*Butor*]

BRODAN

A Knight of the Round Table who embarked with the others on the Grail Quest. [*PostQuest*]

BROKEN SWORD [*Espee Brisiee*]

A weapon which struck Joseph of Arimathea in the thighs when he wandered into a Saracen castle in the forest of Broceliande. Half of the sword broke away and remained in the wound. After Joseph converted the castle and its lord, Matagran, he removed the broken piece from his thighs, and proclaimed that the two halves would not be rejoined until Galahad found them during the Grail Quest. Meanwhile, the piece which had been stuck in Joseph dripped blood constantly. After Gawain, Perceval, and Bors failed, Galahad successfully mended the sword at the end of the Grail Quest. Galahad gave it to Bors. Its tale recalls the GRAIL SWORD and the BLEEDING LANCE. [*VulgQuest, VulgEst*]

BRON [*Boon, Brom, Brons, Gron, (H)ebron*]

The FISHER KING and MAIMED KING in Robert de Boron's Grail Cycle (Robert's *Joseph* and the Didot-*Perceval*). Bron married Enygeus, the sister of Joseph of Arimathea, and accompanied Joseph on his trek from Judea to Britain. Joseph appointed him keeper of the Grail, and he earned his title as the "Rich Fisher" or "Fisher King" after he caught a fish which God multiplied into thousands. His piety was reflected by the fact that he was able to sit in the Perilous Seat at the Grail Table. He had a dozen sons, one of whom was named Alain the Large. Perceval was Bron's grandson. He fell ill when Perceval arrogantly sat in the Round Table's Perilous Seat, and could be cured only by the GRAIL QUESTION. Perceval failed in his first visit to Bron's castle, but returned for a successful second visit. Bron was healed, passed the Grail on to Perceval, and died three days later.

The author of the Vulgate Cycle, recognizing the centuries between Joseph of Arimathea's time and Arthur's reign, makes Bron an ancestor, but not the grandfather, of Perceval and Galahad. The distinction of Fisher King is transferred to Bron's son, Alain. The Vulgate *Estoire del Saint Graal* names another of Bron's sons as Joshua, and the Prose *Tristan* names two more as Naburzadan and Sador.

The longer version of his name, Hebron, belongs to both a biblical city in Israel and a son of Kohath, whose family was responsible for care of the Ark of the Covenant. Proponents of a Celtic origin for the Grail legend have urged a connection with King BRAN of Welsh legend, who was also maimed, who owned a magical vessel (a cauldron), and who was said, in a Triad, to have brought Christianity to Britain. [*RobertBorJ, VulgEst, VulgMer, ProsTris*]

BRONCONE

A knight encountered by Tristan in *La Tavola Ritonda*. He inhabited the fortress of Sangranar with a knight named Sodoc. The two knights tried to steal Tristan's and Lancelot's horses but were defeated. [*Tavola*]

BRONLLAFYN SHORT BROAD

A knife carried by Osla Big Knife, which was so large that it could be used as a bridge for armies to cross bodies of water. However, it proved to be Osla's doom when, during the hunt for Twrch Trwyth, the sheath filled with water and dragged Osla to the bottom of a river. [*Culhwch*]

BRONNIL [*Brumyng*]

In Robert Mannyng's chronicle, a Saxon lord who allied with Mordred and was slain at the final battle against Arthur. [*Mannyng*]

BROS OF THE HEATH

A knight defeated by Tristan during a joust at Camelot. [*ProsTris*]

BROWN EARL

A ruler who fell in love with Enid when he met her during her distressing journey with Geraint. He threatened to kill Geraint unarmed in order to take Enid, but Enid convinced him to abduct her during the night instead. Then, in their quarters, she warned Geraint of the plan so that they could escape. The Brown Earl pursued them, but Geraint defeated him in combat. He is known in Chrétien's *Erec* as GALOAIN. [*Geraint*]

BROWN FAMILY

A family of mighty knights who thrived in Uther Pendragon's day, each bearing the surname *le brun* ("the Brown"). These knights included Brannor, Bruhault, Brun, Ellain, Galehaut, Hector, Hubaus, Riger, and Segurant. Of these, Galehaut, Hector, and Segurant were the most renowned. The Browns were descended from Brutus, first king of Britain, through Albanact. Their home was in the Brown Valley, though some of them ruled the Savage Realm. [*Palamedes*]

BROWN KNIGHT WITHOUT PITY

A knight that held 30 widows captive in his castle, after he killed all of their husbands. He was finally killed by Sir Gareth, who liberated the castle and sent the ladies to Camelot. He may be a duplicate of BREUS the Pitiless, whose original name was *Brun* ("Brown"). [*Malory*]

BROWN ROCK

A castle in Scotland where Arthur's Sir Fergus defeated a horrible giant—the husband of a hag which Fergus had previously slain. Fergus took up temporary residence in the castle afterwards. [*Guillaume*]

BROWN VALLEY [*Val Brun]

Home of the "Brown" family of mighty knights, including Segurant the Brown and Galehaut the Brown. Tristan and Lancelot traversed the valley during their adventures. Its castle was called Vallebrun. [Palamedes, ProsTris, Tavola]

BROWNSTEEL

Arthur's sword in the English chronicle Arthur. [Arthur]

BRUANT[1]

A king who served Arthur. He ruled the Lost City and was nicknamed "Four Beards." [Meriadeuc]

BRUANT[2]

A knight who stole a golden circlet from a lady named Mariole. Mariole's grandson, Torec, later defeated Bruant to avenge the deed. [Maerlant]

BRUDAN

The nephew of Brian of the Isles, Arthur's enemy. He murdered the noble Meliot of Logres, and was slain in turn by Perceval. [Perlesvaus]

BRUHAUT THE BROWN

Son of Ellain, nephew of Hector the Brown, brother of Hector the Brown and Branor the Brown, and uncle of Segurant the Brown. [Palamedes]

BRUIANT OF THE ISLES

A king and one of King Arthur's knights. He fought well in tournaments at the Castle of Maidens and at Banborc. Bruiant presented Arthur with two splendid thrones, magnificently sculpted and adorned. Arthur, in turn, gave them to Erec upon his coronation as ruler of Nantes. [ChretienE, Renaut, Girart]

BRUMAND THE PROUD [Brumant, Brumart]

A knight in Claudas's service who boasted to his comrades that he was bolder than Lancelot, and that he would prove it by sitting in the Round Table's Perilous Seat, something that Lancelot never dared to do. Brumand later had second thoughts, but kept his word. Barging into a meeting of the Round Table, he placed himself in the Perilous Seat, and was swiftly incinerated by a pillar of fire. He left three brothers named Canart, Cadant, and Alibel. [VulgLanc]

BRUMBANE

A lake, next to which Lähelin captured Gringolet, the horse that became Gawain's steed. [Wolfram]

BRUN[1] ("Brown")

Lord of the Savage Realm. He was a descendant of Brutus, and an ancestor of the famous knights of the "Brun" family (Segurant, Hector, Galehaut). Brun was the son of Arbrun and Vagés, the husband of Lye, and the father of Hector, Brun, Lore, and Ysille. By the daughter of a giant, he also had a second son named Hector. [Palamedes]

BRUN[2]

Descendant of Brutus and ancestor of the famous knights of the "Brun" family. He was the son of Brun and Lye, the husband of Pamphille, and the father of Yrlande and Gialle. [Palamedes]

BRUN[3]

A giant who attacked Britain and was killed by Uther Pendragon. [Palamedes]

BRUN[4]

A knight slain by Gawain. He was the son of Urpin of the Mountain and the brother of the Lady Bloisine. His sister plotted to avenge his death but ended up falling in love with Gawain. [Contin4]

BRUN[5] BRANDALIS

One of Perceval's eleven paternal uncles in Perlesvaus. He was the third son of Gais the Large and the brother of Alain. Both Brun Brandalis and his son were slain at a young age. [Perlesvaus]

BRUN[6] OF BRANLANT [Brus of Bralant]

A vassal of Guiromelant, an enemy of Gawain in the First Continuation of Perceval. When Guiromelant made peace with Gawain by marrying his sister, Brun refused to submit to Arthur's rule. Arthur besieged his castle and eventually subdued him. When he agreed to become Arthur's vassal, Arthur gave him the cities of Quilini and Baradigan. In the Livre d'Artus, he is the seneschal of Lady Lore of Branlant. [Contin1, Renaut, Livre]

BRUN[7] OF GUMIAUS

A knight in Arthur's service. He fought against the Saxons at the battle of Carhaix. [Contin2, Livre]

BRUN[8] OF MOROIS

A knight who abducted Guinevere from Sir Yder, who was escorting the queen unarmed. Brun imprisoned Guinevere in his castle at Morois. Arthur's Sir Durmart tracked him down, fought him, defeated him, and rescued the queen. Brun was sent to Arthur's court to do homage. He became Arthur's vassal. Brun's brother was named Sir Cardroain. [Durmart, Girart]

BRUN[9] OF PICIEZ

A Knight of the Round Table present at the wedding of Erec and Enide. [ChretienE]

BRUN[10] OF THE HEATH

A Cornish knight who abducted the paramour of the Pensive Knight. Gawain tracked him down, rescued the lady, and sent Brun to Arthur's court. Brun became one of Arthur's knights. [Contin2]

BRUN[11] THE FELON

An evil knight from Northumberland who is the father of Breus the Pitiless in *Palamedes*. He is possibly identical to ARROUANS THE FELON, also named as Breus's father. He had a brother named Passehen and another son named Falquidés. Arthur killed him. [*Palamedes*]

BRUNAMORT

A knight who guarded the Ford of the Wood. He fought for King Mark of Cornwall in a tournament at Lancien. [Contin4]

BRUNEHEUT

Having been banished from Mark's court, Tristan returned disguised as a madman so he could see Isolde. As part of his insane rambling, he claims to have a sister named Bruneheut. [*FolieB*]

BRUNFORT

One of Tristan's horses in *La Tavola Ritonda*. The beautiful black stallion was given to him by Morgan le Fay. Its name signifies "brown-strong." [*Tavola*]

BRUNING

A Saxon warrior who fought for Mordred against King Arthur and was killed at the battle of Camel. [*GeoffHR*]

BRUNISSEN

The lady of the Castle Monbrun. She was plagued by the evil knight Taulat, but rescued by Arthur's knight Jaufré, who fell in love with her and married her. [*Jaufre*]

BRUNOR[1] [*Breunor, Brunoro*]

Galehaut's father in the Prose *Tristan* and Malory. He conquered the Castle of Tears from a giant named Mago, and married the Beautiful Giantess, the dead giant's wife. Brunor upheld the evil custom of the castle, which involved the murder of visiting knights and their ladies, if the knights were not as powerful as the lord, and the ladies were not as beautiful as the castle's lady. Galehaut deserted his father because of this custom. Tristan and Isolde stumbled upon the island on their way from Ireland and were imprisoned. In the subsequent combat, Tristan killed Brunor and then, because Isolde was the most beautiful, slew the Beautiful Giantess. Galehaut later sought to avenge his father's death but was defeated. [*ProsTris, TristanoR, Tavola, Conti, Malory*]

BRUNOR[2] THE BLACK

The true name of the GOOD KNIGHT WITHOUT FEAR, who was the father of Brunor the Black and Dinadan. [*Palamedes*]

BRUNOR[3] THE BLACK [*Breunor*]

The real name of the Knight of the Ill-Fitting Coat, first given in the Prose *Tristan* and *Palamedes*. He was a Knight of the Round Table, the son of the Good Knight Without Fear, and the brother of Dinadan and Daniel. Lancelot, who had killed Daniel, is his mortal enemy in *La Tavola Ritonda*, but he undertakes a quest with Lancelot in the Prose *Tristan* and in Malory (see KNIGHT OF THE ILL-FITTING COAT). [*Palamedes, ProsTris, Tavola, Malory*]

BRUNOR[4] THE BROWN

Once named as the father of Sir Segurant the Brown, though in other locations, Segurant's father is HECTOR THE BROWN. There may be some confusion with BRANOR THE BROWN, Hector's brother. [*Palamedes*]

BRUNOR[5] THE PLEASANT

A Knight of the Round Table who participated in the Grail Quest. [*ProsTris*]

BRUNORO THE BROWN

In *La Tavola Ritonda*, a relative of Lancelot who showed up at King Mark's court, secured a promise from the king, and asked for the Hebrew Damsel of Thornbush Ford—a maiden loved by both Mark and Tristan. Brunoro led her away in front of her husband, Lambergus. Tristan tracked him down, challenged him, and fought him to a draw. The maiden chose to return with Tristan. This role is played by BLEOBERIS in the Prose *Tristan*. [*Tavola*]

BRUNZ[1] OF LIS

An Arthurian knight, not identical to BRANDELIS. [*Girart*]

BRUNZ[2] THE PROPHET

Father of Sir Escanor the Handsome, an opponent of Gawain, by the Lady Alienor. Brunz was a king who ruled a land near Ireland. [*Girart*]

BRUSAZ

In Heinrich von dem Türlin's *Diu Crône*, one of several kings who served Arthur. [*Heinrich*]

BRUT

A British castle, built by and named after Brutus, the Greek warrior who first settled Britain. Galahad and Bors lodged a night at Brut during the Grail Quest. The lord's name was Brutus, and his daughter fell in love with Galahad. [*PostQuest*]

BRUTE GREENSHIELD

A prince who, according to Geoffrey of Monmouth, succeeded his father King Ebraucus to the British throne in the eleventh century BC. Brute was succeeded by his son Leil. [*GeoffHR*]

BRUTO [Brito]

Hero of Anthony Pucci's *Bruto di Brettagna*, derived from an episode in Andreas Capellanus's *De Amore*. To win the love of a lady, Brito had to retrieve a hawk, two brachets, and a scroll with the "rules of love" from Arthur's court. After solving several related quests, he fought a duel at Arthur's court for the objects, winning because his lady was the most beautiful. [*PucciB*]

BRUTUS[1] [Britto, Brute]

A Roman consul mentioned by Nennius and Geoffrey of Monmouth. He was a descendant of Aeneas and the son of Silvius, who, pursuant to a prophecy, Brutus accidentally killed with an arrow. For this act, he was driven from Italy. He took his followers to Britain, then called Albion, and he conquered the island from a race of giants. Albion was rechristened Britain in honor of Brutus, and in a similar manner, Brutus's three sons—Camber, Locrine, and Albanact—gave their names to Cambria (Wales), Logres (England), and Albany (Scotland). Since Brutus was said to be Britain's first king, a number of chronicles have *Brut* in their titles (e.g., Wace's *Roman de Brut*). [*Nennius, GeoffHR, Dryden*]

BRUTUS[2]

A descendant of the first Brutus and king of the castle Brut. He was a noble and wealthy lord with many possessions, and one of the most beautiful daughters in Britain. This maiden fell in love with Galahad when he and Bors were lodging at Brut during the Grail Quest. When Galahad rebuffed her advances, she killed herself with his sword. Brutus accused the two knights of murdering her, but after he was defeated in single combat with Bors, he accepted their explanation and made peace. [*PostQuest*]

BRYCHAN

The King of Brecknock in Welsh tales. He might have been a historical figure. The Triads mention him as the father of Urien's mother Nefyn, and as one of the "three saintly lineages of the Island of Britain." In the life of Saint Cadoc, his wife Gwladys is abducted by King Gwynnlyw of Glamorganshire, and she is later lusted after by Arthur. [*Triads, SaintsCad*]

BRYS ("Haste")

A warrior in Arthur's service who was the son of Brysethach. He came from the valley of the black fernery in Scotland. [*Culhwch*]

BRYSETHACH

Father of Arthur's warrior Brys. [*Culhwch*]

BUCIFILASO

A plain surrounding the castle of Lerlinte in North Wales. It was famed as the site where Lancelot and Tristan fought

each other during the war between Kings Alois and Amoroldo. [*Tavola*]

BUDEC [Biducus, Budicius, Budes, Budiz, Dubricius, Pudentius]

The king of Brittany who received Uther and Ambrosius—as children—when they fled Britain in fear of Vortigern. Budec sheltered them in his realm until they had come of age and were ready to retake Britain from Vortigern. Budec's son, Hoel, ruled after him. An actual king named Budic ruled Cornouaille in the early sixth century, about a century later than the time period described by Geoffrey. [*GeoffHR, Wace, Layamon*]

BUELT

A region of South Wales now called Builth. Nennius cites it as one of the wonders associated with Arthur: while Arthur was hunting the boar Troynt in the country, his dog, Cabal, left his footprint on a stone. Arthur piled a heap of stones there as a monument to the event. If any stone was removed and carried away, it would vanish and reappear on the mound the next day. [*Nennius*]

BUEVES

A king who was the brother of Guengasoain, a knight defeated by Gawain. [*Vengeance*]

BUFLOUT

An Arthurian knight found exclusively in the romance of *Yder*. He participated in Arthur's war against Taulas of Rougemont. [*Yder*]

BUHOUT

An Arthurian knight found exclusively in the romance of *Yder*, though he may be a variation of BORS. He participated in Arthur's war against Taulas of Rougemont. [*Yder*]

BUJAN

A city in Ireland where King Lanves, Isolde's father, held his court. [*Povest*]

BUN ("Maiden")

Isolde's sister, according to a Welsh Triad. Their father was named Culfanawyd. She was apparently no more faithful to her husband, Fflamddwyn, than Isolde was to Mark. [*Triads*]

BURGUNDY [Borgoine, Burgoigne, Burgon]

A region of southeast France. In Wace, it is part of Arthur's empire, and is ruled by Ligier (Leodegan). In Layamon, after Arthur wins the war against Lucius, he establishes his European capital in Burgundy. From here, Arthur plans to launch his attack on Rome, but he has to depart the area when he hears of Mordred's treachery. Lucius, according to Malory, pillaged and burned areas of

Burgundy in the war. According to one medieval source, Burgundy was the birthplace of Guinevere. In the Welsh tale of *Geraint*, the father of Arthur's warrior Ondyaw is called the duke of Burgundy. In the Vulgate *Merlin*, Dionas, the Lady of the Lake's father, is a vassal of the duke of Burgundy. [*Wace*, *Layamon*, *VulgMer*, *Geraint*, *Awntyrs*, *ProsMer2*, *Malory*]

BURLETTA OF THE DESERT [*Burlette Della Diserta*]

A knight who fell in love with Gaia Pulcella, the daughter of Morgan le Fay, and kidnapped her from the Castle Paulas. Lancelot came across Burletta trying to rape the maiden and rescued her. Burletta set out to avenge this disgrace, but ran across Tristan before he found Lancelot. Tristan defeated him in combat and ordered him to go to Camelot and to surrender to Lancelot. Rather than surrender to his enemy, Burletta threw himself in a river and drowned. [*Tavola*]

BURLOW-BEANIE

A seven-headed monster owned by King Cornwall in the English ballad "King Arthur and King Cornwall." After breaking all his weapons on it, Arthur's Sir Bredbeddle managed to subdue and tame it by confronting it with a Bible. Arthur and his knights could then conjure and employ it at will. It delivered to them Cornwall's magic artifacts—a wand, horse, horn, and sword, the last of which Arthur used to behead the king. [*KingA&C*]

BURMALT

A figure appearing on the Modena Archivolt frieze. In the context of the carving, it appears that Burmalt serves Mardoc of the Dolorous Tower, and that he is guarding one of the bridges leading into Mardoc's fortress. Mardoc has kidnapped Guinevere, and Burmalt is holding the bridge against Arthur and his knights. Meanwhile, however, Gawain is crossing the other bridge and effecting a rescue. Richard Barber (*King*, 31) thought Burmalt identical to DURMART of French romance. [*Modena*]

BUROIN

The duke of the White Lake. He raised and educated Tybalt, the youth who became Lancelot's first squire. He gave lodging to Lancelot one night as he traveled to Arthur's court. [*UlrichZ*]

BUSIRANE

A sorcerer who imprisoned the maiden Amoret and tried to force her to become his lover. Britomart, the warrior maiden, learned of Amoret's plight from Scudamore, Amoret's lover. Britomart braved the enchantments of Busirane's castle, defeated him, and freed Amoret. [*Spenser*]

BUTICOSTIAUS [*Botincoutiaus*, *Boutincostiaus*]

The lord of Finecoce and one of four Irish robber knights defeated by Lancelot on his way to Rigomer castle. Lancelot sent him to Guinevere as a prisoner. [*Merveil*]

BUTOST

One of Arthur's castles. [*Raoul*]

BUZAFARNAN

A king and brother of the barbarian King Milocrates. When Milocrates's island was invaded by Roman warriors, including a young Gawain, he sent a message to Buzafarnan asking for help. Buzafarnan left immediately, but was held up by storms and arrived too late, meeting the victorious Roman fleet as it was leaving the island. Through the heroics of Gawain, Buzafarnan was killed and his ships were sunk by Greek Fire or captured. Elsewhere in the story, the same character seems to be called EGESARIUS. [*DeOrtu*]

BWLCH ("Gap")

Son of Cleddyf Cyfwlch, brother of Cyfwlch and Syfwlch, and one of Arthur's warriors. He had a sword named Glas, a dog named Call, a horse named Hwyrddyddwg, a wife named Och, a grandchild named Lluched, a daughter named Drwg, and a maid named Eheubryd. He assisted Culhwch in hunting the boar Twrch Trwyth. [*Culhwch*]

BYANNE

A lady who was served and loved by Arthur's Sir Evadeam, known as the Dwarf Knight. [*VulgMer*]

BYLAS [*Bila(ce)s*]

A Saxon warrior who joined the Saxon invasion of Britain in the early days of Arthur's reign. At the battle of Diana Bridge, Yvain slew him. [*VulgMer*, *Arthour*]

C

CABALL [*Cafall, Caval(l)*]

Arthur's hunting dog, found in Nennius and Welsh tales. Nennius claims that while Arthur and Cabal were hunting the boar Troynt in the country of Buelt, Cabal left his footprint on a stone. Arthur later built a heap of stones on the location, calling the monument *Cairn Cabal*. Nennius describes this monument as one of the wonders of Britain, saying that men often take the stone from the monument, but it always reappears there within a day.

In Welsh legend, Cabal accompanied Arthur on the hunts for the boars Ysgithyrwyn and Twrch Trwyth (which is possibly the same boar as Troynt), and killed Ysgithyrwyn himself. He was also instrumental during the hunt for a stag in the Forest of Dean. The dog's name comes from *caballus*, the Latin word for "horse." In *Culhwch and Olwen*, Cabal is also described as belonging to Arthur's warrior Syfwlch. [*Nennius, Culhwch, Geraint, TennIK*]

CABARENTIN [*Cararentis, Esbarantin*]

The good King of Cornwall in the Vulgate *Lancelot*; a vassal of Arthur. He assisted Arthur in the campaign against King Claudas of Gaul, and he led a division against Mordred at the battle of Salisbury. Presumably, he was slain there. [*VulgLanc, VulgMort*]

CABCAFLIN

A king who was the father of Arthur's knight Batewain. [*HartmannE*]

CABRION

The lady of Cabrion was a cousin of Arthur. While traveling to Arthur's court, she witnessed Gawain being kidnapped by Caradoc of the Dolorous Tower. She ordered her knights to attack, but they were defeated, and one of Caradoc's knights came after her. Fleeing into the forest, she encountered Duke Galescalain of Clarence, who successfully defended her against her pursuer. [*VulgLanc*]

CACAMWRI

One of Arthur's warriors who was the half-brother of Hygwydd. Cacamwri had an odd talent and desire for destroying barns that is not quite clear. He participated in the hunt for Twrch Trwyth and helped to trap the boar in the Severn river, but was dragged to the bottom by two millstones. He apparently survived, because he later went with Arthur's party to the cave of the Black Hag in the Valley of Distress. Cacamwri and Hygwydd were sent in first, and were both mauled, stripped, and thrown out of the cave screaming by the Black Hag. [*Culhwch*]

CADAIN

One of Arthur's nobles, listed in Biket's *Lai du Cor*. He helped stop Arthur from killing Guinevere when a magical horn betrayed a trivial infidelity. Cadain's wife was also found to be untrue by the horn. [*Biket*]

CADANT [*Chadians*]

A vassal of King Claudas, whom he served in a war against Arthur. His brothers were Canart, Alibel, and Brumand. [*VulgLanc*]

CADARN ("Strong")

Father of Arthur's warrior Nerth. [*Culhwch, Dream*]

CADBURY

In the sixteenth and seventeenth centuries, writers began to associate Camelot with a Roman hill fort near Cadbury, Somerset, possibly because of a local river called the Camel. John Leland was the first known author to do so. Michael Drayton tells us that "By south Cadbury is that Camelot; a hill of a mile compasse at the top, foure trenches circling it, and twixt every of them an earthen wall; the context of it, within, about 20 acres, full of ruines and reliques of old buildings." Folklore relates that Arthur sleeps in a cave beneath the hill, protected by golden gates which stand open only one night of the year. Another tale says that the ghosts of Arthur and his warriors ride down from the top of the hill on certain nights of the year.

Twentieth-century archaeology has demonstrated the existence of a British hill-fort on top of the hill in the late fifth century. It may have been the headquarters of a British king campaigning against the Saxons, though identifying this hypothetical person with Arthur relies, as Richard Barber pointed out (*King*, 24), on the somewhat questionable theory that Arthur was the only British military figure of note in this area in this time period.

William Camden also identified Cadbury with Cath-BREGION, the site of one of Arthur's battles against the Saxons in Nennius's account. [*Camden, Drayton*]

CADELLIN SILVER BROW

Father of one of Arthur's warriors named Gweir. The same Gweir is later named as the son of LLWCH WINDY HAND. [*Culhwch*]

CADFAN

A Welsh warrior whose death at the hands of Maelgwn is mourned by Merlin in an early Welsh poem contained in the *Black Book of Carmarthen*. [*Myrddin*]

CADGYFFRO ("Battle Tumult")

Father of Arthur's warrior Gilbert. [*Dream*]

CADIOLANT [*Cadoalant, Cadoalens*]

A king of Ireland who served Arthur, present at Arthur's court in Cardigan. He fought at one of the Castle of Maidens tournaments and opposed King Ris in another tournament. [*ChretienE, Contin1*]

CADOC¹

A Welsh "saint," whose life contains an Arthurian episode: Cadoc's father, Gwynnlyw, was harbored by Arthur when he kidnapped the lady Gwladys from her husband. Years later, Cadoc, the Abbot of Llancarfan, harbored a fugitive named Ligessauc who had killed three of Arthur's knights. After seven years, Cadoc was finally able to make Arthur accept a payment of 100 cows for the lives of the three knights. Arthur agreed, but demanded that every cow had to be half-red and half-white. Cadoc, through holy means, transformed the cows into such colors, but the cows later turned into ferns. Arthur, humbled through the experience, named the location Ferntown. A Welsh Triad names Cadoc as one of the three "Just Knights" of Arthur's court, where Cadoc endeavored to uphold the law of the church. [*SaintsCad*]

CADOC²

A knight from Carlisle or Tabriol saved by Erec. Cadoc was kidnapped and tortured by a couple of giants. Erec, on his adventures with Enide, heard Cadoc's lady screaming, and rode to the rescue. Erec defeated the giants, and returned Cadoc to his paramour. Cadoc traveled to Arthur's court and related the episode to Arthur's company. He is called KALVIEL in the Norse *Erex Saga*. [*ChretienE*]

CADOC³

A king who fought in a Castle of Maidens tournament, where he was defeated by Gawain's son Guinglain. [*Renaut*]

CADOR¹ [*Cadwr*]

Ruler of Cornwall and father of Constantine. Geoffrey of Monmouth tells us that Cador was of Roman stock but does not name is father. A Welsh translation of Geoffry makes him the son of Gorlois, Igerne's first husband, and in *Geraint*, his father is called Gwryon. He married a sister or half-sister of Arthur. According to Geoffrey, Guinevere was raised in his household (from which Thomas Hughes seems to assume that he was Guinevere's father). The chronicler John Hardyng makes him the son of Igerne, and therefore Arthur's half-brother.

Cador assisted Arthur in the battles against the Saxons, and killed the Saxon leader Cheldric at the Isle of Thanet. He assisted in the battle against the Scots at Lake Lomond, and later helped Arthur in the campaigns against Gaul and Rome. After the first battle of the war, Cador escorted the prisoners captured to the prison in Paris. The Emperor's men lay in ambush to capture the prisoners, but Cador and Lancelot, with their knights, slew them all. As the commander of the rear guard at the battle of Soissons, Cador helped Arthur to finally defeat Lucius. He was killed fighting Mordred's army at Camlann, and his son inherited Arthur's throne. [*GeoffHR, Layamon, Dream, Geraint, Allit, Malory, HughesT*]

CADOR²

Brother of Guignier, the maiden who married Arthur's Sir Caradoc. He was wounded when a knight named Alardin abducted his sister, and became friends with Caradoc when the latter rescued her. He accompanied Caradoc to Arthur's court and married Ydain, one of the ladies there. [*Contin1*]

CADOR³

A ruler of Northumberland who organized a tournament at Banborc to find a husband for his daughter, Andrivete. When he died, his brother, Ayglin, tried to marry the maiden to a commoner, but Kay saved and wed her. [*Girart*]

CADOVAIN

An Arthurian knight. [*Merveil*]

CADRET

Son of King Aguiflet of Scotland, brother of Cuoi, and a powerful knight. He was present at the wedding of Erec and Enide. He is mentioned in Chrétien's *Erec*, and his counterpart in Hartmann's *Erec* is GOASILROET. [*ChretienE*]

CADRÏEL

A knight of Arthur's court. [*Contin1*]

CADRIETH¹ ("Fair Speech") [*Caydryeith*]

A warrior of Arthur's court who was the son of Seidi. He was the brother of Alun of Dyfed and Cas. Although a young man, he was one of Arthur's most trusted advisors because of his keen intellect. A Welsh Triad tells us that he was one of the three "most courteous to guests and strangers." [*Triads, Dream*]

CADRIETH²

One of Arthur's squires. His father was named Gandwy. Cadrieth held the position of chamberlain and guarded the king's bed. [*Geraint*]

CADWAIN OF CARMURAIN [*Cadowain of Caermurzin, Karadoains*]

A knight freed from the prison of Sir Brandin of the Isles by Lancelot. He later joined Gawain on a quest to locate Lancelot. He may be identical to CARDROAIN of the verse romances. [*LancLac, VulgLanc*]

CADWAL [Cadual]

In Reginald Heber's *Morte D'Arthur*, Guinevere pines over her first love—a forest boy named Cadwal she met during her youth in Derwent. It eventually is revealed that Cadwal was actually LANCELOT in disguise. [*HeberMD*]

CADWALLO LONGHAND [Cadwallo Lewirh, Cadwell, Cadwathlan, Cadual]

A king who Geoffrey of Monmouth names as the ruler of the Venedotians (North Welsh) under Arthur. According to historian John Morris (*Age*, 125), an historical Catwallaun Longhand drove the Irish out of Anglesey in 500. His son was named Maelgwn. [*GeoffHR*]

CADWY [Cado, Cadway, Cato]

Son of Geraint, father of Berth, and one of Arthur's warriors in Welsh legend. In the *Life of St. Carannog*, he is Arthur's contemporary and perhaps his superior, ruling the castle of Dunster. He may be identical to CADOR. [*Culhwch*, *SaintsCar*, *Dream*]

CAE HIR

Named in a Welsh *Tristan* fragment as a man who loved Golwg Hafddydd, Isolde's handmaid. He may be a Welsh version of KAHEDINS who, in some versions of the Tristan legend, loves Brangain, Isolde's servant. [*TrisFrag*]

CÆ THE COURTEOUS

A vassal of Queen Flúrant of Ireland, Isolde's mother in the Icelandic *Saga af Tristram ok Ísodd*. He tried to claim credit from a dragon that Tristan slew on Sukstía mountain, which would have allowed him to marry Isolde. Queen Flúrant wanted to hang him for the lie, but Tristan convinced her to simply banish him from Ireland. His character appears in Gottfried's *Tristan* as an unnamed steward. [*SagaTI*]

CAELENC [Canlang]

A Saxon king who, under Rions, invaded Carmelide in the early days of Arthur's reign. He was slain by Arthur at the battle of Carhaix. [*VulgMer*, *Arthour*]

CAELIA

Mother of the Fairy Knight by Tom a' Lincoln, Arthur's son. She was called the Fairy Queen. [*Johnson*]

CAELLUS

A city in the lands ruled by Galehaut, Arthur's enemy-turned-ally. The castle walls collapsed, foreshadowing Galehaut's coming death. [*LanDoLac*]

CAEN [Caiam, Came]

A city in northwest France. According to Laymon, it was named Chinon, but Arthur canged the name to honor

Kay, who had died in the Roman war and was buried there. [*Layamon*, *Allit*]

CAER BRYTHWCH

A city, probably in Wales, but lost to modern geographers. The only Arthurian association with the city comes in *Culhwch and Olwen*, where Arthur's chief gatekeeper, Glewlwyd, says that he was in Caer Brythwch, and possibly implies some Arthurian involvement. The larger legend to which this remark likely refers is lost to history. [*Culhwch*]

CAER DATHAL

Home of Arthur's warriors Teregud, Caradawg, Sulyen, Bradwen, Moren, and Siawn—all sons of Iaen. [*Culhwch*]

CAER FANDDWY

An alternate name for ANNWN, the Celtic otherworld. The meaning of *fanddwy* is unknown. [*Spoils*]

CAER FEDDWID ("Fortress of Carousal")

A nickname for ANNWN, the Celtic otherworld. [*Spoils*]

CAER GOLUDD

An alternate name for ANNWN, the Welsh otherworld. K. Jackson (Loomis, *Romance*, 16) suggests "Inward City" as a translation. [*Spoils*]

CAER GREU

In Welsh oral tradition, Peredur and Gwrgi were killed fighting Eda Great-Knee at Caer Greu, after their warriors abandoned them. The name may be a variation of *Caer Creu*, meaning "city of blood." [*Triads*]

CAER NEFENHYR NINE-TEETH

A British city, once inhabited or visited by Arthur's chief gatekeeper Glewlwyd. [*Culhwch*]

CAER OCHREN

An alternate name for ANNWN, the Celtic otherworld. [*Spoils*]

CAER OETH

A city probably in Wales. Welsh oral tradition had it that Arthur was imprisoned in Caer Oeth for three days by Gwen Pendragon before he was transferred to another prison. [*Triads*]

CAER PEDRYFRAN

A nickname for ANNWN, the Celtic otherworld. It may signify a four-cornered fortress. [*Spoils*]

CAER RIGOR

Another name for ANNWN, the Celtic otherworld. [*Spoils*]

CAER SE

A British city, once inhabited or visited by Arthur's chief gatekeeper Glewlwyd. [*Culhwch*]

CAER SEINT

The Welsh name for the Roman fort of SEGONTIUM.

CAER SIDDI ("Fairy Fortress")

A nickname for ANNWN, the Celtic otherworld, as told by the Welsh poem *The Spoils of Annwn* and a non-Arthurian poem in the Book of Taliesin. [*Spoils*]

CAER WYDR ("Fortress of Glass")

An alternate name for ANNWN, the Welsh otherworld. [*Spoils*]

CAERGAI

A location on the river Dee in Merioneth, Wales, where Kay was said to have lived (Ashe, *Quest*, 192).

CAERLEON [*Caer Llion, Ca(e)rlion, Carlioun, Ca(y)rlyon, Karlion, Karliun, Kerlioun*]

A town on the River Usk in south Wales. In the chronicles, it is one of the key cities of Arthur's realm. The remains of a Roman fortress and ampitheater at the site demonstrates some importance in Roman and post-Roman times. Locals call the ampitheater the "Round Table." According to Geoffrey of Monmouth, Arthur was crowned king in Caerleon by the Archbishop Dubricius. Geoffrey, who sometimes calls it the "City of Legions," suggests that it was the greatest city in Arthur's realm. In the Vulgate *Merlin*, Arthur's coronation at Caerleon is interrupted by a rebellion, and a battle is subsequently fought and won by Arthur outside the city. A number of other texts, including several Welsh stories, name Caerleon as Arthur's main court, at least until the founding of Camelot.

The Arcbishopric of Caerleon passed from Tremonus, during the reign of Ambrosius, to Dubricius, and then to David. It was also the home of Arthur's fool, Sir Dagonet. [*Culhwch, GeoffHR, VulgMer, Owain, Peredur, Malory*]

CAERLIUDCOIT [*Lindocolinum*]

A city in the country of Lincoln in northern Britain, where Arthur fought a battle against the Saxons under Colgrim. [*GeoffHR*]

CAERNARFON

A city and bay in Gwynedd, North Wales. It lies near Snowdon, and was the site of the Roman fort SEGONTIUM.

CAHORS

A section of Arthur's kingdom ruled by Baron Maurice. [*GeoffHR*]

CAHOT THE RED

Brother of the Red Knight that Perceval killed as a youth. In revenge for his brother's death, Cahot joined the Lord of the Fens in waging a war against Perceval's mother, Yglais, and her castle of Kamaalot. By coincidence, Perceval wandered into Cahot's castle, the Key of Wales, looking for a night's lodging. Cahot recognized him, and Perceval ended up slaying him in battle. [*Perlesvaus*]

CAHUS

One of Arthur's squires in *Perlesvaus*. He was the son of Yvain the Bastard. Arthur announced that he was going to take Cahus on a pilgrimage to the chapel of St. Augustine in the White Forest. On the night before the scheduled journey, Cahus had a dream that he visited a shrine near the chapel, took a golden candle, and was stabbed in the side by a Black Knight. He awoke in Arthur's castle and found to his astonishment that he was holding a golden candle, and had a dagger stuck in his side. He perished of the wound after presenting the candle to his king. A similar story is related about an unnamed attendant of Arthur's in John of Glastonbury's chronicle. [*Perlesvaus*]

CAIAPHAS [*Caiphas, C(h)aÿphas, Chaifas, Chayphas*]

In the Book of Matthew, the high priest of Jerusalem who tried and condemned Jesus, and handed him over to Pilate. In the Grail histories, Caiaphas imprisons Joseph of Arimathea after Joseph entombs the body of Christ. He stuck Joseph in the bottom of a dark well and ordered that he be given nothing to eat or drink. He was therefore astonished when, 42 years later, the Roman Emperor Vespasian delivered Joseph from the prison looking as youthful as the day he was put in (Joseph had been sustained by the Grail). Vespasian tried Caiaphas for his crime, and then set him adrift at sea in a rowboat, with no food or water. God kept him alive, in ravenous hunger and thirst, and he was later met by Galahad, Bors, and Perceval during the Grail Quest. Two sixteenth-century versions of Joseph's life give Caiaphas a confederate named ANNAS. [*RobertBorJ, VulgEst, PostQuest, HereJoA*]

CAICHESTER [*Kaicester*]

A British city ruled in Arthur's time by Cursalem. [*GeoffHR*]

CAIRO

In Malory, this Egyptian city is allied to Lucius, Arthur's enemy in the Roman War. [*Malory*]

CALABRIA [*Kalabrois*]

In the romance of *Yder*, Calabria is named as one of Arthur's courts. Malory gives it as a country allied to Lucius the Roman. The latter reference probably indicates a region of southern Italy. [*Yder, Malory*]

CALAFES [*Kalafes*]

King of the Strange Land (including the city of Malta) in the time of Joseph of Arimathea. He suffered from leprosy, but was cured by the Holy Grail, brought to his kingdom by Alan the Large and his brother Joshua. He converted to Christianity and took the name ALPHASAN. He gave his daughter and lands to Joshua, and he helped Alan and Joshua build the Grail Castle of Corbenic. He was wounded by a holy lance after impiously sleeping in the palace which contained the Grail. He died the next day. [*VulgEst*]

CALAMINE VALLEY [*Galamine*]

A lush Middle-Eastern valley near the castle Hemelian. It was abundant with nard, cinnamon, and balsam. Flegetine traveled through it while seeking her husband, Nascien. [*VulgEst*]

CALCAS [*Kallas*]

Son of Caw, one of twenty brothers, and a one of Arthur's knights. He appears in the Welsh tale of *Culhwch* and the Vulgate *Lancelot*. He performed well in a tournament thrown by King Brandegorre of Estrangorre, and he swore fealty to Brandegorre's daughter. [*Culhwch, VulgLanc*]

CALCYDON [*Calcidoine*]

A Mediterranean kingdom. Its lords were ancestors of King Rions of Ireland, an enemy of Arthur. One of its princes, Tydeus, owned a sword which had belonged to Hercules and was later passed on to Rions. [*VulgMer*]

CALEDFWLCH

Arthur's sword in Welsh legend, analogous to EXCALIBUR, with which it shares the same root. Scholars have identified it with *Caladbolg* ("hard lightning"), the enchanted sword belonging to Cuchulainn in Irish mythology. [*Culhwch*]

CALEDON [*Aledon, Caledonia, Calidoine, Calydon, Celidon, Celyddon, Cylyddon*]

A forest covering northern England and southern Scotland, around the area of Dumfries, Carlisle, and the river Tweed. In Nennius, it is the site of Arthur's seventh victorious battle against the Saxons (see ARTHUR'S BATTLES). This seems rather far north for a fight against the Saxons, and some scholars have conjectured that, if the battle really took place, Arthur was fighting Picts allied to the Saxons rather than the Saxons themselves. Geoffrey names the Saxon leader as Colgrim. Welsh legend has the region ruled by Cilydd. Merlin (and Lailoken) was said to have roamed through Caledon like a wild man after he had gone mad at the battle of Arfderydd. In the Vulgate *Estoire del Saint Graal*, we learn that it was the haunt of the fearsome Papagustes serpent. INGLEWOOD, which seves as the setting of several Middle English poems, was one of the forests in the Caledonian region. [*Nennius, Culhwch, GeoffHR, TennIK*]

CALENDIN THE YOUNGER

A Knight of the Round Table who embarked on the Grail Quest. [*PostQuest*]

CALEPH [*Kaleph*]

A castle in Wales belonging to Duke Ganor, the first British ruler converted to Christianity by Joseph of Arimathea's followers. It was the site of a battle between Ganor and his former overlord, the King of Northumberland. [*VulgEst*]

CALEQUE [*Kalec*]

A castle in Britain ruled by Count Dangis. Fleeing Arthur's court for Joyous Guard, Lancelot and Guinevere lodged at Caleque for one night. Count Dangis, a friend of Lancelot, promised to support Lancelot in his struggle against Arthur, and he placed Caleque at Lancelot's disposal. [*VulgMort, PostMort*]

CALFAUDIN

A Saxon knight killed by Meleagant after Calfaudin issued a challenge to any Briton knight. Calfaudin had hoped to prove his honor in order to marry the daughter of the king of Saxony. [*Prophecies*]

CALFLE

A town on the coast of Wales, to which Perceval's mother fled after the death of her husband, Bliocadran. After organizing her affairs, she left Calfle for the forest, where she raised Perceval in seclusion. [*Bliocadran*]

CALIBURN

The original form of EXCALIBUR, given by Geoffrey of Monmouth. [*GeoffHR*]

CALIDORE

Champion of courtesy, assigned by Gloriana, the Fairy Queen, to capture the Blatant Beast. After a number of adventures, he became fascinated with the life of shepherds and digressed fom his quest to become one of them. He fell in love with the shepherdess Pastorella. When she was abducted by pirates, Calidore rescued her, and discovered along the way that she was a princess. He eventually returned to his quest and captured the Blatant Beast after a struggle. [*Spenser*]

CALIDUS

A Roman soldier who fought in the war against Arthur. Mentioned in the Vulgate *Merlin*, he occurs in the same location as "Catellus VULTEIUS" in Wace's version. [*VulgMer*]

CALIGANTE THE POOR

A Knight of the Round Table who died during the Grail Quest. His brothers, Delimaz the Poor and Asalim the Poor, were also of the Round Table. [*PostQuest*]

CALISTRA

Pagan queen of the realm of Femminoro, seat of all lechery. Five of her descendants—Medeas, Lavina, Agnena, Bresenda, Pulizena—inhabited the castle Crudele and clashed with Tristan. [*Tavola*]

CALIXTES

A hermit who lived in the White Forest, near the chapel of St. Augustine. A murderer and robber most of his life, Calixtes repented at the end and spent his last five years as a holy man. Upon his death, Arthur witnessed a battle in which angels triumphed over devils for the man's soul. [*Perlesvaus*]

CALL ("Wise")

The dog belonging to King Arthur's warrior Bwlch. [*Culhwch*]

CALLES [*Kallés*]

A wealthy duke whose six sons led a revolt against him because they feared that Calles intended to disinherit them. Calles' nephews allied with their uncle, as did Gaheris, Gareth, and Agravain. With their help, Calles almost prevailed, but Lancelot and Lionel, who had been deceived by the Maiden of Many Years and Calles' sons, allied with the sons. Calles was slain by Lancelot. [*VulgLanc*]

CALLIC

Archbishop of Everwic. Arthur summoned him to marry Sir Yder to Queen Guenloie. [*Yder*]

CALLYBURNE

A knight in the service of Lucius the Roman in Malory's *Le Morte Darthur*. He was known as one of the strongest men in Pavia. During the first battle of the Roman War, Callyburne slew many of Arthur's men but was killed by Sir Bors. In the Alliterative *Morte Arthure*, Malory's source, Callyburne appears as an unnamed "paynim of Perse." [*Malory*]

CALOBRUS

Cousin of Perceval and son of Calobrutus. He was captured by Gohart of the Castle of the Whale, chained to a rock, and left to starve. He was sustained by the daughter of the Sick King until Perceval found him and freed him. After Perceval captured Gohart, Calobrus chained his former captive to the same rock and likewise left him to die. [*Perlesvaus*]

CALOBRUTUS

One of Perceval's eleven paternal uncles in *Perlesvaus*. He was the seventh son of Gais the Large, the brother of Alain, and the father of Calobrus. [*Perlesvaus*]

CALOGRENANT [*Calogreuand, Colgreva(u)nce, Kalebrant, Kalocreant, Kalogrenant, Kalogreuant, Kalogrian*]

A Knight of the Round Table from Gorre, introduced by Chrétien de Troyes. In two versions of the Yvain story, Calogrenant's tale of an enchanted fountain in Broceliande prompts Yvain to seek the adventure. His counterpart in Welsh legend, in this respect, is CYNON. In Heinrich von dem Türlin's *Diu Crône*, Calogrenant is present at the Grail Castle when Gawain concludes the Grail Quest, but an enchantment puts him to sleep before he can witness the marvels of the Grail.

According to the Vulgate romances, he joined Arthur's company in the early days of the king's reign, fighting against the Saxons at Carhaix and Aneblayse, and against the rebellious kings at the battle of Bedegraine. He appears as a stock character in other places.

During the Grail Quest, he came to a chapel and found Lionel about to murder Bors. In defense of Bors, Calogrenant dueled with Lionel (Bors was praying and refused to fight) and was eventually killed. He prayed just before Lionel struck the killing blow and achieved holy absolution. When Lionel decapitated him, his blood flowed milky white, spilled on the ground, and caused enchanted flowers to grow perennially in that spot. A hermitage at the location was later named after him.

Malory also recounts his death at the hands of Lionel but later, confusingly, reports that Calogrenant was present at the healing of Sir Urry. Malory gives him a second death outside the chamber of Queen Guinevere, where he was slain by Lancelot after joining Mordred's plan to expose Guinevere's infidelity.

R. S. Loomis (*Tradition*, 273) thought that he was a duplicate of KAY, his name deriving from *Kai lo Grenant* ("Kay the Grumbler"). [*ChretienY, ChretienL, Heinrich, VulgLanc, VulgQuest, VulgMer, Contin3, PostQuest, Ywain, Malory*]

CALOISE

A forest near Corbenic through which Galahad and Perceval's sister rode during the Grail Quest. [*PostQuest*]

CALON

The King of Sicily in *Claris et Laris*. He joined Emperor Thereus of Rome's war against Arthur and was killed in battle against Arthur's knights. [*Claris*]

CALUFER

A Saxon king who joined King Rions' war against Arthur. He fought at the battle of Aneblayse, where King Ban of Benoic slew him. [*VulgMer, Arthour*]

CAM

A name meaning "crooked," borne by a number of rivers in Britain, including one near Cadbury Castle in Somerset. This Cam has been suggested as the site of CAMLANN,

Arthur's final battle. Excavation has revealed signs of a battle at the site. [*Topography*]

CAMALIS [*Camaalis*]

King of Camelot in the time of Joseph of Arimathea, according to the Post-Vulgate *Queste del Saint Graal*. He battled the Christians (led by Mordrain and Nascien) when they arrived in his kingdom and, defeating them, imprisoned them in the Giant's Tower. He then offered to settle the dispute in single combat with Nascien, who had been wounded in the first battle. Nascien was magically healed before the duel, however, and was able to defeat Camalis. Camalis and his kingdom then converted to Christianity. In the Vulgate *Estoire del Saint Graal*, ARGESTES is the early king of Camelot. [*PostQuest, ProsTris*]

CAMANDANS

A king of North Wales who was in King Arthur's service. [*Contin1*]

CAMBENIC [*Ambenic, Cambernic, Canbernic, Candebenet*]

A duchy in northern Britain, described in the thirteenth-century *Lancelot do Lac* as bordering on the kingdoms of North Wales and Estrangorre, although its location is nonetheless mysterious. It contained the city of Clarence. There is perhaps a confusion with Cambria, the medieval name for Wales, or Cumbria, a kingdom bordering on Wales and Scotland. Ruled by Duke Escant during the early days of King Arthur's reign, Cambenic was one of the countries in rebellion against Arthur. It was soon invaded by Saxons, and was the site of an epic battle in which Gawain and his father and brothers showed extraordinary prowess. The Saxons were eventually repelled, and Cambenic made peace with Arthur. Later, Cambenic went to war with its neighbor, North Wales. It may be the origin of the country KANADIC in German literature. [*LanDoLac, VulgLanc, VulgMer, Arthour, Malory*]

CAMBER

Son of Brutus, first king of Britain, and brother of Albanact and Locrine. According to Geoffrey of Monmouth, he gave his name to Cambria, or Wales. [*GeoffHR, Wace, Palamedes*]

CAMBRIA

A medieval name for WALES. Geoffrey of Monmouth traces its etymology to the fictional Camber, son of King Brutus. [*GeoffHR*]

CAMBYNES

An English duke who fought in the tournament at Sorelois. It is probably Malory's mistake for the duke of CAMBENIC. [*Malory*]

CAMEL[1]

A river in Cornwall. It begins in Bodmin Moor and empties into the sea near the town of Padstow. It is given by Geoffrey of Monmouth as the actual location of CAMLANN, where Arthur fought his final battle against Mordred. Constantine and Arthur were the only survivors. Constantine became king of Britain while Arthur was taken to Avalon by Morgan le Fay. Near its source is a town named Camelford, which Layamon specifies as the location of the final battle. Local legend places the battle at Slaughter Bridge, about one mile from Camelford. John Leland says that Arthur and Mordred clashed on the bridge and killed each other. [*GeoffHR, Wace, Layamon*]

CAMEL[2]

A knight from Northumberland. He loved Princess Hermondine of Scotland, but she was hesitant to marry him because of his disconcerting sleepwalking habit. He was eventually slain by Arthur's Sir Meliador, one of Hermondine's other suitors. [*Froissart*]

CAMELFORD

A town on the river CAMEL in Cornwall, named by Layamon as the site of Arthur's final battle against Mordred. This event is called CAMLANN in early Welsh tradition. Layamon erroneously thought that the town was on the River Tamar. It has been suggested as the site of CAMELOT. [*Layamon*]

CAMELON

A location near Falkirk in central Scotland, offered as the site of CAMLANN by proponents of Arthur as a northern hero.

CAMELOT[1] [*Camalahot, Camalat, Camallate, Camalot, Camelotto, Camilot, Damolot, Kama(h)alot, Schamilot*]

The famous court and capital of King Arthur, common in the vernacular due to the Lerner and Lowe play bearing its name, appears first (but only once) in Chrétien de Troyes. In most Arthurian tales, it competes with CAERLEON, CARLISLE, CARDUEIL, and LOGRES for the position of Arthur's chief city.

From the Vulgate *Estoire del Saint Graal*, we learn that an evil pagan king named Agrestes ruled the city in the time of Joseph of Arimathea. He slaughtered many of Joseph's followers at the Black Cross before God drove him mad. The Post-Vulgate *Queste del Saint Graal* provides us with different biblical era king named Camalis, after whom Camelot was named. Following these examples, Tennyson agrees that the city was ancient and was not established by Arthur, in contrast to popular tradition.

In Arthur's time, Camelot served as the location for many tournaments, one of Gawain's battles against the Saxons, and many other adventures. It's main church, St. Stephen's, held the remains of Arthur's greatest warriors.

According to the Post-Vulgate *Mort Artu*, King Mark of Cornwall besieged Camelot during the Grail Quest and, after Arthur's death, returned to destroy it completely. In *La Tavola Ritonda*, it falls to ruin after Arthur's death.

Camelot may be a variation of *Camulodunum*, the Roman name for Colchester. The castle also may have taken its name from any number of rivers with the root *cam*, meaning "crooked," which was probably the source of CAMLANN. Descriptions of its location vary. *Palamedes* places it on the Humber River, and Malory identifies it with WINCHESTER, while writers of the sixteenth and seventeenth centuries began to associate Camelot with an old Roman hill fort south of CADBURY. CAMELFORD in Cornwall and CAMELON in Scotland have also been suggested. In recent years, archaeological investigations into the Cadbury fort have shown that it was occupied by Britons in the late fifth century. Given that Camelot is a place of romance and fantasy, however, any investigation into the location of the "real" Camelot is probably futile. [*ChretienL, Wolfram, Perlesvaus, VulgQuest, VulgLanc, VulgEst, PostMer, PostQuest, PostMort, Tavola, Malory, Camden, Drayton, TennIK*]

CAMELOT² [*Kamaalot*]

A valley and castle ruled by Perceval's father, Alain le Gros, in *Perlesvaus*. The author of *Perlesvaus* clearly makes a distinction between Perceval's Camelot and Arthur's Camelot. After Alain's death, the castle fell to his widow, Yglais. It was attacked by Cahot the Red and the Lord of the Fens, but these knights were eventually slain by Perceval. [*Perlesvaus*]

CAMENGUES [*Camugnes*]

A castle or country in or near Britain. It's lord fought against the Saxon invasion in the early days of Arthur's reign. [*VulgMer*]

CAMILLE¹

The daughter of the pagan British king Orcant of Orkney. She found Peter, a follower of Joseph of Arimathea, wounded near her father's castle. Taking pity on him, she arranged for a Christian in her father's prison to be released long enough to heal Peter. Peter later championed her father against King Luce; his victory secured Orcant and Camille's conversion to Christianity. Camille and Peter married and had a son named Herlan. Gawain was one of their descendants. [*VulgEst*]

CAMILLE²

A Saxon sorceress. See GAMILLE.

CAMILLE³

One of Isolde's maidservants. [*ProsTris*]

CAMILLE⁴ WITH THE WHITE THROAT

In Heinrich von dem Türlin's *Diu Crône*, a lady at Arthur's court who failed a chastity test. [*Heinrich*]

CAMILYARD

Malory's variation of CARMELIDE, Leodegan's kingdom. [*Malory*]

CAMLANN [*Cambala, Camball, Camblan, Cambul(a), Camel, Camelford, Camlan, Kamblan, Kemelen*]

The site of the final battle between Arthur and Mordred, where Mordred was killed and Arthur mortally wounded. The romances tell us that Arthur was carried from the battlefield to be healed at Avalon.

The name comes from Welsh tradition, where its extensive proliferation indicates an actual battle was probably fought at some place with that name. These bardic tales, annotated in the Triads, portray a different conception of Camlann than what we have come to accept through Geoffrey of Monmouth and Malory. One Triad mentions the warrior Alan Fyrgan, who was apparently killed there after his warriors deserted him. Another tells us that it was started when Guinevere's sister, Gwenhwyfach, struck Guinevere. A third suggests that Arthur's defeat could be attributed to the method by which he divided his battalions. Some of these Triads probably developed after the *Annales Cambriae*, in which Camlann is listed in the year 537 as the battle where "Arthur and Medraut fell." The *Annales*, unlike later tradition, do not indicate whether Arthur and Medraut (Mordred) were fighting on opposite sides.

Some of the Welsh *Mabinogion* tales discuss Camlann in more detail. *Culhwch and Olwen* tells us that nine warlords planned the battle, including Gwynn Hyfar—Arthur's seneschal of Devon and Cornwall—and that there were only three survivors: Sanddef (he was so beautiful that the warriors mistook him for an angel and refused to attack him), Morfran (he was so ugly that the warriors thought he was a devil and refused to attack him), and Cynwyl. *The Dream of Rhonabwy* informs us that the battle was caused when Arthur's messenger Iddawg delivered a peace offer from Arthur to Mordred in rude and insulting tones. This is the first mention in Welsh literature of Mordred as Arthur's opponent at Camlann, and it must have been influenced by Geoffrey of Monmouth's account. Nennius failed to pick up the story of the battle, and Geoffrey of Monmouth was consequently the first chronicler to mention it. Wace and Layamon followed this tradition, and the battle of Camlann was soon firmly rooted in Arthurian lore. According to the chronicles, Arthur returned from the Roman War to deal with Mordred's insurrection. During their final battle at Camlann, their armies obliterated each other, Arthur slew Mordred, and Mordred mortally wounded Arthur. Morgan le Fay, Arthur's sister, bore his body away to Avalon in a barge.

The location of the battle has been subject to many interpretations. Geoffrey gave the site of the final battle as the river CAMEL in Cornwall; Layamon specifies the town of CAMELFORD. A majority of scholars seems to accept this identification. Another suggestion involves the river Cam near Cadbury. Since *cam* is the Celtic word for "crooked," it is a root of a number of rivers. A possible source for the name is *Camboglanna*, meaning "crooked bank." Camboglanna belongs to a town in Rheged and has been proposed as the site of Camlann by proponents of Arthur as a northern hero. CAMELON in Scotland is another possibility.

The Vulgate *Mort Artu* substitutes SALISBURY for the location of the final battle, which Malory follows. Counterpart locations in other sources include TRENT, URBANO, the HUMBER, IRELAND, and LYONESSE.

Clearly there are many mysteries surrounding "Arthur's final battle." What does seem clear is that the battle of Camlann was a strife between two warring British factions—not between the British and the invading Anglo-Saxons. As Leslie Alcock points out (363), "[Camlann] must have greatly facilitated the Anglo-Saxon advance. Whatever political history lies concealed here, the result must have been the fragmentation of a *Britannia* united under the sovereignty of a *superbus tyrannus* into a number of small British kingdoms. Most of these disappeared in the course of the next century without leaving the least trace...." [*Culhwch, Triads, GeoffHR, Wace, Layamon, Tavola, Allit, Malory, Camden, HughesT, Boece, Drayton*]

CAMLAS

A knight in Arthur's service. [*Girart*]

CAMPADOINE

A castle ruled by Belchis, an enemy of Arthur's warrior Meraguis of Portlesguez. [*Raoul*]

CANAAN[1]

The King of Baradigan—possibly an ally or vassal of Arthur—who fought in a tournament at the Castle of Maidens. [*Renaut*]

CANAAN[2] [*C(h)anaam, Chanaan*]

One of fourteen brothers who followed Joseph of Arimathea to Britain. Canaan and his brother Simeon were shown to lack faith when they were not served, like the other followers, by the Grail. Jealous, he murdered all of his brothers except for Simeon in the middle of the night. In punishment, the Christians decided to bury him alive. Canaan repented at the last minute, and was granted his request to have his dead brothers buried around him. Later, Canaan's tomb burst into flames, and he suffered inside it for hundreds of years, until he was delivered by Lancelot. [*VulgEst*]

CANAGUES [*Tanagues*]

A knight and nephew of Sir Seguarades. He saw Gawain defeat his uncle in combat. Soon after, he attacked Gawain, but Gawain beat him senseless with his own helmet and made him surrender to the Lady of Roestoc. [*VulgLanc*]

CANAIN

A dwarf who served Felinete, a benefactress of Gawain. [*Girart*]

CANAN

Erec's grandfather. Descended from Greek peasants, Canan struggled to build a kingdom through his prowess. Eventually, he was crowned king of Saloliqui and had two children: Lac (Erec's father) and Dirac. He was poisoned by his own aides, and his young sons were carried to Britain by their tutor. [*VulgQuest*]

CANART [*Chanard*]

A powerful knight who served King Claudas. His brothers were Cadant, Alibel, and Brumand, the last of whom died in the Round Table's Perilous Seat. He fought furiously at the battle of Tower Castle, during Claudas's war with Arthur. [*VulgLanc*]

CANDACES [*Gandaries, Kandiges*]

Tristan's great-great-grandfather. He was the son of King Appollo of Lyoness and Gloriande. His father was murdered by the son of the king of Cornwall, who took Candaces in and raised him as his own. When he came of age, he married the king's daughter, Cressille, and became heir to Cornwall and Lyoness. He had twelve sons, including Crissidés and Baralis, who became the kings of Cornwall and Lyoness, respectively. [*ProsTris, Tavola, Povest*]

CANDENART [*Deriard*]

A Saxon warrior who served Kings Sornegrieu and Sapharin. He fought in the battle of Carhaix against Arthur, where he was slain by Kay. [*VulgMer, Arthour*]

CANEDAM THE THIN

A Knight of the Round Table who embarked with the others on the Grail Quest. [*PostQuest*]

CANEDOR OF THE BEAUTIFUL LOVER

A Knight of the Round Table who participated in the Grail Quest. [*PostQuest*]

CANELENGRES [*Kalegras, Kanelangres*]

The surname of Tristan's father, RIVALIN, in Gottfried von Strassburg's *Tristan*, from Rivalin's capital city of Canoel. In the Norse Tristan sagas, the name is the only one given to Tristan's father. The Icelandic *Saga af Tristram ok Ísodd* says that he was the son of Patrocles and that he served King Hlöòvir of Spain. According to this latter tale, he fell in love with Blenzibly, the sister of King Mark of England, with whom he had Tristan. He returned to Spain to defend it against two invading kings named Seran and Desixtus. He won the war, but received a mortal wound. [*Gottfried, TrisSaga*]

CANET[1] OF BLAY

An Arthurian knight who participated in a quest to learn the fate of Merlin. [*VulgMer*]

CANET[2] OF OCCIRE

A knight who served Uther Pendragon. [*VulgLanc*]

CANGUIN ROCK [*Roche de Canguin, Sanguin*]

A castle in Galloway, constructed by Igerne after the death of Uther Pendragon. While Arthur and the rest of Britain thought that Igerne was dead, she was living in the castle with her daughter and granddaughter, Clarissant. Gawain visited the palace and braved the PERILOUS BED adventure found within. The comparable castle in the First Continuation of Chrétien's *Perceval* and in Wolfram's *Parzival* is known as the CASTLE OF MARVELS. Heinrich von dem Türlin calls it SALIE. [*ChretienP*]

CANHASTYR ("Hundred Holds") HUNDRED HANDS

One of King Arthur's warriors in Welsh legend who owned a special dog collar. As one of his tasks, the warrior Culhwch had to obtain this collar to hold the hound Drudwyn while hunting the boar Twrch Trwyth. [*Culhwch*]

CANODAN

Father of Brions, a Knight of the Round Table. [*ChretienE*]

CANODES

A knight who served Arthur or King Leodegan of Carmelide. He fought against the Saxons at the battle of Carhaix. [*VulgMer, Arthour*]

CANOEL

The capital city of Parmenie, homeland of Tristan. It was a port town, situated on the English Channel. Tristan's father, King Rivalin of Parmenie, took his surname (Canelengres) from it. [*Gottfried*]

CANOR[1]

A vassal of the King of a Hundred Knights. He participated in King Mark's tournament in Lancien. [*Contin4*]

CANOR[2] [*Thanor*]

A heathen king of Cornwall who appears in the tale of Tristan's ancestry. He married Chelinde, whose husband, Sador, was believed to be dead. Canor and Chelinde had a son named Cichoriades. Canor went to war with King Pelias of Lyonesse, who loved Canor's wife. Canor was eventually killed by Apollo, the son of Chelinde and Sador. [*ProsTris*]

CANTERBURY

A city in Kent, in near England's southeast coast. According to Geoffrey of Monmouth, it was founded by King Hudibras in the tenth century BC.

Formerly called *Dorobernia*, Canterbury served as Vortigern's capital and as the Christian seat during Arthur's reign (the Welsh Triads list it as one of the three archbishoprics). According to Geoffrey, Canterbury was managed by Duke Kimmarc in Arthur's time.

In the Vulgate and Post-Vulgate Cycles, and in Malory, the Archbishop of Canterbury is perhaps the chief Christian leader in Britain. The cycles tell us that the archbishop, who was related to Guinevere, threatened to excommunicate all of Logres if Arthur did not restore Guinevere as queen, following the exposé of her affair with Lancelot. Retiring to a hermitage after Arthur's death, he was joined by several former Knights of the Round Table.

The Post-Vulgate *Mort Artu* places him on the field after the battle of Salisbury, where he helped Sir Bleoberis build the Tower of the Dead. The story further relates that King Mark of Cornwall murdered him, and that he was avenged by Sir Paulas.

The Stanzaic *Morte Arthur* says that when Mordred seized the throne of Britain and besieged Queen Guinevere in the Tower of London, the archbishop met him and rebuked him for lying about Arthur's death and tormenting the poor Queen. He threatened to "curse [Mordred] with book, bell, and candle" if he did not abandon his attempts. In response, Mordred tried to kill him, and the archbishop fled to a hermitage in Glastonbury, where he received Arthur's body from Morgan, and had it buried in the churchyard. As in the Vulgate and Post-Vulgate, he was joined by several of Arthur's knights in his retirement.

In Malory, the Archbishop of Canterbury takes on a number of roles given to the Archbishop of BRICE in the Vulgate version, including summoning Britain's nobles to the sword-in-the-stone tournament, supporting Arthur's claim to the throne, and blessing the Round Table. In contrast to the archbishop's murder in the Post-Vulgate, Malory says that King Constantine, who ruled Britain after Arthur, restored the Archbishop of Canterbury to his archbishopric. [*Triads, GeoffHR, VulgLanc, VulgMort, VulgMer, PostQuest, PostMort, Stanz, Malory*]

CAP

According to Geoffrey of Monmouth, a king of Britain in the second century BC. He succeeded King Bledud and was succeeded by King Owen. [*GeoffHR*]

CAPENTRENALLE

A wasteland near Camelot. [*Tavola*]

CAPERNAUM

A city in ancient Palestine, on the sea of Galilee. In the Vulgate *Estoire del Saint Graal*, a knight from Capernaum told Emperor Titus of Rome that Titus's son, Vespasian, could be cured of his leprosy with any artifact that had been touched by Christ. Vespasian was cured, and later freed Joseph of Arimathea from prison. [*VulgEst*]

CAPOIR
According to Geoffrey of Monmouth, a king of Britain in the second century BC. He succeeded King Pir and was succeeded by his son, King Cligueill. [*GeoffHR*]

CAPPADOCIA [*Capados*]
An ancient kingdom, later a Roman province, in East Asia Minor. In the Alliterative *Morte Arthure*, it is subject to Lucius, Arthur's enemy in the Roman War. [*Allit, Malory*]

CAPUA
The capital city of the sorcerer Clinschor, an antagonist of Gawain. [*Wolfram*]

CARADAN
A Knight of the Round Table, brother of the knights Damas and Damcab, who participated in the Grail Quest. He resented Lancelot and his kin for their fame and abilities. [*PostQuest*]

CARADAWG¹ [*Caradawc, Cradawg*]
Son of Iaen, brother of Sulyen, Bradwen, Moren, Siawn, and Teregud. One of King Arthur's warriors in Welsh legend, from Caer Dathal, he was related to Arthur through Uther. The name seems to be the source of the French CARADOCs. [*Culhwch*]

CARADAWG² STRONG-ARM
Son of Llyr of the Sea, father of Cawrdaf, and Arthur's chief advisor in Welsh legend. He rode a horse named Host-Splitter. Caradawg is said to be Arthur's first cousin, but Llyr is never said to be related to Eigyr (Igerne) or Uther. He was adapted by French writers as CARADOC SHORTARM. [*Triads, Dream, Geraint*]

CARADIGAS [*Caradigain*]
A knight of Arthur's service who participated in one of Gawain's quests to locate Lancelot. [*LancLac, VulgLanc*]

CARADOC¹ [*Carados, Carahues, Carodac, Carodas, Carodoc, Carrado, Crad(d)oc(k)(e), Kar(a)dos, Karaduz, Karodas*]
The giant, evil lord of the Dolorous Tower, where he lived with his mother. Testifying as to his popularity as one of the earliest Arthurian villains, Caradoc appears in a sculpture on an archivolt of a cathedral in Modena, Italy, constructed in the early twelfth century. On the sculpture, he seems to serve a Lord Mardoc of the Dolorous Tower, and is involved in a kidnapping of Arthur's Queen Winlogee (Guinevere). He is apparently slain by Gawain during the queen's rescue.

In French romance, he is the son of Aupatris or Mitrides and the father of Karakadin. He is variously called "the Cruel," "the Great," and "the Huge." In contrast to the scene on the Modena relief, Caradoc is an autonomous lord. He imprisons dozens of good knights, including Gawain and Yvain, which prompts Arthur to declare war. Caradoc's forces held Arthur at the Wicked Pass, but Lancelot pressed through and engaged Caradoc in single combat. A lady named Floree, who Caradoc had imprisoned, handed Lancelot a magic sword during the fight, and Caradoc was slain. His brother, Tericam the Impenetrable, gave Arthur and Lancelot similar trouble. Malory tells a subdued version of Caradoc's story, naming him as a knight who Lancelot defeated after catching him in the process of kidnapping Gawain.

The name "Caradoc" enjoyed extensive proliferation throughout French Arthurian romances. The name is Welsh in origin and is represented in Welsh Arthurian literature as CARADAWG. A number of other giants or tyrants, including CARADOC THE THIRTEENTH and KAREDOS recall the character of Carados of the Dolorous Tower. [*Modena, VulgLanc, Malory*]

CARADOC²
The King of Cambria, or Wales. He conquered Ireland and married the king's daughter, by whom he had two children: Meriadoc and Orwen. As he grew old and infirm, he gradually relinquished control of his kingdom to his brother, Griffin, retaining only the ceremonial title for himself. Griffin, however, grew covetous of the throne and had Caradoc assassinated during a hunt. Meriadoc escaped to Arthur's court and later brought justice to Griffin. [*Historia*]

CARADOC³
Son of Catel and one of Arthur's warriors. [*Layamon*]

CARADOC⁴
The King of Nantes and husband of Ysave. His wife engaged in an adulterous affair with a sorcerer named Eliavrés, and gave birth to a son, accepted by Caradoc as his legitimate heir and also named Caradoc. To hide the affair, Eliavres used magic to make Caradoc believe he was making love to his wife when, in fact, he was copulating with various animals. When the younger Caradoc, having become one of Arthur's knights, exposed the affair, King Caradoc imprisoned his wife and forced Eliavres into bestiality with the same animals with which Caradoc had been tricked into sleeping. [*Contin1*]

CARADOC⁵
A knight defeated in combat by Branor the Brown after he kidnapped a maiden. [*Palamedes*]

CARADOC⁶
King of Little Britain and vassal of Lancelot in Jean D'Outremeuse's *Ly Myreur des Histors*. He joins Lancelot

in an invasion of Britain after Arthur's death. They execute Guinevere and defeat Mordred. [*Jean*]

CARADOC[7] SHORTARM [*Carados, Garedas, Karadin, Karadues*]

An Arthurian knight who first appears in Robert Biket's *Lai du Cor*, but who is known best through the *Livre de Caradoc*, an interpolation in the First Continuation of Chrétien de Troyes's *Perceval*.

Caradoc relates that Caradoc was the heir to King Caradoc of Nantes, but was actually the son of Caradoc's wife Ysave and a sorcerer named Elïavrés, with whom Ysave had an affair. He was awarded knighthood at Arthur's court and accepted a challenge from a mysterious stranger to engage in a Beheading Game: each would take a swipe at the other's head, and the one left standing would win. Caradoc went first, and chopped of his opponent's head, but the stranger carefully picked up his severed head and secured it upon his neck again. When the stranger's turn came, he refrained from decapitating Caradoc, revealing himself to be Elïavrés, Caradoc's true father.

Caradoc established a reputation as the best of Arthur's knights through a series of quests, including the rescue of the maiden Guignier from the knight Alardin. He made it a personal duty to punish his adulterous parents, locking his mother in a tower and publicly humiliating Elïavrés. In response, Elïavrés cast a spell upon Caradoc which attached a deadly snake to his arm. Guignier and her brother Cador helped him avoid death, by luring the serpent away from Caradoc to Guinger, and then killing it as it went from one host to the other (a remedy prescribed by Elïavrés after Caradoc and Cador shamed it out of him). Caradoc married Guinger, who became his faithful wife as proven by a chastity test at Arthur's court. This test forms the subject matter of Biket's romance and several later chastity test tales. Biket contends that Arthur granted Caradoc the earldom of Cirencester as a reward for his wife's fidelity.

Caradic explains that his surname, *briefbras* ("shortarm"), derived from the fact that his arm was left shortened by the serpent that for a time was attached to it. Likely, however, the writer of the story simply mistranslated *breichbras* ("strongarm"), the surname of the Welsh character CARADAWG. Another Caradoc Shortarm appears in the Vulgate Cycle as the king of Estrangorre. Other than the similarity in names, however, the characters have nothing in common. [*Biket, ChretienE, Contin1, Mottuls, MantelM, Heinrich,* Boy]

CARADOC[8] SHORTARM [*Karadan*]

The King of Estrangorre, Scotland, or Galencie who appears first in the non-cyclical *Lancelot*, and whose story is expanded by the Vulgate Cycle and by Malory. He was the father of King Aguisant of Scotland. The Vulgate *Merlin* says that he married one of Arthur's half-sisters, although in another source, he is named as Arthur's nephew and is married to Queen Catanance of Ireland. He was a Knight of the Round Table during Uther's reign, but he revolted against Arthur when the young king first came

to power. After Caradoc (with the other rebellious leaders) was defeated by Arthur at Caerleon and Bedegraine, his land was invaded by Saxons, and he had to swear fealty to Arthur in order to expel them. Later, as a Knight of the Round Table again, he fought in Arthur's wars against Rome, King Claudas, King Mark of Cornwall, Lancelot, and Mordred. At the battle of Salisbury, he joined in combat with Mordred's King Heliades, and each was mortally wounded.

Though he bears the same name (and, likely, the same etymology) as CARADOC SHORTARM of the *Livre de Caradoc*, his character shows no other similarities. [*LancLac, VulgLanc, VulgMort, VulgMer, Arthour, Malory, TennIK*]

CARADOC[9] THE THIRTEENTH [*Carados*]

A giant knight from Uther Pendragon's Old Table. He ruled the Torre Vittoriosa and hated the knights of the New Table. He defeated Lancelot, Palamedes, Galehaut, and many others, and hung their shields on his tower. Tristan, hearing of his prowess, visited his tower and conquered him after a day's combat. Caradoc gave him the Torre Vittoriosa and retired to a hermitage in Andernantes. His character was probably suggested by CARADOC of the Dolorous Tower. [*Tavola*]

CARAEL

A castle which served as the site of a tournament, which Lancelot won by defeating knights from Sorelois and the Wasteland. [*PostMort*]

CARAÉS [*Careheuls*]

One of Arthur's knights. He fought in a tournament at the Castle of Maidens. [*Renaut*]

CARAGINALE

A British wasteland where Lamorat and Drian were slain by Gawain and his brothers. [*Tavola*]

CARANGES [*Co(u)ranges, Corente(s)*]

A wealthy Scottish city which was King Angusel's capital. It was besieged by Saxons in the early days of Arthur's reign, but Angusel repelled them with the help of Kings Urien and Bagdemagus. [*VulgMer, Arthour*]

CARANNOG

One of the several Welsh "saints," connected to Arthur in his *Life*. A missionary from Cardigan, he set his holy altar adrift in the Severn river, expecting it to wash up where he was most needed. It floated to Arthur's realm in Dindraithof (the Welsh name for Dunster). Arthur seized it, promising to return it to Carannog if Carannog could drive away a serpent that was terrorizing Arthur's land in Carrum. Through spiritual means, Carannog fulfilled the promise. In the meantime, Arthur had tried to use the altar as a table, but anything he placed on top of it was thrown off. Arthur returned the altar to Carannog, at the same time awarding Carrum to the saint. Carannog then resumed his journeys and founded the town of Carrof. [*SaintsCar*]

CARATON

A noble who served Arthur. Like the other lords at Arthur's court, his wife was found to be at least somewhat unfaithful by a magical horn in Biket's *Lai du Cor*. [*Biket*]

CARAUSIUS

A king of Britain several centuries before Arthur. Nennius says that he was the fourth Roman emepror to come from Rome to Britain, and that he immediately succeeded the dead Severus.

While Bassianus held the throne in Britain, according to Geoffrey's account, Carausius convinced the Roman senate to put many ships and soldiers under his control for the purpose of defending Britain's coast. Carausius used the soldiers, however, to overthrow Bassianus and take the throne of the island for himself. Carausius's rule was tyrranical but brief: upon hearing of his betrayal, the Roman senate sent the war leader Allectus to rectify the situation. Allectus killed Carausius and assumed the kingship.

Both Nennius and Geoffrey are thinking of a late third-century Roman admiral who planned to usurp the Roman emperor Diocletian. Allectus, who murdered him, was his finance minister (Lindsay, 10). [*Nennius, GeoffHR*]

CARCELOIS[1] [*Carteloyse, Cartolius, Chartelos*]

A castle on the borderlands of Scotland. Its lord, Count Ernol, was imprisoned by his sons, who wanted to rape their sister and perform similar sinful acts. Galahad, Perceval, and Bors liberated Carcelois the Grail Quest and freed the count from prison. Ernol lived long enough to meet Galahad and die in his arms. [*VulgQuest, ProsTris, Tavola, Malory*]

CARCELOIS[2] [*Catheloys*]

A Grail King and ancestor of Pelles, Elaine, and Galahad. He was the third king of Corbenic Castle, the son of Aminadap, and the father of Manuel. [*VulgEst*]

CARCOBRA

A city in Britain, near lake Plimozœl, where Perceval's uncle Trevrizent adventured. The Burgrave of the city was generous to both Trevrizent and to Perceval's half-brother Feirefiz. [*Wolfram*]

CARDIFF [*Cardef, Caerdyv, Kardyval*]

A city in southern Wales, near Caerleon-on-Usk, named in some romances as one of Arthur's several courts. The Alliterative *Morte Arthure* and Malory mention one of Arthur's knights called the "Captain of Cardiff," who fought in the war against Rome. [*Allit, Carle, SyrGaw, Malory*]

CARDIGAN [*Caradigan, Kardigan, Karidagan*]

A city on the coast of Dyfed in Wales. In Chrétien de Troyes's romances, and in several other tales, Arthur held his court here. In the tale of *Meriadeuc*, the queen of Cardigan is named Lore. Her city was besieged and captured by King Ris of Outre-Ombre, but she eventually forced him to leave. In the *Livre d'Artus*, it is ruled by Lisanor and is besieged by Saxons during the Saxon invasion at the beginning of Arthur's reign. [*ChretienE, UlrichZ, Livre, Meriadeuc*]

CARDOAS

A knight from Lanvale; one of three who fought against Lancelot in the False Guinevere episode. Cardoas and his companions were champions of the False Guinevere, while Lancelot fought to prove the queen's innocence. Lancelot was victorious. [*VulgLanc*]

CARDOILEN OF LONDON

A good Knight of the Round Table who participated in the Grail Quest. [*PostQuest*]

CARDROAIN THE RED [*Cadeain, Cadro(v)ain, Co(r)drovain*]

A knight killed in a sparrowhawk tournament at Landoc by Arthur's Sir Durmart. Cardroain had been championing the lady Idain of Landoc at the tournament. His brother was Sir Brun of Morois. [*Durmart, Atre*]

CARDUEIL [*Cardeuyle, Cardo(e)(i)l(e), Carduel, Caridoel, Kardeuyle, Karduel, Karedol, Karido(e)l*]

One of the locations frequently named as Arthur's capital, particularly in continental literature. It is almost certainly a variation of CARLISLE in Cumberland, although Cardueil's location is often given as Wales or Brittany. It was the home of Do (Sir Girflet's father, whom Malory confusingly calls "Cardol"), Arthur's niece Lore, and Arthur's knights Asgares the Sad and Briamont. Under Arthur, Meliant administered the city. In *Arthour and Merlin*, it is the site of the first battle between Arthur and the rebelling kings—a skirmish which the Vulgate *Merlin* places at CAERLEON. In the prior *Livre d'Artus*, King Urien torches the city during the rebellion. Arthur rebuilds it, only to have the Saxon King Arrant burn the city again. According to the romance of *Yder*, it was the birthplace of Sir Yder and was outside Arthur's kingdom. [*VulgLanc, VulgMer, Livre, PleierG, Arthour*]

CARDUINO

Hero of the Italian *Cantari di Carduino*, a FAIR UNKNOWN story. After the jealous knight Aguerisse (Gareth or Gaheris) murdered Carduino's noble father, Dondinello (Dodinel), his mother raised him in a remote forest and tied to keep him from becoming a knight. Enticed by the sight of a group of knights, however, Carduino left home for Arthur's court. In subsequent adventures, he avenged his father's murder and freed a city from a sorcerer's hold. He married Beatrice, the lady of the city. The account of Carduino's youth hints of PERCEVAL's childhood, while his later adventures bear a resemblance to the story of GUINGLAIN. [*CantariC*]

CARDYCAN

A castle, possibly CARDIGAN, where Aglovale and Perceval lodged on their quest to find Lancelot. [*Malory*]

CAREMBAUS

A Knight of the Round Table who participated in the Grail Quest. [*ProsTris*]

CARENTIN

One of Arthur's knights. [*Renaut*]

CARGRILO

A knight who joined his father, Margon, in a war against the Sore Pucelle, a lady who was eventually championed by Gawain. He was capturred by the Sore Pucelle's warriors. The Sore Pucelle agreed to exchange him for a knight Margon had captured, but Margon betrayed the agreement by murdering the Sore Pucelle's knight. Enraged, the Sore Pucelle launched Cargrilo to his death with a catapult. [*Contin3*]

CARHAIX [*Camaheu, Carahaix, Carahan, Carahes, Caraheu, Caro(h)aise, Karahes*]

A city in Brittany that appears often in continental Arthurian literature. In Eilhart von Oberge's *Tristrant*, Carhaix is the city ruled by King Havelin, father of Kahedins and Isolde of the White Hands. It was besieged by Count Riole of Nantes when Havelin refused to give Isolde to Riole, but was saved by the arrival of Tristan.

In the Vulgate *Merlin*, Carhaix is a wealthy city in Carmelide (some geographic confusion here; Carmelide is supposed to be in Britain), ruled by King Leodegan (Guinevere's father). Cleodalis was Leodegan's steward of the city. It was besieged by Saxons led by King Rions of Ireland in the early days of Arthur's reign. Arthur, Merlin, King Ban of Benoic, and King Bors of Gannes joined Leodegan's forces there. A combination of the kings' prowess and Merlin's magic helped repel the Saxons. Some time later, Rions returned with greater numbers but was still unable to take the city. The second siege ended when Arthur fought Rions in single combat, and Rions was slain. *Arthour and Merlin* describes action at Carhaix which in the Vulgate *Merlin* takes place at ANEBLAYSE. In other texts, Carhaix is named as the homeland of Gaheris, or as one of Arthur's many courts. [*Eilhart, Gliglois, LancLac, VulgLanc, VulgMer, Arthour*]

CARIADOC

Steward of King Mark of Cornwall. He falsely accused Kahedins, Tristan's brother-in-law, of cowardice and was killed by Kahedins. See MARIADOC. [*Thomas*]

CARIDÉS OF ESCAVALON [*Aridés of Escabalon*]

A malevolent lord who attacked the city of Beaurepaire and besieged the lady Blacheflour, Perceval's sweetheart, within. Perceval, who had previously saved Beaurepaire from Clamadeu and Anguigerron, returned, defeated Caridés, and sent him to Arthur. Caridés eventually became a Knight of the Round Table. [*Contin3*]

CARISMAL

A Knight of the Round Table who was defeated in a tournament between the Round Table and the Queen's Knights. [*VulgMer*]

CARL OF CARLISLE

A giant, churlish (*carl* means "churl") nobleman from Carlisle, famed for his poor hospitality. He kept a bull, a boar, a bear, and a lion as pets. Gawain, Kay, and Baldwin lodged with him after becoming lost during a hunt. The Carl beat Baldwin and Kay after they insulted him. He put Gawain through several tests (including, in one version, a Beheading Game) and was ultimately impressed with his courtliness and his willingness to obey his host. He explained to Gawain that as a youth he had made a vow to test all those who lodged with him, and to kill those who failed. Gawain's nobility freed him from the vow. In reward, he gave Gawain his lovely daughter in marriage. Arthur made him the lord of Carlisle and gave him a seat at the Round Table. The Carl founded an abbey in honor of the many knights he had slain. [*SyrGaw, Carle*]

CARLISLE [*Carl(e)(i)le, Carlill*]

A city in northwest England. According to Geoffrey of Monmouth, it was named after King Leil, who ruled in the tenth century BC. Several authors suggest Carlisle as Arthur's capital, or as one of his courts. The city's original name, Luguvallum, may derive from the Celtic god Lug. In the sixth century, it was the capital of the kingdom of Rheged. Geoffrey of Monmouth names Lot, Gawain's father, as the earl of Carlisle. Continental authors probably intend Carlisle when they mention Arthur's CARDUEIL court. The CARL OF CARLISLE features in two English romances. Malory locates two pivotal events at the city: the healing of Urry and the rescue of Guinevere from the stake. In Sir Walter Scott's *The Bridal of Triermain*, Arthur offers the city to the knight who will marry his daughter, Gyneth. [*GeoffHR, Allit, Malory, Scott*]

CARMADAN [*Karmadan*]

A kind and noble knight who lodged Lancelot after the latter drank from a poisoned spring and fell deathly ill. Carmadan's sister, Amable, healed Lancelot and fell in love with him. [*VulgLanc*]

CARMADOL THE BLACK [*Carmaduc*]

One of Arthur's knights who participated in a quest to learn the fate of Merlin. [*VulgMer*]

CARMARTHEN

A city in Dyfed in Wales, on the river Tywi. It is linked to Myrddin, the prototype of Merlin in Welsh tradition, as the Welsh incarnation of the town's name was *Caer Myrddin*. It is unclear which name came first—the character or the town—but the link between the two reached Geoffrey of Monmouth, who made Carmarthen the site of the young Merlin's encounter with King Vortigern's soldiers, on a quest to find a "fatherless" child. Geoffrey also names Eli as the town provost under the king. Nennius had formerly placed the same events in ELLEDI. In Layamon, we are told that Uther Pendragon's smith, Griffin, had his forge in Carmarthen. [*Nennius, GeoffHR, Layamon*]

CARMELIDE [*Cameliard, Camelide, Camilyard, Carmalide, Carmeli(k)e, Ta(r)meli(r)de*]

The country ruled by King Leodegan (Guinevere's father). It may be a variation of CAMEL or CAMELFORD in Cornwall (Ashe, 74). Cleodalis was its seneschal. Carmelide was the home of Sir Guyanor, one of Morgan le Fay's lovers, and of Arthur's knights Puredes and Landens. Its capital was Zelegrebre. The country was invaded by Saxons led by King Rions in the early days of Arthur's reign, and its two principle cities, Aneblayse and Carhaix, were besieged. Arthur, Merlin, King Ban of Benoic, and King Bors of Gannes traveled to Carmelide and twice helped Leodegan rout the invaders; Arthur himself slew Rions. Tennyson replaces Rions' invasion with one by King Urien. [*VulgLanc, VulgMer, Livre, Arthour, Malory, TennIK*]

CARMOISIM THE GREAT

A Knight of the Round Table killed during the Grail Quest. [*PostQuest*]

CARN GWYLATHYR

An English mountain that contained the "five peaks" region, or PUMLUMON, where Arthur's warriors Cei and Bedwyr slew Dillus the Bearded. [*Culhwch*]

CARNANT [*Karnant*]

The capital and chief castle of Destrigales, from which King Lac and, later, his son Erec, ruled. It is either Carwent in South Wales (R. S. Loomis's proposal) or a conflation of *Caer Nantes* ("city of Nantes"), as Nantes takes the place of Destrigales in other Erec romances. In *Parzival*, Wolfram refers to the land itself as Carnant, and says that Duke Orilus defeated Erec in a tournament there. The nearby Well of Lac was capable of repairing the Grail Sword. [*Erec, Wolfram*]

CARNEDYR

An Arthurian warrior who was the son of Gofynyon the Old. [*Culhwch*]

CARNISY [*Carnisin*]

A castle to which maidens bore the body of a unnamed king slain by Lancelot during a forest encounter. [*VulgLanc*]

CARNWENNAN

Arthur's dagger, which he used to kill the Black Hag. [*Culhwch*]

CARODUANT

A lesser king under Arthur, present at the coronation of Erec and Enide as King and Queen of Nantes. [*ChretienE*]

CAROMAN

A powerful Saxon king who, with others, invaded northern Britain in the early days of Arthur's reign. He led a division at the battle of Estrangort. [*VulgMer*]

CARONE THE GREAT OF GRANCHOLE

According to *La Tavola Ritonda*, the first giant to come to Britain from the faraway islands. His son, Federiel, was the first ruler of Dolorous Guard, the castle conquered by Lancelot. [*Tavola*]

CARRAS

Brother of King Claudas of the Land Laid Waste in the Second Continuation of Chrétien's *Perceval*. He invaded Britain and, in turn, had his own kingdom of Recesse invaded by Arthur. He managed to arrange a reconciliation with Arthur through Gawain. [*Contin2*]

CARRICK

A region of southwest Scotland. It originally belonged to Sir Galleron, but Arthur annexed it and gave it to Gawain. Galleron arrived at a feast and challenged Gawain for ownership of the land. The fight ended in a draw, but Gawain graciously returned the country to Galleron anyway. [*Awntyrs*]

CARRUM

A province in Arthur's realm. It was terrorized by a dragon, but was saved through the assistance of Saint Carannog, to whom Arthur gave the country as a reward. [*SaintsCar*]

CART CASTLE [*Charyot*]

A castle on the border of Gorre, in which Lancelot was imprisoned by several queens, headed by Morgan le Fay. (In the Vulgate *Lancelot*, her co-conspirators are Queen Sedile and the Queen of Sorestan; in Malory, they are the Queen of North Wales, the Queen of Eastland, and the Queen of the Out Isles.) They tried to make him choose a lover from among them, but he refused and was eventually freed by one of their maidservants, who elicited from him a promise to fight for her father, King Bagdemagus, in an upcoming tournament. The castle's name commemorated

Lancelot's ride in the cart during his rescue of Guinevere, as he had passed by the castle on the way. (In Malory, however, his rescue of Guinevere occurs long after his imprisonment by Morgan.) Later, Lancelot returned to Cart Castle to save his deliverer from marriage to an evil knight. Malory says that Morgan owned the castle. [*VulgLanc, Malory*]

CARVAIN [*Karvain*]

The home of Queen Guenloie, the lady loved and married by Arthur's Sir Yder. [*Yder*]

CAS

Son of Seidi, brother of Alun and Cadrieth, and one of Arthur's warriors. [*Culhwch*]

CASAIN

One of Arthur's dukes in the Norse *Erex Saga*. He was present at the wedding of Erec and Enide. [*Erex*]

CASE

A castle five miles from Corbenic where Galahad was conceived by Lancelot and Elaine. Lancelot was drugged and led to the castle by Elaine's maidservant, who told him that Guinevere was waiting for him. [*VulgLanc, Malory*]

CASIBILANT [*Cassibilans*]

The nephew of Duke Calles and brother of Alibel, Dyonis, and Dion. His six cousins revolted against Calles, their father. Casibilant and his brothers assisted Calles in the war, in which they were joined by Agravain, Gaheris, and Gareth. [*VulgLanc*]

CASNAR

A Welsh ruler who was the father of Arthur's warrior Llara. [*Dream*]

CASSIBELAUNUS[1] [*Cassibolon*]

One of Arthur's warriors, killed while fighting Mordred's army at the battle of Camel. [*GeoffHR, Wace*]

CASSIBELAUNUS[2]

In the chronicles, the King of Britain during Julius Caesar's invasion in the first century BC. He ascended to the throne of Britain after the death of his brother, King Lud, whose sons were too young to receive the crown. Cassibelaunus was a magnanimous ruler; though he retained the throne when his nephews came of age, he invested them with lands and cities. Julius Caesar demanded Cassibelaunus's fealty and invaded when Cassibelaunus refused. Cassibelaunus enjoyed several victories against Caesar before his nephew, Duke Androgeus of London and Kent, rebelled against him and joined Caesar's forces. Caesar conquered Britain but was persuaded to leave Cassibelaunus on the throne provided the latter pay an annual tribute to Rome. Cassibelaunus

ruled for seven more years, died, and was succeeded by his other nephew, Duke Tenuantius of Cornwall.

In the *Short Metrical Chronicle*, the chronology of which is confused, Cassibelaunus is succeeded by Uther Pendragon. [*GeoffHR, Wace, Short*]

CASTEL OF THE HEVY SOROW

In *Ywain and Gawain*, the name for the castle that Chrétien de Troyes calls the CASTLE OF MOST ILL ADVENTURE. [*Ywain*]

CASTELL SYBERW ("Proud Castle")

A castle owned by one of Peredur Long Spear's cousins. It held five hundred and sixty-six knights. [*Peredur*]

CASTILE

According to Der Pleier, in *Tandareis and Flordibel*, this kingdom in Spain was allied to Arthur. [*PleierT*]

CASTIS

The King of Wales and North Wales in the days of Uther Pendragon. He married Herzeloyde (later Perceval's mother) from the Grail Family. He died before their marriage was consummated, and Herzeloyde inherited his throne and lands. [*Wolfram*]

CASTLE JOYOUS

A fortress visited by the warrior maiden Britomart. There, she found the Red Cross Knight attacked by six knights. She assisted him, and the two of them defeated the attackers. The lady of the castle, Malecasta, had wanted the Red Cross Knight as her lover. When the Red Cross Knight and Britomart lodged at the castle, Malecasta turned her affections to Britomart, not realizing that Britomart was a woman. This misunderstanding led to another brawl, and Britomart and the Red Cross Knight had to flee the castle. [*Spenser*]

CASTLE OF BOYS

An island castle belonging to King Orians of Amalvi. When Arthur set hundreds of children adrift at sea in a vain effort to destroy his incestuous son, Mordred, the boat washed ashore at Amalvi. King Orians took pity on the children and had them raised secretly in the Castle of Boys. [*VulgMer*]

CASTLE OF DEATH

A castle where Gaheris fought and killed the evil Kaols the Cruel. Gaheris gave the castle to one of Kaols's prisoners. [*Livre*]

CASTLE OF ENCHANTMENTS

A castle in the Scottish borderlands, built by Orpheus the Enchanter, who had once debated with Joseph of Arimathea. This was related to Sir Bors in a song that he heard in Corbenic Castle. [*VulgLanc*]

CASTLE OF JOY

One of the various names given to the GRAIL CASTLE in *Perlesvaus*. [*Perlesvaus*]

CASTLE OF LADIES[1]

A fortress on the opposite site of the Oscure River from the Castle of Maidens. Lancelot participated in a tournament fought between the two. The Castle of Ladies was the home of Arthur's Sir Flaundreus. Scholars often refer to CANGUIN ROCK in Chrétien de Troyes's *Perceval* as the Castle of Ladies, but the text does not use this name. [*VulgLanc, Malory*]

CASTLE OF LADIES[2]

Sagremor killed an evil knight named Greomar and siezed his castle, which Arthur named the Castle of Ladies. Sagremor gave the castle to Sir Laudon and his lady, Helyap. The Formidable Knight, Greomar's brother, later besieged the castle and was defeated by Gawain. [*Livre*]

CASTLE OF MAIDENS [*Castellum Puellarum, Chastel des Puceles*]

A ubiquitous but mysterious location in Arthurian romances, featured earliest by Geoffrey of Monmouth, who says that the fortress of Mount Agned was also called the Castle of Maidens. By Agned, Geoffrey seems to mean Edinburgh in Scotland, which was known as *castellum puellarum* in the Middle Ages. It was built by King Ebraucus, who ruled in the time of David in Israel. Geoffrey does not account for the name of the castle, but in French romance it is explained by its large number of maiden inhabitants, either—depending on the tale—willing residents or prisoners.

In the Second Continuation of Chrétien's *Perceval*, the Castle of Maidens is inhabited by a lady and 100 maidens who test the worthiness of visiting knights. Perceval stops by during his quest for the Grail and is richly received. When he awakens the next morning, he is asleep in the forest and the castle has disappeared. In the Third Continuation, it is besieged by Tallidés of the Marsh, who wants to marry one of its maidens against the will of the castle's mistress. Arthur's Sir Sagremor champions the castle and defeats Tallidés, who is eventually allowed to marry his paramour. In the Fourth Continuation, it is ruled by Lady Ysabel, a relative of Perceval. The castle serves as the site of tournaments in Renaut's *Le Bel Inconnu*, the Vulgate *Lancelot*—in which it is said to lie opposite a river from the Castle of Ladies—and Malory.

Its most important appearance arrives in the Vulgate *Queste del Saint Graal*, which tells us that it was once ruled by a duke named Lynors until seven brothers, lodging at the castle, became lustful for his daughter. They killed the duke and his son, and then made it their custom to capture every maiden that passed by the castle and add her to their harem. Galahad ended this wicked custom during the Grail Quest, when he came upon the castle and liberated it. Gawain, Gareth, and Yvain arrived soon after and killed the seven brothers. Rule of the castle was given to Duke Lynors' surviving daughter.

In the Vulgate *Merlin* it is said to be ruled by a lord named Belias the Amorous. In the romance of *Yder*, it is besieged by a Black Knight. (When Arthur refuses to assist the castle, Yder leaves his court in disgust.) In *De Ortu Waluuanii*, it is besieged by a pagan lord, and Arthur saves it with the assistance of a young Gawain. The *Livre d'Artus* gives its ruler as the Queen of Denmark. In *Palamedes*, it is ruled by a maiden cousin of Guiron the Courteous who is besieged by Sir Golistant but is rescued by Guiron. Following this, the maiden converts the castle to a nunnery. In the Prose *Tristan*, it is the site of a great tournament, and its location is given as a dozen leagues from London. Malory, who repeats the story found in the Vulgate *Queste*, also names it as the home of Arthur's Sir Moryans. There may be more than one castle intended in these varied appearances. [*Renaut, Contin2, Yder, VulgLanc, VulgQuest, VulgMer, Livre, Contin3, Contin4, Palamedes, ProsTris, Historia, Malory*]

CASTLE OF MARVELS [*Chastel de la Mervoille, Schastel Marveile*]

A castle in Galloway, first found in the First Continuation of Chrétien's *Perceval*. It is identical to Chrétien's CANGUIN ROCK and Heinrich von dem Türlin's SALIE. It was inhabited by several ladies related to Arthur and Gawain, including Arthur's mother (Igerne or Arnive), Arthur's sister and Gawain's mother (Morgause or Sangive), and Arthur's nieces and Gawain's sisters (Clarissant, Itonje, and Cundrie). Wolfram says that the castle was built by Clinschor the sorcerer. It contained several adventures, including the PERILOUS BED. Gawain journeyed to the castle in the companionship of the Lady Orgeluse, braved the Perilous Bed, and broke the castle's enchantments. Gawain became the castle's lord. The *Livre d'Artus* says that Merlin brought Igerne to live there, and that Pellinore also retired there. [*Contin1, Wolfram, Livre*]

CASTLE OF SOULS

One of the various names given to the GRAIL CASTLE in *Perlesvaus*. It was so nicknamed because anyone who died within it automatically went to heaven. [*Perlesvaus*]

CASTLE OF TEARS [*Castello del Proro, *Chastel des Pleurs, Doleful City, Pleure*]

A castle on the Giant's Isle ruled by Brunor, Galehaut's father. It had been built by the pagan giant Dialetes in the time of Joseph of Arimathea as a stronghold against Christianity, and a custom was established by which knights and ladies who were less valiant or less beautiful, respectively, than the lord and lady of the castle, were slain by the castle's lord. Tristan and Isolde stumbled upon the island on their way from Cornwall to Ireland; in a subsequent battle, Tristan killed both Brunor and his wife, the Beautiful Giantess. Tristan became lord of the castle and lived there for a while with Isolde. In the Italian *I Due Tristani*, they had two children, also called Tristan and

Isolde, during their sojourn at the castle. Once Tristan abandoned it, it was destroyed, at Galehaut's behest, by the King with a Hundred Knights. [*ProsTris, Conti, Tavola, DueTris, Malory*]

CASTLE OF TEN KNIGHTS [*Castel aux Dix Chevaliers*]

A strong castle in Britain. Its custom was that if a challenger could defeat ten knights and the castle's lord, the castle would be liberated; if the knight could only defeat the first ten, however, he would have to take the position of lord of the castle and remain there. The second scenario befell Erec, who relieved Hector of the responsibility. Gawain later defeated the ten knights, but not Erec, leaving himself to guard the castle for six years. Finally, Lamorat defeated all ten knights plus Gawain, ending the customs for good. Lamorat then voluntarily became lord of the castle and married its lady. [*PostMer*]

CASTLE OF TEN MAIDENS [*Chastel as Dis Puceles*]

A fortress inhabited by ten maidens and their lovers. Its lord was Geogenant, a friend of Arthur's Sir Durmart. The Lady of the castle was called Dyonise. [*Durmart*]

CASTLE OF THE BALL [*Chastel de la Pelote*]

A manor near Cambenic in which Gawain lodged upon returning from his quest for the Grail Sword. Its knights were in the habit of protecting local travelers. [*Perlesvaus, Livre*]

CASTLE OF THE BEARDS

A fortress whose knights would require the beard of any passers-by as a toll; with the beards, they made hair shirts for the local hermits. Lancelot ended the custom by slaying the participating knights. The lady of the Castle of the Beards wished Lancelot as a husband, but he left and did not return. [*Perlesvaus*]

CASTLE OF THE BORDERLANDS

The *Livre d'Artus* refers to an episode in which Gawain fought Guinganbresil at the Castle of the Borderlands. Guinganbresil's sister had given birth to a son begotten by Gawain. She was distressed that her brother and lover were fighting, so she kept placing herself and her child between them. In the First Continuation of Chrétien's *Perceval*, Gawain fights an identical duel against Brandelis, rather than Guinganbresil, at the Castle of LIS. [*Livre*]

CASTLE OF THE DOOR [*Castel du Port*]

A castle visited by Gawain, who learned that the castle's residents were under attack by Gernemant of Northumberland. Gernemant had asked the castle's lord for the hand of his daughter. When the castellan refused, Gernemant said that if the castellan did not provide a champion in a year, he would take the maiden by force and give her to his vilest stable boys. Gawain arrived just

before the year was out, championed the castellan, and slew Gernemant. Gawain fell in love with the maiden, but she would not believe him when he revealed his identity. After Gawain left the castle, the maiden went to Arthur's court, and upon receiving confirmation that her savior was truly Gawain, remained there to wait for him. They were joyously reunited at the end of Gawain's adventures and became lovers. [*Meriadeuc*]

CASTLE OF THE ENCHANTRESS[1]

A castle in Sorelois, the kingdom ruled by Galehaut. [*ProsTris*]

CASTLE OF THE ENCHANTRESS[2]

A castle in Ireland ruled by King Anguish. Anguish called a tournament at the castle, on the fields of Fregolo, which Tristan won. [*Tavola*]

CASTLE OF THE FENS

A castle ruled by King Agravadain the Black, who assisted Arthur in the Saxon Wars. It was visited by Merlin and Ban, the latter of whom, because of an enchantment cast by Merlin, slept with Agravadain's daughter, begetting Hector. During Hector's adventures, he was imprisoned at the Castle of the Fens after he slew Mataliz, the lord's son, which means either that the castle had a change of ownership, or that it occurred at a different castle of the same name. Hector won his freedom by championing the lord's niece, Elaine the Peerless, against her husband. [*VulgMer, VulgLanc*]

CASTLE OF THE FOUR STONES [*Chastel des Quatre Pierres*]

A castle visited by Sir Balan, where he heard news of his brother Balin. It was in Bagdemagus's kingdom. Meleagant's body was borne there after he was slain by Lancelot. [*VulgLanc, PostMort, Malory*]

CASTLE OF THE GALLEYS

A seaside castle in Wales, ruled by the Queen of the Maidens. Perceval saved the castle from an attack by his own uncle, the King of the Castle Mortal. [*Perlesvaus*]

CASTLE OF THE GIANTS

A fortress on the Island of the Elephants, belonging to Perceval's foe, the Knight of the Burning Dragon. [*Perlesvaus*]

CASTLE OF THE GRIFFINS

A fortress visited by Lancelot. Any knight who entered had to propose marriage to the castellan's daughter and then try to pull a spear out of a pillar. All knights failed, and were beheaded by the castle's lord. Lancelot alone succeeded, which enraged the castellan so much that he threw Lancelot into his prison. The daughter helped Lancelot escape past the fierce griffin guards. [*Perlesvaus*]

CASTLE OF THE GUARD [*Chastel de la Garde]

A castle constructed by Arthur and presented to Sir Tor in the First Continuation of Chrétien's *Perceval*. In *Durmart le Gallois*, a castle of the same name is ruled by Felon of the Guard, a knight defeated by Durmart. [*Contin1*, *Durmart*]

CASTLE OF THE HORN[1] [*Castel del Cor]

The fortress ruled by the Lord of the Horn. The name of the castle reflected a horn hanging outside which, when blown, summond the Lord to fight. Perceval blew the horn and defeated the Lord in combat. [*Contin2*]

CASTLE OF THE HORN[2]

A castle in Gaul captured by Arthur during his war with Claudas. Arthur gave it to Bors who, in turn, bestowed it on the (unnamed) husband of the Lady of the Lake. [*VulgLanc*]

CASTLE OF THE LAKE [*Castello del Lago]

The Lady of the Lake's castle in *La Tavola Ritonda*. [*Tavola*]

CASTLE OF THE MILLS [*Chastel des Mollins]

A group of mills in Ireland fortified into a stronghold. It was commanded by Sir Procidas, a servant of Queen Fenise of Ireland. [*Durmart*]

CASTLE OF THE MOORS [*Chastel des Landes]

An Irish castle which belonged to King Anguish, Isolde's father, and was governed by the Maiden of the Moors. It was the site of a tournament, the winner of which was to become the Maiden's husband. Palamedes won the tournament but declined to marry the Maiden. [*ProsTris*, *Malory*]

CASTLE OF THE MOST ILL ADVENTURE [*Chastel de Pesme Aventure]

A castle visited by Yvain in Chrétien's *Yvain* and its adaptations. Finding its inhabitants in tears, Yvain inquired and discovered that the maidens of the castle were doomed to be delivered to a pair of fiends. The castle's custom was that any knight who stopped there had to joust with the fiends, facing death or imprisonment if he lost. One clever king—known in Chrétien as the King of the Island of Maidens and in the Norse *Ivens Saga* as King Reinion—avoided this fate by promising to send 30 of his most beautiful maidens to the monsters each year. Yvain freed the castle of this contract by defeating the fiends. The king of the Castle wanted Yvain to marry his daughter, but Yvain refused and departed. In the Middle-English *Ywain and Gawain*, the castle is called the CASTEL OF THE HEVY SOROW, while *Ivens Saga* calls it the ENCOUNTER WITH ADVENTURE. [*ChretienY*, *Ivens*, *Ywain*]

CASTLE OF THE MOUNT

A castle belonging to Sir Dalam, an enemy of Dinadan. [*ProsTris*]

CASTLE OF THE PASS

A castle in Cornwall. [*ProsTris*]

CASTLE OF THE PLAIN

A fortress where Lamorat won a tournament. [*ProsTris*]

CASTLE OF THE ROCK [*Castel de la Roce]

In the Third Continuation of Chrétien's *Perceval*, a castle ruled by Silimac of the Rock, a knight killed while traveling with Gawain. In the Prose *Tristan*, a castle by this name is on the border between Lyonesse and Cornwall. [*Contin3*, *ProsTris*]

CASTLE OF THE THORN

A castle in northern Britain where two young warriors—Dodinel and Kay of Estral—met and decided to oppose their families by taking service with Arthur. It is also named as the castle ruled by Tericam, the tyrant slain by Lancelot. [*VulgMer*, *Livre*]

CASTLE OF THE TWO SISTERS

A castle where Guiron the Courteous and Danain the Red defeated King Meliadus of Lyonesse and King Lac. [*Palamedes*]

CASTLE OF THE WHALE

An island castle ruled by the malicious lord Gohart. Perceval defeated Gohart in battle, took control of the castle, and awarded it to his cousin, Sir Calobrus. [*Perlesvaus*]

CASTLE OF THREE MAIDENS

A castle besieged by the evil Harpin the Red. Hector of the Fens and the King with a Hundred Knights rescued the castle. [*Palamedes*]

CASTLE PERILOUS

A castle, near the Isle of Avalon, in which Sir Ironside, the Red Knight of the Red Lands, besieged the damsel Lyones and held her prisoner until he was defeated by Sir Gareth. Afterwards, a friendly tournament was held at the castle between King Arthur and a collection of opposing knights. [*Malory*, *TennIK*]

CASTLE WITHOUT A NAME [*Castiel sans Non]

A castle on the Island that Floats, ruled by the enchantress Lingrenote. Guengasoain, Gawain's opponente in *La Vengeance Raguidel*, lodged at the castle and received magical arms from the sorceress. [*Vengeance*]

CASTOR

Nephew of King Pelles of Corbenic. When Lancelot had recovered from a period of insanity and was staying at Corbenic incognito, Castor suspected his true identity and pressed Lancelot about it, until Lancelot rebuked him for un-knightly behavior and shamed Castor into promising to keep Lancelot's secret. [*Malory*]

CATALONIA

A region in northeast Spain, on the Mediterranean. It was allied to Lucius the Roman and consequently joined Lucius's war against Arthur. [*Malory*]

CATANANCE

A queen of Ireland who married King Caradoc Shortarm, one of Arthur's vassals. [*PostQuest*]

CATELL¹

According to Geoffrey of Monmouth, a king of Britain in the third or second century BC. He was the son of King Gerontius and the father of King Coill. [*GeoffHR*]

CATELL²

Father of Arthur's warrior Cathleus in Geoffrey of Monmouth, and of Caradoc in Layamon. [*GeoffHR*, *Wace*, *Layamon*]

CATELLUS

In Layamon, a Roman senator who joined Lucius's war against Arthur. Layamon split Wace's LUCIUS CATELLUS into two characters: Catellus and Lucas. [*Layamon*]

CATENOUSE

A duchy ruled by Duke Marmadus, the son of the Red Knight. G. D. West suggested that it was Caithness in Scotland. [*Contin4*]

CATH PALUG [*Capalu*]

A fearsome monster fought, and perhaps slain, by Cei on the Isle of Anglesey, according to an early Welsh poem known as *Pa Gur yv y Portaur*. Cei visited the island specifically to "destroy lions." *Palug* means "clawing," but it seems to have been interpreted as a personal name: "Palug's Cat" rather than "Clawing Cat."

According to a late Welsh Triad, Cath Palug was born to the enchanted pig Hen Wen. Coll, the pig's keeper, cast it into the sea at Menai Strait, from which it apparenlty found its way to Anglesey and was raised by the sons of Palug, on whom the monster turned.

The story of the Cath Palug was apparently carried to France, where it was called "Chapalu." The author of the Vulgate *Merlin* recalls the tale of Chapalu when he tells of Arthur's battle with a hellish feline on the HILL OF THE CAT. In one version of the French Chapalu tale (*Romanz des Franceis*), Arthur was said to have been slain by the creature, which then took the crown of England for itself.

Finally, in the French romance *La Bataille de Loquifer*, the hero Renoart slays a "Chapalu" in Arthur's kingdom of Avalon. [*WelshPG*, *Triads*, *VulgMer*, *Bataille*]

CATHLEUS

One of Arthur's warriors. He wa the son of Catel. [*GeoffHR*]

CATIGERN [*Categren, Cateyrn, Katiger(n), Katigis*]

In Nennius and Geoffrey, the son of Vortigern who was killed in battle against Hengist's Saxon armies while fighting alongside his brother, Vortimer, at Episford. He slew, and was slain by, Hengist's brother Horsa. Layamon says that Horsa and Catigern wounded each other, but indicates later that Catigern did not die at that battle. Wace calls the same character VORTIGER. [*Nennius*, *GeoffHR*, *Layamon*]

CATOR

King of Libya who served Emperor Filimenis of Constantinople, Floriant's father. [*Floriant*]

CAUCASUS

A mountain range in the south of Russia. Wolfram, who seemed to think that they lay in India (which he calls Tribalibot), says that the city of Thabronit, ruled by Perceval's half-brother Feirefiz, lay at their base. [*Wolfram*]

CAULAS¹ [*Maulas*]

A Saxon chieftain who, with others, invaded Carmelide in the early days of Arthur's reign. At the battle of Aneblayse, his forces were routed by Arthur, Leodegan, Ban, and Bors. Caulas was slain by Arthur. [*VulgMer*, *Livre*, *Arthour*]

CAULAS² THE RED

One of Arthur's knights. He fought against the rebellious kings at the battle of Bedegraine, and he participated in a quest to learn the fate of Merlin. [*VulgMer*, *Malory*]

CAULDRONS

These large pots, used in various rituals by the Celts, become enchanted objects in several episodes in Welsh legend. The nature of the cauldrons and the warriors' quests for them have been seen by some as precursors of the GRAIL and the Grail Quest. The earliest Arthurian poem, called *The Spoils of Annwn*, describes Arthur's expedition to the Welsh otherworld, where he obtains a magic cauldron ("gently warmed by the breath of nine maidens," the maidens here preceding the Grail maidens of later legend) that would not "boil a coward's food." Arthur similarly obtains such a cauldron in *Culhwch and Olwen*, after he invades Ireland and kills Diwrnach the Irishman. Diwrnach's cauldron is mentioned among the

"Thirteen Treasures of the Island of Britain": as suggested by *Annwn*, it would only boil food intended for a brave man (this ability to separate the brave from the cowardly mirrors the Grail's ability to divide the pure from the perfidious). An invasion of Ireland similar to the one in *Culhwch* occurs in the non-Arthurian tale of *Branwen*. Here, the British king is Bran the Blessed. The cauldron he obtains as part of his plunder had the power to resurrect the dead (healing is another property assigned to the Grail). The episodes in *Annwn*, *Culhwch*, and *Branwen* are similar, with Ireland suggesting the otherworld in the latter two. In another legend, the bard Taliesin was said to have been born from a cauldron. Irish legend has its share of cauldrons as well, with the mythological god Dagda owning a cauldron of plenty (similar to the Grail in the First Continuation). [*Spoils*, *Culhwch*, *Triads*]

CAUSUEL

A castle where a tournament was held annually for possession of an enchanted parrot. The prize was supposed to go to the knight with the most beautiful lady. A knight called the Merciless Lion generally won the tournament through brute force, though his lady was ugly. Arthur won the tournament in the name of the Lady Without Pride. The tournament is indebted to the SPARROWHAWK tournament of the Erec romances. [*ChevPap*]

CAUTEROUS OF SOLAZ

An Arthurian knight. [*Heinrich*]

CAVALON

A shorter form of ESCAVALON.

CAVE LEGEND

The belief that King Arthur is asleep in an enchanted cave, to be awakened at his country's time of need. The Cave Legend is found primarily in oral folklore; chronicles and romances have Arthur living not in a cave, but on the island of AVALON. Italian literature places Arthur in Mt. Etna on Sicily, which is identified with Avalon. Caves in which Arthur is said to be sleeping are pointed out by rural dwellers and small town residents all over Britain. Generally, the entrance is said to be hidden or sealed, only revealing itself or opening on certain nights of the year or under certain circumstances. These caves include two ARTHUR'S CAVES in Wales and Anglesey, Cadbury hill in Somerset, an underworld in Glamorgan, a hill in Cheshire, a grotto in Yorkshire, and a cavern in Eildon Hills in Melrose. Accompanying the legend are tales of locals discovering the entrances, wandering into the caves, and finding the sleeping Arthur, along with his knights, his Round Table, or a fabulous treasure. The hapless adventurer generally makes some mistake and is driven from the cave. He is unable to find it when he returns. The Cave Legend is merged somewhat uncomfortably with the Wild Hunt in a number of tales. Though Arthur's body is alive in the cave, his spirit emerges and rides through the woods in a supernatural hunt, which, like the entrance to the cave, can be seen on certain nights of the year. [*Topography*]

CAVE OF LOVERS

An enchanted grotto, built into a Cornish mountain by privacy-seeking, amorous giants in times long before Arthur. It was marked by a bronze door, a spacious interior, and a crystal bed. Tristan and Isolde inhabited it during a banishment from Mark's court. [*Gottfried*]

CAVERON OF ROBERDIC [*Gaveros*]

A Knight of the Round Table. He may be identical to GOVERNAL of Roberdic. [*ChretienE*]

CAW

King of Scotland, and father of Arthur's warriors Dirmyg, Iustig, Edmyg, Angawdd, Gofan, Celyn, Conyn, Mabsant, Gwyngad, Llwybyr, Coch, Meilyg, Cynwal, Ardwyad, Ergyryad, Neb, Gildas, Calcas, Hueil, Gwarthegydd, and Gwenabwy. As one of Culhwch's tasks in *Culhwch and Olwen*, he had to obtain the tusk of the Chief Boar Ysgithyrwyn for the giant Ysbaddaden to trim his beard. Ysbaddaden would allow no one to bring him the tusk except Caw. Culhwch thus faced the additional task of convincing Caw to leave his kingdom and travel to Ysbaddaden's fortress. At the behest of Arthur, Caw accompanied the warriors on the hunt for Ysgithyrwyn, took the tusk, and shaved Ysbaddaden with it personally. He also accompanied Arthur on the search for the Black Hag and, after Arthur had killed her, collected her blood. In the *Life of St. Gildas*, Arthur kills Caw's son Hueil. Caw is said to be a giant. [*Culhwch*, *Caradoc*, *Dream*]

CAWRDAF

One of Arthur's warriors and advisors. His father was Caradawg Strong Arm. A Welsh Triad considers Cawrdaf one of the "Three Chief Officers of the Island of Britain." [*Triads*, *Dream*]

CECORMANUS

One of Arthur's earls. He fought in the Roman War and was killed at the battle of Soissons. Wace inserted his character in the same textual location as RIDDOMARCUS in Geoffrey of Monmouth. [*Wace*]

CEDFYW

A Welsh warrior whose death at the hands of Maelgwn is mourned by Merlin in an early Welsh poem. [*Myrddin*]

CEI

The Welsh hero who became the source of the romantic KAY.

CEIDO [*Ceidiaw*]

The father of Gwenddolau, Merlin's lord in several Welsh sources. [*Annales*]

CELECA

A lake in Britain. Beside it stood a monastery, where Sir Lionel (Lancelot's cousin) was healed after having been wounded during the Grail Quest. [*PostQuest*]

CELEMON

Daughter of Cei (Kay). [*Culhwch*]

CELESTRE

A pagan queen who inhabited the Mad Castle and who loved Perceval. For his sake, she converted to Christianity. For this action, she was persecuted by the heathen Knight of the Galleys, but was saved by Sir Meliot of Logres. [*Perlesvaus*]

CELIAS

King of Apulia who was allied to Emperor Thereus of Rome. During Thereus's war with Arthur, Celias was killed by Sir Claris. [*Claris*]

CELIBE [*Caleise, Collybe*]

A forest near the Corbenic, the Grail Castle, that extended to the sea. Galahad traversed it during the Grail Quest and united with Perceval and Bors at the ocean. Found in the Vulgate *Queste del Saint Graal*, the name is given to the sea itself by Malory. [*VulgQuest, ProsTris, Malory*]

CELICE[1]

A damsel of the Lady of the Lake. She is called SARAIADE in other parts of the same story. [*LancLac*]

CELICE[2] [*Celise, Colice*]

A river in the forest of Darnantes in Britain. Joseph of Arimathea came to it with his followers, but could not find a way to cross. He prayed, and God provided him with a bridge. One follower, Canaan, was still unable to cross, betraying his lack of faith and later sin. The castle of Celis lay on its shores. [*VulgQuest, VulgEst*]

CELICES OF THE DOLOROUS TOWER
   [*Sel(e)yses*]

Nephew of the King with a Hundred Knights and a Knight of the Round Table. He won honor at a tournament at Camelot and fought at the Leverzep tournament. He was infatuated with Isolde. When Lancelot and Guinevere were accused of treason, Celices pledged his support to Lancelot and helped him to rescue Guinevere from the stake. He fought alongside Lancelot when Arthur laid siege to Joyous Guard and, later, Benoic. In return for his support, Lancelot made him the earl of Marsan. [*Palamedes, ProsTris, Malory*]

CELIDOINE[1] [*Cilodormes, Colidoines*]

Son of Nascien and Flegetine, and ancestor of Lancelot and Galahad. When Joseph of Arimathea visited Sarras and surrounding regions, Celidoine converted to Christianity with his father and became a devout believer. After King Mordrains of Sarras disappeared, Nascien and Celidoine, still a boy, were imprisoned by an infidel named Galafre. God lifted Nascien from the prison, for which Galafre tried to kill Celidoine by hurling him from a tower, but the arms of God broke Celidoine's descent and carried him away. He had a number of adventures at sea which served to test his piety. He converted King Label of Persia, and later married Label's daughter. Celidoine preceded his father to Britain, where he performed the first conversion of a Briton ruler: Duke Ganor of Galafort. He was crowned King of North Wales. He learned to interpret messages in the stars, and by doing so managed to save his kingdom from a famine. His son, Narpus, inherited his lands and title. Celidoine was buried at Camelot.

Celidoine's name seems to be some variation of Celidon, or the Caledonian forest in northern England and Scotland. R. S. Loomis (*Grail*, 246) points out that Celidoine's powers of prophecy seem reminiscent of Merlin's, and that Merlin is called "Merlinus Celidonius" by Giraldus Cambrensis. [*VulgEst, Arthour*]

CELIDOINE[2]

Arthur's Sir Floriant freed the inhabitants of Celidoine by killing two giants who terrorized them. G. D. West thought that Celidoine was Calchedon in Bithynia. [*Floriant*]

CELIDON

King of Greece in *Claris et Laris*. He was allied to Emperor Thereus of Rome and was slain during Thereus's war with Arthur. [*Claris*]

CELINANT [*Belinan, Selyvaunt*]

The brother of Sir Bliant. He lived in the White Castle. He helped his brother take in and care for Lancelot, when the latter was insane and roaming the forests as a wild man. He may be identical to King BELINANT. [*VulgLanc, PostMer, Malory*]

CELINAS

A Saxon king and cousin of King Rions. He joined Rions' invasion of Carmelide and fought against Arthur's forces at the battle of Aneblayse. [*VulgMer*]

CELIS [*Celys*]

A castle on the Celice river, from which the castle took its name. It was ruled by King Lac, Erec's father, until he was slain by his nephews. During the Grail Quest, Erec returned to the castle and killed his cousins. The castle's residents swore fealty to Erec, their rightful lord. [*PostQuest*]

CELJE

A city through which Perceval's uncle Trevrizent journeyed during his adventures. [*Wolfram*]

CELLI

One of Arthur's warriors. [*Culhwch*]

CELLIWIG [*Celliwic*]

Arthur's Cornish capital in Welsh legend. Scholars have suggested numerous corresponding locations, including Gweek Wood on the Helford River, Kelly Rounds, and Calliwith near Bodmin (Chambers, 91). *Celli* means "forest." A Welsh Triad tells that Mordred once came to Celliwig, consumed all of Arthur's food and drink, then hauled Guinevere from her throne, belted her, and left. Arthur repaid this insult by performing similar deeds at Mordred's court. The story is unique in suggesting that Mordred and Arthur were equals. [*Triads, Culhwch*]

CELTS

A number of mainland Europe tribes that invaded the British Isles between 1000 and 500 B.C. The Celts settled throughout the Isles and eventually became the races known as Britons, Welsh, Scots, Irish, and Cornish. Control of the British Isles was taken from the Celtic tribes when the Romans invaded in the first century. The Celts known as the BRITONS, who inhabited the southern half of the island, became "Romanized" and were thus left as the ruling race after the Romans withdrew. Arthur is often represented as a member of this race.

CELYN ("Holly")

Son of Caw, one of twenty brothers, and one of Arthur's warriors in Welsh legend. [*Culhwch*]

CERANCE

A stream in Sorelois, the kingdom ruled by Arthur's Sir Galehaut. It flowed past the magnificent fortress Oreguellouse and into the straight of Aussurne. [*VulgLanc*]

CERDIC

A Saxon warrior who followed or allied with Hengist. According to Geoffrey of Monmouth, Cerdic came to Britain with Octa, Ebissa, and thousands of other warriors when King Vortigern was friendly to the Saxons. The *Anglo-Saxon Chronicle* places his arrival in 495, with his son Cynric. They enjoyed victories over the Britons in 508, at which Natanleod, "King of the Britons," was killed; in 519, at Chartford on the river Avene; and in 530 on the Isle of Wight. He died in 534, after giving the Isle of Wight to his cousins Stuf and Wihtgar. His father was named Elesa. There has been much debate and speculation over this character because his name is Celtic, not Germanic. [*Anglo, GeoffHR*]

CEREDIGYAWN

A location in Britain through which Arthur's warriors pursued a piglet named Grugyn during the epic hunt of the boar Twrch Trwyth. [*Culhwch*]

CERENHYR ("King of Kinsmen") [*Cyrenhyr*]

Son of Gereinyawn and father of Arthur's warrior Berwyn. A Welsh triad lists him as one of the three "who could not be expelled from Arthur's court." [*Triads, Culhwch*]

CERETIC [*Keredic, Redic*]

Hengist's interpreter who, at a feast with Vortigern, related Hengist's proposal that Vortigern marry Hengist's daughter, Rowena. [*Nennius, Wace*]

CERIDWEN

Mother of Taliesin in non-Arthurian Welsh legend.

CERON

A giant whose six sons, including Plenorius, were defeated by Lancelot and Brunor the Black in the Straits of Sorelois. Ceron lived in the castle at the Straits during his life and engaged in hostilities with Lord Galehaut of Sorelois. He eventually imprisoned Galehaut, but was attacked and killed by Nestor. [*ProsTris*]

CESAR[1] [*Cesaire*]

Father of Vespasian, Joseph of Arimathea's liberator, in Robert de Boron's *Joseph d'Arimathie*. He is replaced by TITUS in the Vulgate *Estoire del Saint Graal*. [*RobertBor*]

CESAR[2]

An bowman encountered by Arthur's Sir Durmart during his adventures in Ireland. Cesar led Durmart to the city of Limerick, where Durmart's paramour was under siege. [*Durmart*]

CETHTRWM THE PRIEST

A member of Arthur's court. [*Culhwch*]

CEUDAWG HALF-WIT

One of Arthur's warriors in Welsh legend. [*Culhwch*]

CHAEVIERE

A pleasant, bustling town situated along the river Humber, near the castle Dolorous Guard. Arthur and his company lodged here after Lancelot liberated Dolorous Guard. [*LancLac, VulgLanc*]

CHAINS CASTLE

The fortress in which Arthur was imprisoned by the False Guinevere. She charmed him there and would not free him until he swore to recognize her as queen. [*VulgLanc*]

CHALAUNCE

The Duke of Clarence and Knight of the Round Table. He fought in the tournament at Sorelois and appears later at the healing of Sir Urry. [*Malory*]

CHALEHORDINE

A knight who served the Maiden of the Narrow Wood, a damsel who loved Gawain. [*Vengeance*]

CHALON

The region of west central France (Chalon-on-Sâone) ruled by the daughter of King Gloier. Gloier was conquered by Galehaut. [*Livre*]

CHAMPAGNE

A historical region of northeast France which, according to Der Pleier, was allied to Arthur. *Arthour and Merlin* tells us that Uther Pendragon acquired Champagne from Harinan, Igerne's first husband. [*Arthour*, *PleierT*]

CHARITY OF OUR LADY

A religious house where Galehaut was healed after he was wounded while trying to find Lancelot. [*VulgLanc*]

CHARLEMAGNE [*Carlo Magno*]

The Post-Vulgate *Queste del Saint Graal* notes that Charlemagne, emperor of the Holy Roman Empire (800–814), when he conquered England, rebuilt the Castle of Treachery (which had been destroyed during the Grail Quest) and created a magnificent statue of Galahad before it. He also apparently razed Corbenic, the Grail Castle. His coming was foretold to Arthur by a mysterious voice.

According to *La Tavola Ritonda*, Charlemagne visited the castle of Leverzep, where he found statues of Tristan, Palamedes, Amoroldo, Lancelot, and Galahad. Charlemagne and his noblemen took the swords of the knights, which were hung around the statues' necks. [*PostQuest*, *PostMort*, *Tavola*]

CHARMES

A renowned British knight. His son, Rim, gave hospitality to Arthur's Sir Yder. Charmes's grandson, Luguain, became Yder's squire. [*Yder*]

CHAROSQUE

A castle in Benoic, on the border of the forest of Briosque. It was near the home of the Lady of the Lake. [*VulgLanc*]

CHARQUEDON [*Calcedor*]

One of the noble Byzantine warriors that Alexander brought to Britain from Constantinople. He fought for Arthur in the battle against the traitor Angres of Windsor and was slain. Chrétien notes that he came from the "African regions." [*ChretienC*]

CHARROIE [*Charrot*]

A castle which Uther Pendragon wrestled from King Amant. Uther bestowed it on King Bors of Gannes, and Bors gave it either to his brother Guinebal or to the Lord of the Castle of the Fens. When Arthur first came to power and was struggling against the Saxons, Amant tried to recapture Charroie, but he was slain by King Bors. [*VulgMer*, *Livre*]

CHARROT

A castle in France which belonged to Patrice, the uncle of King Claudas. King Ban of Benoic apparently captured it, because he awarded it to the daughter of Agravadain the Black. [*VulgLanc*, *Livre*]

CHARTRES

A city of north central France, which Geoffrey says was ruled under Arthur by Guerin. [*GeoffHR*]

CHASTELAIN [*Chestelayne*]

A young ward of Gawain, killed in the battle against the Duke of Lorraine during the Roman War. Gawain was so enraged by his death that he killed dozens of Roman soldiers. [*Allit*, *Malory*]

CHASTIEFOL

The name of Arthur's sword in *Le Chevalier du Papegau*. [*ChevPap*]

CHASTITY TESTS

This ubiquitous theme is represented first in Arthurian literature in Robert Biket's *Lai du Cor* and the anonymous *La Mantel mautaillié*, two late twelfth-century French lays. In Biket's romance, the object that tests chastity is a drinking horn, while in *Mantel* is a mantle or cloak. These two objects are the most frequently used in later texts, though a crown and a glove also appear. In the Welsh Triads, a chastity mantle is owned by Tegau, a lady at Arthur's court, and it is counted among the "Thirteen Treasures of the Island of Britain." Tegau is also given a horn which may have the same properties as the mantle.

In Biket, a messenger from King Mangon of Moraine brings an enchanted horn, made by a fairy, to a feast at Arthur's Caerleon court, where most of Arthur's nobles are present. A note on the horn says that only a man whose wife is completely faithful in both mind and body can drink from the horn, and that a man with an unfaithful wife will have the contents of the horn spilled upon him. Arthur confidently fills the horn and raises it to his lips, but soon finds himself doused with wine. Furious, he whips out his dagger and lunges for Guinevere, but is held back by Owain, Gawain, and Cadain—who protest that no woman is utterly faithful in both mind and body—while Guinevere explains that the horn has unfairly faulted her for, many years ago, giving a ring to a young knight who had killed a giant. Arthur calms down, forgives his wife, and passes the horn around to the other nobles so that he might not be alone in his embarrassment. Sure enough, the other knights are thoroughly drenched by the horn—except for Sir Caradoc, who manages to drink from the vessel without spilling any liquid, showing that his wife is, apparently, completely faithful. In recognition of his triumph, Arthur appoints Caradoc earl of Cirencester.

A version of this same chastity test is inserted in the First Continuation of Chrétien's *Perceval*, with Caradoc again the hero.

Contemporary to Biket, an anonymous French author wrote *Le Mantel Mautaillié*, which follows the same structure as Biket's romance, but the object that tests the women's chastity is a mantle rather than a horn. While in Biket, the men drink from the horn, in *Mantel*, it is the women who must try on the mantle. Again, it is Caradoc's wife alone who is proven faithful. The third late twelfth century chastity test tale occurs in Ulrich von Zatzikhoven's *Lanzelet*. It also involves a mantle, and Lancelot's lady, Iblis, is the winner. Ulrich's mantle has not only the power to determine chastity, but can also determine the manner in which the woman is unfaithful. The wife of King Guivret, for instance, is embarrassed by his dwarfishness, and the wife of Sir Kailet resented the way he dragged her around on his adventures.

Heinrich von dem Türlin's *Diu Crône* includes two chastity tests, one involving a goblet, and the other a glove, which are obvious replacements for the horn and mantle. The goblet is given to both women and men, and spilling the contents reveals the drinker's own falseness rather than his or her paramour's. Only Arthur is able to drink from it without failure. Even Gawain, the hero of the romance, fails. Kay makes great sport of all who fail, which leads to his embarrassment when his own lady, Galaida, can't even touch the tankard. Guinevere spills only a little wine in her attempt. The glove, delivered to Arthur's court in a later episode, showed worthiness by turning its wearer invisible. Any part of the body that remained visible bespoke a fault—infidelity or otherwise. Only Arthur and Gawain were able to wear it honorably, though no one was shown to be completely guileless.

Chastity tests appear in dozens of other romances, including the Dutch *Wrake von Raguisel* (a mantle proves Guinevere's infidelity; Lancelot therefore develops an irrational rage against all mantles and people who wear them, nearly killing his friend Yder when he sees Yder's lady wearing a mantle); the German *Der Mantel*; the Norse *Mottuls Saga* (only Sir Karadin's lady is faithful); the Shrovetide play *Ain hupsches vasnachtspill und sagt von künig Arthus, wie er siben fursten mit iren weyben zuo seinem hoff geladen het und wie si durch ain horn geschendet worden gar hupsch zuo hören* (the Queen of Zipper sends the horn to Arthur's court and all are embarrassed); the German "Lanethen Mantel" (Arthur's niece Laneth sends a mantle to Arthur's court as part of a rivalry with Guinevere); the English *Romance of Sir Corneus*; the German *Dis ist frauw Tristerat horn von Saphoien* (Tristerat of Savoy sends the horn to Arthur's court, and only the wife of the King of Spain is faithful); the Shrovetide play *Der Luneten Mantel* (a lady named Lunet sends the mantle to Arthur's court; again, only the King of Spain has a faithful wife); another Shrovetide play called *Das Vasnachtspil mit der kron* (a chastity crown sent to Arthur's court by the King of Abian tests the men by having horns grow out of their heads if they are unfaithful to their wives; the crown is ultimately returned to its

sender); and the English ballad "The Boy and the Mantle" (Caradoc, again, is the hero).

In the Prose *Tristan*, Morgan le Fay sends a chastity horn to Arthur's court to reveal the adultery of Guinevere, Morgan's enemy. Sir Lamorat intercepts the horn *en route* and re-directs it to King Mark of Cornwall. (Lamorat previously had a fight with Tristan and wanted to embarrass Isolde.) When Isolde failed the test, Mark forced her into a second type of chastity test involving a hot iron. If anyone holding the iron told a lie, the iron would burn the person's hand. Isolde was able to use a trick of language to avoid telling a lie while leaving the impression that she was chaste. This type of test occurs previously in Béroul's *Tristan*. Morgan also sends the horn to Arthur's court in *La Tavola Ritonda* and Malory's *Le Morte Darthur*.

In Hans Sachs's *Die Ehbrecherbuck*, Arthur builds a magic chastity *bridge* that does not allow adulterers to cross. Though the other ladies at his court fall off the bridge, his wife, Guinevere, is able to pass. Finally, the German ballad *Die Ausgleichung* describes how the women at Arthur's court are tested with a mantle, the men with a horn. All fail except the old knight and fairy who brought the items in the first place.

Without fail, each chastity test occurs in a public setting—generally a court gathering—and each knight's or lady's failure results in humiliation. Many of the romances that include chastity tests display an implicit or explicit critique of Arthurian chivalry. [*Biket, MantelM, UlrichZ, Contin1, Wrake, Heinrich, MantelD, Mottuls, ProsTris, Tavola, Hupsches, Lanethen, DisIst, Luneten, Vasnachtspil, Malory, Boy, Sachs, Ausgleichung*]

CHATELLUS

Son of Chater and one of Arthur's knights. [*Wace*]

CHATER

Father of Arthur's warrior Chatellus. [*Wace*]

CHELDRIC[1] [*Childric, Cordryk*]

A Saxon war leader who came from Germany to help his fellow Saxons—Colgrim and Baldulph—conquer Britain. Geoffrey of Monmouth is the first to mention him. Layamon calls him "emperor" and seems to place him above the other Saxons. Cheldric arrived just in time to save Colgrim from Arthur's siege at York. Arthur defeated him at Lincoln and at Caledon forest, after which Cheldric agreed to leave Britain. Cheldric and the others betrayed Arthur, however, and landed again at Totnes. He conquered Somerset, Devonshire, Dorset, and Wiltshire before Arthur arrived and defeated him at Bath, where Colgrim and Baldulph were killed. Seeing the others fall, Cheldric fled into Scotland, but was pursued by Cador of Cornwall, who killed Cheldric at either the Isle of Thanet or at the river Teign. In an alternate version provided by John Hardyng, Arthur bestowed Cheldric with the country of Wessex after defeating him at Bath. [*GeoffHR, Wace, Layamon, Hardyng*]

CHELDRIC[2] [Cheldrich(us), Cheldrik, Childrik]

A Saxon duke who allied with Mordred and brought thousands of Saxons into Britain to oppose King Arthur. Mordred promised him all lands north of the Humber river, and Kent, in return for his support. Arthur killed him at the battle of Camel. [GeoffHR, Wace, Layamon, Allit, HughesT]

CHELINDE

An ancestress of Tristan. She was the daughter of the King of Babylonia. Shipwrecked on the coast of Britain, she was rescued by Sador, the son of Bron, whom she married. Sador's brother Naburzadan tried to rape her, but Sador killed him. Fleeing from Naburzadan's kin, Chelinde became separated from her husband and believed him to be dead. She re-married King Canor of Cornwall but gave birth to Apollo, Sador's son, whom Canor abandoned in a forest. She had another son by Canor named Cichoriades. She was re-united with Sador, but Apollo—ignorant of his true parentage—killed both Sador and Canor, and then married Chelinde himself. St. Augustine, who converted Lyonesse and Cornwall, revealed the incest between Chelinde and Apollo; Chelinde tried to kill the saint and was struck dead by a lightning bolt. [ProsTris]

CHENEUS [Ceilus, Kineus]

Son of Coil and one of Arthur's warriors. [GeoffHR, Wace, Layamon]

CHENELIUS

A tribe of barbarians who fought against Arthur's forces at the battle of Rigomer. [Merveil]

CHERDICH

A Saxon warrior who came to Britain, at the behest of Hengist, when King Vortigern of Britain was friendly to the Saxons. [GeoffHR]

CHERIN[1]

According to Geoffrey of Monmouth, a king of Britain in the third or second century BC. Cherin succeeded King Porrex and was succeeded by his sons, Fulgentius, Eldad, and Andragius. [GeoffHR]

CHERIN[2] OF LINELLO

A knight present at Uther Pendragon's Urbano tournament. [Tavola]

CHESSBOARD CASTLE

A fortress visited by Perceval in the Second Continuation and the Didot-Perceval. Inside, he found a magic chessboard, against which he played three games and lost each time. He became so angry that he was on the verge of hurling the board out the window, but a maiden came along and dissuaded him. Perceval became infatuated with the maiden and agreed to hunt down a white stag for her.

He got distracted with other adventures and had to plead for forgiveness when he returned. The maiden wanted to make him lord of the castle, but Perceval had sworn to pursue the Grail Quest and was forced to depart. The chessboard itself was given to the lady by Morgan le Fay. A similar sequence of events takes place at the FORTRESS OF MARVELS in the Welsh story of Peredur. Magic chessboards make frequent appearances in Arthurian legends. Gawain plays with one in Perlesvaus. See also FLOATING CHESSBOARD, GUINEBAL, GWYDDBWYLL, and THIRTEEN TREASURES. [Contin2, Didot]

CHESTER [Caistor, Chestre]

A city in northwest England, ruled in Arthur's time, according to Layamon, by Earl Cursalem. It is probably identical with the CITY OF THE LEGION, the site of one of Arthur's battles against the Saxons, though there might be some confusion with CAERLEON. The author of the Middle English Ywain and Gawain contended that Arthur held his court in Chester. In the Elizabethan play The Birth of Merlin, its lord under Ambrosius is Eldol. Launfal defeats an "Earl of Chester" in Chestre's Sir Launfal. [Annales, Layamon, ChestreLvl, Ywain, Birth]

CHESTNUT LONG-NECK

Cei's horse, a "lively steed," according to a Triad. [Triads]

CHEVALIER MALFAIT ("Wicked Knight")

The alias adopted by Lancelot after he recovered from a period of insanity and lived alone on the Joyous Island. After ten years, he was coaxed back to Arthur's court by Hector and Perceval. [VulgLanc, PostMer, Malory]

CHINON [Kinon]

A city and castle built by Kay, which, according to Geoffrey of Monmouth, served as his final resting place after he was killed in the Roman war. Layamon says that the name of the city was changed to Caen in honor of the warrior. Perlesvaus, in contrast to Geoffrey, tells us that Kay fled to the castle after he defected from Arthur's court. [GeoffHR, Wace, Layamon, Perlesvaus]

CHIPRE

A town in Italy where Floriant and Florete once lodged during their adventures. [Floriant]

CHRISTOPHER OF THE GRAY ROCK
[Cristofer, Cristofles]

A knight in the service of either Arthur or King Leodegrance of Carmelide. He fought against the Saxon invasion at the battle of Carhaix, and in the north of Britain. [VulgMer, Arthour]

CHRYSOGONE

A virgin who inhabited Fairy Land. While basking in the sun one day, she was impregnated by a sun god. She gave birth to twin daughters—Belphoebe and Amoret—who were taken and raised by the goddesses Diana and Venus. [*Spenser*]

CHURCH OF THE DEATHS

A church erected in Lyonesse to commemorate the deaths of all the knights killed in the war between Arthur and King Meliadus of Lyonesse. [*Palamedes*]

CHYCORADÉS OF LAVENTIN

A knight in Arthur's service. [*Girart*]

CIBDDAR

Father of Arthur's warrior Drych. [*Culhwch*]

CICAVERNE [*Ticaverne*]

A castle where Gawain defended Sir Manassel against a murder charge brought by Duke Escant of Cambenic, who mistakenly thought that Manassel had murdered his son. [*VulgLanc*]

CICHORIADES

A king in the story of Cornwall. He was the son of King Canor of Cornwall and Chelinde and the half-brother of Apollo. He became king of Cornwall after his father. St. Augustine converted him to Christianity. His wife, Joene, was unfaithful to him. Cichoriades locked her in a tower. When her lover presented himself at the base of the tower, Cichoriades started climbing down on a rope. Joene cut the rope from the top, and Cichoriades fell to his death. [*ProsTris*]

CIDEGAST

The Duke of Logres in Wolfram's *Parzival*. He married the lady Orgeluse (later Gawain's wife) and made her his duchess. He was killed by King Gramoflanz, prompting Orgeluse to devote her life seeking revenge on her husband's killer. [*Wolfram*]

CIDELA

A castle where a tournament was held during the Grail Quest. Lionel encountered his brother Bors at Cidela and quarreled with him over a past episode. Sir Calogrenant and a defenseless hermit were both slain in the scuffle. [*PostQuest*]

CIL COED

Father of Arthur's warrior Llwyd in *Culhwch and Olwen*. There is a forest in the parish of Pembroke named Cil Coed (Gantz, 95). [*Culhwch*[

CILGWRI

In *Culhwch and Olwen*, the Ousel (thrush) of Cilgwri is a mystic animal whose wisdom Arthur sought during his quest to find the imprisoned warrior Mabon. The Ousel directed Arthur to the Stag of Rhedenfire. [*Culhwch*]

CILYDD[1]

Ruler of Caledon, son of Cyleddon, and father of Culhwch. Cilydd married Goleuddyd, sister of Igerne. His wife was mortally wounded giving birth to Culhwch, and on her deathbed she made Cilydd promise not to remarry until he saw a two-headed thorn growing on her grave. He did not see such a thorn until seven years later, at which time he sought another wife. He found a suitable woman in the wife of King Doged. Cilydd killed Doged and brought Doged's wife back to his court. [*Culhwch*]

CILYDD[2] HUNDRED HOLDS

One of King Arthur's warriors in Welsh legend who owned a special chain. As one of his tasks, the warrior Culhwch had to obtain this chain to hold the hound Drudwyn while hunting Twrch Trwyth. [*Culhwch*]

CINGLOR

One of Arthur's knights in Béroul's *Tristan*, present at Isolde's chastity trial. [*Beroul*]

CIRCLE OF GOLD

In *Perlesvaus*, the thorn of crowns worn by Christ was set in gold and bejeweled by the maiden Elyza. This crown was bestowed upon Perceval in reward for his defeat of the Knight of the Burning Dragon. Perceval left the Circle in Elyza's stewardship. It was later stolen by Nabigan of the Rock but recovered by Gawain. For a time, Perceval was known as the Knight of the Circle of Gold. Interestingly, the author of the Vulgate *Estoire del Saint Graal*, describing the adventure that provided him with the *Estoire*, relates how he came across a messenger who said, "My lord, my lady greets you, she who was rescued by the Knight of the Circle of Gold on the day that the person you know saw the great marvel." These allusions are not otherwise explained.

A VALLET OF THE CIRCLE OF GOLD and a MAIDEN OF THE CIRCLE OF GOLD appear in French verse romance, though their names are not explained. The Maiden, appearing in the Fourth Continuation of Chrétien's *Perceval*, is besieged by a Knight of the Dragon whose appearance and activities mirror the Knight of the Burning Dragon. Part of the narrative of Jacob van Maerlant's *Torec* involves the recovery of a magical golden circlet stolen from its owners, and both Pelleas and Morholt are awarded circlets of gold as a tournament prize in Malory's *Le Morte Darthur*. [*Perlesvaus, VulgHis, Contin4, Marelant, Malory*]

CIRCULAR VALLEY

A valley in which rested a castle, guarded by a lion, and ruled by a heathen lord who never let any Christian man leave the valley alive. Peredur came upon the valley during his adventures, killed the lion, and defeated the lord's warriors in combat, killing two of the heathen lord's sons. The lord eventually surrendered to Peredur, and Peredur sent him to Arthur for penance. [*Peredur*]

CIRENCHESTER

The location where Constantine, Arthur's grandfather, held his first council of lords when he arrived from Brittany to save Britain from the barbarian hordes. In Biket's *Lai du Cor* Arthur gives the earldom of Cirencester to Caradoc after Caradoc—through a magical horn—proves himself the only knight at Arthur's court with a completely faithful wife (who was born in Cirencester). Biket claimed that the horn was on display in Cirencester at the time of his writing (1150–1200). [*Wace, Biket*]

CIS OF ARRAGUS

An Arthurian knight. [*Heinrich*]

CISGON

According to Heinrich von dem Türlin, one of several lands conquered by Uther Pendragon. [*Heinrich*]

CISSA

A Saxon warrior who arrived in Britain in 477 with his father, Ælle, and his two brothers, Cymen and Wlencing. Upon landing in Cymensora, they defeated the Britons and, in 492, fought and won another battle against the Britons at Andredsceaster. The *Chronicle* does not link him to Arthurian tradition, but, assuming that Ambrosius and Arthur existed, Cissa would have been their contemporary (and opponent). [*Anglo*]

CITY OF THE LEGION

In Nennius, a city in Britain that was site of Arthur's ninth battle against the Saxons (see ARTHUR'S BATTLES). As in all of the twelve battles, Arthur was victorious. Geoffrey refers to it several times, but means it to be CAERLEON. Nennius's City of the Legion may also have been Caerleon, but was more probably CHESTER, known by the Romans as *Urbs Legionis*. Another possibility of Castleford, which was known as *Legiolium* in Roman times. [*Nennius*]

CITY WITHOUT A NAME [*Citié sanz Non*]

An enchanted city near the Island without a Name. It seneschal was named Sir Meliadus. The city was visited by Arthur's knight Meraugis during the Grail Quest and by Gawain during his adventures. [*Raoul, VulgMer, Livre*]

CLAALANT

A knight from Listenois who fought in Arthur's army against the Saxons. [*VulgMer*]

CLADAIN THE GREEN

Called the Green Knight, Cladain visited Arthur's court at Glastonbury and dueled with Sir Durmart. The fight went badly for Cladain, and Arthur called a halt to it at the request of Cladain's paramour. Cladain joined Arthur's service. [*Durmart*]

CLADINAS

Constable of Lady Halaés, Gawain's lover. [*Livre*]

CLAELLANS [*Claellus*]

Seneschal of King Pelles of Listenois. He joined Arthur's forces during the Saxon wars. [*Livre*]

CLAELLUS OF GREAT NORTHUMBERLAND

An Arthurian knight who fought against the Saxons at the battle of Clarence. [*Livre*]

CLAIRE

In the Fourth Continuation of *Perceval*, a maiden known as the Damsel of the Cart, because she carried the body of her slain lover around in a cart. Her lover had been killed by the Knight of the Dragon. Claire wore her clothing inside-out in mourning. Perceval met her, learned her story, and avenged her lover's death by killing the Knight of the Dragon. Claire then interred her paramour and retired to a hermitage in Claradeure. Her counterpart in *Perlesvaus* is the unnamed lover of ALAIN. [*Contin4*]

CLAIRS

A vassal of the King with a Hundred Knights. He was present at King Mark's tournament at Lancien. [*Contin4*]

CLAMADEU OF THE ISLES [*Clamadam, Clamadeus(s), Camedyus, Clamide*]

An important character in Chrétien's *Perceval* and Wolfram's *Parzival*. His story was expanded to include pre-Perceval events in the Prose *Lancelot*. His land is variously called the Distant Isles, Iserterre, and Brandigan. He fought against the Saxons in the early days of Arthur's reign, but he became Arthur's enemy after Galehaut conquered him.

Clamadeu's most important role comes in the Grail stories. He sent his seneschal, Anguiguerron or Kingrun (who, in one source, is also his brother), to attack the town of Beaurepaire because he desired the lady of the town, Blancheflor or Condwiramurs. Anguiguerron captured most of the knights of the town and put them in Clamadeu's prison. Blancheflor was on the verge of defeat when Perceval arrived and agreed to become her champion. Perceval defeated both Anguiguerron and Clamadeu in combat and sent them to Arthur's court. He was eventually designated a Knight of the Round Table and participated in the Grail Quest. In Wolfram's version, he falls in love with Cunneware and marries her. In the Middle-English *Sir Perceval of Galles*, his character is called GOLOTHERAME. [*ChretienP, Contin2, Wolfram, LancLac, VulgLanc, VulgMer, Livre, PostQuest, PleierT*]

CLAMADON

A king whose daughter, Byanne, loved Evadem, Arthur's Dwarf Knight. He is perhaps to be identified with CLAMADEU. [*VulgMer*]

CLAMADOZ OF THE SHADOWS

A young man knighted by Arthur. His father, the Red Knight of the Forest of Shadows, and his uncle, Cahot the Red, were both killed by Perceval. For this, Clamadoz sought revenge. Encountering Perceval at the Queen of the Pavilions' tournament, Clamadoz challenged him to a duel. Before this fight could take place, however, Meliot of Logres arrived, furious because Clamadoz had slain his pet lion in the Field of the Lion. Clamadoz was mortally wounded in the battle against Meliot, and never was able to seek his revenge. [Perlesvaus]

CLAMEROI

A lady at Arthur's court. Clameroi, her sister Branie, and many other ladies at the court failed a chastity test involving a mantle. [Heinrich]

CLAPOR

Brother of Lady Helaés, Gawain's lover. [Livre]

CLARAAZ

Cousin of King Clarion of Northumberland. He joined Arthur's battles against the Saxons. [Livre]

CLARADEURE

A town containing a hermitage built by the hermit Heracle. It was the final residence of Claire, a woman whose lover's death was avenged by Perceval. [Contin4]

CLARADUS

A knight who fought for King Mark of Cornwall in a tournament between Mark and the King with a Hundred Knights at the city of Lancien. [Contin4]

CLARAHEX

A Saxon king present at the battle of Clarence. Sir Pharien of Gannes, fighting in Arthur's army, killed him. [Livre]

CLARENCE

A city or duchy in northern Britain. The early prose Lancelot tells us that it belonged to King Tahalais, Arthur's great-grandfather. Because of its ancestral significance, "Clarence" became the battle-cry of Uther and Arthur. The continental texts place it on the border of North Wales or South Wales, suggesting that it may be identified with St. Clare (Clears) in Carmarthenshire.

It was besieged by Saxons in the early days of Arthur's reign, and was the site of two decisive battles. In the first, the Saxon kings, led by Hargadabran, were encountered by the forces of ten British kings and a duke: the King with a Hundred Knights, Lot, Escant, Clarion, Nentres, Caradoc, Brandegorre, Yder, Belinant, Tradelmant, Aguisant, and Urien. After a fierce and bloody battle, the Saxons were victorious.

In the second battle, the principle combatants were the same, with one notable exception: the above kings had allied with Arthur, and the latter brought his forces. The Saxons were destroyed, and the few survivors fled Britain. In this respect, Clarence is reminiscent of the BADON of earlier chronicles.

In the Vulgate romances, the duke of Clarence is named Galescalain, while Malory calls him Chaulance. An independent Duke of Clarence appears in Sir Gawain and the Green Knight as one of Gawain's friends. [LancLac, VulgLanc, VulgMer, Livre, Arthour, SirGawain, Malory]

CLARENT

In the Alliterative Morte Arthure, a magnificent sword kept by Arthur in a vault at Wallingford. Other than Arthur, only Guinevere knew of its location; therefore, when Arthur saw Mordred wielding it in battle, he knew that Guinevere had betrayed him. Mordred carried it throughout the war with Arthur, and perhaps killed Arthur with it. [Allit]

CLARES

A Saxon king who joined King Hargadabran in the invasion of Britain in the early days of Arthur's reign. Arthur's Sir Gaswain killed him at the battle of Clarence. [Livre]

CLARETE

Maidservant of Beauté, daughter of the King of the Isles. Clarete carried the sword Honoree. Anyone who drew the sword would be allowed to marry Beauté. Beaudous, Gawain's son, accomplished this task and accompanied Clarete back to Beauté's lands. [RobertBlo]

CLARETTE

The beloved of the Knight of the Sleeve, who won her hand during a tournament at Arthur's court. [Riddere]

CLARIBALD

One of Arthur's knights who fought in the Roman War. [Allit]

CLARIE [Claire]

The sister of Sir Sagremor in Renaut de Bâgé's Le Bel Inconnu. She was abducted from her father's castle by two evil giants who intended to rape her. Before they got a chance, however, Gawain's son, Guinglain, killed the giants and rescued Clarie. Guinglain later defeated and captured a knight from Saie, and made him promise to escort Clarie safely to her home. She is known as VYOLETTE in Thomas Chestre's Lybeaus Desconnus. [Renaut]

CLARIEL [Clarel]

A Saxon king who, at the beginning of Arthur's reign, joined a number of others, led by Rions, in an invasion of Carmelide. Arthur slew him at the battle of Aneblayse. [VulgMer, Arthour]

CLARIET [Claries]

A knight from Gaul who served either Arthur or King Leodegan of Carmelide. He fought against the Saxons at Carhaix. [VulgMer, Arthour]

CLARINE

Lancelot's mother, according to Ulrich von Zatzikhoven. She was the wife of Pant (Ban) of Genewis. When the barons of Genewis overthrew and killed Pant, Clarine ran off, carrying the infant Lancelot, but a water fairy appeared and snatched the child away. She returned to Genewis, where she enjoyed the protection of the noble Duke Aspyol until Lancelot returned many years later and claimed his ancestral property. Clarine is probably a variation of ELAINE, who is usually given as Lancelot's mother. [UlrichZ]

CLARINON

A knight defeated in combat by Gawain at the Clear Fountain of Love. [Contin1]

CLARION[1] [Clariance, Clarions, Claryaunce]

The King of Northumberland in the Vulgate Merlin and its adaptations. He joined roughly a dozen fellow kings in a revolt against Arthur at the beginning of Arthur's reign. Arthur defeated them at the battle of Bedegraine. They were unable to continue the rebellion because Saxons invaded their lands. Clarion returned home and fortified his castle, Belande. As the Saxons plundered Northumberland, Clarion received aid from Duke Escant of Cambenic. Eventually, he was able to repel the Saxons, but he and his companions were later defeated at the battle of Clarence. He allied with Arthur, fought in the final battles against the Saxons, and accompanied Arthur's campaign to Rome. Both Clarion and his son, Espinogrés, became Knights of the Round Table. In Tennyson's Idylls, he is named as Urien's ally in the war against King Leodegan of Carmelide. [VulgMer, Livre, Arthour, Malory, TennIK]

CLARION[2]

A Saxon king who, under King Rions, invaded Britain in the early days of Arthur's reign. He owned a magnificent horse named Gringolet. Gawain took the horse from him in combat, and kept it for himself. King Ban of Benoic slew him at the battle of Carhaix. [VulgMer, Arthour]

CLARIS

Protagonist of Claris et Laris. The son of Duke Edaris, he joined the Round Table with his friend and constant companion, Laris. His numerous adventures included saving Laris from the affections of a fairy named Madoine, and helping Arthur to save King Urien from a siege by King Tallas of Denmark. Claris fell in love with Lidoine, the wife of the king of Gascony and the sister of Laris. After the king died, Claris saved Lidoine from an attack by Savari the Spaniard and married her, becoming the King of Gascony and Spain. [Claris]

CLARISCHANZE OF TENEBROC

A Grail Maiden in Wolfram's Parzival. She lived at the castle of Munsalvæsche and served King Anfortas. Wolfram would have taken her name from CLARISSANT, Gawain's sister. [Wolfram]

CLARISSANT [Klarisanz]

A beautiful, fair-spoken maiden who was loved by Sir Guiromelant, and was Gawain's servant when he stayed at the castle called Canguin Rock (Chrétien de Troyes) or Salie Castle (Heinrich von dem Türlin). Gawain later learned that Clarissant was his sister (the daughter of King Lot and Morchades, and the niece of Arthur), which caused him some distress since he was Guiromelant's enemy. With Arthur's help, she ended the hostilities between Gawain and Guiromelant, and the two lovers were allowed to marry. They had a daughter named Guignier. Wolfram von Eschenbach calls her ITONJE. [ChretienP, Contin1, Heinrich]

CLARISTANT

A knight who was cuckolded by Sir Alaris. He tracked Alaris down and engaged him in combat, but Claristant's amie turned on him and joined Alaris's assault. Claristant was saved by the timely arrival of Kay and Gaswain. [ProsTris]

CLAROT OF THE SPUR

One of Arthur's knights. He participated in a quest to learn the fate of Merlin. [VulgMer]

CLARYUS OF CLERMONT

A Knight of the Round Table who joined Lancelot's defection from Arthur's court and helped Lancelot rescue Guinevere from the stake. In return for his support, Lancelot made him the duke of Normandy. After Arthur's death, Claryus joined Lancelot in an abbey at Glastonbury and lived there as a hermit until Lancelot's death. He assisted in Lancelot's funeral and then returned to his own lands. [Malory]

CLARYVAUS OF THE FOREST SAVAGE

An Arthurian knights who fought at the Battle of Bedegraine. [Malory]

CLAUD

Father of Arthur's knight Regan. [GeoffHR]

CLAUDAS[1] [Claudius]

A French king who was the sworn enemy of Lancelot's father, King Ban of Benoic, and of Ban's brother, King Bors of Gannes. He first appears in Perlesvaus and the Second Continuation of Chrétien's Perceval. Perlesvaus first describes him as Lancelot's enemy, and relates how he joined with Brian of the Isles, Arthur's treacherous seneschal, in an invasion of Scotland, which Arthur repelled. In the Second Continuation, his brother, Carras, also invades Britain but is likewise unsuccessful.

Claudas plays a major role in the Vulgate *Lancelot* and the Vulgate *Merlin*, from which Malory adapts his version of the character. The stories portray him as a noble but rather Machiavellian king. J. D. Bruce (418) is correct in calling him "the most complex character in [the Vulgate *Lancelot*]—a leader of men, astute, avaricious, jealous of power, and full of ruthless energy in the prosecution of his evil ambitions, yet capable of a deep paternal tenderness and acts of generosity towards the youthful foes whom he has wronged."

In the time of Uther Pendragon, he broke faith with his overlord, King Aramont (or Hoel) of Brittany, from whom Claudas held the lands of Bourges and Berry. He transferred his allegiance to the King of Gaul and, by extension, to Rome. In response, Aramont and Uther invaded and laid waste to Claudas's land, which became known as the Land Laid Waste. Claudas fled and remained in exile until the deaths of Uther and Aramont, when he returned to his kingdom and began making incursions into the lands of Benoic and Gannes.

Kings Ban and Bors allied with Arthur. In return for their assistance against the rebellious kings and the Saxons invading Britain, Arthur agreed to help them repel Claudas's invasion. After the Saxon wars, Arthur, Ban, and Bors defeated Claudas, who had allied with Duke Frollo of Germany and the Roman Pontius Anthony, at the battle of Trebe. When Claudas attacked again, however, Arthur was preoccupied with a war in Britain and could not help the brother kings. Claudas managed to conquer both Benoic and Gannes, and Ban and Bors both perished. Claudas considered invading Arthur's lands, but a clandestine visit to Arthur's court convinced him to abandon the plot. Meanwhile, Claudas endured a partially successful rebellion in Gannes. The Lady of the Lake managed to rescue Lionel and Bors, the young heirs of King Bors, from Claudas's prison. The princes killed Claudas's boorish son, Dorin, in the process. Many years later, Arthur renewed the war against Claudas when Claudas imprisoned a messenger sent by Guinevere to the Lady of the Lake. In the second war, Count Alan of Flanders and Lord Serses of Pagon joined Claudas, as did his son, Claudin. Arthur defeated Claudas, and his former lands fell under the control of Lancelot. Claudas himself fled to Rome, and no one heard from him again. His son Claudin became a Knight of the Round Table and participated in the Grail Quest. [*Perlesvaus*, *Contin2*, *LancLac*, *VulgLanc*, *VulgQuest*, *PostMer*, *PostQuest*, *Arthour*, *Malory*]

CLAUDAS² [Ca(u)das, Clewdas, Gludas]

A knight who visited Arthur's court and related the feats of Guinglain, Gawain's son, after he fought in a sparrowhawk tournament against Gyffroun. [*ChestreLyb*]

CLAUDAS³ OF ZELANDE

A friend of Escanor the Handsome, Gawain's opponent. [*Girart*]

CLAUDIAS

In Tennyson, an ally of King Urien against King Leodegan of Carmelide. Leodegan defeated them with Arthur's assistance. Tennyson probably took the character from CLAUDAS. [*TennIK*]

CLAUDIN¹

A maiden saved by Arthur's Sir Tandareis when she was kidnapped by a disgruntled suitor named Count Kalubin. She came from the Beautiful Forest, and was the daughter of Angnie and Moralde. Another lord named Kandalion later tried to rape her, but Tandareis allowed himself to be taken prisoner to save her. She wanted to marry Tandareis, and petitioned Arthur to do so, but lost the right to Flordibel, Tandareis's long-time love. Through Tandareis's mediation, she married Kalubin. [*PleierT*]

CLAUDIN² THE YOUNGER [Claudino, Claudyne]

The son of King Claudas, Arthur's French enemy. He assisted his father in the war against Arthur, killing many of Arthur's soldiers. An excellent and noble knight, he was spared his father's wicked disposition, and he recognized his Claudas's injustice towards Lancelot's family. When Arthur won the war and Claudas fled to Rome, Claudin stayed in Gannes and surrendered it to Arthur personally. When he learned of the Grail Quest in Britain, he traveled there and was eventually made a Knight of the Round Table. He guarded a bridge at the castle Beauregard, but was defeated by Galahad. He was present at Corbenic when Galahad completed the quest, and attended the mass held by Joseph of Arimathea. [*VulgLanc*, *VulgQuest*, *PostQuest*, *ProsTris*]

CLAUDINS OF CLUSTRES

A friend and relative of Escanor the Handsom, Gawain's opponent. [*Girart*]

CLAUDITTE¹

The child daughter of Burgrave Scherules of Bearosche, and friend to Obilot, the daughter of Duke Lyppaut. [*Wolfram*]

CLAUDITTE²

An infidel queen who loved Perceval's half-brother Feirefiz. He forsook her for the Grail Maiden, Repanse de Schoye. [*Wolfram*]

CLAUVEGRIS

The grandfather of Arthur's Sir Floriant was called the King of Clauvegris. [*Floriant*]

CLEAR FOUNTAIN OF LOVE [*Clere Fonteine d'Amors]

A fountain where Gawain defeated Sir Clarinon. [Contin1]

CLEDAUC [Cledauke]

Father of Arthur's warrior Eddelein. [GeoffHR, Layamon]

CLEDDYF CYFWLCH ("Sword Completed")

Son of Cleddyf Difwlch, and father of Arthur's warriors Bwlch, Cyfwlch, and Syfwlch. [Culhwch]

CLEDDYF DIFWLCH ("Sword Continuous")

Father of Cleddyf Cyfwlch and grandfather of Arthur's warriors Bwlch, Cyfwlch, and Syfwlch. [Culhwch]

CLEGES [Clegis]

A Knight of the Round Table in the Alliterative Morte Arthure and Malory, perhaps influenced by Chrétien's CLIGES. He participated in the Roman War. He joined Lancelot's defection from Arthur's court, helping him rescue Guinevere from the stake and fighting in the battles against Arthur at Joyous Guard and Benoic. In return for his support, Lancelot made him the earl of Angen. A knight of the same name appears in the non-Arthurian story Sir Cleges. [Allit, Malory]

CLEI

In Heinrich von dem Türlin's Diu Crône, the Queen of Clei, a lady at Arthur's court, is one of many to fail a chastity test. [Heinrich]

CLEINES

One of Arthur's dukes in the Norse Erex Saga. He was present at the wedding of Erec and Enide. [Erex]

CLEIR OF VOIE

A knight present at the tournament of Sorgarda, which was won by Gawain. [Heinrich]

CLEMEMYL

Father of Rathtyen, a lady at Arthur's court. [Culhwch]

CLEMENT[1]

A prince of Cornwall and father of Arthur's warrior Pedrog Splintered-Spear. [Triads]

CLEMENT[2]

An Arthurian knight who fought in the Roman War. [Allit]

CLEODALIS

The seneschal of King Leodegan of Carmelide. He was married to a beautiful woman who Leodegan coveted for his own. One night, Leodegan raped Cleodalis's wife, begetting a daughter later known as the False Guinevere. Leodegan then locked Cleodalis's wife in a tower and kept her as a concubine for several years. Cleodalis, however, never stopped serving the king faithfully. He assisted Leodegan, and Arthur, in battles against the Saxons at Carhaix and Aneblayse, and he led a battalion in Arthur's war against Rome. [VulgMer, Livre, Arthour]

CLEOLAS

In the Vulgate Merlin, the proper name of the FIRST CONQUERED KING. He joined Arthur's war against the Saxons and had a hand in their crushing defeat at the second battle of Clarence. [VulgMer]

CLEOR

A count who joined Nogant in a war aganst King Fenise of Ireland. Cleor was defeated in combat by Fenise's lover, Sir Durmart. [Durmart]

CLEORA

In Henry Fielding's The Tragedy of Tragedies, a maid in the service of Arthur's Queen, Dollallolla. She loved Noodle, one of Arthur's courtiers. At the chaotic end of the play, she slays either Noodle or Dollallolla, and is slain in return by either the maid Mustacha, or by princess Huncamunca. [Fielding]

CLEREMOND

A knight of Arthur's who fought in the Roman War under Cador of Cornwall. He was killed in the war against Mordred. [Allit, Malory]

CLEREMUS

A knight of Arthur's who fought in the Roman War. [Allit]

CLIACLES THE ORPHAN [Cleades]

One of Arthur's knights. He fought against the Saxons at the beginning of Arthur's reign, and later participated in a quest to learn the fate of Merlin. [VulgMer, Arthour]

CLIAS

A Greek knight at Arthur's court who attempted the adventure at the Castle of Marvels (which Gawain eventually completed) but was defeated by Florant of Itolac. Found in Wolfram's Parzival, he is probably identical to Chrétien's CLIGES. [Wolfram]

CLICE

A servant of the False Guinevere. She brought a message to Arthur's court falsely accusing Arthur of holding the wrong Guinevere as his queen. [VulgLanc]

CLIDRA THE FAIR

In Ulrich's Lanzalet, a beautiful woman from the enchanted island of Thyle. She committed some breach of courtly etiquette and was sentenced to take the form of a dragon until kissed by the best knight in the world. She hunkered in a British forest until Arthur's knight Roidurant came along. Clidra begged him to kiss her, but he instead fled. Later, he related the story to Lancelot, who came to the forest, kissed the dragon, and restored her to her original form. An analog to this story is found in the FEARSOME KISS adventure of *Le Bel Inconnu*. [*UlrichZ*]

CLIGES[1]

Hero of a romance written by Chrétien de Troyes. With only threadbare connections to Arthur, Chrétien seems to have written his *Cliges* as a sort of anti-*Tristan*. The son of a Greek warrior named Alexander and Gawain's sister Soredamor, Cliges was born in Britain during his father's years at Arthur's court. His father and uncle, Alis, ruled the kingdoms of Greece and Constantinople under an agreement by which Alis was to remain single and beget no children, and the throne was to fall to Cliges upon the deaths of the brothers. Alexander died first, however, and Alis broke their pact by marrying Fenice, the daughter of the Emperor of Germany.

Cliges accompanied Alis's entourage to Germany for his uncle's marriage. Cliges and Fenice fell in love with each other at first sight, and Fenice managed to preserve her virginity by serving Alis a potion that made him believe his dreams of passionate nights with Fenice were the real thing. During their return to Greece, they were ambushed by the Duke of Saxony, whom Cliges defeated in single combat.

Tormented by his unrequited love, Cliges left the kingdom for Britain, as his father had urged, to test his prowess at Arthur's court. He entered a tournament in Oxford, defeated Sagremor, Lancelot, and Perceval, and fought Gawain to a draw. After a brief sojourn with Arthur and Gawain, he returned to Greece.

The lovers developed a plan by which Fenice would feign death, escape from her tomb, and live with Cliges in a secluded tower. Cliges's servant, John, constructed a tomb from which the lady could get free. The plot worked as planned, and Cliges and Fenice enjoyed a time of bliss before their ruse was discovered by a knight named Bertrand. Forced to flee, the lovers lived abroad until Alis's death, when they returned to claim their crowns.

The adventures of an Arthurian knight named Cliges are recounted in later French romances, but these may refer to a different character. [*ChretienC, Clies*]

CLIGES[2] [*Clicés, Clies, Clygés*]

Another knight or knights of Arthur's court who bears little resemblance, except in name, to Chrétien de Troyes's Cliges. In the First Continuation of Chrétien's *Perceval*, his father is named as King Lac. In the romance of *Yder*, he serves Queen Guenloie of Carvain, but is expelled from her court after he openly criticizes her obvious affection for Sir Yder. He later encounters Yder, who promises to reconcile him with his mistress. In *Les Merveilles de Rigomer*, he participates in the quest to conquer Rigomer Castle and, on the way, ends the evil customs of the Accursed Cemetery. *Rigomer*, perhaps linking him tenuously to Chrétien's character, says that he was from Greece. In *Claris et Laris*, he carries Arthur's standard in battle. [*Contin1, Yder, Merveil, Claris*]

CLIGUEILL

According to Geoffrey of Monmouth, a king of Britain in the second century BC. He succeeded his father Capoir and was succeeded by his son Hely. His reign was characterized by peace and justice. [*GeoffHR*]

CLIMACHIDES [*Clamacidés*]

The baptismal name of a knight who served the first King Nascien. His hand was sliced off in a battle against King Tholomer of Babylonia, but it grew back when he touched the stump to a cross on King Mordrains' shield. Witnessing this miracle, Climachides, Nascien, and Mordrains immediately converted to Christianity. Climachides followed Joseph of Arimathea towards Britain, but was unable to cross the Channel because of some unspoken sin. Nascien later brought him across in a boat. [*VulgEst*]

CLIMADÉS

A Saxon king who, under King Hargadabran, fought aganst Arthur's forces at Clarence. Leonce of Paierne killed him. [*Livre*]

CLINSCHOR [*Klingsor*]

A powerful sorcerer in Wolfram's *Parzival*, formerly the Duke of Terre de Labur, nephew of Vergil of Naples (author of the *Aeneid*). While a duke, he fell in love with Iblis, the wife of King Ibert of Sicily. When Ibert discovered that his wife and Clinschor were having an affair, he had Clinschor castrated. Clinschor fled to Britain to heal and study the magical arts. His talents made him a startling necromancer, and he used his magic to create the enchanted Schastel Marveile (Castel of Marvels) in Terre Marveile (Land of Marvels). Inside, he placed Lit Marveile (Bed of Marvels or Perilous Bed)—an extremely perilous adventure. He imprisoned Gawain's mother Sangive, Gawain's sisters Itonje and Cundrie, and Arthur's mother Arnive in the castle, where they remained until Gawain braved the Perilous Bed and won. An analogous character appears in Heinrich von dem Türlin's *Diu Crône* as GANSGUOTER. Clinschor also appears in the German compilation *Wartburgkrieg*, where he engages in a poetic competition with Wolfram von Eschenbach himself. [*Wolfram*]

CLODDRUS

A Knight of the Round Table who appears at the healing of Sir Urry. [*Malory*]

CLODIUS

King of nothern Germany who, in one French chronicle, became Arthur's ally in the Roman War. [*Liber*]

CLODOVEUS [Clodvis, Codo]

First king of Cornwall in the Prose *Tristan*, apparently based on Clovis, the first Christian king of the Franks. *Tristan* makes him the ancestor of Tristan. He had a son named Anzilere and a daughter named Cressille. His son killed King Appollo of Lyoness, for which Clodoveus executed him. King Clodoveus adopted King Apollo's orphaned son, Candaces. When Candaces came of age, Clodoveus married him to his daughter and made him heir to Cornwall. [*ProsTris, Tavola*]

CLOFAUT [Clefaut]

One of Arthur's warriors. [*GeoffHR*]

CLOTAR

A tyrant who, in Blackmore's *King Arthur*, ruled France with an iron fist. Responding to please for justice from Clotar's vassals, Arthur traveled to France and killed the king. A certain King Clothair ruled the Franks in the middle of the sixth century. [*BlackmoreK*]

CLOTEN

According to Geoffrey of Monmouth, a king of Britain in the third or second century BC. Cloten succeeded King Eliduc and was succeeded by King Gurgintius. [*GeoffHR*]

CLOWDMUR

A knight in Arthur's service who fought in the Roman War. [*Allit*]

CLOWN

Merlin's uncle in the Elizabethan play *The Birth of Merlin*. He tried to assist his sister, Joan Go-too't, in identifying Merlin's father. He became a companion of Merlin after his birth. [*Birth*]

CLOYES

A land in Galehaut's kingdom. The Duke of Cloyes recommended King Bagdemagus of Gorre when Galehaut needed a temporary ruler for Sorelois. [*VulgLanc*]

CLUSE¹

A mountain near the city of Bearosche which was one of the sites of the battle of Bearosche, in which many of Arthur's knights were captured by King Poydiconjunz. [*Wolfram*]

CLUSE²

A land in Der Stricker's *Daniel*, conquered by Daniel of the Blossoming Valley and King Arthur. Its lord, Matur, demanded Arthur's fealty, using two invulnerable giants as his primary threat. Daniel vanquished the giants, and Arthur slew Matur. After they defeated Cluse's seven armies, Daniel married Danise, Matur's widow, becoming king of the land, subject to Arthur. Arthur appointed Beladigant as Cluse's duke. Reminiscent of the enchanted otherworlds of Welsh legend, it was completely encircled by mountains (like SYRIA in Wirnt's *Wigalois*) and could only be entered through a narrow passageway. It was blessed with bold knights, beautiful maidens, constant revelry, and exotic beasts, including elephants and the Babian bird. For Cluse's name, Der Stricker could have used Wolfram's CLUSE, the Latin *clausus*, meaning "closed," or any of several locations called "Kluse" in the German Alps. [*Stricker*]

CLUST ("Ear")

Son of Clustfeinydd and one of Arthur's warriors. He shared the responsibility of Arthur's gatekeeper with seven to nine other warriors, commanded by the chief gatekeeper Glewlwyd Strong Grip. [*Culhwch, Geraint*]

CLUSTFEINYDD ("Hearer") [Clustfeinad]

Father of Arthur's warrior Clust. [*Culhwch, Geraint*]

CLYDNO ("Famous")

A warrior from Edinburgh who fathered Arthur's warriors Eurneid and Cynon. A historical Clydno was a leader of northern Britain in the sixth century (Gantz, 148n). [*Culhwch, Owain*]

CNYCHWR

An Arthurian warrior who was the son of Nes. He is borrowed from an non-Arthurian Irish hero named Conchobar son of Ness. [*Culhwch*]

COCH ("Red")

Son of Caw, one of twenty brothers, and one of Arthur's warriors. [*Culhwch*]

COCTA

In Wace, a Roman senator who joined Lucius's war against Arthur. Geoffrey of Monmouth mentions a GAIUS METELLUS COTTA, who Wace seems to have broken into three separate people. [*Wace, Layamon*]

COCU

A race of men who were part of the defense of Rigomer Castle. They were overcome by Arthur's knights. [*Merveil*]

CODIAS LONGHAND

A Knight of the Round Table who participated in the Grail Quest. [*PostQuest*]

COEL

The duke of Colchester who, according to Geoffrey of Monmouth, took the throne of Britain from King Asclepiodotus in the early fourth century. He acquiesced to the power of Rome on the condition that he be allowed to keep the crown. However, he died soon afterwards. His daughter Helena married the Roman warrior Constantine, who became king in Coel's place. He is often seen as

Arthur's ancestor. His historicity is uncertain. King Coel, oddly, is remembered best in the children's rhyme "Old King Cole." [*Henry, GeoffHR, Wace*]

COGUILLANT OF MAUTIREC

A knight who participated in a tournament, won by Lancelot, at Noauz. [*ChretienL*]

COIL [*Coitt*]

Father of Arthur's warrior Cheneus. [*GeoffHR, Wace*]

COILL[1]

According to Geoffrey of Monmouth, a king of Britain in the third or second century BC. He was the son of King Catell and the father of King Porrex. [*GeoffHR*]

COILL[2]

A first or second century king of Britain in Geoffrey's chronicle. The son of King Marius, Coill was raised in Rome and he dutifully recognized Rome's sovereignty over Britain. He was succeeded by his son, Lucius the Glorious. [*GeoffHR*]

COLCHESTER [*Doleceste*]

A city in southeast England, in Essex. The Romans called it Kaercolun or Camulodunum. The latter name has been suggested as the source of CAMELOT. According to Geoffrey of Monmouth, Colchester was ruled in the fourth century by Coel and was probably named after him. According to Chrétien, Count Branles was the ruler of Colchester in Arthur's time. [*GeoffHR, ChretienE*]

COLEDAWG ("Cultivation")

In one of the Welsh Triads, Coledawg, son of Gwynn, is annotated as one of the "three who could not be expelled from Arthur's court." The larger legend to which this remark refers is lost to modern literature. [*Triads*]

COLGRIM [*Colgrin, Colgrym*]

A Saxon duke, brother of Baldulph, who assumed leadership of the Saxons after the deaths of Hengist, Octa, and Eosa. Colgrim invaded Britain in the early days of Arthur's reign. Arthur defeated him at the river Douglas and pushed him back to York, where he was saved by the arrival, from Germany, of Duke Cheldric and another brigade of warriors. Arthur returned to defeat Colgrim's army in the forest of Caledon, and the Saxons agreed to return to Germany. They broke the treaty, however, and sailed south to conquer Totnes. They marched north, ravaging the land, and besieged Bath. Arthur arrived in Bath and killed Colgrim and Baldulph. [*GeoffHR, Wace*]

COLIVRE THE PROUD

Brother of Brun (Breus) the Pitiless. He was killed in combat by Kay. [*Girart*]

COLL

An enchanter in Welsh legend who studied under Gwythelyn the Dwarf. He was said to have tended the magical pig Henwen, which gave him the designation of one of the "powerful swineherds of Britain." His name is attached to Arthur's in a revised Welsh Triad, in which Arthur tries to hunt down and kill Henwen. He is otherwise non-Arthurian, but his name was used by some Middle-English romance writers, including Chaucer. [*Triads*]

COLLEVAL OF LETERBE

A lord defeated by Perceval. [*Wolfram*]

COLLOCAULAS [*Ancalus, Colocaulnus*]

A Saxon chieftain who participated in the siege of Aneblayse (in Leodegan's kingdom) in the early days of Arthur's reign. Arthur's forces routed the Saxons, and Sir Nascien killed Collocaulas. [*VulgMer, Arthour*]

COLOGIA

In *La Tavola Ritonda*, a castle visited by Tristan and Lancelot during the Grail Quest. Count Sebio of Cologia threw a tournament, offering his daughter to any knight who could defeat him and a hundred of his soldiers. Tristan and Lancelot won the tournament and gave Sebio's daughter to Richevie Ventura, the son of the vavasor who had lodged them. Lancelot and Tristan then had the town baptized. [*Tavola*]

COLOGNE [*Coloine*]

A city on the Rhine River in Germany. In Chrétien de Troyes's *Cliges*, it is the site of Emperor Alis's marriage to Fenice. In the Vulgate *Lancelot*, Cologne is named as the home of the scribe Arodian and the sage Agnatices. *Claris et Laris* puts it in the realm of Emperor Henry of Germany, Claris's father-in-law. Malory tells us that Lucius the Roman besieged and won a castle in Cologne during his campaign against Arthur. [*ChretienC, VulgLanc, Malory*]

COLOMBE

The paramour of Sir Launceor in Malory's *Le Morte Darthur*. After Launceor was killed by Balin, Colombe, overcome with grief, threw herself on his sword. King Mark of Cornwall arrived, buried Launceor and Colombe, and erected a tomb on which he wrote their story and the circumstances of their deaths. The Post-Vulgate calls the same woman LIONE. [*Malory*]

COLUMBINE

"Heroine" of Aaron Hill's 1760 play *Merlin in Love, or: Youth Against Magic*. Stolen from her lover, Harlequin, by Merlin's enchantments, an offended Columbine takes Merlin's wand, turns him into a donkey, and returns to her paramour. [*HillA*]

COLURMENT

Heinrich von dem Türlin's *Diu Crône* contains an allusion to Gawain having picked Lady Fortune's flowers on the field of Colurment, and presenting them to a lady named Leigomon. This was considered a brave act. [*Heinrich*]

COMBE [*Escombes*]

A British forest where Gawain encountered Girflet while on a quest to find Lancelot. The two knights dueled, but stopped when they realized each other's identities. They then met two lovely maidens who guided them to further adventures. [*VulgLanc*]

COMMINGES

One of Lancelot's French lands. He made Sir Hebes earl of Comminges in return for Hebes' support in the conflict against Arthur. [*Malory*]

COMPOSTELA [*Composterne*]

A Spanish land conquered and converted to Christianity by King Flualis, as predicted by Merlin. [*VulgMer*]

CONAIS THE WHITE

A Knight of the Round Table who embarked with the others on the Grail Quest. [*PostQuest*]

CONAL

A non-Arthurian Celtic hero who becomes one of Arthur's warriors in Richard Hole's *Arthur, or the Northern Enchantment in Seven Books* (1789). [*Hole*]

CONAN[1]

The name bestowed by Layamon upon the King of South Wales who, in Geoffrey of Monmouth, was Merlin's maternal grandfather. [*Layamon*]

CONAN[2]

Nephew of King Constantine, Arthur's successor to the throne of Britain, in Geoffrey of Monmouth's *Historia*. Conan murdered his uncle and poisoned all of Constantine's sons so that he could take the throne. After several years of tyrannical rule, he fell off a horse and died. In his sixth-century diatribe, Gildas reproaches a certain Conan of Powys, accusing him of falsehood, fornication, adultery, and murder. This is probably the historical prototype for Geoffrey's character. [*Gildas, GeoffHR*]

CONAN[3]

A nobleman who urged Mordred, after he usurped the throne of Britain, to reconcile with Arthur. Mordred ignored his advice. [*HughesT*]

CONAN[4] MERIADOC

A nobleman in Roman Briton who desired to succeed his uncle, Octavius, to the British throne. When Octavius chose Maximus, a Roman senator, Conan became enraged and declared war. Faced with little support from the other noblemen, however, he eventually made peace. In return, Maximus gave him the kingdom of Brittany and the lady Ursula, the daughter of King Dionotus of Cornwall. One of Conan's descendants, Constantine, was Arthur's grandfather. [*GeoffHR, Wace*]

CONAN[5] THE BOLD

One of Arthur's knights. He participated in one of Gawain's quests to find Lancelot. [*LancLac, VulgLanc*]

CONART

An Irish country traversed by Lancelot on his way to Rigomer Castle, probably the land of Connaught. [*Merveil*]

CONDWIRAMURS

In Wolfram's *Parzival*, Perceval's wife, the daughter of King Tampenteire, and the niece of Gornemant. Perceval came to her rescue when her land of Brobarz was invaded and her city of Belrepeire was besieged by Clamide and Kingrun. The two were defeated by Perceval. Afterwards, Perceval and Condwiramurs were married, but it wasn't long before Perceval set off in search of further adventures. Condwiramurs was constantly on his mind, but he wasn't able to return to her for five years, at which time he found that she had bore him two sons: Kardeiz and Loherangrin. Perceval brought her to Munsalvæsche to become his Grail Queen. Her counterpart is BLANCHEFLUR in Chrétien's *Perceval* and LUFAMOUR in *Sir Perceval of Galles*. [*Wolfram*]

CONISBROUGH [*Cunungeberg*]

A British castle—formerly called Kaerconan—controlled by the Saxon leader Hengist. It was the site of Hengist's last stand against Ambrosius Aurelius. Eldol, Earl of Gloucester, personally captured Hengist at the battle. It was apparently named after CONAN Meriadoc. [*GeoffHR*]

CONMAINS

A knight in Arthur's service. [*Girart*]

CONON[1] [*Kahenin*]

A duke. He gave a castle to two giants who had rescued him from prison. The castle was later conquered by Lancelot. [*VulgLanc*]

CONON[2]

In Dryden's *King Arthur*, the duke of Cornwall under Arthur. His daughter, Emmeline, became Arthur's wife. [*Dryden*]

CONRAD

A Roman bishop who accused Merlin of heresy. Merlin met him in Rome before Pope Gregorio and exposed Conrad's own sins, exonerating himself. [*VitaMer*]

CONSTANCE

Wife of Yonet, a servant of the Lady Andrivete, Kay's bride. [*Girart*]

CONSTANS [*Constance, Constant(ine)*]

Son of the British King Constantine and brother of Ambrosius Aurelius and Uther (and thus, Arthur's uncle). Constans was raised in the church of Amphibalus and became a monk in Winchester, but was pushed by Vortigern, Earl of Gwent, to become King of Britain after his father's death (both of Constantine's other children were too young to assume the throne). Dizzy with the power, Constans accepted and fled the monastery, and Vortigern forced the abbot to unconsecrate him. It was Vortigern himself who laid the crown upon Constans head; he was made king without approval of the bishops. Constans became a puppet king, controlled by Vortigern. At Vortigern's request, Constans invited a number of Picts to stay at his court, to serve as ambassadors from the Pictish tribes in Gaul. Vortigern craftily caused the Picts (led by Gille Callaet) to despise Constans, and they eventually cut off his head while he was sleeping. Vortigern then assumed the throne.

Called MAINE by the Vulgate *Merlin*, Constans is based on a historical figure—the son of "Constantine III" of Britain. He did, in fact, leave a monastery when his father launched a war against Rome. After helping his father conquer Gaul and Spain, Constans was killed by Roman forces. [*GeoffHR, Wace, Layamon*]

CONSTANTIA

In the Elizabethan play *The Birth of Merlin*, the daughter of Lord Donobert and a maiden at Aurelius Ambrosius's court. She was betrothed to Cador of Cornwall until her sister, Modestia, convinced Constantia to join her in a nunnery. [*Birth*]

CONSTANTINE[1] [*Constantin(s), Constantius, Custenhin*]

Arthur's grandfather, found earliest in Geoffrey of Monmouth. Constantine was the brother of Aldroen—ruler of Brittany—and the father of Constans, Ambrosius Aurelius, and Uther Pendragon (or Maine, Pendragon, and Uther, as Robert de Boron and the Vulgate *Merlin* have it). His father may have been named Tahalais, though Baudin Butor makes him the son of Londres. Butor is the only writer to name Constantine's wife: Ivoire, sister of King Ban.

When Guethelin, Archbishop of London, came to Brittany to seek help in driving the Picts and Huns from Britain, Constantine agreed to accomplish the tasks. He traveled to Britain and destroyed the barbarians. Then, since their was no other suitable candidate, he was crowned king at Silchester. In the original accounts, Constantine ruled for ten years before he was assassinated by one of his servants—a Pict named Cadal (or, in some texts, by Vortigern himself); but the Vulgate *Merlin* purports that he died of old age. After his death,

Vortigern, the Earl of Gwent, foisted Constans to the throne.

Constantine is based on a historical Roman army soldier who served in Britain. His story is given by Bede. In 407, his troops elected him "Emperor Constantine III" of Rome—despite the existence of a legitimate Roman emperor named Honorius—and he embarked for the continent on a war of acquisition. After conquering Gaul and Spain, he surrendered to the legitimate Roman army and was soon murdered. Like the fictional Constantine, he apparently had a son named Constans who left a monastery, but who was already dead at the time of Constantine's murder. The historical character survives in the accounts of Nennius and William of Malmesbury, and in a second Constantine mentioned by Geoffrey of Monmouth, but with legendary embellishments. Nennius thought that he was the King of Britain before Vortigern, though he gives a fairy accurate account of his continental exploits and his death. Geoffrey's second King Constantine, who preceded Arthur's grandfather, actually managed to conquer Rome from the Emperor Maxentius, but found his British throne usurped by Octavius. [*GeoffHR, Wace, LancLac, VulgMer, Butor, Pierre*]

CONSTANTINE[2] [*Constantyn, Co(n)staunce, Costauns*]

The king of Britain who succeeded Arthur. A son of Cador of Cornwall, he was a Knight of the Round Table and Arthur's cousin or nephew. Arthur left him as regent of Britain when he left to fight the Roman War, and Constantine was therefore in position for the crown when Arthur died without an heir. Geoffrey of Monmouth says that Arthur gave him the crown after the battle of Camlann, of which Arthur and Constantine were the only survivors. In Jean D'Outremeuse's *Ly Myreur des Histors*, it is Lancelot who places Constantine on the throne. Malory reports that he was a good king, restored the Archbishop of Canterbury to his diocese, and restored order to the realm. Geoffrey says that he faced problems with the Saxons and with the two sons of Mordred, but was able to overcome them. When Mordred's sons took refuge in churches, Constantine pursued them and killed them before the altars. "Smitten by God's judgment" for this sacrilege, Constantine was killed by his nephew Conan, who succeeded him.

Constantine is based on a historical king of Devon and Cornwall who Gildas upbraided for tyranny in *De Excidio Britanniae*. [*Gildas, GeoffHR, Wace, Layamon, Boccaccio, Allit, Malory*]

CONSTANTINE[3] [**Custenhin, Custennin*]

Son of Mynwyedig and father of Goreu in *Culhwch and Olwen*. Constantine was the shepherd of Ysbaddaden, the giant father of Olwen, and he gave lodging to Culhwch and his party during their visit to Ysbaddaden's realm. He was apparently married to one of Culhwch's aunts. Ysbaddaden had slain twenty-three of his sons, so he kept the last, Goreu, hidden in a chest. The Triads call him Arthur's cousin. This identification plus his residence in

Cornwall suggests that he is a Welsh prototype of CONSTANTINE[2]. [*Culhwch, Triads, Dream*]

CONSTANTINE[4] [*Custenhin*]

Farther of Erbin and grandfather of Geraint. [*Geraint*]

CONSTANTINOPLE [*Constantinenoble, Costentineoble*]

A seaport in northwest Turkey founded in 600 BC as the capital of the Roman Empire in the east (Byzantium), which continued to flourish for nearly 1000 years after the fall of Rome. Its original name was Byzantium, changed to Constantinople in AD 330. after the Roman Emperor Constantine the Great. The present name of the city is Istanbul.

From AD 457 to 474, Constantinople was ruled by Emperor Leo I. From 474 to 491, it was ruled by Emperor Zeno, who sent the Ostrogoths under Theodoric I into Italy to drive out the Germans. Zeno was followed by Anastsius (491–518) and Justin I (519–527). Between 527 and 565, which would encompass the Arthurian period as given by the early chronicles and the *Annales Cambriae*, the empire was governed by Justinian the Great, who restored a great many of the territories lost to the German tribes, including Italy itself.

Saving the appearance of Leo in Geoffrey of Monmouth's chronicle as Arthur's enemy during the Roman War, none of the Arthurian tales that include Constantinople reflect its actual history during the Arthurian period. An "Empress of Constantinople" makes an appearance in the Welsh tale of *Peredur*. While visiting Britain, she chanced to see the noble Peredur in a tournament. Peredur fell in love with the Empress at first sight, and he sent all of the men he defeated in the tournament to do honor to her. Later the two met, and the Empress revealed herself to be the same woman who had earlier given Peredur an enchanted stone, which had enabled him to defeat the monster that plagued the King of Suffering and his sons. In gratitude and love, Peredur accompanied the Empress to Constantinople and ruled for fourteen years before returning to Britain.

In Chrétien de Troyes's *Cliges*, the empire of Constantinople and Greece is ruled in succession by Emperor Alexander, Emperors Alis and Alexander, and Emperor Cliges. In the Vulgate *Merlin*, it is the birthplace of Sir Sagremor; Emperor Hadrian is his grandfather or uncle. The Vulgate *Lancelot* tells us that Helain the White—the son of Sir Bors—eventually became its emperor. *Floriant and Florete* gives the empire to Emperor Filimenis, who went to war with Arthur. Sir Floriant married Florete, Filimenis's daughter, and inherited the empire. [*ChretienC, Peredur, VulgLanc, VulgMer, PostMer, Floriant*]

CONYN ("Stalk")

Son of Caw, one of twenty brothers, and one of Arthur's warriors. [*Culhwch*]

COPPER TOWER

A monolith in the Trial Castle. It was inhabited by demons and was worshipped by the castle's populace. Perceval destroyed the tower and expunged paganism from the castle. [*Perlesvaus*]

CORBALAIN

The lady of Corbalain was Sir Galescalain's aunt. Her daughter encountered Galescalain during his adventures and steered him toward the adventure of the Dolorous Tower. [*VulgLanc*]

CORBANIA

La Tavola Ritonda tells us that Lancelot's unnamed daughter lived in the forest of Corbania, doing penance for an unspecified sin. [*Tavola*]

CORBENIC [*Carbonek, Corlenot, Corbenich(e), Corbierc, Corbyn, Orberique*]

The GRAIL CASTLE in the Vulgate, Post-Vulgate, and Malory. It was constructed in Listenois, or the Strange Land, by Alan and Joshua, followers of Joseph of Arimathea, and by King Calafes, who the brothers had converted to Christianity. The Grail was kept in the Palace of Adventures inside the castle. Joshua was the first king of Corbenic, followed by Aminadap, Carcelois, Manuel, Lambor, Pellehan, and Pelles, who was king during Arthur's reign. Pelles lived in Corbenic with his daughter, Elaine (the mother of Galahad) and his son, Eliezier. Other residents included Sir Ulphyne and the Maimed King.

Some time during its history, Tanabos the Enchanter ensorcelled Corbenic in such a way that no one could find it, except by chance—no matter how many times he had been there. Its infrequent visitors would often dine with Pelles, and would witness the Grail Procession. Over the years, it was visited by knights such as Lancelot, Gawain, Lamorat, Hector, Gaheris, and Palamedes. Although the importance of the Grail Procession and the Grail Question are somewhat dubious in these romances, the visiting knights generally failed to recognize the Grail for what it was. Lancelot, during his several visits, rescued Elaine from a boiling tub, killed a serpent, and recovered from a period of insanity. Gawain (the first knight to visit Corbenic in Arthur's time) was expelled in humiliation after his lustful eyes were drawn away from the Grail and to the beautiful maiden carrying it.

Galahad, Perceval, and Bors completed the Grail Quest at Corbenic, and attended a holy mass held there by Joseph of Arimathea (or his son, Josephus). Helain the White, Arthur the Less, Meraugis, Claudin, Lambeguez, Pinable, and Persides were allowed to look on. After the Grail was taken to Sarras by Galahad, the Grail Castle lost its enchantments, but remained standing until the time of Charlemagne, who razed it when he invaded England.

The third continuation of Chrétien's *Perceval*, which is part of an earlier Grail tradition but which was written after the Vulgate Cycle, shows the influence of the Vulgate romances by naming Corbenic as the Fisher King's kingdom. It fell to Perceval after the Fisher King's death. When Perceval retired to a hermitage, he bestowed it upon the King of Maronne.

The Vulgate *Estoire del Saint Graal* claims that *Corbenic* means "holy vessel" in Chaldean. The French author hardly needed to visit the Chaldean language for a source, as *cors benoit* is French for "blessed body." R. S. Loomis (*Grail*, 242–4) thought that the authors had confused *cor benoit* ("blessed horn") for *cors benoit*, and he proposed that the name ultimately went back to the magical horn owned by Bran the Blessed in Welsh literature (see THIRTEEN TREASURES). J. D. Bruce, however, noted the existence of a town named *Corbeni* in Picardy, not far from the monestery where he believed the author of the Vulgate *Queste* lived (Bruce, 394n). [*VulgLanc, VulgQuest, VulgEst, Contin3, PostQuest, Malory, TennIK*]

CORBON [*Corbans*]

In the French romance *La Bataille de Loquifer*, the illegitimate son of the hero Renoart and Morgan le Fay. [*Bataille*]

CORCECA

A blind woman who lived with her mute daughter, Abessa. The lady Una lodged with them after she was abandoned by the Red Cross Knight. [*Spenser*]

CORDANT

A Saxon warrior who, under King Rions, opposed Arthur and King Leodegan of Carmelide at the battle of Carhaix. Arthur's Sir Brithael slew him there. [*VulgMer, Arthour*]

CORDELIA

Daughter of King Lear and sister of Regan and Goneril. When asked by her father to quantify her love, Cordelia answered honestly that she loved him just as any daugher loved a father. Her sisters lied and cajoled Lear. Lear divided Britain between Regan, Goneril, and their husbands, and exiled Cordelia to France, where she married King Aginappus. Eventually, after he had been dispossessed and humiliated, Lear came to realize his mistake. He traveled to France, reconciled with Cordelia, and amassed an army to retake Britain from his daughters and sons-in-law. The expedition was successful. When Lear died, Cordelia succeeded him to the throne. She ruled five years before her nephews, Margan and Cunedag, rebelled against her and imprisoned her. She took her own life in prison. [*GeoffHR*]

CORDOVA [*Cordewa*]

A city in Spain that was allied, according to the Alliterative *Morte Arthure*, with the Roman Procurator Lucius. The "Captain of Cordova" was captured by Arthur's Sir Clegis during the Roman War. [*Allit*]

COREUSEUS ("Fury") [*Courechouse, Couroucese*]

The sword used by Ban, Lancelot's father. [*VulgMer*]

CORFIL BERFACH

One of King Arthur's warriors in Welsh legend. He is taken from the Irish character Conall Cernach. [*Culhwch*]

CORIS

One of Arthur's knights in Béroul's *Tristan*, present at Isolde's chastity trial. [*Beroul*]

CORK [*Corque*]

A country on the southern coast of Ireland. A man named Garras is given as the King of Cork by Chrétien de Troyes, while in *Les Merveilles de Rigomer*, Cork's king is named as Frion, whose daughter was saved by Lancelot. [*ChretienE, Merveil*]

CORNALIS

A Saxon king who, under King Hargadabran, fought aganst Arthur's forces at Clarence. Agravain killed him. [*Livre*]

CORNAN

The horse belonging to Arthur's warrior Peredur. [*Triads*]

CORNASIN

A castle in Cornwall where Tristan recuperated there after he was wounded with a poisoned arrow. [*Tavola*]

CORNETO [*Cornette*]

A city or land allied to Lucius the Roman. During the Roman War, the "Captain of Corneto" was captured by Arthur's forces. [*Allit*]

CORNEUS

A duke and father of Arthur's Sir Lucan the Butler. [*Malory*]

CORNICAS

King of Turkey in *Floriant et Florete*. He was allied to Emperor Filimenis of Constantinople. Floriant killed him during Floriant's war with Filimenis. [*Floriant*]

CORNICANS

One of the many Saxon kings to invade northern Britain in the early days of Arthur's reign. Arthur defeated his forces at the battle of Clarence, and Cornicans fled. [*VulgMer, Livre*]

CORNIX

One of the noble Byzantine warriors that Alexander brought to Britain from Constantinople. He fought for

Arthur in the battle against the traitorous Angres of Windsor. [*ChretienC*]

CORNU

A race of men who were part of the defenses at Rigomer Castle. They were overcome by Arthur's knights. [*Merveil*]

CORNWALL [*Cornewaile, Cornewall(e), Corn(e)well, Cornoaille, Cornouaille, Cornovaglia, Cornwaile, Kornoval*]

A region of Britain, at the southwest tip, including all areas west of the Tamar River. Geoffrey attributes the land's name to Corineus, a warrior of King Brute's. In Arthurian times, Cornwall was united with Devon to form the kindgom of Dumnonia. In French romance, Cornwall is sometimes confused with Cornouaille in Brittany.

Cornwall's chief castle in many legends is Tintagel. The Duke of Cornwall—in most stories named Gorlois—made war against Uther and was slain by him. Gorlois's widow, Igerne, married King Uther and became the mother of King Arthur. In the Tristan and Vulgate romances, Mark is the king or duke of the land. According to *La Tavola Ritonda*, it was divided among Lancelot, Amoroldo, Mordred, and Governal after Mark's death. In other legends, rulers of Cornwall are variously given as Yder, Cador, Cabarentin, and Clement. Welsh legend makes Gwynn Hyfar steward of Cornwall and Devon for Arthur. It was one of the lands that Arthur offered to Mordred in a peace that was never reached. Arthur's final battle at Camlann may have been fought within its borders.

In the English ballad "King Arthur and King Cornwall," the King of Cornwall is a sorcerer and the richest king in the world. He had once lived in Arthur's kingdom (in Brittany) and had fathered a daughter on Guinevere. Guinevere needled Arthur with tales of Cornwall's splendor until Arthur embarked on a quest to find the land. Arthur and his knights managed to tame a fiend called the Burlow-Beanie, which Cornwall owned, and they used it to gain possession of Cornwall's magical items. Arthur used an enchanted sword to behead the king. [*Culhwch, Thomas, VulgLanc, VulgMer, ProsTris, Stanz, Malory, KingA&C*]

CORRANT [*Conrat, Garaunt*]

A knight of Carmelide, and a cousin of Queen Guinevere. He was sent by Morgan le Fay with three others to kill the young Alexander the Orphan, but Alexander defeated them. [*ProsTris, Prophecies, Malory*]

CORS HUNDRED CLAWS

One of Arthur's warriors in Welsh legend. Cors owned an special leash. As one of his tasks, the warrior Culhwch had to obtain this leash to hold the hound Drudwyn when hunting Twrch Trwyth. Arthur himself retrieved the leash on the behalf of Culhwch. [*Culhwch*]

CORSABRIN[1]

A Saracen knight who loved the daughter of King Baudac. The lady did not return Sir Corsabrin's love, so Corsabrin began telling people that she was insane. Baudac's daughter convinced Palamedes to fight Corsabrin, hoping to get rid of him. The combat was held during the tournament at Sorelois. Palamedes defeated Corsabrin. In the Prose *Tristan*, Corsabrin commits suicide rather than surrender, and a devil takes away his soul. In Malory, Palamedes cuts off Corsabrin's head, and a horrible stench emits from his body as his soul leaves, for Corsabrin had not been christened. The knights and lords at attendance took this as a sign, and begged Palamedes to be christened, but Palamedes said he would not until he had completed "seven true battles for Jesus's sake." Corsabrin was the son of Aristot and the brother of Rechaux. [*ProsTris, Malory*]

CORSABRIN[2]

King of Turkey in *Claris et Laris*, alled to Emperor Thereus of Rome. During Thereus's war against Arthur, Corsabrin was slain by Yvain. [*Claris*]

CORSAPIN

A vavasor in the service of Nascien and Flegetine. He left with Flegetine and his son Elicanor for Britain, where he joined with Joseph of Arimathea's followers. [*VulgEst*]

CORSIDARES

A Knight of the Round Table who participated in the Grail Quest. [*PostQuest*]

CORTAINE ("Shortened") [*Cortana*]

The name Charlemagne gave to Tristan's sword when he found it hanging around the statue of Tristan in front of Leverzep. Charlemagne found the sword too heavy, so he had it shortened. [*ProsTris, Tavola*]

CORTOIS OF HUMBERLAND

A knight slain by Orguelleus the Fay and Sir Gomeret because they believed him to be Gawain, their enemy. When they realized their mistake, Orguelleus, a sorcerer, resurrected him. [*Atre*]

COSEN

Father of Brangain, Isolde's handmaid. [*SagaTI*]

COSIGNANO

A castle awarded by Arthur to a squire after the squire brought him some good news. [*Tavola*]

COTATRE [*Cotovatre*]

The town of the smith Trabuchet in Chrétien de Troyes's *Perceval*. Perceval had to travel there to repair the Grail Sword. It becomes a castle in the Fourth Continuation of *Perceval* and a kingdom in Girart d'Amiens's *Escanor*. R. S.

Loomis (*Tradition*, 408) identified it with "Scottewatre," indicating the Firth of Forth. [*ChretienP*, *Contin4*, *Girart*]

COUARS ("Coward") [*Forcoars*]

A Saxon king who opposed Arthur and King Leodegan of Carmelide at the siege of Aneblayse. Arthur killed him in battle. [*VulgMer*, *Arthour*]

COUNSELOR KNIGHTS

A triad of warriors in Arthur's court: Cynon, Aron, and Llywarch. They counseled Arthur on political matters. [*Triads*]

COUNT OF THE BROCHES

A knight who opposed King Narboac in a tournament. Gawain fought on the count's side but was defeated by Sir Hector, battling for Narboac. [*VulgLanc*]

COUNT OF THE PASS [*Earl de Pase*]

An count who owned the castle Fair Guard. Queen Morgan le Fay occupied the castle and kept Sir Alexander the Orphan prisoner there. When the Count discovered this, he had the castle burned to the ground so that Morgan could no longer use it for her evil activities. [*ProsTris*, *Malory*]

COUNT OF THE PLAINS [*Earl de Playns*]

A nobleman who held a tournament against King Hervyn or the lady of the castle Tubele during the Grail Quest. Bors arrived at the tournament and met his brother Lionel, whom Bors had believed dead. [*VulgQuest*, *Malory*]

COUNT OF THE PLANK [*Earl de la Planche*]

An count who made war on King Esclabor, father of Palamedes and Safir. Safir challenged him in combat before King Arthur and killed him. [*ProsTris*, *Malory*]

COUNT OF THE VALLEY [*Earl de Vale*]

A nobleman who invaded the lands of a young knight named Agaran. Agaran and his uncle, a holy man, defeated the Count, but the Count's nephews later killed Agaran's uncle in his cloister. The story was related to Lancelot during the Grail Quest. [*VulgQuest*, *Malory*]

COUNTESS OF THE FEATS

A duchess of a small castle, so named because she had three hundred knights who would tell of their adventures nightly. Any knight who overcame all of the Countess's knights would be allowed to sit with the Countess at dinner. Peredur—on his way to defeat the Black Serpent of the Barrow—accomplished this task. During the dinner conversation, the Countess confessed her love for the knight Edlym Red Sword, and Peredur delighted her by informing her that Edlym was in fact his traveling companion. The Countess and Edlym were united and eventually married. [*Peredur*]

COVEROX

A knight in Arthur's service. [*Contin1*]

COWARD KNIGHT

A cowardly knight in the service of the Maiden of the Cart. He carried arms and armor only because he dreaded the thought of being attacked unprotected, and he refused to fight anyone. Every time he encountered a knight, he inquired nervously from a distance if the knight intended him any harm, and he fled at the first sign of danger. When Gawain met him, he had his armor on wrong and rode backwards; Gawain later learned that the Coward Knight symbolized the backwardness of religion prior to Christianity. The Coward Knight eventually met Perceval, who was so disgusted with the him that he forced the Coward Knight to accompany him in search of adventure. They came upon a Robber Knight attacking two maidens, and Perceval forced the Coward Knight into battle. At first, the Coward Knight sat still, shaking, but after the Robber Knight wounded him, he became sufficiently annoyed to fight back, and he astonished himself by winning. Realizing the joy and honor that accompanies victory, the Coward Knight cast off his cowardice and was re-dubbed the BOLD KNIGHT. He was later killed fighting Aristor of Amorave. [*Perlesvaus*, *Contin3*]

CRADDOC [*Craddok*]

One of Arthur's warriors in *Arthour and Merlin*; he participated in the battles against the Saxons at Carhaix. His name resulted from a corruption of GORNAIN CADRUS in the Vulgate *Merlin*, which the author of *Arthour* split in to two characters, although it may have been influenced by CARADOC. The Alliterative *Morte Arthure* includes Craddoc as the knight who, at the conclusion of the Roman War, brought news of Mordred's treachery to Arthur. [*Arthour*, *Allit*]

CRAIDANOS

A Knight of the Round Table who departed with the others on the Grail Quest. [*PostQuest*]

CRASINE [*Clarysyn*]

In the Alliterative *Morte Arthure*, a city in Lorraine, captured by Arthur during the Roman War. After defeating the Duke of Lorraine in combat, Arthur prepared to conquer the city by assault, but the Countess of Crasine convinced him to take it peacefully. Malory gives the name to the countess herself. [*Allit*, *Malory*]

CRAUSEN

A knight slain by Tristan in *La Tavola Ritonda*. Crausen and Lamorat visited King Mark's court, made fun of the Cornish knights, and defeated them all in combat. To avenge Cornwall's shame, Tristan armed himself and jousted with the two knights, killing Crausen. In the Prose *Tristan*, Crausen's place is occupied by DRIANT. [*Tavola*]

CREACANFORD

A location in Kent where, according to the *Anglo-Saxon Chronicle*, the Saxon invader Hengist and his son Æsc won a battle against the Britons in 456, killing 4,000 men. We may assume from a previous entry that Hengist and his son were fighting Vortigern or his men. [*Anglo*]

CREIDDYLAD [*Creiddylat*]

A lady at Arthur's court. She was the daughter of Lludd Silver Hand. Creiddylad was considered the most beautiful girl in the British Isles, and she was loved by Gwythyr and Gwynn. The warriors fought terrible battles over her, but Arthur intervened and the war came to a draw. Creiddylad remained unmarried, and both of her would-be paramours were forced to fight every May Day for her love, until Judgment Day. [*Culhwch*]

CRENEFORT

A castle whose lord, Grandalis, was the father of one of Arthur's Yvains. [*VulgMer*]

CREOMAS

A knight from Sorelois who joined Arthur's battles against the Saxons at Clarence and Vambieres. [*Livre*]

CREON

A Saxon king who joined the invasion of Britain at the beginning of Arthur's reign. He was slain by Arthur's Sir Galescalain at the battle of Diana Bridge. [*Livre*, *Arthour*]

CRESSIA OF IRONE

One of several Arthurian ladies to fail a chastity test in Heinrich von dem Türlin's *Diu Crône*. [*Heinrich*]

CRESSILE [*Trasfilas*]

The daughter of King Clodoveus of Cornwall, an ancestor of Mark and Tristan. Cressile married Candaces, the son of the murdered King of Lyonesse. She had twelve sons, including Crissidés, who inherited Cornwall. [*ProsTris, Tavola*]

CRISSIDÉS [*Zersides*]

Son of King Candaces of Cornwall and Cresille. He became king of the country when his father died. He was an ancestor of King Mark of Cornwall. [*ProsTris, Tavola*]

CRETE

An island in the Mediterranean Sea, ruled in Arthur's time by Hippolytus, an ally of the Roman Procurator Lucius. [*GeoffHR, Allit*]

CRIMSON HEATH

The home of Perceval's uncle Fortimes, and the location of a tournament attended by Perceval and Gawain. The victor of the tournament was given the task of avenging the death of the knight Alain against the Knight of the Burning Dragon. Perceval was the chosen victor. [*Perlesvaus*]

CRINIDES THE BLACK

A Knight of the Round Table, related in some way to Lancelot. He participated in the Grail Quest. [*PostQuest*]

CRISEA [*Ocise*]

The wife of King Lac and mother of Erec. She was a skilled sorceress, and she enchanted Erec in such a way that he could never be affected by magic. [*PostMer*]

CRISEUZ THE BEAUTIFUL GOOSE

The maiden of Sir Garsallas, a knight defeated by Perceval. [*Contin2*]

CRISTAMANS

A Saxon king who, under King Hargadabran, fought aganst Arthur's forces at Clarence. Arthur killed him. [*Livre*]

CRISTANS

One of the many Saxon kings to invade Britain when Arthur was struggling to establish power. [*Livre*]

CROP-EARED DOG

In an Irish tale, Alexander, the son of the King of India was enchanted in the form of a dog with no ears and no tail. Alexander's brothers were in a similar form. This had been done by Alexander's step-mother, Queen Libearn, who wanted her own son, called the Knight of the Lantern, to inherit the realm of India. The Crop-Eared Dog went to Arthur's court and received assistance from Bhalbhuaidh (the Irish version of Gawain) in defeating the Knight of the Lantern, who was forced to return Alexander to his true form. Alexander duly inherited his father's kingdom. [*IrishD*]

CROS

A castle where Gawain was taken after his death. [*PostMort*]

CROSS

A hermitage in the forest of Breckham. Sir Hector (Lancelot's brother) lodged there during an adventure. [*VulgLanc*]

CROSS OF THE FOUNTAIN

A landmark where Palamedes ran into Yvain and Gaheris. [*ProsTris*]

CROSSELEME

A Knight of the Round Table who appears at the healing of Sir Urry. [*Malory*]

CROSSING

Yet another hermitage in the Breckham forest. [*VulgLanc*]

CROSSROADS

A heath in the forest of Breckham. It was known as a place of adventures, and was visited by Hector and Gawain. [*VulgLanc*]

CROWNED LION OF LIBYA

A mysterious lion with a crown growing from its head that Sir Lionel was fated to destroy. Lionel, Lancelot's cousin, was born with a birthmark in the shape of a lion. It was said that after he had slain the Crowned Lion of Libya, the birthmark would disappear. Upon achieving knighthood, Lionel went to Arthur's court, where a lady appeared leading the Crowned Lion. Lionel fought it, killed it, and presented its skin to Sir Yvain, who was thereafter known as the Knight with the Lion. As foretold, Lionel's birthmark disappeared. [*LancLac*]

CRUDEL ("Cruel") [*Coudel*]

The pagan king of North Wales in the time of Joseph of Arimathea. He imprisoned Joseph and his followers because they were Christians. King Mordrains, in Sarras, was shown a vision of his friends in Crudel's prison. Mordrains traveled to Britain, raised an army, and encountered Crudel's forces near Longtown. Crudel was slain by Duke Ganor, and his army was destroyed. Mordrains freed the Christians and gave North Wales to Celidoine, Nascien's son. [*VulgEst*]

CRUDELE

A castle on the island of Perfida, visited by Tristan and a maiden named Tessina during Tristan's adventures in Logres. Tristan was imprisoned and forced to fight the castle's champion, Lamorat. Lamorat had assumed the position after slaying the previous champion. By custom of the castle, one of the two knights would have to die in the combat, but Tristan feigned death and they were both able to escape later. Tessina was beheaded because her beauty did not match that of Medeas, the castle's pagan queen. [*Tavola*]

CRUDENS

Son of King Hector of the Savage Realm. He married the daughter of the king of Gaul and inherited the kingdom. He had a son named Febus. [*Palamedes*]

CRYSTAL ISLE

The realm of Arthur's vassal Lord Moloas, according to Hartmann von Aue. Chrétien de Troyes calls it the ISLAND OF GLASS. [*HartmannE*]

CUALL ("Foolish")

The dog belonging to Arthur's warrior Cyfwlch. [*Culhwch*]

CUBERT

Son of Daere and one of Arthur's warriors in *Culhwch and Olwen*, borrowed from the Irish folk character Cú Roí, son of Daere. [*Culhwch*]

CUCHULAINN

A hero of Irish mythology who may be a prototype of GAWAIN. He was the son of the god Lug, who some scholars have seen as the orign of Lot, and of the lady Dechtire. Like Gawain, his strength reached its peak at noon. In origin, he may have been a solar deity. He possessed a sword called Caladbolg, which—transferred through the Welsh Caledfwlch—might be the origin of Excalibur. In the Irish tale of *Bricriu's Feast*, he undergoes a Beheading Game that Gawain inherits in *Sir Gawain and the Green Knight*.

CUCUMERLAND

The kingdom of Ither of Gaheviez, Arthur's cousin. [*Wolfram*]

CUDINELLO

A knight defeated by Lancelot and Tristan in the Savage Valley during the Grail Quest. His father was named Estorm de Rivello. [*Tavola*]

CUEL

One of Arthur's warriors. [*Culhwch*]

CUER DE PIERRE ("Heart of Stone")

A malevolent knight who ruled a castle called the Rock. He imprisoned Arthur and some Knights of the Round Table, but King Meliadus of Lyonesse slew him. [*Palamedes*]

CULFANAWYD ("Slender Awl")

An Arthurian warrior who was the son of Gwryon. [*Culhwch*]

CULHWCH [*Cilhwch*]

Hero of *Culhwch and Olwen*, a Welsh tale from the eleventh century or earlier. Culhwch was the son of Cilydd and Goleuddydd, Arthur's aunt. His mother died while giving birth to him in the middle of a herd of pigs, and Culhwch's name—"pig pen"—reflects the circumstances of this birth. His father remarried, and his stepmother commanded that Culhwch marry Olwen, daughter of the giant Ysbaddaden. Culhwch fell in love with her at the mere mention of her name.

Culhwch traveled to Arthur's court at the height of its glory, and demanded his cousin's assistance in finding Olwen. Arthur assigned Cei, Bedwyr, Cynddylig the Guide, Gwrhyr Interpreter of Languages, Gwalchmei, and Menw—the greatest of his warriors—to go with Culhwch to the fortress of Ysbaddaden. Upon arriving, the companions learned that Ysbaddaden was fated to die upon his daughter's marriage, and that Olwen would not marry without her father's permission.

Ysbaddaden tried to slay the party but was injured, so he consented to allow Olwen to marry Culhwch—if Culhwch would perform a list of forty tasks. The tasks involved obtaining magic artifacts from a plethora of fearsome monsters, obtaining the assistance of certain renowned warriors, tending to vast parcels of Ysbaddaden's land in a short period of time, and a number of other impossible deeds. About half of them involved retrieving a set of shears and a comb from between the ears of Twrch Trwyth, an enchanted boar. Ysbaddaden placed numerous conditions on the hunt for Twrch Trwyth: certain warriors had to accompany the party, certain hounds had to be employed, certain leashes were needed to hold the hounds, certain warriors were needed to hold the leashes, and so on.

Culhwch agreed to accomplish all the tasks. He returned to Arthur's court, invoked Arthur's promise to help him, and sat back while Arthur and his men scrambled to meet all of Ysbaddaden's requirements. Among the more interesting of the subsequent adventures are Arthur's trip to Ireland to obtain a cauldron from Diwrnach, the slaying of the boar Ysgithyrwyn, the assault on the cave of the Black Hag, and the epic hunt for Twrch Trwyth.

Though the story only notes the completion of half of the tasks, Culhwch apparently satisfied all the requirements, because he returned to Ysbaddaden and demanded his prize. Ysbaddaden handed over Olwen, remarking bitterly that Culhwch would not have been able to complete even one of the tasks without the assistance of Arthur. Culhwch and Olwen lived together for the rest of their days. [*Culhwch*]

CUMBRIA

A region of Britain on the Irish Sea, just south of Scotland, that includes the cities of Penrith and Carlisle. In the generation after Arthur, it was ruled by Rhydderch the Generous. [*GeoffVM*]

CUMMOCK

A region of southwest Scotland. It originally belonged to Sir Galleron, but Arthur annexed it and gave it to Gawain. Galleron arrived at a feast and challenged Gawain for ownership of the land. The fight ended in a draw, but Gawain graciously returned the country to Galleron anyway. [*Awntyrs*]

CUNDRIE[1]

A sorceress who served as messenger for the Grail family in Wolfram's *Parzival*. She spoke all languages and had mastered the sciences. She came from a race of men with boar-like features that lived in an area near the River Ganges in the kingdom of Tribalibot. Cundrie and her brother, Malcreatiure, were sent by Queen Secundille of Tribalibot to Anfortas, the Grail King, as servants. Cundrie went to Arthur's court and berated Perceval for

failing to ask the Grail Question during his first visit to the Grail Castle. After Perceval proved himself worthy of a second chance, Cundrie led him back to the Grail Castle for the completion of the quest. [*Wolfram*]

CUNDRIE[2] [*Gundrie*]

Daughter of Lot and Sangive and sister of Gawain, Beacurs, Soredamor, and Itonje. She was trapped with her mother and Itonje in the Castle of Marvels until released by Gawain. She then married Duke Lischois Gwelljus of Gowerzin. [*Wolfram, PleierM*]

CUNEDAG

According to Geoffrey of Monmouth, king of Britain in the eighth century BC. With his cousin Margan, he rebelled against Queen Cordelia, his aunt, imprisoned her, and took her throne. Cunedag and Margan divided the island between them, but Margan eventually attacked Cunedag and was slain. Cunedag became king of all Britain and ruled for 33 years. He was succeeded by his son Rivallo. [*GeoffHR*]

CUNEDDA

A northern British chieftan (ruler of the Votadini) who, according to Nennius, drove the Irish out of Wales in the fourth century. Cunedda's sons were part of the expedition. Cunedda appears in other sources, and may have been a real person, though Nennius's dating seems too early; Cunedda would have fought the Irish in the early to mid-fifth century, possibly in the service of Vortigern. He may have descended from Roman nobility. In Welsh texts, a number of saints trace their pedigrees back to Cunedda, and one Welsh history makes him the maternal great-grandfather of Arthur. [*Nennius*]

CUNNEWARE OF LALANDER

Sister of Orilus of Lalander and Lähelin in Wolfram's *Parzival*. A duchess, she served at Arthur's court. It was said that she would never laugh until she beheld the best knight in the world. When Perceval came to court, she broke out into joyous laughter. Her laughter offended the arrogant Kay, who beat her and also abused a dwarf who came to her rescue. Perceval promised to punish Kay for this assault, and later broke his arm in a joust. Clamide, a knight defeated by Perceval, fell in love with Cunneware, married her, and made her the queen of Iserterre and Brandigan. Her character appears unnamed in Chrétien de Troyes's *Perceval* and as the MUTE MAIDEN in the Post-Vulgate version. [*Wolfram*]

CUNNINGHAM

A region of southwest Scotland. It originally belonged to Sir Galleron, but Arthur annexed it and gave it to Gawain. Galleron arrived at a feast and challenged Gawain for ownership of the land. The fight ended in a draw, but Gawain graciously returned the country to Galleron anyway. [*Awntyrs*]

CUNOMORUS [Welsh: *Cynfawr*]

A historical sixth-century king of Cornwall who is named on a Cornish tombstone as the father of "Drustanus," a version of "Tristan." In Wrmonoc's Life of St. Paul Aurelian, Cunomorus is identified with King MARK of the Tristan legends. [*TrisStone*]

CUNYN COF [*Cimin Cof*]

Son of Alun of Dyfed and father of Arthur's warrior Dalldaf. [*Culhwch*]

CUOI

The son of King Aguiflet of Scotland, and the brother of Cadret or Goasilroet. He was present at the wedding of Erec and Enide. [*ChretienE*]

CUPARIA

A fountain near the castle of Joyous Guard where Tristan spied the Questing Beast. [*Tavola*]

CUROI

In Irish mythology, a giant warrior slain by Cuchulainn, Gawain's Irish counterpart. Curoi had abducted a maiden named Blathnat. The Arthurian figures MELWAS and MELEAGANT inherited some of his characteristics.

CURSALEM [*Curfalain, Cursa(l)(e)(n), Curselin, Gursal*]

The Earl of Caichester or Chester. He served Arthur. He was also known as the Warden of the Marches of Wales. He fought for Arthur in the war against Rome. He led half a legion of troops at the battle of Soissons and was killed there. [*GeoffHR, Wace, Layamon*]

CURSESALYNE

A Knight of the Round Table who joined Mordred and Agravain in their plan to expose the affair between Lancelot and Guinevere. Twelve knights cornered Lancelot in the queen's chamber. Cursesalyne was slain by Lancelot in the subsequent duel. [*Malory*]

CURSIN

The unwilling seneschal of King Godonas of Terrandes, a tyrant. He befriended Meleranz, Arthur's nephew, and was pleased when Meleranz slew Godonas. Meleranz appointed Cursin steward of Terrandes. [*PleierM*]

CVITAZIJA

The wife of Liburn of Kesarija. She was desired by both Lancelot and Tristan, and her husband had to defeat both of these knights to save her honor. [*Povest*]

CWM CAWLWYD

A glen where lived the magical Owl of Cwm Cawlwyd. Arthur visited the owl to consult his wisdom during his quest to find the missing warrior Mabon in *Culhwch and Olwen*. The Owl of Cwm Cawlwyd directed Arthur to the Eagle of Gwernabwy. A Welsh Triad lists the Owl as one of the "three Elders of the World." [*Culhwch, Triads*]

CWM CERWYN

A valley or glen, probably in western England, where the boar Twrch Trwyth made a stand against Arthur's warriors during the epic hunt, and killed Gwarthegydd, Tarawg, Rhun, Ysgonan, Gwydre, Garselid, Glew, and Ysgawyn. [*Culhwch*]

CYFARCH

Father of Urien of Rheged, and of Arthur's knights Llew and Aron. [*Triads, Culhwch*]

CYFWLCH ("Complete")

Son of Cleddyf Cyfwlch, brother of Bwlch and Syfwlch, and one of Arthur's warriors in Welsh legend. Cyfwlch had a sword named Glessig, a dog named Cuall, a horse named Drwgddyddwg, a wife named Garym, a grandchild named Neued, two daughters named Gwaeth and Eheubryd, and a maid named Gorasgwrn. As required by Culhwch's tasks, Cyfwlch helped in the hunts for the boars Ysgithyrwyn and Twrch Trwyth. [*Culhwch*]

CYLEDDON

Father of Cilydd and grandfather of Culhwch. He ruled Caledon, from which his name is likely derived. [*Culhwch*]

CYLEDYR THE WILD

An Arthurian warrior who was the son of Nwython. Cyledyr was loyal to the warrior Gwythyr, and joined Gwythyr's army during a war against Gwynn son of Nudd. He and his father Nwython were taken prisoner by Gwynn. Gwynn killed Nwython and forced Cyledyr to eat his father's heart, which drove Cyledyr mad. He was freed when Arthur intervened and liberated the fortress. Cyledyr was present during the hunting of Twrch Trwyth, and it was he who seized the shears from between the boar's ears at the river Severn. [*Culhwch*]

CYMBELINE

According to Geoffrey of Monmouth, the king of Britain in the time of Christ. He succeeded his father, King Tenuantius, and was succeeded by his son, Guiderius. [*GeoffHR*]

CYMOCHLES

Brother of Pyrochles and lover of the sorceress Acrasia. Upon hearing of his brother's "death," he sought to avenge him against Sir Guyon, but he was "captured" on the way by the enchantress Phaedria. He eventually freed himself and was reunited with his still-living brother. Guided by the evil magician Archimago, the brothers found Guyon half-conscious and decided to steal his armor. Prince

Arthur arrived, challenged the brothers, and killed them both. [*Spenser*]

CYMRY

The Welsh name for the Britons who descended from the men of Troy. The Cymry were said to have the divine rights to the island. Arthur was among the members of this race. [*Triads*]

CYN WAS CWRYFAGYL

One of King Arthur's warriors in Welsh legend. He owned a number of cattle that were killed by the boar Twrch Trwyth while the boar was hunted by Arthur and his warriors. [*Culhwch*]

CYNAN

Father of Arthur's warrior Cynlan. [*Culhwch*]

CYNAN GARRWYN

Father Selyf, a warrior in the service of Owain. His surname may mean "white shank" or "white chariot." He is based on a historical figure from the early seventh century. [*Dream*]

CYNDDYLIG THE GUIDE

One of Arthur's warriors in Welsh legend. As a guide, he accompanied Culhwch and other knights of Arthur on Culhwch's adventure to the fortress of the giant Ysbadadden. [*Culhwch*]

CYNDEYRN GARTHWYS

The chief bishop of Arthur's northern kingdoms, according to a Welsh Triad. [*Triads*]

CYNDRWYN

Son of Ermid, brother of Gwynn, and one of Arthur's warriors. [*Culhwch*]

CYNDUR

A Welsh warrior who was apparently killed in a battle against Maelgwn. His death is mourned by Taliesin and Merlin in an early Welsh poem. [*Myrddin*]

CYNEDYR THE WILD

One of Arthur's warriors. He was the son of Hetwn Silver Brow. As one of his tasks, Culhwch had to obtain Cynedyr's help in hunting the boar Twrch Trwyth. Cynedyr was needed to manage the hounds Aned and Aethlem. [*Culhwch*]

CYNFELYN

Father of Gwaeddan, a lady at Arthur's court. An early Welsh poem suggests that he took part in the battle of Arfderydd. [*Culhwch, Myrddin*]

CYNFERCHIN

Perhaps a variation of CYNFARCH, Owain's grandfather. Owain somehow came in possession of three hundred swords that had belonged to Cynferchin. [*Owain*]

CYNLAN

One of Arthur's warriors in Welsh legend. He was the son of Cynan. He was killed at the battle of Aber Tywi by the boar Twrch Trwyth. [*Culhwch*]

CYNON

One of Arthur's three "Counselor Knights," found in the Welsh Triads and other Welsh texts. He was the son of Clydno. While young, arrogant, and in search of adventure, Cynon entered a strange earldom and was directed to an enchanted fountain. Performing a certain ritual at the fountain caused a hailstorm so strong it could kill anyone caught outside, and brought the lord of the region to the fountain to do battle with the brash warrior who had dared to cause the storm. Cynon performed the ritual, and was defeated by the ruler in combat. When he returned to Arthur's court, his tale, inspired Owain to set out in search of the same adventure. (This role is taken by CALOGRENANT in other versions.) The early Scottish poem *Y Gododdin* places Cynon at the Battle of Catraeth around 600 and lists him as one of the few survivors. A Triad says he fell in love with Urien's daughter Morfudd. A Welsh poem puts his grave at Llanbadarn. [*Gododdin, Triads, WelshSG, Owain*]

CYNRIC [*Cenric*]

A Saxon warrior and ruler. The son of the Saxon warrior Cerdic, he arrived with his father in Britain in 495. They won a battle against the Britons in that year, at Cerdicesora; in 508, at which a British king named Natanleod was killed; in 519 at Charford on the river Avene; in 527 at Cerdicesleag; in 530 at the Isle of Wight; and in 552 at the town of Salisbury. Cyrnic had a son named Ceawlin. He would have been a contemporary (and adversary) of Ambrosius, Uther, or Arthur. [*Anglo*]

CYNWAL HUNDRED HOGS

Son of Caw, father of Gwenn Alarch, one of twenty brothers, and one of Arthur's warriors. Cynwal son of Caw and Cynwal Hundred Hogs may actually be two separate characters. [*Culhwch*]

CYNWYL

One of Arthur's warriors, titled "Saint," in Welsh legend. He fought at the battle of Camlann, where he was the last to leave Arthur. He rode a horse named Hen Groen. [*Culhwch*]

CYNYR FAIR BEARD

One of Arthur's warriors in Welsh legends. He is named as the father of Cei, a status transferred to ANTOR in French romance. When he found that his wife was pregnant, he made a number of predictions about the marvelous powers Cei would possess. His predictions proved to be accurate. [*Culhwch*]

CYPRUS [*Cypirs, Cyprese, Syprus*]

According to the Alliterative *Morte Arthure*, the Mediterranean nation was allied to Lucius the Roman, and warriors from Cyprus participated in Lucius's war against Arthur. In the Middle English *Sir Degrevant*, Cyprus is named as the home of Sir Sere, Degrevant's enemy. [*Allit, SirDeg, Malory*]

CYRIONS OF CUITENÏAC

A knight in Arthur's service. [*Contin1*]

CYRWRYD

A ruler or knight from Gwent. He fathered one of the three Guineveres that were married to Arthur in a Welsh Triad. [*Triads*]

CYSTAINT

A companion of Arthur who is named as the son of Bannon. His name is a variation of the Latin CONSTANTINE. [*WelshPG*]

D

DACIA

The region of southern Europe that is now primarily Romania. Geoffrey mentions that Arthur conquered Dacia after pacifying Britain. [*GeoffHR*, *Boccaccio*]

DADWEIR BLIND HEAD

One of King Arthur's warriors in Welsh legend. [*Culhwch*]

DAERE

Father of Arthur's warrior Cubert, from the Irish folk character DÁIRE. [*Culhwch*]

DAGON

A demon who gave powers of enchantment to King Pelles' magician. When Galahad was in the magician's presence, the powers were ineffective. Eventually, the demon consumed the magician. [*PostQuest*]

DAGUENET [*Dagenet, Dagonet, Danguenes*]

A witless knight introduced in the Prose *Lancelot*. He becomes Arthur's beloved court jester in Malory and Tennyson. His epithets include "the Coward," "the Fool," and "the Craven." *Palamedes* says that Daguenet went insane after his wife was abducted by Helior of the Thorn, whom Daguenet eventually killed. Daguenet was a somewhat Walter Mittyish knight, imagining and presenting himself as a fearless warrior when in fact he was prone to flee at the slightest provocation. He would damage his own shield so that it looked as if he had been in combat. Other knights used him to play jokes on their enemies. Kay arranged for Daguenet to face Sir Brunor on Brunor's first joust, thus depriving Brunor of the honor of defeating a true knight in his first combat. In another episode, some of Arthur's knights identified Daguenet as Lancelot to King Mark. Daguenet performed some comical blustering which caused Mark to flee, screaming, into the forest. Lancelot once found himself dubbed "Daguenet's Prisoner" after Daguenet approached Lancelot, who was in a deep reverie, "captured" him by taking hold of his bridle, and led him to Guinevere as his "prisoner." The poor fool was thrashed by Tristan when the latter went insane and was living like a madman in Cornwall. Gawain adopted Daguenet's name as an alias during one of his adventures. In the *Prophecies de Merlin*, Daguenet assumes administration of Arthur's court during the False Guinevere episode, and the place falls apart. Daguenet kills Fole, Arthur's treasurer, when the latter reproves Daguenet for expending all of the funds in the royal treasury. [*LancLac, VulgLanc, VulgMer, Livre, Palamedes, ProsTris, Prophecies, Malory, TennIK*]

DAHAMORHT

A knight killed by Gawain in a tournament at the city of Baldac in Babylonia. Dahamorht's brother, Angaras of Karamphi, tried to slay Gawain for the incident, but was himself defeated. [*Heinrich*]

DAIRE[1]

Father of Yvain of the White Hands in *Palamedes*. The Good Knight Without Fear freed him from a prison in North Wales. [*Palamedes*]

DAIRE[2]

A fairy king. In an Irish tale, his daughter, the Grey-Hammed Lady, married Arthur. He becomes DAERE in Welsh legend. [*IrishL*]

DALAM

Lord of the Castle of the Mountain. Dinadan rescued Dalam from Sir Breus the Pitliess. When Sir Dalan learned that his rescuer was Dinadan, he alleged that Dinadan had killed his father and attacked him. Dinadan, however, won the battle. [*ProsTris, Malory*]

DALIDES

A good knight and friend of Gawain. Galahad and Yvain the Bastard lodged at his father's house during the Grail Quest. Dalides arrogantly and rashly attacked Galahad and was defeated. In shame, he killed himself with his own sword, prompting his father to likewise commit suicide. His body was taken to the Strange Castle, owned by Dalides' paramour. Gawain, learning of the incident, tried to take revenge on Galahad, but failed. [*PostQuest, ProsTris*]

DALLDAF

Son of Cunyn Cof and one of Arthur's warriors. [*Culhwch*]

DALON

A kng of Larise who joined his ally, Emperor Thereus of Rome, in a war against Arthur. [*Claris*]

DAMAS[1] [*Domas*]

A castellan who engaged his brother, Sir Ontzlake, in a land dispute, but avoided personal combat because he lacked confidence in his own fighting skill. He asked every knight who passed his castle to fight as his champion, but none would do so, so he threw all who refused into prison. He eventually made an alliance with Morgan le Fay, who transported Arthur to Damas's dungeon. Damas secured Arthur's promise to champion him against Ontzlake. Meanwhile, Morgan arranged for Sir Accalon of Gaul, with Excalibur, to fight at Ontzlake's champion. With the assistance of Ninniane or Nimue, Arthur defeated Accalon and exposed Morgan's scheme. The Vulgate *Lancelot* says that Damas was reconciled with his brother, but in Malory's version Arthur orders Damas to yield all his lands to Ontzlake, and to repay all the imprisoned knights. Damas was slain fighting Lancelot and his men when Lancelot rescued Guinevere from the stake. [*PostMer, Malory*]

DAMAS² OF DESERT

A Knight of the Round Table and brother of Damcab and Caradan. Damas hated Lancelot's family because of their fame and skill. With four knights of similar opinions, he attacked Galahad and Bleoberis during the Grail Quest, and was slain by Bleoberis. [*PostQuest, ProsTris*]

DAMASCUS [*Damaske*]

The present capital of Syria features in Wolfram von Eschenbach's *Parzival* as a location where Perceval's father Gahmuret traveled, and in Wirnt von Grafenberg's *Wigalois* as a location of a battle fought by several of Wigalois's companions. In the Alliterative *Morte Arthure* and Malory, the city is allied to Lucius the Roman. [*Wolfram, Wirnt, Allit, Malory*]

DAMATAL OF DESERT [*Damadas*]

A Knight of the Round Table who hated Lancelot's family for their fame and skill. With four cousins, he attacked Galahad and Bleoberis during the Grail Quest. He was badly wounded by Galahad. [*PostQuest, ProsTris*]

DAMCAB

Knight of the Round Table and brother of Damas and Caradan. He participated in the Grail Quest. [*PostQuest*]

DAME D'AMORE

In Thomas Chestre's *Lybeaus Desconus*, the fairy of the Golden Isle who loved Guinglain, Gawain's son. She broke with Guinglain when he refused to give up worldly life for her, and he eventually married a princess. In Renaut de Bâgé's *Le Bel Inconnu*, she is called the MAIDEN OF THE WHITE HANDS. [*ChestreLyb*]

DAMEN [*Thamer*]

A mountain in northern Britain where Uther Pendragon defeated the Saxons Octa and Eosa in his second battle against them. The battle went poorly for Uther, until he and his warriors, in a small, force, descended upon the Saxon camp in the middle of the night. He captured and imprisoned the two Saxon leaders, temporarily ending the Saxon threat. [*GeoffHR*]

DAMIETTA [*Damiet*]

A seaport in north Egypt, on the east Nile delta. According to the Alliterative *Morte Arthure*, it was allied to Lucius the Roman, Arthur's enemy. [*Allit, Malory*]

DAMON THE GOOD JOUSTER

An Arthurian knight who was the son of Amant, possibly related to AMANT THE GOOD JOUSTER. [*Palamedes*]

DAMSEL OF THE WHITE HEATH

A maiden loved by Gareth, Gawain's brother. [*VulgLanc*]

DAMSEL SAVAGE [*Damsel of the Wilds*]

An obscure woman who appears in Chrétien's *Yvain* and the Middle English poem *Ywain and Gawain*. She sends a message to the Lady of the Fountain, warning her that Arthur is approaching the Lady's lands. The message prompts the Lady to marry Yvain for protection. [*ChretienY, Ywain*]

DANADOR

A vassal of Emperor Filimenis of Constantinople, father of Sir Floriant. [*Floriant*]

DANAIM [*Daname*]

A knight and nephew of Sir Daras. He guarded Daras's castle against interlopers. They lodged several renowned knights of Arthur's court, including Lancelot, Palamedes, and Tristan. Danaim hated Lucan the Butler and challenged him twice, but Lucan was victorious on both occasions. [*ProsTris, Malory*]

DANAIN THE RED

Friend of Guiron the Courteous in *Palamedes*. He was married to the Lady of Malehaut, who loved Guiron. Danain's wife and friend nearly engaged in an affair, and Danain nearly slew them for it. Instead, he abducted Bloie, Guiron's damsel. They clashed in combat over the woman, and Guiron was victorious. The two knights reconciled when Danain saved Guiron from a murderous knight named Helain. Danain fell in love with a maiden named Albe and became involved in a complicated feud between Albe's family and the clan of Helyom. Eventually, he participated in a tournament at Camelot, received a mortal wound, and died at Malehaut. [*Palamedes*]

DANDRANE

Daughter of Alain the Large and Yglais, and sister of Perceval in *Perlesvaus*. She sought her brother to save her castle, Camelot, from a siege by Cahot the Red and the Lord of the Fens. She was kidnapped by Aristor of Amorave, who intended to marry and behead her, but she was rescued by Perceval. She lived out her days as a maiden in the Grail Castle. She is not the same sister of Perceval who appears, unnamed, in the Vulgate *Queste del*

Saint Graal and as AGRESIZIA in *La Tavola Ritonda*. [*Perlesvaus*]

DANE HILL

In John Hardyng's chronicle, the location of Arthur's first victory against the Saxons led by Octa and Eosa. This occurs at the river GLEIN in Nennius's chronicle. [*Hardyng*]

DANEMON

A knight who joined King Tallas of Denmark in a siege on King Urien. [*Claris*]

DANED

One of Arthur's warriors. He was the son of Oth. [*Dream*]

DANGIS

The count of Caleque Castle. He pledged himself to Lancelot when the latter saved Guinevere from the stake and fled with her to Joyous Guard. [*PostMort*]

DANIAUS

A knight in Arthur's service. [*Contin2*]

DANIDAIN THE PROUD

A knight from Lyonesse. He was the cousin of Breus the Pitiless, whose evil disposition he shared. Lancelot killed him. [*Palamedes*]

DANIEL¹ OF THE BLOSSOMING VALLEY

Hero of Der Stricker's *Daniel von dem blühenden Tal*. Equal in prowess to the likes of Gawain and Perceval, he stands out among other French and German heroes for his cunning, which when paired with his valor made him a potent foe. The son of King Mandogran, Daniel took service with Arthur just before King Matur of Cluse demanded Arthur's fealty. Matur had two giants with impenetrable skin, but Daniel nonetheless set out ahead of Arthur's own army to reconnoiter Matur's lands. Along the way, he liberated the Dark Mountain from an evil dwarf named Juram, and he freed the Bright Fountain from the terror of a demon. In the former adventure, he won a sword capable of slaying Matur's giants, which he employed to that end. Arthur killed Matur, and Daniel fought bravely in the ensuing battles with the armies of Cluse, defeating the majority of them by turning their own magical weapon against them. Later, he saved the Green Meadow from a monster and rescued Arthur from the father of the slain giants. Arthur crowned him the King of Cluse, and Daniel married Queen Danise, Matur's widow. His character is adapted liberally by Der Pleier as GAREL. [*Stricker*]

DANIEL² THE BELIEVER

A Knight of the Round Table who embarked with the others on the Grail Quest. [*PostQuest*]

DANIELLO

The Italian romance *La Tavola Ritonda* makes an interesting departure from the traditional Arthurian story when it places the discovery of the affair between Lancelot and Guinevere near the beginning or middle of Arthur's reign, rather than at the end. Here, their betrayer is not Mordred or Agravain, but Daniello, the cowardly brother of Dinadan and Brunor the Black. Daniello conspired to expose the affair, and roused thirty knights to capture Lancelot in Guinevere's bedchamber. Lancelot slew Daniello and eight others, sparking a feud between Lancelot and Daniello's brother, Brunor the Black. [*Tavola*]

DANISE

The Queen of Cluse in Der Stricker's *Daniel*. Her husband, King Matur, challenged Arthur and was slain. Arthur then took over Cluse. Danise mourned for Matur but agreed to marry Daniel of the Blossoming Valley, a noble knight of Arthur's who had made the conquest possible. M. Resler suggests that Der Stricker chose her name because it corresponds phonetically with "Daniel." Der Stricker may also have derived it from DYONISE of *Durmart le Gallois*. [*Stricker*]

DANIUS

According to Geoffrey of Monmouth, king of Britain in the fourth or third century BC. He was the son of King Sisillius and the brother of King Kimar, who he succeeded. Danius took a concubine named Tangustela and had a son named Morvid, who became king of Britain after Danius's death. [*GeoffHR*]

DANOR

A good knight whose sister gave birth to Arthur's son, Arthur the Less. Danor's father, Tanas, lusted for Danor's wife. Tanas eventually killed Danor and took her. Tamas then disposed of the rest of his family to conceal the murder. [*PostQuest*]

DANUBRE THE BRAVE [*Darubre*]

A Knight of the Round Table and brother of Acorant the Agile. He was related in some way to Lancelot. Danubre and Acorant were attacked by Agamenor, Arpian, and Amatin—three knights who hated Lancelot's family—during the Grail Quest. All five knights were killed or mortally wounded in the brawl. [*PostQuest, ProsTris*]

DARAS

An old knight who lived with his nephew, Danaim, and harbored sick and injured knights in his castle, including Tristan, Mordred, and Palamedes. While Tristan was healing there, Daras discovered that Tristan had slain three of his sons at the Castle of Maidens tournament, and had maimed his other two. Enraged, he threw Tristan, Palamedes, and Dinadan into his prison. When Tristan grew deathly ill, Daras relented and released him on

Tristan's pledge of friendship. He later became a Knight of the Round Table. [*Malory*]

DAREL

A prince of Medarie and Belakun; companion of princes Gamer and Ariun. His lord, Schaffilun, was killed by Wigalois (Gawain's son), to whom Darel transferred his fealty. He accompanied Wigalois in a campaign against King Lion of Namur. [*Wirnt*]

DARENTH [*Darent, Dereuent, Derwent*]

A river in Britain that was the site of the first battle between Vortimer's Britons and Hengist's Saxons. Nennius says that Vortimer won the battle, and pushed on to fight the second at Ryhd yr afael. Layamon claims that all three of Vortigern's sons—Vortimer, Pascentius, and Catigern—fought Vortigern, Hengist, and Horsa, and pushed the Saxons back to Thanet. Darenth is an actual stream that gives its name to Dartford. [*Nennius, GeoffHR, Wace, Layamon*]

DARIAN

A Saxon warrior slain by Arthur's Sir Galescalain at the battle of Diana Bridge. [*Arthour*]

DARIL

A Saxon warrior. He was the son of King Bramangue and the brother of Haram and Orient. He assisted his brother Haram with the siege of Arundel in the early days of Arthur's reign. [*Arthour*]

DARK CASTLE [*Chastel Tenebreus*]

A castle where Lancelot completed an unspecified adventure. At his wish, the inhabitants of the castle changed its name. [*PostQuest*]

DARK MOUNTAIN

A land terrorized by the evil dwarf Juran, who had slain its lord and wanted to marry the lord's daughter. Daniel of the Blossoming Valley, one of Arthur's knights, slew the dwarf and freed the land. The lady of the Dark Mountain later marred Arthur's Sir Belamis. [*Stricker*]

DARK RIVER [*Tembre*]

A broad, deep, muddy river that formed the border between Wales and the perilous land of Gorre. [*VulgLanc*]

DARK VALLEY [*Valle Scura*]

A valley visited by Tristan and Lancelot during the Grail Quest. There, they slew the pagan lord Fellone. [*Tavola*]

DARNANTES [*Andernantes, Arnante(s), Darvances, Dornantes, Nerlantes*]

A British forest that appears in several French romances. The name may be simply an extension of NANTES. The

Vulgate *Lancelot* puts it on the border between Sorelois and the sea of Cornwall, and says that it was the forest where the Lady of the Lake entrapped Merlin. The Prose *Tristan* names its location as the border of Logres and North Wales. The Italian *La Tavola Ritonda* places the forest near Camelot, and says that it served as the proving grounds for the Knights of the Round Table. In *Tavola*, it is a savage wilderness, full of robbers and enchantments. Lancelot, Bors, and Hector retired to a hermitage there after Arthur's death. [*VulgLanc, VulgEst, ProsTris, Tavola*]

DARSENOIS

A knight who Arthur freed from the castle Causuel when he defeated the Merciless Lion, Darsenois's jailer. In return, Darsenois gave Arthur a charger. [*ChevPap*]

DATIS[1]

King of Tuscany who joined Emperor Thereus of Rome's war against Arthur. He was killed during the war by Sir Gaheris. [*Claris*]

DATIS[2]

A knight who joined Arthur's Sir Claris and Sir Laris in their adventures. [*Claris*]

DATOIS

King of Babylon who joined Emperor Thereus of Rome in a war against Arthur. He was slain in battle by Sir Claris. [*Claris*]

DATON

A knight who joined his cousin, Nador, in an attack on Queen Blanche. The besiegers were driven away by Claris and Laris. [*Claris*]

DAUPHINE [*Dalfindede*]

A city in France. In the Alliterative *Morte Arthure*, it is ruled by the Duke of Lorraine, an opponent of Arthur during the Roman War. [*Allit, Malory*]

DAVALON THE PROUD

One of Arthur's knights in Heinrich von dem Türlin's *Diu Crône*. The name is corrupted and split from GUIGOMAR d'Avalon, found in Chrétien's *Erec*. [*Heinrich*]

DAVID[1]

The patron saint of Wales, glorified in legend. Among many churches that he established in Wales was a monestary in the city of Mynyw or Menevia. The city was later re-named St. Davids, and his shrine became a popular destination for pilgrims in the Middle Ages. St. David is connected to Arthur in the Welsh *Life of St. Cadoc* and in Geoffrey of Monmouth's *Historia*. In the former, he joins St. Teilo and St. Cadoc in mediating a dispute between Arthur and a warrior named Ligessauc. The saints successfully convinced Arthur to accept 100 cows in return for the lives of three knights slain by Ligessauc. Geoffrey of Monmouth says that he was Arthur's uncle and that Arthur appointed him to the arcbishopric at Caerleon after St. Dubricius, the former archbishop, retired. [*SaintsC, GeoffHR, Giraldus*]

DAVID[2]

The biblical king of Israel and Judah; son of Saul and father of Solomon. The Vulgate romances purport that Lancelot, through his maternal grandmother, was David's descendant. David's sword, enhanced by Solomon, was later called the Sword of the Strange Hangings and was owned by Galahad. [*VulgQuest, VulgEst*]

DAVID[3] OF TINTAGEL [*Davit*]

One of Arthur's noblemen who was present at the wedding of Erec and Enide. Apparently, David had an excellent control over his temper and emotions. [*ChretienE, Heinrich*]

DAVIS

A knight who fought with his brother, Alain. Claris, Laris, and Bedivere found them fighting and forced them to reconcile. [*Claris*]

DAWN

A forest through which Galahad and Perceval traveled during the Grail Quest. [*VulgQuest*]

DEAN

A Welsh forest, north of Caerleon and south of Hereford. In Welsh legend, Arthur's chief forester in Dean was Madawg son of Twrgadarn. The Welsh story of *Geraint* begins with a great hunt for a magnificent stag in the forest. In Tennyson, it is named as a forest through which Pelleas rode during his adventures. [*Geraint, TennIK*]

DECHTIRE

In Irish legend, the sister of Conchobar, the king of Ulster. With the god Lug, she had a son named Cuchulainn. Cuchulainn is often considered Gawain's Irish counterpart, and Lug may be the origin of Lot. Dechtire, therefore, is, loosely, the counterpart of ANNA or MORGAUSE.

DEDYNE

One of Arthur's knights, mentioned in the medieval romance *Ywain and Gawain*. The name is probably a corruption of DODINEL, mentioned by Chrétien in *Yvain*. [*ChretienP*]

DEEP VALLEY

The lord of the Deep Valley was one of the kings who fought against the Saxons in the early days of Arthur's reign. He was defeated in the battle of Clarence. [*VulgMer*]

DEGRANE WITHOUT VILLANY

A Knight of the Round Table present at the healing of Sir Urry in Malory's *Le Morte Darthur*. Malory notes that he once fought the Giant of the Black Lowe, an adventure not recounted in existing legend. [*Malory*]

DEGREVANT [*Degreevant, Degrevance, Degrevans, Degrevuaund, Degrivaunce, Degrivaunce, Degrivuant, Degryvaunt, Egrivaunt*]

A Knight of the Round Table who is the hero of the Middle English *Sir Degrevant*. Described as Arthur's nephew, his name may derive from a corruption of AGRAVAIN. While Degrevant participated in a crusade, his neighbor, Earl Sere, invaded and ravaged his lands. Upon receiving word of this invasion, Degrevant returned and defeated the earl in combat. At the earl's castle, Degrevant met and fell in love with Melidor, the earl's daughter. He defeated the Duke of Gerle, one of Melidor's suitors. Degrevant and Melidor enjoyed a year-long secret romance before the earl learned of the affair and tried to ambush Degrevant. The plot failed, and in the aftermath the earl decided to reconcile with the knight. Degrevant and Melidor married and had thirty years together before Melidor died. Degrevant then returned to the crusades, in which he perished. Malory mentions him among the knights present at Lancelot's healing of Sir Urry. [*SirDeg, Malory*]

DELAMORE

A country where Arthur had a castle called Flatting. It may be the region of Delamere north of Chester (Hahn, 331). [*Grene*]

DELECTABLE ISLE [**Isle Delitable*]

An island off the east coast of England. It contained the Red City, where Palamedes avenged the death of a king. [*ProsTris, Malory*]

DELEKORS

A courageous and chivalrous knight in Arthur's court who was defeated in joust by Sir Tristan. [*Eilhart*]

DELEYN FITZDAVID

A knight present at one of Arthur's Easter feasts in the English *Arthur*. [*Arthur*]

DELICE [*Dalis*]

Galehaut's sister in the Prose *Tristan*. She lived in the Castle of Tears with her parents, Brunor the Brown and the Beautiful Giantess, or Bagotta. Tristan slew Delice's parents, conquered the castle, and allowed Delice to leave with the corpses of her father and mother. In *I Due Tristani*, the sister of Galehaut is named RICCARDA. [*ProsTris, Tavola*]

DELIMAZ THE POOR

A Knight of the Round Table and brother of Anseliam the Poor and Caligante the Poor. He participated in the Grail Quest. [*PostQuest*]

DELIS

A Spanish knight defeated in combat by Laris. [*Claris*]

DELVELIN [*Develin*]

The town in Ireland where, in the Middle-English *Sir Tristrem*, Tristan landed on his first visit. It is probably Dublin. [*SirTris*]

DEMAGUL

Named as the King of Logres in the Serbo-Russian *Povest' O Tryshchane*. [*Povest*]

DEMEDY

An Irish land visited by Lancelot on his way to Rigomer Castle. Its viscount was terrorized by a neighbor, who Lancelot defeated. Its capital city was called Pavingay. [*Merveil*]

DEMETIA [*Dimetia*]

A country in South Wales on the river Teifi. According to Geoffrey, Merlin's grandfather was the king of Demetia. Vortigern built the fortress of Vortigern here, and retreated here after the Saxons invaded eastern Britain. After four days at the fortress, a holy fire engulfed it and killed Vortigern. It was later ruled, under Arthur, by Stater. The Welsh call the region Dyfed. In non-Arthurian Welsh legend, it is ruled by Pwyll and, later, his son Pryderi. [*Nennius*, *GeoffHR*]

DEMETIUS

Merlin's grandfather in Thomas Heywood's *The Life of Merlin*. Demetius's daughter was impregnated by an incubus, Merlin's father. Heywood has created a personal name—whether deliberately or accidentall—out of DEMETIA, the country which Merlin's grandfather was said to rule. [*Heywood*]

DENIS

A hermit who baptized the survivors of the heathen Trial Castle, after Perceval destroyed the castle's Copper Tower and freed the inhabitants from the grip of paganism. [*Perlesvaus*]

DENMARK [*Danemarc(h)e*, *Danmark*, *Denmarch*, *Denmarke*]

During the Arthurian period, Denmark was populated by collections of Scandinavian clans. The united country of Denmark (*Dane-marche*, "borderland of the Danes") did not exist until the ninth century. No such history prevents the "kingdom of Denmark" from appearing in the Arthurian legends, however. According to Geoffrey of Monmouth, Arthur conquered Denmark and gave it to Aschil, one of his noblemen. In Wace, Aschil is the ruler of Denmark already, but subjugates himself to Arthur's rule in order to avoid a hopeless war. Geoffrey Gaimar's chronicle has Arthur conquer Denmark by killing King Gunter, whose brother, Odulf, subsequently claimed the throne. Welsh legend also makes Arthur ruler of Denmark, naming Yder as one of his Danish warriors. The Didot-*Perceval* names its king as Guillac, who assists Arthur in the Roman War. In the Vulgate *Merlin*, on the other hand, Denmark is ruled by the Saxon kings Aminaduc, Rions, and Bramangue, who are defeated by Arthur. In the Post-Vulgate *Merlin* continuation and in Malory, an unnamed King of Denmark (who is the brother of the King of Ireland) invades Britain with four other rulers, and is killed at the battle of the Humber. In the Welsh Triads, the King of Denmark is the father of Arthur's warrior Nasiens. In *Claris et Laris*, Denmark's king, Tallas, besieges King Urien but is defeated by Arthur's knights. A Queen of Denmark, who hates the Round Table, is the ruler of the Castle of Maidens in the *Livre d'Artus*. [*GeoffHR*, *Wace*, *Didot*, *VulgMer*, *Livre*, *PostMer*, *Dream*, *Malory*]

DENOALEN

An evil baron who served King Mark of Cornwall. He knew of the affair between Tristan and Isolde, and he conspired with two other barons to expose it to Mark. For a long time, Mark wavered between believing the barons and believing Tristan—and alternately banishing from his court one or the other. Finally, while laying another trap for the lovers, Denoalen was attacked and slain by Tristan. [*Beroul*]

DEORTHACH [*Dewrarth*, *Dorath*]

Father of Arthur's warrior Rhufawn Bebyr. [*Culhwch*, *Dream*]

DER KAL ("The Torment")

A river which flowed around the Schatel le Mort, the castle owned by Mabuz the enchanter. [*UlrichZ*]

DERUDICANORO

The fortress ruled by the pagan lord Fellone, a knight defeated by Tristan. [*Tavola*]

DESERT

A city in Logres that was the home of five Knights of the Round Table: Taulat, Senela, Baradam, Damas, and Damatal. [*PostQuest*]

DESERTED FOREST

A wood where Galahad, Palamedes, and Perceval encountered the Questing Beast during Grail Quest. They began pursuit of it, and Palamedes soon slew it. [*PostQuest*]

DESIXTUS

A knight slain by Kalegras, Tristan's father, after Desixtus and his brother Seran invaded Spain, Kalegras's country. [*SagaTI*]

DESOLATE CITY

The name given to SNOWDON, Queen Esmeree the Blonde's capital in Wales, after it was ruined by two sorcerers named Mabon and Evrain. Once the sorcerers were defeated by Gawain's son Guinglain, the city was restored. [*Renaut*]

DESPAIR

An evil monster who inhabited a cave in Fairy Land. He talked visiting knights into killing themselves by convincing them that their lives were too miserable to go on living. One knight, Trevisan, escaped from Despair and encountered the Red Cross Knight. Seeking to slay the monster, the Red Cross Knight visited Despair's cave. Despair reminded the Red Cross Knight of his failures and nearly lured him into suicide, but Una, the Red Cross Knight's *amie*, intervened and took him to safety. [*Spenser*]

DESSEMOUME

An Irish kingdom composed of Cork and Kerry. It was ruled by King Frion, whose daughter was saved from kidnappers by Lancelot. [*Merveil*]

DESTRIGALES [*(D)estregales, Testregeis*]

Literally, "Right Wales," probably indicating South Wales. Chrétien de Troyes names it as the land of Erec and his father, Lac. It's capital was Carnant, which may be Caruent in South Wales. In later romances, Erec's land is NANTES. [*ChretienE, HartmannE*]

DETORS

The king of Northumberland. He served Arthur. [*Claris*]

DEU GLEDDYF ("Two Swords")

Arthur's hunt for the boar Twrch Trwyth took him through this town in Wales, where the boar and it's piglets slew the town's men and animals. [*Culhwch*]

DEVIL'S ROAD [*Chemins au Deable*]

A road which led through the Forest of Misadventure and into the Valley of No Return. Galescalain, Arthur's duke of Clarence, traveled the road despite various warnings, and later had to be rescued by Lancelot. [*VulgLanc*]

DEVON

An area of southwest England, between the Bristol Channel and the English Channel, abutting Cornwall. It is usually included within Arthur's realm. In Welsh legend, Gwynn Hyfar is given as steward of Devon and Cornwall for Arthur. Geraint is also named as its king. Layamon says it was conquered in the early days of Arthur's reign by Cheldric the Saxon, but Arthur liberated it. In Tennyson, it is the homeland of Geraint. [*Culhwch, Layamon, TennIK*]

DEWI

Arthur's chief bishop in the city of St. David's (Mynyw) in Wales, according to an annotation in the Welsh Triads. [*Triads*]

DIALETES [*Devlites, Dialantes, Dialicies*]

A pagan giant who ruled in the Distant Isles in the time of Joseph of Arimathea. His sons all converted to Christianity, so Dialetes killed them and every other Christian he could find. He built the Castle of Tears on the Giant's Isle as a stronghold against Christianity, which retained its evil customs until destroyed by Tristan. This account first appears in the Prose *Tristan*; *La Tavola Ritonda* expands on it and asserts that Dialetes slew Joseph of Arimathea himself. [*ProsTris, Tavola*]

DIANA [*Dyan(n)e*]

The Roman goddess of the hunt. According to the Vulgate *Merlin*, it was her enchantment, given to Dyonas, that caused Viviane (the Lady of the Lake) to be so alluring to Merlin. The Vulgate *Lancelot* tells us that she was the Queen of Sicily, but considered a goddess by her foolish pagan subjects. The Post-Vulgate *Merlin* continuation describes how she murdered her lover in order to be with another man, but then was beheaded by this man for being a murderess. This occurred at a lake in France, and was thereafter called the Lake of Diana. This lake was the home of the Lady of the Lake, and was the place where Lancelot was raised, giving him his epithet. Diana is mentioned several times in Spenser's *The Faerie Queene*. She raised the huntress Belphoebe, who became the paramour of Arthur's squire, Timias. [*LancLac, VulgLanc, VulgMer, PostMer, Spenser*]

DIANA BRIDGE [*Drian, Drien*]

A bridge spanning the lake of DIANA. It was the site of a battle between a group of Arthur's young warriors, led by Gawain and Yvain, and the Saxons, led by King Soriondes. Arthur's forces were victorious. Although the Lake of Diana is mentioned elsewhere as lying in France, this battle seems to occur in Britain. [*VulgMer, Arthour*]

DIANFER

A fortress in the waste land of Lionferfo, ruled by a giant named Lucano the Great, whom Tristan killed. [*Tavola*]

DIARMAID

TRISTAN'S counterpart in Irish legend. Diarmaid, under the influence of a love potion, fell in love with Grainne, the wife of his uncle Finn. Diarmaid and Grainne eventually fled from Finn's court. Finn pursued them. They remained celibate at first, but eventually succumbed to their desires.

DIASBAD ("Outcry")

Wife of Arthur's warrior Syfwlch. [*Culhwch*]

DIGON ("Enough")

One of Arthur's warriors who was the son of Alar. [*Culhwch*]

DILIANFER [*Rilanfer*]

The king of Ireland during Uther Pendragon's reign. He attacked Felix, the king of Cornwall and Lyonesse, and sacked the fortress of Tintagel. Through his victory, he established the custom by which Cornwall paid an annual tribute to Ireland. This custom ended when Tristan slew Morholt, Dilianfer's son. [*Tavola*]

DILLUS THE BEARDED

A bearded man whose whiskers were needed by the warrior Culhwch to make a leash to hold the pups Aned and Aethlem during the hunting of the boar Twrch Trwyth. According to the giant Ysbaddaden, who assigned Culhwch this task, the beard had to be plucked while Dillus was alive, and Dillus naturally would likely not take kindly to the procedure. Arthur's warriors Cei and Bedwyr found Dillus in Pumlumon. They waited for him to eat his fill of a pig and to go to sleep. When he was asleep, the two warriors plucked his beard and then killed him. [*Culhwch*]

DIMILIOC

A castle in Cornwall ruled by Gorlois, duke of Cornwall. When King Uther Pendragon declared war against Gorlois over Igerne, Gorlois' wife, Gorlois sheltered her in Tintagel, his strongest castle, while Gorlois himself holed up in Dimilioc. Gorlois was eventually slain in a battle outside the castle. Malory changes the castle's name to TARABEL. [*GeoffHR*]

DIN TYWI

A location in western England through which Arthur's warriors hunted a piglet named Grugyn Silver Bristle. [*Culhwch*]

DINABUC [*Dynabrok, Dynabus*]

The name give by Wace to the giant of MONT ST. MICHEL slain by Arthur. The English ballad known as "The Legend of King Arthur" says that Dinabuc inhabited St. Bernard's Mount instead. [*Wace, Mannyng, Legend*]

DINABUTIUS [*Dabutius, Dinaburt, Dinabus*]

A royal youth who lived in Carmarthen. Envoys from King Vortigern—searching for a boy without a father—rode through Carmarthen and overheard Dinabutius chiding another boy for having no father. This other boy was Merlin, and he was soon summoned to Vortigern's court. [*GeoffHR, Wace*]

DINADAN [*Dinadam, Dinadano, Dinadeira, Divdan, Dynadan*]

A Knight of the Round Table who appears first in the Post-Vulgate *Queste del Saint Graal* as one of the knights embarking on the Grail Quest. His first significant appearance is in the Prose *Tristan*. Reputed as a humorist and a practical joker, Dinadan questioned the conventions of knighthood, including the idea of courtly love and the notion of knights battling for no reason other than one challenging the other or insulting his honor ("Shame is a bad thing, but a wound is worse," he says in *La Tavola Ritonda*). Nevertheless, he was known as a noble and courageous warrior who did not hesitate to use his sword to right wrongs and to uphold the values of the Round Table.

His brother, Brunor the Black, was the famous Good Knight Without Fear; and his brother, also called Brunor the Black, was known as the Knight of the Ill-Fitting Coat. The Italian *La Tavola Ritonda* assigns him another brother named Daniello, who betrays Guinevere and Lancelot to Arthur. While *Tristan* and Malory tend to use Dinadan for comic relief, in *Tavola*, he is darkly critical of his companions' behavior and struggles bitterly against love of any kind.

Most of his adventures are had in the company of Tristan. Though the latter's actions did not escape Dinadan's ridicule, Dinadan recognized him as one of the noblest knights. He had few enemies, though he was contemptuous of King Mark of Cornwall, and in fact wrote a popular song insulting the monarch. A victorious encounter with Mordred and Agravain sparked a resentment that led to Dinadan's murder by these brothers during the Grail Quest. Palamedes buried him in Camelot. [*PostQuest, Palamedes, ProsTris, Girart, Tavola, Malory*]

DINADAS [*Dinados*]

A Knight of the Round Table from Garlot. He participated in the Grail Quest. [*PostQuest*]

DINAL [*Dinaus*]

One of Arthur's knights. [*Renaut*]

DINAN [*Dinas*]

A land ruled in Arthur's time by Lord Dinas, a vassal of Mark of Cornwall. Eilhart von Oberge calls it LITAN. [*Beroul*]

DINAS[1] [*Dinasso, Dynas, Tinas*]

In the Tristan legends, the lord of Dinan and the seneschal of Cornwall under King Mark. He was a good and loyal friend of Tristan, and counseled Mark to ignore the rumors of Tristan and Isolde's affair and to keep his friendship with the knight. When Tristan was banished, he assisted the lovers by frequently arranging trysts. His son, Liaz, was a count of Cornwall.

The Prose *Tristan* and Malory have him playing a very active role against Mark, defecting and organizing a resistance when Tristan is thrown into prison, and eventually freeing Tristan and imprisoning Mark, allowing Tristan and Isolde to flee Cornwall together. Later, when Tristan received a poisoned wound from Mark, he found succor, until he expired, in Dinas's castle. Dinas organized a second revolt against Mark, which successfully unseated the evil king. *La Tavola Ritonda* says that he became lord of Cornwall after Mark's death, but in the Prose *Tristan* he refuses the position.

According to Malory, Dinas traveled to Camelot and became a Knight of the Round Table, although he left Arthur when Arthur went to war with Lancelot. He fought for Lancelot at the sieges of Joyous Guard and Benoic. For his support, Lancelot made him the Duke of Anjou.

The Italian *La Vendetta Che Fe Messer Lanzelloto de la Morte di Miser Tristano*, uniquely, names Dinas as the brother of Sir Sagremor. Dinas's name may have originally been a place name; *dinas* is the Welsh word for "fortress." [*Beroul, Eilhart, Wolfram, ProsTris, Tavola, Vendetta, Malory*]

DINAS²

A Knight of the Round Table; brother of Meles the Tall. [*PostQuest*]

DINAS EMRYS ("Fort of Ambrosius") [*Dinas Emreis*]

The mountain in the SNOWDON mountain range (North Wales) where King Vortigern sought to build a fortress to stand against the Saxons, only to find that each day's construction kept disappearing overnight. The king's advisors told him to locate a fatherless boy, sacrifice him, and wet the castle's foundation with his blood. Vortigern's messengers turned up such a child. Nennius calls the child Ambrosius (Welsh: Emrys), but Geoffrey of Monmouth replaces him with Merlin. The child managed to prevent his own execution by showing Vortigern the true reason for the tower's collapse: a pool hidden beneath the mountain. Draining the lake revealed a red and white dragon, whose subsequent battle portended Vortigern's eventual defeat. Vortigern gave the castle to Ambrosius and fled to the north. The Welsh called the mountain ERYRI, and legends of Merlin's treasure, buried deep within the mountain, survive to this day. Archaeology has shown occupation of Dinas Emrys in the fifth century, including a household that actually did contain a pool. [*Nennius, GeoffHR*]

DINASDARÉS

An enemy of Gawain in the first *Perceval* continuation. He accused Gawain of killing his father. After an indecisive duel in the forest, they agreed to postpone their combat until they met at a court. They encountered each other at the castle of Escavalon, where Gawain was already slated to fight a knight named Guigambresil. The king of Escavalon decreed that Gawain would have to fight Dinasdarés and Guigambresil together, but Arthur intervened and stopped the battle, and Gawain and Dinasdarés made peace. Dinasdarés married the lady Beatris, the niece of the King of Escavalon. [*Contin1, Contin4*]

DINASDARON [*Di(a)nazarun, Disnadaron*]

One of Arthur's courts. Chrétien de Troyes places it in Wales, while Wolfram von Eschenbach locates it in the country of Löver. It was the site of Sir Urjans' rape of a maiden and Gawain's capture of Urjans. It is probably a conflation of *Dinas d'Aron*, *dinas* being the Welsh word for "Castle." Aron is either Aaron, the patron saint of Caerleon, or the river Arun in West Sussex. [*ChretienP, Wolfram, VulgLanc, PleierG*]

DINDRAITHOF

Arthur's residence along the Severn river, according to the *Life of St. Cadoc*. [*SaintsCad*]

DINIFOGAR

A queen who threw a tournament in which Wigamur, one of Arthur's knights, excelled. [*Wigamur*]

DINISORDRES

Son of Salandres and brother of Menastide, Nastor, Gogonne, and Aristes. Dinisordres, his father, and all of his brothers were defeated in combat by Perceval. They went to Arthur's court as prisoners. [*Contin3*]

DIOCENAR

An unfortunate knight who was cuckholded by Galehaut the Brown. Having lost his lovely wife, Diocenar died from heartbreak. [*Palamedes*]

DIODICIAS

King of Syria in ancient times. With his four wives, he had thirty-three daughters and three sons. One of his daughters, Albine, first populated and gave her name to Albion (Britain). [*Palamedes*]

DION [*Dyonz*]

The nephew of Duke Calles and brother of Alibel, Dyonis, and Casibilant. His six cousins revolted against their father, Duke Calles. Dion and his brothers assisted their uncle in the war, in which they were joined by Agravain, Gaheris, and Gareth. [*VulgLanc*]

DIONIDO

Named in *La Tavola Ritonda* as the Pope during Arthur's reign. When he heard of Tristan's death, he offered indulgences to anyone who would pray for Tristan and his country. The text notes that he was succeeded by Pope Agabito. No known Popes correspond with these names, except perhaps Pope Donus and Pope Agatho, who ascended to the papacy in 676 and 678, respectively. [*Tavola*]

DIONISE

The Queen of Rigomer Castle. She was bound to marry the knight who eventually conquered her kingdom. Gawain achieved this feat but declined to wed her, promising instead to match her with another worthy knight. [*Merveil*]

DIONOTUS

Brother of the Cornish king Caradoc. Dionotus assumed the kingship of Cornwall upon his brother's death. Maximus made him the ruler of Britain in his place when he went to conquer Gaul. Dionotus became an ally of Conan Meriadoc—ruler of Brittany—when Conan married his daughter Ursula. Dionotus helped Conan import thousands of British woman to "Other Britain" to help spread British influence throughout Gaul. [*GeoffHR*]

DIRAC

Uncle of Erec, son of Canan, and brother of Lac. Canan was assassinated, so Dirac and Lac had to flee their ancestral land of Aloliqui for Britain. Arthur found them and eventually knighted them. Dirac later became a king, and his sons murdered Lac. Erec and Meraugis killed Dirac's sons. [*PostQuest*]

DIRLANTES

A Cornish forest surrounding the Tower of Enchantments, where the Wise Maiden imprisoned Tristan's father, King Meliadus. It may be a variation of DARNANTES. [*Tavola*]

DIRMYG ("Contempt")

Son of Caw, one of twenty brothers, and one of Arthur's warriors. [*Culhwch*]

DISSETHACH

A Welsh poem indicates that Arthur once "pierced the cudgel-head in the halls of Dissethach." [*WelshPG*]

DISTANT ISLES [*Far Isles, Foreign Isles, *Lontai(g)nes Iles, Remote Isles, Strange Isles*]

An archipelago near the country of Sorelois, mentioned several times in the Vulgate romances. Galahad, Joseph of Arimathea's son, married the daughter of their king. Later, in Arthur's time, they was ruled by Clamadeu, and were conquered by Galehaut. One of Distant Isles was the Giant's Isle, which held the Castle of Tears and was conquered by Tristan. In the Post-Vulgate *Merlin* continuation and in Malory, the King of the Distant Isles was one five kings who invaded Britain, and who were slain by Arthur's men at the battle of the Humber. The Distant Isles were also the home of a Knight of the Round Table named Balynor. Some have attempted to identify the Distant Isles with the Hebrides or the Isles of Scilly. [*VulgLanc, VulgEst, PostMer, ProsTris*]

DISTANT KNIGHT

In *La Tavola Ritonda*, Tristan's alias during his stay in Ireland. In most versions, he uses the name TANTRIST. [*Tavola*]

DISUS

A bodyguard of Queen Flúrant of Ireland. He told Tristan about the dragon of Sukstía mountain, prompting Tristan to travel there and slay the creature. [*SagaTI*]

DITAS

King of Hungary in *Claris et Laris*. He joined Emperor Thereus of Rome in a war against Arthur and was killed. [*Claris*]

DIWRNACH [*Dyrnwch*]

A Irish giant. He was steward of Odgar of Ireland. Diwrnach owned a magic cauldron, which would only boil if the meat placed in it was intended for a brave man. It was listed in Welsh lore among the "Thirteen Treasures of the Island of Britain." As one of his tasks, Culhwch had to obtain this cauldron from Diwrnach for boiling meat at Olwen's wedding feast. When Arthur, on the behalf of Culhwch, requested the cauldron, Diwrnach refused. At this refusal, Arthur's warrior Llenlleawg killed Diwrnach and took the cauldron, which Arthur's warriors filled with Ireland's treasure before returning to Britain. [*Culhwch, Triads*]

DO [*Deon, D(i)eu, Does, Doon, Due*]

The son of Ares and the father of Arthur's Sir Girflet. He served as Arthur's castellan of Cardueil and, later, London. He fought against the Saxon invasion at the beginning of Arthur's reign. Malory calls him "Cardol," confusing his home with his name. [*ChretienE, Contin1, VulgMer, Arthour, Malory*]

DOCHEL

In Heinrich von dem Türlin's *Diu Crône*, Gawain, in a list of his greatest exploits, mentions that he "took many a drink from the Fountain of Youth" in the Garden of Dochel. This episode is not found in any existing romance. [*Heinrich*]

DODALIS

A Saxon king who participated in the Saxon invasion of northern Britain in the early days of Arthur's reign. He was killed by Agravain at the battle of Cambenic. [*VulgMer*]

DODINEL [*Dedinet, Didoine, Didones, Dinodes, Dodinal, Dodin(i)aus, Dodine(i)s, Dodynas, Dondanix, Dondi(j)el, Dondinax, Dondinel, Dondinello, Dondonello, Oddinello*]

A Knight of the Round Table, first mentioned by Chrétien de Troyes, and given the epithet "the Savage," "the Wild," "the Wildman," or "the Fierce," due to a love of hunting or because, in some stories, he lives in the wilds (in Ulrich's *Lanzelet*, he has a home near the perilous Shrieking Marsh). In the Didot-*Perceval*, he is called the son of the Lady of Malehaut. In Wolfram von Eschenbach's *Parzival*, Dodinel has a brother named Taurian the Wild.

The Vulgate *Merlin* and *Lancelot* gives him a full biography: He was the son of King Belinant of South Wales and Belinant's niece. He participated in the wars against the Saxons in the early days of Arthur's reign, joining the young warriors Gawain and Yvain. He was knighted by Arthur for his service, and became one of the Queen's Knights before he was eventually promoted to the Round Table. His adventures consist primarily of various imprisonments: in Dolorous Guard, the Castle Langree, the Forbidden Hill, and in Meleagant's castle. He was rescued from most of these by Lancelot.

The Prose *Tristan* and Malory give him an impotent role as a knight defeated by Morholt and Tristan (for making fun of him). In French romance, Dodinel perishes during the battle against Mordred's army at Salisbury Plain.

In the *Chantari di Lancellotto*, Dodinel joins Mordred and Kay in accusing Lancelot and Guinevere of treason. In *Il Cantari di Carduino*, he dies at the hands of Gawain's brother, Aguerisse (Gareth or Gaheris), and his death is avenged by his son, Carduino. [*ChretienE, Wolfram, Didot, LancLac, VulgLanc, VulgMer, PostQuest, PostMort, ProsTris, CantariC, Chantari, Malory*]

DODONE

The castle in the forest of Beforet, inhabited by Iweret, Lancelot's opponent in Ulrich's *Lanzelet*. It was beautifully constructed, richly adorned, and masterfully situated on a mountain top. After Lancelot defeated Iweret, the castle fell under his rule. [*UlrichZ*]

DOG-HEADS

An early Welsh Arthurian poem says that, "On the mount of Eidyn [Edinburgh], they [Arthur and presumably Cei] found with Dog-heads; by the hundred they fell." [*WelshPG*]

DOGED

A king who was killed by Culhwch's father Cilydd. Cilydd then stole Doged's wife for his own. [*Culhwch*]

DOL

A British city of which Samson and Teliau served as archbishops during Arthur's time. [*GeoffHR*]

DOLANZIE

A Scottish knight in the service of lord Galehaut. Galehaut left him as viceroy of the Giant's Isle after Tristan conquered it and slew Galehaut's parents. [*Tavola*]

DOLDAVIUS [*Doldanim, Doldamer, Doldan, Doldau, Dolmad*]

The King of Gothland or Jutland who surrendered to King Arthur rather than be conquered by him. He later assisted Arthur in the conquest of France and in the Roman War. [*GeoffHR, Wace, Layamon*]

DOLDAYS

A count who rivaled Arthur for the affections of the Lady of the Blonde Hair. He attended a tournament at the Amorous City, at which Arthur defeated him in personal combat. [*ChevPap*]

DOLFIN

A hunting dog which belonged to Ivor, the tutor of King Meriadoc of Wales. [*Historia*]

DOLLALLOLLA

Arthur's queen in Henry Fielding's parody *The Tragedy of Tragedies*. She loved the diminutive warrior Tom Thumb, and tried to prevent his marriage to her daughter Huncamunca. In the end, she is slain by Noodle, a courtier, or by Cleora, one of her maidservants. [*Fielding*]

DOLOROUS FIELD

The field where Erec was slain by Gawain, and where Hector and Meraugis found Erec's body. [*PostQuest*]

DOLOROUS GUARD [**Dolereuse Garde*]

Castle conquered by Lancelot in the Prose *Lancelot* and its adaptations. It was on the river Humber. *Lancelot* names its original ruler as Brandin of the Isles, while *La Tavola Ritonda* calls him Federiel. The castle was magically enchanted so that any knight who wished to enter had to fight two sets of ten knights—one set at each of two gates—one by one until he defeated them all. He then would have to kill the ruler or stay in the castle for forty days before the enchantments could be lifted and the people freed. The names of the knights that had tried the adventure were written on gravestones within the inner wall of the castle, and their "heads" were next to the stones, but in actuality, the knights were imprisoned in the DOLOROUS PRISON. Many knights lost their freedoms in this manner. Lancelot defeated the twenty knights through the help of some magical shields from the Lady of the Lake, but Brandin fled before Lancelot could fight him. The people of the castle became restless when Lancelot kept leaving, because he was interrupting the forty-day cycle and preventing their freedom. Finally, he went into the depths of the castle, braved a difficult adventure, and returned with the key to the enchantments, which freed the residents. Lancelot them renamed the castle JOYOUS GUARD. He held on to the castle, lived there from time to time, hosted his companions there, and interred his friend Galehaut in its cemetery. When Lancelot rescued Guinevere from the stake, he brought her to the castle. When he was forced out of Britain by Arthur, he changed the castle's name back to Dolorous Guard. In some versions, Lancelot is brought to Dolorous Guard after his death and is buried with Galehaut. In the Post-Vulgate *Mort Artu*, we are told that King Mark of Cornwall exhumed their bodies and destroyed them. [*LancLac*, *VulgLanc*, *VulgMort*, *PostMort*, *ProsTris*, *Tavola*, *Malory*]

DOLOROUS MOUNT [*Mount Dolereus*]

An enchanted hilltop, possibly in Scotland. At the top was a pillar, adorned with 15 crosses, to which only the best knights could tie their horses. Any other knight would be driven insane. Merlin had constructed the test at the behest of Uther Pendragon in order to find worthy knights for Arthur's table. Kahedins vowed to travel there in Chrétien's *Perceval*, but it is Perceval who tests himself at the pillar and succeeds in the Second Continuation. Merlin's daughter inhabited the mountain and explained the adventure to Perceval. [*ContinP*, *Contin2*]

DOLOROUS PRISON [*Dolereuse Chartre*]

A dungeon owned by Brandin of the Isles, lord of DOLOROUS GUARD, but in a separate castle from Dolorous Guard. Every knight who attempted the adventure at Dolorous Guard and failed was thrown into the Dolorous Prison; their names, however, appeared on tombstones at Dolorous Guard, as if they were dead. These knights included Yder, Guivret, Yvain of Leonel, Cadoain, Kehedin, Kay of Estraus, Girflet, Dodinel, Taulas, Mador, Galegantin, and Arthur's son Loholt. Gawain was tricked into the prison by Brandin after Lancelot liberated Dolorous Guard, but the lot of knights were eventually freed by Lancelot. Loholt and Galegantin developed serious illnesses while in the prison; Loholt later died, but Galegantin was healed by the Hermit of the Thicket. [*LancLac*, *VulgLanc*, *Livre*]

DOLOROUS STROKE [*Dolereus Coup*]

The fateful blow which, in the Grail romances, created the Waste Land. The Grail Quest was needed to heal the results of the Dolorous Stroke. The term is used to describe two separate events: the slaying of King Lambor (an early Grail King) by King Varlan, and the maiming of King Pellehan by Sir Balin the Savage. The former appears in the Vulgate *Queste del Saint Graal*, the latter is related in the Post-Vulgate *Suite du Merlin*, and both appear in Malory. In both versions of the Dolorous Stroke, a Grail King is attacked with a forbidden holy weapon.

In the *Queste* episode, King Lambor of Listenois, a Grail King, is at war with King Varlan of Wales. Varlan, forced to flee from Lambor, came across the Ship of Solomon, which contained the magnificent Sword with the Strange Hangings, intended for only the most pure knight. Disregarding the warning on the sheath, Varlan drew the sword and used it to slay King Lambor. This unholy blow turned both Listenois and Wales into the Waste Land, and Varlan was struck dead for his profanity when he returned the sword to the sheath.

In the *Suite* story, Sir Balin the Savage arrives at King Pellehan's court hunting Sir Garlon, an invisible marauder who was Pellehan's brother. Balin killed Garlon in Pellehan's hall. Pellehan, enraged, attacked Balin, shattering Balin's sword. Balin ran from room to room in Pellehan's castle, trying to find some other weapon, with Pellehan at his heels. In one room, he found a corpse in a bed and a long spear (the Bleeding Lance) resting on a nearby table. Balin did not know that the corpse was that of Joseph of Arimathea, and that the spear was the most holy of weapons—the very lance that pierced the side of Jesus Christ on the cross. Thus ignorant, Balin hefted the spear and struck Pellehan, which immediately caused Pellehan's castle to crumble and the land of Listenois to become the Waste Land. Pellehan's wound led to his identification as the Maimed King, and he remained ill until healed during the Grail Quest by Galahad.

A Grail king maimed in combat first appears in the earliest Grail story, Chrétien de Troyes's *Perceval*. Though not called the "Dolorous Stroke," a blow has been delivered to the Fisher King, leaving him infirm. (The circumstances behind this wounding vary from text to text.) We also learn from Chrétien that the Bleeding Lance, found in the Fisher King's castle, will one day "destroy the realm of Logres." Also, in the first continuation of Chrétien's *Perceval*, Gawain is told by the Fisher King that the Grail Sword was used to strike a blow that laid the country of Logres to waste. (In Celtic mythology, similarly, King Bran is wounded in the foot by a poisoned spear, causing his land to suffer.) Thus, the idea of a weapon's blow, whether struck against the Fisher King or elsewhere, causing the destruction of a kingdom, appears in the earliest Grail legends, though the term "Dolorous Stroke" is not used until later.

The Fisher King is not the only figure to be maimed through the thighs in the Grail legends. In the Vulgate *Estoire del Saint Graal*, the characters can barely walk from one place to another without being thrown to the ground by some heavenly blow. An angel shoves a lance through the thighs of Josephus, son of Joseph of Arimathea, when he impiously abandons the conversion of some pagans to Christianity in order to save from death a group of pagans who refuse to convert. The angel later removes the lance and heals Josephus. In another episode, Nascien is injured by a flaming sword that appears out of nowhere when Nascien is too slow to alight from the holy Ship of Solomon (God was angry with Nascien because he had previously used the Sword with the Strange Hangings to kill a giant). Finally, Joseph of Arimathea himself is wounded in the thighs by a sword, which breaks, drips blood continually from the tip, and is thereafter called the Broken Sword. [*ChretienP*, *Contin1*, *Wolfram*, *VulgQuest*, *VulgEst*, *Livre*, *PostMer*, *Malory*]

DOLOROUS TOWER

The castle inhabited by the evil giant Caradoc. In one of the earliest stories of Guinevere's abduction (found on the Modena Archivolt), it was ruled by Mardoc, who had Caradoc kidnap Guinevere. The castle could be entered only by two bridges, which were guarded by the warriors Burmalt and Caradoc. Gawain managed to penetrate the fortress and rescue the Queen.

In later stories, the Dolorous Tower belongs wholly to Caradoc, Guinevere's abduction is removed, and Lancelot becomes Caradoc's killer. In lieu of the queen, in these stories, Caradoc kidnaps many good knights and imprisons them in his squalid, rodent-infested jail. After Lancelot conquered it, he gave it to a maiden who had been imprisoned there. Malory mentions it as the home of Sir Selyses. [*Modena*, *VulgLanc*, *Malory*]

DOLPHIN

A knight slain by Gawain during the Roman War. [*Allit*]

DOMBART

A son of Albanact, the first king of Scotland. Dombart's brothers were Arbrun and Embrunt. [*Palamedes*]

DOMOROT OF LOKVA

Father of Lancelot and Hector in the Serbo-Russian *Povest' o Tryshchane*. [*Povest*]

DÔN

Father of Arthur's warriors Amathaon and Gofannon. He has several other sons in non-Arthurian Welsh legend. He is originally an Irish god. [*Culhwch*]

DONA AVVENTURA

A young knight baptized and dubbed by Lancelot and Tristan. He married the daughter of the vavasour of Cologia. [*Tavola*]

DONADIX

Brother of King Bagdemagus of Gorre. He was killed by Gawain during the Grail Quest. [*PostQuest*]

DONADORD

A heathen warrior slain by Gaheris (Gawain's brother) at the battle of Diana Bridge. [*Arthour*]

DONAS

A knight killed by Claris. Claris and Laris were helping Sir Caradoc protect his paramour from King Ladas, Sir Donas's liege. [*Claris*]

DONAUT [*Donand(er)*, *Dunwale*]

In Geoffrey of Monmouth, a warrior in Arthur's service who was the son of Papo. Geoffrey adopted his name from Welsh mythology (Fletcher, 77). [*GeoffHR*, *Wace*, *Layamon*]

DONÍSUS

The Emperor of Saxony when Tristan served as the King of Spain. Donísus asked for Tristan's help in combating a king named Amilías, who was making frequent raids in Donísus's country. Tristan killed Amilías, and Donísus rewarded him with many lands and treasures. Later, Tristan's son, Kalegras, married Lilja, Donísus's daughter. [*SagaTI*]

DONOBERT

In the Elizabethan play *The Birth of Merlin*, a nobleman at Aurelius Ambrosius's court. He betrothed his daughters, Constantia and Modestia, to Cador of Cornwall and Sir Edwin, but they both decided to enter a nunnery instead. [*Birth*]

DOODLE

In Henry Fielding's parody *The Tragedy of Tragedies*, one of Arthur's several courtiers. In the chaotic ending of the play, Doodle slays Huncamunca, Arthur's daughter, and is in turn slain by either Dollallolla, Arthur's queen, or Mustacha, one of Dollallolla's maidservants. [*Fielding*]

DOORM

In Tennyson, a lord whose lands Geraint and Enid entered during their journey. His vassals called him "the Bull." He came across an unconscious Geraint and a destitute Enid. Bringing them to his castle, he tried to convince Enid that Geraint was dead and that she should accept his favors. When she refused, he beat her. Her screams awakened Geraint, who jumped up and slew Doorm. Doorm is known in Chrétien's *Erec* as ORINGLE and in the Welsh *Geraint* as LIMORS. [*TennIK*]

DORCHIN [*Derquin*]

A vassal of the King with a Hundred Knights. He participated in King Mark's tournament at Lancien. [*Contin4*]

DORE

Atop a hill in Cornwall lie the remains of Castle Dore (possibly from *d'or*, or "gold"), built probably in the third century B.C., and occupied and fortified by the Britons during the post-Roman period. Nearby, the TRISTAN STONE is found, which is a monument to "Drustanus" (Tristan), son of "Cunomorus." Cunomorus, a sixth-century Cornish king, may have lived in the castle. Cunomorus, furthermore, is identified with King Mark in the *Life of St. Paul Aurelian*. [*Topography*]

DORILAS[1] [*Darrilas*]

A Saxon warrior who participated in the Saxon invasion of Britain at the beginning of Arthur's reign. He was slain by Arthur's Gornain Cadrus at the battle of Carhaix. [*VulgMer*, *Arthour*]

DORILAS[2] [*Dorilan*]

A Saxon king slain by King Bors of Gannes at the battle of Aneblayse. [*VulgMer*, *Arthour*]

DORILAS[3]

The nephew of King Nentres of Garlot. He fought with his uncle against the Saxons at the battles of Broceliande and Clarence. [*VulgMer*]

DORIN [*Dorens*]

King Claudas's arrogant son, and the heir to Berry and the Land Laid Waste. Claudas delayed knighting him for fear he would revolt. Dorilas ravaged his own lands and slew his own people for pure amusement. Claudas finally knighted him, and on that very night Dorin was killed by Lionel and Bors—the two sons of the slain King Bors—when they escaped from Claudas's prison. [*LancLac*, *VulgLanc*]

DORMADAT

One of seven brothers, including Ayaò and Albaò, who usurped the throne of Tristan the Stranger, ruler of Jakobsland. Tristan the Stranger sought out his famous namesake, and the two of them returned and slew the seven brothers. [*SagaTI*]

DORSET [*Dorchester*]

A county in southwest England, on the English Channel. It was conquered by Cheldric the Saxon in the early days of Arthur's reign, but Arthur liberated it. It was later ruled in Arthur's time by Earl Jonathal. [*GeoffHR*]

DOUGLAS

A Knight of the Round Table, badly wounded by Gawain in a tournament between the Round Table and the Queen's Knights. [*VulgMer*]

DOVER [*Do(u)vre*]

A seaport in the region of Kent, on the shore of the English Channel. Dover was invaded by Saxons in the early days of Arthur's reign. As the closest city to mainland Europe, it was the site of troop departures and arrivals in Arthur's various wars. Arthur landed in Dover on the way back from his war with Lancelot, and Arthur's forces encountered Mordred in the first of their various battles. Gawain was slain in the combat, and was buried, according to Malory, in a chapel in the city. [*VulgMort*, *VulgMer*, *Stanz*, *Malory*]

DOWARD [*Cloar(d)(icus)*, *Droac*]

A mountain in the country of Archenfield in Wales. It was the site of Vortigern's castle, Ganarew. [*GeoffHR*, *Wace*]

DRAGAN [*Dagarius*]

A Knight of the Round Table from Scotland who fell in love with Isolde while staying with Tristan and Isolde at Joyous Guard. When Dragan petitioned Isole for her love, Tristan became incensed and killed him. Dragan's Round Table seat was taken by Helain the White. [*PostQuest*, *ProsTris*]

DRAGONEL THE CRUEL [*Dragoniaus*]

A malevolent knight who abducted the lady Rohais from the knight Arguisiaus of Carhaix, wounding Arguisiaus in the process. Dragonel intended to force Rohais into marriage, but Perceval encountered him, defeated him, and sent him to Arthur's court. [*Contin4*]

DREM ("Sight")

A warrior of Arthur's court who was the son of Dremidydd. Drem shared the duties of gatekeeper in Caer Llion (Caerleon) with seven to nine other warriors. His master was the chief gatekeeper Glewlwyd Strong Grip. His name means "sight" and, according to the tales, Drem's vision was such that he could see a fly in Scotland from Cornwall. [*Culhwch*, *Geraint*]

DREMIDYDD ("Sighter")

Father of Arthur's warrior Drem. [*Culhwch*, *Geraint*]

DRIADAM

A cousin of Erec who was slain by Mordred, prompting a feud between Erec and Mordred. [*PostMer*]

DRIAIGUE

A location where Urien took Guinevere after he kidnapped her during the rebellion against Arthur. [*Livre*]

DRIAN[1] [*Adrian*, *Brian*, *Dornar*, *Doryan*, *Drians*, *Driant*, *Durnor*, *Tryan*]

Son of Pellinore, brother of Perceval, Lamorat, Aglovale, Alain, and Tor. The bulk of his adventures are found in the Prose *Tristan*. With his brother Alain, he guarded a bridge and jousted with all passers-by. He defeated King Mark of Cornwall in combat. He visited Mark's court with his brother Lamorat and defeated all of Mark's knights except for Tristan. An ongoing feud between Pellinore's clan and Gawain's family eventually led to Drian being attacked by Agravain, Mordred, and Gawain. After Drain defeated the first two, he was mortally wounded by Gawain. His brother Lamorat died trying to avenge him.

Malory calls him "Durnor," but includes two other knights named "Drian" and "Tryan," to whom he gives the adventures above, seemingly unaware that they are all the same person. "Durnor" is killed by Gawain's kin; "Drian" visits Mark's court with Lamorat and is eventually killed when Lancelot rescues Guinevere from the stake; and "Tryan" guards the bridge with his brother Alain. [*PostMer*, *ProsTris*, *Malory*]

DRIAN[2] [*Briant*]

A knight from the Wild Forest or Perilous Forest who helped fight the Saxons and the rebellious kings in the early days of Arthur's reign. He was called "the Merry" or "the Gay." His father was Trahan the Gay, the lord of the

Gay Castle, and his brother was Melian the Gay. He was wounded by Caradoc of the Dolorous Tower, and was imprisoned in a coffin from which only the best knight could remove him. Those who failed had to fight Caradoc, and Caradoc's prison population thus rose dramatically. Lancelot managed to pull him from the coffin and later defeat Caradoc. [*VulgLanc*, *VulgMer*, *Livre*, *Malory*]

DRIANT OF THE ISLE

A knight and friend of Tristan. [*ProsTris*]

DRIUS

An Arthurian knight. [*Merveil*]

DROMÉS

An Arthurian knight in the romance of *Yder*. He participated in Arthur's war against Taulas of Rougemont, a rebelling vassal. [*Yder*]

DRUAS THE CRUEL

The lord of the Hill of Wretches. He slew every knight who adventured his way, but was eventually killed by Agravain. Druas's brother, Sorneham of Newcastle, learned of the incident and, in revenge, he defeated and imprisoned Agravain. [*VulgLanc*]

DRUDWAS

Son of Tryffin, brother of Erdudfyl, and one of King Arthur's three "Golden-Tongued Knights." [*Culhwch*, *Triads*]

DRUDWYN

A hound that belonged to Greid. As one of his tasks, the warrior Culhwch had to obtain this hound to hunt the boar Twrch Trwyth. In addition, the hound had to be managed by the houndsman Mabon, and had to be held with the leash of Cors Hundred Claws, the collar of Canhastyr Hundred Hands, and the chain of Cilydd Hundred Holds. Arthur himself obtained the hound on Culhwch's behalf, and used him in the hunting of the boars Ysgithyrwyn and Twrch Trwyth. [*Culhwch*]

DRUIDAIN[1]

A loathsome hunchbacked dwarf, to whom Gawain gave the false lady Ydain after she tried to leave Gawain for another knight. Druidain's eventual possession of Ydain had been foretold by an oracle in the dwarf's youth. Druidain's father was named Drulias. [*Vengeance*]

DRUIDAIN[2]

A knight who joined Arthur's forces in the battle against the Saxons at Vambieres. [*Livre*]

DRULIAS

Father of the dwarf Druidain. [*Vengeance*]

DRUIS

A priest and philosopher who counseled Arthur. [*Hilton*]

DRULIOS OF THE HAMLET [*Drukins*]

One of Arthur's knights who fought in a tournament against the warriors of King Ban and King Bors. [*VulgMer*, *Arthour*]

DRUST

A eighth-century Pictish king whose father was called Tallorc. He may be the origin of TRISTAN, as in Welsh legend, Tristan's father is called "Tallwrch." However, DRUSTANUS, the name on the Tristan Stone, precedes Drust. In the Irish tale *The Wooing of Emer*, Drust appears as a companion of Cuchulainn, the Irish counterpart of Gawain. Aspects of Drusts's adventures in *Emer* are echoed in the early Tristan legends.

DRUSTANUS

The man commemorated by the TRISTAN STONE near the Castle Dore in Cornwall. The inscription on the stone, written probably in the sixth century, reads, "Here lies Drustanus, son of Cunomorus." Cunomorus is identified with Mark in Wrmonoc's *Life of St. Paul Aurelian*, and the Tristan legend is usually localized in Cornwall, so Drustanus may be the origin of TRISTAN (he precedes the Pictish king DRUST). If Cunomorus is Mark, the identification of Tristan as his son is unusual, though in one Welsh Triad, "Drystan" is called the son of "March."

DRWG ("Bad")

Daughter of Arthur's warrior Bwlch. [*Culhwch*]

DRWGDDYDDWG ("Evil Bringer")

The horse belonging to Arthur's warrior Cyfwlch. [*Culhwch*]

DRWST IRON FIST

One of King Arthur's warriors in Welsh legend. [*Culhwch*]

DRY ISLAND [*Ille Seche*]

An island where Brandeban, the Duke of Tannings, dueled Meliadus the Black. [*VulgLanc*]

DRY ISLAND WITH THE GREEN PINE [*Ille Seche du Pin Vert*]

A later name for the ISLAND OF JOY, where Lancelot lived for a time after a bout with insanity. Its name was changed after the formerly lush land was laid waste. [*VulgLanc*]

DRYCH

One of Arthur's warriors, and the second handsomest man in Britain, behind Arthur himself. His father's name was Cibddar. A Welsh Triad lists him as one of the "three enchanters of the Island of Britain." [*Culhwch*, *Triads*]

DU ("Black")

A horse belonging to Moro Battle Leader. As one of his tasks, the warrior Culhwch had to obtain this horse as a mount for Gwynn son of Nudd. [*Culhwch*]

DUACH

Son of Gwawrddur Hunchback, and brother of Brathach, Nerthach, and the lady Gwenwledyr. He was one of King Arthur's warriors. Duach and his brothers were "sprung from the Highlands of Hell." [*Culhwch*]

DUBGLAS [D(o)uglas]

A river in Britain which was, according to Nennius, the site of Arthur's second, third, fourth, and fifth battles against the Saxons (see ARTHUR'S BATTLES). The name means "blue-black" or "black stream." As in all of the twelve battles, Arthur was victorious. Nennius places the river in Linnuis, which may be the province of Lindsey in Lincolnshire, though no river by this name is known there. There are scattered rivers with similar names in Scotland, including a Dunglas in Lothian, which may be meant by Linnuis, but it is unlikley that Arthur would have fought the Saxons so far north. He may have been fighting Picts. Geoffrey of Monmouth includes the fight—condensing Nennius's four battles into one—and seems to identify it with the River Duglas in Lancashire. The Saxons fled to the nearby city of York after their defeat. [*Nennius, GeoffHR, TennIK*]

DUBLIN [Duvel(l)ine]

The present-day capital of Ireland is also given as the capital city of King Gurmun of Ireland (Isolde's father) in Gottfried's *Tristan*. Tristan traveled to Dublin to be cured of a poisoned wound received at the hand of Morholt of Ireland. In *Durmart le Gallois*, it is ruled by Earl Enor. [*Gottfried, TrisSaga, Dumart*]

DUBRIC [Dubricius]

A Welsh saint who lived in the late sixth and early seventh centuries. Glorified in Welsh legend, Dubric is made an archbishop and the first leader of the British Church. The *Annales Cambriae* say that he died in about 612. Geoffrey of Monmouth places his life nearly a century earlier and connects him with Arthur. According to Geoffrey, King Ambrosius appointed Dubric to the see of Caerleon. Later, Dubric crowned Arthur king of Britain. Dubric proved to be an important spiritual leader during Arthur's reign, inspiring Britons to fight for their land and to accept Arthur as their true leader. Dubric was so holy that he could cure any disease. According to Tennyson, he married Arthur and Guinevere. He eventually stepped down from his position to become a hermit, and Archbhisop David was appointed as his successor. The Vulgate *Merlin* calls Dubric the Archbishop of BRICE, misinterpreting the first syllable ("Du") of his name for the French word meaning "of." [*Annales, GeoffHR, Wace, TennIK*]

DUESSA

An evil, ugly witch in Spenser's *The Faerie Queene* who allegorically represents Mary Queen of Scots and Catholicism. Appearing in the guise of a beautiful maiden named Fidessa, she lured the Red Cross Knight from the quest assigned to him by Gloriana, the Fairy Queen. Just after she seduced him, however, the giant Orgoglio captured them both, threw Red Cross in a dungeon, and made Duessa his mistress. Arthur eventually stormed Orgoglio's castle, killed the giant, and stripped Duessa, exposing her as a disgusting hag. She later became the *amie* of the knight Paridell. She was eventually convicted of attempting to overthrow a queen named Mercilla, and she was executed. [*Spenser*]

DUGUM

Father of Arthur's opponent Mil the Black. [*Culhwch*]

DUICHE

A castle on the banks of the Targejure river, visited by Galehaut, Lionel, and Yvain on a quest to find Lancelot, after Morgan le Fay led them to believe that Lancelot was dead. [*VulgLanc*]

DUKE DE LA ROUSE

An enemy of Arthur whom Gareth defeated and forced to pay homage to the king. Through his fealty to Gareth, the Duke reconciled with Arthur, and he was eventually appointed to the Round Table. [*Malory*]

DUKE OF DUTCHMEN

A leader of a battalion of soldiers in the Duke of Lorraine's brigade, fighting for the Roman army in Arthur's war with Rome. The Duke of Dutchmen led his soldiers into a trap set by Sir Gawain and Sir Florence in north Italy. The soldiers were killed and the Duke fled the field. Malory alone mentions this character, which seems to correspond to ALGERE of the Alliterative *Morte Arthure*. [*Malory*]

DUKE OF THE SWORDPOINT

A nobleman who owned property near Camelot. [*PostMer*]

DUKE OF THE WHITE THORN

A nobleman present at a tournament in *Claris et Laris*. [*Claris*]

DULCEFLUR[1]

A princess of Trefferin and Karedonas whose father, King Gediens, was slain by the heathen King Verangoz of Sorboreste. Her lands were saved by Meleranz, Arthur's nephew, who later married her cousin, Tydomie. At Meleranz's recommendation, Dulceflur was wed to King Libers of Lorgan. [*PleierM*]

DULCEFLUR[2]

The daughter of King Atroclas. She wed Wigamur, an Arthurian knight. [*Wigamur*]

DULCEMAR

Father of Arthur's Sir Tandareis. He ruled Tandernas and was married to Queen Anticoni. Arthur went to war with him, besieging Tandernas, to avenge a wrong committed by Tandareis. Dulcemar and Gawain managed to broker a peace. Through his son, Dulcemar later became overlord of Malmontan and Mermin. [*PleierT*]

DUMBARTON

Capital of Strathclyde, also called ALCLUD. In Geoffrey of Monmouth's *Historia*, Uther Pendragon reclaims it from the Saxons and pacifies it. In Arthur's time, it was besieged by Picts and Scots. A very ill Hoel of Brittany had to hold off the invaders until Arthur returned from the battle of Bath. Arthur later made Eleden Archbishop of the city. In *Culhwch and Olwen*, Dumbarton is named as the home city of Arthur's warrior Tarawg. [*Culhwch*, *GeoffHR*, *Layamon*]

DUMFRIES

Tristan considered seeking harbor with the King of Dumfries when he was faced with imminent banishment from Mark's court. [*Beroul*]

DUMNONIA

A kingdom in Britain composing the countries of DEVON and CORNWALL. It had been a Roman territory. In the sixth century, it was apparently ruled by a King Constantine, who becomes Arthur's successor on Geoffrey of Monmouth. [*Gildas*]

DUN

A castle ruled by Patrice, a vassal of King Claudas. Later, the castle was re-named Issoudun, after Patrice's son Issout. [*VulgLanc*]

DUNBAR

A town in Scotland named in one chronicle as King Lot's home. [*Hardyng*]

DUNE

Warriors from the city of Dune, commanded by Falliers, fought for Lord Madoines in the battle against Beaudous, Gawain's son. [*RobertBlo*]

DUNEWALL

A Welsh nobleman. With others, he tried to save the life of Meriadoc, heir to the throne of Wales, from the murderous intentions of King Griffin. His diplomacy failed, but Meriadoc escaped to Arthur's court anyway. Dunewall later organized a revolt and helped Arthur defeat Griffin. [*Historia*]

DUNFREMLINE

A city in Scotland, visited by Arthur's Sir Fergus in his travels. [*Guillaume*]

DUNOSTRE [*Dunottre*]

A castle in Scotland, embedded in a rock off the coast. It was approachable only by a bridge guarded by a horrible hag wielding a scythe. The castle contained an enchanted white shield, guarded by a dragon, which prevented its bearer from death. Arthur's Sir Fergus learned of the castle from a dwarf, and he ventured there to obtain the shield. He emerged with it after slaying both the hag and the dragon. There is an actual castle called Dunottar in Kincardineshire. [*Guillaume*]

DUNSTER

Called "Dindraithof" by the Welsh, Dunster Castle, near the Bristol Channel in Somerset, is named as Arthur's residence in the *Life of St. Carannog*. Arthur seems to rule the castle jointly with a ruler called Cadwy (possibly Cador). The castle was apparently occupied by Britons in the post-Roman period. [*SaintsCar*]

DUNWALLO MOLMUTIUS [*Denewold*]

An early king of Britain (c. fifth century BC) in Geoffrey of Monmouth. He was the son of King Cloten of Cornwall. When he was born, Britain was fragmented, having crumbled after the death of Porrex. Dunwallo conquered King Pinnier of England, King Ruduac of Wales, and King Stater of Scotland, unifying the island of Britain again. In his forty years on the throne, he established law, order, and justice. When he died, his sons, Belinus and Brennius, contended for the kingdom.

According to the fourteenth-century *Short Metrical Chronicle*, which has a confused chronology, Merlin served Dunwallo and built Stonehenge in his honor. [*GeoffHR*, *Short*]

DURARLS

A heathen warrior slain by Gawain at the battle of Diana Bridge. [*Arthour*]

DURHAM

A county of northern England, on the North Sea. In Béroul's *Tristan*, Arthur seems to have a court there. [*Beroul*]

DURIAN

A priest who Arthur promoted to the archbishopric of Winton. [*GeoffHR*]

DURKAN

A wicked giant. Durkin and his brothers, Margan and Ulian, served Lord Karedoz of Malmontan. All three of the giants were slain Sir Tandareis, one of Arthur's knights. [*PleierT*]

DURMART

Hero of the French romance *Durmart le Gallois*. He was the son of King Jozefent of Wales and Denmark and Queen Andelise. As a youth, Durmart had an affair with the wife of his father's steward. After realizing that the woman was too base for him, he decided to give his love to Fenise, the queen of Ireland, instead. Although he had never seen her, he had been privy to tales of her great beauty, and embarked on a quest to find her. He won a sparrowhawk tournament and bestowed the prize upon the queen without realizing who she was. His further adventures caused him to rescue Guinevere from an abductor named Brun of Morois, and to win a tournament at the Blanches Mores. Offered a place at the Round Table, he declined until he found his love. Finally, he made it to Ireland and rescued the queen from the evil Nogant, who had been besieging her castle in Limerick. Fenise and Durmart were married, and Durmart became king of Ireland. His further adventures took him to Rome, where he fought a horde of pagans attacking the city. [*Durmart*]

DUSBERGO

A court ruled by Lord Arigie where Lancelot battled Brunor the Black, his mortal enemy. [*Tavola*]

DUSCONTEMEDON

A heathen land in the kingdom of Perceval's half-brother Feirefiz. [*Wolfram*]

DUZABEL

A princess from Turtus, kidnapped and held for ransom by a giantess named Fidegart. She was rescued by Arthur's Sir Garel. Her parents were King Amurat and Queen Klarine. She later married Duke Klaris of Argentin. [*PleierG*]

DWNN ("Brown")

One of Arthur's warriors in Welsh legend. He is known as "the Vigorous Chief." [*Culhwch*]

DYABIAUS

A cousin of Perceval and his brothers. He served King Pelles of Corbenic. [*VulgQuest*]

DYAGENNE

A lady loved by Uther Pendragon, although she was married to knight named Argon. She engaged in an affair with Uther and was killed by her husband when he discovered it. [*ProsTris*]

DYFED

A region and former kingdom in southwest Wales, called DEMETIA by the Romans. It contains the cities of Cardigan, Carmarthen, and St. David's, which have various Arthurian associations. Dyfed was settled by Irish tribes during the traditional Arthurian period (fifth and sixth centuries). See ARTHUR OF DYFED and VORTIPORE.

DYFFRYN AMANW

An English valley (presumably next to the mountain Mynydd Amanw) where Arthur's warriors fought one of their many battles against Twrch Trwyth and his piglets. Two of the piglets—Banw and Benwig—were killed before Twrch Trwyth fled on to Llwch Ewin. [*Culhwch*]

DYFFRYN LLWCHWR

A valley in England where Arthur's warriors fought two of Twrch Trwyth's piglets—Grugyn Silver Bristle and Llwydawg the Killer. The piglets escaped after killing many warriors. [*Culhwch*]

DYFGYFLWNG

One of Arthur's warriors. [*Culhwch*]

DYFNWAL

One of Arthur's warriors. [*Culhwch*]

DYFYNARTH [*Dunarth*]

One of Arthur's warriors who was the son of Gwrgwst Half Naked. Dyfynarth was called "King of the North." He was loyal to the warrior Gwythyr, and joined Gwythyr's army when he opposed Gwynn son of Nudd. He was taken prisoner by Gwynn and was not released until Arthur intervened. [*Culhwch*]

DYFYR[1]

An Arthurian warrior who was the son of Alun of Dyfed. Dyfyr was an advisor to Arthur and a companion to Geraint. [*Dream, Geraint*]

DYFYR[2] GOLDEN HAIR

One of the "three splendid maidens of Arthur's court," according to a Welsh Triad. [*Triads*]

DYGYNNELW

Owain's bard, according to a Welsh Triad. [*Triads*]

DYNAUNT

A Cornish knight who was attacked by the giant Taulurd, but was rescued by an insane, naked Tristan. His account of the story at Mark's court led to the discovery that Tristan, who had been presumed dead, was still alive. He is probably identical to DINAS. [*Malory*]

DYOGLIS

The seneschal of King Maglory the Saxon. In the early days of Arthur's reign, he invaded northern Britain with other Saxons. He was killed at the battle of Clarence by Sir Eliezer, King Pelles' son. [*VulgMer*]

DYOFLÊ

A wealthy British town. Nearby was Judgment Field, where Lot of Lothian and Gurnemans fought a tournament in Ulrich's *Lanzelet*. Lancelot, who participated in the tournament, lodged in Dyoflê. [*UlrichZ*]

DYONAS [*Dionas*]

The father of Viviane, the Lady of the Lake in the Vulgate *Merlin*. As a youth, he befriended Diana, the Roman goddess of the hunt, who bestowed upon him a special gift: that his daughter would be loved by the most powerful magician in the world (Merlin). As an adult, he was a strong and likable knight. He served the Duke of Burgundy, whose daughter he married. As a present, the duke bestowed the forest of Briosque on Dyonas, and Viviane was born there. He later served King Ban of Benoic (Lancelot's father), and helped him in the struggle against Claudas. He also fought in some of Arthur's battles against the Saxons, participating in their crushing defeat at the second battle of Clarence. [*VulgMer, ProsMer2*]

DYONIS

Brother of Alibel, Dion, and Casibilant, and nephew of Duke Calles. His six cousins revolted against their father. Dyonis and his brothers assisted Calles in the war, in which they were joined by Agravain, Gaheris, and Gareth. [*VulgLanc*]

DYONISE

A lady who ruled the Castle of Ten Maidens with her lover, Sir Geogenant. Dyonise and Geogenant were friends of Sir Durmart. [*Durmart*]

DYWEL

Son of Erbin, and brother of Geraint and Ermid. One of King Arthur's warriors in Welsh legend, he was apparently killed in a battle against Maelgwn. [*Culhwch*]

E

EALING

Part of SALISBURY plain in England, near Amesbury. It was the site of a battle between Vortigern's Britons and Hengists's Saxons. [*Layamon*]

EASTLAND

The Queen of Eastland was a friend of Morgan le Fay. She was one of the four queens who kidnapped Lancelot and brought him to Cart Castle. The queens tried to make Lancelot choose one of them as his lover, but Lancelot escaped. [*Malory*]

EBALATO

An ancestor of Palamedes in the Italian *I Due Tristani*. A pagan king who secretly became a Christian, he was overthrown an imprisoned, but was kept alive in prison through the miracle of God. His character, as well as his name, seems to be a combination of EVALACH in the Vulgate *Estoire del Saint Graal* and ESCLABOR, Palamedes' father (Gardner, 297). [*DueTris*]

EBEL [*Hebal*]

Servant of the late King Armant of the Red City. Ebel met Palamedes when Palamedes was on his way to avenge Armant's death. Ebel told Palamedes the entire story and directed him to the two traitors who had killed Armant. [*ProsTris, Malory*]

EBRAUCUS

A king of Britain in the eleventh century BC, according to Geoffrey of Monmouth. He ascended to the throne after his father, Mempricius, was killed by wolves. During his reign, he plundered Gaul and founded the city of York, which was named after him, Dumbarton, and Mount Agned. Ebraucus had 20 sons. One of them, Brute Greenshield, became king after him. [*GeoffHR*]

EBRON

A lord who was defeated by Arthur and was forced to free his prisoners. [*Palamedes*]

EBROX

King of Gomeroit. He served Arthur. [*Contin1*]

ECHEL PIERCED THIGH

One of Arthur's warriors in Welsh legend, killed by the boar Twrch Trwyth at Llwch Ewin during the epic hunt. Echel's father was named Gobrwy. [*Culhwch, Dream*]

ECHION [*Ession, Ethion*]

The ruler of Boeotia who was subservient to the Roman Procurator Lucius, and was called upon to join Lucius in the war against Arthur. [*GeoffHR, Wace, Layamon*]

ECHYMEINT

A Welsh triad holds that Arthur was imprisoned for three nights in a magical prison under the Stone of Echymeint by Gwen Pendragon. He was rescued by the warrior Goreu. [*Triads*]

ECTOR [*Hector*]

Arthur's foster-father in the Post-Vulgate *Merlin* continuation and in Malory. In Robert de Boron's *Merlin* and the Vulgate *Merlin*, he is called ANTOR. He was also the father of Arthur's seneschal, Kay. Merlin, who considered him a good and honorable man, gave him the infant Arthur, and told Ector to raise him as his own son. Uther gave Ector great wealth for this favor. When Arthur was sixteen, Ector took him and Kay to the Sword-in-the-Stone tournament, where Arthur accidentally removed the sword, proving his true heritage. Kay tried to take credit for the deed, but Ector compelled Kay to reveal the truth. He asked Arthur to make Kay his seneschal, and Arthur complied. Ector assisted Arthur in the battle of Bedegraine against the rebelling kings, and in the war against the Saxons. [*PostMer, Malory*]

EDA GREAT KNEE

A Welsh Triad tells us that the warriors Peredur and Gwrgi—elsewhere given as Arthur's warriors—were killed fighting Eda Great-Knee at Caer Greu. This defeat was attributed to the desertion of Peredur's and Gwrgi's warriors just prior to the battle. Eda's character is likely based on an actual eighth-century Northumbrian king. [*Triads*]

EDARIS

Father of Arthur's Sir Claris. Edaris was a duke. [*Claris*]

EDDELEIN [*Aedlin*]

Son of Cledauc and one of Arthur's champions. [*GeoffHR, Wace*]

EDELPERT

The son of the Lord of Escalot in the Hebrew *Melekh Artus*. His brother was named Karavoç. Edelpert befriended Lancelot during a tournament at Escalot. [*Melekh*]

EDELTHRED

Attendant to Rowena, wife of Vortigern, in Thelwall's *The Fairy of the Lake*. [*Thelwall*]

EDEN

Another name for the GRAIL CASTLE, as related in *Perlesvaus*. [*Perlesvaus*]

EDERN

An Arthurian warrior in Welsh legend who was the son of Nudd. He was the leader of Arthur's Danish warriors and was Geraint's opponent in the Knight of the Kestrel tournament. Edern appears in French literature as YDER. [*Culhwch, Geraint*]

EDINBURGH

A city in the Lothian region of Scotland, now the capital. In Roman times, it was called *Castellum Puellarum*, leading to an identification with the CASTLE OF MAIDENS. John Major, the Scottish chronicler, thought that Edinburgh was Arthur's capital. The city appears in French romance as TENEBROC. It may be indicated by AGNED in Nennius. [*Major*]

EDISSON OF LANZESARDIN

An infidel count and vassal of Feirefiz, Perceval's half-brother. [*Wolfram*]

EDITONS

In Heinrich von dem Türlin's *Diu Crône*, Gawain mentions an episode in which a knight named Editons betrayed and deserted Sagremor, leaving him in the hands of a wild woman. Gawain apparently defeated Editons in combat. This scene is not found in existing legend. [*Heinrich*]

EDLYM RED SWORD

An earl from an unnamed eastern land who developed a kind of hero-worship for Peredur Long Spear. Edlym caught up with Peredur during Peredur's adventures and asked to become his loyal compatriot. Peredur agreed and Edlym accompanied him to the Mournful Mound where Peredur killed the Black Serpent of the Barrow. After the battle, Peredur gave the Serpent's magical stone to Edlym and sent Edlym to be with his lover, the Countess of the Feats. [*Peredur*]

EDMOND

A knight of Lord Golagros in the Middle Scots poem of *Golagros and Gawain*. In the war between Golagros and Arthur, Edmond was killed by Yvain. [*Golagros*]

EDMYG ("Fame")

Son of Caw, one of twenty brothers, and one of King Arthur's warriors in Welsh legend. [*Culhwch*]

EDOLANZ

A knight who, in the German romance bearing his name, rescued Gawain by slaying a giant, protected a besieged town, and won a sparrowhawk tournament at Arthur's court. [*Edolanz*]

EDWARD[1] OF CARNAVRON

A Knight of the Round Table—brother of Sir Hectymere and Sir Pryamus—who appeared at the healing of Sir Urry. His home is a town in Wales. [*Malory*]

EDWARD[2] OF ORKNEY [*Adoart*]

Cousin of Gawain and brother of Sadoc who fought for Arthur at the Leverzep tournament. He was later made a Knight of the Round Table and was present at the healing of Sir Urry. [*Palamedes, ProsTris, Malory*]

EDWARD[3] OF THE RED CASTLE

A knight who, with his brother Sir Hugh, stole lands from the Lady of the Rock. Yvain, championing the lady, called for a duel against one of the brothers, but the brothers insisted that Yvain fight them both at the same time. Yvain won the battle, killing Edward and wounding Hugh. [*Malory*]

EDWIN

In the Elizabethan play *The Birth of Merlin*, the son of the Earl of Gloucester. He was a member Aurelius Ambrosius's court. He wanted to marry Modestia, the daughter of Lord Donobert, but she decided to enter a nunnery. [*Birth*]

EFFIN

A island country ruled by King Flois. It contained the castle of Alverne, which was besieged by two giants named Galaas and Assiles. Flois sent for assistance from Arthur's court, and Gawain arrived to slay the giants and save the kingdom. [*Heinrich*]

EFFLAM

A Breton saint who, through spiritual means, drove a dragon out of Brittany after Arthur failed to do so through military means.

EFRDDYL [*Erfddf*]

Twin sister of King Urien of Rheged, daughter of Cynfarch and Brychan, and aunt of Owain. [*Triads*]

EFREI

Father of Arthur's warrior Gwrddywal. [*Culhwch*]

EFROI

A knight present at the Sorgarda tournament, which was won by Gawain. His brother was named Melde. [*Heinrich*]

EGBRICHT [Egbert, Egbright]

A Saxon warrior who fought for Mordred against King Arthur and was killed at the battle of Camel. [GeoffHR, Wace]

EGESARIUS

A Mediterranean king. When Egesarius's brother, the barbarian king Milocrates, was invaded by Roman warriors, including a young Gawain, he sent a message to Egesarius asking for help. Egesarius left immediately, but was held up by storms and arrived too late, meeting the victorious Roman fleet as it was leaving the island. Through the heroics of Gawain, Egesarius was killed and his ships were sunk by Greek Fire or captured. Elsewhere in the story, the same character seems to be called BUZAFARNAN. [DeOrtu]

EGLATINE

The wife of King Brandegorre of Estrangorre. Eglatine was the daughter of King Machen of the Lost Island, and the half-sister of King Nentres of Garlot. Sir Dodinel, one of Arthur's knights, was raised as her "son," even though Dodinel had actually been born to Brandegorre and Brandegorre's niece. [VulgMer]

EGROP

An unknown location associated with Arthur in "Culhwch and Olwen." Arthur's chief gatekeeper remarks that he was in Egrop with Arthur. [Culhwch]

EGYPT [Egyte]

The Vulgate Estoire del Saint Graal says that King Evalach (later Mordrains) of Sarras was able to defeat the Egyptians, led by King Tholomer the Fugitive, with the help of Joseph of Arimathea, who brought the power of Christianity. As a result, Evalach converted. In Arthur's time, according to Geoffrey of Monmouth, Egypt was allied with Rome, and King Pandrasus of Egypt joined the Roman Emperor's war against Arthur. Malory says that this king, who was also king of Ethiopia, was slain at the battle of Soissons. In Claris et Laris, Egypt is ruled by King Eleazar, an ally of Emperor Thereus of Rome. Egypt is one of the many lands that Arthur conquers in Jean D'Outremeuse's Ly Myreur des Histors. [GeoffHR, VulgEst, Claris, Jean, Allit, Malory]

EGYPTIAN MAID

Subject of a poem by Wordsworth in which Merlin, his jealous ire provoked by its splendor, blasts a glorious ship called the Water Lily out of the sky. The ship had come from Egypt, and was bearing the Egyptian Maid, a princess sent by her father, the King of Egypt, to marry one of Arthur's knights. At the command of Nina, the Lady of the Lake, Merlin brought her body to Arthur's court, where a succession of knights tried to resurrect her but failed. Finally, the pure Galahad touched her hand and restored her life. The two married. [Wordsworth]

EHANGWEN ("Wide and Spacious")

Arthur's hall in Welsh tales, built by Gwlyddyn. [Culhwch]

EHEUBRYD

Daughter of Cyfwlch and maid of Bwlch. [Culhwch]

EHKUNAT

A count who was the brother of Mahaute and brother-in-law of Gurzgri. He killed Kingrisin of Ascalun by running him through with a lance—a deed that, for a time, was attributed unjustly to Gawain. [Wolfram]

EIDDILIG THE DWARF

One of the three "Enchanter Knights" in Arthur's court. He apparently had the ability to shape-shift. [Triads]

EIDDOEL [Eidoel]

Son of Ner. One of Arthur's warriors Welsh legend. As one of his tasks, the warrior Culhwch had to obtain Eiddoel's help in finding the huntsman Mabon, who happened to be Eiddoel's cousin. Arthur and his warriors, assisting Culhwch, found Eiddoel held captive in Glini's fortress. Glini surrendered his prisoner to avoid having his fortress destroyed. Eiddoel then accompanied Arthur's warriors on the (successful) mission to find Mabon. [Culhwch]

EIDDON THE MAGNANIMOUS

One of King Arthur's warriors in Welsh legend. [Culhwch]

EIDDYL THE TALL

One of Arthur's warriors in Welsh legend. Eiddyl accompanied Arthur to the cave of the Black Hag in the Valley of Distress, in order to obtain the Black Hag's blood for Culhwch. Eiddyl and Amren the Tall were the second pair of warriors to enter the cave; both were beaten within an inch of their lives. [Culhwch]

EIDYN

A Welsh poem notes that Arthur's warriors fought against Dog-heads on the mount of Eidyn. Eidyn may be EDINBURGH. [WelshPG]

EIGRUN

The fortress home of Galaas the Mighty, a tyrannical giant defeated by Gawain. Eigrun housed many prisoners, whom Gawain liberated. [Heinrich]

EIGYR

The Welsh form of IGERNE.

EILADAR

A warrior in Arthur's court who was the son of Penn Llarcan. [Culhwch]

EINAGUIS

In the Post-Vulgate *Mort Artu*, a knight who hated Lancelot, and who participated in Agravain's plot to expose Lancelot's affair with Guinevere. He was in the group of knights that surprised Lancelot in Guinevere's chamber, and was the first to fall under Lancelot's blade. In Malory, this knight is CALOGRENANT. [*PostMort*]

EIRYAWN PENLLORAN

One of Arthur's warriors, killed at Pelunyawg by the boar Twrch Trwyth. [*Culhwch*]

EIRYN THE SPLENDID

A servant of Arthur who was the son of Peibyn. Eiryn, an ugly, red-haired man, owned a magical mantle named Gwenn. Anyone who wore the mantle was rendered invisible. [*Dream*]

EISSYWED ("Need")

Grandchild of Arthur's warrior Syfwlch. [*Culhwch*]

EKUBA

The Saracen Queen of Janfuse. She loved Perceval's brother Feirefiz, who rejected her in favor of Queen Secundille of Tribalibot and the Grail Maiden Repanse de Schoye. [*Wolfram*]

EKUNAVER

In Der Pleier's *Garel,* the King of Kanadic who went to war with Arthur because Uther Pendragon had slain Ekunaver's father. He sent his giant Karabin to deliver a message of his hostile intentions, and he promised to invade Arthur's lands after a year. During the year, Garel, one of Arthur's knights, raised his own army and defeated Ekunaver in Kanadic. Arthur was surprised to find that the war had been won without his participation. Arthur forgave Ekunaver and gave him a seat at the Round Table. Ekuanver received his land from his wife, Queen Kloudite. His capital was Belamunt. His allies included kings Angenis of Iserterre, Salatrias of Kalde, Helpherion of Nasseran, Rubert of Gandin, and Ardan of Rivelanze. His name is reminiscent of ESCANT of Cambenic in the Vulgate Cycle. [*PleierG*]

ELADINAN

A Knight of the Round Table who participated in the Grail Quest. His brother, Hecuba, was also of the Round Table. [*PostQuest*]

ELAF [*Elafius, Elays*]

A Saxon warrior who fought for Mordred against Arthur and was killed at the battle of Camel. [*GeoffHR, Wace*]

ELAIN

Lord of the Red Castle. When he died, his maiden daughter inherited his castle. She was besieged by Yvain the Black but was rescued by Guiron the Courteous. [*Palamedes*]

ELAINE[1] [*Helaine*]

Lancelot's mother; the wife of King Ban of Benoic. Her name has several variations, including Ulrich's CLARINE. She is known as GOSTANZA in *La Tavola Ritonda.* Ulrich considers her the sister of King Arthur, but the later romances, although professing that Arthur had a sister named Elaine, do not equate Arthur's sister with this Elaine. She was descended from David and Solomon of Israel. Her father was named Galegantin, and her sister, Evaine, married Ban's brother, King Bors of Gannes.

King Claudas besieged her castle of Trebe when Lancelot was still a baby. Taking Elaine and Lancelot, Ban fled Trebe to seek help from Arthur. When they were some distance away, they saw Trebe burning, and Ban's heart burst, killing him. As Elaine grieved over her husband, a water-sprite sprang from a nearby lake (the Lake of Diana) and snatched away her child.

Calling herself the "Queen of Great Sorrows," Elaine sadly committed herself to the Royal Minster nunnery while King Claudas captured her husband's former land. She was soon joined by her sister Evaine, who had also lost her children and husband. Evaine, before her death, had a vision of her sons and Elaine's son growing up together in a fairy land under the guidance of the Lady of the Lake. She related this to Elaine, bringing joy to her heart at last. During the Grail Quest, she appeared to Lancelot in a dream and warned him to repent for his affair with Guinevere.

A French variation of HELEN, the name ultimately derives from Greek mythology (e.g., Helen of Troy). [*UlrichZ, LancLac, VulgLanc, PostQuest, Malory*]

ELAINE[2]

In the Didot-*Perceval*, either Gawain's sister and the daughter of Lot, or Gawain's cousin and the daughter of King Viautre of Galerot. She became infatuated with Perceval when he first arrived at Arthur's court. She is mentioned in the Prose *Tristan.* [*Didot, ProsTris*]

ELAINE[3] [*Elayne*]

Galahad's mother, by Lancelot, in the Post-Vulgate and Malory. She is called AMITE in the Vulgate *Lancelot.* She was the daughter of King Pelles of Corbenic, the Grail King. As a young woman, she was placed in a boiling bath by Morgan le Fay, and she suffered in agony there until Lancelot freed her. She fell in love with Lancelot and, knowing that their child would be the Grail Hero, she conspired to lure him to her bed. Her father and her servant, Dame Brisen, befuddled Lancelot with a potion, and told him that Guinevere was waiting for him at Case Castle. Lancelot stumbled to the castle, slept with the woman he found there, and awoke to find that it was Elaine. Lancelot barely spared her life for her treachery.

She was loved by other men, such as Sir Brinol of the Hedged Manor, but she denied them her affections because she truly loved Lancelot. When Galahad was born, she brought him to Camelot. She showed Galahad to Lancelot but Lancelot, ashamed, would barely speak to her. Relations between Elaine and Guinevere were understandably tense. Brisen tricked Lancelot into Elaine's bed again. This time, Guinevere discovered the tryst and banished Lancelot, driving him mad. A few years later, when Lancelot, insane and naked, came into Corbenic, Elaine recognized him and had her father heal him with the Grail. She nursed him back to health and cared for him until he left. During the Grail Quest, Elaine died in an unknown manner. [*PostQuest*, *Malory*]

ELAINE[4] [*Elayne*]

A daughter of Duke Gorlois and Igerne and a sister of Morgause and Morgan le Fay in Malory's *Le Morte Darthur*. Elaine was married to King Nentres of Garlot. In origin, she may have been the same Elaine that appears as Lancelot's mother. The Vulgate *Merlin* calls her BLASINE. [*Malory*]

ELAINE[5] [*Elayne*]

Known as "Fair Maiden of Astolat" in Malory and the "Lily Maid" in Tennyson. She appears nameless in the Vulgate *Mort Artu* and the Stanzaic *Le Morte Arthure*. The daughter of Sir Bernard of Escalot and sister of Sir Tirre and Sir Lavaine, she was considered one of the most beautiful maidens in England. She fell desperately in love with Lancelot when he stayed at her home before the tournament at Camelot. At her request—mostly because he wanted a disguise—Lancelot wore her red sleeve in the tournament. He was badly wounded, and Elaine came to care for him at the house of Sir Baldwin of Brittany.

When Lancelot was well, and prepared to leave for Camelot, Elaine asked him if he would marry her. Lancelot replied that he would never marry. Elaine then asked if he would be her lover, and Lancelot again refused, saying it would be ignoble. She pleaded with him, saying she would die for his love, but Lancelot departed.

Afterwards, she fell sick. Dying, she dictated a letter to Lancelot, which her father wrote down. Then, at her request, she was placed in a rich bed in a barge, and floated down the river Thames to Camelot, where Arthur, Guinevere, and Lancelot found her body and the letter, which asked Lancelot to pray for her soul. They buried her at Camelot. [*Malory*, *TennIK*]

ELAINE[6] THE PEERLESS [*Heleine*]

The lady of the castle Gazevilte, considered one of the most beautiful women in Arthur's realm. Her husband, Persides, locked her in Gazevilte when she claimed that she was more beautiful than he was valiant. Persides told her he would let her out when either a more beautiful woman or a more valiant knight happened along. Elaine's sister brought Sir Hector (Lancelot's brother) to the castle, and by defeating Persides, Hector decided the dispute in Elaine's favor. She was freed from her captivity. [*LancLac*, *VulgLanc*]

ELAM [*Elamet, Elmaye*]

An ancient kingdom in southwest Asia, at the head of the Persian Gulf. According to the Alliterative *Morte Arthure*, it was subject to Rome, and warriors from the land joined Lucius's war against Arthur. [*Allit*, *Malory*]

ELAMIE

In Wirnt von Grafenberg's *Wigalois*, a Queen of Tyre who entered a kind of "sparrowhawk" tournament and won, for she was the most beautiful. As she was receiving her prizes—a splendid horse and a parrot—Count Hojir of Mannesvelt appeared, stole the awards, and gave them to his own, undeserving, lady. No knight would stand up to Hojir until Elamie encountered Wigalois (Gawain's son), who defeated Hojir and gave the prizes to their rightful owner. After Wigalois became the king of Korntin, Elamie rewarded him by introducing him to a band of female warriors, who accompanied Wigalois in his campaign against King Lion of Namur. Roughly the same character is introduced in Renaut de Bâgé's *Le Bel Inconnu* as MARGERIE. [*Wirnt*]

ELAUTH

Father of Arthur's warrior Kegein. [*Layamon*]

ELCAN

Father of the Biblical Samuel. Elcan ruled the city of Arimathea—home of Joseph of Arimathea—at the time of Christ's death. [*VulgEst*]

ELDAD[1]

According to Geoffrey of Monmouth, a king of Britain in the third or second century BC. A son of King Cherin, Eldad succeeded his brother, King Fulgentius, and was succeeded by his other brother, King Andragius. [*GeoffHR*]

ELDAD[2] [*Aldadus, Eldaldus*]

The Bishop of Gloucester and the brother of Eldol, Earl of Gloucester. A moral and pious man, Eldad buried the British warriors who died at the battle of Ambrius's Monastery. He advocated the execution of Hengist (which was carried out by Eldol), and the granting of mercy to Octa and Eosa. He advised Ambrosius Aurelius to give the barren Scotland to the Saxons as a peace offering. [*GeoffHR*, *Wace*, *Layamon*]

ELDOL[1]

According to Geoffrey of Monmouth, a king of Britain in the second century BC. He succeeded King Arthinail and was succeeded by King Redion. [*GeoffHR*]

ELDOL[2] [*Aldolf, Edof, Eldoll*]

The Earl of Gloucester or Chester, and the brother of Eldad. He first appears in Geoffrey of Monmouth. He led a contingent of warriors under Vortigern. He fought bravely with rocks and tree limbs against the Saxon betrayers at Ambrius's monastery in Salisbury. The Britons were defeated, and Eldol swore to exact his vengeance on Hengist the Saxon for the betrayal. When Ambrosius Aurelius invaded Britain, Eldol—disgusted at Vortigern's policy toward the Saxons—joined Ambrosius's army and helped Ambrosius defeat Vortigern at Ganarew. Eldol again fought heroically at the battle of Conisbrough. Here, he finally found his chance to defeat Hengist, and the two fought a tremendous battle before Eldol finally grabbed Hengist by his helmet and dragged him into the Britons' ranks, thus capturing him. Later, Eldol personally beheaded Hengist before Ambrosius, ending—for the time being—the Saxon threat. He appears as Ambrosius's general in the Elizabethan play *The Birth of Merlin*. Geoffrey's complimentary portrayal was almost certainly meant to please Robert, the earl of Gloucester in Geoffrey's time (Loomis, *Romance*, 86). [*GeoffHR*, *Wace*, *Layamon*, *Birth*]

ELEAZAR

King of Egypt in *Claris et Laris*. He joined his ally, Emperor Thereus of Rome, in a war against Arthur, and he was killed in battle by Arthur himself. [*Claris*]

ELEBRANS

An Arthurian knight. [*Merveil*]

ELEDEN

A priest who Arthur appointed Archbishop of Dumbarton. [*GeoffHR*]

ELEMMIE OF HOLMTAROR

A king who conquered Spain with his brother Soran, slaying King Hlööver. Elemmie was slain by Patrocles, Tristan's grandfather. Soran and Elemmie's other brother, Desixtus, later invaded Spain again. [*SagaTI*]

ELEI

A companion of Arthur's named in the Welsh poem *Pa Gur yv y Portaur*. [*WelshPG*]

ELENA

The cousin of Enide, Erec's wife, and the daughter of Earl Tracon of Acusborg in the Norse *Erex Saga*. She was the sweetheart of Mabonagrain, with whom she lived in the castle of Brandigan. To test his love, she elicited a promise from Mabonagrain to slay any knight that passed by their residence. The adventure became known as the Joy of the Court, and persisted until Erec defeated Mabonagrain. Chrétien de Troyes's *Erec* includes her character but does not name her. [*Erex*]

ELERGIA

A sorceress who entraps Arthur in *La Tavola Ritonda*. She was the daughter of Lady Escorducarla of Avalon. Her mother created the palace of Grande Disio for her. She found Arthur in the forest of Darnantes and slipped an enchanted ring on his finger, which caused him to lose his memory. One of the Lady of the Lake's servants summoned help from Tristan, who went to Grande Disio and slew Elergia's four brothers. Arthur himself beheaded the sorceress. Escorducarla plotted revenge on Arthur but failed. Malory calls her AUNOWRE. [*Tavola*]

ELFLAND

According to the Norse saga of Tristan, the origin of Petitcrieu, a dog given to Isolde by Tristan. [*TrisSaga*]

ELGAN

A Welsh warrior, connected in genealogies with the country of Dyfed, who was apparently slain in a battle against Maelgwn. His passing is lamented by Myrddin and Taliesin in an early Welsh poem. [*Myrddin*]

ELI[1]

One of Arthur's chief huntsmen. Eli participated in the hunt for Twrch Trwyth, where he helped to manage the hound Drudwyn. The name is listed twice and may signify two different warriors. [*Culhwch*]

ELI[2]

The provost of Carmarthen during the reign of King Vortigern. At the demand of Vortigern's envoys, Eli brought Merlin and his mother before the king at Snowdon. [*Layamon*]

ELIADAS

A knight defeated in combat by Laris. Claris and Laris were helping Sir Caradoc protect his paramour from King Ladas, Sir Eliadas's liege. [*Claris*]

ELÎADUS[1] [*Eliadeus*]

A castellan who lodged Perceval and the Fair Unknown during their adventures. His father was named Elideus. [*Contin2*]

ELIADUS[2]

King of Sicily and father of Floriant, an Arthurian knight. He was murdered during a hunt by his treacherous seneschal, Maragoz, who desired Eliadus's wife. Floriant avenged Eliadus's death many years later. [*Floriant*]

ELIAN OF MONTFORZ

A nobleman in Arthur's service. [*Heinrich*]

ELIANS [*Eliant, Elianz*]

A Knight of the Round Table from Ireland. He occupied Lancelot's vacant seat at the Round Table after Lancelot and Guinevere fled Arthur's court for Benoic. [*VulgMort*, *PostMort*]

ELIAS[1]

A duke—perhaps a vassal or ally of Arthur—who fought in a Castle of Maidens tournament. [*Renaut*]

ELIAS[2] [*Helyas*]

The leader of a Saxon force that invaded the lands of King Mark of Cornwall. Mark was forced to send for Tristan to assist in repelling the invasion. After Tristan led a battle against Sir Elias and destroyed much of Elias's force, Elias offered to fight any knight Mark could offer, one-on-one, to decide the conflict. Whichever side lost would have to pay an annual tribute to the other side. Tristan met Elias in the challenge. Elias proved to be an excellent knight, as good as Tristan, and it was only thoughts of Isolde that caused Tristan to win the battle and to mortally wound Elias. Elias's men fled Cornwall, and his Saxon tribe paid an annual tribute to Cornwall thereafter. [*ProsTris, Malory*]

ELÏAVRÉS

A knight and sorcerer who engaged in an adulterous affair with Ysave, the wife of King Caradoc of Nantes. He substituted animals, in the form of women, in King Caradoc's bed, while he took his pleasure with Caradoc's wife. Their affair produced a son named Caradoc Shortarm. After his son became one of Arthur's knights, Elïavrés visited Arthur's court and challenged Caradoc to a deadly Beheading Game, but stopped short of killing him. Upon discovering his true parentage, Caradoc Shortarm informed King Caradoc, who locked his wife in a tower and forced Elïavres to copulate with a bitch, a sow, and a mare, by which Elïavres fathered, respectively, Guinalot, Tortain, and Lorigal. The adulterers conspired to kill their son with a serpent, but were unsuccessful. [*Contin1*]

ELIBEL [*Elyzabel*]

A cousin, servant, and messenger of Guinevere. While delivering a message to the Lady of the Lake, she was captured by King Claudas. Claudas's failure to release her led to a war between him and Arthur. [*VulgLanc*]

ELICANOR

The son of Corsapin. Corsapin was a vavasor in the service of Nascien and Flegetine. Elicanor accompanied his father to Britain, where they joined with Joseph of Arimathea's fellowship. [*VulgEst*]

ELIDEUS

Father of Eliadus, one of Perceval's hosts. [*Contin2*]

ELIDIR STOUT AND FAIR

The father of Arthur's warrior Llywarch the Old. [*Triads*]

ELIDUC

According to Geoffrey of Monmouth, a king of Britain in the third or second century BC. Eliduc succeeded King Eliud and was succeeded by King Cloten. [*GeoffHR*]

ELIDUR

A son of King Morvid of Britain who, according to Geoffrey of Monmouth, succeeded his brother Arthgallo to the throne. He ruled with justice, but he was deposed by his two younger brothers, Iugenius and Peredur, and thrown in prison. After his brothers' deaths, Elidur was released and given the throne again. He was succeeded by his nephew Regin. Elidur's son, Gerontius, eventually became king. [*GeoffHR*]

ELIDUS [*Helidus*]

King of Ireland. He served Arthur. Coming across two knights fighting, he asked the cause of their quarrel. The dueling knights stopped fighting each other and attacked Elidus instead. The skilled Elidus defeated both of them, learned that they had been fighting over a woman, visited the lady's castle, and avenged himself on the knights by spending the night with the lady. [*Claris*]

ELIDYR THE GUIDE

One of Arthur's warriors. [*Culhwch*]

ELIE

A maidservant of Leander, son of the Red Knight. After Perceval dueled, then reconciled with Leander, Elie tended to Perceval's battle wounds. [*Contin4*]

ELIEDUS [*Eliteus*]

One of the heathen kings who, under King Oriel, ravaged northern Britain in the early days of Arthur's reign. [*Arthour*]

ELIES[1]

A lord who was a member of Arthur's court. [*Contin1*]

ELIES[2] OF LANDUZ

An Arthurian knight. [*Heinrich*]

ELIEZIER[1] [*Eliezer, Elyazar, Elyezer*]

The son of King Pelles of Corbenic, brother of Elaine, and maternal uncle of Galahad. As a youth, Eliezier left his homeland, Listenois, for Logres, to help in King Arthur's struggle against the invading Saxons. He joined a party of youths led by Gawain. Eliezier served as Gawain's squire and was eventually knighted by Gawain. Eliezier fought in several battles against the Saxons, including their defeat at Clarence. Later, he carried the broken pieces of the Grail Sword. During the Grail Quest, Eliezier held a tournament against a lord named Argustus. Lancelot came upon the tournament in progress, and joined Argustus's side, as they were losing. Argustus's knights were sinful, however, and Lancelot was defeated. Eliezier was at Corbenic when Galahad completed the Grail Quest. Later, he supported Lancelot in the wars against Arthur. [*VulgLanc, VulgQuest, VulgMort, VulgMer, Livre, PostMer, PostQuest, Malory*]

ELIEZIER[2]

A pagan king in Britain, converted to Christianity by Joseph of Arimathea. He left his kingdom in the Scottish borderlands to wander the country, dedicating himself to holy deeds. After thirty years of this asceticism, God appeared to him in a dream and told him to return to his kingdom and live a life of splendor. Joining his son, Lanvalet, he returned. An abbey in his lands, called the Small Charity, where he had received help, was later visited by Lancelot. [*VulgLanc*]

ELIEZIER[3] THE STRONG

A mighty knight who earned fame as a member of Uther Pendragon's court. [*Palamedes*]

ELIFFER [*Efrawg, Efrog, Eladur, Elidur, Elifert, Evrawg*]

The father of Peredur, Perceval's counterpart in Welsh legend. He had several other sons, one of whom was named Gwrgi. A Welsh Triad calls him "Eliffer of the Great Retinue." We are told in the *Annales Cambriae* that his sons fought against Gwenddolau in the battle of Arfderydd in 573, and were victorious. Layamon names him as one of Arthur's earls. In the Welsh story of *Peredur* we learn that Eliffer and most of his sons were slain in battle, prompting his wife to raise Peredur bereft of teachings about knights and battles. [*Annales, GeoffHR, Triads, Layamon*]

ELIFRI RICH IN ARTS

Arthur's head groom in Welsh legend. He became a loyal companion of the warrior Geraint. [*Geraint*]

ELIMAN

The father of Ligessauc, who murdered three of Arthur's knights. [*SaintsCad*]

ELIMAR[1]

A Duke of Argentin, slain by the giant Purdan. His son, Klaris, was captured by the giant and was rescued by Sir Garel. His wife, Klarine, died of sorrow. [*PleierG*]

ELIMAR[2]

A count from Averre who served Arthur's Sir Garel. He bore Averre's standard in the war against King Ekunaver of Kanadic. [*PleierG*]

ELIMAS[1]

A cleric from Radole in Hungary in the service of Arthur. He accompanied Master Elias to Galehaut's court, and helped Galehaut interpret a disturbing dream. [*VulgLanc*]

ELIMAS[2]

A warrior from Argardas, present at the tournament of Sorgarda, which was won by Gawain. [*Heinrich*]

ELIN THE FAIR OF GRAIE [*(H)el(u)in(s)*]

The lord of Graie and vassal of the knight Bleoberis. When Bleoberis was defeated in combat by Gawain's son Guinglain, he ordered Elin and two other knights—the knight of Saie and William of Salebrant—to track down Guinglain and defeat him. Guinglain made short work of these knights, and Elin's arm was broken in the combat. [*Renaut*]

ELINADAS [*Climades*]

A knight in the service of King Leodegan of Carmelide. He led an echelon of soldiers against King Rions the Saxon at the battle of Aneblayse. His aunt was the Wise Lady of the Forest of No Return. [*VulgMer, Livre, Arthour*]

ELINAN OF THE ISLES [*Belinans*]

A knight whom Gawain had to defeat before he could enter Sorelois, Galehaut's land. Gawain sent him to Arthur's court, where Elinan took service. [*VulgLanc*]

ELINANT

One of Perceval's eleven paternal uncles in *Perlesvaus*. He was the sixth son of Gais the Large and the brother of Alain. He ruled Escavalon, had a son named Alain, and died at an early age. [*Perlesvaus*]

ELIS OF CLIMON

One of Arthur's knights. [*Heinrich*]

ELIUD

According to Geoffrey of Monmouth, a king of Britain in the third or second century BC. Eliud succeeded King Urian and was succeeded by King Eliduc. [*GeoffHR*]

ELIWLOD [*Eliwlad*]

One of Arthur's three "Golden-Tongued Knights," according to Welsh tradition. His father was named Madog, and his grandfather was, oddly, Uther. This would make him Arthur's nephew, although only here is Arthur given a brother. In a Welsh poem called the *Dialogue of Arthur and the Eagle*, Arthur encounters the spirit of Eliwlod in the body of an eagle. [*Triads*]

ELLAIN THE BROWN

Father of Hector the Brown, Branor the Brown, and Bruhault the Brown; brother of Hector the Brown. [*Palamedes*]

ELLEDI [*Ælecti, Electi, Elleti, Gledi*]

A town in the region of Glevesing. Here, King Vortigern's men first became alerted to the child Emrys, when they heard another boy taunt him about having no father. This interested the soldiers, for they had been sent by Vortigern to search for a boy with no father, in order to sprinkle his blood on the foundation of Snowdon. [*Nennius*]

ELLIT [*E(s)lis*]

A knight of Arthur's court. He was defeated in combat by Sir Meriadeuc. [*Contin2, Meriadeuc*]

ELLYLW

A lady at Arthur's court who was the daughter of Neol Hang Cock. She lived for three generations. [*Culhwch*]

ELMET

A British kingdom in the Pennine hill area of modern Yorkshire, roughly corresponding to modern West Riding. Britons continued to rule this area after the Saxon invasion in the sixth century (Ashe, *Quest*, 234).

ELOIDES [*Clochides*]

A strong and cruel knight who roamed the borderlands of Scotland in the days of Uther Pendragon. He wed the daughter of Esclamor of the Red City, even though her father forbade it. Retreating with his wife to the Forbidden Hill, he protected her by killing any knight who dared approach. He was slain by Bors, but not before he extracted an oath from Bors to continue the traditions of the Forbidden Hill. Bors was eventually defeated by Lancelot, and Eloides's prisoners were liberated. [*VulgLanc*]

ELPHIN

Son of Gwyddno. One of Arthur's warriors, he was known as a "perverse and over-anxious" young man. [*Dream*]

ELSAM [*Elsie, Islie*]

The Duchess of Brabant who married Loherangrin, Perceval's son, after he saved her from a forced marriage to her steward, Friedrich of Dundramunt. Loherangrin made her promise never to ask his name or lineage, but she was coerced to do so by the Countess of Kleve. In response, Loherangrin left her and returned to his own kingdom, though Elsam had borne him two children. (In the German *Lorengel*, Loherangrin does not leave and they live happily ever after). [*Lohengrin, Lorengel*]

ELVES

Sprites found in Germanic mythology. They appear only rarely in Arthurian legends. Layamon says that elves blessed Arthur after he was born, and that Argante, the enchantress who brought Arthur to Avalon, was a "radiant elf." Layamon also says that Witege, the smith who made Arthur's armor, was also an elf. In Spenser's *The Faerie Queene*, elves formed the original ruling class of Fairy Land. [*Layamon, Spenser*]

ELYAB [*Elyap*]

The wife of Joseph of Arimathea, and mother of Josephus and Galahad. After Joseph was imprisoned, she refused to re-marry and remained faithful. After 42 years passed,

Joseph was freed. Elyab traveled with him to Sarras and then to Britain, where she died. [*VulgEst*]

ELYABEL [*Eliabel(la), Eliobela, Elizabeth*]

Tristan's mother in the Prose *Tristan* and its adaptations. She replaces BLANCHEFLOR from earlier romances. *Tristan* makes her the daughter of Felix and the sister of King Mark of Cornwall and Pernehan, but in the Italian *La Tavola Ritonda*, she is the daughter of King Andremo and Felice, and is only Mark's sister-in-law. She married King Meliadus of Cornwall, who was imprisoned by an enchantress during Elyabel's pregnancy. Setting out in the wilderness to look for him, she went into labor and delivered her child in a forest. She was mortally wounded during childbirth, and perished after naming her son "Tristan," signifying the sadness of the situation. [*ProsTris, Tavola, Malory, Povest*]

ELYAM

A king who imprisoned Sir Hector of the Fens. Gawain defeated him and released Hector. [*VulgLanc*]

ELYAS ANAÏS

The proper name of the HERMIT KING, Perceval's uncle, in the Fourth Continuation of Chrétien's *Perceval*. [*Contin4*]

ELYGOS

A king who fought for King Mark of Cornwall in the tournament at Lancien. [*Contin4*]

ELYN

Lot's father and Gawain's grandfather in the Prose *Brut*. [*ProsBrut*]

ELYNARD THE REDOUBTED

A knight in the famous "Brown" lineage. [*Palamedes*]

ELYZA

The baptismal name of a maiden who awarded Perceval the Circle of Gold after Perceval slew her enemy, the Knight of the Burning Dragon. Perceval left the crown in her stewardship, from which it was stolen by Nabigan of the Rock. Gawain recovered the artifact and returned it to her. [*Perlesvaus*]

ELYZABEL

Guinevere's cousin. While bearing a message from Guinevere to the Lady of the Lake, she was captured and imprisoned by King Claudas, sparking Arthur's second and final war against Claudas. [*VulgLanc*]

EMBLIE

The ladylove of Lohenis, a malicious knight who stole Gawain's horse. She was the son of a king named Emil. [*Heinrich*]

EMBRUNT

A son of Albanact, first king of Scotland. Embrunt's brothers were Dombart and Arbrun. [*Palamedes*]

EME

The daughter of an Irish shepherd named Heudins, with whom Lancelot lodged on his way to Rigomer Castle. Her father's godson, Herbert, was her lover. [*Merveil*]

EMENIDIS

The father of Flois, one of Arthur's noblemen. [*Heinrich*]

EMERAUSE

A knight who fought for King Arthur at the Battle of Bedegraine. His name is probably a variation of the French "Amiraut," or "Emir." [*Malory*]

EMERIT

A knight present at the Sorgarda tournament, which was won by Gawain. He was a vassal of the Duke of Aram. [*Heinrich*]

EMHYR [*Emyr*]

Father of Howel (Hoel) of Brittany in the Welsh *Dream of Rhonabwy*. Geoffrey claims, however that Hoel's father was BUDICIUS. "Emhyr" seems to have been a generic name, signifying "emperor," which the Welsh applied to several characters. [*Dream, Geraint*]

EMIL

A king who fathered the lady Emblie. [*Heinrich*]

EMMELINE

The blind daughter of Duke Conon of Cornwall. Oswald, the Saxon king of Kent, loved her, but she preferred Arthur. This caused a war between Arthur and Oswald. During the war, Emmeline wandered into a forest and was kidnapped by Oswald, whose sorcerer, Osmond, made an attempt to seduce her. Merlin and his spirit Philildel visited her in prison and cured her sight with a magic elixir. Arthur eventually rescued and married her. [*Dryden*]

EMPERUSE

A land ruled by Duke Kandalion under King Bagdemagus of Gorre. [*PleierT*]

EMRYS

The Welsh form of AMBROSIUS, as he appears in Nennius. An early Welsh poem notes that "before the lords of Emrys, Cei did great deeds"—a statement which is rather unclear. [*Nennius, WelshPG*]

ENAUDER

A king in Arthur's service. [*Renaut*]

ENCHANTED ISLE[1]

A fictional location invented by Morgan le Fay in an attempt to kill Arthur. A servant arrived at Arthur's court with a mantle, saying that the Lady of the Enchanted Isle had sent it to Arthur. Arthur, who had been forewarned by the Lady of the Lake, made the servant don the mantle, and she burned to ashes. [*PostMer*]

ENCHANTED ISLE[2]

The location of Arthur's afterlife according to Guillem Torroella's *La Faula*, which scholars have identified with Sicily. Arthur lived on the island, analogous to AVALON, with his sister Morgan. The Grail sustained them. [*Torroella*]

ENCHANTER KNIGHTS

A trio of Arthur's knights—Menw, Tristan, and Eiddilig the Dwarf—mentioned in Welsh legend, who were capable of shape-shifting. [*Triads*]

ENDALAN

A Knight of the Round Table who participated in the Grail Quest. [*PostQuest*]

ENDELIT OF LUNDIS

One of Arthur's various kings. [*Heinrich*]

ENEUAWG

Daughter of Bedwyr. She was a lady at Arthur's court. [*Culhwch*]

ENFAEL ADRANN

Father of Arthur's warrior Greidyawl Enemy-Subduer. [*Triads*]

ENFEIDAS

In Heinrich von dem Türlin's *Diu Crône*, Arthur's aunt, a goddess, and the queen of Avalon. Uther was her brother. [*Heinrich*]

ENFRIE

A knight present at the Sorgarda tournament, which was won by Gawain. [*Heinrich*]

ENGLAND [*Eng(e)lond(e), Engleterre, Ingl(e)and(e), Inghiltarre, Inglaterra, Inglond(e), Yngland(es)*]

Although Arthur is often thought of as the King of England, the designation "England" (signifying "Angle-Land") for the country below Scotland and east of Wales was not used until after the Anglo-Saxon conquest in the sixth and seventh centuries. Prior to this, the area now thought of as "England" was called LOGRES. (In the Prose *Brut*, the name is derived from "Engist," the Saxon leader.) Since "England" was in general usage when a good part of the Arthurian romances were written, however, the name appears quite often, indicating all or some portion of Britain. Malory, for instance, uses "England" without reservation. Usually, it is named as Arthur's kingdom, although there are some notable exceptions. In Wirnt von Grafenberg's *Wigalois*, for instance, the King of England wages war on Arthur, whose kingdom is in Brittany. In the Middle-English *Sir Tristrem* and the Norse and Icelandic Tristan sagas, it is Mark's kingdom. [*Wirnt, TrisSaga, ProsBrut, SirTris, SagaTI, Malory*]

ENGRES

King of Ireland and brother of Isolde in the Icelandic *Saga af Tristram ok Ísodd*. Though his name is similar to the ANGUISH of other Tristan stories, part of his character seems to be based on the traditional MORHOLT. His mother was Queen Flúrent. Engres was a pirate who often raided King Mark's England. Tristan slew him in battle, but not before Engres left a piece of his sword stuck in Tristan's head, which later identified Tristan to Engres's mother and sister. [*SagaTI*]

ENGRI

A knight present at the Sorgarda tournament, which was won by Gawain. [*Heinrich*]

ENIDE[1] [*Enid, Enite, Evida, Nida*]

The beautiful daughter of an impoverished nobleman who figures into Chrétien's *Erec*, the Welsh *Geraint*, and their adaptations. She is the wife of the hero. In Chrétien's romance, her father's name is Licorant and her mother's name is Tarsenesyde. In Welsh legend, her father is the Earl Niwl. Hartmann calls her father Koralus and her mother Karsinefite.

Her future husband (either Erec or Geraint, but referred to throughout the rest of this entry, for convenience, as Erec) met her when he came to her father's humble home (in Lut, Laluth, or Tulmein) during a sparrowhawk tournament. Erec was intent on entering the tournament to exact revenge on Yder, who had insulted Queen Guinevere. As all knights entering the tournament had to be accompanied by a lady, Erec received Enide's father's permission to use Enide for this purpose, and he won the tournament. During these events, Erec fell in love with Enide. They returned to Arthur's court together, married, and retired to Erec's homeland.

In time, Erec grew so domesticated, preferring to spend all his time with Enide, that his people grew discontented. One night, while she thought Erec was asleep, Enide lamented that he had lost his valor. In some versions, her words also cause Erec to believe her unfaithful. Angered, Erec forced Enide to accompany him on a series of dangerous adventures, culminating in a combat with three giants that left him unconscious. A local nobleman (variously called Oringle, Limwris, or Doorm) found them and brought them to his castle, but began to make advances on Enide. When she refused him, he abused her. Erec awoke at her screams and killed the nobleman.

Realizing the folly of his actions, Erec apologized to Enide, and the two returned to Erec's kingdom to live out their days.

The Prose *Tristan* tells a variant version of Erec and Enide. Enide is the daughter of the duke of Huiscam, who has been killed by Sir Senehar. Senehar is besieging Enide when Erec arrives with Galahad, Bleoberis, and Hector. Arthur's knights defeat Senehar and Erec marries Enide. [*ChretienE, HartmannE, Erex, Wolfram, Geraint, ProsTris, TennIK*]

ENIDE[2]

Gawain's girlfriend in Ulrich's *Lanzalet*. [*UlrichZ*]

ENNIAUN

According to Geoffrey of Monmouth, a king of Britain in the third or second century BC. He was the son of King Arthgallo. He succeeded his brother, King Margan. He ruled tyrannically, was deposed by his own nobles, and was succeeded by his cousin Idwallo. [*GeoffHR*]

ENOR

Count of Dublin in *Durmart le Gallois*. He fought in a tournament. [*Durmart*]

ENQUIRY

A castle on the edge of the Fisher King's lands, inhabited by priests. Pious knights customarily stopped at Enquiry to make a confession before approaching the Grail Castle. [*Perlesvaus*]

ENROÉS

A Knight of the Round Table who participated in the Grail Quest. [*ProsTris*]

ENRYDREG [*Enrhydreg*]

A lady at Arthur's court who was the daughter of Tuduathar. [*Culhwch*]

ENTREFERICH

A knight who held a tournament against Arthur, in which Erec excelled. [*HartmannE*]

ENYGEUS [*En(n)igeus, Enyseus, Haningnes, Havingues*]

The sister of Joseph of Arimathea, the wife of Bron, and the mother of Alain, Joshua, Nascien, Sador, Naburzadan, and several other sons. Enygeus and Bron accompanied Joseph on his journey from Judea to western lands, eventually arriving in Britain. Her descendants were the Grail Kings. In a brief interpolated ending to one manuscript of the First Continuation of *Perceval*, she is named as the wife—rather than the mother—of Alain, and as the mother of Perceval. [*RobertBorJ, Didot, VulgMer, Arthour*]

EOPA [*Appas*]

A Saxon who learned the language and manners of the British, as well as the art of medicine. While King Gilloman of Ireland and Pascentius, son of Vortigern, fought at Saint David's to defeat Uther Pendragon and conquer the kingdom, Eopa (one of Pascentius's men) offered to go to Winchester, pose as a Christian doctor, and poison King Ambrosius Aurelius. Pascentius promised Eopa fortune and fame if he were to accomplish this, and Eopa did succeed in assassinating Ambrosius. Pascentius, however, was killed at Saint David's by Uther, and the Irish-Saxon alliance was smashed. [*GeoffHR*, *Wace*, *Layamon*]

EOSA [*Cosa, Ebissa, Eisc, Os(s)a, Oysa, Tosa*]

A cousin or son of the Saxon leader Hengist. Hengist brought him to England with Octa and other Saxon warriors when Vortigern, King of Britain, was friendly to the Saxons. The Saxons eventually went to war with the British, and Eosa and Octa became their leaders. King Ambrosius defeated Eosa at the battle of York and—as a peace offering—gave him a section of Scotland. Eosa and Octa returned, however, to fight Uther after Ambrosius's death. Uther captured them at the battle of Mount Damen and imprisoned them, but they escaped to Germany, raised an army, and returned again. The two Saxons were finally killed at the battle of Saint Albans (or Verulam). Eosa is probably identical to the son of Hengist mentioned by the *Anglo-Saxon Chronicle* as ÆSC. Wace gives two versions of his name—Ebissa and Osa—which Layamon understood as two separate characters. [*Nennius*, *GeoffHR*, *Wace*, *Layamon*]

EPISFORD [*Aylesford, Epsford*]

The Saxon name for the location known by the Britons as *Rhyd yr afael*, a ford where King Vortigern's son, Vortimer, defeated Hengist's Saxon armies in his second such battle. Hengist's brother, Horsa, died in the battle, as did Vortigern's son Catigern. This battle is analogous to the one that the *Anglo-Saxon Chronicle* claims was fought at Ægelsthrep in 455. [*Nennius*, *GeoffHR*, *Wace*]

EPISTROPHUS [*Epistrod, Epistrophius*]

The King of Greece who was subservient to the Roman Procurator Lucius, and was called upon to join Lucius in the war against Arthur. [*GeoffHR*, *Wace*, *Layamon*]

EQUINOT

One of Arthur's Knights of the Round Table who was the son of Haterel. [*HartmannE*]

ERBIN

Son of Constantine and father of Arthur's warriors Geraint, Ermid, and Dywel. Erbin ruled a Cornish kingdom, which he had to turn over to his son Geraint when he became ill. Geraint returned rule of the land briefly to Erbin when Geraint left for a series of adventures, but he eventually came back and took the crown from his aging and grateful father. His counterpart in the French romances, as Erec's father, is LAC. [*Culhwch*, *Geraint*]

ERCING

A region of Britain where Arthur was said to have slain his son, Amr. [*Nennius*]

ERDIN

Brother of Isolde of the White Hands in the Serbo-Russian *Povest' o Tryshchane*, slain by Tristan at a tournament in Baroh. Tristan was badly wounded during the fight and may or may not have recovered at the hands of Isolde, Mark's wife. His name bears a resemblance to KAHEDIN, Isolde of the White Hands' brother in other sources. [*Povest*]

ERDUDFYL

Daughter of Tryffin, sister of Drudwas, and a lady at Arthur's court. [*Culhwch*]

EREC [*Arecco, Arech, Arrake, Arrok, Erech, Erés, Errak(e), Erex, Eric, Heret*]

A Knight of the Round Table who is the hero of Chrétien de Troyes's *Erec* and its adaptations. The first legends in which he appears recount his marriage to Enide and their subsequent adventures. Later, the Prose *Erec* (part of the Post-Vulgate *Merlin* continuation) describes an entirely different set of adventures in which Enide is absent. In Welsh legend (and in Tennyson), he is called GERAINT.

The son of a king named Lac, Erec's homeland is variously noted as Nantes, Destregales, or Carnant. The source of his name may be *Guerec* or *Weroc*, a Breton name which belonged to a tenth-century count of Nantes. Guerec, in turn, may have a relation with GWEIR of Welsh legend whose father, Llwch, like Lac, means "lake." Wolfram von Eschenbach gives him a sister named Jeschute, while in the Post-Vulgate his sister is unnamed. We learn from the latter source that his mother, Crisea, had taken precautions to protect Erec against all forms of enchantment.

Chrétien relates Erec's story as follows: Erec came to Arthur's court as a youth and proved himself a superior knight, perhaps second only to Gawain. During Arthur's ceremonial hunt for the white stag, Erec embarked on a quest to revenge an insult done to Guinevere and himself. His quest took him to the town of Laluth, where he caught up with the insulting knight—Yder, son of Nut. Erec found lodging at the humble home of an impoverished nobleman named Licorant. There, he fell in love with Licorant's daughter Enide. Erec learned from Licorant that Yder was in the town for an annual sparrowhawk tournament. Entering the tournament with Enide, Erec defeated Yder and forced him to surrender to Arthur. Erec returned to Arthur's court where he was honored for his victory, and was given Enide's hand in marriage.

Erec soon brought Enide back to his own kingdom of Nantes, but he was so in love with her that he lost his interest in arms and combat. He spent all of his time with his wife, and his reputation began to suffer as a result. Hearing grumbling from Erec's subjects and comrades, Enide became disconsolate. She eventually confronted Erec with the situation. Angered and embarrassed, Erec decided to embark on more adventures—with his unfortunate wife in tow, but with no other warriors. Erec badly treated Enide, who was forced to watch as bands of rogues attacked her husband. During this series of adventures, Erec defeated a nobleman who fell in love with Enide, defeated and befriended King Guivret the Small, and overcame Sir Kay. Erec was eventually wounded to unconsciousness by a pair giants, whom he killed in order to save Sir Cadoc of Carlisle. The evil Count Oringle, who ruled the nearby town of Limors, found Erec and Enide, and brought them back to his court. Mistaking Erec's unconscious state for death, Count Oringle tried to force himself on Enide. When she screamed, Erec awoke, slew the count, and made up with his wife.

On the way back to Arthur's court, the party came across the beautiful town of Brandigan, ruled by Evrain, where Erec engaged in a dangerous adventure, known as the Joy of the Court, and won, defeating the giant Mabonagrain. His story is capped by a triumphant return to Arthur's court and by Erec's investiture with the throne of his father's kingdom.

The Prose *Tristan* describes a variant version of Erec's meeting with Enide in which Erec, aided by Galahad, Hector, and Bleoberis, saves Enide from an oppressor named Senehar.

The version of Erec's story found in the Post-Vulgate is also entirely different. Knighted just prior to the Grail Quest, Erec proved his prowess by conquering the Castle of the Ten Knights, and by rescuing Bors from the castle of Nabon the Enchanter. Arthur awarded him a Round Table seat, following which Erec embarked on the Grail Quest. He adventured with Meraugis and Hector, who helped him to free his sister and to conquer the Castle Celis, where Lac had been murdered. Soon afterwards, however, Erec slew his sister in order to keep a promise he had rashly made to a lady. In further adventures, he killed Yvain of the White Hands and incurred the enmity of Gawain and his brothers. Gawain killed him, and he was buried at Camelot by Meraugis and Hector. The Alliterative *Morte Arthure* describes his death during Arthur's final battle with Mordred. [*ChretienE, HartmannE, Erex, Wolfram, PostMer, PostQuest, ProsTris, Allit*]

ERGYRYAD ("Attacker")

Son of Caw, one of twenty brothers, and one of Arthur's warriors. [*Culhwch*]

ERI

Father of Arthur's warrior Greid. [*Culhwch*]

ERIANN

One of Arthur's knights. [*Renaut*]

ERIM

Father of Arthur's warriors Uchdryd, Eus, Hen Was, Hen Beddestyr, and Sgilti Light Foot. His sons were bestowed with special gifts of speed. [*Culhwch*]

ERMALEÜ

Gawain's cousin. He is called the son of the king of Orkney. The daughter of the king of Montabor promised him her love if he could defeat twenty knights in a row. After conquering 19, he faced Beaudous, Gawain's son, and was defeated. Beaudous sent him to Arthur's court as a prisoner. [*RobertBlo*]

ERMID

Son of Erbin, brother of Geraint and Dywel, father of Gwynn and Cyndrwyn, and one of King Arthur's warriors. [*Culhwch*]

ERMYNGALL [*Herygall, Heryndale*]

One of Arthur's knights who, according to the Alliterative *Morte Arthure*, was killed during the Roman War. Malory seems to place him on the side of the Emperor Lucius. [*Allit, Malory*]

ERNANT

A knight who was taken prisoner, with his paramour Amelide, by the giant Trudet. They were freed when Guiron the Courteous killed Trudet. [*Palamedes*]

ERNOL [*Arnauld, Arnault, Erveus, Herno(u)l, Hernox*]

A count and vassal of Arthur who ruled the castle Carcelois on the Scottish borderlands. His three sons raped and murdered his daughter, then threw him in prison when he tried to punish them. The castle gained a reputation for murder and lechery. It was visited by Galahad, Perceval, and Bors during the Grail Quest; they slew the sons and liberated Ernol from prison. Ernol, who had been granted a vision of the liberation, died in Galahad's arms after bidding a hermit to warn Arthur of Lancelot and Guinevere's treason. [*VulgQuest, PostQuest, ProsTris, Tavola, Malory*]

ERRANT'S HERMITAGE

A British hermitage where Yvain lodged during an adventure. From the hermit, he learned of the evil wrought by Malduit the Giant, and set out to slay the giant. [*VulgLanc*]

ERRITH

A Welsh warrior who was apparently killed fighting King Maelgwn of Gwynned. His death is lamented by Myrddin and Taliesin in an early Welsh poem. Another warrior killed, Gwrrith, may have been a brother or comrade. [*Myrddin*]

ERROR

Half-woman, half-dragon monster slain by the Red Cross Knight in his first adventure. [*Spenser*]

ERW ("Acre")

Father of Arthur's warrior Llawr. [*Culhwch*]

ERWM THE TALL

One of Arthur's warriors in Welsh legend. He had an enormous appetite, and could eat all the food from three cantrevs (counties) in one sitting. His companion was Atrwm the Tall, who had a similar appetite. [*Culhwch*]

ERYRI [*(H)erir(i), Heremi, Heremus, Reir*]

A mountain in the Snowdon range where Vortigern sought to build a fortress. It is also called DINAS EMRYS. It may be related to the mountain ARAVIUS, where Arthur slew the giant Ritho. According to Tennyson, it was rumored that the infant Arthur had been found by a forester on the mountain. [*Nennius, Layamon, TennIK*]

ESCADUOR

Cousin of Escanor the Handsome, an opponent of Gawain. He led Escanor's soldiers at the tournament of Banborc after Escanor was injured. [*Girart*]

ESCALOINE

A seaside city in Sorelois. [*Palamedes*]

ESCALON THE DARK

A British castle that was shrouded in an evil enchantment after its lord raped a maiden (or a knight raped the daughter of the lord) in the castle's church. It was said that only the best knight alive in the world could open the church door, and thus free Escalon from the spell; the same knight, it was said, would also liberate the Dolorous Tower. After Galescalain and Yvain both attempted the adventure and failed, Lancelot succeeded, returning light to the castle and church. [*VulgLanc, Livre*]

ESCALONE

A land within Arthur's domain. [*VulgLanc*]

ESCALOS

King of Wales and ally of Escanor the Handsome, an opponent of Gawain. [*Girart*]

ESCALOT [*Ascolot, Askalot, Astolat, Scalliotto, Scalot, Shallot*]

A town near Camelot which was the home of Bernard, Tirre or Torre, and Lavaine. The Maiden of Astolat, called ELAINE by Malory, fell in love with Lancelot when he visited her father's town in preparation for a tournament. When Lancelot did not return her love, the maiden committed suicide after arranging for her body to be floated down the river to Camelot in a rich barge. Malory identifies the town with Guildford. Its name may derive from ALCLUD, a ford on the river Clyde. Tennyson's famous "Shallot" is a variation. [*VulgMort, Stanz, Malory, TennLS, TennIK*]

ESCANOR[1] THE HANDSOME

King of the White Mountain and nephew of Escanor the Large. Gawain defeated him in combat after Escanor tried to abduct Sir Girflet. Consequent of this defeat, Gawain obtained Escanor's horse, Gringolet, which had been given to Escanor by his lover, the fairy queen Esclarmonde. Later, Escanor wrongly accused Gawain of his cousin's murder. Gawain at first refused to fight him, so Sir Galantivet, Gawain's squire, ambushed and defeated Escanor. When Escanor and Gawain finally met in combat, Gawain had the upper hand and would have killed his opponent, but a fairy named Felinete, who had once helped Gawain, interceded and convinced Gawain to spare Escanor's life. The two knights reconciled and became friends. Escanor retired to a hermitage after his wife died. [*Girart*]

ESCANOR[3] THE LARGE

Son of a giant and a witch, brother of Alienor, and uncle of Escanor the Handsome, with whom Escanor the Large is sometimes confused. Escanor the Large was born at the same time as Gawain, and he shared Gawain's power by which his strength waxed and waned with the sun. He held an enduring hatred for Gawain, who had once defeated him. He kidnapped Arthur's female cupbearer while she was under Gawain's protection. Gawain tracked him down and killed him in combat, rescuing the maiden. [*Atre, Girart*]

ESCANT [*Escan, E(u)stas*]

The Duke or Earl of Cambenic in the early days of Arthur's reign. With a number of other kings, he revolted against Arthur, and suffered a defeat at the battle of Bedegraine. The rebellion was eventually curtailed by the Saxon invasions. Escant fought alongside King Clarion of Northumberland and had a few successes, but a crushing defeat at the battle of Clarence led him to ally with Arthur so that the kings could expel the Saxons for good. Escant had a hand in their defeat at the second battle of Clarence. During the Roman War, Escant led a battalion of Arthur's soldiers at the battle of Soissons. He may have influenced King EKUNAVER of Kanadic in German romance. [*VulgMer, Arthour, Malory*]

ESCARANT THE POOR

A valiant, excellent knight who fought bravely for Galehaut in the latter's war against Arthur. When Arthur and Galehaut made peace, Escarant joined Arthur's court. [*LancLac*]

ESCAVALON [*Acabalon, Cabalon, Cavalon, Cavillon, Escabalon, Escarvalon, Escavellon, Eschavalon, Kavillon, Quevalon*]

A land mentioned in several romances; there is an obvious connection with AVALON. Wolfram von Eschenbach calls it ASCALUN. In Chrétien's *Perceval* and its First Continuation, Gawain has to fight a duel at Escavalon against Sir Guigambresil. A bit of confusion caused the king of Escavalon to postpone the duel between Gawain and Guigambresil for a year, provided that Gawain spend that year looking for the Bleeding Lance. In the Second Continuation of *Perceval*, Escavalon seems to be one of Arthur's courts, located in Wales. In *Perlesvaus*, it is ruled by Perceval's paternal uncle Elinant, and then by Elinant's son Alain. In Raoul de Houdenc's *La Vengeance Raguidel*, the King of Escavalon's daughter, Lidoine, is loved by two knights: Meraugis and Gorvain Cadrut. In the Vulgate *Lancelot*, King Arguel is mentioned as the ruler. Escavalon was the birthplace of Galescalain, the duke of Clarence. [*ChretienP, Contin1, Contin2, Perlesvaus, Raoul, VulgLanc*]

ESCLABOR THE UNKNOWN [*Astlabor, Escalibore, Esclabort, Scalbrino, Scalabrone*]

A pagan king from Babylon or Galilee who journeyed to Rome as a tribute from his homeland. While in Rome, he saved the life of the emperor. He eventually traveled to Britain, where he also saved the life of King Pellinore. He entered Arthur's service and fathered Palamedes, Safir, Seguarades, nine to eleven other sons (including, possibly, Sir Suziano), and the maiden Florine. He had a brother named Aphasar. Arthur gave him his epithet after he discovered that Esclabor was a heathen (Arthur had assumed that he was Christian). Esclabor was eventually baptized. All of his sons, except those named above, were slain by the fearsome Questing Beast. He had an enemy called the Count of the Plank, but the Count was killed by Safir. During the Grail Quest, he adventured with Palamedes and Galahad, helping to repel King Mark's first invasion of Logres. He committed suicide after Palamedes was slain by Gawain. [*PostQuest, Palamedes, ProsTris, Tavola, Malory*]

ESCLADOR

A vassal of the King with a Hundred Knights. He fought at King Mark's tournament at Lancien. His daughter was called the Maiden of the Circle of Gold. [*Contin4*]

ESCLADOS THE RED [*Ascalun, Salados, Sodal*]

A lord who guarded an enchanted fountain in the forest of Broceliande in Chrétien's *Yvain* and its various adaptations. Yvain heard of his fountain when Calogrenant related how Esclados had defeated him. His interest piqued, Yvain journeyed to Broceliande and slew Esclados in combat, then married his widow, Laudine. [*ChretienE, HartmannI, Ivens, Ywain*]

ESCLAMOR[1]

A giant knight, related distantly to Lancelot, who was raised by King Claudas of the Land Laid Waste. He fought in Claudas's second war against Arthur, and performed great military feats. He participated in the Grail Quest. [*VulgLanc, ProsTris*]

ESCLAMOR[2]

The ruler of the Red City. He forbade a knight named Sir Eloides from marrying his daughter. Eloides did so anyway and, to protect her from Esclamor, he established the Forbidden Hill, which was eventually conquered by Lancelot. [*VulgLanc*]

ESCLANOR THE BLACK

Father of the Good Knight Without Fear and grandfather of Dinadan. [*Palamedes*]

ESCLARMONDE [*Esclarmondine*]

A fairy sorceress, taught by Virgil, who ruled Inglecele. She became the mistress of Escanor the Handsome and Briant of the Isles. She gave the steed Gringolet, later Gawain's horse, to the former. [*Girart*]

ESCOCE

The northeast section of Scotland, above the Firth of Forth, but often used in Arthurian romance to indicate all of SCOTLAND.

ESCORANT [*Escorante, Escoras, Estorause*]

The pagan king of Sarras who, at the conclusion of the Grail Quest, threw Galahad, Perceval, and Bors into prison. There, they were sustained by the Grail, and Escorant, who became deathly ill, released them after a year. He died after receiving their forgiveness. Galahad succeeded him as king of Sarras. [*VulgQuest, PostQuest, Tavola, Malory*]

ESCORDUCARLA

A sorceress who loved Merlin. She created the palace of Grande Disio in the forest of Darnantes, intending to live with Merlin there, but he banished her to the island of Avalon, and the palace fell to her daughter, Elergia. Her daughter Elergia tried to ensnare Arthur, leading to the deaths of Elergia and of Escorducarla's four sons at the hands of Arthur and Tristan. Escorducarla tried to exact revenge on Arthur by sending her brother, Lascanis, to Camelot with magic weapons and armor. Her plan was that Lascanis would defeat all of the Knights of the Round Table, imprison them, and burn the prison. Tristan defeated Lascanis and foiled the plan. Escorducarla was the original owner of Petitcrieu, the lap dog that Tristan eventually presented to Isolde. [*Tavola*]

ESCOSE [*Escolte*]

A city in Northumberland, where the King of Northumberland rallied his armies in preparation for war against Duke Ganor, the first Briton ruler converted to Christianity by Joseph of Arimathea. There seems to be a confusion with ESCOCE. [*VulgEst*]

ESEALT THE TALL

A nimble, polite giant that served King Arthur. With his help, Lancelot and his men were able to enter the stronghold of the wizard Malduc, and rescue Erec and Gawain, who were imprisoned there. [*UlrichZ*]

ESKILABON THE WILD

Duke of Belamunt and the Beautiful Forest. For the love of the lady Klaretschanze of Portugal—and because of the treachery of Prince Frians of Ponterteis—he was forced to guard a flower garden, and to imprison any knight who picked the flowers or who wanted to marry his sister, Flordiane. He was eventually defeated by Arthur's Sir Garel, who freed his prisoners and made Eskilabon swear fealty. Eskilabon then fought alongside Garel in Arthur's war against King Ekunaver of Kanadic, for which Arthur gave him a seat at the Round Table. [*PleierG*]

ESMEREE THE BLONDE

Daughter of King Guingras, from whom she inherited the kingdom of Wales. The sorcerers Mabon and Evrain entered her kingdom, laid waste to her city of Snowdon (thereafter called Desolate City), and turned her into a serpent until either she agreed to marry Mabon or a knight rescued her by defeating the sorcerers and enduring a kiss from her in serpentine form—called the Fearsome Kiss. Esmeree's servant, Helie, traveled to Arthur's court to find a knight to rescue her, and Helie came back with Gawain's son, Guinglain. Guinglain defeated the two wizards and reluctantly allowed the snake to kiss him, thus ending the curse. Esmeree wanted to marry Guinglain, but Guinglain, having fallen in love with the Maiden with the White Hands during the journey, made an excuse to leave, promising to rendezvous with Esmeree at Arthur's court. When she reached Arthur's court and failed to find Guinglain, Arthur—who approved of the marriage—called a tournament at the Castle of Maidens, knowing that Guinglain, who never missed a chance to win honor, would show. Guinglain's participation made him lose the love of the Maiden with the White Hands, and he was thus free to marry Esmeree. The two were wed in Wales, and Guinglain became King of Wales. [*Renaut*]

ESNI

Father of Arthur's warrior Gwynn. [*Culhwch*]

ESOTIL

The head nun in a convent where Yder recovered after Kay tried to murder him. [*Yder*]

ESPINOBLE

One of Arthur's knights. [*Contin2*]

ESPINOGRÉS [*Epynogrys, (E)(s)pi(n)(g)nogre(s), Spinagrus, Spynagrose*]

A knight, sometimes a Knight of the Round Table, who shows up in a number of romances, mostly French, beginning with Raoul de Houdenc's *Meraugis de Portlesguez*. In *Meraugis*, he is the son of Belchis. His father kidnaps the lady Lidoine, hoping to force her into marrying Espinogres, but Lidoine's lover, Meraugis, forces Belchis to release her. In the Third Continuation of Chrétien's *Perceval*, he is a king who slays his mother, Brangemore of Cornwall, in the chapel of the Black Hand. He has a nephew named Partinal who is an enemy of the Grail family. In *L'Atre Périlleux*, Gawain forces him to return to a paramour he deserted. He shows up in the Prose *Tristan*, *La Tavola Ritonda*, and Malory's *Le Morte Darthur* as a companion of Tristan and Dinadan. He was the son of King Clarion of Northumberland and the nephew of Bagdemagus of Gorre. He ruled the fortress of Prougno. Tristan convinced him to have his daughter attempt to vamp the pragmatic Dinadan as a practical joke. Later, Espignogrés fell in love with the daughter of the King of Wales, and became an outstanding fighter by virtue of his love. Sir Helyor le Preuse abducted his paramour, but Palamedes helped Espignogrés retrieve her. In the Scottish tale of *Golagros and Gawain*, he provides information on Lord Golagros, whose castle Arthur passed on the way to Rome. [*Raoul, Palamedes, Contin3, ProsTris, Atre, Tavola, Malory, Golagros*]

ESPINOIE ("Thicket")

A forest in Cornwall where King Mark was wont to hunt. [*ProsTris*]

ESQUYRIS [*Esqwyris*]

A poor but noble knight who served first Galehaut and then Arthur. [*LancLaik*]

ESSCOL [*Escol*]

Son of Alcus, King of Iceland. Alcus voluntarily subjugated himself to Arthur in return for Arthur's promise to make Esscol a knight. [*Layamon*]

ESSELYT SLENDER NECK

A lady at Arthur's court listed in *Culhwch and Olwen*. She may be related to ISOLDE of the Tristan legends. [*Culhwch*]

ESSELYT WHITE NECK

A lady at Arthur's court. [*Culhwch*]

ESSEX [*Eastsex*]

A region of eastern England. Nennius says that it was given to the Saxons as a ransom for the life of King

Vortigern, whom they had kidnapped. Malory says that the province allied with Mordred during his rebellion against Arthur. [*Nennius, Malory*]

ESTERBURY

The site of a battle between 30 of Arthur's knights and an army of Saxons and Irish. Arthur's knights triumphed, driving their opponents to the river Vargonche, where Sagremor slew the Saxon king Brandegue. [*VulgLanc*]

ESTOREL THE POOR

A bold knight who served Galehaut in the war against Arthur, but who later became one of Arthur's companions. [*VulgLanc*]

ESTORGANS

A vassal of the King with a Hundred Knights who participated in King Mark's tournament at Lancien. [*Contin4*]

ESTORM OF RIVELLO

Father of Cudinello, a knight defeated by Tristan and Lancelot during the Grail Quest. [*Tavola*]

ESTORRI OF SOBOLIS

A knight present at Uther Pendragon's Urbano tournament. [*Tavola*]

ESTOUT THE PROUD [*Estu(l)t*]

An evil knight from the Castle Fer in France. He kidnapped the wife of Tristan the Dwarf and held her in his castle. Tristan the Dwarf enlisted the help of the knight Tristan, and both Tristans faced Estout and his brothers in combat. Estout and his brothers were vanquished, but Tristan the Dwarf was killed, and Tristan received a poisoned, fatal wound. [*Thomas*]

ESTRAKE

A region in France, owned by Sir Lancelot. Lancelot made Sir Urry the earl of Estrake in return for Urry's support in the battles against King Arthur. [*Malory*]

ESTRAL [*(D)estraus*]

A castle and land owned by Arthur's Sir Kay (not the seneschal). It was also inhabited by Sir Galeres. [*ChretienE, Heinrich, VulgLanc*]

ESTRALES

A duchess in *The Knight of the Parrot*. Hearing of Arthur's exploits in the guise of the Knight of the Parrot, she declared her love for him. One of her suitors, the Knight-Giant, grew angry at this and promised to bring her Arthur's right hand. The Knight-Giant was slain in the battle, and his brother, the Redoubtable Giant of the Sure Keep, took revenge on Estrales by cutting of the hand of one of her ladies, the countess Bliandois. [*ChevPap*]

ESTRANGARÉ

A king who ruled the city of Pelle and served Arthur in *Meriadeuc*. Estrangaré sounds like the name of a place, while Pelle is a person's name. Some author evidently reversed the two. [*Meriadeuc*]

ESTRANGORRE [*(E)strangore, (E)strango(r)t, Estregor*]

One of the several kingdoms in rebellion against Arthur in the early days of his reign. It bordered on North Wales and Cambenic. The Vulgate *Merlin* gives two separate rulers of the city-state: Caradoc Shortarm and Brandegorre; and the Vulgate *Lancelot* calls the King with a Hundred Knights its lord. This confusion may be resolved by making Estrangorre a country and Estrangort a city, but the names are not used this way consistently. Arthur became overlord by treaty. It was also the home of the knight Gaswain. [*ChretienE, LancLac, VulgLanc, VulgMer, Arthour, Malory*]

ESTRAVAGAOT

One of King Arthur's Knights of the Round Table. [*HartmannE*]

ESTREMORES

Castle ruled by Raolais, an enemy of Arthur. It is the surname of Sir Belias. Both Raolais and Belias are called the Red Knight of Estremores. [*VulgMer, Livre*]

ESTRIGUEL

One of Arthur's castles in *Les Merveilles de Rigomer*. [*Merveil*]

ESUS

One of King Arthur's Knights of the Round Table. [*HartmannE*]

ETHELINA

Daughter of Octa the Saxon who married Arthur as a token of peace between the Britons and the Saxons. She died tragically at a young age. [*BlackmoreP, BlackmoreK*]

ETHELWOLD

A earl and leader of a battalion of soldiers in the Duke of Lorraine's brigade, fighting for the Roman army. Earl Ethelwold led his soldiers into a trap set by Sir Gawain and Sir Florence in north Italy. The soldiers were killed and Ethelwold fled the field. Named in Malory's version of the Roman War, he seems to correspond to Earl ANTELE of the Alliterative *Morte Arthure*. [*Malory*]

ETHIOPIA [*Ethyope*]

An ancient kingdom in Africa on the Red Sea, corresponding to the current locations of Ethiopia and Sudan. According to Heinrich von dem Türlin, the King of Ethiopia, Noir, was one of Arthur's knights, but in Malory, its king, who is also the king of Egypt, is allied to Lucius the Roman, and is killed at the battle of Soissons by Arthur's knights. [*Heinrich, Malory*]

ETHNISE

A heathen city along the Tigris River, known for its fine fabrics. A warrior from Ethnise wounded King Anfortas (Wolfram's Fisher or Grail King) in the scrotum during a joust, but was himself killed. [*Wolfram*]

ETNA

Italian folklore has Arthur reclining upon a royal couch on Mount Etna ever since his final battle with Mordred. See SICILY.

ETTARD [*Ettarre*]

The beautiful but evil maiden loved by Pelleas in Malory and Tennyson. She appears in the Post-Vulgate Cycle as ARCADE. Pelleas awarded her the crown at a tournament in which he defeated sixty knights. Because he was of low birth, however, she rebuked him, called him "Sir Baby," and forbade him from entering her land, known as the Plain of Adventures or Arroy. Pelleas disobeyed her command repeatedly. On each occasion, she sent ten knights against him. Each time, he defeated all the knights, but let them capture him anyway, so that he might catch a glimpse of Ettard on the way to her prison. Pelleas would be released the following day, only to repeat the cycle.

Gawain learned of Pelleas's plight and suggested that he could assist Pelleas by taking his armor to Ettard's court, claiming to have slain him in combat. The plan went off as expected, with Ettard joyously receiving the news that Pelleas was dead. Gawain, however, found himself unexpectedly enamored with Ettard, and she similarly fell in love with Gawain. They swiftly consummated their relationship—both of them losing their virginity in the process—and became lovers. An impatient Pelleas eventually came looking for them and found them sleeping together. Rather than kill them, he laid his sword across their throats. When Ettard awoke and saw Pelleas's sword, she realized that Gawain had lied.

The enchantress Nimue, who had taken pity on Pelleas, cast a spell on Ettard to make her love the knight. The disillusioned Pelleas, however, rejected his former beloved, and she lived out the rest of her life in heartbreak. Tennyson says that her treachery drove Pelleas mad. [*Malory, TennIK*]

EUMENIDES

One of four miscreant brother knights killed by Gawain in Heinrich von dem Türlin's *Diu Crône*. His brothers were Gameranz, Bandarab, and Belianz. [*Heinrich*]

EUPHRATES

According to the Vulgate *Estoire del Saint Graal*, the Euphrates river was the only home of the magical

Cartenans fish, whose rib formed half the hilt of the Sword with the Strange Hangings. [*VulgEst*]

EUPUTTAGLEGGE

A knight who guarded a bridge in the forest of Darnantes. He was wounded by Kay. [*Tavola*]

EURNEID

A lady at Arthur's court who was the daughter of Clydno of Edinburgh. [*Culhwch*]

EUROLWYN

A lady at Arthur's court who was the daughter of Gwydolwyn the Dwarf. [*Culhwch*]

EUROPE THE LARGE

A kingdom allied to Lucius, Arthur's enemy in the Roman War. [*Allit, Malory*]

EUS

Son of Erim, one of five brothers, and one of Arthur's warriors. [*Culhwch*]

EUSTACE

Malory's spelling for Duke ESCANT of Cambenic.

EVADAIN

A British king whose seneschal, Flamus, fought in Arthur's war against the Saxons. [*VulgMer*]

EVADEAM[1]

The son of King Brandegorre of Estrangorre. He was named after the British King Evadeam. A young sorceress turned him into an ugly, misshapen dwarf after Evadeam would not reciprocate her love. He later fell in love with Byanne, whom he served. Byanne brought him to Arthur's court and asked Arthur to knight him. Arthur did so, amidst his knights' jives and guffaws, and Evadeam was called the Dwarf Knight. He surprised his companions with his prowess. When he turned 22 years old, the spell wore off (having been temporarily transferred to Gawain) and he took back his normal, handsome countenance. [*VulgMer*]

EVADEAM[2]

A British king after whom Evadeam was named. He had a son named Tradelment. [*VulgMer*]

EVAINE [*Anayne, Evainne*]

Daughter of King Galegantin, wife of King Bors of Gannes, and mother of Lionel and Bors (Lancelot's cousins). She joined her sister Elaine in the Royal Minster nunnery after Bors died of an illness and King Claudas seized Gannes. She gave her sons to the noble Pharien to look after. Her health declined in the nunnery, where she constantly worried about her sons. She died after being blessed with a vision of Lionel and Bors, along with Lancelot, in the safe care of the Lady of the Lake. [*LancLac, VulgLanc, PostQuest*]

EVALACH [*Evalac, Evelak(e)*]

The King of Sarras, who was converted to Christianity by Joseph of Arimathea. Upon his conversion, he took the name MORDRAINS and joined Joseph's companions in Britain. His name may be a variation of AFFALACH, a Celtic god connected with Avalon. [*VulgEst, Malory*]

EVALACHIN [*Alongines, Valacin*]

King Evalach's strongest castle, well-situated and virtually impregnable. It was besieged by King Tholomer of Babylonia. Evalach encountered him there but was defeated in battle, and was forced to retreat to La Choine. [*VulgEst, Joseph*]

EVALUS

An emperor of Rome who, according to *Perlesvaus*, mounted a sacred stone in the pommel of the Grail Sword. [*Perlesvaus*]

EVANDER¹ [*Ewander*]

King of Syria. He owed his allegiance to Rome, and he therefore joined Emperor Lucius's war against Arthur. Evander, with three others, was assigned by Lucius to liberate the Roman prisoners being taken by Arthur's warriors to a prison in Paris. The Britons won the battle thanks to the timely arrival of Duke Guitard, but Evander killed Earl Borel of Maine. Evander himself was captured or killed when the Romans began to flee (the Vulgate *Merlin* says he was killed by Yder). The Alliterative *Morte Arthure* names Evander and the King of Syria as two separate characters; Evander becomes simply an earl of the Orient. [*GeoffHR, Wace, Layamon, VulgMer, Allit*]

EVANDER²

Son of the Red Knight and brother of Leander, Marmadus, and Meliadas. Perceval killed Evander's father, but Evander and his brothers eventually forgave Perceval. [*Contin4*]

EVENING STAR

In Tennyson, one of four brothers defeated by Gareth in his quest to free the lady Lyonors. His brothers were the Morning Star, the Noonday Star, and Death. His armor was bright red, though he corresponds with the GREEN KNIGHT in Malory. [*TennIK*]

EVERWIC

In the romance of *Yder*, Arthur summons Archbishop Callic of Everwic to marry Yder and Queen Guenloie. WARWICK, the most plausible location, has never had an archbishop. The author may have intended YORK. [*Yder*]

EVIERAN OF GANAOR

A Knight of the Round Table who participated in the Grail Quest. [*PostQuest*]

EVRAIN¹ [*Effuen, Evrains*]

The King of Brandigan who gave hospitality to Erec at the end of Erec's adventures with Enide. Brandigan was the site of an extremely perilous adventure called the Joy of the Court, supervised by Evrain's nephew Mabonagrain, and Evrain tried to dissuade Erec from assuming the adventure. Erec, however, took on the quest and proved victorious. Afterwards, Evrain threw a celebration in his honor. His name may be a variation of YVAIN or URIEN. [*ChretienE, Erex*]

EVRAIN² THE CRUEL [*Jrayn*]

A sorcerer who, with his brother Mabon, entered Wales and laid waste to the city of Snowdon, ruled by Queen Esmeree the Blonde, whom they turned into a snake. He was defeated in combat and was put to flight by Gawain's son Guinglain. [*Renaut, ChestreLyb*]

EWMOND

A knight of Lord Golagros in the Middle Scots poem of *Golagros and Gawain*. During the war between Golagros and Arthur, Ewmond defeated and captured Arthur's Sir Owales. [*Golagros*]

EXCALIBUR [*Caliborne, *Caliburn, Esc(a)labor, Esc(h)alibor(c), Estalibore, Excalibar, Excalibor*]

King Arthur's sword, called CALIBURN in earliest accounts and CALEDFWLCH in Welsh legend. According to Geoffrey of Monmouth, it was "best of swords," and "was forged within the Isle of Avalon." Other tales add that no armor could withstand it, that it blazed with fire when drawn, and that it instantly killed anyone it touched. Robert de Boron and the Vulgate romances name Excalibur as the same sword that Arthur drew from the stone, proving his right to rule Britain. In French romance, Gawain is often seen with Excalibur, and the Vulgate *Merlin* clears this discrepancy by saying that Arthur used the sword for a while, but bestowed it upon Gawain after Arthur won a better sword: Marmiadoise, the sword of King Rions, which had first belonged to Hercules. Gawain lent Excalibur to Lancelot once, and in another episode, Arthur let Meliadus borrow it.

In the Post-Vulgate *Merlin* continuation and in Malory, Arthur receives Excalibur from the Lady of the Lake. (The Sword-in-the-Stone is a separate weapon. Malory varies, saying in one location that Arthur drew Excalibur from the stone, and in another that the Lady of the Lake gave it to him.) Merlin showed Arthur Excalibur held by a hand, protruding from the waters of a lake. Arthur rowed out and took the sword, but had to promise to grant the Lady of the Lake a favor in the future. Arthur also received the sword's scabbard, which was more valuable than the sword itself, for no knight could lose any blood while wearing it. Tennyson says that the Lady bestwoed the sword upon Arthur so that he could drive the heathen out of Britain.

In one episode from the Post-Vulgate and Malory, Arthur entrusts the sword to Morgan le Fay. She made a counterfeit and gave the real one to her lover, Accalon, while returning the copy to Arthur. Wishing Arthur dead, she arranged a fight between Accalon and her brother, but the Lady of the Lake arrived in time to stop Arthur's demise. In the aftermath, Morgan stole the scabbard and threw it into a deep lake. A note in the Post-Vulgate says that a fairy named Marsique recovered the scabbard and gave it to Gawain, for use in a battle against Mabon the Enchanter.

The Vulgate *Merlin* says that its name meant "cuts through iron and steel and wood," while Malory gives the simpler translation "cut steel." Certainly, as Norris Lacy argues, its root seems to be the Latin *chalybs*, meaning "steel." Tennyson claims that on one side of the sword was written, in the oldest tongue, "take me," while the other side read, in modern language "cast me away."

After the final battle with Mordred, Arthur, mortally wounded, commanded one of his knights (Girflet in the Vulgate and Post-Vulgate, Bedivere in the Stanzaic *Morte Arthur* and Malory, Gawain in the Middle English *Parlement of the Thre Ages*, Lucan in the English ballad "King Arthur's Death," and a nameless squire in *La Tavola Ritonda*) to throw Excalibur into a nearby lake. The knight balked at the idea of disposing of such a fine sword but, after twice hiding the sword and lying about having thrown it in to the lake, he complied. As Excalibur sailed to the water, a hand thrust itself up through the surface and caught the sword. The hand waved the sword three times, and then pulled it under the water. Over half a dozen lakes and ponds in Britain—most of them in the southeast—claim to be the location of this event.

In 1191, King Richard the Lionheart supposedly presented "Caliburnus" to his ally, Tancred of Sicily. We may assume that a sword was "discovered" some time during the reported discovery of Arthur's body at Glastonbury. [*Culhwch, GeoffHR, Wace, ChretienP, Didot, VulgMer, PostMer, PostMort, Palamedes, Tavola, Stanz, Parlement, Hardyng, Malory, KingAD, TennIK*]

EZIER

Son of Helianor, a famous knight of Uther's court. His brother was Finoés. [*Palamedes*]

F

FAÉRIE

One of Arthur's courts in the French *Huon de Bordeaux*. It was the object of a struggle between Arthur and Huon. It is the setting of the adventures in Spenser's *The Faerie Queene*—see FAIRY LAND. [*Huon, Spenser*]

FAIR GUARD [*Belle Garde, Belle Regarde*]

A castle occupied by Morgan le Fay. She made Alexander the Orphan promise to remain at the castle for a year, intending to keep him as her lover. When the owner of the castle, the Count of the Pass, learned of Morgan's lecherous activities, he had the castle burned to the ground. To satisfy his promise to stay there, however, Alexander guarded the spot on which the castle had stood for a year. [*ProsTris, Prophecies, Malory*]

FAIR HEATH [*Landebele*]

A forest in which Agravain tried to rape a maiden but stopped and berated her when he saw that she was covered with scabs. She exacted revenge by giving him the plague, which Gawain eventually cured. [*VulgLanc*]

FAIR UNKNOWN [*Biau Desconneü, *Le Bel Inconnu, Lybeaus Desconus, Lybius Disconyus*]

In Renaut de Bâgé's *Le Bel Inconnu* and its adaptations, the name given to Gawain's son GUINGLAIN when he came to Arthur's court, ignorant of his name and paternity. As the "Fair Unknown," Guinglain completed a number of adventures before his name was revealed to him in the Desolate City. In Robert de Blois's *Beaudous*, the true name of the character is BEAUDOUS.

As a theme, the "Fair Unknown" encompasses the numerous instances in which a knight arrives at Arthur's court ignorant of—or unwilling to divulge—his own name, generally because he (or his guardian) wishes to win honor through his prowess, and not simply because of his lineage. Typically, the Fair Unknown's name is revealed to both the hero and the court after the knight is victorious in a series of adventures. The "Fair Unknown" theme occurs in the early tales of PERCEVAL, some of the stories of LANCELOT, the Italian romance of CARDUINO, and in Malory's tale of GARETH. [*Renaut, Contin2, RobertBlo, CantariC, Lybeaus*]

FAIRIES' FOUNTAIN [*Fontaine as Fées*]

A fountain visited by Guinevere, Lancelot, Dodines, Kay, and Sagremor. From here, each of the knights departed on an adventure. [*VulgLanc*]

FAIRY ISLE

An enigmatic island populated by fairies. The Queen of the Fairy Isle sent a chaplet of magic roses to Gaheris, after he was knighted at Arthur's court. [*VulgLanc*]

FAIRY KNIGHT

Arthur's grandson. He was the son of Tom a' Lincoln and Caelia, the Fairy Queen. [*Johnson*]

FAIRY LAND

Realm ruled by the Gloriana the Fairy Queen, and the setting for all the adventures in Spenser's *The Faerie Queene*. True to its name, it was characterized by an abundance of fairies, satyrs, fauns, giants, witches, goblins, dragons, monsters, and knights on quests. Prince Arthur, before he learned his lineage and became king of Britain, came to Fairy Land seeking Gloriana. The early rulers of Fairy Land included gods and elves. [*Spenser*]

FAIRY QUEEN

The title held by CAELIA in *Tom a Lincolne* and GLORIANA in *The Faerie Queene*. [*Johnson, Spenser*]

FAIRY ROCK

A town ruled by Orguelleus the Fay. [*Atre*]

FAIRYLAND

The home of Pulzella Gaia, Gawain's lover in Italian romance. [*Pulzella*]

FALCONARDO THE READY

Lord of the city of Nuscaligi, brother of Federon the Red, and uncle of Tessina. Falconardo's niece was saved by Tristan. [*Tavola*]

FALCONE

A knight who served King Mark of Cornwall. He was defeated in joust by Perceval when the latter rescued Tristan from Mark's prison. [*Tavola*]

FALERNE [*Palerne, Salergne, Salerno*]

A city in northwest Britain that was the home of Sir Breus the Pitiless. Falerne's lord fought against the Saxon invasion in the early days of Arthur's reign. This lord owed allegiance to both the Duke of Cambenic and the King of North Wales. Falerne was caught in the middle when North Wales and Cambenic went to war. [*LancLac, VulgLanc, VulgMer*]

FALLIERS

Count of Dune. Allied to King Madoines, he joined Madoines in battle against Beaudous, Gawain's son. [*RobertBlo*]

FALONORSA

A plain near Arthur's castle at Leverzep. [*Tavola*]

FALQUIDÉS

Brother of Sir Breus the Pitiless. He was killed by Galehaut the Brown. [*Palamedes*]

FALSABRE [*Fusabre*]

A Saxon king who participated in the Saxon invasion of Britain in the early days of Arthur's reign. He battled King Nentres of Garlot. [*VulgMer, Livre*]

FALSARON [*Fansaron*]

A Saxon king who joined King Rions' invasion of Carmelide at the beginning of Arthur's reign. He was wounded at the battle of Aneblayse by King Bors of Gannes. [*VulgMer, Arthour*]

FAMAGUSTA [*Famacoste*]

A city in Cyprus, named in the Alliterative *Morte Arthure* as the home of Arthur's Sir Florent. [*Allit*]

FANOYEL

The King of Syria in the time of Joseph of Arimathea. His wife had an affair with another man, and Fanoyel killed him, prompting the brother of the murdered man, King Label of Persia, to declare war. Label was traveling to the war when he met Celidoine, Nascien's son, and converted to Christianity. [*VulgEst*]

FARADÏEN

A knight who convinced Perceval's cousin, Ysmaine, to sleep with him by promising to marry her. Perceval defeated Faradïen in combat and forced him to keep his promise. [*Contin4*]

FARAM THE BLACK [*Pharan*]

A Knight of the Round Table related to Erec. He met Galahad in the Uther Pendragon Abbey, where the latter was recuperating from a successful battle against King Mark of Cornwall. As Faram chatted with Galahad, Mark sneaked in and poisoned drinks meant for the two knights. God allowed Galahad to survive, but Faram perished. [*PostQuest, ProsTris*]

FARAMON [*Ferramonte, Peremont, Pharamon(d)*]

King of France or Gaul who held his land from Uther Pendragon. He may be the same character as ARAMONT. He is based on a semi-legendary fifth-century Frankish king. According to the French *Palamedes*, he was born a serf but was freed by his master. He later usurped the French throne, which actually belonged to the lineage of Guiron the Courteous, and became Arthur's enemy. Tristan, as a youth, took service in his court. (Faramon had been an ally of Tristan's father, Meliadus). Faramon's daughter, Belide, fell in love with Tristan and accused him of rape when he rejected her. Faramon prepared to execute Tristan, but eventually learned the truth. He offered his daughter and half his kingdom to Tristan, but Tristan left his court for Cornwall. According to the Serbo-Russian *Povest' o Tryshchane*, he later threw a tournament at which Lancelot and Tristan championed a poor woman. They won, and their lady married Faramon's son. [*VulgLanc, Palamedes, ProsTris, Tavola, Malory, Povest*]

FARAN [*Pharien*]

A pagan giant from the Foreign Port, slain by Nascien on his way to Britain. [*VulgEst*]

FARASAN

A heathen giant slain by Arthur's Sir Galescalain at the battle of Diana Bridge. [*Arthour*]

FARINIOCH

A castle, presumably in Wales, to which Vortigern fled after Ambrosius and Arthur defeated his army and slew Hengist. [*Thelwall*]

FARJELASTIS OF AFRICA

An infidel duke who served Perceval's half-brother Feirefiz. [*Wolfram*]

FASCINIA

A sorceress encountered by Arthur on the island of Pamona. She tempted him to carnal lust, but the angel Gabriel visited him and caused him to flee. [*BlackmoreK*]

FAUEL

A heathen slain by Arthur's Sir Sagremor in the battle at Diana Bridge. [*Arthour*]

FAUKAIN OF MT. ESPERANT

A maid who served Queen Guinevere. [*Meriadeuc*]

FAUNUS

A French king's son who became the lover of Diana, the Roman goddess. She murdered him for love of another man named Felix. The Lady of the Lake later used Faunus's tomb to lock up Merlin. [*PostMer*]

FAUSTUS

Son of Vortigern and brother of Vortimer, Catigern, and Pascentius. Faustus was Vortigern's son by Vortigern's own daughter. He was baptized and raised by Saint

Germanus, and he eventually founded a monastery on the banks of the river Riez. [*Nennius*]

FAUVIEL

Gawain's horse in *Les Merveilles de Rigomer*, from the French word "fauve," meaning "beast." Gawain lost the horse when he was robbed and imprisoned at the castle Fors Graviers, but recovered it when he slew Lord Bauduins of Wanglent, who had somehow come into possession of it. The episode mirrors Gawain's loss and recovery of GRINGOLET in the Grail romances. [*Merveil*]

FAVEL [*Faunel*]

A Saxon warrior slain by Gareth in a skirmish near Camelot, during the Saxon invasion of Britain. [*VulgMer*]

FAVELHAND

A steed owned by Sir Ironside, one of Arthur's knights in *Sir Gawain and the Carle of Carlisle*. The name probably derives from French word "fauve," meaning "beast" (cf. FAUVIEL). [*SyreGaw*]

FAVIDA

The name of a lady saved from two giants by Erec in the Norse *Erex Saga*. She appears, unnamed, in Chrétien's *Erec*. She was the daughter of Earl Ubbi of Bouderisborg. Her husband, Cadoc of Tabriol, was kidnapped by the giants but was also saved by Erec. [*Erex*]

FAWNELL

The Frisian steed belonging to Arthur's Sir Florent. [*Allit*]

FEARED SEAT [*Sieges Redoutez*]

A seat at the Grail Table reserved for Josephus, Joseph of Arimathea's son. It swallowed up anyone else who sat there. Although analogous to the Round Table's PERILOUS SEAT, it is distinct from the Perilous Seat at the Grail Table, in which no one could sit. [*VulgQuest*]

FEARLESS KEEP

A castle in the Kingdom of Damsels, where Queen Flor de Mont was imprisoned by a wicked marshall. Arthur, in his quest to rescue the queen, defeated the Knight of the Passage and the marshall's standard bearer before the castle. He enjoyed a quick sojourn there before he continued on to the marshall's Perilous Castle. [*ChevPap*]

FEARSOME KISS

The adventure achieved by Gawain's son Guinglain in Renaut's *Le Bel Inconnu*. Guinglain accepted the quest at Arthur's court and, led by Helie, he traveled to the ruined Desolate City (formerly Snowdon) in Wales, where two sorcerers had invaded and turned the queen, Esmeree the Blonde, into a snake. Guinglain had to defeat the two wizards and then endure a kiss from the snake, resisting the urge to cleave the snake in two. After the vile kiss had been delivered, Esmeree the Blonde was restored to her true form and the curse was lifted. An analog is found in Ulrich von Zatzikhoven's story of CLIDRA THE FAIR, and in the Italian tale of Carduino and BEATRICE. The theme is relatively common in folklore. [*Renaut*]

FEBRUE THE BROWN

A knight defeated by Uther Pendragon during a tournament at the castle of Urbano. [*Tavola*]

FEBUS[1] [*Febusso*]

A famous king of France, descended from Clodoveus, who pre-dated Arthur by several generations. He was the son of King Heuderis or Crudens of Gaul. He married Florine and fathered Altan, Niatar, Lannor, Argons, and Siraouc. Guiron the Courteous was his great-grandson. In *Palamedes*, Sir Breus the Pitiless literally falls into his tomb and learns his story from one of his descendants. A mighty warrior, he had a number of adventures in Logres before he fell in love with the daughter of the king of Northumberland. She at first scorned Febus's love, and sent him on a series of near-impossible tasks, all of which he completed. He fell sick for love of the maiden, she relented and accepted him, and he died in her arms. [*Palamedes, Febusso*]

FEBUS[2]

A knight defeated by Sir Guiron at the Perilous Pass, and by Segurant the Brown at Uther Pendragon's Urbano tournament. He was the son of Galehaut the Brown. Meliadus eventually killed him. [*Palamedes, Tavola*]

FEDERIEL

In *La Tavola Ritonda*, the giant pagan ruler of Dolorous Guard. His father was Carone the Great, and his wife was called Nonfizata. Lancelot conquered the castle by defeating him in combat and slicing off his hand. Federiel surrendered, and Lancelot sent him to Camelot. Federiel journeyed to Mount Nervana, where he found Arthur and his army in the midst of a battle with King Meliadus of Lyonesse. Federiel leapt into the battle and slew ten of Arthur's men before he was cut down. Dolorous Guard's original ruler is called BRIAN OF THE ISLES in the Prose *Lancelot*. [*Tavola*]

FEDERION THE RED

In *La Tavola Ritonda*, a mortally wounded knight who showed up at Arthur's court just after Lancelot's knighting. Lancelot accepted the quest to avenge Federion, but he does not complete the quest in the *Tavola*. Federion's mother, named Tessina, was later saved by Tristan. A similar knight appears in the Vulgate *Lancelot* as MELIAN THE GAY. [*Tavola*]

FEDERON THE RED

Father of Tessina, a lady saved by Tristan. His brother was named Falconardo the Ready, lord of Nuscaligi. [*Tavola*]

FEDERUMGOTTO

A counselor to King Mark of Cornwall in *La Tavola Ritonda*. He accused Tristan and Isolde of treason. Mark investigated the accusations, and was fooled into believing them false. He banished Federumgotto from Cornwall. [*Tavola*]

FEIMURGAN [*Famorgan*]

A variation of MORGAN LE FAY. Wolfram von Eschenbach, in *Parzival*, reverses the name Morgan le Fay (Feimurgan) of Terre de la Joie to make Terdelaschoye of Feimurgan—in Wolfram, therefore, Feimurgan is Terdelaschoye's homeland. [*Wolfram*]

FEIREFIZ

Perceval's heathen half-brother—the son of Gahmuret and his first wife, Queen Belacane of Zazamanc. Since he had one White and one Black parent, Feirefiz was a pie-bald. Appropriately, his name seems to be a variation of *vairs fiz*, meaning "partly-colored son" (Loomis, *Grail*, 217). Feirefiz, being one of the House of Anjou, was a magnificent knight. While Perceval was winning honor and acclaim in Britain, Feirefiz was enjoying a comparable set of adventures in Heathendom, saving lands—such as Janfuse and Thabronit—winning the love of queens—such as Ekuba and Secundille—and assembling an impressive suite of kings, counts, and dukes in his service. In time, he traveled to Britain to find his father, not aware that his father had been dead for some time. He encountered Perceval and the two fought a magnificent, exhausting battle before Perceval's sword broke, pausing the duel long enough for the two warriors to identify each other and rejoice at their acquaintance. Feirefiz accompanied Perceval to the Grail Castle of Munsalvæsche and was in attendance when Perceval was anointed the Grail King. At the ceremonies, it was discovered that Feirefiz could not see the Grail because he was a heathen; Feirefiz decided to receive baptism so that he might see the Grail and so that he might be worthy to marry the Grail Maiden Repanse de Schoye. After he was Christened, he and Repanse were married. The two departed to rule India, where they had a son—the legendary Prester John. [*Wolfram*]

FELELOLYE

Sister of Sir Urry, who accompanied him from land to land until he was finally healed by Lancelot. After the healing, she married Sir Lavaine. [*Malory*]

FELICE¹

Arthur's sister in *La Tavola Ritonda*. She married King Andremo the Old of Sobicio. Her daughter, Elyabel, was Tristan's mother. [*Tavola*]

FELICE²

The son of a sorceress named Sargia, sent by his mother to serve Tristan's son, Tristan the Younger. [*DueTris*]

FELINETE

An enchantress who was the daughter of Lady Felinors. She was served by a dwarf named Canain. She helped Gawain make his horse, Gringolet, take food and water by removing a bag of powder from the horse's ear. Later, when Gawain was winning a duel against Escanor the Handsome, Felinete compelled Gawain to spare Escanor's life. [*Girart*]

FELINORS

Mother of the Lady Felinete. [*Girart*]

FELITOÉ

A vassal of Emperor Filimenis of Constantinople. He ruled Antioch in Syria. [*Floriant*]

FELIX¹

The Roman governor of Judea and Syria in the time of Joseph of Arimathea. The Roman Emperor Vespasian, searching for a leprosy cure, charged Felix to find an artifact which had belonged to Christ. As a young knight, King Evalach (later Mordrains) of Sarras served in Felix's court. [*VulgEst*]

FELIX² [*Felissi, Filicie, Pelis*]

In the Prose *Tristan*, the father of King Mark, whom he preceded as ruler of Cornwall. He also had a son named Pernehan. In *Tristan*, his daughter, Elyabel, becomes Tristan's mother, while Italian romance says that Felix was the father of Meliadus, Tristan's father. *Tristan* characterizes him as an evil, ruthless ruler who was condemned in the church of Norholt. Italian romance provides an opposite description, calling him a good king. The second son of King Baralis of Cornwall and Lyonesse, Felix became heir to the former when his older brother, Feriando, died as a youth. He was attacked by King Dilianfer of Ireland, who sacked Tintagel, causing Felix to die from heartbreak. [*ProsTris, TristanoR, Tavola, Povest*]

FELIX³

A Knight of the Round Table who participated in the Grail Quest. [*ProsTris*]

FELLONE

The pagan Lord of Derudicanoro in the Dark Valley. Tristan and Lancelot came to his fortress during the Grail Quest. Both fought with him and were overwhelmed by his strength. Lancelot was imprisoned while Tristan was left for dead. Upon regaining consciousness, Tristan pursued Fellone into castle Derudicanoro and was able to defeat him by swearing before God that he would not sin again with Isolde. Fellone agreed to be baptized and to swear allegiance to Arthur. [*Tavola*]

FELON¹ CASTLE

See TREACHEROUS CASTLE. [*ProsTris*]

FELON[2] OF ALBARUA

A monster knight with an enormous head. Arthur's Sir Jaufré found him terrorizing the fairyland of Gibel. Jaufré killed him. [*Jaufre*]

FELON[3] OF THE GUARD

An evil knight who ruled the Castle of the Guard. He abducted Sir Gladinel, but Sir Durmart the Welshman, Gladinel's friend, defeated him and forced him to release his prisoners. [*Durmart*]

FELOT OF LISTENOIS

A knight defeated in joust by Arthur's Sir Marhaus. [*Malory*]

FELTEMOUR [*Feldenak*]

In the Alliterative *Morte Arthure* and Malory, a Roman warrior who, seeking to avenge the death of his comrade Gaius, tried to kill Gawain. Gawain slew him. He is known in the earlier chronicles as MARCELLUS MUCIUS. [*Allit, Malory*]

FENICE

Heroine of Chrétien de Troyes's *Cliges*, endowed with a number of characteristics of Isolde, though Fenice explicitly wishes to avoid Isolde's fate. The daughter of the Emperor of Germany, Fenice was courted by the Duke of Saxony, but her father agreed to marry her to Alis, the Emperor of Greece and Constantinople. When Alis came to meet her in Cologne, Fenice fell in love with Alis's nephew, Cliges, who had won fame at Arthur's court. To preserve her virginity, she had her servant Thessala create a potion to give to Alis. The potion caused Alis to believe that, each night, he was making love to Fenice when in fact he was only dreaming.

Fenice and Cliges eventually confessed their love for each other and developed a plan: Fenice would fake her own death, and Cliges would retrieve her from her tomb after burial. While Cliges had a special tomb made for the occasion, Thessala concocted another potion which would give Fenice the appearance of death. The potion worked, but three physicians arrived from Salerno who doubted Fenice's death. They tortured the poor maiden with fire and whips to rouse her, until they were hurled out a high window by a force of Fenice's lady servants.

Fenice was buried as planned, and Cliges rescued her. The wounds she had received from the physicians were mended by Thessala. Cliges and Fenice lived together in a tower for some time in bliss, but they were eventually discovered by Alis's warrior Bertrand. Cliges and Fenice were forced to flee Greece to escape Alis's wrath. When Alis died, they returned and were crowned emperor and empress of Greece and Constantinople. [*ChretienC*]

FENISE

Queen of Ireland in *Durmart le Gallois*. Sir Durmart fell in love with her after hearing of her great beauty. At the city of Landoc, Durmart won a sparrowhawk tournament and presented the prize to Fenise without knowing her identity. Dumart's opponent in the tournament, Nogant, later besieged Fenise in her castle at Limerick, but Durmart arrived and saved her. Fenise and Durmart were married. [*Durmart*]

FER ("Fire")

A French castle owned by the evil Estout the Proud, where he kept the kidnapped wife of Tristan the Dwarf until her husband and the other Tristan rescued her. [*Thomas*]

FERAMANS

A count who was a companion of Lord Formis on the Turning Isle. Urien defeated him when Arthur and his knights fought Formis's knights. [*Livre*]

FERAUNT [*Ferawnte, Ferrand*]

A Spanish knight in the Roman army that fought against Arthur in the Roman War. Feraunt led a force of soldiers under the Duke of Lorraine. He was slain by Gawain's soldiers in an ambush. [*Allit, Malory*]

FERCOS

One of Arthur's warriors. He was the son of Poch. Taken from the Irish hero named Fergus, he may be the source of the later Arthurian knight FERGUS. [*Culhwch*]

FERELOIS

The castle ruled by Abastunagio, son of Galehaut. Abastunagio threw a tournament at Ferelois during the Grail Quest, which Galahad won. Its name is probably a variation of SORELOIS, Galehaut's kingdom. [*Tavola*]

FERGUS[1] [*Ferguut*]

Hero of Guillaume le Clerc's *Fergus*. Raised as a peasant plowman by his father, Soumillet, in the coastal region of Pelande, Fergus's noble blood (from his mother's side) was stirred by the sight of Arthur's knights returning from a hunt. Against the wishes of his parents, he departed for Arthur's court, bearing rusty armor and weapons. At his request, he was knighted by Arthur. Kay sarcastically suggested that, as his first quest, he defeat the fearsome Black Knight, to whom many of Arthur's knights had fallen. Fergus assumed the quest against Arthur's wishes. On the way to the Black Mountain, Fergus stayed at the Castle Lidel and fell in love with Lady Galiene of Lothian, the castellan's niece. Promising to return to her, he set out again. Arriving at the Black Mountain, he defeated the Black Knight and won a magic horn and wimple. These he sent to Arthur, with the Black Knight as his prisoner. He returned to Lidel but found that Galiene had returned to Lothian. Fergus enjoyed more adventures in Scotland, slaying robbers, a pirate crew, and a giant. His most significant quest led him to kill a hag and dragon at the castle Dunostre, thus winning a magical white shield (and later earning the nickname "the Knight with the Fair Shield"). Finally arriving in Lothian, he discovered that Lady Galiene was besieged in Castle Roucebourc. Galiene's servant, Arundele, asked Fergus champion the castle against the invading king and his nephew, Arthofilaus. Fergus agreed, killed Arthofilaus, and sent the king to Arthur. Arthur called a tournament at Gedeorde, which Fergus won. Afterwards, he was married to Galiene and awarded the lands of Lothian and Tudiele by Arthur. His *enfances* bear an obvious resemblance to the early stories of PERCEVAL. His name may be adapted from the Welsh character FERCOS. [*Guillaume, Ferguut*]

FERGUS[2]

An earl whose lands were saved from Taulas the Giant by Sir Marhaus. Fergus later became a Knight of the Round Table and a companion of Tristan. He helped effect a reconciliation between Tristan and Isolde after a quarrel. [*ProsTris, Malory*]

FERGUSSIN

An evil knight who imprisoned Guiron the Courteous and the Good Knight Without Fear after they came to his manor seeking lodging. King Ban of Benoic and King Bors of Gannes rescued them. [*Palamedes*]

FERIANDO

Eldest son of King Baralis of Cornwall and Lyonesse. When he died in childhood, his brother Felix (King Mark's father) took his place as heir. [*Tavola*]

FERMORACCO DELLA PIEMONTANA

In *La Tavola Ritonda*, the fortress ruled by Urgan the Hairy, a giant slain by Tristan. [*Tavola*]

FERNAGU [*Venegus*]

A noble knight who was killed by Mabonagrain while he was attempting the deadly Joy of the Court adventure, which was eventually completed by Erec. [*ChretienE*]

FERNTOWN

A village established by Arthur after a herd of 100 cows, which Arthur had wrongfully obtained, were turned into bundles of ferns. The consecration of the town marked the impact of the holy lesson on Arthur. [*SaintsCad*]

FERNVAIL

King Vortigern's father, according to Nennius. A historical figure named Fernvail may have ruled Gwent or Monmouth. [*Nennius*]

FEROLIN OF SALONIKA

One of the noble Byzantine warriors that Alexander brought to Britain from Constantinople. He fought for Arthur in the battle against the traitor Angres of Windsor. [*ChretienC*]

FEROZ

The husband of the hag Ruel. He was drowned by Sir Flojir, driving Ruel to seek revenge against any knight she saw—one of whom was Wigalois (Gawain's son). [*Wirnt*]

FERRAGUNZE THE COURTLY

Foster-father and teacher of Elyabel, Tristan's mother and Arthur's niece in *La Tavola Ritonda*. Ferragunze claimed that his three virtues were honesty, bravery, and the absence of jealousy of his wife, Verseria. Through a series of amusing tests, Arthur and Meliadus verified these traits. In reward, Meliadus appointed him as viceroy of Sobicio. His ordeal is reminiscent of BALDWIN's in *The Avowing of Arthur*. [*Tavola*]

FERRAMONTE

King of North Wales during Uther's reign, killed at the Urbano tournament by Brunor the Brown. [*Tavola*]

FERRANT[1]

The steed belonging to Gliglois, Gawain's squire. [*Gliglois*]

FERRANT[2]

One of the knights who murdered the Good Knight Without Fear. His companion was Briadan. [*Palamedes*]

FERRER

A warrior who, in the service of the Duke of Lorraine, battled Arthur during the Roman War. [*Allit*]

FEURES OF RAMIDE

An Arthurian knight who preferred war to peace. [*Heinrich*]

FFLAM ("Flame")

Son of Nwyfre, brother of Gwynn, and one of Arthur's warriors. [*Culhwch*]

FFLAMDDWYN ("Flame Bearer")

A warrior who killed Owain (Yvain) or was killed by Owain. A Welsh Triad tells us that his wife, Bun, was unfaithful. [*Triads*]

FFLERGANT

King of Brittany and father of Arthur's warrior Ysberin. [*Culhwch*]

FFLEWDWR FFLAM [*Fleudur Flam*]

Son of Naw, brother of Gwenwynwyn, and one of Arthur's warriors. [*Culhwch, Dream*]

FFOTOR

A British city, once inhabited or visited by Arthur's chief gatekeeper Glewlwyd. [*Culhwch*]

FIACHA

A non-Arthurian Celtic hero who becomes one of Arthur's warriors in Richard Hole's *Arthur*. [*Hole*]

FIDEGART

A giantess who married the giant Purdan. Fidegart and Purdan terrorized their lands, slew knights, and imprisoned maidens. They were both finally slain by Arthur's Sir Garel. [*PleierG*]

FIDELAS

A knight present at the Sorgarda tournament, which Gawain won. [*Heinrich*]

FIDESSA

Alias used by the evil witch Duessa while she was deceiving the Red Cross Knight. [*Spenser*]

FIELD OF THE LION [*Champ del Lion*]

A property between two mountains, owned by Arthur's knight Meliot of Logres. Meliot allowed his pet lion to roam free in the field. It terrorized passers-by and was finally slain by Clamadoz of the Shadows—for which Meliot later exacted revenge. [*Perlesvaus*]

FIELD OF THE SILKS

The location of a tournament attended by Gawain, Lancelot, and Arthur. Arthur won the tournament. [*Perlesvaus*]

FIELD OF THE TENT

The location of a tournament attended by Gawain and Arthur. Gawain won, and his victory allowed him to reclaim the Circle of Gold, which Nabigan of the Rock had stolen from Perceval. [*Perlesvaus*]

FIERS OF ARRAMIS

A knight from Heinrich von dem Türlin's *Diu Crône* who bore a griffin's claw as his symbol. He was engaged to lady Flursensephin of Sorgarda Castle, where Fiers was expected to win a tournament. When Flursensephin quarreled with her little sister Quebeleplus, however, the latter asked Gawain to defeat Fiers. Gawain did so, and compelled Fiers to surrender to the little girl. Essentially the same character appears as MELIANT of Lis in Wolfram von Eschenbach's *Parzival*. In French, the knight's first name means "proud." [*Heinrich*]

FILIMENIS

The emperor of Constantinople and Greece who joined Maragoz, ruler of Sicily, in a war against Arthur. During the war, Filimenis's daughter, Florete, fell in love with Floriant, one of Arthur's knights. The war ended when Floriant defeated Maragoz in single combat. Floriant and Florete wed. Filimenis left his lands to his son-in-law. [*Floriant*]

FILLEDAMOR

The fair, well-mannered sister of King Guivret the Small, Sir Erec's diminutive friend. Filledamor led an idyllic life with her sister Guenteflur in Guivret's city of Penefrec. [*HartmannE*]

FILLEDUCH

A lady at Arthur's court. As the beloved of Sir Gales, Filleduch, along with the other court ladies, failed a chastity chest. [*Heinrich*]

FILONES OF HIBERBORTICON

An infidel count who owed his allegiance to Feirefiz, Perceval's half-brother. [*Wolfram*]

FIMBEUS [*Finbeus*]

The lord of Sardin in the country of Angiez. He was married to a goddess named Giramphiel, who had Lady Fortune supply him with a special belt. This belt, garnished with enchanted stones, made its wearer not only strong and brave, but also handsome and charming. During a visit to Arthur's court, Fimbeus lent the belt to Queen Guinevere, who coveted it so much that she ordered Gawain to fight Fimbeus for it. Gawain reluctantly complied, and won. Giramphiel later managed to steal from Gawain the stone that was the source of the belt's power. She returned it to Fimbeus. Gawain embarked on a quest to recover the victory stone for Arthur's court, the culmination of which brought him to Sardin, where he again defeated Fimbeus, recaptured the stone, and obtained Fimbeus's fealty. [*Heinrich*]

FINC OF SEMINIS

A knight present at the tournament of Sorgarda, which was won by Gawain. [*Heinrich*]

FINECOCE

A seaside castle in Ireland, near castle Rigomer. Lancelot defeated Buticostiaus, its lord, in combat. [*Merveil*]

FINN

The Irish counterpart of King MARK of Cornwall in a legend known as *Diarmaid and Grainne*. His nephew, Diarmaid, and his wife, Grainne, fell in love, eloped, and began an affair.

FINOÉS OF THE MOUNTAIN

Son of the mighty Lyanor of the Mountain. He fought with his father—neither knowing the other's identity—and was killed. [*Palamedes*]

FIR FOREST [*Sapine*]

A castle in northwestern Britain, passed by Gawain and his brothers on their way to battle the Saxons in Scotland. [*VulgMer*]

FIRST CONQUERED KING [*Roi Premier Conquis]

A vassal of Galehaut. He fought in the battles against Arthur before Galehaut and Arthur made peace. Lancelot defeated him in combat. The First Conquered King was so named because he was the first of many kings whose lands (the Borders of Galone) Galehaut conquered. The Vulgate *Merlin* gives him the proper name of CLEOLAS. [*LancLac, VulgLanc, Livre*]

FIRUS BAHANDIN

An Arabian potentate who, along with two others, challenged Arthur to a tournament at Baghdad in Babylon. This tournament is recounted by Gawain in Heinrich's *Diu Crône*. [*Heinrich*]

FISH-KNIGHT

A monster slain by Arthur in *Le Chevalier du Papegau*. It lived in the sea. It's armor, helmet, shield, horse, and sword were all part of its natural body. It had been terrorizing the Lady of the Blonde Hair of the Amorous City, and she summoned Arthur's help. A violent sea storm followed the Fish-Knight's death. [*ChevPap*]

FISHER KING [*Roi Pescheor*]

The keeper of the Grail, sometimes called the Rich Fisher or Angler, generally identical to the GRAIL KING. Chrétien de Troyes's *Perceval*, the first text to mention him, tells of a wound in the thighs or groin that left him infirm and infertile. According to Chrétien and most other writers, the Fisher King received the wound in battle, but in certain variations wound results from the Fisher King fooling around with the broken Grail Sword, which had killed his brother Goondesert (third continuation of Chrétien); or from a battle against the Hags of Gloucester (*Peredur*); or from the Fisher King's disbelieving the Grail (*Livre d'Artus*); or from Perceval's failure to ask the Grail Question (*Perlesvaus*); or from Perceval sitting in the Round Table's Perilous Seat (Didot-*Perceval*). In any event, this injury made him unable to engage in any sport except fishing; hence, his name. In the Robert de Boron Grail romances, and their adaptations, the king is called the "Rich Fisher" because he caught a single fish that fed thousands at the Grail Table. This man later became keeper of the Grail, and successive Grail Kings inherited the nickname. The *Livre d'Artus* reverts to the original explanation of the name.

As to his true name, the stories differ greatly: Chrétien does not bestow a proper name on him; the author of *Perlesvaus* calls him MESSOIS; Wolfram von Eschenbach names him ANFORTAS; in Robert de Boron's *Joseph*, he is called BRON, while in the Vulgate *Estoire del Saint Graal*, he is Bron's son, ALAIN. In the Vulgate romances, the Fisher Kings after Alain include JOSHUA, AMINADAP, CARCELOIS, MANUEL, LAMBOR, and PELLEHAN; and in Arthur's time, the designation belongs to ALAIN, PELLES, or PELLINORE, the three sons of Pellehan. The non-Arthurian *Sone de Nausay* identifies him with JOSEPH OF ARIMATHEA. Most of the Grail legends describe the Fisher King as the uncle or grandfather of the Grail hero (Perceval or Galahad). He ruled the Grail Castle, called Corbenic in the Vulgate romances.

In the early tales, the injured Fisher King awaited Perceval's arrival for healing. To accomplish this, Perceval had to ask the Grail Question, either "Who does the Grail serve?" or "What ails you?" Because of his innocence, Perceval failed to ask the question on his first visit, causing distress, but on his second arrival he successfully cured the king and became the new Grail King himself. In the Vulgate romances, on the other hand, the Fisher King remains king of Corbenic even after the Arthurian knights accomplish the Grail Quest.

His role is complicated in some romances (including Chrétien) by the existence of a separate MAIMED KING, usually the Fisher King's father. In *Perceval*, both kings suffer from the same malady, while in the Vulgate romances, it seems that the Maimed King alone is injured. In many stories, the Maimed King has been wounded by the DOLOROUS STROKE.

The Fisher King may be an derivative of Bran the Blessed, a wounded King of Britain in Welsh texts. Scholars arguing for a Christian origin for the Grail legend have seen the Fisher King as an allegory for Christ, corresponding with the Grail as a symbol of the Eucharist. As some Grail stories link the Fisher King's health—and particulary, as his wound is often described as occurring in the groin, his sexual potency—with the prosperity of his land, other critics have seen him as a spirit figure in an elaborate fertility myth. [*ChretienP, RobertBorJ, Contin1, Contin2, Perlesvaus, Wolfram, VulgLanc, VulgQuest, VulgEst, VulgMer, Livre, PostQuest, Peredur*]

FIVE KINGS

Five rulers—the King of Ireland, the King of Denmark, the King of the Valley, the King of Sorelois, and the King of the Distant Isles—who waged war against Arthur after the establishment of the Round Table. Arthur, Gawain, Kay, and Girflet killed all of them at the battle of the Humber River. [*PostMer, Malory*]

FJALLSHARFIR

A giant slain by Yvain in the Norse *Ivens Saga*. He appears in Chrétien's *Yvain* as HARPINS. "Fjallsharfir" seems to mean "Mountain-Harfir" or "Harfir of the Mountain." [*Ivens*]

FLAMUS

Seneschal of King Evadain. He fought in Arthur's ranks against the Saxons at the battle of Carhaix. [*VulgMer*]

FLANDERS [*Flaundrys*]

A country encompassing what is now parts of France and Belgium, across the sea from Britain. In Geoffrey, Arthur conquers it as part of his invasion of Gaul and defeat of Frollo. Later, King Holdin ruled it under Arthur. In the Vulgate *Lancelot*, he wrestles it from Count Aran, who ruled it under Claudas. A knight named Bloyas came from this region. [*GeoffHR, Wace, VulgLanc, Malory*]

FLANDRIN [*Flaundreus, Flaundrin(s)*]

A knight of Arthur's court who fought against the rebellious kings and the Saxons. He is variously called "the White," "the Noble," and "the Short." Malory says that he came from the Castle of Ladies. [*VulgMer, Arthour, Malory*]

FLANDRISBORG

A city in Flanders that was the home of Earl Gorgun and his brothers Garse and Jentaneon, who were all knights at Arthur's court. [*Erex*]

FLEGETINE [*Fragatine*]

The wife of Nascien, mother of Celidoine, and daughter of the King of Midians. Her husband journeyed to Britain to join Joseph of Arimathea; in a dream, he beckoned her to follow him. Taking her servants Corsapin and Elicanor, she joined him there. [*VulgEst*]

FLEVENTAN

A Welsh forest where Ivor the Huntsman raised Meriadoc, heir to the throne of Wales, and protected him from his murderous uncle, Griffin. After growing up in the forest, Meriadoc was taken to Arthur's court by Kay. [*Historia*]

FLOATING CHESSBOARD

A magic artifact desired by Arthur and sought by Gawain in a Dutch romance. It was owned by King Wonder, who would only relinquish it if Gawain brought him the Sword with Two Rings. This sent Gawain on a long series of interlocking quests, culminating in his return to Wonder's court with the sword. Wonder completed the trade, and Gawain returned to Arthur's court with the Floating Chessboard. [*Penninc*]

FLOEGO

A castle where Lancelot successfully defended the sister of Meleagant, who had been accused of complicity in Meleagant's death. [*VulgLanc*]

FLOIS

The king of Alverne on the Green Island, whose land was routinely invaded by a terrible giant named Assiles. Eventually, Assiles destroyed all of Flois' land except for Effin castle. Flois sent his page Giwanet to Arthur's court to ask for assistance. It arrived in the form of Gawain, who slew the giant. In reward, Flois offered Gawain his crown, but Gawain refused and embarked for further adventures. [*Heinrich*]

FLOJIR

A knight from Belamunt who killed Feroz, the husband of Ruel the hag. [*Wirnt*]

FLOR¹ DE LIS

A maiden who served Morgan le Fay. When Morgan kidnapped the child of Lord Berengier and extorted Berengier's love, Flor de Lis offered to help Berengier and his child escape, provided Berengier would marry her. Berengier agreed, and the three of them fled to Berengier's land of Gomeret. [*Prophecies*]

FLOR² DE MONT

Queen of the Kingdom of Damsels, which she inherited from her father, King Beauvoisin. Her father's wicked steward usurped the kingdom and imprisoned Flor de Mont in the Fearless Keep. One of Flor de Mont's ladies sought out Arthur, who was disguised as the Knight of the Parrot. Arthur slew the steward at his Perilous Castle and restored Flor de Mont to her throne. [*ChevPap*]

FLOR³ DESIREE

Daughter of the Viscount of Pavengay in Ireland. One of the viscount's brutish neighbors, Lord Savari of Ruiste Valee, intended to take Flor Desiree for his concubine, but Lancelot—who happened to lodge with the viscount on his way to Rigomer—slew Savari and saved Flor Desiree from this fate. Flor Desiree's birth name was INGLE. [*Merveil*]

FLORAETE

Tristan's foster-mother, married to Rual li Foitenant. She posed as his real mother during his upbringing in order to shield him from the wrath of Duke Morgan, who had been an enemy of Tristan's father. She died of unknown circumstances during Tristan's life. [*Gottfried*]

FLORANT OF ITOLAC

A knight who served Duchess Orgeluse of Logres. He was titled "the Turkoyt," the meaning of which is uncertain. Like his companion Lischois Gwelljus, he frequented the area around the Castle of Marvels and fought knights to test their worth. Gawain was one of the few knights to defeat him, which helped Gawain to win Orgeluse's love. Florant married Gawain's mother, Sangive. [*Wolfram*]

FLORDEMUNT

A castle in Karmerie, ruled by Lady Tydomie, who married Arthur's nephew Meleranz. [*PleierM*]

FLORDIANE

The sister of Duke Eskilabon of Belamunt. All knights who desired her had to contend with Eskilabon and were invariably defeated and imprisoned—until Arthur's Sir Garel conquered Eskilabon and ended the custom. Garel seemed to engage himself to Flordiane, but he later married Queen Laudamie of Averre. [*PleierG*]

FLORDIBEL

Heroine of Der Pleier's *Tandareis and Flordibel*. The daughter of the King of India, she was sent to Arthur's court as a child to serve Guinevere. Sure that she would never love a man willingly, she asked Arthur for his promise to slay any man who succeeded in winning her love. Over the next ten years, however, she fell deeply in love with one of her servants: a page named Tandareis. Fearing Arthur's vow, the two lovers fled court for Tandareis's home castle of Tandernas, which Arthur subsequently besieged. Peace was reached, but on the condition that Tandareis leave for foreign lands until he could prove his honor. Despondent, Flordibel returned to Arthur's court and waited. After he had won fame through a series of adventures, Arthur invited Tandareis back to court, and he and Flordibel were wed. She became Queen of Malmontan and Mermin, two kingdoms that Tandareis had conquered. [PleierT]

FLOREE[1]

A lady kidnapped by Sir Caradoc of the Dolorous Tower. Caradoc also kidnapped Guinevere. When Gawain came to rescue Guinevere, Floree gave him Caradoc's sword—the only weapon which could kill the giant knight. Caradoc died cursing her name.

FLORÉE[2]

Daughter of King Alain of Escavalon. She was loved by Guinganbresil, one of her father's knights. While traveling through the forest of Breckham, a group of Saxons siezed her, but Gawain rescued her. Later, Gawain stayed at the Castle Brion (which belonged to Alain), slept with Florée, and begot an unnamed son. Florée later married Meliant of Lis. [Livre]

FLORÉE[3]

A cousin and friend of Princess Hermondine of Scotland. She organized five tournaments to find Hermondine a husband, which produced Arthur's Sir Meliador. Agravain wooed and won her during a tournament at Camelot. [Froissart]

FLOREMUS

Seneschal of King Lac of Great Orkney. He joined Arthur's forces against the Saxons at the battles of Clarence and Vambieres. [Livre]

FLORENCE

One of Gawain's sons in Malory. His mother was the sister of Sir Brandelis. A Knight of the Round Table, he was one of the twelve knights who sought to catch Lancelot and Guinevere in an act of treason. Lancelot killed him and his compatriots in the attempt. [Malory]

FLORENT[1]

An Arthurian knight from France who participated in the Roman War. During a mission to procure supplies in northern Italy, Florent and Gawain learned of a nearby Roman brigade, led by the Duke of Lorraine. With only a small force of seven hundred, Gawain and Florent

managed to rout the Romans, who numbered in the thousands. Florent also led a battalion at the final battle at Soissons. [Allit, Malory]

FLORENT[2]

A great sword wielded by Sir Lionel, a cousin of Lancelot. [Allit]

FLORENTIN

Father of Isolde of the White Hands in the Middle-English Sir Tristrem. His counterpart in most of the Tristan romances is HOEL. [SirTris]

FLORENZ

The constable of Cardigan. He joined Arthur's early wars against the Saxons. [Livre]

FLORES [Floire]

A duke from France—perhaps an ally or vassal of Arthur—who fought in a tournament at the Castle of Maidens and was defeated by King Angusel of Scotland. [Renaut]

FLORETE

Daughter of Emperor Filimenis of Constantinople. She fell in love with Floriant, one of Arthur's knights, during a war between Filimenis and Arthur. She defected from her father's camp to be with Floriant. At the end of the war, the lovers were married and Florete became Queen of Sicily. They had a son named Froart. Florete accompanied her husband on several adventures and helped him to kill a dragon. When her father died, Floriant and Florete became the rulers of Greece and Constantinople. At the end of their lives, the joined Morgan le Fay (Floriant's foster-mother) in her otherworldly castle. [Floriant]

FLORI

Guinevere's sister in Heinrich von dem Türlin's Diu Crône. Named as Gawain's sweetheart, she (along with the other ladies at Arthur's court) failed in a chastity test. She had another sister named Lenomie of Alexandria. [Heinrich]

FLORIANT

A knight, briefly of Arthur's court, who is the hero of the thirteenth century French romance Floriant et Florete. His father, King Eliadus of Sicily, was murdered by a treacherous seneschal, Maragoz, while Floriant was still in his mother's womb. Floriant's mother, fleeing from Maragoz, gave birth to Floriant in a forest. Morgan le Fay spirited the child to safety and raised him in her castle at Mongibel (an enfances that parallels that of LANCELOT). When he came of age, he left Mongibel to seek adventure. He saved Queen Alemandine of the White City from a monster, rescued a collection of Arthur's knights from the prison of the tyrant Moradas, killed some giants, and had several other adventures, culminating in his victory at a tournament at Arthur's court. Eventually, he learned that his mother was still under siege from Maragoz, and he convinced Arthur to assist in the rescue. Maragoz secured the alliance of Emperor Filimenis of Constantinople. The armies met in Sicily. Floriant fell in love with Florete, Filimenis's daughter. Defeating Maragoz in single combat, Floriant ended the war and saw his father's murderer executed. Floriant and Florete married, became king and queen of Sicily, and had a son named Froart. Accused of inactivity (like EREC), Floriant abandoned his throne and embarked with his wife on another series of adventures, ending with the rescue of Rome from a Saracen invasion. When Filimenis died, Floriant became Emperor of Constantinople and Greece. At the end of their lives, Floriant and Florete joined Morgan le Fay in her enchanted castle, where Arthur was to be brought after the final battle. [*Floriant*]

FLORIDAS[1]

Lord of the Narrow Borderlands. He joined Arthur's early war against the Saxons. [*Livre*]

FLORIDAS[2]

A knight who fought in Arthur's campaign to take the city of Rome. He accompanied Sir Florence and Gawain on their supply mission which turned into a full battle against a Roman brigade. During the capture of Rome, Sir Floridas led a battalion of soldiers against the Roman armies. [*Allit, Malory*]

FLORIE[1]

In Wirnt von Grafenberg's *Wigalois*, the wife of Gawain and mother of Wigalois. A Syrian queen, she lived with her uncle Joram, who brought Gawain from Arthur's court. Gawain fell in love with Florie immediately, and married her. After remaining with her for several months, he left to return to Arthur's court. When he tried to find his way back to Florie, he lacked a magical belt necessary to enter the land, and was never able to return to her. Florie raised Wigalois virtuously. After he left her to seek adventures, she died from heartbreak at the loss of her husband and son. Her counterpart in Renaut de Bâgé's *The Fair Unknown* is BLANCHEMAL. [*Wirnt*]

FLORIE[2]

The Queen of Kanadic, loved by Ilinot, Arthur's son. When Ilinot was killed in her service, Florie died of sorrow. Her land was inherited by her sister, Queen Kloudite. [*Wolfram, PleierG*]

FLORIE[2] OF LUNEL

A beautiful maiden who served the Grail Family. [*Wolfram*]

FLORIEN

One of Arthur's knights. [*Renaut*]

FLORIMELL

A maid whom Arthur, Britomart, and Guyon saw pursued by a lustful forester. Arthur and Guyon set out to rescue her. During her flight, she sought refuge in the cottage of a witch. The witch's son tried to rape her, but she escaped. The witch then sent a monster after her, but she eluded it by rowing out into the ocean. The owner of the boat, a fisherman, was asleep in the boat. He awoke and tried to rape Florimell. Her screams brought the assistance of the sea god Proteus, who took her to the bottom of the ocean. When Florimell refused to become Proteus's mistress, he imprisoned her. She was freed from the prison by her true love, Marinell, and was joyously united with him.

The witch's monster had taken Florimell's girdle, which the witch used to create a "False Flormiell" out of snow. The False Florimell became the *amie* of the witch's son, but she was carried away by a peasant named Braggadocchio, who became her "champion." She caused jealousy and dissention among several knights and friends. She eventually melted when she stood next to the real Florimell. [*Spenser*]

FLORINCA

A lady saved by Tristan the Younger (Tristan's son) from her cad of a husband. [*DueTris*]

FLORINE[1]

Great-grandmother of Sir Guiron the Courteous. She was the wife of Febus and the mother of Lannor, Niatar, Altan, Siraouc, and Argons. [*Palamedes*]

FLORINE[2]

Sister of Palamedes and daughter of Esclabor the Unknown. The Knight of the Castle of Three Roses died for her love. [*Palamedes*]

FLORIS

A knight captured and imprisoned, along with his brother Alexander, by Eskilabon of Belamunt. He was rescued by his uncle, Gilan, and Arthur's Sir Garel. In reward, he fought alongside Garel in a war against King Ekunaver of Kanadic. His father was Duke Retan of Pergalt. [*PleierG*]

FLORISDELFA

A sorceress taught by Merlin who became enamored of Tristan. She sent him wondrous presents, such as a herd of enchanted horses and a crystal tower drawn across the sea by elephants that breathed fire from their eyes. When she was how beautiful Isolde, her competition, was, she threw herself from the tower to her death. [*DueTris*]

FLOUDEHUEG

A seaport in Britain where, in the old French Lancelot tales, Lancelot arrived as a young man to be knighted by King Arthur. Suggestions for the location of Floudehueg include Hudan Fleot and Weymouth. [*LancLac, VulgLanc*]

FLOWER OF LYONESSE

The name by which Merlin, predicting the knight who would free the valley Servage, referred to Sir TRISTAN. [*Palamedes*]

FLOWERS OF THE WILDERNESS

A duchy ruled by Duke Ammilot under King Ekunaver, Arthur's enemy. [*PleierG*]

FLUALIS

A Saracen king in Jerusalem. He was the husband of Subine. Merlin visited him, invisible, and helped him interpret a disturbing dream. Merlin predicted correctly that he would be conquered by Christians, would covert, and would become the grandfather of scores of Christian knights. [*VulgMer*]

FLURATRONE

The kingdom ruled by a fairy who married Sir Gauriel. [*Konrad*]

FLURDAMURS

Perceval's paternal aunt; daughter of Gandin and Schoette; and sister of Galoes, Gahmuret, and Limmire. Flurdamurs married King Kingrisin of Ascalun and became the mother of King Vergulaht and Antikonie. [*Wolfram*]

FLÚRENT

Mother of Isolde and King Engres of Ireland in the Icelandic *Saga af Tristram ok Ísodd*. She wanted to marry her daughter to Tristan, but Tristan insisted that she marry King Mark. In other romances, she is called ISOLDE. [*SagaTI*]

FLURSENESEPHIN

The daughter of King Leigamar of Sorgarda and the beloved of Sir Fiers of Arramis. During a tournament at Sorgarda, she boasted of Fiers's prowess to Quebeleplus, her younger sister. To humble her sister, Quebeleplus begged Gawain, who was attending the tournament, to defeat Fiers in combat. Gawain complied. Flursenesephin was offered to Gawain, who went on to win the tournament, but Gawain convinced Leigamar to award her to Sir Quoikos, one of Gawain's comrades. She later failed a chastity test at Arthur's court. Her counterpart in Wolfram von Eschenbach's *Parzival* is named OBIE. [*Heinrich*]

FOITENANT

The nickname of Tristan's foster-father RUAL. It signifies "one who keeps faith." [*Gottfried*]

FOIX

A region in France owned by Lancelot. Lancelot made Sir Plenorius the earl of Foix in return for Plenorius's support in the battles against King Arthur. [*Malory*]

FOLE

Arthur's royal treasurer. During the False Guinevere episode, Sir Daguenet, Arthur's fool, took over the administration of Arthur's court. Daguenet depleted the funds in the royal treasury. When Fole reproved Daguenet for overspending, Daguenet killed him. [*Prophecies*]

FONTANE LA SALVÆSCHE ("Wild Fountain")

A forest fountain, next to which Perceval defeated Duke Orilus of Lalander in combat. It was the residence of Perceval's hermit uncle, Trevrizent, who received and educated Perceval. [*Wolfram*]

FOODLE

In Henry Fielding's parody *The Tragedy of Tragedies*, one of Arthur's attendants. He joined a rebellion against Arthur led by Lord Grizzle. [*Fielding*]

FORBIDDEN HILL

A fortress near the Perilous Forest. The Forbidden Hill was established by Sir Eloides, a cruel knight who kidnapped and wed the daughter of Esclamor of the Red City. The Forbidden Hill was her protection, and Eloides killed any knight who tried to approach. His victims were buried in the Small Charity abbey. Eloides was eventually slain by Sir Bors, but not before he extracted a promise from Bors to continue defending the Forbidden Hill. Bors agreed, on the condition that he imprison rather than slay any Knight of the Round Table. Against his will, Bors defeated and imprisoned Gawain, Yvain, and roughly a dozen other Round Table companions, before he was finally defeated—and relieved of his duty—by his cousin Lancelot. [*VulgLanc*]

FORD OF ADVENTURES [*Gué d'Aventures*]

The location of a tournament won by Gawain. Gawain received such honor for his victory that the Maiden of the Narrow Passage, who had never seen Gawain, fell in love with him. [*Vengeance*]

FORD OF BLOOD [*Gués del Sanc*]

A ford in Scotland where a relatively small number of Arthur's men, led by Sir Lancelot, defeated a large force of Saxons and put them to flight. The Saxons were led by King Hargadabran. Lancelot fought like a man possessed in the battle, and Hargadabran's brother, Atramont, was captured. [*LancLac, VulgLanc*]

FORD OF THE FOREST [*Aigue de la Forest*]

A ford where Bors, after stealing Arthur's horse, defeated Sagremor, Bedivere, Lucan, and Kay, taking their horses as well. [*VulgLanc*]

FORD OF THE WOODS

A ford that Sir Garengaus the Strong vowed to guard in the service of King Brandegorre's daughter. [*VulgLanc*]

FORDUCORZ

A knight present at the tournament of Sorgarda, which Gawain won. [*Heinrich*]

FOREI

A country ruled by the Lord of Serre, who died with no male heir. Inheritance of Forei became the subject of a feud between the Lord's daughters, Sgoidamur and Amurfina. Gawain eventually decided the conflict in Sgoidamur's favor. [*Heinrich*]

FOREIGN LAND [*Terre Forraine*]

See STRANGE LAND.

FOREIGN PORT

The home of Faran, a giant slain by Nascien. [*VulgEst*]

FOREST OF ADVENTURES

The forest near Cardigan, mentioned by Chrétien, where Arthur's held his annual hunt for the white stag. The thirteenth-century *Lancelot do Lac* says that a false report was circulated that Lancelot had been killed in the Forest; this report caused the death of Lancelot's friend, Galehaut. Another Forest of Adventures, also called ARROY, is mentioned by Malory. [*ChretienE, LancLac*]

FOREST OF BRAMBLES [*Forest de l'Espinoie*]

A wood by the city of Caranges in Scotland. Gawain, his father Lot, and his brothers Agravain, Gaheris, and Gareth crossed it on the way to fight Saxons in Arestel. [*VulgMer*]

FOREST OF MISADVENTURES

A dangerous forest along the Devil's Road. Arthur's Duke Galescalain of Clarence transversed the forest on his way to the Valley of No Return. [*VulgLanc*]

FOREST OF NO RETURN [*Forest Sans Retour*]

A wood called the PERILOUS FOREST until Guinebal (Lancelot's uncle) fell in love with a local lady and created the Magic Dance, which trapped all passers-by. The lady, called the Wise Lady of the Forest of No Return, was the mother of Agraveil and aunt of Elinadas, two knights in Arthur's service. The forest was also called the LOST FOREST. [*VulgMer*]

FOREST OF SERPENTS

A British forest abundant in snakes. It contained the Giant's Tower and the Spring of Healing, where Palamedes defeated Sir Atamas and rescued Gawain. In another adventure in the forest, Perceval saved a maiden from Sagremor and the Ugly Hero. [*PostQuest*]

FOREST OF SHADOWS

The home of the Red Knight slain by Perceval. [*Perlesvaus*]

FOREST OF THE PINE

A wood where Arthur hunted. [*Contin1*]

FOREST OF THE THREE PERILS

A forest in Gorre visited by Lancelot during his quest to rescue Guinevere from Meleagant. [*VulgLanc*]

FORMIDABLE KNIGHT [*Outredouté*]

An evil knight in *Meraugis de Portlesguez* and the *Livre d'Artus* whose evil brother, Greomar, was killed by Sagremor. In response, the Formidable Knight besieged the Castle of Ladies, which Sagremor had taken from Greomar and given to Sir Laudon. Gawain defeated the Formidable Knight and lifted the siege. The Formidable Knight then apparently resumed his custom of attacking ladies and murdering knights. Finally, the Formidable Knight defeated and removed an eye from Sir Laquis of Lampagrés. Meraugis of Portlesguez, Laquis's friend, tracked the Formidable Knight down and killed him. [*Raoul, Livre*]

FORMIS OF ARMS

A duke who ruled the Turning Isle. Formis and his four knights guarded the lady Abinors, Formis's lover, who had been imprisoned on the island by Merlin. Arthur, Gawain, Yder, and Urien came to the Turning Isle and defeated Formis and his companions in combat. [*Livre*]

FORS GRAVIERS

An Irish castle in which Gawain, during his quest to conquer Rigomer castle, was robbed and imprisoned by Lord Gaudionés. After four days, he was freed by Lorie, his fairy girlfriend. [*Merveil*]

FORTIMES

One of Perceval's eleven paternal uncles in *Perlesvaus*. He was the ninth son of Gais the Large, the brother of Alain, and the lord of the Crimson Heath. [*Perlesvaus*]

FORTRESS

The rather banal name for the castle owned by the Count of Valigues, whose daughter was championed by Hector. [*VulgLanc*]

FORTRESS OF MARVELS

A British fortress in which Peredur had an adventure. Peredur was lead to the fortress by one of his cousins, who was in the guise of a hag. Upon reaching the fortress, Peredur found it deserted except for an enchanted *gwyddbwyll* set (a chess-like game) which he threw into a river after it continually defeated him. Peredur's cousin showed up again in various disguises and eventually pointed him to the Hags of Gloucester, whom Peredur was fated to destroy in revenge for the death of another cousin. A similar event takes place in the Didot-*Perceval* at CHESSBOARD CASTLE. [*Peredur*]

FORTUNE[1]

Fortune is often personified as a woman in Arthurian romance; "Lady" Fortune and "Lady" Love are often named as the controllers of knights' destinies. In Heinrich von dem Türlin's *Diu Crône*, however, Lady Fortune appears as a corporeal being. She ruled the land of Ordohorht along with her son, Luck. Gawain visited her splendid palace and found her sitting on a rotating wheel. She provided Gawain with a magic ring that, as long as Arthur wore it, would protect his court from all harm. Her magic also fashioned a belt worn by Sir Fimbeus but later taken by Gawain. She employed a burgrave named Aanzim. [*Heinrich*]

FORTUNE[2]

A castle in Wales where Lancelot slew a knight. [*ProsTris*]

FOUCAIRE [*Forcaire*]

A pirate who inhabited the Rock of the Perilous Port. He was slain by Pompey. His former abode was used by Mordrains during an adventure at sea. [*VulgEst*]

FOUCHIER

A squire present at King Mark of Cornwall's tournament at Lancien. [*Contin4*]

FOUL HEATHEN

A malevolent pagan lord in the Serbo-Russian *Povest' o Tryshchane*. He was known to greet cordially any knight who arrived at his island. At night, however, the Foul Heathen would viciously torture him. Tristan learned of these customs and traveled to the Foul Heathen's island. When the Foul Heathen discovered the identity of his visitor, he did not enforce the custom. Later, he reconsidered, and had his knights seize Tristan, who was unarmed. Palamedes happened by and gave Tristan a sword. The two knights together slew all of the Foul Heathen's warriors. The Foul Heathen himself escaped by fleeing into a church. [*Povest*]

FOUNTAIN OF ADVENTURES

A fountain in the forest of Darnantes. Tristan and Kahedins fought Lamorat next to the fountain. [*Tavola*]

FOUNTAIN OF INFERTILITY [*Fontaine Brahaigne*]

A magical spring in Logres which sterilized any woman drinking from it. It was once visited by Merlin and Governal. An inscription on the stone foretold a meeting of Galahad, Lancelot, and Tristan at the fountain, where they would see the Questing Beast. [*ProsTris*]

FOUNTAIN OF MARVELS[1] [*Fontaine des Merveilles*]

A fountain where Arthur's Sir Meriadeuc found an enchanted sword. The sword was stained with blood that would not come clean. A knight named Gaus, who languished nearby, had been wounded with the sword and would only heal when struck a second time by the purest of knights. Meriadeuc eventually healed him in this manner, and when he did so, the sword came clean and Meriadeuc found his own name (he had previously been called the Knight with the Two Swords) written on the blade. [*Meriadeuc*]

FOUNTAIN OF MARVELS[2]

A magical spring on the Island of the Fountain in the Prose *Tristan*, identical to the fountain in the forest of Broceliande in Chrétien's *Erec*. The Fountain of Marvels was guarded by Pharant, who was killed at the fountain by Tristan. [*ProsTris*]

FOUNTAIN OF THE DRAGON

A fountain in desert of Medilontas in Lyonesse, where Meliadus met a sorceress called Wise Damsel and was kidnapped. The location appears in the Prose *Tristan* but is not named except in *La Tavola Ritonda*. Merlin erected a stone by the fountain and prophesied that Lancelot, Tristan, and Galehaut would gather there. [*Tavola*]

FOUNTAIN OF THE LION

A Cornish fountain that was the site of several unfortunate episodes involving Tristan's family. The fountain was named after Cichoriades, an ancestor of Tristan, saw a lion dive into the fountain and emerge dry. The Fountain of the Lion was the site where King Mark of Cornwall murdered his brother Pernehan; where Tristan killed his cousin Archeman; where Mark abandoned his infant son Meraugis; and where Lancelot fought Bleoberis. [*ProsTris*, *TristanoR*]

FOUNTAIN OF THE PINE

A spring where Calinan, son of Guiron the Courteous, defeated several of Arthur's knights. Shortly afterwards, Calinan was killed by Palamedes. [*Palamedes*]

FOUNTAIN OF THE SHADE

A Cornish fountain where Tristan dueled the King with a Hundred Knights. [*ProsTris*]

FOUNTAIN OF THE STAG

A spring in Cornwall that was often visited by Isolde. [*ProsTris*]

FOUNTAIN OF THE YOUTH

During a speech in Heinrich von dem Türlin's *Diu Crône*, Gawain alludes to an adventure in which he drank from the Fountain of Youth in the garden of Dochel. [*Heinrich*]

FOUR BEARDS

The nickname of Bruant, a king who served Arthur. [*Meriadeuc*]

FRAGUS

Father of Guiron the Courteous. He was the son of Argons and the grandson of Febus. [*Palamedes*]

FRAIDONS

A heathen warrior who fought against King Angusel of Scotland in the battle of Caranges. [*Arthour*]

FRANCE [*Francia, Fraunce, Frauns*]

France becomes the playing field for a number of important events in Arthurian romance. In most legends, France is used synonymously with GAUL.

Before Rome subjugated Gaul in the first century BC, France was a collection of independent territories ruled by Celtic clans. There were literally hundreds of different tribes of varying origins. The lack of a Gaulish "high king," or centralized ruler, was to Rome's advantage. Caesar oversaw the conquest of France in 58 BC. Rome ruled France for the next 500 years, building a vast infrastructure and protecting the territory from barbarian invasions.

With the collapse of the Roman empire in the fifth century came legions of Frankish, Gothic, and Burgundian invaders. France was splintered, united, and splintered again.

During the Arthurian period, the Franks had established themselves as the most prominent rulers. These included King Childeric I and his son King Clovis I. The latter ruled from 481 to 511, which would place him in the "Arthurian period." After Clovis's death, France again collapsed into numerous territories that were not re-united until the time of Charlemagne in the eighth century.

According to Geoffrey of Monmouth, Arthur conquered France from Frollo during his reign. A number of other texts likewise tell us that it was under the rule of Arthur, and indeed, it seems that Arthurian heroes spent as much time here as anywhere. Many knights and kings that owed allegiance to Arthur came from Brittany. King Ban of Benoic, King Bors of Gannes, King Claudas of the Land Laid Waste, and the knights Lancelot, Hector, Blamor of Gannes, and Bleoberis of Gannes, as well as many others, all came from French lands. Arthur fought his war with the Lucius the Roman on French soil, in Normandy and Burgundy. The Prose *Tristan* features a King Faramon of France who apparently owed his allegiance to Uther Pendragon. In the Stanzaic *Morte Arthur* and in Malory, the country seems to belong to Lancelot, since he appoints Lionel its king when Arthur and Lancelot go to war.

In Welsh legend, three of Arthur's warriors are named as the "King of France": Iona, Paris, and Gwilenhin. Arthur apparently has command of the country, for he summons all France's warriors before the epic hunting of Twrch Trwyth. Der Pleier calls France's king Linefles. [*Culhwch, GeoffHR, Layamon, ProsTris, Stanz, Malory*]

FRANCHEGEL

One of the noble Byzantine warriors that Alexander brought to Britain from Constantinople. He fought for Arthur in the battle against the traitorous Angres of Windsor. [*ChretienC*]

FRANGILES

A Saxon duke who led a battalion of soldiers against Arthur at the battle of Clarence. [*VulgMer*]

FREDERIK

The King of Friesland who allied with Mordred during the latter's rebellion against Arthur. [*Allit*]

FREELENK [*Frelent*]

A Saxon warrior slain by Arthur at the battle of Carhaix. [*VulgMer, Arthour*]

FREGOLO

A field in front of the Castle of the Enchantresses in Ireland where Anguish (Isolde's father) called an Easter Tournament during Tristan's first visit to the country. [*Tavola*]

FREGULLA VITTORIOSO

The fortress belonging to Oris l'Aspro, a knight slain by Tristan. It was encircled by a deep river called the Tendorubia. [*Tavola*]

FRENICAS [*Ferican, Fernicans*]

A Saxon king who joined Rions in the invasion of Camilyard. Arthur killed him at the battle of Aneblayse. [*VulgMer, Arthour*]

FRES MARÉS ("Fresh Pond")

A large Irish castle belonging to a knight named Bedionés. Lancelot lodged at the fortress on his way to the castle of Rigomer. [*Merveil*]

FRIAM OF VERMENDOYS

A duke and an ally or vassal of Gawain's wife, Orgeluse. He was captured by Arthur's knights at the battle of Logres. [*Wolfram*]

FRIANS

A boorish and treacherous prince of Punterteis in Der Pleier's *Garel von dem blühenden Tal*. He was apparently once involved in the theft of Gawain's horse. He could have freed Duke Eskilabon of Belamunt from an obligation to guard a garden, but did not keep his word. Der Pleier may have taken his name from Wolfram's FRIAM, although the theft of Gringolet to which he alludes is committed in Wolfram by URJANS. [*PleierG*]

FRIESLAND [*Fres, Frisia*]

A province of the north Netherlands, on the North Sea. Wace says that it was part of Arthur's empire, and Layamon adds that it was ruled by Kailin. The Alliterative

Morte Arthure names its king as Frederik, who joined Mordred's rebellion against Arthur. [*Wace, Layamon, Allit*]

FRIGENE

A Knight of the Round Table. [*PleierG*]

FRIMUTEL

Perceval's maternal grandfather. Frimutel was the son of Titurel, the brother of Rischoyde, and the father of Anfortas, Trevrizent, Repanse de Schoye, Schoysiane, and Herzeloyde. Like his father and his eldest son (Anfortas), Frimutel was a Grail King, but he abandoned his post to seek adventure. He died in a joust over a woman. [*Wolfram*]

FRION [*Frisons*]

The King of Dessemoume in Ireland in the French *Les Merveilles de Rigomer*. Lancelot rescued Frion's daughter, Martha, from a pack of kidnappers, for which Frion offered Lancelot the girl and the kingdom. When Lancelot refused, Frion attempted to trick him into remaining in Dessemoume, but Lancelot recognized the ruse and departed. Frion later helped Arthur's men conquer Rigomer castle. [*Merveil*]

FRISTINES

An infidel count of Janfuse who served Feirefiz, Perceval's half-brother. [*Wolfram*]

FRIULI

A European city near Acquilea through which Perceval's uncle Trevrizent traveled. [*Wolfram*]

FROART

Son of Sir Floriant and Lady Florete. [*Floriant*]

FROCIN

A mischievous little hunchback dwarf who lived at the court of Mark of Cornwall. He seemed to have a fair knowledge of astronomy and ability with prophecy. He knew of Tristan's and Isolde's affair and took care to make Mark aware of it, deriving glee from the trouble he caused. He twice set up the lovers to be caught by Mark—both times, Mark came to disbelieve the dwarf in favor of his wife and nephew. The dwarf eventually got drunk, announced that Mark had the ears of a horse, and had his head swiped off by Mark as a result. He appears in Eilhart's *Tristrant* as ACQUITAIN and in Gottfried's *Tristan* as MELOT. [*Beroul*]

FROLLE OF THE OUT ISLES

A knight was rescued by Lamorat from four knights who had attacked him all at once. Frolle left in a huff when Lamorat refused to reveal his name. Gawain abducted Frolle's lady and was defeated in combat by Frolle.

Lamorat, witnessing Gawain's defeat, engaged Frolle to protect the honor of the Round Table. Frolle was killed in the duel. His brother Bellyas tried to avenge his death and failed. [*Malory*]

FROLLO [*Floires, Flollo, Follon, Freol, Froles, Froll(e)(s), Thomas Flollo, Fullon*]

In Geoffrey of Monmouth's *Historia*, the steward of France under Emperor Leo of Rome. When Arthur decided to conquer Gaul, Frollo raised an army to oppose him but suffered a crushing defeat. Arthur beat him back to Paris and would have starved Frollo's army, but he agreed to Frollo's proposal to decide the war in a single combat between Frollo and Arthur. The battle was long and difficult, and Arthur was very nearly defeated, but he eventually killed Frollo with Excalibur. Arthur then subjugated Gaul. In the *Gesta Regum Britanniae*, it is Merlin's magic that saves Arthur during his fight with Frollo. Robert of Gloucester places the battle between Arthur and Frollo on an island.

The Vulgate *Merlin* and *Lancelot* locate this story in a larger saga of Arthur's battles against King Claudas and the Roman Pontius Anthony. Here, Frollo, the emperor or duke of Germany, Lamahna, or Gauna, join Anthony and Claudas in a war against Arthur, Ban and Bors. Arthur was victorious. Much later, Frollo challenged Arthur for control of Gaul with the results given by Geoffrey. Frollo's son, Samaliel of Gauna, was knighted by Galahad. *Palamedes* names Frollo's father as Ariohan. [*GeoffHR, Wace, Layamon, VulgLanc, VulgMer, PostQuest, Palamedes, ProsTris, Gesta, RobertG*]

FRONIA

In Thomas Hughes' *The Misfortunes of Arthur*, a lady in Guinevere's service who dissuaded the queen—who had committed bigamy with Mordred—from a plot to murder Arthur. [*HughesT*]

FULBERTA

According to *La Tavola Ritonda*, when Charlemagne came to Britain, he found a statues of Galahad, Amoroldo, and other warriors in front of Leverzep. One of his noblemen took the sword hanging around Amoroldo's statue and named it "Fulberta," meaning "well-sharpened." [*Tavola*]

FÚLCUS

A heathen king who led raids into King Mark's England in the Icelandic *Saga af Tristram ok Ísodd*. Tristan met him in combat, but with a small force. Near defeat, Tristan swore before God to end his affair with Isolde if he should prevail. Fúlcus was soon dead, and Tristan left England for good to assume the throne of Spain. [*SagaTI*]

FULGENTIUS

According to Geoffrey of Monmouth, a king of Britain in the third or second century BC. He succeeded his father, King Cherin, and was succeeded by his brothers, Kings

Eldad and Andragius. According to John of Fordon, Fulgentius was an ancestor of Lot and Gawain. [*GeoffHR*, *JohnF*]

FULGIN

A heathen king slain by Arthur's Sir Galescalain at the battle of Diana Bridge. [*Arthour*]

FUROR

A madman whose mother, Occassion, encouraged him to attack passing knights. Sir Guyon came across Furor beating the squire Phedon. Guyon bound and gagged Occassion, and captured Furor. Guyon later allowed the brash knight Pyrochles to free Furor, who beat Pyrochles to unconsciousness. [*Spenser*]

G

GABARINS OF ASSIGARZIONTE

An infidel count who served Feirefiz, Perceval's half-brother. [*Wolfram*]

GABENIS

A prince from Punturteis, and thus probably a vassal of King Brandelidelin. Perceval encountered him in a forest, and Gabenis directed Perceval to the residence of Perceval's uncle, Trevrizent. [*Wolfram*]

GABRIONELLO

An old knight of Uther Pendragon's order who inhabited Castle Sidravalle in the Perilous Valley. He was subject to two tyrannical giants whom Tristan and Lancelot slew, freeing Gabrionello from their rule. [*Tavola*]

GADARA

One of the many lands allied with Lucius the Roman, Arthur's opponent in the Roman War. [*Allit*]

GADIFFER

An Arthurian knight. [*SyreGaw*]

GADRAN

A Knight of the Round Table, related somehow to Lancelot. He participated in the Grail Quest. [*PostQuest*]

GADRAS THE BLACK

A knight slain by Gawain. He was the uncle of Caradoc of the Dolorous Tower. When Caradoc captured Gawain, Caradoc's mother made Gawain suffer for Gadras's death. [*VulgLanc*]

GADRASOLAIN [*Gadresalain*]

The lover of the sorceress Gamille, with whom he lived in the Saxon Rock in Scotland. Gadrasolain had been in love with another woman before Gamille, but Gamille threw her into a prison and took Gadrasolain for herself. When Lancelot conquered the Saxon Rock, he killed Gadrasolain and freed Gadrasolain's former paramour. [*LancLac, VulgLanc*]

GAFFAR THUMB

In Henry Fielding's parody *The Tragedy of Tragedies*, the father of Arthur's warrior Tom Thumb. Merlin created Tom for Gaffar and his wife when the couple were unable to conceive a child of their own. [*Fielding*]

GAGUNNE

The homeland of Kuraus with the Brave Heart. [*UlrichZ*]

GAHALANTYNE

A Knight of the Round Table and relative of Lancelot. In a tournament against King Bagdemagus, Gahalantyne fought on the side of the King of North Wales. Lancelot, on Bagdemagus's side, beat Gahalantyne bloody. When Mordred and Agravain accused Lancelot and Guinevere of treason, Gahalantyne pledged his support to Lancelot and helped him to rescue Guinevere from the stake. In return for his support, Lancelot made him duke of Auvergne.

After Arthur's death, Gahalantyne joined Lancelot in the abbey of Glastonbury and lived as a hermit until Lancelot's death. Following Lancelot's interment, Gahalantyne returned to his own lands. [*Malory*]

GAHART

A castle ruled by Giramphiel, a goddess who hated Gawain. The unsuspecting Gawain lodged at Gahart one night, and Giramphiel sent him into a perilous combat against a dragon. [*Heinrich*]

GAHERIS[1] [*Agavez, Ahariés, Caherihés, Gaciés, Gadriet, Gahereit, *Gaheriet, Gaherjet, Gaherss, Galeres, Galerot, Gariens, Gar(r)iés, Kaheret, Keheriet, Waheriés*]

Gawain's brother. He was the son of King Lot and either Belisent and Morgause, and his other brothers included Agravain, Gareth, and Mordred. In Der Pleier's *Meleranz*, his parents are Anthonje and the King of Gritenland. The earliest form of his name is so similar to the earliest form of GARETH that the two brothers may have originally been the same character. Chrétien de Troyes is the first writer to mention him, although scholars have suggested a derivation from the Welsh GWEIR. In Wolfram, he is a cousin rather than a brother to Gawain. The Vulgate romances are the first to give Gaheris a series of his own adventures, which are expanded in the Post-Vulgate and in Malory.

The Vulgate legends describe him with a prowess that rivals or exceeds Gawain's. In the Vulgate *Merlin*, he defects with Gawain and his brothers from Lot's court to Arthur's, battling hordes of Saxons along the way. In the Post-Vulgate and Malory, however, he arrives at Arthur's court as Gawain's squire and serves his brother in his first quests. Either way, Arthur eventually knighted him, and he enjoyed a number of adventures, some of which were prophesied by a madman at Arthur's court named Marins. Gaheris freed his brothers from Lord Sorneham of

Newcastle, liberated Gawain and Morholt from the Rock of Maidens, killed a giant named Aupatris, befriended Perceval, and supported Tristan against King Mark of Cornwall. He sometimes quarreled with his brothers Agravain and Mordred, who lacked his nobility. Malory says that he married the damsel Lynet.

His noble deeds were offset by a number of regrettable murders, including those of King Pellinore, who had killed King Lot; of his own mother Morgause, when he found her in bed with Pellinore's son Lamorat; and of Lamorat. In the slaying of Pellinore and Lamorat, he was joined by Gawain.

Gaheris unsuccessfully attempted to dissuade Mordred and Agravain from exposing the affair between Lancelot and Guinevere. However, he dutifully stood guard when Guinevere was to be burned at the stake. As Lancelot rescued her, he killed Gaheris and Gareth, prompting Gawain's later hatred for Lancelot. [ChretienP, VulgLanc, VulgQuest, VulgMer, PostMer, PostQuest, PostMort, Arthour, Stanz, Malory]

GAHERIS[2]

An Arthurian knight from the city of Carhaix. His entire career seems to consist of being imprisoned in various places—the Dolorous Prison, the Valley of No Return, and in the Dolorous Tower—and eventually being freed from each by Lancelot. He was put out of his misery when he ate an apple poisoned by Sir Avarlan, intended for Gawain. Guinevere, who had hosted the dinner, was accused of murder by Gaheris's brother, Mador of the Gate, but was acquitted by Lancelot. The poisoning death is transferred to PATRICE by Malory. [LancLac, VulgLanc, VulgMort]

GAHERIS[3]

A knight from North Wales who occupied his the Round Table seat of his slain namesake, Gaheris of Orkney, and who fought for Arthur during the war with Lancelot. [PostMort]

GAHEVIEZ

The home of Ither, Arthur's cousin. A forge in Gaheviez produced a stout sword wielded by Ither and then by Perceval. The sword shattered in Perceval's combat against Feirefiz. [Wolfram]

GAHILLET OF HOCHTRUASCH

A Knight of the Round Table. [HartmannE]

GAHMURET [Gachmuret]

Perceval's father in Wolfram's Parzival. He was the son of King Gandin and Queen Schoette of Anjou, and the brother of Galoes, Flurdamurs, and Limmire. When Gandin died and Galoes inherited the kingdom, Gahmuret set out in search of adventure. He traveled to Arabia—where he served the Baruc of Baghdad in the war against Ipomidon and Pompeius of Babylon—throughout Africa,

and finally to the nation of Zazamanc. There, he rescued Queen Belacane from an invasion of Scotsmen, apparently provoked because King Isenhart of Azagouc, their friend, had died for her love. During the war, Gahmuret fell in love with Queen Belacane—despite the fact that she was a Moor—and married her. They had a pie-bald son named Feirefiz.

Eventually, Gahmuret grew tired of domestic life with Belacane and sought adventure again. He deserted his wife and traveled to Wales, where he won honor in a tournament. For his victory, Queen Herzeloyde of Wales demanded him as her husband. Gahmuret's brother had recently perished, and Gahmuret's heart belonged to Ampflise, the Queen of France. Ampflise sent pages to Wales to woo Gahmuret back to France. However, a tribunal insisted that it was his duty to marry Herzeloyde, and he complied. After living with her for a brief time, he again—with her permission—left in search for adventure. When he departed, his wife was pregnant. He returned to the Baruc of Baghdad to defend him from another Babylonian invasion, and was killed by King Ipomidon of Niniveh.

His death was mourned by everyone, and nearly drove Herzeloyde mad. She gave birth to Perceval several weeks later. Because of the fate that befell her husband, Herzeloyde raised Perceval ignorant of chivalry and its perils.

Gahmuret's essential story is a retelling of the tale of BLIOCADRAN. As Perceval's father, he is replaced in later romances by ALAIN and PELLINORE. His name may be a variation of GOMERET, a land found in Chrétien's Erec (Bruce, 314n). [Wolfram]

GAHOR

A king who was a vassal of Arthur. Like the other lords at Arthur's court, his wife was found to be at least somewhat unfaithful by a magical drinking horn. [Biket]

GAIDOU [Gaidon]

A Saxon king who joined King Rions' invasion of Carmelide. He was slain by King Bors of Gannes at the battle of Aneblayse. [VulgMer, Arthour]

GAILAIN OF CORNWALL

One of five knights who tried to murder Agravain but were defeated by Agravain's brother, Gawain. [Contin3]

GAIN

Father of Arthur's knight Lernfras. [HartmannE]

GAIS THE LARGE [*Gais le Gros]

Perceval's grandfather in Perlesvaus. He inhabited the Hermits' Cross. His sons were Alain the Large (Perceval's father), Gosgallian, Brun Brandalis, Bertoles the Bald, Brandalus of Wales, Elinant of Escavalon, Calobrutus, Meralis, Fortimes of the Crimson Heath, Meliarman of Albanie, Galerian of the White Tower, and Aliban of the

Waste City. As Alain's father, he replaces BRON from the Robert de Boron cycle. [*Perlesvaus*]

GAIUS [*Caius*]

One of the Roman senate leaders who joined the army of Lucius mustering to oppose the arrival of King Arthur. The name probably resulted from a confusion in Geoffrey's list of senators: he mentions a GAIUS METELLUS COTTA, which Wace seems to have broken into three separate names and people. [*Wace, Layamon*]

GAIUS METELLUS COTTA

One of the Roman senators who became a war leader in Lucius's campaign against Arthur. He led a force of soldiers at the battle of Soissons. Found in Geoffrey of Monmouth, he is split by Wace in to GAIUS, METELLIUS, and COCTA. [*GeoffHR*]

GAIUS QUINTILLIANUS [*Gaynus, Gayous, Quintilian(us), Quencelin, Quyntalyn*]

A Roman warrior who was the nephew of the Roman Emperor Lucius. At the beginning of the war between Arthur and Rome, Arthur sent Gawain, Boso, and Guerin (or Gawain, Bors, Lionel, and Bedivere) as peace envoys to Lucius. During the talks, however, Gaius Quintillianus remarked that Britons were more skilled at bragging and threatening than at battle. Gawain, enraged at these comments, sliced off Gaius's head, thus starting a battle and the war. Gawain later killed Marcellus Mucius, a friend of Gaius, and bade him to tell Gaius, when he met him in hell, that there were indeed no people who were better at bragging than the Britons. The Vulgate *Merlin* calls him TITILIUS. [*GeoffHR, Wace, Layamon, Allit, Malory*]

GAL OF GALEFROI

A knight in Arthur's service. [*Meriadeuc*]

GALAAS

A fearsome giant, surnamed "the Moor" or "the Mighty," found in Heinrich von dem Türlin's *Diu Crône*. Galaas and his foster-father, a giant named Assiles, liked to terrorize surrounding countries, including the land owned by King Flois of the Green Island. On his way to assist Flois, Gawain defeated Galaas at his castle of Eigrun, freed Galaas's prisoners, and secured the giant's oath of fealty. He may be related to the giant GALAPAS found in other texts. [*Heinrich*]

GALABES [*Alaban*]

A fountain in the Welsh country of Gwent, near which Merlin had a home. The Galabes here is perhaps an allusion to the giant GALAPAS; it has also been suggested that Galabes is a variation of Galava, a northern province. Layamon calls it "Alaban," which suggests "Albany," an old name for Scotland. [*GeoffHR, Layamon*]

GALACIA

According to Malory, a land allied with Lucius the Roman. Warriors from Galacia participated in Lucius's war against Arthur. Malory may be indicating the ancient kingdom of Galatia in Asia Minor or the province of Galicia in Spain. [*Malory*]

GALADES OF CANELLE

A lady at Arthur's court who, like many others, failed a chastity test. [*Heinrich*]

GALAFORT [*Galefort*]

The first Christian stronghold in Britain. Celidoine, Nascien's son, converted Duke Ganor of Galafort, and the castle became a home for Joseph of Arimathea's followers. It was named after Galahad, Joseph's son, who was born there. It served as the home of the Grail until Alan and Joshua left Galafort and founded Corbenic. It the Vulgate *Lancelot*, it is owned by Meleagant's sister, although this may be a different castle. [*VulgLanc, VulgEst*]

GALAFRÉ[1] [*Calafer*]

A cruel pagan king who inhabited the land of King Mordrains. He resisted conversion to Christianity. When Mordrains disappeared, Galafré accused Nascien of murdering him, and he imprisoned Nascien and Nascien's young son, Celidoine. When God delivered Nascien from the prison, Galafré tried to kill Celidoine by hurling him from a tower. God's hands broke Celidoine's fall, and a lightning bolt swiftly incinerated Galafré and his castle. Galafré is a name common to non-Christian warriors in medieval sources. [*VulgEst*]

GALAFRÉ[2]

An Arthurian warrior found in Thomas Chestre's *Sir Launfal*. [*ChestreLvl*]

GALAGANDREIZ

The lord of the castle of Moreiz. He received the knights Kuraus, Orphilet, and the young Lancelot as his guests for a night's lodging. He was of uneven disposition, however—liable to fly into a rage at the slightest provocation—and for this reason, Kuraus and Orphilet were on edge. Thus, when Galagandreiz's young daughter offered herself to Kuraus and Orphilet, they declined. Lancelot, however, accepted gladly, and consequently incurred the lord's rage. Galagandreiz challenged Lancelot to a battle, in which each would take turns throwing daggers at the other until one of them died. Lancelot agreed, but was wounded in the arm from Galagandreiz's first throw. Unable to throw accurately on account of his wound, Lancelot instead rushed Galagandreiz and stabbed him with the dagger, killing him. Galagandreiz's daughter convinced his knights to recognize Lancelot as her husband and their new lord, but Lancelot remained at the castle only a short time.

It is probable that Galagandreiz comes from Hartmann's GALAGAUNDRIS, which, in turn, may be derived from Chrétien's GALEGANTIN. [UlrichZ]

GALAGAUNDRIS [Galarantins]

One of King Arthur's Knights of the Round Table, mentioned first by Hartmann von Aue. It is probable that he comes from Chrétien's GALEGANTIN, and he is probably the origin of Ulrich von Zatzikhoven's GALAGANDREIZ. [HartmannE, Heinrich]

GALAHAD¹ [Galaad, Galaç, Galade, Galas(so), Galat(h), Galeas, Galeatto, Galeazzo, Galeotto]

Son of Lancelot. He replaced Perceval as the Grail hero. As a knight, he embodied purity and virtue. The writer of the Vulgate *Queste del Saint Graal* probably invented him because no existing Arthurian knight could fit the lofty description that the author assigned to the Grail Knight— the divine warrior. It is widely accepted that the name came from *Galaad* or *Gilead* found in Genesis 31:48—the heap of rocks marking the boundary between the lands of Laban and Jacob, and signifying a kind of spiritual covenant. R. S. Loomis (*Grail*, 180) thought that the name may have been influenced by a variation of GAWAIN such as "Galaain."

Raised in a nunnery but considered the best knight in the world, Galahad represents a fusion of knighthood and theology; a warrior-monk whose only peer in Arthurian literature might be St. ILLTUD.

Galahad's basic story varies little from the Vulgate *Queste* to the Post-Vulgate to Malory. His arrival was prophesied from the time of Joseph of Arimathea. It was said that he would complete the Grail Quest and would end the other spiritual adventures in Britain. Descended from Nascien, Galahad was born after Elaine or Amite, the Fisher King's daughter, tricked Lancelot into sleeping with her. The episode caused a rift between Lancelot and Guinevere, and Lancelot therefore remained absent through most of Galahad's childhood.

Galahad spent his infancy in Corbenic, the Grail Castle, but was raised in an abbey in the forest of Camelot. When he came of age, Lancelot was summoned to the abbey to knight him. Galahad arrived at Camelot in the midst of miracles. He sat in the Round Table's Perilous Seat, and he pulled a sword (which had belonged to Sir Balin) from a block of marble. The Grail visited Arthur's companions, and the Grail Quest began. Galahad began the quest by finding a holy shield that had belonged to Joseph of Arimathea and King Mordrains.

He had innumerable adventures during the Grail Quest. In some of the most prominent, he ended the wicked customs of the Castle of Maidens, freed the castle Carcelois, destroyed the Castle of Treachery, helped repel King Mark of Cornwall's siege of Camelot, freed Moses (a former follower of Joseph of Arimathea) from a burning tomb, and performed several healings. As several hermits and sages predicted, he surpassed his father in both knightly prowess (defeating, among others, Lancelot, Gawain, Bors, Perceval, and Palamedes) and spirituality (he remained a sinless virgin all his life). He befriended a number of Knights of the Round Table, including Tristan and Palamedes. He spent six months on a barge with his father.

During the quest, he joined with Perceval and Bors, who were destined to become the other two successful Grail knights. The three knights found the ship of Solomon, where Galahad received the marvelous Sword with the Strange Hangings, which had belonged to King David of Israel. In time, the Grail knights were summoned to Corbenic, the Grail Castle, where Galahad repaired the Grail Sword and attended a Grail mass held by Joseph of Arimathea or his son Josephus. After he healed the Maimed King with some blood from the Bleeding Lance, Galahad and the others departed with the Grail for Sarras, a Middle-Eastern kingdom. There, the pagan King Escorant imprisoned them but freed them after a year. Escorant died, and the reluctant Galahad was chosen as the new king. After ruling a year, he witnessed spiritual marvels within the Grail and asked to die. God granted his wish: Galahad fell dead, and the Grail and Bleeding Lance were taken into heaven.

In a notable alternative to the tradition story of Galahad as a virgin, Wordsworth says that he resurrected and married the Egyptian Maid, a beautiful visitor to Arthur's court who had been wounded by Merlin.

Though considered by the *Queste* author the greatest knight of the Round Table, many critics have seen Galahad as characterless. He is less a man than a symbol in most romances, aloof from his Round Table fellows. His sole purpose is to complete the Grail Quest, and his success is pre-ordained. Galahad's pursuit of the quest therefore lacks suspense (by contrast, the adventures of Bors and Perceval are full of tests and perils). Because of these reasons, and because Galahad's spiritual code replaces the code of chivalry, which was the meat and drink of medieval audiences, later authors found it more of an obligation than a pleasure to write of Galahad. The author of *La Tavola Ritonda* remarks: "Everyone receives grace as a reward, but God also gave [Galahad] free grace...So before his shield had received one blow, he was called the best knight in the world because of the grace and works of God." In Tennyson, Galahad's complete spirituatlity is his failing, for Tennyson's ideal seemed to be the unification of the spiritual and the secular. [VulgLanc, VulgQuest, VulgEst, PostMort, PostQuest, Tavola, Malory, Wordsworth, TennIK]

GALAHAD²

Son of Joseph of Arimathea and Elyab who became the first Christian king of Wales. He was conceived after Joseph arrived in Britain, and was born in the Christian stronghold of Galafort, which was named after him. He grew up to be an excellent knight, and his brother Josephus invested him with the kingdom of Hoselice, which was renamed Gales, or Wales, in his honor. He married the daughter of the King of the Distant Isles and fathered Lyanor. According to the Vulgate *Estoire del Saint Graal*, his descendants were Urien and Yvain, but the thirteenth-century *Lancelot do Lac*, he is named as the ancestor of Ban, Lancelot, Pelles, and Alan. He was apparently buried outside of Wales; during his quest to rescue Guinevere from Meleagant, Lancelot found Galahad's tomb and raised the slab, and monks took Galahad's body to Wales. Lancelot fulfilled the prophecy that whoever opened the tomb would end the evil customs of Gorre. [*LancLac, VulgLanc, VulgEst*]

GALAHAD³

The birth name of LANCELOT. The Vulgate *Lancelot* tells us that Lancelot "lost" the name because of his affair with Guinevere, but passed it on to his pure son. Malory says that his name changed when he was christened by the Lady of the Lake. [*LancLac, VulgLanc, Malory*]

GALAHAD⁴

The Saxon king of the Land of the Grazing-Grounds, who joined King Rions' invasion of Carmelide. After Arthur defeated Rions' army at Aneblayse, Merlin wove a magical fog which made Galahad's army collide with the forces of Amant, another enemy of Arthur. The two armies decimated each other. [*VulgMer, Arthour*]

GALAHAD⁵

Son of the British King Hipomenes. Galahad was loved by his own sister. When he rejected her, she fell under the power of a demon, was impregnated, and accused Galahad of rape. Hipomenes executed Galahad, and the Questing Beast was later born of Galahad's sister. [*PostQuest*]

GALAHAD'S FOUNTAIN

A spring in the Perilous Forest. Before it was known by that name, it boiled constantly, and contained the head of King Lancelot, Lancelot's grandfather. Lancelot removed the head, but the fountain continued to boil until the Grail Quest, when Galahad plunged his hands into it and, because he had never known lust, caused it to cool. [*VulgQuest*]

GALAHAD'S MIRACLE

An abbey, formerly the UTHER PENDRAGON ABBEY but re-named during the Grail Quest. While Galahad was recuperating at the abbey, King Mark of Cornwall poisoned his drink. Another knight named Faram died, but Galahad miraculously survived. [*PostQuest*]

GALAHAL

A king who served Arthur. His sister married Sir Caradoc. [*Biket*]

GALAIDA

Kay's sweetheart in Heinrich von dem Türlin's *Diu Crône*. She failed two chastity tests, which humbled Kay, who had been making great sport of the other ladies who failed. Her sister and brother were the Duke and Duchess of Landrie. [*Heinrich*]

GALAIN OF RONNES

A duke who served Galehaut. Galain lent Gawain his shield to use in a battle against the Saxons in Scotland. [*LancLac, VulgLanc*]

GALAMANASAR [*Gabanasar*]

A pagan king, related to King Priam of Troy, who constructed a castle in Britain, dubbed the Treacherous Castle by St. Augustine. Galamanasor and his people remained steadfast pagans while Joseph of Arimathea converted the rest of Britain to Christianity. [*PostQuest, ProsTris*]

GALAMIDE

Sister of Gasozein of Dragoz. Her brother challenged Arthur for Guinevere. Galamide was a powerful fairy, and she supplied Gasozein with magnificent arms from the land of Lansgei. [*Heinrich*]

GALANGELLE OF KLUMESTER

During a speech in Heinrich von dem Türlin's *Diu Crône*, Gawain tells of how he slew Galangelle the giant. This episode, however, does not exist in surviving Arthurian romance. [*Heinrich*]

GALANTINS

A knight who joined Arthur's battle against the Saxons at Clarence. [*Livre*]

GALANTIVET [*Galentivet*]

Brother of Girflet and cousin of Lancelot. Gawain took him as his squire and protégé. When Sir Escanor the Handsome brought an accusation of murder against Gawain, and Gawain was reluctant to defend himself, Galantivet ambushed Escanor and wounded him. [*Girart*]

GALANTON [*Garanton*]

A castle where, in one of his first adventures, Perceval rescued Sir Patrides, who was chained to a block of stone. [*VulgLanc*]

GALANTYNE

Gawain's sword, according to Malory, which he used in the Roman War. The Alliterative *Morte Arthure* calls it GALUTH. [*Malory*]

GALAPAS [*Golapas*]

A giant that Arthur killed at the battle of Soissons (the final battle of the Roman War). When Galapas engaged Arthur, Arthur wielded Excalibur and cut off both of Galapas's legs at the knees, thus lowering him to an adequate height for beheading. His literary roots may cross paths with the giant GALAAS and the fountain of GALABES. [*Allit*, *Malory*]

GALARDONN

A young knight accidentally killed by Lancelot during a joust. [*Malory*]

GALAT

A lady at Arthur's court in Heinrich von dem Türlin's *Diu Crône*. Along with many others, she failed a chastity test. [*Heinrich*]

GALATH

A Welsh form of GALAHAD.

GALEC

Lancelot's son in the Serbo-Russian *Povest' o Tryshchane*. Though his name is similar to GALAHAD, he shares none of Galahad's characteristics or adventures. Lancelot and Tristan tried to rob him of his horse and armor, but he defeated Lancelot in combat. When he discovered that he had beaten his father, he retired to a monastery for the rest of his life. [*Povest*]

GALEDE [*Galide*]

A river flowing past the castle of Galedon. Bors, seeing a maiden in distress, spurred his horse across the river, even though he would have drowned under the weight of his armor if his horse had stumbled. [*VulgLanc*]

GALEDON

A castle on the Galede river where Bors rescued a maiden. [*VulgLanc*]

GALEGANTIN¹ [*Galegaudinz, Galegentix, Galerantis, Galygantynis, G(u)allega(n)tins*]

One of Arthur's Knights of the Round Table, from Wales. He is first mentioned by Chrétien de Troyes. He may be the origin of Hartmann's GALAGAUNDRIS and Ulrich's GALAGANDREIZ. He fought in Arthur's wars against the Saxons, appears in a number of tournaments, and was imprisoned in both the Dolorous Prison and the Forbidden Hill. He contracted an illness in the former and nearly died, but was healed by the Hermit of the Thicket. After participating in the Grail Quest, he was killed by Mordred at the battle of Salisbury. [*ChretienE, LancLac, VulgLanc, Livre, ProsTris*]

GALEGANTIN²

Lancelot's maternal grandfather; the father of Elaine and Evaine. After his daughters were married, Galegantin retired to a seaside hermitage and became a holy man. Lancelot visited him during the Grail Quest, on his way to Corbenic, and Galegantin tried to persuade him to end his affair with Guinevere. [*PostQuest*]

GALEGUINANT [*Galys Gwynans*]

An illegitimate son of King Urien, half-brother of Yvain, and brother of Yvain the Bastard. He fought bravely for Arthur in Arthur's wars against the Saxons and against Lord Galehaut. [*LancLac, VulgLanc, Livre, LancLaik*]

GALEHAUT¹ [*Galahalt, Galahos, Galahot, Galaiotos, Galaous, Galehot, Galeotto, Galeus, Galiot, Galot, Galyot*]

A noble, imperialistic knight from the early French Lancelot romances. He has a significant role in the first half of the Vulgate *Lancelot*, which is somewhat muted in the Prose *Tristan*, and then changed markedly by Malory.

Galehaut's lands are variously called Sorelois, Estregor, and the Distant Isles. His mother was called the Beautiful Giantess (named in *La Tavola Ritonda* as Bagotta), and his father (supplied by the Prose *Tristan*) was a giant named Brunor. His sister was called Delice or Riccarda. Brunor inhabited the Castle of Tears on the Giant's Isle, the customs of which drove Galehaut away from home to seek his own kingdom. He conquered a number of kings including Bagdemagus, the King with a Hundred Knights, the First Conquered King, the King from Beyond the Borders of Galone, and King Gloeir of Sorelois. Gloeir he killed, seizing Sorelois, but he looked after Gloeir's orphaned daughter. Tristan slew his father, for which Galehaut tried to seek revenge but later relented.

In time, he decided to conquer Arthur, and attacked the land of Selice, which was under Arthur's protection. Arthur had difficulty summoning all of his men to the battle site, but a mysterious "Red Knight" (Lancelot in disguise) and Gawain saved the day for Arthur. In the meantime, Galehaut realized that he would defeat Arthur from sheer force of his numbers, and decided to give Arthur a year to gather his entire army before attacking again. A year later, the two kings met again in battle, but Galehaut still had the greater number of men, and would have won almost immediately if it were not for Gawain and a "Black Knight" (Lancelot, again, in disguise) fighting on Arthur's side. Galehaut so admired the deeds of the Black Knight that he met him after the battle and begged him to lodge with him that night. Lancelot agreed after extracting a promise from Galehaut to surrender to Arthur the following day. Galehaut consented, and peace was made between the two kings.

Lancelot and Galehaut became fast friends, accompanying each other on a series of adventures both in Arthur's lands and Galehaut's. When Lancelot was made a Knight of the Round Table, Galehaut requested the same honor so that he might remain Lancelot's companion. Journeying through his own land, however, Galehaut noticed that all his castles were crumbling. He had a disturbing dream, which his sages interpreted as meaning that Lancelot would cause his death. Eventually, Galehaut received a false report that Lancelot had been killed in the Forest of Adventures. He was so depressed from this report that he wasted away and died. Galehodin became his heir.

Later romances tended to minimize the importance of his character. The Italian *Tristano Riccardiano* says that he died of wounds received in his fight with Tristan at the Castle of Tears. In contrast to the earlier romances, Malory gives Galehaut the "High Prince" a somewhat wicked character, eliminating his friendship with Lancelot and, indeed, including a plot by Galehaut and Bagdemagus, jealous of Lancelot's prowess, to kill him. In Malory, he opposes Arthur in two tournaments, at Sorelois and Leverzep. [*LancLac, VulgLanc, ProsTris, Conti, TristanoR, Tavola, Malory*]

GALEHAUT² [*Galhaut*]

A knight in the Brown Family. Galehaut was the son of Brun and Lye, the brother of Hector, Brun, Lore, and Ysille, and the father of Hector the Brown. [*Palamedes*]

GALEHAUT³ THE BROWN

A knight of the "Brown" lineage, which won fame in the generation before Arthur and the Knights of the Round Table. He was the son of Hector or Mailhot, the brother of a second Hector, and the father of a third Hector. He cuckolded a knight named Diocenar and, with Diocenar's wife, had a son named Febus. Galehaut enjoyed numerous adventures before a knight named Armond set upon him with fifty warriors. Though unarmed, Galehaut managed to kill Armond and eighteen of his attackers before he fell under their swords. In Italian romance, Galehaut the Brown is often confused with the first GALEHAUT. [*Palamedes, Prophecies*]

GALEHAUT⁴ THE BROWN

Uncle of the above Galehaut the Brown, brother of Hector the Brown, and father of another Hector the Brown. With his brother, he left Britain to avoid King Vortigern's wrath but was marooned on an island. [*Prophecies*]

GALEHÉS

Uncle of the Lady of Montesclaire. When his niece's city was besieged by marauders, Galahés sought out Gawain and directed him to the afflicted castle. [*Contin1*]

GALEHODIN [*Galaodin, Galihodin, Galyhodyn*]

Nephew, godson, and heir of Galehaut of Sorelois. Galehodin was the grandson of the King of North Wales. In the Vulgate *Lancelot,* he becomes lord of the town of Penning and hosts a tournament there, which Lancelot wins. He was a noble knight who treated Arthur's companions well, although Malory tells a story in which he tries to kidnap Isolde, but is defeated by Palamedes. Galehodin supported Lancelot in the war against Arthur by helping to rescue Guinevere from the stake, and by fighting in the battles at Joyous Guard and Benoic. In return for his support, Lancelot made him Duke of Saintonge. After the death of King Arthur, Galehodin joined Lancelot in the abbey at Glastonbury and lived

there as a hermit until Lancelot's death. With Lancelot's other knights, he took Lancelot's body to Joyous Guard and buried it. He then returned to his own lands. Galehodin is found in *La Tavola Ritonda* as ABASTUNAGIO. [*VulgLanc, Melekh, Girart, Malory*]

GALEHOUS

A knight in Arthur's service. [*Floriant*]

GALENICE [*Galence*]

A British castle in the Vulgate *Merlin*. Its castellan fought against the Saxons with King Belinant of South Wales. *Arthour and Merlin* names its lord as Caradoc. [*VulgMer, Arthour*]

GALENIN [*Kahenin*]

A British duke. Bors championed the lady of Galway against Mariale, Galenin's son. [*VulgLanc*]

GALERIAN

One of Perceval's eleven paternal uncles in *Perlesvaus*. He was the eleventh son of Gais the Large and the brother of Alain. Known as the lord of the White Tower, and he died at a young age. [*Perlesvaus*]

GALES¹ [*Gale(t)(z), Galoes, Galys, Glois*]

A variant spelling of WALES, used by many writers, some of whom were confused into making it a kingdom separate from Wales. Gottfried von Strassburg, for instance, erroneously believed that it was populated by Saxons, and that the name of England (Eng*land*) was derived from it. The Vulgate romances purport that the name came from its first king, Ga*lah*ad—prior to this, it was called HOSELICE. [*Gottfried, LancLac*]

GALES² THE BALD [*Gales Lithauz, Wales li Caus*]

An Arthurian knight first mentioned in Chrétien's *Erec*. He has little significance until the Fourth Continuation of Chrétien's *Perceval*, in which the author names him as the father of Perceval by the lady Philosofine, replacing ALAIN from Robert de Boron's cycle and PELLINORE from the Vulgate Cycle. According to the Vulgate *Merlin*, he fought in Arthur's battles against King Rions and the Saxons. In Heinrich von dem Türlin's *Diu Crône*, his beloved, Filleduch, fails a chastity test. In *Claris et Laris*, Gales avenges a knight's murder by slaying his killer. [*ChretienE, Contin1, HartmannE, Heinrich, LancLac, VulgLanc, VulgMer, Contin4, Claris*]

GALES³ THE GAY

A good and handsome knight of Arthur's court who fought for Arthur in a war against the King with a Hundred Knights and the King from Over the Borders of Galone. His brother was Arthur's knight Helis the Blond. [*LancLac, VulgLanc*]

GALESALAIN

A Knight of the Round Table who fought against the Saxons in the early days of Arthur's reign. He is distinct from GALESCALAIN. [*Livre*]

GALESCALAIN [*Galaas, Galathin, Galesc(h)in*]

Arthur's nephew, named as the son of King Nentres of Garlot and Blasine (Arthur's half-sister) in the Vulgate *Merlin*, and as the son of the king of Escavalon in the Vulgate *Lancelot*. Although his father rebelled against Arthur, Galescalain dreamed of becoming one of Arthur's knights. He deserted his father and joined with the young Gawain, his cousin. They headed for Arthur's court, fighting several battles against the Saxons along the way, in which they were assisted by Merlin. Arthur knighted Galescalain for his brave service, and he became one of the Queen's Knights. Arthur later made him the duke of Clarence. He fought in the war against King Claudas. Later, while on a quest to rescue Gawain from Caradoc of the Dolorous Tower, he saved the Lady of Cabrion and liberated the castle of Pintadol. In other adventures, he was imprisoned in the Valley of No Return, the Dolorous Tower, and the Forbidden Hill, but was rescued from all three by Lancelot. [*VulgLanc, VulgMer, Livre*]

GALESCONDE [*Galescounde*]

One of Arthur's knights who fought in the battles against the Saxons and King Rions. He later became a frequent companion of Gawain. [*VulgLanc, VulgMer, Livre, Arthour*]

GALIADAN

A Knight of the Round Table who participated in the Grail Quest. [*PostQuest*]

GALIAG

A knight in King Mark's service who was a companion of Isolde. He was the son of the count of Miliag. [*Eilhart*]

GALIAINS

A Cornish knight defeated in combat by Gawain. [*Contin3*]

GALICIA [*Galice, Galise*]

A historical kingdom in northwest Spain. Wolfram says that Perceval's uncle Trevrizent held fortresses there. In *Claris et Laris*, it is ruled by King Jonas, who is defeated by Claris and Laris. [*Wolfram, Claris*]

GALIEN[1]

A knight who fought in the wars against the Saxons, alongside the rulers in rebellion against Arthur. [*VulgMer*]

GALIEN[2]

An enemy of King Label, a pagan king converted to Christianity by Celidoine. [*VulgEst*]

GALIEN[3]

Son of Brien of the Gastine. His father was an evil man who had invaded the Blanquemore Valley and the Lac as Jumeles. When his father was slain by Arthur's Sir Meriadeuc, whose family owned the land, Galien pressed his father's former conquests and besieged Meriadeuc's family in the castle of Tygan. Gawain eventually joined the defenders and killed Galien. [*Meriadeuc*]

GALIEN[4]

A knight slain by Galahad during the Grail Quest. Galien was trying to abduct a maiden. [*ProsTris*]

GALIENA

The tortured, troubled wife of Sir Breus the Pitiless—the enemy of all Knights of the Round Table—in La Tavola Ritonda. Breus was insanely jealous of her and refused to let any visitors to his castle look upon her. [*Tavola*]

GALIENE

The Lady of Lothian. While staying with her uncle at Lidel Castle, she met Arthur's knight Fergus, and immediately fell in love with him. Distressed to discover that Fergus was planning to face the Black Knight, she returned to her own land, where she was besieged in her castle of Roucebourc by a malevolent king. She promised Arthofilaus, the king's nephew, a champion to fight within eight days, and then sent her lady Arondele to find one. Arondele returned with Fergus himself, who defeated Arthofilaus and the king, thus permanently sealing Galiene's love. Fergus disappeared shortly, but Galiene met with him again at the Gedeorde tournament, and they married soon afterwards. Arthur awarded the happy couple the lands of Lothian and Tudiele. [*Guillaume*]

GALIGANT [*Galigans*]

A rich castle-town ruled by Lampart. Lampart instituted a custom by which he fought personally against any knight entering the town. If Lampart lost, the knight would receive the best lodging, but if the knight lost, the townspeople would get to cover the knight with filth. Gawain's son Guinglain came to the town and defeated Lampart. [*Renaut*]

GALILEE

A historical region of northern Israel. Residents of Galilee were among the followers of Joseph of Arimathea. It was also the home of Esclabor the Unknown, Palamedes' father. In two romances—*Claris et Laris* and the Alliterative *Morte Arthur*—it is allied to Arthur's Roman enemies. *Claris* names its king as Marbrin. [*VulgEst, PostQuest, Claris, Allit*]

GALINAN THE BLACK [*Calinan, Galinas*]

Son of Guiron the Courteous and Bloie. He was raised by the lord of the castle where his parents were imprisoned when he was born. His foster-father named him after himself. He grew up with Guiron's prowess but with his foster-father's wicked disposition. He defeated Arthur and several Knights of the Round Table at the Fountain of the Pine. Conquered by Lancelot during the Grail Quest, he was eventually slain by Palamedes. [*Palamedes*, *Tavola*]

GALLEMAN

One of Arthur's knights in the German story of *Antelan*. He is defeated in combat by King Antelan. [*Antelan*]

GALLERON [*Galaron, Galeron*]

A Scottish knight in *The Awntyrs of Arthur* whose lands were annexed by Arthur and given to Gawain. Angry, Galleron appeared at Arthur's feast at Rondoles Hall and challenged any of Arthur's knights to a duel. Gawain fought with him at Plumpton. Galleron proved strong and seemed to be winning at the beginning. When Gawain made a comeback, Galleron killed Gawain's horse, Grissel. They fought for hours longer, and both were wounded severely but neither proved the victor. Finally, Galleron yielded to Gawain and ended the combat. For his bravery, Gawain bestowed upon Galleron all the lands that Arthur had annexed. Galleron was then made a Knight of the Round Table. Malory names him as one of the twelve conspirators who sought to catch Lancelot and Guinevere *in flagrante* and expose their affair to Arthur. Lancelot killed him in the battle outside Guinevere's chambers. [*Awntyrs, SyreGaw, Malory*]

GALLGOID

One of Arthur's warriors. [*Culhwch*]

GALLGOIG

One of Arthur's warriors. Whenever he entered a town, he kept all the townsfolk awake until his desires were fulfilled. [*Culhwch*]

GALLIDÉS [*Galindes*]

The lord of the White Caste. He conquered the lands of his niece, the lady of Hungerford Castle, when she refused to marry his seneschal. The lady of Hungerford, on the verge of defeat, was able to retain the services of Bors, who defeated many of Gallidés' knights and, eventually, Gallidés himself. He forced Gallidés to return the stolen lands to the lady, and Gallidés was reconciled with his niece. [*VulgLanc*]

GALLIGAR THE RED [*Galagars, Galligars*]

A knight of Arthur's court who was promoted to the Round Table, on the recommendation of King Pellinore, after the battle of the Humber. [*PostMer, Malory*]

GALLIN

A knight whose brother, Gallinor, was imprisoned by Baudon of Avarlan. Gallin challenged Baudon for

Gallinor's freedom, but was badly wounded before the duel could be fought. Coming upon a party of Arthur's knights, he related his story, and Gaheris agreed to fight against Baudon in Gallin's stead. Gaheris was victorious, and Gallinor was freed. [*PostMer*]

GALLINOR

A knight imprisoned by Baudon, the son of the Duke of Avarlan, in a misunderstanding over a woman. His brother, Gallin, arranged to duel Baudon, but was injured, so Gaheris (Gawain's brother) fought in his place. Gaheris defeated Baudon, and Gallinor was freed and reconciled with his former enemy. [*PostMer*]

GALLOWAY [*Galeway, Galoee, Galvoie, Walweitha*]

A province of southwest Scotland, which, in Layamon, Arthur pacified in the early days of his reign. Chrétien de Troyes describes it as a "harsh and cruel land, where the people are faithless." It was guarded by Orguelleuse of the Narrow Passage, who vowed to never let any knight leave the country alive. Gawain had a number of adventures in the land, most notably at the palace called Canguin Rock (Wolfram von Eschenbach places this in a fictional land called TERRE MARVEILE). It was the homeland of an Arthurian knight named Galleron, who challenged Gawain for the ownership of several properties nearby. Gawain's associations with Galloway in these romances may preserve some memory of a legend in which Gawain was its ruler, a notion that appears in William of Malmesbury. In *Escanor*, it is ruled by Count Brandis. [*WilliamM, Layamon, ChretienP, Girart, Malory*]

GALLUC [*Galauk*]

One of the earls of Salisbury under King Arthur. Galluc fought for Arthur in the war against Rome. He participated in the battle of Soissons and was killed there. [*GeoffHR, Bek*]

GALOAIN [*Milon*]

A count who met Erec and Enide during their adventures in Chrétien's *Erec*. He desired Enide and tried to convince her to abandon Erec for him. Enide warned Erec of Galoain's intentions, and they hurried away. When Galoain followed them, Erec beat him unconscious. His counterpart in the Welsh *Geraint* is the BROWN EARL. Renaut places him at the Castle of Maidens tournament, where he was defeated by Guinglain. [*ChretienE, Renaut, Erex*]

GALOBRUS OF THE RED GLADE

A kinsman of Lancelot. One manuscript of *Perlesvaus* says that, in a later continuation of the story, Galobrus will assist Lancelot against Claudas (Loomis, *Romance*, 263).

GALOES[1]

A Knight of the Round Table. [*HartmannE*]

203

GALOES[2] [*Galwes*]

Perceval's paternal uncle, whose name Wolfram probably borrowed from Hartmann's GALOES. The son of King Gandin and Queen Schoette, Galoes inherited the kingdom of Anjou. Galoes's brother, Gahmuret, set out in search of adventure despite Galoes's pleas for him to remain at court. Galoes loved the lady Annore, Queen of Averre, and he died in her service at Muntori. His slayer was Duke Orilus of Lalander. [*Wolfram*]

GALOGANDRES OF GIPPONES

A duke who served King Clamadeu and was killed fighting against the army of Perceval and Condwiramurs at Beaurepaire. [*Wolfram*]

GALOPAMUR

A Knight of the Round Table who was the son of Isabon. [*HartmannE*]

GALOPEAR

A duke from Greece who fought for King Lion of Namur against Wigalois (Gawain's son) in a war sparked by a murder committed by Lion. In the battle, Galopear killed Marine, a female knight, and was in turn killed by Count Adan of Alarie, Marine's grandfather. [*Wirnt*]

GALOPES

Son of King Mark of Cornwall in Jean D'Outremeuse's *Ly Myreur des Histors*. To avenge his father's death at the hands of Arthur, he convinces the Emperor of Rome to invade Britain. Arthur defeats the emperor and chases him back to Rome, during which Mordred usurps the throne. [*Jean*]

GALOT OF YBERGE [*Galos*]

A duke in Arthur's service. Galot fought in Arthur's war against the King with a Hundred Knights and the King from Over the Borders of Galone. [*LancLac, VulgLanc*]

GALUTH

Gawain's sword in the Alliterative *Morte Arthure*. Malory calls it GALANTYNE. [*Allit*]

GALVAN

A count in the service of King Ekunaver of Kanadic, who went to war with Arthur. Galvan guarded a fortress at the edge of Kanadic, where he was slain by Arthur's Sir Garel. [*PleierG*]

GALVARIUN

One of Arthur's warriors, depicted on the Modena Archivolt as part of a troop who rode to rescue Guinevere from Marduc of the Dolorous Tower. The name is possibly a variation of GAWAIN, but another character named Galvagin—more properly identified with Gawain—appears on the same sculpture. Galvariun has also been identified with GALLERON. [*Modena*]

GALWAY[1] [*Gallway, Galvoie*]

A region of Ireland on the west of the island. According to Wace, it was part of Arthur's empire. In *Les Merveilles de Rigomer*, it is ruled by an ally of Arthur's named Lot (not Gawain's father) and his son Midomidas. In Meriadeuc, a knight in Arthur's service named Blidoblidas is called the son of the King of Galway. The region is sometimes confused with GALLOWAY, an area in Scotland. [*Wace, Merveil*]

GALWAY[2]

A castle near Corbenic, the Grail Castle. Its lady was plagued by Mariale, the son of Duke Galenin, in a land dispute. She was championed by Bors, who defeated Mariale. She introduced Bors to King Pelles of Corbenic. [*VulgLanc*]

GALYHUD [*Galehod, Galyhod*]

A Knight of the Round Table, related somehow to Lancelot, who rescued Galyhud from the dungeon of the giant Tericam. When Lancelot and Guinevere were accused of treason, Galyhud joined Lancelot's camp and helped him rescue Guinevere from the stake. He fought in the battles against Arthur at Joyous Guard and Benoic. In return for his support, Lancelot made him the earl of Périgord. After Arthur's death, he joined Lancelot in a Glastonbury abbey. He attended Lancelot's burial at Joyous Guard and then returned to his own lands. [*Stanz, Malory*]

GALYNDES

A Knight of the Round Table who participated in the Grail Quest. [*ProsTris*]

GALYRAN

A knight of Arthur's court slain in the war against Mordred in the Alliterative *Morte Arthure*. His name may be a variation of GALLERON. [*Allit*]

GAMER

A prince of Medarie and Belakun; companion of princes Darel and Ariun. His lord, Schaffilun, was killed by Wigalois (Gawain's son), to whom Gamer transferred his fealty. He accompanied Wigalois in a campaign against King Lion of Namur. [*Wirnt*]

GAMERANZ LE PELU

One of four evil "toll collectors" slain by Gawain. [*Heinrich*]

GAMILLE [*Camille, Canile, Carmile, Cramile*]

A Saxon sorceress who inhabited the Saxon Rock in Scotland. She seduced a knight named Gadresalain, and threw his lady into her prison. King Arthur became enamored of Gamille when he entered Scotland to repel a Saxon invasion. Gamille's brother, Hargadabrant, was a Saxon king. For her brother's sake, Gamille used Arthur's affections to manipulate him into her prison, where he remained until rescued by Lancelot. After Lancelot took over the Saxon Rock, he had Gamille's books of sorcery burned, causing Gamille to threw herself off a cliff. She survived with injury. [*LancLac*, *VulgLanc*, *Arthour*]

GAMON

A locality in Ireland that was the home of Llenlleawg the Irishman. [*Culhwch*]

GAMOR

Co-leader, with Maladors, of an army of Saracens who fought Ambrosius and Uther Pendragon at Bristol. [*Arthour*]

GAMUR THE SARACEN

An Arabian ruler who, along with two other potentates, challenged King Arthur to a tournament at Baghdad in Babylon. This tournament is recounted by Gawain in Heinrich von dem Türlin's *Diu Crône*. [*Heinrich*]

GANADAL

A Knight of the Round Table who embarked with the others on the Grail Quest. [*PostQuest*]

GANAREW [*Generth, Generon, Genoreu*]

A castle on Mount Doward in the country of Archenfield in Wales. The castle sat along the river Wye. According to Geoffrey of Monmouth, King Vortigern fled to this castle when pursued by Ambrosius Aurelius and Uther, who had come from Brittany to conquer the land. Vortigern fortified himself, but Ambrosius simply set the castle on fire and burned Vortigern alive. Nennius calls the same castle VORTIGERN. [*GeoffHR*, *Wace*]

GANATULANDER

A Knight of the Round Table. [*HartmannE*]

GANDAZ THE BLACK

A Knight of the Round Table who participated in the Grail Quest. His brother was Sir Gandin of the Mountain. [*PostQuest*]

GANDELUS [*Gandaluz, Ganedlu*]

A Round Table knight who fought in a Castle of Maidens tournament in *Le Bel Inconnu* and whose wife failed a chastity test in *Diu Crône*. [*ChretienE, Renaut, Heinrich*]

GANDILUZ

One of Gawain's pages. He was the son of Gurzgri and Mahaute, and thus was the grandson of Perceval's tutor, Gornemant. [*Wolfram*]

GANDIN[1]

The king of Anjou, son of Addanz, husband of Schoutte, father of Galoes, Gahmuret, Limmire, and Flurdamurs, and grandfather of Perceval. He appointed his daughter Limmire Queen of Styria. When he died in battle, his son Galoes inherited the kingdom. [*Wolfram, PleierG*]

GANDIN[2]

In Gottfried's *Tristan*, a mischievous knight from Ireland who was enamored with Isolde. Skilled in playing the rote (a type of stringed instrument), he traveled to Mark's court and entertained Mark with his music. Mark was led to make a rash promise to grant Gandin anything he wished, and Gandin chose Isolde herself. Mark had little choice but to let Gandin carry her off. Tristan followed the pair and tricked Gandin—by playing his harp—into giving Isolde back. Gottfried may have taken the name from Wolfram's character. In the Prose *Tristan*, this abduction is replaced with one by PALAMEDES. [*Gottfried*]

GANDIN[3] OF THE MOUNTAIN

A Knight of the Round Table who participated in the Grail Quest. His brother was Sir Gandaz the Black. [*PostQuest*]

GANDINE

A river in Europe that Wolfram von Eschenbach says was named after Perceval's grandfather Gandin. [*Wolfram*]

GANDWY [*Gadw*]

One of Arthur's gatekeepers. His son was named Cadrieth. [*Geraint*]

GANELON[1]

A baron who served King Mark of Cornwall. He conspired with two compatriots, Godoine and Denoalen, to expose the affair between Tristan and Isolde. [*Beroul*]

GANELON[2]

A traitorous servant of Charlemagne, whom he accompanied to Britain in the eighth or ninth century. They visited the Tower of the Dead, which Arthur's knights had erected on the plain of Salisbury, with Mordred's head hanging in the wind. Ganelon, perceiving that the Tower was a warning to all traitors, had the head cut down and buried in an undisclosed location. [*PostMort*]

GANGES

Wolfram von Eschenbach says that the region around this Indian river was populated by a sub-human race with the features of boars. Cundrie the Sorcerer and her brother Malcreatiure were two of this race. [*Wolfram*]

GANGIER OF NERANDEN

A Knight of the Round Table. His brother was named Scos. [*HartmannE*]

GANIEDA

Merlin's sister in Geoffrey's *Vita Merlini*. She was married to King Rhydderch of Cumbria, but was unfaithful to him. She despaired when Merlin went insane, and sent out knights to find him. When Merlin was brought to court, he told Rhydderch of Ganieda's adultery, but Ganieda managed to convince her husband that nothing Merlin said could be trusted because of his madness. After her husband died and Merlin was restored to her wits, she went to live with her brother in the forest of Caledon. There, she developed, like Merlin, the ability to prophecy. She appears in Welsh legend as GWENDDYDD. [*GeoffVM*]

GANLIDAS [*Galidas*]

A knight defeated by Laris. Claris and Laris were helping Sir Caradoc protect his paramour from King Ladas, Sir Ganlidas's liege. [*Claris*]

GANNES [*Gaines, Ganys, Gaunes, Gausnes, Gawnes*]

A French land ruled by King Bors, and also the chief city within the land. Its creator may have intended Vannes in Brittany. It is said to have bordered the kingdom of Benoic (ruled by Bors' brother King Ban) and the land of King Claudas. Claudas invaded Gannes upon Bors' death and assumed rulership, forcing Bors' widow to flee to a nunnery. The people of Gannes organized an only partially successful revolt against Claudas, but a later campaign by Arthur drove out Claudas and established Sir Bors (King Bors' son) as its king. (The Stanzaic *Morte Arthur* says that Bors was appointed to the throne by Lancelot.) In Malory, Bleoberis (King Bors' godson) eventually becomes its king. Other knights, including Blamor and Lionel, called Gannes their homeland. The province's abbey served as a healing place for Sir Lucan the Butler after he was injured by Tristan. [*LancLac, VulgLanc, ProsTris, Stanz, Malory*]

GANOJE

A British king who harbored Tristan during one of Tristan's exiles from Mark's court. [*Eilhart*]

GANOR[1]

A Knight of the Round Table from Scotland. He was mortally wounded by Lancelot during a tournament at Camelot. King Bagdemagus took his Round Table seat. [*VulgLanc*]

GANOR[2] [*Gaynor*]

The Duke of Galafort in the time of Joseph of Arimathea. He was converted to Christianity by Celidoine, the son of Nascien, and he allowed his city to be used as the first Christian stronghold in Britain. By doing this, he broke faith with his overlord, the King of Northumberland, and was attacked. With the help of the Christian knights, he was victorious. He fought to liberate Joseph and his followers from King Crudel, who had imprisoned them.

He recommended Galahad, Joseph's son, for the crown of Wales. [*VulgEst*]

GANSGUOTER OF MICHOLDE

In Heinrich von dem Türlin's *Diu Crône*, Igerne's second husband, with whom she eloped after the death of Uther Pendragon. Gansguoter won her through his skill at fiddling. He constructed magical palaces for his wife, stepdaughters, and nieces (Amurfina and Sgoidamur). His own castle was called Madarp. During Gawain's quest to retrieve a magic bridle, Gansguoter engaged him in a beheading game and, as happens with this theme, spared Gawain's life. He later assisted Gawain in a quest to recover several artifacts stolen from Arthur's court. His sister, a goddess, aided Gawain during his Grail Quest. Gangsguoter is analogous to Wolfram von Eschenbach's CLINSCHOR. [*Heinrich*]

GANSONAIS

A Knight of the Round Table. During the Grail Quest, he and two other knights were escorting a lady to her brother's castle when they were set upon by ten of the lady's enemies. Gansonais survived the battle, but his two companions were killed. Tired and wounded, he happily passed the woman on to Perceval when the latter happened along. [*PostQuest*]

GANTITIERS OF JASTUNS

A knight at Arthur's court. [*Heinrich*]

GANVES [*Gamvis, Kanves*]

One of Lancelot's lands in Der Pleier's romances. Although similar to GANNES of French romance, it is most likely a corruption of GENEWIS, Lancelot's land in Ulrich von Zatzikhoven's *Lanzelet*. [*PleierG*]

GAR OF THE MOUNTAIN

A Knight of the Round Table who participated in the Grail Quest. [*PostQuest*]

GARADIGAS

One of Arthur's courts in Heinrich's *Diu Crône*. [*Heinrich*]

GARANHON [*Saranhon*]

Son of Glythfyr. He was one of Arthur's warriors and a companion of Geraint. [*Culhwch, Geraint*]

GARANWYN ("White Shank")

Cei's son. He was one of Arthur's warriors. [*Culhwch*]

GARBANO

A castle in Logres where Tristan and Lancelot recovered after battling each other without knowing each other's identities. [*Tavola*]

GAREL[1]

An Arthurian knight whose story, *Garel von dem blühenden Tal*, was written by Der Pleier in the thirteenth century. His native land was Styria, but he had been awarded the Blooming Valley by Arthur. He was the son of Meleranz and Limmire, and was a maternal cousin of Perceval. Present at Arthur's court when King Ekuanver of Kanadic delivered a declaration of war, Garel accepted a mission from Arthur to scout Kanadic and report on Ekunaver's forces. Along the way, he was sidetracked by a number of adventures: he saved the castle Merkanie from a malicious attack; he liberated the prisoners of Duke Eskilabon of Belamunt; he slew the giants Purdan and Fidegart; and he saved Queen Laudamie of Averre from the demon Vulganus. After this last trial, he married Laudamie and became the king of Averre. During each adventure, he gained allies and subjects, all of whom pledged their support in the war against Ekunaver. By the time he reached Kanadic, his army was large enough to defeat Ekunaver before Arthur's forces even arrived. For this, he was richly rewarded by Arthur. He settled down in Averre with Laudamie and became a noble and generous king.

Der Pleier seems to have gained inspiration for Garel from Der Stricker's DANIEL of the Blooming Valley, although Garel's name first appears in Hartmann's *Erec* and Wolfram's *Parzival* as a Knight of the Round Table. He may be connected with GREU of the French *Livre d'Artus*. [HartmannE, Wolfram, PleierG]

GAREL[2]

The King of Mirmidon. He was slain by the evil King Roaz of Glois who, in turn, was killed by Gawain's son Wigalois. [Wirnt]

GARELES

One of Arthur's Knights of the Round Table. [HartmannE]

GARENGAUS THE STRONG [Garingans]

A peer of Sir Bors. He was one of the knights victorious in a tournament at Estrangorre. He swore fealty to King Brandegorre's daughter, promising to guard the Ford of the Woods and to send her the shields of all the knights he defeated. [VulgLanc]

GARETH [Carahés, Charahes, Charehes, Charheries, Gaheret(h), Gaheriet, Gariet(te), Garrett, Generez, *Guerrehet]

Gawain's brother. He was the son of King Lot and either Belisent or Morgause. Gareth's other brothers included Agravain, Gaheris, and Mordred. The earliest form of his name is so similar to the earliest form of GAHERIS that the two brothers may have originally been the same character. He first appears in Chrétien de Troyes's *Perceval*. His name may be an adaptation of the Welsh GWEIR. His first significant adventure comes in the First Continuation of *Perceval*, in which he avenges a knight named Brangemuer by slaying the Little Knight. His story is expanded in the Vulgate Cycle, and Malory attaches to him a FAIR UNKNOWN story (which is particularly reminiscent of Renaut de Bâgé's GUINGLAIN).

The Vulgate *Merlin* and Malory offer two differing tales of his *enfances*. *Merlin* tells us that, with his brothers, he defected from Lot's house and took service with Arthur. He battled the early Saxon invasion and participated in the war against King Claudas. He was knighted either by Arthur or his brother Gaheris.

According to Malory, Gareth arrived at Arthur's court under unusual circumstances at a Pentecost feast, refusing to identify himself. His brothers had not seen him in many years and did not recognize him. Arthur, impressed with the young man's physique and demeanor, put him under the supervision of Kay, who bullied and scorned Gareth, forcing him to work in the kitchens and giving him the nickname "Beaumains," or "fair hands." After a year of this, a maiden named Lynet came to court requesting assistance for her sister Lyones, besieged in her castle by Sir Ironside, the Red Knight of the Red Lands. At Gareth's request, Lancelot knighted him and Arthur assigned him the quest, much to the dismay of Lynet, who wanted a knight, not a kitchen page. Kay, also incredulous, challenged Gareth and was defeated. Despite the constant demonstration of his honor and skill in the subsequent journey, Lynet constantly insulted him, calling him a vile kitchen knave and forcing him to keep down wind. In succession, Gareth defeated the brothers Perard (the Black Knight), Pertylope (the Green Knight), Persaunt (the Blue Knight), and finally Ironside. He spared the latter's life and sent him to Camelot. Gareth and Lyones held a great tournament at the Castle Perilous which proved Gareth's prowess to Arthur's kingdom. After another series of adventures, Gareth married Lyones at Kynke Kenadonne.

In the Vulgate *Lancelot*, the Post-Vulgate, and Malory, Gareth has several other minor adventures which generally proved him a cut above his brothers. He prevented Gawain and Aggravain from killing Gaheris in revenge for Morgause's death, condemned his brothers for the murder of Lamorat, and attempted to dissuade Aggravain and Mordred from exposing the affair between Lancelot and Guinevere. Unsuccessful in this last endeavor, Gareth was eventually slain by either Lancelot or Bors when Lancelot rescued Guinevere from the stake. This led to Gawain's later hatred towards Lancelot. [ChretienP, UlrichZ, VulgLanc, VulgMort, PostMer, PostMer, PostQuest, PostMort, Malory]

GAREZ

A king of Libya. His successor, Amire, was married to Liamere, Garez's daughter. His brother was King Lar of Korntin, and his niece, Larie, married Gawain's son Wigalois. [Wirnt]

GARGALCO

A wilderness near Joyous Guard where Tristan once encountered Kay and Dodinel. Kay took Tristan unaware and knocked him off his horse, then pleaded for Tristan's forgiveness. [*Tavola*]

GARGANTUA

A mythological giant in sixteenth-century French literature, found in a number of texts. Two of these so-called "Gargantuan Chronicles" are Arthurian. Gargantua's father, Grandgosier, had been created by Merlin from whales' bones and Lancelot's blood. His mother, Gargamelle, was created similarly from Guinevere's finger nails. Merlin raised Gargantua and brought him to Arthur's court, where the giant served Arthur for two centuries. At the end of his career, Gargantua was taken to Avalon by Morgan le Fay. [*Gargantuan*]

GARGELOAIN

A lady loved by Tristan's brother-in-law, Kahedin or Ruvalen, in one manuscript of the Prose *Tristan* and in *Palamedes*. Tristan helps arrange a tryst between Gargeolain and his brother-in-law, for which Gargeolain's husband, Bedalis, later tracked Tristan down and mortally wounded him with a poisoned lance. When Gargeloain saw her lover killed, she fell down dead. Eilhart von Oberge tells the same story, calling the lady GARIOLE. [*Palamedes, ProsTris*]

GARIN[1]

The son of Berte and father of Bertrand. Garin, a resident of Tintagel, gave lodging to Gawain when Gawain came to witness the tournament between Tiebaut of Tintagel and Meliant of Lis. [*ChretienP*]

GARIN[2]

A squire present at King Mark of Cornwall's tournament at Lancien. [*Contin4*]

GARIN[3]

A knight who joined Mordred's rebellion against Arthur and was slain by Gawain. [*Allit*]

GARIOLE

The wife of lord Nampentenis in Eilhart's *Tristrant*. She was loved by Tristan's half-brother Kahedins. Nampentenis kept her locked in a castle tower surrounded by walls and moats; however, she made wax impressions of the keys and gave them to Kahedins, who fashioned duplicate keys and used them to gain access. When Nampentenis found out about their tryst, he attacked Kahedins and Tristan, killing the one and mortally wounding the other. She is known in *Palamedes* as GARGELOAIN. [*Eilhart*]

GARIOSSO OF MAGANZA

Lord of the city of Pontiere. Guiron the Courteous stole a lady from him. Gariosso went to Uther's court, claiming the reverse: that Gariosso had stolen the woman from Gurion. The lady corroborated the lie. As was the custom with cuckolds in Uther's court, Guiron was dragged by horses. [*Tavola*]

GARIS OF LAMBALE

A Knight of the Round Table who died during the Grail Quest. His uncle was named Hernars. [*ProsTris*]

GARLES

A city in northern Britain, fortified against the Saxons by the kings in rebellion against Arthur. It may have a relation to GARLOT. [*VulgMer*]

GARLIN OF GALORE

An honorable king in Heinrich von dem Türlin's *Diu Crône*. His son, Count Gotegrin, was a knight at Arthur's court and was named as Guinevere's brother. Though Garlin is not called Guinevere's father, this can perhaps be inferred. [*Heinrich*]

GARLON THE RED [*Garlan*]

Brother of King Pellehan of Listenois (a Grail King) who appears in the Post-Vulgate *Merlin* continuation, Malory, and Tennyson. He loathed Arthur and the Knights of the Round Table. With the power to turn himself invisible, he enjoyed killing other knights by thrusting lances through their backs. Two of his victims were Sir Harlews and Sir Peryn. The populace thought there was a fiend on the loose. Arthur's Sir Balin the Savage, investigating these killings, tracked Garlon to King Pellehan's castle, where he joined a feast in Pellehan's hall. Balin was hesitant to confront Garlon in the castle, but he became enraged when Garlon either slapped him in the back of the head (Post-Vulgate and Malory) or insulted Queen Guinevere (Tennyson). Balin stood up and clove Garlon through the head. Pellehan, enraged, insisted on fighting Balin, which led to the Dolorous Stroke. Tennyson says that Garlon was a lover of Vivien. [*PostMer, Malory, TennIK*]

GARLOT

A kingdom, castle, or city in northern Britain, near Clarence. The Vulgate *Merlin* mentions both Urien and Nentres as its rulers; Malory gives it entirely to the latter. It was one of the lands in rebellion against Arthur in the early days of his reign. Garlot was invaded by Saxons, and served as the site of several important battles. [*VulgMer, PostMer, Arthour, Malory*]

GARNALDO

A Knight of the Round Table who participated in the Grail Quest. His brother was Guares the Black. [*PostQuest*]

GARNANTZ

The domain that Ulrich von Zatzikhoven assigns to Gawain, although it is not found in any other story. It may be a corruption of KARNANT, which Hartmann von Aue gives as the kingdom of Erec's father, King Lac. [*UlrichZ*]

GARNO

A valley visited by Tristan and Tessina. [*Tavola*]

GARNOT

A Knight of the Round Table found in the Serbo-Russian *Povest' o Tryshchane*. As one of Arthur's knights, and as a friend of Morholt of Ireland, he shares the position occupied by GAHERIS in the Prose *Tristan*. Garnot, however, is named as Arthur's son rather than his nephew. [*Povest*]

GARNYSH OF THE MOUNT

In Malory, a knight encountered by Balin after he delivered the Dolorous Stroke to King Pellehan. Garnysh was sitting by a tree, crying because his lady, daughter of Duke Harmel, had not kept a rendezvous. Sir Balin stopped him from killing himself with his sword and took him to Duke Harmel's castle to find his lady. There, they found the lady sleeping in the arms of another knight, at which Garnysh killed them both, cursed Balin for showing him the sight, and killed himself. The story appears in the Post-Vulgate *Suite du Merlin*, but the knight is unnamed. [*Malory*]

GARRADAINS

An Arthurian knight who accompanied Gawain on his quest to conquer Rigomer castle. [*Merveil*]

GARRAS OF CORK [*Carniz of Schores, Gartes of Nomeret*]

A king present at the wedding of Erec and Enide. [*ChretienE, HartmannE, Heinrich*]

GARREDOMECHSCHIN

A Knight of the Round Table. [*HartmannE*]

GARSALLAS [*Carsalas*]

A knight who stole a stag's head and brachet from Perceval while Perceval was fighting the Knight of the Tomb, Garsallas's half-brother. Perceval later encountered and defeated him, and sent him to Arthur's court. Garsallas's father was the duke of Geneloie, and his paramour was named Riseut. [*Contin2*]

GARSCHILOYE

A servant in the Grail Castle and maiden in the Grail Procession. She came from Greenland. [*Wolfram*]

GARSE

One of Arthur's noblemen. His brothers were Earl Gorgun and Jentaneon. [*Erex*]

GARSELID [*Garselit*]

One of Arthur's warriors in Welsh legend. He was an Irishman and an expert houndsman. As one of his tasks, the warrior Culhwch had to obtain Garselid's help in hunting the boar Twrch Trwyth. Garselid did attend the hunt, and was killed by the boar at Cwm Cerwyn. [*Culhwch*]

GARSIDIS

King of Karmerie and husband of Lambore. He died at a young age, which caused his wife to die of grief. His daughter, Tydomie, married Arthur's nephew Meleranz. [*PleierM*]

GARTH GRUGYN

An English hill, site of the last stand of the piglet Grugyn (after whom the hill was evidently named). During the epic hunt of Twrch Trwyth, Arthur's warriors pursued Grugyn Silver Bristle here and killed him, but Rhuddfyw Rhys and many other men were lost in the battle. [*Culhwch*]

GARWEN ("Fair Leg")

One of Arthur's three mistresses, according to a Welsh Triad. Her father was Henin the Old. [*Triads*]

GARWLWYD

In a Welsh poem, a warrior of whom Arthur says "Fierce was his nature with sword and shield." [*WelshPG*]

GARWY THE TALL

Father of Arthur's mistress Indeg. [*Culhwch*]

GARWYLI

Son of Gwyddawg Gwyr. One of King Arthur's warriors, he was killed by the boar Twrch Trwyth at Llwch Ewin during the epic hunt. [*Culhwch*]

GARYM ("Shout")

Wife of Arthur's warrior Cyfwlch. [*Culhwch*]

GASADIN

One of Arthur's dukes in the Norse *Erex Saga*. He was present at the wedding of Erec and Enide. [*Erex*]

GASAN [*Gazan*]

One of the two cities flanking the enchanted Merlin's Tower. The other was the White Castle. [*VulgLanc*]

GASCHIER

A nobleman from Normandy who invaded the Arabic kingdom of Zazamanc. He was defeated in single combat by Perceval's father Gahmuret, who was fighting for Zazamanc. His capital was Rouen. His maternal uncle was King Kaylet of Spain. [*Wolfram*]

GASCONY [Gascoigne, Gascoyne, Gaskoyne]

A territory in southwest France. According to Geoffrey of Monmouth, Duke Hoel conquered it as part of Arthur's campaign in Gaul. Rulers in other sources include Hardiz (Wolfram), Aramont (Prose *Lancelot*), Ladon (*Claris et Laris*), Bors (Welsh Triads), and the Hunting Knight (Irish tale). According to *Arthour and Merlin*, Uther Pendragon acquired it from Harinan, Igerne's first husband; in Heinrich von dem Türlin's *Diu Crône*, Gascony is also represented as part of Uther's kingdom. [*GeoffHR, Triads, Wolfram, Layamon, LancLac, Heinrich, Arthour, Claris, IrishL*]

GASOUDENC [Gasaudenc]

An Arthurian knight in the romance of *Yder*. He participated in Arthur's war against Taulas of Rougemont, a vassal in rebellion, and was defeated in combat by Yder. [*Yder*]

GASOZEIN OF DRAGOZ

A powerful knight who presented himself at Arthur's court, claiming that Guinevere actually belonged to him. In conversation with Arthur, Guinevere had alluded to a past relationship with Gasozein, so his claim seemed to have credit. Arthur gave the matter to Guinevere, and the queen denied any knowledge of Gasozein's ludicrous assertion. Gasozein left court in a rage. Guinevere's brother, Gotegrin, thought the queen had done wrong and kidnapped her. As Gotegrin was about to kill her, Gasozein himself rescued her, but the rescue became an abduction when he tried to kidnap and rape her. Gawain arrived in the midst of this, defeated Gasozein in combat, and returned him to Arthur's court, where he admitted that he had no valid claim to the queen. Gawain then arranged an engagement between Gasozein and Sgoidamur, Gawain's sister-in-law. Gasozein is found in French romance as GASWAIN. [*HartmannE, Heinrich*]

GASSA

An emperor of an unknown land, who procured a magnificent garment from Morgan le Fay and gave it to Guinevere. [*ChretienE*]

GASTINEL

An Arthurian knight in the romance of *Yder*. He participated in Arthur's war against Taulas of Rougemont, a vassal in rebellion. [*Yder*]

GASWAIN [Gasoain, Gasosin, Gosenain, Goswain]

A Knight of the Round Table from the land of Estrangorre. We learn in the Vulgate *Merlin* that as a young man, he fought with Gawain against the Saxons invading Britain, and was knighted by Arthur for his service. He apparently quarrelled with Gawain after one accused the other of being a traitor. Later, he accompanied Gawain on a mission to check on a report that the castle

Dolorous Guard had been liberated by Lancelot, and he was captured and imprisoned in the Dolorous Prison by Brandin of the Isles. Lancelot rescued him from here, and also from the prison of the evil Tericam. He may appear in Heinrich von dem Türlin's *Diu Crône* as GASOZEIN OF DRAGOZ. [*LancLac, VulgMer, Arthour*]

GATUAIN BATEWAIN

One of Arthur's knights who was the son of King Cabcaflin. [*HartmannE*]

GAUDIFER

One of Arthur's knights. [*Golagros*]

GAUDIN[1]

A region near Arthur's Caerleon court. [*Heinrich*]

GAUDIN[2] OF THE WHITE SHIELD

A castellan who once gave lodging to Perceval. [*Contin4*]

GAUDIN[3] THE BROWN OF THE MOUNTAIN
[Gaud(u)i(ns)]

One of Arthur's knights, first mentioned by Chrétien de Troyes (in *Erec*). Renaut de Bâgé calls him the King of Ireland. In *Les Merveilles de Rigomer*, he joins Gawain's quest to conquer Rigomer castle. Along the road, he left the company and rescued a maiden (whom he eventually married) from four giants. Arriving at Rigomer alone, he was imprisoned until freed by Gawain. [*ChretienE, Renaut, Merveil*]

GAUDIONÉS

The malevolent lord of Fors Graviers, an Irish castle. Gawain happened to visit Gaudionés castle on his way to conquer the castle Rigomer. Gaudionés, knowing of Gawain's prowess, sent a group of maidens to disarm him, knowing that Gawain would not attack them. He threw Gawain in a prison, instructing his sister to torture and starve the knight. Gaudionés's sister, however, helped Gawain to escape. Gawain later encountered Gaudionés, defeated him, and took him prisoner. [*Merveil*]

GAUL [Galijus, Gallya, Gawl]

A vast region of western Europe—including France and Germany—inhabited by a number of of Teutonic tribes in Arthur's day. According to Geoffrey, it was conquered in the fifth century by Maximus, and later by Arthur, who had to take it from the Roman leader Frollo. The thirteenth-century *Lancelot do Lac* says that King Claudas, Lancelot's enemy, transferred his allegiance from King Aramont of Brittany to an unnamed King of Gaul. In Malory, King Bors is given as King of Gaul, but this is unlikely since the region was so large, and it encompassed many other kingdoms, including his own brother's. If Bors had truly been King of Gaul, his power would have surpassed Arthur's, and other legends more reasonably make Bors' kingdom Gannes. Sir Accalon also came from this region. In most Arthurian legends, Gaul can be considered synonymous with FRANCE.

An unnamed King of Gaul appears in *Meriadoc* as an opponent of the Emperor of the Alemanni. As part of a peace treaty, he was betrothed to the Emperor's daughter, but he rejected her when he found that King Meriadoc of Wales had already slept with her. After Meriadoc slew the Emperor, the King of Gaul awarded him numerous lands. In *Meriadoc*, the King of Gaul may refer to Clovis, the King of the Franks, who won a battle against the Alemanni in 506 A.D. [*GeoffHR*, *Meriadoc*, *LancLac*, *Malory*]

GAULIIEN

A knight defeated by Perceval after he abducted the lover of Sir Dodinel the Savage. He was forced to release the maiden and to go to Arthur's court, where he became a Knight of the Round Table. [*Contin3*]

GAUNA

The birthplace of the son of King Frollo of Gaul. [*PostQuest*]

GAURIEL OF MONTABEL

A knight who married a fairy, but lost her (and his own handsome features) when he revealed her existence to others. To reclaim her, he had to journey to Arthur's court, defeat three knights, and take them to her land of Fluratrone. He managed to capture Walban, Gawain, and Yvain, and he was thereby reconciled with his wife. In a further adventure at Arthur's court, he rescued the Count of Asterian's daughter from a kidnapper. He was accompanied in his adventures by a pet ram. [*Konrad*]

GAURIUN

A continental land in which Perceval's uncle Trevrizent once sought adventure. [*Wolfram*]

GAUS

A knight healed by Meriadeuc. Gaus, the son of the King of Norval, set out on adventures when he was young. He eventually met the spectre of a former Knight of the Round Table. The two knights fought, and Gaus was deeply wounded by the spirit's sword. The spirit left the sword with Gaus and promised Gaus that he would be healed when a nameless knight of great valor came along and struck Gaus with the sword again. Meriadeuc, having found the sword at the Fountain of Marvels, fulfilled the prophecy. [*Meriadeuc*]

GAUTERE [*Gaunter*]

A knight from Cornwall who was the brother of Sir Arnold. He was one of three unfortunate knights who attacked a knight that they thought was Kay. It was actually Lancelot, disguised in Kay's armor, and the trio got the surprise of their lives. As a condition of his surrender, Lancelot made him go to Camelot and surrender to Guinevere. He was made a Knight of the Round Table, fought at the Castle Perilous tournament, and appeared at the healing of Sir Urry. He was killed fighting Lancelot and his men when Lancelot rescued Guinevere from the stake. [*Malory*]

GAVONY

Lancelot's birthplace in *Les Merveilles de Rigomer*. Traditionally, Lancelot's place of birth is named as BENOIC. [*Merveil*]

GAVÏEN

A knight who abducted the lover of Sir Dodinel the Savage. Perceval chased him down, defeated him, and sent him to Arthur's court, where he became a Knight of the Round Table. [*Contin3*]

GAWAIN[1] [*Calliano, C(h)alvano, Ga(u)gain(s), Galvagin(us), Galwainus, Galwan, Gaoulbanos, Gauan, Gauvain(s), Gauve(i)(n)(s), Gavain(s), Gavaon, Gaven, Gavion, Gawa(i)ne, Gawains, Gawan, Gaw(a)yn(e), Gawe(i)n, Gawin, Gowin, Grion, Gualgua(i)nus, Gualwanus, Valven, Walewein, Walgan(nus), Waluuanii, Walwa(i)n(us), Walwe(i)n, Walwin, Wawain, Wawayne*]

Nephew of Arthur and one of his most famous knights. He is the quintessential knight errant and lover of maidens. In contrast to other prominent knights, such as Perceval or Yvain, no author ever wrote a archetypal romance of Gawain. Although his life spans the great chronicles of Geoffrey of Monmouth and Malory, and a number of Middle English romances feature him, but he has no definitive *Roman de Gawain* in the manner of Chrétien's *Erec* or *Yvain*.

His first significant appearances are in Geoffrey of Monmouth's *Historia* and Chrétien de Troyes's *Perceval*. His character is inconsistent. Early French romance considered him the pearl of worldly knighthood, but the Vulgate and Post-Vulgate Cycles somewhat besmirched his character, turning him into a brash bully who murders knights during the Grail Quest and contributes to Britain's downfall by egging Arthur into a war with Lancelot. Middle-English romance rejects this portrayal and again elevates him to the epitome of chivalric virtue, the most famous example being *Sir Gawain and the Green Knight*. Malory, however, follows the Vulgate interpretation and, consequently, Gawain is a less significant character to modern audiences.

Like Arthur, the figure of Gawain was born long before the Arthurian legends were written in verse or prose. He comes from the hazy realm of oral tradition, and by the time the Latin Chronicles or the French romances were written, their authors felt it sufficient to simply allude to his adventures. Thus, William of Malmesbury—who wrote the earliest existing reference to

Gawain—simply mentioned his relation to Arthur and his tomb in Galloway.

Gawain has no obvious origin in existing early Celtic legend, but he appears Geoffrey of Monmouth's chronicle, and Geoffrey drew his Arthurian characters almost exclusively from Celtic tradition. Another Celtic feature is Gawain's strength, which supposedly waxed in the morning and waned in the afternoon, indicating that in some murky origin, Gawain may have been a sun deity. Though his origins are uncertain, Gawain does have two predecessors or counterparts. The first, Cuchulainn, is an early Irish hero whose adventures (such as the Beheading Game) were assigned to Gawain, in modified form, in French and Middle-English literature. Gawain's other counterpart is GWALCHMEI, a Welsh hero who, like Gawain, is the nephew of Arthur. Gwalchmei is substituted for Gawain in later Welsh adaptations of French literature. Some scholars see Gwalchmei as Gawain's direct origin, but R. S. Loomis rejected this argument in favor of a theory that makes Gawain (orignal form: Gualguainus) a derivation of *Gwallt-afwyn* ("wild hair"), the sobriquet of the Welsh warrior Gwrfan.

Prior to his role in Geoffrey of Monmouth's chronicle, Gawain has a few existing appearances which only hint at his adventures in early oral legend. William of Malmesbury (1125) says he was Arthur's nephew and that he ruled Galloway, which was apparently named after him, and that his grave was discovered in Pembroke in Wales (there seems to be some confusion with an obscure St. Govan, who has a church in Pembroke). On the cathedral archivolt in Modena, Italy (c. 1135), he appears to rescue Guinevere from her abductors, Mardoc and Caradoc.

Geoffrey of Monmouth (c. 1138) sketches a brief biography of his life, naming his parents as King Lot of Lothian and Anna, Arthur's sister. During the time of Arthur's conquests, Gawain is raised in Rome, in the service of Pope Sulpicius. He eventually returns to Britain and becomes one of Arthur's warriors. When Arthur and Rome prepare for war, Gawain is part of a peace envoy sent to the camp of the Roman Emperor Lucius. Gawain takes offense to some comments by one of Lucius's soldiers, cuts off his head, and starts the war. Gawain dies at Richborough, in the first battle between the forces of Arthur and Mordred, Gawain's brother.

Gawain made the transition from chronicle to romance in Chrétien de Troyes's *Perceval* (c. 1190). Though the romance is primarily about the title character, Gawain's adventures occupy the last third of the uncompleted manuscript. Already, we find in Chrétien a portrayal of Gawain as a noble knight, quick with his sword (Excalibur) and with the maidens. While Perceval tries to unravel the mysteries of the Grail and to repair his previous blunder at the Grail Castle, Gawain must go to Escavalon to defend himself against a murder charge brought by Guingambresil. We witness him charm the sister of the king of Escavalon, and then fight his way out of the situation when the king's guards arrive. Later, we see him kindly championing the little daughter of Duke Tiebaut of Tintagel in a tournament, and winning the

tournament through his skill in arms. He endures the vicious tongue of Lady Orgelleuse of Logres, who leads him to Canguin Rock, a mysterious castle inhabited by ladies. He braves the Perilous Bed inside the castle, slays a lion, and apparently ends the castle's enchantments. Chrétien seems to be contrasting the worldly adventures of Gawain with the spiritual education of Perceval.

Chrétien's story ends soon afterwards, and it is unclear how or if he intended to draw Gawain into the Grail Quest. Chrétien's first continuator (c. 1200) focused on Gawain to the exclusion of Perceval, describing Gawain's visit to the Grail Castle, but other continuators retained Perceval as the Grail hero. A notable exception is Heinrich von dem Türlin (c. 1230), who has Gawain complete the Grail Quest and heal the Fisher King.

Throughout the thirteenth century—the golden age of French and German Arthurian romance—Gawain appears in dozens of romances, but rarely in his own adventures. Already established as the greatest of Arthur's knights, Gawain acts as a mentor to young warriors and as a yardstick by which to measure the prowess of other knights. In an often-employed formula, a young knight first arrives at Arthur's court and enters a tournament or joust to prove his prowess. The hero overthrows most of the Knights of the Round Table, but not Gawain, who fights the hero to a draw. In this manner, authors demonstrated the skill of their characters without having them defeat Arthur's greatest knight. Some of these young heroes, such as Guinglain and Wigalois, are Gawain's own sons; Gawain, known as the "Knight of Maidens," has multiple *amies* and, it seems, multiple children.

Among these romances, we have, for the first time, two accounts of Gawain's youth: *Les Enfances Gauvain* and *De Ortu Waluanniii Nepotis Arturi*, which are apparently based on Geoffrey of Monmouth's assertion that Gawain was raised in the service of Pope Sulpicius:

Born illegitimately in the court of Uther Pendragon, Gawain was sent away by his mother in order to avoid any potential problems. She gave him to a knight named Gawain the Brown, who baptized the infant with his name. With only a ring and parchment attesting to his lineage, the infant Gawain was handed to some wealthy merchants (or rescued by fishermen), who took him to Gaul. Leaving him alone on their ship, they docked and entered the town of Narbonne. A poor fisherman named Viamundus happened along, plundered the ship, and took Gawain with him. In time, he journeyed to Rome and raised Gawain there, in the service of the Roman Emperor and Pope Sulpicius. Ignorant of his parentage and true name, Gawain was first called the Boy with No Name and then the Knight of the Surcoat. Knighted by the Emperor of Rome, Gawain claimed the right to the next single combat against Rome's enemies, and was accordingly sent to Jerusalem when Rome went to war with Persia. On the way, the Roman fleet was blown off course and landed on a barbarian island, where Gawain and the Romans defeated the barbarian King Milocrates.

Continuing to Jerusalem, he defeated the Persian warrior Gormundus and settled the dispute.

Having thus served Rome, Gawain decided to journey to the court of the famous King Arthur. The Roman Emperor gave him a box containing the ring and parchment, which he was to present to King Arthur without opening himself. After Gawain defeated Arthur in a joust near his court in Caerleon, Arthur begrudgingly told Gawain that he could join his court if he proved himself worthy. Gawain soon had the chance when Arthur set out to liberate the Castle of Maidens, and Gawain proved himself the only knight able to defeat the pagan king who had captured it. Following this service, Arthur rewarded Gawain by informing him of his name and lineage, and by welcoming him into his service as his knight and nephew.

Other French romances to feature Gawain include a pair of parodies called *La Mule Sans Frein* and *Le Chevalier à l'Épée*, *La Vengeance Raguidel* (Gawain avenges the muder of a knight named Raguidel against Sir Guengasoain), *L'Atre Périlleux* (Gawain rescues a maiden kidnapped by Escanor), *Les Merveilles de Rigomer* (Gawain conquers Rigomer castle after many of Arthur's other knights, including Lancelot, fail). Also notable are Heinrich von dem Türlin's *Diu Crône* (c. 1230), a German romance that makes Gawain the Grail Hero, and Penninc and Pieter Vostaert's *Roman van Walewein* (late thirteenth century), in which Gawain embarks on multiple interlocking quests with the ultimate goal of obtaining the Floating Chessboard from King Wonder.

The great prose cycles written in the early thirteenth century offer the first and only detailed biography of Gawain's life, intertwined with the epic tale of Arthur's rise and downfall. This model was to serve as the source of Malory's Gawain and, consequently, of the modern conception of Gawain. Gawain, though still a significant character, is eclipsed in importance by Lancelot. The Vulgate *Queste del Saint Graal* is the first romance to make Gawain a sinner; the portrayal in the Post-Vulgate romances is even darker; and in the Prose *Tristan*, he is thoroughly evil. The account given by Vulgate and Post-Vulgate romances is summarized as follows:

Gawain is born to King Lot of Lothian and Arthur's half-sister (Belisent or Morgause). He is a descendant of Peter, a follower of Joseph of Arimathea. His brothers are Agravain, Gareth, Gaheris, and Mordred. Gawain's father joins a rebellion against Arthur shortly after Arthur is first crowned. When Gawain, a young man, hears that Arthur is his uncle, he leaves his father's household and swears never to return until Lot submits to Arthur.

Joined by his brothers and cousins (Galescalain and the Yvains), Gawain goes to seek out Arthur, who is embroiled in a war against the invading Saxons. Along the war, Gawain and his companions encounter forces of Saxons, which they defeat at the battles of Logres and Diana Bridge, among others. Merlin assists Gawain in these fights. Eventually, Gawain and his companions find Arthur and are knighted for their brave service. Arthur gives Gawain Excalibur when he receives a better sword. Gawain participates in Arthur's war with Lucius of Rome and begins the first battle as in Geoffrey of Monmouth.

After Arthur has pacified Britain, Gawain has innumerable adventures, some of which are a credit to his character, some of which shame him. He embarks on several quests to find Lancelot, who always seems to be missing. Gawain defends Roestoc against an attack by Seguarades. He supports the true Guinevere duirng the False Guinevere episode. He is imprisoned for a time by Caradoc of the Dolorous Tower, but is liberated by Lancelot. He becomes king of the Castle of Ten Knights for six years.

He gets into his usual scrapes over women: he is attacked by the king of North Wales after sleeping with the king's daughter; and he betrays Pelleas by sleeping with Arcade. He allows himself to become ensorcelled by the ladies on the Rock of Maidens and has to be freed by his brother Gaheris.

In the Post-Vulgate version, Pellinore has killed Lot, so Gawain and his brothers kill Pellinore and Pellinore's sons Lamorat and Drian.

Gawain visits the Grail Castle, but is unable to mend the Grail Sword. He is unable to deliver the daughter of King Pelles from her tub of boiling water. In another visit to Corbenic, he sees the Grail, but his eyes are drawn away from the holy vessel to the beautiful maiden carrying it. He is driven from the castle in a cart, surrounded by peasants pelting him with dung.

When the Sword in the Stone arrives at Camelot, Gawain is unable to draw it, and it is predicted that he will receive a wound for having tried. Gawain is the first to announce his commitment to the Grail Quest when the Grail appears to the Knights of the Round Table. During the quest, Gawain, Gaheris, and Yvain kill the seven brothers whom Galahad has exiled from the Castle of Maidens. In other adventures, Gawain kills his cousin Yvain the Bastard, King Bagdemagus, and sixteen other knights. He is told by a hermit that he cannot achieve the Grail because he lacks humility, patience, and abstinence. Eventually, he is wounded by Galahad in a tournament (by the same sword that Gawain had tried to draw from the stone) and is laid up for the rest of the quest. Afterwards, Arthur chastises him for having killed so many knights during a holy quest.

Gawain remains neutral during the discovery of Lancelot's affair with Guinevere until Lancelot accidentally kills Gaheris and Gareth while rescuing Guinevere from the stake. Gawain's fury forces Arthur into a war with Lancelot, and Gawain refuses any compromise or surrender or apology from

Lancelot. Finally, in Benoic, he fights Lancelot in single combat and receives a serious head wound. The Romans attack Arthur while Arthur is in France, and Gawain's wound is aggravated during the battle. Arthur's army returns to Britain to deal with Mordred's treachery. Gawain, on his deathbed, relents and says, "I am sadder about not being able to see Lancelot before I die than I am about the thought of dying. If I could only see the man I know to be the finest and most courteous knight in the world and beg his forgiveness for having been so uncourtly to him recently, I feel my soul would be more at rest after my death." Gawain perishes of his wound a few days later and is buried in a tomb with his brother Gaheris.

Though this version of Gawain's life and character survives in Malory (1470), Gawain briefly reclaims his heroic, pure status in the Middle English romances of the fourteenth century. These include *Syre Gawene and the Carle of Carlyle* (by passing a test of nobility, Gawain transforms the Carl of Carlisle and marries his daughter), *The Avowing of King Arthur* (Gawain rescues a maiden from Menealf), *The Awntyrs off Arthure* (Gawain defeats Lord Galleron of Galloway in a battle before Arthur), *The Weddyng of Syr Gawen* and "The Marriage of Sir Gawain" (Gawain marries the loathly lady in order to save Arthur), and, of course, *Sir Gawain and the Green Knight*, in which Gawain demonstrates virtues while braving a beheading game at the hands of the supernatural Green Knight.

Again, Malory, using the Post-Vulgate characterization, makes Gawain a knight whose human failings are all too evident, though his final letter of forgiveness to Lancelot ("By a more noble man might I not be slain") is a magnanimous and moving moment. Gawain is not the main character in any of Malory's eight books, though some of them feature Gawain in chapters. The ultimate effect of Malory's treatment was to relegate Gawain to second-class status. In later romances, including modern fiction and film, Gawain's character is eclipsed by the Lancelot-Guinevere affair. Tennyson mentions him only briefly.

In Hughes' *The Misfortunes of Arthur*, Gawain survives until the battle of Camlann. The Middle English *Parlement of the Thre Ages* is unique in saying that Gawain survived the Mordred wars and threw Excalibur into a lake. [Modena, WilliamM, GeoffHR, Wace, ChretienE, ChretienC, ChretienY, ChretienP, Contin1, Wirnt, PleierG, RobertBlo, Historia, Ywain, Stanz, Awntyrs, SirGawain, SyreGaw, Allit, Marriage, Weddyng, Malory, KingA&C, HughesT, HeberMG, TennIK]

Relations: Gawain's family, wives, and kinsmen are named below. More information can be found under their respective entries.

Father: Usually, King Lot of Lothian (and, sometimes, Orkney); Jascaphin in Heinrich von dem Türlin

Mother: Arthur's sister, variously called Albagia, Anna, Belisent, Morgause, Orchades, Sangive, Seife

Wives and Lovers: Amie, Amurfina, Arcade, Beauté, Blanchandine, Blanchemal, Bloiesine, Ettard, Flori, Florée, Florie, Guenloie, Guilorete, Gwendolen, Halaés, Lorie, Orguelleuse, Pulzella Gaia, Ragnelle, Tanrée, Venelas, Ydain

Sons: Beaudous, Florence, Guinglain, Henec Suctellois, Lionel, Lovell, Wigalois

Brothers: Agravain, Aguerisse, Beacurs, Gaheris, Gareth, Gwidon, Mordred

Sisters: Clarissant, Cundrie, Elaine, Itonje, Soredamor

See Also: Beheading Game, Brandelis, Cuchulainn, Grail, Green Knight, Gringolet, Guinganbresil, Guiromelant, Gwalcmei, Loathly Lady, Rigomer

GAWAIN² THE BROWN [*Gauvain le Brun]

The first foster-father of Gawain, entrusted with the child by Morgause and Lot. He named the baby after himself and eventually set him adrift on the ocean. The infant washed up on shore and was rescued by a fisherman. [*Enfances*]

GAWANIDES THE STRONG

Gawain's grandson; the son of Wigalois and Larie. Wirnt von Grafenberg, in *Wigalois*, tells us that he was a noble and powerful knight who had many adventures, and that many tales were told about him. [*Wirnt*]

GAWDELYN

A bad knight and ravisher of ladies who was killed by Sir Aglovale. Gawdelyn's brother, Sir Goodwyn, later tried to avenge this death by attacking Aglovale, but Goodwyn was himself killed. [*Malory*]

GAY CASTLE [*Gais Chasteaus]

A lively, splendid castle on the Thames river, ruled by Trahan the Gay, and inhabited by Trahan's sons Melian the Gay and Drian the Gay, the latter of whom was rescued by Lancelot from a coffin. Afterwards, Lancelot attended a celebration at the Gay Castle. An unnamed Lord of the Gay Castle was one of Arthur's allies against the Saxons. Arthur gave a castle of the same name to Morholt of Ireland. [*VulgLanc, Livre, ProsTris*]

GAY GALLANT [Gais Galantis, Gay Galantin]

One of Arthur's knights who, among many others, joined Gawain in a quest to investigate the Dolorous Guard, and in another to find Lancelot. [*LancLac, VulgLanc*]

GAYNOR

A variation of GUINEVERE found in many Middle English romances.

GAZEL

A castle, probably in northern Britain. Its castellan fought against the Saxons in the early days of Arthur's reign, along with the rulers in rebellion against Arthur. [*VulgMer*]

GAZEVILTE [*Gazewilté*]

The castle of the knight Persides. Persides locked up his wife, Elaine the Peerless, in the castle when she claimed that she was more beautiful than he was valiant. He agreed to let her go as soon as a more valiant knight or a more beautiful woman came along, thus settling the argument. Arthur's knight Hector came to the castle and, through combat with Persides, decided the conflict in favor of Elaine. [*LancLac*, *VulgLanc*]

GECRON

The son of the Babylonian King Micipsa, who fought against Arthur's army at the battle of Soissons. He saw his father fall to the sword of Earl Leir of Boulogne, and he slew Leir in revenge. [*Layamon*]

GEDEORDE

A forest in Arthur's lands that was the site of a white stag hunt and a tournament in Guillaume le Clerc's *Fergus*. The tournament was called specifically to flesh Fergus out of hiding, and he proved the victor. Guillaume, who had a fair knowledge of Scottish geography, may have been referring to Jedburgh in Roxburghshire. [*Guillaume*]

GEDIENS

The King of Karedonas and Trefferin who was treacherously slain by King Verangoz of Sorboreste. His daughter, Dulceflur, found Sir Meleranz, Arthur's nephew, to avenge him. [*PleierM*]

GEER

The Count of Geer was the son of the King of the Island of the Gate and the brother of an Irish knight at Arthur's court. The Irish knight slew the Count of Geer along with the rest of his family, and then fell burning from a tower at Camelot. [*PostQuest*]

GEJES

A knight of Arthur's court in the Serbo-Russian *Povest' o Tryshchane*. [*Povest*]

GELDRAS OF DUNEILE

A king who was a vassal or ally of Arthur. He participated in a tournament at the Castle of Maidens. The name of his land may be a variation of *Dunveline*, or Dublin. [*Renaut*]

GENDAWD

The father of Gwyll, Arthur's mistress. [*Triads*]

GENES

A ship's captain who was a friend of Tristan. When Tristan was mortally wounded, he sent Genes to bring Isolde from Cornwall to heal him, but Genes and Isolde arrived too late; Tristan was already dead. Genes's daughter was also named Isolde. Genes is found in the Prose *Tristan*; in other romances, this ship's captain is generally not named. In some texts, it is KAHEDINS, Tristan's brother-in-law. [*ProsTris*]

GENELOIE

The Duke of Geneloie was the father of Garsallas, a knight defeated by Perceval. [*Contin2*]

GENER OF KARTIS

A mysterious lady encountered by Gawain during the Grail Quest in *Diu Crône*. She saved him from drowning in a river on the way to the Grail Castle by turning it into hard ground. Her brother, Humildis, was a renowned knight. [*Heinrich*]

GENEWIS

The kingdom belonging to Pant (Ban), Lancelot's father, in Ulrich's *Lanzelet*. Although identification with Gwynedd in Wales and Guenet in Brittany have been suggested, it is most likely a variation of BENOIC, Ban's traditional kingdom in other Lancelot stories. It may have influenced Der Pleier's GAMVIS. [*UlrichZ*]

GENGEMOR

An Arthurian knight defeated in joust by Daniel of the Blossoming Valley. [*Stricker*]

GENNES [*Genes*]

A land in Arthur's domain. Its king was one of Arthur's knights, and he accompanied Gawain on two quests to find Lancelot. [*LancLac*, *VulgLanc*]

GENOA [*Gene*]

A seaport in northwest Italy. Genoese soldiers were considered among the best in the Emperor of Rome's armies, and Lucius brought many of them, including a number of giants, to France when he waged war against King Arthur. [*Allit*, *Malory*]

GENTIS

A knight present at the tournament of Sorgarda, which Gawain won. [*Heinrich*]

GEOFFREY OF MONMOUTH

Arthur finds a copy of his *Historia Regum Britanniae* in the House of Temperance, ruled by Alma. The book is unnamed but is identified by its contents. Arthur's version of the book, naturally, breaks off after the reign of Uther Pendragon. [*Spenser*]

GEOGENANT

Ruler, with the Lady Dyonise, of the Castle of Ten Maidens. He was a friend of Arthur's Sir Durmart. [*Durmart*]

GEORGE

The true name of the RED CROSS KNIGHT in Spenser's *The Faerie Queene*. He is St. George, the patron saint of England. [*Spenser*]

GERAINT [*Gereint*]

As the hero of the Welsh legend bearing his name, he is the counterpart of EREC in French romance. He appears in several early Welsh poems, including one which describes his great deeds at the battle of Llongborth. The substitution of his name for Chrétien's Erec is not entirely unfounded phonetically, as *Erec* is itself a derivative of *Guerec*. Several historical figures named Gerontius are known in Britain—particularly in the south—in and around the Arthurian period, and any of them (or, perhaps more likely, a conflation of them all) could have inspired the character.

Geraint was the son of King Erbin of Devon and Cornwall, the brother of Ermid and Dywel, and the father of Cadwy. As a young warrior, Geraint avenged an insult to Queen Gwenhwyfar (Guinevere) committed by the warrior Edern (Yder) by defeating Edern in a sparrowhawk tournament. During the quest, Geraint lodged with Earl Niwl in Cardiff and fell in love with the earl's daughter, Enid. After settling the score with Edern, Geraint returned to Arthur's court where he was honored for his victory, and was given Enid's hand in marriage.

In time, his father grew infirm, and Geraint returned to Devon to assume the responsibilities of a ruler. Though always deemed the best warrior in jousts and tournaments, Geraint grew bored with feats of arms and preferred to spend his time with his wife in their chambers. Rumors began to circulate concerning Geraint's worthiness as a ruler. The grumbling reached Enid's ears, and one morning in bed, when she thought Geraint was asleep, she lamented about the growing scandal. Geraint misinterpreted her words and perceived that she had been unfaithful. He forced his wife to accompany him on a series of dangerous adventures, culminating when, Geraint having been knocked unconscious by some giants, an earl named Limwris tried to force himself on Enid. Geraint awoke at Enid's screams and killed the earl. Realizing that Enid was faithful after all, Geraint asked for, and received, his wife's forgiveness.

The Welsh poem that praises Geraint's deeds at Llongborth may imply, but does not explicitly say, that he died there. Tennyson alone describes his death fighting heathens on the northern sea. [*Gododdin, WelshGer, Geraint, TennIK*]

GERARD[1]

An Arthurian knight from Wales slain by the giant Jolyan during the Roman War. [*Allit, Malory*]

GERARD[2] LE BREUSE

Brother of Sir Arnold le Breuse. On his quest to defeat the Red Knight of the Red Lands, Gareth encountered the brothers at a passage over the river Marcosia. In a brief battle, both brothers were killed. [*Malory*]

GEREINYAWN THE OLD

Father of Arthur's warrior Cerenhyr. [*Triads*]

GEREMIE[1]

King of Hungary in *Floriant et Florete*. He served Emperor Filimenis of Constantinople, who joined a war against Arthur. The war ended in a truce. Geremie's daughter, Blanchandine, married Gawain, and Gawain inherited Geremie's kingdom. [*Floriant*]

GEREMIE[2]

King of India in *Claris et Laris*. He joined Emperor Thereus of Rome in a war against Arthur and was slain in battle by Sir Laris. [*Claris*]

GERES THE LITTLE

One of Arthur's knights. [*Mottuls*]

GERFLET

King Arthur's fool in the Norse *Möttuls Saga*. He is probably related in origin to the knight GIRFLET. [*Mottuls*]

GERHART OF RIVIERS

A prince who attacked the castle Merkanie because King Tjofabier of Merkanie refused to allow Gerhart to wed Sabie, Tjofabier's maiden daughter. In the ensuing battles, he killed Gilbert, Tjofabier's son. Arthur's Sir Garel ended the conflict by defeating Gerhart and Rialt, Gerhart's kinsman. As a condition of Gerhart's surrender, Garel made him pledge support to Arthur's war against King Ekunaver of Kanadic. [*PleierG*]

GERLE

In the Middle English *Sir Degrevant*, the Duke of Gerle was a suitor of Melidor, the maiden loved by Sir Degrevant (a Knight of the Round Table). Degrevant defeated the Duke of Gerle in combat twice, forcing him to relinquish his claim to Melidor's love. Gerle was apparently in France. [*SirDeg*]

GERMANUS

A saint who lived from 378 to 448. He was a Roman official who presided in Gaul before, in 418, he was appointed bishop of Auxerre. He traveled to Britain at least twice. His second visit, in 447, becomes material of legend in Nennius's *Historia Brittonum*, partly adapted from Germanus's *Life*. Nennius says that Germanus came to Britain at the request of King Vortimer. Christianity had been damaged during the reign of Vortigern, whom Vortimer had deposed. When Vortigern reclaimed the throne, Germanus condemned him for marrying his own daughter. When Vortigern ignored Germanus's pleas to break the union, his castle (in one account) was destroyed in a holy fire. [*Nennius, GeoffHR*]

GERMANY

Historically, the Saxons who invaded Britain in the sixth century came from Germany, and Geoffrey of Monmouth according lists Hengist and Horsa as German natives. Though the country was divided by number of Teutonic tribes in the fifth and sixth century, several "dukes" or "emperors" of Germany appear in various Arthurian romances. Among them are an Emperor of Germany whose daughter, Fenice, is the love of Cliges in Chrétien de Troyes's *Cliges*; another Emperor of Germany who joins a tournament at Camelot in the Vulgate *Lancelot*; and Emperor Henry of Germany, who is named as the father of Arthur's Sir Laris in *Claris et Laris*. An Emperor of the ALEMANNI figures into the tale of *Meriadoc*. Duke Frollo, who rules Gaul in Geoffrey of Monmouth's chronicle, is the ruler of Germany (owing his allegiance to Rome) in the Vulgate *Merlin*, and the Germans join Frollo, Emperor Lucius, and King Claudas in a series of aggressions against Arthur. Frollo had stolen the dukedom from a Duke Mathem. [*GeoffHR, ChretienC, VulgLanc, VulgMer, Claris, Historia*]

GERMIONS [*Gremions*]

One of Arthur's knights in *Les Merveilles de Rigomer*. Germions joined Gawain's quest to conquer Rigomer castle. [*Merveil*]

GERNEMANT OF NORTHUMBERLAND

A knight who loved the maiden of the Castle of the Door. When she refused to marry him, he besieged the the castle. He eventually abandoned the siege, after arranging with the Lord of the Castle of the Door that if the maiden could not find a champion within a year, Gernemant would take her by force and give her to his vilest stable boys. Just before the end of the year, Gawain visited the Castle of the Door and agreed to champion the maiden. Gawain killed Gernemant. [*Meriadeuc*]

GERNEMUE

An island on which the fairy Blanchemal resided. [*Contin4*]

GEROAS

A knight in the service of King Ban of Benoic and King Bors of Gannes. Girflet wounded him in a tournament between the brother kings' knights and Arthur's warriors. [*VulgMer*]

GERONTIUS

According to Geoffrey of Monmouth, a king of Britain in the third or second century BC. Gerontius was the son of King Elidur. Gerontius succeeded his cousin, King Runno. Gerontius's son, King Catell, succeeded him. Gerontius is a popular name in British history. See GERAINT. [*GeoffHR*]

GERTHMWL

Arthur's chief elder in his northern lands, according to a Welsh Triad. [*Triads*]

GERVAIS THE SLENDER [*Ieroas*]

A knight who fought in Arthur's battles against King Rions at Carmelide. [*VulgMer, Arthour*]

GERYNE LE GROSS

A knight. Alexander the Orphan, King Mark's nephew, arranged for Geryne to be married to a young maiden who had wanted to marry Alexander. [*Malory*]

GEUN OF TURIE

A fairy who lived in Maiden Land, the island where Lancelot was raised. When Lancelot prepared to depart the island, Geun made him a splendid shield. [*UlrichZ*]

GIAFREDI

In the *Tristano Panciaticchiano*, the brother of Mador of the Gate who was poisoned at Arthur's court. Guinevere, who had hosted the feast at which he died, was accused of murder by Mador, but Lancelot championed her and she was exonerated. The same character is called GAHERIS in the Vulgate *Mort Artu* and PATRISE in Malory. [*TristanoP*]

GIALLE

A lady in the ancestry of the Brown Family. She was the daughter of Brun and Pamphille and the sister of Yrlande. [*Palamedes*]

GIANT WITHOUT A NAME [*Jaiant sans nom*]

A giant baptized and knighted by Arthur. The son of a dwarf, the Giant was suckled by a unicorn as a child, which turned him into a beast. Stupid and perpetually hungry, he killed men and animals indiscriminately. The Giant and his father were stranded on an island for twenty years until Arthur happened to land there and rescue them. [*ChevPap*]

GIANT'S CROSS

A monument near Camelot, along the Montignet Road. It served as a meeting place. [*VulgLanc*]

GIANTS' DANCE

A legend apparently invented by Geoffrey of Monmouth to explain STONEHENGE. The Giants' Dance was a circle of giant stones which had been carried out of Africa by a race of giants and placed on Mount Killaraus in Ireland. When Ambrosius Aurelius desired to build a monument in Amesbury for fallen British warriors, Merlin suggested bringing the Giants' Dance from Ireland. Ambrosius laughed at the idea of transporting such heavy stones, but Merlin was able to accomplish the task through magic and ingenious engineering. Merlin's party—led by Uther—encountered resistance from the Irish under King

Gilloman, but they were victorious. Merlin brought the stones to the plain of Ealing near Amesbury and set them up in a ring. Ambrosius Aurelius, Uther Pendragon, and later kings were buried at the Giant's Dance. The fourteenth-century *Short Metrical Chronicle* has Merlin building the Dance for King Dunval, not Ambrosius. [*GeoffHR, Wace, Short*]

GIANT'S FOUNTAIN

A Cornish spring where Isolde caught Palamedes spying on her. Palamedes had kidnapped Brangain, Isolde's servant. [*ProsTris*]

GIANT'S ISLE [*Giant's Rock*]

One of the Distant Isles, ruled by the giant Brunor, father of Galehaut. The Castle of Tears, which was liberated by Tristan, was situated on the island. [*ProsTris*]

GIANT'S KNOLL

A hill in Britain, two days from Camelot. It was visited by Joseph of Arimathea and his followers. [*VulgEst*]

GIANT'S ROCK

A rock on the Island of Servage, visited by Lamorat during his stay there. [*ProsTris*]

GIANT'S TOWER[1] [**Tour aux Geants*]

A tower near the Spring of Healing, ruled by Atamas, who was also known as the Knight of the Tower. Atamas used the healing powers of the Spring to defeat all knights who came his way, imprisoning them in the Tower. Among its prisoners were Gawain, Gaheris, Bleoberis, and Sagremor. The Giants' Tower was liberated by Palamedes, who defeated Atamas during the Grail Quest. In Joseph of Arimathea's days, the Tower had been ruled by King Camalis, who imprisoned Nascien and Mordrains. [*PostQuest*]

GIANT'S TOWER[2]

The entrance to Arthur's palace in Caerleon. He rallied his warriors there at the beginning of the Roman War. [*GeoffHR, Bek, Allit*]

GIBEL

A fairy land visited by Arthur's Sir Jaufré after he fell through an enchanted fountain. The land was attacked by a horrid monster called Felon of Albarua, but Jaufré killed it. The lady of Gibel rewarded Jaufré with a banquet. MONTGIBEL is Morgan le Fay's residence in some romances, and the lady of Gibel is probably identical to Morgan. [*Jaufre*]

GIEUS

A Knight of the Round Table wounded when Lancelot rescued Guinevere from the stake. [*Tavola*]

GIGAMEC

A malicious knight in Heinrich von dem Türlin's *Diu Crône*. He killed the brother of Sir Aamanz, who was called "the Other Gawain" due to his striking similarity to Arthur's nephew. Aamanz pursued Gigamec in revenge, and the two knights encountered Gawain himself. In a confusing melee, Gawain defeated Aamanz and gave him to Gigamec, who, with another knight named Zedoech, murdered "the Other Gawain" as soon as the real Gawain had left. Gigamec then brought Aamanz's head to Arthur's court, representing it as Gawain's, causing great distress until the truth was discovered. [*Heinrich*]

GILAN

Duke of Swales who, in Gottfried's *Tristan*, harbored Tristan during one of Tristan's exiles from King Mark's court. Gilan owned a little dog named Petitcreiu, which had been given to him by a lady from Avalon. He gave the dog to Tristan as a reward for Tristan's killing of the troublesome giant Urgan. He is known as BRAMANTE in *La Tavola Ritonda*. In the Pleier's *Garel*, he appears as a knight defeated in combat by Garel. Each was so impressed with the other's prowess that they became fast friends. Garel helped Gilan rescue his nephews, Alexander and Floris, from Eskilabon of Belamunt. Gilan returned the favor by fighting alongside Garel in Arthur's war against King Ekunaver of Kanadic. Arthur later awarded him a Round Table seat. [*Gottfried, PleierG*]

GILANEIER

A variation of GUINEVERE, Arthur's wife, found in the French romance of *Jaufre*. [*Jaufre*]

GILBERT[1]

Son of Cadgyffro. He was one of Arthur's warriors and advisors in Welsh legend. A Welsh Triad lists him as one of the "three Slaughter-Blocks of the Island of Britain." He rode a horse named Red Wolf-Tread. The name Gilbert is Norman, and was borne by several British rulers in the twelfth century; the particular progenitor of the name was likely Gilbert of Clare (Loomis, *Romance*, 41). [*Triads, Dream*]

GILBERT[2]

The valiant son of Tjofabier of Merkanie, slain in the his father's war against Gerhart of Riviers. He was avenged by Arthur's sir Garel. [*PleierG*]

GILBERT[3] [*Gylbart, Gylbert*]

Father of a maiden upon whom Gawain begot a child in *The Jeaste of Sir Gawain*. When Gilbert learned that Gawain had slept with his daughter, he challenged him to combat and was defeated, as were his three sons, Gyamoure, Tyrry, and Brandelis. He is known as NORROIZ in the first continuation of Chrétien's *Perceval*. [*Jeaste*]

GILDAS

A Welsh cleric or monk who lived c. 500–570. He is known as the author of *De Excidio et Conquestu Britanniae* (c. 540), considered the earliest "Arthurian" text for the glimpse of post-Roman British history that it provides (Arthur is not mentioned, but Ambrosius and Vortigern appear). Gildas longed for the golden days when Rome ruled Britain, and he lambastes contemporary British rulers (Cuneglas, Constantine of Devon, Aurelius Caninus, Maelgwn of Gwynedd, and Vortipore of Dyfed) for their tyranny and lechery.

Gildas is called the "wisest of Britons" in the *Annales Cambriae*, and he was revered by the Irish and Welsh as a saint. He appears in Welsh legend as the son of Caw, one of 20 brothers, and one of Arthur's warriors. His *Life*, written in the early twelfth century by Caradoc of Llancarfan, recounts how "Saint" Gildas's many brothers resisted Arthur's reign, but Gildas supported the king. Arthur eventually killed Gildas's brother Hueil. Arthur received Gildas's forgiveness and performed great penance for the slaying. Later, Gildas and the Abbott of Glastonbury convinced King Melwas of the Summer Region to release Guinevere, whom Melwas had kidnapped. After Arthur's death, Gildas apparently went to Brittany and set himself up as a teacher. One of his students was Taliesin. According to the *Annales Cambriae*, Gildas visited Ireland in 565 and died in 570. In Hughes' *The Misfortunes of Arthur*, Gildas laments the state of Britain after Arthur's death. [*Annales, Culhwch, Caradoc, GeoffVM, HughesT*]

GILHEDIS

An Arthurian knight in the romance of *Yder*. He fought in Arthur's war against Taulas of Rougemont, a vassal in rebellion, during which he was defeated by Sir Yder. [*Yder*]

GILIERCHINO

Tristan's father-in-law in *La Tavola Ritonda*, in which he replaces HOEL. The king of Solona in Brittany and father of Isolde of the White Hands, Gilierchino went to war with his nephew, Count Albroino of Gippa. When Tristan saved his lands by defeating Albroino, Gilierchino forced him to accept the crown of Brittany. [*Tavola*]

GILIMAR

A noble knight who lodged Lancelot, Gawain, Gareth, and Tristan on their way back from the castle Pluris adventure. Gilimar was thought to be mute; in truth, his wife simply made him refrain from speaking for long periods of time in penance for his excessive blathering about love. [*UlrichZ*]

GILLA¹

One of Arthur's warriors in Welsh legend, who could leap three hundred acres in a single bound. For this reason, he was called "stag shank." [*Culhwch*]

GILLA²

In Thomas Hughes' *The Misfortunes of Arthur*, a British earl who joined Mordred's treason against Arthur. Mordred offered him Cornwall for his support. Hughes may have taken him from Geoffrey's GILLAPATRIC, GILLASEL, or GILLARN. [*HughesT*]

GILLAPATRIC [*Gilpatric, Gylopayk*]

An Irish warrior who fought for Mordred against King Arthur and was killed at the battle of Camel. [*GeoffHR, Wace*]

GILLARN

An Irish warrior who joined Mordred's rebellion against King Arthur and was killed at the battle of Camel. [*GeoffHR, Wace*]

GILLASEL [*Gilloscop, Syllatel*]

An Irish warrior who fought for Mordred against King Arthur and was killed at the battle of Camel. [*GeoffHR, Wace*]

GILLE CALLAET

A Saxon warrior and member of King Constans' court. Vortigern caused Gille Callaet and other Saxons to despise King Constans, and they eventually entered his room and assassinated him, allowing Vortigern to take the crown. [*Layamon*]

GILLMOR [*Gilmarium, Gylomar*]

An Irish warrior who joined Mordred's rebellion against King Arthur and was killed at the battle of Camel. [*GeoffHR, Wace*]

GILLOMAN [*Gillomaurus, Gillomanius, Gillomen, Guillomer*]

The King of Ireland when King Ambrosius Aurelius ruled in Britain. Gilloman heard that Uther and Merlin had landed in Ireland to take away the Giants' Dance (Stonehenge) from Mount Killaraus. Enraged, Gilloman assembled his soldiers and attacked Uther's party as they headed toward the Mount Killaraus, but Uther was victorious. Gilloman later allied with Vortigern's son, Pascentius, in an attempt to conquer Britain from Ambrosius. They met Uther at Saint David's (or at Menevia) in Wales, and both Gilloman and Pascentius were killed in the battle. [*GeoffHR*]

GILLOMAUR¹ [*Gillamaur, Gillamore, Guillamurius*]

The King of Ireland several generations before Arthur. He allied with the Huns and Picts—led by Guanius and Melga—to invade Britain. Gillomaur's Irishmen were driven out by the Romans, under Febus, and then—for good—by Constantine of Brittany. [*GeoffHR, Wace, Layamon*]

GILLOMAUR² [*Colman, Guillamure, Gwyl(o)mar, Villamus*]

The King of Ireland in the early days of Arthur's reign. He came to the aid of the Scots and Picts, whom Arthur was fighting at Lake Lomond, but Arthur defeated him and sent him back to Ireland with a depleted army. After pacifying the island of Britain, Arthur invaded Ireland and captured Gillomaur, forcing the rest of the country to surrender. As his subject, Gillomaur assisted Arthur in the invasion of Gaul and in the Roman War. In Hughes' *The Misfortunes of Arthur*, Gillomaur joins Mordred's treason against Arthur and is slain at the battle of Camlann. [*GeoffHR, Wace, HughesT*]

GIMAZET

A knight present at the tournament of Sorgarda, which Gawain won. [*Heinrich*]

GIMILE

A lady at Arthur's court who, along with most of the other ladies, failed a magical chastity test. [*Heinrich*]

GINAINS

An Arthurian knight who joined Gawain's quest to conquer Rigomer castle. [*Merveil*]

GINEMANS [*Graemans, Guinemans*]

One of four Irish robber knights defeated by Lancelot on his way to Rigomer castle. [*Merveil*]

GINGAMORS

An Arthurian knight who joined Gawain's quest to conquer Rigomer castle. [*Merveil*]

GIOT

One of Arthur's knights. When Lancelot wanted to pursue a claim on his ancestral land of Genewis (Benoic), Giot and Yvain traveled to the land to gauge the moods and inclinations of the various noblemen there, finding that they were favorable toward Lancelot. [*UlrichZ*]

GIPPA

In *La Tavola Ritonda*, a city ruled by Count Albroino, the enemy of Tristan's father-in-law, King Gilierchino. When Albroino was slain in combat, Gilierchino, with Tristan's help, besieged and conquered it. Gilierchino gave it to Tristan, who in turn bestowed it on a knight named Statuano. The name may be a corruption of AGRIPPE, the name of the count himself in the Prose *Tristan*. [*Tavola*]

GIRAMPHIEL

A goddess who hated Gawain because he had stolen a magic belt from her husband, Sir Fimbeus. When Gawain visited her castle, she maliciously told him of an adventure to be found in the country of Aufat—in truth, the "adventure" was a terrible dragon, which Gawain nonetheless managed to defeat. Her second plot involved sending a magical glove, which revealed a woman's infidelities, to Arthur's court. The glove caused great consternation, as no lady was able to pass the chastity test. At the same time, one of Giramphiel's vassals stole magic artifacts from Arthur. In a third scheme, she equipped Fimbeus with enchanted armor and sent him into battle against Gawain, but Arthur's nephew was still victorious. Gawain forced Giramphiel to swear fealty and to return Arthur's treasures. A final plan to circulate a rumor that Gawain was dead proved equally unsuccessful. [*Heinrich*]

GIRFLET [*Gerflet, Gif(f)let, Girfles, Girflez, Gofrei, Grifles, Griflet, Grimfles, Gryflet(te)*]

A Knight of the Round Table, son of Do, and brother of Lorete who first appears in Chrétien de Troyes's *Erec*. He is a ubiquitous character, but rarely a central one. He may have origins in the non-Arthurian Welsh hero called Gilfaethwy, son of Don. The Arthurian knights JAUFRÉ and JOFRIT are probably derivatives. His first notable adventure is provided by Chrétien's *Perceval*, in which Girflet sets out to find adventure at the Castle Orgeluse. He apparently failed and was taken prisoner, because in the First Continuation of *Perceval*, Arthur and his knights embark on a mission to rescue him from the castle.

In Renaut de Bâgé's *Le Bel Inconnu*, Girflet is noted as the lord of Becleus and overseer of a sparrowhawk tournament (Thomas Chestre calls him GYFFROUN). The most beautiful woman was supposed to win the sparrowhawk, but Girflet used his skill at arms to continually defeat every challenger and award the prize to his lady, Rose Espaine, who was unattractive. Guinglain, Gawain's son, eventually defeated him in the name of the lady Margerie.

In Girart d'Amiens's *Escanor*, he has a brother named Galantivet, who serves as Gawain's squire. He becomes captive, and then husband of the Queen of Traverses, who dies shortly after their marriage.

A combination of episodes from the Vulgate and Post-Vulgate romances provides the following biography: Girflet joined Arthur's service at the beginning of the king's reign. Arriving at Arthur's court as a squire, he requested knighthood to avenge the death of his former master, Mylis, at the hands of King Pellinore. He failed in this quest but earned a reputation as a valiant knight afterwards. He fought against the rebellious kings and the Saxons. After the battle of the Humber, Arthur promoted him to the Round Table. His subsequent adventures consisted largely of various imprisonments, leading Gawain to remark that "there never was a man so frequently taken prisoner as Girflet has been." He was betrothed to one of Guinevere's maidservants. During the Grail Quest, Palamedes, Galahad and Samaliel all defeated and wounded Girflet. Girflet and Lucan were the only warriors to survive the battle of Salisbury, and they bore the mortally wounded Arthur to the Ancient Chapel. Arthur ordered Girflet to throw Excalibur into a lake and, after twice hiding the sword and lying about it, Girflet complied. He saw Arthur's body carried away by Morgan le Fay. Later finding Arthur's "grave" at the chapel, he ordered it exhumed and found it empty. He died within a few weeks.

Malory says that Lancelot killed Girflet while rescuing Guinevere from the stake; Girflet's role after the battle of Salisbury is taken by BEDIVERE. [*ChretienE*, *Beroul*, *Renaut*, *LancLac*, *VulgLanc*, *VulgMort*, *VulgMer*, *Livre*, *PostMer*, *PostQuest*, *PostMort*, *Girart*, *Malory*]

GIRIDA

One of Isolde's ladies-in-waiting in *La Tavola Ritonda*. She is known as BESSILLE in the Prose *Tristan*. She fell in love with Tristan, but when he did not reciprocate her affection, her love turned to hate and she conspired with Andred to expose the affair between Tristan and Isolde. [*Tavola*]

GISMIRANTE

Hero of Antonio Pucci's romance bearing his name, Gismirante, the son of a former Knight of the Round Table, left his home in Rome for Arthur's court after his father, on his deathbed, bade him to make the journey. Gismirante served Arthur for seven years before he received a chance to prove himself. Arthur's custom was to refuse dinner until he had heard news of an adventure. Over one particularly boring weekend, no such news came, and Arthur's court began to starve to death. Setting out, Gismirante learned from a fairy the plight of a beautiful princess who was forced by her father to go to church naked. Anyone who gazed upon her was decapitated. Recounting this story satisfied Arthur's requirement. Gismirante then embarked to find the princess. On the way, he saved a griffin from a dragon, gave food to a starving eagle, and rescued a hawk. He saved the princess from her tyrannical father, but lost her to a giant. In the quest to reclaim her, he was assisted by the animals he befriended. He eventually returned to Arthur's court with the princess and married her there. [*PucciG*]

GISORS

A country in Uther Pendragon's kingdom. [*Heinrich*]

GITEDRANO

A fortress in the country of Listenois. Tristan killed Lucanoro, the son of its castellan, during the Grail Quest. Tristan later happened upon the castle looking for lodging. When the castellan realized the identity of his visitor, he seized him and planned to execute him. Palamedes caught them in the act and saved Tristan, killing the castellan and his company. Palamedes took control of the castle. [*Tavola*]

GIUBERC

An Arthurian knight in the romance of *Yder*. He participated in Arthur's war against Taulas of Rougemont, a vassal in rebellion, and was defeated by Sir Yder. [*Yder*]

GIURIANDO

Tristan's horse, according to *La Tavola Ritonda*. It was given to him by Inamante of the Brown Valley. [*Tavola*]

GIURIANO

Nephew of the king of Scotland, present at Arthur's tournament at the Hard Rock. [*Tavola*]

GIWANET

A page to King Flois of the Green Island. When Flois's land was besieged by a giant named Assiles, Giwanet carried a plea for assistance to Arthur's court. [*Heinrich*]

GLAALANT

A Saxon king who fought under King Aminaduc at the siege of Vambieres. Arthur's forces countered and defeated the Saxons. [*Livre*]

GLADET

During a speech in Heinrich von dem Türlin's *Diu Crône*, Gawain refers to an episode in which, at Gladet, he "destroyed the enchantment that nearly burned my friend Sir Lanzelet to death." [*Heinrich*]

GLADINEL

A knight freed from the prison of Felon of the Guard when Sir Durmart defeated Felon. [*Durmart*]

GLADOAIN [*Gladoains*]

In *Perlesvaus*, a good knight from the Isles of Mores. He assisted Lancelot when the latter was attacked four knights at once. Upon receiving a wound, he left the battle to find help, returning with Gawain. He perished of his wound. In return for his service, Lancelot helped Gladoain's brother, the Knight of the Green Shield, expel an invader from Gladoain's castle. He is also listed a knight of Arthur's court and a companion of Gawain in *Les Merveilles de Rigomer*. [*Perlesvaus*, *Merveil*]

GLADOR ESLIS

A vassal of the King with a Hundred Knights present at King Mark's tournament at Lancien. [*Contin4*]

GLADOVAINZ OF HAVERNUEC

A knight present at the tournament at Banborc, which Kay won. [*Girart*]

GLAIS

A king who was one of the two principal combatants in the Jaschune tournament, in which many of Arthur's knights participated. [*Heinrich*]

GLAIT CASTLE

A castle on the Island of Servage, ruled by Nabon the Black, who was slain by Tristan. [*ProsTris*]

GLAKOTELESFLOYER

A knight defeated by Wigamur, an Arthurian knight. [*Wigamur*]

GLAMORGAN [*Glamour, Glomorgan*]

A Welsh country, containing Caerleon, along the river Usk. The *Life of St. Cadoc* notes its king as Gwynnlyw, who was once protected by Arthur. It is named as one of Arthur's courts in *Meriadeuc* and other texts. A Middle English poem says that Arthur gave the land to Gawain after Gawain fought a great duel against Galleron of Galloway. [*SaintsCad, Meriadeuc, Awntyrs*]

GLAS

The sword wielded by Arthur's warrior Bwlch. [*Culhwch*]

GLASGOW

The Scottish city was said to be a haunt of the mad prophet Lailoken (identified with Merlin). It makes marginal appearances in several Arthurian romances.

GLASS BRIDGE

A bridge crossed by Perceval during his quest for the Grail. It crackled and shattered under him, but later reconstructed itself. [*Contin2*]

GLASTONBURY [*Glas(h)enbury(e),*
Glassthenbery, Glastonbery, Glastynbury]

A small town in the county of Somerset in southwestern England. It contains an abbey whose monks, during the Middle Ages, may have been involved in a succession of propaganda intended to bolster the abbey's reputation. Claims found in various twelfth and thirteenth century texts include the assertions that it was founded by St. Patrick or by Joseph of Arimathea (who in some accounts was buried there); that it carried pieces of the holy sepulchre or the crown of thorns; that the Grail was kept there in an enchanted well; and—most striking of all—that, in 1191, the monks discovered the remains of Arthur and Guinevere along with a marker identifying them. The "discovery" was reported by Giraldus Cambrensis (Gerald of Wales) in *De Principis Instructione* a few years later. (See ARTHUR'S GRAVE.) Casting a shadow of fraud on the entire episode is the fact that the abbey suffered a ruinous fire seven years prior, and that the discovery of "Arthur's grave" could be expected to swell the abbey's coffers with offerings from pilgrims. However, twentieth century excavations have lent credence to the description of the grave site, and in the end there is no compelling evidence to prove or disprove a deliberate forgery on the part of the Glastonbury monks.

The identification between Glastonbury and the island of AVALON may have existed prior to the monks' "discovery," but Giraldus's report certainly reinforced the link. Glastonbury can be considered an "island" in the sense that it is surrounded by marshes. Giraldus further states that the name of the town derives from "Glass Island," though it more likely comes from *Glaestings*, a family name (Bruce, 199). The "Glass Island" assertion is found elsewhere, and the evocative nature of the name probably supported the Avalonian identification.

Subsequent writers showed the influence of the monks' report in their descriptions of Arthur's death. Where in the early chronicles his end was shrouded in mystery, encouraging the hope of his eventual return, these later tales offer no such promise. Arthur's body is borne away by Morgan le Fay, supposedly to Avalon, but is then returned to Glastonbury by Morgan and her servants, their attempts to heal him having failed. The finality of this ending is mitigated by some authors who suggest that the body returned by Morgan may not have been Arthur's.

Aside from the identification with Avalon, Glastonbury appears in Arthurian romance as part of the kingdom of Melwas, who kidnapped Guinevere; as the hermitage to which the Archbishop of Canterbury and several Arthurian knights retired after Arthur's death; and as one of Arthur's courts. One manuscript of the English *Arthour and Merlin* names it as Ambrosius's burial place, which in most texts is at Stonehenge. The name seems to appear almost exclusively in legends written in England and Wales; most French texts, including the Vulgate romances, do not mention the town at all, using an ANCIENT CHAPEL to take the place of Glastonbury as Arthur's burial site. [*Caradoc, Giraldus, Durmart, Arthour, Short, Stanz, Allit, Malory, TennIK*]

GLASTONBURY THORN

A thorn tree on Wearyall Hill in Glastonbury, said to be descended from a tree that was sprung from the staff of Joseph of Arimathea, which Joseph had driven into the earth. The tree blossomed twice a year: in the spring, and at Christmas time. An elaborated version of the legend claims that Joseph of Arimathea's staff was cut from a tree grown from the Crown of Thorns worn by Christ. The original Glastonbury Thorn was apparently destroyed by a Puritan fanatic, though legends tell of grievous injury to others who tried to harm the Thorn. The existing descendant is of Mediterranean origin, and some have speculated that the original tree was brought from Arabia by a returning crusader. [*LyfeJoA, Topograhy*]

GLASTONBURY TOR

A hill in GLASTONBURY that shows traces of occupation in Roman times. Various local legends connect the Tor to Arthur. One legend names the hill as the haunt of Gwynn son of Nudd, who appears as Arthur's warrior in *Culhwch and Olwen*. It has been suggested as the location of the fortress of King Melwas of the Summer Region, Guinevere's abductor in the *Life of St. Gildas*. [*Topograhy*]

GLAUDEZ

A Saxon king who fought under King Arrant at the siege of Cardigan. Arthur's forces countered and defeated the Saxons. [*Livre*]

GLEIN [Glem, Gleni]

A river in Britain that was the site of Arthur's first battle against the Saxons. As in all of the twelve battles, Arthur was victorious. Possible locations include the Glem in Lincolnshire, the Glen in Northumberland, and the Glyme in Oxfordshire (Chambers, 202). The first is most probable, since Nennius places another of Arthur's battles in a country called Linnuis, and Linnuis is likely Lindsey, in Lincolnshire. [Nennius, TennIK]

GLEIS

A warrior once defeated by Arthur. [Culhwch]

GLEISYAD [Gleisad]

The sword wielded by Arthur's warrior Syfwlch. [Culhwch]

GLESSIG [Glesing]

The sword wielded by Arthur's warrior Cyfwlch. [Culhwch]

GLEVEDIN

One of King Mark's Cornish castles, visited by Tristan on his first journey to Mark's kingdom. [ProsTris]

GLEVESING [Glywysing]

A region of Britain which contained the village of Elledi, home of the child Ambrosius. It is a district between the rivers Usk and Rumney, in Monmouthshire. [Nennius]

GLEW

One of Arthur's warriors who was the son of Ysgawd. He was killed at Cwm Cerwyn by the boar Twrch Trwyth. [Culhwch]

GLEWLWYD MIGHTY GRIP

An obstructive gatekeeper in the early Welsh poem Pa Gur yv y Portaur and in Culhwch and Olwen. In the former, he refuses Arthur entry into some keep, which prompts Arthur and his companions to recount the various adventures of Arthur's warriors (a theme also found in Irish tales). In Culhwch, he becomes Arthur's chief gatekeeper, blocking Culhwch's admission to Arthur's court during a feast. We learn from Culhwch that he was served by Gryn, Gogyfwlch, Gwrddnei Cat Eye, Drem, Clust, Llaesgymyn, Huandaw, Gogigwr, and Penpingyon. Glewlwyd participated in the hunt for Twrch Trwyth, where he lost all of his servants except for Llaesgymyn. A Welsh Triad names him as one of the three "Offensive Knights" of Arthur's court, for he was so large, strong, and savage that no one dared refuse him anything he asked for. [WelshPG, Culhwch, Triads, Geraint, Owain]

GLEX [Glez]

An Arthurian knight defeated in joust by Sir Yder. [Yder]

GLIGLOIS

Gawain's squire, and later a Knight of the Round Table, in a thirteenth-century French romance bearing his name. The son of a German nobleman, he came to Arthur's court at Caridoel and presented himself to Gawain, who immediately accepted him as a squire. He was praised highly for his service, skill, and knowledge. He soon fell in love with the lady Beauté of Landemore, a maid of Guinevere who was also loved by Gawain. Torn between loyalty to his master and love for Beauté, he finally confessed his feelings to the maiden, but she rebuked him. Persistent, he followed Beauté and a knight named Aharer to the Castle Orgueilleux tournament, running behind their horses until his feet bled. Beauté, who was showing excessive cruelty towards him, finally dispatched him to her sister at Landemore with a sealed message. Upon delivering the message to Beauté's sister, Gliglois learned that Beauté in fact loved him, and had wanted to test his devotion. He was knighted at Landemore and then sent to fight in the tournament on his steed, Ferrant. He was proclaimed the victor at Orgueilleux, and Beauté awarded him her love. Gawain graciously relinquished his own claim on Beauté, resolving Gliglois's conflict. [Gliglois]

GLINI

A warrior who held Eiddoel captive in his fortress. The warrior Culhwch had to obtain the services of Eiddoel as one of his tasks, so he persuaded Arthur to besiege Glini's castle. Glini turned over his prisoner and swore allegiance to Arthur to avoid losing his property. [Culhwch]

GLINYEU [Glifieu]

An Arthurian warrior who was the son of Taran. Glinyeu was loyal to the warrior Gwythyr, and he joined Gwythyr's army when Gwythyr opposed Gwynn son of Nudd. Glinyeu was taken prisoner by Gwynn and was not released until Arthur intervened. In the non-Arthurian Welsh tale of Branwen, Glinyeu is one of only seven British warriors to survive King Bran's successful invasion of Ireland. [Culhwch]

GLITEN

One of the eight sisters of Morgan le Fay. She lived on the island of Avalon. [GeoffVM]

GLITON

A sister of Morgan le Fay who lived on the island of Avalon. [GeoffVM]

GLITONEA

One of the eight sisters of Morgan le Fay. She lived on the island of Avalon. [GeoffVM]

GLOADAIN

The seneschal of Cambenic who was defeated in duel by Gawain. [VulgLanc]

GLOALÉS

A duke who was a companion of Lord Formis on the Turning Isle. Arthur defeated him when Arthur and his knights fought Formis's knights. [*Livre*]

GLOAS

A Saxon king who fought under King Aminaduc at the siege of Vambieres. He bore the Saxon banner. Arthur's forces countered and defeated the Saxons, and Gaheris killed Gloas. [*Livre*]

GLOCEDON [*Glocedoine, Glocedun*]

A castle mentioned in the Vulgate romances. It was situated in northern Britain on the forest of Gloeven. Its lord fought with other regional rulers against the Saxons. Much later, it was visited by Bors, who rescued its lady, Blevine, from a group of peasants and a knight. According to *Arthour and Merlin*, it belonged to Lot. [*VulgLanc, VulgMer, Arthour*]

GLODOALAN [*Glecidolan*]

A dwarf who served King Bilis, lord of the dwarves. He was one of the warriors present at the wedding of Erec and Enide. [*ChretienE*]

GLOEVEN

A forest traversed by Bors. The castle of Glocedon, where Bors rescued a maiden, lay on one of Gloeven's borders. [*VulgLanc*]

GLOIER [*Gloyer*]

The King of Sorelois before the land was conquered—and Gloier killed—by Lord Galehaut. Gloier had inherited Sorelois from his father, King Loholt. After Gloier's death, Gloier's young children were orphaned, but Galehaut took care of them and betrothed a daughter to Galehodin, Galehaut's nephew. Gloier's uncle had been the King of Northumberland. Another of Gloier's daughters was the queen of Chalon. [*LancLac, VulgLanc, Livre*]

GLOIS

A kingdom mentioned in several German texts, probably a variation of GALES or WALES, although Wirnt von Grafenberg, in *Wigalois*, seems to place it in the Middle East. It's king, Roaz, was killed by Wigalois (Gawain's son). [*Wirnt*]

GLORIANA

Queen of Fairy Land in Spenser's *The Faerie Queene*, allegorically representing England's Queen Elizabeth. Gloriana was the daughter of Oberon and was originally named Tanquill. In the poem, Gloriana presides over a magic court and sends knights of her Order of Maidenhead on righteous quest: the Red Cross Knight to free a land from a dragon, Sir Guyon to destroy the lecherous Bower of Bliss, Sir Artegall to slay the giant Grantorto, and Sir Calidore to capture the ravaging Blatant Beast. Prince Arthur saw Gloriana in a dream, fell in love with her, and journeyed to Fairy Land to find her. In the unfinished poem, Arthur never meets the Fairy Queen, but had Spenser completed it, they presumably would have been united. [*Spenser*]

GLORIANDE

Daughter of King Gonosor of Ireland. She married King Apollo of Lyonesse and had a son named Candaces. A son of King Clodoveus of Gaul lusted after her and kidnapped her. Gloriande killed herself rather than submit to him. [*ProsTris*]

GLORIANT [*Gloiant*]

A Saxon king who joined King Rions' invasion of Carmelide in the early days of Arthur's reign. King Bors of Gannes killed him at the battle of Aneblayse. [*VulgMer, Arthour*]

GLORINDE

A forest near the Humber river, bordering on Galehaut's land of Sorelois. [*VulgLanc*]

GLOTIGARAN

An Arthurian knight. [*Heinrich*]

GLOUCESTER [*Caer Loyw*]

A city in southwest England, on the Severn river. In Ambrosius's time, according to Geoffrey of Monmouth, it was ruled by Earl Eldol, and the bishop was his brother Eldad; later, the Earl of Gloucester was Morvid. In the Vulgate *Merlin*, an unnamed Earl of Gloucester fights in Arthur's army in the Roman War. In *Culhwch and Olwen*, Arthur's warriors rescue the huntsman Mabon from a Gloucester prison. The English ballad "King Arthur's Death" names Arthur's Sir Lucan as Gloucester's duke. [*Culhwch, GeoffHR, Wace, KingAD*]

GLOVEIN

A king who served Arthur. Like the other lords at Arthur's court, Glovein's wife was found to be at least somewhat unfaithful by a magical horn in Biket's *Lai du Cor*. [*Biket*]

GLUMDALCA

In Henry Fielding's *The Tragedy of Tragedies*, a giantess defeated and captured by Arthur's warrior Tom Thumb. She fell in love with the diminutive warrior; Arthur, in turn, fell in love with her. She was slain while fighting alongside Tom Thumb against an insurrection led by Lord Grizzle. [*Fielding*]

GLUNPLOUCH

A port in Saxony that Vortigern captured during his war against the Saxons. [*Butor*]

GLYNN YSTUN

A region of south Wales that abuts the Bristol Channel. Arthur's hunt for the boar Twrch Trwyth crossed this country [*Culhwch*]

GLYTHFYR LEDEWIG

Father of Arthur's warrior Garanhon. Glythfyr owned two special hounds. Arthur sought the hounds while helping the warrior Culhwch complete his forty tasks. Curiously, however, the chief giant Ysbaddaden, who assigned Culhwch's tasks, did not ask for these dogs. [*Culhwch, Peredur*]

GOALAN

A king in Arthur's service. [*Renaut*]

GOASILROET

The son of Arthur's vassal, King Angwisiez of Scotland, in Hartmann's *Erec*. Chrétien de Troyes names the same character as CADRET. [*HartmannE*]

GOBRWY

One of Arthur's warriors. He was the son of Echel. [*Culhwch, Dream*]

GODARRE

A location in Scotland, probably near the country of Galloway, bordering the area where King Arthur and the King from Over the Borders of Galone fought a battle. [*LancLac*]

GODEGRAINS [*Gotegrin, Gundregoas*]

A count in King Arthur's service. Godegrains first appears in Chrétien de Troyes's *Erec* as a guest at Erec's wedding. In Heinrich von dem Türlin's *Diu Crône*, he becomes Queen Guinevere's brother and the son of King Garlin of Galore. Godegrains kidnapped his sister from Arthur's court when he felt that she had behaved basely in an incident involving Sir Gasozein of Dragoz. Intending to kill the queen, he was apprehended in the act by Gasozein himself, and was defeated. [*ChretienE, HartmannE, Heinrich*]

GODELAKE

A knight in Arthur's service who fought at the Castle Perilous tournament. [*Malory*]

GODELONTE

A narrows in Scotland through which an army of Saxon invaders fled after they were defeated by Arthur's army, led by Lancelot. The Saxon warrior Hegadabrant was captured at this battle. Lancelot wished to pursue the Saxons through the narrows, but he was held back by his cousin Lionel, who warned him that he would be killed. [*LancLac, VulgLanc*]

GODEZ [*Godoé*]

A knight from the Land Beyond the Borders who was defeated by Lancelot at the Pomeglai tournament. [*VulgLanc*]

GODILNA

In the Norse *Erex Saga*, the sister of King Guivret, a friend of Erec. She could cure any wound, and she used her talents to heal Erec after he had been wounded in a joust with Kay. Unnamed in Chrétien's *Erec*, her character appears as either FILLEDAMOR or GUNETEFLUR in Hartmann von Aue's version. [*Erex*]

GODOINE

A baron of King Mark of Cornwall. Godoine and his compatriots, Ganelon and Denoalen, conspired to expose the affair between Tristan and Isolde to King Mark. Tristan caught him spying through the window of Isolde's chambers and killed him with an arrow through the head. [*Beroul*]

GODONAS

The ruthless king of Terrandes who commanded a force of robber giants. He was killed by Meleranz, Arthur's nephew, who assumed the throne of Terrandes and befriended Cursin, Godonas's seneschal. [*PleierM*]

GODORSON [*Godorsone*]

A river which ran parallel to the River Maine. It flanked a battlefield where Arthur fought the King of the Land Beyond the Borders of Galone. [*VulgLanc*]

GODRAS THE FELON

An evil knight who tried to murder King Lac, Erec's father. Guiron the Courteous and Danain the Red stopped him. [*Palamedes*]

GODROUÉS

A knight who fought on the side of the King with a Hundred Knights at King Mark's tournament at Lancien. [*Contin4*]

GOFAN

Son of Caw, one of twenty brothers, and one of Arthur's warriors. [*Culhwch*]

GOFANNON

Son of Dôn and brother of Amathaon. As one of his tasks, the hero Culhwch had to get Gofannon to deliver irons to the headlands of the giant Ysbaddaden. The character is adopted from Irish legend, where he is Goibniu, the god of the forge (Chambers, 69). [*Culhwch*]

GOFYNYON THE OLD

Father of Arthur's warrior Carnedyr. [*Culhwch*]

GOGFRAN THE GIANT

Guinevere's father in Welsh legend. In the Triads, he is the father of only one of three queens named Guinevere, but a Welsh translation of Geoffrey of Monmouth's *Historia* makes him the father of *the* Guinevere. [*Triads*]

GOGIGWR

A gatekeeper at King Arthur's court and a servant of the warrior Glewlwyd Strong Grip. He was killed by the boar Twrch Trwyth during the epic hunt. [*Culhwch*]

GOGONNE

Son of Salandres and brother of Dinisordres, Nastor, Aristes, and Menastide. Gogonne, his father, and his four brothers were defeated in combat by Perceval, who sent them to Arthur's court. [*Contin3*]

GOGULOR[1]

A giant who, in a fragment of a romance, tried to marry a maiden against her will. He was challenged by one of Arthur's knights to prevent this injustice. Like Gawain, Gogulor's strength increased as the day progressed. [*Gogulor*]

GOGULOR[2]

A knight who fought on the side of the King with a Hundred Knights at King Mark's Lancien tournament. [*Contin4*]

GOGYFWLCH

One of Arthur's warriors who shared the duties of gatekeeper in Caer Llion (Caerleon) with seven to nine other warriors. His master was the chief gatekeeper Glewlwyd Strong Grip. [*Geraint*]

GOHART

Lord of the Castle of the Whales. He captured Perceval's cousin, Calobrus, and chained him to a rock to starve. Perceval found Calobrus and freed him. To avenge his torture, Calobrus captured Gohart and chained him to the same rock to starve. [*Perlesvaus*]

GOHENBERT

A count of Germany who brought his army to Arthur's court, intending to subjugate the king. In the king's household, Gohenbert played a game of chess against Guinevere that turned into a fight. Lancelot killed him. Gohenbert's warriors rose up and attacked Arthur's knights. Arthur's forces prevailed but suffered many losses. [*Prophecies*]

GOHENET

The land ruled by King Hoel in Renaut de Bâgé's *Le Bel Inconnu*. Hoel's kingdom is generally given as BRITTANY. [*Renaut*]

GOIT

Father of Arthur's warrior Gorbonian. [*GeoffHR*]

GOLAGROS [*Golagras, Golagrus, Gologras(e), Gologrus*]

One of the title characters in the Middle Scots poem called *The Knightly Tale of Gologras and Gawain*. Arthur saw Golagros's magnificent castle during a pilgrimage to Rome. Upon learning that Golagros served no master, Arthur vowed to subjugate him. Arthur's knights besieged the castle on the return trip. After a number of losses, Golagros agreed to decide the battle through a single combat between himself and Gawain. When Gawain defeated him, Golagros asked to die. Gawain balked, and Golagros said he would only consent to live if Gawain surrendered to him. Gawain agreed and Gologras, impressed with Gawain's nobility, swore fealty to him and to Arthur. Arthur, however, having learned his own lesson in nobility, freed Golagros from his vow. [*Golagros*]

GOLDEN DRAGON

The standard carried by King Arthur at the battle of Soissons against the Roman Procurator Lucius. [*GeoffHR*]

GOLDEN EAGLE

The standard carried by Lucius at the battle of Soissons against King Arthur. [*GeoffHR*]

GOLDEN ISLE [*Ile d'Or*]

The island and castle belonging to a fairy, called the Maiden of the White Hands in Renaut de Bâgé's *Le Bel Inconnu* and the Dame d'Amour in Thomas Chestre's *Lybeaus Desconus*. The Maiden decreed that any potential suitor would have to guard the island for seven straight years before she would marry him. For five years, the guardian was Malgier, but he was killed by Gawain's son Guinglain. The Maiden so loved Guinglain that she lifted the seven-year requirement for him. [*Renaut, ChestreLyb*]

GOLDEN-TONGUED KNIGHTS

A trio of Arthur's knights—Gwalchmei, Drudwas, and Eliwlod—who were able to complete their quests and achieve their desires through their particularly able use of speech. [*Triads*]

GOLEUDDYDD ("Bright Day")

Daughter of Amlawdd, sister of Igerne, wife of Cilydd, and mother of Culhwch. When she became pregnant with Culhwch, Goleuddydd went mad and lived outdoors, but she returned to sanity before she gave birth. She delivered in the midst of some pigs, and her son was thus name "Culhwch," or "pig pen." She was mortally wounded giving birth, and died soon afterwards. Before she died, she made her husband promise not to remarry until he saw a two-headed thorn growing from her grave. She then summoned her confessor and told him to trim the grave every year, so that nothing would grow upon it. The confessor forgot his promise after seven years, and Cilydd remarried. [*Culhwch*]

GOLISTAN THE BLACK

A knight who guarded the Bridge of the Giant and was defeated there by Segurant the Brown. [*Palamedes*]

GOLISTANT¹ [*Gulistante*]

Lancelot's uncle. Tristan appointed him viceroy of Joyous Guard. He was slain when King Mark of Cornwall besieged Joyous Guard to reclaim Isolde from Tristan. [*ProsTris, Tavola*]

GOLISTANT² THE STRONG [*Gulistante*]

Son of Morholt who appears in *Palamedes* and the Prose *Tristan*. His father was killed by Tristan. He became the squire of Sir Segurant the Brown and was knighted at his master's hand. Golistant fell in love with a maiden at the Castle of Maidens and besieged the castle when she rebuked him. Guiron the Courteous, the maiden's cousin, defeated Golistant in combat, and Golistant died of wounds he received in the fight. The Italian *La Tavola Ritonda* gives a different account of his life, saying that Tristan knighted him and changed his name to AMOROLDO. [*Palamedes, ProsTris, Tavola*]

GOLROTHERAME [*Gollerothirame*]

In the Middle English *Sir Perceval of Galles*, a Saracen Sultan who besieged the Lady Lufamour in Maidenland, intending to force her into marriage. Perceval challenged, fought, and killed him. One of his brothers, a giant, tried to avenge his death and failed. The same character is known as CLAMADEU in Chrétien's *Perceval*. [*SirPerc*]

GOLWG HAFDDYDD

Isolde's handmaid in a Welsh fragment of a Tristan story. She was loved by a man named Cae Hir. [*TrisFrag*]

GOMERET¹ [*Gomet, Gomor(r)et*]

The land ruled by King Ban, according to Chrétien de Troyes. R. S. Loomis thought it was a variation of GWYNEDD in Wales. Most other writers give Ban's realm as BENOIC. In *Perlesvaus*, Gomeret is a castle ruled by Marin the Jealous. Hartmann von Aue notes Beals as Gomeret's lord, and in the Prose *Tristan*, it is the homeland of Morgan le Fay's knights Helianz and Kaz. [*ChretienE, Perlesvaus, HartmannE, ProsTris, Malory*]

GOMERET² THE IMMODERATE
   [*Go(u)mere(t)*]

A knight who, with his companion Orguelleus the Fairy, killed Sir Cortois of Humberland, believing his victim to be Gawain. When they realized their mistake, Orguelleus resurrected Cortois. [*Atre*]

GONEREUS

One of Arthur's knights who joined Gawain's quest to conquer Rigomer castle. [*Merveil*]

GONEREYS

An evil knight who stole lands from a maiden. Palamedes championed the damsel and killed Gonereys, winning back her lands. Gonereys's brother, Sir Archade, tried to avenge his death, but was also killed. [*Malory*]

GONOSOR

King of Ireland. His daughters, Gloriande and Joene, married the kings of Lyonesse and Cornwall. In exchange for Gonosor's assistance in the war against Lyonesse, King Canor of Cornwall agreed to pay an annual tribute to Ireland. Generations later, Tristan freed Cornwall of this tribute by killing Morholt. [*ProsTris*]

GONTIER OF THE THORN

A knight who participated in the tournament at Banborc and was defeated by Sir Bruians of the Isles. [*Girart*]

GOOD ADVENTURE [*Biele Adventure*]

An abbey that King Arthur erected near the Humber River, at the site of his victory over five kings who opposed him in the early days of his reign. [*PostMer, Malory*]

GOOD DEED

A monastery on the edge of the forest of Breckham, in northern Britain. It was an ancient hermitage, greatly expanded under the support of Duke Escant of Cambenic. Gawain lodged there during his adventures. [*VulgLanc*]

GOOD KNIGHT¹ [*Bon Chevalier*]

The banal epithet given to the Grail Hero in *Perlesvaus* and in the Vulgate Cycle. In the former, it refers to PERCEVAL, while in the latter it means GALAHAD. Certain references in the Vulgate also apply it to LANCELOT. Various prophecies heralded the coming of the "Good Knight," who would solve the Grail adventures and advance Christianity in Britain. [*Perlesvaus, VulgLanc, VulgQuest*]

GOOD KNIGHT² WITHOUT FEAR

Son of Esclanor and father of Dinadan and Brunor the Black. The Good Knight's true name, seldom used, was also BRUNOR THE BLACK. He was known as a great knight in his day, and Uther Pendragon awarded him the realm of Estrangorre for his valor.

Among his many adventures, he journeyed to the valley of Servage to rescue his friend, Ludinas of North Wales, from a giant called Nabon the Black. He defeated Nabon's son Nathan, but was betrayed by a maiden and imprisoned in Nabon's prison, where he went mad. He was eventually freed by Tristan, and he recovered his senses with the help of Baucillas, the king's doctor.

A story in the Italian *Novellino* relates how the Good Knight Without Fear told his own soldiers, who did not recognize him, that King Meliadus of Lyoness, his mortal enemy, was a better knight than he. For this "insult," he was seized by his own troops, only to be rescued by Meliadus. He was eventually murdered, as an old man, by two knights named Ferrant and Briadan. [*Palamedes*, *Novellino*]

GOOD SOLDIER

A nickname of Joseph of Arimathea, commemorating his retrieval of Christ's body from the cross. [*Perlesvaus*]

GOODWYN

A knight whose brother was Sir Gawdelyn. When Gawdelyn was killed by Sir Aglovale, Goodwyn swore revenge. He captured one of Aglovale's squires and killed him. Aglovale avenged the murder by slaying Goodwyn. [*Malory*]

GOON DESERT [*Goon Sert, Goot Delsert*]

Brother of the Fisher King and uncle of Perceval in the Third Continuation of Chrétien de Troyes's *Perceval*. One of Goon Desert's daughters was a Grail maiden. Called the lord of the Desert (the Waste Land), Goon Desert ruled the castle of Quingragan, which was besieged by Espinogres and his nephew Partinal. Partinal killed Goon Desert with the Grail Sword, which broke. Perceval, during his visit to the Grail Castle, saw Goon Desert's body on a bier. After learning the story, Perceval avenged Goon Desert's death by killing Partinal. A similar episode is recounted in the Welsh *Peredur*, where the head of Peredur's cousin is seen floating in a dish in the Grail Castle, though the murderers in this case are the Hags of Gloucester. [*Contin3*]

GOOSEWHITE [*Goswhit*]

Arthur's helmet. It was made of steel, bound with gold, and adorned with gems. It had belonged to his father, Uther, and Arthur wore it at the battle against the Saxons at Bath. [*Layamon*]

GOOTH

A castle in which Sir Perceval lodged during the Grail Quest. [*Malory*]

GORANGON [*Garagon, Garengan, Gwyrangon*]

The earl of Kent in the time of Vortigern. Gorangon suddenly found himself without a kingdom when Vortigern—without Gorangon's knowledge—handed Kent to Hengist and the Saxons. [*Nennius*, *GeoffHR*, *Wace*, *Layamon*]

GORASGWRN ("Big Bone")

Daughter of Nerth and maid of Arthur's warrior Cyfwlch. [*Culhwch*]

GORBODUG

According to Geoffrey of Monmouth, king of Britain in the sixth or fifth century BC. He was the son of King Gorbodug, the husband of Queen Iudon, and the father of Ferrex and Porrex. Ferrex and Porrex went to war over their inheritance, and Gorbodug's kingdom crumbled. [*GeoffHR*]

GORBONIAN[1]

According to Geoffrey of Monmouth, Gorbonian succeeded his father, King Morvid, to the throne in the third century BC. His reign was a prosperous one, characterized by the restoration of temples. When he died, his brother Arthgallo succeeded him. Gorbonian's son, Regin, eventually became king. [*GeoffHR*]

GORBONIAN[2]

One of Arthur's champions who was the son of Goit. [*GeoffHR*]

GOREU

Son of Constantine. His father was shepherd for the chief giant Ysbaddaden, and the giant had killed twenty-three of Constantine's sons. Constantine kept Goreu, his last, hidden in a chest to protect him. When Culhwch and a party of Arthur's knights came to Ysbaddaden's fortress seeking Olwen, Cei (Kay) took Goreu under his wing and allowed the boy to accompany him on the subsequent adventures, in which he won the respect of Arthur's men. He participated in the hunt for Twrch Trwyth. Upon completion of Culhwch's tasks, Goreu returned to Ysbaddaden and decapitated him, thus fulfilling the Ysbaddaden's own proclamation that he must die when Olwen wed. Goreu later became one of Arthur's warriors and advisors. One tale states that he was a squire, given the duty of guarding Arthur's bed. A Welsh Triad tells us that he rescued Arthur from imprisonment at the hand of Gwen Pendragon beneath the Stone of Echymeint. Goreu's name translates as "best," but might be a variation of *Gorneu* or *Corneu*, which is roughly Welsh for "Cornishman." [*Culhwch*, *Dream*, *Geraint*]

GORGARI

A knight who kidnapped the Lady of Malehaut. Her brother, Margon, chased him down and rescued the lady. [*Contin3*]

GORGUN

Arthur's Earl of Flandrisborg in the Norse *Erex Saga*. He was present at the wedding of Erec and Enide. His brothers were named Garse and Jentaneon. [*Erex*]

GORHAN

A Saxon king who fought under King Arrant at the siege of Cardigan. Arthur's forces countered and defeated the Saxons, and Arthur personally killed Gorhan. [*Livre*]

GORLAGON

A king whose wife used a magic wand to turn him into a wolf. As a wolf, Gorlagon served Arthur. When Arthur learned Gorlagon's story, he obtained the magic wand and restored Gorlagon to his true form. [*Arthur&G*]

GORLOIS [*Gorlais, Gorlens, Gorloys, Gothlois*]

The duke of Cornwall and the husband of Igerne. He became a vassal of Ambrosius when the latter invaded Britain. He proved his prowess at the battle of Conisbrough against Hengist's Saxons, and at Mount Damen against Octa and Eosa.

When Uther Pendragon ascended to the throne after his brother's death, he called a feast of all his nobles at which he first laid eyes upon Gorlois's wife. He immediately fell in love with her. Igerne, sensing Uther's attentions, convinced her husband to take her back to Cornwall. Uther, enraged at Gorlois's departure, laid siege to the duke's two castles: Tintagel, in which Gorlois had placed Igerne, and Dimiloc (or Tarabel), which housed Gorlois. Uther convinced Merlin to disguise him as Gorlois, so he could enter Tintagel and spend the night with Igerne. As Uther enjoyed Gorlois's wife, Gorlois was slain in a battle against Uther's soldiers. Igerne later gave birth to Arthur.

Tradition gives Gorlois three daughters named Morgause, Elaine, and Morgan le Fay. A Welsh adaptation of Geoffrey of Monmouth's *Historia* makes him the father of Cador of Cornwall, whose relation to Gorlois is uncertain in other texts.

In *Culhwch and Olwen*, his counterpart as Igerne's first husband is RICA. Gorlois may be identical to GWRYON found in the Welsh *Geraint*. The Vulgate *Merlin* calls his character HOEL, and *Arthour and Merlin* calls him TINTAGEL.

Thomas Hughes' *The Misfortunes of Arthur* has the ghost of Gorlois condemn Arthur for Uther's sin. Arthur's fatal conflict with Mordred seems to be the instrument of Gorlois' revenge. "Mordred," says Gorlois, "shall be the hammer of my hate." [*Nennius, Culhwch, GeoffHR, Wace, Malory, HughesT, TennIK*]

GORMANT ("Excess')

One of Arthur's warriors who was the son of Rica and Eigyr (Igerne) prior to Eigyr's later marriage to Arthur's father. Gormant was therefore Arthur's half-brother. [*Culhwch*]

GORMUNDUS

A Persian warrior assigned to champion Persia against Rome in a dispute over Jerusalem. For its champion, Rome presented a young Gawain (not yet in the service of Arthur). Gawain, although young and strong, seemed little match for the gigantic, courageous, and experienced Gormundus; however, after a battle that lasted three days, Gawain delivered a mighty blow to Gormundus's head, killing him. [*DeOrtu*]

GORNEMANT OF GOHORT [*Gormans, Gornemans, Gornimans, Gurnemans of Gorhaut, Gurnemanz of Groharz*]

A Knight of the Round Table who tutored the freshly-knighted Perceval, teaching him the proper use of weapons and armor and the code of knightly conduct. Gornemant first appears in Chrétien de Troyes's *Perceval*, though an appearance in Ulrich von Zatzikhoven's *Lanzelet* (at a tournament against King Lot of Lothian) suggests that Gornemant belongs to an older Arthurian tradition. One of the pieces of advice he gave to Perceval was not to talk too much. Perceval misinterpreted the advice and consequently failed to ask the Grail Question at the castle of the Fisher King.

Wolfram von Eschenbach gives Gornemant three sons named Schenteflurs, Lascoyt, and Gurzgri, and a daughter named Liaze. Gornemant would have had Perceval marry Liaze, but Perceval declined. [*ChretienE, ChretienP, UlrichZ, Wolfram*]

GORRE [*Goirre, Gore, Gors*]

A wild northern kingdom first featured in Chrétien de Troyes's *Lancelot*. In the tales, it borders on North Wales or Scotland, and is surrounded by water. It could only be entered by two perilous bridges: the Sword Bridge and the Underwater Bridge. Its inaccesibility lends it an otherworldly aura. Chrétien's geography suggests an identification with Anglesey or the Isle of Man.

We learn in the Vulgate *Lancelot* that Uther Pendragon went to war with Gorre's first king, Urien, hoping to subjugate the land. Eventually, he captured and imprisoned Urien, but Urien's nephew, Bagdemagus, traded the land to Uther for Urien's life. In time, Urien retook the land and placed Bagdemagus on the throne. To repopulate the land, which had been depleted under Uther's reign, Bagdemagus instituted a custom by which any British knights and ladies who wandered into Gorre had to remain. Because of other conflicts, Arthur overlooked Gorre until Meleagant, Bagdemagus's son, kidnapped Guinevere and brought her there. This prompted Lancelot's quest to free the queen (recounted by both Chrétien and the Vulgate) and the other captives of the land, in which he succeeded.

Attempts have been made to identify Gorre with the peninsula of Gower in Wales. It is more likely a corruption of "Glass," either through the Welsh *gutr* or the French *voire* (Bruce, 202n). The Island of Glass is the realm of King Melwas, Meleagant's counterpart in Welsh legend. [*ChretienL, Wolfram, VulgLanc, VulgMer, PostMer, Arthour, Malory*]

GORRIENDE

A forest near Arthur's Carlisle court; the site of a white stag hunt in Guillaume le Clerc's *Fergus*. The hunt concluded in Ingegal, Scotland, and Perceval was the victor. Scholars have suggested Geltsdale as the possible geographic location. [*Guillaume*]

GORRUN

The most important city in the land of Gorre, which took its name from the city. It was visited briefly by Lancelot during his quest to rescue Guinevere from Meleagant. [*VulgLanc*]

GORVAIN CADRUT [*Gornain(s) Cadrus, Gernan, Gornenis*]

In Raoul de Houdenc's *Meraugis de Portlesguez*, one of two knights who loved a beautiful maiden named Lidoine. Gorvain Cadrut loved her for her beauty, in contrast to Meraugis, who loved Lidoine for her courtesy. Queen Guinevere and a court of maidens decided the matter in favor of Meraugis. Gorvain Cadrut subsequently left Arthur's court in a rage, but he eventually reconciled with Meraugis.

In *Hunbaut*, Gorvain becomes a Knight of the Round Table after he kidnaps Gawain's sister, is defeated by Gawain, and is sent to Arthur's court as a prisoner.

He appears in the Vulgate *Merlin* as a knight who fights in Arthur's battles against King Rions at Carmelide. He slew the Saxon warrior Dorilas at the battle of Carhaix. The *Livre d'Artus* adds further battles to Gorvain's credit, including the defense of the Waste Land against Agrippe. *Arthour and Merlin* splits his character into two warriors: Gornain and CRADDOC.

A Welsh Arthurian warrior named GWRVAN may be Gorvain's origin. His surname suggests the Welsh *cadrauc*, meaning "strong" (Loomis, *Romance*, 374). [*Raoul, VulgMer, Livre, Hunbaut, Arthour*]

GOSENAIN

A variation of GASWAIN.

GOSENGOS

Son of King Amant of Lambal (an enemy of Arthur) and ruler of Tharmadaise. While marching to attack Arthur, Amant was slain by King Bors of Gannes, and Gosengos inherited Lambal. Gosengos and his seneschal, Nabunal, joined Arthur in opposing the Saxon invasion, and also in the war against Rome. Arthur made him a Knight of the Round Table. He harbored a secret love for Guinevere, who, before her marriage to Arthur, had been infatuated with him. [*VulgMer, Livre, Contin4*]

GOSGALLIAN

One of Perceval's eleven paternal uncles in *Perlesvaus*. He was the second son of Gais le Gros and the brother of Alain. [*Perlesvaus*]

GOSTANZA

Lancelot's mother in *La Tavola Ritonda*. Unlike her counterpart in most romances, ELAINE, Gostanza was still pregnant with Lancelot when her husband, King Ban of Benoic, died. In her distress over her husband's death, she delivered Lancelot two months early and died herself after a few days. [*Tavola*]

GOT

A castle inhabited by a cousin of Galahad. Perceval visited Got during the Grail Quest. [*VulgQuest*]

GOTHARDELEN

A loyal Knight of the Round Table. [*HartmannE*]

GOTHLAND [*Gotland, Guthland*]

Part of Arthur's empire. It's king, Doldavius, surrendered to Arthur rather than be conquered. The king later participated in Arthur's wars against France, Rome, and Mordred. [*GeoffHR, Wace, Allit*]

GOUDRI

A locksmith who lived in Brittany. He provided Tristan and Tristan's brother-in-law, Runalen, with a key that allowed them to sneak into the castle of Lord Bedalis, so that Runalen could enjoy a tryst with Bedalis's wife. [*ProsTris*]

GOVERNAL [*Curvenal, Gorvenal, Gouvernal, Governail, Governayl(e), Govomar, Kurvenal*]

An educated man who tutored Tristan as a youth and then became his loyal squire. The Prose *Tristan* tells us that Governal was appointed the post of Tristan's guardian by Merlin. He had been forced to flee his home in Gaul after he killed a knight. When Tristan's father died, Governal spirited him to France to protect him from his enemies. According to some texts, it was partially Governal's negligence that allowed Tristan and Isolde to drink the fateful love potion. Governal accompanied Tristan on most of his adventures, and, with Isolde's maidservant Brangain, arranged in many instances to allow Tristan and Isolde to meet together. In the Prose *Tristan*, Tristan crowns him King of Lyonesse and he marries Brangain. Upon Tristan's death, Governal joined Arthur and Lancelot in a war against King Mark of Cornwall. [*ChretienL, Eilhart, Gottfried, ProsTris, Palamedes, TristanoR, Tavola, Malory*]

GOWEIR

A heathen warrior slain by Gareth at the battle of Diana Bridge. [*Arthour*]

GRACE

In the Alliterative *Morte Arthure*, a city or land in Arthur's empire. The author may have intended Greece, or the city of Grasse in southern France. [*Allit*]

GRADOANS

An Arthurian knight. [*Heinrich*]

GRADASSO OF SANSOGNA

A king whose mortal enemy, Count Lombardo, was slain by Lancelot. [*Tavola*]

GRAELENT[1] [Grailenc]

A Saxon king who participated in the Saxon invasion of Britain in the early days of Arthur's reign. He was struck down at the battle of Clarence by King Caradoc of Estrangorre. [*VulgMer*]

GRAELENT[2]

Hero of an early thirteenth-century Breton lay. His adventures parallel those of LANVAL in Marie de France's tale, though *Graelent* is not explicitly Arthurian, including no Arthurian characters.

GRAIER [Grayer]

Lord of the Castle of the High Wall. Under King Bors of Gannes, he fought in Arthur's wars against the Saxons. King Claudas took over the lands of Bors and King Ban of Benoic, causing their deaths in the process. Graier collaborated with a knight named Lambegue in a plot to assassinate Claudas. Their plan was foiled by Sir Pharien. [*LancLac, VulgLanc, Livre*]

GRAIL [Graal, Gra(a)us, Graaux, (San)Gradale, Graï, Grasal, (San)Greal, Grëaus]

The bowl or chalice mentioned by Chrétien de Troyes in *Perceval* as a beautiful golden dish with some mysterious properties. Robert de Boron connected it with the chalice used by Christ at the Last Supper, granting it enduring fame as the *Holy* Grail. The Grail stories can be divided neatly into two classes: the early tales, in which Perceval is the Grail hero; and the post-Robert de Boron romances, in which Galahad becomes the successful Grail knight. Contrary to popular belief, the Grail does not appear in the scriptures. The Gospels do mention a bowl from which Christ at the Paschal lamb at the last supper, and a cup which he shared with his disciples. Later writers identified the Grail with these objects, but the Bible attaches no special significance to them as holy relics.

About 1180, Chrétien de Troyes wrote *Perceval*, or *Le Conte del Graal* (*The Story of the Grail*), a story which he claimed to have adapted from a Latin book given to him by Count Phillip of Flanders. There is no compelling reason to disbelieve that Chrétien had a written source for the story, though this source has since been lost. Chrétien's tale concerns the adventures of Perceval—the most important of which seems to be his visit to the castle of the enigmatic, wounded Fisher King. The Fisher King invites Perceval for dinner and, during the meal, Perceval beholds a procession of squires who walk through the room carrying a Bleeding Lance and a set of candelabra. These squires are followed by a maiden carrying a *graal*, a wide dish made of gold, adorned with precious jewels, radiant with a brilliant light. Three times the procession passed in front of Perceval, but Perceval, warned by his tutor not to talk too much, refrained from asking about the *graal* or who it served. When he woke up the next morning, he found the castle deserted and he departed. He soon came across his maiden cousin, who rebuked him for failing to ask about the Grail, for by doing so, he would

have cured the Fisher King. Later, he visited his uncle in a hermitage, who provided further information about the Grail: it contained a single mass wafer which was served to the Maimed King, the Fisher King's infirm father. Shortly after these revelations, Chrétien's story turns to the adventures of Gawain and never returns; Chrétien apparently died before reaching a conclusion.

Chrétien's story is simultaneously stirring and frustrating in its mystery. What are the Grail's origins? What is its significance? Would Perceval have returned the Fisher King's castle? Was Perceval or Gawain destined to complete the adventure? Perhaps most important of all, how closely did Chrétien follow his source? What material was contained in the book given to him by the count of Flanders?

The enigma surrounding Chrétien's *graal* and the intended conclusion of its *conte* inspired four Continuations, two prologues (*Bliocadran* and the *Elucidation*), and four adaptations (*Perlesvaus*, Wolfram's *Parzival*, Heinrich von dem Türlin's *Diu Crône*, and the Welsh *Peredur*) over the next half century. In each of these tales, we learn new, and sometimes contradictory, things about the Grail and the residents of the Grail castle.

The First Continuation of *Perceval* first tells us that the Grail provided food and wine for the Fisher King's company, a notion which appears in later Grail romances but not, as some believe, in Chrétien. Both the Second Continuation and *Perlesvaus* say that it contained the blood of Christ, either reflecting or forecasting the influence of Robert de Boron's *Joseph*. The First Continuation is also the first to link the Fisher King's injury with the transformation of his kingdom into the Waste Land, which is found later in the Vulgate romances.

Wolfram von Eschenbach thought that the Grail was a stone, perhaps confusing *graal* for the French *grais*, meaning "sandstone" (Bruce, 328n), or perhaps confusing the stones adorning the Grail (as in Chrétien) with the Grail itself. The Grail had fallen from heaven during Lucifer's war with the angels. Instructions to the Grail Family appeared on the stone's surface. As in the First Continuation, it provided its keepers with unlimited food and drink, and anyone who gazed upon it could not die within the following week. Wolfram describes the Grail as a gift from God to the elite Grail Family—spiritual agents in the world of man.

In Heinrich's *Diu Crône*, we learn that the entire Grail company is in fact dead, and that the Grail Question is needed not to cure the Fisher King, but to free the inhabitants of the Grail Castle from a living death.

In the tales that reach a conclusion, Perceval visits the Grail Castle a second time, asks the Grail Question, heals the Fisher King, and becomes the new Grail King himself (an exception is *Diu Crône*, in which Gawain becomes the Grail hero but returns to Arthur's court). The Grail is generally carried away to heaven upon Perceval's death.

Around the turn of the thirteenth century, Robert de Boron wrote *Joseph d'Arimathie*, the tale which shaped almost all future Grail romances. Identifying the Grail with the bowl or chalice in which Christ instituted the Eucharist at the Last Supper, Robert turned the Grail into the "Holy" Grail. As early as a decade later, Robert's story was reworked and expanded into the Vulgate *Estoire del Saint Graal*. These "Grail histories" describe the migration of the Grail from Jerusalem to Britain in the hands of Joseph of Arimathea, a figure who appears briefly in each of the four Gospels. Joseph, a soldier of Pontius Pilate and a disciple of Christ, sought to preserve artifacts touched by Christ for future generations. He went to Christ's house and retrieved the Grail. Taking it to the crucifixion site, he caught Christ's blood in the bowl. After he obtained and entombed Jesus's body, the Jews threw him in a prison to rot, but the Grail sustained him for over forty years. Upon his release, he embarked for western lands with a sizable company of followers. His followers ate supper around a GRAIL TABLE, which anticipated the Round Table. Once in Britain, the Grail was entrusted to the sons of Bron, who constructed Corbenic, the GRAIL CASTLE. Bron's descendants acted as keepers of the Grail until the coming of the GRAIL HERO, who would complete all the spiritual adventures in Britain.

In Robert, the Grail does not provide food and healing, themes which probably come from a Celtic origin. Instead, it is a means of providing spiritual glory to Joseph's fellowship, a means of identifying the sinners among the group, and of communicating with God. It fills and satisfies their spirits rather than their stomachs. It is a symbolic representation of Christ among the fellowship.

Robert de Boron also wrote a *Perceval*, which is now lost but was adapted into the French Didot-*Perceval*. According to this version, Perceval caused the Fisher King's sickness by arrogantly sitting in the Round Table's Perilous Seat. Both of these tales preserved Perceval as the Grail Hero but were eclipsed by the Vulgate *Queste*, which replaces Perceval with Galahad, Lancelot's son and the best knight in the world. In all Grail tales prior to the *Queste*, Perceval literally stumbles upon the Grail Castle. Neither Arthur nor any of his other knights are involved in the proceedings. The Vulgate *Queste* scraps these previous versions and introduces the Grail "Quest," in which all of Arthur's knights participated for the express purpose of finding the Holy Grail. The Post-Vulgate Cycle, the Prose *Tristan*, and Malory faithfully adapted this version.

The quest commenced after the Grail appeared to Arthur's knights during the Pentecost feast. Galahad's success had been pre-ordained since Joseph's time, and only the purest of Arthur's other knights had any hope of achieving it with him. In the end, only two of them—Perceval and Bors, who God tested vigorously—measured up, although another dozen or so knights were allowed to witness the quest's completion. Lancelot, to his despair, was denied fulfillment because of his sin with Guinevere, though he was allowed a vision of his son's success. Other knights, such as Gawain and Hector, learned that their lustful and murderous ways had excluded them as well. The quest itself involved a number of episodes which, together, ended all the spiritual adventures in Britain. It culminated when Galahad, Perceval, and Bors attended a mass held in Corbenic by the spirit of either Joseph of Arimathea or his son Josephus. Galahad healed the Maimed King with blood from the Bleeding Lance, and

the three knights embarked with the Grail for ancient city of Sarras. There, another holy mass ended with the Grail lifted into heaven by the hand of God. Galahad and Perceval died in Sarras, but Bors returned to Camelot, where Arthur learned that a good number of his knights had been killed in the adventures. In addition to depleting the ranks of Round Table, the Grail Quest also left a spiritual vacuum which contributed to Arthur's eventual downfall.

It should be pointed out that neither the early Perceval Grail Quest nor the later Galahad Grail Quest circled around the objective of finding the Grail and gaining possession of it, or of bringing it back to Camelot. There is no question of removing the Grail from the Grail Castle. The goal, in both versions, is to *understand* the Grail, to grasp its meaning. Success depends on the knight's spirituality and purity rather than his dedication or prowess.

It has been widely accepted that the word *Grail* and its early variations—*graal*, *greal*, and *grazal*—derive from the Low Latin word *gradalis* or *cratalis*, meaning "bowl." Some writers of Grail romances tried to link it with the French *agreer* ("agreeable"), as the Grail was agreeable to all who saw it (Bruce, 254–5). After Robert de Boron called it the Holy Grail, *Saint Grail* or *Sangreal*, some authors caused confusion by dividing the word in the wrong place, producing *Sang Real*, or "royal blood," referring to the contents of the Grail rather than the Grail itself (Bruce, 255n). This incorrect division has produced far-flung theories of the Grail's origin even in modern times.

Studies into the origin of the Grail have focused on three theories: a Christian origin, a Celtic origin, and an origin in pagan fertility ritual. Adherents to the Christian origin theory point to the Eucharistic properties of the Grail even in Chrétien, noting that it contained a wafer or *Corpus Christi* and that the description of the Grail Procession recalls a report of a Byzantine mass written in the seventh or eighth centuries. The Fisher King is to be identified with Christ himself, as allegories of Christ as a fisherman abound in biblical literature. Christian origin theorists note that shortly after Chrétien's *Perceval*, the Bleeding Lance was linked to the spear that pierced Christ's side, and that the Grail itself was said to contain the blood of Christ.

Proponents of the Celtic origin theory look for progenitors of the Grail in the Welsh CAULDRON tales. In *The Spoils of Annwn*, Arthur retrieves a magic cauldron from the otherworld; in *Culhwch and Olwen*, he brings it back from Ireland; and in the non-Arthurian *Branwen*, King Bran the Blessed also takes it from the Irish king. Among these cauldrons' properties are the ability to separate heroes from cowards (represented in Robert's *Joseph* when the Grail separates the pious from the sinners), the power to provide unlimited food and drink to its owner (as the Grail does in the First Continuation of *Perceval* and Wolfram), and the capability to restore life to the dead. Bran, represented in Robert de Boron as Bron, is to be identified with the Fisher King, as he also receives wound which causes his land to waste. Another possible origin of the Grail in Welsh legend is the *dysgl* ("dish") of Rydderch the Generous, listed among the "Thirteen Treasures of the Island of Britain," which also provided food and drink to worthy warriors. Yet another theory revolves around the Horn of Bran, also mentioned in the "Thirteen Treasures," which has the same food-providing properties as the cauldron and *dysgl*.

The ritual theory identifies the Grail legends with the ancient myth of the Vegetation Spirit, represented in the Egyptian tales of Osiris and the Greek stories of Demeter. It focuses on the link between the Fisher King and the Waste Land, noting that the Fisher King's wound is located in the thighs or groin. His infirmity therefore implies a loss of fertility which is connected with the destitution of the Waste Land: flowers fail to blossom, crops do not grow, and rivers run dry.

Each theory has merit, and it is likely that the earliest Grail legends combined elements from Christian, Celtic, and pagan myth to achieve the most alluring of the Arthurian themes. [*ChretienP, Contin1, Contin2, RobertBorJ, Perlesvaus, Wolfram, VulgQuest, VulgEst, Contin3, Contin4, Heinrich, PostMer, PostQuest, Malory*]

GRAIL CASTLE

The castle of the Fisher King, where the Grail was kept. It stood in the heart of the GRAIL KINGDOM. It is called MUNSALVÆSCHE in Wolfram's *Parzival*, ILLES in *Diu Crône*, and CORBENIC in the Vulgate and Post-Vulgate Cycles. In *Perlesvaus,* the Grail Castle was approachable only by a number of perilous bridges, guarded by two stone lions who mauled the unworthy. After the Fisher King's death, it was conquered by the King of the Castle Mortal. All its holy artifacts disappeared until it was re-conquered by Perceval. A chapel outside the castle held the body of Joseph of Arimathea. It was also called Eden, the Castle of Joy, and the Castle of Souls. Anyone who died there went to heaven. After Perceval re-conquered it, Joseus the hermit served as its steward. Eventually, it crumbled to ruin, although the chapel remained in perfect condition. [*Perlesvaus, Wolfram, VulgQuest*]

GRAIL FAMILY

The elite clan of nobles in Wolfram's *Parzival* who were charged to keep and protect the Grail. The eldest son from each generation was chosen to be Grail King—the first Grail King was Titurel, followed by his son Frimutel. After Frimutel, it fell to Anfortas (Wolfram's Fisher King), to Perceval, and lastly to Perceval's son Loherangrin. Other members of the Grail Family included Perceval's mother, aunts, and uncles: Herzeloyde, Trevrizent, Schoysiane, and Repanse de Schoye. The tradition of the family was that the members not chosen to be the Grail King would disperse from Munsalvæsche and become rulers of various lands. The family was in command of a group of Grail Knights called Templars. In *Diu Crône*, Heinrich von dem Türlin re-interpreted the Grail Family as a cursed clan who Gawain saves from a living death. [*Wolfram, Heinrich*]

GRAIL HERO

The knight who seeks the Grail and, generally, becomes its new keeper upon achieving it. In the earliest stories of Chrétien, Wolfram, and their adapters, the Grail Hero is PERCEVAL (or, in Heinrich von dem Türlin's *Diu Crône,* GAWAIN). The Vulgate *Queste del Saint Graal* and later stories, however, give the primary honor to GALAHAD and put Perceval in a secondary position, along with BORS. [*ChretienP, Wolfram, Heinrich, VulgQuest*]

GRAIL KING

The leader of the family who kept charge of the Grail, called the FISHER KING by some writers, but sometimes given as a separate ruler. In Wolfram, the succession of Grail Kings is given as Titurel, Frimutel, Anfortas, Perceval, and Loherangrin; in the Vulgate romances, they are Joshua (a follower of Joseph of Arimathea), Aminadap, Carcelois, Manuel, Lambor, Pellehan, and Pelles. Sometimes the Grail King is the same as, or becomes, the MAIMED KING. The Grail King ruled the GRAIL KINGDOM from the GRAIL CASTLE. [*Wolfram, VulgQuest, VulgEst*]

GRAIL KINGDOM

The land which contained the GRAIL CASTLE. The land was called TERRE SALVAESCHE by Wolfram, and the STRANGE LAND, or LISTENOIS, by the Vulgate romances. In the Vulgate sources, it became the WASTE LAND when the Fisher or Maimed King received his wound. [*Wolfram, VulgQuest, VulgEst*]

GRAIL KNIGHTS

In Wolfram's *Parzvial*, an elite group of knights, sometimes called TEMPLARS, charged with guarding the Grail Castle. [*Wolfram*]

GRAIL MAIDEN

Any of a number of maidens who lived at the Grail Castle and were part of the Grail Procession witnessed by Perceval. The chief Grail Maiden was in charge of bearing the Grail. In Wolfram, this is Repanse de Schoye. [*ChretienP, Wolfram*]

GRAIL PROCESSION

The entourage of servants witnessed by Perceval (and other various knights) in the castle of the Fisher King. One of the servants, usually a maiden, carried the Grail. Described in almost every Grail romance, the Grail Procession generally begins with a Bleeding Lance or spear (identified in some texts with the lance with which the Roman soldier Longinus stabbed Christ). Other objects carried in the procession variously included candelabra, trestles, candles, stones, bowls, platters, and utensils. *Peredur,* which does not feature a Grail *per se,* culminates with a bowl filled with blood in which floats the decapitated head of Perceval's uncle. The procession is first mentioned by Chrétien de Troyes, who includes the Bleeding Lance, a candelabra, the Grail, and a silver platter. The items in Chrétien's Grail Procession recall the description of a Byzantine mass found in a seventh or eighth century manuscript. The Procession in Arthurian romance, however, lacks a priest (Loomis, *Romance*, 278). [*ChretienP, Wolfram, Heinrich, Peredur*]

GRAIL QUESTION

The question that Perceval needed to ask the Fisher King in order to free him from his suffering. Essentially, the quest knight needed to inquire about the wonders witnessed at the Grail Castle and in the Grail Procession. In Chrétien de Troyes's *Perceval*, the Question is "Who does the Grail serve?" Wolfram von Eschenbach alters the question to "What ails you [the Grail King]?" In Heinrich von dem Türlin's *Diu Crône*, Gawain frees the Grail company from a living-death by bellowing "For the sake of God and His majesty, tell me the meaning of this large assembly and miracle!"

Perceval failed to ask the Grail Question on his first visit because he had been warned by his tutor, Gornemant of Gohort, not to talk too much. In some texts, Perceval rectifies his mistake during his second appearance at the castle and completes the adventure. In the First Continuation of Chrétien's Perceval, Gawain partially heals the Fisher King's land by asking about the Bleeding Lance, but he falls asleep before he can ask about the Grail. In *Perlesvaus*, Perceval's failure to ask the Question seems to cause, rather than merely prolong, the Fisher King's suffering. In the post-Robert de Boron Grail romances, the Grail Question, as well as the need for it, disappears. The theme, of a land under a spell which could only be broken by the asking of a certain question, is common in fairy tales and folklore. [*ChretienP, Wolfram, Didot, Perlesvaus, Contin3, Heinrich*]

GRAIL SWORD

In each Grail romance, the Grail appears as the most important of three objects associated with the Fisher King: the Grail, a Bleeding Lance, and a sword. The sword is perhaps the most mutable of the three. In Chrétien's *Perceval*, the sword was fashioned by the smith Trabuchet and given to Perceval by the Fisher King. The magnificent blade had a hilt of ruby. In Chrétien's version, Perceval is warned that it will shatter if he uses it in battle, and that it will have to be repaired by Trabuchet in Cotatre. In Wolfram's *Parzival*, Sigune tells Perceval that the sword is good for one blow, but that it will shatter on the second and would have to be repaired by immersing it in the spring near Karnant called Lac. Perceval shattered it in a duel and did manage to mend it in the spring.

In both the First and Second Continuations of *Perceval*, it is said that the perfect Grail Knight could mend the sword, which had become broken through unknown means. Gawain is unable to join the pieces in the First Continuation (nor in the Vulgate *Lancelot*). Gawain learns that the Grail Sword was once used to strike a blow that "laid the whole country of Logres to waste," perhaps alluding to the role of the SWORD WITH THE STRANGE HANGINGS in the Vulgate texts. In the Second Continuation, Perceval is able to put the sword together, but the hairline fracture that remains bespeaks Perceval's failure to achieve complete perfection. We learn in the Third Continuation that it was broken when a knight named Partinal used it to kill Goondesert, the Fisher King's brother. In the Fourth Continuation, Perceval is finally able to mend it completely.

In *Perlesvaus*, the Grail Sword is identified with the sword which beheaded St. John the Baptist. Gawain needed it to enter the Grail Castle, and he recovered it from King Gurguran as a reward for dispatching a terrible giant plaguing Gurguran's land. The sword was subsequently stolen by the King of the Watch, but was returned. Gawain delivered it to the hands of the Fisher King, which somewhat alleviated his subsequent failure to ask the Grail Question.

In Heinrich von dem Türlin's *Diu Crône*, the Grail Sword is simply awarded to Gawain upon completion of the Grail Quest. In the Vulgate *Queste del Saint Graal*, it is called the BROKEN SWORD, having been shattered when it struck Joseph of Arimathea, and it is mended by Galahad at the conclusion of the Grail Quest. However, in the Vulgate romances, the importance of the Grail Sword is eclipsed by the magnificent SWORD WITH THE STRANGE HANGINGS; Galahad's mending of the Grail Sword is simply one episode in a long line of tests that serve to prove Galahad as the greatest knight. [*ChretienP, Contin1, Contin2, Perlesvaus, Wolfram, Heinrich, VulgQuest, Contin3, Contin4*]

GRAIL TABLE

A precursor to the Round Table, modeled after the table of the Last Supper and used by the followers of Joseph of Arimathea. When the crops of the Grail fellowship failed (signifying unworthiness within the company), Joseph had the table constructed to weed out the sinners among the group. Bron, later known as the Rich Fisher, caught a fish that was multiplied into thousands in the presence of the Grail. The unworthy, however, found themselves unable to physically sit at the Grail Table.

The Grail Table was made of silver. Like the Round Table, it had a Perilous Seat that destroyed anyone who sat in it. It also had a Feared Seat reserved for Josephus, Joseph of Arimathea's son. The fate of the Grail Table after Joseph's time is unclear, but at the conclusion of the Grail Quest, Galahad, Perceval, and Bors were served mass at the table. In an Irish version of the Grail Quest story, the table is last found in the ship the bore Lancelot and the body of Perceval's sister. [*RobertBorJ, VulgQuest, VulgEst*]

GRAINNE

The Irish counterpart of ISOLDE. She was the wife of the Irish chieftan Finn. Under the influence of a potion, she fell in love with Diarmaid, Finn's nephew. The lovers eloped and began an affair.

GRAM

An Arthurian knight. [*Heinrich*]

GRAMOFLANZ

A king in Wolfram's *Parzival* who ruled the fortress city of Sabins after his father Irot. His counterpart in Chrétien de Troyes's *Perceval* is GUIROMELANT. Gromflanz's prowess was so great that he refused to fight less than two knights at any one time. In one battle, he killed Duke Cidegast of Logres. Cidegast's widow, Orgeluse, then dedicated her life to finding a new husband who could exact revenge on Gramoflanz. She eventually settled on Gawain, and Gawain challenged Gramoflanz to a duel by stealing a garland from one of Gramoflanz's trees. They arranged to fight on the field at Joflanze. At the scheduled date, Gawain fought a long battle with Perceval, thinking he was Gramoflanz, and the real duel had to be rescheduled while Gawain recovered. Later, Gramoflanz fought against Perceval, thinking it was Gawain, and lost. Exasperated, he demanded—and rescheduled for the third time—a fight with the real Gawain.

Meanwhile, Gramoflanz had fallen in love with Gawain's sister Itonje, who was recently released from her imprisonment at Castle of Marvels. He courted her through letters and gifts, and she eventually reciprocated his love. Realizing that any outcome of the Gawain/Gramoflanz battle would result in sorrow for Itonje, Itonje's lady Bene (who had been acting as a go-between for Itonje and Gramoflanz), Arthur, and King Brandelidelin (Gramoflanz's maternal uncle) conspired to convince Orgeluse, Gawain, and Gramoflanz to drop the feud. They succeeded, and Gramoflanz and Itonje were happily married. Gramoflanz appears in the stories of Der Pleier as one of Arthur's knights, and his credits include the war against King Ekunaver of Kanadic and the siege of Tandernas. [*Wolfram, PleierG, PleierT*]

GRANDALIS

Castellan of Crenefort and father of Arthur's Sir Yvain of Lionel. [*VulgMer*]

GRANDE DISIO

A palace in the forest of Darnantes, where a sorceress named Elergia entrapped Arthur. After Tristan freed Arthur, Arthur tried to have it razed, but the workmen could not pull it down. Merlin had prophesied that the palace would stand until the end of the world. [*Tavola*]

GRANDES

A king of Gaul. Three of his kin were present at the culmination of the Grail Quest. [*Tavola*]

GRANDINES THE CRUEL

An evil knight who was killed by Galahad during the Grail Quest. [*ProsTris*]

GRANDOINE OF THE DISTANT ISLE

A count who was a companion of Lord Formis on the Turning Isle. Yder defeated him when Arthur and his knights fought Formis's knights. [*Livre*]

GRANDOME [*Grandomes*]

A Saxon warrior who participated in the Saxon invasion of Britain. He was defeated and captured by Gawain in a skirmish near Logres. [*VulgMer*]

GRANDON

One of Arthur's knights. [*SyreGaw*]

GRANTORTO

A giant who attacked the kingdom of the maiden Irena. Artegall killed him and saved the kingdom. [*Spenser*]

GRANWEN

One of Arthur's warriors and advisors. He was the son of Llyr. [*Dream*]

GRASSLANDS AND GIANTS

The land ruled by King Rions, an enemy of Arthur, in the Vulgate *Merlin*. It is perhaps the same as the Land of the GRAZING GROUNDS. Elsewhere, Rions is called the King of Ireland and Denmark. [*VulgMer*]

GRATIAN[1] MUNICEPS

The king of Britain prior to Constantine (Arthur's grandfather). He had previously been a general under the British king/Roman emperor Maximus, and had proved his prowess by driving the Picts and Huns off the island. As a king, however, he was tyrannical, and was assassinated by his own noblemen. Afterwards, the kingdom fell into ruin until the arrival of Constantine from Brittany. Giovanni Boccaccio, the Italian author of *The Fates of Illustrious Men*, thought that Constantine obtained the kingdom from Gratian. [*GeoffHR, Wace, Boccaccio*]

GRATIAN[2] THE PALE [*Grastian the Castellan*]

A steward of King Ban of Benoic (Lancelot's father). He took care of the city of Trebe in Ban's absence. When Ban allied with Arthur, Gratian joined their struggle against the rebellious kings and Saxons, and he apparently became a Knight of the Round Table. His son Banin was Ban's godson and also a Knight of the Round Table. [*VulgMer, Livre, Arthour, Malory*]

GRAUSEN

A deserted manor near Camelot where Lancelot hid while waiting to rescue Guinevere from the stake. [*Tavola*]

GRAUSIN

A Knight of the Round Table killed during the Grail Quest. [*Tavola*]

GRAVADAIN OF THE STRONG CASTLE

A British nobleman who opposed the Saxons in the early days of Arthur's reign. He fought under King Clarion of

Northumberland in the battles in northern Britain. He may be identical to one of the AGRAVADAINs. [*VulgMer*]

GRAY STONE [*Llech Las*]

A location in Scotland where Iddawg, one of Arthur's warriors, performed penance after his lack of diplomacy caused the battle of Camlann. [*Dream*]

GRAZING GROUNDS

A land ruled by King Rions, probably identical to the land of GRASSLANDS AND GIANTS. Galahad and Alipansin, vassals of Rions, are also mentioned as kings of the Grazing Grounds. [*VulgMer*]

GREAT FOOL

A nephew of Arthur in an Irish tale. His adventures owe something to Perceval or Peredur. He was raised ignorant of his nobility because his family was Arthur's enemy. When he came of age, he proved himself a skilled fighter by visiting Arthur's court and defeating Gawain, as well as three obscure knights known as the Red Knight, the Purple Knight, and the Speckled Knight. [*IrishF*]

GREECE

Greece became part of the Byzantine Empire when, in the third century, Diocletian divided the Roman Empire in two. The succession of emperors with authority over Greece is covered under CONSTANTINOPLE. By the Arthurian period, the western empire had fallen to the Vandals and the eastern empire was under attack by other barbarians. Greece was invaded by Huns, Slavs, and Goths.

Arthurian legend fails to recognize this history. In *Culhwch and Olwen*, Arthur has conquered Greece along with most of western Europe. Geoffrey of Monmouth has a king of Greece, Epistrophus, allying with Lucius of Rome in a war against Arthur. Chrétien de Troyes correctly makes it part of the empire of Constantinople and gives its succession of emperors as Alexander, Alis, and Cliges. The Post-Vulgate *Queste del Saint Graal* tells us that Erec was a descendant of Greeks; his grandfather, Canan, had been the King of Saloliqui. Finally, in *Floriant et Florete*, Greece is ruled by Emperor Filimenis and is later inherited by Sir Floriant. [*Culhwch, GeoffHR, ChretienC, Wace, PostQuest, Floriant, Malory*]

GREEN CHAPEL

The chapel where Sir Gawain had promised to meet the Green Knight (Bertilak) exactly one day after New Year—one year after the Beheading Game challenge that Gawain accepted at Camelot. Gawain searched long for the location, and finally met the Green Knight on the settled day. There, the Green Knight spared Gawain's life and revealed his true identity. [*SirGawain, Grene*]

GREEN ISLAND

The realm of King Flois, one of Arthur's vassals. It contained the castles of Effin and Alverne. The island was besieged by a giant named Assiles, but was saved by Gawain. [*Heinrich*]

GREEN KNIGHT[1] [*Vert Chevalier*]

The alias of Cladain the Green, who joined Arthur's court after he was defeated by Sir Durmart. [*Durmart*]

GREEN KNIGHT[2]

The title character of the Middle English poem *Sir Gawain and the Green Knight*. The Green Knight showed up at King Arthur's court during the New Year's feast and presented a Beheading Game challenge to the knights present: any knight would be allowed to take a swing at the Green Knight with an axe while the Green Knight stood perfectly still and offered no defense. In return, that warrior would have to stand still before the Green Knight one year later while the Green Knight took a swing at him.

None of Arthur's warriors rose to the challenge. Arthur was about to do it himself when Gawain stepped forward and took the axe. Confident that the Green Knight would not survive the blow—and would thus be unavailable for the second part of the challenge—Gawain swung the axe and chopped off the Green Knight's head. The Green Knight, however, calmly picked up his head, mounted his horse, and told Gawain to meet him in a year and a day in the Green Chapel.

As the next New Year's approached, Gawain set off to find the Green Chapel, much to the distress of his comrades who expected never to see him again. He lodged for Christmas with a lord who had a castle called Hutton near the Green Chapel. When the lord offered him lodging, the two knights agreed that for the three days that Gawain was there, each knight would give to the other whatever he had obtained that day. On the first day, the lord went out hunting while Gawain hung around the castle. While the lord was gone, his wife tried to bed Gawain, but succeeded in only getting a kiss. When the lord returned, he presented Gawain with a freshly killed deer; true to his word, Gawain gave to the lord the kiss he had received from the lord's wife. The second day went much the same. On the third day, the lord's wife gave up on trying to seduce Gawain, and presented him with her girdle, which she said would protect him. When the lord came home, Gawain gave him the kiss but kept the girdle.

The next day, Gawain left for the Green Chapel. He met the Green Knight there and prepared to receive his blows. The Green knight gave him two feinted blows and lightly nicked his neck on the third one. The Green Knight then revealed himself to be Gawain's host: the lord of the castle Hutton, named Bertilak of the High Desert. He explained that the two feinted blows were for the days that Gawain faithfully turned over the kisses, and the nick was for not turning over the girdle. The Green Knight then told Gawain that he had been sent to Arthur's court by Morgan le Fay—whose enchantments had spared Bertilak's life after the decapitation—as a ploy to distress Guinevere. Gawain returned to Camelot, where he was honored for his adventure.

A later poem known as *The Grene Knight* offers a similar story, but changes the Green Knight's true name to BREDBEDDLE. [*SirGawain*, *Grene*]

GREEN KNIGHT[3]

A knight of King Arthur's court who was the son of Sir Ironside. [*SyreGaw*, *Carle*]

GREEN KNIGHT[4]

The guise adopted by the knight PERTYLOPE, who was defeated by Gareth. [*Malory*]

GREEN MEADOW

A land terrorized by a diseased monster who had to bathe in a vat of blood each week. The creature slew a good portion of the Green Meadow's population before Daniel, one of Arthur's knights, overcame the monster's spells and beheaded him, thus rescuing his friend, the Count of the Bright Fountain. Sandinose, the maiden of the Green Meadow, later married Arthur's Duke Beladigant. [*Stricker*]

GREEN WOOD [*Bois Verdoyant, Busco Verdulant*]

The castle owned by Sir Guiron the Courteous, a knight of Uther Pendragon's time. [*Palamedes*, *Tavola*]

GREENLAND

The giant island enters Arthurian romance in Wolfram's *Parzival*: Wolfram says that warriors from Greenland joined in King Vridebrant of Scotland's invasion of Zazamanc, which was repelled by Perceval's father Gahmuret. It was the home of the Grail maiden Garschiloye. In *Meriadeuc*, its king, Amangon, is one of Arthur's subjects, and Der Pleier also names it as one of Arthur's allies. [*Wolfram*, *Meriadeuc*, *PleierT*]

GREGORIO

A cardinal who ascended to the papacy in the *Vita di Merlino*. Merlin had predicted Gregorio's ascension. Merlin was later brought to trial for heresy before Gregorio, by a bishop named Conrad, but Merlin was exonerated. The author may have been thinking of Pope Gregory I (590–604), the earliest Gregory and the closest to the traditional Arthurian period. However, there were twelve other Gregories between Gregory I and *Merlino*. [*VitaMer*]

GREGORY

The name of three priests who presented a holy bell to King Gurguran (Gawain's ally) and bade him bring it to the Grail Castle. [*Perlesvaus*]

GREID

One of Arthur's warriors who was the son of Eri. Greid owned a hound named Drudwyn. As one of his tasks, the warrior Culhwch had to obtain this hound to help hunt the boar Twrch Trwyth. Greid was loyal to the warrior Gwythyr, and joined he Gwythyr's army against Gwynn son of Nudd. Greid was taken prisoner by Gwynn and was not released until Arthur intervened. [*Culhwch*]

GREIDAWL ENEMY-SUBDUER [*Greidyawl*]

One of Arthur's warriors and advisors in Welsh legend. He was the son of Enfael Adrann and the father of Gwythyr. A Welsh Triad tells us that his granddaughter, Gwenhwyfar, was one of Arthur's three queens bearing that name. "Greidawl" may signify "passionate." [*Culhwch*, *Triads*, *Dream*]

GREINGRADOAN

An Arthurian knight in Heinrich von dem Türlin's *Diu Crône*. He scolded Kay for making sport of ladies who failed a chastity test. [*Heinrich*]

GREINS

A knight present at the tournament of Sorgarda, which Gawain won. [*Heinrich*]

GRELOGUEVAUS

Perceval's father in the First Continuation of Chrétien's *Perceval*. He was a descendant of Joseph of Arimathea. His counterparts in texts contemporary to the First Continuation include BLIOCADRAN, GAHMURET, and ALAIN. [*Contin1*]

GREMINÉS

An Arthurian knight who joined Gawain's quest to conquer Rigomer castle. [*Merveil*]

GREOMAR

A malevolent knight who was the brother of the Formidable Knight and the cousin of Caradoc. He enjoyed imprisoning knights, beating them, and forcing them into combat with his warriors. Sagremor eventually killed him. [*Livre*]

GREOREAS [*Creoreas*]

A robber knight who abducted and raped a maiden in Chrétien de Troyes's *Perceval*. Greoreas was defeated by Gawain and was forced to eat with hounds for a month as punishment. Greoreas extracted his revenge on Gawain by stealing Gawain's horse, Gringolet. He later sent his nephew to kill Gawain, but Gawain was victorious, reclaiming his horse in the process. After he was defeated in combat by Sir Durmart, Greoreas shunned his evil ways and humbly presented himself at Arthur's court. In the *Livre d'Artus*, Greoreas is among Arthur's warriors in the battle against the Saxons at Vambieres, though he still dislikes Gawain because of Gawain's conflict with Greoreas's cousin, Guinganbresil. [*ChretienP*, *Contin1*, *Durmart*, *Livre*]

GRESLEMUEF OF FINISTERRE [*Grahelens*, *Gresmurs*]

One of Arthur's noblemen present at the wedding of Erec and Enide. His brother was Guinguemar of the Isle of Avalon. [*ChrétienE*, *HartmannE*]

GRESOWN

In *Lancelot of the Laik*, a knight of Arthur's who fought in the war against Galehaut. He appears no where else in Arthurian romance, although his name occurs in the same place as GIRFLET's in the Vulgate *Lancelot*. [*LancLaik*]

GRESSAMANT

An Arthurian knight defeated in joust by Daniel of the Blossoming Valley. [*Stricker*]

GREU OF ALENIE

A Knight of the Round Table found exclusively in the *Livre d'Artus*. He was the son of the King of Alenie, and he apparently joined Arthur's service during the Saxon wars. He embarked on the quest to remove the Ugly Appearance from a Libyan river when a maiden arrived at Arthur's court and announced the adventure. Greu was successful, thanks to the assistance of the Wise Lady of the Forest of No Return. Afterwards, he married the Wise Lady's niece, the messenger who had brought him to the adventure. Der Pleier's GAREL has some similar adventures, and the names may be related. [*Livre*]

GREY-HAMMED LADY

A otherworldly woman, bearing the true name of Ailleann, who visited Arthur's court in an Irish romance. In the form of a deer, she was pursued by the King of Gascony. After being hunted for three days, she resumed her human form and came to court. The ladies at court eventually became jealous of her beauty, and when she revealed her nickname, "Grey Ham," to one of the ladies, her confidant immediately betrayed her to the rest of court, saying she had a tuft of grey hair on her inner knee. When the ladies at court were examined, however, it was discovered that the "Grey-Hammed Lady" was the only one who did *not* have this tuft of hair. The other ladies were punished and exiled, and the Grey-Hammed Lady awarded them new wives from the otherworld. The Grey-Hammed Lady herself married Arthur. [*IrishL*]

GRIBALO

A dwarf who served King Bilis, lord of the dwarves, in Chrétien's *Erec*. He came to the wedding of Erec and Enide. Hartmann von Aue calls the same character GRIGORAS. [*ChrétienE*]

GRIFFIN¹ [*Griffith*]

The King of Wales after Caradoc, his brother. As Caradoc grew old and infirm, he gradually relinquished more power to his brother, but Griffin coveted the entire throne. Eventually Griffin had Caradoc murdered during a hunt. The noblemen of Wales were suspicious, but Griffin kept them silenced through fear. He tried to murder Caradoc's children, Meriadoc and Orwen, but they were saved by Ivor, their foster-father, and taken into hiding. Meriadoc eventually arrived at Arthur's court and, after winning favor, convinced Arthur to summon Griffin for trial. Griffin refused and fortified himself in Snowdon, but a domestic revolt combined with Arthur's siege led him to surrender. He was properly tried and executed, and his kingdom was given to Meriadoc. [*Historia*]

GRIFFIN²

A smith from Carmarthen who made weapons for Uther Pendragon, including a magnificent spear which was used by Arthur to defeat Frollo. [*Layamon*]

GRIFFINE

A Knight of the Round Table. [*SirLamb*]

GRIFFON

The knight of the Treacherous Pass. He once lent Lancelot some armor, and later demanded Lancelot's armor in repayment. Griffon rode around, displaying the armor, leading everyone to believe that Lancelot was dead. He defeated and imprisoned Kay, but became scared when a body of Arthur's knights set out after his head. He released Kay to Aglovale and stopped bothering Arthur. [*VulgLanc*]

GRIFFONET

One of Guinevere's Queen's Knights. He opposed the Knights of the Round Table in a tournament at Carhaix. [*VulgMer*]

GRIFUZ [*Griffin*, *Grifud*, *Gryffitz*]

One of Arthur's knights who was the son of Nogoid. [*GeoffHR*, *Wace*]

GRIGORAS [*Gligoras*]

A dwarf who served King Bilis of the dwarves. He came to the wedding of Erec and Enide. He is identical with the character called GRIBALO by Chrétien de Troyes. In *Diu Crône*, he fails a "chastity test." [*HartmannE*, *Heinrich*]

GRIGORZ

King of Ipotente and cousin of Perceval's enemy Clamadeu. Grigorz provided Clamadeu with a Castillan war horse named Guverjorz. [*Wolfram*]

GRILL

A knight who had succumbed to the temptations of the Bower of Bliss and had been turned into a swine. When Sir Guyon destroyed the Bower and restored the knights within to their true form, Grill complained that he had enjoyed being a pig. [*Spenser*]

GRIMAL

Hero of the *Histoire de Grimal*, a non-Arthurian French prose romance that elaborates on the characters appearing in the Vulgate *Estoire del Saint Graal*. Grimal was the son of Mordrain and Gratille. After his parents and relatives went to Britain, Grimal became king of Babylonia.

GRIMARK

One of Arthur's warriors who was the son of Kinmark. [*Layamon*]

GRIMBALD

An earth fiend in the service of Osmond, a Saxon sorcerer. He tried several times to lure Arthur to his grave, but he was foiled by Philadel, an air spirit. [*Dryden*]

GRIME

An Arthurian knight who participated in the Roman War. [*Allit*]

GRIMSBY

A seaport on the eastern coast of England, at the mouth of the Humber river. Arthur landed here upon returning from his conquest of Iceland. [*Layamon*]

GRINGALAS THE STRONG

A Knight of the Round Table who participated in the Grail Quest. [*ProsTris*]

GRINGOLET [*Gringalet, Gringuljete, Winwalite*]

Gawain's magnificent horse, first named by Chrétien de Troyes in *Erec*. Wolfram von Eschenbach, who gives it the epithet "with the Red Ears," says that it came from the Grail Castle of Munsalvæsche and was originally owned by the Grail Knight Lybbeals of Prienlascors. King Lähelin won the horse when he killed Lybbeals in a joust; Lähelin gave the steed to his brother Duke Orilus who, in turn, gave it to Gawain. It was stolen by Urjans, won from him by Lischois Gwelljus, and returned to Gawain when he defeated Lischois. It was stolen at another point by Kay, who was knocked off it by Erec. At still another time, Greoreas—who was any enemy of Gawain—stole it, but Gawain recovered it when he defeated Greoreas's nephew.

The Vulgate *Merlin* names Gringolet's first owner as the Saxon king Clarion, one of the many Saxon rulers who invaded Britain in the early days of Arthur's reign. Gawain took Gringolet from Clarion after defeating him in a skirmish on the plains of Roestoc. Finally, in Girart D'Amiens' *Escanor*, Gawain obtains the steed from Escanor the Large, who had received it as a gift from the fairy Esclarmonde. The animal would not eat or drink in the absence of its former master, until a maiden named Felinete helped Gawain cure Gringolet by removing a bag of powder from one of the horse's ears.

The horse's name probably comes from the Welsh *Gwyngalet*, meaning "white-hard." The horse of Gwalchmei, Gawain's counterpart in Welsh legend, is called Kincaled. [*ChretienE, ChretienP, Wolfram, VulgMer, Girart*]

GRISANDOLES

The alias of AVENABLE, a maiden assisted by Merlin when she came to Julius Caesar's court dressed as a man. [*VulgMer, ProsMer2*]

GRISONSTINO

A hermit who lived in the wilderness of Darnantes. He hosted Tristan and Kahedins during their adventures there. [*Tavola*]

GRISSEL ("Grey")

Gawain's horse, which was killed by Sir Galleron during a duel. [*Awntyrs*]

GRISWOLD

A knight who joined Mordred's rebellion against Arthur. Gawain killed him in battle. [*Allit*]

GRITENLAND

According to Der Pleier's *Meleranz*, the King of Gritenland married Anthonje, Arthur's sister. He fathered Gaheris. [*PleierM*]

GRIZZLE

In Henry Fielding's parody *The Tragedy of Tragedies*, a nobleman at Arthur's court. He loved Huncamunca, Arthur's daughter, and became enraged when Arthur betrothed her to the diminutive warrior Tom Thumb. In the original play *Tom Thumb*, he kills Tom Thumb's ghost after the little man iss eaten by a cow, for which Grizzle is slain by Huncamunca. In the revised *Tragedy of Tragedies*, Tom Thumb kills Grizzle in battle. [*Fielding*]

GROADAIN

A dwarf who served the lady of Roestoc. He led Hector and Gawain on several adventures, and procured the latter's promise to duel the knight Seguarades on his lady's behalf. Groadain treated both knights cruelly, and was censured by the lady of Roestoc for it. His niece fell in love with Hector. [*LancLac, VulgLanc*]

GROING POIRE MELE ("Pear Muzzle") [*Gremporemole*]

A knight with a minuscule nose. He led an echelon of Arthur's soldiers against King Rions at the battle of Aneblayse. [*VulgMer, Arthour*]

GROMER SOMER JOUR [*Gromerson Erioure, Grommer Grummerson*]

A knight who appears in several Middle English romances, probably first in *The Wedding of Sir Gawain and Dame*

Ragnelle. Gromer captures an unarmed King Arthur in Inglewood forest and forces Arthur to promise to return in one year, either to divulge what women most desire, or to forfeit his life to Gromer. Gawain eventually obtains the answer from Gromer's sister, Ragnelle, and Arthur is saved.

Malory (who may have written *Wedding*) includes Gromer as a Knight of the Round Table. As one of the knights who joined Agravain and Mordred in their attempt to catch Lancelot and Guinevere *in flagrante delicto*, Gromer was slain by Lancelot. Earlier in *Le Morte Darthur*, Gromer is said to be Scottish.

In *The Turke and Sir Gawain*, a later verse romance, Gromer, bewitched into the form of a "turke," or churl, shows up at Arthur's court and challenges one of the assembly to an exchange of blows. After delivering one to Gawain, he asks to postpone the reciprocal strike. The turke then leads Gawain on a series of spectacular adventures, culminating in a visit to the Isle of Man, where Gawain, with the turke's help, slays the pagan king and his giant attendants. The turke then asks Gawain to behead him, which results in his rebirth in the form of Gromer, a Christian knight. In the denouement, Arthur appoints Gromer the King of Man. [*Wedding, Malory, Turke*]

GRONOSIS

An Arthurian knight who was the son of Kay. [*ChretienE, Heinrich*]

GROVE

A forest visited by Gaheris during a quest to find Lancelot. He met a maiden who he championed against her brother-in-law, Count Guidan. [*VulgLanc*]

GROWING LOOKOUT

An enchanted hill in Britain, probably in Wales. The Growing Lookout had a mysterious property of growing by about fifty times its normal size without warning, and from the top of it, a person could see the entire island of Britain. Lancelot rode by it on the way to Arthur's court to fight Valerin, but could not stop and examine it because of his haste. [*UlrichZ*]

GRUGYN SILVER BRISTLE

One of the boar Twrch Trwyth's warriors, who had been turned into a piglet. Grugyn and Twrch Trwyth's other piglets fought against Arthur and his warriors, killing many men at the battle of Dyffryn Llwchwr. Grugyn separated from Twrch Trwyth and made a final stand at Garth Grugyn. He was killed after slaying Rhuddvyw and many of Arthur's other warriors. [*Culhwch*]

GRYN

One of Arthur's warriors who shared the duties of gatekeeper in Caer Llion (Caerleon) with seven to nine other warriors. His master was the chief gatekeeper, Glewlwyd Strong Grip. [*Geraint*]

GRYSINDE

A lady who became the subject of dispute between Mabon the Black and Mennonas. Tristan and Isolde came to help Mabon. When Mennonas saw that Grysinde was not as beautiful as Isolde, he beheaded her. [*ProsTris*]

GUALAGNE

The King of Gualagne participated in Arthur's tournaments at the Hard Rock and the castle of Leverzep. He had previously been an enemy of Arthur, but was subdued. [*Tavola*]

GUANIUS [*Wanis*]

King of the Huns. Three generations before Arthur, he allied with King Melga of the Picts and King Gillomaur of Ireland to invade Britain. He plagued Kings Maximus and Gratian before he was driven away for good when Constantine, Arthur's grandfather, arrived from Brittany to assume Britain's throne. [*GeoffHR, Wace*]

GUARES THE BLACK

A Knight of the Round Table, known as the "Ugly, Burned One." Guares and his brother, Garnaldo, both participated in the Grail Quest. [*PostQuest*]

GUASCOGNA

In *La Tavola Ritonda*, the King of Guascogna was slain by Lancelot during Arthur's tournament at Leverzep. The name is a variation of GASCONY. [*Tavola*]

GUELGUEZINS OF HOHE BOIS

A duke in Arthur's service. [*HartmannE*]

GUENDEBORC

A field situated between the Castle of Maidens and the Castle of Ladies. The two fortresses held a tournament at Guendeborc, in which Lancelot participated. [*VulgLanc*]

GUENDOLEN

The half-Djinn queen of a magic castle visited by Arthur in Sir Walter Scott's *The Bridal of Triermain*. Arthur fell in love with Guendolen and stayed with her for three months. Before returning to his own lands, he promised Guendolen that should a daughter come of their union, Arthur would wed her to his best knight. Guendolen later gave birth to Gyneth. [*Scott*]

GUENDOLOENA[1]

Merlin's wife. A beautiful Welsh woman, she despaired after Merlin went mad at the battle of Arfderydd. In one of his moments of rationality, Merlin sent a message to Guendoloena, telling her to give him up and to remarry. He lapsed back into insanity, however, came to Guendoloena's wedding, and killed her prospective husband with a pair of stag's horns. [*GeoffVM*]

GUENDOLOENA² [Gwendoloena]

Arthur's queen in *De Ortu Waluuanii*, probably a variation of GUINEVERE. Unique to this story, she is given prophetic powers which allow her to predict Gawain's arrival at court. [*DeOrtu*]

GUENGASOAIN [(Guen)gasouains]

A treacherous knight who murdered the noble knight Raguidel. Guengasoain's benefactress, Lingrenote the sorceress, made him so powerful that no single knight could defeat him. He kept a ferocious bear as a companion in case more than one knight should engage him. Gawain and Yder, seeking to avenge Raguidel's death, nevertheless killed Guengasoain. Yder married his daughter, Trevilonete. Guengasoain's uncle was King Aguissant (Angusel) of Scotland. His brother was named King Bueves. [*Contin1, Vengeance*]

GUENLOIE¹ [G(u)eneloie]

In the romance of *Yder*, the queen of Carvain. She fell in love with Yder when he lodged at her court. Proud, she sent him away to prove himself. She came to regret her decision and set out to locate him. In time, the two were reunited and married. Her name is similar to a form of GUINEVERE, and in an earlier version of the story, Yder's mistress may have been Arthur's queen. [*Yder*]

GUENLOIE²

Gawain's lover in *Meriadeuc*. She was the son of King Amangon of Greenland. Gawain abandoned her in favor of the maiden of the Castle of the Door. [*Meriadeuc*]

GUENTEFLUR

The fair, well-mannered sister of King Guivret, Erec's diminutive friend. She led an idyllic life with her sister Filledamor in Guivret's city of Penefrec. [*HartmannE*]

GUERDON

Earl of Winchester under Arthur. [*Wace*]

GUERELIÉS

An Arthurian knight. [*Yder*]

GUERGUINT [Gurguint, Gwergound]

Earl of Hereford under Arthur. [*Wace, Layamon*]

GUERIN¹ [Gerin(s), Geryn]

The ruler of Chartres under King Arthur. He brought the Twelve Peers of the Gauls to Arthur's coronation in Caerleon, and later brought soldiers to accompany Arthur in his campaign against Rome. He was one of the three messengers that Arthur sent to meet with the Roman Emperor Lucius—an effort that resulted in ruin when Gawain killed a Roman warrior. Guerin fought for Arthur throughout the Roman campaign, and was a key player at the final battle at Soissons. [*GeoffHR, Wace, Layamon*]

GUERIN² [Geryne]

A knight defeated by Lamorat at the tournament of Sorelois. [*ProsTris, Malory*]

GUERREHET

See GARETH.

GUES OF STRAUZ

A Knight of the Round Table. [*HartmannE*]

GUETHELIN [Gosselyn, Guencelin]

The Archbishop of London in the fifth century. When the Romans were departing Britain for good, Guethelin made a rousing speech to the British people in which he encouraged them to develop a national pride, train themselves as warriors, and defend their country. Nevertheless, Britain fell to ruin and was invaded by Huns and Picts, led by Guanius and Melga. Guethelin traveled to Brittany to seek help. He ordained Constantine, brother of Aldroen, as King of Britain, and brought him back to the island to drive out the barbarians. After Constantine pacified the land once again, Guethelin raised two of Constantine's children: Ambrosius Aurelius and Uther Pendragon. [*GeoffHR, Wace, Layamon*]

GUHU

A knight of Arthur's court. He participated in Arthur's war against a rebellious vassal named Taulas of Rougemont. [*Yder*]

GUI OF CARMELIDE [Guy]

One of the knights sent by Morgan le Fay to kill Alexander the Orphan at the castle Fair Guard. Alexander defeated him. [*ProsTris, Prophecies, Malory*]

GUIDABAN

A knight who fell in love with Isolde and plotted to kill Tristan. Joined by his brother, they set out to attack Isolde's lover, but before they could do so, they met Palamedes, who killed Guidaban. [*ProsTris*]

GUIDAN

A lord who stole the land of Valigues from his sister-in-law, murdering her fiancée. Gaheris (Gawain's brother) championed the maiden against Guidan in a duel at Roestoc. When it became apparent that Guidan would lose the combat, he jumped into a river and drowned. [*VulgLanc*]

GUIDERIUS

According to Geoffrey of Monmouth, Guiderius succeeded his father, Cymbeline, as king of Britain in the first century AD. His brother was named Arviragus. Britain had been paying tribute to Rome for several generations when Guiderius took the throne, and Guiderius decided to stop the practice. As a result, Rome invaded Britain. Guiderius died fighting the Romans, but his brother Arviragus continued the fight and was victorious. [*GeoffHR*]

GUIENNE [*Gyane*]

A region of southwest France, named as part of Arthur's kingdom in the Alliterative *Morte Arthure*. Malory says that Lancelot ruled it, and that he gave it to his brother Hector in return for Hector's support in the war against Arthur. [*Allit, Malory*]

GUIFAS

A heathen king killed by King Clarion of Northumberland in the battle of Rockingham. [*Arthour*]

GUIGAR

A Knight of the Round Table who participated in the Grail Quest. [*PostQuest*]

GUIGENOR [*Aguigenor, Guingenor*]

Arthur's grand-niece in the First Continuation of *Perceval*. Guigenor was the daughter of Guiromelant and Clarissant and the niece of Gawain. She married a knight named Alardin. [*Contin1*]

GUIGNIER [*Guiner*]

A maiden who married Sir Caradoc, one of Arthur's knights, in the First Continuation of Chrétien de Troyes's *Perceval*. Caradoc rescued her from a knight named Alardin, who had abducted her after wounding her brother, Cador. Caradoc married her at Arthur's court. In a later episode, Caradoc's evil parents attached a deadly serpent to his arm. Placing Caradoc in a vat filled with vinegar and herself in a vat filled with milk, Guignier caused the snake to unwind itself from the knight and to pursue the sweeter host. As it leapt between them, Cador cleaved off its head, but he accidentally caught part of Guignier's breast in the stroke. A magic shield provided by Alardin bestowed a golden breast its place. A chastity test at Arthur's court, involving a horn, showed that she was the only faithful wife of the Round Table knights. [*Contin1*]

GUILLAC

King of Denmark in the Didot-*Perceval*. He assisted Arthur in the Roman War. He was killed fighting Mordred's army at Winchester. [*Didot*]

GUILLADON

Sister of Taulas of Rougemont, a vassal in rebellion against Arthur. [*Yder*]

GUILLAMAR

In Dryden's *King Arthur*, a friend of the Saxon king Oswald. He may represent GILLAMAUR of Ireland found in Geoffrey of Monmouth. [*Dryden*]

GUILLANT

A great-grandson of Brutus and grandson of Albanact. It is unclear whether his father was Dombart or Embrunt. He joined his cousin Illbrint in a war against King Brun of the Savage Realm, their cousin, hoping to subdue him. Guillant killed Silhaut, Brun's brother, but was in turn slain by Brun. [*Palamedes*]

GUILODIEN

A horse ridden by Gawain. [*Contin1*]

GUILORETE

A maiden upon whom Gawain fathered Lionel. She was the daughter of Norrois of Lis and the sister of Brandelis and Meliant. Found in the First Continuation of Chrétien's *Perceval*, she is usually unnamed in other sources. [*Contin1*]

GUINABLE

A count in King Arthur's service. [*ChretienL*]

GUINALOT

Product of a union between the sorcerer Eliavres and a bitch. Guinalot was conceived after King Caradoc of Nantes, discovering that the sorcerer had been sleeping with Caradoc's wife, forced Eliavres to copulate with the hound. [*Contin1*]

GUINAN THE PALE [*Guina(n)s, Gwinas*]

A knight in Arthur's service in the Vulgate *Merlin*. He fought at the battle of Bedegraine, against the kings in rebellion against Arthur. He was saved from death by Sir Lucan the Butler. Malory says that he came from the city of Bloy. [*VulgMer, Arthour, Malory*]

GUINARD

A physician who healed Arthur's Sir Yder after Kay had tried to murder Yder with a sword thrust through the back. Guinard inhabited a convent administered by a nun named Esotil. [*Yder*]

GUINAS[1]

A count who sought to test himself against Gawain. He set up a special pavilion for the unscheduled duel, waiting for Gawain to wander along, but he was defeated first by Gaheris, Gawain's brother, and was sent to Gawain as a prisoner. [*VulgLanc*]

GUINAS[2] OF BLAKESTAN

A cruel and arrogant knight. His cousin Ladomas accidentally slipped into bed with Guinas's lady, and Guinas attacked him for this mistake, nearly killing him. Guinas then rejected his own paramour. Arthur's Sir Hector came along in the middle of this, and Guinas—in a foul temper—pressed him into combat. Hector defeated

Guinas twice and refrained from killing him so that Guinas could be reconciled with his lady and cousin. [*LancLac*, *VulgLanc*]

GUINAT

A heathen warrior slain by Agravain at a battle near Camelot. [*Arthour*]

GUINCEL [*Ginses*]

A warrior who fought at the tournament of Tenebroc, where he was unhorsed by Gawain. [*ChretienE*]

GUINCEMAIN

A knight who, during the Grail Quest, besieged the castle of Lord Boncenes. Galahad came upon the siege, just as Guincemain was about to start catapulting his prisoners into the castle. Galahad killed Guincemain and put an end to the siege. [*ProsTris*]

GUINDARD

A heathen warrior slain by Arthur's Sir Sagremor at the battle of Diana Bridge. [*Arthour*]

GUINEBAL¹ [*Guimbaut, Guinebaut, Gwenbaus*]

The older brother of Kings Ban and Bors and the uncle of Lancelot. He was a wise cleric, a skilled fighter, an amateur magician, and a tutor for his brothers as youths. Bors gave him the castle of Charroie. Guinebal became fast friends with Merlin when his brothers joined Arthur's wars against the Saxons and the rebellious kings. Merlin was impressed with Guinebal's knowledge, and added to his repertoire of magic. Guinebal fell in love with the lady of the Inhospitable Land Upheld when he met her in the Perilous Forest. For her love, he created a number of marvels, including the Magic Dance, which ensnared any passers-by, and a magic chessboard which moved its own pieces against any willing player, and invariably defeated him. Because of his enchantments, the forest was re-named the Forest of No Return. Guinebal died after teaching the lady some magic. [*VulgMer, Arthour, Malory*]

GUINEBAL² [*Guinbat(ing)*]

A Saxon warrior slain by Agravain at a battle in Logres. [*VulgMer, Arthour*]

GUINEMANT

One of the many Saxon kings who invaded Britain in the early days of Arthur's reign. He was slain by Gawain in a skirmish at Logres. [*VulgMer*]

GUINEMARS

Arthur's queen in *Les Enfances Gauvain*. It is probably a variation of GUINEVERE, though unlike Guinevere, Guinemars is described as a loyal and chaste wife. [*Enfances*]

GUINEVERE¹ [*Gainor, Gainovere, Ganora, Gaynor(e), Genever, Genievre, Genoyre, Ginevra, Ginover, Guanhumara, Guendoloena, Gueneour, Gueneuora, Guenevera, Guenevere, Guenievre, Guenivere, Guenloie, Guenore, Gunnore, Gven(e)our(e), Gwendoloena, *Gwenhwyfar, Gwennor, Gwenore, Gwinore, Jenover, Ntzenebra, Vanour, Velivera, Wanore, Waynor, Wenneveria, Zenevra, Zenibra, Zinevra*]

The wife of King Arthur. Her character varies greatly between legends. In the most common version of the Arthurian saga, Guinevere contributes to the downfall of Arthur's kingdom by engaging in an affair with Lancelot. Mordred took her (or tried to take her) as his own wife when he rebelled against Arthur. In the aftermath of the final battles that destroyed Arthur's kingdom, Guinevere sought refuge in a nunnery.

She appears first in the Welsh *Culhwch and Olwen* (c. 1080). The Welsh version of her name, Gwenhwyfar, means "white ghost." A Welsh Triad says that Arthur had three wives of this name—the daughters of Cywyrd, Gwythyr, and Gogfran—which may have inspired the French tradition of the True and False Guineveres. (The cross discovered at "Arthur's Grave" in Glastonbury identifes Guinevere as his second wife.) Another Triad calls her one of the "faithless wives" of the Isle of Britain. A third Triad talks of an episode in which Mordred visited Arthur's court and beat Gwenhwyfar, and a fourth says that the battle of Camlann (Arthur's last battle) somehow began over a feud between Gwenhwyfar and her sister, Gwenhwyach.

Geoffrey of Monmouth (1138) latinized her name as "Guinevere." He tells little about her, except to say that she was raised in the house of Cador of Cornwall and was ravishingly beautiful. Guinevere and Arthur were married after the Saxon wars. When Mordred revolted against Arthur while Arthur was fighting the Roman War, he took Guinevere as his wife, and Guinevere seemed to be a willing collaborator. Arthur returned, and as the battles between Mordred and Arthur raged, Guinevere fled to Caerleon and took the veil.

Two major themes follow Guinevere throughout the development of the Arthurian legend: her infidelity, and her abductions. In many texts, these themes are intertwined, with her rescuer becoming her lover. Chrétien de Troyes, in his *Lancelot* (C. 1180), is the first to mention her affair with Lancelot, which may have been invented by Marie de Champagne, Chrétien's patroness. The acceptance of Andreas the Chaplain's *De Amour*—which glorified adultery—in Marie's court may explain Chrétien's ability to portray Guinevere as both a noble queen and an unfaithful wife. On the other hand, Celtic queens were free to take lovers at their pleasure, and the affair may therefore have a Celtic origin, with the element of tragedy inserted by authors of different sensibilities.

Though her most famous affair is with Lancelot, Guinevere's earliest lover, as we've seen, seems to have been Mordred, with whom she is a willing consipirator in the chronicles. In Marie de France's *Lanval* (c. 1170) as well, she is said to have a number of lovers, and she propositions Sir Lanval. In several romances, she fails a variety of chastity tests, suggesting affairs with any number of other knights. In the romance of *Yder* (c. 1225–50), her infatuation with Yder and his subsequent marriage to a woman named Guenloie (a variation of Guinevere) may indicate an earlier tradition in which Guinevere and Yder were lovers. There is allusion to this tradition in the *Folie Tristan* of Berne (c. 1190). According to the Vulgate *Merlin* (c. 1230), she apparently had a dalliance with a knight named Gosengos before her marriage to Arthur.

Even the earliest Arthurian bards seem to have attached an abduction story to Guinevere. Such a tale is represented on an cathedral archivolt in Modena, Italy (c. 1135): Guinevere is abducted by Carados of the Dolorous Tower, who gives her to Mardoc, his master. Arthur gathers his knights and mounts a rescue, and it appears to be Gawain who successfully retrieves the queen, though Yder is also present. Another depiction appears in Caradoc of Llancarfan's *The Life of St. Gildas* (c. 1130), where Guinevere's kidnapper is King Melwas of the Summer Region (probably the origin of Meleagant). Although Arthur (presented in the tale as a tyrant) rouses warriors from Devon and Cornwall to pursue, it is the Abbott of Glastonbury and St. Gildas who shrewdly win her freedom.

In Ulrich's *Lanzelet* (c. 1200), Guinevere's abductor is King Valerin of the Tangled Wood. Valerin had lost, in combat against Lancelot, a claim that Guinevere should be his because of a promise of marriage made when Guinevere was a girl. Unsatisfied with his loss, Valerin kidnapped Guinevere and hauled her back to his fortress of the Tangled Wood. Arthur besieged the magic fortress—an effort that proved futile until he enlisted the aid of the wizard Malduc, who destroyed the palace's defenses and allowed Arthur and his knights to seize the castle. Guinevere's son Loüt played an important role in the rescue.

Heinrich von dem Türlin (c. 1230) presents an interesting abduction tale: Gasozein of Dragoz arrives at Arthur's court claming that Guinevere is actually his wife. Guinevere refutes his claim, but her brother Gotegrin believes her wrong and kidnaps her, intending to kill her for her wickedness. Gasozein rescues her, but then kidnaps her himself and tries to rape her. She is finally saved by Gawain, who forces Gasozein to confess the falseness of his claim.

In *Durmart le Gallois*, she is kidnapped by Brun of Morrois and rescued by Durmart. Finally, in the *Livre d'Artus* (c. 1240), she is kidnapped and briefly held by King Urien during the war between Arthur and the rebellious kings.

The version told by the French prose cycles (c. 1215–1240) and subsequently by Malory (1470) builds on Geoffrey's account and forms the basis for most modern tales of Guinevere:

Guinevere is the daughter of King Leodegan of Carmelide. She has an identical half-sister, also named Guinevere, who is the daughter of Leodegan and his seneschal's wife. The two Guineveres are distinguished only by a crown-shaped birthmark on the legitimate Guinevere's back.

Merlin has predicted her marriage to Arthur. Arthur comes to her father's land shortly after his coronation because King Rions and the Saxons have invaded. Arthur falls in love with Guinevere and marries her as soon as he has achieved victory. On their wedding knight, enemies of Leodegan attempt to kidnap Guinevere and substitute Guinevere's half-sister in Arthur's bed, but Arthur's knights foil the plan.

Guinevere forms her own body of knights called the Queen's Knights, whose ranks include Gawain, Yvain, and other young warriors.

When Lancelot arrives at court, he falls in love with the queen at first sight. She presents him with a sword. He falls into trances of rapture whenever he gazes upon her. At first she is amused by his adoration. After Lancelot ends Arthur's war with Galehaut, Galehaut brings about a meeting between Lancelot and Guinevere, and Lancelot confesses his love. Guinevere rewards him with a kiss.

Saxons invade Britain and Arthur opposes them at Saxon Rock. Guinevere goes with him. Lancelot also arrives. One night, while Arthur is sleeping with Gamille, a Saxon enchantress, Lancelot visits Guinevere's chambers and their affair begins.

Guinevere the False, Guinevere's half-sister, sends a message to Arthur claiming to be the true queen, as if the wedding-night ruse had worked. The false Guinevere enchants Arthur and he accepts her as the true queen. The real Guinevere is exiled and goes to live in Sorelois, Galehaut's land. The ruse is eventually discovered, the false Guinevere dies or is executed, and the queen returns to court.

Morgan le Fay learns of the affair between Lancelot and Guinevere and tries to reveal it to Arthur. Her plans are never entirely successful. Morgan hates Guinevere because Guinevere has ended an affair between Morgan and Sir Guiomar, Guinevere's cousin.

Meleagant abducts Guinevere from Arthur's court and takes her to his castle in Gorre. Bagdemagus, Meleagant's father, prevents Guinevere from being mistreated. Lancelot arrives and fights Meleagant to a draw. One night, he enters Guinevere's chambers in Meleagant's castle and spends the night with her. He has a wound, and he leaves blood on the bed. When Meleagant sees the blood, he believes the queen has slept with Kay, who is wounded and sleeping in the queen's outer room. Lancelot schedules a duel with Meleagant at Arthur's court to prove her innocence.

Lancelot enters the tournament at Pomeglai, and Guinevere is present. To test his love, she tells him to act like a coward, and he does. At Arthur's court,

Lancelot kills Meleagant. In a later adventure, it appears that Lancelot is dead, and Guinevere is heartbroken. She rejoices when she learns he is alive.

Lancelot is triked into sleeping with the daughter of King Pelles twice; once at her castle, once at Camelot. He believes he is sleeping with Guinevere. Guinevere discovers him in bed with the lady, believes his actions to be deliberate, and banishes him from her sight forever. Lancelot goes mad. He is eventually cured by the Grail and is reconciled with Guinevere.

After the Grail Quest, Guinevere believes that Lancelot has fallen in love with the maiden of Escalot. She banishes him again. During a dinner, a knight named Avarlan tries to arrange for Gawain to eat some poisoned fruit. Guinevere innocently gives the fruit to Gaheris of Carahew instead, and he dies. Gaheris's brother, Mador of the Gate, accuses Guinevere of murder. Meanwhile, the body of the maiden of Escalot arrives at Camelot in a boat, and Guinevere learns that Lancelot did not love her. Lancelot arrives in time to defend Guinevere against the charge. He exonerates her, and the lovers are reconciled.

Agravain and Mordred learn of the affair between Lancelot and Guinevere. Arthur begins to suspect. Arthur goes on a hunting party but makes Lancelot stay behind. Lancelot goes to Guinevere's chambers. Agravain rouses a band of knights and catches the lovers *in flagrante*. Lancelot battles his way free and promises to return to rescue the queen.

Guienvere is condemned to execution. On the morning she is to be burned, Lancelot returns with a body of knights and rescues her from the stake. Guinevere and Lancelot flee to Joyous Guard and are pursued by Arthur. The Pope intervenes and forces Arthur to restore Guinevere as queen. Arthur continues the war against Lancelot, however, pursuing him to France.

While Arthur is gone, Mordred usurps the throne. He falls in love with Guinevere and asks her to marry him. Guinevere flees to the Tower of London and Mordred besieges her there. Arthur returns to Britain with his army and Mordred abandons the siege. Guinevere flees to Amesbury and, after she hears of Arthur's death, takes the veil. She soon dies.

The are a number of notable variations to the version of Guinevere's last days presented by Geoffrey of Monmouth and the prose cycles. In *Perlesvaus* (c. 1200), she dies of grief after learning of her son Loholt's murder by Kay, and she is buried in Avalon. In *La Tavola Ritonda* (c. 1325–50), she falls down dead upon hearing of Arthur's death. In Jean D'Outremeuse's *Ly Myreur des histors* (c. 1350), she is slain by Lancelot and entombed with a living Mordred, who feasts on her flesh but eventually starves. In the Middle English tale of *Sir Launfal* (c. 1380), Guinevere, a wicked, adulterous floozy, is magically blinded by the sorceress Triamour. Finally, in Hector Boece's *Scotorum Historia* (1527), following the final battle between

Mordred and Arthur, she is kidnapped by the Picts (who supported Mordred) and lives out her days as a prisoner.

Reginald Heber's *Morte D'Arthur* (1812) includes a tale of Guinevere's youth in which she falls in love with a forester named Cadual. Later married to Arthur, she longs for her former love and comes to realize that Cadual was in fact Lancelot in disguise.

According to Tennyson, Guinevere fell in love with Lancelot when he first escorted her from her home to Arrthur's court for her marriage (in the Vulgate Cycle, Lancelot is not yet born when Arthur marries Guinevere). She is seduced by his warmth and humor and liveliness and, when she reaches Camelot, she is repelled by Arthur, who is "high, self-contained, and passionless." Her affair with Lancelot contributes to Arthur's downfall not only at the end: during his entire reign, her infidelity sets a poor example and undermines with sin Arthur's lofty ambitions. News of her adultery contributes to the madness of Balin and Pelleas. In the end, when she sees what destruction her actions have caused, she is repentant and ashamed to the point of groveling, realizing too late that she needn't have looked any further than Arthur for the ideal husband and lover. [*Culhwch*, *Caradoc*, *GeoffHR*, *ChretienE*, *ChretienL*, *UlrichZ*, *Perlesvaus*, *FolieB*, *Wolfram*, *Layamon*, *VulgLanc*, *VulgQuest*, *VulgMort*, *VulgMer*, *Livre*, *PostQuest*, *PostMort*, *ProsTris*, *DeOrtu*, *Tavola*, *Jean*, *Stanz*, *ChestreLvl*, *Awntyrs*, *Malory*, *KingA&C*, *Boece*, *HughesT*, *Thelwall*, *TennIK*]

Relations: Guinevere's family and kinsmen are named below. More information can be found under their respective entries.

Father: Cador, Garlin of Galore, Gogfran, Leodegan of Carmelide, Rions, Vortigern

Children: Although she is generally described as childless, a number of authors give her a son named Loholt, whose murder in *Perlesvaus* leads to her own death. In Wolfram's *Parzival*, she and Arthur have a son named Ilinot who also dies a premature death, and in the Alliterative *Morte Arthure*, she is the mother of Mordred's two sons. The English ballad "King Arthur and King Cornwall" says that she had a daughter by the king of Cornwall. In the *Livre d'Arts*, she raises the illegitimate daughter of Sagremor and Senehaut. In Tennyson, she tries to raise an infant girl called Nestling that Arthur and Lancelot found in an eagle's nest, but the child dies.

Brothers: Gotegrin, Mordred (in an interpolation in one manuscript of Wace's *Roman de Brut*)

Sisters: Angharad, Flori, Guinevere the False, Gwenhwyach, Lenomie

See Also: Agravain, Arthur, Arthur's Grave, Avalon, Chastity Tests, Dolorous Tower, Guenloie, Guinevere the False, Lancelot, Meleagant, Melwas, Mordred, Queen's Knights, Wadling Lake

GUINEVERE²

An ancestor of Perceval, known as the "lady of the chapel." Her daughter's lover murdered Guinevere's husband and framed Guinevere for the murder. Guinevere's four sons walled her up in a chapel. God made the tomb holy, and all who visited it were healed of wounds or disease. Galahad, Perceval, and Bors visited the chapel at the conclusion of the Grail Quest. [PostQuest]

GUINEVERE³ THE FALSE

The identical half-sister of Guinevere, fathered by Leodegan on the wife of Cleodalis, his seneschal. Leodegan's enemies conspired to replace the true Guinevere with the false Guinevere on Arthur's wedding night, but Merlin learned of the plan and commissioned Sir Ulfin and Sir Bretel to stop it. Years later, Guinevere the False formed an alliance with Bertelay, an old knight who had been expelled from Leodegan's court for murder. They sent a message to Arthur proclaiming that Guinevere the False was the true queen, and that Arthur had been living with an impostor since his wedding night. Arthur decreed a judicial trial between Gawain and Bertelay, but before it could take place, the False Guinevere captured and imprisoned Arthur. Arthur succumbed to a love potion, returned to court, and proclaimed Guinevere the False queen. Lancelot championed the real queen against three of Bertelay's knights to prove her innocence. In the non-cyclical *Lancelot do Lac*, Bertelay and the False Guinevere then admit their guilt and are burned. According to the Vulgate *Lancelot,* Lancelot and the true Guinevere fled Arthur's court for Sorelois, where they lived for several years before Guinevere the False perished of an illness, confessing on her death bed. [*LancLac, VulgLanc, VulgMer*]

GUINGAN OF DOLAS

A knight to whom Arthur gave command of the Castle of the Elms. [*Contin1*]

GUINGANBRESIL [*Gui(n)gambresil*]

A proud lord who, in Chrétien's *Perceval*, accuses Gawain of murdering Guinganbresil's master. Guinganbresil and Gawain scheduled a duel before the king of Escavalon. Arthur intervened, however, and the two knights made peace. Guinganbresil then married Tancree, the niece of the king of Escavalon. In Wolfram's *Parzival*, he is known as KINGRIMURSEL. In the *Livre d'Artus*, Guinganbresil appears among Arthur's forces in the Saxon wars. As in *Perceval*, he is hostile to Gawain, but because Gawain has slept with Florée, a maiden loved by Guinganbresil, as well as with Guinganbresil's sister, begetting a child with each of them. [*ChretienP, Contin1, VulgMer, Livre*]

GUINGLAIN [*Giglain, Gyngalyn, Gyngelayne, Gyngolyn, G(e)ynleyn*]

Son of Gawain and a Knight of the Round Table. He is the hero of Renaut de Bâgé's *Le Bel Inconnu* and Thomas Chestre's *Lybeaus Desconus*. His mother was a fairy named Blanchemal who raised him in ignorance of his true name and paternity, so he was called *le bel inconnu*, or the FAIR UNKNOWN. He joined Arthur's court and soon accepted a quest to free Queen Esmeree the Blonde of Wales, whose city of Snowdon had been laid waste by two sorcerers.

Blond Esmeree's lady, Helie, who had come to Arthur's court seeking help, was furious when she learned that Arthur had assigned a young and inexperienced knight to the task. Guinglain changed her thinking during the journey to Snowdon, as he conquered the evil Sir Bleoberis; rescued the lady Clarie from two giants; defeated three attackers named Elin, William, and the knight of Saie; won a sparrowhawk tournament against Sir Girflet in honor of the lady Margerie; and defeated Malgier, the guardian of the Golden Isle.

In this last adventure, Guinglain fell in love with the fairy ruler of the Golden Isle, known as the Maiden with the White Hands. The Maiden loved Guinglain in return and wished to marry him, but Guinglain was forced to sneak away from her in the middle of the night in order to complete his quest.

He traveled to the Desolate City of Snowdon and defeated the two sorcerers—Mabon and Evrain—who had cursed the city and who had turned Esmeree the Blonde into a snake. He was then approached by the snake, which had to kiss him in order to return to her true form. Guinglain fought the urge to cleave the snake in two, kissed it, and completed the adventure. A voice (which turned out to be the Maiden with the White Hands) then informed him of his true name and paternity. Esmeree the Blonde fell in love with Guinglain and wished to marry him, but Guinglain's love for the Maiden led him to return to the Golden Isle, where he found the Maiden incensed at his earlier departure. She eventually accepted him back, but he lost her love for good when he sneaked away to attend Arthur's tournament at the Castle of Maidens. He married Esmeree the Blonde and became the king of Wales.

The Wedding of Sir Gawain calls him the son of Ragnelle rather than Blanchemal. He appears in the Post-Vulgate *Queste del Saint Graal* as a knight defeated by Arthur the Less. In Malory, he joins Mordred and Agravain in their plot to catch Lancelot and Guinevere *in flagrante delicto*, and he is slain by Lancelot. His character becomes BEAUDOUS in Robert de Blois's romance, and his adventures are given to CARDUINO in an Italian *cantare*. [*Renaut, Contin1, Contin2, PostQuest, ProsTris, Wedding, Malory*]

GUINGRAS [*Gringras*]

The good and kind King of Wales in Renaut's *Le Bel Inconnu*. His daughter, Esmeree the Blonde, inherited his kingdom and married Gawain's son, Guinglain. [*Renaut*]

GUINGUEMAR [*Gimoers, Gryngamore, Guigomar, Guingamuer, Gwinganiers*]

A knight who Chrétien de Troyes calls the Lord of the Isle of Avalon. Morgan le Fay was his lover. He had a brother named Greslemuef of Finisterre and, in Malory, two sisters named Lynet and Lyones. He became Gareth's brother-in-law and companion. He shows up at the tournament of the Castle of Maidens in Renaut de Bâgé's *Le Bel Inconnu* and at the Castle Perilous tournament in Malory. In the First Continuation of Chrétien's *Perceval*, his fairy lover is named Brangepart, and he has a son by her named Brangemuer. Guinguemar has his own non-Arthurian lay in which falls in love with an unnamed fairy, possibly Morgan. He may be connected with GUIOMAR, Morgan's lover in the Vulgate romances. [*ChretienE, HartmannE, Renaut, Contin1, Heinrich, Malory*]

GUINIACALC

Father of Arthur's Sir Alardins. [*Contin1*]

GUINIER [*Aguinier*]

A vassal of Galehaut. Guinier lent Arthur's Sir Hector a shield to use in battle against the Saxons in Scotland. [*LanDoLac, VulgLanc*]

GUINLAIN [*Guinlains*]

An Arthurian knight who ruled the castle of Tintagel in Renaut de Bâgé's *Le Bel Inconnu*. [*Renaut*]

GUINNON [*Gurnion*]

A fortress in Britain that was the site of Arthur's eighth battle against the Saxons. In this battle, we are told, Arthur "carried the image of the holy Mary, the everlasting Virgin, on his shield, and the heathen were put to flight on that day, and there was a great slaughter upon them." Possible locations include castles in Cornwall, Winchester, and fortress of Garionenum in Norfolk. Geoffrey and the *Annales Cambriae* adopt the image of Arthur's shield from this battle for the battle of BADON. [*Nennius, TennIK*]

GUINOCH

The castle in Saxony where Sardoine, Hengists's daughter, lived before she married Vortigern. [*Butor*]

GUIOMAR [*Gogenar, Goiomar, Goionar(d), Guyamor*]

Cousin of Guinevere and brother of Sadoine in the Vulgate *Merlin*. He fought alongside Leodegan and Arthur against the Saxons. He fell in love with Morgan le Fay. Guinevere discovered their affair and ended it, sparking the famous hatred between Morgan and the queen. Morgan later gave birth to Guiomar's son, who became a noble knight. The origin of his name and character are probably found in GUINGUEMAR of Chrétien's *Erec*. [*VulgLanc, VulgMer, Livre, Arthour, Malory*]

GUIOMARC

An ally of Arthur in the Roman War. He was killed fighting Mordred's army. [*Didot*]

GUIONCE [*Guionences*]

Seneschal of King Cleolas, King Alain of Escavalon, or King Pelles of Corbenic. He fought with Arthur's forces against the Saxon invasions. [*VulgMer, Livre*]

GUIOT

A duke from Listenois who besieged the sister and niece of King Pellinore in the castle of Belloé. Branor the Brown defeated him in combat and brought about a marriage between Guiot and the niece. [*Palamedes*]

GUIRLANDOT

In *La Tavola Ritonda*, the knight who rescued Isolde after she was kidnapped by Palamedes. He hid her in his tower, Madrana, and later died in combat with Palamedes. The same knight appears unnamed in the Prose *Tristan*; Malory calls him ADTHERPE. [*Tavola*]

GUIROMELANT[1] [*Geromelant, G(u)iremelanz, Grinomelant*]

A knight who ruled the town of Orquelenes in Galloway or the land of Janphis. His story comes from Chrétien's *Perceval* and the First Continuation. He loved Gawain's sister Clarissant but hated Gawain. Gawain encountered him after freeing Clarissant from Canguin Rock. They arranged to meet in combat at Arthur's court in Orcanie to settle their differences. Arthur intervened, canceled the duel, and allowed Guiromelant to marry Clarissant. As a wedding present, Arthur gave him the country of Nottingham or Madarp. He appears in Wolfram von Eschenbach's *Parzival* as GRAMOFLANZ. In the *Livre d'Artus*, he joins Arthur's war against the Saxons but dislikes Gawain because of Gawain's conflict with Guinganbresil, Guiromelant's brother or cousin. [*ChretienP, Contin1, Livre, Heinrich*]

GUIROMELANT[2]

An aide to King Amant of Lambal, Arthur's enemy. When Amant was slain by King Bors, Guiromelant vowed never to serve Arthur. [*VulgMer*]

GUIRON THE COURTEOUS [*Girone, Guron(e), Gyron*]

Hero of the French *Palamedes*. A peerless knight, he was descended from King Clovis of France on the side of his father (Fragus) and from Joseph of Arimathea on his mother's side. R. S. Loomis though that his character came from GWYRON in the *Mabinogion* tales. He ruled the Green Wood. He was an ally of Tristan's father Meliadus, whom he aided in a war against Scotland. According to *La Tavola Ritonda*, he became an enemy of the Round Table after suffering disgrace at Uther Pendragon's court: a lady whom he had abducted from Gariosso of Maganza lied to Uther, saying that Gariosso had stolen her from Guiron. Uther had Guiron dragged around the fields of Urbano from a cart, as was the punishment for cuckolds.

Guiron loved the lady of Malehaut, who happened to be married to Danain the Red, Guiron's best friend. When she was entrusted to Guiron's care, he nearly had an affair with her, but some noble words written on his sword (which had belonged to Hector the Brown) shamed him to the point of near suicide. In revenge for Guiron's intentions, Danain abducted Bloie, Guiron's *amie*. Guiron rescued her and reconciled with Danain when Danain saved him from a knight named Helin. Guiron and Bloie were later imprisoned by a wicked lord named Galinan. Bloie died in the prison after giving birth to Guiron's son, whom Galinan raised and named after himself. Lancelot eventually freed Guiron from the prison. In another adventure, he was imprisoned by the giant Nabon the Black until rescued by Tristan. The Fountain of Guiron the Courteous commemorated Guiron's rescue of King Arthur from the giant Hebusan. After many other adventures, Guiron retired to the tomb of Febus, his renowned ancestor, where he died. [*Palamedes*, *Tavola*]

GUIRRÉS

A knight who fought on the side of the King with a Hundred Knights at King Mark's Lancien tournament. [*Contin4*]

GUISINANT

A castle that belonged to the Good Knight Without Fear. [*Palamedes*]

GUITARD [*Guitardus, Gwitard*]

The Duke of the Poitevins or Poitou who was conquered by Duke Hoel at the behest of Arthur, as part of Arthur's campaign to subjugate all of Europe. Guitard later became loyal to Arthur and fought for him in the Roman campaign. During the war, Guitard learned that a Roman force was planning to liberate Roman prisoners when they were being escorted to a Paris prison. Guitard arrived just in time and saved Arthur's men from defeat. He also commanded a company of soldiers in the final battle at Soissons, and there killed King Munstensar of Africa. His name probably comes from the Welsh GWITART. [*GeoffHR*, *Wace*, *Layamon*]

GUITHELIN

According to Geoffrey of Monmouth, king of Britain in the fourth century BC. He succeeded King Gurguint Barbtruc. He married Marcia and fathered Sisillius, who succeeded him. [*GeoffHR*]

GUITSHIRE

The location in Arthur's realm governed by Earl Balluc. [*Wace*]

GUITTONIA

The name of Arthur's wife given by Giovanni Boccaccio in *De Casibus Virorum Illustrium*. Mordred married her when he seized Arthur's throne. [*Boccaccio*]

GUIVRET[1] OF LAMBALE [*Gimires*]

An Arthurian knight who fought in the Saxon Wars. He was imprisoned in both the Dolorous Prison and the Forbidden Hill, and was freed from both by Lancelot. In the war with Mordred, he led a battalion at Salisbury and was presumably killed there. [*VulgLanc*, *VulgMer*, *VulgMort*, *Arthour*]

GUIVRET[2] THE SMALL [*Cuiret, Gimires, Guimar, Guiret, Guivres, Guivrez, Gvires, Gwiffred, Guyart, Gyvreiz*]

The diminutive King of Ireland in the Chrétien de Troyes's *Erec* and the Welsh *Geraint*, also known as the LITTLE KING. His rich castle was called Pointure or Penefrec. His two sisters were named Filledamor and Guenteflur.

Erec and Enide entered Guivret's land uninvited during their journey, for which Guivret challenged Erec to combat. Though Guivret was a fierce warrior—his size made him agile and hard to strike—Erec eventually overcame him. The two knights became fast friends. When Guivret heard of Erec's imprisonment at the hands of Count Oringle, he set out to liberate his friend, finding upon his arrival that Erec had already killed the count. Guivret accompanied Erec back to Arthur's court after a sojourn in the city of Brandigan, where Erec completed the Joy of the Court adventure.

In Ulrich's *Lanzelet*, a magical mantle brought to Arthur's court reveals that Guivret's wife hates him because of his dwarfish size. In the Prose *Tristan*, he appears at the tournament of Sorelois. [*ChretienE*, *UlrichZ*, *HartmannE*, *Erex*, *Geraint*, *ProsTris*]

GUIVRET[3] THE YOUNGER

A Knight of the Round Table who was the son of Arthur's Sir Pelleas and the lady Arcade. He may be identical to GUIVRET THE SMALL. [*PostMer*]

GUIZ THE PUNY

A knight whom Galahad rescued from Mordred. [*ProsTris*]

GULISTARDO

Tristan's first war-horse in *La Tavola Ritonda*. It was given to him by Bellices, the daughter of the king of Gaul. [*Tavola*]

GUNDEBALD

In *Meriadoc*, the King of the Land From Which No One Returns. He waged war against the Emperor of the Alemanni and kidnapped the Emperor's daughter, treating her like a princess. His brother was named Guntrannus. He was slain by King Meriadoc of Wales, a protégé of Kay. [*Historia*]

GUNDEFLÉ [*Gondeffles*]

One of many Saxon kings who invaded Britain at the beginning of Arthur's reign. His brother was Transmaduk. He was one of the few survivors of the great Saxon slaughter at Clarence. Arthur's forces chased him to his galleys and forced him back to Saxony. [*VulgMer*, *Arthour*]

GUNES

An Arthurian knight who came from Worcester. [*Renaut*]

GUNTEL

A page who served Melleranz, Arthur's nephew. [*PleierM*]

GUNTER

King of Denmark in Geoffrey Gaimar's chronicle. He withheld tribute from Arthur. Gunter's treacherous brother, Odulf, sent a message to Arthur telling him of Gunter's decision. Arthur conquered Denmark, killed Gunter, and appointed Odulf to the throne. Gunter had another brother namd Ascil. This episode is found in Geoffrey Gaimar's chronicle; other chronicles mention Arthur's conquest of Denmark but do not name its king. [*Gaimar*]

GUNTRANNUS

The brother of Gundebald, the King of the Land From Which No One Returns. He served his brother in a war against the Emperor of the Alemanni. [*Historia*]

GUNVASIUS [*Goneweys, Gonfal, Gonwais, Gunfasius, Gunphar*]

King of the Orkneys who chose to voluntarily subjugate himself to Arthur rather than have Arthur conquer him. Arthur left him at his post. He later assisted Arthur in the conquest of King Frollo and Gaul. [*GeoffHR, Wace, Layamon*]

GUOS

A heathen warrior slain by Gareth at the battle of Diana Bridge. [*Arthour*]

GURES THE YOUNGER

A Knight of the Round Table who participated in the Grail Quest. [*PostQuest*]

GURGINTIUS

According to Geoffrey of Monmouth, a king of Britain in the third or second century BC. Gurgintius succeeded King Cloten and was succeeded by King Merian. [*GeoffHR*]

GURGUINT BARBTRUC

According to Geoffrey of Monmouth, king of Britain in the fourth century BC. He was the son of King Belinus. During his reign, he subjugated Denmark and allowed the Basques to populate the barren Ireland. He was succeeded by King Guithelin. [*GeoffHR*]

GURGURAN [*Gurgurant*]

A heathen, cannibal king in *Perlesvaus* who possessed the sword that had beheaded St. John the Baptist. His son was kidnapped by a giant, which made Gurguran forsake his pagan religion. Gawain came to Gurguran's kingdom in Scotland seeking the sword, and he accepted the challenge of rescuing Gurguran's son. Gawain killed the giant, but was unable to save the prince's life. Gurguran nevertheless gave Gawain the sword as a reward. Gurgurant cooked his son's body and fed it to his followers. Gurguran then had himself baptized, taking the Christian name ARCHIER. Three priests named Gregory later gave Gurguran a holy bell to take to the Grail Castle. [*Perlesvaus*]

GURGUSTIUS

According to Geoffrey of Monmouth, king of Britain in the eighth or seventh century BC. He was the son of King Rivallo and the father of King Sisillius. [*GeoffHR*]

GURMUN THE GAY

King of Ireland, husband of Queen Isolde, and father of Isolde in Gottfried's *Tristan*. As a bitter enemy of King Mark of Cornwall, he sent his best knight, Morholt, to menace Cornwall and collect a tribute. Tristan traveled to Ireland under the name "Tantris" and killed a dragon. When Gurmun learned of this noble deed—and then of Tristan's true identity—he agreed to peace between Ireland and Cornwall and he gave his daughter to Mark. Gottfried says that Gurmun's father was the King of Africa. His character in other romances is called ANGUISH. [*Gottfried*]

GURZGRI

Son of Perceval's tutor Gornemant, brother of Shcenteflurs, Lascoyt, and Liaze, husband of Mahaute, and father of Gandiluz. He traveled to the town of Brandigan to try his hand in the Joy of the Court adventure. He failed, and was killed by the warrior Mabonagrain. [*Wolfram*]

GUSG

A warrior in Arthur's service. He was the son of Achen. [*Culhwch*]

GUVERJORZ

A Castillian war horse belonging to King Clamadeu, an opponent of Perceval. The horse was given to Guverjorz by a relative, King Grigorz of Ipotente. [*Wolfram*]

GUYNGLAFF

A marginally-sane magician who was encountered by Arthur in a Breton text. Guynglaff roamed the woods and spouted cryptic prophecies, identifying him with MERLIN. Most of his prophecies involved tragedies to befall Britain in the sixteenth century. [*Dialog*]

GUYON

Representative of temperance sent by Gloriana, the Fairy Queen, to destroy the Bower of Bliss, the garden belonging to the evil enchantress Acrasia, where many knights were lured to their lecherous dooms. On the way, he was attacked, tempted, and robbed, but was victorious in each of his encounters. He was eventually assailed, while in a weakened condition, by two knights named Pyrochles and Cymochles, but he was rescued by Prince Arthur. Guyon and his mentor, the Palmer, continued to the Bower of Bliss, where they were assaulted on all sides by sensual delights. Resisting them, they captured the sorceress Acrasia and destroyed the Bower. Guyon had further adventures in Arthur's company. [*Spenser*]

GUZILAGNE

The kingdom ruled by the King with a Hundred Knights in *La Tavola Ritonda*. [*Tavola*]

GWADYN ODDEITH ("Sole Blaze")

An Arthurian warrior. Hot, bright sparks shot from the soles of his feet when he struck something hard. His was thus given the task of clearing away unwanted vegetation when Arthur was on the march. [*Culhwch*]

GWADYN OSOL

An Arthurian warrior who was so heavy that if he were to stand on the highest mountain in the world, it would become a level plain under his feet. His first name means "sole." [*Culhwch*]

GWAEDDAN

Daughter of Cynfelyn and maid of Arthur's warrior Syfwlch. [*Culhwch*]

GWAETH ("Worse")

Daughter of Arthur's warrior Bwlch. [*Culhwch*]

GWAETHEF OLL ("Worst of All")

Daughter of Arthur's warrior Syfwlch. [*Culhwch*]

GWALCHMEI [*Gwalchmai*]

Counterpart of GAWAIN in Welsh legends. He was the son of Gwyar, the brother of Gwalhafed, and the nephew of Arthur. One of Arthur's best warriors, he is described as noble, brave, and courteous. His character bears a relation to the Irish hero CUCHULAIN. The root of his name, *Gwalch*, means "hawk," and *mei* may indicate "May," as in "Hawk of May." He was Arthur's best rider, and accompanied Culhwch and other warriors in Arthur's service on Culhwch's quest to find Olwen. He also accompanied the search for Owain when he was missing. Gwalchmei was one of the knights that Peredur saw as a youth, prompting Peredur to become a knight himself. Gwalchmei owned a magnificent brocade given to him by the Earl of Anjou's daughter. A Welsh Tristan fragment calls to him "Gwalchmei Golden-Tongue," referring to his negotiating skills. A Welsh stanza places his grave at Peryddon. [*Culhwch, WelshSG, Dream, Geraint, Peredur, TrisFrag*]

GWALHAFED

Son of Gwyar and brother of Gwalchmei. He was one of Arthur's warriors. Some have suggested him as the origin of GALAHAD. [*Culhwch*]

GWALLAWG

In the Welsh *Geraint*, a warrior of Arthur's court who was the son of Lleanawg. A historical King Gwallawg existed in the late sixth century. [*Geraint*]

GWARAE GOLDEN HAIR

One of Arthur's warriors in Welsh legend who accompanies Arthur on the search for the two dogs of Glythvyr Ledewig. The name must be closely related with Gwri Golden Hair, a name given to the infant Pryderi in the non-Arthurian Welsh story of *Pwyll*. He is probably also connected with GWRFAN WILD HAIR. In Welsh, "golden hair" is *gwallt-euryn*, which R. S. Loomis suggests as the origin of the name GAWAIN. [*Culhwch*]

GWARTHEGYDD

Son of Caw, one of twenty brothers, and one of Arthur's warriors. He accompanied Arthur on the hunt for Twrch Trwyth and managed the two hounds of Glythvyr Ledewig. The boar killed him at Cwm Cerwyn. [*Culhwch, Dream*]

GWASAWG

A warrior and supporter of the Welsh lord Rhydderch, who apparently opposed Gwenddolau at the battle of Arfderydd. Merlin fought on Gwenddolau's side and thus made an enemy of Gwasawg. [*Myrddin*]

GWASTAD ("Level")

Father of Arthur's warrior Gwefyl. [*Culhwch*]

GWAWRDDUR[1]

The British warrior whose prowess is compared to Arthur's in *Y Gododdin*: "he glutted black ravens [slew his enemies] on the ramparts of the stronghold, though he was not Arthur." This passage refers to a battle fought at "Catraeth" (possibly Catterick) in about AD 600. In the battle, the British were destroyed by the Angles. The passage in question signifies that though Gwawrddur was mighty, he was not as mighty as Arthur. This is the earliest existing appearance of Arthur's name. Clearly, the audience of the poem was expected to know the identity of "Arthur"; conventional scholarship holds that the reference alludes to the famed battle-leader of a century prior, but some scholars (e.g., Richard Barber, *Figure*, 21–34) have argued that the passage refers to Arthur of Dalriada, a northern figure who lived contemporary to the writing of *Y Gododdin*, and in close geographic proximity to its writer and audience. Some have suggested, too, that the passage is a later interpolation in the poem, subsequent to Arthur's fame. [*Gododdin*]

GWAWRDDUR[2] HUNCHBACK [Gwaredur]

Father of three of Arthur's warriors—Duach, Brathach, and Nerthach—and Gwenwledyr, a lady at Arthur's court. [Culhwch]

GWEDDW

Owner of the horse Gwynn Dun Mane, which the warrior Culhwch had to obtain as one of his tasks. [Culhwch]

GWEFYL ("Lip")

A warrior in Arthur's service who was the son of Gwastad. When he was sad, he would let his lower lip droop to his navel, and would pull his upper lip over his head like a hood. [Culhwch]

GWEIR[1]

A warrior who was the son of Geirioedd. He was imprisoned in Annwn, the Welsh otherworld, and may have been rescued by Arthur.

The name belongs to a number of warriors in Welsh legends, and can mean "hay," "collar," "circle," "loop," or "bend." It may be the source of the Breton Guerec, or EREC, and may also be the origin of GAHERIS. [Spoils]

GWEIR[2]

One of four brothers, all named Gweir, who were Arthur's maternal uncles. He is called "Gweir son of Cadellin Silver Brow," but is also named as the son of Llwch Windy Hand in the same sentence. [Culhwch]

GWEIR[3]

One of Arthur's warriors and advisors. His father was Gwestyl. He was one of the three knights that Peredur saw as a youth, prompting him to begin his own career as a knight. [Dream, Peredur]

GWEIR[4] FALSE VALOR

One of four brothers in Welsh legend, all named Gweir, who were Arthur's maternal uncles. Their father was Llwch Windy Hand. [Culhwch]

GWEIR[5] GREAT VALOR

An Arthurian warrior named as one of the three "Enemy Subduers of the Island of Britain" and a "stubborn man" in the Welsh Triads. [Triads, Geraint]

GWEIR[6] SERVANT OF BIRDS

One of four brothers, all named Gweir, who were Arthur's maternal uncles. Their father was Llwch Windy Hand. Gweir had a daughter named Tangwen. [Culhwch]

GWEIR[7] WHITE SHAFT

One of four brothers in Welsh legend, all named Gweir, who were Arthur's maternal uncles. Their father was Llwch Windy Hand. [Culhwch]

GWEN PENDRAGON

An enchanter who imprisoned Arthur in Caer Oeth, in Anoeth, and in an enchanted prison under the Stone of Echymeint. Arthur was rescued by Goreu. [Triads]

GWENABWY

Daughter of Caw, sister of twenty brothers, and mother of Arthur's warrior Gwydre by Llwydeu. [Culhwch]

GWENDDOLAU

Son of Ceido and patron of Myrddin (Merlin) in Welsh texts. Geoffrey says he was the King of Scotland. He was killed at the battle of Arfderydd in 573, fighting a combined force of the sons of Eliffer (Gwrgi and Peredur) and King Rhydderch of Cumbria. Events at the battle drove Merlin insane. Gwenddolau's warriors continued the battle for a month and a half despite their lord's death. Another Welsh source lists him as the owner of a magical chess board. [Myrddin, Annales, Triads, GeoffVM]

GWENDDYDD

Sister of Myrddin (Welsh prototype of Merlin) in early Welsh lore. Her son apparently fought at the battle of Arfderydd, where he was killed by Myrddin, after which Gwenddydd disavowed her brother. Myrddin was driven insane by the killing. Several poems include conversations between Gwenddydd and Myrddin. Geoffrey of Monmouth calls her GANIEDA. [Myrddin]

GWENDOLEN[1]

An early queen of Britain. She was the daughter of Corineus of Cornwall. She married Locrine, king of Britain. Locrine eventually cast her away in favor of the German princess Estrildis. Gwendolen returned to Cornwall, raised an army, and attacked Locrine. Locrine died in the fighting. Gwendolen deposed Estrildis, became queen of Britain, and ruled for 15 years. She eventually gave the throne to her son Maddan. [GeoffHR]

GWENDOLEN[2]

A lover of Merlin. Merlin turned her into a hag after she rebuked him for his demonic powers. Gawain later married her and, when he kissed her, she returned to her beautiful form. [HeberG]

GWENHWYACH

Sister of Gwenhwyfar (Guinevere) in Welsh legend. She lived at Arthur's court. Two Welsh Triads say that the battle of Camlann somehow began when Gwenhwyach struck Gwenhwyfar. [Culhwch, Triads]

GWENHWYFAR

The original form of GUINEVERE, found in Welsh legend. According to a Welsh Triad, Arthur had three queens of this name, who were the daughters of Cywyrd, Gwythyr, and Gogfran. [Culhwch, Triads]

GWENN[1] ("White") [Gwen]

A white mantle owned by Arthur's servant Eiryn the Splendid. The mantle rendered its wearer invisible. [Dream]

GWENN[2] ALARCH ("White Swan")

A lady at Arthur's court. She was the daughter of Cynwal Hundred Hogs. [Culhwch]

GWENN[3] LLIANT ("White Flood")

A fair and generous lady at Arthur's court. [Culhwch]

GWENT

A region of southeast Wales, on the Severn river, ruled at one time by Octavius, and later by Vortigern. Geoffrey calls it Merlin's country, and says that Merlin lived there for a time at the fountain of Galabes. [GeoffHR]

GWENWLEDYR

Daughter of Gwawrddur the Hunchback, sister of Duach, Brathach, and Nerthach, and a lady at Arthur's court. [Culhwch]

GWENWYNWYN[1]

Son of Naw and brother of Fflewdwr. In Culhwch, he is called Arthur's greatest warrior. [Culhwch, Dream]

GWENWYNWYN[2]

Son of Naf and brother of Atlandor. He is one of Arthur's warriors in Welsh tales, listed as one of the "three Seafarers of the Island of Britain." [Culhwch, Triads]

GWERNABWY

The Eagle of Gwernabwy is the fourth wise animal that Arthur's warriors consulted on their quest to find the imprisoned Mabon. The Eagle sent them on to the Salmon of Llyn Llyw. In the Triads, the Eagle is listed among the "three Elders of the World." [Culhwch, Triads]

GWERTHMWL

A ruler who served Arthur. [Dream]

GWERTHRYNION

A region of Britain named after King Vortigern. Vortigern fled there after the Saxons took over much of the eastern part of Britain. After Vortigern's death, Gwerthrynion fell to Vortigern's son, Pascentius. [Nennius]

GWESTYL

Father of Arthur's warrior Gweir. [Dream]

GWGAWN RED SWORD

A warrior who served Owain. [Dream]

GWGON GWRON

Son of Peredur, listed as one of the "three Prostrate Chieftains of Britain" in the Welsh Triads. [Triads]

GWIAWN CAT EYE

An Arthurian warrior who possessed remarkable visual perception. [Culhwch]

GWIDON

Brother of Gawain in the Hebrew Melekh Artus. As the son of Lot and Arthur's sister, he occupies the place given to GARETH in other tales. [Melekh]

GWILENHIN

One of Arthur's warriors in Welsh legend. He was titled "King of France," although the same distinction is given to Iona and Paris in the same stories. As one of his tasks, the warrior Culhwch had to obtain Gwilenhin's help in hunting the boar Twrch Trwyth. Gwilenhin did attend the hunt, and was killed by the boar at Aber Tywi. [Culhwch, Dream]

GWILYM

One of Arthur's warriors and advisors in Welsh legend. He was the son of the "ruler of France." He became a companion of the warrior Geraint. Gwilym is a variation of the English "William." [Dream, Geraint]

GWIRNESIS

An Arthurian knight. [Heinrich]

GWITART

Son of Aedd, brother of Odgar, and one of Arthur's warriors in Culhwch. He appears in Geoffrey of Monmouth as GUITARD. [Culhwch]

GWLADYS

The wife of King Brychan of Brecknock. She was abducted by King Gwynnlyw of Glamorgan, who, while fleeing from Brychan, encountered Arthur. Arthur desired Gwladys, but Cei and Bedwyr persuaded him to follow his nobler instincts, to give harbor to Gwynnlyw, and to leave Gwladys alone. Gwladys and Gwynnlyw had a child named Cadoc, who became a saint, and in whose hagiography this story appears. [SaintsCad]

GWLGAWD OF GODDODIN

Owner of a magical wine horn. As one of his tasks, Culhwch had to obtain this horn from Gwlgawd for Olwen's wedding feast. [Culhwch]

GWLWLWYD CHESTNUT HAIR

Owner of the Yellow Pale-White Ox and the Spotted Ox. As one of his tasks, Culhwch had to obtain these oxen from Gwlwlwyd. [Culhwch]

GWLYDDYN THE CARPENTER [Glwyd(d(yn]

Arthur's master architect and builder. He constructed Arthur's dining hall, called Ehangwen. He was slain by the boar Twrch Trwyth during the epic hunt. [Culhwch]

GWRDDNEI CAT EYE

One of Arthur's warriors who shared the duties of gatekeeper in Caer Llion (Caerleon) with seven to nine other warriors. His master was the chief gatekeeper Glewlwyd Strong Grip. Gwrddnei could see as well at night as he could by day. [Geraint]

GWRDDYWAL

A warrior in Arthur's service who was the son of Efrei. [Culhwch]

GWRES

A warrior from Rheged who served Owain. He carried Owain's banner in battle. [Dream]

GWRFAN WILD HAIR

An Arthurian warrior in Culhwch and Olwen. His epithet in Welsh is gwallt-afwyn, which R. S. Loomis suggests as an origin for the name GAWAIN. Almost certainly related in origin to GWARAE GOLDEN HAIR, he may also be the origin of GORVAIN CADRUT. [Culhwch]

GWRFODDW THE OLD

Brother of Eigyr (Igerne), uncle of Arthur, and one of Arthur's warriors. He was killed by the piglet Llwydawg the Killer at the battle of Ystrad Yw. [Culhwch]

GWRGI[1]

Son of Eliffer and brother of Peredur and Arddun. He is mentioned in the Annales Cambriae, which imply that he fought the battle of Arfderydd against Gwenddolau in 573. According to the Annales, this would have been 36 years after the death of Arthur, but Peredur appears later in Welsh legend as Arthur's contemporary. Gwrgi may be identical with GWRGI SEFERI, a huntsman mentioned in Culhwch and Olwen. The Annales say that he died in 580. The Welsh Triads add that his death took plalce at Caer Greu, where he and his brother Peredur fought Eda Great-Knee. Gwrgi and Peredur were both killed after their warriors abandoned them. [Annales, Triads]

GWRGI[2] SEFERI

A huntsman enlisted by Arthur to help track the boar Twrch Trwyth. [Culhwch]

GWRGWST HALF NAKED

An Arthurian warrior who was the father of Dyfynarth.. Gwrgwst was loyal to the warrior Gwythyr, and joined Gwythyr's army against Gwynn son of Nudd. Gwrgwst was taken prisoner by Gwynn and was not released until Arthur intervened. [Culhwch]

GWRHYR[1] FAT CATTLE

An Arthurian warrior. [Culhwch]

GWRHYR[2] INTERPRETER OF LANGUAGES

One of Arthur's warriors and advisors. Gwrhyr was said to know all languages and, as an interpreter, he accompanied Culhwch and other knights of Arthur on Culhwch's quest to find Olwen. He communicated with the piglet Grugyn Silver Bristle, and learned of the boar Twrch Trwyth's refusal to hand over the comb and shears that he possessed. [Culhwch, Dream, Geraint]

GWRRITH

A Welsh warrior who was apparently killed fighting King Malegwn of Gwynned. His death is lamented by Myrddin and Taliesin in an early Welsh poem. Another warrior killed, Errith, may have been a brother or comrade. [Myrddin]

GWRYON

Father of Arthur's warriors Culfanawyd, Huabwy, Cador, Uchei, and Seidi in various Welsh tales. GORLOIS, the father of Cador in a Welsh adaptation of Geoffrey of Monmouth, may be a variation of his name. [Culhwch, Triads, Geraint]

GWYAR ("Blood")

Father of Arthur's warriors Gwalchmei and Gwalhafed. He is, loosely, the counterpart of LOT. [Culhwch, Dream, Geraint]

GWYDDAWG[1]

A warrior in Arthur's service who was the son of Menestyr.. Gwyddawg killed Cei (Kay), which lead to a feud between Arthur and Gwyddawg, in which Gwyddawg and his brothers were killed. [Culhwch]

GWYDDAWG[2] GWYR [Gwythawg Gwyri]

A warrior in Arthur's court. He had a son named Garwyli. [Culhwch]

GWYDDBWYLL

A Welsh board game, analogous to chess, played by a number of characters in Welsh legend, including Arthur and Owain in The Dream of Rhonabwy. In the game, one player's king attempts to escape from the board, while the other player attempts to capture the king. Peredur encounters an enchanted gwyddbwyll set in Peredur which parallels Perceval's adventures at CHESSBOARD CASTLE in Chrétien's Perceval. See also THIRTEEN TREASURES. [Rhonabwy, Peredur]

GWYDDEN THE DIFFICULT

One of Arthur's warriors. His mother was an enchanted hound named Rhymi. He had a brother named Gwyddrud. [Culhwch]

GWYDDNO[1]

Father of Arthur's warrior Rhufawn the Radiant. [*Triads*]

GWYDDNO[2] LONG SHANK

Father of Elphin and the owner of a magical basket, which always contained the foods enjoyed most by those who ate from it. As one of his forty tasks, the warrior Culhwch had to obtain the basket from Gwyddno, so that the giant Ysbaddaden could eat from it during his daughter's wedding feast. [*Culhwch*]

GWYDDRUD

One of Arthur's warriors. His mother was a magical hound named Rhymi. He had a brother named Gwydden. [*Culhwch*]

GWYDOLWYN THE DWARF [*Gruddlwyn*]

An Arthurian warrior who fathered the lady Eurolwyn. As one of his tasks, Culhwch had to obtain a magical bottle from Gwydolwyn, which would keep warm any liquid poured into it. Culhwch had to use the bottle to carry the blood of the Black Hag. [*Culhwch*]

GWYDRE[1]

One of Arthur's warriors who was the son of Llwydeu and Gwenabwy. His uncle, Hueil, stabbed him, which led to a feud between Arthur and Hueil. [*Culhwch*]

GWYDRE[2]

A son of Arthur killed at the battle of Cwm Cerwyn by the boar Twrch Trwyth. [*Culhwch*]

GWYL ("Modest")

One of Arthur's three mistresses. She was the daughter of Gendawd. [*Triads*]

GWYN GODYFRON [*Gwyn Godybrion*]

An Arthurian warrior. [*Culhwch, Dialogue*]

GWYN LLOGELL GWYR

A magistrate at Arthur's court who became a faithful companion of the warrior Geraint. [*Geraint*]

GWYNEDD

A country in northwest Wales, known as VENEDOTIA by the Romans. Vortigern arrived here looking for a place to build a fortress as a defense against the Saxons. He found a spot in the mountains of Eryri, or Snowdon. The *Annales Cambriae* tell us that Maelgwn was the king of Gwynned until 537, when he died of a plague. [*Annales, Nennius*]

GWYNESSI

A region of northern Britain where Vortigern built the castle of Gwyretheyrn after abandoning his attempt to construct a fortress at Snowdon. [*Nennius*]

GWYNGAD

Son of Caw, one of twenty brothers, and one of Arthur's warriors. [*Culhwch*]

GWYNGELLI

One of Arthur's warriors who participated in the hunt for Twrch Trwyth. [*Culhwch*]

GWYNIARTE OF BLOY

A knight in Arthur's service who fought at the battle of Bedegraine and was unhorsed by the King with a Hundred Knights. [*Malory*]

GWYNLLIW THE BEARDED

Father of Arthur's warrior Cadog. [*Triads*]

GWYNN[1] ("White")

Originally a Celtic deity, probably of the otherworld, who appears as one of Arthur's warriors in *Culhwch and Olwen*. Even in *Culhwch*, however, he is a supernatural character, vested with the powers of the demons of Annwn (the Celtic otherworld), of which he is sometimes presented as king. He loved a lady named Creiddylad, and he became enraged when he learned that another warrior named Gwythyr had kidnapped her from the home of her father, Lludd Silver Hand. Gwynn rescued Creiddylad from Gwythyr's fortress and took her to his own home. Gwythyr raised an army to oppose Gwynn. Eventually, Arthur intervened and returned Criddylad to her father. Thereafter, Gwynn and Gwythyr were destined to fight every May Day until Judgment Day.

Gwynn is named as the son of Nudd (originally Nodens, another god), and the brother of Edern (Yder) and Owain (Yvain). In folklore, he is said to haunt Glastonbury Tor. [*Culhwch*]

GWYNN[2]

An Arthurian warrior who was the son of Esni. [*Culhwch*]

GWYNN[3]

Son of Nwyfre, brother of Fflam, and one of Arthur's warriors. [*Culhwch*]

GWYNN[4]

Son of Ermid, brother of Cyndrwyn, and one of Arthur's warriors. [*Culhwch*]

GWYNN[5]

An Arthurian warrior who was the son of Tringad. He was killed at the battle of Pelunyawg by the boar Twrch Trwyth. [*Culhwch, Geraint*]

GWYNN[6] DUN MANE

A horse belonging to the warrior Gweddw. As one of his tasks, Culhwch had to get this horse for the huntsman

Mabon to ride while hunting Twrch Trwyth. Arthur obtained the horse on the behalf of Culhwch. [*Culhwch*]

GWYNN[7] IRASCIBLE

Arthur's steward of Devon and Cornwall. He had a hand in planning the battle of Camlann. [*Culhwch*]

GWYNNAN

Father of Arthur's warrior Teithi the Old. [*Culhwch*]

GYNNLYW [*Gynnlym*]

The King of Glamorgan in the *Life of St. Cadoc*. He abducted Gwladys, the wife of King Brychan of Brecknock, and fled with her. He encountered Arthur on a hilltop. Arthur desired Gwladys, but was persuaded by Cei and Bedwyr to follow his nobler instincts and give harbor to Gwynnlyw. Gwynnlyw and Gwladys later produced a son, St. Cadoc. [*SaintsCad*]

GWYS

One of Twrch Trwyth's piglets, killed in battle against Arthur's warriors at Mynydd Amanw. [*Culhwch*]

GWYSTYL ("Hostage")

Son of Nwython, brother of Rhun and Llwydeu, and one of Arthur's warriors. [*Culhwch*]

GWYTHYR

One of Arthur's warriors in *Culhwch and Olwen*. He was the son of Greidawl. Gwythyr helped Culhwch by collecting the bottles of Linseed Oil requested by the Chief Giant Ysbaddaden. The bottles were given to Gwythyr by a hill of ants after he saved the ants from a fire. Gwythyr also participated in the search for the Black Hag in the Valley of Distress

Gwythyr loved the lady Creiddylad, daughter of Lludd Silver Hand, and he took her from her father's house. Before he could consummate their relationship, Gwynn son of Nudd rescued her from Gwythyr. Gwythyr raised an army to oppose Gwynn but was defeated. Meanwhile, Arthur intervened and returned Creiddylad to her father's house. After this, Gwynn and Gwythyr were forced to fight on every May Day until Judgment Day for their love.

A Welsh Triad names Gwythyr as the father of one of Arthur's three wives named Gwenhwyfar. [*Culhwch, Triads*]

GYAMOURE

A knight whose sister slept with Gawain in her forest pavilion. With his father, Gilbert, and brothers, Tyrry and Brandelis, Gyamoure tracked Gawain down, but Gawain defeated the entire family. [*Jeaste*]

GYERYES

An Arthurian knight. [*ChestreLvl*]

GYFFROUN LE FLOWDOUS

In Thomas Chestre's *Lybeaus Desconus*, the knight opposed by Guinglain (Gawain's son) at a sparrowhawk tournament. He is known as GIRFLET in Renaut de Bâge's *Le Bel Inconnu*. [*ChestreLyb*]

GYFLET [*Gy(r)flet(te), Gylet, Jeffelot, Jurflete*]

Squire of Guinglain (Gawain's son) in Thomas Chestre's *Lybeaus Desconus*. Possible sources include Chestre's own GYFRE, from *Launfal*, and the knight GIRFLET. [*ChestreLyb*]

GYFRE

Servant of Arthur's Sir Launfal; a present from the lady Triamour, Launfal's lover. He assisted his master in a battle against Sir Valentyne of Lombardy. [*ChestreLvl*]

GYLBERT THE BASTARD

A knight slain by Sir Meliot of Logres. Earlier, Gawain had cut off one of Gylbert's hands during a duel. When Meliot killed Gylbert, Gylbert's lover cast an enchantment on Meliot that left him with an incurable, festering wound. The wound could only be cured if some knight braved the adventure of the Chapel Perilous, retrieved a sword from within, and ran the sword over the wound. Lancelot completed the adventure and cured Meliot. [*Malory*]

GYLLYMER

Brother of Gautere and Raynold. Believing him to be Kay, Gyllymer and his two brothers attacked Lancelot, who was dressed in Kay's armor, and got the surprise of their lives. Sent by Lancelot to Arthur's court, he later became a Knight of the Round Table. He was killed fighting Lancelot's men when Lancelot rescued Guinevere from the stake. [*Malory*]

GYMELE OF SCHITRIELE

A maiden who served Isolde. Tristan's brother-in-law Kahedins lusted after her. Isolde gave her to Kahedins for a night but gave Gymele a magical pillow that, once slipped under Kahedins' head, caused him to fall asleep immediately, before he could take Gymele's maidenhood. [*Eilhart*]

GYNETH

Arthur's daughter in Sir Walter Scott's *The Bridal of Triermain*. She was the product of a brief fling between Arthur and Guendolen, a half-Djinn queen. When she came of age, she visited Arthur's court, as Arthur had promised Guendolen to wed Gyneth to his best knight. She charmed almost all of Arthur's knights with her wiles, and the tournament that was supposed to produce her future husband turned into a slaughter. After a young knight named Vanoc died at her feet, Merlin ended the fighting. To punish Gyneth for her vanity, he put an enchantment on her that caused her to fall asleep for several centuries. She was awakened when Sir Roland de Vaux discovered her castle in the Valley of St. John. [*Scott*]

GYROMALANCE

One of Arthur's knights in the Scots poem of *Golagros and Gawain*. He may be connected to either of the GUIROMELANTs of French romance. [*Golagros*]

H

HADRIAN [*Adrian, Ludranes*]

Roman Emperor from 117 to 138. Britain was under Roman occupation during his reign, and he commissioned a stone wall across northern England, from Solway Firth to the Tyne, to protect southern Britain from the northern tribes.

In the Vulgate *Merlin*, Hadrian is introduced as the Emperor of Constantinople in Arthur's time. His daughter married King Brandegorre of Estrangorre. Arthur's Sir Sagremor was Hadrian's grandson, and the intended heir to Hadrian's throne. As Hadrian grew old and infirm, he faced a revolt from his Greek barons. [*VulgMer, Livre, Arthour*]

HAGS OF GLOUCESTER

In *Peredur*, a pack of NINE WITCHES that killed one of Peredur's cousins and maimed an uncle. Peredur saw the head of his slain cousin on a platter (this cousin corresponds to the murdered GOONDESERT in the Third Continuation of Chrétien's *Perceval*), and he learned that he was fated to destroy the Hags for these actions. Peredur was eventually led to their lair by another cousin in disguise, and he killed the Hags with the help of Arthur's other warriors. [*WelshPG, Peredur*]

HAGUENIAX

A knight in Arthur's service. [*Contin1*]

HAINAULT [*Hainaut*]

A province of southwest Belgium. According to Wace, it was part of Arthur's empire. Wolfram says that it was ruled by King Lambekin in the time of Uther. [*Wace, Wolfram, Allit*]

HAIRY CARL

A monster who abducted the maiden Amoret but was defeated and killed by Arthur's squire Timias and the huntress Belphoebe. [*Spenser*]

HALL OF STATUES

A chamber that Tristan built in a grotto that, in Thomas's *Tristan*, he had captured from a giant named Moldagog. The Norse *Tristrams Saga ok Ísöndar* says that the Hall of Statues was on Mont St. Michel, in a cave formerly belonging to the giant slain by Arthur. Two of the statues were of Isolde and Brangain. Tristan consoled himself in his lover's absence by speaking to her statue. When Kahedins, Tristan's brother-in-law, confronted Tristan for not consummating his marriage to Kahedins' sister, Tristan showed him Isolde's statue. Kahedins fell in love with Brangain upon seeing her image, and he forced Tristan to take him to Britain to meet her. [*Thomas, TrisSaga*]

HALLOLKIS

A knight in Arthur's service. [*Golagros*]

HANDSOME CAD [**Biaus Mauvais*]

The name given to Sir Bors by the people of Estrangorre when Bors refused to marry King Brandegorre's daughter, who was very beautiful. [*VulgLanc*]

HANDSOME COWARD [**Biaux Coars*]

A noble Knight of the Round Table found in Chrétien's *Erec*, alongside the UGLY HERO. He may have a relation to the COWARD KNIGHT of *Perlesvaus*. In the second *Perceval* continuation and the Didot-*Perceval*, he loves an ugly woman named Rosete, and he fights Perceval when Perceval insults her honor. Rosete later became beautiful at Arthur's court. According to the Prose *Tristan*, he participated in the Grail Quest. [*ChretienE, Contin2, Didot, ProsTris*]

HANDSOME FOUNDLING

The nickname given to LANCELOT by his adopted mother, the Lady of the Lake, in order to avoid revealing his real name to him. [*LancLac, VulgLanc*]

HANDSOME PRISONER

An alias adopted by Sir BRIAN OF THE ISLES after Gawain defeated him and sent him to Arthur's court. [*Meriadeuc*]

HANDSOME YOUNG MAN

Earliest name of MERIADEUC, who was ignorant of his own name, during his early service at Arthur's court. When he was knighted, he took the name the KNIGHT OF THE TWO SWORDS. [*Meriadeuc*]

HANGUIS

One of Lancelot's squires. [*VulgMort*]

HANSAC

A port in King Hoel's Brittany. [*ProsTris*]

HANTE

A land ruled by Nautenis, an enemy of Tristan's father-in-law Jovelin. In view of its proximity to Jovelin's Arundel, it may represent the county of Hampshire. [*Gottfried*]

HARAM [Harans]

One of the many Saxon kings who invaded Britain as the young Arthur was struggling to establish power. Haram laid waste to most of Lothian and besieged Arundel. [VulgMer, Arthour]

HARD ROCK [*Dure Roche, Rocca Dura]

In Perlesvaus, the castle occupied by Brian of the Isles, Kay, and Meliant when they invaded Britain and waged war against Arthur. In the Prose Tristan, it is a castle owned by Arthur, where the king and Guinevere held a tournament in the heyday of Arthur's reign, between Arthur and the kings of Scotland and Ireland. Tristan won the tournament. [Perlesvaus, ProsTris, Malory]

HARDIANT [Hardians]

A Saxon king who, with many others, invaded Britain at the beginning of Arthur's reign. [VulgMer]

HARDIFIUS

A knight present at the tournament of Sorgarda, which Gawain won. [Heinrich]

HARDIZ

The King of Gascony in the time of Uther. He gave his sister Alize in marriage to Duke Lambekin of Brabant, and thus gained a valuable ally. He participated in a tournament at the Welsh city of Kanvoleis, thrown by Perceval's mother Queen Herzeloyde, and was defeated by Gahmuret. [Wolfram]

HARDOLF

A knight who participated in Arthur's conquest of Rome. When Arthur returned to Britain to deal with Mordred's insurrection, he left Hardolf in command of some the lands he had conquered. [Allit]

HARGADABRAN [Bardogabran, Bordogabron, Hardogabran, Hargadabrant, Hargodabran(t)]

A mighty, gigantic Saxon king who was one of the principal invaders of Britain at the beginning of Arthur's reign. He answered to Aminaduc, the Saxon high king who was his uncle. Hargadabran took advantage of Britain's political turmoil by leading his armies into the northern kingdoms while all their rulers were battling Arthur at Bedegraine. He led a defeat of the northern kings at Clarence, but was himself defeated there after the rebelling kings united with Arthur. On the tails of this defeat, Hargadabran fled back to Saxony.

Hargadabran led a second invasion, in Scotland, many years later, conspiring with his sister, Gamille of Saxon Rock, to capture and imprison Arthur and Gawain. Lancelot foiled the plan. Arthur's forces defeated the Hargadabran's Saxons at the battle of Godelonte Narrows, and Lancelot cut off Hargadabran's leg. Hargadabran was subsequently taken prisoner by Yvain, and, grieving over

his defeat and maiming, he killed himself. [LancLac, VulgLanc, VulgMer, Livre]

HARINAN

In Arthour and Merlin, Igerne's first husband. Uther conquered him and won from him the lands of Gascony, Normandy, Bologna, Paito, Champagne, and Anjou. After his death, Igerne married Hoel. (Uther was her third husband.) The author of Arthur may have taken his name from ARAMONT, mentioned in the Vulgate Lancelot—which, however, identifies Aramont and Hoel as the same person. [Arthour]

HARLEQUIN

Merlin stole his lover, Columbine, but she returned to Harlequin after using Merlin's wand to turn Merlin into a donkey. [Hill]

HARNIEL [Harmel]

In the Post-Vulgate Merlin continuation and in Malory, Balin agrees to help a knight (called Sir Garnysh of the Mount by Malory) reconcile with Duke of Harniel's daughter. Upon finding the girl sleeping with another knight, Balin's companion murdered the girl and her lover and then killed himself. [PostMer, Malory]

HARP CASTLE

A castle belonging to King Bagdemagus of Gorre. [VulgLanc]

HARPIN[1] OF THE MOUNTAIN [Harpyns]

An evil giant in Chrétien's Yvain who wished to marry the daughter of a king. The king refused, and Harpin slaughtered two of his sons, kidnapped another four, and then ransomed the four sons for the king's one daughter. The king was saved when Yvain arrived and—with the assistance of his lion—killed Harpin. Harpin appears in the Norse Iweins Saga as FJALLSHARFIR. [ChretienY, Ywain]

HARPIN[2] THE RED

A knight who broke faith with Arthur after he was sentenced to execution for a crime. As Arthur's enemy, he besieged the Castle of Three Maidens. Sir Hector of the Fens and the King with a Hundred Knights came to the castle's defense, and Hector killed Harpin in combat. [Palamedes, ProsTris]

HARRAHOARS

A Saxon warrior present at the battle at Vambieres between the Saxon King Aminaduc and King Arthur. [Livre]

HARRY LE FYSE LAKE

A Knight of the Round Table in Malory's Le Morte Darthur. When Lancelot and Guinevere were accused of treason, Harry pledged his support to Lancelot and helped him rescue Guinevere from the stake. His name may be a corruption of EREC le fils Lac (Erec son of Lac). [*Malory*]

HASART

The seneschal of the King of the Barren Wasteland. He was accused of murdering the king's son. Gawain agreed to represent him in judicial combat, and met the king's champion in battle. Gawain called off the duel when he realized that his opponent was Gaheris, his brother. [*VulgLanc*]

HATEREL

A count who fathered Arthur's Sir Equinot. [*HartmannE*]

HATLAYNE

In the Middle English *Sir Perceval of Galles*, the chamberlain of Lufamour, who became Perceval's wife. His name is probably a variation of the French *chatelain*, meaning "castellan." [*SirPerc*]

HAUD OF SCHUWAKE

The name of Lancelot's father in the English ballad "Sir Lancelot du Lake." In most stories, Lancelot's father is named BAN. [*SirLanc*]

HAUDEBOURC [*Antebourc, Handeborc*]

The Duke of Haudebourc captured and imprisoned Arthur and some of his knights. He was slain by Morholt, who freed the prisoners. [*Palamedes, ProsTris*]

HAUPT

A wandering squire who, with his companion Blat, made his way to Cornwall on the heels of Tristan's near-capture: Tristan had been chased through the woods, after leaving a tryst with Isolde, by Mark's knight Andred. Tristan escaped by jumping into a boat and paddling off down a river. Isolde commissioned Haupt and Blat to assist in the matter by claiming it was they who Andred had chased, thus fooling Andred and Mark into thinking that Tristan had not been there. [*Eilhart*]

HAVELIN

The noble king of Karahes and the father of Kahedins and Isolde of the White Hands in Eilhart's *Tristrant*. He refused to marry his daughter to Count Riole of Nantes, so Riole attacked him in revenge. Karahes was besieged and would have fallen if not for the timely arrival of Tristan, who defeated Riole, befriended Kahedins, and married Isolde. He is represented in Gottfried's *Tristan* as the similar sounding JOVELIN, and is replaced in later Tristan legends by HOEL. [*Eilhart*]

HEAD OF ANNWN

In *The Spoils of Annwn*, Arthur travels to his realm and steals his magic cauldron. Six hundred of Arthur's warriors were slain in the expedition. In non-Arthurian Welsh tales,

the Head of Annwn is variously named as Arawn, Hagan, and Pwyll. [*Spoils*]

HEBES THE FAMOUS [*Berbes, Habé, Ebes*]

A Knight of the Round Table who was originally Tristan's squire. He was related somehow to Lancelot. He first met Tristan in France, where Hebes served King Faramon. Later, he encountered Tristan in Ireland, at the Castle of the Moors tournament, when the latter was using the alias "Tantrist." Hebes swore to keep Tristan's identity secret, but inadvertently betrayed him when he kneeled down before him, and Isolde realized that "Tantrist" must be of nobility. Tristan knighted Hebes, and Hebes later saved Tristan from Isolde's mother, the Queen of Ireland.

Hebes eventually took service with Arthur and was promoted to the Round Table. According to the Post-Vulgate, he was slain by Tristan, during the Grail Quest, in a tragic misunderstanding; Tristan thought Hebes was Palamedes, whom Tristan wanted to slay because of his love for Isolde. Palamedes had earlier defeated Hebes in joust and had exchanged shields with him. Seeing Hebes riding towards him, Tristan lowered his lance and charged, despite Hebes' cries to stop, and pierced his chest. Hebes was buried by Gaheris.

Malory gives a different account, saying that when Lancelot and Guinevere were accused of treason, Hebes pledged his support to them and helped Lancelot rescue Guinevere from the stake. He fought for Lancelot in the wars against Arthur, and in return for his support, Lancelot made him the earl of Comminges. [*PostQuest, ProsTris, Malory*]

HEBRIDES

A group of islands off the western coast of Scotland. According to Wace, they were a part of Arthur's empire. They may be intended as the home of any number of knights with the sobriquet "of the Isles." [*Wace*]

HEBRON

The longer form of BRON.

HEBUSAN

A giant who captured and imprisoned Arthur. Guiron the Courteous defeated him and freed Arthur. To commemorate the occasion, Arthur christened the Fountain of Guiron the Courteous. [*Palamedes*]

HECTOR[1]

An ancestor of the "Brown" family who ruled the Savage Realm. He was the son of Brun and Lye, the brother of Brun, Galehaut, Lore, and Ysille, and the father of Crudens. [*Palamedes*]

HECTOR[2] OF THE FENS [*Astor(e), Ector, (H)estor(e), Jastor*]

Lancelot's half-brother. The bastard son of King Ban of Benoic, Hector was conceived when Merlin caused Ban to fall in love with the daughter of Lord Agravadain of the Castle of the Fens. Agravadain raised Hector until he was old enough to take service with Arthur. Hector became a Knight of the Round Table, and his adventures occupy a large part of the Vulgate *Lancelot* and the Post-Vulgate Cycle. (In Girart d'Amiens's *Escanor*, he is called the son of Ares, but there is probably some confusion with TOR.)

Ector's deeds included saving Elaine the Peerless from her irrational husband, helping Arthur repel a Saxon invasion of Scotland, and saving his own *amie*, Perse, from a forced married to Lord Zelotés. After Lancelot's period of insanity, Hector and Perceval found Lancelot at Bliant's Castle and brought him back to Camelot. Hector was originally a friend of Gawain, but he later declared hatred of Gawain for the death of Sir Erec. Meraugis and Arthur the Less became his frequent companions. During the Grail Quest, Hector joined company with Galahad to destroy the Castle of Treachery. He fought Perceval, and both were mortally wounded, but the appearance of the Grail cured them. Nascien the Hermit told him that he would be unsuccessful in the quest because of his sins, and, indeed, he was later denied entry to Corbenic, the Grail Castle. When Lancelot broke with Arthur over Guinevere, Hector joined his brother and fought Arthur at the battles of Joyous Guard and Benoic. In return for his support, Lancelot made him king of Benoic and Guienne.

In the Vulgate and Post-Vulgagte *Mort Artu*s, Hector, following Arthur's death at the battle of Salisbury, joined Lancelot, Bleoberis, and the Archbishop of Canterbury in a hermitage, where he died after four years. Malory says that after he stabilized his own lands, he, Bleoberis, Blamor, and Bors traveled to Jerusalem, where they died fighting the Turks. [*LancLac, VulgLanc, VulgQuest, VulgMort, VulgMer, Contin3, ProsTris, PostMer, PostQuest, PostMort, Stanz, Malory*]

HECTOR[3] THE BROWN

A famous, unsurpassed warrior of the generations before Arthur. He was the brother of Galehaut the Brown and Ellain the Brown, and the father of another Galehaut the Brown. The other Hector the Brown was his nephew. Hector fled Britain with his brother Galehaut to avoid the wrath of King Vortigern, but he was shipwrecked and stranded on an island. [*Palamedes, Prophecies*]

HECTOR[4] THE BROWN

Another famous knight of the "Brown" lineage; the son of Galehaut the Brown, Ellain the Brown, or Brun; the brother of Branor the Brown and Bruhalt the Brown; and the father of Segurant the Brown. There is a confusion among relationships here, and this Hector the Brown might be more than one character. [*Palamedes, Prophecies*]

HECTOR[5] THE NOBLE

A knight slain by Guiron the Courteous at the Levegnic tournament. His brother, Hermenor, was also killed by Guiron. [*Palamedes*]

HECTYMERE

A Knight of the Round Table who was the brother of Sir Edward of Carnavron and Sir Pryamus. [*Malory*]

HECUBA

A Knight of the Round Table who participated in the Grail Quest. His brother was Sir Eladinan. [*PostQuest*]

HEDGED MANOR[1]

The residence of the Hermit of the Hedge. Lancelot recuperated there after he was wounded by the King with a Hundred Knights during a tournament. [*VulgLanc*]

HEDGED MANOR[2]

The home of Brinol, who hated the Queen's Knights and was defeated before his residence by Lancelot. [*VulgLanc*]

HEDOR [*Hector*]

Gawain's paternal grandfather. His son was Lot, who succeeded him as the king of Orkney. He was descended from Joseph of Arimathea through Peter. Hedor's father was Argustes, and his wife was the daughter of the King of North Wales. [*VulgEst*]

HEFEYDD ONE CLOAK [*Hyfeidd*]

One of Arthur's warriors. [*Culhwch, Dream*]

HEGLAN [*Egglane*]

A knight in Arthur's court from Camelot, defeated in duel by King Pellinore. [*PostMer, Malory*]

HEIMET

A knight present at the tournament of Sorgarda, which Gawain won. [*Heinrich*]

HELA

The Queen of Hell in Norse mythology. She appears in Thelwall's *The Fairy of the Lake*, attended by frost giants and other supernatural creatures. Rowena, Vortigern's wife, seeks her assistance in seducing Arthur. [*Thelwall*]

HELAÉS OF LIMOS

A countess who became Gawain's lover. She had offered her love to an invader, Oriolt, if he could defeat Gawain in combat, but Gawain was victorious. Helaés's brother was named Clapor and her uncle was Meleagar. [*Livre*]

HELAIN[1] [*Helake, Helyus*]

One of the two peasant brothers who were protégés of King Armant of the Delectable. They treacherously killed the king and seized his kingdom. Palamedes killed Helain and avenged King Armant's death. Helain is first found in the Prose *Tristan*, where his brother is unnamed. Malory gives variations of the name—Helake and Helyus—to both brothers. In *La Tavola Ritonda*, Helain is called

PASSAUVER. His name is a variation of ALAIN, and the spellings are interchangeable. [*ProsTris*, *Malory*]

HELAIN[2] THE BLACK

A participant in the tournament at the Pine of the Giant. His uncle was the king of Ireland. [*Palamedes*]

HELAIN[3] THE BROWN

A brief companion of the Good Knight Without Fear. He was a weak knight. [*Palamedes*]

HELAIN[4] THE DRAGON

One of Arthur's knights. He fought for Arthur in a battle against the King with a Hundred Knights and the King from Over the Borders of Galone. [*LancLac*]

HELAINE[1]

A squire from Taningues who dreamed that he was injured by Gawain, and that Gawain promised to make it up to him. Helaine's mother made Helaine promise that he would not be knighted by anyone except Gawain; however, every time he sought Gawain at Camelot, Gawain was away on adventures. Eventually, the Lady of Rosetoc, who Helaine served, insisted that he be knighted. Helaine witnessed an unknown knight defeat Seguarades in combat, and decided that he would be knighted by the victor. He was delighted when he found out that the victor was in fact Gawain, and he was able to keep his promise to his mother. [*LancLac*, *VulgLanc*]

HELAINE[2]

A king who imprisoned Sir Hector. He was defeated by Gawain and forced to release Hector and his other captives. [*VulgLanc*]

HELDIN

King of Denmark in *Claris et Laris*. He joined Emperor Thereus of Rome in a war against Arthur. He was apparently succeeded by King Tallas. [*Claris*]

HELEDD

A man mentioned in a Welsh Triad as one of the "three unrestricted guests of Arthur's court, and three wanderers." Another Triad calls him a "violent one," and a third reaffirms his role as a "wanderer" of Arthur's court. [*Triads*]

HELEN [*Ele(y)ne*, *(H)elaine*, *(H)elena*]

The daughter, niece, or wife of King Hoel of Brittany (excepting the Vulgate *Merlin*, where she is the niece of Lionel of Nanteuil, and the Norse *Saga of Tristram*, where she is Duke Orsl's daughter). She was kidnapped by the Giant of Mont St. Michel. Arthur, on his way to wage war against Lucius of Rome, heard of her plight and traveled to the mountain with Kay and Bedivere. They arrived to find the lady dead—either from rape or from suicide to avoid rape—but Arthur avenged her by killing the giant. A tomb was later erected on Mont St. Michel in her memory. [*GeoffHR*, *Wace*, *Layamon*, *VulgMer*, *TrisSaga*, *Malory*]

HELES

A Knight of the Round Table who appears at the healing of Sir Urry. [*Malory*]

HELIADES

An ally of Mordred. Mordred appointed him king of Scotland when he usurped Arthur's throne. Heliades fought against Arthur's forces at the battle of Salisbury, where he killed, and was killed by, King Caradoc. [*VulgMort*]

HELIANS OF GOMERET [*Elyas*]

A knight in the service of Morgan le Fay. Sir Helians was sent by Morgan with three others, including his brother Kaz, to kill the young Alexander the Orphan at the behest of King Mark of Cornwall. All three were defeated. [*ProsTris*, *Prophecies*, *Malory*]

HELIAS[1]

The duke of Rognes who joined Arthur's battles against the Saxons at Clarence and Vambieres. His kingdom was later conquered by Galehaut. [*Livre*]

HELIAS[2] OF TOULOUSE [*E(ng)lias*]

A sage and scribe who served Merlin and Arthur. He helped Galehaut interpret a disturbing dream, and he predicted the birth of Galahad. He died during the Grail Quest after reciting some of Merlin's prophecies to Perceval. [*VulgLanc*, *Livre*, *VitaMer*, *Prophecies*]

HELIE[1] [*Elene*, *Elias*, *(H)elie(s)*, *Helyes*]

The lady-in-waiting for Queen Esmeree the Blonde of Snowdon. When Esmeree's city was cursed by two sorcerers, Helie traveled to Arthur's court to find a knight to save her lady. She was infuriated when Arthur gave her the young, inexperienced Guinglain (Gawain's son), who at that time was called simply "Fair Unknown." Helie and her dwarf, Tidogolains, rode off in a huff, but Guinglain pursued them and convinced them to let him try the adventure. Helie realized she had been mistaken about Guinglain when Guinglain proved himself worthy in a number of combats, and when he eventually completed the adventure and freed Esmeree. [*Renaut*, *ChestreLyb*]

HELIE[2]

A knight who served King Urien during Urien's rebellion against Arthur. [*Livre*]

HELIE[3] OF RAGRES

A noble knight in the service of Galehaut. He asked for and received the privilege of guarding the North Wales Bridge—one of the only passages in to Galehaut's land of

Sorelois—after Gawain defeated the prior guardian in combat. [*LancLac, VulgLanc*]

HELIENT

The daughter of the King of North Wales. While lodging at their castle, Gawain enjoyed a night with the lady. The king found out and tried to have Gawain killed, but Gawain skillfully escaped. [*VulgLanc*]

HELIFER

A knight defeated by Sir Gurion at the Perilous Pass after he revealed his love for Guiron's *amie*. [*Palamedes*]

HELIN¹

Son of Helin the Red and brother of Alibon and Marran. He and Alexander the Orphan mortally wounded each other. [*Palamedes*]

HELIN² THE RED

A murderous knight born in incest. Rescued from two knights by Sir Guiron, he betrayed Guiron by tying him to a tree in the middle of winter, leaving him to freeze. Guiron was rescued by his friend, Danain the Red. Helin had sons named Alibon, Marran, and Helin. [*Palamedes*]

HELIOR OF THE THORN

A knight who abducted the wife of Sir Daguenet, Arthur's fool. Daguenet eventually killed him. [*Palamedes*]

HELIOT [*Elyot*]

A renowned harpist. When Dinadan wrote an insulting song about King Mark of Cornwall, Dinadan taught the song to Heliot who, in turn, taught it to every harpist in England, Wales and, especially, Cornwall. He eventually was called upon to sing the song in front of Mark himself (Tristan had sworn he would protect Heliot). Mark banished him from Cornwall forever. [*ProsTris, Malory*]

HELIS¹

A knight who fought in Arthur's forces against the Saxons. He was the steward of the Castle Roestoc and the brother of Mabonagrain. [*Livre*]

HELIS² [*Elyse*]

A cousin of Arthur. When his father, Ardan, was defeated by Palamedes in joust, Helis swore revenge. Helis, however, was also defeated. [*Palamedes, ProsTris, Malory*]

HELIS³ THE PALE [*Helain, Helys*]

A knight who assisted Gawain in saving the lady of Nohaut from an attack by the King with a Hundred Knights. He later fought for Arthur in battles against the King with a Hundred Knights and the King from Over the Borders of Galone, and against Agrippe in the Waste Land. He participated in one of Gawain's quests to find Lancelot. [*LancLac, VulgLanc, Livre*]

HELIZ THE BLACK [*Elys*]

A knight, subservient to Duke Chalaunce of Clarence, who fought in the tournament at Sorelois. [*ProsTris, Malory*]

HELIZABEL

The daughter of Pelles and mother of Galahad in the Vulgate *Lancelot*. The story notes that although her name was Helizabel, she was called AMITE. The Post-Vulgate changes her name to ELAINE. [*VulgLanc*]

HELL

A rocky, perilous river which flowed past the Trial Castle and into the sea. Perceval had the bodies of pagans hurled into the river after he converted the castle. [*Perlesvaus*]

HELLAWES THE SORCERESS

An enchantress from the castle Nygramous who created the fearsome Chapel Perilous. Lancelot braved the chapel to retrieve a sword and discovered that its terrifying properties were simply illusions. Hellawes appeared before him and asked him for a kiss in exchange for the sword, but Lancelot refused. It turned out that Lancelot would have perished from the kiss had he consented. Hellawes had tendencies toward necrophilia, and she would have rather had Lancelot as a dead lover than to have lived without him. Lancelot hurried away, and Hellawes died a few weeks later from sorrow. [*Malory*]

HELP FOR THE POOR [*Secors as Povres*]

The former name of the SMALL CHARITY abbey, which was visited by Lancelot. [*VulgLanc*]

HELPHERICH OF NASSERAN

A king who, allied with King Ekunaver of Kanadic, went to war with Arthur. Ekunaver was defeated by Garel, and Helpherich was given a seat at the Round Table. [*PleierG*]

HELY

According to Geoffrey of Monmouth, a king of Britain in the second or first century BC. He succeeded his father Cligueill. He had three sons, Lud, Cassibelaunus, and Nennius, the first of whom succeeded him. [*GeoffHR*]

HELYAN THE PALE

A Knight of the Round Table who was either the uncle or great-uncle of Sir Sagremor. His brother, Hadrian, was emperor of Constantinople. [*Palamedes*]

HELYAS

A knight who was forced to flee Cornwall with his brother, Assar, after their sister was raped by King Mark. They settled on the Island of Two Brothers. Later, Helyas abducted Assar's wife and started a war. Assar received the assistance of Tristan, who slew Helyas in single combat. [*ProsTris*]

HELYOR

A knight who abducted the paramour of Sir Espinogrés. Palamedes, responding to Espinogrés's laments, vowed to rescue her, but Sir Safir, Palamedes's brother, accomplished the deed first by defeating Helyor in combat. [*ProsTris*, *Malory*]

HELYS THE RED

A knight whose nephew, Taulas, was killed by Arthur's knights. Afterwards, Helys attacked any knights of Arthur's service that he came across. [*Palamedes*]

HEMELIAN [*Emelyant*]

A castle on the border of the Middle-Eastern duchy of Orberica, ruled by Nascien. [*VulgEst*]

HEN BEDDESTYR ("Old Walker")

Son of Erim, one of five brothers, and one of Arthur's warriors. He was faster than any man, on horseback or on foot. [*Culhwch*]

HEN GEDYMEDDEITH ("Old Comrade")

An Arthurian warrior. [*Culhwch*]

HEN GROEN ("Old Skin")

The horse belonging to Saint Cynwyl, one of Arthur's warriors who survived the battle of Camlann. [*Culhwch*]

HEN WAS ("Old Servant") THE SWIFT

Son of Erim, one of five brothers, and one of Arthur's warriors. He could ran faster than any animal. [*Culhwch*]

HEN WYNEB ("Old Face")

One of Arthur's warriors in Welsh legend. [*Culhwch*]

HENDRIS [*Ho(n)dri(s)*]

King of Slavonia. He joined his ally, Emperor Thereus of Rome, in a war against Arthur. He was killed by Gawain. [*Claris*]

HENEC SUCTELLOIS

A Knight of the Round Table who was the son of Gawain. [*HartmannE*]

HENETE

One of Arthur's knights. Henete was one of many to ride after Meleagant when Meleagant kidnapped Guinevere, but he was defeated. [*HartmannI*]

HENGIST [*Algis, Angis, Ang(u)ys, Engis(t), Hanguist, Hengest, Hengistus*]

A semi-legendary Saxon chieftain credited in the *Anglo-Saxon Chronicle* with the impetus for the Saxon conquest of Britain. He has an important role in the Arthurian chronicles, and is mentioned by Bede, Nennius, and Geoffrey of Monmouth, among others. Bede traces his descent from a Saxon god, and names his father as Wihtgils. In Arthurian chronicles, he has a son named Octa and another son, or cousin, named Eosa. The *Anglo-Saxon Chronicle* gives him a son named Æsc, who may be identical to Eosa. In Dryden's *King Arthur*, he has a son named Oswald.

Hengist, his brother Horsa, and their warriors were welcomed into Britain by the British King Vortigern. Vortigern hoped to employ them as mercenaries against the Picts and the Irish. Hengist had other plans. Seeking the kingdom of Britain for himself, he gave his daughter Rowena (or, in one source, Sardoine) to Vortigern in exchange for the country of Kent, to which he summoned a large Saxon army. Vortigern allowed the immigration because he believed that Hengist's Saxons would help protect Britain from Ambrosius and Uther Pendragon, who were poised to invade from Brittany. The Triads call Vortigern's decision to admit Hengist to Britain one of the "Three Unfortunate Counsels of the Island of Britain."

Eventually, Vortigern (and the rest of Britain) became aware of Hengist's plan. Vortimer, Vortigern's son, led an army of Britons to drive Hengist and the Saxons off the island. Vortimer succeeded, but died soon afterwards. Hengist returned and told Vortigern that he wished to make peace. At the signing of a treaty at Ealing or Ambrius, however, Hengist and his men drew daggers and slaughtered Vortigern's men. Hengist took Vortigern prisoner and ransomed his life for the countries of Essex, Sussex, and Middlesex.

According to Nennius, Hengist died soon after this conquest and was succeeded by his son Octa. Geoffrey, however, contends that Hengist lived to plague Ambrosius when he became king, but was finally defeated and captured at the battle of Conisbrough. He was then executed by Eldol, the Earl of Gloucester. In the Vulgate *Merlin*, Hengist tries to murder Uther in his tent, at night, during a lull between battles. Uther, warned of the plot by Merlin, was armed and ready, and he slew Hengist after a short struggle. *Merlin* does not mention Octa, but says that Hengist's kinsmen, led by Aminaduc, invaded Britain during Arthur's reign. In Richard Hole's *Arthur*, Hengist is alive during Arthur's reign. Aided by the three Fatal Sisters, he adopts Arthur's likeness and tries to rape Inogen, Arthur's wife. He is attacked and slain by his own warriors, believing him to be Arthur.

An interesting variation occurs in the fourteenth-century *Short Metrical Chronicle*, where Hengist is praised as one of Britain's most noble kings. According to this text, he ruled Britain for 150 years, united the island, and conquered parts of France. His reign is placed between those of King Belinus and King Lear. In the Prose *Brut*, "England" is derived from his name. [*Bede, Anglo, Nennius, Triads, GeoffHR, Wace, VulgMer, Butor, ProsBrut, Arthour, Short, Dryden, Hole*]

HENIN THE OLD

Father of Arthur's mistress Garwen. [*Triads*]

HENRI[1] OF THE BORDERLANDS [*Harvys, Herni, Hervi*]

A knight who challenged Sir Alexander the Orphan for the former castle Fair Guard and was defeated. He fought against the Saxons when they invaded Britain. [*ProsTris, Prophecies, Malory*]

HENRI[2] THE COURTEOUS

A knight who brought a force of soldiers to Jerusalem to save it from an attack by the King of Baghdad. [*Prophecies*]

HENRY[1]

The Alliterative *Morte Arthure* once names Henry as Yvain's father, probably intending URIEN. [*Allit*]

HENRY[2]

Emperor of Germany, king of Cologne, and father of Arthur's Sir Laris. Henry's daughter, Lidoine, married Sir Claris. [*Claris*]

HENRY[3] II

According to Etienne de Rouen, author of *Draco Normannicus*, the famed English monarch (1154–1189) corresponded with Arthur, who was immortal and living in an antipodal kingdom. Henry was in the process of conquering Brittany from Count Rollandus when Arthur sent a letter to Henry in an attempt to intervene on Rollandus's behalf. Arthur supposedly granted stewardship of Britain to Henry II, but retained ultimate sovereignty for himself. Henry ignored the letter and evidently suffered no consequences. The Post-Vulgate *Merlin* continuation notes that Henry II removed statues of Perceval and Clamadeu from the battlefield at Beaurepaire and stored them in his treasury at St. Lorent. According to Giraldus Cambrensis, it was Henry who told the Glastonbury monks where to find Arthur's body. Henry had apparently learned of the location from a bard. [*Etienne, Giraldus, PostMer*]

HENWEN

An enchanted pig in Welsh legend, tended by the magician Coll. The stories and Triads in which Henwen appears are non-Arthurian—with the exception of a single re-written Triad, in which Arthur chases and tries to destroy Henwen because it has been prophesied that her offspring will worsen the state of the world. After giving birth to several piglets, she dove into the ocean. This hunt is reminiscent of his pursuit of TWRCH TRWYTH in *Culhwch and Olwen*. [*Triads*]

HER

Son of Yder. Her was one of King Arthur's barons who fought for Arthur in the war against Rome. Her was part of the escort taking Roman prisoners to Paris. The prisoner train was attacked by the Romans, and Her was killed. [*GeoffHR*]

HERAUT [*Barant*]

The real name of the KING WITH A HUNDRED KNIGHTS in the Prose *Tristan* and in Malory. [*ProsTris, Malory*]

HERAWDE

A "great lord" from Rome, killed fighting Arthur's warriors in the Roman War. [*Malory*]

HERBERT

The godson of a hostler named Heudins, with whom Lancelot lodged on his way to Rigomer castle. Herbert loved Heudins' daughter, Eme. [*Merveil*]

HERCULES

In the Vulgate *Merlin*, Arthur comes to possess Marmiadoise, the Sword of Hercules, forged by Vulcan and passed from heir to heir until it was owned by Rions, Arthur's enemy. The conception of Hercules (or, more properly, Heracles) in Greek mythology precedes that of Arthur: Zeus visited the lady Alcmene in the form of her husband, Amphitryon, much as Uther Pendragon seduced Igerne in the form of her husband, Gorlois. [*VulgMer*]

HEREFORD [*Herford*]

A city in west central England, on the Wye river. Wace says that Earl Guerguint governed the city under King Arthur. [*Wace, Layamon*]

HERENC

An Arthurian knight who joined Gawain's quest to conquer Castle Rigomer. [*Merveil*]

HERGIN

The region of Wales that contains Mount Droac, on which Vortigern built a castle. [*Wace*]

HÉRI THE CLEVER

In the Icelandic *Saga af Tristram ok Ísodd*, one of King Mark's counselors. He advised Mark of the affair between Tristan and Isolde. He had previously served Philippus, Mark's father. [*SagaTI*]

HERLAN[1] [*Herlans*]

The grandson of Joseph of Arimathea. He inherited the kingdom of Orkney from his father, Peter. He married the King of Ireland's daughter and had a son named Meliant. Herlan was an ancestor of Lot and Gawain. [*VulgEst*]

HERLAN[2] OF BENOIC

A knight present at the Sorelois tournament. [*ProsTris*]

HERLAN[3] THE BEARDED [*Harlews le Berbeus, Herlaus*]

A knight defeated by Alexander the Orphan at the castle of Fair Guard. Malory gives this name to the knight, unnamed in the Post-Vulgate *Suite du Merlin*, who is killed by the invisible Sir Garlon while in the company of Sir Balin. [*PostMer*, *ProsTris*, *Malory*]

HERLEN [*Harlon*]

Father of Argustes, a knight aided by Lancelot during the Grail Quest. [*VulgQuest*, *Malory*]

HERLINDE

A lady loved by King Vridebrant of Scotland. On her account, Vridebrant killed King Hernant. This story was related to Perceval's father Gahmuret when he came to the kingdom of Zazamanc. [*Wolfram*]

HERLION [*Helyois*]

A king defeated by Lancelot in a tournament at Pomeglai. His brother was King Clarion of Northumberland. [*VulgLanc*]

HERMAN

Arthur's Count of Triple. He was killed in the Roman War. [*VulgMer*]

HERMIT KING [*Hermit Uncle*]

Perceval's uncle. Perceval came across his forest cloister after having failed to ask the Grail Question during his first visit to the Fisher King's castle. The Hermit King gave Perceval additional information about the Grail and the Grail keepers. The character first appears in Chrétien de Troyes's *Perceval*, though he has no name or designation. In *Perlesvaus*, he is given the proper name of King PELLES; Wolfram von Eschenbach names him TREVRIZENT; and the Fourth Continuation of Chrétien's *Perceval* calls him ELYAS ANAÏS. There is some confusion as to whether he is Perceval's maternal uncle (and therefore the brother of the Fisher King) or his paternal uncle (the brother of Alain the Large). [*ChretienP*, *Contin2*, *Didot*, *Perlesvaus*, *Wolfram*, *Contin4*]

HERMIT OF THE HEDGE

A knight-turned-hermit who lived in the Hedged Manor, near the castle Dolorous Guard and the Dolorous Prison. He gave lodging to Lancelot and Gawain when they came to liberate the Dolorous buildings, and he administered the Extreme Unction to two of Arthur's knights—Loholt and Galegantin—when they were sick in the Dolorous Prison. [*LancLac*, *VulgLanc*]

HERMIT'S CROSS

The home of Gais the Large, Perceval's grandfather. [*Perlesvaus*]

HERMIT'S SPRING [**Fontaine a 'Ermite*]

A fountain where Hector had his armor stolen by a treacherous squire, as part of the Lord of the Fens' plan to capture Hector. [*VulgLanc*]

HERMITAGE OF THE HEDGE

A location where Kay was released to Aglovale after having been imprisoned by Griffon. [*VulgLanc*]

HERMITAGE OF THE MOUNT

An abbey where Yvain recovered from wounds received while helping a maiden recover a sparrowhawk. [*VulgLanc*]

HERMOINE THE HERMIT

A holy man from Tarsus who baptized Sarrassinte, King Mordrain's wife, as a child. He died in Orberica. After Joseph of Arimathea converted Mordrains, he re-interred Hermoine's body in a holy tomb in Orberica. Nascien later encountered Hermoine's spirit during an adventure at sea. [*VulgEst*]

HERMONDINE

Daughter of the King of Scotland. She was loved by a knight named Camel, but was unnerved by his sleepwalking habit. She offered to marry the knight who displayed the greatest prowess in a series of five tournaments, which were organized by her cousin Florée. When Meliador, one of Arthur's knights, learned of her pledge, he set out to win her. He killed Camel and proved himself to Hermondine by winning the tournament at Roxburgh against 1,566 knights. Hermondine married him. [*Froissart*]

HERNANT[1]

A king killed by King Vridebrant of Scotland for the love of Herlinde. In revenge, Hernant's allies and kinsmen invaded Scotland. These events occurred during the reign of Uther in Britain. [*Wolfram*]

HERNANT[2] THE YOUNG

A squire of Sir Guiron the Courteous. [*Palamedes*]

HERVI OF RIVEL [*Harvy, Hernil, Herui(s), Herv(i)eu, Hervis*]

An Arthurian knight named in the romance of *Yder* as a king and the father of one of Arthur's Yvains. According to the Vulgate romances, he served Uther Pendragon before Arthur. He participated in the Saxon wars, the campaign in Gaul, the war against Galehaut, the struggle against Rions and Nero, and the battle of the Humber. Arthur appointed him to the Round Table after the Humber. He was still serving as Arthur's knight when he was 80 years old. [*LancLac*, *VulgLanc*, *VulgMer*, *Livre*, *PostMer*, *Arthour*, *Malory*]

HERVYN

In Malory, a nobleman who held a tournament against the Count of the Plains during the Grail Quest. Bors arrived at the tournament and met his brother Lionel, whom Bors had believed dead. In the Vulgate *Queste del Saint Graal*,

Hervyn's place is occupied by the lady of the Castle TUBELE. [*Malory*]

HERVYSE DE LA FOREST SAVAGE

A Knight of the Round Table, possibly identical to HERVI. [*Malory*]

HERYAN THE BROWN

A squire to Sir Guiron the Courteous who was knighted for his service. [*Palamedes*]

HERYLL

A knight in the service of Cador of Cornwall. He participated in Arthur's war against Rome. [*Allit*]

HERZELOYDE

Queen of Wales and mother of Perceval in Wolfram's *Parzival*. Herzeloyde was a member of the enigmatic Grail Family, the daughter of Frimutel, and the sister of Anfortas, Trevrizent, Schoysiane, and Repanse de Schoye. As was the custom in the Grail Family, Herzeloyde was sent away from Munsalvæsche, the Grail Castle, to become the wife of a noble lord; in her case, this lord was Castis, the King of Wales and North Wales. Their marriage was unconsummated due to Castis' untimely death, and Herzeloyde, as a maiden, inherited Castis' kingdom.

She threw a tournament at her city of Kanvoleis, promising herself and her lands to the knight who won the tournament. The noble Gahmuret was the victor, and thus found himself bound to marry Herzeloyde, even though it was not his wish. After their marriage, Gahmuret secured permission from Herzeloyde to seek adventure, and was killed fighting in the Middle East.

Herzeloyde went slightly mad and soon gave birth to Perceval, who she saw as the reincarnation of her husband. She raised him in seclusion, ignorant of knighthood and chivalry, in order to protect him from the same fate that befell his father. While she was living in this sequestration, King Lähelin entered and conquered her lands. Perceval eventually found out about knighthood from some passing knights, and insisted on going to the court of King Arthur. When he left, Herzeloyde died from a broken heart.

Herzeleide is German for "heart sorrow," and Wolfram probably created the name to express the queen's sorrow for losing her husband. Her character is unnamed in Chrétien de Troyes's *Perceval*. [*Wolfram*]

HETTOR

A knight present at King Uther Pendragon's Urbano tournament. He was defeated by King Lot. This name often appears as a variation of HECTOR. [*Tavola*]

HETWN

Father of Arthur's warrior Cynedyr the Wild. He has two epithets: "Silver Brow" and "the Leper." [*Culhwch*]

HEUDINS

An Irish shepherd with whom Lancelot lodged on his way to Rigomer castle. During Lancelot's stay, a pack of robbers besieged Heudins' hostel, but Lancelot drove them off. Heudins had a daughter named Eme and a godson named Herbert. [*Merveil*]

HEW¹

A knight who served Lord Golagros. During the war between Golagros and Arthur, Hew was captured by Arthur's knights. [*Golagros*]

HEW² DE LA MONTAYNE

A knight from North Wales who jousted with Lancelot prior to the tournament at the Castle of Maidens. Hew lost. [*Malory*]

HEWIN

A duke who governed Guiens under King Arthur. [*Pierre*]

HEWIS

An Arthurian knight. [*Golagros*]

HIGH MOUNTAIN [*Haute Montai(n)gne*]

"He of the High Mountain" was a nobleman present at the wedding of Erec and Enide. [*ChretienE*]

HIGH ROCK

One of the Arthur's Castles. It was seized by Montenart of the Hidden Island, but was returned to Arthur's control when Erec killed Montenart. [*PostMer*]

HIGH WALLS [*Haut Mur*]

A castle in Benoic. It's lord, Grayer, was one of King Ban's stewards. [*VulgLanc, VulgMer*]

HIGH WILD FOREST

Pellinore's domain in the Post-Vulgate. In other references, it is LISTENOIS or the WASTE LAND. [*PostMer*]

HIGHLANDS OF HELL

The sons of Gwawrddur Hunchback were "sprung from the Highlands of Hell." The Highlands also contained the Valley of Distress, in which the White Hag and Black Hag lived. [*Culhwch*]

HILDIFONSUS

A Welsh bishop who King Mark commissioned to conduct an ordeal in which Isolde would have to prove her fidelity. On the way to the ordeal, a "beggar" (Tristan in disguise) helped Isolde cross a patch of mud, and Isolde was able to swear before God that no man had come near her except Mark and the "beggar." [*SagaTI*]

HILL CASTLE

The lair of Malduit, a giant slain by Yvain. [*VulgLanc*]

HILL OF THE CAT [*Mons du Chat*]

A knoll next to Lake Lausanne in France or Italy where Arthur slew a giant devil cat in the Vulgate *Merlin*. The evil cat, which had been born when a fisherman broke a promise to God, had terrorized the region for many years. Prior to Arthur's defeat of the cat, the hill was called the Hill of the Lake. The monster defeated by Arthur recalls the CATH PALUG of Welsh legend. The author of *Merlin* may be referring to Cat's Tooth, a hill in Savoy. [*VulgMer*]

HILL OF THE SPRING

The location of Sir Tericam's prison, which held such knights as Hector, Lionel and Gaheris, before Tericam was killed by Lancelot. [*VulgLanc*]

HILL OF WRETCHES [*Tertre as Caitis*]

The residence of Druas the Cruel, who made a tradition of slaying passing knights. It was renamed AGRAVAIN'S HILL when Agravain killed Druas and ended the hill's customs. [*VulgLanc*]

HIPOMENES [*Ypoménés*]

The grandfather of the Questing Beast. He was a king in Britain, and his daughter loved her brother, named Galahad. She was impregnated by a demon. Under the demon's influence, she falsely accused Galahad of rape. Galahad was executed, and the Beast was born of Hipomenes's daughter in due time. Realizing that the monster couldn't have sprung from a human, Hipomenes tortured the truth from his daughter and then had her executed. [*PostQuest, ProsTris*]

HIPPOLYTUS

The ruler of Crete who owed his allegiance to Rome, and was called upon to join Lucius in the war against Arthur. [*GeoffHR, Wace*]

HIRELGLAS[1]

The Baron of Periron or Peritum under King Arthur who fought for Arthur in the war against Rome. Hirelglas was part of the escort taking Roman prisoners to Paris. The prisoner train was attacked by the Romans, and Hirelglas was killed. [*GeoffHR, Wace*]

HIRELGLAS[2] [*Herupeys, Hire(s)lg(l)as*]

Nephew of Bedivere and a knight of Arthur's court in Geoffrey of Monmouth's *Historia*. During the Roman War, he saw his uncle killed by King Boccus of Media, and he became enraged. He avenged Bedivere's death by slaying Boccus. The French *Liber de Compositione Castri Ambaziae* renames him BILLEIUS and the Vulgate *Merlin* calls him SEGART. [*GeoffHR, Wace*]

HIRTACIUS

The King of Parthia. He owed his allegiance to Rome, and he joined Lucius's war against King Arthur. He led a battalion of soldiers at the battle of Soissons. [*GeoffHR*]

HIUTEGER

A Scottish duke who served King Vridebrant of Scotland. Hiuteger accompanied Vridebrant on a campaign to conquer the Arabain kingdom of Zazamanc. When Vridebrant returned to Scotland, Hiuteger continued the assault. To decide the conflict, Hiuteger agreed to face Gahmuret (Perceval's father, who was championing Zazamanc) in single combat. Hiuteger lost. [*Wolfram*]

HLÖOVIR

A king of Spain who was served by Tristan's father and grandfather. His land was invaded by two kings named Seran and Elemmie, and Hlöòver was killed by Elemmie. Patrocles, Tristan's grandfather, later re-conquered the country and took the throne. [*SagaTI*]

HOEL[1] [*Horel, Howel(l), Ohel*]

King of Brittany or Nantes. He was an ally of Arthur, who was either his uncle or cousin. In Welsh legend, his father is named Emhyr, but Geoffrey of Monmouth calls him the son of Budec. In some of the Tristan romances, he is Tristan's father-in-law. Welsh legend names him as one of Arthur's three "Royal Knights," and says that he was handsome, wise, and skilled at arms.

In Arthur's early days as king, Hoel assisted his kinsman against the Saxon invaders led by Colgrim. Hoel became sick during the campaign, and Arthur was forced to leave him in the city of Dumbarton. While Arthur was defeating the Saxons in Bath, Picts and Scots attacked Dumbarton, and Hoel had to weakly hold them off. Eventually, Arthur returned and rescued Hoel from defeat. Hoel, in turn, helped Arthur win the war against the Scots at Lake Lomond. During the campaign against Gaul, Hoel accompanied Arthur and, with a division of soldiers, conquered much of the region, including Aquitaine and Gascony. Hoel also pledged himself and a force of soldiers to Arthur at the beginning of the campaign against Rome. Before they embarked, however, they received word that Hoel's niece Helen (or, in Malory, his wife—the Duchess of Brittany) had been carried off by the giant of Mont St. Michel. Arthur and his knights attacked and killed the giant, but were too late to save the woman's life. (In the Vulgate *Merlin*, the Helen's uncle is LIONEL of Nanteuil; and in the Norse *Tristrams Saga*, the character is called ORSL.)

Despite the loss, Hoel went with Arthur to Rome and proved one of the best warriors Arthur had, leading a battalion of soldiers at Soissons. In Geoffrey's account, Arthur sends Hoel on to conquer Rome while Arthur returns to Britain to deal with Mordred's insurrection.

In the Prose *Tristan*, Hoel becomes the father of Isolde of the White Hands, Kahedins, and Ruvalen (replacing HAVELIN or JOVELIN from earlier texts). Another (unnamed) daughter married King Meliadus of Lyonesse and became Tristan's step-mother. Tristan came to Hoel's court and ended up saving Hoel from a tyrannical neighbor named Agrippe. In return, Hoel married Tristan to Isolde of the White Hands.

A ruler named Hoel governed Brittany in the time of William the Conqueror and was one of William's allies. Geoffrey of Monmouth may have used adopted Hoel's name in order to flatter his Norman patrons (Bruce, 23). [*GeoffHR*, *Triads*, *Wace*, *VulgMer*, *ProsTris*, *Dream*, *Geraint*, *Prophecies*, *Malory*]

HOEL²

The King of Gohenet who was an ally or vassal of Arthur. He participated in a tournament at the Castle of Maidens. [*Renaut*]

HOEL³

The other name of King ARAMONT of Brittany, possibly identical to the first HOEL. [*VulgLanc*]

HOEL⁴

The duke of Cornwall in the Vulgate *Merlin* and *Arthour and Merlin*. In the former, he takes the role usually assigned to GORLOIS, while in the latter he precedes TINTAGEL as Igerne's husband. *Arthour* names him as Igerne's second husband, after Harinan. His daughters were Blasine, Belisent, and Brimesent. [*VulgMer*, *Arthour*]

HOELAÉS

A Saxon warrior who was part of the Saxon army fought by Arthur at the siege of Vambieres. [*Livre*]

HOJIR OF MANNESVELT

A count called the "Red Knight" because of his crimson hair and beard. In a version of the "sparrowhawk" tournament found in Wirnt von Grafenberg's *Wigalois*, Hojir wrongfully gave a parrot—which had been intended for the most beautiful lady at the tournament—to his own lady. None of the knights at the tournament were willing to stand up to him. The rightful victor left and found Wigalois (Gawain's son), who accompanied her back to the tournament, defeated Hojir in combat, and awarded the parrot to its rightful owner. Hojir and his lady were forced to travel to Arthur's court as prisoners. Hojir later became a friend of Wigalois. His counterpart in Renaut de Bâge's *The Fair Unknown* is GIRFLET. [*Wirnt*]

HOLDIN [*Holden, Holdyne, Howeldin*]

One of Arthur's nobles, to whom Arthur gave either Flanders (in Geoffrey of Monmouth) or Boulogne (in Wace). Holdin assisted Arthur in the Roman war. He led a company at the Battle of Soissons, where he and King Alifatma of Spain mortally wounded each other. Arthur had him buried in his city of Thérouanne or Tervanna. In the Prose *Brut*, he is Arthur's chamberlain. Thomas Bek

calls him the "King of the Ruteni." [*GeoffHR*, *Wace*, *ProsBrut*, *Bek*]

HOLLAND

Part of Arthur's empire according to the Alliterative *Morte Arthur*, Holland did not exist as a country until the tenth century. [*Allit*]

HOLOFERNES

King of Sarras. He made war on King Tholomer of Babylonia. He was killed and succeeded by King Evalach. [*VulgEst*]

HOLY CEMETERY

A graveyard and church, so named because it contained the bodies of Galahad, a son of Joseph of Arimathea, and Simeon, a follower. In the "Knight of the Cart" episode from the Vulgate *Lancelot*, Lancelot raises the stone on Galahad's tomb, proving that he has the mettle to rescue Guinevere from Meleagant. Lancelot failed to raise Simeon's tombstone—an adventure completed by his son Galahad during the Grail Quest. [*VulgLanc*]

HOLY GRAIL

The GRAIL, after it became identified with the chalice or dish used by Christ at the Last Supper.

HOLY LANCE

A name used in the Post-Vulgate *Suite du Merlin* for the Lance of LONGINUS, which a Roman soldier stuck in the side of Jesus Christ. See BLEEDING LANCE. [*PostMer*]

HONOREE

The King of the Isles decreed that any knight who was able to draw Honoree, a magnificent sword, from its sheath would marry Beauté, the king's daughter. Clarete, Beauté's maidservant, carried the sword around until Beaudous, the son of Gawain, managed to draw it. [*RobertBlo*]

HONORIUS

The Roman Emperor during Arthur's war with Rome, according to one French source. Lucius was his general. In most sources, the Emperor is LEO or LUCIUS himself. An historical Emperor Honorius ruled Rome in the late fourth and early fifth centuries. [*Liber*]

HONTZLAKE

A knight from Wendland who, at the Round Table's first feast, rode into Arthur's hall and abducted Nimue. Arthur assigned King Pellinore to retrieve the lady and bring back the knight. Pellinore came upon Hontzlake fighting Nimue's cousins, Mellot and Bryan. Pellinore challenged Hontzlake to combat, and Hontzlake responded by killing Pellinore's horse. This enraged Pellinore so much that he killed Hontzlake with a single blow to the head and returned Nimue to Camelot. [*Malory*]

HORN

Hengist's brother in the Prose *Brut*; probably a corruption of HORSA. He built a castle called Horn Castle which was destroyed by Vortigern. [*ProsBrut*]

HORSA [*Horse, Horsus*]

A Saxon leader and a brother of Hengist welcomed into Britain by the King Vortigern. Bede, the first to mention Horsa, traces the brothers' decent from a Saxon god, and names their father as Wihtgils. Horsa led part of the Saxon army in Britain. He was killed fighting one of Vortigern's sons (Vortimer, Catigern, or Vortiger) during Vortimer's war against Hengist, but managed to mortally wound his killer. The site of Horsa's death is variously given as Episford or Æglestherp. [*Bede, Anglo, Nennius, GeoffHR, Wace, Layamon*]

HOSELICE[1] [*Haucelice, Hoceliche, Sorelice*]

An early name of WALES, according to the Vulgate romances. It was renamed in honor of Galahad, son of Joseph of Arimathea. Galahad was its first Christian king. Its finest city was Palagre. [*LancLac, VulgEst*]

HOSELICE[2] [*Hoschelice*]

A Saxon kingdom ruled by Ammaduc, who led an invasion of Britain at the beginning of Arthur's reign. [*VulgMer*]

HOSSENT

The castle ruled by Assar, an enemy of King Mark of Cornwall. [*ProsTris*]

HOST-SPLITTER

The horse belonging to Arthur's warrior Caradawg Strong-Arm. [*Triads*]

HOUSE OF HOLINESS

A spiritual house where the Red Cross Knight recuperated—physically and spirituatlly—before his battle with a dragon. The lady presiding over the house was named Coelia. [*Spenser*]

HOUSE OF PRIDE

A palace visited by the Red Cross Knight after he was seduced by Duessa, an evil witch. It's queen was Lucifera, and her counselors were the seven deadly sins. The Red Cross Knight encountered Sansjoy, the brother of a knight (Sansfoy) he had slain. Sansjoy and the Red Cross Knight met in single combat, but when the Red Cross Knight seemed to be winning, a black cloud carried Sansjoy away. [*Spenser*]

HOWE

A nephew of Arthur and brother of Jon. Howe and Jon accompanied Sir Launfal when Launfal fled to Caerleon to escape Guinevere's disfavor. When Launfal fell into poverty and depravity in Caerleon, Howe and Jon returned to Arthur's court. [*ChestreLvl*]

HRÍNGR

Earl of Spain and brother of Sigurðr and Isolde the Dark. He gave his sister to Tristan when the latter conquered Spain. [*SagaTI*]

HUABWY

An Arthurian warrior who was the son of Gwryon. [*Culhwch*]

HUANDAW

A gatekeeper at King Arthur's court. He served Glewlwyd Strong Grip and was killed by the boar Twrch Trwyth during the epic hunt. [*Culhwch*]

HUARWAR

An Arthurian warrior who was the son of Aflawn. He had such an enormous appetite that he became a virtual plague in the countries of Devon and Cornwall until his stomach was sated. [*Culhwch*]

HUBAUS THE BROWN

One of the knights of the "Brown" lineage. [*Palamedes*]

HUDIBRAS

According to Geoffrey of Monmouth, a king of Britain in the tenth century BC. Hudibras was the son of King Leil and the father of King Bladud. During Hudibras's reign, he founded the cities of Canterbury and Winchester. [*GeoffHR*]

HUEIL

Son of Caw, one of twenty brothers, and one of Arthur's warriors who "never submitted to a lord's hand." According to *Culhwch and Olwen*, Hueil became Arthur's enemy by stabbing Gwydre, Hueil's nephew and one of Arthur's warriors. Caradoc's *Vita Gildae* recounts how Hueil, who had aspriations for the British throne, led raids into Britain from Scotland. Arthur tracked him down and killed him at the island of Minau, then had to beg for the forgiveness of St. Gildas, Hueil's brother. [*Culhwch, Caradoc*]

HUELINS OF BEDIGAN

A knight who joined Arthur's battles against the Saxons at Clarence and Vambieres. [*Livre*]

HUET

A squire present at the tournament at Lancien, thrown by King Mark of Cornwall. [*Contin4*]

HUGE YELLOW

The horse belonging to Urien's son Pasgen. [*Triads*]

HUGH OF THE RED CASTLE

A knight who was the brother of Sir Edward of the Red Castle. Hugh and his brother stole lands from the Lady of the Rock. Yvain championed the lady, fought the two brothers at the same time (as they had insisted), killed Edward, and defeated Hugh. Yvain ordered Hugh to return the Lady of the Rock's lands and to report to Arthur's court. [*Malory*]

HUGON [*Hewgon*]

A knight defeated in combat by Sir Alexander the Orphan at Fair Guard. [*ProsTris, Malory*]

HUISCAM

The Duke of Huiscam is named as Enide's father in the Prose *Tristan*. He was killed by Senahar. Erec avenged the duke's death by imprisoning Senahar. [*ProsTris*]

HUMBER

A river in northeast England, often appearing as the northern border of Arthur's kingdom. According to Geoffrey of Monmouth, the river was named for Humber, king of the Huns, who drowned there while fighting the sons of Brutus. The Vulgate romances locate a number of fortresses on the Humber—including Galafort, Dolorous Tower, Dolorous Guard, King's Fortress, Queen's Ford, and the town of Chanviere—but they seem to think that the river is in Wales. The *Livre d'Artus* locates one of Arthur's battles against the Saxons on the river. According to the Post-Vulgate *Merlin* continuation, Arthur battled the Kings of Ireland, Denmark, the Valley, Sorelois, and the Distant Isles at the Humber, killing all of them (in the Vulgate *Lancelot*, seven kings were said to have opposed Arthur in the battle). Kay showed particular valor in the fight. Arthur erected the Abbey of the Good Adventure along the river to commemorate the battle, and Guinevere dubbed a nearby ford the Queen's Ford. In Hector Boece's *Scotorum Historia*, the Humber is the site of Arthur's final battle with Mordred, a fight that earlier texts place at SALISBURY or CAMLANN. [*GeoffHR, VulgLanc, VulgMort, VulgEst, VulgMer, Livre, PostMer, Malory, Boece*]

HUMILDIS

The renowned brother of Gener of Kartis, a maiden who helped Gawain during his Grail Quest. [*Heinrich*]

HUNBAUT

A Knight of the Round Table who Arthur sent, with Gawain, to the court of the King of the Isles. Gawain and Hunbaut were supposed to demand the king's submission to Arthur. After delivering their message, they fled the king's court. On the return trip, Hunbaut became separated from Gawain. He rescued a knight from a pack of robbers before returning to Arthur's court. [*Hunbaut*]

HUNCAMUNCA

The daughter of Arthur and Queen Dollallolla in Henry Fielding's parody *The Tragedy of Tragedies*. She loved the diminutive warrior Tom Thumb, to whom Arthur betrothed her. This enraged Lord Grizzle, another of her suitors. In the original play, *Tom Thumb*, Grizzle kills Tom Thumb's ghost, for which Huncamunca kills him; in the revised *Tragedy of Tragedies*, Huncamunca slays Cleora, her maidservant. Doodle, one of Arthur's courtiers, kills Huncamunca in return. [*Fielding*]

HUNES

An Arthurian knight who joined Gawain's quest to conquer Rigomer castle. [*Merveil*]

HUNESON [*Hemison, Onesun*]

The lover of Morgan le Fay, with whom she had a daughter called Pulzella Gaia. He was killed by Tristan on the mountain of Petrosa, for which Morgan cursed Tristan to die with his own lance. Morgan somehow obtained the lance used by Tristan to kill Huneson, poisoned it, and sent it to King Mark of Cornwall, who used it to kill Tristan. [*ProsTris, Tavola, Malory*]

HUNGARY [*Hungri(e)*]

The Vulgate *Merlin* tells us that Sagremor's father was the King of Hungary and Vlask. In *Claris et Laris*, it is ruled by King Ditas and then by King Saris. In Malory, it is listed as the home of Sir Urry, the knight healed by Lancelot. Hungary did not exist as a country until the late tenth century, when Stephen I became its first king. During the Arthurian period, it was made up of the old Roman provinces of Pannonia and Dacia. [*VulgMer, Arthour, Malory*]

HUNGERFORD [*Hongrefort*]

A castle in the Vulgate *Lancelot*, possibly the actual Hungerford in Berkshire. The Lady of Hungerford was the daughter of Count Alout of the Land of the Heather and the sister of Amide. When Alout died, his brother Gallidés tried to force the lady of Hungerford into a marriage with his seneschal. When she refused, Gallidés went to war with her and besieged Hungerford. Amide brought Sir Bors to champion the lady against Gallidés, and Bors was victorious. [*VulgLanc*]

HUNS

A collection of warlike Asiatic tribes that invaded eastern and central Europe in the fourth and fifth centuries. Geoffrey of Monmouth says that the Huns, led by Guanius, invaded Britain in the fifth century, during Maximus's absence, but were driven out by Gratian Municeps. They returned upon Gratian's death, and were finally defeated by Arthur's grandfather Constantine. [*GeoffHR*]

Hunting Knight

The alias used by the King of Gascony during a visit to Arthur's court. [*IrishL*]

Hunting Maiden [*Damoiselle Cacheresse*]

The alias adopted by NINIANE or NIMUE during her first visit to Arthur's court, when she was abducted by a knight and rescued by Pellinore. [*PostMer*]

Huon

Hero of *Huon de Bordeaux*, an early thirteenth century French Carolingian romance. Huon enjoyed the protection of Morgan le Fay. Oberon, the fairy king, gave Huon the realm of Faérie. Arthur, who had been living there since his "death," thought that the land was rightfully his. Arthur tried to seize it from Huon, but Oberon intervened and stopped him. [*Huon*]

Hurbise

A forest in which a dragon devoured Arnoullant the Fair, a companion of Segurant the Brown. [*ProsTris*]

Husdent [*Hiudan, Hodain, Hudenc, Idonia, Utant*]

Tristan's dog. In some texts, it is given to him by the daughter of King Faramon of France. Several sources maintain that the hound licked some of the love potion that bound Tristan and Isolde, making him unusually loyal to the lovers. When Tristan and Isolde were forced to flee from Mark into the forest of Morrois, Husdent followed them. Tristan then trained him not to bark so that he would not attract attention. When the lovers had to part again, Tristan gave Husdent to Isolde, and the hound later identified Tristan to Isolde when Tristan came to court disguised as a fool or insane. The dog died on top of the lovers' grave three days after they were buried. [*Beroul, Gottfried, FolieB, FolieO, ProsTris, Tavola, SirTris*]

Hutton

The castle owned by Bertilak of the High Desert, also called the Green Knight. Gawain lodged at Hutton while waiting for the day on which he was scheduled to fight the Green Knight at the Green Chapel. [*SirGawain, Grene*]

Hwyrddyddwg ("Late Bringer")

The horse belonging to Arthur's warrior Bwlch. [*Culhwch*]

Hygwydd

A servant of Arthur assigned the task of bearing the magical cauldron that Arthur seized from Diwrnach the Irishman. Hygwydd later accompanied Arthur's party to the cave of the Black Hag in the Valley of Distress. Hygwydd and his brother Cacamwri were the first warriors to enter the cave, and they were both mauled, stripped, and thrown out of the cave screaming by the Black Hag. [*Culhwch*]

Hyrcania [*Ertayne, Irritaine*]

An ancient Persian province on the Caspian sea, allied, according to the Alliterative *Morte Arthure*, to Lucius the Roman, Arthur's enemy. [*Allit, Malory*]

I

IACO

A knight at King Uther Pendragon's Urbano tournament. He was defeated by King Ban of Benoic. [*Tavola*]

IAEN

Father of Arthur's warriors Teregud, Sulyen, Bradwen, Moren, Siawn, and Caradawg. He came from Caer Dathal, and was related to Arthur through Uther. [*Culhwch*]

IAGO

According to Geoffrey of Monmouth, king of Britain in the seventh century BC. He was the nephew of King Sisillius. He was succeeded by Kinmarch, Sisillius's son. [*GeoffHR*]

IAGUVIUS [*Jaguz*]

Baron of Ballon under King Arthur. He fought and died against the Romans at the battle of Soissons. [*GeoffHR, Wace*]

IAPHINE

During a speech in Heinrich von dem Türlin's *Diu Crône*, Gawain refers to an episode in which he "avenged Lady Andeclis, whose lover was slain by Iaphine." [*Heinrich*]

IBARITUN

One of the lands ruled by King Malloas, a friend of Arthur's nephew Meleranz. [*PleierM*]

IBERT

The King of Sicily some time before Arthur. He discovered that his wife, Iblis, was having an affair with Duke Clinschor. In revenge, he had Clinschor castrated. [*Wolfram*]

IBLIS¹ [*Ibelis, Yblis*]

The daughter of the great and evil warrior Iweret. She lived with her father in the castle Dodone in the wood called Beforet. She fell in love with Lancelot after seeing him in a vision, but was distressed when she learned that Lancelot intended to combat Iweret. Despite his own love for Iblis, Lancelot engaged in the battle and won. He and Iblis were then married. A magical mantle brought to Arthur's court showed her to be completely true to Lancelot in both mind and body. She and Lancelot happily ruled Genewis and Dodone together and had three sons and a daughter. [*UlrichZ*]

IBLIS²

Wife of King Ibert of Sicily. She was loved by a duke named Clinschor. She rewarded Clinschor with a pavilion in which the two slept together. When Ibert discovered their affair, he had Clinschor castrated. [*Wolfram*]

ICELAND [*Yselond, Ysland*]

It was the ninth century before Iceland was settled by Norse explorers. It had not been discovered during the Arthurian period but, according to Geoffrey of Monmouth, Arthur conquered from King Malvasius. Layamon calls the conquered king Alcus, and says that Malvasius ruled it later. Warriors from Iceland assisted Arthur in the invasion of Gaul and in the Roman War. In *Meriadeuc*, the Queen of Iceland is the sweetheart of King Ris of Outre-Ombre, Arthur's enemy. Ris conquered nine kings in her honor and made a mantle for her out of their beards. She asked Ris to conquer Arthur for the final beard, but Ris was unsuccessful. The Queen's sister was the Lady of the Isles. In some romances, Iceland is confused with IRELAND. [*GeoffHR, Wace, Layamon*]

IDAIN OF LANDOC [*Ide, Ydain*]

An unattractive woman whose lover, Cardroain, championed her in a sparrowhawk tournament at Landoc. The sparrowhawk was to go to the most beautiful woman present, but Cardroain expected to win it for Idain through force of arms. Arthur's Sir Durmart, however, won the tournament. [*Durmart*]

IDDAWG

Son of Mynyo. As a warrior and messenger for King Arthur, Iddawg deliberately caused the Battle of Camlann between Arthur and Mordred when he delivered a peace message from Arthur to Mordred in rude and insulting tones. For this, he became known as "the Churn of Britain." After the fateful battle, he did penance in Scotland for his deeds. Rhonabwy met Iddawg in his epic dream, and Iddawg became his guide in the times of Arthur, seven hundred years before Rhonabwy's life. [*Dream*]

IDEUS

An Arthurian knight whose wife was proven unfaithful by an enchanted mantle. [*Mottuls*]

IDŒL

Father of Arthur's knight Johfreit. [*Wolfram*]

IDRES

A variation of YDER used by Malory, who calls him the king of Cornwall. [*Malory*]

IDUMEA

An ancient kingdom in southwest Asia, south of the Dead Sea. It was ruled by Serses in Arthur's time. Serses was an ally of the Roman Procurator Lucius, and brought Idumean soldiers to fight against Arthur in the Roman war. [*Wace*]

IDWALLO

According to Geoffrey of Monmouth, a king of Britain in the third or second century BC. He was the son of King Iugenius. Idwallo ascended to the throne after his cousin, King Enniaun, was deposed. He ruled with justice and was succeeded by his cousin Runno. [*GeoffHR*]

IELS

One of Arthur's vassals. He was the king of Galoes. [*HartmannE*]

IGANGSOL

During a speech in Heinrich von dem Türlin's *Diu Crône*, Gawain refers to an episode in which he "wrestled with the fierce Matleide at Igangsol." This adventure is not recounted in existing Arthurian literature. [*Heinrich*]

IGER

A prince present at the tournament of Sorgarda, which Gawain won. [*Heinrich*]

IGERNE [*Agyana, *Eigyr, Hierna, Igraine, Igrayne, Igern(a), Izerla, Izerna, Ugerne, Ygerne, Ygraine, Yguerne*]

King Arthur's mother. Uther, Arthur's father, fell in love with her when she and her husband, the Duke of Cornwall (variously called Gorlois, Hoel, and Tintagel) attended a feast at Uther's court. Igerne chastely rebuked Uther's advances and convinced her husband to return with her to Cornwall—an action that enraged Uther, prompting him to invade Cornwall and besiege the duke's castles. Merlin magically transformed Uther into the semblance of the duke, spiriting him into Tintagel castle so that he could spend the night with Igerne. Arthur was conceived on this occasion. Meanwhile, the duke was slain fighting Uther's men, and Uther swiftly married Igerne, who was confused about the identity of Arthur's father. Upon Arthur's birth, Merlin took him away to be raised in secret, and Igerne did not meet him until his coronation many years later.

Igerne first appears as EIGYR in the Welsh *Culhwch and Olwen*, in which she is the daughter of Amlawdd. In Welsh texts, she has a son named Gormant. Her seven brothers include Gwrvoddw, Llygadrudd Emys, and five warriors named Gweir. She also has a sister called Goleuddyd. The English *Arthour and Merlin* gives her three husbands before Uther: Harinan, Hoel, and Tintagel. With her various husbands, she had between one and five daughters—variously called Anna, Morgan le Fay, Morgause, Elaine, Blasine, Belisant, and Brimesent—who were Arthur's sisters or half-sisters.

According to Chrétien de Troyes, Igerne traveled to the land of Galloway after Uther's death—with all of her treasure—and constructed the castle called Canguin Rock. While everyone, including Arthur, thought she was dead, Igerne served as the ruler of the castle for many years. Gawain discovered her during his adventures there. Heinrich von dem Türlin tells a similar story, having Igerne marry an enchanter named Gansguoter and retire to his castle of Salie with her maiden daughters. In the Vulgate romances, she dies of unknown causes shortly before Uther Pendragon's death, or shortly after Arthur's coronation. Her counterpart in Wolfram's *Parzival* is named ARNIVE. [*Culhwch, GeoffHR, ChretienP, Heinrich, VulgMer, Arthour, Malory*]

IGNARO

A servant of the giant Orgoglio, who was killed by Arthur. [*Spenser*]

IGNAURES

A British knight who fought at the tournament at Noauz. [*ChretienL*]

IGRES

A land near Lancelot's castle of Joyous Guard, ruled by King Amoroldo of Ireland. [*Tavola*]

IGUEDON [*Engredan*]

A Saxon warrior killed by Sir Ulfin at the battle of Carhaix. [*VulgMer, Arthour*]

ILAMERT OF LANOEIR

In Heinrich von dem Türlin's *Diu Crône*, Gawain required a magic skein of thread to cross a river. This he obtained by defeating the brother of its owner, Lady Ilamert of Lanoier. [*Heinrich*]

ILAS

In a fragment of a twelfth-century French romance known as *Ilas et Solvas*, two companions named King Ilas of Ireland and King Solvas renounce their loyalty to Arthur and challenge him to combat. The result of these actions have not survived in the existing fragments. [*Ilas*]

ILE

A lady at Arthur's court who, with the other court ladies, failed a chastity test. [*Heinrich*]

ILET THE HARD-HANDED

A king in Arthur's service. [*Heinrich*]

ILINOT[1] [Elinot]

Arthur's son by Guinevere in Wolfram's *Parzival*. He loved the lady Florie of Kanadic and was killed in her service, causing Florie to die of sorrow. Wolfram may have borrowed him from Chrétien's LOHOLT. [*Wolfram, PleierG*]

ILINOT[2]

A prince who served Arthur's Sir Garel. [*PleierG*]

ILL-SPEAKING MAIDEN [*Demoiselle Mesdisant, Maledisant*]

A maiden who arrived at Camelot seeking a champion to avenge the death of a knight in the Straight of Sorelois. She was hoping to find Lancelot, but she reluctantly accepted Arthur's appointment of Sir Brunor the Black, or the Knight of the Ill-Fitting Coat, to the task. Throughout their journey to Sorelois, she insulted the poor knight, who proved himself lousy at jousting but superior at swordplay. Other knights witnessed her behavior toward Brunor and chastised her for being such a shrew. She later revealed that she truly loved Brunor, and that she had only scorned him in hope that he would abandon the dangerous adventure. Lancelot renamed her BIEN PENSANT. After the quest, Brunor married her and called her BEAU VIVANT. [*Malory*]

ILLANT

The Duke of Illant was one of Arthur's vassals. [*Heinrich*]

ILLBRINT

Great-grandson of Brutus and grandson of Albanact. It is unclear whether his father was Dombart or Embrunt. He joined his cousin, Guillant, in a failed attempt to subdue their cousin, King Brun of the Savage Realm. [*Palamedes*]

ILLES

The GRAIL CASTLE in Heinrich von dem Türlin's *Diu Crône*. Gawain traveled there with Kay, Calogrenant, and Lancelot to complete the Grail Quest by questioning the castle's inhabitants about its marvels. [*Heinrich*]

ILLESGALERON

A prince of Wales who joined Arthur's battle against the Saxons at Vambieres. He is found exclusively in the *Livre d'Artus*. His cousin, Guinganbresil, was an enemy of Gawain. When Illesgaleron did not show sufficient hatred for Gawain, Guinganbresil turned on him. There is a twelfth-century non-Arthurian French romance called *Illes et Galeron*. [*Livre*]

ILLTUD [*Illtyd*]

One of the several Welsh "saints" whose *Life* includes an encounter with Arthur. The son of Bicanus and Rieingulid, Illtud was apparently the cousin of Arthur, whom he served before founding a monastery and school in Glamorgan. St. Gildas was his pupil. As an unusual combination of warrior and monk, St. Illtud may anticipate GALAHAD. Nennius mentions Illtud and his holy altar, but does not connect them with Arthur. [*Nennius, SaintsI*]

ILLYRICUM

A land whose queen was abducted by the barbarian King Milocates. She was rescued from Milocates' island by Gawain, who returned her to the King of Illyricum. [*DeOrtu*]

IMAIN

Duke of Tulmein and brother-in-law of Enide's father Koralus. He held the annual sparrowhawk tournament in Tulmein, which was won by Sir Erec. [*HartmannE*]

IMANE OF BEAFONTANE

A lady abducted by Meleagant in Wolfram's *Parzival*. She was rescued by Karnahkarnanz of Ulterlec. Meleagant's usual victim is Guinevere. [*Wolfram*]

IMILOT

A wise old knight in whose care Garel (Arthur's king of Averre) placed his wife, Laudamie, when he went to war with King Ekunaver of Kanadic. [*PleierG*]

IMPENETRABLE FOREST

The roving grounds of Sir Tericam, an evil knight slain by Lancelot. [*VulgLanc*]

INAMANTE

A friend of Tristan. Tristan made him viceroy of Ponteferno, a castle he had conquered. Inamante presented Tristan with a horse named Giuriando. [*Tavola*]

INBALT [*Humbald, Imbaltus*]

The Gaulish duke of Armorica (Brittany) before his realm was conquered—and he was killed—by Maximus. Inbalt's land was given to Conan Meriadoc. [*GeoffHR*]

INCUBUS [*Ekupedes*]

An evil spirit or demon who was thought in medieval times to enter the bedchambers of sleeping women and to copulate with them as they slept. Such a demon supposedly impregnated the daughter of the King of South Wales, who later gave birth to Merlin. A "frozen demon" named Incubus appears in Thelwall's *The Fairy of the Lake* as the servant of Hela, Queen of Hell. A braggart in life, he fled when confronted with his first battle and died of apprehension. The Saxon Rowena called upon his help in her plan to seduce Arthur. [*GeoffHR, Wace, Thelwall*]

INDEG

One of Arthur's three mistresses in Welsh legend. She was the daughter of Garwy the Tall. [*Culhwch, Triads*]

INDIA [Inde]

The Welsh *Culhwch and Olwen* seems to suggest that Arthur once campaigned in India, for Arthur's chief gatekeeper Glewlyd says that he was once in "India the Great" and "India the Lesser." Wolfram, who calls the land TRIBALIBOT, says it was ruled by Queen Secundille, then by Perceval's half-brother Feirefiz, and then by Feirefiz's son Prester John. In the Vulgate *Merlin*, "Greater India" is ruled by King Lac, whose seneschal, Minoras, assisted Arthur in the battles against the Saxons. In the Alliterative *Morte Arthure* and Malory, the land is allied to the Roman emperor Lucius, and soldiers from India participate in the war against Arthur. A similar situation is found in *Claris et Laris*, in which the ruler is Geremie. In the Irish tale *Eachtra an Mhadra Mhaoil*, Gawain assists the Crop-Eared Dog, the son of the King of India, to regain human form. [*Culhwch, Wolfram, VulgMer, Claris, Allit, Malory, IrishD*]

INGAGEL

A Scottish forest where Perceval concluded a white stag hunt in Guillaume le Clerc's *Fergus*. [*Guillaume*]

INGLECELE

Home of the fairy Esclarmonde, mistress of Escanor the Handsome. It is probably ANGLESEY. [*Girart*]

INGELES

One of Arthur's knights. [*SyreGaw*]

INGLE

The baptismal name of FLOR DESIREE, a maiden rescued by Lancelot. [*Merveil*]

INGLEWOOD [Englewood, Ingleswood]

A forest south of Carlisle that was the site of adventures in Middle English Arthurian texts, including *The Awntyrs off Arthure at the Terne Wathelyne*, *The Avowing of King Arthur, Sir Gawain, Sir Kay, and Baldwin of Britain* and *The Wedding of Sir Gawen and Dame Ragnelle*. The forest is in the CALEDONIAN region. It was farmed and developed out of existence over the last 200 years. [*Awntyrs, Wedding, Avowing*]

INGLIART WITH THE SHORT EARS

A magnificent war horse from the Grail Castle of Munsalvæsche. It belonged to Gawain until it strayed away from him in the battle at Bearosche and was captured by Perceval, who retained ownership. [*Wolfram*]

INGRES

The king of Ingres came to Arthur's tournaments at the Hard Rock and the castle of Leverzep. [*Tavola*]

INGUSE OF BAHTARLIEZ

A lady whose medicine saved the life of Gawain after King Lähelin defeated him in a joust. [*Wolfram*]

INHOSPITABLE LAND SUSTAINED [*Terre Estrange Soustenue]

The lady of this land was loved by Guinebal, an uncle of Lancelot. In her service, Guinebal created the Magic Dance and a magic chessboard in the Forest of No Return. Guinebal also instructed the lady in the magical arts, which had been taught to him by Merlin. [*VulgMer*]

INOGEN

Merlin's daughter in Richard Hole's *Arthur*. She fled Britain with her father after Hengist's Saxon invasion. Arthur fell in love with her, saved her from rape by Hengist, and married her. [*Hole*]

INPRIPALENOT

A Knight of the Round Table. [*HartmannE*]

INSCRIBED STONE

A stone mentioned by Nennius. It lay in a field by the Gallic Sea and marked the site of Vortimer's third battle against Hengist's Saxons. [*Nennius*]

IONA

One of King Arthur's warriors in *Culhwch and Olwen*. According to the tale, Iona was king of France, although the title is also given to Paris and Gwilenhin in the same story. [*Culhwch*]

IONEKE

A knight in the service of Duke Cador of Cornwall. He fought for Arthur in the Roman War. [*Allit*]

IPOMIDON

A ruler from Babylon. His brother was named Pompeius. The brothers' ancestral city of Niniveh was seized by the Baruc of Baghdad. In response, Ipomidon and Pompeius invaded the Baruc's country, where they had to contend with Gahmuret, Perceval's father, who was serving the Baruc. In their second invasion, Ipomidon killed Gahmuret in combat. [*Wolfram*]

IPOTENTE

A land ruled in Arthur's time by King Grigorz. It was in the northern part of Britain. [*Wolfram*]

IRELAND [Erlandi, Irlaunde, Irlonde, Orlandeia, Yrland(e), Yrlond]

Ireland is often named as a kingdom subject to Arthur. Historically, Ireland was divided into a number of Celtic kingdoms during the Roman and Arthurian periods. The Romans never conquered Ireland, and Celtic culture continued to flourish in Ireland after the Saxons invaded Britain. There were no Irish "high kings" during the Arthurian period; the basis of the Irish political system was the independent *tuatha*, of which more than 100 existed, each with its own ruler. Nevertheless, various characters called the "King of Ireland" appear in Arthurian texts.

The early chronicles tend to portray the Irish as a people aligned with the barbarian Picts and Scots to oppose Arthur at the beginning of his reign. Geoffrey of Monmouth asserts that it was ruled by King Gilloman during the reign of Ambrosius. Gilloman was later killed by Uther, and Arthur conquered the island from Gilloman's successor Gillomaur.

In Irish and Welsh legend, Aedd (Áed) and his son Odgar were kings of the island, but they would have ruled some time before or after Arthur. Welsh legend typically has Ireland being invaded and plundered by the British; this occurs in *Branwen* and *Culhwch and Olwen*, and both invasions result in the capture of a magic cauldron. In *Culhwch*, Arthur and his party began their hunt for the boar Twrch Trwyth in Ireland. Twrch Trwyth had destroyed much of the island when the hunt commenced.

The Vulgate *Estoire del Saint Graal* names King Marahant as it's ruler in Joseph of Arimathea's time. Contemporary to Arthur, the Vulgate Cycle names its various kings as Thoas, Plarion, Sorengrieu, Rions, Mahaglant, Margan, and Yon. All but the last were Saxons, killed or defeated by Arthur at the beginning of his reign. In the Post-Vulgate, an unnamed King of Ireland, who is the brother of the King of Denmark, invades Britain and is slain by Arthur at the battle of the Humber. It should be noted here that French romances are often confused as to the location of Ireland; some of them seem to make the country part of Scotland, or otherwise contiguous to Britain.

In the Tristan legends, Ireland is the home of Isolde, whose father, called Gurmun or Anguish, is the king. Texts that integrate the Tristan saga with Arthur's history deal with the issue of Ireland's rulership uncomfortably. Malory, for instance, gives the kingdom to Anguish, Rions, and Marhalt at the same time.

Assorted romances give a wide variety of Irish rulers: Guivret in Hartmann's *Erec*, Cadiolant in the First Continuation of Chrétien's *Perceval*, Fenice in *Durmart le Gallois*, Gawain in Robert de Blois's *Beaudous*, Ilas in *Ilas et Solvas*, Caradoc in *Meriadoc*, Alfred in *Yder*, Cador and Elidus in *Claris et Laris*, and Angiron in Heinrich von dem Türlin's *Diu Crône*. The French tale called *Les Merveilles de Rigomer* is set in Ireland, described as a "strange land with broad and deep forests, marshes, and heaths," which render it wild and almost uninhabitable. In the Didot-*Perceval*, Arthur's final battle with Mordred is fought in Ireland. [*Culhwch, GeoffHR, Contin1, HartmannE, Yder, Gottfried, LancLac, VulgLanc, VulgEst, VulgMer, Durmart, PostMer, Merveil, Ilas, RobertBlo, Historia, Claris, Malory*]

IRENA

A maiden whose kingdom was attacked by a giant named Grantorto. Gloriana, the Fairy Queen, assigned the knight Artegall to free the kingdom. Artegall killed the giant and restored Irena to her lands. [*Spenser*]

IRION

A king whose daughter, Martha, married Tristan's son Ysaie. [*Ysaie*]

IRISH BRIDGE

One of the two bridges by which someone could enter Galehaut's land of Sorelois. The other was the North Wales Bridge. It is unclear why the bridge was called the "Irish Bridge"—it certainly could not have connected Sorelois to Ireland, although it was said to be exceedingly long. Parts of it went underwater. The description of it is reminiscent of the UNDERWATER BRIDGE of Chrétien's *Lancelot*. [*LancLac, VulgLanc*]

ÍRÓN

In the Norse *Tristrams Saga*, the Roman emperor who went to war with Arthur. He is called LUCIUS by most sources. [*TrisSaga*]

IRONSIDE

A Knight of the Round Table who first appears in the Middle English *Sir Gawain and the Carl of Carlisle*. The romance notes that he was famed as a giant and dragon slayer, that he owned a steed named Favelhand, and that his son, by the lady of Blancheland, was called "The Knyght of Armus Grene," perhaps referring to the Green Knight. He was called "Ironside" because he was always armed.

Ironside enters Malory's tale of Sir Gareth. Nicknamed the "Red Knight of the Red Lands," he laid siege to the Castle Perilous, ruled by the lady Lyones, in hopes of drawing Lancelot, Tristan, Gawain, or Lamorat into combat with him. Lyones's sister, Lynet, traveled to Camelot to find a knight to save the castle. Gareth, Gawain's brother, under the name "Beaumains," took the quest and accompanied Lynet to the Castle Perilous. He defeated many knights along the way and finally met Sir Ironside. The battle between them lasted an entire day from morning to night. Sir Ironside might have defeated Gareth, but Gareth beheld the face of the lovely Lyones in a castle window and doubled his strength. He overcame Ironside, who asked for mercy, explaining that he only had opposed Arthur's knights because he promised a lady to do so after her brother had been killed by either Lancelot or Gawain. Gareth spared his life, and Ironside went to Camelot to tell all of the deeds of Sir "Beaumains." He later served as carver at Gareth's wedding feast. [*SyreGaw, Carl, SirLamb, Malory*]

IROT

A king. He was the father of King Gramoflanz by the sister of King Brandelidelin. Gramoflanz inherited Irot's lands when Irot was slain by Gawain's father, King Lot. [*Wolfram*]

ISABON

Father of Arthur's Sir Galopamur. [*HartmannE*]

ISAIAH [*Lysays, Ysaïes*]

A king descended from the first Nascien. His father was Alain the Large and his son was called Jonah. His descendants included Lancelot, Bors, and Galahad. [*VulgQuest, VulgEst, Malory*]

ISAIAS

A Knight of the Round Table who participated in the Grail Quest. [*PostQuest*]

ISAJES

Uther Pendragon's chief Marshal. After his death, his son Maurin was appointed to the office. [*Wolfram*]

ISAZANZ

During a speech in Heinrich von dem Türlin's *Diu Crône*, Gawain refers to an episode in which he "helped the lovely maiden Isazanz to escape from Anfroihin when he tried to abduct her." [*Heinrich*]

ISCAMBRINELLO

A king who came to Uther Pendragon's tournament at Urbano. He was defeated by Sir Segurant the Brown. [*Tavola*]

ISEL OF CLAMEROI

A lady at Arthur's court who failed a chastity test. [*Heinrich*]

ISENHART

A Saracen lord from the Middle East or Africa who loved Belacane, Queen of Zazamanc. She did not reciprocate his love, and he died in a battle against one of her princes. In revenge, Isenhart's allies and friends—led by his cousin Vridebrant of Scotland—attacked and besieged Belacane's kingdom. Belacane was saved by Perceval's father Gahmuret, who assumed the throne of Isenhart's former kingdoms. Isenhart's father's name was Tankanis. [*Wolfram*]

ISENLAND

According to Der Pleier, a land allied to Arthur. [*PleierT*]

ISETERRE [*Iserterre*]

In Wolfram's *Parzival* the land of King Clamadeu, foe of Condwiramurs of Brobarz. Clamadeu was forced to abandon Iseterre when he was defeated by Perceval and sent to Arthur's court for his penance. In the Pleier's *Garel*, Iseterre is ruled by King Angenis. [*Wolfram, PleierG*]

ISLAND OF BATTLES

The location where Arthur killed Frollo according to the Vulgate *Lancelot*. In the chronicles, this fight occurs outside Paris. [*VulgLanc*]

ISLAND OF BEAUTIFUL MAIDENS [*Ile as Puceles Beles*]

An island ruled by Queen Alemandine. Its capital was the White City. The island was terrorized by a monster that swallowed the beautiful maidens, but Arthur's Sir Floriant killed it. [*Floriant*]

ISLAND OF FAIRIES [*Isle aux Phees*]

The Lady of the Island of Fairies, possibly identical to the Queen of FAIRY ISLE, was the sister of Pellinore. Enraged at her brother's murder by Gawain, she made all knights who visited the island swear to kill Gawain. [*Palamedes*]

ISLAND OF GLASS [*Isle de Voirre*]

An otherworldly island, ruled in Welsh legend by King Maelwys, who abducted Guinevere. Chrétien de Troyes names its ruler as Baron Moloas, which is probably a variation of Maelwys. According to Chrétien, the Island of Glass never had storms, was devoid of toads and snakes, and always had a perfect temperature. This description evokes an image similar to the Isle of AVALON, and it therefore supports the identification of Avalon with GLASTONBURY, which some writers though was once called the Island of Glass. In the Vulgate *Lancelot*, the Island of Glass is the home of Sir Mador the Black. [*Dialogue, ChretienE, VulgLanc*]

ISLAND OF HONEY

An early name of Britain, according to Welsh legend. It had previously been called Myrddin's Precinct. It was later conquered by Prydein son of Aedd, and became known as Prydein, or Britain. [*Triads*]

ISLAND OF JOY [*Isle de Joie*]

An island in King Pelles' realm, to which Lancelot retired from the world in shame after enduring five years of insanity. Calling himself the Wicked Knight (*Chevalier Malfait*), he lived in the Tower of Giants, the Castle Blank, or Bliant's Castle, and jousted with any knight that happened along. In some romances, he co-habitates with Elaine of Corbenic. It was called the Island of Joy because Lancelot hung his shield from a tree outside the castle, and maidens sang and danced around it daily. After ten years, Lancelot was coaxed back to Arthur's court by Hector and Perceval. Following his departure, the Island of Joy was laid waste and was renamed the DRY ISLAND. [*VulgLanc, ProsTris, PostMer*]

ISLAND OF MARVELS[1] [*Isle de Merveilles*]

An enchanted island which held, among other things, Merlin's Bed. Mordred was once imprisoned in a tower there, but was rescued by Gawain. [*VulgLanc*]

ISLAND OF MARVELS[2]

An alternate name for MERLIN'S ISLAND. [*PostMer*]

ISLAND OF MAIDENS [Isle of Virgins]

In Chrétien's *Yvain* and the Welsh *Owain*, a king who is plagued by a pledge to send thirty maidens a year to the Castle of the Most Ill Adventure, where they were imprisoned. Yvain eventually rescued them. In the medieval poem *Ywain and Gawain*, this location is changed to MAIDENLAND; the Norse *Ivens Saga* names the King of the Isle of Maidens as REINION. [*ChretienY*, *Owain*]

ISLAND OF NEED [*Isle Souffroitose*]

An island lacking anything pleasant. Perceval was warned that kings of the ISLAND OF PLENTY who failed to prove their worth were banished to the Island of Need. [*Perlesvaus*]

ISLAND OF PLENTY [*Isle Plenteürose*]

An otherworldly island abundant in riches, food, and pleasantness. It tolerated no unworthy kings, and dispatched inadequate rulers to the ISLAND OF NEED. *Perlesvaus* suggests that Perceval became king of the Island of Plenty at the consummation of his adventures. [*Perlesvaus*]

ISLAND OF THE ELEPHANTS

The home of the demonic Knight of the Burning Dragon, who was slain by Perceval. Its chief castle was the Castle of Giants. [*Perlesvaus*]

ISLAND OF THE FOUNTAIN

Location of the Fountain of Marvels, where Tristan killed Pharant. [*ProsTris*]

ISLAND OF THE GATE

The King of the Island of the Gate was the father of one of Arthur's Irish knights. The Irish knight slept with his mother and sister, slew his father, murdered the rest of his family, and then fell burning from a tower at Camelot. His suicide was one of the marvels surrounding Galahad's arrival at court. [*PostQuest*]

ISLAND OF TWO BROTHERS

Named after the brothers Assar and Helyas, who fled to the island from Cornwall after King Mark raped their sister. [*ProsTris*]

ISLAND THAT FLOATS [*Ille Qui Flote*]

An island ruled by Queen Lingrenote, a sorceress. Her castle was called the Castle Without a Name. Her lover, Guengasouain, was Gawain's enemy. [*Vengeance*]

ISLAND WITHOUT A NAME [*Ile sans Nom*]

An enchanted island whose resident, a sorceress, bewitched unsuspecting knights to defend the island against all visitors. Gawain, who came to the island seeking the Sword with the Strange Hangings, was one of her victims.

Trapped on the island, he was forced to fight his friend, Sir Meraugis. He was finally able to escape by feigning death. [*Raoul*]

ISOLDE[1] [*Essyltt, Isalde, Isal(d)t, Isall, Isaot(t)a, Iseo, Iseu(l)t, Iseus, Ísodd, Ísól, Isol(d)t, Ísönd, Ísot, Isotta, Isoud(e), Ixolta, Izonda, Izota, Yseu(l)t(e), Ysodd, Yso(l)t, Ysonde]

The wife of King Mark of Cornwall and tragic lover of Tristan, often called "Isolde the Beautiful" or "Isolde the Blonde" to distinguish her from ISOLDE OF THE WHITE HANDS. Although married to Mark, she engaged in an adulterous affair with Tristan because the two lovers were unable to resist the affects of a love potion.

An early form of her name, *Esseylt*, is found in a list of ladies in the Welsh tale *Culhwch and Olwen*, and her character may be Celtic in origin. Her counterpart in Irish folklore is called Gráinne. The origins of the Tristan and Isolde legend is covered under the entry for TRISTAN.

The daughter of the King of Ireland (either Anguish or Gurmun), she first met Tristan when he arrived in Ireland incognito to be healed of a wound given by Isolde's uncle or brother, Morholt, whom Tristan slew in a combat between Ireland and Cornwall. The legends disagree as to the extent of Tristan and Isolde's attraction prior to the consumption of the potion: in Gottfried's version, for instance, she hates Tristan for slaying her uncle, while in the Prose *Tristan*, they both feel an initial attraction.

Tristan made his second visit to Ireland to bring Isolde back to Cornwall to marry King Mark, Tristan's uncle. On their voyage from Ireland to Cornwall, Tristan and Isolde accidentally drank a love potion that was intended for Isolde and Mark and had been entrusted to Isolde's servant Brangain. They fell helplessly in love and began their affair. On her wedding night, Isolde substituted Brangain in Mark's bed in order to hide her loss of virginity. She later tried to have Brangain killed to hide the secret, but the attempt failed and she and Brangain were able to reconcile. (Malory omits this episode.)

King Mark suspected the two lovers, having received intelligence from his vassals, but through a number of tricks and ruses, the lovers managed to instill in the king a sense of doubt as to their guilt, which created an uncomfortable situation at court but managed to keep them together. Though Mark often banished them or sentenced them, he was generally persuaded to receive Isolde as his queen again before long.

In the traditional version of the story, Tristan, having been banished from Mark's court, marries another woman named Isolde of the White Hands. He receives a mortal wound and sends for Isolde of Cornwall to heal him. Isolde sails to Brittany, but Tristan's wife, jealous of their love, tells him that Isolde is not coming, and Tristan dies. Isolde perishes of sorrow upon finding him.

In the revised version of the legend, found in the Prose *Tristan* and Malory, she eventually flees from Mark's court and lives with Tristan in Joyous Guard, Lancelot's castle, until Tristan is slain by Mark. As in the original tale, she dies on top of his body and is buried in the same grave.

In the Prose *Tristan*, Isolde is also loved by Palamedes the Saracen, who abducts Brangain to get close to her. Other than Palamedes, competing suitors included Kahedins, who died for her love, Dragan, who was killed by Tristan, and the King with a Hundred Knights. The prose cycles say that she was a close friend of Queen Guinevere, whose situation was similar to Isolde's. [*MarieC, Thomas, Beroul, Eilhart, FolieO, FolieB, Gottfried, UlrichT, TrisSaga, ProsTris, PostQuest, PostMort, SirTris, Tavola, SagaTI, Malory, TennIK*]

ISOLDE[2]

In Gottfried's *Tristan*, the Queen of Ireland, wife of King Gurmun of Ireland, and mother to Tristan's lover Isolde. She cleverly convinced her husband to make peace with Cornwall and to give their daughter to King Mark. She concocted the fateful potion, intended for Mark and Isolde, which bound Tristan and Isolde in love. In most other versions, her character is unnamed. [*Gottfried*]

ISOLDE[3]

God-daughter of Tristan. She was the daughter of Genes, the seafarer who brought Isolde of Cornwall to the mortally wounded Tristan's bedside. Isolde told Isolde of the White Hands that Isolde of Cornwall was coming, which sparked the jealousy that led to Tristan's premature death. [*ProsTris*]

ISOLDE[4]

The daughter of Tristan and Isolde in the Italian *I Due Tristani*. She was born along with Tristan the Younger during Tristan and Isolde's sojourn at the Castle of Tears. Raised by foster-parents, she grew into a beauty. Palamedes, who had loved her mother, tried to abduct her and was slain by Palante, Tristan's cousin, in the process. She later married King Juan of Castille, whom her brother served. [*DueTris*]

ISOLDE[5] OF THE WHITE HANDS

Tristan's wife. He married her as a substitute for Isolde of Cornwall, Mark's wife. Her home country was Brittany, and her father—alternately Havelin, Jovelin, Gilierchino, or Hoel—is usually said to have been embroiled in some kind of war or insurrection, from which he was rescued by Tristan. Tristan, despondent over his banishment from Mark's court and his inability to possess the other Isolde, re-targeted his love to this Isolde, prompted by both her beauty and her name. He came to his senses on their wedding night and declined to consummate their relationship, telling Isolde (in some versions) that he was castrated. Her brother Kahedins became a loyal companion of Tristan. Gottfried calls her mother Karsie. She had another brother named Ruvalen. In the Prose *Tristan*, she accompanies her husband to an adventure on the Island of Servitude. In the legends, Tristan at best treats her indifferently, and often treats her cruelly.

In the traditional story, Isolde of the White Hands genuinely loves Tristan but she becomes enraged when she discovers his love for the other Isolde. When Tristan received a poisoned wound and sent for Mark's wife Isolde to cure him, Isolde of the White Hands exacted her revenged by reporting to Tristan that the returning ship bore black sails—which signified the other Isolde was not on board—when it actually flew white sails—signifying that she was in fact on the ship. Tristan died in distress. In the Prose versions, however, this episode is excluded and Isolde of the White Hands simply disappears from the story, or perishes from sorrow, when Tristan leaves Brittany to return to Cornwall. [*Thomas, Eilhart, Gottfried, ProsTris, Tavola, Malory, TennIK*]

ISOLDE[6] THE DARK

Tristan's wife in the Icelandic *Saga af Tristan ok Ísodd*, essentially the same character as ISOLDE OF THE WHITE HANDS. The sister of Earls Sigurðr and Hríngr of Spain, she was offered to Tristan when he conquered the kingdom. They had a son named Kanelgras who eventually became king of England. Like Isolde of the White Hands in the traditional legend, Isolde the Dark was jealous of Tristan's love for her namesake in England. Tristan was eventually wounded in combat, and he sent to England for the other Isolde (an experienced healer), telling the shipmaster to fly white sails during the return voyage if she was on board, and black sails if she was not. Isolde the Dark, seeing the ship returning with white sails, lied to Tristan and said they were black. Tristan died immediately from sorrow. [*SagaTI, TrisKv*]

ISSOUDUN [*Dun-Issout, Esordes*]

A castle in King Claudas's lands, formerly called simply DUN, but renamed in honor of Issout, its castellan. [*VulgLanc*]

ISSOUT [*Essent*]

Son of Patrice. A vassal of King Claudas, Issout became the lord of the Castle Dun, which was renamed Issoudun in his honor. [*VulgLanc*]

ITARC [*Irtac*]

The King of Turkey who was subject to Rome. The Roman Emperor Lucius Hiberius summoned Itarc to fight in the war against Arthur. [*Wace, Layamon*]

ITHER

The King of Cucumerland or Gaheviez. He is first mentioned by Hartmann von Aue as one of Arthur's knights. In Wolfram von Eschenbach, he takes on the role of the RED KNIGHT from Chrétien's *Perceval*: Once the squire of Perceval's uncle Trevrizent, he became a noble Knight of the Round Table. He was a cousin of both Arthur and Perceval, and he was the lover of Perceval's aunt Lamiere.

Ither went before Arthur to claim his inherited lands, but he accidentally offended Arthur by spilling some wine on Guinevere (in contrast to Chrétien's Red Knight, with whom the offense is deliberate). While waiting outside Arthur's court for Arthur to send a knight to avenge the deed, the young Perceval, on his way to Arthur's court, encountered him. Perceval admired his red armor and, once he was in the presence of Arthur, asked for it. Kay sarcastically told Perceval to go ahead and take the armor. When Perceval went back outside and demanded the armor, and Ither refused, Perceval hurled a well-aimed javelin through Ither's visor, killing him. Perceval then took the armor, as well as Ither's sword, and became the new "Red Knight." Later, when Perceval had become more mature and knowledgeable, and after several people rebuked him for it, Perceval regretted the killing of such a skilled warrior. [*HartmannE, Wolfram*]

ITOLAC

A land ruled in Arthur's time by King Onipriz. The powerful knight Florant also came from the country. [*Wolfram*]

ITONJE [*Itoni*]

Daughter of Lot and Sangive in Wolfram's *Parzival*. She was the daughter of Lot and Sangive, and the youngest sister of Gawain, Beacurs, Soredamor, and Cundrie. She was trapped in the Castle of Marvels under the magic of the sorcerer Clinschor until freed by Gawain. Through correspondence—via her servant Bene—she fell in love with King Gramoflanz, but was distressed to find that Gawain and Gramoflanz were scheduled to fight a mortal duel. Through a collaboration of Itonje, Bene, Arthur, and Brandelidelin, the fight was called off and Itonje and Gramoflanz were happily married. [*Wolfram, PleierM*]

ITUREA

A land ruled by Serses, an ally of Lucius the Roman. [*GeoffHR, Layamon*]

IUGENIUS

A son of King Morvid of Britain. He joined his brother Peredur in deposing his elder brother, King Elidur. Iugenius became king of the southern half of Britain. He died after seven years and was succeeded by Peredur. Iugenius's son, Idwallo, eventually became king himself. [*GeoffHR*]

IUSTIG

Son of Caw, one of twenty brothers, and one of Arthur's warriors. [*Culhwch*]

IVAIN

A leper from the city of Lantayn in Cornwall. He attended what was to be Isolde's burning at the stake for her affair with Tristan. He convinced Mark that a better punishment for Isolde would be to turn her over to him and the other lepers. Mark agreed and gave Isolde to the lepers. Tristan showed up and beat them away before they could take advantage of her. [*Beroul*]

IVENANT [*Ivenans*]

A king with whom Yder lodged at the beginning of his adventures. Ivenant agreed to knight Yder if the young man could refuse his wife's advances. Yder succeeded and Ivenant dubbed him. [*Yder*]

IVOINE

A variation of MAINE, Arthur's slain uncle.

IVOIRE

Sister of King Ban of Benoic. She married King Constantine of Britain, Arthur's grandfather. Her first son was Ivoine or Maine. She died giving birth to her twin sons Uther and Pendragon. [*Butor*]

IVOR

A Welsh huntsman who served King Caradoc of Wales. When Caradoc was slain by his brother, Griffin, Ivor became the foster-father of Caradoc's children, Meriadoc and Orwen. He saved their lives when Griffin plotted to kill them. Ivor, the children, and his wife Morwen went into hiding in the forest of Fleventan. In time, Meriadoc was kidnapped by Kay, and Orwen was taken by King Urien of Scotland, but Ivor was reunited with them at Arthur's court. [*Historia*]

IWELL [*Iwill*]

A knight in Arthur's service. [*Golagros*]

IWERET

Called the best knight in the world in Ulrich's *Lanzelet*, Iweret lived in the castle of Dodone in the forest of Beforet. He stole the lands of Mabuz, the son of the fairy queen who raised Lancelot, and the queen thus ordained that Lancelot would have to defeat Iweret before Lancelot could find out his own name. At a battle in Beforet, Lancelot killed Iweret, and was suitably rewarded—both with his name and with Iweret's daughter Iblis. Various suggestions have linked Iweret with *Ywerit*, the father of Bran the Blessed in one Welsh text; *Y Werydd*, which is Welsh for "the ocean"; and GUIVRET, a dwarf king in Chrétien de Troyes's *Erec*. [*UlrichZ*]

J

JACK THE GIANT KILLER

A popular fairy-tale hero whose story was probably first developed in the Elizabethan age, though it has only reached us in complete form from publications in the eighteenth century. It was said that Jack was born in Cornwall, the son of a farmer, during the reign of King Arthur. Cornwall was, at the time, terrorized by a giant who lived on a mountaintop. Hearing that anyone who slew the giant would have all his treasures as a reward, Jack dug a pit for the monster and buried a pick-axe it its head when it tumbled in. Word of his accomplishment spread, and he was commissioned to slay a number of other giants, which he always accomplished through wit, skill, and trickery. Jack eventually fell in to the company of Arthur's son, saved him from a devil, visited Arthur's court, and, for his bravery, was appointed to the Round Table. Thereafter, Jack sent the heads of all the giants he killed to the King Arthur. Eventually, Jack married the daughter of a duke, retired to a house built for him by Arthur, and lived happily ever after (Opie, 47–65).

JACOB OF ESTRIGUEL

A knight who fought on the side of King Mark of Cornwall during Mark's tournament at the city of Lancien. [*Contin4*]

JAFFA [*Jaffe*]

A port in Israel, named in the Alliterative *Morte Arthure* as the home of some of the pagans in the Roman army defeated by Arthur. According to the Middle English *Sir Degrevant*, Arthur's knight Degrevant was slain there during a Crusade. [*Allit*, *SirDeg*]

JAIDONS

An Arthurian knight who joined Gawain's quest to conquer Rigomer castle. [*Merveil*]

JAKOBSLAND

Home of Tristan the Stranger, who was deposed by seven wicked brothers. Tristan the Stranger sought out his famous namesake, and the two were able to re-conquer the land. [*SagaTI*]

JANDREE

A pagan princess who was the sister of King Madaglan of Oriande. Madaglan suggested that Arthur take Jandree as his queen after Guinevere's untimely death. Jandree loved Arthur but despised his religion; Arthur likewise balked at the thought of marrying a heathen. Because of these religious differences, the match never took place. After her brother died, and after Perceval began to destroy paganism in her lands, Jandree began to question her own faith. She received a holy vision and subsequently converted to Christianity, taking the baptismal name SALUBRE. She lived out the rest of her days in penitence and died in a hermitage. [*Perlesvaus*]

JANDUZ OF LANN

A lady at Arthur's court who failed a chastity test. [*Heinrich*]

JANFRÜEGE

A castle ruled by the mighty warrior Laamorz. The castle had the power to render any knight who entered helpless to Laamorz's will. Gawain was led there through the deception of a malevolent goddess named Giramphiel, but advice given by Lady Fortune allowed Gawain to avoid the enchantment and to defeat Laamorz in single combat. [*Heinrich*]

JANFUSE

An African kingdom ruled in Arthur's time by Queen Ekuba, a lover of Perceval's brother Feirefiz. Later, through Feirefiz's appointment or through some other means, Count Fristines became the ruler of the land. [*Wolfram*]

JANPHIE

Lancelot's sweetheart in Heinrich von dem Türlin's *Diu Crône*. With the other ladies at Arthur's court, she failed a chastity test. [*Heinrich*]

JANPHIS

The kingdom ruled by Guiromelant, Gawain's brother-in-law. [*Heinrich*]

JAPHITE

The faithful and devoted wife of the evil King Roaz of Glois. She was a beautiful Asian woman. When Wigalois (Gawain's son) killed her husband, she died from sorrow. Her brothers, Zaradech and Panschavar, came from Asia to retrieve her body, and they became Wigalois's companions. [*Wirnt*]

JARE WITH THE GOLDEN HAIR

In *Diu Crône*, a lady at Arthur's court who, with all the other ladies, failed a chastity test. Her sister was named Amerclie. [*Heinrich*]

JASCAPHIN OF ORCAINE

Father of Gawain and Clarissant in Heinrich von dem Türlin's *Diu Crône*. His wife was Queen Morcades (Morgause). When King Jascaphin died, his brother banished Morcades from Orcaine. Gawain's father is usually named as LOT. [*Heinrich*]

JAUFRÉ

One of Arthur's knights, perhaps identical to GIRFLET, who avenged a wrong done against Arthur by the evil knight Taulat. In the course of this adventure, he fell in love with Lady Brunissen of the Castle Monbrun—who had been oppressed by Taulat—and married her. Another adventure took him through an enchanted fountain to the fairyland of Gibel, where he killed a monster called Felons of Albarua. [*Jaufre*]

JECOINE OF THE CLEARING

A loyal knight who served King Evalach (Mordrains) of Sarras in the war against King Tholomer of Babylonia. [*VulgEst*]

JECONIAS

A Knight of the Round Table whom Yvain, his cousin, appointed as the seneschal of Vambieres. He joined Arthur's war agains the Saxons. [*Livre*]

JEMSETIR

The land that Tristan, calling himself "Pro," claimed as his homeland when he first arrived in Ireland. He knew Ireland and Cornwall were at war and he could thus not claim to be from Cornwall. [*Eilhart*]

JENEPHUS OF ANGUS

A duke in Arthur's service. [*Heinrich*]

JENOVER OF BEUMONT

One of Arthur's noblemen. [*Heinrich*]

JENTANEON

A nobleman in Arthur's service. His brothers were Earl Gorgun of Flandrisborg and Garse. [*Erex*]

JERAPHIN

A land next to the Red Sea ruled by King Rial. It was seized by the evil King Roaz of Glois. When Wigalois (Gawain's son) killed Roaz, he won the rights to the kingdom, and he returned it to Rial. [*Wirnt*]

JERNEGANZ OF JEROPLIS

A duke who served Perceval's brother, Feirefiz. [*Wolfram*]

JERNIS OF RYL

A count who served Arthur. His daughter, Ampflise, was a Grail Maiden. [*HartmannE, Wolfram*]

JERUSALEM

As an extension of its biblical role, Jerusalem is the setting for the early Grail history, including the origins of the Grail, the adventures and trials of Joseph of Arimathea, the Roman Emperor Vespasian's campaign to avenge Christ's death, and, eventually, Joseph's departure for western lands. Christians from Jerusalem followed Joseph of Arimathea and populated Britain.

In the Vulgate *Merlin*, Merlin visits Jerusalem and accurately depicts the Saracen King Flualis's defeat at the hands of Christians, followed by his own conversion to Christianity. In *De Ortu Waluuanii*, Jerusalem serves as the site of Gawain's first triumph: the city became the object of a dispute between Rome and Persia, and it was ruled that the matter would be decided by a single combat. The Persians put forth their best warrior, Gormundus, while the Emperor of Rome sent the young and untried Gawain. After a three-day battle, Gawain killed Gormundus and settled the conflict in Rome's favor.

Jerusalem is one of the many cities and lands that Arthur conquers in Jean D'Outremeuse's *Ly Myreur des Histors*. [*VulgMer, VulgEst, DeOrtu, Jean*]

JESCHUTE

Daughter of King Lac and sister of Erec in Wolfram's *Parzival*. She married Duke Orilus of Lalander. A young Perceval visited her pavilion in the forest of Brizljan. Misinterpreting advice given to him by his mother, he kissed her and took one of her rings. When Orilus came home and found out Perceval had been there, he ignored his wife's protests and accused her of adultery. He forced her to embark on a grueling ride with him, without allowing her to change her clothes or her mount for months. When they finally encountered Perceval again, Perceval defeated Orilus in a duel and forced him to reconcile with his wife. The same character appears in Chrétien's *Perceval* but is unnamed. [*Wolfram*]

JESMELADANT

A knight who served Arthur in the wars against King Rions. [*VulgMer*]

JETAKRANC OF GAMPFASSACHE

An infidel count who served Perceval's half-brother Feirefiz. His land was known for its fine fabrics. [*Wolfram*]

JOACHIM

A duke of Manaheim whom Erec saved after he had been kidnapped by seven robbers. Joachim's brothers, Juben, Perant, and Malcheus, were also abducted and freed. Erec sent them to Arthur's court to relate the adventure. [*Erex*]

JOAN GO-TOO'T [*Jone*]

Merlin's mother in the Elizabethan play *The Birth of Merlin*. She was impregnated by the Devil, who came to her in human form. She was convinced that the father was a nobleman at Aurelius Ambrosius's court until the Devil revealed himself again to her. Her brother was named Clown. [*Birth*]

JOENE

Wife of King Cichoriades of Cornwall. Her husband locked her up in a tower because she was adulterous. Joene's lover appeared at the foot of the tower, and Cichoriades started climbing down the tower from a rope in order to fight with him. The crafty Joene cut the rope from the top, and her husband fell to his death. With her lover, she fled to North Wales. Joene's father was King Gonosor of Ireland and her sister was Queen Gloriande of Lyonesse. [*ProsTris*]

JOFLANZE

A dueling ground where Gawain and King Gramoflanz agreed to fight a duel. The meadow lay between the Sabins and Poynzaclins rivers near the city of Roche Sabins. Perceval and Gawain, and then Perceval and Gramoflanz, fought here, but the duel between Gramoflanz and Gawain was called off through the intervention of Arthur. [*Wolfram*]

JOHENIS

During a speech Heinrich von dem Türlin's *Diu Crône*, Gawain talks of an episode in which he "defeated twenty knights in freeing Johenis from the dungeon." This episode is not found in existing Arthurian texts. [*Heinrich*]

JOHFRIT [*Joferit, Jofreit*]

Lord of Liez, son of Idœl, and maternal relative of Arthur. Johfrit encountered Lancelot shortly after Lancelot arrived in the world of men from the enchanted island of his upbringing. Lancelot was inexperienced in horseback riding and was faring rather poorly. Johfrit met and befriended him, and showed him the proper way to use the reins. He gave lodging to Lancelot at his castle, and his wife sponsored a tournament in which Lancelot participated. His name is probably a variation of JAUFRE or GIRFLET, who, according to R. S. Loomis, comes from the Welsh Gilfaethwy. Interestingly, as Loomis points out, Welsh tradition has Gilfaethwy or his brother Gwydion teaching Lleu how to ride a horse. (Lleu may be a literary precursor of Lancelot.) [*UlrichZ, Wolfram*]

JOHN[1]

Servant of the Greek knight Cliges. John built the special tomb in which Cliges' love, Empress Fenice, was buried after she faked her own death. The tomb was designed to keep Fenice alive until Cliges could excavate her. John then gave Cliges and Fenice asylum in his tower. Later, John was captured by Cliges's uncle (and Fenice's husband) Alis, after Alis learned of the trick. John protested his innocence, saying that he had only been doing the bidding of his master. Alis agreed and pardoned him. [*ChretienC*]

JOHN[2] THE BAPTIST [*Jehan*]

The biblical priest who baptized Jesus Christ and was beheaded by Herod. The sword used in this decapitation is identified with the Grail Sword in *Perlesvaus*. [*Perlesvaus*]

JOLI

A page who served Blanchandine, a princess who married Gawain. [*Floriant*]

JOLIES OF TINTAGEL

A knight who fought on the side of King Mark of Cornwall during Mark's tournament at the city of Lancien. [*Contin4*]

JOLÏETE

A maidservant of Bloiesine, Gawain's lover. [*Contin4*]

JOLYAN [*Jubaunce*]

A Genoese giant who fought against Arthur's forces in the Roman War. He served the Duke of Lorraine. In battle, he slew Arthur's Sir Gerard. [*Allit, Malory*]

JON

A nephew of Arthur and brother of Howe. Jon and Howe accompanied Sir Launfal when Launfal fled to Caerleon to escape Guinevere's disfavor. When Launfal fell into poverty and depravity in Caerleon, Jon and Howe returned to Arthur's court. [*ChestreLvl*]

JONAH [*Jona(an)s*]

An ancestor of Lancelot and Galahad, descended from Joseph of Arimathea. His father was named Isaiah, and his son, Lancelot, was Sir Lancelot of the Lake's grandfather. He was a noble and valiant king. He married the daughter of King Maronel of Gaul, inherited the kingdom, and established his posterity in France. [*VulgQuest, VulgEst, Malory*]

JONAP [*Ionap(es)*]

A Saxon giant who joined King Rions' invasion of Carmelide. Arthur wounded him at the battle of Aneblayse. [*VulgMer, Arthour*]

JONAS[1]

A hermit priest encountered by Perceval in a forest. His companion was named Alecys. [*Perlesvaus*]

JONAS[2]

King of Tiberias and ally of Emperor Filimenis of Constantinople, Floriant's father. [*Floriant*]

JONATHAL [*Ionas, Jonathan, Jonathas*]

Earl of Dorset or Dorchester under King Arthur. He fought for Arthur in the Roman War and led half a legion of warriors at Soissons. [*GeoffHR, Wace, Layamon, Allit*]

JORAM[1]

A wise man and sage who served Vortigern. When Vortigern was having problems building his fortress at Snowden, it was Joram who advised him to sprinkle the foundation with the blood of a child with no father. This led to the arrival of Merlin, who humiliated Joram by showing Vortigern the real reason for the fortress's failure. [*Layamon*]

JORAM[2]

The King of Syria. He arrived at Arthur's court at Caridoel and offered Guinevere a magical belt. When Guinevere refused the gift, Joram challenged all of Arthur's knights. Through the powers of the belt, he defeated all of the Knights of the Round Table in turn. Gawain was the last to fall. Joram took Gawain prisoner and led him back to Syria. There, Gawain married Joram's niece, Florie, and their union produced Wigalois. [*Wirnt*]

JORANS LI FEBLES

The Irish champion of Rigomer castle, also known as the Knight of the Triple Arms. He guarded a heath at the entrance to Rigomer, and was defeated by both Lancelot and Gawain during their attempts to conquer the castle. [*Merveil*]

JORANZ OF BELRAPEIRE

A nobleman in Arthur's service. [*Heinrich*]

JORAPHAS

A castle in the country of Korntin. It was ruled by Count Moral and Countess Beleare. Wigalois (Gawain's son) recovered at Joraphas after defeating a dragon named Pfetan, and before fighting the evil King Roaz of Glois. [*Wirnt*]

JORDAIN

Son of the King of Spain, killed by Gawain or Bedivere in the Roman War. [*Didot*]

JORDAN [*Iordains, Iurdains, Jordanus*]

Chamberlain of Gorlois, the Duke of Cornwall. Merlin magically disguised either himself or Ulfin as Jordan to help sneak Uther and Ulfin into the castle of Tintagel so that Uther Pendragon could sleep with the Duke's wife, Igerne. Jordan eventually became one of Arthur's knights and participated in the war against the Saxons. [*GeoffHR, Wace, Layamon, VulgMer, Malory*]

JOREL

A king of Korntin who received a magical suit of armor from a knight named Brian. Jorel passed the armor on to Count Moral of Joraphas, who in turn gave it to Wigalois (Gawain's son) for use in a battle against King Roaz of Glois. [*Wirnt*]

JOSEFENT [*Josephent, Jozefent*]

King of Wales. He married Andelise, queen of Denmark, and fathered Sir Durmart, who became an Arthurian knight. [*Durmart*]

JOSEPH OF ARIMATHEA [*Giuseppe, Iosepes, Josep*]

A former soldier of Pontius Pilate who brought the Grail to Britain. His story is told in Robert de Boron's *Joseph d'Arimathie* and the Vulgate *Estoire del Saint Graal*. Each of the four Gospels mentions Joseph of Arimathea, a rich man and member of the Council of Sadducees who secretly became a disciple of Christ. He obtained Jesus's body from Pontius Pilate and had it entombed. The Grail histories, drawing on some information from the Christian apocrypha (e.g., *The Gospel of Nichodemus*), enhanced the status of this minor Biblical character.

After the crucifixion, Joseph sought to preserve the artifacts that the Savior had touched. The most important of these was the Grail—the cup or bowl used by Christ at the Last Supper—in which Joseph caught some of Jesus's blood. Some stories say that he also obtained the Bleeding Lance, with which a Roman soldier named Longinus had stabbed Christ in the side.

He was thrown in prison by the Jews and left to rot, but the Grail sustained him for over forty years. He was freed by the Roman Emperor Vespasian, who had come to Jerusalem to avenge Christ's death. (This is based in part on the *Gospel of Nichodemus*, in which Joseph is imprisoned but is freed by the risen Christ, allowing him to return to Arimathea.)

Joseph gathered a sizable number of followers and departed with the Grail for western lands. Along the way, they stopped at the kingdom of Sarras. Joseph converted King Evalach (later Mordrain) and Duke Seraphe (later Nascien) to Christianity, and they later joined his fellowship in Britain. Lancelot was Nascien's descendant. Another follower, Peter, was an ancestor of Gawain. To separate the sinful from the pious among his fellowship, Joseph founded the Grail Table, modeled after the table of the Last Supper and precursor to Arthur's Round Table.

In Robert de Boron's romance, he remains childless, but in the Vulgate *Estoire del Saint Graal*, he has two sons by his wife Elyab: Josephus, the first Christian bishop and Joseph's successor as Grail keeper; and Galahad, the first king of Christian Wales. Urien and Yvain descended from Joseph through Galahad. His sister Havingues married Bron, whose sons became the Grail Kings.

Robert de Boron says that after entrusting the Grail to Bron, Joseph returned to Arimathea while his followers journeyed to Britain. In the Vulgate *Estoire* and later versions, however, he arrives in Britain himself and begins converting the local rulers. Duke Ganor, his first convert, provided a home for his followers in the city of Galafort. Imprisoned for a time by the pagan King Crudel, he was rescued by his friend Mordrain. With his followers firmly rooted in Britain, Joseph passed on, leaving the Grail to his son Josephus. In the Italian *La Tavola Ritonda*, he is slain by a pagan giant named Dilantes. The French *Perlesvaus* tells us that he was buried in a tomb at the Grail Castle, while in the Vulgate *Estoire* he is entombed in Scotland. In the Post-Vulgate and Malory's *Le Morte Darthur*, his body occupies an enchanted chamber in the Grail Castle, along with the Bleeding Lance and the Grail.

Centuries later, the spirit of either Joseph or Josephus presided over a mass held in the Grail Castle, attended by Galahad, Perceval, and Bors. He instructed the knights to take the Grail to Sarras, where he again appeared at a mass the culminated in the Grail's ascension into heaven.

Aside from the Grail stories, there are a number of traditions concerning Joseph of Arimathea as a missionary in England. According to one, he founded the abbey at Glastonbury after King Arviragus gave him the land. Another, found in an interpolation in William of Malmesbury's chronicle, says that St. Phillip, who was spreading Christianity in Gaul, sent him to Britain. Various continental legends have him chumming about with Mary Magdalene and Lazarus. In one notable non-Arthurian romance, *Sone de Nausay*, Joseph is the Fisher King himself, having ascended to the throne of Norway after conquering the heathens there and marrying the country's princess. [*RobertBorJ, Perlesvaus, LancLac, VulgLanc, VulgQuest, VulgEst, Joseph, Malory, DeSancto, HereJOA, LyfeJOA*]

JOSEPHUS [*Giosefette, Josafas, Josaphas, Josephe(s), Josephet*]

The son of Joseph of Arimathea, introduced in the Vulgate *Queste del Saint Graal* and *Estoire del Saint Graal*, in which he takes on many of the characteristics assigned to Joseph by Robert de Boron. The author of the *Queste* probably invented him to provide a pure, virginal precursor to Galahad. Joseph's wife Elyab bore him while his father languished in a Jewish prison for four decades. After his father's release, the family led an expedition to western lands. Josephus became the first Christian bishop and the leader of Joseph's followers. He sat in the Perilous Seat at the Grail Table. Josephus helped convert the kingdom of Sarras, in which he baptized Mordrain and Nascien, and the various sovereignties in Britain. He died unmarried and childless after passing the Grail onto the sons of Bron. At the culmination of the Grail Quest, the spirit of either Josephus or his father presided over a mass held for Galahad, Perceval, and Bors—the successful Grail Knights. [*VulgQuest, VulgEst, PostQuest*]

JOSEUS [*Josep(h)(s), Josex*]

In *Perlesvaus*, the son of King Pelles. His mother told him that he would be a monk rather than a king, which made Joseus so angry that he killed her. He spent the rest of his life as a hermit, doing penance for this crime, although he would have been a great knight. Lancelot helped him clear his forest of robber knights. Joseus picked up arms only once, to help Perceval re-conquer the Grail Castle from the evil King of the Castle Mortal. He became the caretaker of the Grail Castle and died there. [*Perlesvaus*]

JOSHUA [*Joseus, Josué*]

Son of Bron, brother of Alain, and follower of Joseph of Arimathea in the Grail histories. With Alain, he journeyed to the Strange Land, converted King Calafes, and established Corbenic, the Grail Castle. He inherited the land upon Calafes's death, and became the first Grail King. He married Calafes's daughter and passed the throne to his son, Aminadap. His descendants included Pellehan, Pelles, Elaine, and Galahad. John of Glastonbury makes him an ancestor of Arthur himself, through Igerne. [*VulgEst, JohnG*]

JOSIMAS

A holy man, formerly a knight, who lodged Perceval and Gawain in his hermitage. [*Perlesvaus*]

JOVEDAST OF ARLES

A knight defeated in combat by Perceval. [*Wolfram*]

JOVELIN

Father of Kahedins and Isolde of the White Hands (Tristan's wife) in Gottfried's *Tristan*. As the Duke of Arundel, he was attacked by enemies, but was saved by Tristan. In return, he encouraged the marriage between Tristan and his daughter. He appears in Eilhart's *Tristrant* as the similar-sounding HAVELIN, and in later legend as HOEL. [*Gottfried*]

JOY OF THE COURT [**Joie de la Cort, Schoydelakurt*]

An extremely dangerous adventure in King Evrain's town of Brandigan. It is found in Chrétien's *Erec* and its adaptations. No knight who ever sought the adventure returned alive. Erec decided to assume the adventure when he came to the town at the end of his journey with Enide, much to the distress of Enide and Evrain. Making his way past a row of heads spiked on spears, Erec entered a wooded area. He followed a path and found a lady (called Elena in the Norse *Erex Saga*) sleeping on a bed under a sycamore tree. Shortly thereafter, the lady's knight, Mabonagrain, arrived and challenged Erec to a fight. After a long battle, Erec defeated Mabonagrain, who gratefully told Erec his story: long ago, he had foolishly promised the lady to come to the spot and guard it with his life until he was finally defeated in combat. Thus, Mabonagrain had killed every knight who came that way. Since Erec had defeated him, however, he was free. Having won the adventure, Erec blew a horn, thus altering the town of his victory. The court rejoiced, and King Evrain threw a celebration in Erec's honor. The ladies of the town composed a song about the adventure called the Lay of Joy. It's odd name may be a corruption of *jeu del cor*, or "game of the horn" (Loomis, *Romance*, 196). Wolfram von Eschenbach transformed the name into *Schoydelakurt*, which he seems to think is a land, once ruled by Mabonagrain and eventually by Erec. [*ChretienE, HartmannE, Wolfram, Erex*]

JOYOUS GUARD [*Gioiosa Guardia*, **Joieuse Garde*]

Lancelot's castle, formerly called DOLOROUS GUARD, but renamed after Lancelot conquered it. In the Prose *Tristan* and its adaptations, Lancelot allows Tristan and Isolde to live in the castle after their flight from King Mark's court. During the Grail Quest, when Tristan was away, Mark attacked Joyous Guard and took back Isolde. Lancelot returned the castle to its former name (Dolorous Guard) after his affair with Guinevere was exposed and he was expelled from Camelot. Arthur besieged the castle until Lancelot returned to France. Some sources say that Arthur had Joyous Guard razed. As for its location, the Vulgate *Mort Artu* places it in Northumberland, and Malory more specifically suggests the castle of Bamburgh. Bamburgh sits upon the ruins of an earlier British castle. [*LancLac*, *VulgLanc*, *ProsTris*, *Tavola*, *Stanz*, *Malory*]

JUAN OF CASTILLE

The king whom Tristan the Younger, Tristan's son, eventually served. Tristan the Younger married Infanta Maria, Juan's daughter, after rescuing her from the Moors. Juan married Isolde, Tristan the Younger's sister. [*DueTris*]

JUBEN

A duke of Forckheim who Erec saved after he had been kidnapped by seven robbers. His brothers, Joachim, Perant, and Malcheus, were also abducted and liberated. Erec sent them to Arthur's court to relate the adventure. [*Erex*]

JUDAS MACCABEES

A biblical figure who successfully revolted against the Syrians around 175 B.C. and reclaimed Palestine for the Jews. Medieval legend also names him as the inventor of falconry. In *Perlesvaus*, Gawain obtains a splendid shield which had supposedly belonged to Judas, and in the First Continuation of Chrétien's *Perceval*, he is named as the original owner of the fabulous Sword with the Strange Hangings. In the Vulgate *Merlin* and the *Livre d'Artus* he is said to have established the adventure of the Ugly Appearance in either the Land of the Grazing Grounds or the realm of the Wise Lady. [*Contin1*, *Perlesvaus*, *VulgMer*, *Livre*]

JUDGEMENT FIELD

A tournament field near the town of Dyoflê. It was an extremely versatile field, designed for any number of sports. Lot of Lothian and Gurnemans fought a tournament here, in which Lancelot participated. [*UlrichZ*]

JUGEIN [*Iuegyn*, *Vigenin*, *Wigein*]

The Earl of Leicester under King Arthur. He fought in the Roman war and led half a legion of troops at the battle of Soissons. [*GeoffHR*, *Wace*, *Layamon*]

JULIAN[1]

A Knight of the Round Table who participated in the Grail Quest. [*PostQuest*]

JULIAN[2]

An Arthurian knight who joined Gawain's quest to conquer Rigomer castle. [*Merveil*]

JULIAN[3]

A knight who, at the inisistance of a lady, swore to slay any knight who passed his castle. He was conquered by Floriant, the foster-son of Morgan le Fay, and became Floriant's companion. The two knights helped to save Rome from a siege by Saracens. Afterwards, Julian visited Arthur's court and became a Knight of the Round Table. [*Floriant*]

JULIUS[1]

A Roman senator and warrior who joined King Claudas's second war with Arthur. [*VulgLanc*]

JULIUS[2] CAESAR

History holds that Julius Caesar led the first Roman conquest of Britain, subduing the tribal chief Cassivellaunus, in roughly 54 B.C. Nennius, among other chroniclers, recognizes this fact but places the date in 44 A.D. Nevertheless, in the Vulgate *Merlin*, Caesar is Arthur's contemporary. King Claudas became Caesar's vassal in return for Roman reinforcements in the wars against Arthur, Ban, and Bors. Caesar, with his eye on Benoic, sent Pontius Anthony and an army to aid Claudas. Despite his aid, Claudas was defeated by Arthur. Merlin visited him and exposed the lechery of Caesar's wife (she had a dozen male concubines, disguised as women), whom Caesar then executed. On Merlin's advice, Caesar married Avenable, a maiden who had come to his court seeking help. His daughter married Patrick, Avenable's brother. Within a few chapters of this episode, however, Lucius is the Emperor of Rome, and Caesar is mentioned, correctly, as a figure in distant history. In the French *Huon de Bordeaux*, Caesar has a son by Morgan le Fay named Huon. [*Nennius*, *VulgMer*, *Huon*, *ProsMer2*]

JULIUS[3] THE MARTYR

According to Geoffrey of Monmouth, Guinevere fled to the nunnery of Julius the Martyr in Caerleon after Arthur's death. [*GeoffHR*, *Wace*]

JURAN

An evil dwarf in Der Stricker's *Daniel*. Armed with a magic sword that defied all armor, Juran terrorized the land of the Dark Mountain. He wanted to marry the maiden of the Dark Mountain, so he killed her father. No knight could oppose him. Daniel of the Blossoming Valley, one of Arthur's knights, cunningly convinced Juran to show his true prowess by fighting him without the sword, and Juran was slain. Daniel used his sword to kill the two giants of Cluse. [*Stricker*]

JURANS OF BLEMUNZIN

An infidel count who served Perceval's half-brother Feirefiz. [*Wolfram*]

JUST KNIGHTS

A trio of Arthur's knights—Blaes, Cadog, and Pedrog—who appear in Welsh legend. They were noted for enforcing justice in Arthur's realm, each in his own fashion: Blaes endeavored to uphold secular law; Cadog preserved canonical law; and Pedrog defended military law. [*Triads*]

JUSTIN I

Ruler of the Byzantine Empire from 519 to 527. He succeeded his father, Anastsius, and was succeeded by Justinian the Great. In Jean D'Outremeuse's *Ly Myreur des Histors*, he invades Britain and is defeated by Arthur. [*Jean*]

JUTE

A member of ancient Germanic tribes, living in what is now Denmark and northern Germany, who invaded southeast England in the fifth century, settling in Kent.

JUTLAND

A peninsula of northern Europe, forming the mainland of Denmark and part of what is now northern Germany. (Geoffrey calls this area GOTHLAND.) The King of Jutland, Doldavius, voluntarily subjugated himself to Arthur in exchange for Arthur's protection from invasion. Arthur commandeered warriors from Jutland for the invasion of Gaul and the Roman War. [*GeoffHR, Wace, Layamon*]

JUVENAL¹ [*Juveneaus*]

A Christian bishop appointed to King Nascien's Orberica by Joseph of Arimathea. [*VulgEst*]

JUVENAL²

A doctor who healed the wounds that Gawain and Brandelis inflicted upon each other in combat. [*Contin1*]

K

KAHADINST OF LANPREBOIS

A duke present at a tournament thrown by Arthur at the Castle of Maidens. There is perhaps a connection with KAHEDINS. [*Renaut*]

KAHANIN [*Kehamans, Kehenans*]

A Saxon king who, in the service of King Rions of Ireland, fought King Arthur and King Leodegan at the battle of Carmelide. Arthur killed him at the battle of Aneblayse. [*VulgMer, Arthour*]

KAHEDINS[1] [*Caerdin, Ch(a)edino, Ganhardin, Gheddino, Ghedin, Kaedin, Kahedins, Kahedrin, Kaherdin, Kardín, Kehedins, Kehenis, Kehydyns*]

Brother of Isolde of the White Hands and son of Havelin, Jovelin, or Hoel. He became a loyal friend and companion, and then brother-in-law, to Tristan, but became enraged when he learned that Tristan had not consummated his marriage with Isolde of the White Hands. Tristan took Kahedins to see the other Isolde (or her statue), and Kahedins understood his predicament. He fell in love with Isolde's maidservant, Brangain or Gymele. In Thomas's version, his affair with Brangain was ended when she heard (untruthfully) that he had fled from combat with a cowardly knight named Mariadoc. He later killed Mariadoc in a joust. In the Prose *Tristan*, he falls in love with Isolde herself, causing his friendship with Tristan to end angrily (and causing Tristan to go insane); the tale says he died of grief after he confessed his love to Isolde and she cruelly rebuked him. In Eilhart von Oberge's version, he loves Ganoje, the wife of lord Nampetenis, and he breaks into Nampetenis's castle to sleep with her. When Nampetenis found out, he chased after Kahedins, killed him, and mortally wounded Tristan. In other versions, Kahedins survives to captain the ship that is supposed to bring Isolde to a mortally wounded Tristan's bedside, or he joins Palante, Tristan's cousin, in an invasion of Cornwall after Tristan's death. A Welsh character called CAE HIR (Cae the Tall) may be identical. [*Thomas, FolieB, Eilhart, ProsTris, Tavola, TrisSaga, DueTris, Malory*]

KAHEDINS[2] [*Kehedins*]

One of Arthur's knights, variously called "the Small" and "the Fair." He is said to be a cousin of Gawain and Yvain. He had a sister named Ydain. His uncle was Sir Kay of Estral. As a squire, he participated in the struggle against the Saxons and was knighted by Arthur for his service. He fought in the Roman War, in the first campaign against Claudas, and in the battle against Caradoc of the Dolorous Tower. In other adventures, Kahedins was imprisoned in the Dolorous Prison and the Valley of No Return, and was freed from both by Lancelot. [*ChretienP, Contin1, LancLac, VulgLanc, VulgMer, Arthour*]

KAHETI

In Wolfram's *Parzival*, a land in the realm of King Poydiconjunz (Bagdemagus) of Gorre. Horse-archers from Kaheti fought in the battle of Bearosche against Duke Lyppaut. [*Wolfram*]

KAILET

One of Arthur's knights. A magical mantle brought to Arthur's court revealed that Kailet's wife was displeased with the way he always took her with him wherever he went. Ulrich probably took the name from Hartmann von Aue's GAHILLET. The name was taken by Wolfram as KAYLET. [*UlrichZ*]

KAILIN

The king of Friesland who served Arthur. [*Layamon*]

KAIRENZA

According to the Hebrew *Melekh Artus*, one of Arthur's half-sisters (the daughter of Igraine) was married to the Duke of Kairenza. [*Melekh*]

KALEGRAS

The name of both Tristan's father and Tristan's son in the Icelandic *Saga af Tristram ok Ísodd*, from CANELENGRES, Tristan's father's surname in German romance. Tristan's son, whose mother was Isolde of the White Hands, was raised by King Mark after the deaths of Tristan and Isolde. Mark eventually bestowed the throne of England on him. Kalegras married Lilja, the daughter of Emperor Donísus of Saxony. They had two sons, named Patrocles and Mórodd, and a daughter named Mollina. [*SagaTI*]

KALOT ENBOLOT

The location—perhaps in Sicily—where the sorcerer Clinschor was castrated by King Ibert of Sicily. [*Wolfram*]

KALUBIN

A count defeated by Arthur's Sir Tandareis. He loved the maiden Claudin and served her faithfully for many years. Fed up with her continual dismissals, he kidnapped and abused her. Tandareis encountered them and defeated

Kalubin to save the maiden. Later, through Tandareis's negotiations, Kalubin and Claudin were wed. [*PleierT*]

KALVIEL OF FOLKBURG

In the Norse *Erex Saga*, a duke from Karinlisborg who, along with his wife Favida, was attacked by two giants in a forest. While his wife escaped, Kalviel was beaten and tied. Favida managed to find Erec, who slew the giants and rescued Kalviel. He appears in Chrétien's *Erec* as CADOC. [*Erex*]

KAMAALOT

A variation of CAMELOT, given in *Perlesvaus* as the home of Perceval's family. [*Perlesvaus*]

KAMELIN [*Kamelins*]

A Knight of the Round Table and son of King Alfred of Ireland. Kamelin, his father, and his brother Miroet found Yder, after he had been poisoned by Kay, and helped restore him to health. [*Yder*]

KAMERIE

The land ruled by Queen Tydomie, who married Meleranz, Arthur's nephew. The court was at Flordemunt. [*PleierM*]

KAMPHIES

One of the many knights forced to swear allegiance to Gawain. [*Heinrich*]

KANADIC [*Kanedic*]

A land in German Arthurian texts which may derive from CAMBENIC. In Wolfram's *Parzival*, it is the location of a sparrowhawk tournament, where Duke Orilus of Lalander defeated eight Knights of the Round Table. According to Der Pleier, in *Garel*, the land was ruled first by Queen Florie, who died from grief following the slaying of her lover Ilinot, Arthur's son. It fell to the hands of Kloudite, Florie's sister, who married King Ekunaver. The latter went to war with Arthur and was defeated in Kanadic by Garel of the Blooming Valley. [*Wolfram*, *PleierG*]

KANAHIN [*Kanahins*]

One of Lancelot's squires. As Arthur and Lancelot went to war over Guinevere, Kanahin, at Lancelot's command, hung Lancelot's shield in the church of St. Stephen's in Camelot, to commemorate Lancelot's knightly deeds in happier times. [*VulgMort*]

KANCOR

A renowned scientist and artisan in Arthur's time. [*Wolfram*]

KANDALION

The bold but wicked Duke of Montikluse. He made it his hobby to imprison knights in his Malmort Tower, leaving them to starve. He captured Arthur's Sir Tandareis when the latter was defending a maiden named Claudin against a force of Kandalion's knights. Unlike his previous victims, Tandareis was kept alive through the graces of Antonie, Kandalion's sister, and was released three times to attend, incognito, tournaments at Arthur's court, in which he defeated Kandalion. Kandalion eventually released Tandareis to claim a reward offered by Arthur for his return. [*PleierT*]

KANÚEST

The chief huntsman of King Mark of Cornwall. He came across Tristan and Isolde, living in exile in a Cornish forest. His inaccurate observations of their cohabitation, which he thought was chaste, led to Mark's acceptance of the lovers back to his court. [*TrisSaga*]

KANVOLEIS [*Kanvoleiz*]

The capital city of Queen Herzeloyde's Wales where Herzeloyde threw a tournament. Gahmuret won the tournament and thus won the right and duty to marry Herzeloyde. The city was later ruled by their son Perceval and then his son Kardeiz. [*Wolfram*]

KAOLS THE COMPASSIONLESS

A lord killed by Gaheris in combat. Kaols had ruled the Castle of Death, in which he imprisoned knights and their ladies. [*Livre*]

KARADAS

In *Diu Crône*, Gawain's host during his visit to the Castle Salie, where he met his grandmother, Igerne. Karadas's counterpart in Wolfram's *Parzival* is PLIPPALINOT the Ferryman. [*Heinrich*]

KARADOS

A variation of CARADOC.

KARAHES

A variation of CARHAIX.

KARAKADIN

Son of Lord Caradoc of the Dolorous Tower. [*ProsTris*]

KARAMPHI

A castle visited by Gawain in Heinrich von dem Türlin's *Diu Crône*. In a previous tournament, Gawain had killed one of Karamphi's princes, named Dahamorht. In revenge, Dahamorht's brother Angaras attacked him. The lord of Karamphi stopped the fight, but Gawain had to embark on the Grail Quest as a condition of the truce. In Wolfram's *Parzival*, these events occur at ASCALUN. [*Heinrich*]

KARAMPHIET

A dwarf who served Amurfina, Gawain's wife. [*Heinrich*]

KARDEFABLET OF JAMOR

A duke who lived in Arthur's time. Kardefablet's wife was the sister of Duke Lyppaut of Bearosche. As his brother-in-law's ally, Kardefablet fought for Lyppaut in the battle of Bearosche against King Meliant of Lis. [*Wolfram*]

KARDEIZ[1]

Perceval's son by the lady Condwiramurs. He was the twin brother of Loherangrin. Kardeiz was tutored in his youth by Duke Kyot of Katelangen. Kardeiz inherited Perceval's secular lands of Brobarz, Anjou, Wales, and North Wales while Loherangrin became the new Grail King. [*Wolfram*]

KARDEIZ[2]

Brother of Condwiramurs, Perceval's wife. He was the son of King Tampenteire. He was killed for the love of a lady. [*Wolfram*]

KAREDONAS

A land whose king, Gediens, was slain by a heathen warrior called Verangoz of Sorboreste. The king's daughter, Dulceflur, asked for a champion from Arthur's court, and Meleranz, Arthur's nephew, saved the kingdom. [*PleierM*]

KAREDOS [*Karidos*]

The giant lord of Malmontan and Mermin in Der Pleier's *Tandareis and Flordibel*, probably modeled (and named) after CARADOC, the giant slain by Lancelot in French romance. Karedos commanded an army of robber knights who attacked unsuspecting knights traveling through the land. He was slain by Tandareis, who assumed control of his lands. [*PleierT*]

KAREIS

The King of Kareis was the brother-in-law of Prince Gabenis of Punturteis in Wolfram's *Parzival*. [*Wolfram*]

KARET

A knight present at the Sorgarda tournament, which Gawain won. [*Heinrich*]

KARFODYAS OF TRIPPARUN

A count defeated in combat by Perceval. [*Wolfram*]

KARINLISBORG

The birthplace of Kalviel, a duke saved from two giants by Erec. [*Erex*]

KARKE

The chief castle of Arundel, land of Tristan's father-in-law Jovelin. It was besieged by Jovelin's enemies but was rescued by Tristan. [*Gottfried*]

KARMIL

A beautiful town in Mermin. It served as the court of Tandareis, one of Arthur's knights. [*PleierT*]

KARMINAL

King Arthur's hunting lodge in the forest of Brizljan. He sometimes kept court here. [*Wolfram*]

KARNAHKARNANZ OF UTERLEC

Perceval, as a youth, encountered him in the wilds of Soltane, where Perceval had been raised in seclusion by his mother. Perceval had never seen a knight before, and was fascinated by Count Karnahkarnanz. Karnahkarnanz was on a mission to rescue the lady Imane from her abductor, Meleagant, but before he departed he told Perceval that King Arthur made knights and that Perceval was of hardy enough stock to become one himself. This inspired Perceval to leave Soltane, much to the distress of his mother. [*Wolfram*]

KARNEIS

The land ruled by Count Liander, who was rescued from Eskilabon's prison by Arthur's Sir Garel. [*PleierG*]

KAROES

A knight of Arthur's court. [*Heinrich*]

KARONICA

A river in Arthur's land of Löver, flowing past the castle Sabins. [*PleierT*]

KARRABEL

A city on the border of Egypt, in Nascien's kingdom. Karrabel's lord pretended to be a good Christian, but had actually murdered his own father. When the lord of Karrabel rebuked a knight named Nabor, who had betrayed Nascien, God tired of his hypocritical, impious behavior and blasted him to ashes with a thunderbolt. [*VulgEst*]

KARRIOZ

A dwarfish, beast-like, pagan knight in the service of King Roaz of Glois. His bones had no marrow, doubling their strength. He guarded the path to Roaz's castle, and Wigalois (Gawain's son) had to contend with him when he traveled to Glois to kill Roaz. Much feared for his prowess, Karrioz was nevertheless defeated by Wigalois. Fleeing from Wigalois, he ran headlong into a poisonous swamp fog and was killed. [*Wirnt*]

KARSIE

Duchess of Arundel in Gottfried's *Tristan*. She was the wife of Duke Jovelin and the mother of Isolde of the White Hands and Kahedins. [*Gottfried*]

KARSINEFITE [*Karsnafite*]

Enide's mother according to Hartmann von Aue and Wolfram von Eschenbach. Chrétien de Troyes gives the name as TARSENESYDE. [*HartmannE, Wolfram*]

KATELANGE [*Katelangen*]

A duchy in Arthur's realm. The ruler is noted by Hartmann von Aue as Malivliot and by Wolfram von Eschenbach as Duke Kyot. [*HartmannE, Wolfram*]

KATERAC

A ford near the Grail Castle. [*Heinrich*]

KAVOMET

A famous knight present at the Sorgarda tournament, which Gawain won. [*Heinrich*]

KAY[1] [*Cai(e), Caius, Cay, *Cei, Che, Cheudo, Chieso, Cheix, Coi, Gues, Kæ, Kaye, Kaynus, Kayous, Kazin, Kenis, Kei(e), Keii, Keis, Ke(u)(l)(s), Ke(u)x, Keuz, Key(e), Keys, Koi(s), Ky, Qes, Quei(s), Ques, Qui, Quoi(s)*]

Arthur's seneschal and, in later legends, his foster-brother. He was transferred to romance from Welsh legend, where he appears as CEI, though the Welsh may have adopted the name from the Roman *Caius*. Almost all of the legends in which he appears—from the Welsh tales to the French and German romances to Malory—give him a rude, brash, and insulting temperament. In Welsh legend, he backs up his tongue with a number of unique abilities, but most stories portray him as an inferior warrior. A small number of texts depict him as a essentially noble knight who often falls victim to his own tongue and temper. With no romance of his own, he appears as a supporting—and generally antagonistic—character in the stories of other knights such as Perceval, Lancelot, and Yvain.

We first meet Cei in the Welsh *Culhwch and Olwen* and in several short poems. His father's name was Cynyr, and he had a son named Garanwyn and a daughter named Celemon. Coldness and stubbornness were prophecized for Cei before his birth. Cei had a number of supernatural skills, including the ability to hold his breath underwater for nine days, to go without sleeping for the same period, to grow as tall as a tree, to generate enough heat to light a fire, and to deliver an incurable wound with his sword. In addition, he was the handsomest of Arthur's warriors. "Vain was an army compared to Cei in battle," says a Welsh poem, which describes his victories against nine witches and the fearsome Cath Palug. In *Culhwch*, he accompanies Culhwch on his quest to find Olwen, and he accomplishes several of Culhwch's tasks, including the slaying of Wrnach the Giant, the rescuing of Mabon, and the theft of the beard of Dillus the Bearded. After Cei killed Dillus, Arthur made up an insulting rhyme about the incident, causing a rift between Arthur and Cei that lasted until Cei's death. Cei was killed by another of

Arthur's warriors—Gwyddawg—whom Arthur killed in revenge.

Geoffrey of Monmouth brought his character, Latinized as Kay, into the Arthurian section of *Historia Regum Britanniae*, which was adapted by Wace and Layamon. After Arthur ascended the throne of Britain, he gave Anjou to Kay. Later, Kay and Bedivere helped him kill the giant of Saint Michael's Mount. After distinguishing himself in the Roman war, Kay was killed by King Sertorius of Libya at the battle of Soissons. Arthur had him buried in the castle of Caen or Chinon, which Kay had built. According to Layamon, Arthur changed the name of the castle's town to Caen.

Kay became known to Chrétien de Troyes probably through Wace's *Roman de Brut*. Chrétien gave him roles in his *Erec, Lancelot, Yvain*, and *Perceval*. Hartmann von Aue, in turn, included him in his *Erec* and *Iwein*, as did Wolfram von Eschenbach in *Parzival*. Through Wolfram, he became known to other German authors such as Der Stricker (*Daniel*) and Der Pleier (*Garel*).

Kay's role in these romances is rarely flattering. He goads other knights, abuses women and dwarves, wheedles his way into adventures (in which he fails), and maliciously sends young knights off on dangerous quests—only to be humiliated when they succeed. It became *de rigueur* in these French and German romances to include an episode in which Kay scorned or offended the hero, only to later be repaid for his insolence. In Chrétien's *Lancelot*, he coerces Arthur into letting him try to rescue Guinevere from Meleagant, and then is defeated and imprisoned by Meleagant. In *Yvain*, he makes fun of Yvain for setting out on an adventure, and later is defeated in combat by Yvain, who has won the adventure. In *Perceval* and its adaptations, Kay's abuse of a dwarf and a lady results in a broken arm and collar bone when Perceval avenges them. Malory notes how he bullied Gareth and Brunor only to be humiliated by their successes.

In a number of tales, however, Kay is described as a brave and valiant warrior who often falls victim to his brash tongue. Of Kay, *Les Merveilles de Rigomer* says: "The seneschal was very valiant, and had never been a coward or confused; but he did say a lot of stupid things. Some of the other knights were more laudable, although not more brave, than Kay, who often lost respect due to station because of his brash way of speaking." Similarly, Heinrich von dem Türlin says, "Although Keii might be unpleasant and quite mannerless, he still had not lost the pride of nobility. Indeed, he was so brave that he wouldn't avoid any monster."

In several French romances, on the other hand, Kay is evil in earnest. In *Perlesvaus*, he murders Loholt, Arthur's son, in his sleep, and then claims credit for a giant which Loholt had slain. When this crime is exposed, Kay flees Arthur's court for Brittany and joins forces with Brian of the Isles, Arthur's enemy. The two knights lead an army against Arthur, but are defeated at the battle of Cardueil. Kay is wounded, and he flees to Chinon to live out his days as a fugitive. In *Yder*, he tries twice to murder the noble Sir Yder by poison. The First Continuation of Chrétien's *Perceval* includes an episode (resolved in the

Third Continuation) in which Kay murders Sir Silimac and is defeated in judicial combat by Gawain for this homicide. The Dutch *Walewein ende Keye* also portrays him in an extremely unflattering manner, and he is eventually run out of Arthur's court after slandering Gawain.

In the Vulgate Cycle, we find the biography of Kay that will last through the remainder of the Arthurian legends, including the Post-Vulgate Cycle and Malory's *Le Morte Darthur*. He was the son of Antor or Ector, Arthur's foster-father. When the infant Arthur came to Antor's household, he was suckled by Antor's wife, while Kay was nursed by a peasant wet-nurse, which was responsible for his evil tongue. Arthur was originally intended as Kay's squire. This all changed after Uther Pendragon's death, when a certain Sword in a Stone appeared outside a church in Logres or London. Attending the tournament there, Kay lost his sword. Arthur, unable to find it, drew the sword from the stone and presented it to Kay. Kay, realizing the significance of the sword, originally claimed that he drew it, but revealed the truth under his father's interrogation. Arthur then acquiesced to Ector's request that Kay become his seneschal. Kay proved himself worthy—if still ill-mannered—during the following wars against the rebellious kings, the Saxons, King Claudas, King Rions, and the five kings who met with Arthur at the battle of the Humber. As in the chronicles, Kay accompanied Arthur to Mont St. Michel and to the Roman War, where—in an important variation from the chronicles—he survived the battle of Soissons. He then returned to Britain with Arthur and became the bullying, inferior knight described in the romances. If he was not particularly noble, however, neither was he particularly wicked. He acquitted himself well in several adventures and earned his place at the Round Table. He was eventually killed in the second Roman War, just after Arthur's war with Lancelot.

Chrétien gives him a son named Gronosis, and Heinrich von dem Türlin names his sweetheart as Galida. In the First Continuation of Chrétien's *Perceval*, he is in love with Lady Lore of Branlant. In Girart D'Amiens' *Escanor*, he wins a tournament at Banborc and falls in love with the lady Andrivete, whom he eventually marries. [*WelshPG, Culhwch, GeoffHR, Wace, ChretienE, ChretienL, ChretienY, ChretienP, RobertBorM, Layamon, Perlesvaus, Contin1, Wolfram, ProsMer1, VulgLanc, VulgMort, VulgMer, PostMer, PostQuest, PostMort, Arthour, Stricker, PleierG, Heinrich, Merveil, Walewein, Girart, Malory*]

KAY[2] OF ESTRAL [*Kay Destran, Kes, Kex, Key, Ques*]

A minor Knight of the Round Table who first appears in Chrétien's *Erec*. In the Vulgate *Merlin*, he is one of the young nobleman that Gawain leads against the Saxons; Arthur knights him in gratitude. In the Vulgate *Lancelot*, he is one of knights that Lancelot frees from the Dolorous Prison. He lived in the Valley of No Return, having pledged to his wife to remain there until the Valley was destroyed. The Post-Vulgate *Mort Artu* says that he was

killed fighting Mordred's army at the battle of Salisbury. [*ChretienE, LancLac, VulgLanc, VulgMer, PostMort*]

KAY[2] THE STRANGE

A Knight of the Round Table who fought for Arthur at the Leverzep tournament in Malory. He also appeared at the healing of Sir Urry. He may be the same character as KAY OF ESTRAL, Malory having misread *Kay D'Estral* as *Kay l'Estrange*. [*Malory*]

KAYLET OF HOSKURAST

The King of Spain and Castille during the reign of Uther in Britain. He was prompted by his uncle Schiltunc to join King Vridebrant of Scotland's invasion of the African kingdom of Zazamanc. He was defeated in the invasion, with the others, by Perceval's father Gahmuret, who also happened to be Kaylet's maternal cousin. Kaylet had once loved Alize, sister of King Hardiz of Gascony. Hardiz, however, gave Alize to King Lambekin of Brabant instead. Kaylet then married the lady Rischoyde. Kaylet was also the maternal uncle of Killijacac. [*Wolfram*]

KAZ OF GOMERET [*Car*]

A knight in the service of Queen Morgan le Fay. Sir Kaz was sent by Morgan with three others, including his brother Helians, to kill the young Alexander the Orphan at the behest of King Mark of Cornwall. Kaz was outjousted and defeated by Alexander. [*ProsTris, Prophecies, Malory*]

KEGEIN

One of Arthur's warriors who was the son of Elauth. [*Layamon*]

KENT

A country in southeast England. Ruled by Aldolf in Octavius's reign and by Gorangon in King Vortigern's time, it was granted to the Saxon leader Hengist, and Saxons continued to occupy it throughout Arthur's reign. King Vortimer fought a battle against Hengist in Kent, and Horsa and Vortigern's son Vortiger were slain. Many years later, when Mordred seized the throne of England, most of Kent allied with him. Arthur offered it to Mordred as part of a peace treaty that was never achieved. Kent was a hotly contested piece of land during the time in which Arthur was said to thrive. It was one of the first to fall under the control of the Saxons. The non-Arthurian *Anglo-Saxon Chronicle* says that Hengist's son Æsc ruled it starting in 512. In Dryden's *King Arthur*, it is ruled by Oswald, Arthur's Saxon enemy. [*Anglo, Nennius, Wace, Malory, Dryden*]

KENTIGERN

The patron saint of Glasgow, Scotland who is described in his twelfth-century *Life* as the son of Yvain and the grandson of Urien. John Major's chronicle makes him the son of Thametes, the grandson of Lot, and the nephew of

Gawain. Scottish tales describe St. Kentigern's encounters with Lailoken, a Scottish counterpart of Myrddin or Merlin. [*Major*]

KESARIJA

An ancient city visited by Tristan and Lancelot. It was ruled by a great knight named Liburn. Tristan and Lancelot desired Liburn's wife, but Liburn defeated both of them for her honor. [*Povest*]

KEY OF WALES

A castle on the border of Wales, ruled by the tyrannical Cahot the Red. It was liberated by Perceval. [*Perlesvaus*]

KIBOUENE PITS

The name of the prison in Rigomer Castle, where all of the knights who failed in their attempt to conquer the castle were kept. Lancelot was one of its residents until freed by Gawain. [*Merveil*]

KILGWRI

The Ousel (thrush) of Kilgwri was the first animal whose assistance was sought by Arthur's warriors in their quest to find Mabon, an imprisoned huntsman. The Ousel of Kilgwri sent them on to the Stag of Rhedenfre. [*Culhwch*]

KILIMAR

A nobleman from Montikluse. He helped Antonie, Duke Kandalion's sister, arrange for Tandareis, Arthur's imprisoned knight, to attend tournaments at Sabins. [*PleierT*]

KILLARAUS [*Killare, Hilomar*]

An Irish mountain, where the Giants' Dance was located before it was removed to Salisbury plain by Merlin. It is probably the real mountain of Kildare, an identification made by Giraldus Cambrensis. [*GeoffHR*]

KILLIRJACAC

A very handsome count from Champagne. His uncle was Kaylet, the King of Spain. Killirjacac served Duke Gaschier of Normandy and accompanied Gaschier on his invasion of Zazamanc, the land of Queen Belacane. He was defeated with the other invaders by Perceval's father Gahmuret, who was fighting for the queen. Killirjacac later participated in the tournament at Kanvoleis. [*Wolfram*]

KIMAR

According to Geoffrey of Monmouth, king of Britain in the fourth or third century BC. He was the son of King Sisillius and the brother of King Danius, who succeeded him. [*GeoffHR*]

KIMBELIN [*Cinbelin*]

A figure from Welsh myth that Geoffrey adopted as one of Arthur's warriors. He was the son of Trunat. [*GeoffHR*]

KIMMARC [*Kinmare, Kynmar, Rimarec*]

A duke or earl who governed Canterbury under King Arthur. [*GeoffHR, Wace, Layamon*]

KIMMARCOCH [*Chinmark, Kinnard*]

The earl of Tréguier who fought for Arthur in the campaign against Rome. He died at the battle of Soissons. Layamon alters his name and kingdom to Kinard of Striguil. [*GeoffHR, Wace, Layamon*]

KINCAR [*Ringar*]

One of Arthur's champions who was the son of Bangan. He appears first in Geoffrey of Monmouth, who seems to have adopted his name from Welsh mythology. [*GeoffHR, Wace, Layamon*]

KING OF LOVE

An enigmatic figure in Andreas's *De Amore*. The King of Love wrote the thirty-one "Rules of Love" onto a parchment, which fell into the hands of an unnamed "Briton" knight when he won a hawk from Arthur's court. Like Father Time or Mother Nature, the "King of Love" is more metaphorical than corporeal. [*Andreas*]

KING OF SUFFERING

A potentate of an unnamed land. He was so called because each day, one of his sons had to be sacrificed to a cave-dwelling beast. After their deaths, they would be revived, only to be killed again only a few days later. The King and his sons were relieved of their torment when Peredur killed the beast and ended the ritual. [*Peredur*]

KING OF THE ISLES

A lord who Arthur decided to subjugate. He sent Gawain and Sir Hunbaut to the King of the Isles' court to demand the lord's submission. The two knights delivered their message and left hastily. [*Hunbaut*]

KING OF THE LAKE

In Malory, a knight appointed by Arthur to the Round Table after the battle of the Humber. The same character is called LACH by the Post-Vugate *Suite du Merlin*. [*Malory*]

KING OF THE RED CITY

A nobleman who fought at Arthur's tournament at Tenebroc. He was defeated in combat by Erec. [*ChretienE*]

KING OF THE VALLEY

One of five kings that invaded Britain at the begging of Arthur's reign. Arthur's forces slew him and his allies at the battle of the Humber River. [*PostMer, Malory*]

KING OF THE WATCH

A nobleman who lodged Gawain while the latter was on a quest for the Grail Sword. The King made Gawain promise to return and show him the sword once Gawain had obtained it. When Gawain kept his promise, the King of the Watch stole the sword, but priests made him return it. [*Perlesvaus*]

KING WITH A HUNDRED KNIGHTS [*Roi des Cent Chevaliers*]

A valiant and bold king who plagued Arthur at the beginning of Arthur's reign. He first appears in the Prose *Lancelot*, although Ulrich von Zatzikhoven mentions a king named RITSCHART, who is said to have 100 knights. The King's actual name varies from story to story: *Lancelot* calls him MALAGUIN; the Third Continuation of Chrétien's *Perceval* gives him the name MARGON; in the Prose *Tristan*, his proper name is HERAUT. Malory tells us that although his knights numbered only 100, but he kept them "extremely fine in appearance at all points."

Variously identified as the sovereign of Malehaut, Estrangorre, Guzilagne, Piacenza, or part of Logres, the King with a Hundred Knights was one of the rebellious kings that Arthur defeated at Bedegraine. He eventually allied with Arthur in order defeat the invading Saxons, and he participated in Arthur's war against Rome. Later, however, he was conquered by lord Galehaut, and he joined Galehaut's war against Arthur. When Arthur and Galehaut forged a truce, the King again submitted to Arthur's rule and became a Knight of the Round Table. He had a son named Maranz and a daughter named Landoine, both of whom were saved from a pack of robbers by Sir Bors. He loved the Queen of North Wales and Isolde. The Italian *I Due Tristani* says that he married Riccarda, Galehaut's sister. *La Tavola Ritonda* describes his death at the battle of Lerline, fighting alongside King Amoroldo of Ireland. [*LancLac, VulgLanc, VulgMer, ProsTris, Tavola, DueTris, Malory*]

KINGDOM OF DAMSELS

A beautiful island kingdom saved by Arthur in *Le Chevalier du Papegau*. It's queen, Flor de Mont, was overthrown and imprisoned by the wicked steward of her late father, King Beauvoisin. The steward imprisoned her in the Fearless Keep and retired himself to the Perilous Castle. Arthur, responding to the queen's entreaties, slew the steward and saved the kingdom. [*ChevPap*]

KINGDOM OF NO RETURN

A nickname for GORRE, Sir Meleagant's land. [*VulgLanc*]

KINGDOM OF THE ISLES

A kingdom that was the home of Brien of the Isles, an enemy of Gawain. It was ruled by the Lady of the Isles, and its capital was Rades. [*Meriadeuc*]

KINGRIMURSEL

Prince of Ascalun in Wolfram von Eschenbach's *Parzival*. He was the landgrave of Schanpfanzun, the nephew of Ascalun's slain King Kingrisin, and the cousin and vassal of Kingrisin's son Vergulaht. Kingrimursel, blaming Kingrisin's death on Gawain, challenged Gawain to a duel at Schanpfanzun and promised him safe passage through Ascalun until the duel. King Vergulaht, however, became irate when he saw Gawain flirting with his sister, and he summoned his men to attack Gawain. Kingrimursel, enraged that Vergulaht had broken his word, fought alongside Gawain against Vergulaht's men until Vergulaht relented. They set a new time and place for the duel, but before it could take place, Gawain was exonerated of the death of Kingrisin. Kingrimursel is known in Chrétien's *Perceval* as GUINGANBRESIL. [*Wolfram*]

KINGRISIN

King of Ascalun and husband of Flurdamurs, with whom he fathered Vergulaht. Kingrisin was slain by Count Ehkunat, and Vergulaht inherited his kingdom. For some reason, Kingrisin's death was blamed on Gawain, and his nephew Kingrimursel challenged Gawain to a duel in revenge. Gawain was eventually exonerated. [*Wolfram*]

KINGRIVALS

The capital of North Wales, ruled by Queen Herzeloyde, Perceval's mother. [*Wolfram*]

KINGRUN

The seneschal of King Clamide (Clamadeu). With Clamide, he invaded the land of Brobarz and besieged Belrepeire, castle of the lady Condwiramurs. Clamide and Kingrun would have succeeded but for the arrival of Perceval, who defeated them both in combat. Kingrun had killed Schenteflurs, the son of Gornemant, and for this reason he refused when Perceval ordered him to report to Gornemant. Rather than kill Kingrun, Perceval sent him to King Arthur instead. Kingrun's counterpart in Chrétien de Troyes is ANGUIGUERRON. [*Wolfram*]

KING'S FORTRESS

A Frankish castle on the Humber river, near the border of Sorelois, where Lancelot and Galehaut once lodged. [*VulgLanc*]

KINKENART [*Quinquenart*]

One of many Saxon kings who invaded Britain at the beginning of Arthur's reign. He raided and plundered northern Britain, plaguing King Brandegorre of Estrangorre. Sagremor killed him. [*VulgMer, Livre*]

KINLITH [*Kinlint*]

Son of Nwython, brother of Rhun, and one of Arthur's champions. [*GeoffHR, Wace*]

KINMARCH

According to Geoffrey of Monmouth, king of Britain in the sixth century BC. He was the son of King Sisillius and the father of King Gorbodug. [*GeoffHR*]

KINMARK

Father of the warrior Grimarc. [*Layamon*]

KLAMORZ

A knight present at the Sorgarda tournament, which Gawain won. [*Heinrich*]

KLARETSCHANZE

A lady from Portugal loved by Duke Eskilabon of Belamunt. In her service, he defeated and imprisoned many knights, until he himself was defeated by Arthur's Sir Garel. [*PleierG*]

KLARINE[1]

Duchess of Argentin and wife of Duke Elimar. Her husband was slain by the giant Purdan. Arthur's Sir Garel saved her son, Klaris, from the giant's prison, but Klarine died from grief over the loss of her husband. [*PleierG*]

KLARINE[2]

Queen of Turtus and wife of Amurat. Her daughter, Duzabel, was kidnapped by the giant Purdan and was rescued by Sir Garel. [*PleierG*]

KLARIS

The duke of Argentin who Sir Garel saved from the giant Purdan's prison. His father, Elimar, had been slain by the giant, and his mother, Klarine, died of grief. In gratitude to Garel, Klaris pledged his support in Arthur's war against King Ekuanver of Kanadic. Arthur later made him a Knight of the Round Table. [*PleierG*]

KLERDENIS

A knight present at the Sorgarda tournament, which Gawain won. [*Heinrich*]

KLEVE

In *Lohengrin*, the Countess of Kleve convinced Duchess Elsam of Brabant to ask Loherangrin, Perceval's son and Elsam's husband, his name and lineage. Loherangrin had forbidden the question and he left Elsam when she asked it. [*Lohengrin*]

KLIMBERKO

A knight defeated by Tristan at a tournament at Baroh in Pazareia. [*Povest*]

KLOUDITE

The wife of King Ekunaver of Kanadic, an enemy of Arthur. She inherited the land of Kanadic from her sister, Florie. [*PleierG*]

KNIGHT OF LADIES [*Chevalier as Dames*]

An alias adopted by Arthur's Sir MERIADEUC when traveling incognito. [*Meriadeuc*]

KNIGHT OF MAIDENS[1] [*Chevalier as Damoisels*]

A nickname for Gawain, alluding originally to his reputation as a playboy. However, in the Post-Vulgate *Suite du Merlin*, Gawain adopts the name after he accidentally kills a the maiden lover of Blamoure and swears to help all damsels in distress from then on. [*Raoul, PostMer*]

KNIGHT OF MAIDENS[2]

When Guiron the Courteous first arrived at King Uther Pendragon's court, he was accompanied by over a dozen young maidens, thus earning himself this nickname. [*Palamedes*]

KNIGHT OF THE BRIDGE

Former ruler of the Dolorous Guard, the castle Lancelot conquered. He may be identical to BRANDIN OF THE ISLES. His was called the "knight of the bridge" because he guarded a bridge and attacked all Queen's Knights, for he harbored a hate for Guinevere. [*ProsTris*]

KNIGHT OF THE BURNING DRAGON

A demonic lord who, in *Perlesvaus*, inhabited the Castle of Giants on the Island of the Elephants. The Knight carried a shield which was possessed by a devil, and which spouted bursts of flame on command. He terrorized Arthur's lands, and crispened many good knights, including Perceval's cousin Alain. Perceval sought to avenge the deed. Protected by his own magic shield, Perceval journeyed to the Knight's castle and defeated him in combat. The Knight's shield turned on its master and blasted him to cinders. A similar character is called the KNIGHT OF THE DRAGON in the Fourth Continuation of Chrétien's *Perceval*. [*Perlesvaus*]

KNIGHT OF THE CART[1] [*Chevalier de la Charrete*]

A name given to LANCELOT during his quest to rescue Guinevere from Meleagant of Gorre. In his haste to rush after the Queen, Lancelot rode his horse to death. Looking around for more transportation, he found a churl who was willing to give him a ride in a cart. Lancelot hesitated briefly and then dove in. Since riding in a cart was considered disgraceful for a knight—such a mode of transportation was reserved for criminals on their way to be hanged—shame followed Lancelot throughout the adventure. First told in Chrétien de Troyes's *Lancelot*, versions of this story contained in the Vulgate *Lancelot* and Malory serve to lessen Lancelot's humiliation and to make his ride in the cart a clever, pragmatic tactic. In one passage in the Vulgate *Lancelot*, the title refers to BORS. [*ChretienL, LancLac, Malory*]

KNIGHT OF THE CART[2] [*Chevalier del Car*]

An alias given to Sir RAGUIDEL after his body floated up to Arthur's court in a cart on a boat. [*Vengeance*]

KNIGHT OF THE CASTLE OF THREE ROSES

This knight died for the love of Florine, Palamedes's sister. [*Palamedes*]

KNIGHT OF THE DRAGON[1]

An alias for Sir Segurant the Brown, a great knight of Uther's court, who pursued a dragon throughout his career. [*Palamedes*]

KNIGHT OF THE DRAGON[2]

A fearsome warrior in the Fourth Continuation of *Perceval*, almost identical to the KNIGHT OF THE BURNING DRAGON in *Perlesvaus*. The Knight of the Dragon ruled a city of pagans in the Islands of the Sea. His name reflected the dragon's head which was attached to the front of his shield. At the Knight's command, the head would breathe fire and scorch the Knight's opponents. In this manner, the Knight killed the lover of the lady Claire. Perceval met Claire and learned the circumstances of her lover's death. Perceval tracked down the Knight of the Dragon, who was besieging the city of Montesclaire. Mortally wounded in the subsequent combat, the Knight of the Dragon allowed Perceval to baptize him before he died. [*Contin4*]

KNIGHT OF THE FIELD

A Knight of the Round Table who embarked with the others on the Grail Quest. [*PostQuest*]

KNIGHT OF THE GALLEY

A heathen knight who roamed the sea and murdered Christians. He was killed by Arthur's Sir Meliot of Logres. [*Perlesvaus*]

KNIGHT OF THE GOLDEN ARMS

A designation given to GAWAIN during a tournament in which he won the Circle of Gold. [*Perlesvaus*]

KNIGHT OF THE GOLDEN QUILT

One of Arthur's nights. [*Merveil*]

KNIGHT OF THE GREEN SHIELD

A warrior from the Mores Isles in *Perlesvaus*. Lancelot helped him expel an invader, the Lord of the Rock, after the Knight's brother, Gladoain, was slain in Lancelot's service. In *Palamedes*, Brunor the Black is known by this alias. [*Perlesvaus, Palamedes*]

KNIGHT OF THE HIGH MOUNTAIN

A knight who participated in a tournament thrown by Arthur at the Castle of Maidens. [*Renaut*]

KNIGHT OF THE HORN [*Chevalier au Cor*]

An Arthurian knight found in two French romances. [*ChretienE, Merveil*]

KNIGHT OF THE ILL-FITTING COAT

A Knight of the Round Table whose true name in some romances is BRUNOR THE BLACK. It appears that he was the subject of a now lost French romance. A fragment, called *Le Vallet à la Cote Mal Tailliée*, relates how he arrives at Arthur's court but is rejected for a place in Arthur's service. After the Knight departs, Gawain speaks in his favor and sends a courier to bring him back. Given the style of similar romances, including the Knight's story in the Prose *Tristan*, we may assume that in the original, the messenger failed to convince the Knight of the Ill-Fitting Coat to return, spurring Arthur to send a group of knights after him. The Knight would have then defeated Arthur's knights, embarked on a series of adventures, proven his merit, and returned to find an open seat at the Round Table. In any event, he is listed among Arthur's knights in Renaut de Bâgé's *Le Bel Inconnu*, the Second Continuation of Chrétien's *Perceval*, and *Les Merveilles de Rigomer*.

His original story, probably modified, is inserted into the Prose *Tristan*. We learn from this and other sources that he was the brother of Dinadan and Daniello. We hear in *La Tavola Ritonda* that he hated Lancelot because Lancelot had slain Daniello. The two knights fought to a draw at the castle Dusbergo.

The Knight of the Ill-Fitting Coat has a chapter in Malory's book of Tristan, expanded from a shorter version in the Prose *Tristan*. When he first arrived at Arthur's court wearing his misshapen coat, Kay scoffed at him. The coat had belonged to Brunor's murdered father (the Good Knight Without Fear), and Brunor had vowed to wear the coat until his father's death was avenged. Arthur knighted him, and he soon proved his merit by rescuing Guinevere from a lion that had escaped from the king's menagerie. Kay humiliated him by arranging for Brunor's first joust to be with Daguenet, Arthur's fool.

Responding to the request of Ill-Speaking Maiden, Arthur sent Brunor to avenge the death of a knight in Sorelois. He was miserably defeated in joust against Bleoberis and Palamedes along the way, but it turned out that Brunor only lacked skill in joust. On foot, he slew a dozen knights at the castle Orguellous. He befriended Lancelot (in contrast to *Tavola*), who rescued him from the Castle Pendragon. Together, they went to Sorelois and defeated six brothers named Playne de Fors, Playne de Amors, Plenorius, Pillounes, Pellogris, and Pellandis, completing the quest. On the return to Camelot, Lancelot evicted Brian of the Isles from the Castle Pendragon and gave the fortress to Brunor. Brunor married the Ill-Speaking Maiden, whose name he changed to Beau Vivant. Arthur eventually promoted him to the Round Table. [*Vallet, Renaut, ProsTris, PostQuest, Malory*]

KNIGHT OF THE LANTERN

Step-son of the King of India. To insure that the Knight of the Lantern would inherit the kingdom, his mother enchanted the King's own sons into the form of dogs. One of these sons, Prince Alexander, was known as the Crop-Eared Dog. The Knight of the Lantern went to Arthur's court and offended the king, which led Gawain on a quest to avenge the insult. With the Crop-Eared Dog's assistance, Gawain tracked the Knight of the Lantern down, defeated him, and forced him to restore Alexander to his human form. [IrishD]

KNIGHT OF THE LITTER

An alias for LANCELOT, which he used after he was wounded during his early adventures, but before he knew his real name. [VulgLanc]

KNIGHT OF THE MILL

The name given to PEREDUR Long Spear when he fought in a tournament before the Empress of Constantinople. Peredur was lodging with a miller at the time. [Peredur]

KNIGHT OF THE PARROT

King Arthur's alias in the French romance Le Chevalier du Papegau. Arthur adopted the name after winning a magic parrot in a tournament at the Castle Causuel, in which he championed the Lady Without Pride. The parrot was intelligent: it sang, recounted Merlin's prophecies, and advised Arthur during his adventures. Served by a dwarf, it was kept in a golden, bejeweled cage. Arthur enjoyed several adventures under this pseudonym. [ChevPap]

KNIGHT OF THE PASSAGE

A knight defeated by Arthur in front of the Fearless Keep in the Kingdom of Damsels. The Knight of the Passage lodged Arthur following his defeat. [ChevPap]

KNIGHT OF THE SLEEVE

Hero of a Dutch romance. His mother was a queen, but he was raised in a monastery. During his numerous adventures, in which he overcame knights, giants, and beasts, he carried the sleeve of his paramour, Clarette, on the tip of his lance. He embarked on a successful quest to find his father. He eventually won the right to marry Clarette during a tournament at Arthur's court. His true name was MIRAUDIJS. [Riddere]

KNIGHT OF THE SPRING

An alias for Sir ATAMAS, a knight who guarded the Spring of Healing and was defeated by Palamedes. [PostQuest]

KNIGHT OF THE SURCOAT

The nickname given to GAWAIN after he was knighted by the Emperor of Rome. Ignorant of his real name during his upbringing, he was first called the Boy with No Name, but was dubbed the Knight of the Surcoat after his fellow knights were surprised to see him wear a tunic over his armor—a custom then unknown in Rome. [DeOrtu]

KNIGHT OF THE TOMB

An adventure encountered by Perceval in the Second Continuation of Chrétien's Perceval and the Didot-Perceval. Perceval came across a tomb in his quest to hunt a white stag for the lady of Chessboard Castle. The Knight of the Tomb, also known as the BLACK KNIGHT, who came from the forest of Argonne, lived in the tomb at the behest of his paramour. In the Second Continuation, the Knight of the Tomb emerges and fights with Perceval, is defeated, and must return to the tomb. In the Didot-Perceval, Perceval frees him, and the ungrateful Knight of the Tomb shoves Perceval into the tomb and locks it. However, the Knight of the Tomb, who didn't have a mount, was unable to get Perceval's enchanted mule to move. He was forced to release Perceval from the tomb and to resume his place.

During the battle between Perceval and the Knight of the Tomb, Garsallas, the Knight of the Tomb's half-brother, ran off with Perceval's hound and the head of a stag Perceval had slain, sending Perceval on a series of quests that prolonged his return to Chessboard Castle. [Contin2, Didot]

KNIGHT OF THE TOWER

An alias for Sir ATAMAS, who inhabited the Giant's Tower and was defeated by Palamedes. [PostQuest]

KNIGHT OF THE TWO SWORDS

The name adopted by MERIADEUC during his early adventures at Arthur's court. Ignorant of his true name, he was called Handsome Young Man until knighted by Arthur. He received sword froms both Arthur and his future wife, Lady Lore of Cardigan, for which Kay gave him this alias. [Meriadeuc]

KNIGHT OF THE VALLEY [*Chevalier de la Vale

An ugly knight defeated in combat by Arthur's Sir Brandelis. [Claris]

KNIGHT OF THE WHITE SHIELD

The name assigned to PERCEVAL during the tournament at the Red Land, in which Perceval bore a white shield. See also WHITE KNIGHT. [Perlesvaus]

KNIGHT OF TRIPLE ARMS [*Chevalier as Armes Trebles]

The champion of Rigomer Castle whose real name was JORANS LI FEBLES. [Merveil]

KNIGHT OF TWO SHIELDS [*Chevalier as Dous Escus]

An alias for Sir BEAUDOUS, Gawan's son, referring to his custom double-shield. [RobertBlo]

KNIGHT WITH THE BLACK SHIELD

The name given to Sir TRISTAN at the Castle of Maidens tournament when Tristan would not reveal his own name. [Malory]

KNIGHT WITH THE EAGLE

A nickname for Sir WIGAMUR, an Arthurian knight who saved an eagle from a vulture and thus gained a loyal companion. [*Wigamur*]

KNIGHT WITH THE LION

In Chrétien's *Yvain* and its adaptations, the alias given to YVAIN after he rescued a lion from a serpent. The lion became Yvain's friend and guardian and refused to leave his side. In the Prose *Lancelot*, this designation is given to Yvain after Sir Lionel gives him the skin of the Crowned Lion of Libya. [*ChretienY, LancDoLac, Owain, Ivens*]

KNIGHT WITH THE STRANGE BEAST

A nickname of King PELLINORE, referring to his ceaseless hunt for the elusive QUESTING BEAST. [*ProsTris, Malory*]

KNIGHT WITH TWO SWORDS

An alias of Sir BALIN the Savage, who once carried two swords. [*PostMer, Malory*]

KNIGHT-GIANT

A character in *Le Chevalier du Papegau*. He loved the Lady of Estrales. She, in turn, was infatuated with Arthur, called the Knight of the Parrot, and an incensed Knight-Giant swore to bring her Arthur's dismembered hand. He encountered Arthur in the forest and was mortally wounded after a long battle. Before he died, he apologized to Arthur and gave him his magic breast plate. His brother, the Redoubted Giant of the Sure Keep, tried to avenge his death but failed. [*ChevPap*]

KNIGHTS OF BATTLE

A trio of Arthur's knights—Cador, Lancelot, and Owain—mentioned in Welsh legend. They were exceptionally noble and brave in combat. [*Triads*]

KNIGHTS OF THE WATCH

A group of Arthur's knights who were brave and honorable, but were inferior to the Knights of the Round Table. It is first mentioned by Chrétien in *Perceval*. The Prose *Lancelot* tells us that it seated 150 knights, which may be the origin of Malory's assertion that the Round Table sat 150. An order of a similar nature is called the TABLE OF ERRANT COMPANIONS in the Post-Vulgate. [*ChretienP, LancLac, VulgLanc*]

KOLLR

A swineherd who served Queen Flúrent of Ireland, Isolde's mother. His sty was by the sea, and he was thus in a position to report immediately to his queen any news from the ocean, including Tristan's first arrival. [*SagaTI*]

KORALUS

The name of Enide's father according to Hartmann von Aue. He is called LICORANT by Chrétien de Troyes. Once a wealthy nobleman, he was wrongfully dispossessed, and was forced to live in abject poverty with his wife (Karsinefite) and daughter in the city of Tulmein, which belonged to Koralus's brother-in-law, Imain. Despite his dire situation, he gave good hospitality to Erec when Erec came to Tulmein to compete in the sparrowhawk tournament, and he lent Erec a suit of armor, a sword, and his daughter Enide for the occasion. After Erec and Enide married, Erec's father Lac made Koralus the lord of the castles Montrevel and Roadan. [*HartmannE*]

KORNTIN

A land ruled by King Lar and Queen Amire. Korntin was seized by the evil King Roaz of Glois. King Lar was killed, and Queen Amire was driven to the castle of Roimunt on the edge of the kingdom. Korntin was wrongfully held by Roaz for ten years before Wigalois (Gawain's son) arrived to answer Amire's call for help. He killed Roaz and became the King of Korntin. Lamire, the daughter of Lar and Amire, was his queen. [*Wirnt*]

KULIANZ THE FOOL

Heinrich von dem Türlin's name for the character called ANTANOR by Wolfram—the mute fool who spoke upon Perceval's arrival at Arthur's court. [*Heinrich*]

KURAUS WITH THE BRAVE HEART

A British knight from Gagunne, encountered by Lancelot early in his adventures. Lancelot came across Kuraus and Orphilet fighting in a clearing. They were both ready to collapse from exhaustion, and Lancelot made them stop fighting. The three knights went together to the castle of Moreiz, where they enjoyed the hospitality of Lord Galagandreiz. Galagandreiz was of uneven disposition, and Kuraus feared him. For this reason, he declined to sleep with Galagandreiz's daughter when she offered herself to him. At the end of their adventure, Kuraus invited Lancelot back to Gagunne, but Lancelot declined.

R. S. Loomis thought that *Kuraus* is a derivation of *cuars*, meaning "coward." His character is an allusion to the French tale (found in Manessier's continuation of *Perceval* and in *Perlesvaus*) of the coward knight who later turns out to be brave, and is thus given a new name—hence "with the Brave Heart." [*UlrichZ*]

KURION

A malicious knight who attacked Queen Albiun of the Wild Mountain, intending to steal her lands. He was defeated by Arthur's Sir Tandareis, ending the assault. [*PleierT*]

KUSAN

In the Serbo-Russian *Povest' o Tryshchane*, a vassal of the Queen of Ireland who, by bringing his queen Tristan's sword, identified Tristan as the knight who slew Morholt. He appears as an unnamed youth in the Prose *Tristan*. [*Povest*]

KYLE

A region of southwest Scotland. It originally belonged to Sir Galleron, but Arthur annexed it and gave it to Gawain. Galleron arrived at a feast and challenged Gawain for ownership of the land. The fight ended in a draw, but Gawain graciously returned the country to Galleron anyway. [*Awntyrs*]

KYLLICRATES OF CETRIUN

A vassal of Feirefiz, Perceval's half-brother. [*Wolfram*]

KYMBELYN

One of Arthur's knights in the English *Arthur*, present at one of Arthur's Easter feasts. He was the son of Gryffith. [*Arthur*]

KYNKE KENADONNE [*Kynkenadon*]

An castle near the border of Wales. Arthur held his Pentecost feast here one year. Gareth was married in the castle. [*Malory*]

KYOT

A titular duke of Katelangen who gave up his fief in order to enter into spiritual service. He was the brother of Tampenteire and Mampfilyot, the husband of Schoysiane, the father of Sigune, and the paternal uncle of Perceval's wife Condwiramurs. When Condwiramurs' country was invaded, Kyot and his brother Mampfilyot assisted her as well as possible, but they needed Perceval to save the duchy. When Perceval was anointed as Grail King, Duke Kyot escorted Perceval's wife and sons to the Grail Castle to join Perceval. [*Wolfram*]

L

LA CHOINE

A castle in Sarras ruled by King Evalach. It was the site of a battle between Evalach and King Tholomer of Babylonia. With Joseph of Arimathea's help, Evalach won. Great feats of arms were performed by Seraphe (Nascien) and a mysterious, God-sent, White Knight. [*VulgEst*]

LA ROCHELLE

A French city on the English Channel, where Arthur landed on his way to battle Claudas. [*VulgMer*]

LAAMEZ OF BABYLON

A knight present at the Sorgarda tournament, which Gawain won. [*Heinrich*]

LAAMORZ

A terrible knight who inhabited the castle of Janfrüege in Heinrich von dem Türlin's *Diu Crône*. His castle was enchanted to render any knight who entered powerless. A malicious goddess named Giramphiel sent Gawain to the castle, hoping to destroy him, but Lady Fortune warned Gawain of the danger. As a result, Gawain refused to enter Janfrüege, but insisted that Laamorz meet him outside. Gawain won the combat and secured Laamorz's fealty. Laamorz recalls MABUZ in Ulrich von Zatzikhoven's *Lanzalet*. [*Heinrich*]

LABEGUES

In Paolino Pieri's *La Storia di Merlino*, one of two messengers from Vortigern who, seeking a boy without a father, found Merlin in Northumberland. His companion was called Ruggieri. [*Pieri*]

LABEL

A pagan King of Persia, converted to Christianity by Celidoine, the son of Nascien. Label, who had been knighted by King Evalach of Sarras, was traveling to a war against King Fanoyel of Syria when he encountered Celidoine. He died soon after his baptism, and his men, who had refused to convert, put Celidoine out to sea in a small boat with a hungry lion. Celidoine survived and later married Sarrasinte, Label's daughter, who became a follower of Joseph of Arimathea. A variation of the name, LABELL, is given to a king's daughter in two English versions of Joseph of Arimathea's story. [*VulgEst*]

LABELL

Probably from a confusion of LABEL, a maiden who appears in the English *Here Begynneth the Lyfe of Joseph of Armathia* as the daughter of the Welsh king who imprisoned Joseph of Arimathea and his followers when they first arrived in Britain. The king was besieged by Mordrain, to whom he offered Labell as a peace offering. Labell and Mordrain married. She appears in the *Lyfe of Joseph of Armathy* as Celidoine's wife. [*HereJOA, LyfeJOA*]

LABIGADES

A knight in Arthur's service. [*Heinrich*]

LABIUS

A British earl who was killed fighting the Romans at the battle of Soissons. [*Layamon*]

LABOR

Guinevere's first cousin. He gave the queen advice on how to protect herself during Mordred's uprising. [*VulgMort*]

LAC[1] [*Ilax, Lake*]

Erec's father, who, like his son, first appears in Chrétien de Troyes's *Erec*. He is variously called the king of Nantes, Destregales, Celis, Seland, Carnant, or the Black Isles. In Wolfram's *Parzival*, he has a daughter named Jeschute, the Post-Vulgate *Queste del Saint Graal* credits him with another unnamed daughter, and in *Palamedes*, he has a second son named Brandelis. He bestowed the cities of Motrevel and Roadan on Enide's father when she married Erec. In the early *Erec* tales, he dies peacefully, and his son inherits his throne.

The Post-Vulgate *Queste* gives a tale of Lac (and Erec) at odds with previous stories. Here, Lac is the son of King Canan of Salolliqui in Greece. His father was assassinated, forcing Lac and his brother Dirac, both still children, to flee Greece for Britain. There, they were found, raised, and knighted by a young Arthur, and both became kings. Lac married King Pelles's sister, Crisea. Dirac's sons eventually became jealous of Lac's greater fame and killed him, seizing his castle. Erec avenged the murder.

Lac's name means "lake" in French. In origin, he may be the Welsh LLWCH, which also means "lake." According to Wolfram, he took his name from a spring near Karnant. [*ChretienE, Erex, Wolfram, Heinrich, PostQuest, Palamedes*]

LAC[2]

Father of Sir Cliges, a knight at Arthur's court. [*Contin1*]

LAC[3]

A spring near Karnant from which King Lac received his name. According to Wolfram, the water of the spring could mend the Grail Sword if it was shattered. After

Perceval broke the sword in a duel, the spring was able to repair it. [*Wolfram*]

LAC⁴

A king of Great India in Arthur's time, according to the Vulgate *Merlin*. He sent his seneschal, Minoras, to help Arthur in the Saxon Wars. [*VulgMer*]

LAC⁵

King of Greater Orkney. Galehaut conquered him. [*Livre*]

LAC⁶

The son of Erec and Enide, named after King Lac. Both Lac and his brother Odus became kings. [*Erex*]

LAC⁷

Yvain's brother, Tristan's friend, and Arthur's knight. [*Tavola*]

LACEN [*Lacene*]

A British forest where Gawain, Agravain, and Mordred killed Drian and Lamorat, the sons of Pellinore, in a blood quarrel. In Malory, this event occurs near Sorelois. [*PostMer*]

LACH

In the Post-Vulgate *Merlin* continuation, a king appointed by Arthur to the Round Table after the battle of the Humber. This is perhaps the same person as King LAC, Erec's father. Malory calls this character the KING OF THE LAKE, as his name means "lake" in French. [*PostMer*]

LADAS

A king who fell in love with Sir Caradoc Shortarm's ladylove. He tricked Caradoc into agreeing to fight against eight of Ladas's knights with only two other knight's fighting on Caradoc's side. Caradoc chose Claris and Laris as his companions, and the three knights were victorious. Ladas was killed. [*Claris*]

LADIANA [*Labiane*]

The niece of King Mark of Cornwall. Her brother, Aldret (Andred), was Mark's adviser. Mark raped her, begetting Meraugis, who later became a Knight of the Round Table. Mark locked Ladiana in a tower when he discovered that she was pregnant. After she gave birth to Meraugis, Mark slew her and left her body to be eaten by wild beasts. [*PostQuest*]

LADINAS¹

A knight from Benoic who accompanied his master, King Ban, to Britain, when Ban allied with Arthur. Ladinas fought in the battle of Bedegraine, against the kings in rebellion against Arthur, and at the battle of Carhaix, against King Rions's Saxons. [*VulgMer, Arthour, Malory*]

LADINAS²

A young knight from North Wales who fought alongside Gawain in some early Saxon skirmishes. [*VulgMer*]

LADINAS³

A knight defeated and captured when Meleagant kidnapped Guinevere. [*Malory*]

LADINEL

An early companion of Gawain who fought in the Saxon Wars. [*VulgMer*]

LADIS

King of Lombardie who joined his ally, Emperor Thereus of Rome, in a war against Arthur. [*Claris*]

LADOMAS

A British knight. Ladomas accidentally laid down in the same bed as his cousin's lady. His cousin, Guinas of Blakestan, found him there and wounded him badly in an ensuing skirmish. Arthur's Sir Hector defeated Guinas and made him reconcile with Ladomas. Hector had unknowingly killed Ladomas's brother Mataliz while defending Mataliz's enemy. When Ladomas discovered this, he let Hector go to repay him for his service with Guinas, but warned him that they would fight if they met again. [*LancLac, VulgLanc*]

LADON

King of Gascony who married Lidoine, the sister of Arthur's Sir Laris. He was past his prime when the marriage took place and he soon died, allowing Lidoine to marry Sir Claris, her true love. [*Claris*]

LADY OF THE BLONDE HAIR

Arthur's paramour in *Le Chevalier du Papegau*. The Lady was the fairy sovereigness of the Amorous City, and she was plagued by a horrible creature known as the Fish-Knight. Arthur slew the monster after the Lady's servant, Beauty Without Villany, came to Arthur's court looking for assistance. The Lady of the Blonde Hair fell in love with Arthur, but angered him by making him promise to act as "the worst knight in the world" during a tournament at her castle. Arthur was so furious at this humiliation that he beat the Lady. Later, the two made up and became lovers. [*ChevPap*]

LADY OF THE FOUNTAIN

Wife of the Lord of the Fountain. When Owain killed her husband she married Owain, but renounced him when he spent a year away from her at Arthur's court. After a number of grueling adventures, Owain was able to return to her graces. She is known as the Lady, or Countess, of the Fountain in the Welsh *Owain*, and as LAUDINE in other tales. [*Owain*]

LADY OF THE ISLES

Queen of the Kingdom of the Isles. She swore to only marry the best knight in Britain, whom she perceived as Gawain. One of her vassals, Brian of the Isles, set out to defeat Gawain, thereby proving himself the best knight and earning the right to marry the Lady. Brian returned to the Kingdom claiming that he had slain Gawain, and the Lady prepared to marry him, but Gawain showed up on their wedding day and ended the marriage. The Lady's sister was the Queen of Iceland. [*Meriadeuc*]

LADY OF THE LAKE

An enigmatic fairy credited with imprisoning Merlin, raising Lancelot, giving Excalibur to Arthur, and bearing Arthur's body to Avalon. Some of these roles are given to MORGAN LE FAY in some versions, and it is likely that the two characters emerged from the same Celtic goddess, called MODRON. The Italian *La Tavola Ritonda* says that Morgan was her sister. Some texts, such as the Post-Vulgate *Suite du Merlin* or Malory's *Le Morte Darthur*, have more than one character bearing this title. Her proper names include NINIANNE, VIVIANE, NINA, and NIMUE, all seemingly scribal variants of each other.

Her first role seems to have been Lancelot's foster-mother; in Chrétien de Troyes's *Lancelot*, we learn that Lancelot has a magical ring given to him by his foster-mother, and that "this lady was a fairy...who had cared for him in infancy." In Ulrich von Zatzikhoven's *Lanzelet*, we see Lancelot's upbringing by the Queen of MAIDENLAND. The Queen also has a son named Mabuz, who probably owes his character to the Welsh Mabon, son of Modron.

Neither of these romances call Lancelot's guardian the "Lady of the Lake," though the character is roughly identical to the Lady specifically named in the Vulgate *Lancelot*, which continues the tradition. Here, her home was an invisible island in the Lake of Diana in Brittany. Both Ulrich and *Lancelot* tell how the Lady, or one of her servants, took the infant Lancelot from his mother after his father's kingdom fell to an invasion or revolt. In Ulrich, her nurturing of Lancelot was part of a larger plan to revenge herself on Iweret, a powerful lord who wronged her son Mabuz. She raised Lancelot until he was old enough to depart for Arthur's court. According to *Lancelot*, she accompanied him to Arthur, who knighted the boy at her request. She left him after bestowing upon him the magic ring mentioned by Chrétien. *Lancelot* says that she also raised Lionel and Bors, Lancelot's cousins. She assisted Lancelot throughout his adventures, providing magic weapons and armor when needed, and curing him of insanity after he went mad in a Saxon prison. In similar ways, she also provided assistance to Lionel and Bors.

It is also in the Vulgate *Lancelot* that we first find the assertion that she imprisoned Merlin, which apparently occurred before Lancelot's birth. The Lady used Merlin's love to learn his craft, then—after she had learned enough—she sealed him in a pit in the forest of Darnantes, where he remained forever. The Lady's treatment of Merlin in *Lancelot* is difficult to reconcile with her more noble behavior towards Lancelot. The Vulgate *Merlin* (and its English translation, called the Prose *Merlin*) handles this conflict by giving Merlin a more romantic end. *Merlin* also provides additional details about the Lady: The daughter of a nobleman named Dyonas, her birth was blessed by Diana, the goddess of the woods. Merlin met her in the forest of Briosque and fell in love with her at first sight. He courted her by dazzling her with enchantment. After learning his magic, she imprisoned him in a tower in the forest of Broceliande, where she visited him often, but never allowed him to leave.

In the *Suite du Merlin* and in Malory, the Lady (called Ninniane or Nimue) first arrives at Arthur's court in pursuit of a white stag. In short time, she and her hound were abducted by Sir Hontzlake of Wentland and Sir Abelleus. Arthur sent Gawain after the stag, assigned Tor to retrieve the hound, and dispatched Pellinore to rescue the Lady. The latter two knights were successful and, in gratitude, the Lady agreed to stay at Arthur's court, where Merlin fell in love with her. According to the *Suite*, the Lady secretly hated Merlin. Again, after learning his spells, she sealed him in a cavern tomb. Malory has her imprison him by placing a stone over the mouth of his cave. She then took Merlin's place as Arthur's advisor. She saved Arthur from his own sword in a battle against Accalon, from a poisoned cloak sent to him by Morgan le Fay, and from a sorceress named Aunowre or Elergia. She also vindicated Guinevere in the murder of Gaheris or Patrise. Malory adds that she married the noble Sir Pelleas. In her final service to Arthur, according to Malory, she was one of the four queens who bore his body from the plain of Salisbury to the Isle of Avalon.

In the *Suite* and Malory, however, the title of the Lady of the Lake also belongs to a woman who gives Excalibur to Arthur in return for a future gift. She later arrived at Arthur's court to claim the gift: the head of Sir Balin, who had killed her brother. Arthur was in the process of refusing the request when Balin showed up and beheaded her, saying that she had killed his mother. In these stories, Ninianne (or Nimue) is presented as the Lady of the Lake's servant; after the Lady's death, Ninianne earns the title herself.

She appears as the title character in Thelwall's *The Fairy of the Lake*, in which she saves Arthur from the Saxon Queen Rowena's seduction, and saves Guinevere from the incestuous plans of her father, King Vortigern. In the *Prophecies de Merlin*, in addition to Lancelot and his cousins, she also raises Tristan's half-brother, Meliadus the Younger, who becomes her lover. [*ChretienL, UlrichZ, LancLac, VulgLanc, VulgMer, PostMer, ProsTris, Prophecies, Tavola, ProsMer2, Malory, VitaMer, Thelwall*]

LADY OF THE LANDS

See MAIDEN OF THE MOORS.

LADY OF THE ROCK

A lady whose lands were stolen by Sir Edward of the Red Castle and Sir Hugh of the Red Castle. When she lodged Sir Yvain during his adventures, he heard her tale and became furious at the injustice. He called for a meeting with the two knights and challenged them to a duel for the lady's lands. He defeated them both at once, killing Edward. Hugh gave the lands back to the Lady. [*Malory*]

LADY OF THE RULE

Mother of Alyne by King Pellinore. [*Malory*]

LADY WITHOUT PRIDE

A sister of Morgan le Fay rescued by Arthur from an attacker called the Knight of the Wasteland. Arthur won a tournament at the Castle Causuel in her honor, winning a parrot. [*ChevPap*]

LÆHTAMRIS

A forest where Perceval defeated King Vergulaht of Ascalun and ordered Vergulaht—as a term of his surrender—to assume a quest for the Grail. Vergulaht later transferred this duty to Gawain. [*Wolfram*]

LAHEDUMAN OF MUNTANE

A vassal of King Poydiconjunz (Bagdemagus). He fought for King Meliant of Lis in the battle of Bearosche and was defeated by Gawain. [*Wolfram*]

LÄHELIN

A king who conquered Wales and North Wales from Queen Herzeloyde, Perceval's mother, in Wolfram's *Parzival*. His brother was Duke Orilus of Lalander and his sister was Cunneware of Lalant. He stole a strong horse named Gringolet from the Grail Knight Lybbeals, and the horse eventually was owned by Gawain. His name may be a variation of the Welsh *Llewellyn* (Bruce, 333n). [*Wolfram*]

LAHIFILIROST

The Burgrave of the city of Patelamunt in Queen Belacane's land of Zazamanc. Lahfilirost welcomed Perceval's father Gahmuret when he arrived and supported him in repelling the invasion of Zazamanc. For his assistance, Gahmuret bestowed upon Lahfilirost the duchy of the slain Duke Prothizilas. [*Wolfram*]

LAILOKEN

A mad prophet from Scottish legend who supposedly lived in the late sixth century, and who many writers identify with MYRDDIN or MERLIN. In a Welsh Myrddin poem known as "The Prophecy of Myrddin and Gwenddydd," Gwenddydd, Myrddin's sister, says, "I ask my *Llallogan* Myrddin, a wise man, a prophet...." *Llallogan* is general translated as "twin brother."

Lailoken's legend is very similar to Myrddin's: Lailoken was said to have participated in a battle between the towns of Lidel and Carwannock. His side suffered enormous losses, and an apparition in the sky blamed Lailoken for the deaths. This episode parallels Myrddin's experience at Arfderydd. Lailoken went insane and ran off

to live in the forest like a wildman, where he spewed random prophecies of his own "triple" death and of the downfall of Britain. King Meldred hauled him into his court for amusement, but was decidedly unamused when Lailoken divined the adultery of Meldred's wife. Lailoken was befriended by Saint Kentigern, who gave Lailoken his Last Rites at Lailoken's request, even though Lailoken's prophecy of his own death seemed impossible: he claimed he would die from a beating of sticks and stones, then from being impaled through the heart with a stake, and then from falling into water. Later, as Lailoken was wandering through a field near Dunmeller, Meldred's shepherds spied him and stoned him. As he began to perish from the beating, he fell off a cliff into the river Tweed— and was impaled through the heart by a protruding stick (Goodrich, 3–11).

LAKE OF IDLENESS

The enchanted residence of the fairy Phaedria, who lured knights to her island with sensual temptations. [*Spenser*]

LAKE OF TWINS [*Lac as Jumeles*]

The homeland of Meriadeuc, a knight of Arthur's court. Meriadeuc inherited the land from his father, Bleheri. Meriadeuc's mother was known as the Lady of the Lake of Twins. [*Meriadeuc*]

LALUTH [*Lalut*]

The city that Erec entered during his pursuit of Yder in Chrétien's *Erec*. In Laluth, Erec stayed with the noble Licorant, met his future wife Enide, and defeated Yder in the sparrowhawk tournament. Hartmann von Aue places these events at TULMEIN, while the Norse *Erex Saga* changes the name to ROSON. [*ChretienE*]

LAMANHA

The birthplace of Frollo, the ruler of Gaul slain by Arthur. [*PostQuest*]

LAMBALE [*Lamba(y)l(e)*, *Lambel(l)e*]

A land ruled by King Amant, an enemy of Arthur. When Amant was slain by King Bors, Lambale fell to Gosengos, Amant's son. It was the home of Arthur's knight Guivret. A "Count of Lambale" appears at the Sorelois tournament in *Palamedes*, but in the Prose *Tristan*, the count himself is named Lambale. [*LancLac*, *VulgLanc*, *VulgMer*, *Palamedes*, *ProsTris*, *Arthour*]

LAMBEGUE [*Lambeguen*, *Lambegues*, *Lambeguez*, *Lanbeguet*]

A Gaulish knight who originally served King Bors of Gannes as a tutor for Bors and Lionel, King Bors' sons. When Gannes was conquered by Claudas, Lambegue unwillingly entered his service. Later, he broke faith, started a revolt, and tried to murder Claudas, but was foiled by the noble Pharien, his own uncle. He eventually reconciled with Pharien. Content that Bors and Lionel were being cared for by the Lady of the Lake, Lambegue left Gannes for Britain, joined Arthur's wars against the Saxons, and became a Knight of the Round Table. Bors saved him from execution in the forest of Roevent. He became a companion of Tristan, and once tried to rescue Isolde from an abduction by Palamedes. He joined the Grail Quest and was present at Corbenic when Galahad completed it. He was killed fighting Lancelot and his men when Lancelot rescued Queen Guinevere from the stake. [*LancLac, VulgLanc, Livre, PostQuest, ProsTris, Malory*]

LAMBEKIN

Duke of Brabant and Hainault in the time of Uther. He married Alize, the sister of King Hardiz of Gascony, and thus became Hardiz's loyal ally. He participated in a tournament at the Welsh city of Kanvoleis, thrown by Perceval's mother, Queen Herzeloyde. [*Wolfram*]

LAMBERGUS

In the Italian *Tristano Riccardiano* and *La Tavola Ritonda*, the husband of the Hebrew Damsel of Thornbush Ford. He found out that his wife and Tristan were having an affair. When he challenged Tristan to combat, he lost. He was also cuckolded by a knight named Blanor or Brunoro, but Tristan returned the woman to Lambergus. In the Prose *Tristan*, the same character is called SEGUARADES. The author of *Tavola* may have confused him with LAMBEGUE, a friend of Tristan in *Tristan*. [*Tavola*]

LAMBETH [*Lambehythe*]

A town in England, across the Thames River from London. Malory names it as the location of Sir Meleagant's castle, which in other legends is in GORRE. [*Malory*]

LAMBOR [*Lambord*]

A Grail King descended from Bron. He ruled Corbenic and the Strange Land. He inherited the post from his father, King Manuel, and passed it on to his son, King Pellehan. He was a man of great Christian faith. His descendants included Pelles, Elaine, and Galahad. Lambor was slain by King Varlan of Wales, who split his head with the forbidden Sword with the Strange Hangings. This was the first Dolorous Stroke, and it created a Waste Land of Wales and the Strange Land. John of Glastonbury's genealogy makes Lambor an ancestor of Arthur through Igerne. [*VulgQuest, VulgEst, PostMer, JohnG, Malory*]

LAMBORC [*Lambor*]

A castle between Camelot and Joyous Guard where Arthur and his knights lodged on their way to wage war against Lancelot. [*VulgMort, PostMort*]

LAMBORE

The Queen of Karmerie who died of sorrow after the untimely passing of her husband, King Garsidis. Her daughter, Tydomie, later married Arthur's nephew, Sir Meleranz. [*PleierM*]

LAMBRION [*Lambrions*]

A castle in Gaul. Its lord was a wise vassal of King Claudas. He stopped an unfortunate duel between Pharien and Lambegue, two worthy knights and relatives who were fighting over Lambegue's plot to kill Claudas. [*VulgLanc*]

LAMBUS

One of the many Saxon kings who, under the Saxon King Hargadabran, fought against Arthur at the battle of Clarence. [*Livre*]

LAMENDRAGOT

A Knight of the Round Table. [*HartmannE*]

LAMER

An Arabian warlord. He invaded and plundered Libya in order to locate a magical suit of armor. His brother Brien later killed him for this armor, which eventually wound up in the possession of Gawain's son Wigalois. [*Wirnt*]

LAMET [*Lamer*]

The baptismal name of ORCANT, an ancestor of Gawain. [*VulgEst*]

LAMIDE

One of Isolde's maidservants. She accompanied Isolde's from Ireland to Cornwall, and later to Tristan and Isolde's exile in the Forest of Morrois. [*ProsTris*]

LAMMIRE

In Wolfram's *Parzival*, Perceval's paternal aunt, the daughter of Gandin of Anjou, and the sister of Flurdamurs, Gahmuret and Galoes. She was appointed by her father as Queen of Styria. She became the wife or mistress of Ither, the "Red Knight" slain by Perceval. In Der Pleier's *Garel*, she is the mother of Garel of the Blooming Valley, having apparently married King Meleranz after her affair with Ither. [*Wolfram, PleierG*]

LAMORAT[1] [*Amorotto, Lamerok, Lamorak, Lamorant*]

A Knight of the Round Table named after his uncle. He was the son of King Pellinore and the brother of Aglovale, Perceval, Alain, Drian, Tor, and Meliodan. His story is related by the Prose *Tristan*, the Post-Vulgate Cycle, and Malory. Among his more noteworthy adventures are the liberation of the Castle of the Ten Knights, his victory at the Sorelois tournament, and the conquest of the Isle of Servage. In this last adventure, he teamed with Tristan. (Tristan and Lamorat had previously been enemies: Tristan once refused to joust with Lamorat, so Lamorat arranged for a magical horn that proved infidelity to be sent to Isolde.) Malory considered Lamorat the third greatest knight in Britain, behind Lancelot and Tristan. *La Tavola Ritonda* says he had a son named Sodoc.

Lamorat's father had slain King Lot, Gawain's father. In revenge, Gawain had slain Pellinore. Lamorat exacerbated this family enmity by having an affair with Morgause, Gawain's mother. Gaheris murdered Morgause when he found them in bed together, and Lamorat was eventually slain by Gawain and his brothers in an unfair fight, just after they killed his brother Drian. Sir Pionel, Lamorat's cousin, tried to avenge Lamorat's murder by poisoning Gawain, but the plan went awry. [*PostMer*, *PostQuest*, *Palamedes*, *ProsTris*, *Tavola*, *Malory*]

LAMORAT² OF LISTENOIS

Brother of Pellinore and uncle of Lamorat[1]. He was a famous knight of Uther Pendragon's day until he was accidentally killed by the Good Knight Without Fear, his companion, while wearing the armor of one of his enemies. [*Palamedes*]

LAMPADES OF THE FLATLAND

A knight who served Arthur in the war against King Rions. [*VulgMer*, *Arthour*]

LAMPART [*Lambard, Lanpar(t), Lupars*]

The lord of Galigan and seneschal of Esmeree the Blonde, Queen of Wales. He instituted a custom in his castle whereby any knight coming to seek lodging for the night would have to joust with him. If the knight knocked down Lampart, he would have the best of lodging, but if Lampart defeated the knight, the knight would be covered with filth and run out of town by the villagers. Gawain's son Guinglain—traveling as the "Fair Unknown"—defeated Lampart and won the right to a good night's lodging. Lampart then accompanied Guinglain to his adventure at the Desolate City. [*Renaut*, *ChestreLyb*]

LAMYEL OF CARDIFF

A Knight of the Round Table present at the healing of Sir Urry. He was apparently a "great lover." [*Malory*]

LANARK

A region of southwest Scotland. It originally belonged to Sir Galleron, but Arthur annexed it and gave it to Gawain. Galleron arrived at a feast and challenged Gawain for ownership of the land. The fight ended in a draw, but Gawain graciously returned the country to Galleron anyway. [*Awntyrs*]

LANBORC

A Knight of the Round Table who participated in the Grail Quest. [*ProsTris*]

LANCASTER [*Lincestre*]

A city on the west coast of northern England. In the Vulgate *Merlin*, the kings in rebellion against Arthur met there to devise a plan for opposing the Saxon invasions. [*VulgMer*]

LANCE OF LONGINUS

See BLEEDING LANCE.

LANCELOT¹ [*Ancalot, Lanç(arote), Lanceloet, Lancelott, Lancelus, Lanchelot, Lancil(l)otto, Lançolot, Lanseloit, Lanselos, Lanselot(os), Lanslate, Lanslod, Lansselos, Lantsloot, Lanzelet, Lanzelot, Lanzilet, Lanziloto, Launcelot, Launselake, Lawnslot*]

The most famous of Arthur's knights. Raised by the Lady of the Lake (and thus called "Lancelot of the Lake"), he joined the court at Camelot and became Arthur's best and bravest—until his tragic affair with Guinevere, Arthur's wife, precipitated the collapse of Arthur's kingdom. Lancelot's son, Galahad, completed the Grail Quest.

Though an important and certainly famous character, Lancelot's story is not subject to the same discrepancies and inconsistencies that plague Gawain or Yvain. Essentially, there is only one version of his *estoire*, found in the Vulgate Cycle (c. 1215–30). Most later versions, including Malory's, are based upon it, and the earliest Lancelot romance, by Chrétien de Troyes, fits neatly within it. The only particularly significant exception is Ulrich von Zatzikhoven's *Lanzelet*, which is summarized momentarily.

Chrétien de Troyes wrote the earliest romances still in existence to mention Lancelot, but Ulrich's *Lanzelet*, written shortly after Chrétien and without Chrétien's influence, suggests that Chrétien did not invent the character. Ulrich claimed to have a French source, and this archetypal *Lancelot* was probably the source of Chrétien's *Lancelot* and the Prose *Lancelot*. This hypothetical ur-*Lancelot* would have been written about 1150. Lancelot's character cannot definitively be traced earlier than that. R. S. Loomis argued that Lancelot originated with the Welsh warrior LLWCH LLENLLEAWG, who himself is a derivation of an Irish god named Lug. "Llwch" is the Welsh word for "lake," and would have provided Lancelot with his sobriquet, "of the Lake." "Llenlleawg," meanwhile, according to this theory, was altered to "Lancelot," perhaps under the influence of the common name "Lancelin." The Welsh Triads mention an Arthurian knight named Lawnslot, but this is more likely a Welsh adaptation of the French Lancelot than an original Welsh character.

Lancelot appeared briefly in Chrétien's *Erec* and *Cliges* before Chrétien featured him in his own romance, *Lancelot*, or *The Knight of the Cart* (c. 1175). *Lancelot* does not provide a biography of Lancelot, but rather features a piece of Lancelot's career: his rescue of Guinevere from Meleagant and his subsequent affair with the queen. This story is summarized as follows:

> Meleagant of Gorre arrives at Arthur's court and challenges Arthur to send Guinevere into the forest escorted by only one knight. Kay coerces the right to act as this escort. Kay is defeated, and both Kay and

Guinevere are kidnapped by Meleagant and taken to Gorre.

Gawain immediately sets out to rescue Guinevere, accompanied by an unnamed knight who we learn only much later to be Lancelot. It is clear that Lancelot loves the queen desperately. Lancelot rides ahead of Gawain but his horse dies from exhaustion. A dwarf driving a cart tells Lancelot to get in the cart if he wants to find Guinevere. Lancelot hesitates for two steps before diving into the cart. Riding in a cart is a form of humiliation reserved for criminals, and Lancelot is immediately branded the "Knight of the Cart" and is subject to public scorn.

Lancelot and Gawain learn that Guinevere has been taken to Gorre, which is only accessible by two bridges: the Sword Bridge and the Water Bridge. Lancelot heads for the first, while Gawain decides to try the latter. Gawain fails, nearly drowns, and is removed from the action. Lancelot manages to cross the Sword Bridge but is badly cut by the blade.

Lancelot has a few other adventures on the way to Meleagant's castle. We learn that he was raised by a water fairy who gave him a ring that protects him from spells.

Lancelot arrives at Meleagant's castle and is greeted by Bagdemagus, Meleagant's noble father. Bagdemagus cures Lancelot's wounds. Lancelot and Meleagant meet in battle. Lancelot gains the upper hand, and Bagdemagus calls a truce, arranging for Guinevere to be freed. Guinevere is angry at Lancelot for hesitating before entering the cart—he put his honor above his love for her—but she eventually forgives him.

Lancelot comes to the barred window of Guinevere's chamber at night. She tells him he can enter and spend the night with him. He bends the bars and climbs through, but cuts his hand in the process. He leaves in the morning after a night of passion, and Meleagant discovers drops of blood in Guinevere's bed. He accuses her of sleeping with the wounded Kay, whose bed is in the next room. Lancelot duels Meleagant to prove the queen's innocence, but Bagdemagus again calls a halt, and another fight is planned at Arthur's court.

Lancelot enters the tournament at Noauz. To test his love, Guinevere, orders him to fight as badly as possible, and Lancelot obiediently acts like a coward. On the next day, Guinevere tells him to fight his best, and Lancelot wins the tournament.

Meleagant imprisons Lancelot in a tower, but Meleagant's sister releases him. Lancelot shows up at Arthur's court and finds that Gawain is about to fight Meleagant in Lancelot's stead. Lancelot dons his armor, fights Meleagant, and kills him, thus acquitting the queen.

Chrétien claimed to have been given his source material by his patroness, Countess Marie of Champagne, who might have suggested the romance between Lancelot and Guinevere. There is no hint here of the tragedy, caused by the affair, to befall Lancelot, Arthur, and Guinevere as in the Vulgate *Mort Artu*.

Chrétien's source may be similar to the one used by Ulrich von Zatzikhoven to write *Lanzelet* (c. 1200), which is summarized below. Ulrich provides a much more extensive biography of Lancelot but omits the affair with Guinevere.

Lancelot, the son of King Pant of Genewis and Queen Clarine (Arthur's sister) is spirited away from his mother by a water fairy after his tyrannical father is overthrown and slain by his own nobles. Lancelot is raised in an otherworldly land called Maiden Land, where he learns courtesy and chivalry from the ladies and deeds of arms from visiting mermen. Thus armed, he ventures into the world of men. He is ignorant of his parentage and name, having been told he will learn these once he has slain Iweret—a powerful knight who has wronged the son of the queen of Maiden Land.

Lancelot's first two adventures involve the winning of a maiden, through combat, from her tyrranical father or uncle. The first maiden, the unnamed daughter of Galagandreiz, he eventually abandons because she chose him last out of three knights; the second maiden, Ade, daughter of Linier, abandons him when he falls under a spell that makes him cowardly. During this time, he wins two castles and proves himself noble at a tournament, and word of his fame reaches Arthur. Arthur dispatches Gawain to retrieve Lancelot, but Lancelot declines to venture to Arthur's court.

Eventually, Lancelot finds Iweret and falls in love with his daughter, Iblis. In a long battle, Iweret is killed and his castle (Dodone) and lands fall into Lancelot's possession. As promised, a messenger arrives and tells Lancelot his name and ancestry. Lancelot and Iblis are married. Lancelot then decides to go to Arthur's court and discovers, on his arrival, that Arthur is being challenged by King Valerin of the Tangled Wood for Guinevere. Lancelot requests permission to fight the combat, and Arthur allows it; Valerin is defeated.

Searching for more adventure, Lancelot travels to the castle of Pluris, where he wins a contest, but is then entrapped by the lady there. She holds him as her concubine for a time, but he manages to cleverly escape with the help of several Knights of the Round Table.

Returning to Arthur's court, Lancelot finds that Guinevere has been abducted by Valerin and Valerin's defenses prove too strong for Arthur's men to breach. At the behest of Arthur, Lancelot travels to the fortress of the wizard Malduc to ask for help. Malduc agrees to destroy Valerin's defenses, but in return, Arthur must deliver to him his old enemies: Gawain and Erec. The exchange is made and Guinevere is rescued. In time, Lancelot leads a rescue expedition to Malduc's palace, rescues his fellows, and kills the necromancer.

Finally, Lancelot's thoughts return to his ancestral lands, and he travels to Genewis. The nobles there gladly turn over the kingdom to Lancelot's rule, and he and Iblis are crowned king and queen in two separate ceremonies: one at Genewis, and one at Dodone.

Ulrich's *Lanzelet* failed to spark any later traditions, but we see in the story analogues to Chrétien's *Lancelot* and the Prose *Lancelot* that suggest a common source or sources. Lancelot's father, Pant of Genewis, is identical to King Ban of Benoic. The Queen of Maidenland is later called the Lady of the Lake. Other analogues are more tenuous: Valerin for Meleagant, Malduc for Merlin, and the queen of Pluris for Morgan le Fay.

Perhaps the earliest Arthurian prose romance is the French *Perlesvaus*. Lancelot is the third knight, after Perceval and Gawain, to venture to the Grail Castle. Unlike his predecessors, however, Lancelot is not allowed a vision of the Grail because of his affair with Guinevere, which he refuses to recognize as a sin, and for which he refuses to repent. Lancelot has a number of other adventures in the story, including a version of the Beheading Game in the Waste City. His exploits help Perceval to finally achieve the Grail.

In the early thirteenth century, Lancelot's story was recast into prose, in the non-cyclical *Lancelot do Lac* and shortly thereafter in the vast prose corpus known as the Vulgate Cycle. Lancelot is so prominently featured in all three branches of the original cycle—the *Lancelot*, the *Queste del Saint Graal*, and the *Mort Artu*—that the work is often known as the Lancelot-Grail Cycle. The Vulgate romances contain themes found in both Chrétien and Ulrich, though its real origin was probably the lost *Lancelot* that preceded these two authors.

Among the Vulgate *Lancelot*, *Queste del Saint Graal*, and *Mort Artu*, we find the model Lancelot story, destined to last into modern times via Malory's *Le Morte Darthur*:

Lancelot is born to King Ban of Benoic and Queen Elaine. He is descended from Nascien, a follower of Joseph of Arimathea. He has an older, illegitimate brother named Hector. King Claudas, Ban's neighbor, attacks Ban's castle at Trebe. Ban flees with his wife and son but he soon falls dead. The Lady of the Lake appears, takes Lancelot from Elaine, and brings him to her enchanted, otherworldly homeland.

Lancelot grows up to be a great hunter and warrior. He is full of courtesy. He is raised with his younger cousins Lionel and Bors. When he reaches the age of eighteen, the Lady of the Lake instructs him on knighthood and chivalry. She brings him to Arthur's court so that he may become a knight. Lancelot is knighted, and he falls in love with Guinevere at first glance. He soon succeeds in his first quest: the deliverance of the lady of Nohaut from an oppressor.

With the help of enchanted arms from the Lady of the Lake, Lancelot accomplish a near-impossible feat: the liberation of the enchanted castle known as Dolorous Guard. He has several other adventures that win him honor and fame. (In Malory's version, the foundation for Lancelot's fame is formed by his extraordinary feats of arms during the Roman War— which occurs before Lancelot's birth in the Vulgate *Merlin*.)

Arthur is attacked by Galehaut of Sorelois. Lancelot has been imprisoned by the Lady of Malehaut, but he is allowed to leave to join Arthur's army. His deeds impress Galehaut. During the second part of the war, Galehaut is so amazed by Lancelot's prowess that he agrees to surrender to Arthur if Lancelot will become his companion. Lancelot agrees, the war ends, and the two knights become fast friends. After several adventures together, they are both appointed to the Round Table. Galehaut arranges a meeting between Lancelot and Guinevere, and Lancelot confesses his love. Guinevere reciprocates.

Saxons invade Scotland. Lancelot joins Arthur's army there and spends his first night in Guinevere's chambers. While trying to free Arthur from a Saxon prison, Lancelot is captured. He goes mad but is cured by the Lady of the Lake, who approves of his romance with Guinevere. With Lancelot's help, Arthur drives away the Saxons.

Lancelot breaks with Arthur when Arthur recognizes Guinevere the False as the true queen. Eventually, they are reconciled. Lancelot liberates the prisoners of Morgan le Fay's Valley of No Return. He is imprisoned by Morgan le Fay but is allowed to leave on furlough. He kills Caradoc and liberates the Dolorous Tower. Lancelot returns to Morgan's prison but is eventually released. When he arrives at Arthur's court, he finds that Galehaut, believing him dead, has died of sorrow. Lancelot has him buried in Joyous Guard (the re-named Dolorous Guard).

Meleagant abducts Guinevere and Lancelot rescues her in the manner described by Chrétien de Troyes.

Lancelot visits Corbenic, the Grail Castle, and rescues Amite, King Pelles's daughter, from an enchanted boiling bath. Pelles, knowing that Lancelot will father Galahad, gets him drunk and convinces him that Guinevere is waiting for him at Case Castle. Lancelot goes to the castle and sleeps with Amite, believing her to be Guinevere. Galahad is conceived.

Lancelot enjoys many further adventures with his cousin Lionel as his squire. He helps Arthur expel King Claudas from Gaul. At Camelot, he is again tricked into bed with Amite. Guinevere discovers the tryst and banishes Lancelot from her sight. Lancelot goes mad and runs into the forest. He lives like a wild man, attacking everyone he comes across. He is taken in by King Bliant of the White Castle and stays with him for two years. Eventually, he wanders to Corbenic, and King Pelles heals him with the Grail. Lancelot returns to Camelot and is reunited and reconciled with Guinevere.

The Grail Quest begins. Galahad arrives at court and is knigthed by Lancelot. During the adventure, Galahad overthrows his father. Lancelot confesses his sins to a hermit and promises to end his affair with Guinevere and to preform acts of penance. Despite his virtue, Lancelot is unable to succeed in the quest because of his sin with Guinevere and because he is unable to renounce his chivalric values in favor of spiritual ones. However, he is allowed a vision of Galahad, Perceval, and Bors completing the quest. When he tries to approach the Grail, he is knocked unconscious. When he awakens twenty-four days later, the quest is over.

Lancelot forgets or ignores his promise and begins his affair with Guinevere anew. They quarrel briefly when Guinevere believes that that Lancelot loves the lady of Escalot. Lancelot defends Guinevere against a murder charge brought by Mador of the Gate and is victorious. The lovers conduct themselves indiscreetly, and Arthur suspects their infidelity. While Arthur is hunting, Agravain and Mordred rouse a band of knights and catch Lancelot and Guinevere *in flagrante*. Lancelot fights his way free and promises to return if Guinevere is sentenced to execution. Many of Arthur's knights, most of them Lancelot's kin, defect along with Lancelot.

Arthur sentences Guinevere to be burned at the stake. Lancelot shows up with his knights and rescues her. Many of Arthur's knights fall, including Gaheris and Gareth, Gawain's brothers. Lancelot takes Guinevere to Joyous Guard, and Arthur, egged on by a vengeful Gawain, pursues them. The pope intervenes and forces Arthur to take Guinevere back. Lancelot returns her and departs for the continent. Gawain urges Arthur to war, and Arthur crosses to France and besieges Lancelot in Benoic. Lancelot offers to go into exile for ten years if he can rejoin Arthur's court when he returns. Gawain rejects the proposal and demands single combat against Lancelot. The two knights meet, and Gawain receives a serious wound.

The Romans invade Gaul, and Arthur abandons Benoic to fight them. Then Mordred usurps the British throne. Arthur's forces return to Britain. Gawain dies from his head wound after forgiving Lancelot on his death bed. Mordred and Arthur meet in battle and both are killed. Guinevere enters a convent and dies.

Lancelot returns to Britain to deal with Mordred's sons. He kills them in battle, then joins the Archbishop of Canterbury, his cousin Bleoberis, and his brother Hector in a hermitage. Lancelot dies after several years and is buried in Joyous Guard next to Galehaut. According to Malory, Lancelot died in the Odor of Sanctity. The Post-Vulgate *Mort Artu* says that King Mark of Cornwall disinterred Lancelot's body and destroyed it.

Lancelot was a French hero, and as the heyday of French Arthurian romance began to wane, so did the character. The Post-Vulgate Cycle (c. 1235) eliminates the Vulgate's *Lancelot* and reduces Lancelot's importance in the Grail legend. French romances throughout the remainder of the thirteenth century returned their focus to Gawain and a spattering of new Arthurian knights. (*Les Merveilles de Rigomer*, one romance that does include Lancelot in some detail, has him fail in his quest to conquer Rigomer Castle; Gawain succeeds.) Italian authors wrote about him through the thirteenth and fourteenth centuries in *La Tavola Ritonda* and a number of *cantares*, but their influence did not reach France or England. Other than the Italian texts, between the Post-Vulgate Cycle and Malory's *Le Morte Darthur*, the only significant text to feature Lancelot was the Stanzaic *Le Morte Arthur* (c. 1400), which recounts the downfall of Arthur's kingdom and Lancelot's involvement as in the Vulgate *Mort Artu*. Middle English romance almost excludes Lancelot completely, focusing on Gawain as the embodiment of chivalry, courtliness, and valor.

Malory's *Le Morte Darthur* was responsible for Lancelot's revival. By bringing the love triangle to the forefront, by making Lancelot Arthur's best friend as well as his greatest knight, and by humanizing the character, Malory guaranteed Lancelot's enduring fame. [*ChretienE, ChretienC, ChretienL, UlrichZ, Perlesvaus, LancLac, VulgLanc, VulgQuest, VulgMort, ProsTris, PostMer, PostQuest, PostMort, Merveil, Stanz, Tavola, Chantari, Allit, Malory, LancLaik, Povest, TennIK*]

Relations: Lancelot's family, wives, and kinsmen are named below. More information can be found under their respective entries.

Father: Ban of Benoic, Domorot of Lokva, Haud of Schuwake, Pant of Genewis

Mother: Clarine, Elaine, Gostanza

Wives and Lovers: Ade, Amite, Elaine, Guinevere, Iblis, Janphie, Martha, queen of Pluris

Children: unnamed maiden of Corbania, Galahad, Galec, unnamed son of Martha

Brother: Hector of the Fens

See Also: Ban, Benoic, Claudus, Dolorous Guard, Elaine, Escalot, Galahad, Galehaut, Guinevere, Joyous Guard, Lady of the Lake, Lionel, Meleagant, Melehan

LANCELOT[2]

The grandfather of Lancelot of the Lake. Descended from Nascien, he was the son of Jonah and the father of Kings Ban (Lancelot of the Lake's father), Bors, and Guinebaus. Born the heir to Gaul, he doubled his kingdom by marrying the daughter of the King of Ireland. While drinking from a chapel fountain one day, his cousin, the Duke of the White Fortress, who was also the husband of King Lancelot's mistress, sneaked up behind him and beheaded him, sending his head into the fountain. The fountain boiled, burning the Duke, and continued to boil until the Grail Quest, when Galahad put his hand into the fountain. Lancelot of the Lake found his grandfather's body and buried it next to his grandmother's. [*VulgLanc, VulgQuest, VulgEst, Malory*]

LANCHA

One of Arthur's knight. [*Tavola*]

LANCIEN [*Lantayn, Lencien*]

A city in Cornwall where King Mark often held court in Béroul's *Tristan*. It was the home of the leper Ivain. In the Fourth Continuation of Chrétien de Troyes's *Perceval*, Mark holds a tournament in Lancien against the King with a Hundred Knights. In this day, the name belongs to a forest and a farm in Cornwall, near the River Fowey. [*Beroul, Contin4*]

LAND BEYOND THE BORDERS OF GALONE

A northern land in rebellion against Arthur in the early days of his reign. The King of the Land Beyond the Borders of Galone was joined in his rebellion by King Aguissant of Scotland and King Yon of Little Ireland. Arthur defeated all of them. The King later joined forces with the King with a Hundred Knights and resumed the war; again, he was defeated. He became the vassal of the lord Galehaut and joined Galehaut in his war against Arthur, but was defeated a third time when Galehaut— through the design of Lancelot—yielded to Arthur. [*LancLac, VulgLanc*]

LAND FROM WHICH NO ONE RETURNS

The kingdom ruled by King Gundebald in *Meriadoc*. It was a lake of tar with an island of solid ground in the center. Unwary visitors often sank into the pit, giving the land its name. King Meriadoc of Wales journeyed to the Land From Which No One Returns and defeated Gundebald there. [*Historia*]

LAND OF GIANTS

A country on the border of Gorre. The Castle Passing marked the border. [*VulgLanc*]

LAND OF MAIDENS

During an episode in *Diu Crône*, Gawain lodges at the castle of Rohur in the Land of Maidens. [*Heinrich*]

LAND OF THE HORN [**Landes del Cor*]

The area ruled by the Lord of the Horn, who was defeated by Perceval. It contained the Castle of the Horn. [*Contin2*]

LAND THAT TRISTAN FREED

A name for the valley or island of SERVAGE, after Tristan killed Nabon the Black, the evil giant who ruled it. Its lord was Sir Sagremor. [*ProsTris*]

LANDALIS

A Saxon warrior who participated in the Saxon invasion of Britain at the beginning of Arthur's reign. He commanded three galleys upon which a handful of Saxons escaped Arthur's Saxon slaughter at Clarence. [*VulgMer*]

LANDEMORE [*Landesmores, Landemeure*]

A Scottish castle and land found in several French romances. In Guillaume le Clerc's *Fergus*, Perceval hunts a white stag in the region. In *Gliglois*, it us the home castle of Beauté, a maiden loved by both Gawain and his squire, Gliglois. At Beauté's request, Gliglois was knighted at Landemore, and he became lord of the castle upon marrying her. Both *Meraugis de Portlesguez* and *La Vengeance Raguidel* mention a Lady of Landemore, present at several tournaments. All texts may refer to a series of foothills south of the Firth of Forth known as the Lammermoor Hills. [*Raoul, Vengeance, Guillaume, Gliglois*]

LANDENS OF CARMELIE [*Laudons*]

A Knight of the Round Table wounded fighting the Saxons at the battle of Clarence. [*VulgMer, Livre*]

LANDO

A knight defeated by Erec in a tournament. [*HartmannE*]

LANDOC

An Irish city where Sir Durmat won a sparrowhawk tournament for Queen Fenise of Ireland. The expected victor, Lord Cadroain, loved Lady Idain of Landoc. [*Durmart*]

LANDOINE[1]

The daughter of the King with a Hundred Knights. Near Penning, Landoine and her brother, Maranz, were saved from a pack of ruffians by Sir Bors. [*VulgEst*]

LANDOINE[2]

A nobleman in the service of King Argestes, who ruled Camelot in the time of Joseph of Arimathea. An evil man, Landoine helped Argestes force the Christians in Camelot to revert to paganism. [*VulgEst*]

LANDON

A Saxon warrior killed by King Bors at the battle of Carhaix. [*VulgMer*]

LANDONE

A forest through which Sir Bors traveled on his way to an adventure at Hungerford Castle. [*VulgLanc*]

LANDREAS [*Landon, Laudon*]

A knight from Carmelide who served Arthur in the war against King Rions. He led an echelon of soldiers at the battle of Aneblayse. Landreas was the nephew of the seneschal of Leodegan of Carmelide. [*VulgMer, Arthour*]

LANDRES OF LYONESSE

One of Tristan's uncles, killed while helping Tristan and Lancelot defend Joyous Guard against Arthur. [*Tavola*]

LANDRIE [*Siandre*]

In Heinrich von dem Türlin's *Diu Crône*, Galaida, Kay's beloved, is called the sister of Duchess Leimas and the Duke of Landrie. [*Heinrich*]

LANDUNAS

A knight who brought word to Arthur that King Mark of Cornwall had been overthrown and that the land was without a ruler. Elsewhere, he is said to be king of the Red City. [*Palamedes, ProsTris*]

LANER[1]

A Knight of the Round Table, related to Lancelot, who participated in the Grail Quest. [*PostQuest*]

LANER[2]

A location in southwest Scotland, probably in the country of Galloway. After Sir Galleron and Sir Gawain fought each other to a draw, Gawain, in admiration, gave all the lands "from Laner to Layre" to Galleron. The lands had originally belonged to Galleron but were annexed by Arthur and given to Gawain. [*Awntyrs*]

LANETH

A niece of Arthur's who, to revenge an infidelity accusation made by Guinevere, sent a magical chastity mantel to Arthur's court. The mantel proved Guinevere adulterous. [*Lanethen*]

LANFATE

A knight slain by Arthur's Sir Suziano of the Valiant Heart while guarding a bridge. Lanfate's fiancee, Losanna, convinced Suziano to assume the post for a year. [*Tavola*]

LANGALIF

A duke in Arthur's service, present at the wedding of Erec and Enide. [*Erex*]

LANGREE

A castle whose lord imprisoned Sir Dodinel after finding him lying by a river, half-drowned. Sir Hector eventually killed the lord and freed Dodinel. [*VulgLanc*]

LANGRES

A city near the vale of Soissons, in which Arthur fought his epic final battle against Lucius's Romans. [*GeoffHR, VulgMer*]

LANGUEDOC [*Langueduk*]

A region in south France owned by Lancelot. Lancelot made Sir Safir the earl of Languedoc in return for Safir's support in the battles against King Arthur. It was also the home of Sir Phelot. [*Malory*]

LANIURE OF SERRE

A lord once defeated in combat by Gawain in Heinrich von dem Türlin's *Diu Crône*. When he died, his daughters, Amurfina and Sgoidamur, vied for a magic bridle which gave the owner the rights to Serre. Gawain eventually settled the matter in Sgoidamur's favor, though he married Amurfina. H. Sparnaay notes that the corresponding character in Chrétien de Troyes's *Yvain* is called "li sire de *la Noire* Espine," or the LORD OF THE BLACK THORN (Loomis, *Romance*, 441). [*Heinrich*]

LANNOR

Son of Febus and Florine, and brother of Argons, Niatar, Altan, and Siraouc. [*Palamedes*]

LANOIS OF ZIEBE

A king in Arthur's service. [*Heinrich*]

LANOR

A Saxon duke of Batingues who, with many other Saxon rulers, invaded northern Britain at the beginning at Arthur's reign. He led a battalion at the battle of Clarence, was defeated by Arthur's forces, and fled to the sea. [*VulgMer*]

LANORIO

An abbey in Logres where the King with a Hundred Knights had the heads of Bagotta and Brunoro (Galehaut's parents) buried after they were slain by Tristan. [*Tavola*]

LANPHUHT

In Heinrich von dem Türlin's *Diu Crône*, the queen of Lanphuht is one of several ladies at Arthur's court to fail a chastity test involving a goblet. [*Heinrich*]

LANTRIS

Tristan's squire, whose name was changed from ALCARDO when Tristan knighted him. He was Isolde's cousin. He accompanied Tristan on his adventures in Logres. He was slain when King Mark of Cornwall besieged the castle of Joyous Guard to reclaim Isolde from Tristan. [*Tavola*]

LANVAL[1] [*Lam(be)well, Landevale, Landevall, Lanfal, Launfal(le), Lenval, Linval*]

The hero of several poems and lays, beginning with Marie de France's *Lanval* (late twelfth century). Curiously, he does not appear in any of the chronicles or cycles, save one mention in the Vulgate *Merlin* as a knight who fights in a tournament at Carhaix. Marie's *Lanval*, or its source, was adapted in the early fourteenth century as *Sir Landeval*, by Thomas Chestre in the late fourteenth century as *Sir Launfal*, and in the sixteenth century as *Sir Lambewell* and *Sir Lamwell*.

Lanval was a gracious and generous knight who was appointed as "steward" of Arthur's other knights. Lanval disliked Queen Guinevere for her numerous infidelities, and she overtly returned the disdain. He made an excuse to leave Arthur's court and went to Caerleon, where he lived for a year but fell into debt. Eventually, he became so poor and depraved that everyone in Caerleon made fun of him, and he left Caerleon to seek adventures. He came upon a pavilion in a forest where he met a beautiful and mysterious maiden named Triamour, and he immediately fell in love with her. Triamour gave him a horse, a servant, a banner, an unlimited amount of gold, a suit of armor, and an enchantment which insured that Lanval would not be harmed in joust or duel. In return, Lanval had to love Triamour exclusively, and had to agree not to tell anyone about their relationship. When Lanval returned to Caerleon rich and powerful, he suddenly found himself with a lot of friends. A tournament was held in his honor, which he won. A knight in Lombardy named Valentyne heard of Lanval's prowess and offered a joust; Lanval traveled to the city of Atalye in Lombardy and killed Valentyne. Throughout all of these adventures, Lanval continued his relationship with Triamour, whom he had to meet in secret.

Eventually, Arthur heard of his knight's adventures and asked him to come back to court. Lanval complied and returned to merriment at Arthur's court in Cardiff. While he was there, Queen Guinevere tried to seduce him. Lanval rebuked her advances and said that he loved a fairy woman whose ugliest servant was more beautiful than Guinevere. Guinevere, furious, went to Arthur, told of Lanval's boast, and said that Lanval had made advances on her. Arthur swore to kill Lanval. Meanwhile, all of the items and enchantments that Lanval had received from Triamour disappeared, as he had broken his promise by telling Guinevere of his love for the enchantress. Arthur captured Lanval and set up a royal court to judge the knight, but the court decided that Guinevere was probably at fault. They said that Lanval simply had to bring his lover to the court and prove her existence; otherwise, he would have to be hanged. They gave him a year and two weeks to find Triamour and bring her back to Cardiff.

Lanval was unable to find Triamour in the given time. When he returned to Cardiff, Arthur demanded that he be hanged, but members of his court argued instead that Lanval should be sent into exile. As they debated, Triamour arrived at court with her servants, and their radiant beauty proved that Lanval's claim had been a true one. Lanval and Triamour left together for Triamour's land, where they lived happily ever after.

Lanval's story was grafted onto another knight in the non-Arthurian Breton lay of *Graelent*, and to Gawain in the Italian *La Pulzella Gaia*. Echoes of the tale appear in Der Pleier's *Meleranz*. [*MarieL*, *VulgMer*, *Stricker*, *ChestreLvl*, *SirLand*, *SirLamb*]

LANVAL[2]

In the Hebrew *Melekh Artus*, the lord of Astolat, father of Edelpert, Karavoç, and presumably—though she is not named in the text—Elaine. This character appears unnamed in the Vulgate *Mort Artu* and as BERNARD in Malory. The author may have adopted the name from the popular French hero. [*Melekh*]

LANVENIC

A city near the Roevent forest, where Sir Bors rescued his former tutor, Lambegue, from an unjust execution. [*VulgLanc*]

LANVERNIS [*Lanerv*]

A city in Scotland, near Caranges, ruled by King Aguisant and plundered by Saxons in the early days of Arthur's reign. [*VulgMer*, *Arthour*]

LANVERUNZ [*Lanveranz*]

In Wolfram's *Parzival*, a land ruled in Arthur's time by Duke Astor. The name is given to the duke himself in one instance, probably a mistake. [*Wolfram*]

LANZIDANT

A knight from Greenland who served as a page to Ampflise, the Queen of France. He was sent to Wales by Ampflise—along with Liadarz and Liahturteltart—to woo Gahmuret (Perceval's father) back to France. Gahmuret, however, married Herzeloyde, the Queen of Wales. [*Wolfram*]

LAPSIT EXILLIS

A Latin-sounding name given to the Grail in Wolfram's *Parzival*. Its meaning is uncertain, though "valueless stone" and "small stone" have been suggested. There is probably some connection with *lapis exilir*, the philosopher's stone. [*Wolfram*]

LAQUIS OF LAMPAGRÉS

A knight who was defeated and maimed by the Formidable Knight. In response, Meraugis of Portlesguez, Laquis's companion, killed the Formidable Knight and brought his severed hand to Laquis. [*Raoul*]

LAR

King of Korntin, husband of Queen Amire, and father of Lamire. He was killed by King Roaz of Glois, who seized his land and drove his family into exile. Lar's ghost, sometimes in the form of a beast, wandered Korntin for ten years, until Wigalois (Gawain's son) arrived to destroy Roaz. Lar guided Wigalois through Korntin and told him of a horrible dragon named Pfetan that needed to be vanquished. Lar provided Wigalois with a magic lance to accomplish this feat. Lar also revealed that Gawain was Wigalois's father. Wigalois eventually avenged Lar's death and allowed his spirit to rest. Lar's brother, Garez, was a king of Libya. [*Wirnt*]

LARDANS

A knight who fought for the rebellious kings at the Battle of Bedegraine. [*Malory*]

LARGINA

The unchaste mother of Suziano, one of Arthur's knights. By seducing two kings, Esclabor and Amorotto, she came to possess the rich cities of Tarsena and Latinale. [*Tavola*]

LARIE

In Wirnt von Grafenberg's *Wigalois*, the daughter of King Lar and Queen Amire of Korntin. Her father was killed by King Roaz of Glois, who drove Larie and her mother to the border of their own kingdom. She was raised in the castle of Roimunt and was promised to any knight who could vanquish Roaz. Wigalois (Gawain's son), answering the challenge, fell in love with Larie at first sight. After Wigalois killed Roaz, he and Larie were married. They happily and justly ruled Korntin for the rest of their days, and had a valiant son named Gawanides. Larie's counterpart in Renaut de Bâgé's *The Fair Unknown* is ESMEREE THE BLONDE. [*Wirnt*]

LARIS [*Lairis, Larris, Larys, Layris*]

One of the heroes of *Claris et Laris*. An Arthurian knight, he was the son of Emperor Henry of Germany and the best friend of Claris. He fell in love with Marine, sister of Yvain and daughter of King Urien. This enraged his previous paramour, the fairy Madoine, with whom Laris already had a child. Madoine imprisoned Laris, but Claris rescued him. With Claris and Arthur, Laris saved Urien from a siege by King Tallas of Denmark, another of Marine's suitors, but Laris was captured and imprisoned by Tallas. Merlin guided Arthur's Sir Brandaliz to Laris's prison, and Brandaliz freed him. Laris married Marine and became the king of Denmark, which Arthur had stripped from Tallas. Laris's sister, Lidoine, married Claris. [*Claris*]

LASANCIS [*Lansansissa*]

Brother of Escorducarla, a sorceress whose daughter was slain by Arthur. To revenge herself on the king, Escorducarla gave Lascancis enchanted weapons and armor, and told him to go to Arthur's court. Lasancis planned to defeat each knight, including Arthur, place them in a prison, and burn the prison. Tristan, the last knight to face Lasancis, managed to steal his magic lance and to overcome his magic armor with a heavy mace. Lasancis surrendered and was imprisoned for the rest of his life. [*Tavola, Cantare*]

LASCOYT

The second son of Gornemant, Perceval's tutor. He was a count. Lascoyt was killed by Yder in a sparrowhawk tournament. [*Wolfram*]

LAST SUPPER

According to later Grail tradition, beginning with the texts of Robert de Boron, the Grail was the chalice or dish used by Christ at the Last Supper (and later used by Joseph of Arimathea to catch Christ's blood on the Cross). Biblical tradition holds that Christ and his disciples used a round table for the Last Supper, which inspired Joseph's Grail Table and Arthur's Round Table. [*RobertBor J, VulgQuest, VulgEst*]

LATINALE

A rich city given to Largina by King Amorotto, her lover. [*Tavola*]

LAUDAMIE

Queen of Averre, which she inherited from King Avenis and Queen Anfole. She had a sister named Anfole. Her land and castle, Muntrogin, were terrorized by a horrible demon called Vulganus. She was saved by Arthur's Sir Garel, whom she married. [*PleierG*]

LAUDELET

A lake on the border of Ordohorht, where Gawain visited Lady Fortune. [*Heinrich*]

LAUDINE [*Analida, Alundyne*]

The Lady of the Fountain who became Yvain's wife after Yvain killed her husband, Esclados. She is first mentioned in Chrétien de Troyes's *Yvain*. She was the daughter of Laudunet. She married her husband's killer to ensure that her lands would be protected. When Yvain stayed away from her for over a year, she renounced him. After a series of adventures, Yvain was able to return to her favor. According to Heinrich von dem Türlin, she later failed a chastity test at Arthur's court. [*ChretienY, HartmannI, Heinrich, Ywain*]

LAUDON OF RONNES

A knight to whom Sagremor gave a castle that he had conquered from Sir Greomar. Arthur called the castle the Castle of Laides. Laudon's lover was named Helyap. [*Livre*]

LAUDUNAL OF PLEYEDUNZE

A lord defeated in combat by Perceval. [*Wolfram*]

LAUDUNET [*Landuit*]

Father of Laudine, Yvain's wife, in Chrétien's *Yvain*. The Middle-English *Ywain and Gawain*, he is called the Duke of Landuit. Chrétien's version may refer to LOTHIAN in Scotland. [*ChretienY, Ivens, Ywain*]

LAUNCEOR [*Lanceor*]

A knight from Ireland who served Arthur. He left Arthur's court to avenge the death of the Lady of the Lake on Sir Balin, who had beheaded her. Balin killed him in the joust, leading Launceor's lover, Lione or Colombe, to kill herself in sorrow. King Mark of Cornwall had the lovers entombed, and erected a monument to their tragic tale. Tristan and Lancelot later fought a fierce duel at Launceor's tomb. [*PostMer, Malory*]

LAUNDES

A region of France owned by Lancelot. Lancelot made Sir Bellangere the earl of the Laundes in return for Bellangere's support in the battles against King Arthur. [*Malory*]

LAUREL

Agravain's wife. She married Agravain at the same time her aunts, Lyones and Lynet, married Gareth and Gaheris. [*Malory*]

LAUSANNE

A lake in Switzerland where Arthur slew a devil cat, at the Hill of the Cat. [*VulgMer*]

LAVAINE [*Lavayne*]

Son of the Bernard of Escalot and brother of Sir Tirre and the lady Elaine. He became a companion of Lancelot during the tournaments at Camelot and followed the knight faithfully, even after his sister died for Lancelot's love. Lavaine married Felelolye, the sister of Urry. Arthur assigned him to the Round Table, but he defected from Arthur's court when Lancelot rescued Guinevere from the stake. In return for his support, Lancelot made him earl of Armagnac. [*Malory, TennIK*]

LAVAL

The duke of Laval was slain by Sir Morholt. The duke's son, in revenge, later nearly killed Morholt. [*PostMer*]

LAVINA

The sister of Medea, the lecherous queen of Crudele castle. Her other sisters included Agnena, Bresenda, and Pulizena. [*Tavola*]

LAWENOR

A British castle, said to be about sixty-five miles from Camelot. Lancelot and the Lady of the Lake lodged there on their way to Arthur's court, where Lancelot was to be knighted. [*LancLac, VulgLanc*]

LAWNSLOT

A Welsh variation of LANCELOT.

LAY OF JOY

A song composed by the ladies of Brandigan, telling of the victory of Erec at the Joy of the Court adventure. [*ChretienE*]

LAY OF TEARS[1] [**Lai de Plors*]

A story of Joseph of Arimathea's encounter with Orpheus the Enchanter, played to Sir Bors on his first visit to Corbenic. [*VulgLanc*]

LAY OF TEARS[2] [**Lai de Plors*]

A story written by Tristan after he was poisoned during his fight with Morholt. [*ProsTris*]

LAY OF THE LOVE POTION

A story written by Tristan about the potion taken by Tristan and Isolde. [*ProsTris*]

LAYRE

A location in southwest Scotland, probably in the country of Galloway. After Sir Galleron and Sir Gawain fought each other to a draw, Gawain, in admiration, gave all the lands "from Laner to Layre" to Galleron. The lands had originally belonged to Galleron and were annexed by Arthur and given to Gawain. [*Awntyrs*]

LAZALIEZ[1] [*Lazeliez*]

Great-great-grandfather of Perceval, father of Addanz, and uncle of Uther Pendragon. His brother was named Brickus. His parents, Mazadan and Terdelaschoye, were both fairies. [*Wolfram*]

LAZALIEZ[2]

The son of Meleranz (Arthur's nephew) and Queen Tydomie of Karmerie. He had a brother named Medanz and a sister named Olimpia. [*PleierM*]

LE

A Knight of the Round Table. [*HartmannE*]

LE MANS

A city in west central France. Arthur gave it to his knight Borel to rule. [*Wace*]

LEANDER

Son of the Red Knight, brother of Evander, Meliadas, and Marmadus, and husband of Ysmaine. Leander's father was killed by Perceval. Leander fought with Perceval twice to avenge his father's death. Pereceval defeated him, and Leander and his brothers forgave Perceval. [*Wace*]

LEAR

The tragic king made famous by Shakespeare first appears in Geoffrey of Monmouth's *Historia Regum Britanniae*. He succeeded his father, King Bladud, to the throne of Britain in the ninth century BC. He fathered three daughters: Goneril, Regan, and Cordelia. In trying to determine how to divide his kingdom among them, he asked each of them how much they loved him. Only Cordelia gave an honest answer, which Lear interpreted as insulting. Lear married Cordelia without a dowry to King Aganippus of Gaul. and divided Britain between his other daughters, marrying them to regional noblemen. Goneril, Regan, and their husbands dispossessed, ill-treated, and humiliated Lear, making him realize how foolish he had been to exile Cordelia. Eventually, he traveled to France and reconciled with his faithful daughter. Lear, Cordelia, and Aganippus roused soldiers from Gaul, led them into Britain, and reclaimed the island from the evil sisters. Lear died after three years, leaving the island to Cordelia. [*GeoffHR*]

LEDE

The name given by Heinrich von dem Türlin to a maiden at Arthur's court who could not laugh until she beheld the best of knights. When Perceval arrived at court, she broke into gales of laughter, foretelling Perceval's successes. Wolfram von Eschenbach calls her CUNNEWARE, the Post-Vulgate names her the MUTE MAIDEN, and she appears in Chrétien de Troyes's *Perceval* unnamed. [*Heinrich*]

LEGNIS

A Roman general who served Emperor Lucius. [*GeoffVM*]

LEICESTER [*Leyccer*]

A city in central England, governed by Earl Jugein under King Arthur. [*GeoffHR*, *Wace*, *Layamon*]

LEIDEBRON OF REDUNZEHTE

A duke once defeated in combat by Perceval. [*Wolfram*]

LEIGAMAR

Count of Sorgarda. He threw a tournament at his castle to decide who would marry his daughter, Flursensephin. Gawain won the tournament but declined to wed the maiden. At his suggestion, Flursensephin was awarded to Sir Quoikos, a friend of Gawain. Analogs to Leigamar appear in Chrétien's *Perceval* as TIEBAUT and in Wolfram's *Parzival* as LYPPAUT. [*Heinrich*]

LEIGORMON

A maiden for whom Gawain endured great peril by plucking Lady Fortune's flowers on the plain of Colurment. Gawain relates this episode during a speech in in Heinrich von dem Türlin's *Diu Crône*, but the adventure is not found in existing texts. [*Heinrich*]

LEIL

According to Geoffrey of Monmouth, a king of Britain in the tenth century BC. He was the son of King Brute Greenshield and the father of King Hudibras. The city of Carlisle (Caer Leil) was named after him. [*GeoffHR*]

LEIMAS OF LIANDRE

The sister of Galaida, Kay's beloved. [*Heinrich*]

LELAS OF RUVHO

A Knight of the Round Table, related to Lancelot, who embarked with the others on the Grail Quest. [*PostQuest*]

LELLIUS OF HOSTIA

A Roman warrior who led a force of soldiers under against Arthur at the Battle of Soissons. [*GeoffHR*]

LENDRIE

The homeland of Arthur's Sir Wigamur, ruled by Wigamur's father, King Paldriot. [*Wigamur*]

LENNOX

A region of southwest Scotland. It originally belonged to Sir Galleron, but Arthur annexed it and gave it to Gawain. Galleron arrived at a feast and challenged Gawain for ownership of the land. The fight ended in a draw, but Gawain graciously returned the country to Galleron anyway. [*Awntyrs*]

LENOMIE OF ALEXANDRIA

Guinevere's sister in Heinrich von dem Türlin's *Diu Crône*. She was a queen. She had another sister named Flori. [*Heinrich*]

LEO [*Leomye*]

The Emperor of Rome during Arthur's reign, according to Geoffrey of Monmouth. Leo had appointed Frollo the ruler of Gaul. Leo commissioned Lucius Hiberius to lead the war against Arthur. After Arthur defeated and killed Lucius, he planned to march on Leo in Rome, but he was recalled to Britain to deal with Mordred's rebellion. A historical Emperor Leo I ruled the eastern empire (Constantinople) between 457 and 473. Another Leo ruled in 474. Pierre de Langtoft calls him Pope rather than Emperor, referring to St. Leo I, who held the papacy from 440 to 461. Most chronicles drop Leo and make Lucius the emperor of Rome. In the Alliterative *Morte Arthure*, Leo becomes Lucius's soldier rather than his superior. [*GeoffHR*, *Pierre*, *Allit*]

LEODEBRON

One of the many Saxon kings who invaded Britain in the early days of Arthur's reign. [*VulgMer*, *Arthour*]

LEODEGAN [*Ladugan, Leodegan(e)s, Leodegar, Leodegon, Leodegran(ce), Lodegreance*]

Guinevere's father. He was the king of Carmelide. His earliest existing mention is in the Prose *Lancelot*, though he may be identical to Geoffrey of Monmouth's LEODEGAR. At the beginning of Arthur's reign, Leodegan was attacked by the forces of King Rions, a Saxon giant. Arthur, Merlin, King Ban of Benoic, and King Bors of Gannes journeyed to Carmelide and, incognito, offered their assistance to Leodegan. The combined forces of the kings led to the defeat of Rions at Carhaix and Aneblayse, two of Leodegan's cities. Arthur revealed his identity to Leodegan, who offered him Guinevere. Leodegan had also fathered the False Guinevere on the wife of his seneschal, Cleodalis, and he had a son who was killed in combat. Leodegan's enemies tried to replace Guinevere with the False Guinevere on Arthur's wedding night, but Arthur's knights thwarted the plot. As a wedding present, Leodegan gave Arthur the Round Table and one hundred knights, which he had acquired from Uther Pendragon. He died soon after his daughter's marriage. In Tennyson, he is named as the brother of Urien, who besieges his kingdom in place Rions. [*LancLac*, *VulgLanc*, *VulgMer*, *PostMer*, *Palamedes*, *Arthour*, *Malory*, *TennIK*]

LEODEGAR [*Laeyer, Leger, Lier, Ligier*]

Earl of Boulogne or Burgundy, or both, under Arthur. He assisted Arthur in the war against Rome. At the battle of Soissons, he killed the Babylonian king Micipsa, and was killed either by Micipsa or by Micipsa's son, Gecron. Arthur had him buried in Boulogne. He may be identical with LEODEGAN, Guinevere's father in French romance. [*GeoffHR*, *Wace*, *Layamon*]

LEOLIN [*Leonin, Joelin*]

Father of Maximus the Great, the British king who became the Roman Emperor. Leolin helped Constantine the Great conquer Rome and shared the duties as co-emperor. [*GeoffHR*, *Wace*]

LEONCE [*Leonche, Lyonses*]

A nobleman from Paierne in the service of King Ban of Benoic and King Bors of Gannes. Leonce was awarded the stewardship of Benoic when Ban and Bors left to join Arthur's war against the rebellious kings. Leonce visited Britain briefly to join Arthur's forces in the Bedegraine battle, and he later returned to help fight the Saxons. When Benoic and Gannes were seized by Claudas, Leonce entered into an uncomfortable service with his masters' enemy. He brought comfort to the people of Gannes by reporting that its princes, Bors and Lionel, were safe in the care of the Lady of the Lake. [*LancLac*, *VulgLanc*, *Livre*, *Arthour*, *Malory*]

LEONELLE [*Leonele*]

The worthy wife of Blair, a vavasor in Carmelide. The couple lodged Arthur and Merlin during one of their visits to Leodegan's kingdom. [*VulgMer*, *Arthour*]

LEONIÉS

An Arthurian knight who joined Gawain's quest to conquer Rigomer Castle. [*Merveil*]

LEOPLANE

A field near the Welsh city of Kanvoleis. Gahmuret, Perceval's father, set up his pavilion on Leoplane before a tournament thrown by Queen Herzeloyde. [*Wolfram*]

LERLINTE

A castle on the Plain of Bucifalaso. Dispute over ownership of the castle sparked a war between King Amoroldo of Ireland and King Alois of North Wales. A battle between Tristan and Lancelot was supposed to decide the outcome, but Arthur intervened and the battle never took place. [*Tavola*]

LERMEBION OF JARBES

A Knight of the Round Table. [*HartmannE*]

LERNFRAS

A Knight of the Round Table who was the son of Gain. [*HartmannE*]

LESBIA

A cave woman who abducted the infant Wigamur (later an Arthurian knight) from his father, King Paldriot. She reared Wigamur until he was stolen from her by a sea monster. [*Wigamur*]

LESPAR

A castle where, during the Grail Quest, a rally was held against the Knights of the Round Table. Tristan unwittingly arrived in the middle of it, killed the king's brother, and was set upon by 100 knights. Palamedes and Galahad arrived, rescued him, and humbled the king. [*PostQuest*]

LESPIN

A bold Knight of the Round Table. [*HartmannE*]

LEVENET

The lady of the castle of Rohur in the Land of Maidens. She lodged Gawain before the great tournament at Sorgarda. [*Heinrich*]

LEVERZEP [*Leverzerp, Lonazep, Lonezep, Lovezeph, Lovezerp, Verzeppe*]

A castle in the forest of Breckham, along the Humber River. In the Prose *Lancelot*, it is the site of a battle between the duke of Cambenic and the king of North Wales. Gawain participated, fighting for Cambenic, and decided the battle. Arthur later gave the castle to a maiden who brought him news of Lancelot. The Prose *Tristan* and Malory relate a tournament held by Arthur at the castle, which was won by Tristan and Lancelot, with Palamedes earning distinction. Events at the tournament led to a rift between Tristan and Palamedes. *La Tavola Ritonda* says that hundreds of knights were slain at the tournament, keeping it from becoming the greatest tournament in history. Afterwards, Arthur vowed not to allow swords at further tournaments. Statues of Palamedes, Tristan, Lancelot, Amoroldo, and Galahad were erected in front of the castle. Hundreds of years later, the location was visited by Charlemagne. [*LancLac, VulgLanc, ProsTris, Tavola, Malory*]

LEWLIN

An Arthurian knight slain during the Roman War by the King of Lybia. [*Allit*]

LI GWEIZ PRELLJUS

In Wolfram's *Parzival*, a ford on the river Sabins in the land of King Gramoflanz. At the behest of Duchess Orgeluse of Logres, whom he loved, Gawain went to Li Gweiz Prelljus and took a garland from one of Gramoflanz's trees, sparking a feud between the two knights. The name of the ford is a corruption of *le Gué Perellous*, or the PERILOUS FORD, found in Chrétien de Troyes's *Perceval*. [*Wolfram*]

LIADARZ

A page to Queen Ampflise of France. He was the son of Count Schiolarz. He was sent to Wales by Ampflise—along with Lanzidant and Liahturteltart—to woo Perceval's father Gahmuret back to France; Gahmuret, however, married Herzeloyde, the Queen of Wales. [*Wolfram*]

LIAHTURTELTART

A page to Queen Ampflise of France. He was the son two fairies named Beaflurs and Pansamurs. He was sent to Wales by Ampflise—along with Lanzidant and Liadarz—to woo Perceval's father Gahmuret back to France; Gahmuret, however, married Herzeloyde, the Queen of Wales. [*Wolfram*]

LIAMERE

The Queen of Libya, the wife of King Amire, and the daughter of King Garez. She was coveted by a neighboring lord, Prince Lion of Namur. Lion killed Amire and tried to court Liamere. Liamere, however, soon perished in sorrow for her dead husband. The deaths of Amire and Liamere were avenged by Wigalois (Gawain's son), who killed Lion. [*Wirnt*]

LIANDER

A Knight of the Round Table and former subject of Erec, who left Destregales to become the Count of Karneis. He was imprisoned by Duke Eskilabon of Belamunt and freed by Arthur's Sir Garel. [*PleierG*]

LIANTES

A desert in Cornwall which contained the Fountain of the Lion. King Mark of Cornwall killed his brother Pernehan at the fountain. [*ProsTris, Tavola*]

LIAZ

A handsome count from Cornwall and a page to Gawain. His father's name was Tinas. [*Wolfram*]

LIAZE

The daughter of Perceval's tutor Gornemant, and the sister of Schenteflurs, Lascoyt, and Gurzgri. Gornemant wanted Perceval to marry her, but Perceval declined. After leaving, Perceval's mind dwelt on her for a time, but he promptly forgot her upon meeting Condwiramurs, his future wife. [*Wolfram*]

LIBANOR

Daughter of King Ban of Benoic and Sade, and sister of Lancelot. Pendragon, Arthur's uncle, visited her with the aid of a devil and fathered two chilren upon her. [*Butor*]

LIBEARN

Step-mother of Prince Alexander of India. She turned Alexander into the Crop-Eared Dog so that her son, the Knight of the Lantern, would inherit the kingdom. The Crop-Eared Dog received the assistance of Gawain and managed to undo the spell. [*IrishD*]

LIBERS[1]

Count of Traverain and a vassal of Arthur. He is first mentioned by Chrétien de Troyes, but not named until Hartmann von Aue's *Erec*. He came to the wedding of Erec and Enide. [*HartmannE*]

LIBERS[2]

The King of Lorgan. He wanted to marry Queen Tydomie of Karmerie—a match which was sponsored by Tydomie's uncle (and Libers' brother-in-law), Malloas. When she refused, because of her love for Arthur's nephew Meleranz, Libers invaded her lands. He was defeated by Meleranz, who arranged a marriage between Libers and Queen Dulceflur, Tydomie's cousin. [*PleierM*]

LIBRAN

A king who battled and killed an unnamed uncle of Perceval, forcing Perceval's aunt into seclusion. [*VulgQuest*]

LIBURN

A famed knight from the city of Kesarija in the Serbo-Russian *Povest' o Tryshchane*. His famous brothers were Igurn and Marko. He hadn't lifted a lance in forty years when Lancelot and Tristan visited his city and demanded to sleep with his wife, Cvitazija, but he dutifully saddled up, swiftly defeated both knights at the same time, and let them go after slapping them each across the face. [*Povest*]

LIBYA [*Lybia, Lyby*]

The North African kingdom features in several Arthurian texts: Geoffrey of Monmouth says that Arthur killed King Sertorious of Libya, an ally of Lucius the Roman, during the Roman War. The Alliterative *Morte Arthure* says that this king was slain by Cador of Cornwall. In Wirnt von Grafenberg's *Wigalois*, King Amire of Libya is murdered, but his death is avenged by Gawain's son Wigalois. Finally, the Prose *Lancelot* features a mysterious beast called the "Crowned Lion of Libya" that was killed by Lionel. [*GeoffHR*, *Wirnt*, *LancLac*, *VulgLanc*, *Allit*, *Malory*]

LICANOR THE GREAT

A good knight born to a man and woman united by Bors during the Grail Quest. After Arthur's death, Licanor slew Sir Meraugis. [*PostQuest*]

LICAT AMR [*Licat Anir*]

The tomb to Amr, son of Arthur, near a fountain in Ercing. According to Nennius, Arthur buried Amr here after killing him. Every time someone measures the burial mound, Nennius claims, he measures a different length— "sometimes six, sometimes nine, sometimes twelve, sometimes fifteen feet." [*Nennius*]

LICORANT [*Linconaus, Leconuials*]

Husband of Tarsenesyde and father of Enid who had fallen into poverty in the town of Laluth. Licorant gave lodging and armor to Erec when Erec entered the town in search of the insolent warrior Yder. Erec fell in love with Enide and married her. In consideration of the marriage, Erec bestowed two castles upon Licorant—Roadan and Montrevel. Later, Licorant was overjoyed to see his daughter crowned Queen of Nantes. This version of his name is supplied by Chrétien de Troyes. The Welsh *Owain* calls him NIWL and Hartmann von Aue names him KORALUS. I. L. Foster suggests that the name may be a corruption of *li cons uials* ("the old earl") found in Chrétien's lost source (Loomis, *Romance*, 193). [*ChretienE*]

LICORIDON

A knight from whom Gawain saved the Lady Idain. In revenge, Licordion told the homicidal Maiden of the Narrow Wood where to locate Gawain. [*Vengeance*]

LIDAS

A knight killed in combat by Laris. Claris and Laris were helping Sir Caradoc protect his paramour from King Ladas, Sir Lidas's liege. [*Claris*]

LIDDAMUS[1]

A duke and vassal of King Vergulaht of Ascalun. When Gawain committed an offense against Vergulaht, Liddamus argued for Gawain's execution; when Vergulaht refused, Liddamus suggested transferring the obligation to search for the Grail (which had been laid upon Vergulaht by Perceval) from Vergulaht to Gawain, which Vergulaht did. [*Wolfram*]

LIDDAMUS[2] OF AGRIPPE

An infidel count who served Feirefiz, Perceval's half-brother in Wolfram von Eschenbach's *Parzival*. [*Wolfram*]

LIDEL

A Scottish town and castle. In Welsh legend, the prophet Lailoken (identified with Merlin) supposedly went mad at a battle fought between Lidel and Carwannock. In Guillaume le Clerc's *Fergus*, Arthur's knight Fergus met Lady Galiene of Lothian, his future wife, while lodging at Lidel. There is an actual castle in Roxburghshire called Liddel. [*Guillaume*]

LIDOINE[1]

The beautiful daughter of the king of Escavalon, loved by two of Arthur's knights: Meraugis of Portlesguez and Gorvain Cadrut. The former loved her for her personality, and the latter for her beauty. At the tournament of Lindesores, Guinevere ruled that Meraugis had the better claim to her. At Lidoine's command, Meraugis then embarked on a series of adventures, accompanied by Lidoine, to prove himself worthy of her. They eventually became separated, and Meraugis was believed to have been killed. Lord Belchis tried to force her into marriage with Espinogres, his son, but Meraugis showed up in time to prevent the marriage and to claim Lidoine as his own. [*Raoul*]

LIDOINE[2]

Daughter of Emperor Henry of Germany, sister of Sir Laris, and cousin of Arthur. She married King Ladon of Gascony, but she was loved by Claris, Laris's friend. When Ladon died, King Savari of Spain tried to force her into marriage by invading her lands and capturing her, but Claris rescued her, and Claris and Lidoine were wed. [*Claris*]

LIDONAS

The squire of Eliezer, King Pelles' son. He assisted his master in some early skirmishes against the Saxons. [*VulgMer*]

LIEZ

The castle ruled by Johfrit in Ulrich's *Lanzelet*. It is probably related to LIS, a location often found in French texts. [*UlrichZ*]

LIGESSAUC [*Ligessac*]

A knight, the son of Eliman, who murdered three of Arthur's knights. Arthur chased him down, but Ligessauc sought refuge in a church, where he was harbored by the beneficent Saint Cadoc for seven years. Eventually, Saints Cadoc, David, and Telio mediated with Arthur, who agreed to accept one hundred cows in payment for the deaths of his knights. Ligessauc appears in the Triads as one of the "Tree Seafarers of the Island of Britain." [*SaintsCad*, *Triads*]

LIHETRI

The chamberlain of Arthur's Sir Yder. [*Yder*]

LILJA

Daughter of Emperor Donísus of Saxony. She married Kalegras, Tristan's son, and became Queen of England. She had two sons, Patrocles and Mórodd, and a daughter named Mollina. [SagaTI]

LIMANGIN [Limados]

A duke from Camelot who, in Arthur's service, led a battalion of soldiers in the second war against Claudas. [VulgLanc]

LIMERICK [Limeri]

The capital of Ireland in the French Durmart le Gallois. It was besieged by the evil Nogant, but saved by the knight Durmart. [Durmart]

LIMOGES

A city in west central France, known for its fine porcelain. The knight Pilades carried a shield made in the city. [ChretienL]

LIMOR

A city whose bishop was the brother of Sir Sagremor. The Bishop of Limor's other brother was the Bishop of Lumeri. [Contin4]

LIMORS[1] ("Death") [Limwris]

An English town that Erec and Enide entered during their journey. Erec had been injured during the trip, and fell unconscious. The ruler of the town, Count Oringle, thought that Erec was dead, and he began making advances on Enide. When Enide proved difficult, Oringle abused her. Enide's screams awoke Erec, who jumped up and killed Oringle. "Liimors," probably indicating, "death," was corrupted by Welsh storytellers to "Limwris" and given to the count himself. [ChretienE, Geraint]

LIMORS[2]

The castle belonging to lord Linier in Ulrich's Lanzelet. It had a custom that every occupant would attack any knight that approached it without presenting an olive branch. Lancelot was ignorant of this custom, and he was assailed as he rode up to the castle. He fought his way inside, where he was given harbor by Linier's niece (and foster daughter) Ade. Eventually, Linier and Lancelot fought in single combat, and Linier was killed. [UlrichZ]

LIMOS

The Countess of Limos was loved by Sir Oriles, but she loved Gawain. She told Oriles that he could have her if he defeated Gawain in combat. Oriles tried and failed, and the countess gave her love to Gawain instead. [Livre]

LIMOURS

In Tennyson, a knight who had been suitor of Enide when her family was wealthy. Geraint and Enide ended up lodging with Limours during their journey. Limours tried to convince Enide to abandon Geraint. Enide pretended to agree and advised Limours to take her by force in the morning. Returning to Geraint, Enide told her husband what had transpired, and the two fled Limours's house. Limours chased after them but he was knocked unconscious in a fight with Geraint. This figure appears in the Welsh Geraint as the BROWN EARL. An individual named LIMORS appears later in Geraint. Tennyson seems to have taken the character from the former and the name from the latter. [TennIK]

LIMOUSIN

A region of west central France, in the province of Guienne. It was owned by Lancelot, who bestowed it on Sir Blanor of Gannes in return for Blanor's support in the battles against King Arthur. [Malory]

LINCOLN

A shire on the eastern coast of England, south of the Humber River. The city of Kaerliudcoit stood here and was the site of one of Arthur's battles against Colgrim's and Cheldric's Saxons. It contains the region known as LINDSEY, which may be the actual site of LINNUS, the location of Arthur's battles against the Saxons mentioned by Nennius. [GeoffHR, Wace]

LINDESORES

A castle in the forest of Broceliande, ruled by King Belinant of South Wales in the Vulgate Merlin. During the Saxon invasions, the various northern kings rallied their forces at Lindesores. In the Third Continuation of Chrétien's Perceval, Perceval arrives at Lindesores in a magical boat and fights the castle's lord, Mendandre de la Loge, who tries to make him pay a toll. In Raoul de Houdenc's Meraugis de Portlesguez, it is the site of a sparrowhawk tournament in which Meraugis of Portlesguez and Gorvain Cadrut both fall in love with the Lady Lidoine. [Raoul, VulgMer, Contin3]

LINDSEY

The northenmost province of Lincolnshire. In Renaut de Bâgé's Le Bel Inconnu, one of the Yvains is noted as the King of Lindsey. Pierre de Langtoft gives it as Lot's kingdom, which is usually LOTHIAN. Nennius may mean Lindsey when he places four of Arthur's battles against the Saxons in LINNUIS. [Renaut, Pierre]

LINEFLES

The King of France, who married Arthur's sister, Olimpia, and had a son named Meleranz. [PleierM]

LINGRENOTE

A sorceress who was the benefactress of Guengasoain, Gawain's opponent in La Vengeance Raguidel. She ruled the Castle Without a Name on the Island that Floats. She provided Guengasoian with magic arms. [Vengeance]

LINIER

Lord of the castle Limors. He was the brother of Patricius von den Bigen. Linier's niece, Ade, was also his foster-daughter. When he discovered that Ade had given harbor to Lancelot, Linier flew into a rage and demanded that Lancelot accept a challenge involving a giant, two lions, and, eventually, combat with Linier himself. Lancelot agreed, survived the challenge, killed Linier, and made Ade his paramour. [*UlrichZ*]

LINLIGWAN [*Llyn Lliwan*]

A marvelous lake along the river Severn in Wales, which filled and emptied according to the tides. [*GeoffHR*]

LINNUIS

A region of Britain that contained the river Dubglas where, according to Nennius, Arthur won four battles against the Saxons (see ARTHUR'S BATTLES). It may be identical to LINDSEY in Lincolnshire, though no river called Dubglas is known here. Other possibilities are LOTHIAN, which has a river Dunglas, and Lindum in Scotland, which has a river Douglas, though these would be too far north for a fifth-century campaign against the Saxons. Nennius may be preserving some memory of a battle against the Picts instead. [*Nennius*]

LINODAS

A heathen warrior slain by Sir Sagremor at the battle of Diana Bridge. [*Arthour*]

LIODARZ

Son of Prince Teschelarz of Poitou. He was saved from a pack of robbers by Arthur's Sir Tandareis. He became Tandareis's loyal companion and served as his steward of Malmontan. [*PleierT*]

LION

The African Prince of Namur. He killed his neighbor, King Amire of Libya, because he coveted Amire's wife, Lamire. Lamire died of heartbreak, however, leaving Lion in misery. Meanwhile, word of his deed reached King Wigalois of Korntin, the son of Gawain and relative (through his wife) of Lamire. Wigalois raised an army and met Lion in battle. Lion was killed by Gawain. [*Wirnt*]

LIONE

In the Post-Vulgate *Suite du Merlin*, the lover of Launceor, a knight slain by Balin. When Lione found her lover dead, she stabbed herself with his sword. King Mark of Cornwall erected a monument to the lovers' tragic story. Malory calls the maiden COLOMBE. [*PostMer*]

LIONEL[1] [*Lionello*]

A Knight of the Round Table and cousin of Lancelot. He was named after a lion-shaped birthmark, which was fated to disappear once Lionel had slain the Crowned Lion of

Libya, a feat he accomplished shortly after achieving knighthood. His brother was Sir Bors, one of the Grail Knights. His father, King Bors of Gannes, died when King Claudas invaded his lands, and his mother, Queen Evaine, fled to a nunnery. Sir Pharien, one of his father's servants, raised the young princes until Claudas discovered their existence. Lionel and Bors spent a short time in Claudas's care before they were rescued by Sariade, a servant of the Lady of the Lake. The Lady raised them with their cousin Lancelot. When Lionel came of age, the Lady sent him to Britain to become Lancelot's squire. Arthur eventually knighted him and promoted him to the Round Table. He had numerous adventures with his brother and cousin, including his fight against the Crowned Lion.

During the Grail Quest, two knights captured him and beat him with thorns. His brother Bors found him in this state, but chose to rescue an abducted damsel instead. A furious Lionel later tried to kill Bors for this choice, but Bors refused to fight. Lionel, trying to get to Bors, killed a hermit and another knight named Calogrenant before God came between the brothers in a pillar of fire or lightning. Lionel forgave Bors, who departed to find the Grail.

When Lancelot and Guinevere were accused of treason, Lionel pledged his support to Lancelot and helped him to rescue Guinevere from the stake. In return for his support, Lancelot made him the king of Gannes or France. In the Vulgate *Mort Artu*, he is slain during Lancelot's war with Mordred's sons; the Post-Vulgate says that Melehan, Mordred's son, slew him; the Stanzaic *Le Morte Arthur* says that he was killed during Lancelot's war against Arthur; and Malory says that Lionel was slain by disillusioned citizens of Logres after Arthur's death. [*LancLac, VulgLanc, VulgQuest, VulgMort, Contin3, PostMer, PostQuest, PostMort, Stanz, Allit, Malory*]

LIONEL[2] [*Lioniaus*]

Gawain's son in the First Continuation of Chrétien's *Perceval*. His mother was Guilorete of Lis. He was to receive a magnificent shield at the King of Ambervale's wedding. [*Contin1*]

LIONEL[3] OF NANTEUIL

In the Vulgate *Merlin*, Helen, the lady slain by the Giant of St. Michael's Mount, is called the niece of "Lionel of Nanteuil." In most sources, Helen is the niece, wife, or daughter of HOEL of Brittany. [*VulgMer*]

LIONFERFO

A waste land ruled by Lucano, a giant slain by Tristan. [*Tavola*]

LIONS

These creatures make frequent appearances in Arthurian texts. Generally, like dragons, they are monsters to be slain. They are often pets of malevolent lords.

In an early Welsh poem, Arthur recounts how Cei went to the island of Anglesey to destroy lions. Cei contends here with the fearsome Cath Palug, which appears in other Arthurian texts and seems to be a demonic form of lion. In Chrétien de Troyes's *Perceval* and related texts, a lion is one of the perils faced by the knight (generally Gawain) who braves the adventure of the Perilous Bed in the Castle of Marvels. In Ulrich von Zatzikhoven's *Lanzelet*, Lancelot must kill two lions at the house of Lord Linier. In the Second Continuation of Chrétien de Troyes's *Perceval*, Perceval slays two ferocious lions belonging to a knight named Abrioris. In *Perlesvaus*, Melot of Logres has a pet lion that inhabits the Field of the Lion. This lion is killed by Sir Clamadoz of the Shadows, prompting Melot to take vengeance against Clamadoz. In the same romance, Perceval kills the pet lion of the Red Knight of the Deep Forest. The romance of *Tyolet* has Tyolet fighting lions and receiving injury at their claws. According to *Lancelot do Lac*, Sir Lionel, the cousin of Lancelot of the Lake, was born with a lion-shaped birthmark. This mark disappeared when Lionel fought and killed the Crowned Lion of Libya at Arthur's court, presenting its skin to Yvain. In the Vulgate *Lancelot*, Sir Hector of the Fens rescues Angale from a pair of lions owned by Lord Marigart in the castle of Raguidel. In the Welsh story of *Peredur*, Peredur slays a lion that guards the Circular Valley. In *Les Merveilles de Rigomer*, the evil Mal Ostagier owns four lions, and the creatures also inhabit the dangerous Male Gaudine. Lancelot slays a panther in this forest. In the Prose *Tristan*, Brunor the Black (the Knight of the Ill-Fitting Coat) kills a lion that has escaped from Arthur's menagerie and is menacing Guinevere. In *Sir Gawain and the Carl of Carlisle*, the Carl has several pet lions.

On the other side, some of the most significant appearances of lions in Arthurian literature feature them as protectors or loyal companions of knights. This is the case in Chrétien de Troyes's *Yvain*. Yvain, traveling through a forest, finds "a lion, and a serpent which held him by the tail, burning his hind-quarters with flames of fire." Deciding the serpent the evil of the two creatures, Yvain kills it and thus saves the lion. The grateful lion becomes Yvain's constant companion and fierce protector throughout the rest of his adventures, earning Yvain the nickname "The Knight with the Lion."

We find a similar story in the Vulgate *Quest del Saint Graal*: During the Grail Quest, Perceval finds himself on an island populated by wild beasts. He witnesses a serpent carrying away a lion cub. The cub's mother arrives in swift pursuit and engages the serpent in combat. Perceval, regarding the lion "as being the more natural animal and of a nobler order than the serpent," kills the snake. The thankful lion stays with Perceval for the rest of the day.

Finally, in Spenser's *The Faerie Queene*, a lion becomes the protector of the maiden Una after she is abandoned by the Red Cross Knight.

Lions often represent kings or royalty in classical mythology (cf. the Crowned Lion of Libya), but the examples of the lion as a "protector" suggest a symbolism for Christ, who is called "the Lion of the tribe of Judah" in Revelations 5:5. These appearances also echo Aulus Gellius's first-century tale of Androcles, a Roman slave who assisted a lion by drawing a thorn from its paw.

[*WelshPG*, *ChretienY*, *ChretienP*, *Contin2*, *Perlesvaus*, *Tyolet*, *LancLac*, *VulgLanc*, *VulgQuest*, *Peredur*, *ProsTris*, *Merveil*, *SyreGaw*, *Spenser*]

LIORLINGE

A castle given to Isolde by Mark after she passed a chastity test at the enchanted Red Stone. [*Tavola*]

LIPPIDINS OF AGREMUNTIN

An infidel duke who served Feirefiz, Perceval's half-brother. [*Wolfram*]

LIS [*Liz*]

A castle mentioned by Chrétien de Troyes and his continuators as the home of Meliant and Bran. In the First Continuation of *Perceval*, the damsel of Lis, Guilorete, bears Gawain a son. Wolfram called its capital Barbigœl. It probably comes from the Welsh *llys* ("castle"), though other possibilities include the French *lis* ("lily") and a corruption of *iles* ("isles"). [*ChretienE*, *Contin1*, *Wolfram*]

LISANOR [*Lionors*, *Lyonors*]

In the Vulgate Cycle, a young lady with whom Arthur, prior to marrying Guinevere, had a brief fling. Their union produced Loholt (or, in Malory, Borre), who became a Knight of the Round Table. Lisanor was the daughter of Earl Sevain and was born at Quimper-Corentin castle. The *Livre d'Artus* makes her the Lady of Cardigan. In earlier sources, Loholt's mother is Guinevere. [*LancLac*, *VulgLanc*, *VulgMer*, *Livre*, *Arthour*, *Malory*]

LISAVANDER [*Lysavander*]

The burgrave of the city of Beauvais under King Meliant of Lis. He was defeated in a battle at Bearosche by Gawain. [*Wolfram*]

LISCHEIT

The son of Tinas. Tutored in the martial arts by Gawain, he eventually came to rule a land bordering on Cornwall. [*PleierT*]

LISCHOIS GWELLJUS OF GOWERZIN

A duke who served Duchess Orgeluse of Logres. Lischois frequented a river in Terre Marveile near the Castle of Marvels. Orgeluse, seeking a prospective husband and knight servitor would lead any suitors to the location and have them fight Lischois. Lischois was invariably victorious until he encountered Gawain (at the time, he was in possession of Gawain's stolen horse, Gringolet). Gawain defeated Lischois in combat twice; both times, Lischois refused to surrender, preferring death. Gawain refused to kill him and finally turned him over to Plippalinot the Ferryman as a prisoner. Lischois's companion, Florant of Itolac, similarly failed against Gawain. Lischois later married Gawain's sister Cundrie. [*Wolfram*]

LISTENOIS [Lestenois, Listenoise, Listinois, Listonei(s), Lystenoys(e)]

Another name for the GRAIL KINGDOM, as introduced in the Vulgate *Merlin* and Post-Vulgate *Suite du Merlin*. Its relationship with the STRANGE LAND (the Grail Kingdom in the other Vulgate stories) is uncertain. Possibly, they are the same land, or one is a smaller dominion within the other. Listenois became the WASTE LAND after the Dolorous Stroke. The country was ruled by the line of Grail Kings or Fisher Kings, including Pellehan and Pelles. In several instances, Alan and Pellinore are called kings of Listenois, but as they are Pelles' brothers, the statements can be reconciled. The country's main feature was Corbenic, the Grail Castle. Listenois was the home of the knights Eliezer, Claalant, Felot, and Bryan. An unnamed King of Listenois, in Malory, opposes Arthur at the tournament at Leverzep. [*LancLac*, *VulgMer*, *PostMer*, *ProsTris*, *Malory*]

LITAN

The castle inhabited by Dinas, King Mark of Cornwall's seneschal, in Eilhart's *Tristrant* Other writers call it DINAN. [*Eilhart*]

LITTLE BRITAIN

A common alternate name for BRITTANY and, sometimes, NORMANDY.

LITTLE IRELAND

A country ruled by King Yon, who went to war with Arthur at the beginning of Arthur's reign. It may be the Isle of Man. [*LancLac*, *VulgLanc*]

LITTLE KING

Nickname of GUIVRET THE SMALL. [*Geraint*]

LITTLE KNIGHT [*Petit Chevalier]

A dwarfish knight slain by Gareth in the First Continuation of Chrétien's *Perceval*. Gareth was avenging the death of another knight named Brangemuer, as well as his own previous humiliation at the Little Knight's hands. In the Second Continuation, the Little Knight's sister, Tanrée, becomes Gawain's lover. The Little Knight himself attended a tournament in the White Land. He had a magic shield that could only be carried successfully by a knight who was truly loved by his lady. [*Contin1*, *Contin2*]

LLACHEU

Son of Arthur in Welsh legend. He was one of his father's warriors and advisors. He appears in Chrétien de Troyes as LOHOLT. The Welsh storytellers considered him powerful and fearless. An early Welsh poem known as *Mi a Wum* contains the passge: "I have been where Llacheu was slain, son of Arthur, marvelous in songs, when ravens croaked over blood." [*Triads*, *Dream*]

LLAESGYMYN

A gatekeeper at King Arthur's court, and a servant of the warrior Glewlwyd Strong Grip. Apparently, he was not a very good servant: when Glewlwyd's other servants were killed, Glewlwyd despaired because Llaesgymyn was the only one he had left, and Llaesgymyn was "of no use to anyone." [*Culhwch*, *Geraint*]

LLAMREI

Arthur's mare, which he lent to Caw of Scotland for the hunting of the boar Ysgithyrwyn. It was a powerful beast that could carry four men at one time. [*Culhwch*]

LLANBADARN

The resting place of Arthur's warrior Cynon, according to a Welsh poem. [*WelshSG*]

LLANCARFAN

A town in Wales, of which St. Cadoc was the abbott in Arthur's time. [*SaintsC*]

LLANDAFF

The priest Teliau served here before he was promoted to Archbishop of Dol. [*GeoffHR*]

LLANFORFAEL

The site of Yvain's grave in an early Welsh poem. [*WelshSG*]

LLARA ("Meek")

An Arthurian warrior who was the son of Casnar. [*Culhwch*, *Dream*]

LLAWR ("Earth")

One of King Arthur's warriors who was the son of Erw. [*Culhwch*]

LLAWFRODEDD THE BEARDED

One of King Arthur's warriors and advisors. [*Culhwch*, *Dream*]

LLAWGAD TRWM BARGOD EIDYN ("Heavy Battle-Hand of the Border of Eidyn") [Llongad Grwrm Fargod Eidyn]

The warrior who killed Afaon, son of Taliessin, according to a Welsh Triad entitled "Three Unfortunate Assassinations of the Island of Britain." Another Triad notes that Afaon avenged his death from the grave, so Llawgad may have been killed. [*Triads*]

LLEFELYS

King of France, son of Beli, and brother of Lludd, King of Britain, in the non-Arthurian Welsh tale, *Lludd and Llefelys*. At the request of his brother, Llefelys helped to rid three plagues from the island of Britain—one of which was a pair of dragons that his brother buried under the mountain DINAS EMRYS and were, presumably, the same dragons that were later uncovered by Merlin.

LLEMENIG

A Welsh warrior, mentioned in the Triads as both an "unrestricted guest" and a "wanderer" of Arthur's court, and as one of the three "violent ones" of Britain. He may be identical to LLEMINAWG of *The Spoils of Annwn*. [*Triads*]

LLEMINAWG

One of Arthur's warriors who, in *The Spoils of Annwn*, helps Arthur take the enchanted cauldron from the Welsh otherworld. He may be identical to LLENLLEAWG from *Culhwch and Olwen* who has a similar role in a comparable expedition. Either he or his comrade LLUCH LLEAWG may be the origin of LANCELOT. He may be identical to LLEMENIG of the Triads. [*Spoils*]

LLENAWG

Father of Arthur's warrior Gwallawg. [*Geraint*]

LLENLLEAWG

One of Arthur's warriors, from the headlands of Gamon in Ireland. He is called "the exalted one." Llenlleawg accompanied Arthur to Ireland the quest to obtain the cauldron of Diwrnach. Upon Diwrnach's refusal to hand it over, Llenlleawg grabbed Arthur's sword Caledfwlch and killed Diwrnach. He may be identified with either LLUCH LLEAWG or LLEMINAWG from "The Spoils of Annwn," and may be a prototype of LANCELOT. [*Culhwch*]

LLES

The Emperor of Rome who opposed Arthur in Welsh legend. His counterpart in non-Welsh sources is either LUCIUS or LEO. [*Triads*]

LLEW

Son of Cynfarch and one of Arthur's "Golden-Tongued Knights." He apparently had a particular skill with speech. He was the brother of Urien, the father of Mordred, and thus the Welsh counterpart of LOT. In the Welsh translation of Geoffrey's *Historia*, he is also named as the husband of Anna (Arthur's sister) and father of Gwalchmei (the Welsh counterpart of Gawain). He may be identical to LLUCH. [*Triads*]

LLOEGR

An old Welsh name for the region of Britain now called "England." It was transformed into the more common LOGRES.

LLOFAN SEVERING HAND

The slayer of King Urien, according to Welsh tradition. [*Triads*]

LLONGBORTH

The site of an epic battle in early Welsh legend. Geraint, king of Devon, is the hero of the battle, and he may have died there. One line alludes to Arthur, though it is unclear whether it is indicating that Arthur himself was at the battle, or whether only "Arthur's men" were there. Llongborth may be identified with Langport in Somerset or Portchester on the coast of Hampshire. Portchester was the site of a battle between the Saxons and the Britons in 501, according to the *Anglo-Saxon Chronicle*. [*WelshGer*]

LLUBER BEUTHACH

One of King Arthur's warriors in Welsh legend. His name comes from the Irish character "Lóegaire Búadach." [*Culhwch*]

LLUCHED ("Plague")

Grandchild of Arthur's warrior Bwlch. [*Culhwch*]

LLUCH ("Lake") LLEAWG

One of Arthur's warriors, described in the ninth-century Welsh poem *The Spoils of Annwn*. He assisted Arthur in obtaining a magical cauldron from Annwn. He may be related to LLENLLEAWG from *Culhwch and Olwen* who has a similar role in a comparable expedition. Either Lluch Lleawg or his comrade LLEMINAWG may be the origin of LANCELOT, having descended from the Celtic God LUG. [*Spoils*]

LLUDD[1]

The king of Britain in a non-Arthurian Welsh tale, *Lludd and Llefelys*. The son of Beli, Lludd inherited the kingdom after his father's death. Three plagues fell upon his island, and Lludd sent for his brother Llefelys, King of France, to help eradicate them. With his brother's help, he rid himself of the plague—one of which was a pair of dragons that he buried under the mountain Dinas Emrys and were, presumably, the same dragons that were later uncovered by Merlin.

LLUDD[2] SILVER HAND

Father of Arthur's warrior Creiddylad. [*Culhwch*]

LLUDD[3] OF THE BREASTPLATE

One of Arthur's three battle horsemen. [*Triads*]

LLWCH[1] EWIN

An English lake where the boar Twrch Trwyth made a stand against Arthur and his warriors during the grand hunt. Twrch Trwyth killed many men—including Echel Pierced Thigh and Garwyli—before he fled on to Llwch Tawy. *Llwch* is Welsh for "lake." [*Culhwch*]

LLWCH[2] TAWY

An English lake to which the boar Twrch Trwyth fled while pursued by Arthur's warriors. At the lake,

Trwyth and his piglets split up. From here, the boar went on to the Havren River. [*Culhwch*]

LLWCH³ LLAWWYNNAWG

One of King Arthur's warriors in Welsh legend. He is perhaps taken from the Irish folk character LUG (he is mentioned as being from "across the sea"). According to the legend, he fathered a number of sons who became Arthur's warriors, including, probably, Llenlleawg. Several of his sons were named Gweir. His first name means "lake," while his second seems to mean "striking hand." His relationship with LLUCH LLEAWG and LLEMINAWG is uncertain, but he may be identical to either of these characters. He may be the origin of LANCELOT and LOT. [*Culhwch*]

LLWNG

One of Arthur's warriors in Welsh legend. [*Culhwch*]

LLWYBAR ("Path")

Son of Caw, one of twenty brothers, and one of Arthur's warriors. [*Culhwch*]

LLWYD [*Llwydeu*]

An Arthurian warrior who was the son of Cil Coed. Llwyd lived in Porth Cerddin in Dyfed and lodged Arthur and his warriors on their return from the invasion of Ireland. [*Culhwch*]

LLWYDAWG THE KILLER

One of the piglets of the boar Twrch Trwyth. Llwydawg fought alongside Twrch Trwyth during the epic hunt, and killed many of Arthur's warriors at Dyffryn Llwchwr. Llwydawg himself was finally killed at Ystrad Yw, but not before the warriors Peissawg the Tall, Llygadrudd Emys, and Gwrfoddw fell to his tusks. [*Culhwch*]

LLWYDEU

An Arthurian warrior. He was the son of Nwython, the brother of Rhun and Gwystyl, and the father of Gwydre and Gwenabwy. [*Culhwch*]

LLWYFENYDD

A county or city in the kingdom of Rheged, ruled by Yvain, according to a sixth-century elegy in *The Book of Taliesin*.

LLWYR

Son of Llwyryon. He owned a magic cup which always held the best drink. As one of his tasks, Culhwch had to obtain the cup for the giant Ysbaddaden. [*Culhwch*]

LLWYRDDYDDWG

The horse belonging to Arthur's warrior Syfwlch. [*Culhwch*]

LLWYRYON

The father of Llwyr, a warrior who owned a magic cup. [*Culhwch*]

LLYCHLYN

The Welsh word for Scandinavia. In *Culhwch and Olwen*, Glewlwyd, Arthur's gatekeeper, says that "in the contest between the two Ynyrs...twelve hostages were brought from Llynchlyn." A Welsh Triad names the earl of Llychlyn as the father of Arthur's warrior Blaes. [*Culhwch*, *Triads*]

LLYGADRUDD EMYS ("Red Eye Stallion")

Brother of Eigyr (Igraine), uncle of King Arthur, and one of Arthur's warriors. He was killed at Ystrad Yw fighting the piglet Llwydawg the Killer during the great hunt of the boar Twrch Trwyth. [*Culhwch*]

LLYN LLYW

A British lake that was the home of the Salmon of Llyn Llyw, a magical creature that guided Arthur's warriors on their quest to find Mabon, a knight kept prisoner in Gloucester. [*Culhwch*]

LLYR

A euhemerized Celtic sea deity who was the father of Bran, Manawydan, Branwen, Caradawg Strong Arm, Granwen, and others. According to Welsh legend, Llyr was the King of Britain before his son Bran. In one legend, Llyr's son Caradawg is Arthur's first cousin, making Llyr the brother of either Eigyr (Igraine) or Uther, although this relationship is not substantiated in any texts. He is sometimes called "Llyr of the Sea." His counterpart in Irish legend is the sea god Lir. [*Culhwch*, *Dream*]

LLYWARCH THE OLD

One of Arthur's three "Counselor Knights," according to the Welsh Triads. He was so named because he gave precious advice to Arthur. In the Triads, he is also listed as one of the three "unrestricted guests" and "wanderers" of Arthur's court. Llywarch has a larger role in non-Arthurian legend and history, where he is said to be the cousin and contemporary of Urien, a bard, and the father of twenty-four sons. [*Triads*]

LLYN BARFOG

A lake in Merioneth, Wales. According to local tradition, Arthur killed a monster (possibly an AFANC) on the shores of the lake. Arthur's horse left a hoofprint in a rock there (Ashe, *Quest*, 192).

LOATHLY LADY

A term used to describe the ugly woman married by an unnamed Arthurian knight in Chaucer's *The Wife of Bath's Tale*, and by Gawain in "The Marriage of Sir Gawain" and *The Wedding of Sir Gawain*. In *Wedding* and "Marriage,"

Arthur is taken prisoner by Sir Gromer and must return in a year to either tell Gromer the one thing that women desire most or be killed. Arthur enlists Gawain to find the answer, and Gawain finds an ugly hag (named Ragnell in *Wedding*) who promises to provide the answer as long as Gawain marries her. To serve his king, Gawain agrees, and finds that what women desire most is the power to govern themselves and to make their own decisions. On his wedding night, Gawain crawls into bed with his repulsive spouse, and finds that she has become a beautiful woman. She tells him that she can be beautiful for during the day and ugly at night, or fair at night and hideous during the day. Gawain gives the choice to her, effectively granting woman's greatest desire, and she rewards him by becoming constantly beautiful. In Chaucer's tale, the unnamed protagonist has raped a maiden, and it is Guinevere who assigns him the task, in lieu of his execution, of learning what women desire most. Again, he finds the answer from a hag and is forced to marry her. On his wedding night, his choice is whether to have her fair and adulterous or ugly and faithful. By giving the choice to her, he is rewarded with a wife who is both fair and faithful.

A version of the Loathly Lady story is found in Reginald Heber's *The Masque of Gwendolen* (1816). Gwendolen is a former lover of Merlin who Merlin turned her into a hag after she rebuked him for his demonic powers. Gawain later married her and, when he kissed her, she returned to her beautiful form.

Prior to any of these romances, a precursor to the Loathly Lady is loved by the Handsome Coward in the Second Continuation of Chrétien's *Perceval* and in the Didot-*Perceval*. She is named Rosete. Perceval and Kay tease her for her ugliness, and the Handsome Coward defends her honor. We are told that she later became beautiful at Arthur's court, though the stories do not relate the circumstances of her transformation. The theme may ultimately come from Celtic legend; it is found in the Irish tale of the *Adventures of the Sons of Eochaid Mugmedon*. [*Contin2, Didot, Chaucer, Marriage, Wedding, HeberM*]

LOC THE LITTLE

A Knight of the Round Table killed during the Grail Quest. [*PostQuest*]

LOCRINE

A son of Brutus and brother of Albanact and Camber. When Brutus died, the three brothers divided Britain among themselves. The region ruled by Locrine was named "Logres" in his honor.. Locrine drove invading Huns out of Britain and married Gwendolen, the daughter of Corineus of Cornwall, though he did not love her. He kept the German princess Estrildis as a mistress. When Coineus died, Locrine cast Gwendolen away and made Estrildis his queen. Gwendolen went back to Cornwall, raised an army, and attacked Locrine. Locrine was killed. Gwendolen deposed Estrildis and became queen of Britain. [*GeoffHR*]

LODOER

In the romance of *Tyolet*, a knight of Arthur's court who failed in the adventure that Tyolet ultimately completed. His name may be a corruption of *Bedoer* or BEDIVERE (Loomis, *Romance*, 121). [*Tyolet*]

LODONESIA

An early name for LOTHIAN.

LOGRES [*Logereis, Logris, Logroys, Londres, Longres, Lugereis*]

Arthur's kingdom in a large number of texts. Roughly corresponding to the geographic area that we now call "England," the name derives from *Lloegr*, the early Welsh name for England, through the Latin form *gria*. (The name "England," or "Angle-Land," was a product of the Anglo-Saxon invasion of Britain, after the Arthurian period.) Geoffrey of Monmouth, using his typical creative eponomy, says that the kingdom was named after Locrine, son of King Brutus.

"King Arthur of Logres" is a fairly common designation in French and German legends, though the texts are often ambiguous as to whether Logres is a territory or a city. In the Vulgate romances, it is both, with the latter named as Arthur's capital and identified with LONDON. The site of several Saxon battles at the beginning of Arthur's reign, Logres was invested with its own bishop. According to the Post-Vulgate *Mort Artu*, King Mark of Cornwall invaded and destroyed it after Arthur's death.

In German romance, Logres is often noted as Gawain's kingdom, since Wolfram von Eschenbach tells us that Gawain married Duchess Orgeluse of Logres (who, in turn, had inherited it from her late husband, Duke Cidegast). Though Malory refers to Arthur's realm as "England," he gives the surname "de Logres" to several knights. [*GeoffHR, ChretienP, Wolfram, PleierG, VulgLanc, VulgMer, PostQuest, PostMort, Malory*]

LOGRIN

A giant who plagued Arthur. He was killed by Arthur's son, Loholt, but Kay murdered Loholt and took credit for Logrin's demise. [*Perlesvaus*]

LOHENCIS OF OUEIN

One of Arthur's knights in Heinrich von dem Türlin's *Diu Crône*. It is a reversal of YVAIN OF LEONEL. [*Heinrich*]

LOHENIS OF RAHAZ

An evil knight in *Diu Crône*. He raped a noblewoman, for which he was arrested by Gawain, tried at Arthur's court, imprisoned, and exiled in disgrace. As a result, he harbored a hatred for Gawain and later, through trickery, managed to steal Gawain's horse. The same character appears in Wolfram's *Parzival* as URJANS. [*Heinrich*]

LOHERANGRIN [*Lohengrin, Lorengel*]

Son of Perceval and Condwiramurs, twin brother of Kardeiz, and heir to the Grail kingship. Loherangrin's story is told by Wolfram von Eschenbach (in *Parzival*) and the unknown author of the later *Lohengrin*. After his ascension to his father's position, the Grail appointed Loherangrin as a champion to Duchess Elsam of Brabant, and a swan guided him to the country. He later married Elsam and became duke of the Brabant. He was forced to leave and return to the Grail Castle—after fathering several children—when the princess asked his identity, a question that he had forbidden. In the German *Lorengel*, the taboo does not exist and Loherangrin therefore does not leave Elsam. Wolfram may have adopted his name from *Loherenc Garin*, or "Garin of Lorraine," a popular character in a French *chanson de geste*. [*Wolfram, Lohengrin, Lorengel*]

LOHOLT[1] [*Loez, Loholt, Lohoz, Lohut, Loüt*]

King Arthur's son. He was a Knight of the Round Table. The Vulgate Cycle tells us that his mother was the lady Lisanor, but in Ulrich's *Lanzelet* and in *Perlesvaus*, he is the proper son of Guinevere. He is probably derived from the Welsh LLACHEU; Malory calls him BORRE. Ulrich tells us that he was handsome, noble, skilled and a great asset to his father. He helped Arthur and his knights rescue Guinevere from her abductor, Valerin. In *Perlesvaus*, he kills a giant named Logrin in the Perilous Forest, and then goes to sleep on top of the giant's body, as is his custom. Kay found him in this state and murdered him, claiming the credit for the giant's death himself. The murder was later exposed, and Guinevere died from sorrow.

The prose *Lancelot* tales tell us that he died from a disease he contracted in the Dolorous Prison, and Ulrich contends that he accompanied Arthur to an otherworld location (Avalon, in other texts) from which they both will return. Loholot is probably identical to Wolfram von Eschenbach's ILINOT. [*ChretienE, UlrichZ, Perlesvaus, LancLac, VulgLanc, VulgMer*]

LOHOLT[2]

The lord of Sorelois. He fortified his land by ensuring that it could only be entered by two well-guarded causeways: the Irish Bridge and the North Wales Bridge. He left Sorelois to his son Gloier, from whom it was conquered by Galehaut. [*LancLac, VulgLanc*]

LOIFILOL

An Arthurian knight. A magical mantle brought to Arthur's court showed his wife to be somewhat stingy when it came to marriage-oriented favors. [*UlrichZ*]

LOIRE

The prose *Lancelot* tells us that the French river formed one of the borders of King Ban's Benoic. [*LancLac, VulgLanc*]

LOMBARDO [*Limbordo, Liombardo, Lionbordo*]

A count who hated Knights of the Round Table. He was encountered and defeated by a newly-knighted Lancelot, and was forced to surrender to Guinevere. He became one of Arthur's knights, but retained his hate for Lancelot. When Lancelot rescued Guinevere from the stake and took her to Joyous Guard, Lombardo joined Arthur in the siege. [*Tavola, Pulzella*]

LOMBARDY [*Lombardie*]

A region of northern Italy, surrounding Milan, from which great warriors were said to come. An early duke of Lombardy was Gradie, an ally of the Roman Emperor Valentinian. Emperor Lucius of Rome brought many Lombard warriors with him when he made war against King Arthur. Arthur later marched through Lombardy on his way to capture Rome. In Chestre's *Launval*, Lombardy is the home of the giant knight Valentyne. [*Layamon, ChestreLvl, Allit, Malory*]

LOMBLANDA

The daughter of the King of Lomblanda died in the Castle of Treachery, after predicting that Galahad would liberate the castle. [*PostQuest*]

LOMOND [*Lumine, Lumond*]

A loch in west central Scotland, notable for its many islands and rivers, where Arthur—with the help of Cador and Hoel—defeated an army of Picts and Scots. The barbarians fortified themselves on the lake's sixty islands, but Arthur simply surrounded the lake, denied them food, and starved them to defeat. King Gillomaur of Ireland attempted to save the Picts and Scots, but he was also defeated by Arthur. After this battle, the northern barbarians acquiesced to Arthur's power and became his vassals. [*GeoffHR, Wace, Layamon*]

LONDON [*Londen, Londres, Lounde, Lunden*]

In Arthurian legends, London sometimes depicted as Arthur's capital—or at least as one of the cities where Arthur kept a castle, court, and garrison. In several texts, London is equated with LOGRES. Malory says that it was on Christmas in London that Arthur pulled the sword from the stone and thus proved himself the true King of Britain. After his coronation, and before the founding of Camelot, London and Caerleon served as Arthur's capitals. Guinevere fled there when Mordred seized Arthur's throne. Mordred besieged her in the Tower of London until he was called away by Arthur's arrival. [*Arthour, Stanz, Malory*]

LONDON BRIDGE

In one version of *Tristrams Kvæði*, an Icelandic ballad, Tristan receives his mortal wound while battling a "heathen dog" on London Bridge. [*TrisKv*]

LONDRES[1]

A king after whom London was named. Londres was the father of Constantine, Arthur's grandfather. [*Butor*]

LONDRES[2]

In *La Tavola Ritonda*, the capital of King Anguish of Ireland, Isolde's father. In other sources, it is a variation of LONDON. [*Tavola*]

LONELEY FOREST

A wood near Perceval's home of Kamaalot. [*Perlesvaus*]

LONGFIEZ OF TURTELUNZ

A knight once defeated in combat by Perceval. [*Wolfram*]

LONGINUS [*Longis*]

Named first in the First Continuation of Chrétien's *Perceval* and in the Didot-*Perceval* as the Roman soldier who stuck Christ in the side with a spear. This lance, called the BLEEDING LANCE or Avenging Lance, found its way to Britain and became one of the objects in the Grail Procession. It constantly dripped blood from its tip. His name reflects the Greek word for "spear" (Bruce, 257). [*Contin1, Didot, HereJOA*]

LONGTOWN

A British city that was the site of battle between King Crudel's pagans and King Mordrain's Christians in the time Joseph of Arimathea. [*VulgEst*]

LONGUESON

A city near Lancelot's castle, Joyous Guard. [*PostMort*]

LONVEGO [*Longue*]

A forest near Hungerford Castle, where Bors once traveled. [*VulgLanc*]

LORAYNE THE SAVAGE

A "false knight and a coward" who mortally wounded Sir Myles of the Laundis, causing his death and the suicide of Myles's lover, Alyne. [*Malory*]

LORD OF THE BLACK THORN [*Sire de la Noire Espine*]

A nobleman who owned a piece of land in Arthur's realm. When he died, his eldest daughter disinherited his youngest daughter and expelled her from the land. The younger daughter traveled to King Arthur's court to appeal the case. Yvain agreed to champion her cause, and Gawain was assigned as the eldest daughter's champion. After fighting for many hours, the two knights revealed their identities to each other, and both stopped fighting immediately. They both appealed to Arthur to award the judgment to the other. Arthur, recognizing that their self-sacrifice was a sign of love for each other, made an independent judgment in the case, awarding half the land to the wronged younger daughter. [*ChretienY*]

LORD OF THE FENS[1]

A malicious knight who waged war on Alain and Yglais, Perceval's parents. He continued the war after Alain's death, joining forces with Cahot the Red. Gawain defeated him and won Yglais a year's peace, after which the Lord of the Fens was defeated again by Perceval. Perceval drowned him in a pool of his own knights' blood. [*Perlesvaus*]

LORD OF THE FENS[2]

The ruler of the CASTLE OF THE FENS in the Vulgate *Merlin*. His daughter was the mother of Sir Hector of the Fens. He is properly called AGRAVADAIN THE BLACK. [*VulgMer*]

LORD OF THE HORN [*Sires del Cor*]

Presented as the King of Ireland and Norois in the Second Continuation of Chrétien's *Perceval*. He ruled the Castle of the Horn in the Land of the Horn. The "horn" to which his name refers hung outside his castle. Perceval blew it and summoned the Lord to battle. After defeating him in combat, Perceval sent the Lord of the Horn to Arthur's court as a prisoner. [*Contin2*]

LORD OF THE ROCK

An evil knight who siezed the castle of Gladoain after the latter's death. Gladoain's brother, the Knight of the Green Shield, sought help from Lancelot, who had been Gladoain's friend. Lancelot killed the Lord of the Rock. [*Perlesvaus*]

LORE[1]

A lady from Carlisle or Branlant in the service of Guinevere. In the First Continuation of Chrétien's *Perceval*, she is the daughter of Brun of Branlant, but the Prose *Lancelot* makes her Arthur's niece; the daughter of King Clarion of Northumberland and Arthur's unnamed sister. She served as Arthur's wine steward and as Kay's mistress. [*ChretienP, Contin1, LancLac*]

LORE[2]

The Lady of Cardigan and a vassal of Arthur. She was besieged by King Ris of Outre-Ombre, and her city was captured. Lore saw a chance to reclaim her city when none of Ris's knights would venture to the fearsome Waste Chapel. Ris had promised to grant any favor to the knight who accepted the quest. Lore offered to complete the quest. Braving a forest of brambles and beasts, she arrived at the Waste Chapel. She witnessed the burial of a knight named Bleheri, and she took Bleheri's sword. Girding it about her waist, she found that she could not undo the straps. She returned to Cardigan, where Ris was forced to abide by his promise and restore the Lady's city. She went to Arthur's court to find a knight who could undo the sword. After hundreds of knights attempted the feat but failed, a newly-knighted youth called simply Handsome Young Man (he was Bleheri's son, Meriadeuc) undid the sword and girded it over his own, earning himself the title the Knight with the Two Swords. Arthur had promised to marry her to the knight who undid the sword, but Meriadeuc immediately left court to seek adventure. Lore remained at Arthur's court, and Meriadeuc eventually returned. He and Lore were married in great splendor and retired to Cardigan to rule. They had two children. [*Meriadeuc*]

LORE³

A woman in the ancestry of the "Brown" family. She was the daughter of Brun and Lye and the sister of Brun, Hector, Galehaut, and Ysille. [*Palamedes*]

LORE⁴ OF BRANLANT

A lady who takes her name, but not her character from the first LORE. Known as the MAIDEN OF THE NARROW WOOD, she fell in love with Gawain, who had saved her from Waldin of the Fearsome Vales. Lore plots to kill Gawain in order to possess him forever. Brun of Branlant was her steward. [*Livre*]

LORETE¹

Sister of Girflet and daughter of Do. She lived her her father's home in Cardueil, which was burned during the Saxon invasion. [*Livre*]

LORETE² OF THE FAIR HAIR

A lady at Arthur's court, famed for her beauty. [*Raoul*]

LOREZ OF JASSAIDA

A knight present at the Sorgarda tournament, which Gawain won. [*Heinrich*]

LORGAN

The land ruled by King Libers and Queen Dulceflur, who were married at the urging of Meleranz, Arthur's nephew. [*PleierM*]

LORIE

Gawain's fairy girlfriend in *Les Merveilles de Rigomer*. She ruled a land called Roche Florie. In *Rigomer*, she helps to rescue Gawain from the prison of an evil knight named Gaudinoés. Her name recalls FLORIE, Gawain's lover in Wirnt von Grafenberg's *Wigalois* and in Heinrich von dem Türlin's *Diu Crône*. [*Merveil*]

LORIGAL

Son of the sorcerer Eliavres. Lorigal's mother was a mare. Eliavres had been forced to copulate with the mare after King Caradoc of Nantes found Eliavres sleeping with Caradoc's wife. Rachel Bromwich (Grout, 43) suggested *Lluagor* ("Host-Splitter"), Caradoc's horse in the Triads, as an origin. [*Contin1*]

LORRAINE [*Loreyn*]

A region of northeast France. According to Wace, it was part of Arthur's empire. During the Roman War (in the Alliterative *Morte Arthure* and Malory), Arthur's forces marched through Lorraine on their way to Rome. The fought the army of the Duke of Lorraine, who had rejected Arthur's sovereignty. Gawain and Sir Florence, leading only a few hundred warriors, defeated the duke's army of thousands at the battle of Metz. Arthur imprisoned the duke in Dover and appointed Priamus to rule the land. [*Wace, Allit, Malory*]

LOSANNA

The evil sovereigness of the Ancient Tower in *La Tavola Ritonda*. She was the daughter of Trincardo the Mad and the sister of Pinabel and Uriées. Pinabel had slain Uriées so he could marry a maiden named Tessina. Losanna's family swore to avenge the murder, killed Pinabel, and brought Tessina to the Ancient Tower for execution. Tristan saved the lady. Sir Dinadan fell in love with Losanna and tried to reclaim Tessina from Tristan, but failed. [*Tavola*]

LOSIOZ

A knight in the service of Queen Tydomie of Karmerie, who married Arthur's nephew Meleranz. [*PleierM*]

LOST BRIDGE

An alternate name for the UNDERWATER BRIDGE leading to the land of Gorre. [*VulgLanc*]

LOST CITY [*Citié Perdue*]

A city ruled by Bruant, one of Arthur's kings. [*Meriadeuc*]

LOST ISLAND [*Isle Perdu*]

A small island in the straight of Assurne, so named because of its remoteness. It was part of lord Galehaut's lands, off the coast of Sorelois, and was visited by Lancelot. Before Galehaut, it was apparently ruled by a King Machen. It is named as the home of Sir Minadoras and of Galeguinant, its constable [*LancLac, VulgLanc, VulgMer, Livre*]

LOST ROCK [*Roche Perdue*]

The castle in the forest of Broceliande ruled by Matiadas, a knight defeated by Claris and Laris. [*Claris*]

LOT¹ [(A)loth, Los(t), Lote, Lott(o)]

Gawain's father. He married Arthur's sister—Anna, Sangive, Seife, Belisent, or Morgause, depending on the source. R. S. Loomis thought that Lot's origin was the Celtic god LUG, transferred through the Welsh character named LLWCH, but Geoffrey of Monmouth may have simply invented his name to explain LOTHIAN, Lot's kingdom. Another possible origin is a certain Leudonus, who was said to have ruled Lothian in the fifth century. Lot's counterpart in Welsh legend (as the father of Gawain's counterpart, Gwalchmei) is GWYAR.

First found in Geoffrey of Monmouth's *Historia Regum Britanniae* as the dispossessed heir to Norway, King Lot is also described in various texts as the ruler of Lothian, Orkney, Carlisle, Pictland, and the Out Isles. According to the Vulgate romances, he was the son of King Hedor of Lothian. Other than Gawain, Lot's children, in various sources, include Gaheris, Agravain, Gareth, Mordred, Beacurs, Cundrie, Itonje, Soredamor, Elaine, and Thametes. Geoffrey says that Lot, Urien, and Angusel were all brothers, but in later legends they are unrelated except by marriage.

The circumstances surrounding Lot's marriage to Arthur's sister are related in *Les Enfances Gauvain* and *De Ortu Waluuanii Nepotis Arturi*: sent to live in the court of King Uther Pendragon as a hostage after Uther conquered Norway, Lot fell in love with Uther's daughter (whom he served as a page) and engaged in a clandestine relationship, of which Gawain was the illegitimate product.

Geoffrey and other chroniclers give Lot the role of Arthur's supporter and ally. Lot fought against the Saxons during the reigns of Uther and Arthur. In reward, Arthur returned Lothian to him when it had been reclaimed from the Saxons, and later appointed Lot the King of Norway—Lot's hereditary right as the grandson of Sichelm—when it had been conquered from Riculf. Lot later fought for Arthur in the campaigns against Gaul and Rome, and he led a battalion of soldiers at the battle of Soissons. According to the Alliterative *Morte Arthure*, which follows Geoffrey's account, Lot was slain in the war against Mordred. The Didot-*Perceval* gives a similar account of his death.

The Vulgate *Merlin* is the first to name Lot as Arthur's enemy—one of the rebellious kings whom Arthur defeated at Caerleon and Bedegraine. His rebellion was cut short when the Saxons invaded Britain, and Lot had to return to Lothian to defend it. His sons defected to join Arthur's service. Gawain later defeated Lot in combat and forced him to surrender to Arthur. Lot then advocated a truce between Arthur and the other rebellious kings, for the purpose of expelling the Saxons.

In the Post-Vulgate *Merlin* continuation and in Malory's account, Lot never allies with Arthur. After repelling an invasion of Saracens, he joins forces with King Rions and King Nero to invade Arthur's land and to lay siege to the Castle Tarabel. Merlin, realizing that the combined armies will defeat Arthur, goes to Lot's chambers and distracts him by weaving a fascinating tale of prophecy while Nero's army is being destroyed. When Lot learns of the trickery, he leads his army against Arthur's but is killed in battle by King Pellinore, sparking a deadly feud between his descendants and Pellinore's. Arthur has him buried at St. Stephen's in Camelot. [*GeoffHR*, *Wace*, *ChretienE*, *Didot*, *Layamon*, *Enfances*, *Wolfram*, *VulgLanc*, *VulgMer*, *PostMer*, *Arthour*, *DeOrtu*, *Allit*, *Malory*, *Boece*]

LOT²

A Knight of the Round Table who participated in the Grail Quest. [*ProsTris*]

LOT³

The King of Galway in *Les Merveilles de Rigomer*. Lot and his son Midomidas were Arthur's allies. [*Merveil*]

LOTHAN

One of the prisoners of the giant Nabon the Black freed by Tristan. [*Palamedes*]

LOTHIAN [*Leon(e)is, Lodien(t), Loh(e)n(o)is, Lonneys, Loonois, Lothaine, Lyoneis*]

A kingdom in southeast Scotland. In most Arthurian texts, it is ruled by King Lot. Geoffrey says that Arthur restored Lot to the throne of Lothian after reclaiming the country from the Saxons. The connection between Lot and Lothian probably comes from Geoffrey's tendency toward conjectural eponymy. Chrétien de Troyes marks *Loenel* (likely *Loeneis*, or Lothian) as the homeland of one of the three Yvains; Wolfram gives the rule of the land, in Uther's time, to King Riwalin; and in Guillaume le Clerc's *Fergus*, Lady Galiene rules Lothian from her castle Roucebourc. Fergus becomes lord when he marries her. The Vulgate *Merlin* tells us that it was invaded and plundered by Saxons at the beginning of Arthur's reign. LYONESSE, the land of Tristan, may be identical. [*GeoffHR*, *Wace*, *ChretienE*, *Wolfram*, *VulgMer*, *Malory*]

LOTOR

A British city, once inhabited or visited by Arthur's chief gatekeeper Glewlwyd. [*Culhwch*]

LOTA

Isolde's mother in *La Tavola Ritonda;* the wife of King Anguish of Ireland. She was an experienced healer, and she tried to heal her brother Morholt after his battle with Tristan, but she could not save him. When Tristan was in Ireland incognito, Lotta discovered Tristan's identity by matching the broken sword piece found in her brother's head to Tristan's sword. Later, Lotta created the love potion for Mark and Isolde that was consumed by Tristan and Isolde. Lotta's character is unnamed or called ISOLDE in other romances. [*Tavola*]

LOUDUN HILL

A region of southwest Scotland. It originally belonged to Sir Galleron, but Arthur annexed it and gave it to Gawain. Galleron arrived at a feast and challenged Gawain for ownership of the land. The fight ended in a draw, but Gawain graciously returned the country to Galleron anyway. [*Awntyrs*]

LOUIS [*Lupus*]

The Bishop of Troyes. Pope Romanus sent Louis and Saint Germanus to Britain, at the request of King Vortimer, to repair the Christianity had been damaged by King Vortigern. [*Wace*, *Layamon*]

LOUMEDON THE LARGE

An Arthurian knight. [*Heinrich*]

LOUYS THE LOYAL [*Lowes*]

One of Lord Golagros's knights in the Middle Scots tale of *Golagros and Gawain*. During the war between Gologras and Arthur, Louys defeated and captured Arthur's Sir Lionel. [*Golagros*]

LOVEDON

A plain where Arthur's army camped before encountering Mordred in the final battle at Salisbury. [*VulgMort*]

LOVELL [*Lovel*]

A Knight of the Round Table who was the son of Gawain by the sister of Sir Brandelis. He joined the plot of Mordred and Agravain to expose the affair between Lancelot and Guinevere. With a dozen knights, they trapped Lancelot in Guinevere's chambers. Lovell was slain by Lancelot in the subsequent battle. [*Malory*]

LÖVER

One of Arthur's kingdoms in German romance, containing the city of Bems-on-Korcha, and the forest of Briziljan (Broceliande). Its capital was Dinazarun. [*Wolfram, PleierG*]

LOW SPRING

A fountain visited by Yvain during his quest to slay Malduit the Giant. [*VulgLanc*]

LOWER ISLANDS

Galehaut's kingdom in the Serbo-Russian *Povest' o Tryshchane*, called the DISTANT ISLANDS in the Prose *Tristan*. [*Povest*]

LOWES

One of Arthur's knights slain during the war with Mordred. [*Allit*]

LUCAN¹ [*Lacan(u)s, Lukyn*]

Arthur's butler, cupbearer, or wine steward, sometimes called "Lucan the Good," who first appears in the First Continuation of Chrétien's *Perceval*, though not significantly until the Vulgate *Lancelot*. Malory makes him Bedivere's brother, naming his father as Duke Corneus. In Arthur's service, he fought against the rebellious kings at the battle of Bedegraine, and against the Saxons at the battles of Carhaix and Aneblayse. He appears in several tournaments and events throughout Arthur's reign. He fought in Arthur's wars against Lancelot and Mordred. Lucan was one of the few survivors of the final battle at Salisbury. With his cousin Girflet (or, in Malory, his brother Bedivere), he carried the wounded Arthur to the Ancient Chapel. Lucan died there, either because Arthur accidentally crushed him, or because his intestines spilled

out of a previous unnoticed wound. In the English ballad of "King Arthur's Death," Lucan's brother Bedivere dies in the above manner, and Lucan (named as the duke of Gloucester) survives to throw Excalibur, Arthur's sword, into a lake. [*Contin1, VulgLanc, VulgMort, VulgMer, PostQuest, PostMort, Arthour, Stanz, Malory, KingAD*]

LUCAN² [*Leucan*]

A nephew of Joseph of Arimathea, charged with guarding the ark that contained the Holy Grail. He accompanied his uncle to Britain, died, and was buried there. Lancelot visited his tomb on the way to a duel at Nohaut. [*LancLac, VulgLanc, VulgEst*]

LUCAN³ THE PHILOSOPHER

A master of pagan faith who served Duke Ganor, a British ruler, in the time of Joseph of Arimathea. He championed paganism in a debate against Josephus, Joseph's son, for which God immediately struck him dead. [*VulgEst*]

LUCANOR THE GREAT

An insane giant who ruled the fortress of Dianfer in the waste land of Lionferfo. The offspring of a giantess and a lion, his brothers included Urgan the Hairy and the two giants of the Perilous Valley. Tristan slew Lucano, all of his brothers, and his nephew Burletta. [*ProsTris, Tavola*]

LUCANORO

Son of the castellan of Gitedrano. Lucanoro was slain by Tristan during the Grail Quest. Lucanoro's father tried to execute Tristan but was slain in the process by Palamedes. [*Tavola*]

LUCAS [*Luzes*]

A Knight of the Round Table from Camelot killed during the Grail Quest. He was the brother of Alma and Tanadal. [*PostQuest*]

LUCE¹

A giant whose brother, Menedron, was slain by Guiron the Courteous. Luce imprisoned Guiron in his castle in Sorelois for seven years to avenge the death. [*Palamedes*]

LUCE²

A knight in the service of King Mark of Cornwall. He led a battalion of Mark's warriors agains the invading Saxons, led by Helyas. [*ProsTris*]

LUCERNE

A city in Italy, visited by Arthur after the Roman War. [*Allit*]

LUCIABIAUS

A devil trapped by Merlin under a rock. When Perceval happened by, Luciabiaus tried to trick him into freeing him, but was unsuccessful. [*Contin4*]

LUCIENS

One of many Saxon kings who invaded Britain as Arthur's was struggling to establish power. Under King Hargadabran, he participated in the battle of Clarence and was killed by King Bors. [*Livre*]

LUCIFER

Lucifer appears in Blackmore's *Prince Arthur*. He supports the Saxon King Octa against Arthur, but is countered by God's own favor for Arthur. He seems to be the BLACK HERMIT in *Perlesvaus*. There are, of course, numerous metaphorical references to Lucifer throughout the Arthurian romances. [*Perlesvaus, BlackmoreP*]

LUCIFERA

Queen of the House of Pride. Her counselors were the seven deadly sins. The Red Cross Knight visited her palace while under the spell of the evil witch Duessa. [*Spenser*]

LUCIUS¹ [*Luc(i)es, Lucidar, Lucyus*]

The Roman official who began a war with Arthur. Geoffrey of Monmouth gives him the title of procurator or deputy under the Emperor Leo (the emperor is Honorius in another source), but Wace and later sources call him the Emperor of Rome. He is often given the surname "Tiberius" or "Hiberius." Wace tells us that he was born in Spain and was between 30 and 40 years old at the time he went to war with Arthur. The Norse *Saga of Tristam* calls him ÍRÓN. R. S. Loomis (*Literature*, 85) suggests a derivation from the Welsh LLENLLEAWC HIBERNUS (Llenlleawc the Irishman), corrupted to Lucius Hiberus. Other scholars have suggested that Geoffrey of Monmouth took the character from a "Lucerius," named in the chronicle of Sigebert of Gembloux as a western Roman emperor between 469 and 470.

In the early chronicles, Arthur's war with Lucius immediately precedes Mordred's uprising, but beginning in the Vulgate *Merlin*, the war is placed at the beginning of Arthur's reign. It began when Lucius sent envoys to Arthur's court, demanding a tribute. Arthur responded that no tribute was due (or that it was Arthur who was owed a tribute from Rome), and Lucius organized his armies, bringing rulers from Europe, Africa, Arabia, and Asia. Arthur's forces met Lucius's in Gaul, where any hope of peace was destroyed when Gawain killed Lucius's diplomatic envoy. After a number of skirmishes in Gaul and other parts of Europe, Arthur and Lucius met at the valley of Soissons. In an epic battle, Lucius's army was destroyed. Most sources say that Arthur himself killed Lucius, sending his body back to the Roman senate as the "tribute" he had been ordered to pay. Sometimes Gawain is given as Lucius's slayer. In one source, it is Lancelot. In the Alliterative *Morte Arthure* and in Malory's version, Arthur then conquers Rome itself, but in the earlier chronicles, he is summoned back to Britain by Mordred's treachery before the conquest of Rome can be completed. [*GeoffHR, Liber, Wace, Layamon, VulgMer, Pierre, Mannyng, Allit, Malory*]

LUCIUS²

A companion of Arthur. [*BlackmoreP*]

LUCIUS³ CATELLUS [*Lucas*]

In Geoffrey of Monmouth, one of the Roman senators who became a war leader in Lucius's campaign against Arthur. He led a force of soldiers at the Battle of Soissons. Layamon split him into two characters: Lucas and CATELLUS. [*GeoffHR, Wace*]

LUCIUS⁴ THE GLORIOUS

A King of Roman Britain who ruled roughly three and a half centuries before Arthur. He was the son of King Coill. He is highly praised by the chroniclers for converting the island to Christianity—a feat which, according to the Vulgate *Estoire del Saint Graal*, was prompted by Peter, a relative of Joseph of Arimathea, who arrived in Britain during Lucius's reign. Peter befriended Lucius and became his vassal after the latter's conversion. Lucius asked Pope Eleutherius to send Christian bishops to Britain. Under his reign, parishes and dioceses were set up in London, York, and Caerleon, and the old heathen temples were demolished. Those who refused to convert were destroyed. When he died, however, he left no heir, and the Britons and Romans fought over who should be crowned in Lucius's place. The fighting lasted for several generations and resulted in a series of impotent kings before the kingdom was settled briefly under Asclepiodotus. According to Nennius, Lucius received his Baptism in 167, but Geoffrey says that he died in 156, and Layamon places his death in 160. Interestingly, the confused fourteenth-century *Short Metrical Chronicle* places his reign *after* Arthur's. [*Nennius, GeoffHR, Wace, Layamon, VulgEst, Short*]

LUCK

In Heinrich von dem Türlin's *Diu Crône*, the son of Lady Fortune. Gawain visited their castle at Ordohorht and saw Luck sitting with his mother on a golden wheel. [*Heinrich*]

LUG

An Irish sun-god whom some scholars have seen as the origin—through the Welsh LLWCH—of LOT and LANCELOT. He was the father of Cuchulainn, the Irish counterpart of Gawain. He owned a magic spear called the Luin of Celtchar that may precede the Bleeding Lance of the Grail legend.

LUD

According to Geoffrey of Monmouth, a king of Britain in the first century BC. He was the eldest son of King Hely. His brothers were Cassibelaunus and Nennius. During his reign, Lud built cities and palaces all over Britain. One city, London, was named after him. Lud had two sons, Androgeus and Tenuantius, but when he died, they were too young to inherit the throne. Cassibelaunus succeeded him. [*GeoffHR*]

LUDINAS

A good knight from North Wales, imprisoned by the giant Nabon the Black. The Good Knight Without Fear set out to free him but was also imprisoned. Tristan eventually rescued them both. [*Palamedes*]

LUDUFIS

A knight present at the Sorgarda tournament, which Gawain won. [*Heinrich*]

LUFAMOUR

Perceval's wife in the Middle English *Sir Perceval of Galles*, named in other Perceval romances as BLANCHEFLOUR. He married her after he saved her land, called Maidenland, from an invasion by the evil Sultan Golrotherame. She seems to have been a fairy. [*SirPerc*]

LUGUAIN [*Lug(u)ain(s), Lugein*]

In the romance of *Yder*, Sir Yder's squire. He joined with Yder after Yder lodged with his father, Rim. After a period of service, he was knighted. [*Yder*]

LUIN OF CELTCHAR

An enchanted spear owned by the god Lug in Irish mythology. In battle, the weapon tore through the enemy ranks like lightning. After battle, it had to be quenched in a cauldron full of blood to render it safe to handle. When the hero Celtchar hefted it, blood dripped from its tip, landed on his body, and killed him. Proponents of a Celtic origin for the Grail legend have identified the Luin of Celtchar with the BLEEDING LANCE, which also bled from its tip. In addition, the Luin is associated with a CAULDRON, which some advocates see as the origin of the Grail.

LUNETE [*(E)luned, Lunet(a)*]

Servant of the Lady Laudine in Chrétien de Troyes's *Perceval* and its adaptations. Laudine's husband was killed by Yvain after a battle at an enchanted fountain. Lunete fell in love with Yvain, but she had to face the fact that Yvain loved Laudine. She convinced Laudine to marry Yvain. When Yvain apparently abandoned Laudine, Laudine's chamberlains rebuked Lunete for suggesting the match in the first place. Lunete was imprisoned but was eventually rescued by Yvain. Her ring, which had the ability to turn the wearer invisible, is counted in Welsh legend among the "Thirteen Treasures of the Island of Britain."

An episode in the *Livre d'Artus* has Lunete (or another character of the same name) establishing the adventure of the magic fountain in the first place. She was a cousin of Niniane, the Lady of the Lake, who taught her some of the magic she had gleaned from Merlin. Lunete used this magic to create the fountain in the forest of Broceliande, which was first defended by her lover. [*ChretienY, Livre, Ivens, Owain, Ywain*]

LUNETTE

The maidservant of Lady Galiene of Lothian in the Dutch romance of *Ferguut*. She is known as ARONDELE in Guillaume le Clerc's *Fergus*. [*Ferguut*]

LUOGO FRANCO ("French Room")

Tristan's palace in the castle of Tintagel in Cornwall. [*Tavola*]

LUSIN

A castle in Lyonesse ruled by King Pelias. [*ProsTris*]

LUT

A town which, according to Hartmann von Aue, was the birthplace of Erec's wife Enide. It is probably a variation of LALUTH, which is Enide's home and birthplace in Chrétien's *Erec*. [*HartmannE*]

LUTRINHO

A plain in Logres Crossed by Tristan on his way to Joyous Guard. [*Tavola*]

LUXEMBOURG [*Lusheburgh*]

According to the Alliterative *Morte Arthure*, Arthur rested his forces in Luxembourg at the conclusion of the Roman War. [*Allit*]

LYANNE

A talkative maiden at Arthur's court, obsessed with the sight of her own reflection in a mirror. [*Heinrich*]

LYANOR[1]

An ancestor of Urien and Yvain. He inherited the kingdom of Wales from his father, Galahad (son of Joseph of Arimathea). His mother was the daughter of the King of the Distant Isles. [*VulgEst*]

LYANOR[2] OF THE MOUNTAIN [*Helianor*]

A mighty knight from Uther Pendragon's day. He helped King Faramon of France battle the Saxons. He was still fighting when he was 80 years old. He accidentally killed his son, Finoés of the Mountain, when the two fought each other incognito. Eventually, he died at Camelot. [*Palamedes*]

LYAS THE LARGE [*Lyons*]

A knight who went to war with his neighbor, Helyom. Lyas and Helyom mortally wounded each other. Lyas had fifteen daughters who continued the struggle against Helyom's clan. One of the daughters, Albe, became the lover of Danain the Red. [*Palamedes*]

LYBEUS DESCONNUS

See FAIR UNKNOWN.

LYBBEALS

A Grail Knight (Templar) from Prienlascors, killed by King Lähelin. He was the first owner of Gringolet, the noble horse from Munsalvæsche that eventually became Gawain's steed. [*Wolfram*]

LYBIALS

A knight from Roconita whose lady, Sarine, sent him to Arthur's court to win honor. He jousted with Meleranz, Arthur's nephew. His parents were Kardeuz and Deselmiur. [*PleierM*]

LYE

Woman in the famous "Brown" family. She was the wife of Brun and the mother of Hector the Brown, Galehaut the Brown, Brun, Lore, and Ysille. [*Palamedes*]

LYLE[1]

Name of the home of several knights in Malory, always a simple mis-interpretation of the French *l'île* ("the isle"). [*Malory*]

LYLE[2]

A lady of Avalon, named by Malory. She sent a servant to Camelot with a magic sword, saying that only a pure knight could draw it. This feat was accomplished by Balin, who kept the sword despite the servant's warnings, and later slew his brother Balan with it. The visit turned out to be part of an elaborate revenge scheme exposed by Merlin. Her name is Malory's corruption of the French *l'île* ("the isle"), as in *dame de l'île d'Avalon* ("Lady of the Isle of Avalon"), which is the lady's title in the Post-Vulgate *Suite du Merlin*. [*Malory*]

LYNET [*Lynette*]

A maiden known as the Damsel Savage. Appearing in Malory, she is the sister of Lady Lyones and Sir Guinguemar. When her sister was besieged by Sir Ironside, the Red Knight of the Red Lands, Lynet traveled to Arthur's court to find a champion. Arthur assigned Gareth—who called himself "Beaumains"—to the quest, which enraged Lynet, for Gareth had only recently been knighted. On the way to Lyones's castle, Lynet continually insulted and rebuked Gareth, but she finally relented after Gareth overcame a number of knights. Following Gareth's defeat of Ironside, Lynet introduced him to Lyones and attended their marriage. Lynet married Gaheris, Gareth's brother. Tennyson claims that she fell in love with Gareth during their travels. [*Malory, TennIK*]

LYNORS [*Lianour, Lyanoure*]

The original duke of the Castle of Maidens. He was slain by seven visiting brothers who wanted to rape his daughter. After his death, the Castle began its evil customs which were not ended until the Grail Quest. [*VulgQuest, ProsTris, Malory*]

LYONAS

A castle in King Mark's Cornwall. [*Malory*]

LYONES [*Lyonesse, Lyonors*]

The sovereigness of the Castle Perilous. She was the sister of Lady Lynet and Sir Guinguemar. She was besieged by Sir Ironside, the Red Knight of the Red Lands, but was saved by Gareth, whom she then married at the castle of Kynke Kenadonne. [*Malory, TennIK*]

LYONESSE [*Elionois, *Leonois, Liones, Lyoness*]

The ancestral land of Tristan, ruled by his father Rivalin or Meliadus. The Prose *Tristan* describes its history, including Kings Pelias, Lucius, Apollo, and Candaces. It was thought to lie between Cornwall and the Isles of Scilly, and to have sank into the sea. It is perhaps identical to Marie de France's LEON. Despite its given location, the name is probably a variation of LOTHIAN. In some versions of the Tristan legend, Tristan makes his tutor, Governal, king of the land. In Tennyson, it seems to be Arthur's kingdom, and it is the site of Arthur's final battle with Mordred. [*Eilhart, ProsTris, Tavola, Malory, TennIK*]

LYONS

A city in east central France, at the juncture of the Rhone and Saône rivers. The knight Taulas of the Desert carried a shield made in Lyons. [*ChretienL*]

LYPONDRIGAN

A knight who, after suffering defeat at the hands of Arthur's Sir Wigamur, abducted Wigamur's wife, Dulceflur. Wigamur fought and defeated him again, saving the lady. [*Wigamur*]

LYPPAUT

In Wolfra's *Parzival*, the duke of Bearosche and vassal of King Meliant of Lis, whom he raised. His daughters were Obie and Obilot, his brother was Duke Marangliez of Brevigariez. King Meliant fell in love with Lyppaut's daughter Obie. When Obie rejected him, Meliant declared war on Lyppaut. Gawain happened upon Bearosche and agreed to give Lyppaut his aid. In battle, Gawain captured Meliant and delivered him to the girl Obilot. Obilot transferred him to her sister, the two reconciled, and the war ended. Lyppaut's counterparts are TIEBAUT in Chrétien's *Perceval* and LEIGEMAR in Heinrich von dem Türlin's *Diu Crône*. [*Wolfram*]

LYSANDER OF IPOPOTIYCON

An infidel count who served Feirefiz, Perceval's half-brother. [*Wolfram*]

M

MABON[1]

An enchanter and hero from Welsh legend derived from the Celtic god Maponos. He was the son of Mellt and Modron (herself taken from the goddess Matrona). He is named as a servant of Uther Pendragon in an early Welsh poem. In *Culhwch and Olwen*, Culhwch needs his assistance in the hunt for the boar Twrch Trwyth. Mabon, unfortunately, had been abducted from his mother when he was three years old, and no one knew where to find him. In a related task, the warrior Eiddoel, Mabon's cousin, was needed to locate Mabon. Arthur's warriors consulted with several wise animals, including the Eagle of Gwenabwy and the Salmon of Llyn Llew before they located Mabon in a prison in Gloucester, which they besieged and destroyed. Mabon assisted in the hunts of Ysgithyrwyn and Twrch Trwyth while mounted on a horse named Gwynn Dun Mane. During the battle at the Severn river, Mabon seized a razor from between the boar's ears. Mabon is also listed among Arthur's warriors in *The Dream of Rhonabwy*. The First Continuation of Chrétien's *Perceval* names "Mabon the Enchanter" among the knights in Arthur's service. The Anglo-Norman version of his name, MABUZ, is given to a cowardly knight in Ulrich's *Lanzelet*. The other two MABONs are likely derivations of his character. Chrétien's MABONAGRAIN also suggests Mabon's influence. [*WelshPG, Culhwch, Contin1, Dream*]

MABON[2] [*Maboun(nys)*]

A wizard who, with his brother Evrain, plagued Esmeree the Blonde, Queen of Wales. Pretending to be minstrels, they entered the city of Snowdon and cast spells which made the populace go insane. They laid waste to the city of Snowdon, turning it into the Desolate City. Mabon turned Esmeree the Blonde into a snake, saying that she would remain that way until she agreed to marry him, or until a knight rescued her. Esmeree the Blonde's lady, Helie, traveled to Arthur's court and secured the services of Gawain's son, Guinglain. Guinglain traveled to the Desolate City, defeated Evrain in combat, and killed Mabon. [*Renaut, ChestreLyb*]

MABON[3] THE BLACK

An enchanter in the Post-Vulgate *Merlin* continuation and the Prose *Tristan* who learned sorcery from Merlin. There is no reason to doubt that he is derived from the Welsh MABON.

Mabon captured and imprisoned Bors. Fearful of Erec, who by his mother's enchantment was immune to magic, Mabon sent Bors to kill him. Erec defeated Bors and freed him from Mabon's service. In another episode, Gawain apparently fought against Mabon over a fairy named Marisque. Gawain, equipped with the scabbard of Excalibur, was victorious.

Mabon began a rivalry with his friend, Mennonas, for the love of the lady Grysinde. He sent an enchanted ship, called the Ship of Joy, to find Tristan, intending that Tristan should fight Mennonas as Mabon's champion Tristan arrived on the ship, engaged Mennonas in combat, and killed him. [*PostMer, PostQuest, ProsTris*]

MABON[4] ROCK

A castle ruled by King Agrippes and besieged by King Vadalon. Agrippes' daughter ended the siege by poisoning the attacking army's water supply. When Vadalon discovered this, he had the maiden imprisoned in iron bands, from which she was eventually freed by Sir Bors. [*VulgLanc*]

MABONAGRAIN [*Mabanaring, Mabo(n)agrin*]

A large knight in Chrétien's *Erec*, probably a conflation of the Welsh MABON and some other character (EVRAIN has been suggested). He was the nephew of King Evrain of Brandigan. As a youth, he foolishly promised a lady he loved (called Elena in the Norse *Erex Saga*) to grant her every desire. She then bound him by his rash promise to take up residence in a forest in the town of Brandigan, and to kill every knight who came that way. Soon, the city of Brandigan became renowned for this perilous adventure, which was called the Joy of the Court. Mabonagrain was forced to kill many good knights—including Gornemant's son Gurzgri—because of his promise, but he was finally freed from his obligation when Erec undertook the adventure and defeated Mabonagrain. [*ChretienE, Wolfram, Erex*]

MABSANT ("Patron Saint")

Son of Caw, one of twenty brothers, and one of Arthur's warriors found in the Welsh *Culhwch and Olwen*. [*Culhwch*]

MABUZ

The cowardly lord of the Schatel le Mort encountered by Lancelot. His origin is likely MABON, an enchanter knight in Welsh legend. Mabuz was the son of the water fairy (the queen of Maidenland) who had raised Lancelot. Within Mabuz's domain was a beautiful forest called, appropriately, Beautiful Wood or Beforet, but he could not enjoy it because his neighbor, the undefeatable Iweret, had annexed it. For this reason, his mother (the fairy) charged Lancelot to defeat Iweret in combat.

Mabuz so loathed courageous knights that he had his castle enchanted in such a way that any knight who entered uninvited would turn into a complete coward. He imprisoned these bewitched warriors and killed them on occasion, whenever he was in a bad temper. Lancelot happened upon the castle during his adventures and succumbed to the spell. Mabuz beat him and threw him in prison with his other knights.

When Iweret became intolerable, however, and began burning Mabuz's lands, Mabuz went to his prison to look for the most cowardly knight there, knowing that, with the enchantment lifted, that knight would be the bravest. He picked out Lancelot, who agreed to fight Iweret provided that Mabuz refrain from killing any of his prisoners for a year. Mabuz agreed and freed Lancelot, who ended Mabuz's troubles by slaying Iweret. [*UlrichZ*]

MACAROT OF PANTELION

A knight killed by Gawain after he stole an ivory horn from the Maiden of the Ivory Horn, whom Gawain was accompanying. For his service, the Maiden gave Gawain a ring that quintupled his strength. [*Contin1*]

MACCABRUNO

In *La Tavola Ritonda*, Tristan assists his future father-in-law, Gilierchino, in quashing a rebellion led by Gilierchino's nephew, Albroino. Maccabruno was another uncle of Albroino, whom he joined in the war. He commanded the city of Gippa, which he surrendered to Tristan and Gilierchino after Albroino's death. [*Tavola*]

MACEDONE

In the Dutch *Ferguut*, a knight slain by Arthur's Sir Fergus. He takes the place of ARTHOFILAUS in Guillaume le Clerc's *Fergus*. [*Ferguut*]

MACEDONIA

In Godfrey of Viterbo's *Pantheon*, the Saxons who invade Britain during the reign of Vortigern and Uther are identified implausibly with Macedonians. Macedonia also appears in Malory as a land allied with Lucius, Arthur's enemy in the Roman War. [*Godfrey, Malory*]

MACEDOR

A warrior who served Alexander of Constantinople. With Alexander, he joined Arthur's service for a brief time, and he was killed during Arthur's war against the traitor Angres of Windsor. [*ChretienC*]

MACHARS

A Saxon king who, under King Hargadabran, fought Arthur's army at Clarence. [*Livre*]

MACHEN

King of the Lost Island. His daughter, Eglantine, married King Belinant of South Wales. [*VulgMer*]

MACHMERIT

A Knight of the Round Table. [*HartmannE*]

MACKBETH

A Scottish lord who joined King Tollo of Scotland and King Octa the Saxon in a war against Arthur. [*BlackmoreP*]

MACLICLISIER [*Maclisier*]

A dwarf who served Yder in Hartmann von Aue's *Erec*. While traveling with Yder, he insulted and abused Guinevere's servant and the knight Erec, prompting Erec to track Yder down and force an apology. The dwarf appears previously in Chrétien's *Erec* unnamed. [*HartmannE*]

MACOAT

A Saxon king who, under King Hargadabran, fought Arthur's army at Clarence. [*Livre*]

MACOB OF ICRAC

A fearsome Irish knight. He stripped his aunt of the land she had inherited from her late husband. Lancelot, on his way to find adventure at Rigomer Castle, heard of this situation and championed the lady. He defeated Macob after a long combat and sent him off to Arthur's court. [*Merveil*]

MACSEN

The Welsh name for MAXIMUS.

MAD CASTLE

A heathen castle populated by knights bent on murdering Christians. Perceval visited the castle, and his holy presence caused the knights to hack each other to pieces. The lady of the castle, Celestre, converted to Christianity. [*Perlesvaus*]

MADAGLAN

The pagan king of Oriande in *Perlesvaus*. He was related somehow to Guinevere, and he challenged Arthur for possession of the Round Table after Guinevere's death. He tried to convince Arthur to marry his sister, Jundree, but Arthur refused to marry a heathen. Madaglan invaded Scotland, but Arthur's soldiers, led by Lancelot, repelled them. Madaglan invaded a second time, and Arthur's warriors, under Brien of the Isles, were unable to defeat him. A second campaign by Lancelot resulted in Madaglan's death, and Oriande was converted to Christianity. Madaglan's tale, particularly his demand that Arthur relinquish the Round Table, echoes the False Guinevere episode in the Vulgate *Lancelot*, in which Madaglan's counterpart would be BERTELAY. [*Perlesvaus*]

MADAM

A Knight of the Round Table who embarked with the others on the Grail Quest. [*PostQuest*]

MADARP

In Heinrich von dem Türlin's *Diu Crône*, the land ruled by Gansguoter, Igraine's second husband. It contained the castle of Salie, where Gawain encountered his grandmother, mother, and sisters. In Chrétien's *Perceval*, these events occur in GALLOWAY. [*Heinrich*]

MADAWG¹ [*Madog*]

Son of Teithyon, and one of Arthur's warriors. He was killed at Pelunyawg by the boar Twrch Trwyth. [*Culhwch*]

MADAWG²

Father of Arthur's knight Eliwlod. He was a son of Uther, which would make him Arthur's brother. [*Triads*]

MADAWG³

The twelfth-century ruler of Powys whom Rhonabwy served. [*Dream*]

MADAWG⁴

Arthur's forester from the Forest of Dean. He was the son of Twrgadarn. His tale of a magnificent white stag prompted Arthur to organize an epic hunt. [*Geraint*]

MADDAN

Son of King Locrine and Queen Gwendolen of Britain. According to Geoffrey of Monmouth, he succeeded his mother to the British throne in the twelfth century BC. He ruled for 40 years. His sons, Mempricius and Malim, contended each other for the throne after his death. [*GeoffHR*]

MADO

A knight in Arthur's service. [*Contin1*]

MADOC¹

One of Arthur's earls in Layamon, likely adopted from the Welsh MADAWG. [*Layamon*]

MADOC²

The King of Madoc was a knight in Arthur's service. The location of "Madoc" is unknown. [*Contin1*]

MADOINE

A fairy companion of Morgan le Fay. When Arthur's knights Claris and Laris were Morgan's prisoners, Madoine fell in love with Laris. Laris and Madoine had a child together, but Laris eventually fell in love with Princess Marine. Madoine stalked Laris through some of his adventures and eventually abducted him, but he was rescued by Claris. [*Claris*]

MADOINES

A knight who tried to force the lady Beauté to marry him against her will. Beaudous, Gawain's son, defeated Madoines and rescued her. In the battle, Madoines's nephew, Morans, was slain. [*RobertBlo*]

MADOK OF THE MOUNTAIN

A knight of North Wales who jousted with Lancelot prior to the tournament at the Castle of Maidens. Madok lost. Like MADOC, he probably originates with the Welsh MADAWG. [*Malory*]

MADOLAS

A Saxon ally and kinsman of Kion Rions, Arthur's enemy. Madolas was slain by Arthur's forces at the battle of Aneblayse. [*VulgMer*]

MADON

King of Bulgaria and one of the allys of Emperor Thereus of Rome. Madon joined Thereus in a war against Arthur, and he was killed in battle by Arthur's Sir Laris. [*Claris*]

MADOR¹ OF THE GATE [*Amador(e)*]

A Knight of the Round Table who appears usually in tournament lists, although his name suggests that he might have been Arthur's gatekeeper in an earlier legend. He was exceptionally tall. His brother is called Gaheris the White in the Vulgate *Mort Artu*, Giafredi in the *Tristano Panciaticchiano*, and Patrise in Malory. This brother was poisoned by Avarlan or Pionel, but circumstances implicated Guinevere, whom Mador challenged as a murderess. He fought Lancelot in judicial combat and lost; later, when he learned the truth of his brother's death, he apologized to Guinevere and received her forgiveness. He was one of the twelve knights that joined Agravain and Modred in an attempt to catch Lancelot and Guinevere *in flagrante* and thus prove them guilty of treason, but he was killed in his attempt by Lancelot. [*VulgMort, Floriant, TristanoP, Stanz, Malory*]

MADOR² THE BLACK

Brother of Adragain the Dark and resident of the Black Isle. He was a comrade of King Urien. [*VulgLanc*]

MADRANA

A tower in Cornwall belonging to a knight named Guirlandot. Isolde hid in the tower after she ran away from Palamedes, who had abducted her. [*Tavola*]

MADRAS

A squire knighted by Arthur during the war against King Tallas of Denmark. [*Claris*]

MADUC THE BLACK

An Arthurian knight in *La Vengeance Raguidel* and the *Livre d'Artus*. Maduc broke faith with Arthur after Arthur fought a successful war against Raolais, Maduc's brother. Leaving his home in Estremores, Maduc constructed a fortress in the Narrow Wood and used it as a base of operations for a succession of raids against Arthur and his knights. Maduc fell in love with the maiden of the Narrow Wood, but she loved Gawain instead. Maduc besieged her and, after Gawain rejected her, Maduc was able to marry her. [*Vengeance, Livre, Wrake*]

MADULE

Wife of Nicoraut. Nicoraut and Madule found and raised the infant Apollo (an ancestor of Tristan) after King Canor, the child's stepfather, abandoned him in the forest. When Canor discovered that the child had been saved, he killed Madule and her husband. [*ProsTris*]

MADURAS

A knight in the service of Leriador. He was wounded in combat with Lord Agravadain of the Castle of the Fens. [*VulgMer*]

MAEL

One of Arthur's warriors who was the son of Roycol. [*Culhwch*]

MAELDINUS

A Welsh warrior who, while hunting in the mountains of Arwystli, went insane from eating poisoned apples that had been intended for Merlin. He and Merlin (who had gone insane for other reasons) were both cured at a fountain in the forest of Caledon. Maeldinus then chose to live in Caledon with Merlin, Taliesin, and Ganieda. [*GeoffVM*]

MAELGWN

A historical sixth-century king of Gwynned mentioned in several Welsh texts. The Latin version of his name is *Maglocunus* ("Hound Prince"), and a certain "Maglocune" is berated by Gildas in his *De Excidio Britanniae*. The *Annales Cambriae* says that he died in 547 from the plague. In the Welsh Triads, he appears as one of Arthur's chief elders. He has two sons named Rhun and Alser. In another Welsh poem, Taliesin and Myrddin mourn the deaths of many warriors who died in a battle against Maelgwn. [*Gildas, Annales, Myrddin, Triads*]

MAESBELI [*Maisbeli*]

A British field in which the Saxon Hengist sought to set an ambush for Ambrosius Aurelius. Ambrosius heard of the ambush beforehand, and arrived prepared. Ambrosius won the subsequent battle, and pushed Hengist on to Conisbrough. [*GeoffHR*]

MAGAAT

A Saxon king who was one of many to invade Britain at the beginning of Arthur's reign, joining his brothers Aminaduc and Bramangue and his son Arrant. Sagremor killed him at the battle of Vambieres. [*VulgMer*]

MAGANCE [*Magouns*]

A castle in Sussex that, according to Malory, was later called Arundel. When Prince Bodwyne was killed by King Mark of Cornwall, Bodwyne's wife, Angledis, fled to the castle with her young son, Alexander the Orphan. Berengier, a vassal of Agledis's father, Ranner, watched over the lady and her son. Alexander was raised here until he became a knight. Traitorous knights within the castle told Mark of Alexander's existence, however, and later helped Mark in his plots to murder Tristan. [*ProsTris, Prophecies, Malory*]

MAGANO

A kinsman of Tristan who helped murder Meliadus, Tristan's father. He inhabited the castle of Brioda, where he and his brothers were later slain by Tristan. [*Tavola*]

MAGIC DANCE

An enchantment in the Forest of No Return, created by Guinebal (Lancelot's uncle) in the Vulgate Cycle. Guinebal fell in love with the Lady of the Forest of No Return. Seeing that she enjoyed watching some locals engaged in dancing, Guinebal bewitched the area so that the people danced eternally. Passers-by were snared into the festivities. The enchantment was ended by Lancelot. A similar episode occurs in Raoul de Houdenc's *Meraugis de Portlesguez*, and Meraugis is caught in the enchantment. [*VulgLanc, VulgMer, Raoul*]

MAGLAHANT

One of several Saxon kings who joined the Saxon invasion of Britain during Arthur's reign. He was the brother of Mahaglant and Ammaduc and the father of Soriondes. [*VulgMer*]

MAGLOAS

One of King Arthur's knights. He participated in one of Gawain's quests to locate Lancelot. [*LancLac, VulgMer*]

MAGLORY [*Manginoires*]

One of the many Saxon kings to invade Britain at the beginning of Arthur's reign. Maglory and his seneschal, Dyoglis, were killed at the battle of Clarence. [*VulgMer, Arthour*]

MAGNUS

A counterpart of King MARK in the Danish ballad of *Tistram og Isold*. He confronts his wife one morning after she has spent the night in the forest with Tristan, but her handmaid manages to convince him that they have been with a woman in childbirth. [*Tistram*]

MAGO

A giant who ruled the Castle of Tears on the Giant's Isle before he was killed by Brunoro the Brown, Galehaut's father. Mago was the nephew of a great pagan giant named Dialantes. [*Tavola*]

MAGOAT

A Saxon king who, under King Hargadabran, fought Arthur's army at Clarence. He was killed by Galescalain. [*Livre*]

MAGUS

In *Povest' o Tryshchane*, a servant of the wife of Sir Seguarades, who arranged a tryst between Tristan and his lady, but was forced to confess the event to a jealous King Mark. He appears only as a nameless dwarf in the Prose *Tristan*. [*Povest*]

MAHAGLANT [*Maaglan(t)*]

A giant Saxon king of Ireland, and a brother of Ammaduc and Maglahant. He was one of many Saxon kings to invade northern Britain in the early days of Arthur's reign. [*VulgMer*]

MAHARDI

The dead brother of a maiden championed by Gawain. Mahardi was scheduled to fight a warrior named Reimambram of Zadas in order to save his sister, Behalmi, from his clutches. Mahardi perished before the combat could take place, and Gawain, who arrived at their castle of Sempharap just in time, agreed to fight in Mahardi's stead. Gawain was victorious. [*Heinrich*]

MAHAUTE

Wife of Gornemant's son Gurzgri, mother of Gandiluz and Schionatulander, and sister of Count Ehkunat. Her husband was killed at the Joy of the Court tournament in Brandigan, destroying her happiness. [*Wolfram*]

MAIDAIROS

A Knight of the Round Table who participated in the Grail Quest. [*PostQuest*]

MAIDEN OF MANY YEARS

An old woman who led Lancelot on several adventures, ending with Lancelot's unfortunate slaying of Duke Calles. [*VulgLanc*]

MAIDEN OF THE CART

The name of three damsels who served the Fisher King. Their names reflected the cart in which they traveled, which contained some 150 heads in sealed boxes. They included the heads of Adam and Eve. The Maiden of the Cart most often mentioned had gone bald when Perceval failed at the Grail Castle. Afterwards, the Maiden traveled to Britain and tried to rectify the situation by guiding Perceval, Gawain, and Lancelot towards holy quests. Her tasks were completed when Perceval killed the Black Hermit. [*Perlesvaus*]

MAIDEN OF THE CIRCLE OF GOLD [**Pucele au Cercle d'Or*]

A damsel whose castle, Montesclaire, was besieged by the Knight of the Dragon. Perceval rescued her and killed the knight. The Maiden was the daughter of King Esclador. [*Contin4*]

MAIDEN OF THE IVORY HORN [**Pucelle au Cor d'Ivoire*]

A maiden met by Gawain. She owned a magical horn that provided food and drink in unlimited quantities (much like the horn of BRAN in Welsh legend). While she was traveling with Gawain, the horn was stolen by Sir Macarot of Pantelion. Gawain tracked down the thief, killed him, and retrived the artifact. In reward, the Maiden gave Gawain a magic ring tha quintupled his strength. [*Contin1*]

MAIDEN OF THE MOORS [**Demoisele des Landes, Lady of the Lands*]

A cousin of King Anguish of Ireland. The king threw a tournament at the Castle of the Moors, her stronghold, to find her a husband. Palamedes and Tristan were the best knights in the tournament, but neither of them married the Maiden. [*ProsTris*, *Malory*]

MAIDEN OF THE NARROW WOOD [**Pucele del Gaut Destroit*]

A damsel who appears in French romance. She is given the proper name LORE OF BRANLANT in the *Livre d'Artus*. Her castle was besieged by Waldin of the Fearsome Vales, a jilted suitor, and she sent a messenger to Arthur's court for assistance. Gawain, under the alias "Daguenet," delivered her from Waldin and departed. Later learning Gawain's identity, she fell in love with him. She built a trap in her castle designed to behead Gawain on his next visit, either (depending on the text) because he spurned her love or because she wanted to be entombed with him forever. In one text, Gawain visits her castle but manages to escape unrecognized with the help of her servant, Marot. The Maiden's plan never came to fruition, and she eventually married Maduc the Black. A similar character is called ORGUELLEUSE OF LOGRES in *Perlesvaus*. [*Vengeance*, *Livre*, *Hunbaut*]

MAIDEN OF THE WHITE HANDS [**Pucele aux Blanche Mains*]

A fairy who ruled the Golden Isle. She had several suitors, so she declared that she would marry anyone who could defend the Golden Isle against all visitors over a period of seven years. Malgier the Gray, a loathsome knight, was only two years away from winning the challenge when he was killed by Arthur's knight Guinglain (Gawain's son). The Maiden was so pleased by Malgier's death that she abolished the custom and agreed to marry Guinglain immediately. Guinglain was in the middle of a quest to remove a curse from Queen Esmeree the Blonde of Wales, however, and—fearful that the Maiden would try to detain him—he sneaked away from the Golden Isle in the middle of the night. Tortured with love for the Maiden, Guinglain returned as soon as he could. The Maiden had followed his progress on the quest. She scorned him upon his return and befuddled him with enchantments of revenge. Eventually, she accepted him back into her heart, but he lost her love for good when he decided to leave her so he could participate in a tournament at the Castle of Maidens. [*Renaut*]

MAIDENLAND [*Maydenland*]

The enchanted land of fairies where, in Ulrich's *Lanzelet*, Lancelot was raised. It had no men, but Lancelot was able to learn skill with arms from visiting mermen. It is comparable to the island or valley in later legends ruled by the Lady of the Lake. In the Middle English *Sir Perceval of Galles*, Maidenland is the fairy land ruled by the Lady Lufamour. It was attacked by the Saracen Sultan Golrotherame, who wanted to wed Lufamour. Perceval saved Maidenland and married the queen. In this role, its counterpart in earlier Perceval romances is BEAUREPAIRE. Another "Maidenland" appears in *Ywain and Gawain*, taking the place of the ISLAND OF MAIDENS in Chrétien's *Yvain*. [*UlrichZ, SirPerc, Ywain*]

MAIMED KING [**Roi Mahaignié, Wounded King*]

In the Grail romances, a king with a mysterious wound that would not heal. Though not called the "Maimed King" until later, a character of this nature appears in Chrétien's *Perceval*. Named as the father of the FISHER KING, he lies infirm in a chamber in the Grail Castle and is sustained by a single mass wafer served to him from the Grail. His son, the Fisher King, also has a wound, and confusion between the two characters probably led later authors to identify them as the same person. Presumably, the Maimed King would have been healed along with the Fisher King had Perceval asked the Grail Question.

The character called the "Maimed King" comes from the Vulgate romances, and his true name is variously given as PELLEHAN, PELLES, PELLINORE, or ALAN. He was either the father or brother of the Fisher King. He was once a Grail King himself, but he received a supernatural wound which left him physically and spiritually feeble. The wounding occurred during a war in Rome, or when Balin struck him with the Bleeding Lance, or when he doubted the holiness of the Holy Grail, or in punishment for drawing the Sword with the Strange Hangings. He lay ill in the Grail Castle for many years until, during the Grail Quest, Galahad cured him with blood from the Bleeding Lance. He spent the rest of his life in a hermitage.

In the French *Perlesvaus*, there is a suggestion of Arthur himself as a Maimed King: his lapse into inactivity and dishonor occurs congruent with Perceval's failure at the Grail Quest. Arthur is renewed by a visit to the chapel of St. Augustine in the White Forest. *Perlesvaus* also mentions a SICK KING that may have influenced the Vulgate Maimed King. [*ChretienP, Perlesvaus, VulgLanc, VulgQuest, VulgEst, VulgMer, Livre, PostQuest, Malory*]

MAINE[1]

A region of northwest France, south of Normandy. According to Geoffrey of Monmouth, it was part of Arthur's domain, and was ruled under Arthur by Borel. [*GeoffHR*]

MAINE[2]

A river in Scotland, bordering the lands of the King of the Land Beyond the Borders of Galone. Arthur and the King fought a battle near the river. [*LancLac*]

MAINE[3] [*Moine, Moyne*]

In the Vulgate *Merlin*, Arthur's great uncle, who preceded Vortigern as King of Britain. He is called CONSTANS in the chronicles. The son of Constantine and Ivoire, and brother of Uther and Pendragon, Maine was foisted to the throne by Vortigern after his father's death. He was an impotent king, and Vortigern eventually had him assassinated. This alternate name for Constans undoubtedly comes from his title in the chronicles: *le Moine*, or "the Monk." [*VulgMer, Butor, Arthour*]

MAL OSTAGIER

An evil Irish knight who ruled the castle of Mal Ostoir. He owned four lions and a horrible bird that had an appetite for knights' heads. Gaheris, Gawain's brother, heard about his evil customs and challenged him to combat, killing him. [*Merveil*]

MAL OSTOIR

The castle ruled by Mal Ostagier, an evil knight killed by Gaheris. [*Merveil*]

MAL PAS

A particularly muddy stretch of road through a swamp in Cornwall that served an important purpose in Béroul's *Tristan*. Isolde, being taken to a public trial in which she would be forced to deny any affair with Tristan, had to pass through Mal Pas. She arranged for Tristan, disguised as a leprous beggar, to be sitting by the side of the road there. When she arrived with her entourage, she fretted about crossing the swamp and ruining the hem of her skirt. She summoned the "leper" to piggy-back her over the pass. Then, at her trial, she was able to swear before God that no one except Mark and the "leper" had ever been "between her legs." Beroul injects a good deal of humor in the story by having the "leper" direct Mark's advisors—and Tristan's enemies—into the deepest, muddiest parts of the swamp. Mal Pas has been idenfied by scholars with the bog Malpas on the River Truro in Cornwall. [*Beroul*]

MALADOR [*Maladors*]

Co-leader, with Gamor, of an army of Saracens who fought Ambrosius and Uther Pendragon at Bristol. [*Arthour*]

MALAGRIN THE FELON [*Malegryne*]

A knight slain by Alexander the Orphan at the behest of a maiden whom Malagrin had harassed. [*ProsTris, Prophecies, Malory*]

MALAGUIN [*Alguigines, Angvigenes, Maleginis*]

The proper name given to the KING WITH A HUNDRED KNIGHTS in the early prose Lancelot tales. The King is given other names in other sources, and in *Lancelot of the Laik*, Malaguin and the King with a Hundred Knights are two separate characters, although both are kings in the service of Lord Galehaut. MARGON, the King with a Hundred Knights's name in the Third Continuation of Chrétien's *Perceval*, may originate with Malaguin. [*LancLac, VulgLanc, Arthour, Laik*]

MALAGUINE [*Malaguinne*]

A Saxon castle in Scotland, from which the Saxons launched an invasion of Britain during Arthur's reign. They were defeated, mostly through the prowess of Lancelot. [*LancLac, VulgLanc*]

MALAKIN THE CASTELLAN

One of the many Saxon kings who invaded Britain in the early days of Arthur's reign. He led a battalion in the battle of Clarence. [*VulgMer*]

MALAN

A heathen king killed by Gawain at the battle of Diana Bridge. [*Arthour*]

MALAQUIN[1]

A Welsh Knight of the Round Table who won honor in a tournament at Estrangorre. He swore fealty to King Brandegorre's daughter. Later, he participated in the Grail Quest. [*VulgLanc, ProsTris*]

MALAQUIN[2]

In the Vulgate *Lancelot*, Arthur's king of Scotland. He may be the same character as MALAGUIN, the King with a Hundred Knights. [*VulgLanc*]

MALCHEUS

A duke of Manaheim and one of four brothers saved by Erec from seven robbers. His brothers were named Juben, Perant, and Joachim. [*Erex*]

MALCREATIURE

A dwarf with animal features from the land of Tribalibot (India). He was the brother of Cundrie la Surziere. Queen Secundille of Tribalibot sent Malcreatiure and Cundrie to King Anfortas (Wolfram's Fisher King) as a gift, and Anfortas gave him to Duchess Orgeluse of Logres as a squire. Gawain was forced to ride Malcreatiure's nag for a while after his own horse was stolen. [*Wolfram*]

MALDALET [*Maudalet, Maudelec*]

One of the many Saxon kings to invade and ravage northern Britain at the beginning of Arthur's reign. [*VulgMer, Arthour*]

MALDUC

A supreme wizard who lived on the Misty Lake in Ulrich von Zatzikhoven's *Lanzelet*. Malduc was the sworn enemy of King Arthur, since Erec had killed Malduc's father, Gawain had killed his brother, and Arthur had driven him out of Britain. Even so, when Arthur needed help rescuing Queen Guinevere from the clutches of King Valerins of the Tangled Wood, he called on Malduc. Malduc agreed to lift the enchantment prohibiting the entry of Arthur's knights into Valerins' castl—provided that Arthur turn over Erec and Gawain to him. Arthur reluctantly agreed—knowing that Erec and Gawain would give themselves gladly for the queen—and Malduc caused the knot of brambles and branches that surrounded Valerins' fortress to unwind.

Once Malduc had his hands on Erec and Gawain, he locked them in cages and delighted in torturing them daily. Finally, when word of their torment had sickened Arthur's court long enough, Lancelot spearheaded an expedition to rescue the two knights from the wizard's clutches. With the help of the giant Esealt the Tall, Lancelot and his men got into Malduc's sanctuary on the Misty Lake, killed him and his household, and freed their comrades. He had a single unnamed daughter who was allowed to live. [*UlrichZ*]

MALDUIT

A cruel heathen giant, prone to engage in plundering, rape, and murder. Malduit murdered his own parents and became lord of the Hill Castle. After falling in love with a maiden, he promised to cease his wicked activities, but he soon came to regret his vow. Yvain was tricked into battering Malduit's shield, hanging outside of the Hill Castle, giving Malduit an excuse to begin another rampage. Yvain tried to fight him in single combat, but he was imprisoned in the Castle Penning by people furious that he had released the giant in the first place. Eventually, Sir Bors arrived, slew Malduit, and freed Yvain from the dungeon. [*VulgLanc, Palamedes*]

MALE GAUDINE

A forest traversed by Arthur and his company on their way to Quintefuelle. The forest was inhabited by many dangerous creatures including legions of monkeys, poisonous toads, lions, and tigers. Its most fearsome beast was an evil panther which Lancelot slew after an exhausting combat. [*Merveil*]

MALEC [*Malard*]

A Saxon warrior in the service of King Rions. He was slain by Arthur's Sir Lucan at the battle of Carhaix. [*VulgMer, Arthour*]

MALECASTA

Sovereigness of the Castle Joyous, a palace of sexual indulgence. She tried to force the Red Cross Knight to become her lover, but he defeated her knights with the help of Britomart, the warrior maiden. Britomart and the Red Cross Knight lodged at the Castle Joyous. Malecasta turned her affections to Britomart, not realizing that Britomart was a woman. Entering Britomart's chambers at night, Malecasta discovered her mistake and roused her castle. Britomart and the Red Cross Knight were forced to flee. [*Spenser*]

MALEGER

A wretch who led a band of riff-raff in an attack on the castle of the lady Alma. Prince Arthur, defending Alma, encountered Maleger in single combat. Earth was Maleger's mother, and every time Arthur knocked him down to the earth, Maleger arose stronger. Arthur finally picked him bodily off the ground, crushed him lifeless, and threw him into a lake. [*Spenser*]

MALEHAUT [*Malaot, Malehot, Maloalto, Maloant, Maloaut, Malohaut, Malohier, Melyhalt, Mimalto*]

A city in Arthur's Britain. It was part of the realm of the King with a Hundred Knights. The Lady of Malehaut, who was the king's sister, was considered a great beauty in her day. (She is only once given a proper name: Bloie.) She was married to a knight named Danain the Red, but she fell in love with Guiron the Courteous. Only Guiron's purity dissuaded them from having an affair. She was the mother of Dodinel and an unnamed son who was killed by Lancelot. The Lady exacted revenge on Lancelot by imprisoning him, but she eventually freed him. In another episode, she was kidnapped by a knight named Gorgari, but was rescued by her brother.

The Lady of Malehaut became a good friend of Guinevere, and Lancelot and Guinevere arranged a match between the Lady of Malehaut and Lord Galehaut of Sorelois (Danain apparently being dead). When she learned that Galehaut had died, she died of grief. [*Didot, LancLac, VulgLanc, VulgMer, Contin3, Palamedes, Arthour, Tavola*]

MALÉS THE BROWN [*Malot*]

A Knight of the Round Table. He served as a standard-bearer in the battle of Carhaix, where Arthur fought against the vassals of King Rions. [*VulgMer, Arthour*]

MALGAR

A heathen king slain by Gawain at the battle of Diana Bridge. [*Arthour*]

MALGIER THE GRAY [*Malgiers, Maugys, Mauugeys*]

A powerful knight who lusted after a fairy called the Maiden of the White Hands or the Dame d'Amour. The maiden had decreed that any knight who could defend her island for seven years, against any knight who passed that way, could marry her. Malgier set his sights on accomplishing the goal, although he was so loathsome that the Maiden would have found some way to get out of the marriage anyway. After five years, he had killed 140 knights and seemed undefeatable, but he was finally killed by Gawain's son Guinglain. [*Renaut, ChestreLyb*]

MALGLEIRES

A heathen king who served King Rions. He was slain by Arthur at the battle of Aneblayse. [*Arthour*]

MALIFER OF THE BLACK VALLEY

Champion of the Saxons. When the Saxons invaded Gaul, Malifer fought Guiron the Courteous, Gaul's champion, in single combat to decide the war. Malifer was defeated. [*Palamedes*]

MALINGRE

A knight slain by Galehaut the Brown. Malingre was the brother of Mitridés. His nephews, Caradoc and Tericam, plagued the Round Table. [*Palamedes*]

MALIVLIOT

A Knight of the Round Table from Katelange. [*HartmannE*]

MALLIAS OF THE THORN [*Melior*]

A peer of Sir Bors who won honor in a tournament held in the kingdom of Estrangorre. With his companions, he swore fealty to the daughter of King Brandegorre of Estrangorre. [*VulgLanc*]

MALLOAS

King of Aleste and Ibaritun. He was the uncle of Tydomie, a maiden who married Arthur's nephew Meleranz. Before the marriage, Malloas wanted Tydomie to wed King Libers of Lorgan. When she refused in favor of Meleranz, Malloas led an army to invade Tydomie's lands, but he relented when he learned of Meleranz's noble pedigree. [*PleierM*]

MALMONTAN

In the Pleier's *Tandareis and Flordibel*, a castle near Poitou, ruled by an evil giant named Karedoz. It loosely corresponds to the DOLOROUS TOWER of the French Prose *Lancelot*. Tandareis, one of Arthur's knights, had to defeat four giants—Ulian, Margun, Darkion, and Karedoz—to conquer it, thereby freeing its prisoners and ending its wicked customs. Tandareis became lord of the castle (and its neighbor, Mermin) and later awarded it to Dulcemar, his father. [*PleierT*]

MALMORT TOWER

A fortress in Emperuse, ruled by Duke Kandalion. It served as the prison of Sir Tandareis, Arthur's nephew, when he was captured by Kandalion. [*PleierT*]

MALORE

A Saxon warrior in the service of King Rions, slain by Arthur at the battle of Carhaix. [*VulgMer, Arthour*]

MALPIRANT

In the Norse *Erex Saga*, the knight defeated by Erec at the Sparrowhawk tournament. This occurred after Malpirant's dwarf insulted Guinevere. The same knight is called YDER in the other versions of Erec's legend. [*Erex*]

MALPORDENZ

A knight present at the Sorgarda tournament, which Gawain won. [*Heinrich*]

MALRUC OF THE ROCK [*Marec, Ma(u)ruc*]

A duke in the service of King Arthur. He fought against the rebellious kings at the battle of Bedegraine, and he participated in the defeat of the Saxons at the battle of Carhaix. [*VulgMer, Arthour*]

MALSERON

A giant who served King Ekunaver of Kanadic. His companions were Karabin, Zirijon, and Zirdos. He planned to join Ekunaver's war against Arthur, but he was defeated by Arthur's Sir Garel, and the giants were forced to remain neutral. [*PleierG*]

MALTA

A city in the Strange Land, or the Grail Kingdom. It was ruled by Calafés in Joseph of Arimathea's time. [*VulgEst*]

MALVASIUS [*Malverus, Malinus*]

The King of Iceland in Arthur's time. Arthur conquered him and subjugated the island. His name may come from the Welsh MELWAS. [*GeoffHR, Wace*]

MALVERN [*Malverne*]

The forest residence of two giants slain by Yder. Following this combat, Yder was poisoned by Kay and left for dead, but was discovered and healed by King Alfred of Ireland. [*Yder*]

MAMMON

King of the House of Riches. He tried to tempt the knight Guyon away from his quest with great wealth and his daughter, Philotime, but Guyon resisted the temptations and continued his quest. [*Spenser*]

MAMORET

A knight present at the Sorgarda tournament, which Gawain won. [*Heinrich*]

MAN

An island in the middle of the Irish Sea, between England and Ireland. According to Layamon, Arthur conquered and pacified it during the early days of his reign. The island serves as the setting for much of *The Turke and Gowin*. Sir Gromer, enchanted in the form of a turk or churl, brought Gawain to the Isle of Man to contend with its pagan king. With the Turk's help, Gawain killed the king and his giants. Gromer suggested that Gawain become the new king, but Gawain declined and gave the throne to Gromer. [*Layamon, Turke*]

MANAHEIM

A duchy ruled jointly by three brothers: Perant, Joachim, and Malcheus, all of whom were saved by Erec from a pack of robbers. [*Erex*]

MANASSEL [*Manassés, Manessel*]

A knight in the service of the Duke of Cambenic. The duke's seneschal accused Manassel of betraying the duke's son. Manassel had difficulty finding a champion, but his wife convinced Gawain to fight the combat. Gawain won, proving Manessel innocent. [*LancLac, VulgLanc*]

MANASSES [*Manassen*]

One of Arthur's knights. A friend accused Manasses of sleeping with his wife, bound him, and nearly threw him in a well to drown. Manasses was saved by Morgan le Fay, who rescued him because her dead lover, Accalon of Gaul, was Manasses's cousin. After drowning his former friend, Manasses delivered a threatening message from Morgan to Arthur. [*PostMer, Malory*]

MANATHES [*Manachés*]

A follower of Joseph of Arimathea who, in Sarras, was once charged with guarding an ark containing the Holy Grail. His companions were Anascor and Lucan. [*VulgEst*]

MANATUR [*Manartur*]

Brother of King Tholomer of Babylonia, whom Manatur served in a war against King Evalach (Mordrains) of Sarras. Manatur was slain at the battle of Orcaut by Seraphe (Nascien). [*VulgEst*]

MANAWYDAN

Son of Llyr who serves King Arthur in *Culhwch and Olwen* and in an early Welsh poem. Most of the appearances of this character are in non-Arthurian legend. In the Welsh *Branwen*, he is the brother of King Bran the Blessed and one of only seven warriors to survive Bran's conquest of Ireland. He has his own *Mabinogi* tale called *Manawydan son of Llyr* in which he marries Rhiannon, widow of King Pwyll of Dyfed, and contends with a sorcerer named Llywd. In origin, he is an Irish sea god called Mananán mac Lir. [*Culhwch*]

MANCIPICELLE

A malicious maiden who tried to cause Gawain's death by luring him into a battle against the mighty Sir

Guiromelant. The ruse failed, and Mancipicelle later apologized. [*Heinrich*]

MANDIN THE WISE

A Knight of the Round Table who participated in the Grail Quest. [*ProsTris*]

MANDOGRAN

The King of the Blossoming Valley and father of Daniel, an Arthurian knight. [*Stricker*]

MANESET

A Knight of the Round Table. [*HartmannE*]

MANGON OF MORAINE

A king who, in Robert Biket's *Lai du Cor*, sends a magic drinking horn to Arthur's court. The horn spilled its contents on men with "unchaste" wives, which turned out to include every man at Arthur's court (including Arthur) except Sir Caradoc. [*Biket*]

MANIBEL

A resident of Corbenic, the Grail Castle, who did not believe in the Grail. During the Grail Quest, Galahad removed two serpents which had been placed around Manibel's neck as punishment for his blasphemy. Manibel died soon afterwards. [*ProsTris*]

MANPFILYOT

The paternal uncle of Condwiramurs, Perceval's wife. He was the brother of Kyot and Tampenteire. [*Wolfram*]

MANTLES

See CHASTITY TESTS and the THIRTEEN TREASURES.

MANUEL[1] [*Manaal, Manael*]

A Grail King who was the son of Carcelois and the father of Lambor. First mentioned in the Vulgate *Estoire del Saint Graal*, he was a descendant of Bron and an ancestor of Pelles, Elaine, and Galahad. John of Glastonbury makes him an ancestor of Arthur through Igerne. [*VulgEst, JohnG*]

MANUEL[2]

A Greek knight who married Amande, daughter of the King of Spain, at Arthur's Cardueil court. [*Manuel*]

MAPONOS

A Celtic deity who, euhmerized, appears as Arthur's warrior MABON. He was the son of Matrona, who appears as Modron.

MARABRON

Son of King Vagor of the Strange Island. He challenged and imprisoned Sir Lionel for murdering Marabron's

brother. Lancelot championed Lionel against the charge, defeated Marabron, and generously let him live. [*VulgLanc*]

MARADINS

A knight in Arthur's service. [*Contin2*]

MARADOR

A generous knight who once lodged a wounded Sir Bors. [*VulgLanc*]

MARAGINS

A cousin of Lancelot in *La Tavola Ritonda*. With other knights of his family, he attended a tournament in Ireland sponsored by King Anguish. He was poisoned or otherwise slain during the tournament in a mysterious manner, and his kinsmen blamed Anguish. The king was challenged to judicial combat by Brunoro. Anguish enlisted Tristan to fight as his champion and was exonerated. Maragins' story appears in both the Prose *Tristan* and Malory's *Le Morte Darthur*, but his character is unnamed. [*Tavola*]

MARAGON

Brother of the Knight of the Dragon, who was slain by Perceval. [*Contin4*]

MARAGOND [*Margondés, Margondre*]

One of the many Saxon kings to invade Britain during the beginning of Arthur's reign. He was a cousin of Hengist. He was involved in the siege at Vambieres and in a skirmish with King Nentres of Garlot. He was killed by Arthur's forces at the second battle of Clarence. [*VulgMer*]

MARAHANT [*Marehan(t)*]

The King of Ireland in the time of Joseph of Arimathea. His son was murdered, and circumstances led Marahant to accuse King Orcant, the first king of Orkney. Peter, a relative of Joseph's, defended Orcant before King Lucius of Britain. Marahant was slain in the combat. [*VulgEst*]

MARAN

A castle where a group of knights seeking a missing Lancelot, including Bors and Lionel, agreed to meet on St. John's Day to share their news. [*VulgLanc*]

MARANGLIEZ OF BREVIGARIEZ

A duke who was the brother of Duke Lyppaut of Bearosche. He joined his brother when Lyppaut was attacked by King Meliant of Lis. He was defeated and captured by Perceval, fighting for Meliant. [*Wolfram*]

MARANGOZ

The seneschal of King Eliadus of Sicily. Marangoz fell in love with Eliadus's wife and murdered Eliadus during a hunt. He proposed to the queen, but she fled from him and secured herself in the castle of Monreal, which Marangoz besieged for almost 20 years. Eventually, Eliadus's son, Floriant, arrived in Sicily with King Arthur and an army to lift the siege. Marangoz received assistance from Emperor Filimenis of Constantinople. After several battles, the opponents agreed to decide the war in single combat between Floriant and Marangoz. After losing his nose, an ear, and a hand in the fight, Marangoz surrendered and was executed. [*Floriant*]

MARANZ

The son of the King with a Hundred Knights. Near Penning, Maranz and his sister, Landoine, were saved from a pack of ruffians by Sir Bors. [*VulgLanc*]

MARAT OF THE TOWER

A Knight of the Round Table who embarked with the others on the Grail Quest. [*PostQuest*]

MARBRIN

King of Galilee and one of the allies of Emperor Thereus of Rome. Marbrin joined Thereus in a war against Arthur, and he was slain in battle against Claris and Laris. [*Claris*]

MARC

Grandson of Tristan and son of Ysaie the Sad and Martha. Tutored by the dwarf Tronc (Oberon), he fought to bring order and righteousness to an anarchic post-Arthurian Britain. He married Orimonde, a princess from Persia. [*Ysaie*]

MARCELLUS MUCIUS [*Marcel(lus), Marcelle Mutu, Marchel*]

A Roman warrior who was present at the peace talks between Arthur's and Lucius's men. He was enraged when Gawain killed his friend Gaius Quintillianus, and tried to exact revenge for the deed, but he was also killed by Gawain. Thomas of Castelford says he was Lucius's nephew. The Alliterative *Morte Arthure* calls him FELTEMOUR. [*GeoffHR, Wace, Layamon, VulgMer, Bek*]

MARCH [*Marche*]

A castle ruled by Count Bedoin. During the Grail Quest, Galahad besieged March Castle to stop Bedoin from disinheriting his sister. Bedoin was eventually defeated. [*PostQuest*]

MARCHE

Lancelot's paternal grandmother. Lancelot visited her tomb and buried his grandfather, King Lancelot, alongside her. [*VulgLanc*]

MARCHEPIERE

A horse ridden by Guiron the Courteous. It was given to him by King Faramon of France. The steed was slain during Guiron's combat with Malifer. [*Palamedes*]

MARCOISA [*Marcoise, Mortayse*]

A river running through the Waste Forest, dividing it in half. Gareth slew Sir Gerard and Sir Arnold near the river during his adventures. During the Grail Quest, Lancelot visited the river, was defeated by a black knight, and found a magic barge that gave him news of Galahad's adventures. [*VulgQuest, PostQuest, Malory*]

MARCUS

A Roman senate supervisor who joined the army of Lucius Hiberius to oppose King Arthur. The name is found in Layamon and probably resulted from a corruption of Geoffrey's MARIUS LEPIDUS. [*Layamon*

MARDOC

A lord who appears to mastermind the kidnapping of Guinevere on the Modena Archivolt. Caradoc, who served him, abducted the queen, and both Carados and a churl named Burmalt guarded his castle. It appears that Arthur's warriors, led by Gawain, managed to penetrate the defenses and rescue the queen. Some scholars have suggested that he represents MORDRED. [*Modena*]

MAREC

The son of a monk named Alier. Sir Seguarades stole his lands, but Gawain restored them. [*VulgLanc*]

MARÉS

The King of Roestoc in the early days of Arthur's reign. He fought against the Saxons at Margot Rock. [*VulgMer*]

MARESCOS

A knight encountered by Lancelot on his way to adventures at Rigomer Castle. Marescos was in charge of protecting all of the Irish and Scottish—but not British—knights traveling there. [*Merveil*]

MARGALANT [*Margalaunt, Morgalant, Murgalant*]

An evil Saxon or Saracen king. With a number of other kings, he invaded Britain shortly after Arthur assumed the throne. His forces countered with Gawain and his young companions at the battle of Diana Bridge, and Gawain killed him there. [*VulgMer, Arthour*]

MARGAN[1]

According to Geoffrey of Monmouth, a king of Britain in the third or second century BC. He was the son of King Arthgallo. He succeeded his cousin King Regin, ruled in tranquillity, and was succeeded by his brother Enniaun. [*GeoffHR*]

MARGAN[2]

A Saxon king of Ireland, slain by Arthur's Sir Sagremor at the battle of Esterbury. [*VulgLanc*]

MARGANANT [*Marganan*]

A Saxon warrior slain by King Bors of Gannes at the battle of Carhaix. [*VulgMer, Arthour*]

MARGANOR[1] [*Morganor*]

The seneschal of the King with a Hundred Knights. With his lord, he joined the kings in rebellion against Arthur, fighting Arthur at the battle of Bedegraine. Later, he invaded the lands of the Lord of the Narrow Borderland and captured the lord's defenders, Yvain and Sagremor. Marganor was eventually defeated by Sir Hector. [*LancLac, VulgLanc, VulgMer, Arthour*]

MARGANOR[2]

A knight who joined Arthur's battle against the Saxons at Vambieres. [*Livre*]

MARGARIT [*Margaris*]

One of the several Saxon kings to invade northern Britain while all the northern kings were campaigning against Arthur at Bedegraine. His companions were Brandegorre and Hargadabran. [*VulgMer*]

MARGERIE

The sister of King Agloant of Escoce. Her lover was killed by Lord Girflet during a sparrowhawk tournament in the city of Becleus. Margerie fled from the city and ran into Guinglain (Gawain's son), who listened to her story and promised to help her. Together, they returned to Becleus, where Guinglain defeated Girflet and properly awarded the sparrowhawk to Margerie. Margerie returned home under the protection of a knight Girflet provided. [*Renaut*]

MARGOADRAS

A Saxon king who was a cousin of Hengist. He joined King Aminaduc in an attack on Arthur at Vambieres. [*Livre*]

MARGOIL

One of Arthur's knights. [*Wace*]

MARGON[1]

The wine steward of the Saxon King Pignoras. He fought against Arthur's forces at the second battle of Clarence, and was killed there. [*VulgMer*]

MARGON[2]

The KING WITH A HUNDRED KNIGHTS in the Third Continuation of Chrétien's *Perceval*. Before he was known by this name, he led an siege on the castle of the Sore Pucelle in an attempt to force the lady to marry his son. His son, Cargrilo, was taken prisoner by the Sore Pucelle, and was catapulted to his death when Margon killed the Sore Pucelle's lover. Margon was eventually defeated by Gawain, the Sore Pucelle's champion, and sent to Arthur's court. During the journey, he rescued his sister, the Lady of Malehaut, from Gorgari, an abductor. Arriving at Arthur's court with a hundred knights in tow, he was given his more common designation. Arthur appointed him to the Round Table. His name may reflect MALAGUIN, the King with a Hundred Knights in the Vulgate *Lancelot*. [*Contin3*]

MARGON[3]

A wicked giant whose brothers were Ulian and Durkion. The brothers served Lord Karedoz of Malmontan, and all of them were slain by Arthur's Sir Tandareis. [*PleierT*]

MARGONDES

A knight who fought in Arthur's army against the Saxons at Clarence. He is first called the King of Sorelois, a position later given to GALEHAUT. Later, he is named as the seneschal of that country. [*VulgMer*]

MARGONDRE [*Margondes*]

A knight from the Black Castle. In the forest of Sapinoie, Margondre encountered Lancelot and told him that Guinevere was an adulteress. Lancelot took exception to this insult, defeated Margondre in combat, and made him to go Camelot to apologize to Guinevere for slandering her name. Later, Margondre participated in the Grail Quest. [*VulgLanc, ProsTris*]

MARGORAS

A Saxon king, allied to King Rions, killed by King Ban of Benoic at the battle of Aneblayse. [*VulgMer*]

MARGOT[1] [*Margaras*]

A Saxon vassal of King Rions. He fought against Arthur at the battle of Aneblayse. [*VulgMer, Arthour*]

MARGOT[2] ROCK

A location on the river Severn that was the site of a battle between Saxons, led by King Oriel, and Christians, led by King Clarion of Northumberland and Duke Escant of Cambenic, in the early days of Arthur's reign. The Christians were victorious. [*VulgMer*]

MARGRAVES LACBUZ

A knight in the service of Queen Tydomie of Karmerie, who married Arthur's nephew Meleranz. [*PleierM*]

MARGUIS

An Irish king at Arthur's court. [*Contin1*]

MARHALT

In Malory, the King of Ireland and father of Sir Marhaus. Malory's chronology is a bit confusing here: we are told that Marhaus is the son of an Irish King, but Marhalt does not ascend the throne of Ireland until after the death of Marhaus. Like his son Marhaus, Malory probably took his character from MORHOLT. [*Malory*]

MARHAUS

Malory's name for MORHOLT, the Irish knight slain by Tristan. [*Malory*]

MARIA

Daughter of King Juan of Castille whom Tristan the Younger, Tristan's son, saved from the Moors and then married. [*DueTris*]

MARIADOC [*Cariado, Mariadoco, Maríadokk, Marjodoc, Meriadok*]

King Mark's steward of Cornwall. He began as a friend of Tristan, but became jealous and angry upon learning that Tristan and Mark's wife Isolde—both of whom he held in high regard—were having an affair. He began a campaign to expose the lovers to Mark, allying himself with the evil dwarf Melot, which was somewhat successful. In the traditional legend, he falsely accuses Kahedins, Tristan's brother-in-law, of cowardice, for which Kahedins slays him. In *La Tavola Ritonda*, Mark, discovering he is lonely without his wife and best knight, kills Mariadoc for suggesting their exile. [*Thomas, FolieO, Gottfried, SirTris, TrisSaga, Tavola*]

MARIALE [*Marialle*]

The son of Duke Galenin. He challenged a lady for ownership of Galway Castle, but was defeated in judicial combat by Sir Bors. [*VulgLanc*]

MARIEL BRIDGE [*Maruel*]

A location where Lancelot, disguised in Kay's armor, defeated four attacking knights. [*VulgLanc*]

MARIEN

A French nobleman in the service of King Claudas of the Land Laid Waste. He led a battalion in Claudas's war against Arthur, and he was wounded by Arthur's Sir Patrides. [*VulgLanc*]

MARIGART THE RED

The evil, murderous lord of Raguidel Castle. He imprisoned the lady Angale, and developed a custom by which he raped maidens and condemned them as concubines. Marigart was slain, and his castle liberated, by Sir Hector. [*VulgLanc*]

MARIN[1] [*Herminde*]

Brother of King Armant of the Red City. His brother was slain by treacherous vassals. When Palamedes came to the Red City to avenge Armant's death, Marin traveled ahead and heralded Palamedes's arrival. After Palamedes killed the traitors, he gave the Red City to Marin. Marin became a Knight of the Round Table. He was killed fighting Lancelot and his men when Lancelot rescued Guinevere from the stake. [*ProsTris, Malory*]

MARIN[2] THE JEALOUS

Lord of the castle of Gomoret. Gawain lodged in his manor one night during Marin's absence. Upon his return, Marin accused his wife of adultery and murdered her. His son, Meliot, left him in disgust and became a liegeman of Gawain. Marin began a personal vendetta against Gawain, declaring war on anyone who aided him. He was eventually slain by Nabigan of the Rock. [*Perlesvaus*]

MARINAIA

Merlin's mother in Paolino Pieri's *La Storia di Merlino*. She became pregnant with Merlin after her body was violated one night by an Incubus demon. She faced condemnation before a judged named Matteo, but was saved when Merlin revealed the judge's own flawed paternity. [*Pieri*]

MARINE[1]

In Wirnt von Grafenberg's *Wigalois*, a lady from Alarie. She became a knight—one of the only female knights in Arthurian romance—after her grandfather, Count Adan of Alarie, was captured by King Roaz of Glois at a battle in Damascus. Marine collected a troop of female warriors and entered into the service of Queen Elamie. She joined Gawain's son Wigalois (who had rescued her grandfather) in his campaign against Prince Lion of Namur, and she was tragically killed in battle by Duke Galopear of Greece. Adan avenged her death by slaying Galopear. [*Wirnt*]

MARINE[2]

Daughter of King Urien and sister of Yvain in *Claris et Laris*. King Tallas of Denmark besieged her father in an attempt to marry Marine by force. Sir Laris and Arthur's other knights lifted the siege, and Marine married Laris. [*Claris*]

MARINELL

Son of a sea nymph. He guarded a beach. He was fated to be defeated and wounded by a virgin. Because of this, he rejected the love of all women, and specifically of the maiden Florimell, who loved him. Marinell challenged the warrior maiden Britomart when she came to his beach, and she defeated and badly injured him. Marinell's mother spirited him to her undersea kingdom and healed him. There, Marinell discovered that Florimell had been imprisoned by the sea god Proteus. He fell in love with her, freed her, and was joyously united with her. [*Spenser*]

MARINS

A mute madman at Arthur's court. When Gaheris (Gawain's brother) and Agravain first came to court, Marins suddenly recovered the power of speech, told Arthur to knight Gaheris before Agravain, prophesied greatness and tragedy for Gaheris (he had received this prophecy from Merlin), and then died. Arthur had him buried at the church of St. Stephen's in Camelot. [*PostMer*]

MARIOLE

A beautiful maiden who owned a magical golden circlet. She married King Briant of the Red Island. When her circlet was stolen by her brother-in-law, Bruant, she became impoverished and her husband died. In despair, she threw her infant daughter Tristouse into the ocean. Tristouse, who survived, had a son named Torec, who defeated Arthur's knights. [*Maerlant*]

MARIUS[1]

A first-century king of Britain in Geoffrey's chronicle. He succeeded his father, King Arviragus. During his reign, he fought the Picts in Scotland. He was succeeded by his son, Coill. [*GeoffHR*]

MARIUS[2] LEPIDUS

One of the Roman senators who became a war leader in Lucius Hiberus's campaign against Arthur. He led a force of soldiers at the battle of Soissons and was killed there. [*GeoffHR*]

MARK [*Marc, March, Marco, Marcus, Markæs, Marke(s), Markis, Marko(s), Mars, Mórodd*]

King of Cornwall in the Tristan legends. He was Tristan's uncle and Isolde's husband, thus playing the inconvenient third part of the Tristan-Isolde-Mark love triangle. Prior to his marriage to Isolde, he took his young nephew into his court and was greatly impressed by his prowess, particularly when Tristan defeated Morholt of Ireland, thus freeing Cornwall from a tribute. Mark appointed Tristan his steward or chamberlain, and his heir-apparent. He later assigned Tristan the task of bringing Isolde, his betrothed, from Ireland, and on their return trip, Tristan and Isolde accidentally drank a love potion and began their notorious affair, which destroyed the relationship between uncle and nephew. Over the course of years, Mark sometimes banished, sometimes sentenced the lovers, but usually relented—either through their pleas or through pressure from his peers. In the tragic finale of some of the romances, he slays Tristan.

Mark's character varies greatly from one legend to the next. Far from the evil King Mark portrayed in the romances of Malory and Tennyson, Mark's early appearances generally present him as a sympathetic or even noble king who acts fairly towards his wife and nephew, against whom he has a legitimate grievance. Unaware of the love potion, he gives Tristan and Isolde every benefit of the doubt until circumstances compel him to act against them. In some versions, when he later hears of the source of their love, he laments and professes that he would have relinquished his wife had he known.

His character begins to degrade in the Prose *Tristan*, but even here he is a complex figure who, although motivated by lust and pride and insecurity, finds himself tortured over his treatment of Tristan and Isolde. After sentencing them on one occasion, he runs sobbing to his chambers, calling himself "the most worthless king to ever have worn a crown." Meanwhile, the Post-Vulgate introduces an episode in which Mark destroys Arthur's kingdom, securing his fate in later literature as a certain villain. Malory and Tennyson both present him as an utter tyrant.

In Welsh, where he appears as *March*, he is the son of Meirchyawn, a cousin of Arthur, and leader of the Norwegian warriors commanded by Arthur. *March* means "horse," and Béroul tells us that he had horse's ears. The origin of his name is probably the Roman "Marcus." There is evidence for his actual existence. A historical king named Kynvawr ruled Cornwall in the early sixth century. The name, which in Latin form is "Cunomorus," appears on a sixth-century tombstone in Cornwall marking the grave of "Drustanus...son of Cunomorus." Drustanus is often accepted as the origin of Tristan. Mark is connected with Cunomorous in the Life of Saint Paul Aurelian, whose author says that Mark's full Latin name was Marcus Cunomorous. If these facts are true, then the historical Mark was Tristan's father, not his uncle. Interestingly, a Welsh Triad does list "March" as the father of "Drystan," but seems to be the only source to do so.

In the Prose *Tristan*, Mark's father's name is Felix, and he is given a brother named Pernehan, whom he murders. Malory similarly tells us that he slew his brother Bodwyne and, later, Bodwyne's son Alexander. While in the early romances and the Prose *Tristan*, Tristan is the son of Mark's sister (Blancheflour or Elyabel), Italian romance contends that Meliadus, Tristan's father, was Mark's brother. According to the Post-Vulgate, Mark raped his niece and had a son named Meraugis, who became a Knight of the Round Table.

The Prose *Tristan* and Malory relay that Mark's rift with Tristan began not over Isolde, but over the wife of Sir Seguarades, some time before Isolde and Mark were married. Mark is a cowardly knight who always avoids combat or attacks by surprise. His tolerance of Tristan—when he does tolerate him—is spurred not out of magnanimity, but out of fear of Tristan and his friends at Arthur's court, and out of fear that his own knights—most of whom are friends with Tristan—will revolt. Nonetheless, the reports by certain traitorous knights (most notably his nephew Andred) lead him to imprison Tristan three times, to banish him twice, and to try to execute him once. In several of these instances, Arthur and his knights intervene, forcing Mark to relent. Mark develops a hatred for Arthur and at various times plots to murder Yvain, Kay, and Gaheris.

There are numerous accounts of Mark's end. The earliest legends do not describe his death. Tristan and Isolde perish in Brittany, and Mark simply disappears from the story.

The Post-Vulgate *Queste del Saint Graal* and *Mort Artu* tell us that he invaded Logres and besieged Camelot during the Grail Quest. Arthur's knights defeated him, but he returned after Arthur's death, laid waste to Arthur's kingdom, destroyed Camelot, and desecrated the tombs of Lancelot and Galehaut. He tracked down Arthur's remaining knights at a hermitage, murdered the Archbishop of Canterbury, and was himself killed by Arthur's Sir Paulas.

One version of the Prose *Tristan* has Mark slay Tristan with a poisoned lance provided by Morgan le Fay, while another version recounts a more traditional tale of Tristan's death at the hands of a lord named Bedalis. After Tristan's death, Mark is exiled to the Redoubted Island, but he eventually escapes and reclaims his throne. In still another manuscript, Mark is taken prisoner by the sons of Dinas (his former seneschal) is tied to a tree, and is eaten by a bear.

According to the Italian *La Tavola Ritonda*, Arthur, King Amoroldo of Ireland, and King Governal of Lyonesse invaded Cornwall after Tristan's death, and besieged Mark in the castle of Tintagel. Mark was eventually captured and was locked in a tower overlooking Tristan's grave. His captors fed him fattening food and drink until Mark died of gluttony after 32 months.

Malory tells us that he was killed by Bellangere, his great-nephew, who was avenging the deaths of Bodwyne and Alexander the Orphan. In the Italian *La vendetta che fe messer Lanzelloto de la morte di miser Tristano*, he is slain by Lancelot in revenge for Tristan's death. Finally, in the Icelandic *Saga af Tristram ok Ísodd*, he gives England (his kingdom) to Kalegras, Tristan's son, and lives out his days in a hermitage in Jerusalem. Jean D'Outremeuse gives Mark a son named Galopes who avenges Mark's death at the hands of Arthur by inciting the Roman Emperor to invade Britain. [*Triads, Thomas, Beroul, Eilhart, TrisSaga, Dream, ProsTris, PostQuest, PostMort, TristanoR, Tavola, SagaTI, Vendetta, Malory, TennIK*]

MARLAGAN

A knight who imprisoned Calogrenant. Sir Sagremor battled him for Calogrenant's release, and in the midst of the battle, another knight kidnapped Marlagan's lady. Marlagan promised to free Calogrenant if Sagremor would rescue the lady, and Sagremor did so. [*VulgLanc*]

MARLAN [*Merlan*]

The King of the Scottish Borderlands, called "the Simple" or "the Accursed" because of his evil ways. He hanged his own father, imprisoned maidens, and impoverished his own people. He was eventually slain in joust by Lancelot, much to the joy of his subjects. [*VulgLanc*]

MARLIAUS

One of Arthur's knights in the English *Arthour and Merlin*. He distinguished himself at a London tournament. He supplants MEDIAN from the Vulgate *Merlin*. [*Arthour*]

MARLYN

Son of Morgan le Fay and Ogier the Dane. [*Ogier*]

MARMADUS

Son of the Red Knight and brother of Leander, Evander, and Meliadas. Perceval killed Maramdus's father, but Marmadus and his brothers eventually forgave Perceval. [*Contin4*]

MARMANS OF COP

An Arthurian knight who joined Gawain's quest to conquer Rigomer Castle in Ireland. [*Merveil*]

MARMIADOISE [*Marandois(e), Marundois*]

A magnificent sword, forged by the Roman god Vulcan, and originally owned by Hercules. The sword was passed from heir to heir until it came to King Rions, Arthur's enemy. Arthur captured the sword after defeating Rions at the battle of Aneblayse. Since it was better than Excalibur, Arthur loaned the latter to Gawain. [*VulgMer, Arthour*]

MARONAN

A non-Arthurian Celtic hero who becomes one of Arthur's warriors in Richard Hole's *Arthur*. [*Hole*]

MARONEL [*Maronex*]

The King of Gaul some time before Arthur's reign. His daughter married Jonah, an ancestor of Lancelot, and since Maronel had no male heir, Jonas inherited the kingdom, thus establishing Lancelot's roots in France. [*VulgQuest, VulgEst, Malory*]

MARONNE

In the Third Continuation of Chrétien's *Perceval*, the King of Maronne marries the Fisher King's daughter. [*Contin3*]

MAROT

Maidservant of the homicidal Maiden of the Narrow Wood. The Maiden sought to kill Gawain, whom she had never seen. When Gawain visited the Maiden's castle, Marot helped him to keep his identity a secret so that he could escape unharmed. [*Vengeance*]

MARRAMILES

An Arthurian knight. [*KingA&C*]

MARRIEN

A devil-spawned centaur with the head of a dog. It served the evil King Roaz of Glois, and it attacked Sir Wigalois (Gawain's son) when he came to Glois to kill Roaz. Marrien carried a kettle full of magical fire, which could not be quenched, and which he hurled at Wigalois. Wigalois' surcoat and horse were burned away, but he found that the fire could not burn through his magical armor. He advanced, gravely wounded Marrien, and used Marrien's blood to put out the fire. Marrien, meanwhile, fled into a swamp full of poisonous fog and died. [*Wirnt*]

MARRION

A sister of Morgan le Fay. [*Bataille*]

MARROCH

A heathen king who attacked a queen named Ysope. He was defeated by Arthur and Sir Wigamur. [*Wigamur*]

MARROK [*Marrocke, Merrak, Mewreke*]

A Knight of the Round Table who participated in the Roman War and also fought in the war against Mordred's insurrection. Malory tells us that his wife betrayed him, turning him into a werewolf for seven years. Mordred killed him in battle. [*Allit, SyreGaw, Carle, Malory*]

MARS

One of the ancient gods worshipped by the people of Sarras, before Joseph of Arimathea converted them to Christianity. A devil inhabited a statue of Mars in King Evalach's palace, but it was exorcised by Joseph's son, Josephus. In early mythology, Mars was the Roman god of War. [*VulgEst*]

MARSALE

A forest near the Humber river where an army of five kings planned to ambush Arthur. The ruse worked, but Arthur's forces got the upper hand and defeated the five kings at the battle of the Humber. [*PostMer*]

MARSAN

A region in France owned by Lancelot. Lancelot made Sir Selyses the earl of Marsan in return for Selyses' support in the battles against King Arthur. [*Malory*]

MARSION [*Marrion*]

In the *La Bataille de Loquifer*, a sister of Morgan le Fay. She helped her sister bring the hero Renoart to the Isle of Avalon. [*Bataille*]

MARSIQUE

A beautiful fairy, over whom Gawain fought Mabon the Enchanter. Marsique equipped Gawain with Excalibur's scabbard, ensuring Gawain's victory. [*PostMer*]

MARSILLE [*Marsyl*]

The good king of the island of Ponmecainne, who received his island as a gift from Sir Galehaut. He fought against Arthur's warriors at the Sorelois tournament. [*ProsTris, Malory*]

MARTEL OF THE LARGE SHIELD

A Knight of the Round Table who participated in the Grail Quest. [*PostQuest*]

MARTEROL

A castle in Britain, visited by Perceval during the Grail Quest. It lay close to the Rock of Maidens. [*PostQuest*]

MARTHA[1]

The daughter of King Frion of Dessemoume. She was kidnapped by a pack of thieves but was rescued by Lancelot. Frion wanted to marry her to Lancelot, but he

refused and departed. Martha later bore Lancelot's son. [*Merveil*]

MARTHA[2]

Daughter of King Irion. She married Ysaie, son of Tristan, and had a son named Marc. [*Ysaie*]

MARTIN

A blind youth whose sight was restored by Orguelleus the Fairy. [*Atre*]

MARUC THE RED [*Malruc*]

A knight defeated by Arthur's Sir Dodinel in defense of a maiden. He was later killed by the evil Sir Griffon. [*VulgLanc*]

MARVELOUS BALL

A hill in Britain. It had a brass ball on top that appeared—depending on the distance from which it was viewed—as a horse, a mule, a hound, a fox, or just a ball. Lancelot used the Marvelous Ball as the launching point for his expedition to recapture his homeland of Genewis. [*UlrichZ*]

MARVELOUS STONE

The enchanted stone on which Yvain poured water, summoning the lord of the fountain and beginning the events related in the various versions of *Owain* or *Yvain*. Wolfram von Eschenbach gives this name to the stone but does not tell the story. [*Wolfram*]

MASADE

Arthur's Earl of Vera in the Norse *Erex Saga*. He was present at the wedding of Erec and Enide. [*Erex*]

MATABAN THE WHITE [*Matham*]

A famous knight of Uther Pendragon's day. [*Palamedes*]

MATAGRAN [*Mategrant*]

Brother of lord Argon of the Rock. The brothers, who lived in Britain, were converted to Christianity by Joseph of Arimathea. [*VulgLanc, VulgEst*]

MATAILLIÉS ("Misshapen")

A Saxon king in the service of King Rions. He was slain at the battle of Aneblayse by King Bors of Gannes. [*VulgMer, Arthour*]

MATAIN THE CRUEL [*Maten*]

The lord of the White Castle, where Knights of the Round Table were reviled. Lancelot, Bors, Gaheris, and Bagdemagus visited the castle, and found its knights mistreating Mordred. After a long battle against scores of knights, Lancelot killed Matain. [*VulgLanc*]

MATALIZ [*Mat(h)aaliz*]

A knight who was the brother of Sir Ladomas and was the enemy of Synados of Windsor. Mataliz attacked Synados's company of three knights with seventeen of his own, but Arthur's Sir Hector—summoned by Synados's wife—arrived and killed Mataliz. Hector later came upon Mataliz's funeral and was attacked by several knights, but Ladomas called off the attackers and let Hector go. [*LancLac, VulgLanc*]

MATALY [*Matalie*]

An early Knight of the Round Table, injured in a tournament against the Queen's Knights. [*VulgMer*]

MATHAEL

Brother of Brangain (Isolde's maidservant) and Perynin. Brangain presented her two brothers to Tristan as servants. [*ProsTris*]

MATHAMAS¹

The lord of a tower near the Fairies' Fountain. He hated Arthur. While adventuring in the forest with Guinevere, Dodinel and Sagremor embarked on a quest to procure some rations from Mathamas. Dodinel was diverted along the way, but Sagremor entered Mathamas's hall and boldly demanded food. Mathamas responded by ordering his knights to attack Sagremor, and after a exhausting battle, Sagremor was imprisoned. Mathamas's daughter kept Sagremor from starving until Gawain showed up, defeated Mathamas, and forced him to release Sagremor. [*VulgLanc*]

MATHAMAS² OF RECET

A knight who joined Arthur's forces against the Saxons at Vambieres. [*Livre*]

MATHAN¹

A Saxon king who, under Hargadabran, fought Arthur at Clarence. Arthur's Sir Dodinel killed him. [*Livre*]

MATHAN² THE BROWN [*Matto*]

A giant, noble Cornish knight. Gaheris, Gawain's brother, defeated him over a lady, driving Mathan insane. He roamed wild through the forest of Morrois. When Tristan similarly went insane, he was at first mistaken for Mathan. [*ProsTris, Malory*]

MATHANS [*Mathamas*]

One of the many Saxon kings to invade northern Britain at the beginning of Arthur's reign. He fought in the first battle at Clarence. [*VulgMer*]

MATHEM [*Matan*]

Duke of Soane in Germany. His ancestral land was stolen by Duke Frollo, and Mathem was forced to flee to Montpellier. His daughter, Avenable, journeyed to Julius Caesar's Roman court to seek redress. On Merlin's advice, Caesar married Avenable and restored Mathem to his duchy. [*VulgMer, ProsMer2*]

MATIADAS

A knight whose castle, the Lost Rock, was situated in the forest of Broceliande. Matiadas required any knight seeking lodging to fight five of his knights. Claris and Laris defeated Matiadas's five warriors and were allowed to spend the night at the Lost Rock. [*Claris*]

MATILDA

Attendant to Emmeline, Arthur's future wife in Dryden's *King Arthur*. [*Dryden*]

MATIS

A Roman knight in the service of Emperor Lucius, assigned to liberate a prisoner train during the war against Arthur. The attack failed. [*VulgMer*]

MATLEIDE

During a speech in Heinrich von dem Türlin's *Diu Crône*, Gawain tells how he "wrestled with the fierce Matleide at Igangsol." [*Heinrich*]

MATRONA

A Celtic goddess who may be the origin of MORGAN LE FAY through MODRON. She is the mother of the god Maponos, who appears in Welsh legend as Mabon.

MATTEO

In Paolino Pieri's *La Storia di Merlino*, the magistrate who judged Merlin's mother, Marinaia, after she gave birth to the son of a devil. He nearly sentenced her to execution, but relented when Merlin revealed that the judge's own paternity was in question. [*Pieri*]

MATUFER

An island off the coast of Cornwall. The famous Red Stone, at which King Mark tested Isolde's chastity, was located on the island. [*Tavola*]

MATUR

The proud King of the land of Cluse in Der Stricker's *Daniel von dem blühenden Tal*. With two invincible giants as his henchmen, he demanded Arthur's subjugation. Arthur pretended to acquiesce, but only long enough to get his army inside Cluse. Arthur killed Matur in single combat and, with Daniel's considerable help, proceeded to conquer Cluse. Matur's widow, Danise, married Daniel. G. Rosenhagen suggests that his name was meant to mirror *Artûs* (Middle High German "Arthur"), while S. Singer proposes a derivation from the Latin *Maturus*. [*Stricker*]

MATUVANA

A plain crossed by Tristan and Dinadan. It held the castle Fregulla Vittorioisa, where Tristan slew a knight. [*Tavola*]

MAUDINS LI GARDINGNIERS

A knight with whom Lancelot lodged one his way to Rigomer Castle. Though Maudins originally received Lancelot genially, he became enraged when he discovered that Lancelot had killed three of his friends. They fought, but Maudins yielded when he learned Lancelot's name. [*Merveil*]

MAUDIT THE WISE [*Maldis, Malduz, Maldwiz*]

One of Arthur's best Knights of the Round Table, first mentioned by Chrétien de Troyes. A magical mantle brought to Arthur's court revealed that his wife talked too much. [*ChretienE, UlrichZ*]

MAUGAN

A priest who Arthur appointed as Archbishop of Silchester. [*GeoffHR*]

MAUGANTIUS [*Malgantius, Ma(y)gan*]

One of King Vortigern's advisors. He was in attendance when Merlin and his mother were brought before Vortigern, who had been seeking a child without a father so he could sprinkle his blood on the base of Snowdon. Merlin's mother explained that she had been impregnated by a demon. Maugantius confirmed the validity of her story, saying that such demons were known as *incubus*. [*GeoffHR, Wace, Layamon*]

MAUNIS

A Knight of the Round Table. [*HartmannE*]

MAUPAS

A heathen duke slain by Arthur's Sir Craddok at the battle of Carhaix. [*Arthour*]

MAURICE [*Mauricius, Mawrene, Morys*]

The Baron of Cahors under King Arthur who fought for Arthur in the war against Rome. Maurice was part of the escort taking Roman prisoners to Paris. The prisoner train was attacked by the Romans, and Maurice was killed. Malory also places Maurice among Arthur's forces at the battle of Bedegraine. [*GeoffHR, Allit, Malory*]

MAURICIUS SILVANUS

A Roman senator who became a war leader in Lucius Hiberius's campaign against Arthur. He led a force of soldiers at the battle of Soissons. [*GeoffHR*]

MAURIN[1] [*Marran, Mauron*]

A kinsman of Arthur who was serving as a soldier of Baldulph, the Saxon. Apparently deciding that blood was thicker than water, Mauron betrayed his commander and warned Arthur of Baldulph's plan to ambush him. Arthur was able to send Cador to slaughter Baldulph's forces. Arthur later appointed Maurin the Earl of Worcester or Winchester. [*GeoffHR, Wace, Layamon*]

MAURIN[2] OF THE HANDSOME THIGHS

Queen Guinevere's chief Marshal in Wolfram's *Parzival*. The office had been held by his father Isajes before him. [*Wolfram*]

MAURIN[3] OF THE NIMBLE SHANKS

A knight taken prisoner by Lancelot during the tournament at Dyoflê in Ulrich's *Lanzelet*. Ulrich attests to his uncommon speed. Lancelot did not particularly want to take prisoners, but decided to take Maurin to let everyone know that he could have taken more if he had wished. [*UlrichZ*]

MAWRELLE OF MAWNCES [*Maurel*]

A knight in Arthur's service who was killed during Arthur's war against Rome. [*Allit, Malory*]

MAXIMIAN

The name that Geoffrey of Monmouth erroneously gives to MAXIMUS. [*GeoffHR*]

MAXIMUS [*Macsen, Maxen, Maximian, Maximien*]

A Spanish-born Roman general who, in the late fourth century, served the Roman empire as *Dux Britanniarum*, or commander of the Roman army in Britain. He may have led a campaign against the Picts around 370. Maximus's soldiers apparently elevated him as their emperor, and in 383, they convinced him that he had a right to the Roman Empire itself. Maximus crossed the channel into Gaul to begin an invasion. He conquered parts of Europe, and his allies murdered Gratian, the western Roman emperor. Though he had effectively conquered Rome, he never occupied the capital. In 388, while he was camped in Aquileia, he was attacked, captured, and executed by Count Theodosius.

The chronicles style Maximus as a king of Britain. Gildas and Nennius describe his rule as tyrannical, but Geoffrey of Monmouth (who erroneously calls him "Maximian") gives him certain credit for holding back the barbarian invasions. Welsh tradition, too, heroifies Maximus in the character of MACSEN. The chroniclers seem to agree, however, that Maximus's *hubris* led—at least partially—to the downfall of Britain. By siphoning all of Britain's warriors to wars in Gaul, and by then establishing them there, Maximus effectively depopulated the island of its defense, leaving it open to invasions by Picts and continental barbarians.

In the Welsh story called *The Dream of Macsen*, Maximus, who is already the Emperor of Rome, dreams of a glorious island far to the west (Britain) and of a beautiful woman to be found there. Upon awakening, he sets out on a search for the land of his dreams, eventually coming to Segontium in Wales and meeting the woman, Elen of the Hosts. Maximus marries Elen and, as he has conquered Britain in the process of finding her, he bestows the land upon her father, Eudaf. Macsen remains in Britain for seven years, after which the Roman citizens elect a new emperor. Upon hearing of this, Macsen raises an army of Britons—led by Elen's brothers, Cynan and Afaon—travels back to Rome, and, unlike the Maximus of the chronicles, re-captures the empire.

Maximus is credited with various sons, including Victor, St. Peblic, Owain, and Constantine. His daughter, Sevira, married King Vortigern. [*Gildas*, *Nennius*, *GeoffHR*, *Wace*, *Layamon*, *Triads*]

MAZADAN [*Mazedan*]

An ancestor of both Perceval and Arthur—through his sons Lazaliez and Brickus, respectively. He and his wife, Terdelaschoye, were both fairies. [*Wolfram*]

MAZOE

One of the eight sisters of Morgan le Fay. She lived on the island of Avalon. [*GeoffVM*]

MEAUX [*Meau(l)s*]

A city in France, just east of Paris. The Vulgate *Estoire del Saint Graal* calls it the birthplace of King Mordrains. At the time of Mordrains' birth, it was ruled by Count Sevain, who was ordered to send a certain number of male youths to Rome. Mordrains (then called Evalach) was one of these children. According to the Vulgate *Mort Artu*, Arthur once stayed in the city during his war with Lancelot. [*VulgMort*, *VulgEst*]

MEDANZ

The son of Meleranz (Arthur's nephew) and Queen Tydomie of Karmerie. He had a brother named Lazaliez and a sister named Olimpia. [*PleierM*]

MEDARIE

A land ruled by King Schaffilan, who was killed by Gawain's son Wigalois. The three princes of Medarie were Darel, Gamer, and Ariun. [*Wirnt*]

MEDEAS

The lecherous sovereigness of Crudele castle, where Tristan was imprisoned and his companion, Tessina, was beheaded. Medeas's sisters were named Lavina, Agnena, Bresenda, and Pulizena. All were descendants of a pagan queen named Calistra. The name comes from the wife of Jason in classical mythology. [*Tavola*]

MEDELANT [*Medalan, Med(e)lan(e)*]

One of the many Saxon kings to invade northern Britain in the early days of Arthur's reign. He was killed by Gawain in a skirmish near the city of Vambieres. [*VulgMer*, *Arthour*]

MEDIA [*Mede(a)*]

An ancient kingdom in the part of southwest Asia that is now northwest Iran. In the chronicles, the king of Media—

named Boccus or Politetes—joins the Roman emperor Lucius in the war against Arthur. [*GeoffHR*, *VulgMer*]

MEDIAN THE CURLY-HAIRED [*Medians*]

One of Arthur's knights in the Vulgate *Merlin*, present at a tournament between Arthur's knights and the knights of Kings Ban and Bors. *Arthour and Merlin* replaces his character with MARLIAUS. [*VulgMer*]

MEDILONTAS

A desert in Lyonesse. Meliadus, Tristan's father, got lost while hunting there. He came across the Fountain of the Dragon, where he met a sorceress who imprisoned him for a time. [*Tavola*]

MEDINA

A lady who lived with her two sisters, Elissa and Perissa. Her temperance stood in contrast to the asceticism of Elissa and the hedonism of Perissa. [*Spenser*]

MEDRAUT

The Welsh version of MORDRED.

MEDYR ("Aim")

Son of Medryeddyd. One of Arthur's warriors, Medyr had outstanding aim. When in Cornwall, he could reportedly hit a wren in Ireland. [*Culhwch*]

MEDYREDYDD ("Aimer")

Father of Arthur's warrior Medyr. [*Culhwch*]

MEILYG

Son of Caw, one of twenty brothers, and one of Arthur's warriors. [*Culhwch*]

MEIONES OF ATROPFAGENTE

An infidel duke who served Feirefiz, Perceval's half-brother. [*Wolfram*]

MEIRCHYAWN [*Meirchion*]

Father of King Mark in Welsh legend. He may have been a brother of Eigyr (Igraine) or Uther. [*Dream*, *TrisFrag*]

MELALDON [*Aladanc, Meleaudon*]

A knight from Blois who fought for Arthur in the battles against King Rions. [*VulgMer*, *Arthour*]

MELAN

In the Norse *Erex Saga*, Enide's uncle, called IMAIN by Hartmann von Aue. [*Erex*]

MELDE

A knight who fought in the Sorgarda tournament. Melde's brother, Effroi, was also present. [*Heinrich*]

MELDRED

A king of Dunmeller in Scotland. He enjoyed hearing from the "mad prophet" Lailoken (identified usually with Merlin), but was somewhat unamused when Lailoken divined that Meldred's wife was an adulteress.

MELEAGANT [*Meleag(r)aunce, Meliakanz, Meljacanz, Meljaganz, Meljahkanz, Miljanz, Milienc*]

Guinevere's abductor in Chrétien de Troyes's *Lancelot* and the Vulgate *Lancelot*. He probably originates with MELWAS, the king who kidnaps Guinevere in Welsh legend.

Meleagant was the son of King Bagdemagus of Gorre. Gorre had a custom by which any knight or lady that entered became a prisoner. Since Gorre could only be entered by crossing two dangerous bridges—one a sword, and the other underwater—it was not difficult to enforce this custom. Eventually, Meleagant captured Queen Guinevere, sending several of Arthur's knights after him. Some of the would-be rescuers were defeated, Kay was captured, Gawain got lost, and Lancelot became the one who eventually succeeded in the quest and rescued the queen.

Meleagant's father disapproved of his son's actions, and prevented him from harming the Guinevere during the abduction. When Lancelot survived the perilous journey to Bagdemagus's castle, Bagdemagus urged Meleagant to turn over the queen. Meleagant, however, opted to fight and was defeated by Lancelot. He yielded on the condition that they meet again to battle in one year. Meanwhile, however, Lancelot slept with Guinevere in Bagdemagus's castle. He had been injured, and left blood on Guinevere's sheets. Meleagant assumed the blood was from the wounded Kay, and accused Guinevere of treason. Lancelot agreed to champion her at their scheduled fight, but Meleagant had Lancelot captured and imprisoned in a special tower called the Tower of the Fens. At the appointed time, Meleagant went to Arthur's court to fight the battle, expecting to either win by default or to be assigned a lesser knight to fight. Lancelot, however, had been freed from his prison by Meleagant's sister, and arrived just in time. He killed Meleagant in the subsequent duel.

Malory adapted this story for a chapter in *Le Morte D'Arthur*, with a number of differences: first, Meleagant's motivation for capturing the Queen, according to Malory, was not pride, but love. He thought her the most beautiful woman in the world, and nearly fought Lamorat to the death to prove his claim. The second difference is Meleagant's general incompetence as a knight: it had occurred to him to kidnap Guinevere, but he delayed acting on this for many years because he was greatly afraid of Lancelot, and he realized that any attempt to take the queen would be swiftly avenged by her champion. At tournaments, he was generally defeated. Third, Meleagant does not reside in his own land, but is a Knight of the Round Table, and simply holds a castle near Camelot, in Lambeth.

In Wolfram's *Parzival*, Meleagant also abducts a lady named Imane of Beafontane, who is rescued by Karnahkarnanz of Ultertec. Later, he fights in a war declared by King Meliant of Lis on Duke Lyppaut of Bearosche. In Wolfram's mind, Meleagant must have survived the duel with Lancelot because his chronology places the war at Bearosche after Lancelot's rescue of Guinevere. [*ChretienL, VulgLanc, PostQuest, Malory*]

MELEAGAR THE RED

Uncle of the Lady Helaés of Limos and the knight Clapor. He advised Lord Oriol, who conquered Helaés's lands and fell in love with her, to defeat Gawain in order to win Helaés's love. Oriol was unable to prevail against Gawain, and Meleagar's plan failed. [*Livre*]

MELEHAN [*Melian*]

Mordred's eldest son in the Vulgate *Mort Artu*. He vied for control of Britain after Arthur's and Mordred's deaths. Lancelot and his kin met Melehan in battle at Winchester. Melehan was slain by Bors, but not before he killed Lionel. A son of Mordred named MELOU appears in Layamon's *Brut*. [*VulgMort, PostMort*]

MELERANZ[1]

Father of Arthur's Sir Garel. He married Queen Lammire and became king of Styria. [*PleierG*]

MELERANZ[2]

Arthur's nephew and hero of Der Pleier's *Meleranz*. He was the son of Olimpia, Arthur's sister, and King Linefles of France. As an adolescent, he ran away to Arthur's court. On the way, he met a maiden named Tydomie, Queen of Kamerie, bathing under a tree, and the two fell in love. He was knighted by Arthur and had several adventures, culminating in his return to Karmerie to save Tydomie, who was being forced by her uncle to marry King Libers of Lorgan. Meleranz and Tydomie married and ruled Terrandes, which Meleranz had liberated from the giant Godonas. They had a daughter named Olimpia and two sons named Lazaliez and Medanz. [*PleierM*]

MELES THE TALL

A Knight of the Round Table who participated in the Grail Quest. He was the brother of Sir Dinas. [*PostQuest*]

MELGA

King of the Picts. Three generations before Arthur, he allied with King Guanius of the Huns and King Gillomaur of Ireland to invade Britain. He plagued Kings Maximus and Gratian before he was driven away for good when Constantine, Arthur's grandfather, arrived from Brittany to assume Britain's throne. [*GeoffHR, Wace*]

MELIADAS

Son of the Red Knight and brother of Leander, Evander, and Marmadus. Perceval killed Meliadas's father, but Meliadas and his brothers eventually forgave Perceval. [*Contin4*]

MELIADOC [*Meljadoc*]

A knight in Arthur's Britain, who fought at the tournament at Tenebroc. [*ChretienE*]

MELIADOR

The son of the Duke of Cornwall. He was one of Arthur's knights. He heard that Hermondine, the daughter of the King of Scotland, would marry the knight who was the victor in a series of tournaments. Meliador traveled to Scotland and killed Camel, one of Hermondine's suitors. He was victorious in a tournament at Roxburgh against over fifteen hundred knights, and he was able to marry the princess. He had a sister named Phenonee. [*Froissart*]

MELIADUS¹ [*Maliaduc*]

A Saxon king who joined the Saxon invasion of northern Britain in the early days of Arthur's reign. He participated in the siege of Vambieres and the second battle of Clarence. [*VulgMer, Arthour*]

MELIADUS² [*Meliodas, Melyodas*]

Tristan's father in the Prose *Tristan* and its adaptations. As such, he replaces RIVALIN from earlier legends. The King of Lyonesse, Meliadus was considered one of the best knights in the world in his time. He is a central character in the French *Palamedes*, in which he abducts the beautiful queen of Scotland and has a son with her named Meliadus the Younger. As a result of this abduction, he went to war with Scotland and its allies, including Arthur. He lost and was imprisoned by Arthur at Camelot until Arthur needed his services to help against a Saxon invasion, led by Aliohan, whom Meliadus defeated in single combat. In *La Tavola Ritonda*, Meliadus refuses to submit to Arthur's rule and goes to war with the king, but surrenders when his ally, Lord Galehaut, yields.

Meliadus married Elyabel, Mark's sister (although in Italian romance, Meliadus is Mark's brother, the son of Felix). He was imprisoned in the Rock of the Cornishwoman by an enchantress at the same time that his wife gave birth to Tristan and died. He was rescued by Merlin. He eventually re-married the daughter of King Hoel of Brittany (called Agia in *La Tavola Ritonda*), who tried to murder Tristan but ended up poisoning her own child by Meliadus. Meliadus spared her life at Tristan's request, but forever resented her. Meliadus was murdered by vassals of the count of Norholt, or by his own kinsmen. Tristan fled Lyonesse to serve at King Faramon of Frances's court, but he later returned and avenged Meliadus's death. In Malory's version, Meliadus is still alive some time after Tristan's return from Gaul. [*ProsTris, Palamedes, TristanoR, Tavola, VitaMer, Povest, Malory*]

MELIADUS³

A knight who served as the seneschal of the City Without a Name. [*Raoul*]

MELIADUS⁴ THE BLACK [*Melyadus*]

The lord of the Hedged Manor. Meliadus hated Guinevere's knights. He battled Sir Sagremor on the Dry Island. After badly wounding Sir Dodinel, he was defeated by Lancelot, who forced Meliadus to go to Guinevere and apologize. Arthur took Meliadus into his service, and Meliadus became a good friend to Lancelot. He participated in the Grail Quest. When the affair between Lancelot and Guinevere was exposed, Meliadus helped Lancelot rescue Guinevere from the stake; in the process, however, Meliadus was slain by Gaheris. [*VulgLanc, VulgMort, PostMort, ProsTris*]

MELIADUS⁵ THE PALE [*Meliadus, Meliard*]

A knight in the service of King Ban of Benoic. He fought for Arthur against the rebellious kings at Bedegraine. [*VulgMer, Arthour*]

MELIADUS⁶ THE WHITE

A Knight of the Round Table who participated in the Grail Quest. [*ProsTris*]

MELIADUS⁷ THE YOUNGER

Tristan's half-brother in the *Prophecies de Merlin*. Born to King Meliadus of Lyonesse and the queen of Scotland, whom Meliadus had abducted, he was raised by the Lady of the Lake with Lancelot, Bors, and Lionel. When he grew up, he became the Lady of the Lake's lover. He convinced the Lady to bring him to Merlin's tomb, where he wrote down the prophecies spoken by Merlin's ghost. [*Prophecies, VitaMer*]

MELIAN¹

A Knight of the Round Table who participated in the Grail Quest. [*PostQuest*]

MELIAN² THE BLOND

Nephew of King Meliadus of Lyonesse. During the war between Arthur and Scotland, Melian and a Scottish knight named Tarsan killed each other. [*Palamedes*]

MELIAN³ THE GAY

A knight from the Gay Castle; brother of Drian the Gay and son of Trahan the Gay. One of Lancelot's first quests was to avenge wounds given to Melian by the son of the Lady of Malehaut or by Caradoc of the Dolorous Tower. (There is some manuscript confusion as to whether Lancelot avenges Melian or his father TRAHAN.) Later, Melian pointed Lancelot to the adventures at the Dolorous Tower and, after Lancelot conquered it, Melian married a lady who had been imprisoned there. [*VulgLanc, Livre*]

MELIANT[1]

A nephew of King Faramon of France in the Prose *Tristan*. He was accused of theft at the same time that Faramon's daughter, Belide, falsely accused Tristan of rape. Faramon offered Belide a choice of saving either Meliant or Tristan; when she chose Tristan, he knew she was lying about the crime. The same character is named BRANO in *La Tavola Ritonda*. [*ProsTris*]

MELIANT[2] [*Melianus*]

An ancestor of Gawain, descended from Peter. Meliant inherited the kingdom of Orkney from is father, Herlan, and passed it to his son, Argistes. [*VulgEst*]

MELIANT[3]

Arthur's lord of Cardueil who led a battalion in the second war against Claudas. [*VulgLanc*]

MELIANT[4] OF DIANARCA [*Meleagant, Meliagante, Melyan(t), Melyas*]

A young knight from Dianarca, Lyle, or Denmark. He was knighted by Galahad at the beginning of the Grail Quest. He was soon badly wounded because he did not make a full confession before embarking on the Quest, because he proudly took a dangerous road, and because he covetously stole a crown. He recovered, and was present at Corbenic when Galahad completed the Quest. Arthur appointed him to the Round Table, but Meliant pledged his support to Lancelot when the latter's affair with Guinevere was exposed. He helped rescue the queen from the stake, and fought against Arthur at the battles of Joyous Guard and Benoic. In return for his support, Lancelot made him the earl of Tursan. [*VulgQuest, PostQuest, ProsTris, Malory*]

MELIANT[5] OF LIS [*Melian(s), Mel(l)ianz, Meljanz of Liz, Miljanz*]

The King of Lis and one of Arthur's Knights of the Round Table, according to Chrétien de Troyes and Wolfram von Eschenbach. He was raised by a lord named Tiebaut or Lyppaut, and he fell in love with his foster-father's daughter, Obie. When Obie rejected his love, Meliant became enraged and declared war on Lyppaut, summoning many knights—including his uncle Bagdemagus and his cousin Meleagant—to his aid. Gawain joined Lyppaut's defense. Gawain captured Meliant in the battle and made him the prisoner of Obie's sister Obilot. Obilot, in turn, gave him to her sister. Meliant and Obie reconciled, and the war was ended. Later, as an ally of Arthur, Meliant was captured in a battle at the castle of Logres.

In *Perlesvaus*, we learn that Meliant's father, the lord of the Waste Manor, was killed by Lancelot. Here, Meliant is presented as an antagonist to Arthur who harbors hate for all of Arthur's court. He joined forces with Brien of the Isles and Kay, who were at war with Arthur. Meliant was mortally wounded by Lancelot at the battle of Pennevoiseuse.

The Prose *Lancelot* credits him with being one of only five men to ever cross the perilous North Wales Bridge into Sorelois. In the *Livre d'Artus*, he marries Florée, daughter of King Alain of Escavalon.

Meliant of Lis could easily be the origin of any of the other MELIANTs. A character similar to Wolfram's Meliant appears in Heinrich von dem Türlin as FIERS OF ARRAMIS. [*ChretienE, ChretienP, Perlesvaus, Wolfram, LancLac, VulgLanc*]

MELIANT[6] OF MELIADEL

A knight whose sister, Melie, was assisted by Arthur's Sir Meriadeuc. [*Meriadeuc*]

MELIANUS

A knight whose lands were protected from Nabor by the Good Knight Without Fear. [*Palamedes*]

MELIARMAN

One of Perceval's eleven paternal uncles in *Perlesvaus*; the tenth son of Gais le Gros and the brother of Alain. He lived in Scotland and died in combat. [*Perlesvaus*]

MELIDAN THE MERRY [*Meldons*]

A peer of Sir Bors who distinguished himself at a tournament in Estrangorre. He swore fealty to the daughter of King Brandegorre of Estrangorre. [*VulgLanc*]

MELIDOR [*Melydor, Mildor(e), Mylder*]

The daughter of Earl Sere, a nobleman who went to war with Arthur's Sir Degrevant. She fell in love with Degrevant, and the two enjoyed a year-long affair before the earl discovered it. Melidor and her mother pressured the earl to make peace with Degrevant, and he finally acquiesced. Melidor and Degrevant married. [*SirDeg*]

MELIE

A lady whose sweetheart, Menelais, was slain by the evil Brian de la Gastine. Before he died, he asked Melie to bear his body to the perilous Waste Chapel—a feat that Melie was unable to accomplish alone. Meriadeuc found her in the forest and assisted her in interring her lover. Meriadeuc later discovered that she was his cousin. [*Meriadeuc*]

MELIGOR

A knight in the service of Lord Golagros, Arthur's opponent in the Middle Scots tale of *Golagros and Gawain*. [*Golagros*]

MELION

A British knight who possessed an enchanted ring which allowed him to change between human and werewolf form. His wife stole the ring while he was in his werewolf state, trapping him there until her treason was detected. The knight's name is probably a variation of MELIANT. [*Melion*]

MELIOR

An alias used by MERLIN. [*Butor*]

MELIOT[1]

A castle near the location where Balin began a quest that eventually led to the Dolorous Stroke. [*PostMer*]

MELIOT[2] OF LOGRES [*Melyot*]

A Knight of the Round Table, sometimes called Meliot of the Rock. He appears in *Perlesvaus* and in Malory. In the former, his father, Marin the Jealous, murders his mother. Meliot fled from his father to a hermitage owned by his uncle. He was later knighted, and he inhabited a property called the Field of the Lion. He killed Clamadoz of the Shadows in revenge for the death of his pet lion. Meliot's father was killed by Nabigan of the Rock, who then tried to deprive Meliot of his lands. Gawain championed him against Nabigan and succeeded. Meliot repaid this service by rescuing Gawain and Arthur when they were besieged by Anurez the Bastard. He was wounded in the battle (or, in Malory, after fighting Gylbert the Bastard), and could not be healed until Lancelot traveled to the Perilous Chapel and brought back a holy sword or cloth. Meliot later killed the pagan Knight of the Galley and rescued Gawain from execution by heathens. *Perlesvaus* relates that he was murdered by Sir Brudan, but in Malory he is killed—with ten other knights—by Lancelot when they trapped Lancelot in Guinevere's chamber. He may be identical with MELLOT of Logres, also found in Malory. [*Perlesvaus, Malory*]

MELIS

A knight in Arthur's Britain who fought at the tournament at Tenebroc. [*ChretienE*]

MELIUS

Merlin's maternal grandfather in Baudin Butor's romance. His daughter was named Optima. Optima at first wanted to name Merlin Melius. [*Butor*]

MELLIC OF THE HILL [*Melyon de la Mountaine*]

A knight from Tartare encountered by Bors, Hector, and Lionel during their quest to find Lancelot. Bors asked Mellic to bear news of the quest to Camelot. Mellic became one of Arthur's knights, and he joined Mordred and Agravain in their plot to catch Lancelot and Guinevere *in flagrante*. Lancelot killed him. [*VulgLanc, Malory*]

MELLOT OF LOGRES

A knight who was the brother of Sir Brian of the Isles and the cousin of Nimue in Malory's *Le Morte Darthur*. Mellot and Brian tried to free Nimue when she was abducted by Hontzlake of Wendland, but they could not defeat him. Their battle, however, delayed Hontzlake long enough to allow Pellinore to catch up to him and slay the abductor. He may be identical to MELIOT OF LOGRES. [*Malory*]

MELLT

Father of the huntsman Mabon by Modron. [*Culhwch*]

MELODIAM

Pellinore's eldest son, according to a reference in the Post-Vulgate *Suite du Merlin*, which says that he was slain by Gawain. Melodiam does not appear again, and his character seems to have been transferred to LAMORAT. [*PostMer*]

MELOT

An evil little dwarf from Acquitain who plotted—with Mark's steward Mariadoc—to expose the affair between Tristan and Isolde. He was somewhat successful. He appears in Béroul as FROCIN. Eilhart calls him ACQUITAIN, which suggests that they both had a common source but that Eilhart confused Melot's homeland with his name. [*Gottfried*]

MELOU

One of the two sons of Mordred in Layamon's *Brut* (the other is unnamed) who opposed King Constantine after the deaths of Mordred and Arthur. Constantine defeated Mordred's sons, and cut off Melou's head at the church of Saint Amphiball in Winchester. Melou may be related to MELEHAN, a son of Mordred in the Vulgate *Mort Artu*. [*VulgMort*]

MELWAS [*Maelwys*]

The King of the Summer Region or the Island of Glass. He was Guinevere's abductor in one of her earliest kidnapping tales. He is thus probably the origin of MELEAGANT. He is represented in Chrétien de Troyes's *Erec* as MOLOAS. His name has been translated as "prince of death," "young prince," and "noble pig." He is named as one of Arthur's warriors in *Culhwch and Olwen*, where he is the son of Baeddan. The story of his abduction of Guinevere is told in Caradoc of Llancarfan's *Vita Gildae* and in a Welsh poem called "The Dialogue of Arthur and Gwenhwyfar." Following Melwas's kidnapping of the queen, Arthur and his knights hunted Melwas to Glastonbury. Arthur was unable to secure her release. St. Gildas and the abbot of Glasontbury intervened and convinced Melwas to free his prisoner. [*Caradoc, Dialogue*]

MELYOS

A Knight of the Round Table who participated in the Grail Quest. [*ProsTris*]

MEMORY OF BLOOD [*Memoire de Sanc, Mover of Blood*]

The scabbard which held Galahad's SWORD WITH THE STRANGE HANGINGS. It was made of wood from the Tree of Life in Eden, and looking at it reminded one of Abel's murder under that tree. It had been fashioned by King Solomon of Israel, and was covered with the skin of a serpent. Only the best knight in the world (Galahad) could draw the sword from the scabbard and escape injury. [*VulgQuest*, *Malory*]

MEMPRICIUS

A king of Britain in the twelfth century BC. When Mepricius's father, King Maddan, died, Mempricius killed his brother Malim to secure the throne for himself. He ruled in tyranny and lechery until he was killed by a pack of wolves while hunting. His son, Ebraucus, succeeded him. [*GeoffHR*]

MENABLES OF THE TABLE

A knight defeated in combat by Perceval. He went to Arthur's court as a prisoner and became a Knight of the Round Table. [*Contin3*]

MENADOC

A king who served Arthur. [*Contin1*]

MENAGLAAS

A Saxon who, under King Aminaduc, fought Arthur and his knights at Vambieres. [*Livre*]

MENAGORMON OF EGLIMON [*Margon of Glufion, Margue Gormon*]

A lord in the service of King Arthur. He was present at the wedding of Erec and Enide. [*ChretienE*, *HartmannE*, *Heinrich*]

MENALUS

King of Africa and one of the allies of Emperor Thereus of Rome. Menalus joined Thereus in a war against Arthur, and he was slain in battle against Claris and Laris. [*Claris*]

MENANDRE OF THE LOGE

An inhabitant of the country of Lindesores and a vassal of Sartuz of the Loge. He tried to collect a "toll" from Perceval when he landed in Lindesores, but Perceval defeated him and sent him to Arthur's court. He eventually became a Knight of the Round Table. [*Contin3*]

MENASTIDE

Son of Salandres and brother of Dinisordres, Nastor, Aristes, and Gogonne. Menastide, his father, and his four brothers were defeated by Perceval and sent to Arthur's court. [*Contin3*]

MENDAMP [*Menadap*]

A Saxon warrior in the service of King Rions. He was slain by Arthur's Sir Girflet at the battle of Carhaix. [*VulgMer*, *Arthour*]

MENEALFE OF THE MOUNTAIN

A knight who, in the Middle English *Avowing of King Arthur*, kidnapped a maiden. Kay challenged him and was defeated; Gawain succeeded in rescuing the maiden and avenging Kay. His character may have been inspired by MELEAGANT, though his name is likely a fusion of "man" and "elf" (Hahn, 156). [*Avowing*]

MENEDUKE OF MENTOCHE [*Menaduke*]

A Knight of the Round Table related to Lancelot. Malory says that he joined Lancelot's defection from Arthur's court and participated in the battles against Arthur at Joyous Guard and Benoic. In return for his support, Lancelot made him earl of Rouerge. The Alliterative *Morte Arthure* says that he was slain during the war against Mordred. [*Allit*, *Malory*]

MENELAIS

Lord of the Perilous Castle. He served Lord Brian of the Gastine, but his sweetheart, Melie, was the niece of Bleheri, Brien's enemy. Menelais sneaked away with his lover, but Brian tracked him down and killed him in his sleep. Menelais's last request to Melie was that she inter him in the Waste Chapel, which she did with the help of Arthur's Sir Meriadeuc. [*Meriadeuc*]

MENESTYR

Father of Arthur's warrior Gwyddawg. [*Culhwch*]

MENEVIA

An early name of the city of SAINT DAVID'S.

MENNON THE SMALL [*Mecio, Nanowne le Petite*]

A Knight of the Round Table imprisoned and murdered by the giant Nabon the Black on the Island of Servage. He was a cousin of Perceval and Lamorat. Hearing of his death, Tristan and Lamorat journeyed to Nabon's fortress and killed Nabon in revenge. [*ProsTris*, *Palamedes*, *Malory*]

MENNONAS

A knight who rivaled his friend, the sorcerer Mabon the Black, for the love of the lady Grysinde. Mabon sent for Tristan to help him in the situation. Tristan arrived with Isolde, and when Mennonas saw that Grysinde was not as beautiful as Isolde, he killed her. Tristan then fought Mennonas in single combat and beheaded him. [*ProsTris*]

MENW

Son of Teirwaedd and father of Anynnawg. In Welsh legend, Menw was one of Arthur's sorcerers and advisors. In *Culhwch and Olwen*, Arthur sends him to accompany Culhwch and other warriors on Culhwch's quest for Olwen, in case Menw's magical abilities (particularly his skill for invisibility) are needed. During the hunt for the boar Twrch Trwyth, Menw changed himself into a bird and flew at the boar, trying to seize the razor, shears, or comb between its ears. He missed, and was struck by the boar, wounding him. The wound left him weak for the rest of his life.

An odd Welsh Triad says that Uther Pendragon taught Menw one of the three "Great Enchantments" of Britain. Another Welsh source calls him one of Arthur's three "Enchanter Knights," who had the ability to shape-shift. Some have seen him as a prototype for MERLIN. [*Culhwch*, *Triads*, *Dream*]

MEOCHIDE [*Meotide*]

An Arabian or African kingdom, visited by Flegetine in her search for her husband Nascien. [*VulgEst*]

MEODRAS

The Emperor of Spain in Layamon's chronicle. He was a vassal of Rome and he joined the Roman Lucius's war against Arthur. Geoffrey of Monmouth gives the title of king of Spain to ALIFATIMA. [*Layamon*]

MEON

Guinevere's page. [*Mottuls*]

MERALIS

One of Perceval's eleven paternal uncles in *Perlesvaus*; the eighth son of Gais le Gros and the brother of Alain. [*Perlesvaus*]

MERANPHIT

A knight present at the Sorgarda tournament, which Gawain won. [*Heinrich*]

MERAUGIS OF PORTLESGUEZ [*Maraghise*, *Mera(u)gys*, *Meralgis*]

A Knight of the Round Table who is the hero of Raoul de Houdenc's *Meraugis de Portlesguez*. He vied with his friend Gorvain Cadrut for the love of the lady Lidoine, whom they both met at the torament of Lindesores. A court of maidens chaired by Guinevere ruled that Meraugis, who loved Lidoine for her courtesy, was more deserving than Gorvain Cadrut, who loved her for her beauty. At Lidoine's behest, Meraugis embarked on a series of adventures designed to make himself worthy of her. During the adventures, Meraugis became separated from Lidoine, and rumors circulated of his death. He reunited with Lidoine in time to prevent her forced marriage to Sir Espinogres. Meraugis eventually reconciled with Gorvain.

The Vulgate *Merlin* lists him among Arthur's companions who fought against King Rions and the Saxons. In the Post-Vulgate, we learn that Meraugis is the son of King Mark of Cornwall and Ladiana, Mark's niece. Mark slew Ladiana after she gave birth, and he left the infant Meraugis hanging in the woods. A forester found and raised him, baptizing him with the name "Meraugis of Portlesguez" after a local knight. Meraugis joined Arthur's service and, during the Grail Quest, he helped Erec to avenge Erec's father's death by conquering the castle of Celis. He buried Erec's body in Camelot when Erec was slain by Gawain. At Camelot, he took Erec's seat at the Round Table and learned of his true lineage. He embarked on more adventures with Galahad and Hector, with whom he conquered the Castle of Treachery. After Arthur's death at Salisbury, he joined the Archbishop of Canterbury in a monastery. He was eventually slain by Sir Licanor the Great, who served King Mark. [*Raoul*, *Vengeance*, *VulgMer*, *PostQuest*, *PostMort*, *Arthour*]

MERAUGUINS

An Irish king who was a member of Arthur's court. [*Contin1*]

MERCILESS LION

Owner of the Castle Causuel, known as the Maulvais Garcon ("Bad Boy") as a child. He ran a crooked tournament out of his castle, in which a parrot was the prize. The lord of the most beautiful lady at the tournament was supposed to win. The Merciless Lion always presented an ugly woman, but he used force to win anyway. He robbed and imprisoned many knights, before Arthur, fighting on behalf of the Lady Without Pride, cut off his arm and defeated him. At Arthur's command, he freed his prisoners and made restitution to his victims. [*ChevPap*]

MERIADEUC

Hero of *Meriadeuc*, or *Le Chevalier aux deux épées*, a thirteenth-century French Arthurian romance. He was the son of Bleheri, a knight slain unwittingly by Gawain in the service of Brien de la Gastine. When he came of age, he went to Arthur's court and became Gawain's squire. Ignorant of his real name, he was called "Handsome Young Man." When Lady Lore of Cardigan came to court wearing a sword (that had belonged to Bleheri) that no knight could unbuckle, Meriadeuc asked Arthur to make him a knight, attempted the test himself, and succeeded. Fastening Lore's sword over the one bestowed by Arthur, he earned the name the KNIGHT WITH THE TWO SWORDS. He departed immediately to seek adventure, despite the pleas of Lore, whom Arthur had promised to wed to the knight who could pass the test. Meriadeuc soon proved his prowess by defeating King Ris, one of Arthur's enemies. He traveled with Gawain for a time, but upon learning that Gawain had killed his father, he shunned Gawain's company. Arriving at his family's home at the Lake of Twins, he learned the true story of his father's death. He avenged his father by slaying Brien de la Gastine. His mother brought about a reconciliation between Meriadeuc and Gawain. He healed a knight named Gaus at the Fountain of Marvels by striking him with a magic sword, and found his true name written on the sword. After defeating the Red Knight of the Perilous Valley, another enemy of Arthur, Meriadeuc returned to Arthur's court, where he married Lore. He became the King of Cardigan and had two children with his wife. [*Meriadeuc*]

MERIADOC

The King of Cambria (Wales) in the anonymous romance bearing his name. His father, King Caradoc of Wales, was murdered by Griffin, Caradoc's brother, who then assumed the throne for himself. Griffin plotted to kill Meriadoc and Orwen, Meriadoc's sister, but the children were taken to safety by their foster-father Ivor. From Ivor, Meriadoc was kidnapped by Kay, who took him to Arthur's court. Under Kay's tutelage, Meriadoc grew into a powerful warrior, and he championed Arthur against the Black, Red, and White Knights. Arthur rewarded him by giving justice to Griffin, which allowed Meriadoc to claim the throne of Wales. He turned Wales over to the stewardship of King Urien, his brother-in-law, and left Britain for Europe. There, he joined the forces of the Emperor of the Alemanni against King Gundebald of the Land From Which No One Returns, who had kidnapped the Emperor's daughter. He braved a number of supernatural adventures and finally slew Gundebald. He rescued the Emperor's daughter, fell in love with her, and returned with her to the Emperor. The Emperor, however, wanted to betroth his daughter to the King of Gaul, so he betrayed and imprisoned Meriadoc. With his lover's assistance, Meriadoc escaped and slew the Emperor. Meriadoc was awarded lands by the King of Gaul and ruled them nobly for the remainder of his life, with the Emperor's daughter as his queen. [*Historia*]

MERIAN

According to Geoffrey of Monmouth, a king of Britain in the third or second century BC. Merian succeeded King Gurgintius and was succeeded by King Bledud. [*GeoffHR*]

MERÏEN

Perceval married his cousin, the daughter of Goondesert, to Lord Merïen. [*Contin3*]

MERIN

Father of Gleis, an opponent of Arthur. [*Culhwch*]

MERKANIE

A castle ruled by King Tjofabier. It was besieged by Gerhart of Riviers, who wanted to marry Sabie, Tjofabier's daughter. The war was ended by Arthur's Sir Garel, who defeated Gerhart in combat. In reward, Tjofabier pledged support to Arthur's war against King Ekunaver of Kanadic. [*PleierG*]

MERLIN [*Marlyn, Mellin(s), Merdhin, Merlino, Merlins, Merlion, Merlun, Merlyn(g)*]

Wizard and adviser to four kings of Britain: Vortigern, Ambrosius, Uther and Arthur. A number of legends endow him with the ability to shape-shift, which is fitting, for his figure changes greatly throughout the Arthurian saga. In the best-known version of the Arthurian cycle, he disguises Uther Pendragon so that Uther can spend a night with Igerne, wife of the Duke of Cornwall, begetting Arthur; he supports Arthur's claim to the throne of Britain and advises him through the wars against the rebellious kings and the Saxons; and he falls in love with the Lady of the Lake, who uses his own magic to seal him in a forest tomb or cave.

Geoffrey of Monmouth, the first writer to mention Merlin, adapted him from MYRDDIN, a warrior and "mad prophet" in Welsh legend. Geoffrey probably modified the name to avoid an unpleasant association with the French *merde*, meaning "excrement."

In *Historia Regum Britanniae*, Geoffrey assigns to Merlin the role given to Emrys, or AMBROSIUS, in Nennius's *Historia*. Merlin's mother was the daughter of the King of South Wales (who Layamon calls Conan). She was impregnated by an *incubus* demon, who appeared to her in the guise of a man, and who was the source of Merlin's supernatural powers. Warriors of King Vortigern of Britain, seeking a fatherless child whose blood was needed to slake the foundations of Snowdon, his new fortress, found Merlin in Carmarthen, where they heard another youth named Dinabutius taunt Merlin for having no father. They hauled Merlin and his mother before Vortigern, where the story of his birth was related. Merlin saved himself from execution by offering to show Vortigern the true reason that the tower walls on Snowdon kept collapsing. Leading them to a cave inside the mountain, Merlin pointed out a lake that he advised Vortigern to drain. Within the lake, the company discovered a white dragon and a red dragon. The two serpents battled, and the white dragon was victorious. Merlin then recited a long series of prophecies (which actually formed Geoffrey's *Prophetiae Merlini*, written prior to *Historia*) that foretold Vortigern's death at the hands of Ambrosius, the coming of Arthur, the conquest of Britain by the Saxons, and the conquest of the Saxons by the Normans. Merlin's words caused Vortigern to flee Snowdon for Ganarew, where Ambrosius destroyed him. (In Thomas Heywood's version, alternately, Merlin stays at Vortigern's court for a considerable time, entertaining the king with his tricks and talents.)

When King Ambrosius Aurelius wished to create a monument in Amesbury to the British warriors who died against the Saxons, the bishop Tremorinus advised him to seek out "Vortigern's Prophet" to construct it. Finding him at the fountain of Galabes in Gwent, Ambrosius summoned Merlin to his side. Merlin agreed to travel to Ireland, with Uther and a contingent of soldiers, to bring the Giants' Dance back to Salisbury. Through magic and skill, he constructed a contraption to lift the heavy stones, and—after some resistance from the Irish—the quest was accomplished. Merlin set up the stones in a circle, and the site became known as Stonehenge. On the way back to Britain, Merlin foresaw the poisoning death of Ambrosius, and said that Uther would be king in his place.

Some years later, Uther—like his predecessors—had occasion to call on Merlin for assistance. Uther was in love with the Igerne, the wife of Gorlois, duke of Cornwall. At the advice of Sir Ulfin, Uther asked Merlin to help him break into the castle of Tintagel in Cornwall, so he could sleep with Igerne. Merlin was able to sneak him into the castle of Tintagel by magically disguising him as Gorlois, while Merlin himself took on the guise of either Jordan or Brithael, both knights of the duke. The next morning, Merlin came and fetched Uther away.

After Geoffrey wrote his *Historia*, he apparently learned new information about the Welsh Myrddin, which he then incorporated into his *Vita Merlini*. The action of the *Vita* takes place after Arthur's death. Merlin and Taliesin apparently helped bring Arthur's body to the Island of Apples (Avalon). Later driven mad by a vision in the sky at the battle of Arthuret, Merlin fled into the Caledonian forest and spouted mysterious prophecies to all who saw him. He told his wife, Guendolena, to re-marry, but then killed her prospective husband. A magical fountain eventually allowed him to regain his senses, but he remained in the forest, living with his sister Ganieda and with Taliesin. The differing accounts of Merlin found in Geoffrey's books and in Welsh texts apparently confused some later writers. Giraldus Cambrensis recognized two Merlins: Merlin Ambrosius, who prophesied at Vortigern's court, and Merlin Celidonius or Merlin Silvester, who lived in Arthur's time and went mad at the battle of Arthuret.

Geoffrey does not make Merlin a figure at Arthur's court, since his last acts occur during the reign of Uther Pendragon. Consequently, Chrétien de Troyes does not mention Merlin at all. We owe our conception of Merlin as Arthur's magician to Robert de Boron, who wrote a verse *Merlin* of which only a small portion survives. Robert's romance was adapted by other French writers into a Prose *Merlin*, a Vulgate *Merlin*, and a Post-Vulgate *Merlin*, which together form the basis of Malory's story of Merlin and thus provided the modern portrayal of the character.

Robert elaborated on the circumstances of Merlin's birth. Satan had apparently intended him as a kind of Anti-Christ, but a holy man named Blaise, who later raised and tutored the child, divined the plot and foiled it by baptizing Merlin moments after his birth. Although the evil was purged, Merlin still inherited supernatural powers from his demon father.

When Arthur was born, Merlin spirited him away from his parents, baptized him, and gave him to a lord named Antor or Ector for rearing. He continued to serve Uther, advising the king to establish the Round Table. After Uther's death and the following anarchy, Merlin persuaded the Archbishop of Brice or Canterbury to summon the lords and knights of Britain to the Sword-in-the-Stone tournament. Arthur succeeded in drawing the sword, and Merlin supported his claim to the throne. Though a number of kings rebelled against the young Arthur, Arthur defeated them with the assistance of Merlin (portrayed here as a competent warrior and tactician as well as a magician), who advised the king to ally with Kings Ban of Benoic and Bors of Gannes.

In subsequent episodes, Merlin accompanied Arthur in his battles with King Pellinore, in his retrieval of Excalibur from the Lady of the Lake, in his wars against Lot and Rions, and during his foundation of the Round Table at Camelot. Merlin's prophecies told of the Grail Quest, of Arthur's downfall and death, and of his own imprisonment by the Lady of the Lake.

Merlin's imprisonment and death in the Vulgate romances ignore Geoffrey's *Vita Merlini*. Melin fell in love with the Lady of the Lake (called Ninniane, Vivien, or Nimue) and doted upon her. When she had learned all or most of his magic, she became bored with him and lured him into a cave, tomb, tower, or tree, and sealed him inside with his own spells. Presumably he suffocates or dies of starvation, but in some versions, the Lady of the Lake vists him frequently and they continue to share their love; she has only put him in a prison, not a tomb.

A notable variation occurs contemporary to the Vulgate Cycle in the Didot-*Perceval*, in which Merlin builds an *esplumoir* ("bird cage"?) near the Grail Castle, enters, and is never seen again, though he is fated to remain alive until the end of the world. Late Welsh legend has Merlin surviving in an invisible fortress of glass, guarding the Thirteen Treasures of the Island of Britain. The notion of Merlin as the young Arthur's tutor is relatively new—perhaps stemming from T. H. White's *The Sword in the Stone*—but is found in Spenser's *The Faerie Queene*.

A note on the nature of Merlin's magic is appropriate. In Geoffrey of Monmouth's chronicle, Merlin performs three great feats of enchantment: his prophecies, his movement of the Giant's Dance from Ireland, and his transformation of Uther (through drugs) into the likeness of Gorlois. Throughout these episodes, Geoffrey calls him "Merlin the Prophet." Though he seems to have some power with alchemy, and knowledge of engineering (he lifts the great stones from Ireland not by magic, but by "assembling his own machinery"), he is by no means the wizard or sorcerer that later legend was to make him.

In the French prose cycles, we learn the source of his magic: his devil father. The nature of his enchantments are more diverse. He continues to demonstrate prophecy, as well as mystic insight into events occurring before him (e.g., he knows when the king's envoys are seeking him). He can change his own form, appearing as a giant churl or as a small child, and he has the power to control the lusts and loves of men (e.g., King Ban and the daughter of Agravadain of the Fens). He can enchant objects and locations with a variety of spells. Thus, he is several times called "magician" or "wizard" by his associates.

Not, however, until the seventeenth century does Melrin become a sorcerer in full mythological glory. Dryden (1691) has him descending from the heavens, surrounded by spirits, in a chariot drawn by dragons. *The History of Tomb Thumb* (1621) describes him as "a diuell or spirit, cunning in all Arts and Professions, all sciences, secrets, and discoueries, a coniurer, an inchanter, a charmer, hee consorts with Elues and Fayries, a Commander of Goblins, and a worked of Night-wonders...." Though the tendency of subsequent legend was to scale back Merlin's powers, it is the portrayal of the supernatural Merlin, who consorts with fairies and spirits and devils, that found its way into fantasy and folklore. [*GeoffHR*, *GeoffVM*, *Giraldus*, *RobertBorM*, *ProsMer1*, *VulgLanc*, *VulgMer*, *PostMer*, *Malory*, *Spenser*, *Dryden*, *Heywood*, *TennIK*]

Relations: Merlin's family, wives, and kinsmen are named below. More information can be found under their respective entries.

Mother: Joan Go-too't, Marinaia, Optima, unnamed daughter of the King of South Wales

Wives and Lovers: Columbine, Escorducarla, Guendoloena, Gwendolen, Lady of the Lake, Morgan le Fay, Viviane

Daughters: unnamed maiden of the Dolorous Mount, Inogen

Sister: Ganieda

See Also: Arfderydd, Avalon, Balin, Blaise, Gregorio, Guinebaut, Gwenddolau, Gyneth, Lailoken, Meliadus, Merlin's Stones, Morgan le Fay, Myrddin, Phildabel, Round Table, Silence, Sword in the Stone, Taliessin, Uther, Viviane, Vortigern

MERLIN'S BED

A marvel encountered by Gawain at the Island of Marvels. Laying on the bed made a man temporarily lose "mind and memory." [*VulgLanc*]

MERLIN'S CASTLE

A castle where Yvain brought an injured Mordred after a tournament at Penning. Its connection with Merlin is uncertain. [*VulgLanc*]

MERLIN'S CAVE

A cavern in Cornwall supposedly haunted by Merlin. It lies under the promontory atop which Tintagel Castle rests. [*Topography*]

MERLIN'S HILL

A hill near Carmarthen in Dyfed (southwest Wales) said to be Merlin's birthplace. Local legend places the cave of his imprisonment at the base of Merlin's Hill, and it is said that a careful listener can hear him groaning within. [*Topography*]

MERLIN'S ISLAND

The island where Balin and Balan killed each other. Merlin created many marvels on the island, including the second Sword-in-the-Stone, which floated up to Camelot before the Grail Quest. The island was also known as the ISLAND OF MARVELS. [*PostMer*]

MERLIN'S ROCK

A rock where Merlin killed two enchanters. It is named only in the Vulgate *Lancelot*, although the episode itself occurs in the Post-Vulgate *Suite du Merlin*. [*VulgLanc*]

MERLIN'S STONE

The stone from which Arthur drew the Sword in the Stone. [*ProsTris*]

MERLIN'S STONES

Six stones erected by Merlin across Britain. Each had a series of prophecies written on it. The first was in Lyonesse; the second in Cornwall, where Tristan and Lancelot battled; the third in Logres, in which the sword drawn by Galahad at the beginning of the Grail Quest was fixed; the fourth in the Perilous Valley; the fifth in the Dark Valley, where Tristan and Lancelot fought again; and the sixth in North Wales, where Lancelot and Tristan had a third combat. One of these latter stones appears in an Italian cantare as the ROCK OF MERLIN. [*ProsTris Tavola*]

MERLIN'S TOWER[1]

An enchanted tower between the White Castle and the town of Gasan. It was prophesied that only Lancelot would end the enchantments. [*VulgLanc*]

MERLIN'S TOWER[2]

A tower on the Turning Isle once inhabited by Merlin. [*Livre*]

MERLIN'S WILDERNESS

According to *La Tavola Ritonda*, the original name of the Forest of DARNANTES, an enchanted wood where Arthur's knights could find numerous adventures. [*Tavola*]

MERLOENS

A plain in the kingdom of Affraudis, crossed by Tristan and Dinadan. [*Tavola*]

MERMIN

A land ruled—and terrorized—by the giant Karedoz of Malmontan, until he was defeated by Arthur's Sir Tandareis. Tandareis assumed the throne and ruled from Karmil, although he made his father Dulcemar the symbolic overlord. [*PleierT*]

MESSOIS

The name of the FISHER KING in *Perlesvaus*, probably a reference to the biblical Messiah. This particular Fisher King was Perceval's maternal uncle, the brother of Yglais, Pelles, and the King of the Castle Mortal. [*Perlesvaus*]

MESSUR Y PEIR ("Measure of the Cauldron")

The name bestowed upon the harbor formerly called Porth Cerddin after Arthur and his warriors, returning from their invasion of Ireland bearing an enchanted cauldron, landed there. [*Culhwch*]

METELLIUS

One of the Roman senate leaders who joined Lucius's war against Arthur in Wace's *Brut*. The name probably resulted from a confusion in Geoffrey's list of senators: he mentions a GAIUS METELLUS COTTA, which Wace seems to have broken into three separate names. [*Wace, Layamon*]

METTEVA

A city where Lancelot knighted Sir Turinoro, brother of the Pope. [*Tavola*]

METZ [*Meyes, Moyses*]

A city in Lorraine, where Arthur's forces battled the Duke of Lorraine after the Roman War. Sir Priamus, a knight in Arthur's service, killed the Marquis of Metz in the battle. [*Allit, Malory*]

MICHEL

A priest in the land of Karahes. He was a vassal of King Havelin. Michel welcomed Tristan upon his arrival in Karahes, and explained to Tristan the war between Havelin and Count Riole of Nantes. [*Eilhart*]

MICIPSA [*Maeptisas, Misappa*]

The king of Babylon who was subject to Rome, and was called upon to join Lucius in the war against Arthur. He fought at the battle of Soissons and was killed there by Earl Leir (Leodegar) of Boulogne. Wace says that Leir and Micipsa mortally wounded each other, while Layamon claims that Micipsa's son Gecron killed Leir in revenge. [*GeoffHR, Wace, Layamon*]

MIDDLESEX

A district of southeast Britain, near London. King Vortigern yielded Middlesex and other districts to the Saxons under Hengist in exchange for his life after Hengist captured him. [*Nennius*]

MIDOMIDAS [*Midolas*]

The son of King Lot of Galway. Midomidas arrived at Arthur's court after the conquest of Rigomer Castle. He immediately requested the right of combat against Miraudiaus, a knight against whom Arthur was pledged to send a champion. Arthur granted his request, but Midomidas relinquished the right to Lancelot when the latter arrived. [*Contin4, Merveil*]

MIERIIEN

King of Lanval. He married Perceval's cousin, the daughter of Goondesert. [*Contin3*]

MIGLORAS

A knight captured by Gaheris in a tournament at Carhaix. [*VulgMer*]

MIL THE BLACK

Son of Dugum. He was conquered by Arthur. [*Culhwch*]

MILAN [*Meloine*]

The Alliterative *Morte Arthure* says that this Italian city surrendered and sent tribute to Arthur after Arthur conquered Rome. [*Allit, Malory*]

MILIAG

The homeland of King Mark's knight Galiag. [*Eilhart*]

MILL CASTLE

The site of a sparrowhawk tournament sponsored by King Narbaoc. Hector and Gawain participated. [*VulgLanc*]

MILLEMARGOT

One of the many knights who chased after Meleagant when Meleagant kidnapped Guinevere. He was defeated by Meleagant. [*HartmannI*]

MILOCATES

A barbarian island king who abducted the wife of the King of Illyricum. Gawain and a fleet of Romans blew ashore on their way to Jerusalem and immediately came into conflict with Milocates when Gawain killed one of his stags. Milocates sent for help from his brother, named either Egesarius or Buzafarnan. Milocates was killed in the ensuing war, his island was occupied by Romans, and the Queen of Illyricum was returned to her home. [*DeOrtu*]

MILON OF NOMADJENTISIN

An infidel king who served Feirefiz, Perceval's half-brother. [*Wolfram*]

MIMALTO

A variation of MALEHAUT found in *La Tavola Ritonda*.

MINADAP

A Saxon king and vassal of King Rions in the Vulgate *Merlin*. He was slain fighting Arthur's forces at the battle of Aneblayse. TRIOMADAC, his name in *Arthour and Merlin* is a corruption of "Roi Minadap." [*VulgMer*]

MINADORAS[1]

Duke and seneschal of King Pallas. He joined Arthur's battle against the Saxons at Clarence. [*Livre*]

MINADORAS[2]

Another knight who joined Arthur in the battle against the Saxons at Clarence. [*Livre*]

MINADORAS[3]

Seneschal of the First Conquered King. He joined Arthur's battle against the Saxons at Clarence. [*Livre*]

MINADORAS[4] OF THE LOST ISLAND

A knight present among Arthur's forces at the battle at Vambieres. [*Livre*]

MINADOS [*Sinargos*]

A Saxon king in the service of King Rions. He was slain by Arthur's forces at Aneblayse. [*VulgMer, Arthour*]

MINAP [*Minape*]

A Saxon king who served King Rions. He was slain in the battle of Aneblayse, against Arthur's army, by King Ban of Benoic. [*VulgMer, Arthour*]

MINARDES

A heathen warrior slain by Yvain at the battle of Diana Bridge. [*Arthour*]

MINAU

An island where Arthur killed Hueil, the brother of St. Gildas. [*Caradoc*]

MINODALES

A knight who defeated Merlin, and was defeated by Gawain, in a tournament at Carhaix. [*VulgMer*]

MINORAS[1]

The seneschal of King Lac of Great India. Lac sent him to Britain to assist Arthur in the Saxon Wars. [*VulgMer*]

MINORAS[2]

A Knight of the Round Table who participated in Arthur's war against the Saxons. [*Livre*]

MINORAS[3] THE FORESTER

The castellan of New Castle under King Clarion of Northumberland. He sheltered Lot and Gawain for a night during the Saxon Wars. [*VulgMer*]

MINORAS[4] THE WICKED

A Knight of the Round Table who engaged in a silly rivalry with the Queen's Knights. He was badly wounded when he attacked Sir Galescalain. [*VulgMer*]

MIRABEL[1]

A heathen king slain by Duke Escant of Cambenic at the battle of Rockingham. [*Arthour*]

MIRABEL[2] OF AVENDROYN

A king. He was the brother of King Schirniel of Lirivoyn. He was defeated in a battle at Bearosche by Perceval. [*Wolfram*]

MIRALDO

A British nobleman convinced by Satan to revolt against Arthur when Arthur was in France. Arthur quelled the rebellion and granted amnesty to Miraldo and his allies. [*BlackmoreK*]

MIRANGEL

A baron in the service of King Dulcemar of Tandernas. He led a battalion of soldiers in Dulcemar's battle against Arthur. [*PleierT*]

MIRAUDE

The most beautiful maiden in the world. She agreed to marry Sir Torec if he would defeat all the Knights of the Round Table, which he did. [*Maerlant*]

MIRAUDIAUS

A knight who tried to force a lady to marry him against her will. She requested, and received, a champion from Arthur's court. Miraudiaus fell ill because he was terrified of Gawain, whom he assumed Arthur would appoint. Gawain, ignorant of the circumstances, showed up at Miraudiaus's castle looking for lodging. Miraudiaus imprisoned him. He then headed to Arthur's court for the duel. When he discovered that his opponent was to be Lancelot, he immediately surrendered and freed Gawain. Arthur appointed him to the Round Table. [*Merveil*]

MIRAUDIJS

The true name of the KNIGHT OF THE SLEEVE, hero of a Dutch romance. [*Riddere*]

MIRMIDON

A land ruled by King Garel until Garel was killed by King Roaz of Glois. The land was reclaimed by Gawain's son Wigalois when he slew Roaz. [*Wirnt*]

MIROET [*Miroez*]

A Knight of the Round Table and son of King Alfred of Ireland. Miroet, his father, and his brother Kamelin discovered Yder left for dead in a forest after he had been poisoned by Kay. The three knights managed to return Yder to health. [*Yder*]

MISTY LAKE

The enchanted home of the wizard Malduc. It was surrounded by the perilous Shrieking Marsh and the Steaming Path. Malduc kept Gawain and Erec prisoner at the Misty Lake, torturing them daily, until Lancelot led an expedition to rescue them. Lancelot's men were able to cross the lake and enter the fortress with the help of the giant Esealt the Tall. [*UlrichZ*]

MITARZ OF ANSGEWE

A knight present at the Sorgarda tournament, which Gawain won. His homeland is probably a variation of ANJOU. [*Heinrich*]

MITRIDES

King of the Dolorous Tower. He was the father of Caradoc and Tericam, two giants who plagued Arthur, in *Palamedes*. His brother was named Malingre. He is called AUPATRIS in the Post-Vulgate *Suite du Merlin*. [*PostMer*]

MOADAS

A knight who fought on the side of King Mark of Cornwall during Mark's tournament at Lancien. [*Contin4*]

MOAP

A Saxon "emir" who, under King Aminaduc, fought Arthur's forces at the battle of Vambieres. Sagremor wounded him. [*Livre*]

MODESTIA

In the play *The Birth of Merlin*, the daughter of Lord Donobert and a maiden at Ambrosius's court. Her father wanted to wed her to Sir Edwin, but she was resolved to dedicate her life to religion. She eventually convinced her sister, Constantia, to join her in a convent. [*Birth*]

MODRON

In Welsh legend, the mother of Mabon the Enchanter. She is in origin the Celtic goddess MATRONA. She was said to be the daughter of Affalach and the mother of another son named Owain and a daughter named Morfudd. Several scholars point to her as the origin of MORGAN LE FAY, Owain's mother in later romance. She may also be the origin of the LADY OF THE LAKE. [*Culhwch*, *Dream*]

MOHAMMED [*Mahom(m)et, Mahommé*]

In the Vulgate *Estoire del Saint Graal*, Mohammed is one of four gods worshiped by the pagans in Britain, before they are converted to Christianity by Joseph of Arimathea. The other three gods were Jupiter, Apollo, and Tervagant. [*VulgLanc*, *VulgEst*]

MOHANADAP

A Saxon king who, under King Hargadabran, fought Arthur's forces at the battle of Clarence. [*Livre*]

MOHIANAPUS

A Saxon king who was the uncle of King Rion and King Aminaduc. He opposed Arthur's forces at the battle of Vambieres. [*Livre*]

MOLDAGOG

A giant from Brittany who was defeated by Tristan near Mont St. Michel. Tristan took his castle and built his Hall of Statues nearby. [*Thomas*, *TrisSaga*]

MOLLINA

Tristan's granddaughter. She was the daughter of King Kalegras of England and Queen Lilja. [*SagaTI*]

MOLOAS [*Maheloas, Maloans*]

One of Arthur's barons in Chrétien's *Erec*, from the Welsh MELWAS. He was the lord of the Glass Isle or the Black Isle. Heinrich von dem Türlin conflates him with Chrétien's Count of Treverain, calling him Maloans of Treverain. [*ChretienE*, *Heinrich*]

MÔN

The Welsh name for ANGLESEY.

MON MEROUAC

The King of Mon Merouac was an ally of Rigomer Castle, and was therefore an opponent of Arthur. [*Merveil*]

MONACLIN

One of many Saxon kings who invaded Britain at the beginning of Arthur's reign. He was slain by Gawain in a skirmish on the plains of Roestoc. [*VulgMer*]

MONAQUIN

A Saxon king slain by Gawain at the battle of Roestoc. [*VulgMer*]

MONBRALAN

A forest in which Perceval fought the Fair Unknown. [*Contin2*]

MONEVAL

A Knight of the Round Table who took a friendly rivalry between the Round Table and the Queen's Knights too far. He was badly wounded when he attacked Sir Galescalain, a Queen's Knight. [*VulgMer*]

MONJARDIN

The city in Spain in which the Lady Lidoine was held captive by King Savari until rescued by Claris. [*Claris*]

MONJOIE

A mountain range on the border of Burgundy, through which Arthur and his army traveled on their way to the Roman War. [*VulgMer*]

MONMELITIRE

An Irish land whose king was allied to Rigomer Castle, which Gawain conquered. The king held his lands from a lady named Qrainglaie. [*Merveil*]

MONREAL

A castle in Sicily, near Palermo, where Sir Floriant's mother was besieged by Maragoz until Arthur intervened and lifted the siege. Its seneschal was named Omer. [*Floriant*]

MONT ST. MICHEL

A hill in Brittany that served as the lair of a Spanish giant who kidnapped Helen, the daughter, niece, or wife of Hoel of Brittany. Wace names the giant Dinabuc. Arthur and his knights, on their way to fight the Roman War, heard of the abduction and rode to rescue the lady. Arthur, Kay, and Bedivere arrived to find the lady dead (either killed by the giant or by herself to avoid rape). They crept to the giant's lair and found him roasting children (or, in Geoffrey, piglets) on a spit. Arthur challenged and killed him. Arthur later ordered a church built at this site. In the Norse *Saga of Tristram and Ísönd*,

Tristan builds his famous Hall of Statues in the giant's former cave. According to the Middle English *Parlement of the Thre Ages,* Arthur fought a dragon, rather than a giant, on Mont St. Michel. The Prose *Brut* calls the location SAINT BERNARD'S MOUNT. [*GeoffHR, Wace, Layamon, VulgMer, TrisSaga, Allit, Parlement, Malory*]

MONTAGU

A city and land in which Arthur sometimes held court. The Duke of Montagu was one of Arthur's allies. [*RobertBlo, Claris*]

MONTE ALBRANO

In *La Tavola Ritonda,* a castle where Tristan and Isolde lived during one of their several banishments from King Mark's court. This episode occurs at the same point as their banishment to the forest of MORROIS in the Prose *Tristan.* [*Tavola*]

MONTEGIBEL [*Mongibel*]

The home of Morgan le Fay in *Floriant et Florete* and *Le Chevalier du Papegau.* In the former, it is said to be in Sicily. Floriant retires at Montegibel with his wife Florete at the end of their lives. Folklore identifies it with Mt. Etna. [*Floriant, ChevPap*]

MONTELEI

A castle at Orkney where Arthur's knights participated in a tournament. [*Heinrich*]

MONTENART OF THE HIDDEN ISLAND

An arrogant knight who stole the Castle of the High Rock from Arthur. Sagremor challenged Montenart for the castle but, before the duel could be fought, Montenart was slain by Erec in revenge for an unrelated past wrong. [*PostMer*]

MONTEREVEL [*Montrevel*]

A castle in King Lac's kingdom of Destregales. It was given to Enide's father to rule when Lac's son Erec married Enide. [*ChretienE, HartmannE*]

MONTESCLAIRE [*Montescler*]

A mountain or village somewhere in Britain. A beautiful maiden was besieged inside, and it was said that whoever rescued her could possess the enchanted Sword with the Strange Hangings. The quest was assumed by Gawain in the First Continuation of Chrétien de Troyes's *Perceval.* Gawain saved the maiden and received the sword. In the Third Continuation, however, it is Perceval who saves the maiden, called the Maiden of the Circle of Gold, from the Knight of the Dragon, though there is no mention here of the Sword with the Strange Hangings. A Red-Haired Knight of Montesclaire is named as a knight who appears at the Castle of Maidens tournament. [*ChretienP, Contin1, Contin3*]

MONTESOAVE ("Sweet Mountain")

A castle in Ireland where the King with a Hundred Knights and the King of Scotland held a tournament. Tristan was in Ireland recovering from poison and participated. Palamedes the Saracen won. [*Tavola*]

MONTIGNET [*Montiguet*]

A castle near Camelot, visited on various occasions by Lancelot and Bors of Gannes. [*Vulglanc*]

MONTIKLUSE

A castle in the land of Emperuse, ruled by Duke Kandalion under King Bagdemagus of Gorre. Featured in the Pleier's *Tandareis and Flordibel,* it was probably inspired by Der Stricker's KLUSE. [*PleierT*]

MONTLAIR

A castle in the kingdom of Gannes. It was the court of King Bors (Lancelot's uncle). Sir Placidas was its steward. It was the last castle to fall during the invasion of King Claudas. [*LancLac, VulgLanc, VulgMer*]

MONTOR

A city in King Pellinore's lands. [*PostMer*]

MONTPELLIER

A wealthy city in Provence, where Duke Mathem of Soane took refuge after his land was stolen by Duke Frollo. (On Merlin's advice, Julius Caesar restored Mathem to his duchy.) [*VulgMer, ProsMer2*]

MOPADES

The bard who served King Hoel of Brittany. [*BlackmoreP*]

MORADAS

A tyrannical knight who captured and imprisoned many of Arthur's knights before he was conquered by Sir Floriant and sent as a prisoner to Arthur. [*Floriant*]

MORAL

Count of Joraphas, husband of Countess Beleare, and brother of Bejolare of Leodarz. He was attacked and carried away by a dragon named Pfetan, but was rescued by Wigalois (Gawain's son). He later joined Wigalois in a campaign against Prince Lion of Namur. [*Wirnt*]

MORALDE

The lord of the Beautiful Forest. He was married to lady Angie. His daughter, Claudin, was kidnapped by a count but saved by Arthur's Sir Tandareis. [*PleierT*]

MORANS

A knight killed by Beaudous, Gawain's son, when Beaudous rescued the lady Beauté from Madoines, Morans's nephew. [*RobertBlo*]

MORAT [*Moras*]

A Saxon warrior who served King Rions in the war against Arthur. He was slain by King Ban of Benoic at the battle of Carhaix. [*VulgMer, Arthour*]

MORAY [*Mureif, Murray, Murreve*]

A region of northeast Scotland where Arthur defeated a collection of Picts and Scots at the beginning of his reign. From here, he pushed the barbarian hordes on to the lake called Loch Lomond. Arthur later restored the rule of Moray to King Urien. [*GeoffHR, Wace, Layamon*]

MORCADES [*Orcades*]

The first version of MORGAUSE, mother of Gawain, Agravain, Gaheris, Gareth, Mordred, Clarissant, and Soredamor. She is found in the First Continuation of Chrétien's *Perceval*, in *Les Enfances Gawain*, and in Heinrich von dem Türlin's *Diu Crône*. Her name was probably, originally, a place name, *Orcades* being the Latin designation of ORKNEY, the land traditionally ruled by Gawain's parents. The name became Morcades and then Morgause under the influence of MORGAN LE FAY.

Morcades had an affair with Lot, her page, and gave birth to Gawain, whom, in order to avoid a scandal, she gave up to a knight named Gawain the Brown. After Gawain had grown, he found his mother, grandmother (Igerne), and sisters living in Canguin Rock or Salie. Gawain freed them from the castle's sorcery. Her counterpart in Wolfram's *Parzival* is SANGIVE. Heinrich von dem Türlin calls her husband Jascaphin rather than Lot. [*Contin1, Enfances, Heinrich*]

MORDAUNT

A knight who was seduced by the sorceress Acrasia in the Bower of Bliss. He abandoned his wife, Amavia, and his infant son, Ruddymane. Amavia managed to free him from the Bower, but Acrasia had given him a poison that acted after his release and killed him. His death was avenged, and the Bower destroyed, by Sir Guyon. [*Spenser*]

MORDRAIN [*Mondrames, Mordrains, Mordrayns, Mordrayous*]

The baptismal name of EVALACH, the King of Sarras converted by Joseph of Arimathea in the Vulgate Cycle. Born in the French city of Meaux, Mordrain, as a youth, took service with Emperor Augustus Caesar of Rome, who put him in the charge of Count Felix of Syria. He killed one of Felix's sons during a quarrel and fled to King Tholomer of Babylonia, with whom he remained until he became King of Sarras. He married Queen Sarrassinte. His lands bordered on Tholomer's, and tensions between the two eventually escalated into war. Joseph of Arimathea and his party arrived during the hostilities, and Mordrain's conversion to Christianity allowed him to win the conflict. Joseph also reconciled him with Seraphe, Mordrain's estranged brother-in-law, who upon conversion became known as Nascien. After Mordrain's

conversion, God tested him by placing him on the Rock of the Perilous Port for several days, but Mordrain's faith did not waver. Joseph and his followers departed for Britain, and some time later, Mordrain had a vision in which he saw Joseph imprisoned there by the pagan King Crudel. Leaving Sarras, he journeyed to Britain with his soldiers and freed Joseph. According to a Middle English romance, he married Labell, the daughter of Crudel. During a mass, he approached the Holy Grail and was struck blind. He asked God to keep him alive until he could meet Galahad. God granted his wish, and Mordrain retired to a hermitage in Britain. (He seems to be a duplicate, in this sense, of the MAIMED KING, and the *Livre d'Artus* specifically calls him by this title.) A few hundred years later, Galahad visited him during the Grail Quest, healed his wounds, and allowed him to die. J. D. Bruce notes that the only other appearance of the name Mordrain is as the name of an abbot who presided over the Benedictine monastery of Corbie in Picardy in the late eighth century, leading him, among other things, to conclude that the author of the Vulgate *Queste* was a monk in Corbie. [*VulgQuest, VulgEst, Livre, PostQuest, Malory, HereJOA*]

MORDREC

In the romance of *Yder*, the gatekeeper of Taulas of Rougemont, a vassal of Arthur who rebelled. [*Yder*]

MORDRED[1] [*Medraut, Medrawd, Medrod, Mo(r)d(d)red(e), Mo(r)dret, Mordarette, Mordered, Mordrech, Mordrés*]

The knight who rebelled against Arthur and caused Arthur's final downfall. In the earliest legends, he is Arthur's nephew, but starting with the Vulgate Cycle, he also becomes Arthur's son, adding an element of incest and sin to the tragic tale.

The first appearance of his name occurs in the *Annales Cambriae*, which say that both Arthur and "Medraut" died at the battle of Camlann in 537. This is the only information provided about Mordred in the *Annales*, and the text does not even say that Mordred and Arthur were on opposite sides. In the Welsh Triads, where he is the son of Llew (Lot, Arthur's brother-in-law), he is one of Arthur's "Royal Knights," described as handsome, wise, and skilled at arms.

In another Triad, we hear how Mordred showed up at Arthur's court in Celli Wig in Cornwall, ate all of Arthur's food, drank all of his wine, and dragged Guinevere off her throne and beat her. Arthur repaid Mordred's insult by visiting his court and similarly taking all the food and mead. This is the first portrayal of Mordred in Welsh as Arthur's enemy. Though we must consider the influence of Geoffrey of Monmouth as a possibility, it seems unlikely since, other than the fact that Arthur and Mordred are antagonists, the accounts found in Geoffrey's *Historia* and the Welsh Triads have no common elements. A third Welsh text, *The Dream of Rhonabwy*, makes Arthur and Mordred opponents at the battle of Camlann, though it was written well after Geoffrey.

It is in Geoffrey of Monmouth, then, that we first find a complete account of Mordred's life and rebellion. He was the son of Lot and Anna, Arthur's sister. Gawain was his brother. (One line in Wace, almost certainly an interpolation, makes Mordred Guinevere's brother.) He became a warrior in Arthur's court, elevating himself to a position of power by capitalizing on the reputation established by his brother Gawain. When Arthur left Britain to fight the Roman War, he left Mordred as regent. Mordred declared that Arthur was dead, married Arthur's wife Guinevere (who seems to have been a willing complicitor in the rebellion), and made alliances with the Saxons, Picts and Scots. When Arthur returned from the continent, Mordred's army met him at Richborough, where Gawain was killed. Mordred and Arthur's armies battled all the way into Cornwall, where Mordred and Arthur perished at the battle of Camel (Geoffrey's version of Camlann). Mordred had two sons who plagued King Constantine, Arthur's successor, and Layamon calls one of them Melou.

The story outlined by Geoffrey of Monmouth is followed fairly faithfully throughout the chronicles and the prose romances (including Malory), with only slight alterations. His character is ignored in Chrétien de Troyes's romances (but is echoed in the traitorous ANGRES of Windsor). He is introduced in the Vulgate *Lancelot* as the youngest and most evil of Gawain's brothers, and his first adventure involves sleeping with a married woman and defeating the woman's husband when he discovers them together. Later, while traveling with Lancelot, he murders an old man who says Mordred is not the son of Lot—the first hint of his true paternity. Now and then there are prophecies and hints of the fate to befall Arthur and Mordred.

Mordred's biography in the Vulgate Cycle, the Post-Vulgate Cycle, and Malory can be outlined as follows: Mordred is conceived when Arthur and his half-sister (Morgause or Belisent) sleep together about the time of Arthur's coronation. Arthur does not know his parentage, and therefore does not know that he is committing incest. He finds out later from Merlin. As for the lady's part, in the Vulgate *Merlin*, she believes she is sleeping with her husband Lot, while in the Post-Vulgate *Suite du Merlin* and in Malory, she has uncertain motives for sleeping with Arthur. Afraid of Merlin's predictions for the future, and seeking to destroy his incestuous child, Arthur orders all children born on the day of Mordred's birth to be loaded into a boat and sent out to sea. Though the boat sank, Mordred survived, washed up on an island, was found by a fisherman, and was raised by Lord Nabur the Unruly. He eventually joined Arthur's court and was re-united with his true family. Generally a poor knight, Mordred conspired with his brothers to murder Lamorat, Drian, and Dinadan. He raped and murdered maidens. The circumstances of his rebellion are similar to Geoffrey's account, though it is preceded by an episode in which Mordred and Agravain expose the affair between Lancelot and Guinevere by catching the lovers *in flagrante* in Guinevere's chambers. This leads to a war between Arthur and Lancelot, and it is while Arthur is in France fighting Lancelot that Mordred fakes Arthur's death, usurps the throne, and falls in love with Guinevere. In contrast to the chronicles, Guinevere does not join Mordred, and she flees when he tries to force her into marriage. As in the chronicles, Arthur eventually returns, fights Mordred in a number of battles (Barham Down and Dover) before they clash for the final time at Salisbury (replacing Camlann), where they mortally wound each other in combat. Mordred's son, Melehan, continues the war but is slain by Lancelot.

There are numerous variations found in a number of texts. In Giovanni Boccaccio's *De Casibus Virorum Illustrium*, Mordred is the son of Arthur and a concubine, while in Pierre de Langtoft's chronicle, he is only Arthur's cousin. In *La Tavola Ritonda*, he survives the final battle with Arthur only to be killed by Lancelot at the castle of Urbano. In Jean D'Outremeuse's *Ly Myreur des histors*, Lancelot entombs Mordred, alive, with the body of Guinevere. To survive, Mordred consumes the flesh of the dead queen but eventually starves to death. Tennyson ignores the influence of Malory and returns him to his traditional role as Arthur's nephew, but not his son.

The most interesting variations to Mordred's character occur in Scottish chronicle, most notable the *Chronica Gentis Scotorum* of John of Fordum and the *Scotorum Historia* of Hector Boece. In these chronicles, Mordred is the rightful heir to Britain, being the son of Arthur's sister and King Lot of the Picts. Arthur, presented as a lecherous, treacherous king, refuses to honor his pledge to leave his throne to Mordred. Mordred's rebellion is a righteous attempt to correct this injustice.

Even in the romances in which Mordred is a traitor, he is not always portrayed as vile and corrupt. The Alliterative *Morte Arthure*, among others, endow him with a certain ruthless dignity, much like King Claudas or the early portrayals of Mark. [*Annales*, *Triads*, *GeoffHR*, *Wace*, *Layamon*, *VulgLanc*, *VulgMort*, *VulgMer*, *PostMer*, *PostQuest*, *PostMort*, *Pierre*, *Stanz*, *Tavola*, *Mannyng*, *Jean*, *Boccaccio*, *JohnF*, *Allit*, *Malory*, *Boece*, *TennIK*]

MORDRED²

One of Arthur's knights in Renaut de Bâgé's *Le Bel Inconnu* who fights in the Castle of Maiden's tournament and is defeated by Guinglain (Gawain's son). This does not appear to be the same character as Arthur's nephew, because he is named as a king, because he is given a brother named Segures, and because no mention is made of the relationship between Mordred and Guinglain. On the other hand, Segures is similar to Seguarades, who is Mordred's foster-brother in the Post-Vulgate *Merlin* continuation. [*Renaut*]

MOREIZ

The castle ruled by Galgandreiz. It was inherited by Galagandreiz's daughter after he died fighting Lancelot. The knights of the castle, and the daughter, recognized Lancelot as their new lord, but Lancelot left after a short time. Moreiz may be a variant of MORAY or the forest of MORROIS in Scotland. [*UlrichZ*]

MOREL

The horse that the Greek knight Cliges rode in the tournament at Oxford in Chrétien's *Cliges*. In *Durmart le Gallois*, Sir Sagremor owns a horse of the same name. [*ChretienC, Durmart*]

MOREN¹

An Arthurian warrior from Caer Dathal who was the son of Iaen. His brothers were Sulyen, Bradwen, Teregud, Siawn, and Caradawg. [*Culhwch*]

MOREN² MYNAWG

One of Arthur's warriors who was the son of Bradwen. His last name signifies "the Noble." [*Culhwch, Dream*]

MORES¹

A group of islands inhabited by Gladoain and the Knight of the Green Shield, allies of Lancelot. [*Perlesvaus*]

MORES² OF LYONESSE

A knight who was briefly a companion of Tristan during his adventures. [*ProsTris*]

MORET¹ OF THE WAY

A knight in the service of King Ban of Benoic and King Bors of Gannes. He fought to protect Arthur's lands at the battle of Bedegraine. [*VulgMer*]

MORET² THE NEGRESS

In Heinrich von dem Türlin's *Diu Crône*, one of the many ladies at Arthur's court to fail a chastity test involving a goblet. [*Heinrich*]

MORFRAN ("Great Raven") [*Morfryn*]

Father of Myrddin, the Welsh prototype of Merlin. He was the son of Tegid and was one of Arthur's warriors. He had another son named Rahawd. He fought at the battle of Camlann, but no one struck him because he was so ugly and hairy that the other warriors thought he was a devil. This ugliness earned him the title of one of Arthur's three "Offensive Knights." [*Culhwch, Triads, Dream*]

MORFUDD

Owain's sister in Welsh tradition. She was the daughter of King Urien of Rheged and Modron. She was loved by the warrior Cynon. [*Culhwch, Triads*]

MORGAN¹

The Duke of Brittany in the Thomas of England branch of the Tristan legend. He went to war with Tristan's father, Rivalin or Rouland, who was Morgan's vassal (the stories differ as to who started the war). The initial war was destructive and a truce was called for a year. At the end of the year, the war resumed and Morgan killed Rivalin. Tristan, born soon afterwards, was hidden from the vengeful Morgan by Rual or Rohand, his father's steward; later, Tristan returned to claim his ancestral land of Parmenie, and he killed Morgan when Morgan refused. *Sir Tristrem* gives him three brothers, all killed by Tristan: Morholt, Urgan, and Beliagog. [*Gottfried, TrisSaga, SirTris*]

MORGAN² LE FAY [*Feimurgan, Marguel, Morgaine, Morgana, Morgein, Morghain, Morghana, Morgn, Morg(u)e(n)*]

An enchantress or fairy, probably derived from the Welsh MODRON and, ultimately, from the Celtic goddess MATRONA, and she may have been influenced by an enchantress in Irish mythology called Morrigan. She is generally named as Arthur's half-sister, but she is sometimes his full sister or his niece. Her most important role is to bear Arthur's body to the Island of Avalon after he receives a mortal wound at the battle of Camlann. Incongruously, though, she is often portrayed as Arthur's enemy during his reign. Thus, her character is remarkably inconsistent throughout the Arthurian saga, sometimes described as evil, sometimes as benevolent; somtimes ugly, sometimes beautiful. When she is not a character in a story, she is sometimes mentioned as a metaphorical or mythical figure.

She first appears in Geoffrey of Monmouth's *Vita Merlini* as the queen of the Island of Apples (Avalon), to which Arthur's body is borne after Camlann. Described as beautiful, she is said to have shape-shifting and healing abilities. She has nine sisters including Moronoe, Mazoe, Gliten, Glitonea, Gliton, Tyronoe, and Thitis. Geoffrey, however, does not name her as Arthur's sister.

Morgan does not appear in Geoffrey's *Historia*, nor in Wace's *Roman de Brut*. Layamon includes a variation of her name, ARGANTE, as the elven queen who takes Arthur's body to Avalon. As it is unlikely that Layamon was influenced by Geoffrey's *Vita*, both of these stories can be taken as examples of a widely-held Welsh or Breton oral tradition. Either Chrétien de Troyes or Etienne de Rouen is the first to name her as Arthur's sister. In Chrétien's *Erec*, she is, as in Geoffrey, the ruler of Avalon, and she has a lover named Guinguemar. Her magical healing ointment heals Erec and Yvain in their respective romances. Chrétien does not demonstrate a dependence on the earlier texts, suggesting, again, a wide profusion of her character in oral legend.

In between these early accounts and the Vulgate Cycle are a smattering of contradictory appearances in various French romances, few of which contribute anything meaningful to the evolution of her character. Wolfram von Eschenbach (who, through a reversal of her traditional name, calls her TERDELASCHOYE of Feimurgan) has her as the wife of Mazadan and an ancestor of Arthur. Ulrich von Zatzikhoven's *Lanzelet* features a water fairy who raises Lancelot from infancy. Though not named as "Morgan," the fairy is said to be the mother of Mabuz, probably identical to Mabon son of Modron in Welsh legend. Morgan may have therefore once been the same character as the LADY OF THE LAKE, a role which she is given in *Arthour and Merlin*. She is first mentioned as the mother of Yvain in a minor French romance called *Tyolet*, and she does not assume the role again until the Post-Vulgate *Suite du Merlin*. However, her counterpart, Modron, is named as Owain's mother in Welsh legend.

As with a great many of characters, the Vulgate Cycle is the first group of texts to give Morgan le Fay a complete story, starting with her birth as the daughter of Igerne. Her father is not named. He was most likely Gorlois, Igerne's first husband, but at one point Morgan is called a bastard. Nentres of Garlot took her into his care when her father died, and he assigned her to a nunnery, where she learned to read, write, heal, and interpret the stars. During Arthur's Saxon wars, she met Merlin and increased her knowledge of the magical arts through his teaching. Eventually, she became the lover of Guinevere's cousin, Guiomar. Guinevere ended their affair when she learned of it, causing Morgan's subsequent hatred for Arthur and his knights. Her hate was intensified by her own love or lust for Lancelot, who would have nothing to do with her. She created the Valley of No Return, which entrapped a number of Arthur's warriors; imprisoned Lancelot on three separate occasions and tried to trick Arthur's court into thinking he was dead; and sent hints of Lancelot's affair with Guinevere to Arthur. In the end, however, she dutifully takes Arthur's body from the battlefield of Salisbury without any explanation for her change of heart.

The *Suite du Merlin*, the other Post-Vulgate romances, and the Prose *Tristan* add and change the following facts: She married King Urien, and she had a son by him named Yvain. She later tried to murder Urien but was stopped by her son. Merlin fell in love with her. After she learned Merlin's magic, however, she scorned him and threatened him with death if ever came near her again. In addition to her other plots against Arthur, she made a counterfeit of Excalibur and its scabbard, giving the original to her lover, Sir Accalon of Gaul, while returning the fake one to Arthur. She then arranged for Arthur and Accalon to meet in combat, and it was only through the intervention of Nimue (the Lady of the Lake) that Arthur survived. Afterwards, Morgan managed to throw Excalibur's scabbard into a lake. She sent a mantle to Arthur that would have burned him to cinders had he put it on, but Arthur made her unfortunate servant don it instead. She also sent a magical chastity horn to Arthur hoping to reveal Guinevere's adultery. It was from Morgan that Mordred learned of the affair between Lancelot and Guinevere. She kidnapped Tristan and made him carry an insulting shield depicting Guinevere's infidelity at one of Arthur's tournaments. Later, she sent a poisoned lance to Mark, which Mark used to kill Tristan. She also plotted with Mark to destroy Alexander the Orphan, who for a time become Morgan's prisoner. She had a number of lovers, including Helians, Kaz, Gui, and Corrant. Despite her evil deeds, she again bears her brother's body away from the last battlefield for healing.

Malory's tales are derived primarily from the Vulgate, and he adds only the confirmation of her parentage by Igerne and Gorlois, giving her two sisters named Morgause and Elaine. In *Sir Gawain and the Green Knight* it is revealed that the Green Knight's visit to Arthur's court is yet another of Morgan's plots to distress Arthur. In the French tale of *Huon de Bordeaux*, she has a son with Julius Caesar named Huon, and in *La Bataille de Loquifer*, she has a son with the hero Renoart named Corbon. In Italian romance, she has a daughter named Pulzella Gaia, the Lady of the Lake is presented as her sister, and Uther Pendragon is her father. Some texts have her living on Sicily, in a castle called Montegibel.

Consequent of the growth of her fame, Morgan appears in a number of non-Arthurian or quasi-Arthurian texts as the mother, sister, or benefactress of various characters. [*GeoffVM*, *ChretienE*, *Contin2*, *Wolfram*, *Tyolet*, *VulgLanc*, *VulgMort*, *VulgMer*, *Bataille*, *ProsTris*, *PostMer*, *PostQuest*, *PostMort*, *Arthour*, *Huon*, *Malory*]

MORGAN[3] THE BLACK

One of Arthur's sons in Rauf de Boun's *Petit Brut*. He was Arthur's favorite. His brothers were Adeluf III and Patrick the Red. [*ProsBrut*]

MORGAN[4] THE WISE [*Morgue*]

A wizard who created a jar of magical ointment that was used by the Lady of Norison to heal the insane Sir Yvain in Chrétien's *Yvain*, the Norse *Ivens Saga*, and the medieval tale of *Ywain and Gawain*. Chrétien and *Ivens* call Morgan a female, but the *Ywain* mentions Morgan as a male. Chrétien, the originator of the character, probably had MORGAN LE FAY in mind. [*ChretienY*, *Ivens*, *Ywain*]

MORGAN[5] TUDD

Arthur's chief physician in the Welsh *Geraint*. He treated Arthur's warriors, including Edern (Yder) and Geraint. The author may have simply confused the gender of MORGAN LE FAY. [*Geraint*]

MORGANOR

In *Arthour and Merlin*, an illegitimate son of King Urien. He was the heir to his father's land of Gorre. Yvain was his brother. [*Arthour*]

MORGANORE[1]

A king killed by King Ban of Benoic at the battle of Bedegraine. [*Malory*]

MORGANORE[2]

Knight of the Round Table who was defeated outside Camelot by Tristan. [*Malory*]

MORGANORE[3]

An ally of King Urien of Gorre. He joined Urien in an invasion of King Leodegan's Carmelide, but was repelled by Arthur. [*TennIK*]

MORGAN'S CHAPEL

A chapel, named after MORGAN LE FAY, on the path to the Valley of No Return. [*VulgLanc*]

MORGANT

An Arthurian warrior in Welsh legend. He was the father of Rhyawdd. A Morgant (Morcant) is listed in Nennius as a late sixth century northern king who battled the Saxons with Urien. He is given the title "the Wealthy" or "the Generous." A Welsh Triad calls him one of the three "red ravishers" of Britain; a separate Welsh source tells us that his chariot had the magical ability of immediate transportation. [*Culhwch*, *Triads*, *Dream*]

MORGAUSE [*Morgawse*]

Arthur's half-sister with whom, in Malory's *Le Morte Darthur*, Arthur engages in a brief affair, producing Mordred. As Arthur's sister, and as the mother of Gawain, Gaheris, Aggravain, Gareth, and Mordred, she replaces ANNA, found in Geoffrey of Monmouth, and BELISENT, in *Arthour and Merlin*. Her character is not named in the Vulgate and Post-Vulgate Cycles. The earliest occurrence of her name, Orcades or MORCADES, is found in the First Continuation of Chrétien's *Perceval*, and is a variation of ORKNEY, of which Morgause is generally given as queen.

Her parents are usually named as Gorlois and Igerne. When her widowed mother re-married Uther Pendragon, Morgause married King Lot of Lothian and had several children including Gawain. Her sisters were Morgan le Fay and Elaine. Morgause's husband went to war with Arthur at the beginning of Arthur's reign, but was defeated. Shortly after this defeat, Morgause visited Arthur in his bedchamber and conceived Mordred. (Arthur had been ignorant of Morgause's identity, and of the fact that she was his half-sister.) Eventually, her husband was slain and all her children departed to take service at Arthur's court. She began an affair with Lamorat, the son of King Pellinore, who was a family enemy. When her sons found her in bed with Lamorat, Gaheris killed her. [*Malory*]

MORGUAN

One of Arthur's castles, situated near the city of Cardigan. [*Contin4*]

MORGUENETE

A maiden who served Morgan le Fay. [*Prophecies*]

MORHOLT¹ [*Amurat, Amoroldo, Marhaus, Moraunt, Morold, Morolt*]

An Irish giant or knight who appears in the Tristan legends. He was the uncle or brother of Isolde. His father is called Dilianfer in *La Tavola Ritonda* and Marhalt in Malory. He demanded a tribute from Cornwall—either of money or children—prompting King Mark of Cornwall to summon a young Tristan to fight in Cornwall's defense. In the Prose *Tristan*, he champions his brother-in-law, King Anguish of Ireland, for the tribute, while in other texts he seems to be acting on his own behalf. Mark, unable to find another champion, knighted and sent the untried Sir Tristan to battle on the Isle of Saint Samson. Tristan and Morholt fought for a day, before Tristan's sword finally stuck in Morholt's head and a piece broke off, mortally wounding him. Later, Morholt's sister, the queen of Ireland (called Isolde or Lotta), matched the broken piece with Sir "Tantrist's" sword and swore vengeance against Tristan, but was dissuaded by her family. *Tristan* tells us that Tristan later took Sir Morholt's vacant seat at the Round Table. In French romance, Morholt has a son named Golistant; Italian romance re-names the same son Amoroldo.

The Post-Vulgate *Suite du Merlin* and Malory's *Le Morte Darthur* give Morholt an entire series of adventures prior to his battle with Tristan, claiming that Morholt was a Knight of the Round Table. Morholt joined Gawain and Yvain during their temporary banishment from Camelot, and enjoyed a number of adventures in the Forest of Arroy. He defeated the Duke of the South Marches, who hated Arthur, killed an evil giant named Taulas, rescued a lady in the wood of Plessis, and was imprisoned at the Rock of Maidens until rescued by Gaheris. [*ChretienE, Beroul, Eilhart, Wolfram, Gottfried, Palamedes, ProsTris, PostMer, Malory*]

MORHOLT²

Grandson of the above Morholt. He became the king of Ireland. [*Palamedes, ProsTris*]

MORIEN [*Moriaen*]

The title character of a thirteenth-century Dutch romance. In his original inception, Morien seems to have been the son of Perceval, but the author of the existing text—apparently in light of Perceval's advertised virginity in the Vulgate romances—makes him the son of Aglovale, Perceval's brother. A huge Moor, Morien was born when his father visited his mother, a Moorish princess, in an Arabian kingdom. Aglovale promised to return to her but did not. When Morien came of age, he embarked on a search for his father. His quest led him into contact with Lancelot and Gawain, who at Arthur's behest were searching for Perceval. After saving Gawain's life, Morien reunited his parents and saw his father crowned king of his homeland. Aspects of Morien's story recall FEIREFIZ from Wolfram's *Parzival*. [*Morien*]

MORIN

A giant who invaded the Savage Realm and was killed by Hector, a famous knight of the "Brown" lineage. [*Palamedes*]

MORMONDA

A castle in the valley of Servage ruled by the giant Nabon the Black. Nabon imprisoned many good knights there. They were eventually liberated by Tristan. [*Palamedes*]

MORNING STAR

The first knight defeated by Gareth in his quest to liberate the lady Lyones. Found in Tennyson, he corresponds to the BLUE KNIGHT in Malory. [*TennIK*]

MORO BATTLE LEADER

A Welsh warrior who owned a great horse named Du. This horse was needed by Culhwch for the hunting of Twrch Trwyth. [*Culhwch*]

MOROCCO

In Wolfram's *Parzival*, it is said that Perceval's father Gahmuret had adventures and won honor in this African kingdom. [*Wolfram*]

MÓRODD

A version of MARK found in the Icelandic *Saga af Tristram ok Ísodd*. He was the son of King Philippus and Queen Philippia of England. When he became king after his parents' deaths, his sister Blenzibly (Later Tristan's mother) revolted against him. The short rebellion ended in a truce. Like the early King Mark, he was a noble king, and gave his nephew and wife every benefit of the doubt (and even offered Isolde to Tristan) before he banished them to a cave. He later gave his kingdom to Kalegras, Tristan's son, and lived out the rest of his life at a hermitage near Jerusalem. Kalegras and his queen, Lilja, named their second son after him. [*SagaTI*]

MORONOE

One of Morgan le Fay's sisters in Geoffrey of Monmouth's *Vita Merlini*. [*GeoffVM*]

MOROVEUS

Arthur's Duke of Cornwall in the story of *Meriadoc*. [*Historia*]

MORRIGAN

An Irish warrior goddess who had the ability to shapeshift. Her character seems to have been combined with the Welsh Modron to creat MORGAN LE FAY.

MORROIS [*Morois, Morris, Morroiz*]

A lush forest in Cornwall which serves as the location of several adventures in the Tristan stories. Tristan and Isolde lived there for a time, at the Wise Damsel's Rock, after an escape from execution at Mark's court. Isolde eventually went back to Mark, through the hermit Orgin's mediation (in Beroul) or Mark's kidnapping (in the Prose *Tristan*). Tristan roamed the forest of Morrois during his period of madness. In another adventure, King Mark sent Kay and Gaheris into the forest for an "adventure"—in truth, Mark intended to kill them by the Perilous Lake, but he was unsuccessful. Morrois has been identified with locations in Cornwall and Scotland. [*Beroul, ProsTris, Malory*]

MORTAL [*Marte*]

An evil castle. Its king was Perceval's maternal uncle, but the king's family disavowed him because of his evil ways. The king attacked the Castle of the Galleys and the Grail Castle. The latter belonged to his own brother, the Fisher King. The king fled from Perceval at the Castle of the Galleys. He seized the Grail Castle upon the Fisher King's death, but Perceval re-conquered it. Beholding his own defeat, the King of the Castle Mortal threw himself off the Grail Castle's battlements to his death. [*Perlesvaus*]

MORTAL LAY

A lay composed by Tristan after he discovered Kahedin's love for Isolde. Tristan soon went insane. [*ProsTris*]

MORVID[1]

According to Geoffrey of Monmouth, a king of Britain in the third century BC. He was the son of King Danius and Tangustela, a concubine. "He would have been of highest renown for his prowess had he not given way to exceeding great cruelty, for no man would he spare his wrath, but would slay him on the spot had he any weapon at hand." During his reign, Britain was invaded by Flemmings. Morvid defeated them and brutally executed them. He died fighting a ferocious sea monster who had attacked the island. Morvid had five sons named Gorbonian, Arthgallo, Elidur, Iugenius, and Peredur. Gorbonian succeeded him. [*GeoffHR*]

MORVID[2] [*Mordup, Moreoint, Morice, Morud, Morvith*]

The earl of Gloucester under Arthur. He led a battalion of soldiers in the war against Rome. As commander of the reserve forces at the battle of Soissons, he brought his troops in at a key time, allowing Arthur's forces to finish Lucius's army for good. [*GeoffHR, Wace, Layamon*]

MORWEN

Wife of Ivor and foster-mother of Meriadoc (later the King of Wales) and Orwen. With her husband, she brought the children into hiding when their evil uncle targeted them for assassination. The children were kidnapped from her care, but she was later reunited with them. [*Historia*]

MORYANS OF THE CASTLE OF MAIDENS

A knight Arthur's court who fought at the Battle of Bedegraine. [*Malory*]

MOSES [*Moy(s)(s)és, *Moÿs*]

A son of Simeon and relative of Joseph of Arimathea. Following Joseph to Britain, Moses put on a pious facade, but was in truth guilty of lechery and fornication. He was exposed when Joseph's followers were divided (either at the Grail Table, or at the English Channel). Later, he brashly decided to sit at the Grail Table's Perilous Seat and was either swallowed by the earth (in Robert de Boron) or carried away by hands of fire (in the Vulgate version). In the latter version, he was placed in the Perilous Palace in the forest of Darnantes, where he was destined to burn until freed by Galahad during the Grail Quest. [*RobertBorJ, VulgLanc, VulgEst, PostQuest*]

MOTE OF MARK

A sixth-century hill fort on the southern coast of Scotland with an uncertain connection to King Mark of the Tristan legend. [*Topography*]

MOTLEY KNIGHT

An ally of the evil King Marin the Jealous. He attacked Gawain on Marin's behalf, but was defeated. [*Perlesvaus*]

MOURNFUL MOUND

The hill inhabited by the Black Serpent of the Barrow. Peredur traveled there and killed the beast. [*Peredur*]

MOUREE, THE

A land from which Emperors Filimenis of Constantinople and Thereus of Rome summoned allies during their respective wars against Arthur. Thereus's ally was called King Salatre of the Mouree. The Mouree was the medieval name for Peloponnesus. [*Floriant, Claris*]

MOYDAS

One of many Saxon kings to invade northern Britain in the early days of Arthur's reign. Gawain killed him at the battle of Cambenic. [*VulgMer*]

MUIRCHETACH MAC ERCA

A king who, according to historian John Morris, ruled in southern Ireland from 482 to 532. Morris thought him a contemporary of Arthur, and the dates do seem to fit.

MULE WITHOUT A BRIDLE

Title figure in a late twelfth-century comic French verse romance by Paien de Maisières. The bridal that the mule was missing was magic, and whoever held it held the rights to a kingdom. One sister had seized the bridle from another, and the disinherited sister brought the bridle-less mule to Arthur's court, seeking redress. Kay set out on the quest but failed; Gawain was successful in retrieving the object. Heinrich von dem Türlin adapted the story in *Diu Crône*, giving the sisters the names Sgoidamur and Amurfina. [*Paien*]

MUNSALVÆSCHE ("Wild Mountain")

The GRAIL CASTLE in Wolfram's *Parzival*, inhabited by Anfortas (Wolfram's Fisher King) and the Grail Family. It was located in the land known as Terre de Salvæsche, or "wild land." It was known for producing excellent horses, which were ridden by the Templars, the castle's guardians. One of these horses, Gringolet, was eventually owned by Gawain. Besides the Templars, Munsalvæsche was defended by the simple fact that it was almost impossible to find. Perceval journeyed to Munsalvæsche twice. He completed the quest the second time and became the new Grail King. In German, the castle would be called "Wildenberg," and internal evidence suggests that Wolfram wrote in a German castle called Wildenberg, in the Odenwald. [*Wolfram*]

MUNTORI

A land in an unknown location where Perceval's uncle Galoes was killed in the service of his lady. [*Wolfram*]

MUNTROGIN

The capital of the land of Averre, ruled by King Garel, one of Arthur's knights, and Queen Laudamie. [*PleierG*]

MURGALANT OF TREBEHAM

One of the few Saxon kings to survive the battle of Clarence, where they were crushed by Arthur. [*VulgMer*]

MUSTACHA

In Fielding's *The Tragedy of Tragedies*, a maiden at Arthur's court who loved Doodle, one of Arthur's courtiers. She killed either Doodle or her fellow maidservant, Cleora, and was in turn slain by Arthur. [*Fielding*]

MUSTENSAR [*Mustansar, Ofustesar*]

The King of Africa who was subject to Emperor Lucius, and was called upon to join Lucius in the war against Arthur. He was killed at the battle of Soissons by Arthur's noble Sir Guitard. [*GeoffHR, Wace, Layamon*]

MUTE KNIGHT

The name given to Peredur after he swore not to speak to any Christian man until the lady Angharad Golden Hand professed her love for him. She eventually did so, and he was able to speak to his comrades again. [*Peredur*]

MUTE MAIDEN

In the Post-Vulgate, a maiden of Guinevere's service who led the newly-knighted Perceval from his seat at the Table of Less-Valued Knights to the seat adjoining the Round Table's Perilous Seat., proclaiming it his own. She had been mute before this episode, and died (at her own request) soon afterwards. The same sort of maiden appears unnamed in Chrétien de Troyes's *Perceval*, as CUNNEWARE in Wolfram von Eschenbach's *Parzival*, and as LEDE in Heinrich von dem Türlin's *Diu Crône*. The scene is repeated in Malory, but the maiden is again unnamed. In some tales of Lancelot, a similar "mute" maiden first speaks to Lancelot upon his arrival to Arthur's court, foretelling his greatness. [*PostMer, Tavola*]

MWRHETH

Father of Arthur's warrior Blathaon. [*Dream*]

MYCENAE

An ancient city in the southern part of Greece. Alexander's warrior Nebunal came from this city. [*ChretienC*]

MYCHIN

A knight in the service of Lord Golagros, Arthur's opponent in the Middle Scots tale of *Golagros and Gawain*. [*Golagros*]

MYLES OF THE LAUNDIS

A knight who was engaged to Alyne, Pellinore's daughter. He was mortally wounded by Sir Lorayne the Savage. Alyne screamed for help, but King Pellinore, passing by, was intent in a quest and would not stop. Later, Pellinore found Myles and Alyne dead. [*Malory*]

MYLIS

A knight slain by King Pellinore at Pellinore's forest pavilion. Mylis's squire, Girflet, brought his body to King Arthur's court at Caerleon and pleaded with the king to bury Mylis and to make Girflet a knight so that he might avenge his master's death. [*Malory*]

MYNNEU

A mountain in the Alpine Range where Arthur fought a decisive battle against the Romans, killing Lucius. After this battle, he received word of Mordred's treachery and had to return to Britain. Mentioned in Welsh texts, Mynneu takes the place of SOISSONS in the chronicles. [*Triads*]

MYNWYEDIG

Father of Constantine the Cornishman. [*Culhwch*]

MYNYDD AMANW

An British mountain that was the site of a battle between Arthur's warriors and the boar Twrch Trwyth and his piglets. Two of the piglets—Twrch Llawin and Gwys—were killed before Twrch Trwyth continued his flight to Dyffryn Amanw. [*Culhwch*]

MYNYDD BANNAWG ("Horned Mount")

A mountain in Britain on which two oxen lived: Nynnyaw and Peibyaw. As one of his tasks, the warrior Culhwch had to travel to Mynydd Baannawg and capture the oxen. [*Culhwch*]

MYNYW

The Welsh name for Menevia, later known as SAINT DAVID'S.

MYR

One of Arthur's warriors and huntsmen in Welsh legend. [*Culhwch*]

MYRDDIN

The Welsh bard and enchanter who was the probable source of Geoffrey of Monmouth's MERLIN. He is identified also with LAILOKEN. There are actually two characters in Welsh legend who bear this name. One was a mad prophet, and the other was the son of Morfran and a bard at Arthur's court.

Myrddin's story is related through a series of early Welsh verses, collectively called the Myrddin Poems. He served a king named Gwenddoleu in a war against King Rhydderch of Cumbria. At the battle of Arfderydd, he went insane after he accidentally slew the son of his sister, Gwenddydd. Thereafter, he roamed a northern forest, spouting mysterious prophecies of Britain's future and of his own death.

As to his name, one theory argues that it began with the Roman stronghold of Maridunum in Wales, which means "sea fortress." In time, Maridunum was altered and corrupted into "Merddin" or "Myrddin." With it's original name lost, a *Caer* ("city") was placed in front of the name. Since *Caer Myrddin* would have signified "City of Myrddin," people assumed that "Myrddin" was a personal name, and the Welsh began telling stories of a certain prophetic bard named Myrddin who roamed the forests of northern England and southern Scotland. [*Myrddin, Annales, Triads*]

MYRDDIN'S PRECINCT

According to Welsh legend, the first name of the island of Britain. It was conquered, and became known as the Island of Honey. Ostensibly, the name would seem to refer to MYRDDIN or MERLIN, but one would assume that the earliest name of the island would necessarily precede the sixth-century Myrddin. This suggests that, in origin, Myrddin may have been something more than a warrior or mad prophet. [*Triads*]

MYREOT

An Arthurian knight. [*Golagros*]

MYSENES [*Micenés*]

One of the many Saxon kings to invade northern Britain at the beginning of Arthur's reign. [*VulgMer*]

N

NABAOR

A warrior rescued by Gawain. Nabaor had lived in the realm of Illyricum until the barbarian King Milocrates kidnapped him. When a young Gawain and a Roman fleet landed on Milocrates' island, Nabaor helped them to defeat the king and to take over the island. [*DeOrtu*]

NABIGAN OF THE ROCK

A malevolent lord. He killed King Marin the Jealous and tried to deprive Meliot, Marin's son, of his lands. He also stole the holy Circle of Gold, which belonged to Perceval. Gawain reclaimed the Circle and killed Nabigan in combat. Nabigan's brother, Anurez, later caused trouble for Gawain and Arthur. [*Perlesvaus*]

NABIN

A landless knight in King Claudas's army. He was captured by King Bagdemagus during Claudas's second war with Arthur. [*VulgLanc*]

NABON[1]

A Knight of the Round Table who participated in the Grail Quest. [*ProsTris*]

NABON[2] THE BLACK

One of several giants killed by Tristan. Nabon ruled Glait or Mormanda Castle on the island of Servage, and he hated all of Arthur's knights. He had killed several of them, including Mennon the Small, a cousin of Sir Lamorat. As the result of a shipwreck, Lamorat washed upon Nabon's island just before a tournament which Nabon had declared in honor of his newly-knighted son, Nathan. Determined to slay Nabon, Lamorat entered the tournament, but, although he fared best of the visiting knights, Nabon nearly killed him. Tristan, who had also come to the tournament, stepped in just in time, and killed both Nabon and his son. Tristan awarded Nabon's island to the noble Sir Seguarades. [*ProsTris, Palamedes, Malory*]

NABOR[1]

An old knight in Nascien's service. He betrayed his lord and nearly killed him, but Nascien prayed, and God struck Nabon dead. [*VulgEst*]

NABOR[2]

The son of King Nascor and brother of Aglinda. The devil tricked Nabor into believing that Aglinda was not his real sister, and made Nabor want to rape Aglinda. When he attempted to do so by a spring, Aglinda prayed and Nabor fell dead. In memory of the episode, the spring was called the Spring of the Virgin, and it was enchanted to paralyze visiting non-virginal knights. [*PostQuest*]

NABOR[3]

A giant who tried to steal some lands from a lord named Melianus. The Good Knight Without Fear championed Melianus and killed Nabor. [*Palamedes*]

NABOR[4]

A knight defeated in combat by Claris and Laris. Claris and Laris were helping Sir Caradoc protect his paramour from King Ladas, Sir Nabor's liege. [*Claris*]

NABUDANS

A knight who found Sir Floriant (an Arthurian knight) and Florete (Floriant's wife) asleep in a forest. Desiring Florete, he awoke her with a kiss and tried to abduct her. Her cries wakened Floriant, who conquered Nabudans and sent him to Arthur's court. In *Claris et Laris*, while serving Lord Ladas, Nabudans is killed in combat by Laris. [*Floriant, Claris*]

NABUNAL OF THARMADAISE

The seneschal of Lambale. He first served King Amant, Arthur's enemy, and then King Gosengos, Amant's son. Gosengos allied with Arthur, and Nabunal ended up serving in Arthur's army in battles against the Saxons and the Romans. [*VulgMer, Livre*]

NABUR[1]

The seneschal of King Tholomer of Babylonia, who Nabur served in the war against King Evalach (Mordrains) of Sarras. Evalach defeated Nabur in the battle of La Choine but refrained from killing him at the urging of Seraphe (Nascien). [*VulgEst*]

NABUR[2] THE UNRULY

Mordred's foster-father. Mordred, as an infant, washed up on Nabur's island after Arthur sent him adrift at sea. A fisherman found the child and brought him to Nabur for rearing. Nabur was also the natural father of Sir Sagremor. [*PostMer*]

NABURZADAN

One of the twelve sons of Bron in the Prose *Tristan*. His brothers included Alain the Large and Sador. He fell in love with Chelinde, Sador's wife, and raped her. Sador killed him. [*ProsTris*]

NADIEN

An evil knight from Benoic who served King Claudas against Arthur. [*VulgLanc*]

NADOR

A knight defeated, with his cousin Daton, by Claris and Laris after he besieged Queen Blanche. [*Claris*]

NADUS

King of Syria and one of the allies of Emperor Thereus of Rome. Nadus joined Thereus in a war against Arthur, and he was slain in battle against Claris and Laris. [*Claris*].

NAF

Father of Arthur's warriors Atlendor and Gwenwynwyn. [*Culhwch*]

NAHODOPÉS

A Saxon warrior who, under King Aminaduc, fought against Arthur's forces at the battle of Vambieres. [*Livre*]

NAMANT OF THE PINE

A knight who defeated hundreds of knights at the ford he guarded. He was finally overcome by the Good Knight Without Fear. [*Palamedes*]

NAMPETENIS

Tristan's slayer in Eilhart von Oberge's *Tristrant*. He fought for Count Riole of Nantes in a war against King Havelin (Tristan's father-in-law). Havelin's son Kahedins fell in love with Nampetenis's wife, Gariole. One day, while Nampetenis was out hunting, Kahedins—with Tristan's help—sneaked into Nampetenis's stronghold and enjoyed a pleasant afternoon with Gariole. When Nampetenis found out, he chased after the two warriors with a squad of knights, killed Kahedins, and mortally wounded Tristan with a poisoned blade. He may be the same character as Gottfried's NAUTENIS. [*Eilhart*]

NAMTERSBORG

According to the Norse *Tristrams Saga*, a land conquered by Tristan and Kahedins. [*TrisSaga*]

NAMUR

In Wirnt von Grafenberg's *Wigalois*, an African land ruled by Prince Lion. Gawain's son Wigalois took control of the land when he defeated Lion in a war. The Belgian province may be the source of the name, but Wirnt specifically places it in Heathendom. [*Wirnt*]

NANTES [*Nante*]

A city near the west coast of France, on the Loire river. Wolfram names it as Arthur's court in Brittany. Rulers of Nantes in other texts include Lac and Erec (Chrétien's *Erec*), Riole (Eilhart's *Tristrant*), Rigolin (Gottfried's *Tristan*), Caradoc (First Continuation of *Perceval*), and Hoel (the Vulgate *Merlin*). In the Erec romances, its capital is Carnant, a name which some later authors give to the land itself. [*ChretienE, Contin1, Wolfram, Eilhart, PleierG*]

NAPINS [*Napin*]

A Saxon fleet commander. He was one of only a few Saxons to survive the battle of Clarence, where they were crushed by Arthur. [*VulgMer, Arthour*]

NARANT

Count of Ukerland and father of Bernout de Riviers. He was in the service of King Clamadeu of Iseterre, and he was killed when fighting at Beaurepaire against the army of Perceval and Condwiramurs. Upon his death, Bernout inherited Ukerlant. [*Wolfram*]

NARBADUC

An early pagan ruler of Dolorous Guard. His body was entombed there, but was destroyed when Joseph of Arimathea brought Christianity to Britain. Lancelot used his former tomb to inter his friend Galehaut. [*VulgLanc*[

NARBAOC [*Marboars, Narbouanrs*]

The king of the Mill Castle. He sponsored a tournament in which Gawain and Hector participated. [*VulgLanc*]

NARBONNE

A city in Gaul where the infant Gawain was taken by a group of merchants. Gawain's mother, Anna, had given Gawain to the merchants to avoid problems at court with his legitimacy. Landing their ship near the city, the merchants left Gawain and their wealth unguarded on board, where both were taken by a poor fisherman named Viamundus. [*DeOrtu*]

NARON [*Aaron*]

A knight and a follower of Joseph of Arimathea. He greeted Mordrain when he first came to Britain. [*VulgEst*]

NARPUS [*Nappas, Narpos*]

An ancestor of Lancelot and Galahad. In the Vulgate Cycle, he is called the son of Celidoine and grandson of Nascien, but Malory skips Celidoine and makes him the son of Nascien. Narpus's son was also named Nascien. He ruled North Wales. [*VulgQuest, VulgEst, Malory*]

NARRAN [*Naram*]

An knight who provided intelligence on King Rions when Rions went to war with Arthur. [*PostMer, Malory*]

NARROW BORDERLAND [**Estroit Marche, Narrow March, Strait Marches*]

A castle and land owned by King Belinant of South Wales. It was invaded by Saxons near the beginning of Arthur's reign. Its lord, who presumably held his fief from Belinant, was the brother of King Caradoc. He was attacked frequently by the rulers of North Wales and Cambenic, and by the King with a Hundred Knights. Because of the frequent attacks, the land around the Narrow Borderland was laid waste. The lord instituted a custom by which any knight who entered the castle had to spend the night and fight in the morning against the castle's enemies. Arthur's knight Hector arrived when the castle was being attacked by the King with a Hundred Knights' seneschal, Marganor. Following the custom, Hector fought and defeated Marganor. The lord of the castle wanted Hector to marry his daughter, but Hector left for further adventure. The Narrow Borderland is also named as the home of Sir Floridas, a knight in Arthur's service. [*LancLac, VulgLanc, VulgMer, Livre, Malory*]

NARROW CASTLE [*Chastel E(s)troit*]

A fortress in North Wales where Dinadan had to defend himself against a charge of murder. Brunor the Black, Dinadan's brother, championed Dinadan and acquitted him. The castle seems to be ruled by the Duke of Haudebourc, who presided over the combat. [*ProsTris*]

NARROW WAY

A castle in northern Britain besieged by Saxons in the early days of Arthur's reign. [*VulgMer*]

NARROW WOOD [*Gaut Destroit*]

The castle belonging to the MAIDEN OF THE NARROW WOOD, who is sometimes given the proper name Lore of Branlant. According to the Vulgate *Merlin*, Waldin of the Fearsome Vale conquered it, but the *Livre d'Artus* describes how Gawain successfully defended it from Waldin. [*VulgMer, Livre*]

NASCIEN[1] [*Naciamis, Nacien(s), Nacyanus, Nancien(s), Nasiens, Natianus, Natiien, Necienzo*]

The baptismal name of SERAPHE, the Duke of Orberica converted by Joseph of Arimathea. His sister was named Sarrasinte, and his wife was Flegetine. He had been estranged from his brother-in-law, King Evalach (later Mordrain) of Sarras, but Joseph reconciled them, and Nascien joined Evalach in a war against King Tholomer of Babylonia. Mordrain and Nascien won the war, thanks to their conversion to Christianity. Afterwards, Nascien was blinded for gazing at the Grail, but an angel restored his sight with some of the blood from the Bleeding Lance. After Joseph of Arimathea's departure from Sarras, Nascien and his son Celidoine were imprisoned by a traitorous nobleman named Galafre. God removed Nascien from the prison and stuck him in the middle of the ocean, on the Turning Isle. He had several adventures at sea. In one of them, he boarded the Ship of Solomon and drew the Sword with the Strange Hangings to kill a giant. God punished him for drawing the forbidden sword by wounding him through the thighs. Nascien eventually joined Joseph of Arimathea's followers in Britain, where he died. His son Celidoine became King of North Wales. His descendants included Lancelot, Bors, and Galahad. [*VulgQuest, VulgEst, PostMer, Malory*]

NASCIEN[2]

Son of Narpus, great-grandson of Nascien[1], and father of Alain the Large. [*VulgQuest, VulgEst, Malory*]

NASCIEN[3] [*Na(n)cien*]

A Knight of the Round Table who became a hermit. According to the Vulgate *Merlin*, he was the son of Bron, the first Fisher King, and Havingues (Joseph of Arimathea's sister), which means, to be living in Arthur's time, that he had an *extremely* long life span. His brothers included Alan and Joshua. The *Livre d'Artus* more reasonably makes him a descendant of the first Nasicen. His prowess helped Arthur defeat King Rions at the battle of Aneblayse, the Saxons at the battles of Clarence and Vambieres, and King Claudas at the battle of Trebe. He traded his armor for a robe after he witnessed the Grail carried by a white stag. He retired to a hermitage and became a sage for Arthur's knights during the Grail Quest. He may have tutored Galahad. He was visited by Gawain and Hector, and he told them both that they would not achieve the Grail because of their sins. [*VulgQuest, VulgMer, Livre, PostMer, PostQuest, Malory*]

NASCIEN[4]

In Welsh legend, the son of the King of Denmark, and one of Arthur's three "Royal Knights." He is described as wise, handsome, and skilled at arms. Likely, Welsh storytellers simply borrowed the name from the Grail stories. [*Triads*]

NASTOR

Son of Salandres and brother of Menastide, Dinisordres, Gogonne, and Aristes. Nastor, his father, and all of his brothers were defeated in combat by Perceval. They went to Arthur's court as prisoners. [*Contin3*]

NATALON

King of Syria who served Emperor Filimenis of Constantinople. He joined Filimenis in a brief war against Arthur. [*Floriant*]

NATANLEOD [*Natanliodus*]

A "king of the Britons" who, according to the *Anglo-Saxon Chronicle*, was slain in a battle against the Saxons Cerdic and Cynric in 508. The site of the battle, Netley, was named after him. He would have been a contemporary of Arthur. Henry of Huntingdon's chronicle makes him a general in the service of Uther Pendragon. We learn from Hector Boece that Natanleod had no miliatry experience, and that Uther was mentally ill when he appointed Nataleod commander of his armies. Because of Natanleod's incompetence, much of Britain fell to the Saxons. [*Anglo, Henry, Boece*]

NATHAN

Son of the giant Nabon the Black, slain by Tristan in the Prose *Tristan* and by the Good Knight Without Fear of Estrangorre in *Palamedes*. [*ProsTris, Palamedes*]

NAUBE [*Maube*]

A forest which served as the home of the hermit Seraphe in Joseph of Arimathea's time. [*VulgEst*]

NAUTENIS

The ruler of Hante in Gottfried's *Tristan*. He was an enemy of Duke Jovelin of Arundel, Tristan's father-in-law. With other knights, he besieged Jovelin's castle of Karke, but was defeated by Tristan. He may be the same character as Eilhart's NAMPETENIS. [*Gottfried*]

NAVARRE [*Nauerne*]

An historical area of northeast Spain and southwest France. According to both Der Pleier's *Tandereis* and the Alliterative *Morte Arthure*, it was part of Arthur's domain. [*PleierT, Allit*]

NAW ("Nine")

An Arthurian warrior who was the sun of Seithfed. His brothers included Sinnoch, Wadu, and Bedyw. He was the father of Gwenwynwyn and Fflewdwr. [*Culhwch, Dream*]

NEB ("Someone")

Son of Caw, one of twenty brothers, and one of Arthur's warriors. [*Culhwch*]

NEBEDONS

An Arthurian knight in Heinrich von dem Türlin's *Diu Crône*, resulting from a corruption of Bedoier or BEDIVERE. [*Heinrich*]

NEBUCHADNEZZAR

Wolfram says that King Nebuchadnezzar of Babylon was the maternal uncle of King Pompeius of Babylon—one of two brothers who fought with the Baruc of Baghdad and who Perceval's father Gahmuret died fighting against. If Wolfram intends to indicate the legendary King Nebuchadnezzar who ruled from 605 B.C. to 562 B.C.—and it seems he does—Pompeius must have been a truly ancient man. [*Wolfram*]

NEBUNAL OF MYCENAE

A warrior who served Alexander of Constantinople. With Alexander, he joined Arthur's service for a brief time, and fought against the traitor Angres of Windsor. [*ChretienC*]

NEFYN

Wife of Cynfarch the Old and mother of Urien and Efrddyl. Her father was named Brychan. [*Triads*]

NEILIBURZ

A knight present at the Sorgarda tournament, which Gawain won. [*Heinrich*]

NEINI THE DWARF

One of the many ladies at Arthur's court to fail a chastity test involving a goblet. [*Heinrich*]

NELOTONS

An Arthurian knight. [*Heinrich*]

NENTRES [*Nanter, Nanters, Natres, Neutres*]

King of Garlot. He first appears in the Vulgate *Merlin*, though the Didot-*Perceval*'s VIAUTRE may be the same character. Nentres married Arthur's half-sister (Blasine or Elaine) and also looked after the young Morgan le Fay. Nentres opposed Arthur's claim to the British throne and joined a rebellion against him. Nentres's son, Galescalain, opposed Nentres's revolt and took service with Arthur. Arthur defeated the rebels at the battles of Caerleon and Bedegraine, after which the rebel kings had to return home to deal with a Saxon invasion. Nentres's wife was kidnapped by the Saxons, but Gawain rescued her. After suffering several defeats at the hands of the Saxons, Nentres and the others made peace with Arthur, joined his forces, and crushed the Saxons at the battle of Clarence. Later, during Arthur's war with Rome, Nentres earned distinction by slaying King Alifatima of Spain. Arthur eventually appointed him to the Round Table. [*VulgMer, Livre, Malory*]

NEOL HANG COCK

Father of Arthur's warrior Ellylw. [*Culhwch*]

NEORANGE

A valley along the forest of Briosque in France, near the Lady of the Lake's home. [*VulgMer*]

NERBOIS

The King of Nerbois was slain by Tristan at Arthur's Leverzep tournament. [*Tavola*]

NEREJA

A maidservant of Queen Amena of Korntin in Wirnt von Grafenberg's *Wigalois*. She traveled to Arthur's court to find a champion when Korntin was invaded by King Roaz of Glois. When Arthur appointed Wigalois (Gawain's son) to the task, Nereja was furious because she thought Wigalois too young and inexperienced. As she traveled with Wigalois, however, and watched him win a number of combats, she gradually developed respect for and confidence in him. By the time they reached Roimunt (Amena's castle), Nereja was happy to present Wigalois as her champion. Her counterpart in Renaut de Bâgé's *Le Bel Inconnu* is HELIE. [*Wirnt*]

NERIOLIS

A warrior who served Alexander of Constantinople. With Alexander, he joined Arthur's service for a brief time, and fought against the traitor Angres of Windsor. [*ChretienC*]

NERIUS

A warrior who served Alexander of Constantinople. With Alexander, he joined Arthur's service for a brief time, and fought against the traitor Angres of Windsor. [*ChretienC*]

NERO

A king who was the brother of King Rions, Arthur's enemy. When King Lot of Lothian rebelled against Arthur, Nero joined him. At the battle of Tarabel, Merlin held back Lot's half of the army, and Nero was slain in combat. Arthur had him interred at the church of St. Stephen's in Camelot. [*PostMer, Malory*]

NERONEUS OF THE ISLE

A Knight of the Round Table knighted by Lancelot at the Red Castle. He guarded a bridge called the Bridge of Giants. Lancelot gave him the lands surrounding Pendragon Castle when he conquered the castle from Sir Brian of the Isles. When Lancelot and Guinevere were accused of treason, Neroneus pledged his support to Lancelot and helped him rescue Guinevere from the stake. In return for his support, Lancelot made him earl of Pardiac. [*ProsTris, Malory*]

NERTH ("Might")

One of Arthur's warriors and advisors. He was the son of Cadarn and the father of Gorasgwn. [*Culhwch, Dream*]

NERTHACH

Son of Gwawrddur Hunchback and brother of Duach, Brathach, and the lady Gwenwledyr. He was one of King Arthur's warriors in Welsh legend. According the tales, Nerthach and his brothers were "sprung from the Highlands of Hell." Nerthach was also the name of a city. [*Culhwch*]

NERVANA

A mountain on the border of Logres (Arthur's kingdom) and Lyonesse (Tristan's land). [*Tavola*]

NES

Father of Arthur's warrior Cnychwr, borrowed from the Irish character named Ness. [*Culhwch*]

NESTLING

An infant girl found by Arthur and Lancelot in an eagle's nest. She had a ruby necklace around her neck. Arthur gave the baby to Guinevere to raise, but it died in infancy. Her necklace was later awarded to Tristan as a tournament prize. [*TennIK*]

NESTOR[1] OF GANNES

Father of Bleoberis (a Knight of the Round Table) and brother of King Ban of Benoic. Blanor may have been another of his sons. Nestor killed a giant named Ceron at the Straits of Sorelois, freeing Galehaut from Ceron's prison. Galehaut built the Castle of Nestor in honor of this event. Later, Nestor and Bleoberis encountered each other unrecognized, and Bleoberis accidentally killed his father in combat. [*Palamedes, ProsTris*]

NESTOR[2] OF THE FOUNTAIN

Son of Arthur's Sir Bleoberis. [*ProsTris*]

NETAN CLOFARD

An Arthurian warrior found in Layamon's *Brut*. The name seems to have resulted from a conflation of the names Neton (NWYTHON) and CLOFAUT in Geoffrey's account. [*Layamon*]

NETHAWG

Father of Arthur's warrior Penn. [*Culhwch*]

NETOR

King of Bulgaria who served Emperor Filimenis of Constantinople. He joined Filimenis in a brief war against Arthur. His brother was named Sathan. [*Floriant*]

NEUED[1] ("Want")

Grandchild of Arthur's warrior Cyfwlch. [*Culhwch*]

NEUED[2]

Father of the warrior Tringad. [*Culhwch*]

NEUSTRIA

A former name of NORMANDY.

NEVERN [*Nyfer*]

A river in north Dyfed that empties into the Irish Sea. Arthur fought one of his battles against Twrch Trwyth there. [*Culhwch*]

NEVOIS

A location where Gawain lodged on the way to an adventure in the Kingdom of the Isles. [*Meriadeuc*]

NEW CASTLE[1]

A castle in the northern forest of Broceliande, where two young noble cousins—Galescalain and Gawain—met and decided to oppose their fathers by taking service with Arthur. [*VulgMer*]

NEW CASTLE[2]

A castle in King Clarion's Northumberland, ruled under Clarion by Minoras. [*VulgMer*]

NEW TABLE [*Tavola Nuovo]

Italian literature distinguishes between the Tavola Vecchio ("Old Table") and the Tavola Nuovo ("New Table"); that is, the Round Table fellowships commanded by Uther Pendragon and Arthur. Uther's Old Table seems to have been composed primarily of brawny, brash knights, while Arthur's New Table was known for its justice, courtliness, and virtue. [*Tavola*]

NIATAR

A son of Febus and Florine and brother of Altan, Lannor, Siraouc, and Argons. [*Palamedes*]

NICHODEMUS NOTHING

In the Elizabethan play *The Birth of Merlin*, a courtier at Aurelius Ambrosius's court. [*Birth*]

NICODEMUS [Nichodemus]

In the Gospels, a Roman soldier who helps Joseph of Arimathea remove Christ's body from the cross. This episode is recounted in Robert de Boron's *Joseph of Arimathea*. Nicodemus's own apocryphal *Gospel* inspired part of Robert de Boron's tale. *Perlesvaus* tells us that he was the progenitor of Perceval's paternal lineage. His body was kept at Kamaalot, Perceval's home, before Perceval moved it to the Grail Castle. [*RobertBor J*, *Perlesvaus*, *VulgMer*]

NICORANT[1] THE POOR

A knight loyal to Tristan, whom he assisted throughout the various trials at Mark's court. [*ProsTris*]

NICORANT[2] THE WELL-MADE

A Knight of the Round Table who embarked with the others on the Grail Quest. He was valued for his fine sword work. [*PostQuest*]

NICORAUT

A Cornish knight who raised Apollo, an ancestor of Tristan, after he had been abandoned in the forest by his step-father, Canor. When Canor discovered that Nicoraut had saved the child, he killed Nicoraut and his wife, Madule. [*ProsTris*]

NICOSIA

The Duke of Nicosia joined Sir Maragoz's attack on the mother of Sir Floriant. [*Floriant*]

NIGHT

The fourth knight defeated by Gareth in Tennyson. He corresponds to the RED KNIGHT OF THE RED LANDS in Malory, though Tennyson gives him black armor. He gave a fearsome appearance, adorned with bones, and wearing a skull for a helmet. When Gareth shattered the helmet, however, he discovered that Night was actually an youth, coaxed into his position by his brothers. [*TennIK*]

NIMUE [Nineve, Nymue]

The name of the LADY OF THE LAKE, or one of them, in Malory's *Le Morte Darthur*. She is called NINNIANE in the Post-Vulgate *Suite du Merlin*, Malory's source. She imprisoned Merlin and married Sir Pelleas. [*Malory*]

NINA

The LADY OF THE LAKE in Wordsworth's *The Egyptian Maid*. She commanded Merlin to take the body of an Egyptian princess, whose ship he had destroyed, to Arthur's court for healing. [*Wordsworth*]

NINE WITCHES

In a Welsh poem, Cei (Kay) is said to have "pierced nine witches" in the "uplands of Ystafngwn." The theme of nine enchantresses is recurring in Welsh legend. In the story of *Peredur*, Peredur kills the nine HAGS OF GLOUCESTER to avenge a cousin's murder. In *The Spoils of Annwn*, we learn that a magic cauldron seized by Arthur from the otherworld was "gently warmed by the breath of nine maidens." In Geoffrey of Monmouth's *Vita Merlini*— influenced heavily by Welsh legend—Arthur is taken to the Island of Apples, ruled by nine sorceresses, including Morgan le Fay. The theme seems to have origins in classical mythology. In the first century, Roman geographer Pomponius Mela described and island off the coast of Brittany inhabited by nine enchantresses with the power to heal the sick. [*Spoils*, *WelshPG*, *GeoffVM*, *Peredur*]

NINE WORTHIES

Nine historical figures considered particularly worthy of reverence. First compiled in fourteenth-century French romance, they included three pagans—Alexander the Great, Hector of Troy, and Julius Caesar—three Jews— Joshua, David, and Judas Maccabeus—and three Christians—Charlemagne, Godfrey of Bouillon, and Arthur. Their names are evoked to suggest the transience of worldly life and the power of death, which claims even the mighty and glorious. In the Alliterative *Morte Arthure*, Arthur has a dream in which he sees Fortune's wheel with the other eight worthies upon it, and a place reserved for him. [*Allit*]

NINIVEH [Ninus]

The ancient capital of Assyria. It was the ancestral homeland of the brothers Pompeius and Ipomidon of Babylon—having been founded by their ancestor Ninus— but was seized by the Baruc of Baghdad. In response, the brothers invaded the Baruc's land. Perceval's father, Gahmuret, serving the Baruc, was involved in the ensuing war. [*Wolfram*]

NINNIANE [Nimiane, Niniame]

The LADY OF THE LAKE in the Vulgate *Lancelot* and the Post-Vulgate *Merlin* continuation. She raised Lancelot and imprisoned Merlin. The Middle English Prose *Merlin* says that the name was Hebrew, meaning "I shall not lie." *Arthour and Merlin*, which gives the Lady of the Lake role to Morgan le Fay, names Ninniane as a town near Morgan's residence. Some scholars have favored a Celtic origin for Ninniane, finding it in the lady Rhiannon, wife of Lord Pwyll. Merlin calls her NIMUE. [*VulgLanc*, *Livre*, *PostMer*, *Arthour*]

NIR

Father of Arthur's warrior Eiddoel. [*Culhwch*]

NIWL [*Yniol*, *Yniwl*]

Father of Enide in the Welsh *Geraint* and Tennyson's *Idylls*. Niwl was an unfortunate earl whose lands were stolen by his nephew. Although he was impoverished, he granted lodging to Geraint when Geraint came to the Knight of the Kestrel tournament seeking to exact revenge on Edern (Yder. Niwl agreed to "lend" Geraint his daughter Enide for the tournament (each competitor had to bring his lady in order to enter). Geraint eventually fell in love with Enid and married her. At the urging of Geraint, Niwl's nephew restored to Niwl his former lands. Niwl's counterpart in Chrétien's *Erec* is LICORANT. I. L. Foster sees his name as a corruption of *li cons uials* ("the old earl"), the nobleman's name in *Geraint*'s presumed source (Loomis, *Romance*, 193). Tennyson combines the characters of the unnamed nephew and Yder, making Yder Niwl's nephew and disinheritor. Yder's cruelty towards Niwl stemmed from Niwl's refusal to allow Yder to marry Enide. [*Geraint*, *TennIK*]

NOAUZ

The location of a tournament sponsored the Lady Noauz and the Lady of Pomelegoi. Lancelot, imprisoned by Meleagant, learned that Queen Guinevere would be at the tournament. He convinced one of Meleagant's servants to let him out of the prison—with the promise that he would return to the prison when the tournament was over. Lancelot won the tournament—to the delight of Guinevere—and kept his promise to return. [*ChretienL*]

NOBLE MAIDEN

The beautiful owner of a castle in which Arthur lodged. An experienced healer, she cured him of wounds he received fighting the Knight-Giant. [*ChevPap*]

NODAWL TRIMMED BEARD

An Arthurian warrior. [*Culhwch*]

NOGANT THE TALL

An evil, cowardly knight related to Queen Fenise of Ireland. Seeking to win Fenise in marriage, he entered a sparrowhawk tournament at the city of Landoc, hoping that his size would scare away the other competitors. When this failed to happen, he ran away from the contest. Fenise announced his cowardice to the world, causing him

to attack her in her castle at Limerick, tricking Arthur into joining him. Sir Durmart, seeking to marry Fenise himself, arrived at the battle, and Nogant rode swiftly away on a camel rather than face Durmart. [*Durmart*]

NOGOID [*Nagroil*]

Father of Arthur's warrior Grifuz. [*GeoffHR*, *Wace*]

NOHAUT [*Nohalt*, *Norham*, *Norhant*, *Norhaut*]

A duchy in the northern part of Arthur's Britain, perhaps in Northumberland, named in the Vulgate romances. It was plundered by Saxons, led by King Oriel, in the early days of Arthur's reign. Later, governed under Arthur by the Lady of Nohaut, it was invaded by the King of Northumberland. The Lady traveled to Arthur's court to find a champion to defend the land, and Arthur gave her the newly-knighted Lancelot. After putting Lancelot through several trials—including one involving the giant knight Antoagais—she accepted him, and he proved victorious in personal combat against Northumberland's knights. She became infatuated with Lancelot and cared for him when he was wounded, but she gave up when she saw her love was futile. In *Arthour and Merlin*, the city is named as Urien's capital in Gorre; there may be some confusion with SORHAUT. [*LancLac*, *VulgLanc*, *VulgMer*, *Arthour*]

NOIRS OF ETHIOPIA

A king in Arthur's service. [*Heinrich*]

NONFIZATA

The paramour of Federiel, the pagan lord of Dolorous Guard. She predicted Federiel's battle with Lancelot. [*Tavola*]

NOODLE

One of Arthur's courtiers in Henry Fielding's parody *The Tragedy of Tragedies*. In the chaotic end of the play, he either slays or is slain by Queen Dollallolla. [*Fielding*]

NOONDAY SUN

The second knight defeated by Gareth in Tennyson. His counterpart in Malory is the RED KNIGHT. He wore red armor. [*TennIK*]

NORDELONE

A city in Orkney, Gawain's homeland. [*VulgMort*]

NORDIEN

In the German romance *Wigamur*, the hero helps the Count of Nordien's fiancée, Piomes. [*Wigamur*]

NORFOLK

A region of northeastern England. When Mordred seized the throne of Britain from Arthur, most of Norfolk allied with him. [*Malory*]

NORFOU

A place where Bors met a woman who criticized him for his conduct at the Grail Castle. [*VulgLanc*]

NORHOLT [*Norof*]

In the Prose *Tristan*, a city in Cornwall. The Count of Norholt ordered the death of Meliadus, Tristan's father, because a seer had told him that Meliadus's lineage would destroy the house of Norholt. The prophecy was fulfilled when Tristan, in revenge for his father's death, killed the Count and his family. Norholt later became one of King Mark's courts. In *La Tavola Ritonda*, the city is called BRIODA. In *Palamedes*, Meliadus is slain by vassals of MORHOLT, of which "Norholt" may simply be a variation. It may also be related to the city of NOHAUT. [*ProsTris, Povest*]

NORISON [*Narison*]

When Yvain went insane, he found succor at the home of the Lady of Norison. She cured his madness with a salve made by Morgan the Wise. In return, Yvain helped to defend her land against the invading Earl Alier. [*ChretienY*]

NORMAGA

The lord of Sorelois in the English *Arthour and Merlin*—a title usually assigned to GALEHAUT. [*Arthour*]

NORMANDY [*Normandie, Normandye, Normendie, Normondye*]

A region of France east of Brittany on the English Channel. Geoffrey says that Arthur conquered Normandy and gave it to Bedivere. *Arthour and Merlin* tells us that Uther Pendragon acquired it from King Harinan, Igraine's first husband. In Malory, Lancelot owns the land and appoints Sir Claryus as its duke, in return for Claryus's support in the war against Arthur. Wolfram says that Gaschier was the ruler of Normandy during the reign of Uther. [*GeoffHR, Wolfram, Arthour, Malory*]

NORMELANDA

A knight whose nephew, Sir Breus the Pitiless, was the antithesis of Arthurian knighthood. [*Tavola*]

NOROIS

One of the lands ruled by the Lord of the Horn, whom Perceval defeated in combat. [*Contin2*]

NORROIZ OF LIS [*Norés, Norez*]

Father of Brandelis, Meliant, and of a damsel named Guilorete. Guilorete was seduced by Gawain in a forest pavilion in the First Continuation of Chrétien's *Perceval*. When Norroiz heard of his daughter's disgrace, he tracked Gawain down but was killed. His daughter later bore Gawain's son. In *The Jeaste of Sir Gawain*, he is known as GILBERT. [*Contin1*]

NORT [*Norz*]

A knight called the Youth of Nort was in Arthur's service He joned one of Gawain's quests to locate Lancelot. [*LancLac, VulgLanc*]

NORTH WALES [*Nor(th)gales, Nor(th)galis, Norgoise*]

The northern part of Wales is given as its own kingdom in a large number of Arthurian romances. In the First Continuation of Chrétien's *Perceval*, it is ruled by King Camadans, an ally of Arthur. According the Vulgate *Estoire del Saint Graal*, its first Christian king was Celidoine, the son of Nascien. The Vulgate *Merlin* gives the kingdom, in Arthur's time, to both Belinant and Tradelmant. In the Post-Vulgate *Suite du Merlin* and in Malory, it is one of the kingdoms ruled by Rions. Geoffrey of Monmouth says it was ruled by Peredur after Arthur's death, and the Italian *La Tavola Ritonda* names two kings of North Wales: Alois and Ansilerno. In Malory, the unnamed Queen of North Wales is a companion of Morgan le Fay in her plans to imprison Lancelot in Cart Castle, to trap Elaine of Corbenic in a bath of boiling water, and to bear Arthur's body from the battlefield of Salisbury to Avalon. In the chronicles, the region is called VENEDOTIA. [*GeoffHR, Contin1, VulgEst, VulgMer, PostMer, Tavola, Malory*]

NORTH WALES CAUSEWAY [*Welsh Causeway*]

One of only two bridges connecting Arthur's Britain with Galehaut's kingdom of Sorelois. The other was the Irish Bridge. The North Wales Bridge was submerged in parts, and was defended at the Sorelois end by a strong tower and a stout knight. Only five knights ever made it across alive—these included Gawain, Meliant, Yder, Dodinel, and Arthur. Its description is reminiscent of Chrétien's UNDERWATER BRIDGE. [*LancLac, VulgLanc*]

NORTHMEN [*Northland*]

Yder, an ally or vassal of Arthur, is called the King of the Northmen in the Vulgate *Merlin* and the king of Northland in *Arthour and Merlin*. [*VulgMer, Arthour*]

NORTHUMBERLAND [*Hortoberlande, Norhorbelande, Nortoberlande, Nortumbellande*]

A kingdom in the north of Britain, just south of Scotland. King Clarion of Northumberland was an early enemy of Arthur, but the two eventually allied. Various texts name Northumberland as the home of Blaise, a friend of Merlins, and of the knights Balin and Balan. In Paolino Pieri's *La Storia di Merlino*, it is Merlin's home. In Girart D'Amiens' *Escanor*, Northumberland is ruled by Cador, and *Claris et Laris* names its ruler as Detors. The Vulgate *Merlin* sometimes describes it as a city. In the Vulgate *Lancelot*, its king goes to war with the Lady of Nohaut, but his champion is defeated by Lancelot. In *Meriadeuc*, its king lusts after Guinevere and is promised the queen by his lord, King Ris of Outre-Ombre, but Ris's attempt to conquer Arthur and kidnap the queen is thwarted. [*VulgLanc, VulgMer, Girart, Claris, Arthour, Malory*]

NORVAL

Sir Gaus, a knight healed by Arthur's Sir Meriadeuc, is called the son of the King of Norval. [*Meriadeuc*]

NORWAY

In Welsh legend, Norway is subject to Arthur, and the Norwegian warriors are led by Mark, Arthur's first cousin. In other tales, Norwegian warriors allied with Picts and Saxons and caused problems for Arthur and his predecessors. Geoffrey says that Arthur conquered Norway from King Riculf and gave it to Lot. Lot supposedly had a hereditary right to the kingdom as the grandson of King Sichelm. Later in Geoffrey's account, however, Odbricht is the King of Norway. In any event, Lot and Gawain are often called knights of Norway in later legends. In Der Pleier's romances, Lot's son, Beacurs, is king. In actuality, the kindgom of Norway did not exist until the late ninth century, being a collection of tribes prior to this time. [*GeoffHR, Wace, Layamon, PleierT, Dream*]

NOTTINGHAM [*Nortigean, Notigehan*]

In the First Continuation of Chrétien's *Perceval*, Arthur presents Nottingham to Lord Guiromelant when he marries Clarissant, Gawain's sister. According to the fourteenth-century *Short Metrical Chronicle*, Lancelot built Nottingham to house Queen Guinevere during his civil war with Arthur. [*Contin1, Short*]

NOUQUESTRAN [*No(u)quetrant*]

In Guillaume le Clerc's *Fergus,* a Scottish mountain, also called the Black Mountain, which was inhabited by the fearsome Black Knight. Arthur's knight Fergus journeyed to Nouquestran to obtain a magic horn and wimple from the Black Knight, and he succeeded. Nouquestran was also said to be one of Merlin's haunts. M. D. Legge has suggested Mount Rubers Law as the geographic location that Guillaume had in mind. [*Guillaume*]

NUT [*Niut, Nown, Noyt, Nu(c)(s), *Nudd, Nun, Nus, Nuz*]

Father of Arthur's Sir Yder as well as the warriors Gwynn, Owain, and Dryon. He is a mortal incarnation of the Celtic god Nodens, whose counterpart in Irish mythology is Nuada Argetlam. His father was named Senyllt. The Welsh Triads call him "Nudd the Generous." In the romance of *Yder*, we learn that Nut, the duke of Alemaine in Scotland, abandoned Yder's mother, but left half of a ring with her so that he could someday be identified. Yder set out on a quest for his father when he came of age. They eventually encountered each other and fought a combat before they learned each other's identities and reconciled. At the conclusion of the romance, Nut finally marries Yder's mother. He appears as one of Arthur's kings in Robert Biket's *Lai du Cor*, where his wife is shown to be unfaithful in a chastity test. [*Culhwch, GeoffHR, Biket, ChretienE, Triads, Yder, Geraint*]

NWYFRE ("Firmament")

Father of Arthur's warriors Gwynn and Fflam. [*Culhwch*]

NWYTHON [*Neco, Neton*]

Father of Arthur's warriors Gwystyl, Rhun, Llwydeu, and Kinlith. [*Culhwch, GeoffHR*]

NYGRAMOUS

A castle that was the home of Hellawes, a sorceress defeated by Lancelot. [*Malory*]

NYNNYAW

An ox that lived on the far side of Mynydd Bannawg. Nynnyaw had once been human, but was turned into an ox because of his sins. As one of his tasks, the warrior Culhwch had to capture the ox and yoke it together with another ox from Mynydd Bannawg named Peibyaw. [*Culhwch*]

O

OBERON [*Auberon*]

The dwarf son of Julius Caesar and Morgan le Fay whose adventures are recounted in *Huon de Bordeaux*, *Auberon*, and *Ysaie le Triste*. As a horribly ugly dwarf called TRONC, he served as a mentor and companion to Ysaie and Marc—the son and grandson of Tristan. When these knights completed their quests, fairies rewarded Oberon by making him beautiful and by giving him the throne of the kingdom of Faérie, which Arthur thought belonged to him. Arthur contested Oberon for the kingdom, but Oberon scared Arthur away by threatening to turn him into a wolf. Oberon died having bestowed his lands to Huon de Bordeaux. *Ogier le Danois* calls Oberon Morgan's brother rather than her son. Though originating in French romance, Oberon was popular in Elizabethan England. In Spenser's *The Faerie Queene*, Oberon's daughter, Tanaquill, becomes the Fairy Queen Gloriana. Oberon also appears as the king of fairies in Shakespeare's *A Midsummer Night's Dream*, married to the fairy Titania. [*Huon, Auberon, Ysaie, Ogier, Spenser*]

OBIE

The oldest daughter of Duke Lyppaut of Bearosche in Wolfram's *Parzival*. She was loved by King Meliant of Liz—Lyppaut's sovereign lord—but rejected his affections. Meliant, enraged, declared war on Lyppaut and summoned many lords to assist him. Gawain arrived to fight for Lyppaut. He captured Meliant in battle and gave him to Obie's younger sister, Obilot. Obilot, in turn, transferred Meliant to Obie's command, giving Obie and Meliant a chance to reconcile. The war was ended and Obie and Meliant were engaged. Obie's counterpart in Heinrich von dem Türlin's *Diu Crône* is named FLURSENSEPHIN. [*Wolfram*]

OBILOT

The charming daughter of Duke Lyppaut of Bearosche, sister of Obie, and friend of Clauditte in Wolfram's *Parzival*. Obilot—who was still a child—developed a crush on Gawain when he came to Bearosche to assist Lyppaut in the war against King Meliant. At Obilot's request, Gawain generously consented to become her "knight servitor" and wore her sleeve in battle. When Gawain captured Meliant in battle, he sent him to Obilot as a prisoner. Obilot, in turn, transferred Meliant to her sister Obie. Meliant and Obie reconciled and the war was ended. Obilot's counterpart in Chrétien de Troyes's *Parzival* is called the "maiden with the little sleeves," and in Heinrich von dem Türlin's *Diu Crône*, she is called QUEBELEPLUS. [*Wolfram*]

OC

A land. King Pelles of Corbenic sent a message to the Duke of Oc, and Lancelot encountered the page. [*VulgLanc*]

OCCASION

A hag who encouraged her mad son, Furor, to attack knights. She was captured and bound by Sir Guyon. [*Spenser*]

OCH ("Groan")

Wife of Arthur's warrior Bwlch. [*Culhwch*]

OCTA [*Occa, Ochta*]

Son of Hengist and brother of Ebissa in Geoffrey of Monmouth's *Historia* and the other chronicles. Octa's father, a great Saxon leader, brought Octa to Britain during the reign of King Vortigern, Hengist's brother-in-law. When Hengist's plan to conquer Britain became known, Vortigern and his successors went to war with the Saxons. Octa succeeded his father as the Saxon leader after Hengist was executed by King Ambrosius.

Ambrosius defeated Octa, forced baptism on him, and banished him to Scotland. When Ambrosius died, however, Octa resumed his war against King Uther. He was captured with his kinsman Eosa at Mount Damon by Uther, and was thrown into prison. In time, Octa and Eosa convinced the prison guards to free them, and the lot fled to Germany, where they raised an army and returned. Geoffrey says that Octa was finally killed at Saint Albans (or Verulam) by Uther's army.

In Nennius (whose chronicle predates Geoffrey), it is uncertain whether Octa is the Saxon commander in the battles against Arthur (see ARTHUR'S BATTLES), but the possibility is open. Geoffrey attributes this campaign to Octa's successor, Colgrim.

Richard Blackmore gives Octa a daughter named Ethelina, who married Arthur. Octa may be related to the Welsh character OSLA. [*Nennius, GeoffHR, Wace, BlackmoreP*]

OCTAVIUS [*Octaves*]

An expatriated Roman who ruled Britain several generations before Arthur. Formerly the duke of Gwent, he stole the British throne from King Constantine while the latter was conquering Rome. Constantine sent one of his generals, Trahern, to deal with Octavius, and Octavius was forced to flee to Norway. He put a contract on Trahern's life and, when Trahern was assassinated, he returned to Britain to rule until he died. He was succeeded by Maximus. [*GeoffHR*, *Wace*]

OCURSUS THE BLACK

A Knight of the Round Table, related to Lancelot, who participated in the Grail Quest. [*PostQuest*]

ODABEL

A Roman knight and companion of a youthful Gawain in Rome. He accompanied Gawain to Jerusalem, where Gawain was scheduled to represent Rome in a single-combat challenge against Persia. On the way, they were blown by a storm to a barbarian island, and Odabel was instrumental in the defeat of Milocrates, the barbarian king. [*DeOrtu*]

ODBRICHT

The King of Norway under Arthur, killed at the battle of Camel against Mordred. [*GeoffHR*]

ODELIZ

The lover of Sir Meliant of Lis. [*Raoul*]

ODGAR

King of Ireland in *Culhwch and Olwen*. He was the son of Aedd and the brother of Gwitart. As one of his forty tasks, Culhwch needed Odgar to draw the tusk out of the chief boar Ysgithyrwyn. Culhwch also needed to obtain a magic cauldron from Diwrnach, Odgar's steward. When Diwrnach refused to hand it over, Arthur and his men destroyed Ireland. [*Culhwch*]

ODINIAUS THE FAIR

A knight that Perceval found dead in a forest. He later encountered Odiniaus's lover and was forced to break the bad news. [*Contin2*]

ODUIN

A count in Arthur's service. [*Renaut*]

ODULF

Brother of King Gunter of Denmark. When Odulf learned that his brother was withholding tribute from Arthur, Odulf sent a message to Arthur, who sailed to Denmark, killed Gunter, and appointed Odulf to the throne. Odulf had another brother named Aschil. [*Gaimar*]

ODUS

The son of Erec and Enide in the Norse *Erex Saga*. He was named after Enide's father, whom Chrétien calls LICORANT. The text notes that both Odus and his brother Ilac became kings. [*Erex*]

ODYAR THE FRANK

The steward of Arthur's court in Caerleon. [*Geraint*]

OELEVANT

A castle that King Ban of Benoic gave to the daughter of Agravadain the Black. Warriors from Oelevant participated in Arthur's battle against the Saxons at Cardigan. [*Livre*]

ÓENGUS MAC NAD FRAÍCH

A king of Cashel, Munster (south central Ireland), in the second half of the fifth century. He was a member of the Eóganacht dynasty, which might have been expelled from Wales a few decades earlier. Óengus was believed to have married Ethne Uathach of the Uí Ceinnselaig dynasty, whom he joined in a war aganst the Laigin people. Óengus and his allies lost the battle of Cenn Losnada against the Laigins in 490, and Óengus was killed. Óengus would have been contemporary with Arthur, and some scholars have suggested him as the source of King ANGUISH of Ireland in French prose romance, though a far more likely source is Geoffrey's ANGUSEL. In any event, a number of Irish figures with the name Óengus were known in the fifth, sixth, and seventh centuries (Mac Niocaill, 6–9, 57).

OFFENSIVE KNIGHT [*Outrageus*]

A knight slain in combat by Gawain. Gawain wore the Offensive Knight's armor so he could travel incognito. [*Claris*]

OFFENSIVE KNIGHTS

A trio of Arthur's knights—Morfran, Sanddef, and Glewlwyd—who worked their will through their appearances: Morfran through his hideousness; Sanddef through his angelic beauty; and Glewlwyd through his enormous size, strength, and ferocity. Morfran and Sanddef were said to have survived the battle of Camlann because of their countenances. [*Triads*]

OGIER THE DANE

A hero in Carolingian romance, possibly based on a historical figure named Otker. He is non-Arthurian except for an account in *Ogier le danois* where Ogier is shipwrecked in the Mediterranean. Rescued by angels, he comes to the Island of Avalon, where he finds Morgan, Arthur, and Gawain still alive. He lives with Morgan in her palace for 200 years, begetting two sons upon her, before leaving. [*Ogier, Jean*]

OIGEONES

The standard-bearer for Duke Eskilabon of Belamunt. He fought in Arthur's war against King Ekunaver of Kanadic and was later made a Knight of the Round Table. [*PleierG*]

ÔL ("Track")

An Arthurian warrior who was the son of Olwydd. A superb tracker, Ôl, as an adult, was able to track down a herd of pigs stolen from his father seven months before his birth. [*Culhwch*]

OLD KNIGHT [*Presbys Hippotes*]

A warrior who, in a Greek poem, Lancelot, Palamedes, Gawain, and Tristan were unable to defeat. He is properly called BRANOR THE BROWN in *Palamedes*. [*Presbys*]

OLD TABLE [*Tavola Vecchio*]

Italian literature distinguishes between the *Tavola Vecchio* ("Old Table") and the *Tavola Nuovo* ("New Table"); that is, the Round Table fellowships commanded by Uther Pendragon and Arthur. Uther's Old Table seems to have been composed primarily of strong and crude knights, while Arthur's New Table was known for its justice, courtliness, and virtue. Examples of Old Table knights include Abiron, Branor the Brown, and Caradoc the Thirteenth. [*Tavola*]

OLÉRON [*Olyroun*]

An island off the coast of Britain in Chestre's *Launfal*. The King of Oléron's daughter, Triamour, became the lover of Sir Launfal. She and Launfal eventually went to Oléron, where they remained. Counterparts in other tales are AVALON and AMYLION. [*ChestreLvl*]

OLIMPIA[1]

An infidel queen who loved Perceval's half-brother Feirefiz. Feirefiz rejected her, along with several others, in favor of the Grail Maiden Repanse de Schoye. [*Wolfram*]

OLIMPIA[2]

Arthur's sister. She married King Linefles of France and had a son named Meleranz. [*PleierM*]

OLIMPIA[3]

The daughter of Meleranz and Tydomie, named after her grandmother. [*PleierM*]

OLIMPIAS

A knight who hated the Knights of the Round Table. Arthur's Sir Claris defeated and badly wounded him in combat. [*Claris*]

OLIVIER

A count in the service of Garel, Arthur's king of Averre. He took word of Garel's victory at the battle of Kanadic to Laudamie, Garel's wife. [*PleierG*]

OLWEN ("White Track")

Daughter of the chief giant Ysbaddaden, and object of Culhwch's affection in *Culhwch and Olwen*. She was incredibly beautiful, and it was said that when she walked, white trefoils sprouted behind her. Culhwch's stepmother obliged him to marry Olwen, and his heart swelled at the very mention of her name, even though he had never seen her. After a long journey, he found her at Ysbaddaden's fortress. She said she could not leave with him without her father's permission, but advised Culhwch to ask Ysbaddaden for her, and to accomplish whatever tasks the giant set for him. Culhwch, with the great assistance of Arthur and his warriors, eventually completed the list of tasks, and returned to Ysbaddaden's fortress. As was the decree, Ysbaddaden was killed and Olwen was married to Culhwch. In a non-Arthurian tale called *Einion and Olwen*, Olwen is rescued from the otherworld by a shepherd name Einion, and the two have a son named Taliesin. [*Culhwch*]

OLWYDD ("Tracker")

Father of Arthur's warrior Ol. [*Culhwch*]

OMER

Castellan of the Castle Monreal, where Floriant's mother fled after she was attacked by Lord Maragoz. The siege was eventually lifted by Arthur and Floriant, and Floriant made Omer his seneschal. [*Floriant*]

ONAGE

A wealthy city that belonged to King Evalach (Mordrains) of Sarras. It was captured during Evalach's war with King Tholomer of Babylonia. [*VulgEst*]

ONAM OF GALIOT

A Knight of the Round Table. [*HartmannE*]

ONDYAW

An Arthurian warrior. He was the son of the duke of Burgundy. [*Geraint*]

ONE WITH THE GOLDEN BOW

A Knight of the Round Table in Hartmann von Aue's *Erec*, probaby from Chrétien's VALLET OF THE GOLDEN CIRCLE. [*HartmannE*]

ONE WITHOUT A NAME [*Cil sans Non*]

An alias adopted by GAWAIN during his adventures in *L'Atre Perilleux* after a false report of his death was circulated. [*Atre*]

ONIA

A servant of the Lady of the Lake in *La Tavola Ritonda*. She was married to the King of Scotland. Onia was bringing a shield from the Lady to Lancelot when she was attacked and robbed by Sir Breus the Pitiless. Lancelot slew Breus for this offense. [*Tavola*]

ONIPRIZ OF ITOLAC

A king once defeated in combat by Perceval. [*Wolfram*]

ONORGUE

One of the many ladies at Arthur's court to fail a chastity test involving a goblet. She is described as a mighty fairy. [*Heinrich*]

ONTZLAKE

The younger brother of Sir Damas. Damas stole his lands and refused to fight Ontzlake in personal combat to settle the matter. Morgan le Fay allied with Damas and, as part of her own revenge plot against Arthur, arranged for Arthur to fight as Damas's champion and for Sir Accalon of Gaul to fight as Ontzlake's champion. Though Accalon had Excalibur and Arthur had a counterfeit sword, Arthur defeated Accalon and made Damas surrender all his lands to Ontzlake. [*Malory*]

ORASTE GENTESIN

A swampland in heathendom known for its strong bamboo shafts, good for making spears. The King of Oraste Gentesin in Arthur's time, Thoaris, was a vassal of Perceval's half-brother Feirefiz. [*Wolfram*]

ORBELLANDA¹

An ancestor of Dinadan, Brunor the Black, and Daniel (three of Arthur's knights). Lancelot insulted his memory, aggravating a feud between Lancelot and Brunor. [*Tavola*]

ORBELLANDA²

A land whose king was present at Arthur's Leverzep tournament. [*Tavola*]

ORBERICA [*Orberike*]

The birthplace of Sarrassinte, King Evalach's wife. It was ruled by Nascien, Sarrassinte's brother. Joseph of Arimathea converted Orberica and placed Juvenal in a bishopric there. [*VulgEst, VulgMer*]

ORBRIE

The Duke of Orbrie was defeated by Yvain in a tournament. [*Claris*]

ORCAGE [*Arrage*]

A land allied to Lucius the Roman. Warriors from Orcage participated in Lucius's war against Arthur. [*Allit, Malory*]

ORCANT

An ancestor of Lot and Gawain. He was king of ORKNEY, which was named after him, in the time of Joseph of Arimathea. He was accused of murdering King Marahant of Ireland's son. Before King Lucius of Britain, he was successfully defended against this charge by Peter, a relative of Joseph of Arimathea who had stumbled into Orcant's kingdom. In admiration of Peter, Orcant converted to Christianity, taking the name LUMET. Peter married Orcant's daughter, Camille. [*VulgEst*]

ORCAUT

The richest city in King Evalach's Sarras. It was the site of the final battle between Evalach and King Tholomer of Babylonia. Josephus, Joseph of Arimathea's son, converted the city and exorcised a demon there. [*VulgEst*]

ORDER OF MAIDENHEAD

The order of knights commanded by Gloriana, the Fairy Queen. [*Spenser*]

ORDOHORHT

In Heinrich von dem Türlin's *Diu Crône*, the residence of Lady Fortune and her son Luck. Gawain visited them in Ordohorht and saw them seated on a golden wheel. [*Heinrich*]

ORDUALE BESCO

A castle in Cornwall or Lyonesse where Governal procured supplies for Tristan and Isolde when they were living in exile at the Tower of Enchantments. [*Tavola*]

ORGANIA

In the Italian *La Tavola Ritonda*, King Pelles' country. It could be a variation of either ORKNEY or CORBENIC. [*Tavola*]

ORGIN [*Ogrin, Ugrim*]

A hermit and holy man in Cornwall. He befriended Tristan and Isolde when they were forced to flee from Mark and live in the forest. He acted as their scribe when they desired to reconcile with Mark. [*Beroul, FolieB*]

ORGOGLIO

A haughty giant who encountered the Red Cross Knight with the witch Duessa. Orgoglio made the Red Cross Knight his slave and Duessa his mistress. Una, the Red Cross Knight's *amie*, learned of his plight and found help from Prince Arthur. Arthur stormed Orgoglio's castle and slew him, freeing the Red Cross Knight. [*Spenser*]

ORGUEILLOX THE PROUD

Lord of the Perilous Castle. His castle's enchantments were destroyed by Claris and Laris. [*Claris*]

ORGUELLEUS¹ ("Proud") [*Orguellous*]

A castle, first mentioned by Chrétien de Troyes in *Perceval*. A mysterious ugly woman came to Arthur's court to rebuke Perceval for failing to cure the Fisher King. Almost in passing, she noted that hundreds of men lived in the castle Orguelleus with their maidens, and Girflet vowed to travel there to seek adventure. Chrétien did not finish this plot line, but in the First Continuation, Arthur and his company set out to free Girflet, who was apparently captured and imprisoned in the castle. Gawain conquered the castle by defeating the Riche Soudier. In the Second Continuation, Perceval had to prove his worth at a tournament at the castle (ruled by a knight named Orguelleus) before he could complete the Grail Quest. In *Perlesvaus*, it is inhabited by Orguelleuse of Logres, a murderous maiden who plots to kill Gawain, Perceval, and Lancelot. The castle next appears in the French romance *Gliglois*, as the location of a tournament won by Gliglois,

Gawain's squire, which proves him worthy of marrying the lady Beauté. In Malory, Sir Brunor the Black defeats a dozen knights at the Castle Orguelleus, ending the castle's custom, which had been to take all passing knights prisoner. [*ChretienP*, *Contin1*, *Contin2*, *Perlesvaus*, *Gliglois*, *Malory*]

ORGUELLEUS² OF THE HEATH [*Orilus of Lalander*]

A knight featured in the stories of Chrétien de Troyes and Wolfram von Eschenbach. His first appearance is in Chrétien's *Erec*, as a knight defeated by Erec at the Tenebroc tournament. In Chrétien's *Perceval* and Wolfram's *Parzival*, he owns a forest pavilion in Briziljan or Broceliande. Perceval, on his way to Arthur's court for the first time, visits the pavilion and finds Orguelleus's wife (called Jeschute by Wolfram) alone inside. Misinterpreting advice given to him by his mother, Perceval eats the woman's food, kisses her, and takes a ring from her finger. Orguelleus returns and, finding that another man has been there, becomes enraged, accuses his wife of adultery, and forces her to mount a steed and ride with him, seeking Perceval. Perceval met them some time later. Orguelleus had not allowed his wife to change her dress or her mount in months. Orguelleus challenged Perceval to combat. Perceval was victorious, and he forced Orguelleus to make amends to his wife and to go to Arthur's court.

Wolfram gives Orguelleus a brother named Lähelin and a sister named Cunneware. His wife Jeschute was Erec's sister, yet Orguelleus and Erec frequently combated each other. He was an enemy of the Round Table had had killed Galoies (Perceval's uncle), Schionatulander (Perceval's cousin's lover), and a knight named Plihoplehri (Bleoberis). He seemed to be friends with Gawain, as Gawain had received his horse, Gringolet, from Orguelleus. [*ChretienE*, *ChretienP*, *Wolfram*, *Didot*, *Heinrich*]

ORGUELLEUS³ OF THE NARROW PASSAGE

The guardian of the borders of Galloway, who vowed that no knight that entered the country would escape alive. Gawain defied this vow by defeating Orguelleus in combat at the Perilous Ford. Orguelleus's lover was Orguelleuse of Logres. [*ChretienP*, *Contin1*]

ORGUELLEUS⁴ THE FAIRY

A knight who was an enemy of Gawain. He possessed magical powers and ruled the Fairy Rock. With Sir Goumeret, he killed Sir Cortois of Huberlant, believing him to be Gawain. When the knights realized their mistake, Orguelleus resurrected Cortois. [*Atre*]

ORGUELLEUSE OF LOGRES [*Orgeluse*]

Duchess of Logres found in Chrétien's *Perceval*, Wolfram's *Parzival*, and *Perlesvaus*. In Chrétien, she escorts Gawain through his adventures in Galloway, attempting to lead him into danger at every turn. Her lover was Orguelleus of the Narrow Passage.

Perlesvaus and Wolfram both built on Chrétien's description of the character, but in very different ways. In the former, she is a wicked, marginally-sane woman who prepares tombs in the chapel of her castle (also called Orguelleus) for Gawain, Lancelot, Perceval, and herself. Expecting that if any of these knights came to her castle, they would want to pray in her chapel, she rigged a sharp blade to behead anyone kneeling before the chapel's altar. In this way, she planned to dispatch the three best knights in Britain and entomb herself with them. She made the mistake of revealing the entire plan to Gawain, who was lodging with her incognito, and Gawain warned his comrades to stay away from her castle. A similar character called the MAIDEN OF THE NARROW WOOD appears in *Hunbaut*.

In Wolfram, Orguelleuse inherits the castle of Logres from her late husband, Cidegast, after he is killed in battle against King Gramoflanz. She dedicated her efforts to finding a knight to marry her and exact revenge on Gramoflanz. Many knights failed Orguelleuse's test—which involved pitting her prospective husband against the powerful Duke Lischois Gwelljus. Until Gawain, only Perceval had proved promising, but Perceval shunned Orguelleuse in favor of his wife Condwiramurs and the Grail Quest. Anfortas, Wolfram's Fisher King, was another suitor—and one for whom Orguelleuse seemed to genuinely care—but he was injured in the groin in Orguelleuse's service and had to retire to the Grail Castle. Gawain encountered Orguelleuse and fell in love with her immediately, despite Orguelleuse's cruel treatment and spiteful tongue. Gawain's honor and compassion had no effect on the duchess until he defeated Lischois Gwelljus in combat and won the deadly adventure at the Castle of Marvels. Having accomplished this, and having revealed his identity, Orguelleuse reciprocated Gawain's love and explained her situation. Gawain agreed to fight King Gramoflanz, but was distressed to find that his own sister Itonje was in love with the king. Arthur intervened and convinced Orguelleuse to forgive Gramoflanz and abandon her vendetta. Gawain and Orguelleuse were then married. [*ChretienP*, *Perlesvaus*, *Wolfram*]

ORGUILLUS

A giant from Africa who, in Thomas's *Tristan*, conquered dozens of kings and stole their beards. With the beards, he fashioned a robe, but had a single open space. He demanded King Arthur's beard. Arthur was suitably enraged and, after a long battle, defeated Orguillus. Orguillus's nephew later made a similar demand of the king of Spain, but was defeated by Sir Tristan. Orguillus's role is served by RIONS or RITHO in other tales. [*Thomas*]

ORIAN RUSSELL

In *Arthour and Merlin*, a heathen king slain by Sagremor during a battle at Camelot. The character appears in the

Vulgate *Merlin*, but is unnamed; the name may have been inspired by ORIANCE or ORIEL from *Merlin*. [*Arthour*]

ORIANCE

One of the many Saxon kings who, in the early days of Arthur's reign, invaded parts of northern Britain. He was maimed by Gaheris (Gawain's brother) at the battle of Cambenic. [*VulgMer*]

ORIANDE

A pagan island off the west coast of Scotland, ruled by King Madaglan, an enemy of Arthur. Perceval slew Madaglan and converted Oriande to Christianity. [*Perlesvaus*]

ORIANS

The lord of the Castle Amalvi, on an island near Britain. He came across the shipwreck of the infants that Arthur had set to sea in an attempt to destroy his son, Mordred. Orians built the Castle of Boys to house and raise the infants. His son, Acanor the Ugly Hero, was one of Arthur's knights. [*PostMer*]

ORIEL [*Oriens, Oriol(t)*]

A Saxon king who invaded northern Britain at the beginning of Arthur's reign. He participated in the siege of Vambieres, the plunder of Nohaut, and the invasion of Escavalon. He fought King Clarion and Duke Escant at Cambenic, and Gawain at Camelot. His father, Aminaduc, also participated in the invasion.. [*VulgMer, Arthour*]

ORIENT

Son of the Saxon king Bramangue. He participated in the Saxon invasion of Britain in the early days of Arthur's reign. He was one of the few Saxons to survive the battle of Clarence, where Arthur crushed them. [*VulgMer*]

ORIGGE

A knight in Arthur's service, killed by the King of Libya during the Roman War. [*Allit*]

ORILES

A knight, also called the Green Knight, who fell in love with Lady Helaés of Limos. Helaés refused to return his love until he vanquished Gawain, whom Helaés saw as the world's best knight. Despite the assistance of his mother's enchantments, Oriles was unable to defeat Gawain. Helaés gave her love to Gawain instead. [*Livre*]

ORILUS OF LALANDER

Wolfram von Eschenbach's variation of ORGUELLEUSE OF LA LANDE. [*Wolfram*]

ORIMONDE

A princess from Persia who married Marc, Tristan's grandson. [*Ysaie*]

ORINGLE

Count of the town of Limors in Chrétiend Troyes's *Erec*. Erec and Enide came to the town after Erec had been injured during their journey, and had fallen unconscious. Count Oringle thought that Erec was dead and he made advances on Enide. When Enide rejected Oringle's affections, Oringle abused her. Enide's screams awoke Erec, who jumped up and killed Oringle where he stood. The name of the count's town, LIMORS, is given to the nobleman himself in the Welsh *Geraint*. The Norse *Erex Saga* calls him PLACIDUS and Tennyson names him DOORM. [*ChretienE*]

ORINSCE

A river in Cornwall, in which Isolde tried to drown herself after Palamedes abducted her. She was saved by a Cornish knight. [*ProsTris*]

ORIS THE HARSH

A knight who hosted Tristan and Dinadan in his fortress of Fregulla Vittoriosa on the plain of Matuvana. Tristan had killed his brother, Sigurano. When Oris discovered the identity of his guest, he challenged him to a duel, despite Dinadan's warnings. Tristan mortally wounded him. [*Tavola*]

ORKNEY [*Dorkain(e)(s), Orcaine, Orcania, Orc(h)anie, Orcany, Orkenise, Orkenye, Ortaine*]

A group of islands north of the island of Great Britain, just off the coast of Scotland. Orkney is traditionally part of King Lot's realm, though it is ruled by Gunvasius in Geoffrey of Monmouth and Souenas in the English *Arthur*. Sometimes, it is named as one of Arthur's courts. The Vulgate *Merlin* seems to think it was a city in Lothian, one of Lot's other kingdoms, or that it was next to Wales. A number of other continental romances also locate it in Scotland. In *Merlin* it is attacked by Saxons while Lot is leading a rebellion against Arthur. Lot returned and drove away the invaders. According to the Vulgate *Estoire del Saint Graal*, its name came from King Orcant, an early ruler and an ancestor of Lot. Orkney is in some texts the surname of Gawain, Gareth, Agravain, and Gaheris. [*GeoffHR, Wace, Layamon, Contin1, VulgLanc, VulgEst, VulgMer, Arthour, Malory*]

OROFAISE

A country situated between Sorelois and North Wales. During the Saxon invasion of Britain, the Saxon King Aminaduc's warriors were hard pressed by Arthur and the Knights of the Round Table. Aminaduc's wife sent a Saxon giant to lay waste to Orofaise, hoping that Arthur's knights would be drawn to the adventure and would be slain. Arthur personally responded to the Countess of Orofaise's cries for help. Having defeated the giant in combat, Arthur answered the countess's plea for justice and had the giant drowned in a river. [*Livre*]

ORPHEUS THE ENCHANTER [*Orfeu*]

The founder of the Castle of Enchantments in the Scottish Borderlands. During his visit to Corbenic, Bors heard a song describing a debate between Orpheus and Joseph of Arimathea. [*VulgLanc*]

ORPHILET THE FAIR [*Orp(y)let*]

A Knight of the Round Table in Ulrich von Zatzikhoven's *Lanzelet*. Orphilet was encountered by Lancelot early in his adventures. Lancelot came across Orphilet and Sir Kuraus fighting in a clearing. They were both ready to collapse from exhaustion, and Lancelot made them stop fighting. The three knights went together to the castle of Moreiz, where they enjoyed the hospitality of Lord Galagandreiz. Galagandreiz was of uneven disposition, and Orphilet feared him. For this reason, he declined to sleep with Galagandreiz's daughter when she offered herself to him. At the end of their adventure, Orphilet asked Lancelot to accompany him to King Arthur's court, but Lancelot declined. A knight later in the poem is called TORFILARET, but it is uncertain if Ulrich meant to signify the same knight. If so, than Orphilet is related to TOR of later romance. [*UlrichZ*]

ORRI

A forester in Cornwall. When Tristan had been banished from King Mark's court for a time, Orri gave him refuge in his cellar. From there, Tristan corresponded with Isolde while Mark thought he was in Scotland. [*Beroul*]

ORSL

According to the Norse *Tristrams Saga*, the name of the Duke of Brittany whose wife Helen was kidnapped by the giant of Mont St. Michel. This character is known as HOEL in other versions. [*TrisSaga*]

ORTENAX [*Cortenans, Ertanax*]

A magical species of fish from the Euphrates river. A rib bone from the Ortenax formed one half of the crosspiece on the Sword with the Strange Hangings. Anyone touching the rib would forget all his joys and sorrows until he released it. [*VulgQuest, VulgEst, Malory*]

ORUOGODELAT

A Knight of the Round Table. [*HartmannE*]

ORWEN

The twin sister of King Meriadoc of Wales. Orwen's father, King Caradoc, was murdered by her uncle, Griffin, who then targeted the children for assassination. They were saved by Ivor and Morwen, their foster parents, and taken to hiding in the forest of Fleventan. In time, Meriadoc was taken to Arthur's court and Orwen was kidnapped by King Urien of Scotland, whom she later married. [*Historia*]

OSCURE [*Ocire*]

A wide river separating the Castle of Maidens from the neighboring Castle of Ladies. [*VulgLanc*]

OSESTER OF FLORESBORG

An earl in Arthur's service. [*Erex*]

OSFRAN

A Welsh warrior whose son apparently died at the battle of Camlann. [*WelshSG*]

OSINEDOT

A British port where an army of Saxons landed to join King Mark in an attack on Arthur. [*PostQuest*]

OSLA BIG KNIFE

One of Arthur's warriors in Welsh legend. He carried a knife called Bronllafyn Short Broad, which was so big that it could be used as a bridge for armies to cross bodies of water. Osla accompanied Arthur on the epic hunt for Twrch Trwyth. At the Severn river, Osla lost his knife from the sheath while running after the boar; the sheath filled with water and pulled Osla to the bottom of the river. In a separate tale, oddly, Osla is Arthur's enemy at the Battle of Badon. He is perhaps, then, to be identified with the Saxon OCTA. [*Culhwch, Dream*]

OSMOND

A Saxon magician in the service of King Oswald the Saxon, Arthur's enemy. He commanded a demon named Grimbald and an army of fiends. When Oswald kidnapped Emmeline, Arthur's fiancée, Osmond tried to seduce her but failed. When Arthur rescued Emmeline, he threw Osmond into a dungeon. [*Dryden*]

OSPINEL [*Opinaus*]

One of the knights killed by Mabonagrain in the deadly Joy of the Court adventure, which was eventually completed by Sir Erec. Ospinel was said to never flee from battle, which probably cost him his life. [*ChretienE, HartmannE*]

OSSENET

A Knight of the Round Table who participated in the Grail Quest. [*ProsTris*]

OSTORIUS

The Saxon leader in the Elizabethan play *The Birth of Merlin*. He takes the role of HENGIST from the chronicles. His sister, Artesia, married King Aurelius Ambrosius. Ostorius used his position as the king's brother-in-law to move hordes of his troops to Britain. He then betrayed and murdered Aurelius. He was slain by Uther Pendragon in battle. [*Birth*]

OSWAIN BRAVEHEART [*Osanain, Osenain, Osoman, Ozanna, Suziano*]

A Knight of the Round Table. *Palamedes* says he was the son of Quinados Braveheart, but in *La Tavola Ritonda*, he is the son of Lady Largina and either King Esclabor or King Amorotto of Listenois. He fought in Arthur's wars against King Rions in the Vulgate *Merlin*. Malory lists him among the knights defeated and imprisoned when Meleagant kidnapped Guinevere, and in the Prose *Tristan*, he participates in the Grail Quest.

In *Tavola*, he has to guard a bridge for the love of Lady Losanna of the Anicent Tower, having slain its previous guardian (and Losanna's fiancee), Lanfate. While Oswain was trying to slay a maiden named Tessina, whom Losanna hated, Tristan discovered and killed him. [*VulgLanc, VulgMer, ProsTris, Palamedes, Arthour, Tavola, Malory*]

OSWALD[1]

A nobleman at the court of Aurelius Ambrosius. [*Birth*]

OSWALD[2]

The Saxon king of Kent in Dryden's *King Arthur*. He is named as Hengist's son, taking the place of OCTA in the chronicles. Once Arthur's ally against the Picts, he went to war with Arthur over Britain and over Emmeline, the daughter of the duke of Cornwall. Arthur won the war, but Oswald and his sorcerer Osmond kidnapped Emmeline. Arthur reclaimed her in single combat against Oswald. Arthur let Oswald retain the throne of Kent. [*Dryden*]

OTUN

An earl in Arthur's service. [*Erex*]

OUTER WALES

The kingdom of Lac and Erec, usually called DESTREGALES.

OUT ISLES

A series of islands off the northwest coast of Britain. Malory identifies them with the Hebrides. They were the home of Arthur's Sir Frolle. The Queen of the Out Isles was one of the four queens who kidnapped Lancelot and took him to Cart Castle. [*Malory*]

OWAIN

The original form of YVAIN, found in Welsh legends and belonging to the historical character of that name.

OWALES

An Arthurian knight in the Middle Scots tale of *Golagros and Gawain*. During the war between Arthur and Gologras, Owales was defeated by Golagros's Sir Ewmond. [*Golagros*]

OWEN

According to Geoffrey of Monmouth, a king of Britain in the second century BC. He succeeded King Cap and was succeeded by King Sisillius. [*GeoffHR*]

OWGHRTETH

A lord of Turry who appears in the Alliterative *Morte Arthure*, apparently as one of Arthur's vassals. [*Allit*]

OXEN FORD

Merlin's name for the Castle SINDENART. [*VulgLanc*]

OXFORD [*Osseneford, Oxenford*]

A city in south central England, formerly called Rhydychen, governed by Earl Boso in Arthur's time. According to Chrétien, the Greek knight Cliges won a great tournament in a field south of Oxford, defeating Sagremor, Lancelot, and Perceval, and fighting Gawain to a draw. Medieval tradition had it that Merlin's scribe, Petronius, was the founder of Oxford University. [*GeoffHR, Wace, ChretienC, VulgLanc*]

P

PADARN [*Paternus*]

One of the several Welsh "saints," whose *Life* contains an encounter with Arthur. Arthur is presented as a tyrant in the story. He wanders into Padarn's cloister at Llanbadarn Fawr and demands Padarn's tunic. Padarn calmly causes a crevasse to open in the earth and swallow Arthur. Arthur is not released until he begs forgiveness. This tunic is mentioned among the "Thirteen Treasures of the Island of Britain" in Welsh lore. We may surmise that it was red, since Padarn bears the epithet "Red Coat." [*SaintsP, Triads*]

PAFORT

A knight present at the Sorgarda tournament, which Gawain won. [*Heinrich*]

PAGON

A castle in Gaul. Arthur conquered it from Serses, an ally of King Claudas. [*VulgLanc*]

PALACE OF ADVENTURES

An enchanted section of the castle Corbenic where the Grail was kept. Full of marvels and enchantments, it was considered a sign of bravery to have spent the night there. Both Bors and Lancelot did so—the latter to cure his madness (the presence of the Grail drove a demon out of him). The Palace was constructed by Alan and Joshua in the time of Joseph of Arimathea. King Calafes, the lord of the Strange Land, died after impiously sleeping in the palace. According to the Third Continuation of Chrétien's *Perceval*, Perceval and the Fisher King were buried in the palace. [*VulgLanc, Contin3, Malory*]

PALACE OF THE GARDEN [**Palagio del Giardino*]

A palace in Cornwall, near Tintagel, where Isolde threw a celebratory feast after she and Tristan were welcomed back to Mark's court. Mark changed his mind and sent his seneschal Underigo and other knights to seize them. Lancelot and Tristan killed all of Mark's knights in the palace. [*Tavola*]

PALADEM

A king who served King Rions, Arthur's enemy. [*VulgMer*]

PALADES

An original owner of the Dolorous Guard, the castle conquered by Lancelot. Imprisoned by giants, he ransomed his life by promising to deliver twelve children to them annually. [*Palamedes*]

PALADORE

A lover of Morgan le Fay slain by Arthur, causing a rift between Arthur and Morgan. [*HeberM*]

PALAGRE

The finest city in Hoselice, or Wales, in the time of Joseph of Arimathea. Galahad, Joseph of Arimathea's son, was crowned in Palagre. [*VulgEst*]

PALALUNE

In *La Tavola Ritonda*, the Cornish wilderness where Isolde sent her squires and her maidservant Brangain. Isolde had instructed the squires to slay Brangain because she thought that Brangain might tell Mark of her affair with Tristan. The squires took pity on the woman and spared her. She and Isolde were later reconciled. This episode appears in numerous Tristan romances, but the forest is generally not named. [*Tavola*]

PALAMEDES [*Palamides, Palamidez, Palamidesso, Palomides, Palomydes*]

A Saracen knight whose character was born in thirteenth-century French romance. His first appearances are in *Palamedes*, the Post-Vulgate Cycle, and the Prose *Tristan*. He was commonly known as the "Knight of the Questing Beast," the Questing Beast being demon that Palamedes pursued throughout his career. Palamedes's nobility and prowess were almost unsurpassed.

His father was King Esclabor, and his many brothers included Safir and (in Malory) Seguarades. His sister was named Florine.

Like Tristan, Palamedes loved Isolde, which led to a number of tense situations between the two knights, who otherwise respected and admired each other. Among other offenses, Palamedes kidnapped Isolde after returning Brangain, Isolde's maidservant, whom he had found in a forest (this abduction replaces one by GANDIN in Gottfried's version). On this occasion, as in others, Tristan and Palamedes clashed in battle over Isolde's love. After these battles, the two knights generally reconciled but remained bitter.

In various adventures, Palamedes championed a lady against the evil Sir Gonereys, won the love of the King of Baghdad's daughter by killing a malicious knight named Corsabrin, avenged the murder of King Armant of the Red City, defeated Sir Atamas at the Spring of Healing, freed the Giant's Tower, and helped repel King Mark's invasion of Logres. In the culmination of a life-long quest, he slew the Questing Beast at the Lake of the Beast.

He continually refused baptism until Galahad defeated him and forced him to become a Christian as a condition of his surrender. (In Malory, however, his baptism follows a final battle and reconciliation with Tristan.). He was present at Corbenic for the completion of the Grail Quest.

Accounts of his fate vary. The Post-Vulgate *Queste del Saint Graal* tells us that, shortly after the Grail Quest, he was slain by Gawain, causing his father to commit suicide. In Malory, he helps Lancelot rescue Guinevere from the stake, for which Lancelot makes him the duke of Provence. In the Serbo-Russian *Povest' o Tryshchane*, he receives a mortal wound from Tristan at the castle of the Foul Heathen. In the Italian *I Due Tristani*, he tries to abduct Isolde, the daughter of Tristan and Isolde, and is slain in the attempt by Palante, Tristan's cousin. [*ProsTris, Palamedes, PostQuest, TristanoR, Malory, DueTris, Povest*]

PALANTE

Tristan's cousin. He raised an army in Lyonesse and invaded Cornwall after Tristan's death. Joined by Kahedins, he slew Andred, Mark's treacherous seneschal, and captured Mark. He later killed Palamedes when the pagan knight tried to abduct Isolde, Tristan and Isolde's daughter. He married the duchess of Milan. [*DueTris*]

PALAUS [*Paulas, Pela Orso, Pellaus*]

Morgan le Fay's castle in Italian romance. Morgan imprisoned her daughter, Pulzella Gaia, in the castle's dungeon, after Pulzella Gaia had an affair with Gawain. Gawain rescued her from the prison, and placed Morgan le Fay there in her stead. [*Tavola, Pulzella*]

PALDRIOT

The king of Lendrie who became the father of Wigamur. Wigamur was abducted from Paldriot as an infant and later became an Arthurian knight. Wigamur re-discovered his father when the two nearly fought in single combat years later. [*Wigamur*]

PALE WHITE LIVELY BLACK

The horse belonging to Arthur's warrior Morfran. [*Triads*]

PALERMO

Capital of Sicily. It was the location of a battle between Arthur and Emperor Filimenis of Constantinople. At the conclusion of the war, Sir Floriant became king of Sicily and made Palermo his seat. [*Floriant*]

PALET OF TREBE

A knight in the service of King Ban of Benoic and King Bors of Gannes. He joined Arthur's forces at the battle of Bedegraine. [*VulgMer*]

PALLAS

A king whose seneschal, Minadoras, fought alongside Arthur in the Saxon wars. [*Livre*]

PALMER

Companion of the knight Guyon in his quest to destroy the evil Bower of Bliss. [*Spenser*]

PALMOANO

A vassal of King Meliadus of Lyonesse, Tristan's father. When Meliadus died, Tristan appointed Palmoano regent of Lyonesse while Tristan went to serve King Faramon of France. [*Tavola*]

PAMADAS

A heathen warrior slain by Gaheris at the battle of Diana Bridge. [*Arthour*]

PAMONA

An island in the Orkneys where Arthur was driven ashore by a storm raised by Satan. Satan met him there and led him through several challenges, making him fight a number of fearsome monsters. Arthur survived the trials with the assistance of the angel Gabriel. [*BlackmoreK*]

PAMPHILIA [*Pamphile, Pamphylia*]

An ancient region in south Asia Minor, on the Mediterranean Sea. According to the Alliterative *Morte Arthure*, it was allied to Lucius the Roman, Arthur's enemy. [*Allit, Malory*]

PAMPHILLE

A woman in the ancestry of the famous Brown lineage. She was the wife of Brun and the mother of Yrlande and Gialle. [*Palamedes*]

PANAWR BATTLE LEADER

One of Arthur's warriors in Welsh legend. [*Culhwch*]

PANCRIST

A castle that Arthur presented to either Gawain or Girflet. [*Contin1*]

PANDRASUS [*Pandras*]

The king of Egypt who was subject to the Roman Emperor Lucius. He was called upon to join Lucius in the war against Arthur. He led a force of soldiers at the battle of Soissons. In Malory's account, the "King of Egypt and Ethiopia" is killed at Soissons, but it is unclear if this is the same character. [*GeoffHR, Wace, Malory*]

PANON

Father of Arthur's warrior Ysgawyn. [*Culhwch*]

PANSAMURS

The fairy husband of Beaflurs. His son Liahturteltart was a page to Queen Ampflise of France in the time of Uther. [*Wolfram*]

PANSCHAVAR

An Asian lord. His brother was Zaradech. His sister Japhite died from heartbreak when Wigalois, Gawain's son, killed King Roaz of Glois, Japhite's husband. Panschavar and Zaradech came to Glois to retrieve Japhite's body. Both brothers later joined Wigalois's war against Prince Lion of Namur. [*Wirnt*]

PANT

The tyrannical king of Genewis, named in Ulrich von Zatzikhoven's *Lanzelet* as Lancelot's father. He was overthrown and killed by his own nobles. Pant is manifestly a corruption of BAN, the name traditionally given to Lancelot's father. [*UlrichZ*]

PANTHELIUS [*Pantelion*]

A bold Roman consul who led an echelon of Roman Soldiers in Claudas's second war against Arthur. [*VulgLanc*]

PAPAGUSTES

A fearsome Scottish serpent, the ribs of which conferred upon their holder immunity for heat. One of these ribs formed half of the hilt of Galahad's SWORD WITH THE STRANGE HANGINGS. [*VulgEst*]

PAPIRIS OF TROGODJENTE

An infidel king who served Feirefiz, Perceval's half-brother. [*Wolfram*]

PAPO [*Apies, Po*]

Father of Arthur's warrior Donaut. [*GeoffHR, Wace*]

PAR-LUI-FET

An alias of PERCEVAL in *Perlesvaus*. Given to him by King Pelles, it signified a self-made knight. [*Perlesvaus*]

PARDIAC

A region of France owned by Lancelot. Lancelot made Sir Neroneus the earl of Pardiac in return for Neroneus's support in his war against King Arthur. [*Malory*]

PARENT [*Pharien*]

A follower of Joseph of Arimathea and companion of Peter. He founded a chapel in Britain, in the land of Count Baalan, who Parent converted to Christianity. [*VulgEst*]

PARFOYAS OF LAMPREGUN

A count who was once defeated in combat by Perceval. [*Wolfram*]

PARIS[1]

The "King of France" in Welsh legend, who gave his name to the country's capital. Paris was one of Arthur's warriors. Interestingly, the title "King of France" is given to two other warriors—Iona and Gwilenhin—in the same story. In Jean D'Outremeuse's *Ly Myreur des Histors*, one of Arthur's warriors named Paris of France is given the daughter and lands of the King of Saynes, whom Arthur conquers. [*Culhwch, Jean*]

PARIS[2] [*Parigi, Paryse, Paryss*]

In the chronicles, Arthur fights and kills Frollo in Paris, thus conquering Gaul. While he was pacifying Gaul and beginning the administration of laws, he made Paris his capital. During Arthur's battles with Emperor Lucius of Rome, he sent the prisoners captured to a prison in Paris. In *La Tavola Ritonda*, Paris is King Faramon of France's capital. [*GeoffHR, VulgMer, Tavola, Malory*]

PARK

The Count of Park inhabited a castle near the lair of the giant Tericam of the Impenetrable Forest. Lancelot freed the Count of Park's brother from Tericam's prison, for which the count rewarded Lancelot with horses. [*VulgLanc*]

PARMENIE [**Armenie, Ermenia, (H)ermonie*]

Tristan's ancestral land, ruled by his father King Rivalin and then bequeathed to Tristan. Tristan never ruled the kingdom, but instead commended it to the stewardship of his foster-father, Rual. Upon Rual's death, it was ruled by Rual's sons. Its capital was the city of Canoel. Later writers give Tristan's homeland as LYONESSE. Thomas of England's original version, "Armenie," might be a derivation of "Armorica," an early name for Brittany. Gottfried von Strassburg would have changed it to "Parmenie" to avoid confusion with Armenia. [*Thomas, Gottfried, TrisSaga, SirTris*]

PARMENIDES

A warrior who served Alexander of Constantinople. With Alexander, he joined Arthur's service for a brief time, fighting against the traitor Angres of Windsor. [*ChretienC*]

PARROT

See KNIGHT OF THE PARROT.

PARSAMANT

A knight defeated by Perceval, who ended Parsamant's custom of beating and robbing his prisoners. [*Contin4*]

PARTHIA

An ancient country in southwest Asia, southeast of the Caspian Sea. It was ruled by King Hirtacius in Arthur's time, who was subject to the Emperor Lucius of Rome. [*GeoffHR*]

PARTHIE

One of the many ladies at Arthur's court to fail a chastity test involving a goblet. [*Heinrich*]

PARTINAL

A knight whose death is the object of Perceval's quest in the Third Continuation of Chrétien's *Perceval*. The nephew of Sir Espignogres, Partinal besieged Goondesert, Perceval's uncle, in the castle of Quingragan. The siege was lifted, but Partinal disguised himself as one of Goondesert's knights, sneaked into the castle, and slew Goondesert with the Grail Sword. Perceval learned of the murder from the Fisher King. He tracked Partinal to the Red Tower, Partinal's castle, and killed him after a day-long duel. Perceval then took his head to the Grail Castle. Partinal's role is filled by the HAGS OF GLOUCESTER in the Welsh *Peredur*. [*Contin3*]

PASCENTIUS [*Pascent, Passent*]

Son of Vortigern and brother of Vortimer, Catigern, and Faustus. Nennius mentions that after his father's death, he was granted the rule of Buelt and Gwerthrynion by the new king, Ambrosius. Geoffrey, however, contends that Pascentius fled to Germany, raised an army, and returned to Britain to attack Ambrosius. After one defeat, he allied with King Gilloman of Ireland and tried again. He sent a Saxon assassin named Eopa to kill Ambrosius, and the Saxon succeeded. Uther and his army met Pascentius and Gilloman near St. David's (or at Menevia) and killed them. Wace says that Pascentius hated his father because of his father's dealings with the Saxons. Thomas Heywood erroneously makes him a Saxon. [*Nennius, GeoffHR, Wace, Layamon, Heywood*]

PASGEN

A son of Urien and brother of Owain. The Welsh Triads call him "arrogant," and say that he rode a horse named Huge Yellow. [*Triads*]

PASSAUVER

In *La Tavola Ritonda*, a traitorous knight who killed King Arduano (Arnant) of the Red City. Palamedes, who swore to avenge the king, slew Passauver in the city of Saraziana. Passauver's counterpart in the Prose *Tristan* is HELAIN. [*Tavola*]

PASSBRUEL [*Passabrunello, Passe-Brewel*]

Tristan's horse. It enabled Tristan's friends to recognize him when he was otherwise in disguise. In *La Tavola Ritonda*, it is killed during Tristan's battle with a giant named Urgan the Hairy. [*ProsTris, Tavola, Malory*]

PASSELANDE

King Arthur's horse in Béroul's *Tristan*. [*Beroul*]

PASSING

A castle where Yvain was imprisoned after he accidentally freed a fearsome giant named Malduit, and thus infuriated the castle's residents. He was rescued by Bors, who slew the giant. [*VulgLanc*]

PATELAMUNT

A city in the African or Middle-Eastern kingdom of Zazamanc. It was ruled by Queen Belacane and served as Gahmuret's port of arrival when he came to the kingdom. [*Wolfram*]

PATERNAS

One of Arthur's knights in a Norse legend. His wife was proven unchaste during a chastity test involving a mantle. [*Mottuls*]

PATH OF NO RETURN

The road leading to the enchanted FOREST OF NO RETURN, where Guinebal created the Magic Dance. [*VulgLanc*]

PATREUS

A Knight of the Round Table defeated in a tournament against the Queen's Knights. [*VulgMer*]

PATRICE [*Patriche*]

A vassal of King Claudas. He ruled the castles Charrot and Dun. His son, Issout, inherited the latter. [*VulgLanc*]

PATRICK[1]

A nobleman from Scotland. While Arthur was besieging the Saxons Colgrim and Baldulph at York, Patrick learned that another Saxon—Cheldric—had landed nearby with a force of soldiers. He rode to York and warned Arthur to break off the siege or be destroyed by Cheldric's onslaught. [*Layamon*]

PATRICK[2]

The son of Duke Mathem of Soane and brother of Avenable, Julius Caesar's wife. At Merlin's advice, Patrick married Caesar's daughter. [*VulgMer, ProsMer2*]

PATRICK[3] THE RED

One of Arthur's sons in Rauf de Boun's *Petit Brut*. His brothers were Adeluf III and Morgan the Black. [*ProsBrut*]

PATRICIUS OF THE MOUND

The father of Ade, one of Lancelot's wives in Ulrich's *Lanzelet*. He was a renowned huntsman and tracker. His daughter was raised by his brother Linier, who was eventually killed by Lancelot in combat. Ade introduced Lancelot to him and he approved of the match. [*UlrichZ*]

PATRIDES

A nephew of King Bagdemagus of Gorre, sometimes called Patrides of the Golden Circle. He served as steward of Gorre when Bagdemagus left to seek adventure at Arthur's court. Later, he fought alongside his uncle in Arthur's war against King Claudas and won himself great honor. He became a Knight of the Round Table. In another adventure, Perceval rescued him from an imprisonment at the castle Galanton. Patrides had tried to elope with the castle's lady, for which Galanton's residents chained him to a rock to starve. During the Grail Quest, Gawain killed Patrides while Patrides was trying to avenge Yvain of Cenel's murder. Malory calls him the son of Pellownus. [*VulgLanc, PostQuest, Palamedes, Girart, Malory*]

PATRIGALT

The king and warriors from Patrigalt participated in a tournament at the Welsh city of Kanvoleis, thrown by Perceval's mother, Queen Herzeloyde, in Wolfram's *Parzival*. One of the Grail Templars at Munsalvæsche came from the country. In Der Pleier's *Tandareis and Flordibel*, Patrigalt is a land allied to Arthur. [*Wolfram, PleierT*]

PATRIS OF THE MOUNTAIN

A knight sent to Arthur's court as a prisoner after Agravain defeated him in combat. [*Contin4*]

PATRISE

An Irish knight in Malory's *Le Morte Darthur*. He was the cousin of Sir Mador of the Gate. At a dinner party thrown by Queen Guinevere, Sir Patrise ate a poisoned apple meant for Sir Gawain. The apple had been poisoned by Sir Pionel, in revenge for the death of Sir Lamorat. Patrise had convulsions and died. Mador accused Guinevere of treason, but the truth of the matter was later discovered. His character is called GAHERIS in the Vulgate *Mort Artu*. [*Malory*]

PATRIZ OF THE MOUNTAIN

One of five knights who tried to kill Agravain and were defeated by him. [*Contin3*]

PATROCLES[1]

Tristan's grandfather in the Icelandic *Saga af Tristram ok Ísodd*. He was the father of Kalegras and the vassal of King Hlöövir of Spain. He became the leader of the Spanish after his lord was slain in a battle against an invader named Elemmie. He slew Elemmie, but soon died of wounds received in the battle. His brief rulership helped establish his son and grandson as Spain's heirs. [*SagaTI*]

PATROCLES[2]

Tristan's grandson. He was the son of King Kalegras and Queen Lilja of England. [*SagaTI*]

PAULAS

A knight related to Lancelot. After Arthur's death, he retired to a hermitage run by the Archbishop of Canterbury. King Mark of Cornwall came to the hermitage to destroy the last of Arthur's knights. After Mark killed the archbishop, Paulas killed Mark. [*PostMort, ProsTris*]

PAVENGAY [*Pavongais*]

An Irish castle in the land of Demedy. Lancelot visited the region on his way to adventures at Rigomer Castle, and he rescued the viscount of Pavengay's daughter, Flor Desiree, from a brutish neighbor named Savari. [*Merveil*]

PAVIA [*Pavy*]

A town in northwest Italy, on the Ticino River, that was the home of Sir Callyburne. When Arthur captured Rome, Pavia was one of the many lands to surrender to him and pay tribute. [*Allit, Malory*]

PAWNCE

A city in Lombardy, acquired by Arthur after the Roman War. [*Allit*]

PAYERNE [*Pa(i)erne, Payarne*]

The home of Leonce, one of King Ban's knights. Its lord, perhaps identical to Leonce, fought against the Saxons in the early days of Arthur's reign. [*VulgLanc, VulgMer, Arthour, Malory*]

PAZAREIA

Home of Isolde of the White Hands in the Serbo-Russian *Povest' o Tryshchane*. The story concludes with a tournament at the castle of Baroh in Pazareia. [*Povest*]

PEDRAWD [*Bedrawc*]

Father of Arthur's warrior Bedwyr. [*Geraint*]

PEDROG SPLINTERED-SPEAR

One of the three "Just Knights" in Arthur's court. Pedrog meted justice through the law of arms, in contrast to his fellows, who upheld the law of the earth or the law of the church. [*Triads*]

PEDYVERE OF THE STRAIT MARCHES

A knight who ran afoul of Lancelot. Pedyvere was chasing his wife with a sword, trying to cut off her head, because she had committed adultery. Lancelot stopped him, and the woman begged Lancelot for protection. However, Pedyvere distracted Lancelot by pointing to some imaginary horsemen behind him. When Lancelot was looking in the other direction, Pedyvere cut off his wife's head. He then immediately yielded to Lancelot and would not fight. Lancelot sent Pedyvere to Guinevere, who in turn made him take his wife's body to the pope in Rome to receive penance. After that, Malory tells us, Sir Pedyvere "fell into great goodness and was a holy man and a hermit." Despite the similarity of his name, he is probably not identical to BEDIVERE. [*Malory*]

PEHPIMEROT

A Knight of the Round Table. [*HartmannE*]

PEIBYAW

An ox that lived on the near side of Mynydd Bannawg. Peibyaw had once been human, but was turned into an ox because of his sins. As one of his tasks, the warrior Culhwch had to capture the ox and yoke it together with another ox from Mynydd Bannawg called Nynnyaw. [*Culhwch*]

PEIBYN

Father of Arthur's warrior Eiryn the Splendid. [*Dream*]

PEISSAWG THE TALL

King of Brittany and one of Arthur's warriors. He was killed at Ystrad Yw by the piglet Llwydawg the Killer during the great hunt of Twrch Trwyth. [*Culhwch*]

PELANDE

In Guillaume le Clerc's *Fergus*, the homeland of Arthur's knight Fergus, where he was raised by his father, Soumillet. Guillaume identifies Pelande with Galloway. [*Guillaume*]

PELIAS

An early heathen king of Lyonesse. He fell in love with Chelinde, the wife of King Canor of Cornwall, and imprisoned Canor in his castle Lusin. Sador, Chelinde's first husband, defeated Pelias in combat and forced him to release Canor. Later, Canor and Pelias went to war, and Pelias was killed. His son Luce succeeded him. [*ProsTris*]

PELIAZ THE STRONG

A Knight of the Round Table from Logres, killed by Gawain during the Grail Quest. [*PostQuest*]

PELLANDRIS

Brother of Playne de Amours, Playne de Fors, Plenorius, Pillounes, and Pellogris, all of whom guarded the fortress of Sorelois. By defeating all six brothers, Breunor and Lancelot liberated the fortress and its prisoners. Afterwards, Pellandris joined Arthur's service. [*Malory*]

PELLE

A city ruled by King Estrangaré, who served Arthur. [*Meriadeuc*]

PELLEAS [*Pellias*]

A knight of extraordinary skill and courage, and lord of many islands, who loved the lady named Arcade or Ettard. He awarded her the crown at a tournament in which he defeated sixty knights, but Arcade continually rebuked and scorned him. He followed her to the country of Arroy, where he kept vying for her love. Every day, she sent ten knights against him, and every day he defeated them all but let them capture him anyway so that he might get a glance of Arcade on the way to her prison. Then,

Arcade's men would humiliate him and release him in the forest.

Gawain learned of Pelleas's plight and offered to help him by visiting Arcade. Bringing Pelleas's armor with him, he told Arcade that he had killed Pelleas. Whatever his plan had been, Gawain abandoned it when he saw Arcade's beauty. He slept with her, betraying Pelleas. Pelleas found them together in an outdoor pavilion. After considering killing them, he finally decided to lay his sword across their throats and depart. When Arcade awoke, she realized that Pelleas had been there and that he was still alive.

In the Post-Vulgate *Merlin* continuation, Pelleas prepares to die of grief, but a repentant Gawain brings Arcade to him. Apologies are made, and Pelleas and Arcade marry, producing a son named Guivret the Younger. In Malory's version, however, Nimue, the Lady of the Lake, bewitches Ettard so that she pines for Pelleas for the rest of her life, but Nimue marries Pelleas herself. He becomes a Knight of the Round Table.

Tennyson allows neither of these happy endings for poor Pelleas. Pelleas, discovering that Ettare and Gawain are both false, falls into despair and runs away from the hateful scene. He later encounters Perceval, who tactlessly informs him that Guinevere and Lancelot are also untrue. Having lost all faith in the nobility of Arthur's court and the Round Table, Pelleas goes mad, becomes the "Red Knight," maims innocents, and rapes maidens. He sends a message to Arthur's court telling the king that Pelleas's castle is full of cowards and whores, but that they are more noble than Arthur's court because they do not hide their true nature. Arthur eventually has to lead a phalanx of knights against him. [*PostMer, Malory, TennIK*]

PELLEHAN [*Parlan, Pellam*]

A Grail King of Listenois in the Vulgate romances. The first appearance of his name in the Vulgate *Queste del Saint Graal* suggests that he was Perceval's father, which would make him the origin of PELLINORE (and also, probably, of PELLES). The Vulgate *Estoire del Saint Graal*, however, calls him the son of King Lambor and the father of Pelles and Pellinore, making him Perceval's grandfather and Galahad's great-grandfather. Like all Grail Kings, he inherited the title of FISHER KING from Bron, the first of his lineage. Later, however, he fell ill with a festering wound and became known as the MAIMED KING. The circumstances behind this wound vary: the Vulgate *Estoire* tells us that he received it in a battle in Rome; in the Vulgate *Queste*, we learn that he was struck through the thighs by a holy spear when he tried to draw the Sword with the Strange Hangings, meant only for Galahad.

The Post-Vulgate *Merlin* continuation provides a much longer story. Here, he has a brother named Garlon, an invisible knight who commits murder and is pursued by Balin. Balin eventually slew Garlon during a feast in Pellehan's Perilous Castle, for which Pellehan attacked Balin, shattering the latter's sword. Pellehan pursued Balin throughout his castle as Balin ran from room to room looking for a weapon. Eventually, he found the Bleeding

Lance—the spear that killed Christ—and struck Pellehan through the thighs with it. This blow was called the Dolorous Stroke, and it caused the castle to crumble and turn Listenois into a Waste Land. (In another version, however, the Dolorous Stroke occurs in an episode with Pellehan's father, Lambor.)

Pellehan's wound refused to heal, and he lay ill for many years. At the end of the Grail Quest, Galahad cured him with some blood from the Bleeding Lance, and Pellehan retired to a hermitage.

Tennyson alone names Pellehan as one of the kings who joined Lot's rebellion against King Arthur at the beginning of Arthur's reign. [*VulgQuest*, *VulgEst*, *PostMer*, *Malory*]

PELLES [*Peles, Pellas, Pelleur*]

The Vulgate GRAIL KING. He was the father of Elaine (or Amite) and grandfather of Galahad. His origin may lie with the Welsh characters PWYLL, lord of Dyfed, or BELI, king of Britain. Another possible source for his name is the Cornish *peller*, meaning "enchanter" (Loomis, *Romance*, 267).

Pelles was the son of PELLEHAN (usually the Maimed King) and the brother of PELLINORE, although all three were probably once the same character. According to *Perlesvaus*, in which Pelles makes his first appearance, he was Perceval's maternal uncle. His siblings included Yglais (Perceval's mother, also called the Widowed Lady), Messois the Fisher King, and the evil King of the Castle Mortal. *Perlesvaus* calls him the "HERMIT KING," for he retired to a hermitage after his son, Joseus, killed his wife.

In the Vulgate romances, Pelles is himself the FISHER KING—the king of the land of Listenois (a.k.a the Strange Land) and the Grail Castle, Corbenic. (The Vulgate *Merlin*, however, names Alain as the Fisher King and Pelles as his brother.) He was descended from Bron, the first Fisher King. His son, Eliezer, was one of Arthur's knights. According to the Post-Vulgate Cycle, his two sisters married Lac and Dirac, the father and uncle of Sir Erec.

Pelles was aware of various prophecies that Galahad, the yet-conceived son of Lancelot and Elaine, would complete the Grail Quest and restore the land of Listenois. Thus, he conspired with Brisen, Elaine's maidservant, to get Lancelot into Elaine's bed. When Lancelot was visiting Corbenic, Pelles drugged his wine and told him that Guinevere was waiting for him at Case Castle. Lancelot rode there, climbed into Elaine's bed and, believing he was with Guinevere, fathered Galahad. Some years later, Lancelot went insane and eventually found his way to Corbenic. Pelles took him to the Palace of Adventures, where the Grail was kept, and cured him. At the culmination of the Grail Quest, Pelles received Galahad, Perceval, and Bors in his castle, presented them with the Grail, and led Galahad to heal the Maimed King.

Malory confuses matters by attaching to Pelles a story given in the Vulgate *Queste del Saint Graal* to Pellehan: As a youth, Pelles came across a ship that had been built by King Solomon of Israel. Aboard the ship, he tried to draw the Sword with the Strange Hangings, which was meant only for Galahad, and he received a holy wound through his thighs, rendering him infirm. Thus, in Malory, Pelles also may be identified with the MAIMED KING.

Neither the Vulgate stories nor Malory describe Pelles's death. In *Perlesvaus*, he is slain by Aristor of Amorave, an evil knight who is later killed by Perceval. [*Perlesvaus*, *LancLac*, *VulgLanc*, *VulgQuest*, *PostMer*, *PostQuest*, *Malory*]

PELLINORE [*Pellanor, Pelleore, Pellinor(o)*]

A king of Listenois, Wales, or "the Isles" first mentioned in the Vulgate *Merlin* and the *Livre d'Artus* as the MAIMED KING, who was wounded by a holy lance after he doubted the wonders of the Grail, and who would only be healed at the conclusion of the Grail Quest. He was the son of PELLEHAN and the brother of PELLES (the Fisher King), although all three kings were probably originally the same character. R. S. Loomis thought that the origin of his name was "Beli Mawr" (BELI THE GREAT), a character in Welsh mythology.

The Vulgate *Merlin* says that Pellinore had twelve sons and a second brother named Alain. The Post-Vulgate romances expand and change his role. Pellinore's father, Pellehan, becomes the Maimed King, and Pellinore is given a number of adventures at Arthur's court. He is also named in the Post-Vulgate as the father of Perceval, Lamorat (who is his brother in *Palamedes*), Drian, Aglovale, and Tor—five noted Knights of the Round Table. In *Palamedes*, he has a sister called the Lady of the Island of Fairies. Malory says that he married the Queen of Flanders. Malory reproduces his adventures from the Post-Vulgate, but removes his association with the Grail family.

The *Livre d'Artus*, in an apparent attempt to reconcile conflicting traditions, actually includes two characters named Pellinore. The are cousins. The first is the father of Perceval and 16 other sons. He was wounded in the manner described above and can only find sport in fishing. He is thus both the Maimed King and the Fisher King. Fourteen of his sons were killed when King Agrippe invaded the Waste Land, causing Pellinore to retire to the Castle of Marvels and to await his healing. The second Pellinore is the king of Listenois (the Waste Land) and Corbenic (the Grail Castle). He has twelve sons. Like his cousin, he has been wounded, by the Bleeding Lance, and must await healing from Galahad. The two Pellinores are destined to be healed on the same day. No source beyond the *Livre d'Artus* includes this duplication.

According to the Post-Vulgate *Merlin* continuation, Pellinore pursued the horrid and elusive Questing Beast, giving him the nickname "Knight with the Strange Beast." In his first appearance, Arthur challenges him for the right to pursue the Questing Beast (and for the injury of the young Sir Girflet). Pellinore wins the combat, but Merlin stops him from slaying Arthur. He later enters Arthur's service. At the battle of Tarabel, he kills King Lot of Lothian, sparking a feud between his sons and the sons of Lot (Gawain, Aggravain, Gaheris, and Mordred). Arthur promoted Pellinore to the Round Table. In another adventure, Pellinore, intent on rescuing one maiden from

Sir Hontzlake of Wentland, declined to help another, who later turned out to be Alyne, his own daughter by the Lady of the Rule. She killed herself when she realized that Pellinore would not help her avenge her slain lover. According to the French *Palamedes*, Pellinore conquered Wales and helped Arthur quash a Saxon invasion.

In the traditional legend, Pellinore is slain by Gawain and his brothers in revenge for Lot's death. In the Italian *Chantari di Lancelotto*, however, he is alive at the end of Arthur's reign, and he helps Lancelot defend Joyous Guard against Arthur. [*VulgMer*, *Livre*, *ProsTris*, *Palamedes*, *PostMer*, *PostQuest*, *Palamedes*, *Chantari*, *Malory*]

PELLOGRIS

Brother of Playne de Amours, Playne de Fors, Plenorius, Pillounes, and Pellandris, all of whom guarded the fortress of Sorelois. By defeating all six brothers, Brunor the Black and Lancelot liberated the fortress and its prisoners. Afterwards, Pellogris became a knight Arthur's court. [*Malory*]

PELLOWNUS

An ancient knight who lodged Tristan when Tristan was on his way to the Castle of Maidens tournament. Pellownus had a son named Persides. [*Malory*]

PELOWNES

A castle in northeast England. A party of knights was taking Palamedes to Pelownes to be executed when Lancelot rescued him. [*Malory*]

PELUNYAWG

A locality in England where the boar Twrch Trwyth made his second stand against Arthur's warriors. Madawg, Gwynn son of Tringad, and Eiryawn Penlloran were all killed. The boar then fled to Aber Tywi. [*Culhwch*]

PEMBROKE

A city on the coast of Wales, in Dyfed. Gawain's grave was fabled to have been found in Pembroke. [*WilliamM*]

PEN PALACH ("Cudgel-Head")

A monster slain by Arthur in the halls of Dissethach. [*WelshPG*]

PEN RHIONYDD [*Penrhyn Rhionydd*]

Arthur's northern capital, according to Welsh legend. It may have been in Scotland. Its name suggests that it is a cape, or the tip of a peninsula. [*Triads*]

PENARWAN

The daughter of Culfanawyd. She married Owain, but was unfaithful. Because of her infidelity, Owain abandoned her before she could bear him children. [*Triads*]

PENDRAGON[1] [*Pandragon, Pendragoun*]

The surname of Kings Arthur and Uther, meaning "head dragon" or "dragon's head." As first told by Geoffrey of Monmouth, Uther adopted the symbol of the dragon because of the comet with the dragon's head that Merlin had seen in Wales, heralding the death of King Ambrosius Aurelius, Uther's brother. In Welsh legend, it is also the surname of one "Gwen Pendragon," who once kept Arthur prisoner.

In the Prose and Vulgate *Merlins*, the name Pendragon is given to the character elsewhere called AMBROSIUS AURELIANUS: the son of Constantine and Ivoire, the uncle of Arthur, and the king of Britain between Vortigern and Uther, Pendragon's brother. Pendragon allied with Merlin, defeated Vortigern and Hengist, died fighting the Saxons, and was buried at Stonehenge. Uther is said to have adopted his brother's name as a surname in memory of the slain king. [*GeoffHR*, *Triads*, *ProsMer1*, *VulgMer*]

PENDRAGON[2] CASTLE

A castle ruled by Sir Brian of the Isles in which Sir Brunor the Black was taken prisoner. Lancelot rescued Brunor, kicked Brian out of the castle, gave the castle to Brunor, and gave the land surrounding it to Sir Neroneus of the Isle. [*Malory*]

PENEFREC

A rich island castle in King Guivret's Ireland, according to Hartmann von Aue. It corresponds with POINTURIE, found in Chrétien de Troyes. Erec enjoyed a hospitable stay in Penefrec, which was characterized by abundant surrounding lakes, a well-stocked game preserve, and the best hunting dogs. Guivret's sisters, Filledamor and Guenteflur, were able to enjoy an idyllic existence there. [*HartmannE*]

PENELOI

The nickname or last name of Yvain in Ulrich's *Lanzelet*. The word appears only in Ulrich, and the origins and meaning of it are unknown. [*UlrichZ*]

PENMARC

A port in Brittany. When Tristan was mortally wounded, he waited for the ship carrying Isolde to arrive at Penmarc. [*ProsTris*]

PENN[1]

A warrior in Arthur's service who was the son of Nethawg. Penn was loyal to the warrior Gwythyr, and he joined Gwythyr's army against Gwynn son of Nudd. He was taken prisoner by Gwynn and was not released until Arthur intervened. [*Culhwch*]

PENN[2] LLARCAN

Father of Arthur's warrior Eiladar. [*Culhwch*]

PENNEVOISEUSE

One of Arthur's courts in *Perlesvaus*, on the Welsh coast. It was targeted by Brien of the Isles in his war against Arthur, but Arthur won the battle. E. K. Chambers (165) identifies it with Penzance in Cornwall. [*Perlesvaus*]

PENNING [*Peningue*]

The location of a tournament during Arthur's reign, hosted by Duke Galehodin, the castle's ruler. Lancelot won the tournament. [*VulgLanc*]

PENOR

One of the several kings conquered by Galehaut. [*VulgLanc*]

PENPINGYON

A gatekeeper at King Arthur's court who, according to Welsh legend, "travels on his head to save his feet." He served the warrior Glewlwyd Strong Grip and was killed by the boar Twrch Trwyth during the epic hunt. [*Culhwch, Geraint*]

PENRITH

A city in Cumbria, just southeast of Carlisle. In *The Bridal of Triermain*, Sir Walter Scott names it as one of Arthur's courts. [*Scott*]

PENSIVE KNIGHT [**Pensif Chevalier*]

A knight met by Gawain in the Second Continuation of Chrétien's *Perceval*. He lived in a forest near the Black Chapel. The knight was "pensive" over his lady, who had been abducted by Sir Brun of the Heath. Gawain rescued the woman from Brun and returned her to the Pensive Knight. [*Contin2*]

PERANT

A duke of Manaheim who was one of four brothers saved by Erec from a pack of robbers. Perant's brothers were named Joachim, Malcheus, and Juben. [*Erex*]

PERARD

Known as the "Black Knight of the Black Lands." Perard was the brother of Pertylope, Perymones, and Persaunt. He was the third knight to stand in the way of Sir Gareth on his way to defeat Sir Ironside, the Red Knight of the Red Lands. After a two-hour joust and duel, Gareth killed Sir Perard and continued his adventure. [*Malory*]

PERCEVAL[1] [*Parcefal, Parceval, Parcifal, Parcival, Parsifal, Partzefal, Parzival, Percevalle, Percevas, Percevelle, Perchevael, Perciuales, Percival, Percyvell, Perlesvaus, Persevall, Prenzival, Pressivalle, Prezzivale*]

The original Grail Hero, who cured the Fisher King and succeeded him as Grail King. He first appears in Chrétien

de Troyes's unfinished *Perceval* (c. 1190). Chrétien may have invented his name, although he has a counterpart and possible origin in Welsh texts called PEREDUR. Another progenitor in Welsh may be PRYDERI.

Perceval, which introduced the Grail to the Arthurian saga, inspired four continuations, two prologues (*Bliocadran* and the *Elucidation*), and three adaptations (*Perlesvaus*, Wolfram's *Parzival*, and Robert de Boron's *Perceval*, the last of which has been lost but is represented in prose by the Didot-*Perceval*) within the next half century. All these texts (with the possible exception of the first continuation) retain Perceval as the Grail Hero. His status changed with the Vulgate *Queste del Saint Graal*: Perceval became a secondary hero to the more pure Galahad. Following the influence of the Vulgate Cycle, only the Middle English *Sir Perceval of Galles* (which eliminates the Grail theme) featured Perceval as the central hero.

Perceval's adventures in the earliest romances, beginning with Chrétien de Troyes, can be summarized as follows: His father (variously called Alain, Bliocadran, Gahmuret, Greloguevaus, Gales, and Perceval) and brothers were slain in various combats, leading his mother (Herzeloyde or Yglais) to raise him in a secluded forest (sometimes called the Waste Forest), ignorant of chivalry and its perils. He learned to hunt and became adept with the spear. One day, he sees a group of knights in shining armor in his forest and believes them to be angels. When he learns that they are knights, and that King Arthur "makes knights," he resolves to go to Arthur's court and become a knight himself. His heartbroken mother hastily gives him some advice: to honor and serve ladies, to require only a kiss or a ring for his service, to learn the names of his companions, to travel only with honorable knights, and to pray at churches. As Perceval leaves his mother, he glances behind him and sees her collapsed on the ground, but he continues on his way.

His first adventure brings him to a tent occupied by a married lady (called Jeschute in Wolfram). Bungling his mother's advice, he eats the woman's food, kisses her, steals one of her rings, and leaves. When her husband, Orguelleus, comes home and finds that Perceval has been there, he accuses his wife of adultery. Perceval later has to combat Orguelleuse to exonerate himself and the woman of any wrongdoing.

Arriving at Arthur's court, he is struck by the beauty of the vermilion armor worn by the Red Knight, who has offended Arthur and is waiting outside the castle to be challenged by one of Arthur's knights. Perceval enters Arthur's court and promptly but innocently makes a fool of himself. A somber maiden (called Cunneware or the Mute Maiden) laughs when she sees him. As it has been prophesied that she would only laugh when she beheld the greatest of knights, Kay becomes jealous and beats her. A dwarf or fool (Antanor) who comes to her defense is kicked into a fire by Kay. Perceval later avenges Kay's abuse by breaking his arm in a joust.

Arthur knights the youth at his request, and Perceval immediately asks for the armor worn by the Red Knight. Kay malevolently tells Perceval to go ahead and take it, assuming that the Red Knight will kill him. Perceval leaves the castle and throws one of his spears through the Red Knight's visor, killing him instantly. A squire named Yvonet happens along and shows Perceval how to remove and wear the red armor.

Perceval wanders away and comes to the castle of Gornemant of Gohort, a noble lord who lodges Perceval and shows him how to properly use a sword and a lance. Noticing a tendency towards loquacity in Perceval, Gornemant advises him not to talk too much, so as to avoid offending his companions. Perceval departs and comes to the city of Beaurepaire, where the castle's lady (Blancheflur or Condwiramurs) is besieged by the evil King Clamadeu of the Isles. Perceval defeats Clamadeu and his seneschal, Anguigerron. He falls in love with the lady of Beaurepaire and promises to return to her (in Wolfram, he marries her).

In the most important scene of the story, Perceval then comes to the castle of the enigmatic Fisher King (who, he later learns, is his uncle), who has a wound that has left him infirm. The Fisher King gives him the Grail Sword. Dining in the castle, Perceval witnesses a procession of squires and maidens bearing, among other things, a Bleeding Lance and the Grail. He is curious about these objects, but, mindful of Gornemant's advice, he refrains from asking about them. He determines to inquire about them the next morning, but when he awakens, the castle is empty. Perceval rides into the forest where he finds a woman (named Sigune in Wolfram) weeping over the body of her dead lover. She turns out to be Perceval's cousin, and she admonishes him for failing to ask about the lance and the Grail, saying that if he had asked, the Fisher King would have been cured. After some more adventures, he returns to Arthur's court where he receives the same rebuke from an ugly maiden (named Cundrie in Wolfram). Determined to rectify his mistake, he sets out to find the Fisher King's castle again. He finds his uncle (Trevrizent in Wolfram, the Hermit King in other stories) in a hermitage, and learns more information about the Grail and the Fisher King.

At this point, Chrétien de Troyes's romance turns to the adventures of Gawain and eventually ends without returning to Perceval. Each of Chrétien's continuators finishes the romance in varying ways. The first continuation, itself incomplete, virtually ignores Perceval in favor of Gawain. The second describes Perceval's various adventures as he attempts to return to the Grail Castle. Eventually finding it again, Perceval tries to repair the broken Grail Sword, but it retains a hairline fracture, symbolizing Perceval's failure to achieve perfection. The second continuation, too, ends without a conclusion. In the third, Perceval finally heals the Fisher King and is crowned Grail King. He rules for seven years, retires to a hermitage, and is succeeded by the King of Valoune, who has married the Fisher King's daughter. The fourth continuation recounts a similar success as Perceval returns to the Grail Castle and completely mends the Grail Sword.

Wolfram's *Parzival* follows a similar route. After Perceval's battle with his half-brother, Feirefiz, Cundrie appears and leads him back to the Grail Castle. Perceval asks the Grail Question and heals the Fisher King. He becomes Grail King and rules with his wife, Condwiramurs. Other than the Grail Castle, his kingdoms include Anjou and Wales. Perceval and his wife have two sons named Loherangrin and Kardeiz.

Shortly after Chrétien's *Perceval*, Robert de Boron wrote his cycle of romances, which transformed the Grail into the *Holy* Grail but still showed intention of retaining Perceval as the Grail Hero. Robert may have written a verse *Perceval* which was adapted by the author of the prose Didot-*Perceval*, in which Perceval himself causes the Fisher King's wound by arrogantly sitting in the Round Table's Perilous Seat. He eventually heals the Fisher King by asking the Grail Question and remains in the Fisher King's court. Robert exerted a less direct influence on the author of *Perlesvaus*, which recounts a multitude of Perceval's adventures as he destroys paganism and advances Christianity in Britain. His adventures include the rescue of his family castle, Kamaalot (inhabited by his mother Yglais and his sister Dandrane), from the Lord of the Fens and Cahot the Red; the rescue of the Grail Castle from the King of the Castle Mortal; the obtaining of the Circle of Gold; and the battles against the fearsome Knight of the Burning Dragon and the evil Black Hermit. In the culmination of his adventures, Perceval assumes the kingship of the otherworldly Island of Plenty and retires from the world.

With the Vulgate Cycle, however, Perceval becomes a hero secondary to the noble Galahad, and never again in Medieval literature does he regain his former status. Briefly summarized, the Vulgate romances give Perceval as the son of Pellehan or Pellinore and the youngest brother of Aglovale, Drian, Lamorat, and Tor. Again raised by his mother in seclusion, he eventually leaves with his brother Aglovale and becomes his squire. Knighted at Arthur's court, he is seated at the Table of Less-Valued Knights until the Mute Maiden takes him by the hand, speaks for the first time, and leads him to his proper seat at the Round Table. He embarks on the Grail Quest when it is announced, and he is allowed to succeed with Galahad and Bors after he resists temptation from various fiends and remains a virgin. With the other Grail Knights, he attends a mass at Corbenic and then journeys to Sarras, where he perishes after a year. In these romances, Perceval is simply a less significant version of Galahad, not very necessary to the plot, but probably retained because of his prior status as the original Grail hero. [*ChretienP*, *Contin1*, *Contin2*, *Bliocadran*, *Wolfram*, *Perlesvaus*, *VulgLanc*, *VulgQuest*, *Contin3*, *Contin4*, *ProsTris*, *PostMer*, *PostQuest*, *SirPerc*, *Malory*, *Perchevael*, *TennIk*]

PERCEVAL[2]

A knight who served King Pellinore. Pellinore named his son Perceval after him. [*Palamedes*]

PERCEVAL[3]

Father of Perceval in the Middle English *Sir Perceval of Galles*. He married Acheflour, Arthur's sister. He was killed in battle by the Red Knight, prompting Acheflour to raise Perceval ignorant of knighthood and its dangers. He replaces ALAIN, PELLINORE, and other characters in earlier Perceval stories. [*SirPerc*]

PEREDUR[1]

A character in both Arthurian and non-Arthurian Welsh legend. He is the Welsh counterpart, and perhaps the origin, of PERCEVAL. Peredur himself may have origins in the Welsh hero PRYDERI, though multiple references probably point to a historical figure of that name. His father was called Elidur or Efrawg and he had a brother named Gwrgi. In Welsh, he is often given the surname "Long Spear," and his name phonetically (*peri dûr*) could be taken to mean "hard spear." Another theory holds that *Peredur mab Efrawg* is a corruption of *Praetor ab Eburaco*, a Roman title signifying "an official from York."

Peredur appears in the *Annales Cambriae*, which says that he and Gwrgi defeated Gwenddolau at the battle of Arfderydd in 573. Peredur and his brother were slain in 580 against Eda Great-Knee at the battle of Caer Greu, apparently after their own warriors deserted them. He left a son named Gwgon Gwron. As Arthur's death in the *Annales* occurs in 539, it seems that Peredur was originally a post-Arthurian hero (and possible a historical figure) later drawn, like Urien and Owain, into the Arthurian saga. A Peredur also appears in *Y Gododdin* as one of the British warriors slain by the Angles at the battle of Catraeth (c. 600), though this may be a late interpolation.

Peredur appears briefly in the Welsh Triads and in Geoffrey of Monmouth's *Historia Regum Britanniae*. In Geoffrey's *Vita Merlini*, he becomes the king of North Wales after Arthur's death and, as in the *Annales*, goes to war with King Gwenddoleu of Scotland.

His romance, called *Peredur*, dates from the thirteenth century. It parallels the adventures of Perceval in Chrétien de Troyes's *Perceval*, and it is unclear how much of his story was adapted directly from Chrétien and how much is part of an earlier Celtic or French tradition. The youngest of seven boys who, with their father, were all killed in war and combat, Peredur was raised by his mother ignorant of chivalry and its perils. One day, he saw some knights near his home and decided to accompany them to Arthur's court, causing his mother to die of grief. Arriving at Arthur's hall, he was proclaimed the "flower of knights" by two dwarves, who Cei beat for their insolence to the rest of Arthur's knights. Peredur later avenged Cei's abuse by breaking Cei's arm. In his first combat, he defeated a knight who had offended Gwenhwyfar, Arthur's queen.

Peredur visited the home of his uncle (analogous to the Fisher King in Chrétien), where he saw the head of another uncle floating in a dish. His various adventures led him to slay robbers, reclaim kingdoms, and win tournaments. He had a brief affair with Angharad Golden Hand, conquered the heathens of the Circular Valley, slew the Black Serpent of the Barrow, and killed the Black Oppressor. He won the favor of the Empress of Constantinople, with whom he shared a throne for fourteen years. He then returned to his adventures, and was prompted by his cousin—in disguise—to slay the Hags

of Gloucester, who had murdered the uncle whose head was in the dish. This revenge them parallels Perceval's slaying of Partinal in the third continuation of *Perceval* in order to avenge the death of Goon Desert. [*Gododdin, Annales, GeoffHR, GeoffVM, Triads, Peredur, Geraint*]

PEREDUR[2]

In Geoffrey of Monmouth's chronicle, a son of King Morvid of Britain. He joined his brother Iugenius in a revolt against their elder brother, King Elidur. Elidur was thrown in prison. Peredur and Iugenius divided the island, and Peredur became king of all Britain when Iugenius died. Upon Peredur's death, Elidur was again given the throne. Peredur's son, Runno, eventually became king. These events occurred in the third or second century BC. [*GeoffHR*]

PEREVIDA

Daughter of King Pelles of Corbenic and mother of Galahad in *La Tavola Ritonda*. She is known as AMITE or ELAINE in French romance. [*Tavola*]

PERFIDA ("Wicked")

An island in Britain that held Crudele Castle, where Tristan was imprisoned for a time. [*Tavola*]

PERGALT

A castle ruled by Duke Retan, an ally of Arthur's Sir Garel. [*PleierG*]

PERIES OF ORGANIA

A king present at Uther Pendragon's Urbano tournament, where he was defeated by King Ban of Benoic. [*Tavola*]

PÉRIGORD

An area in France ruled by Lancelot. Lancelot made Sir Galyhud the earl of Périgord in return for Galyhud's support in the battles against King Arthur. [*Malory*]

PERILOUS BED [*Bed of Marvels*]

An enchanted bed encountered by Gawain in Chrétien's *Lancelot*, Chrétien's *Perceval*, Wolfram's *Parzival*, Heinrich von dem Türlin's *Diu Crône*, and the Vulgate *Lancelot*. The heart of the adventure was that any knight who lay on the bed would swiftly find himself assaulted by arrows or flaming lances, and that only by covering himself adequately with armor would he survive. Generally, the missile assault is then followed with an attack by lions, leopards, dragons, or other fiends.

Chrétien places the bed in Canguin Rock in Galloway; Wolfram's Perilous Bed is in the Castle of Marvels in the Terre Marveile; Heinrich names the castle as Salie; and the Vulgate version places it in the Grail Castle. The first three stories also include the additional peril of a fierce lion, which Gawain slays, and his success lifts the enchantments from the castle. The Vulgate version says that Sir Bors also braved the bed, and was wounded by a fiery lance that came out of nowhere. Wolfram tells us that the bed was enchanted by the sorcerer Clinschor. R. S. Loomis (*Tradition*, 42) thought that the Perilous Bed was originally associated with the TURNING CASTLE motif, and that it originated ultimately in Irish legend. [*ChretienP, Wolfram, VulgLanc, Heinrich*]

PERILOUS BRIDGE[1]

Another name for the SWORD BRIDGE leading to the land of Gorre. Lancelot crossed it in his quest to rescue Guinevere. [*VulgLanc*]

PERILOUS BRIDGE[2] [*Pont Perileus*]

A half-finished bridge on the way to the Castle Orguelleus. Perceval had to cross it. When he reached the end, it detached itself from one side of the chasm, turned 180 degrees, and allowed Perceval to keep riding to the other side. This was only to happen when the best of knights rode upon it. [*Contin2, Elucid*]

PERILOUS CASTLE[1]

A manor where Sir Meliot of Logres lay sick until he was cured by Lancelot. [*Perlesvaus*]

PERILOUS CASTLE[2]

A castle Arthur had to conquer in order to free the Kingdom of Damsels from the grip of a tyrant. [*ChevPap*]

PERILOUS CASTLE[3] [*Chastel Paorous*]

A castle ruled by Lord Menelais. It was said that no one passed the castle without seeing or hearing something that would terrify him. [*Meriadeuc*]

PERILOUS CASTLE[4]

A castle whose enchantments were destroyed by Arthur's knights Claris and Laris. Its ruler was Orgueillox the Proud. [*Claris*]

PERILOUS CEMETERY[1]

A haunted graveyard in *Perlesvaus*. Its chapel, the Perilous Chapel, held the shroud that covered Christ, which Perceval needed to defeat the Lord of the Fens. Perceval's sister, Dandrane, braved the horrors of the cemetery to retrieve a piece of the shroud. Lancelot had to perform similarly on a quest to heal Meliot of Logres. A variation of Dandrane's adventure is given to Lore of Cardigan at the WASTE CHAPEL in *Meriadeuc*. [*Perlesvaus*]

PERILOUS CEMETERY[2] [*Atre Périlleux*]

A cemetery visited by Gawain during his quest to rescue Arthur's female cupbearer from Sir Escanor. Gawain spent the night there and learned of a maiden trapped in a tomb by a fiend. He beheaded the devil and freed the damsel. [*Atre*]

PERILOUS CHAPEL[1]

The chapel in the PERILOUS CEMETERY, found in *Perlesvaus* and Malory's *Le Morte Darthur*. In the former, Perceval had to brave the horrors of the haunted cemetery and chapel to retrieve the shroud which had covered Jesus Christ. Perceval's sister, Dandrane, also had to journey to the Perilous Chapel to retrieve a piece of the shroud. Finally, Lancelot was required to face the Perilous Chapel to obtain a sword and cloth in order to heal Meliot of Logres.

It is the latter knight's adventure that Malory embellishes. In *Le Morte Darthur*, the Perilous Chapel is guarded by 30 knights twice the size of any man, and is ruled by Hellawes the Sorceress, lady of the Castle Nygramous. When Sir Meliot de Logres killed Sir Gylbert the Bastard, Gylbert's lover, a witch, cast a spell on Sir Meliot so that his wounds would never be healed unless some knight braved the Perilous Chapel and retrieved a bloody sword within. Lancelot came upon the sickly Meliot and promised to help him. He traveled to the chapel, held his shield before him, and pushed through the ranks of knights into the chapel without incident. Inside, he found the sword on an altar. On his way out, the 30 knights, in unison, told him to replace the sword or perish, and Lancelot bravely chose to risk it and press forward. Again, the knights did not attack. It turned out that the entire Chapel was an elaborate charade created by Hellawes the Sorceress, and Lancelot was the first person to call her bluff. Hellawes appeared before Lancelot and asked him for a kiss in exchange for the sword, but Lancelot refused her. Hellawes then told him that if he had kissed her, he would have fallen down dead. She professed her love for Lancelot, and said that she would have rather had him dead than not have him at all. Lancelot hurried away, and Hellawes died within a fortnight from sorrow. [*Perlesvaus, Malory*]

PERILOUS CHAPEL[2]

A chapel visited by Gawain and Hector during the Grail Quest. Both knights saw visions portending the completion of the quest by Galahad, Perceval, and Bors. The visions signified the unworthiness of both Gawain and Hector. [*PostQuest*]

PERILOUS CHEST

A chest in the castle Dolorous Guard containing the demons that enchanted the castle. Lancelot, upon conquering the stronghold, found the key to open the chest and release the demons, thus ending the enchantments. [*VulgLanc*]

PERILOUS FORD[1] [*Gué Perellos*]

A treacherous ford in the land of Galloway that no knight dared to cross. Gawain reached it during his travels and tried to jump his horse across it, but his horse jumped badly and dumped him into the river. [*ChretienP*]

PERILOUS FORD[2]

A ford defended by the knight Bleoberis. Gawain's son Guinglain defeated Bleoberis at the Perilous Ford and sent him to King Arthur. [*Renaut*]

PERILOUS FORD[3]

A ford where Perceval defeated a knight named Urbain. Urbain, to honor his fairy lover, jousted with all knights who passed the ford. [*Didot*]

PERILOUS FOREST

A name given to several woods in Arthurian romance; it is impossible to differentiate one from the other. *Perlesvaus* names it as a forest near the Grail Castle; the Post-Vulgate locates it between Logres and Gorre; Malory places it in Wales. The Vulgate *Lancelot* says that the lord of Bellegarde Castle (or the White Fortress) murdered King Lancelot, Lancelot's grandfather, by a spring in the Perilous Forest. Lancelot visited his tomb there. Other locations in the Perilous Forest included the Small Charity Abbey, the Spring of the Two Sycamores, and the Forbidden Hill. In the Vulgate *Merlin*, it is the former name of the FOREST OF NO RETURN, which was enchanted by Guinebal, Lancelot's uncle. The Post-Vulgate names it as the forest of Merlin's imprisonment by the Lady of the Lake. Knights who experienced adventures in the Perilous Forest include Galahad, Lancelot, Lamorat, Tristan, Meleagant, Gaheris, and Perceval. [*Perlesvaus, VulgLanc, VulgEst, VulgMer, Malory*]

PERILOUS LAKE

A lake in the Forest of Morrois in Cornwall. King Mark of Cornwall sent Sir Kay on an "adventure" to the Perilous Lake. Mark intended to ambush and kill him. Kay, unbeknownst to Mark, joined with Sir Gaheris on the way. Mark and his nephew Andred defeated Kay, but Gaheris defeated them both. Rather than kill King Mark, Gaheris forced him to revoke Tristan's exile from Cornwall. [*ProsTris, Malory*]

PERILOUS MOUNT

A treacherous mountain that Arthur's Sir Kahedins vowed to climb until he reached the top. [*ChretienP*]

PERILOUS PALACE

In the Post-Vulgate, a castle in the forest of Darnantes where Simeon, a sinful follower of Joseph of Arimathea, was forced to burn until Galahad came and freed him of his torment. Elsewhere, the Perilous Palace is named as the castle of Pellehan, the Grail King, which is usually called the PALACE OF ADVENTURES. [*PostMer, PostQuest*]

PERILOUS PASS [*Passage Perilleux*]

A location with a castle guarded by Lord Febus and a band of twenty knights. Galehaut the Brown established the adventure. Guiron the Courteous defeated Febus and all the knights, completing the adventure. Guiron made Seguarades lord of the castle of the Perilous Pass. [*Palamedes*]

PERILOUS PORT [*Perilous Rock*]

A rock in the middle of the sea, once used as a harbor for a band of pirates. After King Mordrain converted to Christianity, God transported him to the Rock of the Perilous Port to test his faith. Although tempted by a fiend and threatened by storms (which broke the Rock in two), Mordrain resisted his desire to leave the Rock, and thus passed the test. The geography given by the *Estoire del Saint Graal* suggests an identification with the Rock of Gibraltar, although the latter is not in the middle of the ocean. [*VulgQuest, VulgEst, Malory*]

PERILOUS SEAT [*Seggio Periglioso, *Siege Perilous*]

The forbidden seat at the Grail Table and Round Table, meant only for the most pure. It was said to commemorate the seat occupied by Christ at the table of the Last Supper, or the one vacated by Judas at the same table. Robert de Boron was the first writer to mention it. According to the Didot-*Perceval*, it was the thirteenth seat the Round Table, and Merlin had ordained that only the best knight could sit in it. A newly-knighted Perceval jumped into the seat without thought, and it split under him. The seat had been intended for him, but he had sat in it prematurely. As a result, the Fisher King could not be cured and part of Britain became a Waste Land.

The Vulgate romances relate that at the Grail Table, Josephus, the son of Joseph of Arimathea, sat in the Perilous Seat. The Round Table's Perilous Seat was reserved for Galahad. (It was empty for many years until Galahad came to court at the beginning of the Grail Quest.) Any other man who sat in the Perilous Seat was swiftly incinerated, swallowed by the earth, or carried off in flames. This horrid fate befell Moses at the Grail Table, and Brumand and Riger at the Round Table. The seats next to the Perilous Seat were likewise reserved for the best of knights: at the Round Table, they were filled by Perceval and Bors.

Analogs to the Perilous Seat appear in other romances. In *Durmart le Gallois*, Durmart sits in one upon is arrival at Arthur's court. In Wirnt von Grafenberg's *Wigalois*, Wigalois sits on a rock when he arrives at Arthur's court, which astonishes the other knights because it was said that only a pure knight could even approach it. [*RobertBorJ, Didot, Wirnt, Durmart, VulgLanc, VulgQuest, VulgEst, PostMer, PostQuest, Palamedes, Malory*]

PERILOUS VALE

The residence of Morgan le Fay in Chrétien de Troyes's *Erec*. [*ChretienE*]

PERILOUS VALLEY[1] [*Val Perilleus*]

A land ruled by the Red Knight, an enemy of Arthur. Situated on the Sea of Norway, it was ringed by high mountains and could only be entered via a narrow passage. The Red Knight imprisoned many of Arthur's knights in the Perilous Valley until they were freed by Gawain and Meriadeuc. [*Meriadeuc*]

PERILOUS VALLEY²

A dangerous vale from which no knight ever returned alive. Lancelot and Tristan entered the valley during the Grail Quest and slew two savage giants at the castle of Sidravalle. [*Tavola*]

PERINIS [*Paranis*]

Isolde's chamberlain. He acted as a go-between for Tristan and Isolde when they had to be apart. He killed a malicious forester who planned to betray the lovers, and he summoned King Arthur from Scotland to come to Isolde's trial. [*Beroul, FolieB, Eilhart*]

PERIRON [*Peritum*]

A location in Arthur's kingdom that was governed by Baron Hirelglas. [*GeoffHR, Wace*]

PERLESVAUS [*Pellesvaus*]

A variation of PERCEVAL, used in the thirteenth-century French *Perlesvaus*. The author relates that the name signifies "he who has lost the vales," because his father's land, the vale and castle of Camelot, was invaded and conquered by the Lord of the Fens. This alternate form of Perceval's name confused some later authors, and both Perceval and "Pellesvaus" consequently appear in the romance of *Escanor*. [*Perlesvaus, Girart*]

PERNEHAN [*Perna, Pernam, Perlo*]

The younger brother of King Mark of Cornwall in the Prose *Tristan*. He was the smallest and ugliest son of King Felix. He condemned Mark for cowardice in surrendering a tribute to Ireland. In revenge for the insult, Mark slew Pernehan at the Fountain of the Lion while the two were hunting in the desert of Liantes. There is a similar character in Malory named BODWYNE. [*ProsTris, TristanoR, Tavola, Povest*]

PERSAUNT OF INDE

A knight known as the "Blue Knight." He was the brother of Sir Perard, Sir Pertylope, and Sir Perymones. Gareth, on his quest to defeat the Red Knight of the Red Lands, encountered Persaunt at a tournament. Gareth had previously defeated Sir Persaunt's three brothers, and he soon overcame Persaunt himself. Following the battle, Persaunt lodged Gareth. He offered his maiden daughter to Gareth for the night, but Gareth balked at the thought of defiling a virgin. At the next Pentecost feast, Persaunt went to Camelot and gave himself to King Arthur's service. Arthur eventually appointed him to the Round Table. [*Malory*]

PERSE

Paramour of Sir Hector of the Fens. She was the daughter of the Lord of the Narrow Borderland. Her father promised her to Lord Zelotés, but Perse resisted the match because of her love for Hector. Zelotés abducted her. Hector rescued her, killing Zelotés in the process. [*VulgLanc*]

PERSEVAUS

A Knight of the Round Table in Hartmann's *Erec*. The name is likely a variation of PERCEVAL, but Perceval appears in Hartmann as a separate character. [*HartmannE*]

PERSIA [*Perse*]

An ancient empire in southwest Asia, including the area from the Indus River to the west borders of Asia Minor and Egypt. In the Vulgate *Estoire del Saint Graal*, Persia is ruled by King Label in Joseph of Arimathea's time. Wolfram says that magic was invented in the city of Persida in Persia, and that Perceval's father Gahmuret had adventures in the region. *De Ortu Waluuanii* describes a war between Persia and the Roman empire over the city of Jerusalem, in which a young Gawain, in the service of the Roman Emperor, defeated a Persian champion named Gormundus and settled the dispute. The daughter of the King of Persia appears at a "sparrowhawk" tournament in Wirnt von Grafenberg's *Wigalois*. In the Alliterative *Morte Arthure* and Malory's *Le Morte Darthur*, the area seems to be under the command of the Roman Emperor, Lucius; Persian warriors joined Lucius's campaign against Arthur. [*Wolfram, Wirnt, VulgEst, DeOrtu, Allit, Malory*]

PERSIDA

A fabled Persian city in which magic was first invented, according to Wolfram. The sorcerer Clinschor healed himself here after his castration and was introduced to the magical arts. [*Wolfram*]

PERSIDES THE BLONDE¹

A knight who was cuckolded by Tristan. [*ProsTris*]

PERSIDES THE RED²

The lord of the castle Gazewilté. He married the wondrously beautiful Helen the Peerless against the wishes of his family and hers. His uncle chastised him and told him he had abandoned his knighthood because of Helen and had humiliated himself. Helen said that she, too, had given up the admiration of others for the sake of Persides—and that her shame was greater because she was more beautiful than Persides was valiant. Persides, angry, locked Helen in a tower and told her she would stay there until a more beautiful lady or a more valiant knight showed up, settling the matter. In time, Arthur's knight Hector came along and defeated Persides, ending the dispute. [*LancLac, VulgLanc*]

PERSIDOS

A Knight of the Round Table from Calaz, present at Corbenic when Galahad completed the Grail Quest. [*PostQuest*]

PERTYLOPE [*Pertilope*]

The knight known as the GREEN KNIGHT in Malory. He was the brother of Perard, Perymones, and Persaunt. Gareth defeated him as part of a quest to conquer Sir Ironside, the Red Knight of the Red Lands. Pertylope pledged himself to the service of Gareth and Arthur, and Arthur made him a Knight of the Round Table. He was killed fighting Lancelot and his men when Lancelot rescued Guinevere from the stake. His name is similar to BERTILAK, the name of the Green Knight in *Sir Gawain and the Green Knight*. [*Malory*]

PERYDDON

The resting place of Arthur's warrior Gwalchmei. [*WelshSG*]

PERYF

Father of Arthur's warrior Twrch. [*Culhwch*]

PERYMONES

Known as the RED KNIGHT, the brother of Perard, Pertylope, and Persaunt. He was the fifth knight defeated by Gareth on a quest to conquer Sir Ironside, the Red Knight of the Red Lands. Perymones pledged himself to the service of Gareth and Arthur, and Arthur made him a Knight of the Round Table. He was killed fighting Lancelot and his men when Lancelot rescued Guinevere from the stake. [*Malory*]

PERYN¹ OF MONTBELIARD

A knight who joined company with Sir Balin the Savage but was soon slain by the invisible Sir Garlon. Balin had him interred, and a message appeared on his tomb predicting the death of King Pellinore at the hand of Gawain. [*Malory*]

PERYN² OF THE MOUNTAIN

A knight defeated by Sir Alexander the Orphan at the castle Fair Guard. [*Malory*]

PERYNIN

Brother of Brangain (Isolde's maidservant) and Sir Mathael. Brangain presented her to brothers to Tristan as servants. [*ProsTris*]

PERYS OF THE FOREST SAVAGE

A knight with a reputation for murdering maidens. Lancelot learned of his deeds from a lady and killed him. Found in Malory, he is based on an unnamed villain in the Vulgate Lancelot. [*Malory*]

PERSIVES OF LANGAULOS

A Knight of the Round Table who participated in the Grail Quest. [*PostQuest*]

PETER¹ [*Peron, Petr(e)us*]

A follower of Joseph of Arimathea, mentioned by Robert de Boron and the Vulgate *Estoire del Saint Graal*. Robert tells us that he was assigned the task of traveling to the Vale of Avaron (Avalon?) in Britain and to await the coming of the third Grail Keeper (unnamed, but probably Perceval).

In the *Estoire*, Peter is an ancestor of Lot and Gawain. His cousin, Simeon, tried to murder him, but succeeded only in giving him a poisoned wound. As it festered and caused great pain, Peter was sent out to sea to find his fate. He washed up at Orkney, where King Orcant's daughter found a Christian doctor to heal him. In gratitude, Peter championed King Orcant against King Marahant of Ireland. Peter slew Marahant, winning the respect and friendship of Orcant and King Lucius of Britain, both of whom subsequently converted to Christianity. He married Camille, Orcant's daughter, and inherited the kingdom of Orkney, which he passed on to his son, Herland. [*RobertBorJ, VulgEst*]

PETER² OF THE ROCKS

Bishop of Winchester in the early thirteenth century. According to the *Chronicon de Lanercost*, he dined with Arthur in 1216. Before disappearing, Arthur gave Bishop Peter the power to produce a butterfly in his hand at will, so that he could prove having met the legendary king. Peter subsequently became known as the "Bishop of the Butterfly." [*ChroniconL*]

PETERSAND [*Petersaint*]

One of many Italian cities to surrender and send tribute to King Arthur after he had captured the city of Rome. [*Allit, Malory*]

PETIPACE OF WINCHELSEA [*Petipas, Pettypas*]

A knight defeated by Sir Tor during his quest to retrieve a white brachet stolen from Arthur's court. Tor sent him to Arthur, who eventually appointed him to the Round Table. He later joined Mordred and Agravain in their plot to trap Lancelot and Guinevere *in flagrante*. He was slain by Lancelot outside Guinevere's chambers. [*SyreGaw, Malory*]

PETITCREIU [*Pencru, Peticrewe, Peticru, Petit Creü, Petitcriur, Petitto Araviuto*]

A little lap dog, given to Duke Gilan of Wales by a goddess from Avalon. It was the offspring of a brachet and a leopard. Tristan saw the dog when he was staying with Gilan, and thought that it would cheer up Isolde during their separation. Tristan performed a service for Gilan by slaying the troublesome giant Urgan, and asked for

Petitcreiu as a gift. Gilan assented, and Tristan sent it on to Isolde. The dog had a little bell around its neck. The ringing of the bell caused happiness in all who were near. When Isolde realized its magical properties, she ripped it off the dog, so that she would not be happy when her lover was sad. In the Middle-English *Sir Tristrem*, Petitcreiu's original owner is named Triamour. [*FolieO, Gottfried, PleierG, SirTris*]

PETREIUS COTTA [*Peredur, Peter, Petrinus, Petrion*]

A Roman senator who became a general in the war between Arthur and Lucius Hiberius. He was present at the first battle, which began after Gawain cut off a Roman warrior's head during peace negotiations. Gawain and his companions—fearful at how Arthur might react to their actions—concentrated on capturing Petreius Cotta to soothe Arthur's anger when they returned to him; Boso managed to accomplish this arrest. Without their leader, the Roman brigade fell apart. Arthur was indeed pleased with his prisoner, he and threw him into a Paris jail. An attempt by the Romans to rescue him failed. [*GeoffHR, Wace, Layamon, VulgMer, Allit*]

PETRONIUS [*Petrone*]

A scribe who served Merlin. According to Medieval tradition, he founded Oxford University. In the Vulgate *Lancelot*, he helps Galehaut interpret a disturbing dream. [*VulgLanc, Prophecies*]

PETROSA

A mountain near Paulas, Morgan le Fay's castle, where Tristan killed Huneson the Bald, Morgan's lover. [*Tavola*]

PEUL

Father of Teleri, a lady at Arthur's court. [*Culhwch*]

PFETAN

A great black dragon who lived in Korntin and plagued its people. The spirit of the slain King Lar of Korntin enlisted Gawain's son, Wigalois, to slay Pfetan, and he gave him a special lance to accomplish this deed. Lar also presented Wigalois with a sweet blossom, for the dragon's breath was so foul that it could kill a man. On his way to fight the dragon, Wigalois came across Countess Beleare of Joraphas, whose husband, Count Moral, had been carried off by the creature. Arriving at the dragon's lair, Wigalois immediately lanced it through the heart, killing it, but he suffered a terrible injury in the process and fell down half-dead by a lake. Countess Beleare, joyfully reunited with her husband, found him there and brought him back to her castle for healing. [*Wirnt*]

PHAEDRIA

A water fairy who inhabited a the Lake of Idleness. Knights who wanted passage across the lake boarded Phaedria's ferry, but they were seduced and taken to her magical island. Sir Guyon refused to succumb to her temptations and escaped her. [*Spenser*]

PHARANT

Guardian of the Fountain of Marvels on the Island of the Fountain. He was killed by Tristan. Pharant's wife took Pharant's body to Arthur's court, demanding vengeance. Arthur personally challenged Tristan to combat, unaware of Tristan's identity, and was defeated. [*ProsTris*]

PHARAOH [*Pharaen*]

A vassal of King Rions slain by Gawain at the second battle of Carhaix. [*VulgMer*]

PHARIEN [*Farien, Phariaunce*]

A knight from Trebe in the service of kings Ban (Lancelot's father) and Bors. He accompanied his lieges to Britain to assist in Arthur's wars against the rebellious kings and the Saxons. He fought in the battle of Bedegraine. King Bors banished Pharien after Pharien killed another knight to avenge his uncle's death. Pharien took service with King Claudas, the enemy of Ban and Bors, but still retained his loyalty to Bors and his family.

After Ban and Bors died during Claudas's invasion of their lands, Pharien guided Bors's widow to a monastery and then looked after her children, Bors and Lionel, whom he hid from Claudas. Claudas had an affair with Pharien's wife and found out about the princes from her. Claudas agreed to take care of them and made Pharien heir to their lands until they were grown. In time, however, the people of Gannes (Bors's former land) revolted and Pharien found himself in the uneasy situation of protecting King Claudas against his former allies and friends. This led to a temporary rift between Pharien and his nephew, Lambegue. Pharien lived long enough to see Bors and Lionel placed in the care of the Lady of the Lake. [*LancLac, VulgLanc, VulgMer, Arthour, Malory*]

PHEDON

A squire whose "best friend" falsely accused Phedon's fiancée of falsehood. Phedon's "friend" arranged for Phedon to find his fiancées maid, disguised as Phedon's fiancée, in the embraces of another man. Thus deceived, Phedon killed his fiancée. When he learned the truth, Phedon killed his friend and went chasing after the evil maid. He was attacked in the forest by a madman named Furor, but was saved by Sir Guyon. [*Spenser*]

PHELOT OF LANGUEDUK

A knight who served the King of North Wales. He designed a malicious plot to murder Lancelot. Lancelot came upon Phelot's wife, shrieking that she had lost her hawk in a tree and that her husband would kill her if he found out. She coaxed Lancelot into removing his armor and climbing the tree to retrieve the hawk. While Lancelot was climbing, Phelot rode out of a brush and bellowed, "Oh, knight Lancelot, now I have found thee as I wished!"

Refusing to allow Lancelot to don his armor or pick up his sword, Phelot challenged him to combat. Lancelot disarmed Phelot with a branch, took his sword, and killed him. [*Malory*]

PHENONEE

Sister of Arthur's Sir Meliador. She married Agamanor of Normandy. [*Froissart*]

PHILIDEL

An air spirit in Dryden's *King Arthur*. Philidel became a fugitive from hell when she refused to obey the evil commands of Osmond, a Saxon sorcerer. Merlin brought her into his service, and she saved Arthur from the malevolent schemes of Osmond and Grimbald, an enemy earth spirit. [*Dryden*]

PHILIPPÍA

King Mark's mother in the Icelandic *Saga af Tristram ok Ísodd*. She was married to King Philippus of England, and her daughter, Blenzibly, became Tristan's mother. [*SagaTI*]

PHILIPPUS

King of England and father of King Mark in the Icelandic *Saga af Tristram ok Ísodd*. He was married to Queen Philippía, and his daughter, Blenzibly, became Tristan's mother. [*SagaTI*]

PHILLIP

One of Christ's apostles. The Vulgate *Estoire del Saint Graal* tells us that he baptized Joseph of Arimathea and that Peter, one of Joseph's followers, founded a church in Orkney in honor of Phillip. In an English version of Joseph's life, Phillip travels with Joseph from Israel to France, and bids him to go to Britain with the Grail. [*VulgEst, HereJOA*]

PHILSOFINE

Wife of Gales the Bald and mother of Perceval in the Fourth Continuation of Chrétien de Troyes's *Perceval*. A follower of Joseph of Arimathea, she was a member of the party that brought the Grail to Britain. [*Contin4*]

PHOENIX

A bird of fabled beauty in Egyptian mythology. It was said to live in the desert for five or six centuries, then consume itself in flames only to be reborn out of its own ashes, beginning the cycle again. According to Wolfram von Eschenbach, this was accomplished through the virtue of the Grail. [*Wolfram*]

PHRYGIA

An ancient country in west central Asia Minor, ruled in Arthur's time by King Teucer, an ally of the Roman Procurator Lucius Hiberius. [*GeoffHR*]

PIACENZA

The kingdom ruled by the King with a Hundred Knights in the Italian *I Due Tristani*. It is the name of a city in Lombardy. [*DueTris*]

PIANTAGIORNO

A white war-horse given to Tristan by Duke Bramante after his previous horse, Passe-Bruell, was slain by a giant named Urgan. [*Tavola*]

PIBLESUN OF LORNEPARZ

A king once defeated in combat by Perceval. [*Wolfram*]

PICOLS

An alias taken by TRISTAN when he visited Mark's court after his banishment. Tristan was disguised as a madman so he could get close to Isolde. G. D. West (*Verse*, 133) notes J. M. Telfer's suggestion of a connection with a fool named Picol at the court of King John. [*FolieB*]

PICTS

One of the earliest tribes from mainland Europe to invade the British Isles (3000-1000 B.C.). They settled throughout the islands, but were eventually driven into Ireland, Wales, and Scotland by the invading Celtic tribes, with whom they eventually merged. During Roman times, the term "Pict" was used to describe all of the barbarian tribes living in Scotland who were never conquered by the Roman empire. During the Roman occupation of Britain, the Picts were a frequent headache, leading raids over Hadrian's wall and into what is now northern England. When the Romans withdrew from Britain in the early fifth century, leaving a depleted British military, the problem intensified. It appears that in the late 420s or so, a British ruler named Vortigern employed Saxon mercenaries to swell the British ranks and hold back the Pictish invasions. Vortigern's scheme backfired, and the Saxons, perhaps allied with the Picts they were hired to oppose, became the new enemy. In the late fifth century, a new wave of British resistance, begun by Aurelianus Ambrosius and probably continued by Arthur, held back both races. In the meantime, the Scots arrived from Ireland and established their own kingdoms in Picitish lands, and in the sixth century, St. Columba converted the former "barbarians." After several hundred years of hostilities between the Picts and Scots, the two races joined politically in the ninth century, and the Picts, as such, ceased to exist.

Turning to the Picitsh role in Arthurian legend: According to Geoffrey of Monmouth (who says that they arrived from Scythia during the reign of Marius in Britain), Arthur subjugated the Picts in the early days of his reign, after the battles at Moray and Lomond. Contradicting previous chronicles, Hector Boece says that the Picts were Arthur's allies against the Saxons and that Lot was their king. In Richard Blackmore's *Prince Arthur*, Mordred is represented as their king. [*Bede, GeoffHR, Boece, BlackmoreP*]

PIGNARÉS THE WICKED

A count who was a companion of Lord Formis on the Turning Isle. King Nentres defeated him when Arthur and his knights fought Formis's knights. [*Livre*]

PIGNORAS [*Pin(n)ogras, Pongerrens*]

One of the many Saxon kings to invade northern Britain at the beginning of Arthur's reign. Pignoras had a hand in the siege of Vambieres, and he opposed Nentres in a battle at Broceliande. After several other battles, Gawain killed him on the plains of Roestoc. In another version, he is slain by Eliezer at Garlot. His wine steward, Margon, continued the struggle. [*VulgMer, Livre, Arthour*]

PILADES

A knight who fought in the tournament at Noauz. He carried a shield made in Limoges. [*ChretienC*]

PILOISE

A page in the court of King Mark of Cornwall. Isolde employed him to take a message of love and forgiveness to Tristan, after she erroneously accused him of an act of dishonor. On his way back to Cornwall, bearing Tristan's acceptance, he stopped in the city of Saint Michelsstein and enjoyed a fair. [*Eilhart*]

PILLOUNES

Brother of Playne de Amours, Playne de Fors, Plenorius, Pellogris, and Pellandris, all of whom guarded the fortress of Sorelois. By defeating all six brothers, Brunor the Black and Lancelot liberated the fortress of its prisoners. Afterwards, Sir Pillounes became a knight of Arthur's court. [*Malory*]

PINABEL[1]

A warrior who served Alexander of Constantinople. With Alexander, he joined Arthur's service and was killed during Arthur's war against the traitor Angres of Windsor. [*ChretienC*]

PINABEL[2]

A Knight of the Round Table present at Corbenic when Galahad completed the Grail Quest. [*PostQuest*]

PINABEL[3] [*Pinabello*]

A knight in who fell in love with a maiden named Tessina. Tessina's mother, on condition of marriage, made Pinabel kill Uriées, his own brother, who had slain Tessina's uncle Garionne. Pinabel did so, sparking a war between him and his other brothers. They eventually slew him in the valley of Zetro. Tristan had to save Tessina from the family. [*ProsTris, Tavola*]

PINADOS

An early Knight of the Round Table defeated by Gawain in a tournament against the Queen's Knights. [*VulgMer*]

PINADRIANS OF ANGUEFORE

A knight in Arthur's service. [*Girart*]

PINCADOS

A Knight of the Round Table related to Lancelot. He participated in the Grail Quest. [*PostQuest*]

PINCENAR [*Pinc(h)enar(s)*]

A Saxon king killed at the battle of Roestoc by King Ban of Benoic. [*VulgMer, Arthour*]

PINDOLUS

A Knight of the Round Table badly wounded by Gawain in a tournament against the Queen's Knights. [*VulgMer*]

PINE CASTLE

A castle where Tristan was imprisoned for four years by King Mark of Cornwall. Perceval defeated Mark and forced him to release Tristan. [*ProsTris*]

PINNAS

A heathen warrior slain by Gaheris at the battle of Diana Bridge. [*Arthour*]

PINTADOL

A castle conquered by Galescalain, Arthur's duke of Clarence. Galescalain defeated four knights, thus liberating the castle of its evil customs. [*VulgLanc*]

PIOLES

A maiden encountered by Arthur's Sir Wigamur. She was betrothed to the King of Nordien, and Wigamur, although two nights in her presence, did not take advantage of her. Wigamur later re-united her with her fiancée. [*Wigamur*]

PIONEL [*Pyonel*]

In Malory, a knight in Arthur's service who was the cousin of Lamorat. When Lamorat was slain by Gawain and his brothers, Pionel devised a plot to kill Gawain. Guinevere hosted a party, and Pionel poisoned some fruit intended for Gawain. An unlucky knight named Patrise ate the fruit instead of Gawain and died. Sir Mador, Patrise's cousin, accused Guinevere of murder, but Nimue eventually arrived at court and explained the truth. By this time, Pionel had fled the court. The Vulgate *Mort Artu* calls the same character AVARLAN. [*Malory*]

PIOPHAS

A Saxon warrior who, under King Aminaduc, fought Arthur's forces at the battle of Vambieres. [*Livre*]

PIR

According to Geoffrey of Monmouth, a king of Britain in the second century BC. He succeeded King Samuil-Penissel and was succeeded by King Capoir. [*GeoffHR*]

PISA [*Pis(e)*]

According to the Alliterative *Morte Arthure*, this Italian city was acquired by Arthur after the Roman War. [*Allit*]

PLAARIN

A Knight of the Round Table who participated in the battles against the Saxons at Vambieres and Clarence. He may be identical to BLAARIS. [*Livre*]

PLACIDES[1] [*Placidan*]

A Saxon warrior slain by Arthur's Sir Galescalain in a battle at Camelot. [*VulgMer, Arthour*]

PLACIDES[2] THE MERRY

A knight in the service of King Ban of Benoic and King Bors of Gaul. He helped defend his masters' lands against King Claudas while they were assisting Arthur in Britain. Later, he was involved in a quest to learn the fate of Merlin. [*VulgMer, Arthour, Malory*]

PLACIDUS

In the Norse *Erex Saga*, an evil Earl who tried to force Enide into marriage. Erec, whom the earl had thought was dead, awoke from unconsciousness while Placidus was trying to force himself on Enide. Erec slew him. He appears in Chrétien's *Erec* as ORINGLE. [*Erex*]

PLAISSANT OF THE ISLE

Alias assumed by FLORETE while she accompanied her husband, Floriant, on a series of European adventures. [*Floriant*]

PLANTAMOR[1]

A Saxon king slain by Arthur at the battle of Clarence. [*Livre*]

PLANTAMOR[2]

The steed ridden by Arthur during the battle against the Saxons at Vambieres. [*Livre*]

PLARÉS

Nephew of Lord Raolais of Estremors. He joined his uncle's war against Arthur and was killed in the fighting by Galescalain. [*Livre*]

PLARION

A king of Ireland in the service of King Rions, Arthur's enemy. He helped Rions invade Carmelide, and he was defeated by Arthur's forces at Carhaix. [*VulgMer*]

PLATO OF MARGDEIBORG

A duke who was Gawain's nephew. He was carried away by a dragon but was saved by Erec. In return, Plato tried to give Erec his dukedom, but Erec declined. [*Erex*]

PLAYNE[1] DE AMOURS

A knight who guarded a fortress in the land of Sorelois. He was the brother of Playne de Fors, Plenorius, Pillounes, Pellogris, and Pellandris. Sir Brunor the Black defeated the Playnes on his way to liberate their fortress. [*Malory*]

PLAYNE[2] DE FORS

A knight who guarded a fortress in Sorelois. His brothers were Playne de Amours, Plenorius, Pillounes, Pellogris, and Pellandris. He eventually became a Knight of the Round Table. [*Malory*]

PLEASANCE [*Plesaunce*]

One of many Italian cities to surrender to Arthur after he conquered Rome. [*Allit, Malory*]

PLEGRUS

The greatest knight of King Philippus of England, Mark's father. When his lord died, he joined Blenzibly, Philippus's daughter, in her short revolt against King Mark. He was later slain in joust by Kalegras, Tristan's father. [*SagaTI*]

PLEHERIN

A knight and vassal of King Mark of Cornwall. During one of Tristan's exiles, he chased some squires through the forest and mistakenly thought one of them was Tristan. He caused a scandal by reporting that Tristan had fled from him. [*Eilhart*]

PLENORIUS

Son of Ceron and brother of Playne de Amours, Playne de Fors, Pillounes, Pellogris, and Pellandris. He ruled a fortress in the Straits of Sorelois in which many knights were imprisoned. Lancelot and Brunor the Black liberated the fortress by defeating Plenorius and his brothers. They let Plenorius keep the fortress provided he pledge allegiance to Arthur. Plenorius later became a Knight of the Round Table. When Lancelot and Guinevere were accused of treason, Plenorius pledged his support to Lancelot and helped him rescue Guinevere from the stake. In return for his support, Lancelot made him the earl of Foix. [*ProsTris, Malory*]

PLESSIS WOOD ("Deceitful Wood")

A forest where Arthur's Sir Morholt rescued a queen and her dwarf from being burned (the queen's husband had been tricked into thinking that she was committing adultery with the dwarf). Later, he encountered an adventure at the Stone of the Stag. [*PostMer*]

PLIAMIN

A grim Arthurian knight with a macabre sense of humor. He helped Erec and Gauriel rescue the Count of Asterian's daughter from a kidnapper. [*Konrad*]

PLIMIZOEL

A river in Britain near which Arthur often camped and held court. It flowed into a lake in Carcobra and into the sea at Barbigœl. [*Wolfram*]

PLINESCHANZ OF ZAMBRON

A count once defeated in combat by Perceval. [*Wolfram*]

PLIPPALINOT

A knight and ferryman on a river near the Castle of Marvels. Plippalinot had worked out an arrangement by which he received the horse of any knight defeated in combat by Lischois Gwelljus, who guarded the river. Plippalinot and his daughter Bene befriended and lodged Gawain when he came to the area and, after some reluctance, filled him in on the adventures to be had at the Castle of Marvels. [*Wolfram*]

PLOBORZ

A knight present at the Sorgarda tournament, which Gawain won. [*Heinrich*]

PLUINANT

A Saxon king who, under King Hargadabran, opposed Arthur's forces at the battle of Clrence. [*Livre*]

PLUMPTON

A town in Cumberland, about fourteen miles south of Carlisle, where Sir Gawain and Sir Galleron dueled over a group of Scottish lands annexed by Arthur. [*Awntyrs*]

PLURIS

A castle visited by Lancelot in Ulrich von Zatzikhoven's *Lanzelet*. Like the castle PLEURE from Tristan romance, it suggests a "weeping castle." It was ruled by a beautiful woman, who established a tradition by which each visiting knight was given a chance to joust with a hundred knights in a row. Whoever defeated them all would be awarded the lady and her lands. Lancelot defeated the knights and found himself in an awkward position because he was already married to Lady Iblis. He agreed to remain with the Queen of Pluris for a short time, and she disarmed him and surrounded him at all times with forty knights to prevent his escape. Eventually, she allowed him to enter a tournament on the promise that he would return after striking down the first knight. Fortunately, his opponents turned out to be Gareth, Tristan, and Gawain, his comrades. Learning of his promise, they evaded his blows and fled Pluris. Lancelot, who had not struck a blow, pursued them all the way to Arthur's court, where he remained. [*UlrichZ*]

POCH [*Roch*]

Father of Arthur's warrior Fercos in *Culhwch and Olwen*, adopted from the Irish character named Róech. [*Culhwch*]

POIDAS

A prince present at the Sorgarda tournament, which Gawain won. [*Heinrich*]

POINTURIE

In Chrétien's *Erec*, a castle owned by Guivret, the "Little King," where Erec was received and healed after receiving an injury. Hartmann von Aue calls the same castle PENEFREC. [*ChretienE*]

POITIERS [*Paito*]

A city in west central France that was the capital of Poitou. In *Arthour and Merlin,* we learn that Uther Pendragon acquired it from Harinan, Igerne's first husband. The Alliterative *Morte Arthure* names it as part of Arthur's empire. Malory says that Lancelot owned it, and that he made Bleoberis the duke of Poitiers in return for Bleoberis's support in the battles against King Arthur. [*Arthour, Allit, Malory*]

POITOU

A Gaulish duchy ruled by Duke Guitard. It was conquered by Hoel of Brittany—for Arthur—but Guitard was allowed to keep the land as long as he swore allegiance to Arthur. Wolfram says that Schiolarz was the ruler of Poitou during the reign of Uther in Britain; Der Pleier calls its ruler Prince Teschelarz. Its capital was once Poitiers. [*GeoffHR, Wace, Wolfram, PleierT*]

POLAND

According to the Norse *Tristrams Saga*, Tristan, during one of his banishments from Mark's court, served the Duke of Poland. [*TrisSaga*]

POLIDAMAS

Nephew of King Yder of Cornwall. He fought in Arthur's war against the Saxons and helped repel King Agrippe's invasion of the Waste Land. [*Livre*]

POLITETES [*Polipliters, Polydetes, Polydeuces*]

The duke of Bithynia or Mede who was subservient to the Roman Procurator Lucius, and was called upon to join Lucius in the war against Arthur. He led a force of soldiers at the battle of Soissons, where he was killed by Arthur himself. [*GeoffHR, Wace, Layamon, VulgMer*]

POLLIDAMAS [*Domas, Polidamas*]

The nephew of King Tradelmant of North Wales. With his uncle, he fought the Saxons at the battles of Arundel and Clarence. [*VulgMer, Arthour*]

POLLORNIS

The page of Blenzibly, Tristan's mother in the Icelandic *Saga af Tristram ok Ísodd*. [*SagaTI*]

POMELEGOI [Pomeglai]

The location of a tournament entered and won by Lancelot in the Vulgate *Lancelot*. During the tournament, Guinevere tested his love by telling to perform dishonorably, and Lancelot demonstrated his faithfulness by acting like a coward. The Lady of Pomelegoi sponsored the tournament with the Lady of Noauz. Chrétien places the tournament at NOAUZ. [*ChretienL, VulgLanc*]

POMPEIUS

A ruler from Babylon and brother of Ipomidon in Wolfram's *Parzival*. The brothers' ancestral city of Niniveh was seized by the Baruc of Baghdad. In response, Pompeius and Ipomidon invaded the Baruc's country, where they had to contend with Gahmuret, Perceval's father, who was serving the Baruc. Wolfram says that Pompeius's maternal uncle was King Nebuchadnezzar. [*Wolfram*]

PONMECAINNE [Pomytayn]

An island owned by Sir Galehaut. Galehaut gave the island to King Marsyl. [*ProsTris, Malory*]

PONTEFERNO

A castle conquered by Tristan during the Grail Quest. Tristan left a knight named Inamante as viceroy. [*Tavola*]

PONTEFRACT [Ponfret]

A city in Yorkshire that is named as one of Arthur's castles in *Yder*. [*Yder*]

PONTHIEU

A Gaulish duchy ruled by King Arthur. [*GeoffHR*]

PONTIER DEL MONTE

A castle given to Isolde by Mark after she passed a chastity test at the Red Stone. [*Tavola*]

PONTIUS[1] ANTHONY [Pontius Antonius, Poince]

A Roman senator sent to France, by Julius Caesar, to help King Claudas conquer lands belonging to King Ban of Benoic (Lancelot's father) and King Bors of Gannes. Duke Frollo of Germany, Pontius's cousin, was also part of the mission. Arthur and Merlin brought an army to counter the invasion, and defeated Pontius Anthony at the battle of Briosque. He returned to Rome, raised a new army, and invaded Benoic again. Although the attack was successful, Pontius Anthony was slain in battle by King Ban. [*LancLac, VulgLanc, VulgMer*]

PONTIUS[2] PILATE

The biblical Roman procurator of Judea, Samaria, and Idumaea who condemned Jesus Christ to be crucified. According to the Grail legends, Joseph of Arimathea was one of Pilate's knights, before Joseph's conversion to Christianity. Pilate gave Christ's body to Joseph, expecting that Joseph intended to defile it. Joseph, however, placed the body in a holy sepulcher. [*RobertBor, VulgEst*]

PONTREMOLI [Port Tremble, Pount Tremble]

A city in Lombardy, Italy that surrendered to Arthur after the Roman War. [*Allit, Malory*]

POOR KNIGHT

An impoverished nobleman who gave lodging and friendship to Gawain and Lancelot. In reward, the two knights sent horses and treasures recovered from thieves to the Poor Knight. His manor was called the Waste Castle. Perceval and the Coward Knight saved the Poor Knight's two maiden daughters from a Robber Knight. He finally reclaimed his wealth and position after Lancelot braved a Beheading Game in the Waste City. [*Perlesvaus*]

POPE

History records the following popes during the traditional Arthurian period: St. Leo I (440–461), St. Hilary (461–468), St. Simplicius (468–483), St. Felix III (483–492), St. Gelasius I (492–496), Anastasius II (496–498), St. Symmachus (498), Lawrence (an anti-Pope, c. 498–505), St. Hormisdas (514–523), St. John I (523–526), St. Felix IV (526–530).

Popes named during the Arthurian period in legend include Sulpicius (probably Simplicius), who Gawain served; Romanus, who sent bishops to Britain during the reign of Vortimer; Leo, who served during Arthur's war with Rome; Dionido, whose brother, Trionoro, killed Gawain; and Gregorio, who tried Merlin for heresy.

In the Vulgate *Mort Artu* and its adaptations, the pope (unnamed), through the Bishop of Rochester, forces Arthur to restore Guinevere as queen after she runs away with Lancelot, threatening to place Arthur's lands under interdiction if he does not. Arthur complies.

In Malory, the pope crowns Arthur emperor of Rome after the Roman War. In the same story, Pedyvere, who murdered his wife, was sent to the pope after Lancelot defeated him. [*GeoffHR, Layamon, VulgMort, Tavola, VitaMer, Malory*]

POPELICANS

A race of men who fought with honed weapons and defended Rigomer Castle. They were defeated by Arthur's knights. [*Merveil*]

PORREX[1]

According to Geoffrey, a prince of Britain in the sixth or fifth century BC. He was the son of King Gorbodug and Queen Iudon. He contested his brother Ferrx for the British throne after Gorbodug's death. Ferrex received aid from the Franks, but was slain by Porrex. Iudon, who had favored Ferrex, became enraged and killed Porrex. Afterwards, the kingdom of Britain became fragmented until Dunwallo Molmutius reunited it. [*GeoffHR*]

PORREX²

According to Geoffrey of Monmouth, a king of Britain in the third or second century BC. He was the son of King Coill and the father of King Cherin. [*GeoffHR*]

PORRUS

Duke of Athens who served Emperor Filimenis of Constantinople. He joined Filimenis in a brief war against Arthur. [*Floriant*]

PORT LA ROINE ("Queen's Port")

A Scottish seaport through which Arthur's Sir Fergus traveled during his adventures. The location is probably identical to Queensferry. [*Guillaume*]

PORTH CLEIS

A seaport in west Dyfed where the boar Twrch Trwyth and his piglets landed while on the run from Arthur and his warriors. [*Culhwch*]

PORTH CERDDIN

A harbor in Dyfed that was home of Arthur's warrior Llwyd. Arthur and his soldiers landed here upon returning from their invasion of Ireland. They bore the enchanted cauldron of Diwrnach, and the port was renamed *Messur y Peir* ("measure of the cauldron") in honor of the event. [*Culhwch*]

PORTLESGUEZ [*Portleguez*]

A Welsh castle where, according to the Post-Vulgate *Queste del Saint Graal*, Merlin's mother died. It was the surname of Arthur's knight Meraugis, who apparently had no association with the castle, but instead took the name from another knight. [*Raoul, Livre, PostQuest*]

PORTSMOUTH [*Portesmouthe*]

A city on the English Channel where King Ban of Benoic and King Bors of Gannes landed on their way to join Arthur in Britain. [*Arthour*]

PORTUGAL

According to Wolfram, warriors from Portugal participated in a tournament at the Welsh city of Kanvoleis, thrown by Perceval's mother Queen Herzeloyde. In Der Pleier's *Tandareis and Flordibel*, Portugal is allied to Arthur, but in Malory, Portugal is allied to Lucius of Rome. [*Wolfram, PleierT, Malory*]

POSSIZONJUS OF THILER

An infidel count who served Feirefiz, Perceval's half-brother. [*Wolfram*]

POSTEFAR OF LAUDUNDREHTE

A lord once defeated in combat by Perceval. [*Wolfram*]

POWYS

A region in central Wales. It was a kingdom during the Arthurian period, though it is rarely mentioned in Arthurian legend. The bard Taliesin is connected to its court.

POYDICONJUNZ

Wolfram von Eschenbach's variation of BAGDEMAGUS. [*Wolfram*]

POYNZACLINS

A river abutting or inside the realm of King Gramoflanz. It paralleled the Sabins river and flowed into the nearby sea. The town of Roche Sabins lay between the two rivers. [*Wolfram*]

POYTWIN OF PRIENLASCORS

A knight defeated at the tournament of Kanvoleis by Perceval's father Gahmuret. [*Wolfram*]

PRANDIN

A count in the service of King Dulcemar of Tandernas. He led a battalion of soldiers in Dulcemar's battle against Arthur. [*PleierT*]

PRAVERAUS

A Knight of the Round Table. [*HartmannE*]

PRESSELEU

A city or land in Britain, through which Arthur and his warriors chased the boar Twrch Trwyth. [*Culhwch*]

PRESTER JOHN [*Preter John*]

A legendary Asian or African ruler, bastion of Christianity in Heathendom, given by Wolfram von Eschenbach as the son of Perceval's half-brother Feirefiz and the Grail lady Repanse de Schoye. In Richard Johnson's *Tom a Lincolne*, his daughter, Anglitora, marries Tom a' Lincoln and has a son named the Black Knight. His legend was so strong in the Middle Ages that successions of popes attempted to communicate with him for centuries. [*Johnson*]

PRIADAN THE BLACK [*Prydam*]

The champion of an evil woman who tried to steal her younger sister's land. Bors, on the Grail Quest, championed the younger sister and defeated Priadan in combat. He spared Priadan's life, however, and thus passed a spiritual test. [*VulgQuest, Malory*]

PRIAM

In Greek legend, the last king of the fabled city of Troy. The Post-Vulgate *Queste del Saint Graal* tells us that his nephew, Galamanasor, built the Castle of Treachery, which was conquered by Galahad during the Grail Quest. [*PostQuest*]

PRIAMUS¹ [*Pryamus*]

An Italian knight who joined Arthur's service during the Roman War. Gawain met him while foraging for supplies in northern Italy. They fought in single combat, and developed such a respect for each other's prowess that they became fast friends. Priamus provided Gawain with information about the Duke of Lorraine, and he helped Gawain defeat the duke's brigade of Roman soldiers. In reward, Arthur had Priamus baptized, gave him a seat at the Round Table, and appointed him the new duke of Lorraine. Much later, Lancelot killed him while rescuing Guinevere from the stake. He had two brothers named Edward and Hectymere. [*Allit, Malory*]

PRIAMUS² [*Pryamus, Pryan*]

A chaplain who Arthur appointed Archbishop of York after the city was reclaimed from the Saxons. [*GeoffHR*]

PRIBANDRON

A knight in Arthur's service. [*Stricker*]

PRIDE OF THE CLEARING

A pavilion that Peredur visited on his way to Arthur's court in *Peredur*. Peredur's mother had told him to take any riches he found and give them to the poor, take food when it was offered, and to romance ladies. In the pavilion, Peredur found a beautiful lady and an assortment of food. Attempting to comply with his mother's advice, Peredur ate the food, took the lady's ring, kissed her, and left. When the lady's husband returned, he was furious at the thought of another knight in his pavilion, and he chased Peredur. They eventually met in combat and Peredur was victorious. In Chrétien's *Perceval*, an identical episode occurs in the forest of BROCELIANDE. [*Peredur*]

PRIDWEN [*Priwen, Prydwen(ne)*]

In Welsh tradition, Arthur's ship, in which he voyaged to the Annwn, the Welsh otherworld. Geoffrey of Monmouth makes it Arthur's shield. It had an image of the Virgin Mary painted on the inside, and Arthur carried it against the Saxons at Bath. [*Spoils, Culhwch, GeoffHR, Wace, Gesta*]

PRO OF JEMESTIR

The name used by TRISTAN on his first visit to Ireland. He was ill from poison, and had washed up on the Irish shore. Knowing that Ireland was at war with Cornwall, he concealed his identity and represented himself as Pro of Jemestir. "Pro" was cured of his poison by the medicines of Isolde, and he was appointed by the King of Ireland to travel to Britain and obtain food to ameliorate a famine. On his second visit, he used the name TANTRIST. [*Eilhart*]

PROCIDES

The castellan of Limerick who served Queen Fenice of Ireland. He bore Ireland's standard in battle. [*Durmart*]

PROTHIZILAS

A prince under Queen Belacane of Zazamanc (the first wife of Perceval's father Gahmuret). He fought against Isenhart, one of Belacane's suitors, and both warriors were killed in the duel. Gahmuret later gave Prothizilas's duchy to Sir Lahfilirost. [*Wolfram*]

PROUD CASTLE

See ORGUELLEUS.

PROUD FORTRESS

A strong castle belonging to Lancelot's friend Galehaut. It crumbled to the ground—along with all of Galehaut's other castles—portending Galehaut's death. [*LancLac, VulgLanc*]

PROUD KNIGHT

See ORGUELLEUS.

PROVALDINO

A knight that Palamedes left in charge of Tuscia after he had conquered it. [*Tavola*]

PROVENCE [*Provance*]

A region in southeast France, on the Mediterranean Sea. Der Pleier, in *Tandareis and Flordibel*, contends that it was allied to Arthur, as does the Alliterative *Morte Arthure*. Malory says that Lancelot owned it, and that Lancelot made Palamedes the duke of Provence in return for Palamedes' support in the war against Arthur. [*PleierT, Allit, Malory*]

PROXIMUS

In the Elizabethan play *The Birth of Merlin*, a Saxon magician who served King Vortigern. On Joram's advice, Vortigern sought a young Merlin in order to slake the foundation of a castle with the child's blood. Layamon calls this character JORAM. [*Birth*]

PRURIN

Hartmann von Aue tells us that a tournament was held between the cities of Prurin and Tarebron, in which Erec excelled. Wolfram says that Erec defeated his brother-in-law, Duke Orguelleus, at the tourney. [*HartmannE, Wolfram*]

PRUSSIA [*Prussland, Spruysland*]

According to the Alliterative *Morte Arthure*, heathens from Prussia fought against Arthur's forces in the Roman War. [*Allit*]

PRYDEIN

The modern name "Britain" grew out of "Prydein"—the old Welsh term for the island, which sounds like "Britain" when pronounced. According to Welsh legend, the island was called Myrddin's Precinct until it was settled, after which it became known as the Island of Honey. When the Island of Honey was conquered by Prydein, son of Aedd the Great, it was renamed in his honor. [*Triads*]

PRYDERI

A warrior, the son of Pwyll and ruler of Dyfed, who makes an appearance in all of the branches of the *Mabinogi*. Pryderi is not a part of Arthurian literature, but he may have been the origin of PEREDUR, PERCEVAL, or other Arthurian heroes. *The Spoils of Annwn* refers to him and his story. His name may be a variation of PRYDEIN, the Welsh word for Britain. [*Spoils*]

PUERINERO TURPIN

A knight captain in Mark's service. He led Cornish knights against Arthur's men when Arthur besieged Tintagel following Tristan's death. Puerinero was slain in the battle. [*Tavola*]

PUHULIN CASTLE

A fortress belonging to Queen Tydomie of Karmerie, wife of Arthur's nephew Meleranz. [*PleierM*]

PULAZ

A giant who reluctantly served the evil Godonas of Terrandes. He was pleased when Godonas was slain by Meleranz, Arthur's nephew. [*PleierM*]

PULCHRA

A castle ruled by Earl Milan, who tried to abduct Enide from Erec. [*Erex*]

PULIZENA

The sister of Medea, the lecherous female ruler of Crudele castle. Her other sisters included Lavina, Bresenda, and Agnena. [*Tavola*]

PULZELLA GAIA ("Merry Maiden") [*Gaia Donzella, Gaia Pulcella*]

The daughter of Morgan le Fay and a knight named Huneson the Bald. Pulzella Gaia possessed some of her mother's magic. In *La Tavola Ritonda*, Morgan wants to marry her to Tristan, but he refuses. Lancelot later rescues her from a knight named Burletta, who has kidnapped and is trying to rape her. In *La Pulzella Gaia*, Gawain fights against her when she assumes the form of a serpent. She defeats him and becomes his lover, but warns him not to reveal their love. When he does so to spite a jealous Guinevere, she refuses to return to him until Arthur nearly executes him for making false boasts about his beautiful paramour. Pulzella Gaia's mother threw her into a dungeon in the castle of Palaus. Gawain rescued her, and the two lovers were reconciled. (This tale is a variation of the story of *Lanval* in which Pulzella's character is called TRIAMOUR.) [*Tavola, Pulzella*]

PUMLUMON ("Five Peaks")

A region of the mountain Carn Gwylathyr in west central Wales. The warriors Cei and Bedwyr found Dillus the Bearded here and killed him. [*Culhwch*]

PUNT

A town in King Brandelidelin's Punturteis. It was surrounded by water. [*Wolfram*]

PUNTURTEIS [*Ponterteis*]

A land ruled in Arthur's time by King Brandelidelin, a friend of Arthur. The capital was Punt. Gabenis, Urjans, and Frians are all named as princes of Punturteis. [*Wolfram, PleierG*]

PURPLE KNIGHT

A knight of Arthur's court defeated by the Great Fool. [*IrishF*]

PURADES

One of Arthur's knights from Carmelide who participated in a quest to learn the fate of Merlin. [*VulgMer*]

PURDAN

A wicked giant who, with his wife Fidegart, terrorized his lands, killed noble knights, and imprisoned maidens. His victims included Princess Duzabel, Dukes Elimar and Klaris, and the dwarf King Albewin. His reign of terror was ended by Arthur's Sir Garel, who slew the two giants. [*PleierG*]

PWYLL

The ruler of Dyfed in the Welsh tale that bears his name. He was the father of Pryderi. He became, for a time, the ruler of Annwn, having exchanged kingdoms with Arrawn. He is non-Arthurian, though some scholars view him as the origin of PELLES. *The Spoils of Annwn* makes reference to his story. [*Spoils*]

PYGMIES

A race of men who fought with honed weapons and defended Rigomer Castle. They were defeated by Arthur's knights. [*Merveil*]

PYROCHLES

A brash knight who attacked Sir Guyon after he found that Guyon had captured Occasion and Furor, Pyrochles quarry. After defeating Pyrochles, Guyon allowed him to release and fight Furor, but Furor got the upper hand and beat Pyrochles unconscious. Pyrochles was eventually healed by the evil magician Archimago and was re-united with his brother, Cymochles. Guided by Archimago, the two brothers found Guyon unconscious and decided to steal his armor. Prince Arthur arrived during their theft, challenged them, and killed them both. [*Spenser*]

Q

QRAINGLAIE

A beautiful Irish queen in *Les Merveilles de Rigomer*. Sir Sagremor came to her pavilion in a forest. When she refused to return his greetings, he raped and impregnated her. The text notes that Qrainglaie's son, when he came of age, slew his father. [*Merveil*]

QUADOQUENEIS

An Arthurian knight. [*Heinrich*]

QUAHOMAS

A Saxon king who, under King Hargadabran, opposed Arthur at the battle of Clarence. [*Livre*]

QUARCOS

An Arthurian knight. [*Heinrich*]

QUEBELEPLUS

In *Diu Crône*, the young daughter of Lord Leigamar of Sorgarda. When Leigamar scheduled a tournament, Quebeleplus quarreled with her sister, Flursenesphin, over the prowess of the latter's beau, Fiers of Arramis. To get back at her sister, Quebeleplus begged Gawain to defeat Fiers in combat. Gawain complied and delighted the little girl. The same character appears in Wolfram's *Parzival* as OBILOT. [*Heinrich*]

QUEEN OF GREAT SORROWS

The alias used by ELAINE, Lancelot's mother, when she retired to a nunnery after Claudas's invasion of her land, her husband's death, and her son's abduction by the Lady of the Lake. [*LancLac, VulgLanc*]

QUEEN OF THE BLACK THORN [*Reine de la Noire Espine*]

The mother of Urbain, a knight defeated in combat by Perceval. [*Didot*]

QUEEN OF THE MAIDENS

The lady of the Castle of the Galleys. Her castle was besieged by the King of the Castle Mortal, but was saved by Perceval. She fell in love with her champion, but Perceval never returned to her. [*Perlesvaus*]

QUEEN OF THE PAVILIONS [*Roine des Tentes*]

Sister-in-law of Cahot the Red, who was killed by Perceval. She fancied Perceval despite this act, and she unsuccessfully tried to persuade her nephew, Clamadoz of the Shadows, to abandon his quarrel with Perceval. [*Perlesvaus*]

QUEEN'S FORD

A ford on the Humber River named for Queen Guinevere, who was the first to discover it. This was during Arthur's battle at the Humber against five kings or the Saxons. Later, Albyon, the son of the vavasour of Queen's Ford, took it upon himself to guard it, and fought at one point with Lancelot. [*LancLac, VulgLanc, Livre, PostMer*]

QUEEN'S KNIGHTS

A body of knights lesser in status than the Knights of the Round Table (though arguably, at their inception, greater in skill). The Queen's Knights were, for the most part, skilled but unseasoned warriors who had only recently been knighted and wished to win honor. They had an unfriendly rivalry with the Round Table. Queen's Knights carried only plain white shields to signify their position. When a vacancy opened on the Round Table, it was customary to look first to the Queen's Knights to fill it. Lancelot, Gawain, and many other knights served first as Queen's Knights before they were promoted to the Round Table. [*VulgMer, PostMer, Malory*]

QUENEDIC [*Ganedic*]

King Quenedic is named as the father of an unnamed Knight of the Round Table. [*ChretienE*]

QUENUS OF CAEREC [*Quenut*]

An Arthurian knight who joined one of Gawain's quests to find Lancelot. [*LancLac, VulgLanc*]

QUERQUONS DARIEL

A knight in Arthur's service. [*Heinrich*]

QUESTING BEAST [*Barking Beast, Beast Glotisant, Beast Gratisanti, *Beste Glatissant, Bestia Grattisante, Bizarre Beast, Glatissant Beast, Howling Beast*]

A demonic monster with the head of a serpent, the body of a leopard, the buttocks and legs of a lion, and the feet of a hart. It emitted the sound of twenty or thirty hounds questing from its belly, and was often pursued by scores of actual hounds. (A similar unnamed beast appears in *Perlesvaus*, but it is a Christ allegory rather than a demon.)

The Questing Beast was born of a union between a devil and the daughter of King Hipomenes. Upon its birth, most of the attending midwives perished, and the Beast escaped into the forest. The quest to destroy the monster was related somehow to the Grail Quest. It was pursued first by Pellinore, and later by Palamedes, who was known as the Knight of the Questing Beast. During the Grail Quest, it was chased at times by Galahad, Bors, Yvain the Bastard, Perceval, Gawain, Lancelot, and Hector—all of whom fought with Palamedes over the right to pursue it. Despite Pellinore's claim that only his kin could catch it, and despite Merlin's prophecy that Perceval wound kill it, the Questing Beast was finally slain by Palamedes at a lake later known as the Lake of the Beast. As its body sank into the waves, the water boiled.

Palamedes' slaying of the Questing Beast appears in the Post-Vulgate *Queste del Saint Graal*. Some authors, unfamiliar with this text, claim that no one ever caught or killed the monster. [*ProsTris*, *PostMer*, *PostQuest*, *Malory*]

QUILINI

One of Arthur's castles. Arthur gave it to Brun of Branlant after Brun agreed to become Arthur's liege. [*Contin1*]

QUIMPER-CORENTIN [*Aquinparcorentin, Campacorentin, Percorentin*]

One of Arthur's several courts. It is the modern-day Quimper in Finistère. It was the home of Lady Lisanor (the mother by Arthur of Sir Loholt) and Sir Aces. Its chief city in the romances is Beaumont. [*Contin1*, *LancLac*, *VulgLanc*, *VulgMer*]

QUINGRAGAN [*Quikagrant*]

The castle belonging to Goondesert, Perceval's uncle. It was besieged by Partinal, who slew Goondesert treacherously even after he had repelled the siege. [*Contin3*]

QUINOTFIERS OF BAHANZ

A knight in Arthur's service. [*Heinrich*]

QUINCEQUARAINS

One of Arthur's knights in *Les Merveilles de Rigomer* is called the Varlet of Quincequarains. It may be related to the forest QUINQUEROI in Chrétien's *Perceval*. [*Merveil*]

QUINQUEROI ("Five Kings")

A forest that was the home of the Red Knight, who was killed by Perceval. [*ChretienP*]

QUINTAREUS [*Quine*]

A Knight of the Round Table. [*ChretienE*, *Heinrich*]

QUINTEFUELLE [*Quintefoille*]

A rich city distant from Britain. Its lord perished, and his daughter was supposed to inherit the land. Her cousin, however, raised a counterclaim and stole the city from her. The lady traveled to Arthur's court to find a champion. Arthur decided to go himself. The king and his company came to Quintefuelle after passing through several strange and dangerous lands. The king fought the duel himself, killed the lady's cousin, and restored her to her throne. [*Merveil*]

QUINTUS CARUCIUS [*Carrius, Carous*]

One of the Roman senators who became a war leader in Lucius's campaign against Arthur. Quintus, with three others, was assigned by Lucius to liberate the Roman prisoners being taken by Arthur's warriors to a prison in Paris. The Britons won the battle thanks to the timely arrival of Duke Guitard. Quintus later led a force of soldiers at the battle of Soissons. [*GeoffHR*, *Wace*, *Allit*]

QUINTUS MILVIUS

One of the Roman senators who became a war leader in Lucius's campaign against Arthur. He led a force of soldiers at the battle of Soissons and was killed there. [*GeoffHR*]

QUIOLAS

A Saxon king who, under King Hargadabran, fought Arthur's forces at the battle of Clarence and was killed by Adragain. [*Livre*]

QUIOQUES GOMERET

An Arthurian knight in Heinrich von dem Türlin's *Diu Crône*. He occupies the place given to King BAN of Gomeret in Chrétien's *Erec*. [*ChretienE*]

QUIRION OF ORCEL

A king present at the wedding of Erec and Enide. The youngest of Quirion's knights was one hundred years old. [*ChretienE*]

QUOIKOS OF MONTISCHSDOL

A Breton knight who fought alongside Gawain in a tournament at Sorgarda Castle. Though Gawain won the tournament, he awarded the right to marry Flursensephin, the lady of Sorgarda, to Quoikos. Quoikos had a brother named Sempitebruns. [*Heinrich*]

R

RADES

A magnificent, well-fortified city in the Kingdom of the Isles. It was surrounded by lush lands and rivers. Gawain defeated an enemy, Sir Brian of the Isles, in Rades. [*Meriadeuc*]

RADIGUND

Queen of the Amazons. She hated knights and imprisoned and humiliated them at every opportunity. Sir Artegall learned of this injustice and set out to slay her. He challenged her to single combat and defeated her, but when he wrenched off her helmet to behead her, he was overcome by her beauty. Radigund regained herself, and she captured and imprisoned Artegall. Artegall's paramour, the warrior maiden Britomart, heard of his plight, went to the Amazons' kingdom, killed Radigund, and freed Artegall. [*Spenser*]

RADOLE

A city in Hungary that was the birthplace of Master Elimas, one of Arthur's clerics. [*VulgLanc*]

RADURANTS [*Raidurains*]

A good knight present at Arthur's tournament at the Castle of Maidens in Renaut de Bâgé's *Le Bel Inconnu*. He may be identical to ROIDURANT, a knight found in Ulrich von Zatzikhoven's *Lanzelet*. [*Renaut*]

RAFACE

A Knight of the Round Table who embarked with the others on the Grail Quest. [*PostQuest*]

RAGNELLE [*Ragnelle*]

The LOATHLY LADY who becomes Gawain's wife in the medieval poem *The Wedding of Sir Gawain and Dame Ragnelle*. Arthur was captured in the forest of Inglewood by Ragnelle's brother, Gromer Somer Jour. Gromer agreed to release Arthur, but only on the condition that Arthur return in one year and either tell Gromer what women desire most or be killed.

Arthur and Gawain searched in vain for the answer. As the appointed date neared, Arthur met the hideously ugly Ragnelle in Inglewood, she agreed to tell Arthur the answer—that women desire sovereignty over themselves and their men—on the condition that Arthur wed Ragnelle to Sir Gawain.

Arthur returned to Camelot and told Gawain of his adventure, and Gawain agreed to the marriage so that he could save Arthur's life. Guinevere and the court, shocked at the prospect of the fair Gawain marrying the repulsive

Ragnelle, tried to convince Ragnelle to have a quiet wedding in the early morning, but Ragnelle insisted on a large, boisterous wedding at mid-day, with everyone in attendance. At the wedding feast, she disgusted the court by eating an unconscionable amount of food and otherwise exhibiting repellent table manners.

At night, Gawain and Ragnelle went to bed, and Ragnelle demanded the conjugal rights of a married woman. Gawain rolled over to face her and found himself looking at a beautiful young woman. Ragnelle then explained that Gawain could have her beautiful at night and ugly during the day or ugly at night but beautiful during the day. Gawain gave the choice to her, and in doing so bestowed upon her the sovereignty that women most desire. Gawain's reply broke a curse that had been placed upon Ragnelle. In reward, Ragnelle became beautiful all the time. She and Gawain had a son named Guinglain. She died after she had been married to Gawain for five years. There is evidence that her name was taken from a pagan God known to Middle English writers (Hahn, 76). Both Arthur and Gawain refer to her repeatedly as a fiend or devil. [*Wedding*]

RAGUIDEL[1] [*Ragisel*]

A noble knight who was murdered by the knight Guengasoain. His body floated up to Arthur's court in a boat, accompanied by a letter asking some knight to avenge him. On the boat, Raguidel's body lay in a cart, and he was therefore also known as the KNIGHT OF THE CART. By drawing a lance from Raguidel's body, Gawain assumed the task and, with the help of Yder, succeeded. [*Vengeance, Wrake, Atre*]

RAGUIDEL[2]

A castle where Hector, Lancelot's brother, ended a number of evil customs by defeating Lord Marigart the Red and by rescuing lady Angale from a pair of lions. [*VulgLanc*]

RAIMEL OF LOVENTEL

A knight in Arthur's service. [*Heinrich*]

RAINDURANT [*Boidurant, Randurz*]

A nobleman's son from Tergalo who fought at the tournament of Tenebroc. He was unhorsed by Erec. [*ChretienE, HartmannE*]

RAINS

A knight present at the Sorgarda tournament, which Gawain won. [*Heinrich*]

RAMATHAIN

A Middle-Eastern land, beyond the River Jordan, which contained the city of Arimathea, Joseph's birthplace. It was ruled in Joseph's time by Elcan, father of the biblical Samuel. It's name seems to be a variation of ARIMATHEA. [*VulgEst*]

RAMOANO

A wilderness near the castle of the Hard Rock. Tristan defeated Arthur and Yvain in a joust there. [*Tavola*]

RAMURET

A skilled knight slain by Karyet (Gareth) in Ulrich von Zatzikhoven's *Lanzelet*. He could be identified with Wace's ROMAREC or Wolfram's GAHMURET. [*UlrichZ*]

RANCIER THE PILGRIM [*Ansirus*]

Father of Alice the Belle Pilgrim. He was a duke, related to Lancelot, who made a pilgrimage to Jerusalem every three years. [*ProsTris, Prophecies, Malory*]

RANDOL [*Ralidol*]

A Saxon who joined King Rions' invasion of Carmelide in the Vulgate *Merlin*. Later, he became the seneschal of the king of Gaul, and joined Claudas's war against Arthur. He fled the battle of Trebe after he was badly wounded by Gawain. *Arthour and Merlin* says that King Ban of Benoic killed him at the battle of Carhaix, which occurs before the war in Gaul. [*VulgMer, Arthour*]

RANNALD [*Raunald*]

An Arthurian knight in the Middle Scots tale of *Golagros and Gawain*. During the war between Golagros and Arthur, Rannald was slain by Golagros's Sir Rigal. [*Golagros*]

RANNER

King of Miranceis, father of Angledis, and grandfather of Alexander the Orphan. His grandson was raised by his constable, Berengier, in the castle Magance. [*ProsTris, Prophecies*]

RAOLAIS

Lord of Estremors, brother of Maduc, and uncle of Plarés. He was called the Green Knight. Raolais was an enemy of Arthur and, consequently, Arthur invaded his lands. Plarés was killed in the fighting. The war was eventually decided in a single combat between Raolais and Gawain. Gawain was victorious, and Raolais became a Knight of the Round Table, joining Arthur's war against the Saxons. Maduc, disgusted with Raolais's fealty to Arthur, became hostile to his brother. [*Livre*]

RAOLAUS

A Saxon king who, under King Hargadabran, fought Arthur's forces at the battle of Clarence. [*Livre*]

RAOUL OF CHAUX

A very old knight in King Arthur's service. Sir Dodinel offered him, jokingly, as an opponent for Sir Bertelay, the elderly knight who championed the False Guinevere. [*VulgLanc*]

RAPAS

A heathen king who helped King Oriel plunder northern Britain at the beginning of Arthur's reign. [*Arthour*]

RAPHAEL

An angel who guided Arthur through his conquest of the Saxons. [*BlackmoreP*]

RATHTYEN

A lady at Arthur's court who was the daughter of Clememyl. [*Culhwch*]

RATISBONNE

A city in Germany where the Emperor of Germany held a court. [*ChretienC*]

RAYNALD

An Arthurian knight who participated in the Roman War. He was the brother of Richer and the son of Rowlaunde. [*Allit*]

RAYNOLD

A Knight of the Round Table who attacked Lancelot, who was disguised in Kay's armor. Raynold and his companions, Gyllymer and Gautere, who had thought that the inferior Kay was their opponent, received the surprise of their lives. Raynold was later killed fighting Lancelot and his soldiers when Lancelot rescued Guinevere from the stake. [*Malory*]

RAZALIC

A mighty Saracen lord from Azagouc. He ruled a large number of Moors. With allies, he invaded the neighboring country of Zazamanc but was defeated by Perceval's father, Gahmuret. [*Wolfram*]

REBEDINCH

An Arthurian knight in Heinrich von dem Türlin's *Diu Crône*. His name seems to be a variation of ROBERDIC, the name of a place in Chrétien's *Erec*. [*Heinrich*]

RECHAUX THE STRONG

Brother of Corsabrin (a knight killed by Palamedes) and son of Aristot. He married a princess from Iquanz. [*ProsTris*]

RED CASTLE[1]

A castle conquered from Lord Serses by Sir Bors, who established a monastery on the site. [*VulgLanc*]

RED CASTLE²

When a lord named Elain died, he left the Red Castle to his maiden daughter. Yvain the Black wanted to marry the maiden, and he besieged the castle when she refused. Guiron the Courteous came to the maiden's aid, defeated Yvain, and lifted the siege. [*Palamedes*]

RED CASTLE³

The home of the knights Hugh and Edward. [*Malory*]

RED CITY¹

A King of the Red City was defeated by Erec at the Tenebroc tournament in Chrétien's *Erec*. He may have inspired Hartmann's ROIDERODES. [*ChretienE*]

RED CITY² [*Rouge Citié*]

The castle ruled by Sir Partinal, an enemy of Perceval's family. Perceval killed him there. [*Contin3*]

RED CITY² [*Vermiglia*]

A city on the Delectable Isle, off the east coast of Britain, ruled by King Armant. When two of Armant's protégés killed Armant and seized the city, Sir Palamedes avenged the deed, became lord of the Red City, and gave the city to Marin, Armant's brother. [*ProsTris*, *Tavola*, *Malory*]

RED CITY³

A "King of the Red City" appears in *Les Merveilles de Rigomer* as an ally of Rigomer castle. Gawain defeated him during his battle to conquer the castle. [*Merveil*]

RED CROSS¹ [*Croix Roge*]

A landmark outside King Mark's court at Lancien. Mark left a message to Tristan and Isolde, who were living in exile in the forest of Morois, on the cross. [*Beroul*]

RED CROSS²

A landmark visited by Hector, Lionel, Erec, and the Ugly Hero during their adventures. [*PostMer*]

RED CROSS KNIGHT

Representative of holiness in Spenser's *The Faerie Queene*. He carried a shield with a bloody red cross on it. He was commissioned by Gloriana, the Fairy Queen, to accompany Una to the kingdom of her parents and deliver them from a dragon that was scourging their land. On the way, he was tricked by the evil sorcerer Archimago into believing Una a wanton, and he abandoned her. He became infatuated with Duessa, a witch in the guise of a beautiful maiden named Fidessa. He drank from a magic fountain which made him weak, allowing the giant Orgoglio to throw him in a dungeon. Una sought and obtained the help of Prince Arthur, who killed Orgoglio, exposed Duessa, and freed the Red Cross Knight. Eventually, they reached Una's land and the Red Cross Knight slew the dragon in a three-day battle. The Red Cross Knight and Una were betrothed. In a later adventure, the Red Cross Knight joined the warrior maiden Britomart at the Castle Joyous. It is revealed late in Spenser's poem that the Red Cross Knight is St. George, the patron saint of England. [*Spenser*]

RED FOREST

A wood inhabited by the Red Knight. Arthur challenged the Red Knight for proper ownership of the Red Forest. Arthur's Sir Meriadoc decided the issue in Arthur's favor, but persuaded Arthur to relinquish his claim. [*Historia*]

RED GIANT

A giant who killed Aliban of the Waste City, Perceval's uncle. Alain, Perceval's father, avenged Aliban by slaying the Red Giant, but he received a mortal wound in the process. [*Perlesvaus*]

RED KNIGHT¹ [*Knight of the Red Shield*]

A knight from the forest of Quinqueroi who offended Arthur and was killed by Perceval. Wolfram von Eschenbach calls him ITHER. Chrétien de Troyes relates how Perceval noticed his bright red mail suit on his way to Arthur's court. After Arthur had knighted Perceval, Perceval asked for the armor. Kay—seeking to cause trouble—told Perceval that he could go ahead and take it. Perceval rode out to meet the Red Knight and demanded the armor. When the Red Knight—expectedly—refused, Perceval threw a well-aimed spear into the Knight's eye, killing him instantly. With the help of the servant Yonet, he donned the red armor and rode away. Perceval himself was then called the Red Knight for a time.

Presented lightly in Chrétien's version, this episode takes on a tragic air in later stories. In *Perlesvaus*, Perceval slays the Red Knight accidentally while the latter is fighting the White Knight. Perceval had believed that knights in armor were invincible, and he was therefore shocked and saddened when his javelin pierced the Red Knight's visor. The Red Knight, who was the Lord of the Forest of Shadows, had a brother named Cahot the Red and a son named Clamadoz of the Shadows. Both tried to avenge the Red Knight's death but failed. In Wolfram's *Parzival*, Perceval similarly comes to regret the killing.

In the Fourth Continuation of Chrétien's *Perceval*, the Red Knight has four sons: Evander, Marmadus, Leander, and Meliadas. Following their pardon to Perceval for their father's death, the Red Knight's body was buried by St. Brendan.

According to the Middle English *Sir Perceval of Galles*, Perceval killed the Red Knight in revenge for the murder of Perceval's father at the Red Knight's hands. His red armor gave him supernatural powers. [*ChretienP*, *Wolfram*, *Perlesvaus*, *Contin4*, *SirPerc*]

RED KNIGHT²

A king from Montescler who participated in Arthur's tournament at the Castle of Maidens, and was defeated in joust by Tristan. [*Renaut*]

RED KNIGHT³

The nickname of Count HOJIR OF MANNESVELT, because of his crimson hair and beard. [*Wirnt*]

RED KNIGHT⁴

An alias of Lord RAOLAIS, an enemy of Arthur. [*Livre*]

RED KNIGHT⁵

An alias of Sir PERYMONES, a knight defeated by Gareth. [*Malory*]

RED KNIGHT⁶

The name adopted by Sir PELLEAS, after Gawain's treachery and news of Guinevere's infidelity drove him insane and turned him into a marauder. He sent an insulting message to Arthur, and Arthur was forced to rally forces against him. [*TennIK*]

RED KNIGHT⁷

A knight of Arthur's court defeated by the Great Fool. [*IrishF*]

RED KNIGHT⁸ OF THE CLIFF [*Rous de la Faloise*]

A knight who was slain by Gawain while attempting to kidnap the Maiden of the Harp. [*Livre*]

RED KNIGHT⁹ OF THE DEEP FOREST

A knight who killed Perceval's cousin and was slain by Perceval in return. The Red Knight's comrade was a pet lion whom Perceval also killed. [*Perlesvaus*]

RED KNIGHT¹⁰ OF THE PERILOUS VALLEY [*Roux de Val Perilleus*]

A traitorous relative of Arthur who, hearing that Arthur was away on adventures, invaded the land of Cardigan and captured Arthur's castle at Disnadaron. Arthur eventually rallied his forces and marched on the city, and the Red Knight fled, intending to fortify himself in his impregnable castle in the Perilous Valley. He was intercepted along the way by Gawain and Meriadeuc. Meriadeuc defeated him and forced him to surrender to Arthur. [*Meriadeuc*]

RED KNIGHT¹¹ OF THE RED FOREST

A British knight who was challenged by Arthur for ownership of the Red Forest. Sir Meriadoc defeated the Red Knight in combat and decided the issue in Arthur's favor, but convinced Arthur to return the Red Forest to the Red Knight. [*Historia*]

RED KNIGHT¹² OF THE RED LANDS

The alias of Sir IRONSIDE, a knight defeated in combat by Gareth. Like Gawain, his strength waxed and waned with the sun. [*Malory*]

RED MOUNTAIN

During a quest to find Lancelot, Gawain visited the Hermit of the Red Mountain, who directed him to the North Wales Causeway, a bridge to Sorelois. [*VulgLanc*]

RED OLIVE TREE

The location of a hermitage visited by Lancelot and Perceval during the Grail Quest. Lancelot had some disturbing dreams, signifying the sin of his affair with Guinevere, in which he was wounded in the thigh. Perceval was able to cure the wound. Lancelot made a full confession of his sins to Perceval and the hermit. [*PostQuest*]

RED ROSE KNIGHT

The alias adopted by TOM A' LINCOLN, Arthur's illegitimate son, during his years as an outlaw. [*Johnson*]

RED STONE [*Petrone Vermiglio*]

A holy site on the island of Matufer off the coast of Cornwall. Anyone who touched the stone could only tell the truth. Mark brought Isolde there to discover the truth about her affair with Tristan. Tristan, disguised as a pilgrim and a madman, grabbed Isolde and kissed her in front of everyone. Then, Isolde was able to swear that no one had used her body basely except Mark, the "pilgrim," and the "madman." [*Tavola*]

RED TOWER¹

A pagan stronghold. The Lord of the Red Tower captured Gawain and tried to make him fight a lion, unarmed, but Gawain was rescued by Meliot of Logres. [*Perlesvaus*]

RED TOWER²

The stronghold of Partinal, Perceval's uncle. [*Contin3*]

RED TOWER BRIDGE

A bridge built by Argan in rage after having been twice cuckolded, by Uther Pendragon and Sir Hector. It was built near the castle known as Uther's Shame. Any knight who defeated its guardian had to assume the position himself; these unlucky victors included Tor and Hoel. Finally, Hoel, Kay, and Kehedin defeated the fours sons of Argan and ended the custom. [*ProsTris*]

RED WOLF-TREAD

The horse belonging to Arthur's warrior Gilbert. [*Triads*]

REDENZ

A city in King Hoel's Brittany. [*ProsTris*]

REDION

According to Geoffrey of Monmouth, a king of Britain in the second century BC. He succeeded King Eldol and was succeeded by King Rhydderch. [*GeoffHR*]

REDOUBTED GIANT OF THE SURE KEEP

Brother of the Knight-Giant, a knight killed by Arthur in *The Knight of the Parrot*. He attacked Arthur in a forest to avenge his brother's death. Arthur defeated him. As his brother had died trying to prove his valor to the Duchess of Estrales, the Redoubted Giant took vengeance on this woman by cutting off the arm of one of her ladies, the Countess Bliandois. [*ChevPap*]

REDOUBTED ISLAND

An island inhabited by a giant. During inclement weather, the giant lit fires on the island to attract passing ships in need of a port. When the ships arrived, the giant would kill everyone aboard. The giant was eventually killed by Uther Pendragon. Much later, King Mark of Cornwall, after Tristan's death, was deposed and exiled to the Redoubted Island. However, he eventually escaped and reclaimed his kingdom. [*ProsTris*]

REGIN[1]

According to Geoffrey of Monmouth, a king of Britain in the third or second century BC. He was the son of King Gorbonian. He succeeded his uncle, King Elidur, ruled in justice and mercy, and was succeeded by his cousin Margan. [*GeoffHR*]

REGIN[2] [*Regian, Regeym*]

An Arthurian knight, appearing in Geoffrey of Monmouth, who was the son of Abudar or Claud. Welsh mythological genealogies mention a Regin who had a grandfather named Cloten (Fletcher, 77). [*GeoffHR, Wace*]

REIMAMBRAM OF ZADAS

A terrible giant who tried to kidnap lady Behalim of Semphrap but was stopped by her brother, Mahardi. Mahardi and Reimambram scheduled a duel to decide the matter, but Mahardi died before it could be fought. Gawain took his place, defeated Reimambram, and forced him to swear fealty to Behalim. [*Heinrich*]

REINION OF HUNGARY

A king who ruled the Castle of Most Ill Adventure in the Norse *Ivens Saga*. To save his own life, he pledged thirty maidens per year to a giant named Fjallsharfir. Yvain slew the giant and saved him from the pledge. The character appears unnamed in Chrétien's *Yvain*. [*Ivens*]

RENNES

A city in northwest France that was conquered by Maximus in the fifth century. [*GeoffHR*]

RENOART

The hero of the French *La Bataille de Loquifer*, who also appears in the *Chanson de Guillaume* and *Aliscans*. The texts are part of the non-Arthurian William of Orange Cycle, written in France in the thirteenth century.

Loquifer contains a scene in which Renoart, is transported by Morgan le Fay to the Island of Avalon, of which Arthur is king. He has a tryst with Morgan which produces a son named Corbon. [*Bataille*]

REPANSE DE SCHOYE

The Grail bearer in Wolfram's *Parzival*. She was the daughter of Frimutel, the sister of Anfortas, Trevrizent, Schoysiane, and Herzeloyde, and the aunt of Perceval. As a maiden, Repanse had charge of the Grail and carried it in the Grail Procession. After Perceval became the Grail King, Repanse fell in love with Feirefiz, Perceval's pie-bald half brother. Repanse and Feirefiz married and moved to India, where they became the parents of Prester John. [*Wolfram*]

RESCRADDECK [*Rhicaradoch*]

The home of Ulfin, a knight who served both Uther Pendragon and King Arthur. [*GeoffHR, Drayton*]

RESCUE

In the Vulgate *Merlin*, a stronghold near Garlot, to which Queen Blasine of Garlot tried to flee after the Saxons besieged her city. She was captured by Saxons along the way, but later was rescued by Gawain. The fortification supposedly took its name because Vortigern was rescued there from an attack by Hengist, who was slain. This account of Hengist's death conflicts with earlier tales, including one in the same text. [*VulgMer*]

RESTFUL HERMITAGE

An isolated hermitage in Breckham Forest. [*VulgLanc*]

RETAN

The duke of Pergalt. Arthur's Sir Garel saved his sons, Alexander and Floris, from Duke Eskilabon's prison. In return, Retan joined Arthur's war against King Ekunaver of Kanadic and was appointed to the Round Table. [*PleierG*]

RETHENAME

A castle near the border of Orkney, where Gaheris found his mother, the queen of Orkney, *in flagrante* with Lamorat, a family enemy. Gaheris killed his mother and his brothers later slew Lamorat. [*PostMer, ProsTris*]

REVELINE

The Count of Reveline was defeated in a tournament by Yvain. [*Claris*]

REVELLUS

One of Arthur's noblemen in the Norse *Erex Saga*. His brothers were Bilis, the dwarf king, and Brattur. [*Erex*]

REYNEZ

An Arthurian knight who was the son of Colys. [*Arthur*]

RHEDEFRE

The Stag of Rhedenfre was the second "wise animal" that Arthur's warriors encountered on their quest to find the imprisoned warrior Mabon. The Stag sent them to the Owl of Cwm Cawlwyd. [*Culhwch*]

RHEGHED [*Reged*]

A kingdom in northern Britain, ruled by King Urien and his son Owain (Yvain) in legend and, probably, in history. The kingdom no longer exists, and its former borders are uncertain, but it seems to have been situated in northern England or southern Scotland. Sir Walter Scott, in *The Bridal of Triermain*, says that Arthur promised it to whichever of his knights married Gyneth, his daughter. [*Nennius, Culhwch, Scott*]

RHEIDWN ARWY [*Rheiddwn*]

An Arthurian warrior who was the son of Beli. "Arwy" may signify "the Rough." [*Culhwch*]

RHEU RHWYDD DYRYS

One of Arthur's warriors and chief huntsmen. His surnames indicate "easy and difficult." [*Culhwch*]

RHIANNON

As one of his tasks, Culhwch had to capture the two Birds of Rhiannon. It was said that they could "wake the dead and lull the living." In several non-Arthurian *Mabinogion* tales, an otherworldly woman named Rhiannon marries Pwyll, ruler of Dyfed, has a son named Pryderi, and marries Manawydan after Pwyll's death. [*Culhwch*]

RHIOGANEDD

An Arthurian warrior who was the son of the King of Ireland. [*Dream*]

RHIWALLAWN

A son of Urien who fought against the Saxons and enjoyed a number of victories. [*Triads*]

RHODES

A Greek island that joined Lucius the Roman's war against Arthur. [*Allit*]

RHONABWY

One of the soldiers of Madawg, ruler of the country of Powys (Wales) in the twelfth century. While on a mission to capture Iorwerth, Madawg's renegade brother, Rhonabwy and his companions came to the town of Didylstwn in Rhychdir Powys. There, they asked for lodging at the house of Heilyn the Red. After receiving a cold welcome in the dilapidated residence, Rhonabwy went to sleep on a yellow ox skin and had a marvelous dream that he and his companions were in the Britain of Arthur, some seven hundred years before his time. They met the warrior Iddawg, who escorted them to Arthur's camp on the River Severn. There, Rhonabwy and his companions heard of the Battle of Camlann, witnessed a gwyddbwyll game between Arthur and Owain, and saw Arthur make peace with Osla before the battle of Badon. When Rhonabwy awoke, he found he had been sleeping for three days and thee nights. [*Dream*]

RHONGOMYNYAD ("Cutting Spear") [*Rhongomiant, Rhongomyniad*]

Arthur's spear in *Culhwch and Olwen*. Geoffrey of Monmouth shortens the name to RON. [*Culhwch, GeoffHR*]

RHUDDVYW RHYS

An Arthurian warrior killed at Garth Grugyn by Grugyn Silver Bristle, a piglet pursued by Arthur and his warriors. [*Culhwch*]

RHUFAWN THE RADIANT

An Arthurian warrior who was the son of Deorthach or Gwyddno. He is called one of the three "fair princes" and one of the three "golden corpses" of the Island of Britain. [*Culhwch, Triads, Dream*]

RHUN[1]

An Arthurian warrior killed at Cwm Cerwyn by the boar Twrch Trwyth. He was the son of Beli Adver. A Triad calls him one of the "three red ravishers" of Britain. [*Culhwch, Triads*]

RHUN[2] [*Run, Ron*]

An Arthurian warrior who was the son of Nwython and the brother of Gwystyl, Llwydeu, and Kinlith. [*Culhwch, GeoffHR*]

RHUN[3]

An Arthurian warrior who was the son of Maelgwn of Gwynedd. His experience and wisdom were such that everyone always turned to him for advice. [*Dream*]

RHUN[4]

A son of Urien of Rheged and brother of Owain. He became the archbishop of York and assumed the name PAULINUS. According to one manuscript, a compilation of history put together by Rhun was one of Nennius's sources. [*Nennius*]

RHUN[5] RED ADLER

One of Arthur's warriors and huntsmen. [*Culhwch*]

RHYAWDD [*Rahawd*]

One of Arthur's warriors and advisors. He was the son of Morgant. The Welsh Triads call him one of the three "frivolous bards" of Britain. He rode a horse named Spotted Dun. [*Triads, Dream*]

RHYCH SEFERI

An Arthurian warrior in Welsh tradition, known to entertain his comrades with song. He was skilled with a club, and he used his boots as throwing weapons. [*Culhwch*]

RHYDDERCH[1]

According to Geoffrey of Monmouth, a king of Britain in the second century BC. Rhydderch succeeded King Redion and was succeeded by King Samuil-Penissel. [*GeoffHR*]

RHYDDERCH[2] THE GENEROUS [*Rodarchus*]

King of Cumbria in Myrddin legend, probably based on a historical sixth-century ruler of Strathclyde. Nennius names him as one of the kings who fought alongside King Urien against the Saxons in the sixth century. According to the Myrddin poems, Rhydderch was one of the leaders at the battle of Arfderydd, where he fought alongside King Peredur of North Wales, and opposed King Gwenddolau of Scotland. Rhydderch was victorious. Merlin, who had fought on Gwenddolau's side in Welsh legend, and on Rhydderch's side in Geoffrey's *Vita Merlini*, went insane at the battle and fled to the forest of Caledon. Rhydderch's wife, Ganieda, was Merlin's sister. In his moments of insanity, Merlin told Rhydderch that Ganieda was adulterous, but Ganieda managed to convince her husband that Merlin could not be trusted because of his madness. Rhydderch died during Merlin's life, and his widow went to live with her brother in the forest. A Welsh poem places his grave at Abererch. A Welsh text called the "Thirteen Treasures of the Isle of Britain" names one of the treasures as a *dysgl*, or dish, owned by Rhydderch. It was said to provide food and drink to Rhydderch's company and has been seen by some scholars as the origin of the Grail. [*Myrddin, Nennius, GeoffVM*]

RHYDYCHEN

An early name of OXFORD.

RHYFERYS

Arthur's master of hounds in Welsh legend. [*Geraint*]

RHYGENYDD

A cleric whose crock and dish are counted among the Thirteen Treasures of the Island of Britain. The dish produced any food desired by its owner, leading some scholars to connect it to the Grail.

RHYMHI

A magic female dog in Welsh legend. Rhymhi lived in Aber Deu Cleddyf and had two pups that were sought by Arthur and his warriors, on the behalf of Culhwch, for the hunting of the boar Twrch Trwyth. Curiously, the giant Ysbaddaden, who assigned the tasks to Culhwch, did not request these hounds, and it is unclear why Arthur and his soldiers decided that they had to obtain them. Two of Rhymhi's sons—Gwydden and Gwyddrud—were also said to be Arthur's warriors. [*Culhwch*]

RHYNNON STIFF BEARD

The owner of a set of magical bottles in which no liquid ever soured. As one of his tasks, Culhwch had to obtain these bottles for use at Olwen's wedding feast. [*Culhwch*]

RHYS ONE-TOOTH

A Welsh warrior who apparently died in a battle against King Maelgwn of Gwynned. In an early Welsh poem, Myrddin and Taliesin lament his passing. [*Myrddin*]

RIAL

King of Jeraphin. His land was seized by King Roaz of Glois, but was returned to him by Wigalois (Gawain's son). In return, he assisted Wigalois in a war against Prince Lion of Namur. [*Wirnt*]

RIALT

A count and kinsman of Gerhart of Riviers who participated in Gerhart's attack on the castle Merkanie. Defeated by Arthur's' Sir Garel, he was forced to cease hostilities. [*PleierG*]

RIANO

A great palace in Cornwall where Tristan lay ill after his battle with Morholt. [*Tavola*]

RICA

Father of Arthur's warrior Gormant. Welsh legend calls him the "chief elder of Cornwall," and first husband of Eigyr (Igraine), which would make him a counterpart of GORLOIS. [*Culhwch*]

RICART

A brief companion of Agravain in *Les Merveilles de Rigomer*. As a vassal of an Irish nobleman named Robert, Ricart and other knights accompanied Agravain on a quest to find Robert's kidnapped wife. [*Merveil*]

RICCARDA

Galehaut's sister in the Italian romance *I Due Tristani*. She married the King with a Hundred Knights. In *La Tavola Ritonda*, she is called DELICE. [*DueTris*]

RICH FISHER

See FISHER KING.

RICHARD[1] [*Riciers*]

A count in Arthur's service. [*Renaut*]

RICHARD[2]

Arthur's cousin in the Prose *Brut*. Arthur bestowed several Gaulish lands upon him. [*ProsBrut*]

RICHARD³

An Irish count who directed two of Vortigern's messengers, Ruggieri and Labegues, to Northumberland, where Merlin had been born. [*Pieri*]

RICHARD⁴

Son of the king of Jerusalem in Arthur's time. The king of Baghdad invaded his lands. Richard sent to Arthur for aid, and Henry the Couretous arrived with British troops to drive the pagans away. Later, Richard attacked Sarras but was unable to overcome Alchendic, its king. [*Prophecies*]

RICHBOROUGH

A British port where King Arthur landed upon his return from the Roman campaign. Mordred, who had usurped the throne, met him there with an army. Many men fell—including Angusel and Gawain—and Mordred's army was pushed back to the river Camel. Wace places this battle at ROMNEY. [*GeoffHR*]

RICHE SOUDIER

Lord of the Castle Orguellous, where Girflet was imprisoned. Arthur besieged the castle to free Girflet. Gawain fought the Riche Soudier in single combat and won. Arthur captured the castle. [*Contin1*]

RICHER [*Richier*]

An earl in Arthur's service who fought in the Roman War in Geoffrey of Monmouth's *Historia*. His father was named Rowlaunde and his brother was Raynald. Pierre de Langtoft erroneously places him in Lucius's army. [*GeoffHR, Wace, VulgMer, Pierre, Allit*]

RICHEVIE VENTURA

A young man baptized and knighted by Lancelot and Tristan. He married the daughter of Count Sebio of Cologia. [*Tavola*]

RICHIER¹

A brief companion of Agravain in *Les Merveilles de Rigomer*. As a vassal of an Irish nobleman named Robert, Richier and other knights accompanied Agravain on a quest to find Robert's kidnapped wife. [*Merveil*]

RICHIER²

A duke from Wales who, at the tournament of Winchester, fought Mador of the Gate. [*Prophecies*]

RICHIER³ OF THE VALLEY

A squire of Guiron the Courteous. [*Palamedes*]

RICHOMARCH [*Rimar(c)*]

One of Arthur's barons, who fought and died against the Romans at the battle of Soissons. [*GeoffHR, Wace, Layamon*]

RICULF [*Ridulph, Rycolf*]

A king who stole the country of Norway from Lot after the death of Sichelm, Lot's grandfather. After pacifying Britain, Arthur sailed to Norway, killed Riculf, and gave the kingdom back to Lot. [*GeoffHR, Wace, Layamon*]

RIDRAS

In *Arthour and Merlin*, a heathen king slain by King Ban of Benoic at the battle of Aneblayse. The character appears unnamed in the Vulgate *Merlin*. [*Arthour*]

RIDWATHELAN

A nephew of Bedivere in Layamon. He avenged his uncle's death at the Battle of Soissons by killing Boccus, the Roman warrior who had killed Bedivere. Geoffrey of Monmouth and Wace call him HIRELGLAS. [*Layamon*]

RIEINGULID

The daughter of King Amlawdd, husband of Bicanus, and mother of St. Illtud, who was Arthur's cousin. [*Saints*]

RIELEI OF WROWELE

An Irish Knight of the Round Table who was the father of Sir Patrick. During a banquet, he became enraged when a servant brought him the wrong food and drink, and he killed the servant. [*HartmannI*]

RIEZ

A British river, along which Faustus, son of Vortigern, built a great monastery. [*Nennius*]

RIGAL OF RONE

One of Lord Golagros's knights in the Middle Scots tale of *Gologras and Gawain*. During the war between Arthur and Golagros, Rigal slew, and was slain by, Arthur's Sir Rannald. [*Golagros*]

RIGER THE BROWN

A knight, possibly of the "Brown" lineage, who sat in the Perilous Seat. The earth opened beneath him and swallowed him. This occurred during Uther Pendragon's reign. [*Prophecies*]

RIGOLIN

A knight from Nantes and enemy of Duke Jovelin of Arundel. With other knights, he besieged Jovelin's chief city of Karke, but was defeated by Tristan. He probably has the same origins as Eilhart's similarly-named RIOLE of Nantes. [*Gottfried*]

RIGOMER

An enchanted Irish castle that serves as the focus of the thirteenth century French tale of *Les Merveilles de Rigomer* ("the Marvels of Rigomer"). Its name reflects that it was situated on a *rigort de mer*, or "bay of the sea" (Loomis,

Romance, 385). It was guarded by fearsome beasts, scores of soldiers, and numerous enchantments. Its queen, Dionise—who seems to have been half-ruler, half-prisoner—could only marry the knight who could conquer the castle, a feat deemed impossible. Arthur's knights first learned of its existence when a messenger sent by Dionise came to Arthur's court.

The castle had been created by a fairy. It lay on an island off the coast of Ireland, atop a high cliff, with only a single bridge connecting it to the mainland. The bridge was guarded by a horrendous dragon. The heath approaching the bridge, called Vrikevreue, was guarded by three knights called the Unarmed Knight, the White Knight, and the Knight of Triple Arms. Traveling to Rigomer involved a long journey through Ireland, described in the story as a wild and savage land. If a knight did happen to make it past the defenses, he would succumb to the castle's magic, which would steal his wits and scramble his mind.

Lancelot was the first of Arthur's knights to embark on the journey. He completed a number of perilous adventures in Ireland before arriving at the castle. He passed all the defenses, including the dragon, but once inside the fortress, he was tricked into putting on a magic ring, which turned him into a fool. He was thrown into the Kibouene Pits, Rigomer's unholy prison.

When word of Lancelot's imprisonment reached Britain, Gawain raised a battalion of Arthur's knights to conquer Rigomer. Gawain was imprisoned along the way, and the other knights reached it first. The best of them—including Gaheris, Gaudin, Cliges, Bleoberis, and Sagremor—went ahead of the main party. They were all defeated and imprisoned. The rest of the knights challenged Rigomer's armies. They performed valiantly, but were overwhelmed by waves and waves of supernatural forces.

Gawain finally freed himself, arrived at the castle, passed the defenses, and refused to accept the ring. He took the rings off the fingers of his friends, freeing them from Rigomer's magic. Having thus conquered the castle, Gawain declined to marry Dionise, promising to find another worthy husband for her. [*Merveil*]

RIM [*Rens, Rins*]

A knight who gave hospitality to Arthur's Sir Yder. Yder rewarded him by sending him the bounty of his victories. Rim's son, Luguain, became Yder's squire. Rim's father was named Charmes. [*Yder*]

RIMA

A maiden rescued by Tristan from a serpent. [*Tavola*]

RINAL

A land ruled by Uther Pendragon. [*Heinrich*]

RINALT

A count who served King Dulcemar of Tandernas. He tried and failed to arrange a truce when Arthur went to war with Dulcemar over an offense committed by Dulcemar's son. [*PleierT*]

RIODACH

A city in Syria. Queen Florie—the wife of Gawain and the mother of Wigalois—was buried here. [*Wirnt*]

RIOLE

The Count of Nantes in Eilhart's *Tristrant*. Riole loved Isolde of the White Hands, daughter of King Havelin of Karahes (and later Tristan's wife). When Havelin refused an offer of marriage, Riole attacked him. He besieged Karahes and probably would have won the war, but Tristan arrived and, championing Havelin, defeated Riole. When Havelin died, Riole resumed the war against Kahedins, Havelin's son, but was again defeated by Tristan. His counterpart in Gottfried's *Tristan* is RIGOLIN. [*Eilhart*]

RIONS [*Retho, Rhines, Rictor, Rience, Rion(es), Riouns, *Ritho, Riton, Riun, Rostrik, Roy(e)ns, Roystone, Ruiston, Rusten, Ryence, Ryens, Ryon(s), Ryton*]

A giant slain by Arthur. He is variously described as the king of Africa, Denmark, the Land of Grasslands and Giants, the Grazing Grounds, Ireland, the Isles, North Wales, and South Wales. His character undergoes a considerable evolution between Geoffrey of Monmouth and Malory. Geoffrey probably based him on a Welsh giant who was said to inhabit the Mountain of Snowdon. E. K. Chambers thought that his name might preserve some memory of RIOTHAMUS, a historical British ruler. In Thomas Chestre's *Sir Launfal*, he is named as Guinevere's father, and in Spenser's *The Faerie Queene*, he is the father of the warrior maiden Britomart. A variation of Rions is found in *Meriadeuc* as King RIS.

Geoffrey places the battle between Arthur and Rions at Mount Aravius (in Welsh, Eryri, or Snowdon). Rions had fashioned a cloak from the beards of all the kings he had killed, but he needed one more. He sent a message to Arthur demanding that Arthur send his own beard to Rions in penance, or to face Rions' wrath. Arthur challenged Rions to a fight, defeated him, and took the cloak for himself. Many other authors allude to this battle, giving variations of Rions' name and the battle site.

In the Vulgate *Merlin*, Rions becomes a Saxon king who invades Carmelide, Leodegan's kingdom, early in Arthur's reign. With fifteen allied kings, he besieged the castle of Carhaix. Arthur, fresh from his defeat of the rebellious kings at Bedegraine, journeyed to Carhaix with Merlin, King Ban of Benoic, and King Bors of Gannes, and the combined forces of the kings led to Rions' defeat. Rions suffered a second defeat at Aneblayse, another of Leodegan's cities, in which Arthur captured Rions's sword—a magnificent blade called Marmiadoise that had been owned by Hercules. Rions returned to Carhaix again, demanded Arthur's beard as in Geoffrey of Monmouth, and Arthur finally killed him in single combat.

The Post-Vulgate *Merlin* continuation and Malory's *Le Morte Darthur* modify the story: After his defeat at Carmelide, Rions helped the kings in rebellion against Arthur to repel a Saracen invasion. In time, however, he turned on these kings, conquered their lands, and made his famous request for Arthur's beard. With his brother King Nero and King Lot of Lothian, he met Arthur's forces at the castle of Tarabel in Cornwall. Before the battle, however Balin and Balan intercepted and abducted Rions, delivering him to Arthur as a prisoner. Consequently, Arthur was able to defeat the other kings. [*GeoffHR, Wace, Layamon, ChretienP, VulgMer, PostMer, ChestreLvl, Malory, KingR, Spenser*]

RIOTHAMUS [*Rigatamos, Riothimir*]

A British king mentioned in early continental chronicles who in 468, at the request of Emperor Anthemius of Rome (ruled 467–472), brought an army of twelve thousand Britons "by way of the ocean" to Gaul to destroy the Euric the Visigoth. Euric was amassing power and he threatened the crumbling empire's western territories. Arvandus, Rome's traitorous prefect in Gaul, warned Euric of Riothamus's advance, and Euric was able to lay an ambush in Burgundy that decimated the British army. Riothamus reportedly escaped, but it is not known what became of him. The kingdom over which Riothamus ruled is also not known. Some scholars have suggested that he came from Brittany rather than Britain.

Geoffrey Ashe and other scholars have identified Riothamus with Arthur. Riothamus seems to be a variation of the Celtic *rigatamos*, a title meaning "great king," rather than a personal name. Riothamus and a historical Arthur would have lived in the same time frame, and Riothamus's campaign in Gaul is mirrored in Geoffrey of Monmouth's *Historia* by Arthur's conquest of France. The area of Burgundy in which Riothamus was last reported contains a valley known as Avallon, which may be a historical origin for Arthur's final resting place. Other scholars have tried to connect Riothamus with Ambrosius or even Uther. A less controversial theory suggests simply that Geoffrey of Monmouth was inspired by Riothamus's story when he wrote of Arthur's expedition to Gaul. E. K. Chambers thought that a derivation of his name might be found in RITHO (Rions), a giant slain by Arthur in the chronicles.

RIPOSTA

An island in the Uziano Sea ruled by Lasancis, an enemy of Arthur. [*Tavola*]

RIS[1]

A British king who opposed Cadioalant in a tournament at Caerleon. [*Contin1*]

RIS[2]

King of Outre-Ombre ("outer shadows") who defeated nine kings and made a mantle for his paramour, the Queen of Iceland, out of their beards. He sent a message to Arthur's court demanding Arthur's beard. When Arthur refused, he besieged and captured the city of Cardigan. He offered to grant any favor to a knight who would brave the fearsome Waste Chapel. When none of his knights rose to the task, Lady Lore of Cardigan—over Ris's objections—completed the adventure and forced Ris to return her city. Later, Arthur's Sir Meriadeuc defeated Ris and his best knights in combat, forcing them to surrender to Arthur. Ris reconciled with Arthur and became one of the king's knights. Found in the tale of *Meriadeuc*, his character and name were evidently suggested by RIONS. [*Meriadeuc*]

RISCHOYDE

Perceval's great-aunt. She was the daughter of Titurel and the sister of Frimutel. She married Kaylet of Hoskurast, the King of Spain and Castille. [*Wolfram*]

RISEUT

A lady who stole a hound from Pereval. Her lover, Garsallas, stole a white stag's head from Perceval. Their thefts delayed Perceval's return to the Grail Castle. [*Contin2*]

RITHO

The name in Geoffrey of Monmouth of a giant killed at Mount Snowdon. He is generally known as RIONS in other tales. [*GeoffHR*]

RITSCHART[1]

The Count of Tumane who participated in the Dyoflê tournament in Ulrich's *Lanzelet*. He opposed Lot, and fared poorly in the tournament—twenty of his knights were captured—until Lancelot agreed to fight for his side. Ulrich notes that Ritschart had 100 knights in total; he may thus be identical to the KING WITH A HUNDRED KNIGHTS found in later texts. [*UlrichZ*]

RITSCHART[2] OF NAVERS

A count who was an ally or vassal of Duchess Orgeluse of Logres. He joined a battle against Arthur in Logres, and was defeated by Arthur himself. [*Wolfram*]

RIVALIN[1] [*Riwalin*]

A king. Rivalin and his wife, Anzansnuse, cared for Gawain after he had been badly injured in a battle against four "toll collectors." [*Heinrich*]

RIVALIN[2] CANELENGRES [*Riwalin*]

Tristan's father in the early German legends. He is variously given as the king of Lyonesse (or Lohenis), or the lord of Parmenie. Rash and bold, he declared war on his overlord, Duke Morgan, and fought a destructive conflict. During a truce, he traveled to Cornwall to assist King Mark against Mark's Irish enemies. There, he met Mark's sister Blancheflor and fell in love with her. He received a deep wound in battle, but Blancheflor's presence revived him. They married, and Blancheflor died giving birth to Tristan. Gottfried says that Rivalin died soon afterwards, in the renewed war against Morgan, but not before commending Tristan to the care of his steward, Rual. Eilhart says that he lived to raise his son. Upon Rivalin's death, Tristan inherited his kingdom but never ruled it. The Norse *Saga of Tristram and Ísönd* calls him simply CANELENGRES, and the Middle-English *Sir Tristrem* refers to him as ROULAND. His character was supplanted by MELIADUS. [*Eilhart, Wolfram, Gottfried*]

RIVALLO

According to Geoffrey of Monmouth, king of Britain in the eighth century BC. He was the son of King Cunedag and the father of King Gurgustius. During his reign, a plague befell Britain. [*GeoffHR*]

RIVALLD

One of Arthur's dukes in the Norse *Erex Saga*. He was present at the wedding of Erec and Enide. [*Erex*]

ROADAN

A castle in the country of Nantes that Erec gave to Licorant (or Koralus) when he married Licorant's daughter Enide. This gift brought Licorant out of poverty. R. S. Loomis (*Tradition*, 76) identifies it with Castle Rudlan in North Wales. [*ChretienE*]

ROAZ

The pagan king of Glois who sold his soul to the devil and was thus able to use sorcery to take over many lands, including the neighboring kingdom of Korntin. He killed King Lar of Korntin and drove Queen Amena to the border. After holding Korntin for ten years, he was killed in single combat by Wigalois (Gawain's son), who had arrived as Amena's champion. Roaz's wife, Japhite, died from sorrow. [*Wirnt*]

ROBBER KNIGHT

A thief and murderer who kidnapped two maidens from the Waste Castle. Perceval and the Coward Knight caught him in the act, and Perceval forced the Coward Knight to intervene. The Coward Knight killed the Robber Knight, turning himself into the Bold Knight. [*Perlesvaus*]

ROBERDIC

The home of Sir Caveron and Sir Governal, who may be the same character. [*ChretienE, ChretienL*]

ROBERT[1]

The squire of Guinglain, Gawain's son. [*Renaut*]

ROBERT[2]

The lord of castle Sotain Herbert. Agravain met him during Agravain's adventures in Ireland. Robert's lovely wife had been carried off by a violent storm. The lady found her way to the castle of an evil, lustful nobleman, who imprisoned her and forced her to marry him against her will. Agravain and some of Robert's knights managed to rescue her and return her to her rightful husband. [*Merveil*]

ROCCHETTO

The court fool of King Faramon of France. He foretold Morholt's death at the hands of Tristan. [*Tavola*]

ROCEBOURC

In Guillaume le Clerc's *Fergus*, a castle in Lothian, where Lady Galiene of Lothian was besieged by a malicious king. She was rescued by Arthur's Sir Fergus. Guillaume was probably referring to the actual Scottish castle of Roxburgh. [*Guillaume*]

ROCEDON

The daughter of the Duke of Rocedon helped Lancelot escape from Cart Castle when he was imprisoned there by Morgan le Fay and the Queen of Sorestan. In return, Lancelot helped her regain lands which had been stolen by Sorestan. [*VulgLanc*]

ROCHE FLORIE

The home of Lorie, Gawain's fairy girlfriend. [*Merveil*]

ROCHEMONT

A Knight of the Round Table. [*Scott*]

ROCHESTER

A city in Kent. The Bishop of Rochester, on orders from the pope, brought about a reconciliation between Arthur and Guinevere after the queen's affair with Lancelot was exposed. [*VulgMort, Stanz, Malory*]

ROCK CASTLE

A castle converted to Christianity by Joseph of Arimathea. It was ruled by Lord Matagran. [*VulgEst*]

ROCK OF BLOOD [*Roche de Sanc]

A cliff near the city of La Choine, where King Evalach of Sarras fought a battle against King Tholomer of Babylonia. Evalach was nearly defeated, but a holy White Knight appeared and routed Tholomer's forces. The enormous bloodshed at the battle stained the cliff red, giving it its name. [*VulgEst*]

ROCK OF HERMITS [*Roche aux Ermites]

A small island where King Mark of Cornwall, in one of his many attempts to rid himself of Tristan, abandoned his nephew. A knight named Assar, who lived on the nearby Island of Two Brothers, befriended and rescued Tristan. [*ProsTris*]

ROCK OF MERLIN

Merlin's tomb, where Tristan and Lancelot fought a great battle in the Italian *Quando Tristano e Lancielotto Combattettero al Petrone di Merlino*. Merlin had predicted that the two greatest knights in the world would do battle there. Tristan thought he was fighting Palamedes, who had agreed to meet him there but was delayed by injury. Lancelot, for his part, expected to stop a fight between Tristan and his son Galahad. The two knights revealed themselves and ended the fight before they injured each other too severely. This episode appears, in varied forms, in many different romances. In *La Tavola Ritonda*, a number of stones of this nature are collectively called MERLIN'S STONES. [*Quando*]

ROCK OF THE CORNISHWOMAN

A castle where a Cornish enchantress bewitched and imprisoned Meliadus, Tristan's father, on the eve of his son's birth. [*ProsTris*]

ROCK OF THE MAIDENS [*Roche aux Pucelles*]

A high rock on which Merlin imprisoned a lady and her many sisters, after the lady tried to kill Merlin by sorcery. The maidens on the Rock possessed the power of prophecy and correctly predicted the deaths of Arthur, Gawain, Morholt, and Gaheris. Gawain and Morholt were trapped on the Rock after they decided to enjoy the maidens' company. Yvain tried to rescue them, but found that they had no memory of their former lives. They were eventually freed by Gaheris, who defeated the maidens' brother in combat. [*PostMer, PostQuest*]

ROCKINGHAM [*Rok(e)ingham*]

In the English *Arthour and Merlin*, the site of the decisive battle between Arthur and the kings who rebelled against him. The Vulgate *Merlin* places this fight at the forest of BEDEGRAINE. The similarity of Rockingham and "Brekenham," a variation of Bedegraine, may have contributed to the confusion. *Arthour* also places a battle between King Clarion and the Saxons in the forest of Rockingham. [*Arthour*]

ROCKY CRAG

In the Vulgate *Merlin*, the Duke of the Rocky Crag allied with Arthur and pledged support to Arthur's war against the Saxons. [*VulgMer*]

RODDAN

A duke in Arthur's service. [*Erex*]

RODRIC [*Sodric*]

A king of Picts who, during the reign of Marius in Britain, brought a fleet from Scythia and invaded Scotland. Marius conquered him but gave Caithness to the Pictish people. [*GeoffHR*]

ROESTOC

A castle in Arthur's kingdom. According to the Vulgate *Merlin*, its castellan joined the British kings' war against the Saxons. Roestoc plain was the site of a battle between the Saxons and a group of youths led by Gawain. In the Vulgate *Lancelot*, the Lady of Roestoc is attacked by Sir Seguarades, who desires to marry her. She sent one of her vassals—a dwarf named Groadain—to find a champion from Arthur's court to fight Seguarades. Groadain returned with Hector and Gawain, the latter of whom was traveling incognito. Hector's lady refused to let him fight, so the combat was left to the "unknown" knight. After a long battle, Gawain was victorious against Seguarades, and he freed the Lady's lands. [*LancLac, VulgLanc, VulgMer*]

ROEVENT

A British castle owned by the uncle of Sir Kahedins or by Arthur. [*VulgLanc*]

ROGEDAL OF MIRNETALLE

A count once defeated in combat by Perceval. [*Wolfram*]

ROGER [*Ugier*]

A presumptuous knight who came to Uther's court to have Merlin predict the fate of his son. He arrogantly sat in the Round Table's Perilous Seat and was killed. [*VitaMer*]

ROGES

A prince enchanted by his stepmother in the form of a fox. He joined Gawain during Gawain's quest for the Floating Chessboard. Roges could only return to human form if he saw King Wonder, his son, Gawain, and the maiden Ysabele all together in the same place. At the conclusion of the adventure, Gawain returned to Wonder's court, the condition was met, and Roges became a man again. [*Penninc*]

ROGNES

A dukedom conquered by Galehaut from Duke Helias. [*Livre*]

ROGUEDON

A castle ruled by Griffon, an enemy of Arthur. [*VulgLanc*]

ROHAIS

A maiden whose lover, Arguissiaus of Carhaix, was badly wounded by Sir Dragonel the Cruel. Dragonel intended to force Rohais into marrying him, but Perceval arrived, defeated him in combat, and saved Rohais. [*Contin4*]

ROHAND [*Rohant*]

Steward of Rouland, Tristan's father. When Rouland was slain by Duke Morgan, Rohand raised Tristan, calling him "Tantrist," and pretending that the boy was his own son. He is known as RUAL in Gottfried's version. [*SirTris*]

ROHAS

A mountain in the land of Styria—presently called the Rohitscher Berg—where Perceval's uncle Trevrizent had some adventures, fighting battles against the Slovenes, before settling down into a hermitage. [*Wolfram*]

ROHUR

A castle where Gawain found lodging prior to the tournament at Sorgarda castle. The mistress of Rohur was named Levenet. [*Heinrich*]

ROIDERODES

A knight defeated by Erec in a tournament in Hartmann von Aue's *Erec*. He may be identical with either RANDURAZ or the KING OF THE RED CITY in Chrétien's *Erec*. [*HartmannE*]

ROIDES

A knight present at the Sorgarda tournament, which Gawain won. [*Heinrich*]

ROIDURANT

One of Arthur's knights. He encountered a dragon in the forest, who begged him to kiss her. Roidurant fled instead, but related the story to Lancelot, who assumed the adventure and kissed the dragon, turning it into the beautiful Clidra the Fair. [*UlrichZ*]

ROIMUNT ("King's Mountain")

A castle at the edge of the kingdom of Korntin. A strong fortress, it was the only place of refuge for Queen Amena of Korntin after her land was seized by King Roaz of Glois. Amena lived at Roimunt for ten years until Roaz was killed by Wigalois (Gawain's son). [*Wirnt*]

ROLAND DE VAUX

The hero of part of Sir Walter Scott's *The Bridal of Triermain*. On a quest to find a Sleeping Beauty, he located a castle in the Valley of St. John, which contained Gyneth, Arthur's daughter. Merlin had enchanted her into a deep slumber, but Roland woke her with a kiss. [*Scott*]

ROLLANDUS

A twelfth-century pseudo-historical count of Brittany found in Etienne de Rouen's *Draco Normannicus*. Henry II of England was conquering Rollandus's kingdom, so Rollandus sent to Arthur, who was living in a southern paradise, for assistance. Arthur, in turn, sent a message to Henry warning him to leave Brittany alone and to prepare for Arthur's return. Henry ignored the message and Arthur never appeared. [*Etienne*]

ROMANUS

Fictional pope during the reign of King Vortimer (Vortigern's son). At Vortimer's request, Romanus sent two bishops—Germanus and Louis—to help restore Christianity in Britain, which had faltered under Vortigern's rule. [*Layamon*]

ROMAREC [*Rumarek, Rumaret(h)*]

The King of Finland or Wendland in the time of Arthur. He voluntarily subjugated himself to Arthur to avoid being conquered. He sent his son to Arthur's court as a kind of hostage. His son later helped put a stop to a brawl in Arthur's hall. Romarec assisted Arthur in the conquest of France. [*Wace, Layamon*]

ROME [*Romme, Roume*]

Historically, it is known that Roman legions conquered Britain in 43 A.D. The histories proposed by Gildas, Nennius, and Geoffrey follow the same pattern: an initial invasion followed by hundreds of years of uncertain, absentee domination and constant usurpation by British natives or expatriated Romans, an eventual withdrawal, a return—at the pleading of the Britons—to drive away the Picts and Scots, a second departure, and a refusal to return again to help the Britons against the barbarians. The departure takes place in early fifth century. It leaves Britain in anarchy and paves the way for the assumption of the throne by Constantine, Arthur's grandfather. The histories also suggest that Arthur descended from Roman stock (some histories call Ambrosius, Arthur's uncle, a Roman senator). See BRITAIN for a fuller history.

Beginning with Geoffrey of Monmouth, almost all the chronicles include a war between Arthur and Rome that begins when Rome demands Arthur's submission. Geoffrey names the Roman emperor as Leo, but the procurator, who takes charge of the campaign against Arthur, is named Lucius. Following the Romans' demand, Arthur raised an army and met the Romans in Gaul. Both sides convened to discuss a treaty, but during the talks, Gawain became enraged at the insults of a Roman warrior and cut off his head, inciting a battle. Several skirmishes followed, culminating in the final battle at Soissons, in which Lucius was killed and Arthur was victorious. Arthur prepared to march on Rome itself, but he was recalled to Britain to deal with Mordred's insurrection.

Geoffrey and his immediate successors thus locate the Roman War at the end of Arthur's reign. The Vulgate Cycle changes this chronology, placing the Roman War just after Arthur's victories against the Saxons and the rebellious British kings at the beginning of his reign. The Vulgate *Merlin*, in fact, names the Roman Emperor in Arthur's time as none other than Julius Caesar! Caesar sent Roman warriors, under the command of the senator Pontius Anthony, to assist King Claudas of the Waste Land in his war against Arthur, Ban of Benoic, and Bors of Gannes. Claudas was eventually victorious, but Pontius Anthony was killed. Later, *Merlin* follows Geoffrey by naming Lucius as the Roman leader, but *Merlin* (following a tradition begun by the chronicler Wace) eliminates Leo and calls Lucius himself the Emperor of Rome. As in Geoffrey, Arthur kills him at the battle of Soissons and returns home. In the Vulgate *Mort Artu*, the Romans invade Burgundy at the end of Arthur's reign, as Arthur is fighting Lancelot in France. Arthur again slays the Roman Emperor and, as in Geoffrey, returns to Britain to deal with Mordred.

The Alliterative *Morte Arthure* follows Geoffrey's chronology by placing the war against Lucius just before Mordred's insurrection. The text adds, however, a description of Arthur's conquest of the city of Rome itself (an idea found earlier in John Hardyng's chronicle). Malory includes Arthur's occupation of Rome, but reverts to the Vulgate Cycle's chronology, and excludes the Roman invasion of Burgundy.

It is interesting to note that the western Roman Empire fell in AD 476 (see CONSTANTINOPLE for information on the eastern empire), but the Arthurian legends, which take place in the late fifth or early sixth century, refer to Rome as if it still possessed all its glory in Arthur's time. The author of *Floriant et Florete* seems to have at least some knowledge of Rome's problems with the barbarian tribes: in the story, it is besieged by Saracens but saved by the timely arrival of the hero Floriant. [*Gildas, Nennius, GeoffHR, Wace, Layamon, Hardyng, VulgMort, VulgMer, Floriant, Allit, Malory*]

ROMNEY [*Ramsey, Romsey*]

In Wace, the seaport in Britain where Mordred's army met Arthur's on their return from the Roman War. A great battle was fought, and Gawain and Angusel were killed. This parallels Geoffrey's account of the battle of RICHBOROUGH and Malory's description of DOVER. [*Wace, Layamon, Awntyrs*]

RON

Arthur's lance according to Geoffrey of Monmouth. It was one of the finest weapons ever made. Arthur carried it at the battle of Bath against the Saxons. In *Culhwch and Olwen*, Arthur's spear is called RHONGOMYNYAD, of which *Ron* seems to be an abbreviation. [*GeoffHR, Wace*]

RONDOLES HALL [*Rondallsete, Rondol(f)sett(e)*]

A castle in the vicinity of Inglewood Forest where Arthur, Guinevere, and Arthur's knights retired to dinner after an adventure at lake Wadling. Galleron appeared and challenged any of Arthur's knights to a duel to reclaim lands that Arthur had annexed. Rondoles Hall was probably based on a real location; there are records of manors named Randalholme, Randasset, and Randerside in the area of Lake Wadling (Hahn, 213). [*Awntyrs*]

ROOLANT [*Roulyons*]

A vassal of King Rions, Arthur's Saxon enemy. Roolant joined Rions' invasion of Carmelide. [*VulgMer, Arthour*]

ROS

A region of Wales where Gawain's tomb was supposedly discovered during the reign of William I in 1087. [*WilliamM*]

ROSCHE SABINS [*Rogisabens, Roisawenz*]

The capital city of the land ruled by King Gramoflanz, Gawain's enemy. It had previously been owned by Gramoflanz's father, King Irot. The town was well-guarded with numerous moats and towers. It stood near the sea, between the Sabins and Poynzaclins rivers. [*Wolfram, PleierG*]

ROSE ESPANIE

The unattractive ladylove of Girflet, lord of Becleus. Girflet continually entered her in a sparrowhawk tournament, even though she was not beautiful, which was supposed to be a requisite for winning the sparrowhawk. Girflet's own skill as a knight made him the victor. He was finally given his just deserts by Gawain's son, Guinglain, who entered the tournament with Margerie, a truly attractive woman. [*Renaut*]

ROSEAMONDE OF THE NOBLE VALES

Paramour of Sir Semiramin, a knight saved by Perceval. [*Contin4*]

ROSETE LA BLOIE [*Rozain*]

A LOATHLY LADY loved by the Handsome Coward. Perceval encountered them in the forest and laughed at her ugliness. The Handsome Coward attacked Perceval for this insult but lost. Both went to Arthur's court, where Rosete was again teased by Kay. She later became beautiful. [*Contin2, Didot*]

ROSON

In the Norse *Erex Saga*, the location of the Sparrowhawk tournament where Erec met Enide. Chrétien de Troyes calls the castle LALUTH. [*Erex*]

ROTH

Arthur's king of Ireland in one manuscript of Pierre de Langtoft's chronicle; very likely a corruption of "the rich king of Ireland" (*ly ryche* rois *de Irland*). [*Pierre*]

ROUEN

A city in Normandy. Wolfram says it was Duke Gaschier's capital. In the Alliterative *Morte Arthure*, the Duke of Rouen joins Arthur's war against Rome. [*Wolfram, Allit*]

ROUERGE

An area in France owned by Lancelot. Lancelot made Sir Menaduke the earl of Rouerge in return for Menaduke's support in the battles against King Arthur. [*Malory*]

ROUGEMONT [*Rogemont*]

A castle ruled by Lord Taulas in the romance of *Yder*. Taulas rejected Arthur's authority, and Arthur besieged the castle in response. [*Yder*]

ROULAND

Tristan's father in the Middle-English *Sir Tristrem*, analogous to RIVALIN in the romance of Gottfried von Strassburg. After fathering Tristan on Blancheflor, the sister of King Mark, Rouland was slain in a war against Duke Morgan. His steward, Rohand, raised Tristan, and the latter avenged his death. His counterpart in the Prose *Tristan* is MELIADUS. [*SirTris*]

ROULENT

One of Arthur's towns. [*Vengeance, Durmart*]

ROUND PINE

A tree in Orkney where, in the time of Joseph of Arimathea, King Orcant tested knights who wanted to champion him against a murder charge brought by King Marahant of Ireland. By defeating King Orcant himself, Peter, a follower of Joseph of Arimathea, won the right to fight the combat. [*VulgEst*]

ROUND TABLE [*Tavola Ritonda*]

A term applied both to Arthur's fellowship of knights and the actual table at which the fellowship convened. It is first mentioned by Wace in *Roman de Brut*, who says that Arthur seated his knights at a round table to avoid disputes about precedence; since there is no "head" at a round table, no knight can claim superiority over the others by his position at the table. As *The Grene Knight* tells it: "[Arthur] made the Round Table for their behove, that none of them shold sitt above, but all shold sitt as one." In Layamon, the table is constructed by a carpenter who comes to Arthur's court in the days of peace following Arthur's conquest of almost all lands west of the Alps. The carpenter suggested the idea of the Round Table to Arthur after a brawl broke out in Arthur's court over who would get to sit at the head of the (then) rectangular table.

The number of knights who could sit at the table varies from legend to legend, ranging from 13 (Didot-*Perceval*) to 50 (Robert de Boron) to 60 (Jean d'Outremeuse) to 130 ("The Legend of King Arthur") to 140 (Hartmann von Aue) to 150 (Vulgate *Lancelot*) to 250 (Vulgate *Merlin*) to 1600 (Layamon). Layamon's Round Table, with the incredible 1600 seats, was also portable! Béroul mentions that the Round Table "rotate[d] like the Earth," but it is unclear what purpose this would serve. Any table seating more than a dozen knights would be so large in diameter as to be unwieldy, but some artists and late authors depict it as a ring rather than a solid table, with space in the middle for servants and entertainers.

In contrast to Wace, who makes Arthur the founder of the Round Table, Robert de Boron and the Vulgate Cycle assert that Uther established it, after hearing Merlin's tales of the Grail Table in the time of Joseph of Arimathea. Uther apparently gave it to King Leodegan of Carmelide who, in turn, gave it to Arthur as a wedding present when Arthur married Guinevere, Leodegan's daughter. The claim that Leodegan once owned the Round Table is first found in *Perlesvaus*, and in both *Perlesvaus* and the Vulgate

Lancelot, a demand is made upon Arthur to relinquish the Round Table to a relative of Leodegan (Jandree in *Perlesvaus* and Guinevere the False in the Vulgate *Lancelot*).

When Arthur re-established the Round Table in his own court, Merlin designated one of the seats the Perilous Seat, which was destined to be filled by Galahad. Merlin wrote the names of the knights who sat in each seat in magical golden letters, which changed as the occupancy of the seats changed. In the Vulgate, the Round Table is presented as the greatest of Arthur's orders, ahead of the Queen's Knights, the Knights of the Watch, the Table of Errant Companions, and the Table of Less-Valued Knights. Members of the Round Table were bound by a code of honor and service. Malory outlines this code as:

- To never do outrage nor murder
- Always to flee treason
- To by no means be cruel but to give mercy unto him who asks for mercy
- To always do ladies, gentlewomen, and widows succor
- To never force ladies, gentlewomen, and widows
- Not to take up battles in wrongful quarrels for love or worldly goods

See TWELVE RULES OF THE ROUND TABLE for another list.

Italian romance distinguishes between the Round Tables of Uther Pendragon (called the *Tavola Vecchio*, or "Old Table") and Arthur (the *Tavola Nuovo*, or "New Table"). *La Tavola* names four types of seats at Arthur's Round Table: the Perilous Seat, the Royal Seat (reserved for Arthur), the Adventurous Seats (occupied by the majority of knights) and seats for infirm knights.

Welsh warriors traditionally ate and met in circles, which may be an origin of the Round Table theme. Fights over placement and other favors at feasts are common in Irish tales. Romance writers were probably also enticed to develop the Round Table after the tradition that Christ and the apostles sat at a round table at the last supper. In Luke 22:24-6, God chastises his apostles for bickering over precedence, which is echoed in Wace's story of the Round Table's origins. Pilgrims returning from Jerusalem in the eleventh and twelfth centuries reported to have seen the marble round table of the Last Supper. These reports may have influenced the account of Robert de Boron, for whom the Round Table was the third of its kind, following the table of the Last Supper and the Grail Table.

The fate of the Round Table is rarely discussed, but in the Post-Vulgate *Mort Artu*, Mark destroys Camelot and the Round Table with it.

A round table made from oak is kept in Winchester Castle, and it was thought by Caxton, Malory's publisher, to be the authentic Arthurian Round Table. However, it was probably constructed in the thirteenth or fourteenth century for one of the various Arthurian festivals held in the Middle Ages. The Wichester table is 18 feet in diameter, and since 1522 it has displayed the names of 25 knights taken from Malory's *Le Morte Darthur*. [*Wace*,

ChretienE, RobertBorM, Didot, Wolfram, Perlesvaus, Stricker, VulgLanc, VulgQuest, VulgMort, PostMer, PostQuest, PostMort, Tavola, Jean, Boccaccio, Malory, Grene, Legend]

ROWENA [R(h)on(e)wen, Ronix, Rowan, Rowen(ne), Roxiena]

The daughter of the Saxon leader Hengist, given in marriage to King Vortigern of Britain by Hengist in exchange for the country of Kent. She is first found in Nennius. Vortigern's marriage to Rowena horrified many of Vortigern's subjects—as well as the British clergy—because Rowena was a heathen and Vortigern was a Christian, and also because the union cemented an uncomfortable alliance between the British and the Saxons. When Vortigern's son, Vortimer, took the throne from his father and defeated the Saxons, Rowena pretended that she wished to convert to Christianity. She was able to get close to Vortimer, and she then poisoned and killed him, allowing Vortigern to reclaim the throne and the Saxons to return. Her character is found in Godfrey of Viterbo's *Pantheon* as ANGRIA and in Baudin Butor's romance as SARDOINE.

Rowena appears as the main character in Thelwall's *The Fairy of the Lake*. A heathen sorceress, she falls in love with Arthur (here presented as the contemporary of Vortigern and Ambrosius) and embarks on an elaborate scheme to seduce him by magic, calling upon her supernatural allies such as Queen Hela of the Infernal Regions and the demon Incubus. Thwarted by the Lady of the Lake, Arthur's guardian, she murders her husband Vortigern and offers Arthur the crown along with herself. Arthur, horrified at her crime, burns Rowena and her castle to the ground. [*Nennius, GeoffHR, Wace, Layamon, Thelwall*]

ROWLAUNDE

The father of Arthur's knights Raynald and Richer. [*Allit*]

ROXBURGH

A Scottish castle where Arthur's Sir Meliador defeated 1,566 knights for the love of Hermondine, princess of Scotland. [*Froissart*]

ROYAL KNIGHTS

A trio of Arthur's knights—Nascien, Mordred, and Llew—in Welsh legend, who were handsome, wise, and skilled in arms. The inclusion of Mordred in this list is interesting, and this description of him is unique to Welsh legend. [*Triads*]

ROYAL LAY

A story about Tristan written by Arthur. [*ProsTris*]

ROYAL MINSTER

A nunnery in Gaul to which Elaine (Lancelot's mother) fled after her husband died and her land was conquered by King Claudas. She was soon joined by her sister-in-law, Evaine (King Bors's widow) when Claudas conquered Gannes. Evaine died at the Royal Minster after receiving a vision in which she saw her sons, Lionel and Bors, and Elaine's son, Lancelot, in the safe care of the Lady of the Lake. [*LancLac, VulgLanc*]

ROYAL SEAT [*Seggio Reale]

Arthur's seat at the Round Table. [*Tavola*]

ROYCOL

Father of Arthur's warrior Mael. [*Culhwch*]

RUAL LI FOITENANT [Róaldur]

Tristan's noble foster-father in Gottfried's *Tristan*. Rual was the husband of Floraete and the steward of Tristan's father, Rivalin Canelengres. His epithet signifies "one who maintains faith." Rivalin commended Tristan to Rual's care on his death bed. Rual and Floraete raised Tristan as their own son to shield him from Rivalin's former enemies—most notably Duke Morgan of Brittany. Rual embarked on a search for Tristan when Tristan was abducted by some merchants, and he was relieved when he found that Tristan had made his way to his uncle Mark's court. After Tristan re-conquered his ancestral land of Parmenie from Duke Morgan, he gave the throne of the land to Rual, and to Rual's sons after him. Rual and Floraete died from unknown circumstances during Tristan's life. He is called ROHAND in the Middle-English *Sir Tristrem*. [*Gottfried, TrisSaga*]

RUBERT OF GANDIN

A king who joined King Ekunaver of Kanadic's war against Arthur. [*PleierG*]

RUBISCO

A castle in Lyonesse owned by King Meliadus, Tristan's father. [*Tavola*]

RUDDYMANE

The infant son of Amavia and Mordaunt. Sir Guyon carried Ruddymane to safety after his parents' deaths. [*Spenser*]

RUEL

A vicious, hideous hag who inhabited the woods of Glois. Her husband, Feroz, was murdered, which drove her to seek revenge on any knight she saw. One such knight was Wigalois (Gawain's son), who came to Glois on an adventure. Ruel charged him, and he didn't defend himself immediately because she was a woman. Surprising him with her might, she bound him and carried him off like a sack. As she was about to cleave off his head, his horse whinnied. Hearing the noise, Ruel thought that Pfetan, the local dragon, was coming, and she fled, allowing Wigalois to escape. [*Wirnt*]

RUGGIERI

In Paolino Pieri's *La Storia di Merlino*, one of two messengers sent by King Vortigern to find a boy without a father. Ruggieri and Labegues, his companion, found Merlin in Northumberland. [*Pieri*]

RUGIER OF DOLEISE

An enemy of Duke Jovelin of Arundel. He besieged Jovelin in the castle of Karke, but Tristan (Jovelin's son-in-law) arrived and defeated Rugier. [*Gottfried*]

RUISTE VALEE

An Irish mountain castle owned by Lord Savari, a knight slain by Lancelot. [*Merveil*]

RUNNO

According to Geoffrey of Monmouth, a king of Britain in the third or second century BC. He was the son of King Peredur. He succeeded his cousin, King Idwallo, and was succeeded another cousin, King Gerontius. [*GeoffHR*]

RUSSIA

In Layamon's *Brut*, the daughter of Russia's king marries King Alcus of Iceland, a vassal of Arthur. Its kings in *Claris et Laris* are Solifas, who joins Emperor Thereus of Rome's war against Arthur, and Baratron, who joins King Tallas of Denmark in a war against Urien. [*Layamon, Claris*]

RUVALEN

In one manuscript of the Prose *Tristan*, the brother of Kahedins and Isolde of the White Hands. He loved a lady named Gargeolain, and Tristan helped him arrange a tryst with the woman. Later, Gargeolain's husband, Bedalis, tracked down Tristan and Ruvalen and mortally wounded them both with a poisoned lance [*ProsTris*]

RYONS

A king and Knight of the Round Table who participated in the Grail Quest. There is probably no relationship to RIONS, the giant killed by Arthur. [*ProsTris*]

S

SABE

According to Baudin Butor, the wife of King Liban (Ban) and mother of Libanor. She was related to King Claudas of Gaul. [*Butor*]

SABIE[1]

The location of a tournament won by King Lac, Erec's father. [*Palamedes*]

SABIE[2]

The maiden of Merkanie, loved by Gerhart of Riviers. When her father, Tjofabier, refused to grant her to Gerhart, Gerhart launched a war, slaying Gilbert, Sabie's brother. The war was ended by Arthur's Sir Garel, who defeated Gerhart. [*PleierG*]

SABINS

A river running through the land of King Gramoflanz in Wolfram's *Parzival*. Gramoflanz's fortress, standing near it, was called Roche Sabins. The river Poynzaclins paralleled it. Gawain and Perceval and then Perceval and Gramoflanz fought duels near the river. In Der Pleier's *Tandareis*, the name is given to Arthur's castle in Löver on the Karonica river. [*Wolfram, PleierT*]

SACH

A British city once inhabited or visited by Arthur's chief gatekeeper Glewlwyd. [*Culhwch*]

SADALOM

A fashionable Knight of the Round Table slain during the Grail Quest. [*PostQuest*]

SADOC[1]

A Welsh nobleman. With others, he tried to save the life of Meriadoc, heir to the throne of Wales, from the murderous intentions of King Griffin. His diplomacy failed, but Meriadoc escaped to Arthur's court anyway. Sadoc later organized a revolt and helped Arthur defeat Griffin. [*Historia*]

SADOC[2]

A knight overthrown by Beaudous, Gawain's son, during a tournament in Winchester. [*RobertBlo*]

SADOC[3]

A knight who served King Mark of Cornwall reluctantly. Mark assigned him to assassinate Mark's sister-in-law and nephew, Alexander the Orphan. Sadoc refused to complete the task, but told Mark he had done so. When Mark learned of the lie, he tried to have Sadoc killed, but Sadoc slew Mark's henchmen and fled Cornwall. He later rallied Cornish knights to revolt against Mark and to free Tristan from Mark's prison. He eventually came to Arthur's court and became a Knight of the Round Table, but he later joined Lancelot's defection from Arthur's court and helped Lancelot rescue Guinevere from the stake. In return for his support, Lancelot made him the earl of Surlat. [*ProsTris, Prophecies, Malory*]

SADOC[4] OF ORKNEY

Brother of Sir Edward of Orkney and cousin of Gawain. Sir Guiron the Courteous defeated Sadoc in joust. Later, Sadoc fought for Arthur at the Leverzep tournament. [*Palamedes, ProsTris, Malory*]

SADOC[5] THE BLONDE

A Knight of the Round Table who participated in the Grail Quest. [*ProsTris*]

SADOINE [*Sadones*]

Cousin of Guinevere and brother of Guiomar. He served King Leodegan of Carmelide, his uncle, as the castellan of Carhaix or Aneblayse. He helped Arthur and Leodegan defeat King Rions at Aneblayse. He became a Knight of the Round Table and continued to fight in Arthur's war against the Saxons. [*VulgMer, Livre, Arthour*]

SADOR

One of the twelve sons of Bron and nephews of Joseph of Arimathea in the Prose *Tristan*. He was an ancestor of Tristan. He married a Babylonian princess named Chelinde and fathered Apollo. His brother Naburzadan tried to rape his bride, and Sador killed Naburzadan. Chelinde came to believe that Sador was dead and re-married. Sador was eventually re-united with his wife, but was killed by his own son, Apollo, who did not know him. [*ProsTris*]

SAFIR [*Saphar*]

Son of King Esclabor and brother of Palamedes, Florine, and (in Malory) Seguarades. Unlike Palamedes, Sir Safir was christened. In judicial combat at Arthur's court, he killed the Count of the Plank, his father's mortal enemy. He participated in the Grail Quest. He abducted the sweetheart of Sir Espinogrés, but his brother Palamedes convinced him to return her. He joined Lancelot's defection from Arthur's court and helped Lancelot rescue

Guinevere from the stake. In return for his support, Lancelot made him the duke of Languedoc. [*ProsTris, Prophecies, Malory*]

SAFUR

A king in the service of Rions, Arthur's enemy. [*VulgMer*]

SAGARZ

A knight present at the Sorgarda tournament, which Gawain won. [*Heinrich*]

SAGE CLERC

One of Merlin's scribes. He received a book of Merlin's prophecies from Perceval. [*Prophecies*]

SAGREMOR [Sacremors, Sagramor(e), Sagarmour, Sagremore(t), Saigremor(s), Saigremort, Segramors, Segremore, Segremors, Sigamor, Sogremor, Sygramors]

Called "the Desirous," "the Unruly," "the Rash," "the Impetuous," "the Orange," or "of the Desert"; Sagremor is an ubiquitous Knight of the Round Table who first appears in Chrétien de Troyes's *Erec* as a knight who fought alongside Erec at the Tenebroc tournament. According to Wolfram, Sagremor was very skilled and had to be physically restrained to keep him from attacking knights at random. An Italian *cantare* makes him a close friend of Tristan. Renaut de Bâgé gives him a sister named Clarie, and in Italian romance, he has a brother named Dinas. In the Fourth Continuation of *Perceval*, his brothers are the bishops of Limor and Lumeri. In the Third Continuation of *Perceval*, he rescues the Castle of Maidens from a besieger named Tallidés of the Marsh.

Like many Knights of the Round Table, Sagremor is given a full life story in the Vulgate Cycle. Born to the daughter of Emperor Hadrian of Constantinople and the King of Vlask and Hungary, he was raised in Byzantium as the heir to the eastern Roman empire. When his father died, his mother re-married the British King Brandegorre of Estrangorre. When Sagremor was fifteen, he heard tales of the noble King Arthur and the wars against the Saxons, and he left Constantinople for Britain to join the king. Arriving in Dover, he immediately engaged a Saxon army led by King Oriel outside Camelot. Gawain and his brothers joined the battle, and the young heroes were victorious. The youths joined Arthur's company and Sagremor was knighted by Arthur. He continued his service to Arthur in the wars against the Saxons (in which he slew a daunting number of Saxon kings), King Claudas, Rome, and Galehaut. In one adventure, he rescued a maiden named Senehaut from some abductors, slept with her, and begot a daughter who was raised by Guinevere. Later, he became the champion of Queen Sebile of Sarmenie, defended her lands against Baruc the Black, convinced her to convert to Christianity, and became her lover. (Jehan Froissart says he married her.) He had a number of other unremarkable adventures as a Knight of

the Round Table before he was killed by Mordred at the battle of Salisbury.

In the Post-Vulgate *Suite du Merlin*, he is the son of Nabur the Unruly and is Mordred's foster-brother. In Malory, he is a somewhat inferior Knight of the Round Table who is defeated after bullying or brashly attacking knights such as Marhaus, Lancelot, Palamedes, Meleagant, and Tristan. According to *Les Merveilles de Rigomer*, he raped an Irish princess named Qrainglaie and, twenty years later, was killed by his son begotten on that occasion. [*ChretienE, ChretienC, Renaut, Didot, Wolfram, VulgLanc, VulgMort, VulgMer, PostMer, PostQuest, Contin3, Merveil, Vendetta, Froissart, Malory*]

SAGRIS THE SMALL [Sigris]

In the *Tristano Riccardiano* and *La Tavola Ritonda*, a knight who, while visiting Mark's court for healing, learned the Isolde had been abducted by Palamedes. He chased after them, but could not fight well because of his wounds, and was defeated. He was later killed during the Grail Quest. He is called LAMBEGUE in the Prose *Tristan*. [*TristanoR, Tavola*]

SAGUNTIUS

The chief knight of King Gundebald of the Land From Which No One Returns; an opponent of King Meriadoc of Wales. [*Historia*]

SAIE [Saies]

The Knight of Saie was a companion of Sir Bleoberis. When Gawain's son, Guinglain, defeated Bleoberis at a ford, William of Salebrant, Elin of Graie, and the Knight of Saie chased after Guinglain and tried to avenge Bleoberis's injury. All three were defeated. [*Renaut*]

SAINT AARON

A church founded by Arthur in the city of Caerleon. [*Pierre*]

SAINT ALBANS [Albans, Albon]

The location of King Uther Pendragon's last great battle. It is situated north of London and was once called Verulam. In Geoffrey, Uther fights Octa's and Eosa's Saxons here, but Malory makes his enemies a collection of lesser kings seeking to usurp Uther's throne. Uther went out into the field even though he was so sick had to be carried in a horse litter, and was victorious (in Geoffrey, Octa and Eosa were killed). Following the battle, King Uther became more ill and died. Saint Albans was named after the British martyr who died trying to preserve Christianity in Britain when it was being destroyed by the Emperor Diocletian and the warrior Maximianus. [*Gildas, GeoffHR, Wace, Malory*]

SAINT AMPHIBALL

A church in Winchester where Constans, Arthur's uncle, was cloistered until Vortigern foisted him to the throne.

Generations later, King Constantine, Arthur's successor, killed Melou, the traitorous son of Mordred, at the church. [*GeoffHR*, *Layamon*]

SAINT BERNARD'S MOUNT

According to the Prose *Brut*, Arthur fought and killed the giant Dinabuc at Saint Bernard's Mount just prior to the Roman War. Why the author chose to name the hill after Saint Bernard, rather than use the familiar MONT ST. MICHEL, is unclear. [*ProsBrut*, *Legend*]

SAINT CIRRE

A castle in Claudas's kingdom. Its lord was one of Claudas's vassals. It is the name of an actual French town near Versailles. [*VulgLanc*]

SAINT DAVID'S

A coastal city in Wales, formerly called *Menevia*, or *Mynyw* in Welsh. The Irish-Saxon alliance, led by Gilloman and Pascentius, fought their first battle against Uther here in an attempt to take Britain from Uther's brother Ambrosius. Uther won the battle and killed both Gilloman and Pascentius, but before the battle was finished, Pascentius sent a Saxon assassin to Winchester to poison King Ambrosius. Uther had only moments to relish his victory before he heard that his brother was dead. A Welsh Triad lists Saint David's as Arthur's capital in Wales, in which Dewi was the chief bishop and Maelgwn was the chief elder. It was one of the three archbishoprics of the island. [*GeoffHR*, *Triads*]

SAINT JOHN[1]

In the Post-Vulgate *Merlin* continuation, the church in Camelot where Lot and his compatriots were buried following their deaths at the battle of Tarabel. Malory transfers this to SAINT STEPHEN'S. [*PostMer*]

SAINT JOHN[2]

A British valley that features in Sir Walter Scott's *The Bridal of Triermain*. Merlin imprisoned Gyneth, Arthur's daughter, in a castle in the Valley of St. John, placing her in a deep slumber. Sir Roland de Vaux found her and woke her with a kiss. [*Scott*]

SAINT MICHELSSTEIN

A city in Cornwall. Each year, the city held a fair in honor of Saint Michael. Isolde's page, Piloise, traveled to the fair while bearing a message from Tristan to Isolde. [*Eilhart*]

SAINT PETER'S

A nunnery in Carmarthen where Merlin's mother resided. Its provost was named Eli. [*GeoffHR*, *Wace*]

SAINT SAMSON

The Cornish island where, according to Chrétien de Troyes and the Prose *Tristan*, Tristan fought and killed

Morholt in his first duel (Tristan was championing King Mark against Morholt, who had demanded a tribute from Cornwall). It was apparently visible from the mainland. In *La Tavola Ritonda*, the battle takes place on an island called SANZA AVVENTURA. Béroul names Saint Samson as a monastery in King Mark's Cornwall, and, according to Geoffrey Ashe, an actual church named Saint Samson still exists in Cornwall, on a hillside in Golant. There is an island called Saint Samson in the Scilly group. [*Beroul*, *ChretienE*, *ProsTris*]

SAINT SOFFIE

An abbey in Constantinople to which Floriant's mother retired and in which Floriant was crowned emperor of Constantinople. [*Floriant*]

SAINT STEPHEN'S

The chief church in Camelot. It was established by Josephus, the son of Joseph of Arimathea, after God slew Agrestes, Camelot's pagan king. Arthur and Guinevere were married at St. Stephen's. Out of respect for their skill and nobility, Arthur buried Kings Nero and Lot at Saint Stephen's following their deaths at the Battle of Tarabel (though see also SAINT JOHN'S). Other Arthurian knights also rested there, including Erec, Gareth, and Agravain. [*VulgLanc*, *VulgMort*, *VulgEst*, *VulgMer*, *PostMer*, *Malory*]

SAINTONGE

An area of France owned by Lancelot. Lancelot made Sir Galehodin the duke of Saintonge in return for Galehodin's support in the battles against King Arthur. [*Malory*]

SALACH

A British city once inhabited or visited by Arthur's chief gatekeeper Glewlwyd. [*Culhwch*]

SALADIN[1] [*Saleadins*]

King of Carthage and one of the allies of Emperor Thereus of Rome. Saladin joined Thereus in a war against Arthur. [*Claris*]

SALADIN[2] [*Sahaladins, Salhadin*]

Father of King Tallas of Denmark, whom he joined in an attack on King Urien's castle. Arthur came to Urien's aid, and Saladin was slain by Sir Laris. [*Claris*]

SALAMONE

A relative of Joseph of Arimathea, from whom the kings of Cornwall and Lyonesse, including Mark and Tristan, were descended. Possibly the biblical SOLOMON. [*Tavola*]

SALANDRE OF THE ISLES

A knight defeated in joust by Perceval. Perceval also defeated Salandre's five sons: Aristes, Dinisordres, Gogonne, Menastide, and Nastor. All of them were sent to Arthur's court as prisoners. [*Contin3*]

SALATRE

King of the Moree and an ally of Emperor Thereus of Rome. Salatre joined Thereus in a war against Arthur, and he was slain in battle against Claris and Laris. [*Claris*]

SALATRIAS OF KALDE

A heathen king who joined King Ekunaver of Kanadic's war against Arthur. He was slain in the battle of Kanadic by Duke Eskilabon of Belamunt. [*PleierG*]

SALEBRUN [*Salbrons*]

One of the Saxon kings to invade northern Britain at the beginning of Arthur's reign. He fought in the army that opposed Gawain on the plains of Roestoc. Duke Escant of Cambenic killed him at the second battle of Clarence, after he slew Escant's castellan. [*VulgMer, Arthour*]

SALERNO

A seaport in southern Italy, on an inlet of the Tyrrhenian Sea. It was famous in the Middle Ages for its medical school, founded in AD 850. Various Arthurian legends feature physicians from Salerno, including the Alliterative *Morte Arthure*, in which one such doctor tries unsuccessfully to heal Arthur at Avalon. [*Allit*]

SALIE[1]

A land in heathendom, ruled by Counts Urbin and Ambigal—two allies of Gawain's son Wigalois. [*Wirnt*]

SALIE[2]

The castle inhabited by Igerne, Morcades (Morgause), and Klarisanz (Clarissant) in Heinrich von dem Türlin's *Diu Crône*. It was built in the land of Madarp by Gansguoter—Igraine's husband after Uther—through magical means. Gawain was reunited with his grandmother, mother, and sister when he visited the castle and survived the adventure of the Perilous Bed. Chrétien de Troyes called the same castle CANGUIN ROCK, while Wolfram called it CASTLE OF MARVELS. [*Heinrich*]

SALIEL

A murderous knight who killed a relative of Arthur. Arthur swore vengeance on him, and a sorceress offered to lead Arthur to his enemy. Arthur slew Saliel, but was subsequently trapped by the sorceress until freed by Tristan. [*ProsTris, Malory*]

SALIN

A strong warrior who fought for Prince Lion of Namur in a war against Wigalois (Gawain's son). Salin wounded Gawain in the combat. [*Wirnt*]

SALISBURY [*Salesbiri, Salesbury*]

In the chronicles, Salisbury Plain in Wiltshire serves as the location of a battle between King Vortigern and Hengist's Saxons. According to the Vulgate *Merlin*, King Pendragon

and Uther fought a battle against the Saxons there, and Pendragon was killed. Geoffrey says that during Arthur's reign, Anaraut and Galluc served as the earls of Salisbury, while Layamon gives this distinction to Arnold.

In the Vulgate *Mort Artu*, the Post-Vulgate Cycle, the Stanzaic *Morte Arthur*, and Malory, Salisbury Plain is named as the site of the final battle between Arthur and Mordred, in which Mordred was killed and Arthur was mortally wounded. Arthur's knights carried him off the field to the Ancient Chapel, from which he was taken to Avalon by Morgan le Fay. The chronicles place this battle at CAMLANN. [*GeoffHR, Wace, Layamon, VulgMort, VulgMer, PostMort, Stanz, Malory*]

SALMANIDE

An evil "toll collector" slain by Gawain. Salmanide and his brother Ansgavin served a giant named Galaas. [*Heinrich*]

SALUBRE

The baptismal name of Queen JANDREE, after Perceval converted her to Christianity. [*Perlesvaus*]

SALUSTES [*Salust(e)*]

A saint from Orberica. Joseph of Arimathea had him interred in Sarras, giving the newly-christened city a holy body. A church was founded in his name. His spirit appeared to assist King Mordrains of Sarras during his difficult adventure on the Rock of the Perilous Port. [*VulgEst*]

SAMALIEL

The large son of Duke Frollo of Germany. Although he was knighted by Galahad, he opposed Arthur's knights for having defeated his father. During the Grail Quest, he fought and defeated Kay, Gaheris, and Girflet. [*PostQuest*]

SAMSIZ OF THE BLACK ISLAND

Subject of a unique and darkly comical episode in the Serbo-Russian *Povest' o Tryshchane*. Samsiz was a king who arrived at Arthur's camp and challenged all of his knights. He defeated thirteen of them, including Palamedes, Lancelot, and Arthur, and took them as prisoners back to his island. Guinevere sought out Tristan's assistance. After several adventures, Tristan, Guinevere, and Isolde arrived at the Black Island disguised as Venetians. Tristan was forced to protect the ladies from Samsiz's lecherous subjects while devising a plan to free the king. Samsiz himself desired Isolde and offered to either fight Tristan or to play a game of chess for her. Tristan had put on a great show of being a simple merchant, and Samsiz felt he had little to fear. Tristan chose combat, and by the time Samsiz realized his mistake, Tristan had sliced off both of his hands. Tristan freed Samsiz's prisoners. [*Povest*]

SAMSON[1] [*Sampson, Sanxo*]

A Breton saint found in non-Arthurian legends. Geoffrey of Monmouth connects him with Arthur by having King

Ambrosius appoint Samson to the archbishopric of York. He lost his position when York was sacked by the Saxons, but Arthur later gave him the see of Dol in Brittany. Samson was eventually succeeded by Teilo. [*GeoffHR*, *Wace*, *Layamon*]

SAMSON² DRY LIP

An Arthurian warrior. [*Culhwch*]

SAMUIL-PENISSEL

According to Geoffrey of Monmouth, a king of Britain in the second century BC. He succeeded King Rhydderch and was succeeded by King Pir. [*GeoffHR*]

SANADES

An Arthurian knight who was the brother of Sir Arciel. Arciel killed Sanades in a quarrel over a maiden. [*PostQuest*]

SANASESIO

A Knight of the Round Table who participated in the Grail Quest. [*PostQuest*]

SANDINOSE

The maiden of the Green Meadow, whose land was saved by Daniel from a diseased monster. She later married Arthur's Sir Beladigant. [*Stricker*]

SANDDEF ANGEL FACE [*Sandde*]

One of King Arthur's warriors in Welsh legend. He fought at the battle of Camlann, but no man struck him because he was so beautiful that everyone thought he was an angel. He was called one of Arthur's three "Offensive Knights" because of his appearance. [*Culhwch*, *Triads*]

SANDIC

One of the lands owned by Sir Meriadeuc's family. It held the castle of Tygan. [*Meriadeuc*]

SANDWICH

A seaport in Kent, on the southeast coast of England. Arthur passed through the port of Sandwich on his way to fight the Roman War and returned through the port on his way to face Mordred. [*ProsBrut*, *Allit*, *Malory*]

SANEBRON [*Senebruns*]

A knight who served King Clarion of Northumberland and Duke Escant of Cambenic in the early wars against the Saxons. He joined Arthur's forces at the battles of Clarence and Vambieres. He ruled the castle of Falerne. [*VulgMer*, *Livre*]

SANGIVE

Arthur's sister in Wolfram's *Parzival*, replacing ANNA from Geoffrey of Monmouth and predating MORCADES or

MORGAUSE. She was the daughter of Uther Pendragon and Arnive, the husband of Lot, and the mother of Gawain, Beacurs, Itonje, Cundrie, and Soredamor. Der Pleier calls her SEIFE. With her mother and daughters, she was trapped in the Castle of Marvels for many years, under the enchantment of the sorcerer Clinschor, until rescued by her son Gawain. Lot was dead by the time she was freed, so she married Florant "the Turkoyt" of Itolac. [*Wolfram*]

SANGRANAR

A fortress visited by Lancelot and Tristan during the Grail Quest. There, they defeated two knights—Sodoc and Broncane—who tried to take their horses. [*Tavola*]

SANGUEL [*Sangwel*]

One of Lord Golagros's knights in the Middle Scots tale of *Golagros and Gawain*. During the war between Golagros and Arthur, Sanguel was defeated and captured by Arthur's Sir Gyromalance. [*Golagros*]

SANNORIZ

A knight present at the Sorgarda tournament, which Gawain won. [*Heinrich*]

SANDEDOINE [*Sansadonies*]

A castellan from Norhaut who fought alongside King Clarion of Northumberland and Duke Escant of Cambenic in the early wars against the Saxons. [*VulgMer*]

SANSFOY

A pagan knight slain by the Red Cross Knight. Sansfoy had been accompanying Duessa, an evil witch who later seduced the Red Cross Knight. He was the brother of Sansloy and Sansjoy. [*Spenser*]

SANSJOY

Brother of Sansfoy, a pagan knight slain by the Red Cross Knight, and of Sansloy. Encountering the Red Cross Knight at the House of Pride, Sansjoy demanded single combat. Sansjoy received assistance from the evil witch Duessa. When the Red Cross Knight appeared to be winning, however, Sansjoy was carried away in a black cloud. The cloud took him to Hades, where his wounds were treated. [*Spenser*]

SANSLOY

A pagan knight whose brother, Sansfoy, was slain by the Red Cross Knight. He encountered Una, the Red Cross Knight's *amie*, traveling with the evil magician Archimago, disguised as the Red Cross Knight. Seeking to avenge his brother's death, Sansloy attacked Archimago and wounded him, but discovered his true identity when he lifted his helmet. Sansloy then killed the lion protecting Una and abducted her. He tried to rape her in a forest, but a group of satyrs responded to Una's cries and drove him away. [*Spenser*]

SANSOGNA

The king of Sansogna (Saxony) joined King Mark of Cornwall in his attack on Camelot during the Grail Quest. Arthur and his knights defeated the besiegers. [*Tavola*]

SANTIPUS

King of Orcormenie who served Emperor Filimenis of Constantinople. He joined Filimenis in a brief war against Arthur and was killed in the battle by Sir Floriant. [*Floriant*]

SANTO ALOIDO

A city in Lyonesse where Meliadus, Tristan's father, was buried. [*Tavola*]

SANZA AVVENTURA ("Without Adventure")

The island where Tristan fought and slew Morholt, the giant from Ireland who demanded a tribute from Cornwall, in the *Tristano Riccardiano* and *La Tavola Ritonda*. In the Prose *Tristan* and other romances, this battle takes place at the island of SAINT SAMSON. [*TristanoR, Tavola*]

SAPHARIN [*Saphiran*]

A Saxon king who served King Aminaduc, invading northern Britain at the beginning of Arthur's reign. He participated in the siege at Clarence. Later, he joined King Rions' invasion of Carmelide. In one source, Sapharin and Sornegrieu lead the offensive at Carhaix, against Arthur's forces, and Sapharin is slain by Arthur. In another, Sapharin is killed by Gosengos at the battle of Clarence. [*VulgMer, Livre, Arthour*]

SAPIENT OF BAGHDAD [*Sapien of Baudas*]

A scribe who helped record the deeds performed by Arthur and his knights. [*LancLac, VulgLanc*]

SAPINOIE [*Sarpenic*]

A forest in Britain where King Lot, in rebellion against Arthur, laid an ambush for Arthur. Arthur learned of the plot in advance and was ready. In the ensuing battle, Gawain captured Lot and forced him to surrender to Arthur. The forest was also the home of Maduc the Black, an enemy of the Round Table. [*VulgLanc, VulgMer, Livre*]

SARACENS [*Sarazenes, Sarrasins, Sarrazins*]

A generic term for the Arabic tribes of the Middle East, especially Syria. Grail legend holds that the race took its name from the city of SARRAS. *Arthour and Merlin* and Malory replace the Saxon invasion of Britain with an invasion of Saracens, although since both races were not Christians, the authors may have intended the same people. Groups of Saracens also joined Rome's war with Arthur. Other Saracens invaded Cornwall but were repelled by Prince Bodwyne, King Mark's brother. [*VulgEst, Arthour, Malory*]

SARAIDE

A servant of the Lady of the Lake. At the order of the Lady, she rescued the princes Lionel and Bors from the evil King Claudas by enchanting the princes to look like dogs, and two dogs to look like the princes. She was also called CELICE. [*LancLac, VulgLanc*]

SARANT[1]

During a speech in *Diu Crône* Gawain says that "at Bli Maradarf by the sea I slew the devil Sarant, who swallowed the sun." [*Heinrich*]

SARANT[2] OF TRIANDE

An infidel master-weaver from heathen Triande. He produced a number of treasured fabrics, some of which Gawain had an opportunity to wear in his adventure at the Castle of Marvels. [*Wolfram*]

SARAZIANA

A city in Tuscia, where Palamedes avenged the death of King Arduano (Armant) by killing his murderer, Sir Passauver. [*Tavola*]

SARDACIA

King of Damascus in Syria. He married Albine, the daughter of King Diodicias of Syria. Albine and her sisters revolted against their husbands, were defeated, and were exiled to Britain. [*Palamedes*]

SARDIN

A castle ruled by Fimbeus, and enemy of Gawain. Gawain defeated Fimbeus in combat at Sardin. [*Heinrich*]

SARDOINE

The daughter of Hengist who married Vortigern in Bauduin Butor's romance. She is known as ROWENA in previous chronicles. [*Butor*]

SARDUP [*Sadap*]

A Saxon warrior in the service of King Rions, Arthur's enemy. Sir Meraugis killed him at the battle of Carhaix. [*VulgMer*]

SARET

A Knight of the Round Table who embarked with the others on the Grail Quest. [*PostQuest*]

SARGIA

A sorceress who gave her son Felice to Tristan the Younger (Tristan's son) as a squire. [*DueTris*]

SARIS

The king of Hungary who invaded Germany. Laris, the son of Emperor Henry of Germany, killed him in battle. [*Claris*]

SARMEDON [Sormedon]

A king and standard-bearer in the army of King Rions. At the battle of Carhaix, King Bors of Gannes cut off his arm. [VulgMer, Arthour]

SARMENIE

The pagan kingdom ruled by Queen Sebile. Sir Sagremor successfully defended it against an invader, Baruc the Black. Afterwards, Sagremor convinced the populace to convert to Christianity. [Livre]

SARRAS[1] [Sarache]

A legendary city and kingdom in Arabia, bordering the country of Egypt. Sarras was ruled in the Grail histories by King Evalach, whom Joseph of Arimathea converted to Christianity. According to the Vulgate Queste del Saint Graal, the SARACENS took their name from the city. (In truth, the name of the city was likely invented by the author to explain the word Saracen.) Galahad, Perceval, and Bors journeyed to Sarras with the Grail at the end of the Grail Quest, and found that it had reverted to paganism. Its king, Escorant, threw the Grail knights in prison for a year, but released them on his death bed. Galahad, against his will, was chosen king, but he died himself within a year. Its main temple, the Spiritual Palace, served as Galahad's and Perceval's burial place. [VulgQuest, VulgEst, PostQuest, Malory]

SARRAS[2]

A Knight of the Round Table from Logres who first brought news of Galahad's birth to Lancelot. He led Lancelot to the Spring of the Two Sycamores, where they both jousted with Belias the Black. He was killed during the Grail Quest. [VulgLanc, PostQuest]

SARRASINTE[1] [Sagracinte, Sarracinte]

The wife of King Evalach (Mordrain) of Sarras and the sister of Seraphe (Nascien). As a child in Orberica, she was secretly baptized by Hermoine the Hermit. She aided Joseph of Arimathea and his party when they came to Sarras, for she wanted to see her husband and people converted to Christianity. Later, she joined Joseph and her husband in Britain. [VulgEst]

SARRASINTE[2]

The daughter of King Label of Persia. She took the name in honor of Queen Sarrasinte of Sarras when she was baptized by Petrone. Fate brought her to Britain where she joined Joseph of Arimathea's people. She married Celidoine, Nascien's son, became the Queen of North Wales, and gave birth to Narpus, an ancestor of Lancelot. [VulgEst]

SARTINUS OF RIMUL

A king in Arthur's service. [Erex]

SARTUZ OF THE LOGE

Lord of the castle Lindesores. His vassal, Menandre of the Loge, was defeated in combat by Perceval. [Contin3]

SARUZ

A knight present at the Sorgarda tournament, which Gawain won. [Heinrich]

SATELLIE [(Wolf)satellege]

A point in the ocean where the four seas were said to come together. In the Livre d'Artus, Merlin tosses a Gorgon's head (the Ugly Appearance), obtained by Arthur's Sir Greu, into the Gulf of Satellie. In Der Pleier's Garel, the dwarf king Albewin also travels there to sink a Gorgon's head, taken from a demon called Vulganus that had been slain by Arthur's Sir Garel. The seas boiled when Albewin dropped in the head, and it was said that storms perpetually plagued the region afterwards. Both sources may refer to the Gulf of Satalia in Asia Minor (Loomis, Literature, 338). [Livre, PleierG]

SATIPHUS

One of many Saxon kings to invade northern Britain at the beginning of Arthur's reign. In the service of King Aminaduc, he participated in the siege at Clarence and was killed by Arthur. [VulgMer, Livre]

SATOR[1]

Seneschal of King Nador. Nador besieged Queen Blanche, but Claris and Laris saved her, defeating Sator in the process. [Claris]

SATOR[2]

Duke of Venice and one of the allies of Emperor Thereus of Rome. Sator joined Thereus in a war against Arthur. [Claris]

SATRAN

A knight of Arthur's service from the Narrow Borderland. He participated in a quest to learn the fate of Merlin. [VulgMer]

SATYRANE

Half man, half satyr knight who inhabited the woods and protected the maiden Una after the Red Cross Knight abandoned her. Satyrane later fought with a giantess named Argante but was knocked unconscious, only to be saved by a strange knight. He became the companion of the warrior maiden Britomart, Arthur, and Artegall. [Spenser]

SAUSEYSE

A knight who fought Sir Meleagant at the tournament at Sorelois. [Malory]

SAVAGE REALM [*Royaume Sauvage]

A kingdom ruled by descendants of Brutus and ancestors of the "Brown" lineage. It may have been in Scotland. Its first king was Arbrun, who passed it to his son, Brun. Brun's cousins tried to conquer it but were defeated. Later, it was ruled by Hector the Brown. [Palamedes, Prophecies]

SAVAGE VALLEY [*Valle Selvaggia]

A valley visited by Lancelot and Tristan during the Grail Quest. There, they defeated two knights and killed three giants. [Tavola]

SAVARI[1]

An Irish robber baron who owned the castle of Ruiste Valee. He desired a maiden named Flor Desiree, who was the daughter of Savari's neighbor, the viscount of Pavengay. Savari intended to carry her off and keep her as a concubine, but the viscount convinced Lancelot, who was passing through, to defend her. Lancelot challenged Savari and killed him. [Merveil]

SAVARI[2]

King of Spain who besieged Queen Lidoine of Gascony at the castle of Monjardin after the death of her husband, hoping to force her into marriage. The siege was lifted by Arthur's knights, led by Claris, who also loved the queen. Claris killed Savari and succeeded him to the throne of Spain. [Claris]

SAVARIZ

A knight from Carmelide who loved Guinevere the False. After her ploy to replace the real Guinevere failed, and Guinevere the False died, Savariz challenged Arthur to combat. Arthur decapitated him. [Prophecies]

SAWYL HIGH HEAD

One of Arthur's warriors in Welsh legend. The Triads call him an "arrogant" man. [Culhwch, Triads]

SAXONS

A collection of only loosely-unified Germanic tribes that invaded England in the fifth and sixth centuries, and eventually conquered it, holding it until the Normans invaded in 1066. Their own history (in the Anglo-Saxon Chronicle), as well as archaeological evidence, shows their encroachments beginning in the south and east of Britain, shortly after the Roman withdrawal from Britain in the early fifth century, which had left Britain near defenseless. They were closely related to the Jutes and the Angles, who led raids into Britain about the same time as the Saxons. The first conquests of these Germanic invaders included Kent, the Isle of Wight, Wessex (West Saxons), Sussex (South Saxons), Essex (East Saxons), Suffolk, Norfolk, and Northumberland. From these settlements, they led incursions into the territories of the British, Scottish, Cornish, and Welsh, effectively conquering the entire

island within 200 years. In the early legends, Arthur's fame is founded upon his successes in the struggle against the Saxons.

Multiple early sources, including Gildas, Bede, and the Anglo-Saxon Chronicle assert that the Saxons' relentless aggression was stopped for a few decades when the disparate British kings united under a succession of war-leaders and enjoyed a series of military victories against the invaders. Ambrosius seems to have been the first of these generals, and Arthur is given by Nennius as another. In any event, the British were unable to remain united long enough. The Saxon invasions soon resumed and were largely completed by the close of the sixth century.

By the time of Nennius's writing, the history of the Saxon invasion was already becoming tainted with fantastic elements. According to the chronicles, the original Saxon invaders were led by Hengist and his brother Horsa, two characters who appear in the Anglo-Saxon Chronicle and are probably based on historical figures, though they would have only been leaders of a particular tribe of Saxons; there was no "Saxon nation." Vortigern, who was the king of Britain two generations before Arthur, befriended the Saxons and employed them as mercenaries in order to defend Britain against the Picts from the north and against Ambrosius in Brittany. This practice of hiring one barbarian race to defend against another is in keeping with Roman tradition and it is not impossible that a historical British ruler called Vortigern did exactly that, probably in the 440s (Alcock, 108). Sources disagree as to whether Vortigern invited the first Saxons to Britain, or whether they already had encampments on the eastern shore; archaeology seems to favor the latter hypothesis. If, as some historians speculate, Vortigern was anti-Roman, the his plan for the Saxons may have included prevention against a Roman re-occupation (Lindsay, 190).

Continuing with the chronicles' stories, Hengist married his daughter Rowena to Vortigern and was granted the country of Kent. Capitalizing on Vortigern's fear of attack, Hengist brought thousands of Saxon warriors to Britain, covertly plotting to take over the island. When Hengist's plot became clear, Vortimer, Vortigern's son, broke from his father and led an army of Britons against the Saxons, killing Horsa and driving them off the island. When Vortimer died, however, the Saxons returned and reoccupied areas of Kent, Middlesex, Sussex, and Essex. They were driven out again by Ambrosius, only to return to plague Uther Pendragon. Arthur won a final victory against them through a series of seven or 12 battles, culminating in the battle of Badon Hill. A final Briton golden age flourished under Arthur, and the Saxons returned upon his death. Leaders of the Saxon warriors who plagued Ambrosius, Uther, and Arthur are given variously as Octa, Eosa, Colgrim, Baldulph, and Cheldric.

A large portion of the Vulgate Merlin expands upon the Saxon invasion, listing a multitude of Saxon kings from Ireland, Denmark, and Germany who entered Britain and besieged its greatest cities at the beginning of Arthur's reign. The more notable among these dozens of rulers include Aminaduc, Bramangue, Clarion, Galahad,

Hargadabran, Maragond, Oriel, Pignoras, Rions, Salebrun, and Sapharin. Gawain, Yvain, Sagremor, and a number of other young heroes first distinguished themselves in the Saxon wars. Arthur allied with a collection of kings who had been in rebellion against him and, after a number of assorted battles, crushed the Saxons at the battle of Clarence (here replacing Badon). *Arthour and Merlin* and Malory replace this Saxon invasion with an attack by SARACENS. The Vulgate *Lancelot* tells how they again invaded Scotland some twenty years later, but Arthur and Lancelot defeated them at Saxon Rock and drove them away. Mordred was said to have allied with the Saxons when he usurped Arthur's throne, and several Saxon armies participated in the battle of Salisbury, in which Arthur was killed. [*Nennius, GeoffHR, Anglo, LancLac, VulgLanc, VulgMort, VulgMer, Livre, Malory*]

SAXON ROCK

A Saxon outpost in Arestel, Scotland, first occupied by Hengist during the reign of Vortigern. In one tale, it is the location where Uther Pendragon killed Hengist. It served as a base of operations for the various Saxon invasions at the beginning and middle of Arthur's reign. Its lady was Gamille, the sister of the Saxon King Hargadabran. Gamille used her charms to lure Arthur into her prison when Arthur traveled to the Rock to besiege the invading Saxons. Lancelot led an attack on the Rock, captured the castle, and freed Arthur. [*LancLac, VulgLanc, VulgMer*]

SAXONY [*Saxoyne, Sessoi(n)(g)ne, Sessoyne*]

The home of the Saxons. In the Middle Ages, it was the name of a duchy at the base of the Jutland peninsula. The Vulgate *Merlin* calls Brandegorre its king. In the Icelandic *Saga of Tristram ok Ísodd*, its Emperor, Donísus, is an ally of Tristan. In Chrétien de Troyes's *Cliges*, the Duke of Saxony is a nobleman who loves Fenice, the daughter of the Emperor of Germany. Alis, the Emperor of Constantinople and Greece, challenged the Duke of Saxony for Fenice's hand in marriage. They fought a battle in the Black Forest near Cologne, and Alis won the battle through the prowess of Cliges, his nephew. [*ChretienC, VulgMer, Arthour, SagaTI*]

SAYNES

One of many rulers conquered by Arthur. His daughter and kingdom were given to Paris of France, one of Arthur's companions. [*Jean*]

SCANORO THE GREAT

A knight defeated by Lancelot and Tristan in the Savage Valley during the Grail Quest. [*Tavola*]

SCARBOROUGH

A coastal city in Yorkshire where, in the Icelandic *Saga of Tristram ok Ísodd*, Blenzibly established her headquarters during her revolt against her brother, King Mark. [*SagaTI*]

SCARLET CROSS

A landmark in Cornwall where Tristan arranged to meet Governal, his tutor, after they both conducted a search for Isolde, who had been kidnapped by Palamedes. [*ProsTris*]

SCHAFFILOR

The King of Arragon in the days of Uther Pendragon. He participated in a tournament at Kanvoleis in Wales, where he was unhorsed and taken prisoner by Perceval's father Gahmuret. [*Wolfram*]

SCHAFFILUN

The king of Medarie and Belakun. Both Schaffilun and Wigalois (Gawain's son) arrived at the border of Korntin, looking to champion Queen Amena of Korntin against King Roaz of Glois, thus winning the hand of Princess Larie. Wigalois and Schaffilun decided to fight each other for the honor, and Schaffilun was killed. [*Wirnt*]

SCHAITIS

An Arthurian knight. [*Stricker*]

SCHAMILOT

One of Arthur's castles in Wolfram's *Parzival*, obviously a variation of CAMELOT. [*Wolfram*]

SCHANPFANZUN [*Schaffenzun*]

The capital city of King Vergulaht's Ascalun, where Gawain was summoned to fight a duel against Kingrimursel, the city's landgrave. [*Wolfram, PleierT*]

SCHATEL LE MORT ("Castle of the Dead")

The castle owned by Mabuz the Enchanter. It was surrounded by the River Der Kal (River of Torment). The castle was enchanted in such a way that anyone who entered uninvited would turn into a coward; his cowardice, in fact, would be proportional to his prior courage. Lancelot happened upon the castle and succumbed to the spell, causing his companions—his lover Ade and his squire Tybalt—to desert him in disgust. Mabuz kept Lancelot prisoner for a time, but eventually freed him. [*UlrichZ*]

SCHAUT

King of Lis. He was the brother of Poydiconjunz (Bagdemagus) and the father of Meliant, who inherited his crown. [*Wolfram*]

SCHENTEFLURS

Son of Gornemant (Perceval's tutor) and brother of Lascoyt, Gurzgri, and Liaze. He attempted to aid his cousin Condwiramurs when she was attacked by Lord Clamadeu, but he was killed by Kingrun, Clamadeu's seneschal, in battle. [*Wolfram*]

SCHERULES

The burgrave of the city of Bearosche under Duke Lyppaut. His daughter was named Clauditte. He enlisted the assistance of Gawain in a battle against King Meliant of Lis, who was attacking Lyppaut because Lyppaut's daughter Obie had rejected him. Scherules himself fought bravely in the battle. [*Wolfram*]

SCHILTUNC

The uncle of King Kaylet of Spain and the father in-law of King Vridebrant of Scotland. Schiltunc urged Kaylet to accompany Vridebrant on Vridebrant's invasion of Zazamanc, land of Queen Belacane. [*Wolfram*]

SCHIOLARZ

The count of Poitou during Uther's time. Schiolarz participated at a tournament at Kanvoleis in Wales, thrown by Perceval's mother Herzeloyde. His son, Liadarz, was a page to Queen Ampflise of France. [*Wolfram*]

SCHIONATULANDER

A prince and partner in unconsummated love with Perceval's cousin Sigune. He is found in Wolfram's *Parzival* and the later prologue, *Titurel*. Raised by Queen Ampflise of France, Schionatulander fell in love with Sigune. He accompanied Gahmuret, Perceval's father, on his adventures in Baghdad. Later, back in Britain, he was with Sigune in a forest when he happened upon a brachet wearing an ornate leash. Upon the leash was written a story of two lovers named Clauditte and Enkunaht. Before Schionatulander and Sigune could finish the story, the hound broke free and ran off into the forest. Sigune asked Schionatulander to retrieve the hound so she could see how the tale ended. During his quest to retrieve it, Schionatulander encountered Duke Orguelleus of La Lande and was slain in combat. In mourning of his death, Sigune lived in cloister at Schionatulander's tomb and was buried next to him upon her early passing. [*Wolfram*]

SCHIRNIEL OF LIRIVOYN

King of Lirivoyn and brother of King Mirabel of Avendroyn. He fought for Duke Lyppaut of Bearosche when Lyppaut's daughter rejected King Meliant of Lis and Meliant attacked. Perceval defeated him in combat at this battle. [*Wolfram*]

SCHOETTE

Paternal grandmother of Perceval, wife of King Gandin of Anjou, and mother of Galoes and Gahmuret. After Gahmuret left home in search of adventure, and Gandin and Galoes died, Schoette perished from loneliness. [*Wolfram*]

SCHONEBAR

A Knight of the Round Table. [*HartmannE*]

SCHOYSIANE

A member of the Grail Family. She was the daughter of the Grail King Frimutel, and the sister of Anfortas, Trevrizent, Herzeloyde, and Repanse de Schoye. She married Kyot of Katelangen and died giving birth to her daughter Sigune. Prior to this, she raised Condwiramurs, the hereditary Queen of Brabant, who became Perceval's wife. [*Wolfram*]

SCHULDA

In Norse mythology, one of the three Fatal Sisters—the others were Urd and Verandi—who presided over the past, present, and future. In Thelwall's *The Fairy of the Lake*, Rowena, wife of Vortigern, seeks their foresight during her quest to seduce Arthur. [*Thelwall*]

SCHUWAKE

In the English ballad "Sir Lancelot du Lake," the kingdom ruled by Lancelot's father, King Haud. The name was probably chosen because it rhymes with "Lake," as in "I am Lancelot du Lake / Now knight of Arthurs Table Round / King Hauds son of Schuwake." [*SirLanc*]

SCILLY, ISLES OF

A group of more than 100 islands off the tip of Cornwall. Three of them are known as Great Arthur, Middle Arthur, and Little Arthur. Lyonesse, the land of Tristan, was said to have spanned the distance between Cornwall and the Isles of Scilly, but it sank into the sea (Ashe, *Quest*, 189–90).

SCOS

A Knight of the Round Table. He was the brother of Gangier of Neranden. [*HartmannE*]

SCOT

An inhabitant of Scotland, originally referring to the Gaelic tribes who emigrated from Ireland in the fifth century and joined with the native Picts. They are generally presented as a barbarian race who, like the Picts, threatened the southern Britons from the north of Hadrian's Wall. According to Geoffrey, Arthur subjugated the Scots in the early days of his reign, after the battles at Moray and Lomond. The Scottish chronicler John of Fordun appropriately distinguishes between the Picts and Scots and claims that the latter were Arthur's allies against the former. Hector Boece's *Scotorum Historia* presents an alternate version in which the Scots and Picts together become Arthur's allies against the invading Saxons. [*GeoffHR, JohnF, Boece*]

SCOTLAND

The northern half of the island of Great Britain, called ALBANY before the SCOTS arrived from Ireland in the fifth century and established territories there. In early Arthurian tradition—and in history—Scotland was populated primarily by barbarian PICTS who had been driven north by waves of invading Europeans (i.e., Celts and Romans). Geoffrey of Monmouth and the chroniclers describe Arthur's wars against the Scots and Picts. In later Arthurian tradition, however, Scotland seems largely pacified and is generally subject to Arthur's power. Its kings are variously given as Caw (Welsh legend), Angusel and, later, Gwenddoleu (Geoffrey of Monmouth), Malaquin (Vulgate *Lancelot*), Urien (*Meriadoc*), Caradoc (Malory, who also mentions Angusel), and Tollo (Richard Blackmore). Malory also names a separate "King of Scots" who appears in several tournaments. [*Culhwch, GeoffHR, GeoffVM, LancLac, VulgLanc, VulgMer, Historia, Malory*]

SCOTT

A British king in the time of Joseph of Arimathea. His land bordered the forest of Darnantes. [*VulgEst*]

SCOUT

Arthur's squire in Thelwall's *The Fairy of the Lake*. [*Thelwall*]

SCUDAMORE

Lover of the maiden Amoret. He first saw her when she visited the Fairy Queen's court. Scudamore braved the dangers of the temple of Venus, Amoret's guardian, to court her. Britomart, the warrior maiden, found Scudamore lamenting over Amoret, who had been imprisoned by a sorcerer named Busirane. Assisted by Britomart and Arthur, he was re-united with his lover. [*Spenser*]

SEAT OF JUDGMENT

The courtroom and governmental chamber in the Temple of the Sun in King Evalach's Sarras. [*VulgEst*]

SÉBILE

The lovely pagan queen of Sarmenie. Baruc the Black, a jilted suitor, killed her husband and invaded her lands. Sagremor agreed to become her champion. Sébile fell in love with Sagremor and converted to Christianity for his sake. After Sagremor defeated Baruc, Sagremor and Sébile became lovers, and some sources say that they were married. [*Livre, Froissart*]

SEBIO

Saracen count of Cologia. He threw a tournament during the Grail Quest, offering his daughter to any man who could defeat him and a hundred knights. Lancelot and Tristan won the tournament and gave Sebio's daughter to Richevie Ventura, the son of a man who had lodged them. Sebio died of a wound given to him by Lancelot. [*Tavola*]

SECACE [*Sequence, Seure*]

Arthur's sword in the Prose *Lancelot*, used in the battle at Saxon Rock. Although EXCALIBUR is usually named as

Arthur's weapon, *Lancelot* puts the latter sword in the hands of Gawain during this time. [*LancLac, VulgLanc*]

SECKMUR OF ROIS

A Knight of the Round Table. [*HartmannE*]

SECUNDILLE

The infidel queen of Tribalibot (India), and its cities of Thabronit and Thasme. She was fascinated with stories of the Grail, and she sent two of her subjects—Cundrie the Sorceress and Malcreature—to Anfortas, the Grail King, as servants. Later, she fell in love with Feirefiz, Perceval's half brother, and gave him her lands in exchange for his devoted service. He eventually cast off her love, however, in favor of the Grail Maiden Repanse de Schoye, causing Secundille to die of heartbreak. [*Wolfram*]

SEDILE [*Sebile*]

An enchantress queen who was a friend of Morgan le Fay. Sedile, Morgan, and the Queen of Sorestan imprisoned Lancelot in Cart Castle, hoping to make him choose one of them as a lover. Lancelot refused to choose and eventually escaped. Later, Sedile quarreled with Morgan over their mutual love for a knight named Berengier. [*VulgLanc, ProsTris, Prophecies*]

SEGART [*Sebart*]

A knight who fought for Arthur in the Roman War, according to the Vulgate *Merlin*. Avenging the defeat of his uncle, Bedivere, he killed King Boccus of Mede. He is called HIRELGLAS in Geoffrey and Wace. [*VulgMer*]

SEGONTIUM

A Roman fortress in Wales, at the Aber Seint estuary. William Camden thought that Arthur was crowned there. [*Camden*]

SEGOR

A heathen warrior slain by Gawain at the battle of Diana Bridge. [*Arthour*]

SEGRELOS THE FOREIGNER

King Anguish of Ireland's astrologer. He interpreted Anguish's dream portending the affair between Tristan and Isolde, Anguish's daughter. [*Tavola*]

SEGUARADES[1] [*Seguradez, Segwarides*]

An Arthurian knight who appears in the Vulgate romances, the Prose *Tristan*, and Malory, though possibly first appearing as SEGURES in Renaut de Bâgé's *Le Bel Inconnu*. In *Palamedes*, his father is Tarsin of Sorelois. The Vulgate *Merlin* relates how he fought alongside the northern kings in the early Saxon Wars and participated in a quest to learn the fate of Merlin. In *Lancelot*, we learn how he loved the lady of Roestoc and wished to marry her; when she did not reciprocate his feelings, he declared war on her. The Lady of Roestoc was championed by Gawain, who defeated Seguarades in single combat. The Prose *Tristan* says he was married, but was cuckolded by both Tristan and Bleoberis. Both knights defeated Seguarades in personal combat over his own wife, but when given the choice, she chose to return to Seguarades. Malory tells us that he was a moor, the son of King Esclabor, and the brother of Palamedes and Safir. Unlike Palamedes, Seguarades was christened. He fought in the Castle Perilous tournament, and helped Tristan defeat the giant Nabon the Black, ruler of the Isle of Servage. Tristan gave the island to Seguarades. He was killed fighting Lancelot and his men when Lancelot rescued Guinevere from the stake. [*LancLac, VulgLanc, VulgMer, Palamedes, ProsTris, Malory*]

SEGUARADES[2] OF LANVALLE

A knight appointed by Guiron the Courteous to rule the castle at the Perilous Pass. [*Palamedes*]

SEGURANT THE BROWN [*Sigurans*]

Called the Knight of the Dragon, the greatest fighter of Uther Pendragon's Old Table order. The son of Hector the Brown, Galehaut the Brown, or Brunor the Brown, Segurant pursued a dragon from land to land during his career. He finally became king of the country of Abiron. Among his other adventures, he destroyed the Tower of the Copper Marvel and won a tournament at the city of Winchester. The Lady of the Lake tried to ensure that Lancelot never encountered Segurant. During the Grail Quest, however, when Segurant was 160 years old, he defeated Lancelot and jousted Tristan to a draw. He later died from the wound delivered by Tristan. His character has an uncertain connection to SEGUARADES. [*Palamedes, ProsTris, Tavola*]

SEGURES

Named as the brother of Mordred in Renaut de Bâgé's *Le Bel Inconnu*, Segures may be identical to SAGREMOR, Mordred's foster-brother in the Post-Vulgate *Merlin* continuation, or SEGUARADES. [*Renaut*]

SEIDI [*Saidi*]

Son of Gwyron and father of Arthur's warriors Alun of Dyfed, Cadrieth, and Cas. [*Culhwch, Dream*]

SEIFE

Arthur's sister in Der Pleier's *Meleranz*. She was the wife of King Lot and the mother of Gawain. Her sisters included Anthonje and Olimpia. Her name is probably a corruption of Wolfram's SANGIVE. [*PleierM*]

SEIMERET

The sister of Angaras of Karamphi, an enemy of Gawain in *Diu Crône*. Her counterpart in Wolfram's *Parzival* is ANTIKONIE. [*Heinrich*]

SEITHFED ("Seventh")

Father of Arthur's warriors Sinnoch, Wadu, Naw, and Bedyw. [*Culhwch*]

SÊL ("Watch")

An Arthurian warrior who was the son of Sêlgi. [*Culhwch*]

SELAPHAS

A devil exorcised from the city of Orcaut by Josephus, son of Joseph of Arimathea. Previously, Selaphas had caused King Tholomer of Babylonia to kill himself. [*VulgEst*]

SÊLGI ("Watchdog")

Father of Arthur's warrior Sêl. [*Culhwch*]

SELICE

A land in King Arthur's domain. It was invaded by Lord Galehaut, and Arthur was called to defend it. Galehaut and Arthur fought two wars in Selice, which ended in a truce skillfully brokered by Lancelot. [*LancLac*]

SELITUM

A fashionable Knight of the Round Table killed during the Grail Quest. [*PostQuest*]

SELYF[1]

Son of Sinoid. Selyf was one of Arthur's warriors in *Culhwch and Olwen*. His name is a Welsh variation of Solomon. [*Culhwch*]

SELYF[2]

A warrior from Powys who served Owain. He was the son of Cynan White Shank. [*Dream*]

SEMIRAMIS [*Samirami, Semiramin*]

A knight present at the tournament at Noauz, which Lancelot won. In another episode, Semiramis was defeated in combat by Lord Parsamant, whose custom it was to beat, rob, and otherwise ill-treat his captives. Perceval arrived and saved Semiramis from this fate by defeating Parsamant. [*ChretienL, Contin4*]

SEMPHARAP

A castle visited by Gawain. He found its inhabitants distressed because the castle's lord, Mahardi, was scheduled to fight a duel against a fearsome knight named Reimambram of Zadas. Mahardi, however, had fallen deathly ill. The duel was to decide the fate of Behalim, Mahardi's sister, whom Reimambram wanted to obtain. When Mahardi died, Gawain agreed to fight in his place. He defeated Reimambram and saved Behalim. [*Heinrich*]

SEMPITEBRUNS

An Arthurian knight. His brother was Sir Quoikos. [*Heinrich*]

SENAAS

A Saxon who, under King Aminaduc, fought against Arthur's forces at Vambieres. [*Livre*]

SENAHAR

A knight who figures into a variant version of the story of Erec and Enide found in the Prose *Tristan*. Senehar killed the Duke of Huiscam, who was Enide's father, and tried to steal Enide's inheritances. Erec, Galahad, Bleoberis, and Hector defeated Senahar's men, captured him, and imprisoned him for life. [*ProsTris*]

SENAINS OF NORHAUT

The castellan of Norhaut who fought in Arthur's army against the Saxons at the battle of Clarence. [*Livre*]

SENEBALT [*Senebant, Senebaut*]

A Saxon warrior who served King Rions and joined Rions' invasion of Britain at the beginning of Arthur's reign. King Bors of Gannes killed him at the battle of Carhaix. [*VulgMer, Arthour*]

SENEHAUT

Lover of the knight Blios. Blios thought Senehaut was having an affair with her cousin, so he beat the cousin in combat. Though Senehaut and Blios reconciled, relatives of the beaten cousin, to avenge the disgrace, kidnapped Senehaut. Sagremor came upon the abductors and rescued Senehaut, who rewarded her savior by spending the night with him. Eventually reunited with Blios, Senehaut later gave birth to Sagremor's daughter, whom Guinevere raised. [*Livre*]

SENELAS

A Knight of the Round Table from Desert. Senelas, his brother Caulas, and his three cousins set upon Galahad during the Grail Quest and were all killed. [*PostQuest, ProsTris*]

SENIGRAN [*Segrain*]

One of the many Saxon kings to invade northern Britain in the early days of Arthur's reign. He was killed by Galescalain. [*VulgMer, Arthour*]

SENILGORZOF SIRNEGUNZ

A king once defeated in combat by Perceval. [*Wolfram*]

SENNES OF NARJOCLIN

An infidel duke who served Feirefiz, Perceval's half-brother. [*Wolfram*]

SENODALUS

A Saxon king who, under King Hargadabran, fought Arthur's forces at the battle of Clarence. [*Livre*]

SENTRAYLE OF LUSHON

A Knight of the Round Table loyal to Tristan. With Governal and Lambegus, he rescued Tristan after Tristan escaped the treachery of Andred, King Mark's seneschal. [*Malory*]

SEPHAR

A Saxon king who, under King Hargadabran, fought Arthur's forces at the battle of Clarence. [*Livre*]

SERABIL OF ROZOKARZ

A king once defeated in combat by Perceval. [*Wolfram*]

SERAPHE[1] [*Salafres*]

The pre-baptismal name of NASCIEN, a follower of Joseph of Arimathea. [*VulgEst, Contin3*]

SERAPHE[2]

A hermit in Joseph of Arimathea's time who settled in the forest of Naube, driving out the evil serpents which resided there. Seraphe baptized the sister of King Label of Persia. [*VulgEst*]

SERAN

Brother of Elemmie, with whom Seran conquered Spain. He escaped a disastrous battle in which his brother Elemmie was slain. He returned with his other brother, Desixtus, and was slain by the forces of Kalegras, Tristan's father. [*SagaTI*]

SERBIA

In Wirnt von Grafenberg's *Wigalois*, Serbians ally with Prince Lion of Namur against King Wigalois of Korntin (Gawain's son). [*Wirnt*]

SERE OF SYRIA

A British earl who invaded the lands of Degrevant, a Knight of the Round Table. Degrevant, away on the Crusades, learned of the earl's ravagings and returned to meet him in battle. The earl lost the war. Sere's daughter, Melidor, fell in love with Degrevant and began a secret romance. Sere discovered it and tried to ambush Degrevant, but only succeeded in getting many of his knights (including his steward Aymere) killed. Persuaded by his wife and daughter, he reconciled with Degrevant and allowed him to marry Melidor. [*SirDeg*]

SERPENT FOUNTAIN [*Fontana Serpilina*]

A fountain in Cornwall that Tristan was known to frequent during his period of insanity. [*Tavola*]

SERPENT'S DITCH

A deep pit full of poisonous snakes. Perceval rescued a maiden from an evil knight who was going to throw her into it. [*Perlesvaus*]

SERRE

A country ruled by Lord Laniure in Heinrich von dem Türlin's *Diu Crône*. When he died without a male heir, his daughters Amurfina and Sgoidamur vied for control of a magic bridle which gave its owner the rights to the land. Gawain eventually decided the feud in Sgoidamur's favor, though he married Amurfina. Another King of Serre appears in Girart d'Amien's *Escanor* at the tournament of Banborc. [*Heinrich, Girart*]

SERSES [*Sexes, Xerxes*]

The King of Iturea or Idumea who was subservient to the Roman Procurator Lucius. Serses was called upon to join Lucius in the war against Arthur. He led a force of soldiers at the battle of Soissons. [*GeoffHR, Wace, Layamon*]

SERSES[2] [*Xerxes*]

King of the Red Castle and the castle Pagon. He served King Claudas. King Bors of Gannes (Lancelot's uncle) had killed Serses's brother, so Serses became Bors's mortal enemy. When they met in single combat, Bors defeated him and took his crown. Later, his castle at Pagon was conquered by Arthur during Arthur's invasion of Gaul. Serses managed to escape the siege in time to warn Claudas of Arthur's advance. [*VulgLanc*]

SERTORIUS [*Sertor, Sestor, Sextorius, Sextynour*]

The King of Libya who served Emperor Lucius of Rome. He was called upon to join Lucius in the war against Arthur. Sertorius, with three others, was assigned by Lucius to liberate the Roman prisoners being taken by Arthur's warriors to a prison in Paris. The Britons won the battle. Sertorius later led a force of soldiers at the battle of Soissons, where he killed Kay, but was in turn killed by Arthur. [*GeoffHR, Wace, Layamon, VulgMer, Allit*]

SERVAGE ("Servitude")

An island or valley ruled by the evil giant Nabon the Black. Its capital was Glait Castle. Nabon held a tournament there to celebrate the knighting of his son. Lamorat and Tristan both attended, and the latter slew Nabon and his son. Afterwards, it was known as the Land That Tristan Freed, and was given to Sir Seguarades. [*ProsTris, Malory*]

SERVAGAT [*Sernagare*]

A Saxon king from Ireland who was part of the great Saxon invasion at the beginning of Arthur's reign. After plundering areas of northern Britain, he was killed in a skirmish against Gawain. [*VulgMer, Arthour*]

SESOX[1]

A heathen king slain by Gawain at the battle of the Diana Bridge. [*Arthour*]

SESOX[2]

A heathen warrior slain by Agravain at a battle in Logres. [*Arthour*]

SEVAIN[1]

The Roman Count of Meaux in the time of Christ. He was King Mordrain's grandfather, and he sent Mordrain, as a boy, to serve the Emperor of Rome. [*VulgEst*]

SEVAIN[2] [*Sanam, Siwenis*]

Earl of Quimper-Corentin. His daughter, Lisanor, had an affair with Arthur and gave birth to Loholt. [*VulgMer, Arthour, Malory*]

SEVEN ROADS

A heath and crossroads in the forest of Breckham, where Gawain defeated a knight. The knight had been guarding the crossroads for the love of a lady. [*VulgLanc*]

SEVERAUCE LE BREUSE

A Knight of the Round Table who appears at the healing of Sir Urry. The Lady of the Lake once bade Severauce and Lancelot never to fight each other, and they agreed. After that, Severauce never had the desire to fight against any man, but gladly fought giants, dragons, and wild beasts. [*Malory*]

SEVERN [*Hafren, Syvarne*]

An English river. It begins in Central Wales, arcs out through west England, and empties into the Bristol Channel. In *Culhwch*, Arthur's forces battle the boar Twrch Trwyth on the Severn. By driving the boar into the river and trapping him in the currents, the warriors Mabon and Cyledyr the Wild were able to great the needed shears and razor from between the boar's ears. The boar recovered and fled to Cornwall. The river is referenced in continental romance, but the writers are confused about its location. In Malory, the Castle of Maidens is said to lie near the Severn. [*Culhwch, Malory*]

SEVERUS[1]

A Roman senator and general sent by the senate to pacify Britain after the death of King Lucius in the late second century. Nennius says that he was the third Roman emperor to cross to Britain. Severus, leading Romans and Roman-loyal Britons, became immersed in a great war with the Briton duke, Sulgenius. He and Sulgenius were killed in a battle at York; after his death, Severus's sons, Geta and Bassianus, vied for the kingdom. [*Nennius, GeoffHR*]

SEVERUS[2]

A Roman emperor who ruled in Britain after Maximus and before Constantine, Arthur's grandfather. He split his time between Britain and Rome, and he died in Rome. [*Nennius*]

SEVILLANO

A servant of Perceval's father Gahmuret. Sevillano was a ship's captain, and he ferried Gahmuret from Africa to Europe. [*Wolfram*]

SEVILLE

A seaport in southwest Spain. Perceval's uncle Trevrizent traveled through Seville during his adventures. [*Wolfram*]

SGAIPEGAZ

The lovely daughter of Lord Blandukors and Lady Amurelle, who Gawain saved from their service to a terrible giant named Galaas. [*Heinrich*]

SGILTI LIGHT FOOT

One of five sons of Erim. He was an Arthurian warrior, and he was so light that he could run across treetops and along the tips of reeds. [*Culhwch*]

SGOIDAMUR

The younger daughter of Lord Lamuire of Serre, who died without a male heir. Sgoidamur's sister, Amurfina, feuded with her over the rights to their father's land, which was embodied in a magic bridle that Amurfina obtained. Sgoidamur complained to Arthur's court for redress, and Gawain vowed to restore Sgoidamur to her inheritance. During the quest, however, he married Amurfina. After some consequent complications, Gawain arranged for Sgoidamur to marry Gasozein (Gaswain) of Dragoz, a noble knight. Gawain champions a (unnamed) maiden in a similar plight in *La Mule sans Frein*. [*Heinrich*]

SHADY VALLEY [*Valle Ombroso*]

A valley visited by Lancelot and Tristan during the Grail Quest. [*Tavola*]

SHERWOOD

A forest in Nottinghamshire, identified by Malory with the forest of BEDEGRAINE. [*Malory*]

SHIP OF JOY

A magical vessel constructed by Merlin for the king of Northumberland and his friend Agad. The Ship came into possession of Mabon the sorcerer, and he sent it to Tristan so that Tristan could join him in a struggle against Mennonas, an enemy. [*ProsTris*]

SHRIEKING MARSH

A perilous bog that surrounded the Misty Lake, home of the wizard Malduc. Arthur's envoys had to travel through the Shrieking Marsh to find Malduc and enlist his assistance in the rescue of Guinevere from an abductor. The marsh was also inhabited by Sir Dodinel the Wild. Adventurers crossing the marsh were plagued with quicksand, giant fish, boiling waters, enchanted birds, and an occasional heart-stopping shriek. [*UlrichZ*]

SIANIST

The land inhabited by Giramphiel, a goddess who was Gawain's benefactress. [*Heinrich*]

SIAWN

Son of Iaen and brother of Sulyen, Bradwen, Moren, Teregud, and Caradawg. He came from Caer Dathal and was one of Arthur's warriors. He was related to Arthur through Uther. [*Culhwch*]

SIBILIAS OF THE HARD HANDS

A Knight of the Round Table who participated in the Grail Quest. [*ProsTris*]

SICHELM [*Sichelin*]

King of Norway and grandfather of Lot in Geoffrey's *Historia*. When he died, he left his kingdom to his grandson, but a lord named Riculf seized it, prompting Arthur to conquer Norway and restore it to Lot. In *De Ortu Waluuanii*, Sichelm is Lot's uncle rather than his grandfather. Having been conquered by Uther Pendragon, Sichelm was forced to send Lot to Uther's court for rearing. [*GeoffHR, DeOrtu*]

SICILY [*Sesile, Sezile, Suzille, Zezile*]

Italian folklore in the Middle Ages identified AVALON with Sicily and held that Arthur was resting inside Mt. Etna (called Montegibel). This story is represented in *Floriant et Florete*. In *Claris et Laris*, the island is ruled by King Calon, who joins Rome in a war against Arthur. [*Floriant, Claris*]

SICK KING

A leprous potentate whose lands were seized by King Gohart of the Castle of the Whales, but were restored to him by Perceval. His name suggests a relation to the MAIMED KING. [*Perlesvaus*]

SIDRAVALLE

A castle in the Perilous Valley. Its lord, Gabrionello, was subject to two giants. Tristan and Lancelot freed him by slaying the giants. [*Tavola*]

SIEGE PERILOUS

See PERILOUS SEAT.

SIFLOIS

One of the many ladies at Arthur's court to fail a chastity test involving a goblet. [*Heinrich*]

SIGUNE

A cousin of Perceval in Wolfram's *Parzival*, identical to an unnamed lady in Chrétien de Troyes's *Perceval*. Her mother, Scoysiane, died giving birth to her, so she was raised by Queen Herzeloyde of Wales, Perceval's mother.

R. S. Loomis (*Grail*, 205) thought that her name was an anagram of *cusine* ("cousin").

While in the forest of Brizljan with her lover, Schionatulander, she found a hound with an extremely long leash. The leash had a story inscribed upon it, which Sigune only partially read before the hound bolted away, dragging the leash with it. Sigune sent Schionatulander after the hound, and he was killed during the quest by Duke Orguelleus of Lalander. Perceval, on his way to Arthur's court, came across Sigune holding Schionatulander's body in her arms. She paused from her grief long enough to inform Perceval of his lineage.

Perceval met her again some time later, as he was riding away from the Grail Castle, having failed to cure the Fisher King. She related some history of the Grail Family and Grail Sword, but left his presence in disgust when she found out he had failed to ask the Grail Question. Later, Perceval came across her again after Schionatulander had been entombed. Sigune was living a life of constant sorrow and penance over her dead lover's grave. Cundrie the Sorceress, the Grail Maiden, brought her food and drink to sustain her. She tried to point Perceval in the direction of the Grail, but he lost the trail. After several years of this cloistered asceticism, Sigune died hunched over Schionatulander's tomb. When Perceval found her, he opened the tomb and interred her next to her lover. [*Wolfram*]

SIGURANO

A knight slain by Tristan at a tournament in Ireland. Sigurano's brother, Oris the Harsh, tried to avenge him but was also slain. [*Tavola*]

SIGUROR

An earl of Spain who was the brother of Hríngr and Isolde the Dark. He gave his sister to Tristan when the latter conquered Spain. [*SagaTI*]

SILARES

An Arthurian knight mentioned by Heinrich von dem Türlin. His name is a corruption of TOR *fil ares* ("Tor son of Ares"). [*Heinrich*]

SILCHESTER [*Sylchestre*]

A city in Britain in which Constantine, Arthur's grandfather, and Arthur (in some versions) were both crowned. In Arthur's time, Maugan, Baldulph, or Balien served as Silchester's Archbishop. [*GeoffHR*, *Wace*, *Layamon*]

SILENCE

Heroine of the non-Arthurian *Roman de Silence* by Heldris de Cornuälle. Silence, a girl born to Count Cador of Cornwall some time after Arthur's reign, was raised as a boy so that she might escape King Ebain of England's law which prohibited a female from inheriting property. Facing a gender conflict upon reaching puberty, she ran away and joined a group of minstrels. Still disguised as a male, she eventually arrived at Ebain's court, where the king's wife, Eufeme, tried to seduce her, then accused her of rape when she refused. After some further complications—in which Silence displayed much knightly prowess—she was given the task of finding Merlin, which could only be performed by a woman. Silence found Merlin roaming in a forest and brought him back to court. Merlin revealed her true gender to the surprised king, and informed the king of his wife's adultery. After executing Eufeme, King Ebain married Silence and made her Queen of England. The story of GANIEDA in Geoffrey of Monmouth's *Vita Merlini* and the tale of AVENABLE in the Vulgate *Merlin* are echoed in the story of Silence.

SILHAUT

A knight in the ancestry of the "Brown" family. Descended from Brutus, he was the son of Arbrun and Vagés, and was the brother of Brun. He was killed by his cousin, Guillant. [*Palamedes*]

SILIMAC OF THE ROCK

Ruler of the Castle of the Rock. While traveling to the Grail Castle with Gawain, he was killed with a poisoned arrow that seemed to come out of nowhere. Gawain later assisted Sore Pucelle, Silimac's sister, and she divined that Kay was the unseen murderer. Gawain swore to avenge Silimac's death, and he badly wounded Kay in a duel at Arthur's court. [*Contin1*, *Contin3*]

SIMEON [*Symeu*]

A follower of Joseph of Arimathea who was not pure. At a dinner, he was one of only two followers that the Grail would not serve. In envy, he attacked Peter, one of Joseph's pious followers, and badly wounded him. The other followers decided to bury him alive, but before they could perform the task, he was carried away in flames to a tomb in Wales, where he was destined to remain, in agony, until the Grail Quest. Lancelot found the tomb and tried to free him but failed. When Galahad approached, the flames disappeared and Simeon was allowed to die. His son, Moses, also sinned and had to be freed by Galahad. [*VulgLanc*, *VulgQuest*, *VulgEst*, *PostQuest*]

SINADONE

The King of Sinadone was one of Arthur's vassals, and his wife was proven unfaithful by a magic horn in Biket's *Lai du Cor*. Biket may have intended SNOWDON in Wales. [*Biket*]

SINADOS [*Salinas, Synadés, Synados*]

A knight from Windsor in the service of King Leodegan of Carmelide. He fought against the Saxons at Aneblayse. On one adventure, while riding with three knights, Sinados was attacked by Sir Mataliz, who had seventeen knights. Arthur's Sir Hector came to Sinados's rescue and killed Mataliz. When Sinados later heard that Hector had been imprisoned, he launched a rescue expedition. Sinados eventually became a Knight of the Round Table and participated in the Grail Quest. [*LancLac*, *VulgLanc*, *VulgMer*, *Arthour*, *PostQuest*]

SINAGLORRE

A Saxon king who was part of the Saxon invasion of Britain led by King Ammaduc at the beginning of Arthur's reign. He participated in the siege of Clarence. [*VulgMer*]

SINAGON

A Saxon king who, under King Hargadabran, fought Arthur's forces at the battle of Clarence and was killed by Gawain. [*Livre*]

SINARUS

A Saxon warrior maimed by King Lot before the battle of Clarence. [*VulgMer*]

SINDENORT

A castle in Logres. Merlin, who called it OXEN FORD, said that all knowledge would descend upon it. [*VulgLanc*]

SINELANT [*Sinalaut*]

A Saxon warrior killed by Arthur at the battle of Carhaix. [*VulgMer*, *Arthour*]

SINNOCH

Son of Seithfed, brother of Wadu, Naw, and Bedyw, and one of Arthur's warriors. [*Culhwch*]

SINOID

Father of Arthur's warrior Selyf. [*Culhwch*]

SIRAOUC

A son of Febus and Florine. His brothers were Niatar, Lannor, Altan, and Argons. [*Palamedes*]

SISILLIUS[1]

According to Geoffrey of Monmouth, king of Britain in the seventh century BC. He was the son of King Gurgustius. His nephew, King Iago, succeeded him, and his son, Kinmarch, succeeded Iago. [*GeoffHR*]

SISILLIUS[2]

In Geoffrey of Monmouth's chronicle, a king of Britain in the fourth or third century BC. He succeeded his father, Guithelin, when he was only seven. His mother was Queen Marcia. Sisillius was succeeded by his son Kimar. [*GeoffHR*]

SISILLIUS[3]

According to Geoffrey of Monmouth, a king of Britain in the second century BC. He succeeded King Owen and was succeeded by King Bledgabred. [*GeoffHR*]

SKAAREZ

A knight present at the tournament of Sorgarda, which Gawain won. [*Heinrich*]

SMALL CHARITY

An abbey in Scotland, also called HELP FOR THE POOR and TELITE. Lancelot and Sagremor both lodged there during their adventures. Lamorat's body was taken there upon his death. [*VulgLanc*, *Livre*, *PostMer*]

SNOWDON [*Snowden, Synadoun, Synadowne*]

A mountain and mountain range in northwest Wales, called ERYRI by the Welsh, that features in Nennius's and Geoffrey's tale of Vortigern. Vortigern sought to build a fortress on Snowdon as a defense against the Saxons, but each night, all construction completed during the previous day would disappear. Vortigern's advisors told him that the foundation of Snowdon had to be sprinkled with the blood of a fatherless child. The king's emissaries embarked on a search for such a child, and returned with a young Ambrosius (in Nennius) or Merlin (in Geoffrey of Monmouth). The child prevented his own execution by showing Vortigern a lake hidden beneath the foundation of the fortress. Within the lake, the child revealed two worms or dragons, one white, one red. The creatures fought each other, and the white was victorious, which, the child said, foretold Vortigern's eventual defeat. Vortigern fled Snowdon, which became known as DINAS EMRYS. According to the Welsh tale of *Lludd and Llefelys*, the dragons had been buried in Snowdon by Lludd, son of the king of Britain.

Snowdon is named as the capital of Wales in *Historia Meriadoc*. In Renaut de Bâgé's *Le Bel Inconnu*, it is a city at the base of the Snowdén mountains, perhaps to be identified with SEGONTIUM. It was ruled by Esmeree the Blonde, Queen of Wales, but it was laid waste by two sorcerers named Mabon and Evrain. Gawain's son, Guinglain, traveled to the city and lifted the curse by killing the enchanters. [*Nennius*, *GeoffHR*, *Renaut*, *Layamon*, *Historia*]

SOBICIO

A land ruled by Andremo the Old, who married Arthur's sister. Meliadus, Tristan's father, became its ruler when he married Elyabel, Andremo's daughter. Meliadus appointed Sir Ferragunze as its viceroy. After Meliadus's death, its throne was assumed by an unnamed king later slain by Lancelot at Arthur's Leverzep tournament. Another king of Sobicio joined King Mark of Cornwall in his attack on Camelot. [*Tavola*]

SODOC

The son of Lamorat in *La Tavola Ritonda*. He inhabited the fortress of Sangranar with a knight named Broncone. He tried to steal Tristan's and Lancelot's horses during the Grail Quest, for which he was defeated in combat. [*Tavola*]

SOISSONS [*Sessoine, Siesia, So(is)sie, Suize*]
A valley and town in northern France, about fifty miles northeast of Paris. In the Arthurian legends, it is the site of the final battle between Arthur and Lucius, Procurator or Emperor of Rome. Arthur learned of Lucius's advance through the valley and was waiting with his army. An epic battle ensued, in which many knights and kings, on both sides, were slain. Lucius himself was killed, and Arthur's forces were victorious. [*GeoffHR, Wace, Layamon, VulgMer, Allit, Malory*]

SOL
An Arthurian warrior who could stand all day on one foot. [*Culhwch*]

SOLINAS [*Salinas*]
A nephew of King Rions, in whose army Solinas fought against Arthur in Carmelide. [*VulgMer, Arthour*]

SOLOMON
According to the Vulgate *Queste del Saint Graal* and *Estoire del Saint Graal*, this biblical King of Israel learned that Galahad—the end of his lineage—would surpass all others in prowess and piety. Solomon, at the urging of his wife, decided to construct a magnificent ship in order to let Galahad know that his coming had been foretold. He bedecked the ship in all manner of splendor, placing within it a bed adorned with spindles from the Tree of Life in Eden. He also placed the sword of his father, King David, within the ship; this sword later became known as the Sword with the Strange Hangings and could only be wielded by the best knight in the world. Upon completion of the vessel, an inscription appeared on its hull warning the unfaithful from boarding. Solomon, afraid, did not board, and the ship sailed out to sea. Mordrains and Nascien encountered it during their adventures, as did a number of other men, many of whom were punished for drawing the sword. During the Grail Quest, Galahad, Perceval, Bors, and Perceval's sister encountered the ship and boarded it. The ship eventually took the three Grail knights, with the Grail, to the ancient city of Sarras.

Analogs to the Ship of Solomon are known in early Celtic mythology. One is also found in the non-Arthurian lay of *Guigemar*. [*VulgQuest, VulgEst, PostQuest, Malory*]

SOLONA
A city in Brittany ruled by King Gilierchino, father of Isolde of the White Hands. It was besieged by Albroino, Gilierchino's nephew. Tristan joined the battle and killed Albroino. [*Tavola*]

SOLTANE
A secluded wilderness that was Perceval's homeland in Wolfram's *Parzival*. Herzeloyde, Perceval's mother, raised him in this desolate area to keep him away from any knowledge of knighthood, as Perceval's father had died in battle. In French romances, it is called the WASTE FOREST. [*Wolfram*]

SOLVAS
In a fragment of a twelfth-century French romance known as *Ilas et Solvas*, two companions named King Ilas of Ireland and King Solvas renounce their loyalty to Arthur and challenge him to combat. The result of these actions have not survived in the existing fragments. [*Ilas*]

SOMERSET
A county of southwest England on the Bristol Channel. According to Layamon, it was conquered by Cheldric in the early days of Arthur's reign, but Arthur later liberated it. Somerset is the possible location of the SUMMER COUNTRY and the SUMMER REGION, both mentioned in Welsh texts. [*Layamon*]

SOMIÉRE
Father of one of Arthur's Yvains in *Les Merveilles de Rigomer*. [*Merveil*]

SORBARES [*Sorbars*]
One of the many Saxon kings, named in the Vulgate *Merlin*, who invaded and plundered northern Britain at the beginning of Arthur's reign. The story first tells us that he was killed by Pharien at the second battle of Clarence; it later says that he was one of the few Saxons to survive the battle. The *Livre d'Artus* agrees that he was killed at Clarence, by Arthur's Sir Aces of Beaumont. [*VulgMer, Livre, Arthour*]

SORBORESTE
A heathen land ruled by King Verangoz, who was slain by Arthur's nephew Meleranz. [*PleierM*]

SORE PUCELLE OF THE WHITE FOREST
Niece of the Fisher King and cousin of Perceval. She sent the Grail Sword to the Fisher King's castle. She was besieged by Margon, the King with a Hundred Knights. Her knights captured Cargrilo, Margon's seneschal, hoping to trade him for Sore Pucelle's lover, the Lord of the White Land. When Margon killed Sore Pucelle's lover, Sore Pucelle put Cargrilo on a catapult and launched him to his death. Gawain eventually joined Sore Pucelle's forces and defeated Margon. Sore Pucelle then beseeched Gawain to avenge the death of her brother, Silimac, who had been murdered by Kay, and Gawain complied. [*ChretienP, Contin3*]

SOREDAMOR [*Surdamur*]
The daughter of Lot and sister of Gawain. Soredamor was one of Guinevere's servants. She fell in love with Alexander, a Greek warrior who visited Arthur's court. Alexander also became swiftly infatuated with Soredamor. Each was afraid to confess love for the other, but

Guinevere perceived their distress and brought them together. Soredamor and Alexander were married. They returned to Alexander's kingdom of Greece and Constantinople and had a son named Cliges. When Alexander died, Soredamor lived only a few more days before perishing from heartbreak. [*ChretienC*]

SORELOIS [*Soleyse, Sorailes, Sorenlois, Sureluse*]

The kingdom belonging to Sir Galehaut. It had once been ruled by King Loholt, who passed it on to his son Gloier. Galehaut then conquered it from Gloier. Loholt had designed its borders so that it could only be accessed by two perilous bridges—the Irish Bridge and the North Wales Bridge—which were partially submerged and had well-guarded towers at the end. Sorelois was said to lie between North Wales and the Distant Isles (possibly the Hebrides), and was separated from Britain by a strait called Assurne. This geography suggests an identification with Anglesey, the Isle of Man, or even Ireland. R. S. Loomis (*Tradition*, 453) identifies Sorelois with Sorgales (South Wales).

In the Post-Vulgate *Suite du Merlin* and in Malory, another King of Sorelois is one of five kings who invades Britain at the beginning of Arthur's reign and is slain by Arthur's forces at the battle of the Humber. Malory tells of a great Sorelois tournament in which prizes were awarded to Lancelot, Lamorat, Palamedes, and Bagdemagus. The Prose *Tristan* and Malory also gives the name "the Straits of Sorelois" to a fortress where Sir Brunor the Black (the Knight of the Ill-Fitting Cloak), assisted by Lancelot, completed his first quest by defeating six brothers named Playne de Amours, Playne de Fors, Plenorius, Pillounes, Pellogris, and Pellandris, and by liberating the castle of its prisoners. [*LancLac, VulgLanc, VulgMer, PostMer, ProsTris, Malory*]

SORESTAN

A land bordering on North Wales in the Vulgate *Lancelot*. Its queen was a friend of Morgan le Fay, and these two, along with Queen Sedile, once imprisoned Lancelot in Cart Castle, hoping to make him choose one of them as a lover. Its king had been slain by the Duke of Rocedon. The Count of Sorestan is listed among the knights at the Penning tournament. [*VulgLanc*]

SORGARDA

In Heinrich von dem Türlin's *Diu Crône*, a castle ruled by Lord Leigamar. Leigamar threw a tournament at Sorgarda, the winner of which would have the honor of marrying his daughter, Flursensephin. Many knights came to the tournament, including Flursensephin's favorite, Fiers of Arramis. Flursensephin's sister Quebeleplus entreated Gawain to defeat Fiers, however, and Gawain ended up winning the tournament. Since he had no desire to marry, he deferred the honor to his companion, Sir Quoikos. A similar tournament occurs at the city of BEAROSCHE in Wolfram's *Parzival*. [*Heinrich*]

SORGARIT

A knight who fought at the Sorgarda tournament, which Gawain won. His brother, the Count of Bigame, was also present. [*Heinrich*]

SORHALT [*Sorhaus, Sorhens*]

A Saxon king who served King Rions of Denmark, Arthur's enemy. Sorhalt joined Rions in an invasion of Carmelide, Leodegan's kingdom, and he led a battalion of soldiers against Arthur at the battle of Carhaix. [*VulgMer, Arthour*]

SORHAUT [*Schorham, Sorehaut, Sorhaute*]

A British city belonging to Galehaut in the Vulgate *Lancelot* and Urien in the Vulgate *Merlin*. In the latter, it was the capital of Gorre, and it served as a base of operations for the northern kings in their battles against the Saxons. *Lancelot* names it as the chief city of Sorelois. [*LancLac, VulgLanc, VulgMer, Arthour, Malory*]

SORIANO SEA

According to *La Tavola Ritonda*, the sea surrounding the island of Avalon. [*Tavola*]

SORIONDE [*Soriandes, Soriendos*]

A Saxon warrior. He accompanied his father, Maglahant, and his uncle, Mahaglant, to the Saxon invasion of Britain at the beginning of Arthur's reign. He plundered and burned Cornwall. His unit was defeated by Gawain and Yvain at the battle of Diana Bridge. Sorionde was eventually killed by Sir Alier in Malehaut. [*VulgMer, Livre, Arthour*]

SORLOUSE OF THE FOREST

A knight that Gawain encountered in his first quest. Sorlouse was fighting with his brother, Sir Brian of the Forest, over who would chase the hart that Gawain was pursuing. Gawain told them the hart quest was his, and they yielded quickly to him rather than fight him. Gawain sent the two brothers to King Arthur. [*Malory*]

SORNEGRIEU [*So(r)negre(o)ns, Sornegrex*]

A king from Ireland who served King Rions. During Rions's war with King Leodegan of Carmelide, Sornegrieu and Sapharin led the advance at the battle of Carhaix. In the battle, King Ban sliced off Sornegrieu's hand. Later, Sornegrieu participated in a siege at Clarence, where he was killed by the King with a Hundred Knights. [*VulgMer, Livre, Arthour*]

SORNEHAM

The lord of Newcastle. Agravain killed his brother, Druas the Cruel, for which Sorneham imprisoned both Agravain and Gareth. Gaheris defeated him and forced him to free his captives. [*VulgLanc*]

SORROWFUL FIEF

A small monastery in the forest of Beforet, ruled by King Iweret. The monks at the Sorrowful Fief disapproved of Iweret's murderous activities, but they could not deny that the wealth taken from the corpses of warriors slain by Iweret kept the monastery busy and prosperous. Lancelot lodged in the Sorrowful Fief before he fought Iweret in combat. [*UlrichZ*]

SORTIBRAN[1]

A Saxon warrior killed by King Ban of Benoic at the battle of Carhaix. [*VulgMer, Arthour*]

SORTIBRAN[2]

A knight killed by Gawain while trying to abduct a lady. [*VulgMer*]

SOTAIN HERBERT

An Irish castle that belonged to a lord named Robert, whose wife Agravain rescued from a band of marauders. [*Merveil*]

SOUENAS

Arthur's king of Orkney in the English *Arthur*. Orkney is usually represented as LOT's kingdom. [*Arthur*]

SOUMILLET [*Soumeillet, Soumilloit*]

Father of Arthur's knight Fergus. Although he was rich, and married to a noble-born woman, he raised his children as peasants and ploughmen. When Fergus announced his intention to leave their home country of Pelande for Arthur's court, Soumillet's angry fist was sustained only by his temperate wife. [*Guillaume*]

SOUTH MARCHES

The Duke of the South Marches hated Arthur and his knights because Gawain had killed one of his sons. When Arthur's Sir Marhaus happened upon the duke's castle, the duke forced him into combat with the duke's six sons. Marhaus defeated all of them and forced them to go to Arthur's court. [*Malory*]

SOUTH WALES [*Sorgales, Sugales, Surgenale, Sutgales*]

The lower part of Wales, including the kingdoms of DYFED and GLAMORGAN. In the chronicles, Merlin's maternal grandfather (called Conan by Layamon) is the king of South Wales. In the Vulgate *Merlin*, the country is ruled by Belinant, and Marie de France names it as Tristan's birthplace. Spenser names it as the kingdom ruled by Rions. [*GeoffHR, Wace, MarieC, VulgMer, Spenser*]

SPAIN [*Espa(in)gne, Spayn(e), Spyan*]

During the "Arthurian period," Spain was ruled by Visigoths. In the chronicles, Spain is under Roman control, and its king, Alifatima or Meodras, joins Lucius in the war against Arthur. In Wolfram's *Parzival*, it is ruled by King Kaylet. Der Pleier, in *Tandareis and Flordibel*, names Spain as one of Arthur's allies. In *Claris et Laris*, Spain is ruled by Savari and then Sir Claris.

Its most important role comes in the Icelandic *Saga af Tristram ok Ísodd*, where it is named as Tristan's homeland. It's king, Hlöövir, was slain during an invasion. Tristan's grandfather, Patrocles, took control, but was soon killed, leaving it to Kalegras, Tristan's father. Kalegras also died, and Tristan's foster-father, Biring, took the throne. Biring was expelled by a pirate king named Turnes. Eventually, Tristan re-conquered it and served as king until his death. [*GeoffHR, Wace, Layamon, VulgMer, PleierT, Claris, SagaTI, Malory*]

SPARROWHAWK

The name given to Sir Yder after his numerous victories in a SPARROWHAWK TOURNAMENT. [*TennIK*]

SPARROWHAWK TOURNAMENT

A type of tournament first mentioned in Chrétien de Troyes's *Erec*. In the stories that feature Erec or Geraint as the hero, the location of the tournament is variously given as Cardiff, Laluth, Tulmein, or Kanadic. The prize of the tournament was a sparrowhawk (or, in some versions, a kestrel or parrot), and it was supposed to go to the most beautiful lady present. If a dispute arose as to the fairest of the ladies at the tournament, the ladies' knights would fight in single combat until one of them resolved the conflict. As we are introduced to the Sparrowhawk Tournament in each of these stories, an injustice has arisen: a powerful knight has won the tournament several times in a row through force of arms, even though his lady is somewhat plain or manifestly ugly. It is the job of the hero of the story to right this injustice by defeating the knight and awarding the sparrowhawk to the most worthy woman.

In *Erec* and its adaptations, the hero comes across the tournament during his pursuit of the insolent Sir Yder, who, coincidentally, is also the unrighteous victor of the previous tournaments. Erec (or Geraint) "borrows" Enide so that he can enter the tournament and fight Yder. Erec is victorious, and he awards the sparrowhawk to Enide, with whom, in the meantime, he has fallen in love.

In sparrowhawk stories that do not feature Erec or Geraint, the hero of the story generally comes across a weeping lady who should have won the tournament, but was robbed of the distinction by the unjust knight. In Renaut de Bâgé's *Le Bel Inconnu*, Guinglain champions the lady Margerie against the lord Girflet at the castle of Becleus. In Wirnt von Grafenberg's *Wigalois*, Wigalois presents the lady Elamie with the sparrowhawk after defeating Count Hojir of Mannesvelt. In the French *Durmart le Gallois*, Sir Durmart wins the tournament for Queen Fenise of Ireland at the city of Landoc. In *Edolanz*, Sir Edolanz wins such a tournament at Arthur's court. In *Le Chevalier du Papegau*, Arthur wins the tournament in the name of the Lady Without Pride, fighting the

Merciless Lion at the castle of Causuel (in *Papegau*, the prize of the tournament is a magical parrot, which accompanies Arthur on his further adventures). Variations of sparrowhawk tournaments appear in Andreas Capellanus's *De Amore* at Arthur's court, in Raoul de Houdenc's *Meraugis de Portlesguez* at Lindesores, and in the Vulgate *Lancelot* at Mill Castle. Since Andreas and Chrétien, the earliest sparrowhawk writers, both wrote in the court of Marie de Champagne, the theme may have originated there. [*ChretienE, HartmannE, Andreas, Renaut, Wirnt, Raoul, VulgLanc, Durmart, Edolanz, ChevPap*]

SPECKLED KNIGHT

A knight of Arthur's court defeated by the Great Fool. [*IrishF*]

SPECKLED OX

An enigmatic beast mentioned in the Welsh poem *The Spoils of Annwn*. It is unclear if the ox had any connection with Arthur. A Triad names the Speckled Ox as one of the "three prominent oxen" of Britain. It may be related to the SPOTTED OX from *Culhwch and Olwen*. [*Spoils*]

SPINOZA

A forest near Joyous Guard, Lancelot's castle. [*Tavola*]

SPIRITUAL PALACE

A palace in Sarras, where Joseph of Arimathea and his followers lodged during their visit. It had been named by Daniel the Prophet. God named Josephus the first Christian bishop in the palace. The Grail Knights visited it at the end of the Grail Quest. Galahad died and was buried there alongside Perceval's sister, and Perceval himself was later interred there. [*VulgEst, PostQuest*]

SPOLETTO [*Spolet(t)(o)*]

A central Italian city that was one of many to surrender and send tribute to King Arthur after he had captured the city of Rome. [*Allit, Malory*]

SPOTTED DUN

A horse belonging to Arthur's warrior Rhyawdd. [*Triads*]

SPOTTED OX

An ox owned by Gwlwlwyd Chestnut Hair in *Culhwch and Olwen*. As one of his tasks, the warrior Culhwch had to obtain this ox and yoke it together with another of Gwlwlwyd's oxen, the Yellow Pale-White Ox. It may be related to the SPECKLED OX mentioned in *The Spoils of Annwn*. [*Culhwch*]

SPRING OF HEALING

A magical spring in the Forest of Serpents that healed all who drank from it. It was formed when Nascien, a follower of Joseph of Arimathea, stuck his lance into the ground prior to a battle with the evil King Camalis. It

flowed next to the Giant's Tower, and Sir Atamas, also called the Knight of the Spring, ruled them both. Atamas used the power of the spring to defeat any knight who came along: he drank from it in mid-combat, thus invigorating himself while his opponent remained weak. In this manner, he defeated and imprisoned Gawain and many other knights in the Giant's Tower. Palamedes ended the practice by defeating Atamas despite the power of the spring. [*PostQuest*]

SPRING OF MARVELS

A magic spring where Erec defeated Mordred. Its enchantments were ended by Galahad. [*PostMer*]

SPRING OF THE PINE

A spring in a northern forest, at which Hector out-jousted Sagremor, Kay, Girflet, and Yvain. [*LancLac, VulgLanc*]

SPRING OF THE VIRGIN

An enchanted fountain. At the tempting of a devil, a knight named Nabor tried to rape his sister, Aglinda, alongside the spring. The maiden prayed, Nabor was struck dead, and the spring was named in remembrance of the incident. Afterwards, it had the power to paralyze any non-virgin knight who happened along. Erec was frozen in this manner during the Grail Quest. Some maidens found him and lifted him away, restoring his freedom of movement. [*PostQuest*]

SPRING OF TWO SYCAMORES

A spring guarded by Belyas the Black until Lancelot defeated him in combat . [*VulgLanc*]

SPUMADOR

The name given by Spenser to Arthur's horse. [*Spenser*]

STANES

A duke present at the wedding of Erec and Enide. His brother was named Stenes. [*Erex*]

STATER [*Sater*]

King of the Demetians. According to Geoffrey of Monmouth, he served King Arthur. Geoffrey apparently took his name from Welsh mythological genealogies (Fletcher, 76). [*GeoffHR, Wace, Layamon*]

STATUANO

A sculptor in Brittany who created a statue of Isolde for Tristan. The sculpture was so perfect that Tristan knighted the artist and gave him the city of Gippa. [*Tavola*]

STEAMING PATH

A perilous trial, misted by scorching water, on which Arthur's knights had to travel from the Shrieking Marsh to the Misty Lake in order to enlist the assistance of the wizard Malduc. [*UlrichZ*]

STENES

A nobleman in Arthur's service, present at the wedding of Erec and Enide. His brother was Duke Stanes. [*Erex*]

STEVEN

An Arthurian knight. [*Marriage*]

STIPORT

A knight present at the tournament of Sorgarda, which Gawain won. [*Heinrich*]

STIRLING

A castle in Central, Scotland that was one of Arthur's courts in Béroul's *Tristan*. [*Beroul*]

STONE OF HONOR

An enchanted site in Britain, perhaps in Wales. It was big enough for several people to sit on, but "would not endure a man in whom was falseness or malice." Ginover (Guinevere), Gawain, and Lancelot all managed to pass the test of the stone. [*UlrichZ*]

STONE OF THE GIANT [*Perron de la Jaiande*]

With this boulder, Meliadus, Tristan's father, compared his strength with that of a giant. When Meliadus was able to lift the stone, he crushed the giant with it. Tristan was the only other knight able to heft the Stone of the Giant. When Lancelot tried, he failed. [*Palamedes*]

STONE OF THE STAG [*Perron du Cerf*]

A block of marble in the Plessis Wood. An inscription on the Stone of the Stag stated that marvels of the Holy Grail could be seen on the site, but that any knight—save Galahad—who stayed to see them would regret it. Yvain decided to brave the adventure anyway, and awoke the next morning to find himself wounded and his two companions slain. [*PostMer*]

STONEHENGE

A standing-stone monument (megalith) arranged in a circle on Salisbury Plain, probably erected during the Neolithic period. It was once thought that Stonehenge was a Druid temple, but the Druids were not active until about the third century before Christ. In its original inception, it may have been an astronomical observatory, but its architecture was modified considerably between its creation and about 1500 B.C. According to Geoffrey of Monmouth, who calls the megalith the GIANT'S DANCE, Merlin brought Stonehenge from Mount Killarus in Ireland to Britain at the request of King Ambrosius. Other chronicles tell a similar story. Merlin accomplished the transportation of the stones either through feats of engineering, through feats of engineering combined with magic, or through magic alone. On legend holds that Merlin moved the stones with music. Likely, there were numerous local legends describing the origin of the megalith, and Geoffrey simply attached one of them to Merlin. [*GeoffHR*, *Wace*, *ProsMer1*]

STONY PASS

A mountain pass on the road to Gorre. Meleagant's knights guarded it, and Lancelot had to defeat them on his way to rescue Guinevere. [*VulgLanc*]

STRANGE CASTLE [*Chastel Estrange*]

A fortress where Dodinel and Gaswain lodged and healed after wounding each other in a joust. [*Palamedes*]

STRANGE ISLAND

A castle ruled by King Vagor, who once imprisoned Sir Lionel, Lancelot's cousin. [*VulgLanc*]

STRANGE LAND [*Terre Foraine*]

The enigmatic kingdom containing Corbenic, the Grail Castle. It was ruled in Joseph of Arimathea's time by King Calafes, and then by the line of Grail Kings, from Joshua to Pelles. (The Vulgate *Estoire del Saint Graal* says that the second Nascien was its king, but does not later name him as a Grail King.) After the Dolorous Stroke, it became part of the WASTE LAND. It may be identical to LISTENOIS, or it may be a land within that kingdom. In some passages, however, the "Strange Land" refers to the land of GORRE.

In the Vulgate *Mort Artu*, it is said to border on the White Land, which was ruled by Lancelot's grandfather. An unnamed knight from the Strange Land fought for Lancelot in his war against Arthur. This may be a different "Strange Land." [*VulgLanc*, *VulgEst*, *PostQuest*]

STRANGEDORZ OF VILLEGARUNZ

A lord once defeated in combat by Perceval. [*Wolfram*]

STRATHCLYDE

According to Sir Walter Scott's *The Bridal of Triermain*, Arthur promised this western Scottish kingdom to whichever knight married Gyneth, his daughter. In this sixth century, it was ruled by Rhydderch the Generous, who is connected to Merlin in Welsh legend. [*Scott*]

STRENNOLAS OF PICTACON

A duke once defeated in combat by Perceval. [*Wolfram*]

STRONG ROCK [*Rocca Forte*]

A mighty fortress on the edge of the Brown Valley, where Tristan and Lancelot encountered the legendary Segurant the Brown. [*Tavola*]

STYRIA

A duchy in what is now southeast Austria. Perceval's grandfather Gandin, the ruler of Anjou, appointed his daughter Lammire (Perceval's aunt) to rule this land. Lammire married Meleranz, who became king. [*Wolfram*, *PleierG*]

SUFFOLK

A region of eastern England. When Mordred seized the English throne, most of Suffolk allied with him. [*Malory*]

SUGYN ("Suck")

An Arthurian warrior who was the son of Sugynedydd. He could reportedly suck up a sea, leaving nothing but sand. [*Culhwch*]

SUGYNEDYDD ("Sucker")

Father of Arthur's warrior Sugyn. [*Culhwch*]

SUKSTÍA

A mountain in Ireland where Tristan slew a dragon. King Engres of Ireland had sworn that any knight who killed the dragon could marry Isolde. A vassal named Cæ the Courteous tried to claim credit for the battle but was exposed. [*SagaTI*]

SULPICIUS[1] [*Supplicius*]

The Pope during Arthur's time, who, according to Geoffrey, raised Gawain and gave him arms. *De Ortu Waluuanii* names him as a friend of Gawain's foster-father, Viamundus. An actual pope named St. Simplicius held the papacy between 468 and 483. [*GeoffHR*, *DeOrtu*]

SULPICIUS[2] SUBUCULUS

A Roman senator who became a war leader in Lucius's campaign against Arthur. He led a force of soldiers at the battle of Soissons. [*GeoffHR*]

SULTAN [*Soudan*]

The Didot-*Perceval* names "the Sultan" as an ally of the Emperor of Rome. He was slain by Gawain during the Roman War. The Roman Emperor was married to the Sultan's daughter. *Perceval* may be referring to the Sultan of SYRIA, who appears in Geoffrey of Monmouth's version. In one manuscript, he is called the AMIRAUT, or Emir. [*Didot*]

SULYEN [*Sulien*]

A warrior in Arthur's service, related to Arthur through Uther. He was the son of Iaen and the brother of Teregud, Bradwen, Moren, Siawn, and Caradawg. [*Culhwch*]

SUMMER COUNTRY

A land mentioned in Welsh legend, perhaps identical to the SUMMER REGION. Before the epic hunting of Twrch Trwyth, Arthur summoned all the warriors to the Summer Country. Speculation has placed this land near the Mediterranean or in SOMERSET. [*Culhwch*]

SUMMER REGION

The land ruled by King Melwas, Guinevere's abductor in Caradoc of Llancarfan's *The Life of St. Gildas*. As Glastonbury is said to be nearby, the Summer Region is probably SOMERSET. It may have some relation to the SUMMER COUNTRY of *Culhwch and Olwen*. [*Caradoc*]

SUPINABEL [*Syppynabylis*]

A Knight of the Round Table from Brittany, who brought news of Tristan's wedding to Isolde of the White Hands to Camelot, and news of Lancelot's anger towards Tristan back to Cornwall. [*VulgLanc*, *ProsTris*, *Malory*]

SURET

A castle belonging to Duke Escant of Cambenic. [*VulgMer*]

SURLAT

A region in France owned by Lancelot. Lancelot made Sir Sadoc the earl of Surlat in return for Sadoc's support in the battles against King Arthur. [*Malory*]

SURREY

A county in southeast England. When Mordred seized the throne of England, most of Surrey allied with him. [*Malory*]

SUSAVANT

A knight present at the tournament of Sorgarda, which Gawain won. [*Heinrich*]

SUSSEX [*Southsex*]

A region of England that borders the English Channel. It is located just south of the country of Kent. Its name indicates "South Saxons," as it was conquered by the Saxons in the sixth century. It was the site of the Castle Magance, where Alexander the Orphan was raised. When Mordred usurped Arthur's throne, most of Sussex allied with him. [*Malory*]

SUTERE

In the Alliterative *Morte Arthure*, the Sultan of Sutere participates in Lucius's war against Arthur. [*Allit*]

SWAGAR

A knight from Hungary, nearly killed by Sir Lionel, who mistakenly believed that Swagar had slain Lancelot. A maiden interrupted their duel and saved Swagar by promising to show Lancelot, alive, to Lionel. [*VulgLanc*]

SWALES

A corruption of WALES used by Gottfried von Strassburg in *Tristan*. Gottfried names Duke Gilan, a friend of Tristan, as the duke of Swales. [*Gottfried*]

SWEDEN [*Sweben, Swetherwike, Swethland*]

According to Der Pleier and the Alliterative *Morte Arthure*, Sweden was part of Arthur's kingdom. [*PleierT*, *Allit*]

SWIADOS

A Saxon warrior slain by Galescalain at a battle in Camelot. [*VulgMer*]

SWORD BRIDGE

A dangerous bridge that Lancelot had to cross to enter Gorre and rescue Queen Guinevere from Meleagant. The Sword Bridge and the Underwater Bridge served as the only two entrances to Gorre. The bridge was actually a sword—the length of two lances—stretched across a chasm, turned on its edge. Lancelot managed to cross, but wounded himself severely in the process. It was also known as the Perilous Bridge. [*ChretienC, VulgLanc*]

SWORD IN THE STONE

One of the most famous elements of the Arthurian legend, the Sword in the Stone theme first appears in the prose redactions of Robert de Boron's *Merlin*. King Uther Pendragon having died, apparently without an heir, the British lords gathered in Logres or London at the behest of the Archbishop of Canterbury to discuss the appointment of a new king. As if by magic, an enormous stone appeared in a churchyard. The stone had an anvil on top of it, in which a magnificent sword was embedded. This sword is identical to EXCALIBUR in the prose versions of *Merlin*, but is a separate sword in the Post-Vulgate *Suite du Merlin* and in Malory. A message on the pommel of the sword read: "Whoso pulleth this sword out of this stone and anvil is rightfully-born king of all England." All knights present tried in vain to drawn the sword but it remained fixed in the stone despite their best efforts. Arthur arrived in Logres as the squire of Kay, his foster-brother, who was attending his first tournament. Kay forgot his own sword at the first joust, and sent Arthur to retrieve it. Arthur, unable to find it, wandered into the churchyard and found the Sword in the Stone. With the intention of taking it as a substitute for Kay's sword, Arthur drew it from the stone, unwittingly proving himself king of Britain. He had to repeat the feat several times to satisfy the lords present. In the versions in which the Sword in the Stone is *not* Excalibur, Arthur wields it for a while but breaks it during a combat with King Pellinore.

Another Sword in the Stone appears during the Grail Quest. This sword was called the Adventurous Sword. It had once belonged to Sir Balin the Savage, having been given to him by a lady from Avalon. After Balin's death, Merlin fitted it with a new pommel, shoved it into a block of marble, and floated it away on a river. At the beginning of the Grail Quest, it floated up to Camelot. The pommel read: "Never shall a man take me hence save only he by whose side I ought to hang, and he shall be the best knight of the world." Lancelot, Gawain, and Perceval all tried to draw the sword without success. Galahad soon arrived and took the weapon, placing it in an empty scabbard he had brought for that purpose. Galahad later disposed of it in favor of the Sword with the Strange Hangings.

The Sword-in-the-Stone motif is a subset of a larger theme which includes any instance of a knight drawing a weapon from a fixture in order to prove his skill or nobility. In *Perlesvaus*, for instance, Lancelot has to pull a spear from a pillar to survive the Castle of Griffins, and later must pull a bolt from a pillar in Arthur's hall. In *Meriadeuc*, Meriadeuc displays his valor by unbuckling a sword from the waist of Lady Lore of Cardigan. In Robert de Blois's *Beaudous*, Beaudous, Gawain's son, proves his right to marry Beaute by drawing the sword Honoree from its sheath. Finally, in the Post-Vulgate *Suite du Merlin*, Balin proves his prowess by drawing a sword from a sheath carried by a lady from Avalon. This theme is prevalent in classical mythology and may ultimately originate in the Greek tale of Thesus, who proved his paternity by removing his father's sword from under a stone. [*RobertBor], ProsMer1, VulgMer, PostMer, Malory*[

SWORD WITH THE STRANGE HANGINGS
[*Epee as Estranges Renges*]

A magnificent weapon that first appears in Chrétien de Troyes's *Perceval*. It was offered as a reward to anyone who could rescue the maiden besieged in the hill below Montesclaire. Gawain assumed the quest, and won the sword in the First Continuation of *Perceval*. The First Continuation tells us that the Sword had originally belonged to the Jewish patriot Judas Maccabeus. In Raoul de Houdenc's *Meraugis of Portlesguez* as well, Gawain embarks on an adventure to obtain the sword on the Island without a Name.

We learn the full story of the weapon in the Vulgate *Queste del Saint Graal*, in which it assumes the importance of the GRAIL SWORD from the earlier tales. It had once belonged to the biblical King David of Israel and Judah. It was known as the Sword of David. Upon David's death, it passed to his son King Solomon. The sword was adorned with precious jewels, and the crossguard was made of the ribs of two mythical beasts—the Papagustes and the Cortenans. It rested in a scabbard known as the Memory of Blood, made from Eden's Tree of Life, and covered with a serpent's skin. For all its glory, however, its girdle was made only from hemp.

King Solomon placed the sword upon the Ship of Solomon and sailed it out to sea. It was ordained on the pommel of the sword that only the best knight of the world should ever draw it, and many men fell fate to the sword when they tried to draw it themselves. The first was Nascien, who encountered the ship and the sword at the Turning Isle. He drew the sword and used it to slay a giant, for which Nascien was wounded through the thighs by a holy lance, and the sword was broken. King Mordrains later mended the weapon.

On another occasion, some time before Arthur, King Varlan of Wales used it to kill King Lambor of Listenois, the Grail King. This blow was called the Dolorous Stroke, and it turned Wales and Listenois into the Waste Land. Varlan fell dead upon returning the sword to its scabbard. In a third instance, King Pelles, another Grail King, drew the sword and also received a blow through the thighs with a spear. For this he became known as the Maimed King.

Its destined owner, Galahad, found it on the ship during the Grail Quest. Perceval's sister made a new girdle for the sword out of her own virgin's hair. R. S. Loomis thought that this exchange symbolized the replacement of the Old Testament with the New Testament (Loomis, *Romance*, 304). Galahad used it in several battles. Arthur later remarked that the magnificence of Excalibur was second only to the Sword with the Strange Hangings.

According to *La Tavola Ritonda*, the Sword with the Strange Hangings was left hanging around the statue of Galahad in front of the castle of Leverzep. Hundreds of years later, Charlemagne took it from the statue and renamed it Gioisa. In other tales, its fate goes unmentioned. [*ChretienP, Contin1, Raoul, VulgQuest, VulgMort, VulgEst, PostQuest, Malory*]

SWORD WITH THE TWO RINGS

A magic sword that Gawain needed to exchange with King Wonder for the magic Floating Chessboard. It was in the possession of King Amoren, who gave it to Gawain on the condition that Gawain find and bring him the lady Ysabele. The sword ensured victory for anyone who wielded it. [*Penninc*]

SWYNNE

A land named as part of Arthur's empire. [*Allit*]

SWYWON

A companion of Arthur named in an early Welsh poem. [*WelshPG*]

SYFWLCH

Son of Cleddyf Cyfwlch and brother of Cyfwlch and Bwlch. Syfwlch was one of Arthur's warriors. He had a sword named Gleisyad, a dog named Cabal, a horse named Llwyrddyddwg, a wife named Diasbad, a grandchild named Eissywed, a daughter named Gwaethaf Oll, and a maid named Gwaeddan. He was needed by Culhwch, as one of his tasks, to help hunt the boar Twrch Trwyth. [*Culhwch*]

SYMOUND THE VALIANT

A vassal of Galehaut who fought at the tournament of Sorelois. [*Malory*]

SYNOS

A Saxon king who, under King Hargadabran, fought Arthur's forces at the battle of Clarence. [*Livre*]

SYRIA [*Surie*]

The Vulgate *Estoire del Saint Graal* tells us that in Joseph of Arimathea's time, Syria was ruled by Count Felix, and then by King Fanoyel. From Geoffrey of Monmouth, we learn that in Arthur's time, its king, Evander, joined Rome in the war against Arthur and was killed. In Wirnt von Grafenberg's *Wigalois*, Syria is a mountain-enclosed land that can only be entered with a magical belt. Florie, the princess of Syria, becomes Gawain's wife and the mother of Wigalois. Rulers in other texts are given as Tholomé, Natalon, or Nadus. Jean D'Outremeuse, in *Ly Myreur des Histors*, says that Arthur conquered it. According to *Palamedes*, the first inhabitants of Britain—the maiden Albion and her companions—came from Syria, which was ruled at the time by King Diodicias. [*GeoffHR, Wace, Wirnt, Contin4, Palamedes, Floriant, Claris, Jean, Allit, Malory*]

T

TABLE OF ERRANT COMPANIONS
[*Compaignons Errans]
One of the three tables in Arthur's court. The knights of the Table of Errant Companions sought adventures and awaited promotion to the Round Table. Lower than the Table of Errant Companions was the Table of Less-Valued Knights. [PostMer]

TABLE OF LESS-VALUED KNIGHTS
[*Chevaliers Moins Prisiés]
The lowest of Arthur's knightly orders, composed of old, weak, ill, cowardly, or inexperienced knights who did not seek adventures. A rank above the Table of Less-Valued Knights was the Table of Errant Companions. Perceval was originally a Less-Valued Knight before he was more properly seated at the Round Table. [PostMer]

TABRIOL
The homeland of a knight named Cadoc, who was saved by Erec. It is probably a variation of CARDUEIL. [HartmannE]

TADEUS
A knight in Arthur's service who was the son of Reis. [Arthur]

TAILLARS
A knight who fought for the King with a Hundred Knights against King Mark of Cornwall during Mark's tournament at Lancien. [Contin4]

TALIESIN [Talgesin, Taliessin, Talyessin, Teliesin, Thelgesinus]
A famous sixth-century bard from northern Britain who traveled widely. He may have lived at the court of Kings Urien and Owain of Rheged. Several poems attributed to Taliesin survive in *The Book of Taliesin* and other sources, though it is unclear how many of these are authentic. Many of them glorify the lives and lament the deaths of Urien and Owain. He is first connected (anachronistically) to Arthur in *The Spoils of Annwn*, in which Arthur travels to the Welsh otherworld and obtains a magic cauldron. Taliesin, the supposed author of the poem, is one of only seven warriors who survived the expedition. A similar fate befalls him in the non-Arthurian Welsh tale of *Branwen*, in which he is one of seven to survive King Bran the Blessed's conquest of Ireland. In *Culhwch and Olwen*, he is Arthur's "chief bard." The Welsh Triads given him a son named Afaon.

Geoffrey of Monmouth makes him a friend of Merlin and tells us that Taliesin and Merlin took Arthur's body to Avalon after the battle of Camlann. Taliesin came to Merlin's assistance when Merlin went insane and roamed the forest of Caledon. After Merlin was healed, Taliesin remained with him in Caledon.

Taliesin is unknown to Medieval romance, but in Thelwall's *The Fairy of the Lake* and Tennyson's *Idylls*, he resumes his *Culhwch* role as Arthur's chief bard. [Spoils, Culhwch, Nennius, GeoffVM, Triads, Thelwall, TennIK]

TALLAS
King of Denmark and son of King Saladin. He besieged King Urien because he wanted to marry Marine, Urien's daughter. Arthur's knights, led by Claris and Laris, lifted the siege, and Arthur killed Tallas. [Claris]

TALLIDÉS OF THE MARSH [Callidés]
A lord who besieged the Castle of Maidens because he wanted to marry one of the maidens, which the castle's lady refused to allow. Sagremor, championing the castle, fought him in single combat, and Tallidés lost. When he declared his great love for the maiden, however, the lady of the castle relented and the two were wed. [Contin3]

TALLIS
A castle owned by Beauté, *amie* of Beaudous. When Lord Madoines invaded Beautés lands, he besieged Tallis. [RobertBlo]

TALLWCH [Trallwch]
Tristan's father in Welsh legend. An actual king named Talorch, father of Drust, ruled the Picts in the late eighth century. [Triads, Dream, TrisFrag]

TALUS
A man made from iron who became the squire of the knight Artegall. [Spenser]

TAMAR [Tambre]
A river in Cornwall. In Layamon, Arthur fights his final battle with Mordred at Camelford on the Tamar River. Geoffrey of Monmouth calls the location CAMEL, and in Welsh sources, the conflict is called the battle of CAMLANN. [Layamon, Mannyng]

TAMPANIS
Chief squire of Perceval's father Gahmuret. He accompanied Gahmuret on his adventures through Africa

and to Wales, and had the unfortunate duty of informing Gahmuret's wife, Queen Herzeloyde, that Gahmuret had been killed. [*Wolfram*]

TAMPENTEIRE

Father of Condwiramurs, who became Perceval's wife. Tampenteire ruled the land of Brobarz, which he left to his daughter. He had a son named Kardeiz. He was the brother of Kyot and Manpfilyot and the brother-in-law of Gornemant. [*Wolfram*]

TANABOS THE ENCHANTER [*Tanaburs*]

A necromancer who lived in Britain some time between the time of Joseph of Arimathea and Uther Pendragon. He was hailed as the greatest magician ever to reside on the island, save Merlin. To keep a knight from reaching his unfaithful wife, who lived at Corbenic, Tanabos enchanted the Grail Castle in such a way that it could only be found by accident. The enchantment lasted until the time of Charlemagne, who razed Corbenic. [*PostQuest, ProsTris*]

TANADAL

A Knight of the Round Table from Camelot who was killed during the Grail Quest. His brothers were named Alma and Luzes. [*PostQuest*]

TANAGUIN [*Tanaguins, Thanaguis*]

One of the knights in the Vulgate *Mort Artu* who joined Agravain's plan to capture Lancelot and Guinevere *in flagrante* in Guinevere's chambers. He harbored an unexplained hate for Lancelot. He was the first to be killed by Lancelot outside Guinevere's room. In Malory, AGRAVAIN himself takes this distinction. Gawain once assisted a friend of Tanaguin's in the Castle of the Mill tournament. [*VulgLanc, VulgMort*]

TANAS

An evil knight who killed his son, Danor, in order to sleep with his daughter-in-law. To protect himself from witnesses, he also killed his own daughter, on whom Arthur had fathered Arthur the Less. [*PostQuest*]

TANBRUNS LE PREUS

One of several Irish robber knights defeated by Lancelot on his way to Rigomer castle in *Les Merveilles de Rigomer*. [*Merveil*]

TANCREE THE LITTLE

Niece of the king of Escavalon or of Arthur. She married Sir Guinganbresil. [*Contin1*]

TANDAREIS

Hero of Der Pleier's *Tandareis and Flordibel*. The son of King Dulcemar and Queen Antikonie of Tandernas, Tandareis went to Arthur's court as a youth and served as a page. Arthur assigned him to Flordibel, one of Guinevere's maidservants, and over the course of ten years, Tandareis and Flordibel fell deeply in love. Arthur had sworn to kill any man who won Flordibel's love, so the two lovers fled to Tandernas, which Arthur subsequently besieged. After several battles in which Tandareis proved his knightly skill, Dulcemar and Gawain managed to convince Arthur to declare peace. Still angry at Tandareis's offense, Arthur banished him from his court into foreign lands so that Tandareis could establish honor through adventure. Tandareis embarked on a series of quests, during which he liberated the lands of Malmontan and Mermin from the evil giant Karedoz, saved a queen named Albiun from a knight named Kurion, rescued the maiden Claudin from Count Kalubin, and was imprisoned by a malevolent knight named Kandalion. During his imprisonment, he was kept alive by Antonie, Kandalion's sister, who let him out three times so that he could attend tournaments at Arthur's court. Kandalion released him when he learned that Arthur—who had heard of Tandareis's adventures and wanted him back—was offering a substantial reward for news of Tandareis. Tandareis returned to Arthur's court in glory and, after some complications in which Claudin and Antonie both claimed the right to wed him, Tandareis and Flordibel were married. Tandareis graciously bestowed Malmontan and Mermin on his parents, but stayed to rule them as steward and heir. [*PleierT*]

TANDERNAS

The homeland and castle of Tandareis, hero of Der Pleier's *Tandareis and Flordibel*. Ruled by Tandareis's parents, King Dulcemar and Queen Anticoni, it was besieged by Arthur to avenge an offense committed by Tandareis. Dulcemar and Gawain managed to negotiate a peace. The kingdom is first mentioned by Wolfram von Eschenbach in the non-Arthurian *Willehalm*. [*PleierT*]

TANE

One of many ladies at Arthur's court to fail a chastity test involving a magic goblet. [*Heinrich*]

TANGLED WOOD

The fortress occupied by King Valerin. Valerin kidnapped Guinevere and brought her back to the Tangled Wood. The fortress—which is reminiscent of an otherworldly location—was set high upon a mountain, and was cordoned by a tangle of brambles, branches, and snakes that kept out everyone. Arthur could not break the defenses, and only an intervention by the grand wizard Malduc could undo the magic wall. [*UlrichZ*]

TANGWEN

A lady at Arthur's court who was the daughter of Gweir Servitor of Birds. [*Culhwch*]

TANKANIS

Father of the Saracen lord Isenhart. [*Wolfram*]

TANNINGS [*Channing, Taningues*]

A castle near the Severn river, ruled by Duke Brandeban, a friend of Sir Sagremor. Tannings was also the home of Helain, a squire who was knighted by Gawain, and of Alier. [*LancLac, VulgLanc, Livre*]

TANRI

A Knight of the Round Table, related to Lancelot, who participated in the Grail Quest. [*PostQuest*]

TANRÉE

Sister of the Little Knight, a friend of Gawain. She fell in love with Gawain and became his paramour. [*Contin2*]

TANTALIDES

A scribe from Vercelli who served Arthur and recorded the deeds of the Knights of the Round Table. [*VulgLanc*]

TANTALIS

Wife of Alexander (emperor of Constantinople) and mother of Alis and Alexander. Her son Alexander served Arthur for a brief time. [*ChretienC*]

TANTRIST [*Tantris, Tramtrist, Tremtrist*]

An alias adopted by TRISTAN on his visit to Ireland, when he met Isolde. He used the alias so that he would not be recognized as the killer of Morholt, the king's brother-in-law. In some versions, he goes to Ireland to be healed of a poisoned wound received from Morholt. In others, he uses the name PRO on this first visit and "Tantrist" on his second, when searching for a wife for King Mark. Gottfried says that "Tantrist" killed a dragon and thus was forgiven by the royal family, even after Isolde (or her mother) matched the metal fragment found in Morholt's skull to the missing piece of "Tantrist's" sword and discovered the deception. In one source, Tristan is given the alias by Rohand, his tutor, to protect him from Duke Morgan, who killed his father. In others, Tristan adopts the name a second time when disguised as a madman in Cornwall. [*FolieB, FolieO, Eilhart, Gottfried, ProsTris, SirTris, Malory*]

TARABEL [*Terrabyl*]

A Cornish castle. Malory assigns it the role given to DIMILOC by Geoffrey of Monmouth: the castle fortified by the Duke of Cornwall when he went to war with Uther Pendragon (the duke defended Tarabel while placing his wife in Tintagel). When Uther abandoned the siege to enter Tintagel, the duke rode out of Tarabel and was promptly slain by Uther's soldiers. After Arthur became king, King Rions and his brother Nero besieged the castle as part of their campaign against Arthur. Sir Balin captured Rions, and Arthur defeated Nero's army at Tarabel, killing Nero and Lot in the battle. Merlin effected this victory by distracting Lot with a wondrous tale, causing him to enter the battle too late. [*PostMer, Malory*]

TARAN

Father of Arthur's warrior Glinyeu. [*Culhwch*]

TARAQUIN

A castle which was forced, annually, to turn over a dozen maidens to a horrible giant named Aupatris. Gaheris, Gawain's brother, killed the giant and ended the wicked custom. The people of Taraquin erected a monument to the battle; this monument was later destroyed by the sons of Mordred. [*VulgLanc*]

TARAWG

A warrior in Arthur's service from the city of Dumbarton. He was killed at Cwm Cerwyn by the boar Twrch Trwyth. [*Culhwch*]

TAREDD

Father of Twrch Trwyth, an enchanted boar pursued by Arthur in Welsh legend. [*Culhwch*]

TARQUIN

One of Guinevere's messengers. [*VulgLanc*]

TARRABEL

A castle in the land of King Evalach (Mordrain) of Sarras. [*VulgEst*]

TARSAN

Brother of King Bagdemagus of Gorre and nephew of King Urien. Tarsan joined Arthur's war against King Meliadus of Lyonesse. He engaged in combat with Melian, Meliadus's nephew, and the two knights killed each other. [*Palamedes*]

TARSENA

A rich city given to Largina by King Esclabor, her lover. [*Tavola*]

TARSENESYDE

The wife of Licorant and mother of Enide. She lived with her husband in the town of Laluth until Erec married Enide and gave them two castles. [*ChretienE*]

TARSIN

Father of Arthur's Sir Seguarades. Tarsin's wife had a brief affair with Morholt of Ireland. [*Palamedes*]

TARSUS

A city in southern Turkey, near the Mediterranean Sea. It was the birthplace of Hermoine the Hermit, who lived in the time of Joseph of Arimathea. During Arthur's days, it was part of the Roman Empire, and soldiers from Tarsus joined Emperor Lucius's war against Arthur. [*VulgEst, Malory*]

TARTARY [Tartare]

A medieval name for China. According to the Alliterative *Morte Arthure*, Tartary joined Lucius the Roman in his war against Arthur. [*Allit, Malory*]

TARTURIALE

A great giant slain by Morholt. Morholt took his sword, which he later gave to Tristan. [*Tavola*]

TATAIN

Son of Pharien and brother of Anguin. He was raised by the Lady of the Lake and knighted by Sir Lionel. [*VulgLanc*]

TATHAL HONEST DECEITFUL

An Arthurian warrior. [*Culhwch*]

TAUBARINS

King of the Tartars who served Emperor Filimenis of Constantinople. He joined Filimenis in a brief war against Arthur. [*Floriant*]

TAULAT[1] [Taul(l)as]

An evil knight who barged into Arthur's court, killed one of Arthur's knights in front of Guinevere, and promised to return every year to do the same. Arthur's knight Jaufré tracked Taulat down and avenged the insult by killing him. [*Jaufre*]

TAULAT[2] [Caulas]

A giant who terrorized Cornwall. Tristan, who had gone insane, came upon Taulat in the process of killing a knight named Dynaunt. Tristan beheaded the giant. Taulat's brother, Taulurd, had previous been slain by Sir Marhaus. [*ProsTris, Malory*]

TAULAT[3] OF ROUGEMONT [Caulas, Talac, Tallac, Taulas]

A vassal of Arthur who rebelled against the king in *Yder*. In response, Arthur besieged his castle of Rougemont. Sir Yder, who had become disillusioned with Arthur, joined Taulat and the defenders. During the battle, Yder was severely wounded by Kay. This wound dismayed both Arthur and Taulat so much that they reconciled and ended the battle. According to the Vulgate *Merlin*, Taulat was later killed by some Knights of the Round Table, prompting his uncle Helys to attack all knights. [*Yder*]

TAULAT[4] THE GREAT [Caulas, Kollas]

A Knight of the Round Table from Desert who held the title of duke. He fought in the Noauz tournament and was rescued from the Dolorous Prison by Lancelot. Envious of Lancelot's family, Taulat, his brother Senela, and his three cousins set upon Galahad during the Grail Quest. Taulat

was killed by Bleoberis in the battle. [*ChretienE, ChretienL, Contin1, LancLac, PostQuest, ProsTris*]

TAULURD

A giant who plagued the lands of Earl Fergus. Sir Marhaus, a Knight of the Round Table, agreed to deal with the monster. When Taulurd nearly killed Marhaus in combat, Marhaus changed his tactics and fled. Following Marhaus into a river, Taulurd became stuck in the mire. Marhaus stood on the shore with Fergus's men and threw stones at Taulurd's head until the giant died. Marhaus liberated prisoners from Taulurd's castle and made off with a large amount of treasure. Taulurd's brother, Taulas, was later killed by Tristan. [*Malory*]

TAURIAN THE WILD

Brother of Arthur's Sir Dodinel the Wild. He was a friend of Perceval's hermit uncle, Trevrizent. Perceval came across one of his lances, abandoned near Treverizent's abode, and took it. [*Wolfram*]

TAUROC

A castle owned by Arthur. [*VulgMort*]

TAURUS[1]

A Saxon king involved in the plundering of Arundel and the kidnapping of Gawain's mother, Belisent. He later encountered Gawain's forces, and Gawain's brothers literally diced him. [*VulgMer, Arthour*]

TAURUS[2]

A Saxon warrior slain by Gaheris in a skirmish at Camelot. [*VulgMer, Arthour*]

TAURUS[3]

A king in the service of Rions, Arthur's enemy. [*VulgMer*]

TEGAU GOLD-BREAST

A lady at Arthur's court in the Welsh Triads. She possessed an enchanted mantle which, when worn by a woman, would tell if she was faithful or adulterous by appearing, respectively, a perfect fit or too short. Such mantles are used in CHASTITY TESTS throughout Arthurian romance. [*Triads*]

TEGFAN THE LAME

An Arthurian warrior in Welsh legend. [*Culhwch*]

TEGID

Father of Morfran and grandfather of Myrddin. [*Culhwch, Dream*]

TEGYR CUP BEARER

An Arthurian warrior. [*Culhwch*]

TEIFI

A river in west Wales. Vortigern's fortress was situated on the river. [*Nennius*]

TEILO [*Teliau*]

A legendary Welsh Saint. In the *Life of St. Cadoc*, he joins St. David and St. Cadoc in mediating a dispute between Arthur and Ligessauc, in which Arthur agreed to accept payment of 100 cows in return for the deaths of three of his knights at Ligessauc's hands. According to Geoffrey of Monmouth, Teilo was a priest from Llandaff who Arthur appointed as the Archbishop of Dol after Samson, the previous archbishop, left the post. [*SaintsCad, GeoffHR*]

TEIRNON TWRFLIANT

An Arthurian warrior who ruled Gwent Ys Coed. [*Culhwch*]

TEIRTU

The owner of a magical harp that could play by itself. As one of his tasks, Culhwch had to obtain this harp for Olwen's wedding feast. [*Culhwch*]

TEIRWAEDD ("Three Cities")

Father of Arthur's warrior Menw. [*Culhwch, Dream*]

TEITHI THE OLD

An Arthurian warrior who was the son of Gwynnan. According to the legend, the sea flooded Teithi's kingdom and he had to flee to Arthur's court. He was cursed in a manner by which no hilt would remain attached to the blade of his knife. He eventually fell sick and died. [*Culhwch*]

TEITHYON

Father of Arthur's warrior Madawg. [*Culhwch*]

TELERI

A lady at Arthur's court who was the daughter of Peul. [*Culhwch*]

TELITE

An abbey visited by Lancelot, also called the Abbey of the SMALL CHARITY. [*VulgLanc*]

TEMPLARS

The name given by Wolfram to the order of knights assigned to the Grail Castle and commanded by the Grail King. Although they share the same name as the religious-military order established among the crusaders in the twelfth century, no connection should probably be inferred. In the Alliterative *Morte Arthure*, a Templar informs Arthur of the abduction of the duchess of Brittany by the giant of Mont St. Michel. [*Wolfram, Allit*]

TEMPLE OF THE SUN

The most splendid temple in King Evalach's Sarras. It contained the Seat of Judgment and was visited by Joseph of Arimathea and his followers. [*VulgEst*]

TENEBROC [*Daneborc, Taneborc, Taneburgh, Tarebron, Tenabroc*]

A British city in Chrétien's *Erec* at which Arthur called a tournament after the wedding of Erec and Enide. Erec carried the day at the tournament. Wolfram gives the name Clarischanze to the countess of Tenebroc. The name is a French variation of EDINBURGH. It was the location of a tournament in the latter days of Arthur's reign, mentioned in the Vulgate *Mort Artu*. Lancelot was unable to attend because of a wound. Malory places the same tournament at CAMELOT or WINCHESTER. [*ChretienE, HartmannE, Wolfram, VulgMort*]

TENESON

A city ruled by Duke Bramante, a friend of Tristan and ally of Tristan's father. [*Tavola*]

TENUANTIUS

According to Geoffrey of Monmouth, a king of Britain in the first century BC. He was the son of King Lud and the brother of Androgeus. Tenuantius succeeded his uncle, Cassibelaunus, to the throne, having previously been the duke of Cornwall. During his reign, Britain was under Roman rule. Tenuantius was succeeded by his son, Cymbeline. [*GeoffHR*]

TERDELASCHOYE

The fairy wife of Mazadan in Wolfram's *Parzival*. She and her husband were ancestors of both Perceval and Arthur—through their sons Lazaliez and Brickus, respectively. Terdelaschoye came from the mountain of Feimurgan. In creating this name, Wolfram has reversed the elements of the name *Feimurgan de Terdelaschoye*, or MORGAN LE FAY of Terre de la Joie. [*Wolfram*]

TEREGUD

An Arthurian warrior who was the son of Iaen and the brother of Sulyen, Bradwen, Moren, Siawn, and Caradawg. He was related to Arthur. [*Culhwch*]

TERICAM [*Tarquin(e), Teriquam, Terrican*]

Lord of the Impenetrable Forest (also called Terique) and the Castle of the Thorn. Tericam was a giant, cruel knight who captured and imprisoned many good knights, including Hector and Lionel. His usual routine involved stripping them naked, throwing them into his dungeon, and periodically beating them with thorns. He hated Lancelot, who had killed Tericam's brother, Caradoc of the Dolorous Tower. Lancelot eventually slew him and freed his prisoners. Tericam's father is given in one source as Mitrides. [*VulgLanc, Palamedes, Livre, Malory, SirLanc*]

TERIQUE

The forest inhabited by Tericam, a cruel knight slain by Lancelot. [*VulgLanc*]

TERRAGUEL

A castle. A Duke Conon, who originally owned it, gave it to two giants who had rescued him from a prison. The giants ruled in a cruel and tyrannical manner. Lancelot eventually killed them and became lord of the castle himself. [*VulgLanc*]

TERRAMUNT

Castle of Terrandes. It belonged first to the evil Godonas and then to Meleranz, Arthur's nephew. [*PleierM*]

TERRANDES

A land conquered by Meleranz, Arthur's nephew, from the evil knight Godonas. Meleranz and Tydomie later ruled it as king and queen. Its castle was Terramunt. [*PleierM*]

TERRE DE LABUR

The country of the sorcerer Clinschor, whose spells cause Gawain some grief in Wolfram's *Parzival*. In *Floriant et Florete*, it is visited by the title characters during their adventures. It refers to Terra di Lavoro in Italy. [*Wolfram, Floriant*]

TERRE MARVEILE ("Land of Marvels")

A land in which the Schastel Marveile (Castle of Marvels) was situated. In Wolfram's *Parzival*, Gawain braved an adventure at the castle and won the land for himself, an episode that Chrétien de Troyes places in GALLOWAY. Der Pleier names Terre Marveile as Gawain's castle in Logres. [*Wolfram, PleierG*]

TERRE SALVÆSCHE

The "wild land" in which the Grail Castle, Munsalvæsche, was located in Wolfram's *Parzival*. [*Wolfram*]

TERWIN

An unfortunate knight who was talked into killing himself by the monster Despair. Terwin's companion, Trevisan, escaped. [*Spenser*]

TESCHELARZ

A prince of Poitou. His son, Liodarz, was saved from robbers by Arthur's Sir Tandareis. [*PleierT*]

TESSELINE

A castle in Galehaut's kingdom. [*VulgLanc*]

TESSINA

A lady encountered by Tristan and Dinadan in the forest of Cerveroiche. Her father was named Federon the Red. A knight named Pinabel fell in love with her, and her mother made Pinabel kill his own brother, Uriées (who had killed Tessina's uncle, Garionne) as a condition of marriage. This sparked a war with Pinabel's other brothers and sister that led to Pinabel's death and to a death sentence for Tessina. She was captured by Pinabel's brothers at the Fountain of Valesca. Tristan arrived at the Ancient Tower where Tessina's sister-in-law, Losanna, intended to execute her. Tristan defended her, slaying the brothers and freeing her. Dinadan, who felt that Tessina was deserving of death, broke with Tristan over this incident. Tessina was later slain at the Castle Crudele, for she was not as beautiful as the castle's lady. [*Tavola*]

TEUCER[1]

The King of Phrygia who served the Roman Procurator Lucius, and was called upon to join Lucius in the war against Arthur. He led a force of soldiers at the battle of Soissons. [*GeoffHR, Wace, Layamon*]

TEUCER[2]

A Saxon king who, under King Aminaduc, fought Arthur's forces at the battle of Vambieres. [*Livre*]

THABRONIT [*Tabronit*]

A "city of fabled wealth" in Heathendom that was the capital of Queen Secundille's country of Tribalibot. It was situated at the base of the Caucasus Mountains. Populated by Moors, it was known for its fine fabrics and horses. Queen Secundille gave throne to Perceval's half-brother, Feirefiz, out of love. [*Wolfram*]

THAILAIS [*Tahalais*]

Uther Pendragon's grandfather (and Arthur's great-grandfather), as given by Prose *Lancelot*. He ruled the city of Clarence near South Wales, and "Clarence" was thus Arthur's battle cry. [*LancLac, VulgLanc*]

THAMES

A river in south England, flowing east from Gloucestershire, through London, and into the North (Gallic) Sea. The Gay Castle stood on its banks. [*VulgLanc*]

THAMETES

Daughter of Lot, sister of Gawain, and mother of St. Kentigern in John Major's chronicle. [*Major*]

THANET [*Tanet*]

An island off the coast of England occupied by Hengist's Saxon forces during the times of King Vortigern. When the Saxons invaded England, King Vortigern's son, Vortimer, drove them back to Thanet and defeated many of them in subsequent battles. From here, they fled back to Europe to regroup. In Arthur's reign, Cheldric and the Saxons fled to Thanet after suffering a crushing defeat at the hand of Cador of Cornwall. [*Nennius, GeoffHR, Wace*]

THARMADAISE
A country ruled by Gosengos and governed by Nabunal. [*Livre*]

THASME
A metropolis in the country of Tribalibot, ruled by Queen Secundille (the lover of Perceval's half-brother Feirefiz). It was known for its fine fabrics, particularly those made by the master weaver Sarant. [*Wolfram*]

THEBES [*Thebay*]
A city in Egypt, allied, according to the Alliterative *Morte Arthure*, to Lucius the Roman. [*Allit*]

THEREUS
In *Claris et Laris*, a Roman emperor who demanded tribute from Arthur and invaded France when Arthur refused. Arthur's forces decimated Thereus's army—composed of rulers from around Europe, Asia, and Africa—and Thereus fled. He is obviously inspired by LUCIUS from the chronicles. [*Claris*]

THÉROUANNE [*Tervanna*]
A city in Flanders that served as the final resting place of King Holdin of Flanders after he was killed in the Roman war. [*GeoffHR*, *Wace*]

THESSALA
The servant of the lady Fenice, so named because she came from Thessaly in Greece. Thessala had skills at wizardry, and when Fenice—who was engage to be married to Alis, the Emperor of Constantinople and Greece—fell in love with Alis's nephew Cliges, she turned to Thessala for help. Thessala concocted a potion and had Cliges give it to Alis. The potion caused Alis, each night, to think he was making love to his wife when in fact he was sleeping. In this way, Fenice was able to preserve her virginity for Cliges. Thessala later created another potion that allowed Fenice to feign death and escape from Alis. [*ChretienC*]

THIEBAUT OF WINDEN [*Tibaut*]
A Slavic knight who was killed by Mabonagrain in the Joy of the Court adventure (which was eventually completed by Erec). [*ChretienE*]

THIRTEEN TREASURES OF BRITAIN
Thirteen magical artifacts mentioned in Welsh manuscripts. Some of them suggest themes in Arthurian literature, though only one names Arthur directly. The list reflects elements of original Celtic tales as well as the influence of medieval romances imported into Wales from the continent. The full list of treasures includes:

- White-Hilt (*Drynwyn*), the sword belonging to Rhydderch the Generous. It could grant wishes to its bearer. Rhydderch appears as Merlin's master in Geoffrey of Monmouth's *Vita Merlini*.

- The hamper (*Mwys*) of Gwyddno Long-Shank. It could multiply one man's meal into enough food for a hundred men. This food-producing ability is shared with other treasures.

- The (drinking) horn of King Bran the Blessed. A man drinking from it would find that it contained any drink that he desired. R. S. Loomis saw this horn as one of the origins of the Grail, and thought that *cor benoit* ("blessed horn") was the origin of Corbenic, the Grail castle in the Vulgate *Queste del Saint Graal*.

- The chariot of Morgan the Wealthy. It could instantly transport its rider to his desired location.

- The halter (*kebystr*) of Clydno Eiddin, which would produce any horse that its owner desired to ride.

- The knife (*kyllell*) of Llawfrodedd the Horseman.

- The CAULDRON (*pair*) of Diwrnach the Giant. Meat intended for a brave man would boil in the cauldron, but meat to be fed to a coward would not. The cauldron was thus used to separate heroes from knaves. In *Culhwch and Olwen*, Arthur sacks Ireland and returns to Britain with the cauldron, full of Ireland's treasure. This cauldron and others of its kind (appearing in *The Spoils of Annwn* and *Branwen*) have been seen as an origin for the Grail, to which Robert de Boron gives the ability to divide the pure from the perfidious.

- The whetstone (*hogalen*) of Tudwal Tudglyd. A brave man who sharpened his sword on the stone would be able to slay his enemy with one blow, but a coward would get no use from it.

- The coat (*pais*) of PADARN Red-Coat. It would fit a nobly-born man, but would not fit a churl. This ability is shared by the many magic chastity mantles in Arthurian legend, and it echoes in the name of the Knight with the Ill-Fitting Coat. Padarn's hagiography contains an Arthruian episode.

- The crock and dish (*dysgyl*) of Rhygenydd the Cleric. It would produce whatever food its owner desired. This dish has also been suggested as an origin for the Grail, which has a similar ability in the First Continuation of Chrétien's *Perceval*.

- The GWYDDBWYLL board of Gwenddolau son of Ceidio. The pieces would play by themselves. Gwyddbwyll is a Welsh game analogous to chess. Peredur encounters an enchanted gwyddbwyll board in his tale, and magic chessboards of this nature appear in Chrétien's *Perceval*, the Vulgate *Lancelot*, and Vostaert's *Roman van Walewein*.

- The mantle (*llen*) of Arthur in Cornwall. When Arthur wore it, he was invisible. This mantle, called GWENN, also appears in *The Dream of Rhonabwy*.

Some late manuscripts delete at least one of these treasures and add two additional items:

- The mantle of Tegau Eurfon, which revealed whether a woman was chaste or unchaste. Such mantles are prolific in French and German romances that describe CHASTITY TESTS.

- The stone and ring of Eluned (LUNETE), mentioned in Chrétien de Troyes's *Yvain* and the Welsh *Owain*.

THITIS

One of the eight sisters of Morgan le Fay, who ruled with Morgan on the island of Avalon. She could apparently play a stringed instrument called a *citter*, and was popular for it. [*GeoffVM*]

THOARIS OF ORASTEGENTESIN

An infidel king who served Feirefiz, Perceval's half-brother. [*Wolfram*]

THOAS[1]

A knight who fought at the tournament at Noauz, which Lancelot won. [*ChretienC*]

THOAS[2]

A lord who hated the Knights of the Round Table. He imprisoned them whenever he found them. Claris and Laris defeated him and sent him to Arthur's court as a prisoner. [*Claris*]

THOAS[3]

A Saxon king from Ireland who participated in the siege of Clarence at the beginning of Arthur's reign. He was eventually killed by Gawain or by King Ban of Benoic. [*VulgMer*, *Livre*, *Arthour*]

THOLOMER[1]

A scribe who served Merlin. [*Prophecies*]

THOLOMER[2] THE FUGITIVE [*Tolleme*]

King of Babylonia in the time of Joseph of Arimathea. He went to war with King Evalach of Sarras, who had once served Tholomer. Tholomer's brother, Manatur, assisted him in the campaign. Tholomer nearly destroyed Evalach's kingdom, but Joseph of Arimathea converted Evalach to Christianity and thus provided him with the spiritual strength needed to defeat Tholomer. Tholomer besieged the castle of Evalachin and defeated Evalach there, but Evalach won a victory at La Choine and again at Orcaut, where Tholomer was captured. While in Evalach's prison, a devil named Selaphas visited him and tricked him into leaping out a window to his death. His name is

perhaps a variation of Ptolemy, a name which belonged to a number of Egyptian rulers. [*VulgQuest*, *VulgEst*, *PostQuest*, *Malory*]

THOMAS [*Thumas*]

A scribe from Toledo who served Arthur. Thomas and three other scribes were charged with recording the exploits of Arthur and his knights. [*LancLac*, *VulgLanc*]

THONGCEASTER [*Thangcaster*, *Thong Castle*]

The castle known as *Kaercarrei* by the Britons. It was later called Vancaster or Lancaster. The Saxon leader Hengist built it as a stronghold in Britain while he was on friendly terms with Vortigern. According to Geoffrey, it was so named because Hengist measured out the foundation of the castle with a leather thong. The town is now called Caister, and is 23 miles NNE of Lincoln. [*GeoffHR*, *Wace*]

THORBUSH FORD [*Aigua Della Spinna*, *Gué Espine*]

In the Prose *Tristan* and its adaptations (including Malory's) we learn that Tristan and Mark first clashed not over Isolde, but over the lovely wife of another knight—Seguarades in *Tristan* and Malory, and Lambegus in the Italian *Tristano Riccardiano*. This woman loved Tristan instead of Mark, and she sent for him one night when her husband was away. Mark learned of the summons and intercepted Tristan on the road. The two fought a duel, and Mark lost. *Tristan* gives the location of this duel as Thornbush Ford, near the lady's manor. Consequently, *Tristano* calls her the lady of Thornbush Ford (*Aigua Della Spinna*), adding that she was a Jewess. Tristan enjoyed a night with the woman, but left her bed stained with blood from the wounds he had received in the battle against Mark. Her husband discovered this evidence and challenged Tristan, but lost. The same woman was later kidnapped from Mark's court by Sir Bleoberis. In deference to Mark, Tristan delayed rescuing her and thus lost her love. After retrieving her from Bleoberis, Tristan returned her, at her request, to her husband. [*ProsTris*, *TristanoR*, *Tavola*, *Malory*]

THORNY VALLEY [*Valle Spinosa*]

A terrible valley that not even Tristan or Lancelot would enter. It was dark, and full of beasts and savages. [*Tavola*]

THREE DAMSELS

A pine tree in the forest of Darnantes where, as a hermit once told Tristan and Kahedins, many adventures could be found. [*ProsTris*]

THREE (DAMSELS) OF THE CLEAR FOUNTAINS

Three beautiful maidens residing at Arthur's court, possibly with some connection to the CLEAR FOUNTAIN OF LOVE. [*Contin1*]

THREE QUEENS

During Arthur's coronation in Tennyson's *Idylls*, sunlight shining through a stained-glass window falls upon the three queens who, Merlin foretells, will bear Arthur's body to Avalon after the final battle. Merlin etched their images above a portal at Camelot, which became known as the Gate of the Three Queens. The queens are unnamed by Tennyson, but one of them, traditionally, is Morgan le Fay. [*TennIK*]

THYLE

An enchanted island, deep in an unknown sea. The lady-turned-dragon Clidra came from this island, which had marvelously long days in the summer, and extremely short ones in the winter. Some scholars have sought to identify it with the Roman mythological island of Pliny. [*UlrichZ*]

TIBERIAS [*Taubarie*]

A region of Palestine. Its ruler is named as Jonas in *Floriant et Florete* and Daton in *Claris et Laris*. Both were enemies of Arthur. [*Floriant, Claris*]

TIBERIUS[1]

According to Jacob van Maerlant, a Roman Emperor and father of Vespasian, who freed Joseph of Arimathea from a prison in Jerusalem. The Vulgate stories name him TITUS. An Emperor Tiberius I ruled Rome from AD 14 to 37, but six other emperors ruled between Tiberius's reign and Vespasian's.

TIBERIUS[2]

The surname of LUCIUS the Roman in some chronicles, given as his sole name in Hughes' *The Misfortunes of Arthur*. [*HughesT*]

TIBERIUS[3] CAESAR

An Emperor of Rome during Arthur's reign. Claudas asked him for support in his war against Arthur. [*VulgLanc*]

TIDOGOLAIN [*Teandelayn, Teondeleyn*]

A dwarf who served Helie, the lady-in-waiting of Queen Esmeree the Blonde of Wales. He accompanied Helie to Arthur's court to find a champion to remove a curse placed on Esmeree. Helie was furious when Arthur gave her the young, untried Guinglain (Gawain's son), but Tidogolain encouraged Helie to give him a chance. Tidogolain's faith was vindicated when Guinglain proved an excellent knight. [*Renaut, ChestreLyb*]

TIEBAUT

The ruler of Tintagel in Chrétien de Troyes's *Perceval*. He may be identical with Chrétien's THIEBAUT. Tiebaut raised Sir Meliant of Lis, who fought against Tiebaut for Tiebaut's daughter. Tiebaut, a common name at the time of Chrétien's writing, appears in Ulrich's *Lanzelet* as TYBALT. Wolfram calls him LYPPAUT, and Heinrich von dem Türlin calls him LEIGAMAR [*ChretienP*]

TIMIAS

Arthur's brave and faithful squire in Spenser's *The Faerie Queene*. He saved his master's life at the House of Temperance against Maleger. Wounded while pursuing some evil foresters, he was found and nursed by the beautiful huntress Belphoebe. Timias and Belphoebe fell in love. Later, he and Belphoebe rescued the maiden Amoret from a monster, the Hairy Carl. Amoret was wounded during the rescue and Timias, lamenting her injury, kissed her. Witnessing this, Belphoebe accused him of infidelity and left him. Timias became a hermit and lived a life of asceticism until Belphoebe, satisfied as to his devotion, reconciled with him. In Spenser's allegory, Timias represents Sir Walter Raleigh. [*Spenser*]

TIMON

An elderly knight who, according to Spenser, Merlin appointed as Prince Arthur's guardian. This role is usually assigned to ANTOR or ECTOR. [*Spenser*]

TINAS

Father of Lischet, a knight tutored by Gawain. [*PleierT*]

TINTAGEL [*Luntaguel, Til Tomeil, Tindagel, Tindagol, Tintagil, Tintaguel, Tinta(n)jol, Tintegell, Tintoil, Titomeil, Tyntagel, Tyntagill*]

A seaside Cornish castle, ruled by the husband of Igerne, called Duke Gorlois or Duke Hoel (in *Arthour and Merlin*, Tintagel is the name of the duke himself). When Uther Pendragon sought to steal Igerne, her husband secured her in Tintagel, his strongest castle, while he himself holed up in Dimilioc or Tarabel. Though the castle was nigh impregnable by military effort, Uther received Merlin's assistance, was changed into the semblance of the Duke, and was able to enter freely. Once inside, he slept with Igerne, begetting Arthur.

The castle's fate after the death of the duke is unclear. In the Tristan legends, it is ruled by King Mark. In the time of Mark's father, Felix, it was besieged and conquered by King Dilianfer of Ireland. After Tristan's death, Arthur, King Amoroldo of Ireland, and King Governal of Lyoness besieged the castle to capture Mark.

Rulers of Tintagel in other legends include Aliduc (Geoffrey), Tiebaut (Chrétien's *Perceval*), David (Chrétien's *Erec*), and Guinlain (Renaut de Bâgé). In Malory, the castle is conquered by two giants who imprisoned women. They were freed when Lancelot killed the giants, reclaiming the castle in Arthur's name. Tintagel is often given mysterious or supernatural properties. In some legends, it is said to vanish twice a year.

The actual Castle Tintagel rests on a promontory in northern Cornwall. It is an ideal site for a castle, 250 feet above sea level and connected to the mainland by only a thin strip of land that would have been easily defended. The current version of the castle dates only from the mid-twelfth century, but there is evidence of an earlier structure on the site. Archaeological excavations in the Summer of 1998 produced a stone that may connect the castle with Arthur (see. TINTAGEL STONE). [*GeoffHR, ChretienE, ChretienP, FolieO, HartmannE, Renaut, VulgLanc, VulgMer, ProsTris, Tavola, Malory, TennIK, Topography*]

TINTAGEL STONE

Also known as the "Arthur Stone," a small slate piece unearthed by archaeologists at the eastern terraces of Tintagel Castle on July 4, 1998. Hailed by one archaeologist as "the find of a lifetime," the stone holds two inscriptions—one, broken off, is unreadable. The other reads *Pater Coliavifcit Artognov*: "Artognou, father of a descendant of Coll, had this built." Speculation is that the stone, dating from the sixth century, was once part of a wall but was later used as a drain cover.

"Artognou," pronounced "Arthnou," is similar enough to "Arthur" to be an identical person. At the very least, it shows that the name was known to Britons in the sixth century, and that such as person was associated with Tintagel, where King Arthur was supposedly born. "Coll" probably refers to the semi-legendary King COLE mentioned by Geoffrey of Monmouth.

At the time of the final draft of this book, this find had only just been announced in *English Heritage*. Certainly, additional study of the stone and of the Castle Tintagel is mandated.

TINTAZION

One of the lands ruled by Uther Pendragon. [*Heinrich*]

TIRIDE OF ELIXODJON

An infidel duke who served Feirefiz, Perceval's half-brother. [*Wolfram*]

TIRRE [*Torre*]

Son of Sir Bernard of Escalot and brother of Lavaine and Elaine. As Tirre was badly wounded on the day of his knighting, Bernard loaned Tirre's shield to Lancelot to use in a tournament at Camelot. Tirre became angry at Lancelot when Lancelot rejected Elaine's love. [*Malory, TennIK*]

TISBE

A maiden who was a friend of Florete, Sir Floriant's wife. [*Floriant*]

TITILUS

A nephew of Lucius the Roman in the Vulgate *Merlin*. Prior to the Roman War, Arthur sent an envoy to Lucius to discuss possible peace terms. Titilius, who was present, laughed at the Britons' empty threats. Gawain swiftly beheaded Titilius, and the Roman War was underway. Geoffrey introduces this character as GAIUS QUINTILLIANUS. [*VulgMer*]

TITUREL[1]

A Knight of the Round Table in Hartmann's *Erec* whose name was probably the source for Wolfram's Titurel. Hartmann may have taken the name from Tydorel, the hero of a non-Arthurian Breton lay. [*HartmannE*]

TITUREL[2]

The first Grail King in Wolfram's *Parzival*. Wolfram may have adopted the name from Hartmann von Aue's character. Titurel was Perceval's great-grandfather. After receiving the Grail under holy circumstances, Titurel became the patriarch of the Grail Family. His son, Frimutel, was also a Grail King but was slain in a joust. His daughter was named Rischoyde. As a youth, Titurel was an adventurous knight. He fell sick with a laming disease and became bedridden in the Grail Castle of Munsalvæsche. Sustained by the Grail, he lived for several generations to advise his family. He was still alive when Perceval became the new Grail King. [*Wolfram*]

TITUS

The father of Vespasian, the Roman Emperor who freed Joseph of Arimathea from prison in the Vulgate *Estoire del Saint Graal*. Maerlant calls him Tiberius. In the Third Continuation of Chrétien's *Perceval*, Titus brings Joseph of Arimathea to Rome. An actual Emperor Titus ruled Rome from AD 79–81, but his reign came after Vespasian's. [*VulgEst*]

TJOFABIER

The King of Merkanie. He refused to allow Gerhart of Riviers to marry his daughter, Sabie, for which Gerhart made war on him. The war was ended by Arthur's Sir Garel, who defeated Gerhart. In return, Tjofabier pledged his support in Arthur's war against King Ekunaver of Kanadic. Arthur later made him a Knight of the Round Table. [*PleierG*]

TJOFRIT

A knight in the service of Arthur's Sir Garel. He served as an envoy during Garel's campaign against King Ekunaver of Kanadic. [*PleierG*]

TOADAS

A knight who served King Claudas. He led a division of Claudas's troops in a battle against Arthur. [*VulgLanc*]

TOCLIO

A nobleman at the court of Aurelius Ambrosius. [*Birth*]

TODILA

A knight who lodged Tandareis, an Arthurian knight, after the latter was wounded by a pack of robbers. When Tandareis was healed, Todila supplied him with arms and a steed. [*PleierT*]

TODONE

One of Lancelot's kingdoms in Der Pleier's *Garel*. [*PleierG*]

TOLEDO

A city in Spain. According to Wolfram, it was the capital of King Kaylet, Perceval's great-uncle. In the Prose *Lancelot*, it is the home of Arthur's scribe Thomas. [*Wolfram, LancLac, VulgLanc*]

TOLLO

The king of Scotland in Richard Blackmore's *Prince Arthur* who joined Octa the Saxon's war against Arthur. He fought in single combat against Arthur to decide the outcome of the war and was killed. His character and name echo FROLLO from Geoffrey's chronicle. [*BlackmoreP*]

TOLOMEO

One of Merlin's scribes. He had served as one of the pope's chaplains, and he eventually returned to Rome and became a cardinal. [*VitaMer*]

TOM A' LINCOLN

The illegitimate son of Arthur and Angellica, daughter of the Earl of London. He was raised by a shepherd. Known as the Red Rose Knight, Tom led a band of outlaws and interacted with knights such as Lancelot and Tristan. Eventually, he came to Arthur's court and was appointed to the Round Table. He fell in love with Caelia, the Fairy Queen, and had a son named the Fairy Knight. Later, he visited Prester John's kingdom and fell in love with Prester John's daughter, Anglitora. Tom and Anglitora had a son called the Black Knight. When she discovered that Tom was a bastard, Anglitora abandoned him, and he was murdered by her new suitor. He appeared to his son as a ghost and bade him to avenge his death. [*Johnson*]

TOM THUMB

The tiny, adventurous hero whose story appears in the *History of Tomb Thumbe* (1621), probably written by Richard Johnson. (Tom Thumb was well-known prior to this book; various references appear in the sixteenth and seventeenth centuries.) On the title page, Tom Thumb is called "King Arthur's dwarfe." In the story, he is born when his father, Thomas of the Mountain, Arthur's ploughman, sends his barren wife to seek Merlin's help in conceiving a child—any child, "be hee no bigger then my very Thumbe." Merlin translated Thomas's request literally. Tom Thumb's birth was attended by the Queen of the Fairies and her sprites. He grew to manhood in only four minutes. The fairy queen, who became his godmother, later bestowed upon him a hat which taught him all the world's knowledge, a girdle which allowed him to change his form at will, a ring that turned him invisible, and a pair of shoes that almost instantly took him wherever he wanted to go.

Tom's story is full of comical adventures, many of which involve being swallowed—accidentally or deliberately—by various creatures. In one such episode, he was swallowed by a giant, vomited into the ocean, and eaten by a fish, which was caught and served at Arthur's table. Tom was discovered by Arthur, and he so entertained the king that he was appointed a courtier and endowed with great riches.

Tom Thumb is also the title character of two parodies by Henry Fielding: *Tom Thumb* and its revision, *The Tragedy of Tragedies*. Created by Merlin for Gaffar Thumb and his wife, Tom proved himself a noble giant-slayer, for which Arthur rewarded him by betrothing him to his daughter Huncamunca. For Huncamunca's love, Tom had to contend with both Lord Grizzle, another suitor, and Queen Dollallolla, who loved Tom. He survived a murder attempt only to be eaten by a cow during his wedding procession. In the original version, his spirit arose but was slain by Grizzle. [*Fielding*]

TONTAMIDES OF VERNAUS

A scribe in the service of Arthur. Tontamides and three other scribes were charged with recording the deeds of Arthur and his knights. [*LancLac*]

TOR[1] [*Cort, (Es)torz, Thor, Tors*]

A Knight of the Round Table whose earliest appearance is in Ulrich von Zatzikhoven's *Lanzelet* as *Torfilaret* ("Tor fils Aret," or Tor son of Ares) a Welsh prince and companion of Lancelot whose wife was proven unfaithful by a magic mantle. Another character named ORPHYLET may be identical. It is relatively certain that Ulrich took the character from a archetypal French Lancelot tale the formed the basis for *Lanzelet*. R. S. Loomis speculated that his character originated ultimately with the boar TWRCH TRWYTH in Welsh legend (Loomis, *Romance*, 39).

Prior to the Post-Vulgate *Suite du Merlin*, the texts name Tor's father as King Ares. The *Suite*, which contains the longest account of Tor's adventures, tells us that King Pellinore fathered Tor on Ares the Cowherd's wife (making Tor the half-brother of Perceval). Ares, ignorant of this fact, brought Tor before Arthur and asked Arthur to make him a knight. Unlike his twelve brothers in stature and demeanor, Tor had no interest the ways of a laborer. Arthur knighted him, and Merlin revealed his true paternity. His first quest involved the recovery of a white brachet stolen from Arthur's hall by Sir Abelleus, who Tor eventually beheaded. Arthur appointed him to the Round Table after the battle of the Humber. He was killed fighting Lancelot and his men when Lancelot came to rescue Queen Guinevere from the stake. [*ChretienE, UlrichZ, Renaut, Yder, VulgLanc, ProsTris, PostMer, Malory*]

TOR[2] THE STRONG

A warrior who served Alexander of Constantinople. With Alexander, he joined Arthur's service for a brief time, and fought against the traitor Angres of Windsor. [*ChretienC*]

TOREC

Hero of a romance by Jacob van Maerlant. Born to King Ydor and Lady Tristouse, he learned that a magic circlet had been stolen from his grandmother, Mariole. He tracked down the thief, named Bruant, but learned that the circlet was in the possession of Bruant's sister-in-law, Miraude, the most beautiful maiden in the world. She agreed to marry Torec if he could defeat all the Knights of the Round Table. Gawain, Torec's friend, arranged for all of the other knights to release the girths of their saddles so that they would be defeated at the first blow, and Torec was thus able to defeat all the knights except Arthur. Miraude nonetheless allowed him to marry her, and he ascended his father's throne. [*Maerlant*]

TORPLAIN OF THE GREEN PLAIN

An Irish knight with whom Lancelot lodged during his adventures in Ireland. Torplain was the brother of the Viscount of Pavengay, whose daughter Lancelot had saved. [*Merveil*]

TORTAIN

In the First Continuation of Chrétien's *Perceval*, a half-man, half-boar who was the product of a union between the sorcerer Eliavres and a sow. King Caradoc of Nantes had discovered that Eliavres was having an affair with Caradoc's wife, and he forced Eliavres to copulate with the pig as punishment. There is probably a connection to TWRCH TRWYTH of Welsh legend (Bromwich, in Grout, 43). [*Contin1*]

TORVAIN

A race of men who guarded Rigomer castle. They were defeated by Arthur's knights. [*Merveil*]

TOSQUEHAM

A city in Egypt. Messengers seeking Nascien traveled to Tosqueham, where Joseph of Arimathea visited them in a dream and showed them that Nascien was in a ship in the Greek Sea. [*VulgEst*]

TOTNES

A beautiful island off the southern coast of Britain. Constantine, Arthur's grandfather, laid low on the island and trained his army before entering Britain and destroying the barbarian invaders. Later, Totnes was used as a haven for Constantine's sons—Ambrosius Aurelius and Uther—when they came from Brittany to take Britain from Vortigern. During Arthur's reign, Colgrim's Saxons conquered the area in betrayal of a peace treaty they had made with Arthur. [*GeoffHR*]

TOULOUSE

A city in south France, on the Garonne river. According to the Alliterative *Morte Arthure*, it was part of Arthur's empire. The knight Kay of Estral carried a shield, bridle, and breast-strap made in the city. It was also home of Elias, one of Arthur's sages. [*ChretienC, VulgLanc, Allit*]

TOURAINE

A region of west central France, conquered for Arthur by Hoel of Brittany. [*Layamon, Allit*]

TOURNAMENT OF THE DEAD INNOCENCE

The "Last Tournament" in Tennyson's *Idylls of the King*. As Arthur was away from court, Lancelot was appointed its judge. Disillusioned and bored, Lancelot refused to enforce the rules of the tournament or even the basic customs of chivalry, and the festival was a disaster. Tristan was chosen as the winner and, as the crowning calamity, he refused to award the crown to any of the women in the audience—even though his wife, Isolde of the White Hands, was among them—saying that his true love was not present. The tournament marked the beginning of the rapid downfall of Arthur's kingdom. [*TennIK*]

TOURNAMENT OF THE YOUTH

A tournament held by Arthur in Caerleon after the Grail Quest. It was so named because Arthur withheld his seasoned knights from the lists, allowing his new knights a chance to win glory. Pelleas was declared the victor, and he awarded the circlet to Ettare. [*TennIK*]

TOWER CASTLE

A castle in King Claudas's lands, where Claudas organized his armies in preparation for a war against Arthur. Arthur conquered it, and King Bors of Gannes bestowed it on the husband of the Lady of the Lake. [*VulgLanc*]

TOWER OF AMBUSH

The castle belonging to Sir Damas, where Arthur was imprisoned until he agreed to fight Accalon of Gaul. [*PostMer*]

TOWER OF ENCHANTMENTS

In *La Tavola Ritonda*, the castle owned by the Wise Damsel, who ensnared King Meliadus, Tristan's father. Meliadus remained in the Tower of Enchantments until his nobles, at the direction of Merlin, rescued him. Many years later, Tristan and Isolde lived there for a time after they fled Mark's court. Mark eventually stole her back. In the Prose *Tristan*, it is called the ROCK OF THE CORNISHWOMAN. [*Tavola*]

TOWER OF LONDON

A tower made up of several buildings on the Thames River in London. When Mordred, after seizing the throne of Britain, announced his intention to marry Queen Guinevere, she fled to London and secured herself in the Tower of London. Mordred arrived and besieged it, using cannon, but he had to break off the attack to meet the army of King Arthur at Dover. [*Malory*]

TOWER OF MARVELS [*Tor des Mervelles]

A stronghold constructed by Duke Ganor at the behest of Josephus, son of Joseph of Arimathea. It was built on top of the bodies of heathens who had refused to convert to Christianity and were struck dead. It stood until it was destroyed by Lancelot during a battle against Mordred's sons. [VulgEst]

TOWER OF THE DEAD

A monument built upon the plains of Salisbury to commemorate the final battle between Arthur and Mordred. It was constructed by the Archbishop of Canterbury and Sir Bleoberis, who hung Mordred's head from it. [PostMort]

TOWER OF THE FENS

The tower where Meleagant imprisoned Lancelot so that Lancelot could not make his scheduled duel with Meleagant at Arthur's court. However, Meleagant's sister freed Lancelot. [VulgLanc]

TOWER OF THE ROUND PINE [*Tour du Pin Rond]

A castle owned by a belligerent lord. It was named after the pine tree that stood outside, where the owner hung his shield. Knights who wanted a fight would strike the shield and summon the lord. The lord was generally victorious, and he hung the shields of those he defeated on the tower's walls. Palamedes came along, jousted with him, and killed him. [ProsTris]

TOWERS OF JUDGMENT

A pair of towers built on the border of Egypt by Flegetine, Nascien's wife. The towers marked the tombs of the lord of Karrabel, Faran the Giant, and Nabor—three men killed by God for their sins. [VulgEst]

TRABUCHET [Trebuchet, Tribüet]

A noble, masterful, and perhaps magical smith from the town of Cotatre who fashioned the Grail Sword and two knives for the Grail Family. Trabuchet also carved engravings on King Frimutel's sword. Duke Orguelleus of Lalander had a fine helmet crafted by the smith. Perceval was told that Trabuchet was the only one who could repair the Grail Sword once it shattered in combat. Perceval happened upon Trabuchet's smithy while seeking someone to extract a nail from his horse's hoof. Trabuchet repaired the Grail Sword and returned it to Perceval, though he did so reluctantly, as he was fated to die after he had repaired the sword. [ChretienP, Wolfram, Contin3, Contin4]

TRACHMYR

One of Arthur's chief huntsmen in Welsh legend. He participated in the hunt for Twrch Trwyth, during which he helped to manage the hound Drudwyn. [Culhwch]

TRACON OF ACUSBORG

An earl who was the father of Elena, the brother of King Odus, and the uncle of Enide, Erec's wife. [Erex]

TRADELMANT[1] [Cardelmans, Cradlemont]

The King of North Wales who, with other British kings, rebelled against the young Arthur. His brother was King Belinant of South Wales, and his nephews, Dodinel and Pollidomas, took service with Arthur. Arthur defeated Tradelmant and his allies at Caerleon and Bedegraine, after which a Saxon invasion forced the rebellious kings to abandon their revolt and return to their lands. Tradelmant opposed the Saxons at Arundel, Clarence, and other battles. Later, he reconciled with Arthur to expel the invaders, and the Saxons were crushed at Clarence. He further assisted Arthur in the wars against King Rions and Rome. His daughter was loved by Agravain. [VulgLanc, VulgMer, Livre, Malory, Idylls]

TRADELMANT[2]

Godson of King Tradelmant, after whom he was named. He fought unsuccessfully to win Sir Evadeam's lady. [VulgMer]

TRAELUS

A Knight of the Round Table defeated in a tournament against the Queen's Knights. [VulgMer]

TRAEZ OF ANET

A knight who fought in a tournament between Meliant of Lis and Tiebaut of Tintagel. [ChretienP]

TRAHAN THE GAY

Lord of the Gay Castle and father of Drian the Gay and Melian the Gay. When Lancelot was newly knighted, Trahan was borne to Arthur's court. His body contained two spearheads, and a piece of a sword was stuck in his head. By extracting these broken weapons from, Lancelot swore to avenge Trahan's injuries, which had been delivered by a brother of Caradoc of the Dolorous Tower. Lancelot eventually killed Caradoc and his brother—saving Trahan's sons in the process—but for reasons unconnected to this original oath. [VulgLanc, Livre]

TRAHER

An earl in Arthur's service. [Layamon]

TRAMINORE DASTRIE

A knight-captain in King Mark of Cornwall's service. He fought against Arthur's men when Arthur besieged Tintagel. Traminore Dastre was killed in the battle. [Tavola]

TRAMONDO UGHIERE

A servant of Morgan le Fay in La Tavola Ritonda. While taking a magic horn that would expose unchaste ladies to

Arthur's court, he was forced by Lamorat to reroute the item to King Mark of Cornwall. Tramondo appears unnamed in the Prose *Tristan* and Malory's *Le Morte Darthur*. [*Tavola*]

TRANSLAPINS OF RIVIGITAS

An infidel king who served Feirefiz, Perceval's half-brother. [*Wolfram*]

TRANSMADUCK [*Trsnsmaduc*]

A Saxon warrior who fought in the Saxon army against Arthur at the battle of Garlot. His brother was King Gundeflé. [*VulgMer*]

TRASSINO THE WHITE

Son of the King of North Wales. Tristan defeated Trassino in joust twice. [*Tavola*]

TRAVERAIN [*Treverin*]

The Count of Traverain, named Libers, was present at the wedding of Erec and Enide. [*ChretienE, HartmannE*]

TRAVERSES

A wealthy town near Scotland. The King of Traverses was slain by Agravain at the tournament of Banborc. The Queen of Traverses was the sister of Escanor the Handsome. She captured Sir Girflet, with whom she was in love, and kept him prisoner in Traverses until he agreed to marry her. When she died, Girflet returned to Arthur's court. [*Girart*]

TREACHEROUS CASTLE

A pagan stronghold ruled by Arpian. It had been built by King Galamanascor in Joseph of Arimathea's time, and it refused to convert to Christianity with the rest of Britain. St. Augustine gave it its name. The castle imprisoned maidens and slew any knight of Arthur, whom Arpian hated. The lady of the Treacherous Castle suffered from a disease and could only be cured by the blood of a virgin princess. Lancelot visited the castle but could not end the custom. When Arpian imprisoned Galahad, Hector, and Meraugis during the Grail Quest, the castle was destroyed by a holy cataclysm. Arthur kept trying to rebuild it but could not. Much later, Charlemagne successfully reconstructed it and erected a statue of Galahad out front. [*PostQuest, ProsTris*]

TREACEROUS PASS

The region inhabited by Griffon, an enemy of Arthur and the Knights of the Round Table. [*VulgLanc*]

TREBE [*Trebes*]

Chief castle and city of King Ban of Benoic, Lancelot's father. It was situated between the Loire and Arsone Rivers. It was the site of an epic battle in which Arthur, Ban, and Bors fought King Claudas, the king of Gaul,

Frollo, and Pontius Anthony. Claudas was defeated, but he returned years later and conquered all of Benoic except Trebe, which was too well defended. King Ban eventually left the city to seek help from Arthur, and his seneschal immediately betrayed him by opening the gates to Claudas. Claudas razed the city and castle. From a hilltop, Ban saw his beloved city burning and died from heartbreak. Claudas restored the castle. It was re-captured by Arthur's forces just prior to the Grail Quest. [*LancLac, VulgLanc, VulgMer*]

TREE OF LIFE

According to the Vulgate *Queste del Saint Graal*, when Eve took the apple from the Tree of Knowledge, she also took one of the tree's branches. After the expulsion from paradise, she planted the branch, and it grew into a new tree, called the Tree of Life (distinct from the Tree of Life in the book of Genesis that provided eternal life to those who ate its fruit). The Tree of Life, and others grown from its seeds, weathered the great flood and survived until the time of Solomon. Solomon used wood from the Tree of Life to make spindles for the Ship of Solomon, and to create the scabbard for the Sword with the Strange Hangings. The ship and sword eventually came into Galahad's possession during the Grail Quest. [*VulgQuest, VulgEst, PostQuest*]

TREFFERIN

A land whose king, Gediens, was slain by the heathen Verangoz of Sorboreste. The king's daughter, Dulceflur, asked for a champion from Arthur's court, and Meleranz, Arthur's nephew, saved the kingdom. Its capital was Belfortemunt. [*PleierM*]

TRÉGUIER [*Tigel, Striguel*]

A city in Brittany ruled by Kimmarcoch, a vassal of King Hoel of Brittany and, consequently, of King Arthur. [*GeoffHR, Wace, Layamon*]

TREMONOUS [*Tremorius*]

Archbishop of Caerleon during the reign of Ambrosius. When Ambrosius sought to build a monument to fallen British warriors, Tremonous suggested that he seek out Merlin to accomplish the task. [*GeoffHR*]

TRENT RIVER

A river in central England. In the Alliterative *Morte Arthure*, it was the site of the climactic battle between Arthur and Mordred, which other texts place at SALISBURY or CAMLANN. According to Malory, in the early days of King Arthur's reign, most of his enemies lay north of the Trent River. Sir Brastias was appointed warden and was given the job of watching over this area. [*Allit, Malory*]

TREVILONETE

Daughter of Sir Guengasoain. Gawain killed her father to avenge the death of Sir Raguidel, and he therefore had the right to marry Trevilonete. Gawain saw that she was in love with Yder, and relinquished his claim, allowing Yder and Trevilonete to marry. [*Vengeance*]

TREVISAN

A knight encountered by the Red Cross Knight with a rope around his neck. A monster called Despair had convinced Trevisan's companion, Terwin, to kill himself, and was in the process of doing the same to Trevisan when Trevisan fled. Trevisan led the Red Cross Knight to Despair's cave. [*Spenser*]

TREVRIZENT

Perceval's maternal uncle in Wolfram's *Parzival*. He is unnamed in Chrétien's *Perceval*, but he corresponds to the HERMIT KING of Chrétien's continuators. A member of the Grail Family, Trevrizent was the son of Frimutel and the brother of Anfortas, Herzeloyde, Schoysiane, and Repanse de Schoye. As a youth, he had dozens of adventures in exotic kingdoms. After Anfortas received his debilitating wound, Trevrizent retired to a hermitage at the Fontane la Salvæsche where he lived in humble penance. Perceval encountered him there and Trevrizent served as his tutor, educating him on the ways of the Grail and of God. When Anfortas was healed, Trevrizent returned to the Grail Castle to live out his days. [*Wolfram*]

TRIADAN

A vavasor and friend of Sir Lamorat. He lodged Tristan and Lamorat after they had been wounded at the castle Crudele. [*Tavola*]

TRIAL CASTLE [*Chasteaux del Asai*]

One of several heathen castles converted to Christianity by Perceval. Its residents worshipped a Copper Tower, which was full of demons. Perceval cast down the tower and drove the castle's residents out of the castle. Those who refused to convert where smashed with a magic axe as they exited the castle's gates. [*Perlesvaus*]

TRIAMOUR¹ [*Triamore, Tryamour(e)*]

Daughter of the king of Oléron or Avalon. She was an exceedingly beautiful, rich, and mysterious lady that an impoverished Sir Lanval met in a forest. Two of Triamour's ladies brought Lanval to her pavilion, and he immediately fell in love with her. In exchange for his love, Triamour gave Lanval her horse, Blaunchard, her servant, Gyfre, a magical purse which was never empty, a suit of armor, a banner, and an enchantment which ensured that he would never be harmed in joust or duel. In return, Lanval had to agree to forsake all other women, and to keep silent about their relationship. After seven years, Lanval revealed her existence to Guinevere, who had tried to seduce him. Lanval claimed that Triamour's ugliest servant was more beautiful than Guinevere. At this, all of Lanval's enchantments disappeared. Arthur put Lanval on trial to prove his ridiculous claim, but Lanval was unable

to find Triamour. Just as the jury was preparing to order Lanval's execution, Triamour appeared and proved Lanval's boast. Before departing with Lanval to her father's paradisiacal island, Triamour blinded Guinevere. [*MarieL*, *ChestreLvl*, *Johnson*]

TRIAMOUR²

King of Wales in the Middle-English *Sir Tristrem*. He was attacked by the giant Urgan, who wanted to marry Triamour's daughter, Blancheflor. Tristan assisted Triamour by slaying the giant, which Triamour rewarded by giving Tristan a dog named Petitcrieu. He is called GILAN in Gottfried von Strassburg's version. [*SirTris*]

TRIAMOURE

A Knight of the Round Table who was a companion of Tom a' Lincoln, Arthur's illegitimate son. [*Johnson*]

TRIBALIBOT

A heathen country identified by Wolfram von Eschenbach as India. However, its capital, Thabronit, was said to lie at the base of the Caucasus Mountains. The country was ruled by Queen Secundille. She loved Feirefiz, Perceval's half-brother, and eventually gave him the kingdom. A race of half-men with the features of boars were said to live in the country. Cundrie the Sorceress (the Grail Maiden) and her brother Malcreatiure were two of this race. [*Wolfram*]

TRIBUIT [*Trat(h) Tre(u)roit*]

A river in Britain that, in Nennius, was the site of Arthur's tenth battle against the Saxons. As in all of Arthur's twelve battles, Arthur was victorious. Nennius may have intended the river Ribroit in Somersetshire or the river Ribble in Lancashire. A Welsh poem alludes to a fight at a river called TRYFRWYD, which may be identical. [*Nennius*]

TRIDAN [*Triadan*]

A knight from the Hedged Manor defeated in combat by Yvain during the latter's quest to slay Malduit the Giant. As a condition of Tridan's surrender, Yvain forced him to deliver a challenge to Malduit. [*VulgLanc*]

TRIDANZ OF TINODONTE

An infidel king who served Feirefiz, Perceval's half-brother. [*Wolfram*]

TRINCARDO THE MAD

Father of Losanna of the Ancient Tower, a lady who once wronged Tristan. His other children were Pinabel and Uriées. [*Tavola*]

TRINGAD

Son of Neued and father of Gwynn. A resident of Aber Deu Gleddyf, Tringad directed Arthur and his warriors to Rhymhi, a dog that they were seeking. [*Culhwch*]

TRIPLE

A city or land ruled under Arthur by Count Herman, who was slain in the Roman War. [*VulgMer*]

TRISTAN[1] [*Drust(anus)*, *Drystan*, *Thisterum*, *Thistronn*, *Thristrum*, *Tistram*, *Tristan(o)(s)*, *Trist(r)an(t)*, *Tristanz*, *Trist(r)em*, *Tristen(z)*, *Trist(e)ram*, *Tristum*, *Tryshchane*, *Trystan*]

Legendary nephew of King Mark of Cornwall and lover of Mark's wife, Isolde. His life is defined by the tragedy of the love triangle, which eventually caused the lovers' deaths. Though his legend likely originated outside the Arthurian saga, his story was soon grafted onto the Arthurian cycle, and he is often given as a Knight of the Round Table.

We have two possible origins of his name. A sixth century stone in Cornwall marks the grave of a certain *Drustanus*, son of Cunomorous. In Wrmonoc's *Life of St. Paul Aurelian*, Cunomorous is identified with King Mark of Cornwall. Nothing else is stated on the tombstone, and if this Drustanus is truly the origin of Tristan, then it is unknown how much of the Tristan story may be related to Drustanus's actual life. Certainly, the transference of Mark from Tristan's father to his uncle represents a major variation from fact. It is interesting to note, however, that in a Welsh Triad (in which Tristan stops Arthur from stealing one of Mark's swine), Drystan is called the son of March, a variation that occurs nowhere else.

The second possible historical origin concerns a certain Drust, son of King Talorc of the Picts, who ruled in Scotland in the late eighth century. In early Welsh Arthurian texts, Tristan is known as Drystan, son of Tallwch. "Drust" appears in a tenth-century (non-Arthurian) Irish tale called *The Wooing of Emer*, in which Drust's adventures at the court of the king of the Hebrides parallel Tristan's deeds in Ireland in the early Tristan tales.

Whether we are to find Tristan's origins in Drust or Drustanus, neither the Cornish stone nor the early Welsh tales mention the tragic love affair which defines Tristan's life in his saga. This theme may originate in the ninth century Irish tale of *Diarmaid and Grainne*: Diarmaid, the nephew of the Irish chief Finn, falls in love with Grainne, Finn's wife, due to the effects of a spell. Diarmaid and Grainne flee Finn's court and soon become lovers. Whether this story had a direct influence on the Tristan legend, or whether they both sprang from a common source, is uncertain.

The Tristan legend shows its development throughout Britain and Brittany, becoming a mélange of themes found in Welsh, Cornish, Breton, Arabian, and even Oriental folklore. Sometime during the early twelfth century, it appears that a French writer produced an archetypal verse Tristan romance that has since been lost. This *Tristan* prototype became the basis for the French verse *Tristan*s of Thomas of England and Béroul, and the Middle High German *Tristrant* of Eilhart von Oberge, all of which were written in the late twelfth or very early thirteenth century. Chrétien de Troyes apparently also produced a Tristan tale

which no longer exists. The early collection of Tristan tales can be divided into two branches: the realistic, courtly version written by Thomas and followed by Gottfried von Strassburg, the Norse *Tristrams Saga Ok Ísöndar*, and the Middle-English *Sir Tristrem*; and the violent, supernatural version represented by Béroul and Eilhart von Oberge. Though stylistic differences separate each of these tales, the text itself follows a relatively consistent story:

Tristan was born to King Rivalin or Rouland of Parmenie and to Blancheflor, the sister of King Mark. His mother died giving birth to him, and his father died in his infancy or youth. He was raised by Rual, his father's steward, but was kidnapped by merchants as a child. He eventually made his way to Cornwall, where he dazzled King Mark's court with his skill at hunting and music. Rual, who had been searching for Tristan since his abduction, came to Mark's court and was joyously reunited with his ward. Mark (presented in the early tales as a noble king) learned that Tristan was his nephew.

Mark was bound to pay an annual tribute to a giant named Morholt from Ireland. Tristan offered to duel Morholt as Mark's champion, and Mark reluctantly agreed. Tristan killed Morholt, leaving a piece of his sword in Morholt's skull. Having received a poisoned wound himself, Tristan fell ill and eventually departed Cornwall to seek a cure. Arriving in Ireland, he called himself "Tantrist" to disguise his identity as Morholt's killer. Isolde, the daughter of the king of Ireland, cured him. In return, Tristan killed a dragon that had been plaguing the king. Isolde soon discovered Tristan's true identity when the piece of the sword from Morholt's skull was matched with the broken segment on Tristan's sword. The king spared Tristan's life and Tristan returned to Cornwall.

Some time later, Mark was engaged to Isolde, and Tristan went to Ireland to escort her to Cornwall. On the return voyage, they accidentally drank a love potion intended for Mark and Isolde and fell hopelessly in love. Mark suspected their affair, having been informed by various vassals, but he gave them ever benefit of the doubt. Though Tristan and Isolde were, at various times, tried, exiled, or sentenced to death, they always managed to convince Mark of their innocence and return to his favor. Finally, however, Mark banished Tristan from court.

Tristan went to Brittany, where he assisted the king or duke against an attacker. Tristan then married Isolde of the White Hands, daughter of the king. Remembering his true lover on his wedding night, he declined to consummate his marriage.

Tristan was eventually mortally wounded by a poisoned spear (either while assisting Tristan the Dwarf reclaim his kingdom or while helping his brother-in-law, Kahedins, sleep with a married woman). He sent for Mark's wife to heal his wound, telling the ship's captain to fly white sails on the return trip if Isolde was aboard, and to fly black sails if she was not. When the ship returned, Tristan asked Isolde of the White Hands the color of the sails. Jealous of his love for the other Isolde, she told him they were black when in fact they were white. Tristan died of sorrow and Isolde, finding her lover dead, perished on top of his body. They were buried side by side. A vine grew from Tristan's grave and a rose sprung from Isolde's. The plants intertwined, symbolizing the eternal love of Tristan and Isolde.

Sprinkled between these early tales are a collection of lays that describe brief encounters between Tristan and Isolde, often with Tristan in disguise. These include Marie de France's *Chevrefueil* (Tristan and Isolde meet in secret under a tree, where a vision of an intertwined honeysuckle and hazel parallels their own love), the *Folie Tristan*s of Oxford and Berne (an exiled Tristan visits Marks's court in the guise of a fool to see Isolde), and the German *Tristan als Mönch* (Tristan switches identities with a dead knight and, disguised as a monk, attends his own funeral and meets with Isolde). Arthurian elements are slim in these early tales; in the branch of Thomas of England, in fact, his story is set a generation after Arthur's reign.

These early romances were eclipsed in the second quarter of the thirteenth century by the French Prose *Tristan*, which sought to fully integrate the Tristan legend with the Arthurian cycle. *Tristan* formed the basis of most later Tristan romances, including Malory's *Le Morte Darthur*. *Tristan* changes the name of Tristan's parents to Meliadus, King of Lyonesse, and Elyabel. As in the early version, his mother died in childbirth, and his father was slain. His tutor, Governal, spirited him to the court of King Faramon of France to hide him from Meliadus's enemies. After an unfortunate episode in which Faramon's daughter, Belide, fell in love with Tristan and committed suicide when he did not reciprocate, Tristan returned to Cornwall. His adventures at Mark's court—including his duel against Morholt, his voyage to Ireland, his love for Isolde, and his marriage to Isolde of the White Hands— proceed much as in the early Tristan romances, only they are interspersed with innumerable adventures in Arthur's Britain. Notable new elements include his friendship with knights such as Lancelot, Dinadan, and Lamorat, his appointment to the Round Table, his love-hate relationship with Sir Palamedes (who also loved Isolde), his adventures at the Castle of Tears, his period of insanity (caused by his false belief that Kahedins and Isolde were having an affair), and his affair with the wife of Sir Seguarades. The most notable variation from the original legend involves his death which, in most manuscripts of the Prose *Tristan*, occurs at the hands of King Mark, who has been given a poisoned lance by Morgan le Fay. (Morgan hated Tristan because Tristan had killed Huneson, Morgan's lover.)

The Prose *Tristan* influenced a number of Italian works, including a several *cantares*, the *Tristano Riccardiano* (late thirteenth century), the *Tristano Panciaticchiano* (early fourteenth century), the *Tristano Veneto* (fourteenth century), *La Tavola Ritonda* (early fourteenth century), and *I Due Tristani* (mid-sixteenth century). Adaptations also followed in Slavic (*Povest' o Tryshchane*, c. 1580), and Icelandic (*Saga af Tristram ok Ísodd*, fourteenth century, and *Tristrams Kvædi*, fifteenth century). While relatively faithful to their sources, we find some notable variations among these texts. In the Icelandic *Saga*, Tristan, the son of Kalegras and Blezinbly, becomes

the king of Spain, and in the Italian *I Due Tristani*, Tristan and Isolde have two children named Tristan the Younger and Isolde. In the fifteenth century French *Ysaïe le Triste*, his son is called Ysaie. [*TrisStone, MarieC, Thomas, Beroul, Eilhart, Gottfried, TrisMonch, TrisSaga, Triads, ProsTris, Dream, TristanoR, SirTris, TristanoP, SagaTI, Tavola, Ysaie, Malory, DueTris, Povest*]

TRISTAN[2] STONE

A seven-foot tall tomb stone located near Fowey in Cornwall. The stone—which has been moved a number of times—bears a sixth-century Latin inscription: "DRUSTANUS lies here, the son of CUNOMORUS." "Drustanus" is a form of Tristan, and many scholars have thought to identify Drustanus with the Tristan of legend. The *Life of Saint Paul Aurelian* connect Cunomorus with Mark by stating that Mark's full Latin name was Marcus Cunomorus. If these facts are true, history was largely modified by making Mark Tristan's uncle instead of his father. On the other hand, other evidence suggests that Tristan is actually based on the eighth-century DRUST, son of a Pictish King, and not this Drustanus. [*Topography*]

TRISTAN[3] THE DWARF

A nobleman who lived in a castle by the sea in France. His name was a misnomer; he was in fact a giant. His wife was kidnapped by the evil Estout l'Orgillus of the Castle Fer. He traveled to the Blanche Land to find his famous namesake, and to ask him to help rescue his wife. Tristan agreed, and the two Tristans met Estout and his brothers in combat. They were victorious, but Tristan the Dwarf was killed and Tristan was mortally wounded with a poisoned sword. His counterpart in a Icelandic version is TRISTAN THE STRANGER. [*Thomas, TrisSaga*]

TRISTAN[4] THE STRANGER

In the Icelandic *Saga af Tristram ok Ísodd*, the ruler of Jakobsland in Spain. Seven wicked brothers drove him from his land, but his famous namesake, who was king of Spain, helped him to reclaim it, though he received a mortal wound in the process. Tristan the Stranger appears as TRISTAN THE DWARF in other versions of the legend. [*SagaTI*]

TRISTAN[5] THE YOUNGER

Son of Tristan and Isolde in the Italian *I Due Tristani*. He was born, along with a sister named Isolde, during Tristan and Isolde's sojourn at the Castle of Tears. He was raised by foster-parents. Mark, who thought him the son of Isolde of the White Hands, crowned him king of Cornwall. Arthur knighted him and gave him his father's former Round Table seat. He enjoyed the protection of a sorceress named Sergia. Guinevere and the Queen of the Amazons became infatuated with him, and the latter forced herself upon him with enchantments. He eventually entered the service of King Juan of Castille and married Juan's daughter, Maria, whom Tristan saved from Moors. [*DueTris*]

TRISTAN'S LEAP

A stone jutting out from a cliff in Cornwall. After Tristan was caught by King Mark in Isolde's chambers, Mark decreed that Tristan be burned at the stake. To avoid this, Tristan asked to be allowed one last prayer in a cliff-side chapel. Once inside, he jumped out the window that overlooked the cliff and would have been killed in the fall had it not been broken by the well-placed stone. [*Beroul*]

TRISTERAT OF SAVOY

A lady who sent a magical chastity horn to Arthur's court. The horn proved all of the ladies at Arthur's court unfaithful, except for the wife of the king of Spain. [*DisIst*]

TRISTFARDD

King Urien's bard. [*Triads*]

TRISTOUSE

Daughter of King Briant of the Red Island and Mariole. Her mother owned a magic golden circlet and, when it was stolen, Mariole fell into poverty and despair. She cast Tristouse into the sea. Tristouse washed up in the kingdom of King Ydor, whom she married when she came of age. Tristouse and Ydor had a son named Torec, who eventually reclaimed the stolen circlet. Tristouse died shortly after Torec's marriage to the Miraude. [*Maerlant*]

TROIANO

A knight who bet Gawain his head that he could bring a better trophy to Queen Guinevere than Gawain could. Troiano delivered a white doe's head, while Gawain received the head of a great monster from his lover, Pulzella Gaia. Troiano lost the bet, but was apparently not slain by Gawain. [*Pulzella*]

TROIMADAC

In *Arthour and Merlin*, a king who served King Rions and who opposed Arthur at the battle of Aneblayse. His name is a corruption of *roi* MINADAP in the Vulgate *Merlin*. [*Arthour*]

TROIMAN OF GEREIT

A knight in Arthur's service. [*Stricker*]

TROIMAR LO MECHSCHIN

A Knight of the Round Table. [*HartmannE*]

TROMORET

The castellan of Cambenic under Duke Escant. He was killed by the Saxon king Salebrun while fighting in Arthur's forces at the battle of Garlot. [*VulgMer*]

TRONC

The original name of OBERON, a dwarf son of Julius Caesar and Morgan le Fay. [*Ysaie*]

TROYNT

A boar hunted by Arthur and his dog, Cabal, in the country of Buelt. Mentioned by Nennius, the boar is probably to be identified with TWRCH TRWYTH in *Culhwch and Olwen*. [*Nennius*]

TRUEREM

The Count of Truerem was present at the tournament at the Castle of Maidens. [*Renaut*]

TRUANT

Father of Arthur's warrior Kimbelin. [*GeoffHR*]

TRUDET

An evil giant known for raping maidens. Guiron the Courteous killed him. [*Palamedes*]

TRYFAN HILL

The resting place of Arthur's warrior Bedwyr. [*WelshSG*]

TRYFFIN

Father of Arthur's warriors Drudwas and Erdudfyl. [*Culhwch*]

TRYFRWYD

Arthur, describing his warriors' exploits in an early Welsh poem, says "They fell by the hundred before Bedwyr the Fine-sinewed on the strand of Tryfrwyd, fighting with Garwlwyd..." This may be an allusion to the battle of TRIBUIT mentioned by Nennius. [*WelshPG*]

TSCHOVERANZ

A Knight of the Round Table. [*PleierG*]

TUBELE

A castle in a valley where a tournament was held during the Grail Quest between the Count of the Plains and the Lady of Tubele. Bors encountered and battled his brother Lionel at the castle. [*VulgQuest*]

TUDIEL

A land bordering Lothian, which Arthur awarded to Sir Fergus upon completion of Fergus's quests. [*Guillaume*]

TUDUATHAR

Father of Arthur's warrior Enrydreg. [*Culhwch*]

TUDWAL TUDGLYD

His whetstone was one of the THIRTEEN TREASURES of Britain.

TUESMOME

A wild and savage Irish kingdom that Lancelot had to pass through on his way to Rigomer Castle in *Les Merveilles de*

Rigomer. The King of Tuesmome joined with Arthur's army to conquer Rigomer castle. Tuesmome perhaps refers to the historic region of Thormond in Ireland (Vesce, 377). [*Merveil*]

TUGAN

A castle in King Urien's Garlot. Morgan le Fay built a depository in Tugan, in which she hid a magic book given to her by Merlin. The book prophesied the future, telling of the deaths of Arthur and Gawain, but no one could read the book without perishing. [*PostMer*]

TULMEIN

In Hartmann von Aue's *Erec*, the castle where Erec defeated Yder in a Sparrowhawk Tournament and met Enide, his future wife. Tulmein was ruled by Duke Imain. Chrétien de Troyes places these events at LALUTH. [*HartmannE*]

TUMANE [*Tumange*]

The land ruled by count Ritschart in Ulrich's *Lanzelet*. The name does not correspond to any known location. [*UlrichZ*]

TURCANS

King of Armenia who served Emperor Filimenis of Constantinople. He joined Filimenis in a brief war against Arthur. [*Floriant*]

TURINORO

Gawain's killer in the Italian *La Tavola Ritonda*. Turinoro was the count of Cartagina and the brother of the pope. He had been knighted by Lancelot, so when Arthur went to war with Lancelot, Turinoro journeyed to Benoic to help his friend. He encountered Arthur when the king was on the way back to Britain to deal with Mordred's insurrection. Turinoro and his forces engaged Arthur's men. Turinoro slew Gawain, but was killed himself in the fighting. [*Tavola*]

TURKENTALS

A prince and vassal of Queen Herzeloyde of Wales (Perceval's mother). Turkentals was killed when the bold Lähelin invaded and conquered Herzeloyde's lands. [*Wolfram*]

TURKEY

In the chronicles, Turkey is subject to Rome, and its king, Itarc, joins Lucius's war against Arthur. In Wirnt von Grafenberg's *Wigalois*, Turkey allies with Prince Lion of Namur against Wigalois (Gawain's son). [*Wace, Wirnt, Allit, Malory*]

TURNES OF BLAKAMANNAVELLIR

A pirate king who attacked and pillaged Spain, forcing King Biring (Tristan's foster-father) to flee. Turnes kidnapped the young Tristan and sold him as a slave to a band of pirates. The name of his land means "Black Men's Plains" and probably signifies Africa (Hill, 197). [*SagaTI*]

TURNING CASTLE [*Forbidden Castle*]

A tower in the land of the Knight of the Burning Dragon found in *Perlesvaus*. Supposedly designed by Vergil, it spun around on its axis. Copper archers fired bolts from its battlements. Perceval destroyed all its magic by attacking it, and its people were liberated. Castles that rotate on an axis are a common theme in Celtic literature. Guinebal, Lancelot's uncle, sets one spinning in the Perilous Forest in the Vulgate *Merlin*, and another is mentioned in the *Livre d'Artus*. [*Perlesvaus, VulgMer, Livre*]

TURNING ISLE [*Turnaunce*]

An island visited by the first Nascien. It was composed of the waste left over when God separated the four elements. It contained a deposit of iron. The whole mass settled over a lodestone at the bottom of the ocean and the magnetic force caused it to turn perpetually. After spending some time on the island, Nascien left on the Ship of Solomon. During Arthur's reign, Merlin imprisoned the daughter of Duke Abinors, an enemy of Uther, on the island. She remained there, guarded by her lover Formis of Arms, until Arthur and Gawain set her free. Merlin's Tower, which was once inhabited by the wizard, was situated on the island. [*VulgQuest, VulgEst, Livre, Malory*]

TURRY

The city of which Arthur's Sir Owghtreth was lord. [*Allit*]

TURSAN

An area in France owned by Lancelot. Lancelot made Sir Melyas the earl of Tursan in return for Melyas's support in the battles against King Arthur. [*Malory*]

TURTUS

A land ruled by King Amurat and Queen Klarine, whose daughter, Duzabel, was saved from the giant Purdan by Arthur's Sir Garel. [*PleierG*]

TUSCANY [*Tuskane*]

A region of central Italy, surrounding Florence, known for its mighty warriors. Emperor Lucius of Rome brought Tuscan soldiers with him when he waged war against King Arthur. Arthur later marched through Tuscany on his way to sack Rome. After Rome fell to Arthur, Arthur returned and captured all of Tuscany. [*Allit, Malory*]

TUSCIA

A kingdom ruled by King Arduano (Armant) in *La Tavola Ritonda*, analogous to the DELECTIBLE ISLE in the Prose *Tristan*. Its capital was Vermiglia. Palamedes came to rule the land after he avenged Arduano's murder. Palamedes left a knight named Provaldino as regent. [*Tavola*]

TWELVE PEERS[1]

A table in King Brandegorre of Estrangorre's hall. The twelve knights who performed best at one of Brandegorre's tournaments could sit at the table. On one occasion, these twelve included Calcas the Short, Sabilor the Hard-Handed, Arfusat the Fat, Sarduc the Blond, Mallias the Thorn, Agoyer the Cruel, Patrides of the Golden Circle, Melidan the Merry, Garengaus the Strong, Malaquin the Welshman, Agricol the Well-Spoken, and the Ugly Hero. These twelve knights swore fealty to Brandegorre's daughter. [*VulgLanc*]

TWELVE PEERS[2] OF THE GAULS

A group of twelve knights who Guerin of Chartres brought to pay homage to Arthur at his coronation feast in Caerleon. They also joined Arthur for the Roman War. Geoffrey's allusion to the Twelve Peers seems to be an attempt to compare the greatness of Arthur's court to that of Charlemagne in continental romance. [*GeoffHR*, *Wace*]

TWELVE RULES OF THE ROUND TABLE

Giovanni Boccaccio's *De Casibus Virorum Illustrium* enumerates twelve basic rules that formed the Round Table's code of honor and service. [*Boccaccio*]

1. To never lay down arms
2. To seek after wonders
3. When called upon, to defend the rights of the weak with all one's strength
4. To injure no one
5. Not to attack one another
6. To fight for the safety of one's friends
7. To give one's life for one's country
8. To seek nothing before honor
9. Never to break faith for any reason
10. To practice religion most diligently
11. To grant hospitality to anyone, each according to his ability
12. Whether in honor or disgrace, to make a report with the greatest fidelity to truth to those who keep the annals

TWENTY-FOUR KNIGHTS OF ARTHUR'S COURT

A list of Arthur's warriors found in a Welsh manuscript. In the tradition of the Triads, the warriors are separated into eight groups of three. The full list includes Gwalchmei, Drudwas, and Eliwlod as the GOLDEN-TONGUED KNIGHTS; Bwrt (Bors), Galath (Galahad), and Peredur (Perceval) as the VIRGIN KNIGHTS; Cadwr (Cador), Lanslod (Lancelot), and Ywain (Yvain) as the KNIGHTS OF BATTLE; Menw, Trystan (Tristan) and Eiddilig the Dwarf as the ENCHANTER KNIGHTS; Nasiens (Nascien), Medrod (Mordred), and Howel (Hoel) as the ROYAL KNIGHTS; Blaes, Cadog, and Pedrog as the JUST KNIGHTS; Morfran, Sanddef, and Glewlwyd as the OFFENSIVE KNIGHTS; and Cynon, Aron, and Llywarch as the COUNSELOR KNIGHTS. As with the rest of the Triads, this list betrays some influence of the French romances but also preserves elements from authentic Welsh tradition. [*Triads*]

TWRCH[1] ("Boar")

One of Arthur's warriors and advisors. He was the son of Peryf. [*Culhwch*, *Dream*]

TWRCH[2]

An Arthurian warrior who was the son of Anwas. [*Culhwch*]

TWRCH[3] LLAWIN

A ferocious piglet born to Twrch Trwyth. He was killed by Arthur's warriors at Mynydd Amanw. [*Culhwch*]

TWRCH[4] TRWYTH

An Irish king that God turned into a boar as a punishment for his sins. Twrch Trwyth's father's name was Taredd. As one of his tasks, Culhwch had to hunt Twrch Trwyth and take a comb and shears from between the boar's ears. The giant Ysbaddaden had demanded these instruments to groom his hair. Simply killing the boar and taking the items would not suffice, however: Ysbaddaden attached a number of other tasks to this hunt. Culhwch had to hunt the boar with dogs named Drudwyn (who had to be held with a special leash, collar, and chain), Aned, and Aethlem. To be successful in the hunt, Culhwch also had to seek the services of Mabon, Garselid, Cynedyr, Gwynn, Gwilenhin, Bwlch, Cyfwlch, Syfwlch, and, finally, Arthur himself, some of whom had to be mounted on special horses.

Arthur's warriors found Twrch Trwyth in Ireland. Twrch Trwyth had seven piglets that acted as his warriors (six of their names are given—Grugyn Silver Bristle, Llwydawg the Killer, Twrch Llawin, Gwys, Banw, and Benwig). For many days and nights, Arthur's men fought Twrch Trwyth and his piglets. Many of Arthur's men and, eventually, all of the piglets died. In the course of the many battles, they chased the boar out of Ireland into Wales, through England, and down into Cornwall. Finally, Arthur's men trapped the boar in a river, and Mabon got a razor from between his ears, while Kyledyr the Wild took the shears. It took several more battles and losses to retrieve the comb. The warriors succeeded in driving Twrch Trwyth into the sea, where he disappeared, never to be seen again.

It is probably this hunt to which Nennius alludes in the *mirabilia* section of *Historia Brittonum*. Nennius says that Arthur and his dog Cabal hunted a boar named TROYNT in the country of Buelt. Twrch Trwyth's name signifies "king's boar" and the creature is probably identical to *Orc Treith* of Irish legend (Chambers, 72). Twrch Trwyth may also be the origin of TORTAIN in a French legend and has even been suggested as the origin of TOR, son of Ares. [*Culhwch*]

TWRGADARN

Father of Arthur's warrior Madawg. [*Geraint*]

TYBALT

Lancelot's squire, for a short time, in Ulrich's *Lanzelet*. He was the son of Patricius von den Bigen, and the brother of Ade, Lancelot's temporary girlfriend. He had been reared by Buroin, the duke of the White Lake, and taught the art of arms and knightly sportsmanship. Tybalt agreed to be Lancelot's squire after Lancelot killed Liniers—Tybalt's and Ade's uncle—and took possession of his castle, Limors. Tybalt proved a loyal and faithful squire, serving him well at the tournament at Dyoflê. When Lancelot succumbed to the enchantment at the castle Schatel le Mort (which made Lancelot, temporarily, a coward), however, Tybalt abandoned him in disgust. The name is a variant of TIEBAUT, who appears as the Duke of Tintagel in Chrétien de Troyes. [*UlrichZ*]

TYDOMIE

The Queen of Karmerie who married Meleranz, Arthur's nephew. The two met and fell in love when Meleranz was on his way to Arthur's court, and Meleranz eventually rescued her from a forced marriage to King Libers of Lorgan. Her uncle Malloas, who had supported the marriage to Libers, plotted to strip her of her lands, but he relented when he learned of Meleranz's pedigree. Tydomie and Meleranz ruled Karmerie and Terrandes, and had a daughter, Olimpia, and two sons, Lazeliez and Medanz. Tydomie's parents were named Garsidis and Lambore. [*PleierM*]

TYDORIANS

A knight who fought on the side of the King with a Hundred Knights during King Mark's tournament at Lancien. [*Contin4*]

TYGAN CASTLE

The castle owned by the family of Arthur's Sir Meriadeuc. It was besieged by Sir Galien, but Gawain joined the defense and killed Galien. [*Meriadeuc*]

TYMANT

A castle in Genewis (Benoic), Lancelot's homeland, ruled by the good Duke Aspyol. [*UlrichZ*]

TYOLET

A knight whose forest upbringing mirrors that of Perceval. Raised by his widowed mother, he departed for Arthur's court after seeing a knight. His career was punctuated by the retrieval of a white stag's foot for the daughter of the King of Logres, who had promised her hand to any knight that obtained it. He sustained heavy injuries during a fight with two lions that guarded the foot, but he managed to hand the object to another knight before collapsing. The other knight, assuming that Tyolet had died, represented himself as the victor, but was foiled when Gawain—who had discovered the injured Tyolet—exposed him. Tyolet was then able to marry the King of Logres's daughter. [*Tyolet*]

TYRNE

A land ruled by Queen Elamie, who was championed by Wigalois (Gawain's son). [*Wirnt*]

TYRONOE

One of the eight sisters of Morgan le Fay, who ruled with Morgan on the island of Avalon. [*GeoffVM*]

TYRRY

A knight whose sister was violated by Gawain in a forest pavilion. Tyrry, his father Gilbert, and his brothers Gyamoure and Brandelis chased Gawain down to avenge the disgrace, but all were defeated by Gawain in combat. [*Jeaste*]

U

UBBI OF BUDERISBORG

Father of Favida, a woman who was saved from two giants by Erec. Ubbi was an earl. [*Erex*]

UCER

A Saxon king who, under King Aminaduc, fought Arthur's forces at the battle of Vambieres. [*Livre*]

UCHDRYD¹ CROSS BEARD

One of Arthur's warriors. His beard was so long that he could drape it over fifty rafters in Arthur's hall. [*Culhwch*]

UCHDRYD² HOST PROTECTOR

One of Arthur's warriors. He was a son of Erim and one of five brothers. [*Culhwch*]

UCHEI

A son of Gwyron. Uchei is mentioned in the Welsh Triads as a warrior "who could not be expelled from Arthur's court." [*Triads*]

UGLY APPEARANCE [*Laide Semblance*]

An adventure established by Judas Maccabeus. It is found in the *Livre d'Artus*. The "Ugly Appearance" was the image of a fierce creature whose gaze could turn a man to stone. Arthur's knight Greu delivered the realm of the Wise Lady from its terror, and Merlin dumped it into the gulf of Satellie. In Der Pleier's German romances, its counterpart is the head belonging to the demon VULGANUS. [*Livre*]

UGLY HERO [**Lais Hardis, Lais of Lardis*]

A Knight of the Round Table first mentioned in the catalogues of Chrétien de Troyes, next to the HANDSOME COWARD. The Vulgate Cycle provides his biography: a black knight from the castle of Amalvi, the Ugly Hero was properly named ACANOR. Although the Ugly Hero and his father were both Christians, Acanor's dark skin lent him the common nickname. He participated in Arthur's wars against King Rions and King Claudas, and in several quests to find a missing Lancelot. After a tournament in Estrangorre, the Ugly Hero swore fealty to King Brandegorre's daughter. Lancelot freed him from an imprisonment at the Forbidden Hill. Erec defeated him in combat during the Grail Quest. Aside from his deeds in the Vulgate Cycle, he also undergoes a series of knightly adventures in *Claris et Laris*. [*ChretienE, Contin1, VulgLanc, VulgMer, PostMer, Claris*]

UI LIATHAIN

According to historian John Morris, an Irish dynasty that ruled one of the few stable Irish settlements in Britain. Originating from Munster, the Ui Liathains invaded Demetia but were driven out in the Arthurian period by Agricola.

UKERLANT

A land ruled in Arthur's time first by Count Narant and then by Narant's son, Bernout de Riviers. [*Wolfram*]

ULBAN OF SORELOIS [*Ulbawes*]

A Knight of the Round Table who appears at the Sorelois tournament and at the healing of Sir Urry. [*ProsTris, Malory*]

ULFIN [*Ulfines, Ulfius, Ulphin, Ulphyne, Urfin*]

A knight from Rescraddeck who served both Uther Pendragon and Arthur. He first appears in Geoffrey's *Historia*. In Uther's service, he fought in the Saxon Wars, acted as an envoy to Merlin, and participated in the breach of Tintagel (when Uther slept with Igerne). Upon Uther's death, he supported Arthur's claim to the throne, testifying to Arthur's paternity, serving as an envoy to Kings Ban and Bors, and fighting against the rebellious kings at Bedegraine. Arthur awarded him a position as his chamberlain and a seat at the Round Table. His further credits included the wars against Rions, the Saxons, and Claudas, and the thwarting of the first False Guinevere plot. In one episode, he chastised Igerne for not preventing the revolution by admitting she was Arthur's mother; he relented when she protested that she did not know this fact herself. He later became a hermit and lodged Galahad during the Grail Quest. Malory says that he lived in Corbenic in his retirement. Pierre de Langtoft calls him the son of Craddock, but this is probably just a misreading of Rescraddeck, his home. [*GeoffHR, Wace, VulgQuest, VulgMer, Livre, Arthour, PostMer, Pierre, Malory, TennIK*]

ULIAN

A wicked giant who, with his brothers Margan and Durkion, served Lord Karedoz of Malmontan. All of the giants were slain by Arthur's Sir Tandareis. [*PleierT*]

ULSTER HALL

A location in Wales that Arthur gave to Gawain after Gawain fought a duel against Galleron of Galloway. [*Awntyrs*]

ULTIUS

Seneschal of Vortigern. [*Butor*]

UNA

A lovely maiden whose parents' land was attacked by a dragon. Gloriana assigned the Red Cross Knight to go with Una to her land and free it from the dragon. On the way, the Red Cross Knight was tricked by the evil magician Archimago into thinking that Una was a wanton. The Red Cross Knight abandoned her and was thrown in prison by the giant Orgoglio. Una was protected by a lion, satyrs, and the knight Satyrane. They encountered Prince Arthur and convinced him to help. Arthur freed the Red Cross Knight and reconciled him with Una. They continued to Una's lands, the Red Cross Knight killed the dragon, and Una and the Red Cross Knight were married. In Spenser's allegory, Una, meaning "one," stands for the Church of England, the "one" true church. [*Spenser*]

UNARMED KNIGHT [*Chevalier Desarmé*]

One of three guardians of Rigomer Castle. He was defeated in combat by Lancelot. [*Merveil*]

UNBRIDLED HEART

A nickname of Sir LIONEL, Lancelot's cousin. [*VulgLanc*]

UNDERIGO

One of King Mark's seneschals. Mark commissioned him to seize Tristan and Isolde when he suspected them of having an affair. Underigo took a party of knights to the Palace of the Garden, where the lovers were staying, but Underigo and his companions were slain by Tristan and Lancelot. [*Tavola*]

UNDEWATER BRIDGE

One of two dangerous causeways leading to the land of Gorre in Chrétien's *Lancelot*. The other was called the Sword Bridge. The Underwater Bridge was also called the Lost Bridge, and it was actually submerged beneath the sea. Gawain tried to cross it during the quest to rescue Guinevere from Meleagant, but he nearly drowned. The description of the Underwater Bridge is used in the Prose *Lancelot* to explain the IRISH BRIDGE and the NORTH WALES BRIDGE. [*ChretienL, VulgLanc*]

UNFAILING BOW [*Arc Qui Ne Faut*]

A keen booby-trap invented by Tristan. While Tristan and Isolde were forced to hide in the forest of Morrois to escape Mark's wrath, Tristan set up the Unfailing Bow to kill any animal or person that happened by—partially to procure food and partially for protection. [*Beroul*]

URBAIN

A knight defeated by Perceval at the Perilous Ford in the Didot-*Perceval*. His lover was a fairy, and she sent a flock of birds to attack Perceval, but he defeated both Urbain and the birds. The birds spirited Urbain away. Urbain was the son of the Queen of the Black Thorn. His name may be a variation of URIEN [*Didot*]

URBANO

In the Italian *La Tavola Ritonda*, a castle owned by Uther Pendragon and Arthur. *Tavola* opens with a tournament, held by Uther, at the castle. Guinevere holed herself up in the castle when Mordred usurped Arthur's throne. Arthur, returning from his attack on Lancelot in Benoic, engaged Mordred at the castle. During the battle, Yvain was slain and Arthur received his mortal wound—an event that traditionally occurs at CAMLANN. In response to a summons from Guinevere, Lancelot came from France and killed Mordred in front of the castle. [*Tavola*]

URBGENNIUS [*Urbigen(e), Urgain, Urgence, Urgennius, Urgent*]

In Geoffrey of Monmouth, Arthur's earl of Bath. He fought in the Roman War and was killed at the battle of Soissons. His name is a variation of URIEN, which also occurs in Geoffrey. It seems that Geoffrey misinterpreted his sources, identifying two characters instead of one. [*GeoffHR, Wace, Layamon*]

URBINO

A city near Rome where Arthur, in Malory, laid an ambush during the Roman War. The ambush decimated the Roman army, allowing Arthur to take the city of Rome itself. This city is unnamed in the Alliterative *Morte Arthure*. [*Malory*]

URD

In Norse mythology, one of the three Fatal Sisters—the others were Schulda and Verandi—who presided over the past, present, and future. In Thelwall's *The Fairy of the Lake*, Rowena, wife of Vortigern, seeks their foresight during her quest to seduce Arthur. [*Thelwall*]

URGAN THE HAIRY

A troublesome giant who terrorized one of Tristan's friends—Duke Gilan in Gottfried's *Tristan*, King Triamour in the Middle-English *Sir Tristrem*, and Duke Bramante in the Italian *La Tavola Ritonda*. Tristan, visiting his friend, decided to rid him of Urgan's malicious presence in order to claim his friend's dog as a present for Isolde. Tristan's battle with Urgan was difficult, but after blinding him in both eyes and cutting off one hand, Tristan was able to kill Urgan by shoving him off of a bridge into a river. Tristan was also said to have killed a number of Urgan's brothers, including Lucano the Great. [*FolieO, Gottfried, TrisSaga, SirTris, Tavola*]

URGANS [*Hurganet*]

A knight of the Round Table slain by Orguelleus. His death was avenged by Perceval. [*Didot*]

URGLAY

An abbey in Scotland that was the final resting place of Josephus, son of Joseph of Arimathea. He had been buried first in Britain, but the Scots exhumed his body and brought it to Urglay, hoping that its presence would stave off a famine. [*VulgEst*]

URIAN

According to Geoffrey of Monmouth, a king of Britain in the third or second century BC. Urian succeeded his father, King Andragius, and was succeeded by King Eliud. [*GeoffHR*]

URIÉES [*Orices*]

A knight murdered by his brother Pinabel. Uriées had murdered a knight named Garionne, and Pinabel had to slay him in order to wed Garionne's niece, Tessina. The killing sparked a feud between Pinabel, his wife, and his brothers, which ended in Pinabel's death. Tristan had to save Tessina from execution at the hands of Lossana, Uriées's sister. [*ProsTris, Tavola*]

URIEN [*Uria(i)n, Urien(c)e, Uriens, Uriien, Urijan, Urjen, Uryen(s), Vrien, Vrweyn*]

A historical king of Rheged and father of Owain who ruled around 570, but was made Arthur's contemporary by later legends. A number of early Welsh poems glorify his various victories without connecting him to Arthur. In Nennius, he is mentioned as one of the kings who continued the battle against the Angles in the north, but was assassinated by his fellow, King Morcant (Morgant). He first appears as Arthur's warrior in Welsh legend, in which he is the son of Cynfarch and Nefyn, the brother of Efrddyl, Arawn, and Lleu, and the father of Owain, Morfudd, Rhiwallawn, Pasgen, and Run. Owain, his most important son, becomes Yvain in the French romances, and Welsh legend makes him Urien's son by the Celtic goddess Modron. The Triads name Urien's assassin as Llofan Severing Hand.

Geoffrey of Monmouth says that Urien was the brother of Loth (Lot) and Angusel, but most later legends make the three unrelated except by marriage. Geoffrey also makes him King of Moray rather than Rheged. In Geoffrey, Urien is Arthur's supporter, and he assists the king in his campaigns against Gaul and Rome.

Beginning with the Vulgate Cycle, however, he becomes an antagonist to Uther and Arthur. Descended from Joseph of Arimathea, Urien ruled the land of Gorre and the city of Sorhaut. Urien went to war with Uther over Gorre, and Uther was victorious. Urien eventually reclaimed the land, however, and appointed his nephew Bagdemagus to the throne. When Arthur drew the sword from the stone, Urien refused to accept Arthur as his overlord. He joined King Lot and a number of other kings in a rebellion against Arthur. In one source, he kidnaps Guinevere during the revolt. Arthur defeated them at the battle of Bedegraine. The kings had to cancel their rebellion when the Saxons invaded their lands. After experiencing several defeats against the Saxons, Urien and his companions allied with Arthur and crushed the Saxons at the battle of Clarence. Urien swore fealty to Arthur and married Morgan le Fay, Arthur's half-sister. He had two sons named Yvain and Yvain the Bastard. Urien participated in Arthur's war against Rome and in his battle against the five kings at the Humber River before disappearing from the adventures. His death is not described in the Vulgate romances.

Most variations to Urien's Vulgate character involve giving him different kingdoms. In *Meriadoc*, he is the King of Scotland and he becomes steward of Wales upon marrying Orwen, the sister of King Meriadoc of Wales. In *Claris et Laris*, he has a daughter named Marine. In Heinrich von dem Türlin's *Diu Crône*, his land is called Lof, and in *Palamedes*, he conquers Ireland. In Tennyson's *Idylls of the King*, he invades the land of King Leodegan, his brother, taking the role of RIONS in the Vulgate *Merlin*. [*Nennius, Culhwch, GeoffHR, Wace, Layamon, Triads, VulgLanc, VulgMer, Livre, PostMer, Heinrich, Palamedes, Claris, Arthour, Malory, TennIK*]

URJANS

A malicious prince from Punturteis. While at Arthur's court, he raped a visiting noble maiden and fled. Gawain caught him and brought him back to Arthur's court for justice. Urjans was tried and convicted. Arthur and his company were keen on sentencing him to death, but Gawain, moved by a sense of honor, pleaded for his life. Instead, Urjans was sentenced to eat out of a trough with hounds for forty days.

Despite Gawain's intervention on his behalf, Urjans blamed Gawain for his plight, and he found a serendipitous chance to exact his revenge: Gawain came upon Urjans while Urjans was lying on the ground, wounded, after losing a battle on the behalf of Orgeluse, the Duchess of Logres. Gawain, not recognizing the wounded knight, helped to heal him. Urjans repaid him by jumping on Gawain's horse and riding away. Somehow, the horse—called Gringolet—soon fell into the hands of Lischois Gwelljus. Presumably, Lischois killed Urjans, as he was in the habit of doing with other knights. Gawain soon re-acquired the steed. [*Wolfram*]

URPIN OF THE RED MOUNTAIN

A tyrant defeated by Gawain in the Fourth Continuation of Chrétien's *Perceval*, possibly identical to Chrétien's HARPIN. He was the father of Brun and the lady Bloiesine. Bloiesine prevented Gawain from killing her father. [*Contin4*]

URRY OF THE MOUNT

A Hungarian knight who was badly wounded in a tournament in Spain. In the tournament, he killed his opponent, Sir Alpheus. Alpheus's mother was a witch, and she cast a spell on Urry that caused his wounds to eternally fester, only to be cured when the best knight in the world examined them. Urry's mother and sister, Feleloye, carried him from country to country in a litter, hoping to find the knight who could heal him.

Eventually, they came to Arthur's court at Carlisle after the Grail Quest. When Arthur heard Urry's story, he commanded all the knights, dukes, earls, and kings in attendance to attempt to heal the poor knight's wounds. When Arthur attempted it, the wounds closed partially but renewed their bleeding. A hundred and ten other knights gave it their best, but failed. Finally, Lancelot, with reluctance, ran his hands over the wounds. They closed themselves as if they had been healed for many years, proving that God had again granted Lancelot the title of best knight of the world.

Urry became a Knight of the Round Table and was fiercely loyal to Lancelot. When Lancelot and Guinevere were accused of treason, Urry pledged his support to Lancelot and helped to rescue Guinevere from the stake. In return for his support, Lancelot made him the earl of Estrake. [*Malory*]

URSIN

A count of Salie who joined King Wigalois's war against King Lion of Namur. [*Wirnt*]

URSULA

Daughter of King Dionotus (or Athionard) of Cornwall. She married Conan Meriadoc after he became ruler of Brittany, and she helped her husband to spread British influence throughout "Other Britain." [*GeoffHR, Wace*]

URYELLE

A knight of Arthur's who participated in the Roman War. [*Allit*]

UTER OF CAMELOT

A knight in Uther Pendragon's service defeated in combat by Guiron the Courteous. He is apparently a doublet of Uther himself. [*Palamedes*]

UTHER PENDRAGON [*Outeropantragoras, Utepandragon, Utepantragun, Uter(pandragon), Uthir Pen Dragon, Uthur, Uthyr, Utpandragon, Vtere, Vther*]

Father of Arthur and king of Britain before his son. Geoffrey of Monmouth seems to be the first author to make him Arthur's father. In one Welsh poem, Mabon son of Modron is called Uther's man, and in another, Uther claims "a ninth part in the prowess of Arthur," but none of the Welsh texts mentions any relationship between them. One manuscript of Nennius's *Historia* refers to Arthur as "mab uter," which could mean "the terrible," but may have been interpreted by Geoffrey (or his source) as "son of Uter (Uther)."

As Geoffrey tells it, Uther was the son of King Constantine of Britain, who had previously been a prince in Brittany. His mother is unnamed except by Bauduin Butor, who calls her Ivoine. His older brothers were Constans and Ambrosius. Uther's father was assassinated by a Pictish agent, and Earl Vortigern of Gwent foisted Constans to the throne. Uther and Ambrosius were only children at the time, and friends of their father spirited them to safety in the court of King Budec of Brittany. Meanwhile, in Britain, Vortigern arranged Constans's assassination and assumed the throne himself. When Ambrosius and Uther came of age, they amassed an army and invaded Britain. Vortigern was embroiled in a war with the Saxons, led by King Hengist, at the time, and the two brothers managed to defeat and slay both Hengist and Vortigern. Ambrosius became king of Britain. Ambrosius commissioned Merlin to bring the Giant's Dance from Ireland, and Uther led the expedition, defeating King Gilloman of Ireland. In the meantime, Ambrosius was slain by a Saxon, and Britain once again faced a threat from an alliance between King Gilloman of Ireland and Vortigern's son Pascentius. Uther, however, destroyed both these men and assumed the crown of Britain in his brother's place. At his coronation, he was dubbed with the surname "Pendragon" or "dragon's head" in memory of the comet that Merlin had seen in the sky upon the death of Ambrosius. Uther immediately faced a Saxon threat in the form of Octa, the son of Hengist, and Eosa, Octa's kinsman. After a series of battles, Uther defeated and imprisoned the Saxon leaders.

At the feast celebrating his victory over the Saxons, Uther fell in love with Igerne, the wife of Gorlois, Duke of Cornwall. Gorlois sensed Uther's intentions and returned to Cornwall with his wife, who he secured in the castle of Tintagel. Uther declared war on Gorlois and besieged Tintagel and Dimilioc, Gorlois's own castle, but was unable to break the defenses of either. At the suggestion of his knight Ulfin, Uther sent for the assistance of Merlin. Merlin got Uther into Tintagel by magically changing Uther's countenance to match Gorlois. Uther enjoyed a night of passion with Igerne, and Arthur was conceived. Gorlois was soon killed in battle against Uther's soldiers, and Uther married Igerne, with whom he also conceived a daughter named Anna. He fell ill, but nevertheless took to the battlefield of St. Albans, in a litter, to fight Octa and Eosa, who had escaped from prison. After the battle, his sickness grew worse, and he had only enough time to proclaim Arthur his heir before he died. He was buried under the Giant's Dance, next to his brother.

Geoffrey's version of Uther's story is followed relatively faithfully in subsequent texts, with a few notable variations. Wolfram von Eschenbach makes him the son of Brickus, a descendant of fairies, the husband of Arnive (rather than Igerne) and the father of Sangive (rather than Anna). The Welsh Triads give him a second son named Madawg. In Heinrich von dem Türlin's *Diu Crône*, he has a sister named Enfeidas who is the queen of Avalon. *La Tavola Ritonda* makes him the father of Morgan le Fay, who is usually given as his daughter-in-law.

The Vulgate *Lancelot* tells us that Uther was born in Brittany, in the city of Bourges, which would be consistent with Geoffrey's facts if we assume that Uther was already born when Constantine came to Britain. We learn in the same story that Uther assisted King Aramont of Brittany in the destruction of the lands of the treacherous King Claudas, and that he went to war with King Urien over the land of Gorre.

Robert de Boron's *Merlin* and the Vulgate *Merlin* change the names of his brothers to Maine and Pendragon. In contrast to the chronicles, Robert says that Uther invented the Round Table, inspired by Merlin's tales of the table of the Last Supper and the Grail Table. *Merlin* places his death in the midst of a native revolt, not a Saxon invasion.

In the *Short Metrical Chronicle*, he is not Arthur's father, but is a king of Britain whose reign lies between Cassibelan and Vortigern. Finally, Malory changes the facts of his relationship with Gorlois, purporting that Uther had been at war with the duke before meeting Igerne, and that Uther fell in love with Igerne at a feast celebrating a peace between Uther and the duke. [*WelshPG, GeoffHR, Wace, Layamon, Wolfram, LancLac, VulgLanc, VulgMer, Heinrich, ProsTris, PostMer, PostQuest, Butor, Arthour, Short, Tavola, Malory, TennIK*]

UTHER PENDRAGON ABBEY

An abbey constructed by Uther Pendragon. It was renamed GALAHAD'S MARVEL during the Grail Quest. [*PostQuest*]

UTHER'S CASTLE

A castle near Sorelois that Uther Pendragon built. Bleoberis cuckolded the castellan of Uther's Castle. The castle was thereafter an enemy of the Round Table, and knights who strayed there were imprisoned. [*ProsTris*]

UTHER'S SHAME [*Vergogne Uter*]

A castle built by Uther Pendragon for Lord Argan, after the latter discovered that the former was having an affair with his wife, Dyagenne. Argan defeated Uther in combat and made the construction of the castle a condition of his surrender. [*ProsTris*]

UTOLF

A mighty warrior who fought under Lucius the Roman in the war against Arthur. [*Allit*]

UTRENAL

A Knight of the Round Table who embarked with the others on the Grail Quest. [*PostQuest*]

UWAYNE

Malory's version of YVAIN. [*Malory*]

V

VACHOUR
The name Malory once gives to the father of Tor. Tor's father is usually called ARES. [*Malory*]

VADAANS THE BLACK
A large, bold, brutal knight, promoted to the Round Table to replace Hector, who defected to join Lancelot's company. [*PostMort*]

VADALON
The brother of the king of North Wales. He besieged Mabon Rock, ruled by King Agrippe, but his army was destroyed when Agrippe's daughter poisoned its water supply. In revenge, Vadalon imprisoned the girl in a set of iron bands, which caused her extreme pain until she was freed by Sir Bors. [*VulgLanc*]

VAGAN [*Vagon*]
The elderly lord of a castle near Camelot. Vagan gave lodging to the Knights of the Round Table, who were spending their last night together before each departed on a different path on the Grail Quest. [*VulgQuest, PostQuest, Malory*]

VAGÉS
A lady who married Arbrun, a descendant of Brutus, and had two sons named Brun and Silhaut. Her sons were ancestors of the famous "Brown" clan. [*Palamedes*]

VAGOR
King of the Strange Island. Vagor's son, Marabron, accused Arthur's Sir Lionel of murder, and Vagor imprisoned Lionel until the judicial combat could be fought. Lancelot defended Lionel and was victorious. [*VulgLanc*]

VALCOLOR ("Colorful Valley")
A vale where Gawain's son Guinglain—the Fair Unknown—defeated the knights William of Salebrant, Elin of Graie, and the lord of Saie. They had attacked him there to revenge the defeat of their lord, Bleoberis, at Guinglain's hand. [*Renaut*]

VALDOAN [*Vadoan, Valydone, Walydeyne*]
The King of Valdoan was conquered by Lord Galehaut of Sorelois, and he participated in Galehaut's wars against King Arthur. See also AVADOAN. [*LancLac, VulgLanc, Laik*]

VALDONE PASS
A mountain pass near the Waste Forest, in the land owned by Perceval's mother. R. S. Loomis (*Tradition*, 345) read it as SNOWDON, but other scholars have disagreed. [*ChretienP, Contin4*]

VALENCE¹
A city in southern France named in the Alliterative *Morte Arthure* as part of Arthur's empire. [*Allit*]

VALENCE²
A Knight of the Round Table. Vivien, attempting to impugn the purity of the Round Table, recounted to Merlin a rumor which said that Valence had fathered a child on the wife of one of his own kinsmen. Merlin denied the rumor and defended the honor of the Round Table. [*Idylls*]

VALENDON [*Valenton*]
A city near the Castle of Maidens. [*Renaut*]

VALENTYNE
A giant from Lombardy who learned of the fame of Arthur's Sir Lanval and sought to duel with him. He issued a challenge to Lanval, and Lanval traveled to the city of Atalye in Lombardy to accept. During the battle, Valentyne kept knocking Lanval's armor to the ground, but Lanval's servant kept retrieving his master's dropped equipment, allowing Lanval to eventually kill Valentyne. Valentyne's knights sought to kill Lanval in revenge, but Lanval slaughtered them all. [*ChestreLvl*]

VALERIN
King of the Tangled Wood and abductor of Guinevere in Ulrich von Zatzikhoven's *Lanzelet*. After Arthur married Guinevere, Valerin challenged Arthur for the queen, saying that she had been betrothed to him first. Lancelot, newly arrived at Arthur's court, championed Arthur in judicial combat against Valerin and was victorious.

Valerin rescinded his promise to relinquish his claim to Guinevere, and he abducted her while Arthur was hunting. Valerin brought the queen to the Tangled Wood, where he placed an enchantment upon her that caused her to fall into a slumber. Arthur besieged the Tangled Wood but could not penetrate its enchantments. Finally, an intervention by the wizard Malduc destroyed Valerin's defenses. Arthur's army swarmed into Valerin's castle, and Valerin was killed. There are echoes of MELEAGANT's abduction of Guinevere in Valerin's story. See also GAZOSEIN. [*UlrichZ*]

VALFORT

The duke of Valfort was vassal of the Lady of the Blonde Hair, Arthur's paramour. [*ChevPap*]

VALIANT

In the Alliterative *Morte Arthure*, the king of Wales who served Arthur. [*Allit*]

VALINGUES

The Count of Valigues was the father of a lady championed by Gaheris against Guidan. [*VulgLanc*]

VALLEBRUN

A castle in the Brown Valley where members of the Brown Family resided. [*Palamedes*]

VALLET OF THE CIRCLE OF GOLD [*Vallet au Cercle d'Or, Youth of the Golden Circle*]

An Arthurian knight mentioned in lists from at least half a dozen romances. His name is never explained, though it may show some association with the CIRCLE OF GOLD in *Perlesvaus*. In *Claris et Laris*, he is called a king. [*ChretienE, Contin2, Claris*]

VALLEY OF DISTRESS

A valley in the Highlands of Hell, where the Black Hag lived in a cave. As one of his tasks, the warrior Culhwch had to travel here and obtain the Black Hag's blood. [*Culhwch*]

VALLEY OF NO RETURN

An enchanted vale, also called the Valley of False Lovers, created by Morgan le Fay to punish an unfaithful lover. The valley magically entrapped any knight who had ever been unfaithful to his lady. The valley's surrounding forest was called the Forest of Misadventures, and the road leading to it was known as the Devil's Road. Ladies could enter and depart at will. It held some two hundred and fifty captives—including Galescalain, Kehedin, Gaheris of Carahew, and Yvain—before Lancelot, who had never been unfaithful to Guinevere, entered and broke the spell. In retaliation, Morgan kidnapped and imprisoned Lancelot for a spell. [*VulgLanc, Livre, Prophecies*]

VALLTARI

A vassal of Kalegras, Tristan's father. He brought Blenzibly, Kalegras's wife, from England to the mortally wounded Kalegras's bedside. [*SagaTI*]

VALOUNE

The King of Valoune, which apparently encompassed the country of Wales, married the daughter of the Fisher King and succeeded Perceval as the Grail King in the Third Continuation of *Perceval*. [*Contin3*]

VALS OF SORELOIS

A knight who participated in the Sorelois tournament. Rather than a proper name, this was probably originally a surname for another knight. [*ProsTris*]

VALSIN [*Valfin*]

The Count of Valsin was the father of Beauty Without Villany, a messenger to Arthur's court. [*ChevPap*]

VAMBIERES [*Nambire(s), Vandeberes, Wandlesbiri, Wandesborow*]

A city besieged by the Saxons or Saracens in the beginning of Arthur's reign. Vambieres was well-defended and was surrounded by moats. The Saxons burned the city and starved its residents but it was never captured. The siege forced the kings in rebellion against Arthur to abandon their revolt and return home. Arthur and his knights were involved in several skirmishes against the Saxons outside the gates. The Saxons finally abandoned the siege to channel their forces to the battle of Clarence, where they were destroyed. Arthur gave the city to Yvain. [*VulgMer, Livre, Arthour, Malory*]

VAMGAINZIERS

A knight present at the tournament of Sorgarda, which Gawain won. [*Heinrich*]

VANDALIOR

A castle in Cornwall besieged by Saxons in the early days of Arthur's reign. [*VulgMer*]

VANDALIS

A Saxon warrior slain by Gawain in a skirmish at Roestoc. [*VulgMer*]

VANDALS

One of the barbarian Germanic tribes who attacked Rome in the fifth century, sacking the city in 455. They also ravaged Spain and North Africa, conquering the latter and ruling it from 439 to 534, when they were conquered by the Byzantine Empire. The Vandals flourished in a time contemporary to Arthur, and Jean D'Outremeuse says that Arthur subjugated them. [*Jean*]

VANOC

A young knight in Sir Walter Scott's *The Bridal of Triermain*. He was killed in a tournament, hoping to win the hand of Gyneth, Arthur's daughter. His death prompted Merlin to end the tournament and to imprison Gyneth in a centuries long slumber. [*Scott*]

VARGON

A heathen duke who, under King Oriel, fought Kings Urien and Angusel at the battle of Coranges. [*Arthour*]

VARGONCHE

A river near the city of Esterbury where, at the end of a battle, Sir Sagremor killed the Saxon King Brandague and the Irish King Margan. [*VulgLanc*]

VARIENS OF SASIABORG

One of Arthur's kings in the Norse *Erex Saga*. He was present at the wedding of Erec and Enide. [*Erex*]

VARLAN [*Hurlaine*]

A king of Wales, some time before Arthur, who went to war with the Lambor, the Grail King. During one fierce battle, Lambor forced Varlan to flee. The latter came across the Ship of Solomon and found the Sword with the Strange Hangings inside it. The sword was meant for Galahad, but Varlan drew it and used it to slay Lambor. The blow was called the Dolorous Stroke, and it turned Wales and Listenois into the Waste Land. When Varlan returned the sword to its sheath, he was struck dead in punishment for having drawn it. [*VulgQuest*, *VulgEst*, *Malory*]

VARUCH

A Syrian knight present at the tournament of Sorgarda, which Gawain won. Found in Heinrich von dem Türlin's *Diu Crône*, his name may be a variation of the BARUCH, found in Wolfram. [*Heinrich*]

VASPARIANO

Son of a famous knight named Guiron the Courteous. Vaspariano guarded the castle of Crudele, at which he was slain in combat by Sir Lamorat, who had to assume his post. [*Tavola*]

VAUX [*Vance, Vaux*]

In the Post-Vulgate *Merlin* continuation and in Malory, King Rions, Arthur's enemy, took the wife of the Duke of the Vaux ("vales") as his lover. While riding to visit her one night, Rions was intercepted and abducted by the brothers Balin and Balan, who brought him to Arthur. [*PostMer*, *Malory*]

VAWSE

A lady who threw a tournament in the forest of Arroy. Sir Marhaus, a Knight of the Round Table, won the tournament and was awarded a circlet of gold. [*Malory*]

VAYNS

A knight defeated by Sir Alexander the Orphan at the castle Fair Guard. [*Malory*]

VENEDOTIA

The Latin name for NORTH WALES. Geoffrey of Monmouth names Cadwallo Lewirh, a vassal of Arthur, as the king of the Venedotians. [*GeoffHR*]

VENELAS

Gawain's lover. She failed a chastity test involving a magic mantel. [*MantelM*]

VENENSARBORG

A young Tristan, arriving in Cornwall for the first time, was directed to Mark's court by two pilgrim's from Venensarborg. [*TrisSaga*]

VERA

An island paradise ruled by Arthur's Earl Masade. [*Erex*]

VERANDI

In Norse mythology, one of the three Fatal Sisters—the others were Urd and Schulda—who presided over the past, present, and future. In Thelwall's *The Fairy of the Lake*, Rowena, wife of Vortigern, seeks their foresight during her quest to seduce Arthur. [*Thelwall*]

VERANGOZ

The heathen king of Sorboreste, who treacherously slew King Gediens of Karedonas and waged war on Dulceflur, Gediens' daughter. Meleranz, Arthur's nephew, championed Dulceflur and killed Verangoz. [*PleierM*]

VERDOANA

The lady of the castle Aspetta Ventura in *La Tavola Ritonda*. She suffered from leprosy and could only be cured by the blood of a royal virgin. In the quest to heal her, her knights bled hundreds of virgins, most of whom perished. She was finally cured by the blood of Agresizia, Perceval's sister, who subsequently died. She appears in the Vulgate *Queste del Saint Graal* but is unnamed. [*Tavola*]

VERGIL

A famed Roman poet from the first century BC. His most famous work is the epic *Aeneid*, which relates the story of Aeneas as he sails from Greece and founds Rome. The early chroniclers used material from *Aeneid* to form their story of Aeneas and his son, Brutus, the founder of Britain.

Wolfram von Eschenbach, who uses metaphors from *Aeneid* heavily, says that Vergil "of Naples" was the maternal uncle of the sorcerer Clinschor, whose enchantments challenge Gawain *Parzival*. Vergil was the subject of numerous legends in the Middle Ages—most of them false—which are reflected in Wolfram's Clinschor character. Wolfram's assertion that Vergil was from Naples is only marginally accurate: he probably studied in Naples, and may have written part of his *Georgics* there. [*Wolfram*]

VERGULAHT [*Fergulaht, Vergolaht*]

King of Ascalun. He was the son of Kingrisin and his wife Flurdamurs. Vergulaht's cousin, Kingrimursel, accused Gawain of murdering Kingrisin and challenged him to combat in Vergulaht's capital of Schanpfanzun. Vergulaht promised Gawain safe passage until the battle, but became enraged when he found his sister, Antikonie, and Gawain flirting with each other. Vergulaht summoned his guard and attacked Gawain. Gawain fought bravely but would have been defeated if not for the arrival of Kingrimursel, who was furious that Vergulaht had broken his word to leave Gawain unmolested until the combat. Kingrimursel's presence forced Vergulaht to end his attack.

While traveling in the forest of Læhtamris, Vergulaht had been defeated in combat by the Grail-seeking Perceval. As a condition of his surrender, Perceval ordered Vergulaht to join the Grail quest. Vergulaht, as a condition of freeing Gawain, ordered Gawain to relieve him from this obligation by assuming the quest himself. Vergulaht and Kingrimursel rescheduled the combat for a year later at Barbigoel, but before it could take place, Gawain was vindicated in Kingrisin's death. [*Wolfram*, *PleierT*]

VERMIGLIA

The wife of King Amoroldo of Ireland, a friend of Tristan. She died before her husband. [*Tavola*]

VERMILLION KNIGHT

A common translation of the *Chevalier Vermeil*, the RED KNIGHT in Chrétien's *Perceval*. [*ChretienP*]

VERONICA [*Verrine*]

A woman from Jerusalem who lent a cloth to Jesus Christ to wipe his face. Later, the cloth was able to cure Vespasian's leprosy. When Vespasian came to Jerusalem, Veronica told him of all those involved in Christ's death so that Vespasian could execute them. This is Saint Veronica from the Bible. [*RobertBorJ*, *VulgEst*]

VERSARIA

Foster-mother of Elyabel, Tristan's mother. Her husband was named Ferragunze. [*Tavola*]

VERWAINE

A forest along the Thames River in which Gawain was abducted by Lord Caradoc of the Dolorous Tower. [*VulgLanc*]

VESPASIAN [*Vaspasien(s)*, *Vaspasyanus*, *Vaspasyen(s)*]

In the Grail histories, the Emperor of Rome forty years after Christ. He is called the son of Emperor Titus, but the historical emperor Vespasian reigned before Titus, between AD 69 and 79. The Christian apocrypha relates how Vespasian went to Jerusalem to avenge the death of Christ, a tale upon which Robert de Boron and the Vulgate *Estoire del Saint Graal* built: While his father, Titus, was still Emperor, Vespasian suffered from a horrible leprosy and promised riches to anyone who could cure it. Finally, a knight from Capernaum delivered word that an object touched by Jesus Christ might heal him; after searching for such an artifact, Vespasian was cured by

a cloth from Veronica. In gratitude, Vespasian planned to avenge the death of Christ in Jerusalem. He traveled to Jerusalem and executed all people who were involved in Christ's death. He learned of Joseph of Arimathea's imprisonment and freed him. Joseph had him baptized, and he returned to Rome. The Third Continuation of Chrétien's *Perceval* says that Vespasian brought Joseph with him to Rome. Later, Vespasian besieged Jerusalem when it was ruled by Agrippe.

Prior to the Grail histories, Vespasian appears in the chronicles as a Roman general who, under Emperor Claudius I, quelled the revolt of King Arviragus of Britain. [*GeoffHR*, *RobertBorJ*, *VulgQuest*, *VulgEst*, *PostQuest*]

VIAMUNDUS

Gawain's foster-father. He was a poor but nobly-born fisherman living near the city of Narbonne in Gaul. Gawain's mother had given Gawain, as a baby, to some merchants, who docked their ship and left it unattended near Viamundus's home. Viamundus came across the ship, found the infant and a pile of unguarded wealth within, and helped himself to both. Finding no way to spend his ill-gotten gains without arousing suspicion, Viamundus eventually journeyed to Rome with the spoils, representing himself as a noble Roman warlord from Gaul. The ruse worked, and the Roman Emperor awarded Viamundus a manor with in the city, where he lived out his days in relative luxury, raising Gawain to be an honorable and skillful knight. On his deathbed, he repented to the Emperor and to Pope Sulpicius, confessing his crime and deception. The Emperor, who had been his friend, forgave him and buried him in a tomb among the other Roman nobles. [*DeOrtu*]

VIANO

A counselor to Arthur. During Arthur's war with King Meliadus of Lyonesse, Viano advised Arthur to have the court ladies watch over the battle, so that the knights would fight more valiantly. [*Tavola*]

VIAUTRE OF GALEROT

Arthur's brother-in-law in the Didot-*Perceval*. His daughter, Elaine, is named as Gawain's niece or cousin. The Vulgate *Merlin* mentions a certain Neutres (NENTRES) of Garlot, who may be identical to Viautre. Neutres's *wife* is named Elaine in later texts. [*Didot*]

VICTORIOUS TOWER

The stronghold of Caradoc the Thirteenth, a knight defeated by Tristan. Caradoc had hung the shields of all the knights he had conquered from the tower's walls. After his defeat, he gave the tower to Tristan, who in turn gave it to a knight named Arpinello. [*Tavola*]

VIDEBURGH [*Huiteborc*]

A castle in the lands of Lord Galehaut of Sorelois. It bordered the Distant Isles. [*VulgLanc*]

VINNE

A city named as part of Arthur's empire in the Alliterative *Morte Arthure*. [*Allit*]

VILIN

A city in Ireland that served as King Amoroldo's capital. [*Tavola*]

VIOLET THE BOLD

One of many ladies at King Arthur's court to fail a chastity test involving a magic goblet. [*Heinrich*]

VIRGIN KNIGHTS

Three of Arthur's warriors mentioned in Welsh legend (adapted from French romances) who drew their power from their purity. These were Bwrt, Peredur, and Galath, who correspond to Bors, Perceval, and Galahad of the Grail romances. [*Triads*]

VIRGÙ OF LOGRES

A knight-captain in Arthur's service who led Arthur's soldiers at the siege of Tintagel against King Mark of Cornwall. [*Tavola*]

VISTAMARA

Tristan's sword in *La Tavola Ritonda*, called the best sword in the world. [*Tavola*]

VITERBO

An Italian city that was one of many to surrender and send tribute to King Arthur after he had captured the city of Rome. [*Allit*, *Malory*]

VIVIANE [*Viviana, Vivien*]

The proper name of the LADY OF THE LAKE in the Vulgate *Merlin*. It is a variation of NINNIANE, her name in the other Vulgate romances. Merlin met the girl in France, fell in love with her, and taught her his magic. Viviane used the arts learned from Merlin to entrap him in a fortress in the forest of Broceliande, where she visited him frequently.

While love and perhaps jealousy motivate Viviane in *Merlin*, in Tennyson's *Idylls*, she is an evil, pagan witch. Tennyson makes the Lady of the Lake a separate character. Embittered by her father's death at Arthur's hands, she predicts with glee the death of Arthur and the Round Table. She encourages Balin and Balan to kill each other. Once the lover of King Mark of Cornwall, she sets her sights on Merlin after a failed attempt to vamp Arthur. Merlin sees through her wiles but, as he is old and starved for affection, wearily allows her to seduce him. As in *Merlin*, he teaches her a spell that imprisons, and she traps him in a tree. Later, she informs Mordred of the affair between Lancelot and Guinevere, prompting Mordred's accusation and the eventual downfall of Arthur's kingdom. [*VulgMer*, *TennIK*]

VLASK [*Blaske, Blasque*]

The King of Vlask and Hungary was Sir Sagremor's father. After his death, the King's wife (the daughter of Emperor Hadrian of Constantinople) re-married King Brandegorre of Estrangorre. Vlask may refer to the Backa, a territory in present day Serbia, on the border of Hungary. [*VulgMer*, *Arthour*]

VODINUS

The bishop of London who reproved King Vortigern for his marriage to the Saxon princess Rowena. Hengist, father of Rowena and leader of the Saxons, killed Vodinus for this insult. [*Boece*]

VORTIGER

A son of King Vortigern, mentioned by Wace. He split with his father over his father's relationship with the Saxons. Vortiger and the Saxon warrior Horsa killed each other at the battle of Aylesford. He is probably identical to CATIGERN, mentioned in other chronicles but not in Wace. [*Wace*]

VORTIGERN[1] [**Gurthrigern, Gwrtheyrn, Fortager(e)(s), Fortiger(s), Vertaggiere, Vertigier, Vitiglier, Vortiger*]

A British king who ruled several generations before Arthur, famed for bringing misery to Britain by welcoming the Saxons. Bede is the first to mention Vortigern by name, but the figure first appears in Gildas's *De Excidio et Conquestu Britanniae* as the *superbus tyrannus* (generally translated as "proud tyrant," but likely indicating the less pejorative "supreme sovereign") who employed the Saxons against the barbarian Picts and nearly lost the island as a result.

Vortigern is almost certainly a historical figure, though his name seems to be a title, meaning "high king," rather than a personal name. Unfortunately, the earliest source to recount his story in any detail—Nennius's *Historia Brittonum*—is so tainted with legend as to be void of most historical value. A compilation of references from less questionable sources suggests an anti-Roman ruler who came to power in the second quarter of the fifth century, during the chaos that befell Britain after the Roman withdrawal. He seems to have been married to Sevira, the daughter of Magnus Maximus. During his reign, he conflicted with St. Germanus (whose first journey to Britain seems to have been in 429) and with Ambrosius Aurelianus, an apparently pro-Roman general. This period of British history is characterized by a weak British army facing increasing Pictish raids, and Vortigern evidently decided to bolster his military strength by hiring Saxon mercenaries. His plan backfired when the Saxons grew in numbers and power, and began eyeing Britain for themselves. Vortigern's enemy, Ambrosius, began the resistance against the Saxons, and it may have been members of Ambrosius's faction who deposed and killed Vortigern, probably around 450. (This summary is indebted to Jack Lindsay's *Arthur and His Times*.)

We find the following legendary account of Vortigern's life in the chronicles of Nennius, Geoffrey of Monmouth, and their successors:

The son of a man named Fernvail, Vortigern became the earl of Gwent and had sons named Vortimer, Catigern, Pascentius, and Faustas. Upon the death of King Constantine of Britain, Vortigern urged the appointment of Constans, Constantine's eldest son, as king, even though Constans was a monk and was ill-suited to the position. After forcing the abbot of Constans's monastery to release him, Vortigern elevated Constans to the throne. Constans became a puppet king under Vortigern's hand. In time, Vortigern became weary of ruling Britain by proxy, and he crafted to have some Saxons (led by Gille Callaet) assassinate Constans. Vortigern then put the British crown on his own head and established his court in Canterbury. Constantine's other sons, Ambrosius and Uther, both infants, fled Britain for Brittany.

Vortigern was under constant strain for fear of barbarian (Pict and Irish) incursions, a second Roman attack, or an invasion by the sons of Constantine, who were rumored to be building an army in Brittany. To beef up his armies, he welcomed the Saxons, led by Horsa and Hengist, to Britain and employed their services in exchange for land. He married Rowena, Hengist's daughter (in one source called Sardoine), and made Hengist the ruler of Kent. Nennius states that he also took his own daughter as a second wife, and had two children with her, leading the British clergy (and St. Germanus) to condemn him.

Hengist continued ferrying more and more warriors from Saxony to Britain, and by the time Vortigern realized that the Saxons were planning to usurp him, the British had become disgusted with his policies and had replaced him with Vortimer, his son, who began a war against the Saxons. Within a brief time, however, Rowena poisoned Vortimer and Vortigern reclaimed the crown. The Saxons called for a peace treaty to be signed on the plain of Ealing, but they betrayed the Britons, slaughtered Vortigern's army, and took Vortigern captive, ransoming his life for more territories.

Upon acquiring his freedom, Vortigern fled to Wales and laid plans to built a great fortress on Mount Snowdon to defend himself against his numerous enemies. The construction of the fortress hit a snag: each night, all work completed during the previous day disappeared. Vortigern's advisor, Joram, suggested that he find a fatherless child, kill him, and sprinkle his blood over the foundation of the castle. The king's envoys found such a child—Ambrosius (in Nennius) or Merlin (in Geoffrey)—in South Wales. The child scoffed at Joram's suggestion and showed Vortigern the true reason for his fortress's failure: a lake hidden beneath the foundation. Within the lake, the child revealed a pair of dragons, one white and one red. The dragons fought, and the white overcame the red, which, the child prophesied, indicated Vortigern's imminent destruction. Vortigern abandoned Snowdon and fled to his fortress, also called Vortigern. Vortigern and his fortress were either destroyed by a holy pillar of fire (in

Nennius) or by the Greek fire of Ambrosius, who had invaded Britain (in Geoffrey).

The only significant variations to his character are in the *Short Metrical Chronicle* and in Thelwall's *The Fairy of the Lake*. In the former, he rules in Britain *after* Uther Pendragon and he ravages his own land. Arthur, a prince of Wales, drives Vortigern out of Britain and becomes king himself. In Thelwall, he is the father of Guinevere. As in Nennius, he had an incestuous lust for his daughter, but his designs were thwarted by the Lady of the Lake. He was eventually murdered by his own wife, Rowena, who loved Arthur. [*Bede, Nennius, GeoffHR, Wace, Layamon, ProsMer1, Arthour, Short, Thelwall*]

VORTIGERN² [*Guorthegrin, Gwrtheyrnion*]

A fortress built by King Vortigern. Nennius says that it is in North Wales, but he later places it in Dyfed, in South Wales. Geoffrey of Monmouth calls it GANAREW. [*Nennius, Thelwall*]

VORTIGERN'S PROPHET

The name given to MERLIN after his famous series of prophecies before Merlin and his assembly at Mount Snowdon. [*GeoffHR*]

VORITMER

The eldest son of King Vortigern and brother of Catigern, Faustas, and Pascentius. When the lesser kings of Britain became disgusted with Vortigern's open-door policy towards the Saxons, they placed Vortimer on the throne in his father's place. Vortimer proved a much nobler king than his father. He led Briton armies against Hengist and the Saxons, and fought four battles against them, variously given by different authors at Darenth or Derwent, at Episford or Aylesford, by the Inscribed Stone, along the seashore in Kent, and at other unnamed locations. He pushed the Saxons to the isle of Thanet, after which they surrendered and returned to Germany. Nennius claims that Vortimer died from wounds received at the fourth battle; however, Geoffrey says that Vortimer was poisoned by his stepmother Rowena. Layamon says that during his reign, and at his request, two bishops—Germanus and Louis—were sent to Britain to restore Christianity. He was buried in either Lincoln or London. On his death bed, he had requested a monument be erected in his honor, but his barons failed to carry out the request. His father Vortigern was restored to the throne and, hearing of Vortimer's death, the Saxons returned in force. [*Nennius, GeoffHR, Wace, Layamon, Pierre*]

VORTIPORE [*Vortiporous*]

The third King of Britain after Arthur, according to Geoffrey of Monmouth. Vortipore succeeded to the throne after the previous wicked king, Conan, fell off a horse and broke his neck. Vortipore successfully battled off a wave of Saxon invaders and reigned for seven years. Vortipore is a historical figure, though the position attributed to him by Geoffrey is invented. Gildas mentions him as a tyrannical king of Dyfed (Demetia), which he apparently inherited from his father, Agricola. Vortipore had a great-grandson named Arthur of Dyfed. (Chambers, 170). [*Gildas, GeoffHR, Wace*]

VRIDEBRANT

King of Scotland during Uther's reign in Wolfram's *Parzival*. An ally and cousin of the infidel lord Isenhart, Vridebrant invaded the African kingdom of Zazamanc when Isenhart died for the Queen of Zazamanc's love. While in Africa, his own lands were invaded by the kinsmen of Hernant, whom Vridebrant had slain for the love of Herlinde. He had to return to defend Scotland before the invasion of Zazamanc was complete, but he left his lords—Duke Hiuteger, Gaschier of Normandy, and Kaylet of Hoskurast—behind to finish the invasion. These men were defeated by Perceval's father, Gahmuret. Vridebrant was also supported by warriors from Greenland and by Morholt of Ireland. Some time after the war, Vridebrant reconciled with the queen of Zazamanc. His father-in-law was named Schiltunc. [*Wolfram*]

VRIKEVREUE [*Urikeure*]

The name of the land around Rigomer castle in Ireland. It was guarded by three knights—the Unarmed Knight, the White Knight, and the Knight of Triple Arms, all of whom were defeated by Lancelot. [*Merveil*]

VULCAN

According to the Vulgate *Merlin*, this Roman god of the forge fashioned Marmiadoise, a sword owned by Hercules, Rions, and Arthur. [*VulgMer*]

VULGANUS

A hideous half-man, half-horse sea demon that terrorized the land of Averre. He carried a Gorgon's head that turned people to stone. Queen Laudamie of Averre enlisted Arthur's Sir Garel to slay the creature, and he was able to do so after his friend, the dwarf king Albewin, stole the Gorgon's head. After Garel killed Vulganus, Albewin stripped its skin and used it to fashion an impenetrable suit of armor. See also UGLY APPEARANCE. [*PleierG*]

VULTEIUS CATELLUS [*Catellus Vulteius, Catelos, Catenois, Wylters*]

A Roman senator who became a war leader in the campaign against King Arthur. Vulteius, with three others, was assigned by Lucius to liberate the Roman prisoners being taken by Arthur's warriors to a prison in Paris. The Britons won the battle. The Romans took to flight, and Vulteius Catellus was killed. [*GeoffHR, Wace, Layamon, VulgMer*]

VYLLYERS THE VALIANT

A Knight of the Round Table related to Lancelot. When Lancelot and Guinevere were accused of treason, Vyllyers pledged his support to Lancelot and helped him to rescue Guinevere from the stake. In return for his support, Lancelot made him the earl of Béearn. After Arthur's death, Vyllyers joined Lancelot in an abbey at Glastonbury, where he lived as a hermit until Lancelot's death. After participating at Lancelot's interment at Joyous Guard, Vyllyers returned to his own lands. [*Malory*]

VYOLETTE

A maiden rescued from two giants by Guinglain, Gawain's son, in Thomas Chestre's *Lybeaus Desconus*. She is called CLARIE in Renaut de Bâgé's *Le Bel Inconnu*. [*ChestreLyb*]

WADLING [*Wathelan, Wathelyne*]

A lake in Inglewood Forest, ten miles south of Carlisle. It is the setting for the Middle English poem *The Awntyrs off Arthure at the Terne Wathelyne*. While Arthur and his retinue were hunting in the forest, Gawain stayed behind to watch over Guinevere. As they rested in the forest, the sky grew dark, and a spirit—that of Guinevere's mother—appeared. The spirit lamented her own fate: she had been beautiful, powerful, and rich while alive, but in death she was confined to hell where she was chased and beaten by fiends. She warned Guinevere to be kind and generous to the poor, for only by giving money to the poor and having the poor pray for their souls may the rich achieve heaven. She also warned Guinevere against adultery, perhaps alluding to Guinevere's affair with Lancelot. She prophesied the downfall of Arthur and the Round Table, the betrayal of Mordred, and the death of Gawain. The ghost then departed and Guinevere and Gawain retired to Rondoles Hall. Later, Guinevere bade the bishops of Britain to pray for her mother's soul.

Arthur is captured by a baron near the lake in "The Marriage of Sir Gawaine," and must ransom his life by agreeing to return in a year with the answer to the question of what women desire most. It is also the setting for the action in *The Avowing of King Arthur*. [*Avowing, Awntyrs, Marriage*]

WADU

An Arthurian warrior who was the son of Seithfed and the brother of Sinnoch, Naw, and Bedyw. [*Culhwch*]

WALACHIA

A region of eastern Europe in present-day Romania. In Wirnt von Grafenberg's *Wigalois*, warriors from Walachia ally with Prince Lion of Namur against King Wigalois of Korntin (Gawain's son). [*Wirnt*]

WALBAN

A Knight of the Round Table. [*Konrad*]

WALDIN OF THE FEARSOME VALE [*Gaudin*]

A strong knight who assisted his cousin or uncle, King Angusel of Scotland, in repelling an invasion of Saxons. Waldin loved the Lady Lore of Branlant and he besieged her castle, the Narrow Wood, intending to force her into marriage. According to the Vulgate *Merlin*, he managed to conquer it, but the *Livre d'Artus* says that Gawain defeated him and sent him to Arthur's court, where he became a Knight of the Round Table. [*VulgMer, Livre, Arthour*]

WALDOMER

The brother-in-law of the Emperor of the Alemanni. He served as a commander for King Meriadoc of Wales when Meriadoc served the Emperor. [*Historia*]

WALES [*Galays, Galeys, Galis, Galoes, Galys, Gaules, Glois, Valois, Waleis, Walest, Walis*]

A division of Britain, occupying the west central peninsula. Locations in Wales play a large role in Arthurian literature—particularly in Welsh Arthurian literature. Often called CAMBRIA, the country, in both history and legend, is divided into a number of sub-kingdoms. The most basic of these, used in legends with hazy geography, is NORTH WALES and SOUTH WALES. Historically, however, Wales includes the regions of MON, GWYNEDD, POWYS, KEREDIGYAWN, DYFED, YSTRAD TYWI, and GLAMORGAN. Arthur is often named as Wales's overlord, holding his court in either Caerleon or the fictional Cardueil. Its mountain range, Snowdon, places an important role in the tales of Vortigern.

Arthurian legend tends to assign the various divisions of Wales to separate rulers, though a few texts appoint rulers of the entire country. Renaut de Bâgé has Esmeree the Blonde as Wales's queen, having inherited the country from her father, Guingras. Gunglain, Gawain's son, became king when he married her.

In Wolfram von Eschenbach's *Parzival*, we learn that Queen Herzeloyde, Perceval's mother, inherited it from her late husband, King Castis. Gahmuret became king upon marrying Herzeloyde. After Perceval's birth, it was conquered by King Lähelin, but was eventually reclaimed by Kardeiz, Perceval's son.

According to the Vulgate Cycle, the country was called HOSELICE in Joseph of Arimathea's time. Its first Christian king was Galahad, Joseph of Arimathea's son, and its name was changed to Gales or Wales in his honor. Several generations later, Wales was ruled by King Varlan, who struck the Dolorous Stroke against King Lambor of Listenois. The Dolorous Stroke turned both Listeonis and Wales into the Waste Land.

In the *Historia Meriadoc*, Wales is first ruled by King Caradoc, whose life and land are taken by his brother, Griffin. With Arthur's help, the land was eventually restored to Meriadoc, Caradoc's son, who gave it to King Urien to rule in his stead.

Rulers of Wales named in other legends include King Iels (Hartmann's *Erec*), Duke Gilan (Der Pleier's *Garel*), King Triamour (*Sir Tristrem*), and King Valiant (the Alliterative *Morte Arthure*). [*GeoffHR, HartErec, Wolfram, VulgQuest, VulgEst, PleierG, SirTris, Historia, Allit*]

WALLINGFORD

A seaport in southern Britain. According to the Alliterative *Morte Arthure*, Arthur kept a treasury at Wallingford, which included a magnificent sword named Clarent. The treasury was ransacked by Mordred during his insurrection. When Arthur learned of it, he knew that Guinevere had betrayed him, since only Guinevere had known its location. [*Allit*]

WALTER

A knight in Arthur's service who participated in the Roman War. [*Allit*]

WALWERTH [*Walweitha*]

A variation of GALLOWAY give by William of Malmesbury as the land ruled by Walwain (Gawain), after whom it was named. [*WilliamM*]

WANDEHENCHES

A castle on the border of Gorre and the Strange Land. Knights at the castle prevented the prisoners of Gorre from escaping. [*VulgLanc*]

WANGLENT

An Irish castle ruled by Bauduins, an evil knight killed by Gawain. [*Merveil*]

WARWICK [*Cargueit, Guivic, Warguit, Warwyk*]

A county in central England. During Arthur's reign, Arthgal served as the earl of Warwick. [*GeoffHR, Wace*]

WASTE CASTLE

A manor inhabited by the impoverished Poor Knight and his two maiden daughters. It served as lodging for Gawain and Lancelot on one occasion. It was also called the Poor Castle. [*Perlesvaus*]

WASTE CHAPEL[1] [**Gaste Capiele*]

The location of the tomb of Canaan, a follower of Joseph of Arimathea who slew his twelve brothers. The brothers were all buried with their swords on their tombs. After the burial, the swords unexpectedly stood upright and Canaan's tomb became engulfed in flames. Gawain and Hector visited the Chapel, but were driven back by the swords. It was Lancelot's noble presence that finally caused the fire to be extinguished. [*VulgLanc*]

WASTE CHAPEL[2] [**Gaste Capiele*]

A perilous chapel near the city of Cardigan. It was surrounded by all kinds of supernatural perils, beasts, and brambles. King Ris of Outre-Ombre, an enemy of Arthur, braved the chapel and left a cloth on the altar. Later, he offered to grant any favor to the knight who would brave the Waste Chapel by taking a pair of shackles (intended for Arthur when Ris conquered him) to the altar. None of Ris's knights would brave the chapel, but Lady Lore of Cardigan, whose city Ris had conquered, saw a chance to reclaim her sovereignty. She took the shackles to the chapel. Lore saw two dark men in flames tossing around a decapitated head on the way. When she got to the chapel, she was followed by a knight who buried the body of the slain Bleheri, who turned out to be the father of Meriadeuc, the knight Lore eventually married. Lore took a sword from Bleheri's body and later gave it to Meriadeuc. Meriadeuc eventually visited the Waste Chapel and paid homage to his father's body. See also the PERILOUS CEMETERY. [*Meriadeuc*]

WASTE CHAPEL[3]

Another name for the PERILOUS CHAPEL in the PERILOUS CEMETERY in *Perlesvaus*. It shares many characteristics with the WASTE CHAPEL of *Meriadeuc*. [*Perlesvaus*]

WASTE CITY [*Gaste Citié*]

A supernatural, ruined city in *Perlesvaus*. Lancelot visited the Waste City and was challenged to a Beheading Game by one of the residents. By honoring his pledge to return in a year and face death, Lancelot ended a curse and saved the Waste City and its people. In the Fourth Continuation of Chrétien's *Perceval*, the king of the Waste City attacks Gornemant of Gohort, but is driven away by Perceval. [*Perlesvaus*]

WASTE FOREST [*Desolate Forest, *Gaste Forest*]

The forest where Perceval was born and raised by his mother in Chrétien's *Perceval*. One day he encountered some knights, which prompted him to leave the Forest and travel to Arthur's court to become a knight himself, causing his mother to die of grief. In the Vulgate *Queste del Saint Graal*, it is also the home of Perceval's aunt, who Perceval visits during the Grail Quest. It was situated on the edge of the Waste Land and contained the river Morcoise. Wolfram von Eschenbach calls this region SOLTANE. [*ChretienP, Bliocadran, Didot, VulgLanc, VulgQuest, PostQuest*]

WASTE FOUNTAIN

Knights from the Waste Fountain participated in the tournament in which Bliocadran, Perceval's father, was killed. [*Bliocadran*]

WASTE LAND[1] [*Desert, Deserted Land, Land Laid Waste, *Terre Gaste*]

Also known as the STRANGE LAND, the Waste Land was the kingdom destroyed in holy retribution for the DOLOROUS STROKE (or, in one version, for Perceval's failure to ask the Grail Question). To those stories that include it, it is identical to the GRAIL KINGDOM, sometimes called LISTEONIS. The Vulgate *Estoire del Saint Graal* says that it also included WALES. (The country of Dyfed in Wales, interestingly, is laid waste by an enchantment under different circumstances in the early non-Arthurian tale of *Manawydan*.) In the Didot-*Perceval*, the Waste Land encompasses all of Great Britain. The Waste Land's ruler was the Grail King or Fisher King.

The Waste Land is first found in the First Continuation of Chrétien's *Perceval*, where the sickness of the land is linked to the illness and infertility of the Maimed King. (This link forms the most cogent argument of scholars who propose an agrarian ritual origin for the Grail legend.) The Waste Land resulted from use, in combat, of the Grail Sword. Neither the land nor the king could be healed until some knight asked the Fisher King to explain the marvels of the Grail. After Perceval failed to ask the question during his visit to the Fisher King's castle, Gawain partially healed the land and king by inquiring about the Bleeding Lance. The theme of a land under a spell which a question will undo is pervasive in fairy tales and folklore, and the idea that the health of the land and the ruler were one is common in Celtic folktale. We find a particularly relevant example in the Welsh story of *Branwen*, in which Bran, King of Britain, is wounded in the foot by a poisoned spear during an expedition to Ireland. As a result, Britain falls waste. Bran has been viewed by many as the progenitor of the Fisher King.

In the Vulgate *Queste del Saint Graal*, Perceval's aunt is called the "Queen of the Waste Land." She instructs Perceval during the Grail Quest. Malory names her as one of the four queens who takes Arthur's body from the battlefield of Salisbury to the island of Avalon. A "Knight of the Waste Land" is defeated by Arthur in *Le Chevalier du Papegau*. [*Contin1*, *Didot*, *VulgQuest*, *VulgEst*, *PostQuest*, *Tavola*, *ChevPap*, *Malory*]

WASTE LAND[2] [*Land Laid Waste*, **Terre Gaste*, *Terre Desert*]

The region of France ruled by Claudas, the mortal enemy of Lancelot and his family. Orignally called BERRY, the land was renamed after Uther Pendragon and Aramont of Brittany destroyed it and turned it into a desert as part of their campaign against Claudas. [*LancLac*, *VulgLanc*]

WASTE MANOR

An evil residence in Arthur's kingdom. Lancelot killed its lord, so its occupants were prone to attack Arthur's knights. Its prince, Meliant, joined Brian of the Isles in a war against Arthur. [*Perlesvaus*]

WATER LILY

An Egyptian ship seen by Merlin off the Cornish coast, sailing through the air. "Provoked to an envious spleen" by its splendor, he blasted it out of the sky. An Egyptian princess washed ashore. The Lady of the Lake made Merlin carry her body to Arthur's court, where she was resurrected by Galahad. [*Wordsworth*]

WATERFORD

A Welsh territory that Arthur bestowed upon Gawain after Gawain fought a great duel against Galleron of Galloway. [*Awntyrs*]

WAVAIN

A knight of Arthur's who was, according to Wace, dubbed the same day as Gawain. Wace probably used the name after becoming confused by one of the many alternate spellings of GAWAIN. [*Wace*]

WAYFORD

A territory that Arthur bestowed upon Gawain after Gawain fought a great duel against Galleron. [*Awntyrs*]

WAYLAND

An invisible smith in Anglo-Saxon legend. Working in Segontium, he fashioned a series of cups given to Merlin in Geoffrey's *Vita Merlini*. His son, Widia, may be represented in Layamon's *Brut* as WITEGE. [*GeoffVM*]

WECHARD

A knight in Arthur's service who participated in the Roman War. [*Allit*]

WELSH GATE

The gate in Camelot that faced Wales. [*VulgLanc*]

WENDLAND

Layamon says that the king of Wendland—Rumareth—voluntarily subjugated himself to Arthur in fear of Arthur's power. A number of suggestions have been offered for the location of this land, including Finland, Gwynned, and even Vinland, but the most likely is the country of the Wends—which is now an enclave in east Germany. In Malory, the land is the home of Sir Hontzlake. [*Layamon*, *Malory*]

WESSEX

One of the most stable Anglo-Saxon kingdoms, Wessex (in south-western England, roughly modern day Dorsetshire) was one of the first territories settled by the Saxons at the advent of their British invasion. In John Hardyng's chronicle, Arthur gives the area to Cheldric the Saxon after defeating Cheldric at the battle of Bath. [*Hardyng*]

WEST ISLANDS

The realm ruled by the King with a Hundred Knights in the Serbo-Russian *Povest' o Tryshchane*. [*Povest*]

WEST WALES

In Malory, the "Lord of West Wales" pledges thirty thousand soldiers to Arthur's war against Rome. Malory took his character from the King of Wales in the Alliterative *Morte Arthure* who is called VALIANT. [*Malory*]

WESTMINSTER

A town on the Thames River, just west of London. Guinevere was a-maying in the woods and fields near Westminster when Meleagant abducted her. [*Malory*]

WESTPHALIA

Part of Arthur's kingdom in the Alliterative *Morte Arthure*. [*Allit*]

WEXFORD

A seaside city on the southeast corner of Ireland where Gurmun, Isolde's father, sometimes held court. [*Gottfried*]

WHITE CASTLE[1]

The location of a tournament in which Perceval, Gawain, and Meliant of Lis all displayed prowess. [*Didot*]

WHITE CASTLE[2] [*Blanc Castel*]

The stronghold ruled by Bliant and his brother Celinant—the two knights who housed Lancelot during his period of insanity. [*VulgLanc, PostMer, Malory*]

WHITE CASTLE[3] [*Blanc Castel*]

A castle on the border of Gorre that appears several times in the Vulgate Cycle. The Lord of the White Castle was one of the knights who opposed the Saxon invasions at the beginning of Arthur's reign. The Lady of the White Castle is named as the cousin of Galescalain. Another Lord of the White Castle is called Gallides, who was defeated by Bors. [*VulgLanc, VulgMer*]

WHITE CASTLE[4]

A castle in Brittany visited by Arthur after he killed the giant of Mont St. Michel. [*Allit*]

WHITE CITY[1] [*Blance Cité*]

A city saved by Floriant, Morgan le Fay's foster-son, from a terrible monster that ate the city's maidens. The city's queen was named Alemandine. [*Floriant*]

WHITE CITY[2] [*Blanche Cité*]

The Welsh capital of King Jozefent, father of Arthur's Sir Floriant. [*Floriant*]

WHITE CROSS

A landmark at the edge of Camelot Forest. It served as an assembly point for knights on a quest to find Lancelot. [*VulgLanc*]

WHITE FOREST[1]

An enchanted forest near Arthur's Cardueil court. It contained the chapel of St. Augustine, which renewed Arthur's spirits. It was also the haunt of the evil Black Knight, who was slain by Arthur. [*Perlesvaus*]

WHITE FOREST[2]

A wood inhabited by the White Knight. Arthur challenged the White Knight for ownership of the forest. In judicial combat, Sir Meriadoc decided the issue in Arthur's favor, but persuaded Arthur to relinquish his claim. [*Historia*]

WHITE FORTRESS

King Lancelot, Lancelot's grandfather, loved the lady of the White Fortress, who was married to his cousin, a duke. When the Duke of the White Fortress discovered their love, he treacherously murdered King Lancelot—an act for which his castle became shrouded in darkness. The duke was crushed by a crumbling wall. The darkness was to linger at the White Fortress until Galahad's arrival years later. [*VulgLanc*]

WHITE HAG

Mother of the Black Hag, a witch slain by Arthur. [*Culhwch*]

WHITE KNIGHT[1] [*Blans Chevalier*]

A knight defeated by Perceval at the Amorous Ford. The White Knight had guarded the ford for seven years. Perceval sent him to Arthur's court. [*Contin2*]

WHITE KNIGHT[2]

An opponent of the Red Knight. The White Knight was battling the Red Knight when Perceval arrived and accidentally killed the Red Knight. [*Perlesvaus*]

WHITE KNIGHT[3] [*Blanc Chevalier*]

A name assigned to Lancelot before anyone—including Lancelot himself—knew his real name. It was given to him because of his white armor and shield. Lancelot carried the name until he liberated the castle Dolorous Guard and discovered his true name. [*LancLac, VulgLanc*]

WHITE KNIGHT[4] [*Blanc Chevalier*]

A mysterious God-sent warrior who rescued King Evalach of Sarras from certain defeat at the hands of King Tholomer of Babylonia. He appeared when Evalach tore the cloth from the shield that Joseph of Arimathea gave him, revealing the symbol of a cross. After defeating Tholomer's army at the Rock of Blood, the White Knight disappeared. [*VulgEst, Joseph*]

WHITE KNIGHT[5]

One of the three knights who guarded Vrikevreue, the heath surrounding Rigomer castle in Ireland. Lancelot defeated him and his companions. [*Merveil*]

WHITE KNIGHT[6]

A knight who Arthur challenged for ownership of the White Forst. Sir Meriadoc decided the issue in Arthur's favor but convinced Arthur to return the White Forest to the White Knight. [*Historia*]

WHITE LAKE

The property ruled by Duke Buroin in Ulrich's *Lanzelet*. Lancelot lodged here on the way to Arthur's court. [*UlrichZ*]

WHITE LAND[1] [*Blanche Land, Blankenland]

In Thomas's *Tristan*, one of Tristan's homes, in Brittany; in Beroul's version, an area of Cornwall where Tristan and Isolde fled after their exile from Mark's court. [*Thomas, Beroul*]

WHITE LAND[2]

The location of a tournament at which Yder and Arthur were the principal combatants. Gawain and the Little Knight fought on Yder's side and won the tournament. [*Contin1*]

WHITE LAND[3] [*Blance Terre]

The land ruled by King Lancelot, Lancelot's grandfather. It bordered on the Foreign Country. [*VulgLanc*]

WHITE LAND[4]

The King of the White Land is named as an ally of Arthur in *Claris et Laris*. A Queen of the White Land appears in a tournament in *Durmart le Gallois*. [*Durmart, Claris*]

WHITE MOUNTAIN [*Blanche Montaigne]

The kingdom ruled by Escanor the Handsome, an opponent of Gawian. [*Girart*]

WHITE THORN CASTLE [*Blanche Espine]

A castle ruled by Matain the Cruel. Matain hated Arthur's knights, and his people habitually beat and degraded them whenever they happened along. The castle was conquered and destroyed by Lancelot, Bors, Gaheris, and Bagdemagus. Matain was killed by Lancelot. [*VulgLanc*]

WHITE THORN FORD

One of Arthur's estates. [*Merveil*]

WHITE TOWER [Blance Tour]

The home of Galerian, Perceval's paternal uncle. Perceval won a golden cup at a White Tower tournament. [*Perlesvaus*]

WHITEHEAD OF THE HAMLET

A knight who fought in Arthur's army against King Rions in the Vulgate *Merlin*.. [*VulgMer*]

WICHER [Wichere, Wyshard]

A knight in Arthur's service who participated in the Roman War. [*Allit, Malory*]

WICKED CUSTOM [*Malvagia Usanza]

In *La Tavola Ritonda*, an island where Tristan and Isolde washed up on their way from Ireland to Cornwall. The Castle of Tears, owned by the parents of Lord Galehaut, stood on the island, and Tristan had to conquer it in order to leave the island. In the Prose *Tristan*, it is called the GIANT'S ISLE. The "Wicked Custom" was that the visiting knight's lady would be compared to the paramour of the island's lord. Whichever was least beautiful was beheaded. [*Tavola*]

WICKED NEIGHBOR [*Male Voisine]

The name of a horn blown by one of Sir Parsamant's servants in order to summon people to a fight between Parsamant and another knight. Parsamant's treatment of defeated knights was wicked, and Perceval finally ended his custom. [*Contin4*]

WICKED PASS

A pass into the giant Caradoc's lands, where Caradoc's forces battled Arthur's. Lancelot slipped through and went on to the Dolorous Tower to kill Caradoc. [*VulgLanc*]

WIDOWED LADY

A nickname of YGLAIS, Perceval's mother, in *Perlesvaus*. The *Livre d'Artus* also gives her this name, but does not provide a proper name. In *Livre*, her husband is Pellinore, rather than Alain, and she lives in the Waste Forest. [*Perlesvaus, Livre*]

WIGALOIS [Viegloeis, Vigoles, Wigoleis]

Son of Gawain and Princess Florie of Syria. The name itself is similar to GUINGLAIN, his counterpart in Renaut de Bâgé's *Le Bel Inconnu*. GLIGLOIS, the hero of a later romance, recall's Wigalois's name but not his character.

Gawain became separated from Princess Florie before Wigalois's birth, and Florie raised Wigalois alone. The castle in which he grew up featured a wheel of fortune, and his later successes were a curious mix of his own prowess combined with luck.

When Wigalois came of age, he left Syria to seek adventure and to find his father. Arriving at Arthur's court, he astonished the knights by sitting down on a stone that only the most pure could even approach. Arthur knighted him immediately, and presented him to Gawain as a companion. Neither Wigalois nor Gawain were aware of their relationship. Soon after his arrival, the lady Nereja arrived at court, seeking a champion to save Queen Amena of Korntin from the evil King Roaz of Glois. Wigalois asked for, and received, the adventure. This infuriated Nereja, who perceived Wigalois as too inexperienced. Along the road to Korntin, however, Wigalois proved himself to Nereja by defeating several giants and knights. By the time they reached Korntin, Nereja happily presented Wigalois to Queen Amena.

Wigalois soon fell in love with Princess Larie, Amena's daughter, who had been promised to the knight who could rid the land of King Roaz. Wigalois immediately set out to find Roaz, guided by the spirit of the slain King Lar, Amena's husband. Along the way, he defeated a dragon named Pfetan, a hag named Ruel, and a devil named Marrien. Finally arriving in Glois, he fought a long battle against Roaz and killed him. During the quest, King Lar revealed Gawain to be Wigalois' father.

Wigalois returned to Korntin and joyously married Florie. The two were crowned king and queen of the land. News reached Wigalois's wedding feast that an expected guest, King Amire of Libya, had been slain by the evil Prince Lion of Namur. Abandoning his festivities, Wigalois raised an army and marched into Namur. The campaign resulted in the death of Lion, and proved Wigalois as a military leader. He returned to Korntin to live out his days with his wife. [*Wirnt*]

WIGAMUR

An Arthurian knight who is the hero of a German romance bearing his name. The son of King Paldriot of Lendrie, he was abducted as a youth and raised by a series of creatures, including a hag named Lesbia, a sea monster, and Arthur's uncle Yttra. He became known as the Knight with the Eagle after he saved an eagle from a vulture and it became his loyal companion. Finally arriving at Arthur's court, he helped the king save Queen Ysope from a heathen attacker named Marroch. He eventually discovered his paternity, married the lady Dulceflur, and became heir to the kingdom of Lendrie. [*Wigamur*]

WIGHT [*Wyghte*]

An island off the southern coast of Britain. According to the *Anglo-Saxon Chronicle*, the Isle of Wight was conquered by the Saxons Cerdic and Cynric in 530, which is within what many chroniclers identify as Arthur's "reign." The two Saxons gave the island to their cousins, Stuf and Wihtgar, in 534. In the Alliterative *Morte Arthure*, King Valiant of Wales seems to control the island. [*Anglo, Allit*]

WIHTGILS

Father of the Saxons Hengist and Horsa, who invaded Britain during the reign of King Vortigern. [*Bede, Anglo*]

WILD FOREST [**Forest Salvage*]

The residence of the evil Black Hermit slain by Perceval. Also, the home of Claryvaus, Driant, Ladinas, Fergus, and Seguarades. [*Perlesvaus, VulgLanc, VulgMer, Malory*]

WILD MOUNTAIN

The land of Queen Albiun, populated by mountain dwarves. A knight named Kurion tried to conquer it from Albiun, but he was defeated by Arthur's Sir Tandareis. [*PleierT*]

WILD HUNT

A supernatural theme attached in European folklore to a number of legendary and historical heroes, including Arthur. On certain nights of the year, the spirits of these warriors emerge from their resting places and ride through the clouds, forests, and fields, pursuing supernatural game. In Britain, Wild Hunts are sometimes reported near hills associated with Arthur's CAVE LEGEND. The Welsh attach the Wild Hunt to Gwynn son of Nudd.

WILLERIS

An enchanted parrot from Rigomer castle, owned by Queen Dionise. Dionise sent the bird to help Gawain find his way to the castle, which he was destined to conquer. [*Merveil*]

WILLIAM OF SALEBRANT [*William Celebronche*]

A companion of Bleoberis, Elin of Graie, and the lord of Saie in Renaut de Bâgé's *Le Bel Inconnu*. When Bleoberis was defeated in combat by Guinglain (Gawain's son), William, Elin, and the lord tried to avenge Bleoberis's disgrace. Guinglain defeated them all at Valcolor, killing William and wounding the other two. In Thomas Chestre's *Lybeaus Desconus*, William has a stronger role as the guardian of the Perilous Passage. Guinglain defeats him, but does not kill him, instead sending him to Arthur's court. [*Renaut, ChestreLyb*]

WILTSHIRE

A county of southern England. It was conquered in the early days of Arthur's reign by Cheldric the Saxon, but Arthur later liberated it. [*Layamon*]

WINCHESTER [*Goncestre, Gu(i)ncestre, Vinchester, Viscestre, Winc(h)estre*]

A city in Hampshire, south central England. According to Geoffrey of Monmouth, it was founded by King Hudibras in the tenth century BC. Winchester is named by Geoffrey as the location of the second battle between Arthur and Mordred, following the battle of Richborough and preceding the battle at the River Camel. Wace says that Guerdon was Arthur's earl of Winchester; Layamon gives this distinction to Mauron. Chrétien de Troyes and other writers say that Arthur occasionally held court here. The Vulgate *Merlin* describes Winchester as a seaport and says that Ambrosius and Uther landed there on their way to conquer Britain from Vortigern. In the Post-Vulgate, it is fortified by Mordred's two sons after the death of Arthur and Mordred. Lancelot defeated and killed the sons there. In *Palamedes*, it serves as the locale of a tournament won by Segurant the Brown. *Arthour and Merlin* names it as Constantine's burial place, the site of Maine's (Constans') murder, the court where Uther received the crown of Britain, and the location of a battle where Uther and Ambrosius fought Vortigern and Hengist. Finally, in Malory, the city is identified with CAMELOT itself. It was the location of three great tournaments in the waning days of Arthur's reign. Malory's assertion may have been influence by the Winchester ROUND TABLE. [*GeoffHR, Wace, Layamon, ChretienC, Contin2, VulgLanc, VulgMer, PostMort, Palamedes, Arthour, Stanz, Malory*]

WINDSOR [*Guinesores, Vi(n)desores, Windeskore*]

A city in Berkshire, England, near London, on the Thames River. Chrétien says that it was ruled in Arthur's time by the traitor Angres. Arthur's knight Brastias became a hermit near Windsor in his old age. It was also the home of the knight Sinados. In *Le Chevalier du Papegau*, the city is Arthur's chief court. In the *Livre d'Artus*, warriors from Windsor join Arthur's battles against the Saxons. Malory relates a story in which Lancelot, while hunting in Windsor forest, is shot in the buttocks by a misguided arrow from a female hunter's bow. [*ChretienC, LancLac, VulgLanc, Livre, ChevPap, Malory*]

WINDESANT

A city in Gorre that was one of King Bagdemagus's courts. [*VulgLanc*]

WINEHART

A castle in Saxony captured by Vortigern during his war with Hengist. [*Butor*]

WINLOGEE

On the Modena Archivolt, the name of a lady apparently held in a tower by a lord named Mardoc and his knight, Caradoc. Arthur and his knights, including Yder and Gawain, are embroiled in an attempt to rescue her. Her name is a variation of GUINLOIE or GUINEVERE, Arthur's wife. "Guinloie" also belongs to Yder's lover in the French romance of *Yder*. [*Modena*]

WINTON

A city in Britain. Durian served as its archbishop in Arthur's time. [*GeoffHR*]

WIRRAL

A barren wilderness in northern Britain through which Gawain rode in his search for the Green Chapel. [*SirGawain*]

WISE DAMSEL

A sorceress who entrapped Meliadus, Tristan's father, in her fortress, called the Tower of Enchantments or the Rock of the Cornishwoman. She is first found in the Prose *Tristan*. The tower was in the Forest of Morrois in Cornwall. The Wise Damsel used her enchantments to cause Meliadus to lose his memory; he therefore remained with her while his wife gave birth to Tristan and perished. Eventually, Merlin led Meliadus's knights to the tower, where the Wise Damsel was executed. Tristan and Isolde later used her fortress during one of their expulsions from Mark's court. A rock nearby was called the Wise Damsel's Rock. The Italian *Vita di Merlino* relates that she learned her arts from Merlin. [*ProsTris, Tavola, VitaMer*]

WISE LADY OF THE FOREST [*Sage Dame*]

A lady who inhabited the Forest of No Return. Her son Agraveil and her nephew Elinadas both served Arthur. She helped Arthur's Sir Greu defeat the Ugly Appearance adventure by giving him a magical protective ointment. Greu married her niece. [*VulgMer, Livre*]

WISSANT [*Hussidan, Wyndesan*]

A port in France fortified by King Nentres of Garlot during the early Saxon invasions. During Mordred's rebellion, Arthur's army waited in Wissant for the right wind to bring them back to Britain and face Mordred's forces. [*Wace, Layamon, VulgLanc, VulgMer*]

WIT

The name adopted by Tristan in one of his many attempts to meet Isolde during an exile Mark's court. He faked his own death, entered a monastery, and called himself "Brother Wit." Sneaking to his own funeral in Cornwall, he made himself known only to Isolde, who then feigned illness. Representing himself as a physician, Tristan managed to enter Isolde's chamber where they enjoyed a few hours together. [*TrisMonch*]

WITEGE

An elfin smith who fashioned Wygar, Arthur's hauberk, in Layamon's *Brut*. Layamon may be alluding to Widia, the son of the mythological Wayland. [*Layamon*]

WODEN

The chief god in Scandinavian and Germanic mythology. According to Bede, the Saxons Hengist and Horsa were descended from him. The Norse call him Odin. His name was given to the third day of the week (Woden's Day, or Wednesday). [*Bede*]

WOLFRAM VON ESCHENBACH

The author of *Parzival* appears himself as a character in the German compilation *Wartburgkrieg*, in which he engages in a poetic competition with Clinschor, a character who appears in *Parzival*. [*Wartburg*]

WONDER [*Wunder*]

A king who owned the magical Floating Chessboard, which was sought by Gawain for Arthur. King Wonder would only give the chessboard to Gawain if Gawain retrieved for him the magic Sword with Two Rings. This sent Gawain on a series of quests, but he eventually returned to King Wonder with the Sword with Two Rings and exchanged it for the chessboard. [*Penninc*]

WOOD IN THE VALLEY

The rather banal name for a forest in the kingdom of Benoic, belonging to Lancelot's father Ban. It contained lake Diana, where the Lady of the Lake lived. [*LancLac*]

WORCESTER

This city in eastern England was governed by Mauron in Arthur's service. [*GeoffHR*]

WRNACH

A giant who possessed a magical sword, which was the only item that could kill him. Obtaining this sword was the last of the tasks assigned to Culhwch by the giant Ysbaddaden, but it was the first to be accomplished. Culhwch and his party arrived at Wrnach's hall during a feast, and Cei managed to gain entry by claiming to be a sword burnisher. Wrnach turned his sword over to Cei for polishing. After Cei shined the weapon, he thrust it into Wrnach's chest and cut off his head. Culhwch and the warriors of Arthur then plundered Wrnach's kingdom. [*Culhwch*]

WYGAR

Arthur's hauberk, fashioned by the elvish smith Witege, which Arthur wore in the battle against the Saxons at Bath. [*Layamon*]

WYNEBGWRTHUCHER ("Face of Evening")

Arthur's shield in *Culhwch and Olwen*. [*Culhwch*]

WYTHNAINT

One of Arthur's warriors. [*WelshPG*]

Y

YBLÉ

A valley named after the lady Iblis, who married Lancelot. Before her marriage, she made frequent trips to the valley. [UlrichZ]

YDAIN¹

A lady at Arthur's court who married Sir Cador of Cornwall. She was the sister of Sir Kahedins and a cousin of Gawain. [Contin1]

YDAIN² [Ydeine]

A maiden that Gawain rescued from Sir Licoridon. She flirted unabashedly with Gawain, and Gawain fell in love with her. Later, however, she decided to abandon Gawain for a knight with what she perceived to be greater sexual prowess. Gawain defeated this rival knight and then turned Ydain over to a loathsome little hunchback in punishment. Appearing in La Vengeance Raguidel, she is identical to an unnamed character in Le Chevalier a L'Épée. [Vengeance, Wrake]

YDER¹ [*Edern, Edyrn, Hider(us), Hudos, Ide(r)(s), Idres, Idr(o)us, Isder, Itiers, Ridek, Ydes, Ydet, Ydier, Ydras, Ydrus]

A king and Knight of the Round Table who first appears in Culhwch and Olwen. Evidence suggests a widespread popularity of this hero in the before the early thirteenth century, after which his character lost importance. The appearance of Yder on the Modena Archivolt (in the early twelfth century in Italy) testifies as to his early fame. In Welsh texts, we learn only that he was the son of Nudd (probably from Nodens, an Celtic divinity), that he had two brothers named Owain and Gwyn, and that he was the leader of Arthur's Danish warriors. In Geoffrey of Monmouth, he fights, wins honor, and perishes in Arthur's war against Rome. Geoffrey gives him a son named Her.

A passage—almost certainly an interpolation—in William of Malmesbury's Historia Rerum Anglicarum has a young Yder fight three giants on the mountain called Ranae or Brent Knoll. Arthur had embarked with a troop to take care of the ravaging monsters, but Yder went on ahead of the company and encountered them alone. He managed to slay all three giants, but was seriously wounded in the process. Arthur assumed he was dead and made an endowment at Glastonbury for two dozen monks to pray for Yder's soul.

We next meet Yder in Chrétien de Troyes's Erec. During a hunt, Guinevere and Erec come across Yder and his dwarf. Yder's dwarf insults Guinevere and Yder does nothing about it. Intent on avenging the insult, Erec follows Yder to the town of Laluth, where Yder is the annual victor in a SPARROWHAWK TOURNAMENT. Erec enters the tournament, defeats Yder, and sends him to Arthur's court. This story is also related in the Welsh Geraint with identical circumstances. In the Norse Erex Saga, his character is replaced by MALPIRANT.

In the late twelfth or early thirteenth century, a romance of Yder was written in French. In this anti-Arthurian tale, a young Yder sets off on a quest for his vanished father, Nut. During the quest, he visits Queen Guenloie of Carvain and falls in love with her, but is dismissed from her court until he has proven himself. He eventually joins Arthur's court after saving the king from two knights, but is disillusioned with Arthur's behavior and soon departs. He is knighted by a king named Ivenant, and he receives a squire named Luguain from another nobleman. His further adventures again bring him into contact with Arthur, who, along with Kay, tries to murder him. He eventually finds his father, saves Guinevere from a bear, and slays two giants, thus proving himself to Queen Guenloie. Yder and the queen are married at Arthur's court, and Yder becomes a king himself. We must note that "Guenloie" is a variation of "Guinevere," and that Yder is one of Guinevere's rescuers on the Modena Archivolt. It has been suggested that in an early Breton story, Yder was Guinevere's lover, occupying roughly the same role filled by Lancelot in French romance. There is an allusion to this romance in the Folie Tristan of Berne.

In the Vulgate Merlin and in Arthour and Merlin, "Yder of the Dolorous Mount" takes a different role (this Yder is perhaps a different character). Named as the king of Cornwall in the former and the king of Nantes in the latter, he is one of the kings to rebel against Arthur at the beginning of Arthur's reign. After the battle of Bedegraine, in which Yder and his allies are defeated, Yder's land is invaded, ravaged, and plundered by the Saxons. Several defeats against the Saxons lead Yder to swear fealty to Arthur. The Saxons are soon crushed at the battle of Clarence. As in Geoffrey, Yder goes on to serve Arthur in the Roman War and in the war against Galehaut of Sorelois.

We find Yder in a collection of other texts. In the First Continuation of Chrétien's Perceval, he has a son named Yonet. In La Vengeance Raguidel, he helps Gawain avenge the death of Sir Raguidel against Sir Guengasoain. While Gawain duels Guengasoain, Yder fights and slays Guengasoain's bear, which recalls his similar deed in Yder. Yder marries Guengasoain's daughter, Trevilonete. The Alliterative Morte Arthure and Malory, oddly, name him as the son of Yvain, perhaps confusing his relationship to Owain in Welsh texts. He is only an incidental character in Malory, with no hint as to his popularity three to four hundred years earlier. Tennyson returns him to his role as Geraint's Sparrowhawk Tournament opponent, adding that he was Enide's cousin and that he forced Enide's father into poverty when he refused to let Yder wed Enide. Tennyson places his death at the battle of Camlann. [*Culhwch, Modena, WilliamM, GeoffHR, Wace, ChretienE, FolieB, Contin1, Vengeance, VulgLanc, VulgMer, Dream, Geraint, Allit, Malory, TennIK*]

YDER[2]

Count of Meliolant. He lodged Arthur and some Knights of the Round Table during their adventures. [*Contin1*]

YDER[3]

King of the "Land of Northmen" who served Arthur. He led a battalion of Arthur's soldiers against King Rions at the battle of Aneblayse. [*VulgMer, Arthour*]

YDER[4] OF LIS

Named as the father of Brandelis, Meliant, and Guilorete in some manuscripts of the First Continuation of Chrétien's *Perceval*. Gawain killed him in combat. In most manuscripts, his character is called NORROIZ. [*Contin1*]

YDONAS[1]

An early Knight of the Round Table wounded by Gawain in a bloody tournament between the Round Table and the Queen's Knights. [*VulgMer*]

YDONAS[2]

A proud Saxon warrior slain by Gawain at the battle of Cambenic. [*VulgMer*]

YDONE

A lady met by Gawain in a forest pavilion. At her behest, he battled an unidentified knight, and later discovered that his opponent was his brother Gaheris. [*Hunbaut*]

YDOR

A king who found an infant named Tristouse on his shores. When she came of age, he married her and they had a son named Torec, who later defeated Arthur's knights. [*Maerlant*]

YELLOW PALE-WHITE OX

An ox owned by Gwlwlwyd Chestnut Hair. As one of his tasks, Culhwch had to obtain this ox and yoke it together with another of Gwlwlwyd's oxen, the Spotted Ox. The tale, however, does not mention Culhwch completing this task. A Welsh Triad calls it one of the "three prominent oxen" of Britain. [*Culhwch, Triads*]

YGLAIS

Perceval's mother in *Perlesvaus*. When her husband, Alain, died from a combat wound, she became known as the

Widowed Lady. Perceval had left home as a youth, so her castle of Camelot was poorly defended when it was attacked by Cahot the Red and the Lord of the Fens. She sent her daughter, Dandrane, to find Perceval, who eventually returned and saved his mother's land. Yglais and Dandrane lived out their days together. Her brothers were Pelles, the Fisher King, and the King of the Castle Mortal. [*Perlesvaus*]

YNIOL

A variation of NIWL, Enide's father. [*TennIK*]

YNYR

Either of two people or places who fought some kind of contest or battle in the time of Arthur. In *Culhwch and Olwen*, Arthur's chief gatekeeper, Glewlwyd, remarks to Arthur that he was "in the contest between the two Ynyrs, when the twelve hostages were brought from Llychlyn." The larger legend, to which this remark must refer, is lost to us. [*Culhwch*]

YON [*Iom*]

The King of Lesser Ireland, named in the Prose *Lancelot* as one of the rulers who joined the early rebellion against Arthur. He joined forces with the Angusel of Scotland and the King from Land Beyond the Borders of Galone, but Arthur defeated and subjugated him. He later fought for Arthur in the wars against Galehaut and Claudas. Arthur appointed him head of the tribunal which judged and condemned Guinevere after her affair with Lancelot was exposed. Yon later advocated Arthur's war against Lancelot in Benoic, in which his son was killed by Bors. He led a battalion in the final battle against Mordred at Salisbury, where he was killed by a knight from Ireland. [*LancLac, VulgLanc, VulgMort, PostMort*]

YONÉS THE NOVELIERS

A knight in Arthur's service. [*Merveil*]

YONET

A knight who served Lady Andrivete as the castellan of Banborc. When she was besieged by Lord Ayglin, Yonet fought for her until Kay lifted the siege. [*Girart*]

YORK [*Euerwyck, Everwic, Evrevic, Evroïc, Evruïch, Ewrevic, Guevrevic*]

A city in Yorkshire, north central England. According to Geoffrey of Monmouth, it was the site of the first battle between Ambrosius Aurelius and the Saxons, led by Octa and Eosa. Ambrosius was victorious, and he later appointed Samson the archbishop of the city. York was the site of Uther Pendragon's defeat by Octa and Eosa. When Arthur ascended the throne, he fought Colgrim's army at York, but he had to abandon the siege when Saxon reinforcements, led by Cheldric, arrived from Germany. When Arthur eventually reclaimed the city, he appointed Pryamus the new archbishop. [*GeoffHR*]

YRLANDE

A lady in the history of the Brown Family. She was the daughter of Brun and his wife Pamphille. Her sister was named Gialle. [*Palamedes*]

YSABEL

Sovereigness of the Castle of Maidens. Related to Perceval, she was a member of Joseph of Arimathea's fellowship. [*Contin4*]

YSABELE

Maiden daughter of King Assentin. In a series of interlocking quests, Gawain needed to bring her to the court of King Amoraen so he that Amoraen would let him keep the magic Sword with Two Rings, which he needed to trade with King Wonder for a magic chessboard. Arriving at Assentin's court, Assentin imprisoned him but gave him to Ysabele for care. Gawain exerted his traditional charm, and Assentin eventually caught them *in flagrante* and threw them in prison. They were freed by the spirit of a dead knight who Gawain had previously given a burial. On the journey to King Wonder's court, Ysabele was abducted by Sir Estor (Hector), but Gawain saved her. Gawain may have later married her. [*Penninc*]

YSAIE THE SAD

The son of Tristan and Isolde in the French romance bearing his name. He lived in a post-Arthurian Britain characterized by chaos and anarchy, in which Ysaie struggled to promote law and virtue. Raised by a hermit, Ysaie married Martha, the daughter of King Irion. He was assisted in his endeavors by his companion, a dwarf named Oberon, and later by his son Marc. [*Ysaie*]

YSAVE OF CARAHES

A niece of King Arthur who married King Caradoc of Nantes, but committed adultery with a sorcerer named Elïavrés. This affair produced a son, Caradoc, who was recognized by King Caradoc as his legitimate heir. After winning fame as one of Arthur's knights, Caradoc returned to Nantes and locked Ysave in a tower to punish her for her sins. Ysave and Elïavrés conspired to kill Caradoc with a poisonous serpent, but were unsuccessful. [*Contin1*]

YSBADDADEN

"Chief giant" in *Culhwch and Olwen*. He was the father of Olwen, and he owned a fortress in Cornwall. His eyelids were so heavy that they had to be propped up with spears. The warrior Culhwch, who was destined to marry Olwen, came to Ysbaddaden's fortress with Arthur's warriors to ask for the maiden. As Ysbaddaden was fated to die as soon as Olwen was married, the giant refused to relinquish her. After failing to slay the warriors with poisoned spears, which they kept catching and throwing back at the giant, Ysbaddaden laid out a list of about forty nigh impossible tasks for Culhwch to perform as a condition of the

marriage. Arthur, who had promised to assist Culhwch, completed all the necessary tasks. Ysbaddaden, as he had promised, bitterly turned over Olwen, and Goreu, the son of one of Ysbaddaden's servants, killed the giant. [*Culhwch*]

YSBERIN [*Sberin*]

A warrior in the service of King Arthur who was the son of King Fflergant of Brittany. [*Culhwch*]

YSBERYR CAT CLAW

One of Arthur's warriors. [*Culhwch*]

YSGAWD

Father of Arthur's warrior Glew. [*Culhwch*]

YSGAWYN

One of Arthur's warriors who was the son of Panon. He was killed at the battle of Cwm Cerwyn by the boar Twrch Trwyth. [*Culhwch*]

YSGEIR GULHWCH GOVYNCAWN

An Arthurian warrior mentioned in the long list of the members of Arthur's court in *Culhwch and Olwen*. His name translates as "Ridge of Culhwch the Reed-cutter," which makes little sense as a personal name. [*Culhwch*]

YSGEIR OERVEL

A ridge in Ireland where Menw, Arthur's warrior and sorcerer, was wounded by the boar Twrch Trwyth. Arthur's epic hunt for Twrch Trwyth began at Ysgeir Oervel. [*Culhwch*]

YSGITHYRWYN ("White Tusk")

The "chief boar" in *Culhwch and Olwen*. As one of his forty tasks, the warrior Culhwch had to obtain one of Ysgithyrwn's tusks for Ysbaddaden, the "chief giant," to use as a razor. Furthermore, the tusk had to be pulled it out while the boar was still alive, and it could only be drawn by Odgar, son of Aedd. It then had to be entrusted to King Caw of Scotland for delivery to Ysbaddaden. Arthur hunted the boar with his warriors and hounds, and it was Arthur's dog Cabal and Caw who killed the boar. Caw then brought the tusk to Ysbaddaden and personally shaved the giant with it. [*Culhwch*]

YSGONAN THE GENEROUS

One of Arthur's warriors. He was killed at Cwm Cerwyn by the boar Twrch Trwyth. [*Culhwch*]

YSGUDYDD

A servant of Gwenhwyfar (Guinevere). [*Culhwch*]

YSGYRDAF

A servant of Gwenhwyfar (Guinevere). [*Culhwch*]

YSILE

A woman in the Brown Family. She was the daughter of King Brun of the Savage Realm and his wife Lye. She was the sister of Hector, Galhaut, Brun, and Lore. [*Palamedes*]

YSMAINE[1]

Niece of Brun of Branlant, a vassal who rebelled against Arthur. [*Contin1*]

YSMAINE[2]

Perceval's cousin. She slept with the knight Faradien after receiving his promise to marry her. When Faradien deserted her, Perceval defeated him in combat and forced him to keep his promise. [*Contin4*]

YSOPE

A queen attacked by a heathen king named Marroch. She was saved through the intervention of Arthur and Sir Wigamur.]*Wigamur*]

YSTAFNGWN

An early Welsh poem notes that "In the uplands of Ystafngwn, Cei pierced nine witches." Nothing more is said about the incident. [*WelshPG*]

YSTRAD YW

A country in south Wales where Arthur's warriors fought a battle against the ferocious piglets of the boar Twrch Trwyth. On Arthur's side, the warriors Peissawg the Tall, Llygadrudd Emys, and Gwrfoddw were killed, but the warriors managed to kill the piglet Llwydawg the Killer. [*Culhwch*]

YTTRA

An uncle of Arthur in the German romance of *Wigamur*. He tutored the young hero of the story. [*Wigamur*]

YVAIN[1] [*Evrains, Evayn, Evein(s), Eventus, Ewa(i)n, Ewayne, Ewe(i)n, Ewin, Ivan(o), Iven, Iwa(i)n(et), Iwe(i)n, Ovan, *Owain, Owein, Uwayne, Yoain, Yov(a)in, Yvains, Yvein, Ywa(i)n(e)(s), Ywons*]

A Knight of the Round Table who was the son of King Urien. The earliest form of his name is Owain. Urien and Owain are historical figures—opponents of the Anglo-Saxons in the sixth century. He probably succeeded his father as the king of Rheged, just south of Scotland. A number of poems in *The Book of Taliesin* glorify his many victories and lament his death, but do not connect him to Arthur. We learn in the Triads that his wife, Penarwan, was one of the "Three Faithless Wives of the Isle of Britain," that he rode a horse named Cloven-Hoof, and that his mother was Modron, a Celtic goddess who probably became Morgan le Fay. In another poem, we find a mention of his square grave at Llanforfael.

The early twelfth-century chronicles of Geoffrey of Monmouth and Wace are the first texts to mention Yvain as Arthur's contemporary. A thirteenth-century Welsh text called *The Dream of Rhonabwy*, however, shows no influence of the chronicles or the French romances and may suggest an earlier Welsh tradition of Owain as one of Arthur's companions. In this satirical tale, Owain is not only "Emperor" Arthur's contemporary, but seems to be his equal. Owain commands a flock of warrior-ravens. Arthur and Owain play a game of *gwyddbwyll* (a chess-like board game), during which a servant rushes in and reports that Arthur's warriors are slaughtering Owain's chained ravens. When Arthur refuses to stop the murder, Owain orders his ravens released, and the birds begin killing the warriors. Owain refuses to call off the ravens until they have killed a fair number of Arthur's nobles and Arthur, infuriated, crushes the *gwyddbwyll* figures to dust.

Geoffrey of Monmouth says that Yvain succeeded King Angusel of Scotland after Angusel died at the battle of Camlann and that he won many battles afterwards. Wace, however, says that Arthur personally appointed Yvain to the throne of Scotland. In the chronicles, then, he appears late in the Arthurian saga, even as Arthur is fighting his last battles. Contemporary to the chronicles, the *Life of St. Kentigern* names "Ewen" as the father of St. Kentigern, the patron saint of Glasgow.

In the second half of the twelfth century, Chrétien de Troyes wrote the quintessential Yvain romance, called *Yvain*, or *Le Chevalier au Lion*. The Welsh *Owain* is almost identical, and either *Owain* derives from *Yvain* or they both derive from a common source. A Middle English author followed up with *Ywain and Gawain*. Each of these three romances tell essentially the same story: intrigued by Calogrenant's or Cynon's tale of an enchanted fountain in the forest of Broceliande, Yvain, a member of Arthur's court, decides to try the adventure himself. Arriving at the fountain, he pours a basin of water on a stone, which causes a hailstorm to pelt the area. The lord of the fountain, called Esclados, arrives and challenges Yvain, and Yvain kills him. Yvain travels to Esclados's fortress, where he is trapped between two portcullises but is rescued by Lunete, a servant of Esclados's widow, Laudine. Lunete gives him an invisibility ring which allows him to escape. Yvain falls in love with Laudine, and Lunete convinces Laudine to marry him, pointing out that some knight must protect the fountain from Arthur's forces, who are rumored to be on the march. Yvain and Laudine are wed, and Yvain takes his place as the fountain's guardian. When Arthur and his company arrive, Yvain fights with Kay before revealing himself. Desiring to return to court, he asks Laudine for leave, and she allows him to go provided he returns in one year. At court, however, Yvain loses track of time and overstays the year. Laudine sends a messenger to rebuke and renounce him. Yvain goes mad and roams the hills until servants of the Lady of Norison cure him with a magic ointment made by Morgan le Fay. In return for the healing, Yvain helps the countess defend her lands against the Earl Alier. Yvain then makes his way back to his wife. Along the way, he rescues a lion from a serpent. The lion becomes his faithful guardian and refuses to leave his side. Yvain earns the nickname "the KNIGHT WITH THE LION." With his lion, he defeats a giant named Harpin, rescues the denizens of the Castle of Most Ill Adventure, and settles a land dispute between the daughters of the Lord of the Black Thorn. He also rescues the lady Lunete, who has been imprisoned by Laudine's chamberlains as a punishment for Lunete's initial suggestion that Laudine marry Yvain. Yvain eventually reunites and reconciles with Laudine.

In the Vulgate and Post-Vulgate Cycles, he is called "Yvain the Tall" or "Yvain the Great" to distinguish him from the other Yvains, one of whom is Yvain the Bastard, his brother. Descended from Joseph of Arimathea, Yvain is the son of King Urien of Gorre and Arthur's sister, either Brimesent or Morgan le Fay (though the earliest mention of Morgan as Yvain's mother is in the French romance of *Tyolet*). Even as his father participates in a rebellion against Arthur, Yvain follows his cousin Gawain's example and leaves home with his brother to join Arthur's service. On the way to Logres, they defeat armies of Saxons at the battles of Diana Bridge and Arundel. Yvain is knighted by Arthur and he joins Arthur's wars against King Claudas, the Saxons, Rome, and Lord Galehaut. In his many subsequent adventures, he stops Morgan from killing his father, saves the Lady of the Rock from two oppressors, witnesses the Grail marvels at the Rock of the Stag, slays a giant named Malduit, saves Lancelot from drowning, and, with Gawain, kills the seven evil brothers who rule the Castle of Maidens. Some of his adventures occur during a temporary banishment from Arthur's court, brought on by his mother's attempted murder of Arthur. Yvain leads a battalion at the battle of Salisbury (the final battle between Arthur and Mordred), where he kills a Saxon lord named Arcan and the Saxon king who had allied with Mordred. Mordred eventually cleaves him through he brain. Witnessing this slaying, Arthur cries, "Ah! God, why did you allow me to see the worst traitor in the world kill one of the noblest of men?"

Interspersed among the central Yvain romances are a number of tales that offer variations or additions to his story. In *Claris et Laris*, Yvain has a sister named Marine. In *Sir Perceval of Galles*, Yvain's father is called Asoure. *La Tavola Ritonda* says that he died fighting Mordred's army at the siege of Urbano. Malory makes him the father of Yder and equates him with YVAIN OF THE WHITE HANDS, a separate character in the Vulgate Cycle. [*WelshSG, GeoffHR, Wace, ChretienY, Tyolet, VulgLanc, VulgQuest, VulgMort, VulgMer, PostMer, PostQuest, PostMort, Triads, Dream, Owain, Claris, SirPerc, Ywain, Tavola, Arthour, Allit, Malory*]

YVAIN[2]

King of Lindsey who participated in Arthur's tournament at the Castle of Maidens. [*Renaut*]

YVAIN[3]

A Knight of the Round Table who was the son of King Hervi. Found in the romance of *Yder*, he may be identical to the original YVAIN, with "Hervi" being a corruption of "Urien." [*Yder*]

YVAIN[4] [*Yvonet*]

Yet another of Arthur's knights, variously called "the Crooked," "the Buck," "the Deer," and "the Shining." He fought in the Saxon wars and joined one of Gawain's quests to find Lancelot. [*LancLac, VulgLanc, VulgMer, Arthour*]

YVAIN[5] [*Owain*]

An Arthurian warrior in Welsh legend who is the son of Nudd, which would make him the brother of Yder, Gwynn, and Dryon. [*Geraint*]

YVAIN[6]

A knight in Arthur's service who was the son of the Soumière. [*Merveil*]

YVAIN[7] OF CANELONES

A Knight of the Round Table from Germany. He was a cousin to the sons of Urien. He fought in Arthur's forces during the Saxon Wars. During the Grail Quest, while adventuring with Gawain, Yvain ignored a warning and brashly entered a castle, where he was burned alive to avenge the death of Lamorat, who had been killed by Gawain. Yvain's sister, who blamed Gawain for Yvain's death, tried to have Gawain killed but failed. [*VulgMer, Livre, PostQuest*]

YVAIN[8] OF CAVALIOT

One of Arthur's knights mentioned in Chrétien de Troyes's *Erec*. R. S. Loomis notes a twelfth century Welsh chieftain named Owein of Cyveilioc. [*ChretienE*]

YVAIN[9] OF LEONEL [*Iwan of Nonel*]

Another of Arthur's warriors who was knighted by Arthur for his service in the Saxon wars. His father was named Grandalis. Yvain was one of the knights imprisoned in the Dolorous Prison until freed by Lancelot. His other credits include a quest to learn the fate of Merlin and participation in one of Gawain's quests to find Lancelot. Chrétien de Troyes is the first to mention him. His surname may be a variation of *Loeneis*, or LOTHIAN, or it may indicate a "Lionel," or a small lion. As the original Yvain was also called "The Knight with the Lion," this Yvain may have once been the same character. [*ChretienE, Wolfram, LancLac, VulgMer, Arthour*]

YVAIN[10] OF REVEL

A youth knighted by Arthur for his service in the Saxon Wars. [*VulgMer*]

YVAIN[11] OF THE WHITE HANDS [*Yvonet*]

Another Knight of the Round Table who appears in the French prose romance. He is distinct from YVAIN son of

Urien, but Malory merges the two characters. He was the son of Daire. Arthur knighted him in reward for his service in the Saxon Wars. Later, he participated in quests to learn the fate of Merlin and to find Lancelot. He was badly wounded in a fight with King Mark of Cornwall, but was healed at the abbey of the Black Cross. During the Grail Quest, he was slain by Erec, who did not recognize him, for which Erec was later killed by Gawain. His former Round Table seat was taken by Arthur the Less. [*Didot, VulgLanc, VulgMer, Arthour, PostMer, PostQuest, ProsTris, Malory*]

YVAIN[12] THE BASTARD [*Yvain les Avoutres, Yvain of Lafultere, Yvain the Adulterer, Yvonet*]

The illegitimate son of King Urien and the wife of Urien's seneschal, and the half-brother of the first Yvain. He left home with his brother to join Arthur's service, even though his father was involved in a rebellion against Arthur. He fought in the Saxon wars and was knighted by Arthur for his service. He further participated in the wars against Rome, Claudas, and Galehaut. He had a son named Cahus, who died as Arthur's squire. During the Grail Quest, Yvain the Bastard adventured with Gawain and Galahad, and he helped Gawain and Gareth, his cousins, liberate the Castle of Maidens by killing the seven knights that ruled there. Late in the Grail Quest, Yvain was killed by Gawain when they jousted together, unaware of each others' identity. Malory, in an obvious mistake, states that Yvain the Bastard appeared at the healing of Sir Urry, which occurs after his reported death. In the Scottish *Lancelot of the Laik*, Yvain the Bastard and Yvain les Avoutres are two separate characters. [*ChretienE, HartmannE, Perlesvaus, VulgLanc, VulgQuest, VulgMer, PostQuest, Arthour, Malory, Laik*]

YVAIN[13] THE BLACK

A knight who wanted to marry the lady of the Red Castle against her will. He besieged the Red Castle, but Guiron the Courteous championed the lady, defeated Yvain, and ended the siege. [*Palamedes*]

YVONET [*Iwanet, Yonet*]

A servant at King Arthur's court. He was the son of Yder and was related to Guinevere. He appears in Chrétien's *Perceval* and Wolfram's *Parzival*. Yonet greeted the innocent Perceval when Perceval first came to the court to be knighted. He supervised Perceval's fight with the Red Knight, and—after Perceval won—he showed the young knight how to don the dead knight's armor. His name is a diminutive form of YVAIN and is used to describe the various Yvains in the Vulgate *Merlin*. [*ChretienP, Contin1, Wolfram*]

Z

ZARADECH

An Asian lord. His brother was Panschavar. His sister Japhite died from heartbreak when Wigalois, Gawain's son, killed King Roaz of Glois, Japhite's husband. Zaradech and Panschavar came to Glois to retrieve Japhite's body. Both brothers later joined Wigalois's war against Prince Lion of Namur. [*Wirnt*]

ZAZAMANC

A kingdom in Arabia or Africa. It was ruled by Queen Belacane, who was loved by Isenhart. When Isenhart died in a battle for Belacane's love, Isenhart's allies attacked and besieged Zazamanc. Zazamanc was saved by the arrival of Perceval's father, Gahmuret, who beat back the attackers and married Belacane, assuming control of the kingdom. It later fell to Gahmuret's other son, Feirefiz, who gave it to Perceval as a gift. [*Wolfram*]

ZAZANT

During a speech in Heinrich von dem Türlin's *Diu Crône*, Gawain describes how he "came to the aid of Zazant as a dragon was carrying him to its cave." This episode is not found in existing Arthurian literature. [*Heinrich*]

ZEDOECH

One of two knights who murdered Sir Aamanz, who was called "the Other Gawain." [*Heinrich*]

ZELEGEBRE

The capital of Carmelide. It was one of the courts of the False Guinevere. [*VulgLanc*]

ZELOTÉS

An evil king who had been promised the maiden Perse by her father. When Perse refused to marry Zelotés, he abducted her. Hector of the Fens, who loved Perse, went to Zelotés's castle, killed him in combat, and freed Perse. [*VulgLanc*]

ZEROARZ

One of the many Saxon kings to join the Saxon invasion of Britain as Arthur was struggling to establish power. Under King Hargadabran, he fought against Arthur's forces at Clarence. [*Livre*]

ZETRO

A valley where a knight named Pinabel was slain by his brothers. Pinabel's widow was later saved from these brothers by Tristan. [*Tavola*]

ZIDRAS [*Ydraus*]

A Saxon who joined King Rions war against Arthur. He fought Arthur at the battle of Aneblayse but was forced to flee. [*VulgMer, Livre*]

ZIPPER

In a fifteenth-century Shrovetide play, the Queen of Zipper sends a chastity horn to Arthur's court. [*Hupsches*]

ZIRDOS

One of four giants who planned to fight for King Ekunaver of Kanadic in a war against Arthur, but were forced to stay neutral when Arthur's Sir Garel defeated Malseron, the giants' leader. [*PleierG*]

ZIRIJON

One of four giants who planned to fight for King Ekunaver of Kanadic in a war against Arthur, but were forced to stay neutral when Arthur's Sir Garel defeated Malseron, the giants' leader. [*PleierG*]

ZONE

A land ruled by Arthur's Duke Beladigant. [*Stricker*]

ZOROASTER OF ARABIA

An infidel king who served Feirefiz, Perceval's half-brother. [*Wolfram*]

ZYROLAN OF SEMBLIDAC

A king once defeated in combat by Perceval. [*Wolfram*]

Sources

This table cross-references the source codes at the end of each entry with the Arthurian source in which the character, place, object, symbol, or theme appears. The "text" column is a bibliographical annotation of the specific primary text from which I drew information about the Arthurian source. In as many cases as possible, I used a English translation or critical edition of the original source; however, lack of availability of many Arthurian sources (in either critical edition or translation) forced me to use reviews, summaries, and other secondary sources for a number of romances. The annotation "general" in the "text" column indicates that I could find no text that covered the source in adequate detail, and that information in the entries relating to this source comes from general Arthurian references, listed under "general reference" in the Bibliography.

Where no author is given, he or she is anonymous.

Source Code	Author & Title	Date, Form, & Language	Description	Keywords	Text
AlamAvar	Luigi Alamanni *Avarchide*	1548 Italian verse	Arthur and his soldiers besiege Avaricum in Gaul. Modeled on the Trojan War in Greek mythology.	Avaricum	Gardner, Edmund G. *The Arthurian Legend in Italian Literature.* London: Dent, 1930
AlamGyr	Luigi Alamanni *Gyron le Courtois* ("Guiron the Courteous")	1548 Italian verse	The adventures of Guiron, based ultimately on the French *Palamedes*	Guiron	Gardner, Edmund G. *The Arthurian Legend in Italian Literature.* London: Dent, 1930
Allit	Alliterative *Morte Arthure* (Death of Arthur)	c. 1400 English verse	Arthur's Roman War and death	Arthur Lucius Mordred Rome	Benson, Larry D., ed. *King Arthur's Death.* Kalamazoo: Medieval Institute Publications, 1994.
Andreas	Andreas Capellanus (Andreas the Chaplain) *De Amore* ("Of Love")	c. 1185 Latin prose	Treatise on courtly love includes an episode in which a knight wins a hawk at Arthur's court	Bruto King of Love	Andreas Capellanus. *The Art of Courtly Love*, ed. and trans. John Jay Parry. New York: Frederick Ungar, 1941.
Anglo	*Anglo-Saxon Chronicle*	9th c. English chronicle	Chronicle of Saxon events in England includes references to some Arthurian characters	Cerdic Hengist Natanleod Vortigern	Whitelock, Dorothy, ed. *The Anglo-Saxon Chronicle.* New Brunswick: Rutgers University Press, 1961.
Annales	*Annales Cambriae* ("Annals of Wales")	c. 960–980 Latin chronicle	Simple list of dates and events, includes several Arthurian references. First mention of Mordred and Camlann	Arthur Badon Camlann Mordred	Morris, John, ed. *British History and the Welsh Annals.* London: Phillimore, 1980.
Antelan	*Antelan*	late 13th c. or early 14th c. German verse	Dwarf King Antelan of Scotland visits Arthur's court, defeats Arthur's knights, departs	Antelan	General
Arthour	*Arthour and Merlin*	late 13th c. English verse	English adaptation of Vulgate *Merlin*, used by Malory	Arthur, Lady of the Lake Merlin Rockingham	Macrae-Gibson, O. D., ed. *Of Arthour and Merlin*, 2 vols. Oxford: Oxford University Press, 1979.
Arthur	*Arthur*	c. 1428 English verse chronicle	Short chronicle of Arthur's life based on Wace	Arthur Glastonbury	Furnivall, Frederick. *Arthur: a Short Sketch of His Life and History in English Verse.* Oxford: Oxford University Press, 1864.
Arthur&G	*Arthur and Gorlagon*	early 14th c. Latin prose	Arthur meets King Gorlagon, learns his story	Gorlagon	General
Arthur&K	*Arthur and Kaletvwlch*	14th c. Welsh prose	Short tale of Arthur's youth, draws sword Caledfwlch from the stone	Caledfwlch	General
Atre	*L'Atre Perilleux* ("The Perilous Cemetery")	mid-13th c. French verse	Gawain goes on quest to rescue Arthur's abducted cupbearer, braves Perilous Cemetery	Escanor Perilous Cemetery	Woledge, Brian, ed. *L'Atre périlleux.* Paris: Champion, 1936.

Source Code	Author & Title	Date, Form, & Language	Description	Keywords	Text
Ausgleich	"Die Ausgleichung" ("The Adjustment")	1806 German ballad	Chastity test involving both a horn and a mantle. Arthur and Guinevere fail.	Chastity Tests	General
Avowing	*The Avowing of King Arthur, Sir Gawain, Sir Kay, and Baldwin of Britain*	late 13th c. or early 14thc. English verse	During an adventure in Inglewood Forest, all title characters swear various vows, Baldwin emerges honorably	Baldwin Inglewood Menealf	Hahn, Thomas, ed. *The Avowing of Arthur*. In *Sir Gawain: Eleven Romances and Tales*. Kalamazoo: Medieval Institute Publications, 1995
Awntyrs	*The Awntyrs off Arthure at the Terne Wathelyn* ("The Adventures of Arthur at Lake Wadling")	late 14th c. English verse	Gawain & Guinevere encountered the ghost of Guinevere's mother; Gawain battles Galleron of Galloway	Galleron Wadling	Hahn, Thomas, ed. *The Awntyrs off Arthur*. In *Sir Gawain: Eleven Romances and Tales*. Kalamazoo: Medieval Institute Publications, 1995
Bataille	*La Bataille de Loquifer* ("The Battle with Loquifer")	c. 1230 French verse	French hero named Renouart battles a giant, visits Morgan le Fay in the Island of Avalon	Renouart	Barnett, Monica, ed. *La Bataille Loquifer*. Oxford: Blackwell, 1975.
Bede	Bede *Historia Ecclesiastica Gentis Anglorum* ("The Ecclesiastical History of the English People")	731 Latin chronicle	History of Britain drawn partially from Gildas, no mention of Arthur, but includes "Arthurian" characters and places	Ambrosius Badon Vortigern	Bede. *The Ecclesiastical History of the English People*, ed. Judith McClure and Roger Collins. Oxford: Oxford University Press, 1994.
Bek	Thomas Bek of Castleford *Thomas Castleford's Chronicle*	1327 English chronicle	Chronicle of British events drawn partially from Geoffrey of Monmouth	Arthur	Castleford, Thomas. *Thomas Castleford's Chronicle*, ed. Frank Behre. Elanders: Göteborg, 1940.
Beroul	Béroul *Tristan*	late 12th c. French verse	Earliest "common" or "primitive" Tristan legend. Exists only in a Fragment	Isolde Mal Pas Mark Tristan	Béroul. *Tristan*, ed. Norris J. Lacy. In *The Romance of Arthur: an anthology of Medieval Texts in Translation*, ed. James J. Wilhelm. New York: Garland, 1994.
Biket	Robert Biket *Lai du Cor* "Lay of the Horn"	mid to late 12th c. French verse	Chastity test at Arthur's court involving a horn, only Caradoc has a faithful wife	Caradoc Chastity Tests	Biket, Robert. *The Lay of the Horn*. In *Arthur, King of Britain*, ed. Richard L. Brengle. New York: Appleton-Century-Crofts, 1964.
Birth	Attributed to William Shakespeare and William Rowley *The Birth of Merlin, or The Childe Hath Found His Father*	1662 English play	Ambrosius and Uther deal with the Saxons while Merlin's mother tries to locate the child's father	Ambrosius Artesia Clown Joan Go-too't Ostorius	Rowley, William, and William Shakespeare (attributed). *The Birth of Merlin*. In *The Shakespeare Apocrypha*, ed. C. F. Tucker Brooke. Oxford: Clarendon, 1967.
BlackmoreK	Sir Richard Blackmore *King Arthur: An Heroick Poem: In Twleve Books*	1697 English verse	Arthur intervenes in French affairs, slays evil king	Clotar	Merriman, James Douglas. *The Flower of Kings: a Study of the Arthurian Legend in England Between 1485 and 1835*. Wichita: University Press of Kansas, 1973.

Source Code	Author & Title	Date, Form, & Language	Description	Keywords	Text
BlackmoreP	Sir Richard Blackmore *Prince Arthur: An Heroick Poem: in Ten Books*	1695 English verse	A young Arthur tries to reclaim the crown of Britain from the Saxons	Ethelina Tollo	Merriman, James Douglas. *The Flower of Kings: a Study of the Arthurian Legend in England Between 1485 and 1835.* Wichita: University Press of Kansas, 1973.
Bliocadran	*Bliocadran Prologue*	early 13th c. French verse	Prologue to Chrétien's *Perceval.* Perceval's father, Bliocadran, quests and dies	Bliocadran	Wolfgang, Lenora D., ed. *Bliocadran: a Prologue to the Perceval of Chrétien de Troyes.* Tübingen: Niemeyer, 1976.
Boccaccio	Giovanni Boccaccio *De Casibus Virorum Illustrium* ("The Fates of Illustrious Men")	1355–62 Italian chronicle	Arthur's life and death, drawn from Geoffrey of Monmouth	Arthur Round Table	Boccaccio, Giovanni. *The Fates of Illustrious Men,* ed. and trans. Louis B. Hall. New York: Frederick Ungar, 1965.
Boece	Hector Boece *Scotorum Historiae*	1527 Latin chronicle	Chronicle of British history written by a Scottish partisan, portrays Arthur negatively, glorifies Mordred	Arthur Lot Mordred Picts	Fletcher, Robert H. *The Arthurian Material in the Chronicles, Especially Those of Great Britain and France.* Boston: Ginn, 1906.
Boy	"The Boy and the Mantle"	16th c. English ballad	Chastity test at Arthur's court involving a mantle	Caradoc Chastity Tests	Percy, Thomas, ed. "The Boy and the Mantle." In *Relique of Ancient English Poetry.* London: Dent, 1938.
Buchanan	George Buchanan *Rerum Scoticarum Historia*	1582 Latin chronicle	Scottish version of Arthur's life based on Boece, portrays Arthur very negatively	Arthur	Fletcher, Robert H. *The Arthurian Material in the Chronicles, Especially Those of Great Britain and France.* Boston: Ginn, 1906.
Butor	Baudin Butor Unknown	c. 1290 French prose	The pre-Arthurian period, including Vortigern and Pendragon	Ivoire Libanor Pendragon Uther	Thorpe, Lewis. "The Four Rough Drafts of Bauduins Butors." *Nottingham Medieval Studies,* 12 (1968), 3–20; 13 (1969), 49–64; 14 (1970), 41–63.
Camden	William Camden *Britannia*	1586 Latin prose	Survey of British geography, includes many Arthurian locales, identifies Cadbury with Camelot	Cadbury	Camden, William. *Britannia: or, a Chorographical Description of the Flourishing Kingdoms of England, Scotland, and Ireland, and the Islands Adjacent, from the Earliest Antiquity,* trans. Richard Gough. London: John Nichols, 1789.
Cantare	Anonymous, possibly Antonio Pucci *Cantare dei Cantari* ("Song of Songs")	c. 1380 Italian verse	Stories of Arthurian and Carolinian figures	New Table Old Table	Gardner, Edmund G. *The Arthurian Legend in Italian Literature.* London: Dent, 1930.
CantariC	*I Cantari di Carduino* ("The Song of Carduino")	c. 1370 Italian verse	The adventures of Carduino, son of Dodinel	Carduino	Gardner, Edmund G. *The Arthurian Legend in Italian Literature.* London: Dent, 1930.

Source Code	Author & Title	Date, Form, & Language	Description	Keywords	Text
CantariT	*I Cantari di Tristano* ("The Song of Tristan")	mid to late 14th c. Italian verse	A group of texts relating Tristan's adventures; material found in the French Prose *Tristan* and the Italian *La Tavola Ritonda*	Merlin's Stones Palamedes Tristan	Gardner, Edmund G. *The Arthurian Legend in Italian Literature.* London: Dent, 1930.
Caradoc	Caradoc of Llancarfan *Vita Gildae* ("Life of St. Gildas")	c. 1130 Latin hagiography	Biography of St. Gildas, includes his experiences with Arthur and Guinevere's kidnapping by Melwas	Gildas Glastonbury Hueil Melwas	Bruce, James Douglas. *The Evolution of Arthurian Romance from the Beginnings Down to the Year 1300*, vol. 1. Gloucester: Peter Smith, 1958.
Carle	*The Carle off Carlisle* ("The Churl of Carlisle")	early 16th c. English ballad	Gawain's episode with the Carl of Carlisle, adapted from *Syre Gawene and the Carl of Carlyle*.	Beheading Game Carl of Carlisle	Hahn, Thomas, ed., *The Carle of Carlisle*. In *Sir Gawain: Eleven Romances and Tales*. Kalamazoo: Medieval Institute Publications, 1995.
Chantari	*Li Chantari di Lancelotto* ("The Song of Lancelot")	late 14th c. Italian verse	The destruction of Camelot and the Round Table	Escalot Mordred Winchester	Gardner, Edmund G. *The Arthurian Legend in Italian Literature.* London: Dent, 1930.
Chaucer	Geoffrey Chaucer *The Wife of Bath's Tale* in *The Canterbury Tales*	1387 English verse	A knight must learn what women most desire; marries the loathly lady	Loathly Lady	Chaucer, Geoffrey. *The Canterbury Tales: a Selection*, ed. Donald R. Howard. New York: Penguin, 1969.
ChestreLvl	Thomas Chestre *Sir Launfal*	late 14th c. English verse	The adventures of Sir Launfal, adapted ultimately from Marie de France's *Lanval*	Lanval	Chestre, Thomas. *Sir Launfal*. In *Middle English Romances*, ed. Stephen A. Sheperd. New York: Norton, 1995.
ChestreLyb	Thomas Chestre *Lybeaus Desconus* ("The Fair Unknown")	late 14th c. English verse	The adventures of Gawain's son, Guinglain, adapted from Renaut de Bâgé's *Le Bel Inconnu*	Fair Unknown Guinglain Snowdon	Chestre, Thomas. *Lybeaus Desconus*, ed. M. Mills. London: Oxford University Press, 1969.
ChevEpee	Anonymous, possibly Paien de Maisières *Le Chevalier à L'Épée* ("The Knight with the Sword")	late 12th c. French verse	Parody of Gawain adventures.	Ydain	Brewer, Elizabeth, ed. and trans. *The Knight of the Sword*. In *From Cuchulainn to Gawain*. Cambridge: D. S. Brewer, 1973.
ChevPap	*Le Chevalier du Papegau* ("The Knight of the Parrot")	late 14th c. or early 15th c. French prose	A young Arthur goes on adventures, earns the title nickname	Fish-Knight Knight of the Parrot Lady of the Blonde Hair	Vesce, Thomas E., trans. *The Knight of the Parrot*. New York: Garland, 1986
ChretienC	Chrétien de Troyes *Cligés*	late 12th c. French verse	Cligés and his father Alexander, heirs to the empire of Constantinople, have adventures at Arthur's court and at home.	Alexander Alis Cliges Fenice	Chrétien de Troyes. *Cligés*. In *The Complete Romances of Chrétien de Troyes*, ed. and trans. David Staines. Indianapolis: Indiana University Press, 1990.
ChretienE	Chrétien de Troyes *Erec*	late 12th c. French verse	Erec marries Enide, drags her on a series of adventures	Enice Erec Joy of the Court	Chrétien de Troyes. *Erec*. In *The Complete Romances of Chrétien de Troyes*, ed. and trans. David Staines. Indianapolis: Indiana University Press, 1990.

Source Code	Author & Title	Date, Form, & Language	Description	Keywords	Text
ChretienL	Chrétien de Troyes *Lancelot*, or *Le Chevalier de la Charrete* ("The Knight of the Cart")	late 12th c. French verse	Guinevere is kidnapped by Meleagant, Lancelot rescues her and begins an affair with her	Gorre Guinevere Lancelot Meleagant	Chrétien de Troyes. *The Knight of the Cart*. In *The Complete Romances of Chrétien de Troyes*, ed. and trans. David Staines. Indianapolis: Indiana University Press, 1990.
ChretienP	Chrétien de Troyes *Perceval*, or *Le Conte del Graal* ("The Story of the Grail")	late 12th c. French verse	The adventures of the young Perceval, including his visit to the Grail Castle. First appearance of the Grail. Unfinished. Inspired many continuations and adaptations	Blancheflor Bleeding Lance Fisher King Maimed King Grail Grail Sword Perceval	Chrétien de Troyes. *The Story of the Grail*. In *The Complete Romances of Chrétien de Troyes*, ed. and trans. David Staines. Indianapolis: Indiana University Press, 1990.
ChretienY	Chrétien de Troyes *Yvain*, or *Le Chevalier au Lion* ("The Knight with the Lion")	late 12th c. French verse	Yvain slays the Lord of the Fountain, marries his widow, has a series of adventures with a lion	Esclados Knight with the Lion Laudine Yvain	Chrétien de Troyes. *The Knight with the Lion*. In *The Complete Romances of Chrétien de Troyes*, ed. and trans. David Staines. Indianapolis: Indiana University Press, 1990.
ChroniconL	*Chronicon de Lanercost* ("Lanercost Chronicle")	14th c. Latin chronicle	In 1216, Arthur visits and dines with the Bishop of Winchester	Peter of the Rocks	General
ChroniconM	*Chronicon Montis Sancti Michaelis in Periculo Maris* ("Chronicle of St. Michael's Mount")	early 12th c. Breton chronicle	A note that Arthur was king of Britain in 421	Arthur	General
Claris	*Claries et Laris* ("Claris and Laris")	1268 French verse	The adventures and loves of two friends, Claris and Laris	Claris Laris	General
Conti	*Conti di Antichi Cavalier* ("Tales of the Knights of Old")	13th c. Italian prose	One of 20 stories describes the parents of Galehaut and the Castle of Tears	Brunor Castle of Tears Galehaut	Gardner, Edmund G. *The Arthurian Legend in Italian Literature*. London: Dent, 1930.
Contin1	Attributed to Wauchier of Denain First Continuation of Chrétien's *Perceval*	c. 1200 French verse	Continuation of *Perceval* describes adventures of Gawain and Caradoc	Brandelis Brun of Branlant Caradoc Gawain Grail Guiromelant Orguellos	Roach, William, ed. *The Continuations of the Old French "Perceval" of Chrétien de Troyes*, vols. 1–3. Philadephia: University of Pennsylvania Press, 1949–83.
Contin2	Attributed to Gauchier of Donaing Second Continuation of Chrétien's *Perceval*	c. 1200 French verse	Perceval gets tangled in a quest for a white stag's head while trying to return to the Fisher King's castle	Chessboard Castle Grail Knight of the Tomb Little Knight Perceval	Roach, William, ed. *The Continuations of the Old French "Perceval" of Chrétien de Troyes*, vol. 4. Philadephia: University of Pennsylvania Press, 1949–83.
Contin3	Manessier Third Continuation of Chrétien's *Perceval*	c. 1230 French verse	Perceval finally returns to the Grail Castle, is crowned Grail King	Black Hand Bleeding Lance Grail Perceval	Roach, William, ed. *The Continuations of the Old French "Perceval" of Chrétien de Troyes*, vol. 5. Philadephia: University of Pennsylvania Press, 1949–83.

Source Code	Author & Title	Date, Form, & Language	Description	Keywords	Text
Contin4	Gerbert de Montreuil *Fourth Continuation of Chrétien's Perceval*	c. 1230 French verse	Perceval returns to the Grail Castle and mends the Grail sword	Grail Grail Sword Perceval	Gerbert de Montreuil. *La Continuation de Perceval*, ed. Mary Williams. 2 vols. Paris: Champion, 1922–5.
Culhwch	*Culhwch and Olwen*	late 11th c. Welsh prose	Culhwch wants to marry Olwen, seeks Arthur's help to complete tasks necessary to do so. Includes list of some 250 Arthurian warriors.	Cauldron Culhwch Olwen Twrch Trwyth Ysbadadden	Ganz, Jeffrey, ed. and trans. *How Culhwch Won Olwen*. In *The Mabinogion*. New York: Penguin, 1976.
DeOrtu	*De Ortu Waluuanii Nepotis Arturi* ("Of the Rise of Gawain, Nephew of Arthur")	late 13th c. Latin prose	The *enfances* of Gawain, his adventures in Rome, and early exploits at Arthur's court.	Anna Castle of Maidens Gawain Gormundus Milocrates	Day, Mildred Leake, ed. *The Rise of Gawain, Nephew of Arthur*. In *The Romance of Arthur: an Anthology of Medieval Texts in Translation*, ed. James J. Wilhelm. New York: Garland, 1994.
DeSancto	*De Sancto Joseph ab Arimathia* ("Of St. Joseph of Arimathea")	1516 Latin prose	The life of Joseph of Arimathea	Glastonbury Joseph of Arimathea	Skeat, Walter W., ed. *Joseph of Arimathie*. London: Trübner, 1871.
Dialog	*An Dialog Etre Arzur Roe d'an Bretounet ha Guynglaff* ("A Dialogue Between Arthur and Guynglaff")	late 16th c. or early 17th. c. Breton prose	Fragment of a meeting between Arthur and Guynglaff, who spouts Merlinesque prophecies	Guynglaff	Lacy, Norris J. and Geoffrey Ashe. *The Arthurian Handbook*. New York: Garland, 1988.
Dialogue	"Dialogue of Arthur and Gwenhwyfar"	16th c. Welsh verse	Conversation involving Guinevere, Melwas, and Kay	Melwas	General
Didot	Didot-*Perceval*	c. 1220–30 French prose	Adventures of Perceval as he becomes the Grail King, includes a section on the death of Arthur. Based partially on second continuation	Chessboard Castle Grail Perceval Perilous Seat	Roach, William, ed. *The Didot-Perceval*. Philadelphia: University of Pennsylvania Press, 1941.
DisIst	*Dis Ist Frauw Tristerat Horn von Saphoien* ("This is Lady Tristerat of Savoy's Horn")	15th c. German verse	Lady Tristerat of Savoy sends a magical chastity horn to Arthur's court.	Chastity Tests Tristerat	General
Drayton	Michael Drayton *Poly-Olbion*	1612 English verse	The Geography of Britain, including a number of Arthurian locales	Camelot Camlann	Drayton, Michael. *Poly-Olbion*, vol. 4, ed. J. William Hebel. Oxford: Shakespeare Head Press, 1961.
Dream	*Breudwyt Rhonabwy (The Dream of Rhonabwy)*	13th c. Welsh prose	A twelfth-century warrior falls asleep, dreams about meeting Arthur before the battle of Badon	Badon Osla Rhonabwy Yvain	Gantz, Jeffrey. *The Dream of Rhonabwy*. In *The Mabinogion*. New York: Penguin, 1976.
Dryden	John Dryden *King Arthur; or, the British Worthy*	1691 English opera	Arthur battles the Saxon Oswald, marries Emmeline	Emmeline Philadel Oswald	Dryden, John. *King Arthur; or, the British Worthy, a Dramatic Opera*. In *The Works of John Dryden*, ed. Sir Walter Scott. Edinburgh: T. & A. Constable, 1884.
DueTris	*I Due Tristani* ("The Two Tristans")	1555 Italian prose	The story of Tristan and Isolde and their children, also called Tristan and Isolde	Infanta Maria Isolde Juan Tristan	Gardner, Edmund G. *The Arthurian Legend in Italian Literature*. London: Dent, 1930.

Source Code	Author & Title	Date, Form, & Language	Description	Keywords	Text
Durmart	*Durmart le Gallois*	early 13th c. French verse	The adventures of Durmart, who woos and wins Queen Fenise of Ireland	Dumart Fenise Nogant	Gildea, Joseph, ed. *Durmart le Gallois*. 2 vols. Villanova, PA: Villanova University Press, 1965–6.
Edolanz	*Edolanz*	mid-13th c. German verse	Fragment of the adventures of Edolanz, who rescues Gawain and wins a sparrowhawk tournament	Edolanz	General
Eilhart	Eilhart von Oberge *Tristrant*	1170–90 German verse	"Primitive" or "Common" version of the Tristan legend.	Isolde Isolde of the White Hands Mark Rivalin Tristan	Eilhart von Oberge. *Tristrant*, trans. J. W. Thomas. Lincoln: University of Nebraska Press, 1978.
Elucid	*The Elucidation*	13th c. French verse	Prologue to Chrétien's *Perceval*.	Amangon	Thompson, Albert Wilder, ed. *The Elucidation: a Prologue to the* Conte del Graal. New York: Institute of French Studies, 1931.
Enfances	*Les Enfances Gauvain* ("The Youth of Gawain")	early 13th c. French verse	Gawain's infancy and youth, including his trip to Rome	Gawain Gawain the Brown Morcades	Micha, Alexandre. "Miscellaneous French Romances in Verse." In *Arthurian Literature in the Middle Ages*, ed. R. S. Loomis. Oxford: Clarendon, 1959.
Erex	*Erex Saga* ("Saga of Erec")	13th c. Icelandic prose	Adaptation of Chrétien's *Erec* relating the tale of Erec and Enide	Erec Enide	Blaisdell, Foster W. and Marianne E. Kalinke, trans. *Erex Saga and Ívens Saga: The Old Norse Versions of Chrétien de Troyes's* Erec *and* Yvain. Lincoln: University of Nebraska Press, 1977.
Etienne	Etienne de Rouen *Draco Normannicus* ("The Norman Dragon")	c. 1169 Latin chronicle	Arthur and King Henry II exchange letters over the proper rulership of Brittany	Henry II Rollandus	Fletcher, Robert H. *The Arthurian Material in the Chronicles, Especially Those of Great Britain and France*. Boston: Ginn, 1906.
Febusso	*Febusso e Breusso* ("Febus and Breus")	c. 1325–35 Italian verse	Sir Breus the Pitiless stumbles into the cavern tomb of Febus. Based on an episode in *Palamedes*.	Breus Febus	Gardner, Edmund G. *The Arthurian Legend in Italian Literature*. London: Dent, 1930.
Ferguut	*Ferguut*	mid to late 13th c. Dutch verse	Adventures of Fergus, adapted from Guillaume le Clerc's *Fergus*	Fergus	Sparnaay, Hendricus. "The Dutch Romances." In *Arthurian Literature in the Middle Ages*, ed. R. S. Loomis. Oxford: Clarendon, 1959.
Fielding	Henry Fielding *Tom Thumb* and *The Tragedy of Tragedies*	1730 English play	Parody of Arthuriana and tragic theater, involving the diminutive warrior Tom Thumb. Two versions.	Dollallolla Glumdalca Tom Thumb	Fielding, Henry. *The Tragedy of Tragedies*. New Haven: Yale University Press, 1918.
Floriant	*Floriant et Florete* ("Floriant and Florete")	c. 1250–75 French verse	The adventures of Floriant, raised by Morgan le Fay. He weds the daughter of the Emperor of Constantinople	Filimenis Florete Floriant Maragoz	Williams, Harry F., ed. *Floriant et Florete*. An Arbor: University of Michigan Press, 1947.

Source Code	Author & Title	Date, Form, & Language	Description	Keywords	Text
FolieB	*La Folie Tristan de Berne* ("The Madness of Tristan")	late 12th c. French verse	Episode in which Tristan visits Mark's court disguised as a fool so he can meet with Isolde	Husdent Isolde Perinis Tristan	Bédier, Joseph, ed. *Les Deux Poèmes de la Folie Tristan*. Paris: Didot, 1907.
FolieO	*La Folie Tristan d'Oxford* ("The Madness of Tristan")	12th c. French verse	Episode in which Tristan visits Mark's court disguised as a fool so he can meet with Isolde	Husdent Isolde Petitcrieu Tristan	Bromiley, Geoffrey N. *Thomas's Tristan and the Folie Tristan d'Oxford*. London: Grant & Cutler, 1986.
Froissart	Jehan Froissart *Meliador*	1361–69 French verse	Arthur's Sir Meliador wins tournaments for the hand of Lady Hermondine of Scotland	Hermondine Meliador	Micha, Alexandre. "Miscellaneous French Romances in Verse." In *Arthurian Literature in the Middle Ages*, ed. R. S. Loomis. Oxford: Clarendon, 1959.
Gaimar	Geoffrey Gaimar *L'Estoire des Engles* ("The History of the Angles")	c. 1140 French chronicle	The history of the Angles in Britain, contains some Arthurian allusions	Angles Denmark Gunter	Fletcher, Robert H. *The Arthurian Material in the Chronicles, Especially Those of Great Britain and France*. Boston: Ginn, 1906.
Gargantuan	*Les Croniques Admirables du Puissant Roy Gargantua* ("The Admirable Chronicles of the Powerful King Gargantua")	c. 1534 French prose	A mythical giant named Gargantua, whose parents were created by Merlin, serves Arthur for 200 years	Gargantua	Girault, François. *The Tale of Gargantua and King Arthur*, ed. Huntington Brown. Cambridge: Harvard University Press, 1932.
GeoffHR	Geoffrey of Monmouth *Historia Regum Britanniae* ("History of the Kings of Britain")	c. 1138 Latin chronicle	First full version of Arthur's life, his conquests, his war against Rome, his battle against Mordred's rebellion, and his death. Probably the most important Arthurian text ever written. Mostly invented, but presented (and accepted) as history.	Ambrosius Arthur Camel Constantine Guinevere Merlin Mordred Rome Saxons Uther Pendragon Vortigern	Geoffrey of Monmouth. *History of the Kings of Great Britain*, trans. Sebastian Evans. New York: E. P. Dutton, 1958.
GeoffVM	Geoffrey of Monmouth *Vita Merlini* ("The Life of Merlin")	c. 1150 Latin verse	The latter days of Merlin, drawn from the Welsh tales of Myrddin.	Avalon Ganieda Merlin Morgan le Fay Rhydderch Taliessin	Geoffrey of Monmouth. *Vita Merlini*, ed. and trans. Jeffrey Ganz. New York: Penguin, 1976.
Geraint	*Geraint and Enid*	13th c. Welsh prose	Welsh adaptation of same material found in Chrétien's *Erec*, with hero changed from Erec to Geraint	Enide Geraint	Gantz, Jeffrey, ed. and trans. *Geraint son of Erbin*. In *the Mabinogion*. New York: Penguin, 1976.
Gesta	*Gesta Regum Britanniae* ("Deeds of the Kings of Britain")	mid-13th c. Latin	Adaptation of Geoffrey of Monmouth	Arthur Uther	Fletcher, Robert H. *The Arthurian Material in the Chronicles, Especially Those of Great Britain and France*. Boston: Ginn, 1906.
Gildas	Gildas *De Excidio et Conquestu Britanniae* ("Of the Ruin and Conquest of Britain")	c. 540 Latin chronicle	Tirade against the British kings, glorifying the old days of the Roman occupation, mentions Ambrosius, Vortigern, and Badon	Ambrosius Badon Vortigern	Gildas. *De Excidio et Conquestu Britanniae*. In *Six Old English Chronicles*, ed. J. A. Giles. New York: AMS, 1968.

Source Code	Author & Title	Date, Form, & Language	Description	Keywords	Text
Giraldus	Giraldus Cambrensis (Gerald of Wales) *De Principis Instructione* ("On the Instruction of Princes")	c. 1193 Latin chronicle	Includes an account of the discovery of Arthur's body at Glastonbury	Arthur Glastonbury	Wilhelm, James J. "Arthur in the Latin Chronicles." In *The Romance of Arthur: an Anthology of Medieval Texts in Translation*, ed. James J. Wilhelm. New York: Garland 1994.
Girart	Girart D'Amiens *Escanor*	c. 1280 French verse	Kay falls in love; Galantivet defends Gawain against a murder charge.	Andrivete Escanor Galantivet	Micha, Alexandre. "Miscellaneous French Romances in Verse." In *Arthurian Literature in the Middle Ages*, ed. R. S. Loomis. Oxford: Clarendon, 1959.
Gliglois	*Gliglois*	early 13th c. French verse	Gawain and his squire, Gliglois, fall in love with the same woman. She chooses Gliglois.	Beauté Gliglois	Livingston, Charles H., ed. *Gliglois: a French Arthurian Romance of the Thirteenth Century*. Cambridge: Harvard University Press, 1932.
Godfrey	Godfrey of Viterbo *Pantheon*	1169–91 Italian chronicle	Includes the story of Vortigern, Merlin, and Arthur's conception	Merlin Uther Vortigern	Gardner, Edmund G. *The Arthurian Legend in Italian Literature*. London: Dent, 1930.
Gododdin	Aneirin *Y Gododdin* ("The Gododdin")	c. 600 Scottish verse	Earliest Scottish poem contains first reference to Arthur's name, though the poem is not about him	Arthur	Aneirin. "The Gododdin." In *The Earliest Welsh Poetry*, ed. Joseph P. Clancy. London: Macmillan, 1970.
Goeznovii	*Legenda Sancti Goeznovii* (Legend of St. Goeznovius")	1019 Latin hagiography	One section offers a purely historical account of Arthur and Vortigern	Arthur Vortigern	Wilhelm, James J. "Arthur in the Latin Chronicles." In *The Romance of Arthur: an Anthology of Medieval Texts in Translation*, ed. James J. Wilhelm. New York: Garland 1994.
Gogulor	*Gogulor*	13th c. French verse	Fragment of a story in which a young knight battles a giant named Gogulor	Gogulor	General
Golagros	*Golagros and Gawain*	late 15th c. Scottish verse	Arthur sees the castle of Golagros, decides to conquer Golagros, Gawain does so.	Golagros	Hahn, Thomas, ed. *The Knightly Tale of Golagros and Gawain*. In *Sir Gawain: Eleven Romances and Tales*. Kalamazoo: Medieval Institute Publications, 1995.
Gottfried	Gottfried von Strassburg *Tristan*	early 13th c. German verse	Courtly version of the story of Tristan and Isolde, based on Thomas of England's version	Isolde Isolde of the White Hands Mark Tristan	Gottfried von Strassburg. *Tristan*, ed. A. T. Hatto. Harmondsworth: Penguin, 1970.
Grene	*The Grene Knight*	c. 1500 English verse	Inferior adaptation of *Sir Gawain and the Green Knight*	Beheading Game Bredbeddle Green Knight	Hahn, Thomas, ed. *The Grene Knight*. In *Sir Gawain: Eleven Romances and Tales*. Kalamazoo: Medieval Institute Publications, 1995.

Source Code	Author & Title	Date, Form, & Language	Description	Keywords	Text
Guillaume	Guillaume le Clerc *Fergus*	1200–33 French verse	The adventures of Fergus, a Fair Unknown character who joins Arthur's court.	Fergus	Guillaume le Clerc. *The Romance of Fergus*, ed. Wilson Frescoln. Philadephia: William H. Allen, 1983.
Hardyng	John Hardyng *John Hardyng's Chronicle*	1457–64 English verse	Arthur's life as given in Geoffrey of Monmouth.	Arthur Uther Vortigern	Fletcher, Robert H. *The Arthurian Material in the Chronicles, Especially Those of Great Britain and France*. Boston: Ginn, 1906.
HartmannE	Hartmann von Aue *Erec*	late 12th c. German verse	German adaptation of Chrétien de Troyes's *Erec* with some modifications	Enide Erec	Hartmann von Aue. *Erec*, trans. Thomas L. Keller. New York: Garland, 1987.
HartmannI	Hartmann von Aue *Iwein*	late 12th c. German verse	German adaptation of Chrétien de Troyes's *Yvain*	Yvain	Hartmann von Aue. *Iwein*, ed. and trans. Patrick M. McConeghy. New York: Garland, 1984.
HeberMD	Reginald Heber *Morte D'Arthur* ("Death of Arthur')	1812 English prose	Glorious Arthur. Guinevere longs for her past love, Cadual. Mordred plots against Arthur.	Arthur Cadual Mordred	Merriman, James Douglas. *The Flower of Kings: a Study of the Arthurian Legend in England Between 1485 and 1835*. Wichita: University Press of Kansas, 1973.
HeberMG	Reginald Heber *The Masque of Gwendolen*	1816 English prose	Version of the Loathly Lady story	Loathly Lady	Merriman, James Douglas. *The Flower of Kings: a Study of the Arthurian Legend in England Between 1485 and 1835*. Wichita: University Press of Kansas, 1973.
Heinrich	Heinrich von dem Türlin *Diu Crône* ("The Crown")	c. 1230 German verse	Epic Grail story, presents Gawain as the Grail Hero. Includes abduction of Guinevere, Chastity Tests.	Amurfina Chastity Tests Gasozein Gawain Grail	Heinrich von dem Türlin. *The Crown*, ed. and trans. J. W. Thomas. Lincoln: University of Nebraska Press, 1989.
Henry	Henry of Huntingdon *Historia Anglorum* ("History of England")	c. 1129 Latin chronicle	Chronicle of England, lists Arthur's battles against the Saxons.	Arthur	Fletcher, Robert H. *The Arthurian Material in the Chronicles, Especially Those of Great Britain and France*. Boston: Ginn, 1906.
HereJoA	*Here Begynneth the Lyfe of Joseph of Armathia with a Praysing to Joseph*	1520 English verse	Joseph, his quests, and his founding of the abbey at Glastonbury	Glastonbury Joseph of Arimathea	Skeat, Walter W., ed. *Joseph of Arimathie*. London: Trübner, 1871.
Heywood	Thomas Heywood *The Life of Merlin*	1641 English verse	Merlin's life, focusing on his prophecies	Merlin	Heywood, Thomas. *The Life of Merlin*. In *The Romance of Merlin*, ed. Peter Goodrich. New York: Garland, 1990.
Hill	Aaron Hill *Merlin in Love, or: Youth Against Magic*	1740–60 English opera	Merlin falls in love with Columbine. She turns him into a donkey	Columbine Harlequin	Merriman, James Douglas. *The Flower of Kings: a Study of the Arthurian Legend in England Between 1485 and 1835*. Wichita: University Press of Kansas, 1973.

Source Code	Author & Title	Date, Form, & Language	Description	Keywords	Text
Hilton	William Hilton *Arthur, Monarch of the Britons, a Tragedy*	1759 English verse	Dramatic account of Arthur's downfall and death	Arthur	Merriman, James Douglas. *The Flower of Kings: a Study of the Arthurian Legend in England Between 1485 and 1835.* Wichita: University Press of Kansas, 1973.
Historia	*Historia Meriadoci Regis Cambrie* ("Story of Meriadoc, King of Wales")	late 13th c. Latin prose	The adventures of Meriadoc, who joins Arthur's court and claims his heritage, the kingdom of Wales	Griffin Gundebald Meriadoc Orwen	Day, Mildred Leake, ed. and trans. *The Story of Meriadoc, King of Cambria.* New York: Garland, 1988.
Hole	Richard Hole *Arthur, or the Northern Enchantment in Seven Books*	1789 English prose	Arthur obtains the assistance of Merlin in fighting Hengist and the Saxons.	Hengist Inogen	Merriman, James Douglas. *The Flower of Kings: a Study of the Arthurian Legend in England Between 1485 and 1835.* Wichita: University Press of Kansas, 1973.
HughesT	Thomas Hughes *The Misfortunes of Arthur*	1587 English play	Tragedy based on Geoffrey of Monmouth's tale of Arthur's downfall.	Arthur Gorlois Guinevere Mordred	Hughes, Thomas. *The Misfortunes of Arthur*, ed. Brian J. Corrigan. New York: Garland, 1992.
Hunbaut	*Hunbaut*	13th c. French verse	Gawain and Hunbaut have assorted adventures while on a mission for Arthur.	Hunbaut King of the Isles	Winters, Margaret, ed. *Hunbaut.* Leiden: Brill, 1984.
Huon	*Huon de Bordeaux*	early 13th c. French verse	The adventures of Huon of Bordeaux, his tutor Auberon, and their conflict with Arthur	Auberon Huon	General
Hupsches	*Ain Hupsches Vasnachtspill und Sagt von Künig Artus* ("A Pleasing Shrovetide Play About King Arthur")	15th c. German Shrovetide play	The Queen of Zipper sends a chastity testing horn to Arthur's court and it embarrasses all of Arthur's noblemen.	Chastity Tests Zipper	General
Ilas	*Ilas et Solvas* ("Ilas and Solvas")	14th c. French verse	Fragment of a tale in which Ilas and Solvas break allegiance with Arthur.	Ilas Solvas	General
Ivens	*Ivens Saga* ("Saga of Yvain")	13th c. Norse prose	Norse adaptation of Chrétien de Troyes's *Yvain*.	Yvain	Blaisdell, Foster W., ed. and Marianne E. Kalinke, trans. *Erex Saga and Ívens Saga.* Lincoln: University of Nebraska Press, 1977.
Jaufre	*Jaufré*	late 12th c. or early 13th c. French verse	Jaufré, a knight in Arthur's service, slays a giant named Taulat.	Brunissen Jaufré Taulat	Rémy, Paul. "Jaufré." In *Arthurian Literature in the Middle Ages*, ed. R. S. Loomis. Oxford: Clarendon, 1959.
Jean	Jean D'Outremeuse *Ly Myreur des Histors* ("The Mirror of Histories")	c. 1350 French prose	Accounts of the reigns of Uther and Arthur	Caradoc Galopes Guinevere Modred	Fletcher, Robert H. *The Arthurian Material in the Chronicles, Especially Those of Great Britain and France.* Boston: Ginn, 1906.

Source Code	Author & Title	Date, Form, & Language	Description	Keywords	Text
Jeaste	*The Jeaste of Sir Gawayne*	late 15th c. English verse	Gawain sleeps with a maiden in a pavilion, defeats her father and brothers.	Brandelis Gilbert	Hahn, Thomas, ed. *The Jeaste of Sir Gawain*. In *Sir Gawain: Eleven Romances and Tales*. Kalamazoo: Medieval Institute Publications, 1995.
JohnF	John of Fordun *Chronica Gentis Scotorum* ("Chronicle of the People of Scotland")	c. 1385 Latin chronicle	First of the Scottish chronicles to portray Mordred as the rightful heir to the British throne	Mordred	Fletcher, Robert H. *The Arthurian Material in the Chronicles, Especially Those of Great Britain and France*. Boston: Ginn, 1906.
JohnG	John of Glastonbury *Cronica sive Antiquitates Glastoniensis Ecclesie* ("Chronicle of the Antiquities of the Church of Glastonbury")	mid-14th c. Latin chronicle	History of the church at Glastonbury. Describes the discovery of Arthur's body in 1190.	Glastonbury	General
Johnson	Richard Johnson *Tom a Lincolne*	1599–1607 English prose	The adventures of Tom a Lincoln, Arthur's illegitimate son.	Black Knight Tom a Lincoln	Merriman, James Douglas. *The Flower of Kings: a Study of the Arthurian Legend in England Between 1485 and 1835*. Wichita: University Press of Kansas, 1973.
Joseph	*Joseph of Arimathie*	c. 1375 English verse	Account of Joseph of Arimathea's travels based on the Vulgate *Estoire del Saint Graal*	Joseph of Arimathea	Skeat, Walter W., ed. *Joseph of Arimathie*. London: Trübner, 1871.
KingA&C	"King Arthur and King Cornwall"	16th c. English ballad	Arthur and his knights visit the court of King Cornwall and defeat him.	Cornwall	Hahn, Thomas, ed. "King Arthur and King Cornwall." In *Sir Gawain: Eleven Romances and Tales*. Kalamazoo: Medieval Institute Publications, 1995.
KingAD	"King Arthur's Death"	16th c. English ballad	Short ballad about Arthur's death.	Arthur Lucan	Percy, Thomas, ed. "King Arthur's Death." In *Relique of Ancient English Poetry*. London: Dent, 1938.
KingR	"King Ryence's Challenge"	16th c. English ballad	King Ryence demands Arthur's beard	Rions	Percy, Thomas, ed. "King Ryence's Challenge." In *Relique of Ancient English Poetry*. London: Dent, 1938.
Konrad	Konrad von Stoffeln *Gauriel von Muntabel*	late 13th c. German verse	Sir Gauriel must embark on a series of adventures in order to return to the graces of his fairy wife.	Gauriel	General
LancLac	*Lancelot do Lac* ("Lancelot of the Lake")	1215–20 French prose	First biography of Lancelot, his youth with the Lady of the Lake, his earliest adventures at Arthur's court. Incorporated into the Vulgate *Lancelot*	Ban Claudas Dolorous Guard Galehaut Lady of the Lake Lancelot	Corley, Corin, trans. *Lancelot of the Lake*. Oxford: Oxford University Press, 1989.

Source Code	Author & Title	Date, Form, & Language	Description	Keywords	Text
LancLaik	*Lancelot of the Laik*	late 15th c. Scottish verse	Arthur's war with Galehaut and Lancelot's involvement.	Galehaut Lancelot	Lupak, Alan, ed. *Lancelot of the Laik and Sir Tristrem*. Kalamazoo: Medieval Institute Publications, 1994.
Lanethen	"Lanethen Mantel" ("Laneth's Mantle")	15th c. German ballad	Arthur's niece sends a chastity mantle to Arthur and embarrasses his court.	Chastity Tests Laneth	General
Layamon	Layamon *Brut*	late 12th c. to mid-13th c. English verse	English adaptation and expansion of Wace's *Roman de Brut*	Argante Arthur Lucius Mordred Round Table	Layamon. *Brut*, ed. Rosamund Allen. New York: St. Martin's, 1952.
Legend	"The Legend of King Arthur"	16th c. English ballad	Arthur reviews the triumphs and misfortunes of his life.	Arthur Mordred St. Bernard's Mount	Percy, Thomas, ed. "The Legend of King Arthur." In *Relique of Ancient English Poetry*. London: Dent, 1938.
Liber	*Liber de Compositione Castri Ambaziae*	c. 1140 Latin prose	Establishment of the house of Anjou, includes Arthur's war against Lucius.	Billeius Clodius Honorius	Fletcher, Robert H. *The Arthurian Material in the Chronicles, Especially Those of Great Britain and France*. Boston: Ginn, 1906.
Livre	*Le Livre d'Artus* ("The Book of Arthur")	early 13th c. French prose	Continuation of Robert de Boron's *Merlin*, including the adventures of Arthur and Gawain.	Arthur Gawain Greu Pellinore Saxons	Somer, H. Oskar, ed. *The Vulgate Version of the Arthurian Romances*, vol. 7. Washington: Carnegie Institution, 1908–16.
Lohengrin	*Lohengrin*	c. 1283–89 German verse	Adventures of Loherangrin, based on character created by Wolfram von Eschenbach.	Elsam Loherangrin Swan Knight	General
Lorengel	*Lorengel*	15th c. German verse	Adaptation of *Lohengrin*.	Elsam Loherangrin	General
Lovelich	Henry Lovelich *History of the Holy Grail* and *Merlin*	c. 1450 English verse	English verse translation of Vulgate *Estoire del Saint Graal* and *Merlin*.	Joseph of Arimathea Merlin	Ackerman, Robert W. "English Rimed and Prose Romances." In *Arthurian Literature in the Middle Ages*, ed. R. S. Loomis. Oxford: Clarendon, 1959.
Luneten	*Der Luneten Mantel* ("Lunet's Mantle")	15th c. Shrovetide play	Lunet sends a magical chastity mantle to Arthur, embarrasses the court.	Chastity Tests	General
LyfeJoA	*The Lyfe of Joseph of Armathy*	English prose English prose	A version of Joseph of Arimathea's life	Joseph of Arimathea Mordrains	Skeat, Walter W., ed. *Joseph of Arimathie*. London: Trübner, 1871.
Maerlant	Jacob van Maerlant *Torec*	c. 1280 Dutch verse	Sir Torec recovers a family heirloom and defeats Arthur's knights for the love of a maiden.	Mariole Torec	Sparnaay, Hendricus. "The Dutch Romances." In *Arthurian Literature in the Middle Ages*, ed. R. S. Loomis. Oxford: Clarendon, 1959.
Major	John Major *Historia Majoris Britanniae*	1521 Latin chronicle	History of Britain written by a Scot, yet portraying Arthur positively	Arthur	Fletcher, Robert H. *The Arthurian Material in the Chronicles, Especially Those of Great Britain and France*. Boston: Ginn, 1906.

Source Code	Author & Title	Date, Form, & Language	Description	Keywords	Text
Malory	Sir Thomas Malory *Le Morte Darthur* ("The Death of Arthur")	1469–70 English prose	The entire life of Arthur and his court, divided into several sections, including Arthur's ascension (with the assistance of Merlin), the Roman War, the tale of Lancelot, the story of Gareth, the tale of Tristan, the Grail Quest, and Arthur's death. One of the most influential Arthurian works. Based on the Vulgate Cycle, the Post-Vulgate *Suite*, the English *Arthour and Merlin*, the Stanzaic *Le Morte Arthur* and the Alliterative *Morte Arthure*.	Arthur Balin Bedivere Elaine Gareth Gawain Grail Guinevere Lamorat Lancelot Lucius Merlin Morgan le Fay Palamedes Tristan Urry	Malory, Sir Thomas. *Le Morte Darthur*, ed. R. M. Lumiansky. New York: Macmillan, 1982.
Mannyng	Robert Mannyng of Brunne *The Story of England*	1338 English chronicle	Account of Arthur's life based on Wace.	Arthur	Mannyng, Robert. *The Chronicle of Robert Manning of Brunne*, ed. Frederick J. Furnivall. Lessing-Druckerei: Kraus, 1965.
MantelD	Anonymous, possible Heinrich von dem Türlin *Der Mantel* ("The Mantle")	13th c. German verse	Chastity test involving a mantle at Arthur's court.	Chastity Tests	General
MantelM	*Le Mantel Mautaillié* ("The Ill-Fitting Cloak")	late 12th c. French verse	A mantle brought to Arthur's court tests the chastity of the ladies.	Chastity Tests	Bennett, Philip E., ed. *Mantel et Cor: deux lais due 12e siècle*. Exeter: University of Exeter, 1975.
Manuel	*Manuel und Amande* ("Manuel and Amande")	late 13th c. German verse	Fragment of the story of Manuel of Greece, who marries Amande	Amande Manuel	General
MarieC	Marie de France *Chevrefueil* ("The Honeysuckle")	mid to late 12th c. French verse	Tristan and Isolde enjoy a passionate tryst in the forest during Tristan's exile from Mark's court.	Isolde Tristan	Marie de France. *The Honeysuckle*. In *Lays*, trans. Eugene Mason. London: Dent, 1911.
MarieL	Marie de France *Lanval*	mid to late 12th c. French verse	The earliest existing tale of Sir Lanval, and Arthurian knight who falls in love with a fairy.	Lanval	Marie de France. *Lanval*. In *Lays*, trans. Eugene Mason. London: Dent, 1911.
Marriage	"The Marriage of Sir Gawain"	15th c. English ballad	Gawain marries the Loathly Lady to find out what women most desire.	Loathly Lady	Shepard, Stephen H. A., ed. "The Marriage of Sir Gawaine." In *Middle English Romances*. New York: Norton, 1995.
Melekh	*Melekh Artus* ("King Arthur")	1279 Hebrew prose	Two sections from the Vulgate: Uther's seduction of Igerne, and Arthur's death.	Lanval Lancelot Uther	Leviant, Curt, ed. and trans. *King Artus: a Hebrew Arthurian Romance of 1279*. New York: KTAV, 1979.
Melion	*Melino*	c. 1200 French verse	Sir Melion is a werewolf.	Melion	General
Meriadeuc	*Meriadeuc* or *Le Chevalier aux Deux Épées* ("The Knight of the Two Swords")	c. 1225–50 French verse	The adventures of Meriadeuc, called the Knight with the Two Swords, as contrasted with those of Gawain.	Lore Meriadeuc Ris Waste Chapel	Arthur, Ross G. and Noel L. Corbett, trans. *The Knight of the Two Swords*. Gainsville: University Press of Florida, 1996.

Source Code	Author & Title	Date, Form, & Language	Description	Keywords	Text
Merveil	Jehan *Les Merveilles de Rigomer* ("The Marvels of Rigomer")	mid to late 13th c. French verse	Arthur's knights set out to conquer Rigomer Castle in Ireland. Gawain succeeds.	Dionise Quintefuele Rigomer	Jehan. *The Marvels of Rigomer*, trans. Thomas E. Vesce. New York: Garland, 1988.
Modena	N/A The Modena Archivolt	1120–40 Italian sculpture	Sculpture on cathedral in Modena, Italy, depicts Arthur's knights rescuing Winlogee (Guinevere?) from Mardoc and Carrado	Caradoc Mardoc Winlogee Yder	Loomis, Roger S. *Arthurian Legends in Medieval Art*. New York: Modern Language Association of America, 1966.
Moriaen	*Moriaen*	mid to late 13th c. Dutch verse	Morien, son of Sir Aglovale, goes on a quest to find his father.	Aglovale Morien	Weston, Jessie L. *Morien: a Metrical Romance Rendered into English Prose from Medieval Dutch*. London: Nutt, 1901.
Mottuls	*Möttuls Saga* ("Saga of the Mantle")	13th c. Norse prose	A mantle brought to Arthur's court tests the chastity of the ladies.	Chastity Test	Kalinke, Marianne E., trans. *The Saga of the Mantle*. In *The Romance of Arthur: an Anthology of Medieval Texts in Translation*, ed. James J. Wilhelm. New York: Garland 1994.
Myrddin	Various; all Myrddin poems	12th c.–15th c. Welsh verse	A collection of short poems on Myrddin, the prophet and bard in Welsh tradition who anticipated Merlin	Arfderydd Gwenddolau Gwenddydd Myrddin Rhydderch	Bollard, John K. "Myrddin in Early Welsh Tradition." In *The Romance of Merlin*, ed. Peter Goodrich. New York: Garland, 1990.
Nennius	Probably Nennius *Historia Brittonum* ("History of the Britons")	early 9th c. Latin chronicle	Earliest chronicle containing Arthur, describing his 12 battles against the Saxons and his connection to two "miracles." Includes Vortigern, Ambrosius.	Ambrosius Amr Arthur Badon Cabal Octa Snowdon Vortigern	Nennius. *Historia Brittonum*. In *British History and the Welsh Annals*, ed. John Morris. London: Phillimore, 1980.
Novellino	*Il Novellino*	c. 1300 Italian prose	Collection of short stories, including five on Arthurian matters.	Alibano Good Knight without Fear Meliadus	Gardner, Edmund G. *The Arthurian Legend in Italian Literature*. London: Dent, 1930.
Ogier	*Roman d'Ogier le Danois* ("Romance of Ogier the Dane")	14th c. French verse	Ogier the Dane gets shipwrecked on Avalon, becomes Morgan le Fay's lover.	Ogier	Bruce, James Douglas. *The Evolution of Arthurian Romance from the Beginnings Down to the Year 1300*, vol. 1. Gloucester: Peter Smith, 1958.
Owain	*Owain*	13th c. Welsh prose	Story of Owain that contains much of the same material as Chrétien's *Yvain*	Lady of the Fountain Yvain	Gantz, Jeffrey, ed. and trans. *Owein, or The Countess of the Fountain*. In *The Mabinogion*. New York: Penguin, 1976.
Paien	Paien de Maisières *La Mule Sans Frein* ("The Mule Without a Bridle")	late 12th c. French verse	Gawain embarks on a quest to recover a bridle for a maiden.	Beheading Game Sgoidamur	Paien de Maisières. *The Mule Without a Bridle*, ed. and trans. Elizabeth Brewer. In *From Cuchulainn to Gawain*. Cambridge: Brewer, 1973.

Source Code	Author & Title	Date, Form, & Language	Description	Keywords	Text
Palamedes	*Palamedes*	c. 1240 French prose	Two tales—*Guiron le Courtois* and *Meliadus*—relating the adventures of the generation before Arthur. Preserved in the *Compilation* of Rusticiano da Pisa.	Esclabor Febus Guiron Meliadus Palamedes	General
Parlement	*The Parlement of the Thre Ages*	mid to late 14th c. English verse	Debate between young, middle-aged, and old men includes an account of Arthur's life	Excalibur Mont St. Michel	Offord, M. Y., ed. *The Parlement of the Thre Ages*. London: Oxford University Press, 1967.
Penninc	Penninc and Pieter Vostaert *Roman van Walewein* ("Romance of Gawain")	mid to late 13th c. Dutch verse	Gawain seeks the Floating Chessboard, becomes involved in a series of related quests.	Floating Chessboard Sword with the Two Rings Wonder Ysabele	Sparnaay, Hendricus. "The Dutch Romances." In *Arthurian Literature in the Middle Ages*, ed. R. S. Loomis. Oxford: Clarendon, 1959.
Peredur	*Peredur*	13th c. Welsh prose	The adventures of Peredur, related to Chrétien de Troyes's *Perceval*	Black Serpent Fortress of Marvels Hags of Gloucester Peredur	Gantz, Jeffrey, ed. and trans. *Peredur Son of Evrawg*. In *The Mabinogion*. New York: Penguin, 1976.
Perlesvaus	*Perlesvaus*	early 13th c. French prose	Grail romance continuing and adapting Chrétien de Troyes's *Perceval*. Perceval becomes Grail King.	Brien of the Isles Loholt Orgeluse Perceval	Bryant, Nigel, trans. *The High Book of the Grail*. Ipswich: Brewer, 1978.
Pieri	Paolino Pieri *La Storia di Merlino* ("The Story of Merlin")	c. 1300–05 Italian prose	Merlin's youth and early prophecies	Marinaia Matteo Merlin	Gardner, Edmund G. *The Arthurian Legend in Italian Literature*. London: Dent, 1930.
Pierre	Pierre de Langtoft *The Chronicle of Pierre de Langtoft*	c. 1300–07 English chronicle	Chronicle of Britain, including Arthur's life, based on Geoffrey of Monmouth.	Arthur Constantine Leo Lucius Mordred	Pierre de Langtoft. *The Chronicle of Pierre de Langtoft from the Earliest Period to the Death of King Edward I*, 2 vols., ed. Thomas Wright. Lessing-Druckerei: Kraus, 1964.
PleierG	Der Pleier *Garel von dem blühenden Tal* ("Garel of the Blossoming Valley")	1240–70 German verse	Sir Garel embarks on a series of quests, defeats an enemy of Arthur.	Ekunaver Eskilabon Garel Vulganus	Pleier, The. *The Pleier's Arthurian Romances*, trans. J. W. Thomas. New York: Garland, 1992.
PleierM	Der Pleier *Meleranz*	1240–70 German verse	The assorted adventures of Meleranz, Arthur's nephew.	Dulceflur Godonas Meleranz Tydomie	Pleier, The. *The Pleier's Arthurian Romances*, trans. J. W. Thomas. New York: Garland, 1992.
PleierT	Der Pleier *Tandareis and Flordibel*	1240–70 German verse	Tandareis, and Arthurian knight, must complete a series of quests to prove himself worthy of Flordibel.	Flordibel Kandalion Karedos Tandareis	Pleier, The. *The Pleier's Arthurian Romances*, trans. J. W. Thomas. New York: Garland, 1992.

Source Code	Author & Title	Date, Form, & Language	Description	Keywords	Text
PostMer	Post-Vulgate *Suite du Merlin* ("Continuation of Merlin")	1230–40 French prose	Continuation of Prose *Merlin* found in the Post-Vulgate includes the early adventures of Arthur's court, the Dolorous Stroke. Followed by the Post-Vulgate *Queste del Saint Graal*.	Accalon Balin Erec Excalibur Humber Lot Merlin Morgan le Fay Morholt Pelleas Pellinore Tor	Lacy, Norris J., ed. *Lancelot-Grail: the Old French Arthurian Vulgate and Post Vulgate in Translation*, vols. 4 & 5. New York: Garland, 1996.
PostMort	Post-Vulgate *Mort Artu* ("Death of Arthur")	1230–40 French prose	Brief account of Arthur's final days and death, based on the Vulgate *Mort Artu*, follows the Post-Vulgate *Queste del Saint Graal*.	Arthur Arthur the Less Bleoberis Gawain Girflet Guinevere Lancelot Logres Mark Mordred Rome	Lacy, Norris J., ed. *Lancelot-Grail: the Old French Arthurian Vulgate and Post Vulgate in Translation*, vol. 5. New York: Garland, 1996.
PostQuest	Post-Vulgate *Queste del Saint Graal* ("Quest of the Holy Grail")	1230–40 French prose	Account of the Grail Quest, taken in part from the Vulgate *Queste del Saint Graal*. Follows the Post-Vulgate *Suite du Merlini*, precedes the Post-Vulgate *Mort Artu*. Galahad is the Grail Hero. Mark invades Arthur's lands during the Grail Quest, but is defeated. Includes two near-independent romances, *La Folie Lancelot* and the Prose *Erec*.	Arthur the Less Bors Erec Galahad Gawain Grail Lancelot Mark Meraugis Palamedes Pelles Perceval Questing Beast Sword with the Strange Hangings Tristan	Lacy, Norris J., ed. *Lancelot-Grail: the Old French Arthurian Vulgate and Post Vulgate in Translation*, vol. 5. New York: Garland, 1996.
Povest	*Povest' o Tryshchane* ("Romance of Tristan")	c. 1580 Slavic prose	The life and adventures of Sir Tristan, adapted from the French Prose *Tristan*.	Foul Heathen Galec Lancelot Liburn Samsiz Tristan	Dekanic-Janoski, Sonja. "The Serbo-Russian Romance of Tristan and Isolt." In *The Tristan Legend: Texts from Northern and Eastern Europe in Modern English Translation*, ed. Joyce Hill. Leeds: University of Leeds, 1977.

Source Code	Author & Title	Date, Form, & Language	Description	Keywords	Text
Presbys	*Ho Presbys Hippotes* ("The Old Knight")	c. 1300 Greek verse	An Old Knight visits Arthur's court and defeats all of Arthur's knights.	Branor the Brown Old Knight	Martin, R. H., trans. "A Greek Poem About the Deeds of King Arthur, Tristan, Lancelot, Gawain, Palamedes, and Other Knights of the Round Table." In *The Tristan Legend: Texts from Northern and Eastern Europe in Modern English Translation*, ed. Joyce Hill. Leeds: University of Leeds, 1977.
Prophecies	Richart d'Irlande *Les Prophecies de Merlin* ("The Prophecies of Merlin")	1272–79 French prose	Merlin relates a series of prophecies to his scribes.	Alexander the Orphan Merlin	Berthelot, Anne, ed. *Les Prophesies de Merlin.* Cologne: Bodmer, 1990.
ProsBrut	Prose *Brut*	late 13th c. to late 15th c. various chronicles	Group of Anglo-Norman, English, and Latin chronicles ultimately based on Geoffrey of Monmouth.	Arthur Hengist Mordred Rome St. Bernard's Mount	Fletcher, Robert H. *The Arthurian Material in the Chronicles, Especially Those of Great Britain and France.* Boston: Ginn, 1906.
ProsMer1	Prose *Merlin*	early 13th c. French prose	Birth and deeds of Merlin, based on Robert de Boron's verse *Merlin.* Incorporated into the Vulgate *Merlin.*	Antor Merlin Sword in the Stone	Lacy, Norris J., ed. *Lancelot-Grail: the Old French Arthurian Vulgate and Post Vulgate in Translation*, vol. 1. New York: Garland, 1996.
ProsMer2	Prose *Merlin*	mid-15th c. English prose	English translation of the Vulgate *Merlin.*	Merlin Ninniane	Goodrich, Peter, ed. "Middle English Prose *Merlin.*" In *The Romance of Merlin.* New York: Garland, 1990.
ProsTris	Prose *Tristan*	1230–40 French prose	First full integration of Tristan into the Arthurian cycle. Various manuscripts of varying length, some with conflicting accounts.	Alexander the Orphan Dinadan Faramon Governal Isolde Lancelot Mark Meliadus Palamedes Tristan	Curtis, Renée L., trans. *The Romance of Tristan.* Oxford: Oxford University Press, 1994.
PucciB	Antonio Pucci *Gismirante*	1340–80 Italian verse	Gismirante embarks on an adventure to save Arthur's court from starvation.	Gismirante	Gardner, Edmund G. *The Arthurian Legend in Italian Literature.* London: Dent, 1930.
PucciG	Antonio Pucci *Brito di Brettagna*	1340–80 Italian verse	Brito must obtain artifacts from Arthur's court to win the love of a lady.	Brito	Gardner, Edmund G. *The Arthurian Legend in Italian Literature.* London: Dent, 1930.
Pulzella	*La Pulzella Gaia* ("The Merry Maiden")	1350–75 Italian verse	Pulzella Gaia, the daughter of Morgan le Fay, falls in love with Gawain.	Morgan le Fay Pulzella Gaia	Gardner, Edmund G. *The Arthurian Legend in Italian Literature.* London: Dent, 1930.

Source Code	Author & Title	Date, Form, & Language	Description	Keywords	Text
Quando	*Quando Tristano e Lancielotto Combattettero al Petrone di Merlino* ("When Tristan and Lancelot Fought at Merlin's Stone")	late 15th c. Italian verse	Through a misunderstanding, Tristan and Lancelot fight at one of "Merlin's Stones."	Merlin's Stones	Gardner, Edmund G. *The Arthurian Legend in Italian Literature.* London: Dent, 1930.
Raoul	Raoul de Houdenc *Meraugis de Portlesguez*	early 13th c. French verse	Meraugis embarks on adventures to prove himself worthy of Lidoine.	Gorvain Cadrut Island Without a Name Lidoine Meraugis Sword with the Strange Hangings	Raoul de Houdenc. *Meraugis de Portlesguez*, ed. Mathias Freidwagner. Halle: Niemeyer, 1897.
Renaut	Renaut de Bâgé *Le Bel Inconnu* ("The Fair Unknown")	1185–90 French verse	Guinglain, Gawain's son, known as the "Fair Unknown," must save Blonde Esmeree from two sorcerers.	Esmeree Fair Unknown Guinglain Mabon Maiden of the White Hands	Renaut de Bâgé. *Le Bel Inconnu*, ed. Karen Fresco, trans. Colleen P. Donagher. New York: Garland, 1992.
Riddere	*Die Riddere Metter Mouwen* ("The Knight with the Sleeve")	mid to late 13th c. Dutch verse	The adventures of Miraudijs, known as the "Knight with the Sleeve."	Knight with the Sleeve	Sparnaay, Hendricus. "The Dutch Romances." In *Arthurian Literature in the Middle Ages*, ed. R. S. Loomis. Oxford: Clarendon, 1959.
RobertBlo	Robert de Blois *Beaudous*	mid to late 13th c. French verse	The adventures of Gawain's son, Beaudous.	Beaudous Fair Unknown	General
RobertBorJ	Robert de Boron *Joseph d'Arimathie*	1191–1202 French verse	The early history of the Grail and the life of Joseph of Arimathea.	Alain Bron Grail Joseph of Arimathea	Robert de Boron. *Joseph d'Arimathie*, ed. Richard O'Gorman. Toronto: Pontifical Institute of Medieval Studies, 1995.
RobertBorM	Robert de Boron *Merlin*	1191–1202 French verse	Fragment detailing Merlin's association with Arthur.	Merlin Sword-in-the-Stone	General
RobertG	Robert of Gloucester *The Chronicle of Robert of Gloucester*	late 13th c. English verse	Chronicle of Britain, including Arthur's life.	Arthur	Fletcher, Robert H. *The Arthurian Material in the Chronicles, Especially Those of Great Britain and France.* Boston: Ginn, 1906.
Sachs	Hans Sachs *Die Ehbrecherbruck* ("The Adulterer's Bridge")	1545 German verse	Arthur builds a bridge to test Guinevere's chastity; Guinevere passes.	Chastity Tests.	General
SagaTI	*Saga af Tristram ok Isodd* ("Saga of Tristan and Isolde")	14th c. Icelandic prose	The story of Tristan and Isolde	Isolde Isolde the Dark Kalegras Mórodd Spain Tristan	Hill, Joyce, ed. and trans. "The Icelandic Saga of Tristan and Isolt." In *The Tristan Legend: Texts from Northern and Eastern Europe in Modern English Translation.* Leeds: University of Leeds, 1977.
SaintsCad	Lifris Life of St. Cadoc	late 11th c. Latin hagiography	St. Cado saves a murderer from Arthur's wrath.	Cadoc	Chambers, E. K. *Arthur of Britain.* Cambridge: Sidgwick & Jackson, 1927.

Source Code	Author & Title	Date, Form, & Language	Description	Keywords	Text
SaintsCar	Life of St. Carannog	late 11th c. Latin hagiography	St. Carannog helps Arthur drive away a serpent.	Carannog	Chambers, E. K. *Arthur of Britain*. Cambridge: Sidgwick & Jackson, 1927.
SaintsI	Life of St. Illtud	late 11th c. Latin hagiography	The deeds of St. Illtud, Arthur's cousin.	Illtud	Chambers, E. K. *Arthur of Britain*. Cambridge: Sidgwick & Jackson, 1927.
SaintsP	Life of St. Padarn	late 11th c. Latin hagiography	Padarn traps Arthur in a chasm to punish him for insolence.	Padarn	Chambers, E. K. *Arthur of Britain*. Cambridge: Sidgwick & Jackson, 1927.
Sala	Pierre Sala *Tristan*	1525–29 French prose	Prose version of the life of Tristan.	Tristan	Sala, Pierre. *Tristan*, ed. L. Muir. Geneva: Droz, 1958.
Scott	Sir Walter Scott *The Bridal of Triermain*	1804 English verse	Triermain, Arthur's wicked daughter, visits Arthur's court and turns a tournament into a blood-bath. Merlin puts her to sleep.	Triermain	Scott, Sir Walter. "The Bridal of Triermain." In *The Complete Poetical Works of Sir Walter Scott*, ed. Horace E. Scudder. Cambridge: Riverside Press, 1900.
Short	*Short Metrical Chronicle*	1307 English verse	Chronicle of confused chronology, includes Arthur.	Arthur Hengist Uther	Zettl, Ewald, ed. *An Anonymous Short English Metrical Chronicle*. London: Oxford University Press, 1935.
SirCor	*Romance of Sir Corneus*	15th c. English verse	Chastity test involving a drinking horn.	Chastity Tests.	General
SirDeg	*Sir Degrevant*	c. 1400 English verse	The adventures of Sir Degrevant	Degrevant	Casson, L. F., ed. *The Romance of Sir Degrevant*. London: Oxford University Press, 1949.
SirGawain	*Sir Gawain and the Green Knight*	c. 1400 English verse	One of the finest Middle English romances. Gawain is challenged to a Beheading Game by the Green Knight.	Gawain Green Knight	Stone, Brian, trans. *Sir Gawain and the Green Knight*. London: Penguin, 1974.
SirLamb	*Sir Lambewell*	16th c. English verse	Variation of the tale of Sir Lanval.	Lanval	Hales, John W. and Frederick J. Furnivall, eds. "Sir Lambewell." In *Bishop Percy's Folio Manuscript*. London: Trübner, 1867.
SirLanc	"Sir Lancelot du Lake"	16th c. English ballad	Lancelot fights Tarquin.	Lancelot Tericam	Percy, Thomas, ed. "Sir Lancelot du Lake." In *Relique of Ancient English Poetry*. London: Dent, 1938.
SirLand	*Sir Landeval*	early to mid 14th c. English verse	Variation of the tale of Sir Lanval.	Lanval	Sheperd, Stephen A., ed. *Sir Landevale*. In *Middle English Romances*. New York: Norton, 1995.
SirPerc	*Sir Perceval of Galles*	early 14th c. English verse	The adventures of Sir Perceval without the Grail.	Acheflur Perceval	French, Walter H. and Charles B. Hale, eds. *Sir Perceval of Galles*. In *Middle English Metrical Romances*. New York: Russell & Russell, 1964.
SirTris	*Sir Tristrem*	c. 1300 English verse	Full "courtly" version of Tristan's life.	Isolde Mark Morgan Rouland Tristan	Lupack, Alan, ed. *Lancelot of the Laik and Sir Tristrem*. Kalamazoo: Medieval Institute Publications, 1994.

Source Code	Author & Title	Date, Form, & Language	Description	Keywords	Text
Spenser	Edmund Spenser *The Faerie Queene*	1570–99 English verse	"Prince" Arthur tries to find Gloriana, the Fairy Queen, assists a number of knights during his adventure. Poem is incomplete.	Gloriana	Spenser, Edmund. *The Faerie Queen*, ed. A. C. Hamilton. London: Longman, 1977.
Spoils	Attributed to Taliessin *Preiddeu Annwfn* ("The Spoils of Annwn")	c. 900 Welsh verse	Arthur and his warriors visit the otherworld and recover a cauldron.	Annwn Cauldrons Pridwen	Bollard, John K. "Arthur in Early Welsh Tradition." In *The Romance of Arthur: an Anthology of Medieval Texts in Translation*, ed. James J. Wilhelm. New York: Garland, 1994.
Stanz	The Stanzaic *Le Morte Arthur* ("The Death of Arthur")	14th c. English verse	Arthur's death as described in the Vulgate *Mort Artu*, including the Maiden of Escalot, Guinevere's infidelity, and Mordred's rebellion.	Bedivere Escalot Guinevere Lancelot Mador Mordred Salisbury	Benson, Larry D., ed. *King Arthur's Death*. Kalamazoo: Medieval Institute Publications, 1994.
Stricker	Der Stricker *Daniel von dem blühenden Tal* ("Daniel of the Blossoming Valley")	1210–25 German verse	Sir Daniel overcomes Arthur's enemies, becomes a king.	Cluse Daniel Matur	Der Stricker. *Daniel of the Blossoming Valley*, trans. Michael Resler. New York: Garland, 1990.
SyreGaw	*Syre Gawene and the Carle of Carlyle*	c. 1400 English verse	Gawain visits the Carl of Carlisle, acquits himself honorably, marries the Carl's daughter.	Baldwin Carl of Carlisle Gawain	Hahn, Thomas, ed. *Sir Gawain and the Carl of Carlisle*. In *Sir Gawain: Eleven Romances and Tales*. Kalamazoo: Medieval Institute Publications, 1995.
Tavola	*La Tavola Ritonda* ("The Round Table")	1325–1350 Italian prose	Italian adaptation of the Prose *Tristan* and the Vulgate *Queste*.	Dinadan Galahad Lancelot New Table Old Table Palamedes Tristan	Shaver, Anne, trans. *Tristan and the Round Table: a Translation of* La Tavola Ritonda. Binghamton, NY: Medieval and Renaissance Texts and Studies, 1983.
TennIK	Alfred, Lord Tennyson *Idylls of the King*	1859–86 English verse	Collection of poems tracing Arthur's rise and downfall.	Arthur Balin Elaine Gareth Geraint Grail Guinevere Merlin Pelleas Tournament of the Dead Innocence Vivien	Tennyson, Alfred Lord. *Idylls of the King*, ed. J. M. Gray. London: Penguin, 1983.
TennLS	Alfred, Lord Tennyson "The Lady of Shallot"	1832 English verse	Lament of the Lady of Shallot (Escalot) for Lancelot.	Shallot	Tennyson, Alfred Lord. *The Poems of Tennyson*, ed. Christopher Ricks. London: Longmans, 1969.
Thelwall	John Thelwall *The Fairy of the Lake*	1801 English play	Rowena lusts for Arthur. Vortigern lusts for Guinevere. The Lady of the Lake saves them both.	Guinevere Lady of the Lake Rowena	Thelwall, John. *The Fairy of the Lake*. In *Poems Chiefly Written in Retirement*, ed. Johnathan Wordsworth. Oxford: Woodstock, 1989.

Source Code	Author & Title	Date, Form, & Language	Description	Keywords	Text
Thomas	Thomas of England *Tristan*	1170–75 French verse	The earliest "courtly" version of the Tristan legend. Exists only in fragments.	Isolde Isolde of the White Hands Kahedins Mark Tristan	Thomas of Britain. *Tristan*, ed. and trans. Stewart Gregory. New York: Garland, 1991.
Tistram	"Tistram og isolde" ("Tristan and Isolde")	16th c. Danish ballad	Tristan and Isolde enjoy a rendezvous under a linden-tree.	Isolde Mangus Tristan	Bradley, S. A. J. "The Danish Ballads of Tristan and Isolt." In *The Tristan Legend: Texts from Northern and Eastern Europe in Modern English Translation*, ed. Joyce Hill. Leeds, University of Leeds, 1977.
Topography	N/A N/A	N/A Physical topography	Various Arthurian locales in Britain and elsewhere.		Ashe, Geoffrey. *The Landscape of King Arthur*. New York: Holt, 1987.
Triads	Triads of the Island of Britain	11th c. to 14th c. Welsh "Triads"	Indexes of Welsh oral legends, grouped into sets of three (Triads), many of which mention Arthur.	Bran Camlann Guinevere Mordred	Bromwich, Rachel. *Trioedd Ynys Prydein: the Welsh Triads*. Cardiff: University of Wales Press,1978.
TrisFrag	Welsh *Tristan* fragment	c. 1550 Welsh prose	A fragment of a tale of Tristan and Isolde.	Isolde Mark Tristan	Thompson, R. L., trans. "A Welsh Fragment of Tristan." In *The Tristan Legend: Texts from Northern and Eastern Europe in Modern English Translation*, ed. Joyce Hill. Leeds: University of Leeds, 1977.
TrisKv	"Tristrams Kvæði" ("Poem of Tristan")	early 15th c. Icelandic ballad	Account of the death of Tristan.	Isolde Isolde the Dark Tristan	Hill, Joyce. "The Icelandic Ballad of Tristan." In *The Tristan Legends: Texts from Northern and Eastern Europe in Modern English Translation*, ed. Joyce Hill. Leeds: University of Leeds, 1977.
TrisMonch	*Tristan als Mönch* ("Tristan as a Monk")	early to mid 13th c. German verse	Tristan disguises himself as a monk to meet with Isolde.	Isolde Tristan	General
TrisSaga	*Tristrams Saga ok Ísöndar*	1226 Norse prose	First full "courtly" version of the Tristan saga.	Isolde Mark Tristan	Scach, Paul, trans. *The Saga of Tristram and Isond*. Lincoln: University of Nebraska Press, 1973.
TrisStone	N/A Tristan Stone	Erected 6th c. Monolith with inscription	A monolith in Cornwall that commemorates the death of "Drustanus," son of "Cunomorus."	Cunomorus Tristan Tristan Stone	Ashe, Geoffrey. *The Landscape of King Arthur*. New York: Holt, 1988.
TristanoP	*Tristano Panciaticchiano*	early 14th c. Italian prose	Various portions of Tristan's life, derived ultimately from the French Prose *Tristan* and the Vulgate romances.	Giafredi Tristan	Gardner, Edmund G. *The Arthurian Legend in Italian Literature*. London: Dent, 1930.

Source Code	Author & Title	Date, Form, & Language	Description	Keywords	Text
TristanoR	*Tristano Riccardiano*	late 13th c. Italian prose	Italian adaptation of the French Prose *Tristan*.	Brunor Galehaut Mark Meliadus Palamedes Sanza Avventura Tristan	Gardner, Edmund G. *The Arthurian Legend in Italian Literature*. London: Dent, 1930.
TristanoV	*Tristano Veneto*	15th c. Italian prose	Venetian translation of The French Prose *Tristan*.	Isolde Mark Tristan	Gardner, Edmund G. *The Arthurian Legend in Italian Literature*. London: Dent, 1930.
Turke	*The Turke and Gowin*	c. 1500 English verse	A turk (churl) leads Gawain on a series of adventures, ending on the Isle of Man.	Beheading Game Gromer Man	Hahn, Thomas, ed. *The Turke and Gawain*. In *Sir Gawain: Eleven Romances and Tales*. Kalamazoo: Medieval Institute Publications, 1995.
Tyolet	*Tyolet*	late 12th c. French verse	The youthful adventures of Sir Tyolet.	Morgan le Fay Tyolet	Weston, Jessie L. *Guingamor, Lanval, Tyolet, Le Bisclaveret*. New York: AMS Press, 1970.
UlrichZ	Ulrich von Zatzikhoven *Lanzelet*	c. 1200 German verse	Lancelot's early adventures, perils, and wives. Includes an abduction & rescue of Guinevere and a Chastity Test.	Ade Iblis Iweret Lancelot Malduc Pluris Valerin	Ulrich von Zatzikhoven. *Lanzelet*, trans. Kenneth G. T. Webster. New York: Columbia University Press, 1951.
Vallet	*Le Vallet à la Cote Mal Tailliée* ("The Knight of the Ill-Fitting Coat")	13th c. French verse	A fragment. The Knight of the Ill-Fitting Coat arrives at Arthur's court.	Knight of the Ill-Fitting Coat	General
Vasnacht	*Das Vasnachtspil Mit der Kron* ("The Shrovetide Play with the Crown")	15th c. German Shrovetide Play	King of Abian sends a crown to Arthur that tests the fidelity of the men at court.	Chastity Tests	General
Vendetta	*La Vendetta Che fe Messer Lanzelloto de la Morte di Miser Tristano* ("The Revenge of Sir Lancelot for the Death of Sir Tristan")	14th c. Italian verse	Lancelot, avenging Tristan's murder, kills King Mark of Cornwall.	Lancelot Mark Tristan	Gardner, Edmund G. *The Arthurian Legend in Italian Literature*. London: Dent, 1930.
Vengeance	Raoul, possibly Raoul de Houdenc *La Vengeance Raguidel* ("The Avenging of Raguidel")	early 13th c. French verse	Gawain avenges the death of Sir Raguidel, with the help of Yder, by defeating King Guengasoain.	Gawain Guengasoain Raguidel Yder	Raoul de Houdenc. *La Vengeance Raguidel*, ed. Mathias Friedwagner. Halle: Niemeyer, 1909.
VitaMer	*Vita di Merlino con le Sue Profetie* ("The Life of Merlin, with His Prophecies")	c. 1480 Italian prose	Italian translation of the Prose *Merlin*	Gregorio Lady of the Lake Meliadus Merlin	Gardner, Edmund G. *The Arthurian Legend in Italian Literature*. London: Dent, 1930.

Source Code	Author & Title	Date, Form, & Language	Description	Keywords	Text
VulgEst	Vulgate *Estoire del Saint Graal* ("History of the Holy Grail")	1220–35 French prose	Grand history of the Grail based partly on Robert de Boron. Covers Joseph of Arimathea's life, his emigration to Britain, and the founding of the Grail Castle at Corbenic. Followed by the Vulgate *Merlin*.	Alain Bleeding Lance Bron Camelot Celidoine Corbenic Grail Grail Table Joseph of Arimathea Josephus Mordrains Nascien Peter	Lacy, Norris J., ed. *Lancelot-Grail: the Old French Arthurian Vulgate and Post Vulgate in Translation*, vol. 1. New York: Garland, 1996.
VulgLanc	Vulgate *Lancelot*	1215–30 French prose	Long account of Lancelot's birth, rearing, knighting, adventures, love for Guinevere, and rescue of Guinevere from Meleagant. It follows the Vulgate *Merlin* and precedes the Vulgate *Queste del Saint Graal*.	Ban Bors Claudas Corbenic Dolorous Guard Gaheris Galehaut Guinevere Guinevere the False Hector Lady of the Lake Lancelot Lionel Meleagant Saxon Rock	Lacy, Norris J., ed. *Lancelot-Grail: the Old French Arthurian Vulgate and Post Vulgate in Translation*, vols. 2 & 3. New York: Garland, 1996.
VulgMer	Vulgate *Merlin*	1220–35 French prose	Redaction of the Prose *Merlin* with a long continuation describing Merlin's birth and deeds, Arthur's ascension to the throne, the war against the Saxons, and the Roman War. It follows the Vulgate *Estoire del Saint Graal* and precedes the Vulgate *Lancelot*.	Arthur Ban Claudas Gawain Guinevere Lady of the Lake Leodegan Merlin Pendragon Rions Rome Round Table Saxons Sword in the Stone Uther Vortigern Yvain	Lacy, Norris J., ed. *Lancelot-Grail: the Old French Arthurian Vulgate and Post Vulgate in Translation*, vol. 1. New York: Garland, 1996.
VulgMort	Vulgate *Mort Artu* ("Death of Arthur")	1215–30 French prose	The downfall of Arthur's court; the adultery of Lancelot and Guinevere; Arthur's war with Lancelot; Mordred's rebellion; the final battle; Arthur's death. Follows the Vulgate *Queste del Saint Graal*.	Arthur Escalot Gawain Girflet Guinevere Lancelot Mador Mordred Rome Salisbury	Lacy, Norris J., ed. *Lancelot-Grail: the Old French Arthurian Vulgate and Post Vulgate in Translation*, vol. 4. New York: Garland, 1996.

Source Code	Author & Title	Date, Form, & Language	Description	Keywords	Text
VulgQuest	Vulgate *Queste del Saint Graal* ("Quest of the Holy Grail")	1215–30 French prose	The quest to find the Holy Grail. Galahad is the victor, with Bors and Perceval. Gawain is called a murderer. Lancelot is denied spiritual fulfillment because of his affair with Guinevere. Follows the Vulgate *Lancelot* and precedes the Vulgate *Mort Artu*.	Bors Castle of Maidens Corbenic Galahad Grail Lancelot Lionel Perceval Sarras Sword with the Strange Hangings	Lacy, Norris J., ed. *Lancelot-Grail: the Old French Arthurian Vulgate and Post Vulgate in Translation*, vol. 4. New York: Garland, 1996.
Wace	Wace *Roman de Brut* ("Romance of Brut")	c. 1155 French verse	Chronicle of British History based on Geoffrey of Monmouth; first appearance of the Round Table.	Arthur Rome Round Table Saxons	Wace. *Roman de Brut*. In *The Arthurian Chronicles of Wace and Layamon*, ed. and trans. Eugene Mason. London: Dent, 1970.
Walewein	*Walewein ende Keye* ("Gawain and Kay")	mid to late 13th c. Dutch verse	Gawain humiliates Kay.	Kay	Sparnaay, Hendricus. "The Dutch Romances." In *Arthurian Literature in the Middle Ages*, ed. R. S. Loomis. Oxford: Clarendon, 1959.
Wartburg	*Wartburgkrieg*	13th c. Compilation of German poems	Wolfram von Eschenbach debates the sorcerer Clinschor.	Clinschor Wolfram von Eschenbach	General
Wedding	Possibly Sir Thomas Malory *The Wedding of Sir Gawain and Dame Ragnell*	15th c. English verse	Gawain marries the Loathly Lady to find what women desire most in order to save Arthur from a captor.	Gawain Gromer Loathly Lady Ragnelle	Sheperd, Stephen H. A., ed. *The Weddyng of Syr Gawen and Dame Ragnell for Helpyng of Kyng Arthoure*. In *Middle English Romances*. New York: Norton, 1995.
WelshGer	*Geraint filius Erbin*	10th c. or 11th c. Welsh poem	Geraint's deeds at the battle of Llongborth are praised; Arthur or his men were also present.	Geraint Llongborth	Bollard, John K. "Arthur in Early Welsh Tradition." In *The Romance of Arthur: an Anthology of Medieval Texts in Translation*, ed. James J. Wilhelm. New York: Garland, 1994.
WelshGlew	Untitled	10th c. or 11th c. Welsh verse	A dialogue between Arthur and Glewlwyd Mighty Grip. The deeds of Kay and other warriors are mentioned.	Cath Palug Glewlwyd	Bollard, John K. "Arthur in Early Welsh Tradition." In *The Romance of Arthur: an Anthology of Medieval Texts in Translation*, ed. James J. Wilhelm. New York: Garland, 1994.
WelshSG	"The Stanzas of the Graves"	10th c. or 11th c. Welsh verse	The grave sites of a number of heroes are named.	Anoeth Arthur	Bollard, John K. "Arthur in Early Welsh Tradition." In *The Romance of Arthur: an Anthology of Medieval Texts in Translation*, ed. James J. Wilhelm. New York: Garland, 1994.
Wigamur	*Wigamur*	1240–60 German verse	The youth, education, and adventures of Sir Wigamur.	Wigamur	General

Source Code	Author & Title	Date, Form, & Language	Description	Keywords	Text
WilliamM	William of Malmesbury *Gesta Regum Anglorum* ("Deeds of the Kings of England")	1125 Latin chronicle	Chronicle of British history includes a brief mention of Arthur and the first appearance of Gawain. An interpolation contains a story of Yder and Glastonbury.	Arthur Gawain	William of Malmesbury. *William of Malmesbury's Chronicle of the Kings of England*, ed. and trans. J. A. Giles. London: Bohn, 1847.
Wirnt	Wirnt von Grafenberg *Wigalois*	early 13th c. German verse	Wigalois, son of Gawain, liberates an imprisoned country, marries its princess.	Korntin Lion Wigalois	Wirnt von Grafenberg. *Wigalois: the Knight of Fortune's Wheel*, trans. J. W. Thomas. Lincoln: University of Nebraska, 1977.
Wolfram	Wolfram von Eschenbach *Parzival*	1200–1210 German verse	Greatest Middle High German romance adapts Chrétien de Troyes's *Perceval*. Perceval achieves the Grail.	Anfortas Condwiramurs Feirefiz Gahmuret Gawain Grail Grail Family Perceval	Wolfram von Eschenbach. *Parzival*, trans. A. T. Hatto. Harmondsworth: Penguin, 1980.
Wordsworth	William Wordsworth "The Egyptian Maid"	1828 English verse	Merlin destroys a ship and kills an Egyptian Princess. Galahad resurrects and marries her.	Egyptian Maid Nina Water Lily	Wordsworth, William. "The Egyptian Maid." In *The Poems of Wordsworth*, ed. Andrew J. George. Boston: Houghton Mifflin, 1932.
Wrake	*De Wrake van Ragisel* ("The Avenging of Ragisel")	early to mid 13th c. Dutch verse	Dutch adaptation of the French *La Vengeance Raguidel*.	Gawain Raguidel Yder	Sparnaay, Hendricus. "The Dutch Romances." In *Arthurian Literature in the Middle Ages*, ed. R. S. Loomis. Oxford: Clarendon, 1959.
Yder	*Yder*	ealrly 13th c. French verse	The adventures of Yder at Arthur's court. Arthur is portrayed as a tyrant.	Guenloie Kay Yder	Adams, Alison, ed. *The Romance of Yder*. Cambridge: Brewer, 1983.
Ysaie	*Ysaïe le Triste* ("Ysaïe the Sad")	late 14th c. or early 15th c. French prose	Ysaïe (son of Tristan) and his son, Marc, strive to bring justice to an anarchic post-Arthurian Britain.	Auberon Marc Ysaïe	General
Ywain	*Ywain and Gawain*	1310–40 English verse	English adaptation of Chrétien de Troyes's *Yvain*.	Yvain	Sheperd, Stephen H. A., ed. *Ywaine and Gawain*. In *Middle English Romances*. New York: Norton, 1995.